T0140071

# Lecture Notes in Networks and Systems

## Volume 221

The series "Lecture Notes in Networks and Systems" publishes the latest developments in Networks and Systems—quickly, informally and with high quality. Original research reported in proceedings and post-proceedings represents the core of LNNS.

Volumes published in LNNS embrace all aspects and subfields of, as well as new challenges in, Networks and Systems.

The series contains proceedings and edited volumes in systems and networks, spanning the areas of Cyber-Physical Systems, Autonomous Systems, Sensor Networks, Control Systems, Energy Systems, Automotive Systems, Biological Systems, Vehicular Networking and Connected Vehicles, Aerospace Systems, Automation, Manufacturing, Smart Grids, Nonlinear Systems, Power Systems, Robotics, Social Systems, Economic Systems and other. Of particular value to both the contributors and the readership are the short publication timeframe and the world-wide distribution and exposure which enable both a wide and rapid dissemination of research output.

The series covers the theory, applications, and perspectives on the state of the art and future developments relevant to systems and networks, decision making, control, complex processes and related areas, as embedded in the fields of interdisciplinary and applied sciences, engineering, computer science, physics, economics, social, and life sciences, as well as the paradigms and methodologies behind them.

Indexed by SCOPUS, INSPEC, WTI Frankfurt eG, zbMATH, SCImago.

All books published in the series are submitted for consideration in Web of Science.

More information about this series at http://www.springer.com/series/15179

Nancy L. Black · W. Patrick Neumann ·
Ian Noy
Editors

# Proceedings of the 21st Congress of the International Ergonomics Association (IEA 2021)

Volume III: Sector Based Ergonomics

 Springer

*Editors*
Nancy L. Black
Département de génie mécanique
Université de Moncton
Moncton, NB, Canada

W. Patrick Neumann
Department of Mechanical and Industrial
Engineering
Ryerson University
Toronto, ON, Canada

Ian Noy
Toronto, ON, Canada

ISSN 2367-3370          ISSN 2367-3389 (electronic)
Lecture Notes in Networks and Systems
ISBN 978-3-030-74607-0          ISBN 978-3-030-74608-7 (eBook)
https://doi.org/10.1007/978-3-030-74608-7

This Springer imprint is published by the registered company Springer Nature Switzerland AG
The registered company address is: Gewerbestrasse 11, 6330 Cham, Switzerland

# Preface

The International Ergonomics Association (IEA) is the organization that unites Human Factors and Ergonomics (HF/E) associations around the world. The mission of the IEA is "to elaborate and advance ergonomics science and practice, and to expand its scope of application and contribution to society to improve the quality of life, working closely with its constituent societies and related international organizations" (IEA, 2021). The IEA hosts a world congress every three years creating the single most important opportunity to exchange knowledge and ideas in the discipline with practitioners and researchers from across the planet. Like other IEA congresses, IEA2021 included an exciting range of research and professional practice cases in the broadest range of Human Factors and Ergonomics (HF/E) applications imaginable. While the conference was not able to host an in-person meeting in Vancouver, Canada, as planned by the host Association of Canadian Ergonomists/*Association canadienne d'ergonomie*, it still featured over 875 presentations and special events with the latest research and most innovative thinkers. For this congress, authors could prepare a chapter for publication, and 60% chose to do so. The breadth and quality of the work available at IEA2021 are second to none—and the research of all authors who prepared their publication for this congress is made available through the five volumes of these proceedings.

The International Ergonomics Association defines Human Factors and Ergonomics (HF/E) synonymously as being:

*The scientific discipline concerned with the understanding of interactions among humans and other elements of a system, and the profession that applies theory, principles, data and methods to design in order to optimize human well-being and overall system performance.*

*Practitioners of ergonomics and ergonomists contribute to the design and evaluation of tasks, jobs, products, environments and systems in order to make them compatible with the needs, abilities and limitations of people.*

*Ergonomics helps harmonize things that interact with people in terms of people's needs, abilities and limitations.* (https://iea.cc/definition-and-domains-of-ergonomics/)

The breadth of issues and disciplines suggested by this definition gives one pause for thought: what aspect in our lives is not in some way affected by the design and application of HF/E? For designers and managers around the world, a similar realization is growing: every decision made in the design and application of technology has implications for the humans that will interact with that system across its lifecycle. While this can be daunting, the researchers and professionals who participated in IEA2021 understand that, by working together across our disciplines and roles, we can achieve these lofty ambitions. This is especially relevant as we continue our collective journey into an increasingly "interconnected world"—the theme for the 21st IEA Congress. With the rise of a myriad of technologies as promulgated by Industry 4.0 proponents, we need now, more than ever, the skills and knowledge of HF/E researchers and practitioners to ensure that these tools are applied in a human-centric way towards resilient and sustainable systems that provide an enduring and sustainable road to prosperity—as advocated in the new Industry 5.0 Paradigm (Breque et al. 2021). Where the trend of Industry 4.0 aims primarily at encouraging technology purchasing and application, Industry 5.0 includes goals of resiliency and sustainability for both humans and our planet. These proceedings provide examples of research and development projects that illustrate how this brighter, human-centred future can be pursued through "*Ergonomie 4.0*", as stated in the French theme of the Congress.

While the theme of the Congress concerns human interactions within a rapidly evolving cyber-physical world, the devastating impact of the COVID-19 pandemic has given an added dimension to the Congress theme and its delivery model. As the pandemic began to engulf the world, the traditional in-person Congress became increasingly less viable and gave way to the creation of a hybrid model as a means to enhance international participation. In early 2021, it became clear that holding an in-person event would not be possible; hence, the Congress was converted to a fully virtual event. The uncertainty, mounting challenges and turbulent progression actually created new possibilities to engage the global HF/E community in ways that were never previously explored by the IEA. Indeed, one of the scientific tracks of the congress focuses explicitly on HF/E contributions to cope with COVID-19, and readers will find some submissions to other tracks similarly focus on what HF/E practitioners and researchers bring to the world during this pandemic period. This journey epitomizes broader transformative patterns now underway in society at large and accentuates the urgency for resilience, sustainability, and healthy workplaces. No doubt, the notion of globalization will be redefined in the wake of the pandemic and will have far-reaching implications for the connected world and for future society, and with new paradigms emerge a host of new human factors challenges. The breadth of topics and issues addressed in the proceedings suggests that the HF/E community is already mobilizing and rising to these emerging challenges in this, our connected world.

IEA2021 proceedings includes papers from 31 scientific tracks and includes participants from 74 countries across 5 continents. The proceedings of the 21st triennial congress of the IEA—IEA2021—exemplify the diversity of HF/E, and of the association, in terms of geography, disciplines represented, application domains, and aspects of human life cycle and capability being considered. Our diversity mirrors the diversity of humans generally and is a strength as we learn to weave our knowledge, methods, and ideas together to create a more resilient and stronger approach to design than is achievable individually. This is the strength of the IEA congresses, in the past, in the current pandemic-affected 21st occasion, and in the future. There is no other meeting like it.

A substantial number of works were submitted for publication across the Scientific Tracks at IEA2021. This gave us the happy opportunity to group contents by common threads. Each volume presents contents in sections with papers within the track's section presented in alphabetical order by the first author's last name. These proceedings are divided into five volumes as follows:

## VOLUME 1: SYSTEMS AND MACROERGONOMICS (ISBN 978-3-030-74601-8)

Activity Theories for Work Analysis and Design (ATWAD)
Systems HF/E
Ergonomic Work Analysis and Training (EWAT)
HF/E Education and Professional Certification Development
Organisation Design and Management (ODAM)

## VOLUME 2: INCLUSIVE AND SUSTAINABLE DESIGN (ISBN 978-3-030-74604-9)

Ageing and Work
Ergonomics for children and Educational Environments
Ergonomics in Design for All
Gender and Work
Human Factors and Sustainable Development
Slips Trips and Falls
Visual Ergonomics

## VOLUME 3: SECTOR BASED ERGONOMICS (ISBN 978-3-030-74607-0)

Practitioner Case Studies
Aerospace Ergonomics
Agricultural Ergonomics
Building and Construction Ergonomics
Ergonomics in Manufacturing
HF/E in Supply Chain Design and Management
Transport Ergonomics and Human Factors

## VOLUME 4: HEALTHCARE AND HEALTHY WORK (ISBN 978-3-030-74610-0)

Health and Safety
Healthcare Ergonomics

HF/E Contribution to Cope with Covid-19
Musculoskeletal Disorders

## VOLUME 5: METHODS & APPROACHES (ISBN 978-3-030-74613-1)

Advanced Imaging
Affective Design
Anthropometry
Biomechanics
Human Factors in Robotics
Human Modelling and Simulation
Neuroergonomics
Working with Computer Systems

These volumes are the result of many hours of work, for authors, Scientific Track Managers and their reviewer teams, student volunteers, and editors. We are grateful to Springer for making it available to you in book form and are confident you will find these works informative and useful in your own efforts to create a better, more human-centred future.

### References

Breque, M., De Nul, L., Petridis, A., 2021. Industry 5.0: Towards More Sustainable, Resilient and Human-Centric Industry, in: Innovation, E.D.-G.f.R.a. (Ed.), Policy Brief. European Commission, Luxembourg, p. 48. https://ec.europa.eu/info/news/industry-50-towards-more-sustainable-resilient-and-human-centric-industry-2021-jan-07_en

International Ergonomics Association (2021) Definitions and Domains of Ergonomics. https://iea.cc/definition-and-domains-of-ergonomics/; accessed March, 2021

Nancy L. Black
W. Patrick Neumann
IEA2021 Scientific Co-chairs

Ian Noy
IEA2021 Conference Chair

# IEA2021 Acknowledgements

The IEA Congress organizing committee acknowledges many individuals whose contributions to the event have been invaluable to its success.

First and foremost, we acknowledge with deep appreciation the tremendous work of Steve Marlin, CEO of Prestige Accommodations, International Inc. His firm, hired to assist with organizing and executing the Congress, delivered unparalleled service throughout the planning process. Tragically, Steve passed away in early 2021. He provided outstanding support and wise counsel, always with a smile. He is sorely missed. We remain indebted to the Prestige staff, whose expertise and outstanding professionalism guided us through the planning process. In particular, we are grateful to Laurie Ybarra, Sr. Meetings Manager, who oversaw the many diverse aspects of our ever-changing plans and Christine Reinhard, Director of Operations, who skilfully managed the budget, website and registration system. Laurie and Christine's friendly approach, and their unique combination of technical and interpersonal skills, made it a pleasure to work with them. Marie-Hélène Bisaillon, Executive Director of the Association of Canadian Ergonomists/ *Association canadienne d'ergonomie*, supported their work.

The Organizing Committee is also indebted to those contributors who were instrumental in developing and promoting IEA2021. Joanne Bangs, our freelance Communications Specialist, provided engaging news blogs and other promotional collateral to help get the word out about the Congress. Sadeem Qureshi (Ryerson University), Elizabeth Georgiou, Elaine Fung, and Michelle Lam (Simon Fraser University) helped to create widespread awareness of the Congress as well as the HF/E field and profession through creative use of digital and social media. We are also grateful to those who worked diligently to ensure that the Congress provided meaningful opportunities for students and early career researchers, including Daniel P. Armstrong and Christopher A.B. Moore (University of Waterloo), Owen McCulloch (Simon Fraser University), Dora Hsiao (Galvion, Inc.), Chelsea DeGuzman and Joelle Girgis (University of Toronto), and Larissa Fedorowich (Associate Ergonomist, self-employed). The ePoster presentation option, new to IEA triennial congresses in 2021, was defined with care by Anne-Kristina Arnold (Simon Fraser University). Colleen Dewis (Dalhousie University) was key to interpreting our technical submission software and adapting its capacities to our needs. Hemanshu Bhargav (Ryerson University), Rachel Faust (Université de Québec à Montréal), Myriam Bérubé (Université de Montréal), Charlotte Bate, Vanessa DeVries, Caleb Leary, and Marcelo Zaharur (Fanshawe College), Tobi Durowoju (EWI Works), Issa Kaba Diakite, Mariam Keita, Mouhamadou Pléa Ndour, Shelby Nowlan, Faouzi Mahamane Ouedraogo, Jenna Smith, and Israël Muaka Wembi (Université de Moncton), and the aforementioned Larissa Fedorowich assisted with technical submission database verification and clean-up. We are particularly grateful that so many came to us through the Association of Canadian Ergonomists/Association canadienne d'ergonomie, witnessing to the active and motivated ergonomics and human factors community in IEA2021's host country.

The organizers are especially grateful to our sponsors, whose generous contributions made the Congress possible and readily accessible to the global HF/E community. Their recognition of the Congress as a valuable opportunity to advance the field of HF/E, as well as their steadfast support throughout a very trying planning period, was critical to the success of the Congress. The IEA 2021 sponsors include:

*Benefactor Level:*
 Amazon.com, Inc.

*Platinum Level:*
 Anonymous

*Diamond Level:*
 Healthcare Insurance Reciprocal of Canada

*Gold Level:*
 Huawei Technologies Canada
 Institute for Work and Health (Ontario)
 WorkSafe BC

*Silver Level:*
 Fanshawe College
 Simon Fraser University
 Aptima, Inc.

# Organization

## IEA2021 Organizing Committee

### IEA2021 Congress Chair

Ian Noy      HFE Consultant and Forensic Expert, Toronto, Ontario, Canada

### Technical Program Committee Co-chairs

Nancy L. Black      Department of Mechanical Engineering, Faculté d'ingénierie, Université de Moncton, Canada

W. Patrick Neumann      Human Factors Engineering Lab, Department of Mechanical and Industrial Engineering, Ryerson University, Canada

### Media Outreach

Hayley Crosby      Options Incorporated, Canada

### Developing Countries

Manobhiram (Manu) Nellutla      Actsafe Safety Association, Canada

### ePosters Coordinator

Anne-Kristina Arnold      Ergonomics, Simon Fraser University, Canada

### Exhibits Coordinator

Abigail Overduin      Workplace Health Services, The University of British Columbia, Canada

**Early Career Researcher Program Coordinator**

Sadeem Qureshi
Human Factors Engineering Lab, Department of Mechanical and Industrial Engineering, Ryerson University, Canada

**Media Relations**

Heather Kahle
Human Factors Specialist/Ergonomist, WorkSafeBC, Canada

Jenny Colman
Human Factor Specialist, Risk Analysis Unit, WorkSafeBC, Canada

**Events/Social**

Gina Vahlas
Human Factors Specialist/Ergonomist, Risk Analysis Unit, WorkSafeBC, Canada

Era Poddar
Specialist Safety Advisor-Ergonomics, Manufacturing Safety Alliance of BC, Canada

Alison Heller-Ono
CEO, Worksite International, USA

**French Language Coordinator**

François Taillefer
Faculté des sciences, Université de Québec à Montréal, Canada

**Communications Coordinator**

Joanne Bangs
Free-lance consultant, USA

**EasyChair Platform Technical Liaison**

Colleen Dewis
Department of Industrial Engineering, Dalhousie University, Canada

# Scientific Committee of IEA2021

Nancy L. Black (Co-chair)
Université de Moncton, Canada

W. Patrick Neumann (Co-chair)
Ryerson University, Canada

Wayne Albert
University of New Brunswick, Canada

Sara Albolino
Coordinator of the system reliability area for the Center for Patient Safety—Tuscany Region, Italy

Thomas Alexander
Federal Institute for Occupational Safety and Health (BAUA), Germany

Anne-Kristina Arnold
Simon Fraser University, Canada

Pascal Béguin                    Institut d'Études du Travail de Lyon (IETL)-
                                   Université Lumière Lyon 2, France
Tommaso Bellandi                 Northwest Trust - Regional Health Service
                                   of Tuscany, Italy
Klaus Bengler                    Technische Universität München, Germany
Yuval Bitan                      Ben-Gurion University of the Negev,
                                   University of Toronto, Israel
Ivan Bolis                       Universidade Federal da Paraíba, Brazil
Tim Bosch                        TNO, Netherlands
Richard Bowman                   Intertile Research Pty Ltd, Australia
Guy André Boy                    CentraleSupélec (Paris Saclay University),
                                   ESTIA Institute of Technology, France
Karen Bredenkamp                 Magic Leap, USA
Ole Broberg                      Technical University of Denmark, Denmark
Katie Buckley                    University of Melbourne, Australia
Robin Burgess-Limerick           University of Queensland, Australia
Peter Burns                      Transport Canada, Canada
Chien-Chi (Max) Chang            National Tsing Hua University, Taiwan
Andy S. K. Cheng                 Hong Kong Polytechnique University,
                                   Hong Kong
Pieter Coenen                    Amsterdam UMC (VUmc location), Netherlands
Teresa Cotrim                    University of Lisbon, Portugal
Ann Marie Dale                   Washington University in St. Louis, USA
Jonathan Davy                    Rhodes University, South Africa
Enrique De la Vega               TECNM/Instituto Technologico de Hermosillo,
                                   Mexico
Catherine Delgoulet              CRTD, Conservatoire National des Arts et
                                   Métiers (CNAM), France
Michiel de Looze                 TNO, Netherlands
Colleen Dewis                    Dalhousie University, Canada
Clark Dickerson                  University of Waterloo, Canada
Francisco José de Castro         Federal University of Rio de Janeiro, Brazil
  Moura Duarte
Tamsyn Edwards                   San Jose State University, NASA Ames
                                   Research Center, USA
Georg Effenberger                AUVA-Hauptstelle, Austrian Ergonomics
                                   Society, Austria
Echezona Nelson Dominic          University of Nigeria, Nigeria
  Ekechukwu
Antonella Frisiello              LINKS Foundation, Italy
Carlos Manuel Escobar            University of Nottingham, Universidad Peruana
  Galindo                          Cayetano Heredia, Peru
Anindya Ganguli                  Bureau of Indian Standards (BIS), Bharat Heavy
                                   Electricals Ltd. (BHEL), India
Richard Gardner                  Boeing Research & Technology, USA

Rafael E. Gonzalez          Bolivarian University, Petróleos de Venezuela,
                               S.A. (PDVSA), Venezuela
Ewa Górska                  University of Ecology and Management
                               in Warsaw, Poland
Maggie Graf                 International Ergonomics Association -
                               Professional Standards and Education,
                               Certification Sub-committee, Switzerland
Alma Maria Jennifer         De La Salle University—Manila, Philippines
  Gutierrez
Jukka Häkkinen              University of Helsinki, Finland
Gregor Harih                University of Maribor, Slovenia
Veerle Hermans              Vrije Universiteit Brussel, Belgium
Dora Hsiao                  Revision Military, Canada
Laerte Idal Sznelwar        Universidade de São Paulo, Brazil
Rauf Iqbal                  National Institute of Industrial
                               Engineering (NITIE), India
Nicole Jochems              University of Luebeck, Germany
Marie Laberge               Université de Montréal, Centre de recherche
                               du CHU Ste-Justine, Canada
Fion C. H. Lee              UOW College Hong Kong, Hong Kong
Yue (Sophia) Li             KITE, Toronto Rehabilitation Institute—
                               University Health Network, Canada
Peter Lundqvist             SLU - Swedish University of Agricultural
                               Sciences, Sweden
Neil Mansfield              Nottingham Trent University, UK
Márcio Alves Marçal         Universidade Federal dos Vales do Jequitinhonha
                               e do Mucuri, Brazil
Blake McGowan               VelocityEHS, USA
Ranjana Mehta               Texas A&M University, USA
Marijke Melles              Delft University of Technology, Netherlands
Marino Menozzi              Swiss Federal Institute of Technology,
                               ETH Zurich, Switzerland
Francisco Octavio Lopez     TECNM/Instituto Tecnológico de Hermosillo,
  Millan                       Mexico
Karen Lange Morales         Universidad Nacional de Colombia, Colombia
Dimitris Nathanael          National Technical University of Athens, Greece
Yee Guan Ng                 Universiti Putra Malaysia, Malaysia
Jodi Oakman                 La Trobe University, Australia
Udoka Arinze Chris Okafor   University of Lagos, Nigeria
Paulo Antonio Barros        Federal University of Rio Grande do Sul, Brazil
  Oliveira
Vassilis Papakostopoulos    University of the Aegean, Greece
Maria Pascale               Uruguayan Association of Ergonomics
                               (AUDErgo), Uruguay
Gunther Paul                James Cook University, Australia

| | |
|---|---|
| Chui Yoon Ping | Singapore University of Social Sciences, Singapore |
| Ruud N. Pikaar | ErgoS Human Factors Engineering, Netherlands |
| Jim Potvin | McMaster University, Canada |
| Valérie Pueyo | Université Lumière Lyon 2, France |
| Sadeem Qureshi | Ryerson University, Canada |
| Sudhakar Rajulu | NASA - Johnson Space Center, USA |
| Gemma Read | University of the Sunshine Coast, Australia |
| David Rempel | University of California Berkeley; University of California San Francisco, USA |
| Raziel Riemer | Ben-Gurion University of the Negev, Israel |
| Michelle M. Robertson | Office Ergonomics Research Committee, Northeastern University, University of Connecticut, University of California, Berkeley, USA |
| Martin Antonio Rodriguez | Universidad Tecnológica Nacional Buenos Aires FRBA, Argentina |
| Gustavo Rosal | UNE (Spanish Association for Standardisation), Spain |
| Patricia H. Rosen | Federal Institute for Occupational Safety and Health (BAUA), Germany |
| Ken Sagawa | AIST, Japan |
| Paul M. Salmon | University of the Sunshine Coast, Australia |
| Marta Santos | Universidade do Porto, Portugal |
| Sofia Scataglini | University of Antwerp, Belgium |
| Lawrence J. H. Schulze | University of Houston, USA |
| Rosemary Ruiz Seva | De La Salle University, Philippines |
| Fabio Sgarbossa | Norwegian University of Science and Technology, Norway |
| Jonas Shultz | Health Quality Council of Alberta, University of Calgary, Canada |
| Anabela Simões | University Lusófona, Portugal |
| Sarbjit Singh | National Institute of Technology Jalandhar, India |
| John Smallwood | Nelson Mandela University, South Africa |
| Lukáš Šoltys | Czech Ergonomics Association, Czech Republic |
| Isabella Tiziana Steffan | STUDIO STEFFAN—Progettazione & Ricerca (Design & Research), Italy |
| Daryl Stephenson | Occupational Health Clinics for Ontario Workers, Canada |
| Gyula Szabó | Hungarian Ergonomics Society, Hungary |
| Shamsul Bahri Mohd Tamrin | Universiti Putra Malaysia, Malaysia |
| Andrew Thatcher | University of the Witwatersrand, South Africa |
| Giulio Toccafondi | Center for Clinical Risk Management and Patient Safety GRC, WHO Collaborating Center, Florence, Italy |

Andrew Todd                    Rhodes University, South Africa
Judy Village                   University of British Columbia, Canada
Christian Voirol               University of Applied Sciences Western
                                  Switzerland, University of Montreal,
                                  Switzerland
Michael Wichtl                 AUVA-Hauptstelle, Austrian Ergonomics
                                  Society, Austria
Amanda Widdowson               Chartered Institute of Ergonomics and Human
                                  Factors (CIEHF), Thales, UK
Sascha Wischniewski            Federal Institute for Occupational Safety
                                  & Health (BAuA), Germany

# Contents

# Part I: Practitioner Cases (Edited by Ruud N. Pikaar)

# The Virtual World: A Challenge for On-Site Action in Ergonomics

Aline Azambuja Viana[✉], Suzana Lugão, Renata Pinheiro, and Simone Ricart

Workers' Health Coordination, FIOCRUZ, Rio de Janeiro, RJ, Brazil
ergonomia@fiocruz.br

**Abstract.** This article presents the path traveled by a team of ergonomists to adapt the methods they used for ergonomic actions. New ways for performing ergonomic actions were necessary due to the worldwide Covid-19 Pandemic. Face-to-face observation of work activities in development was no longer possible. This study presents the challenges, limitations, and achievements obtained by ergonomists performing their work in a new way.

Activity Ergonomics constitutes the theoretical reference for this work. We present the methodological association used to deal with the challenges derived from the pandemic period. We show results from the association of the Ergonomic Analysis of Work Activity (EAWA) with: the *"paradigm of training in and by the analysis of work, to and by action"*; the Method of Collective Work Analysis (CWA); and the Method of a Workshop of Photography. Those methods also align with the bases of the field of Workers' Health.

We conclude that the strategies adopted were able to conduct a practice in ergonomics that made it possible to achieve its main objectives.

**Keywords:** Activity ergonomics · Ergonomic analysis of work activity · Worker's health · Covid-19 pandemic · Virtual work

## 1 Introduction

### 1.1 The Reasons Why

This article reflects on the strategies developed by an Ergonomics Team facing the impossibility of observing the work in the field, due to the Covid-19 pandemic. The pandemic imposed a health crisis and many restrictions on the movement of people. It generated a challenge to the methodology originally applied in ergonomic work analyses based on activity analysis. This methodology prescribes that the ergonomist observes work on-site and as it is carried out.

Thus, our team of ergonomists, which is a workers' health care team, was in a dilemma. How to access the work situation without infringing a biosecurity standard based on the collective consciousness? How to maintain the dialogical action and participant observation in the face of impediments to proximate contact?

N. L. Black et al. (Eds.): IEA 2021, LNNS 221, pp. 3–12, 2021.
https://doi.org/10.1007/978-3-030-74608-7_1

We, the Ergonomics Team, developed and adopted strategies to face the demands placed upon us. Our team is part of a Worker's Health service at a federal public institution in Rio de Janeiro—Brazil.

The theoretical basis is Activity Ergonomics [1–4]. Its object is the situation where work occurs, and its purpose, the transformation of the system for the better. Transformation occurs through collective construction of proposals for the improvement of working conditions aimed at workers' health and safety [3, 5–7].

## 1.2 The Context

The year 2020 was marked by the global health crisis generated by the SARS-CoV-2 virus. Social distancing and lockdown brought a period of forced reduction in peoples' circulation. This was achieved by the closure of commercial, educational, industrial, banking and service establishments. These measures were necessary due to the high rate of contagion of this virus.

The Pandemic imposed major transformations on production processes [8]. New standards and care procedures were established in the face of increasing contagion: team reduction; changes in workplace hygiene; safe distancing; social isolation; and rotation among workers [9]. In turn, these caused changes to the work scenario, such as: new ways of managing; alternating between remote and face-to-face work; changes in work instruments; and new definitions of production rhythms. Thus, it became necessary to use virtual technologies to maintain working relationships. While remote technologies have become essential means to work, they can be associated with care, but they can also produce illnesses.

Considering these conditions, ergonomic action has also suffered impacts and remodeling. Here we face the dichotomy between prescribed/real work in the ergonomist's task. This occurs because the development of an ergonomic analysis cannot happen under the conditions originally envisaged. Thus, it is essential to develop innovative forms of action with creativity, and to approach new technological resources.

## 2   The Ergonomist Work Transformation

Before the Covid-19 Pandemic, we developed ergonomic action on different fronts: analysis and intervention in work situations; orientation and training of workers; management of indicators; care in the face of health problems. However, due to conditions imposed by the Pandemic, we had to adapt our methodology. In this session, we present our methodological path from pre-pandemic methods to adjustments to cope in the pandemic period.

### 2.1   The Original Methodology

The field of Worker's Health hinges on the concept of work processes as the focal point for understanding the relationship between health and disease at work [10, 11]. This is an advance on the concepts previously used for the study of the health-work relationship when considering "the social and historical dimension of work and Health/Disease" [12].

Our Team is institutionally and referentially included in the field of Worker's Health which is the foundation for ergonomic action. We employ Ergonomic Analysis of Work Activity (EAWA) [6, 7, 13, 14] as a methodological basis. EAWA provides a system to observe and interact with workers to transform work situations for the better. EAWA's strength lays in uncovering how work activity unfolds. Thus, it can confront the prescribed work with actual work.

**The Institutional Practice of EAWA.** The methodology adopted by the team for the development of EAWA in the institution where it operates is structured in 6 stages listed and described below, as explained by Ricart [15, 16]:

*1st stage—Receipt of Demand.* A department of the institution asks us to assist in the resolution of problems related to workers' health and safety. These demands may come from the workers themselves as applicants, from the department managers, or from the institution's worker health and safety team.

*2nd stage—Evaluation Planning.* It involves scheduling and holding a first meeting between us and the team that will be evaluated. Department managers and human resources must also be present. In this meeting, we seek to understand the real demand for the request for an ergonomic analysis. We also seek preliminary information about the main work processes performed; present the methodology and objectives of ergonomic action to the collective; and propose a schedule for the ergonomic action.

*3rd stage—Technical Visits to the Site to be Evaluated.* At this stage, we seek to understand the technical process and the tasks involved in the work activity by going to the department under evaluation, in person. We conduct interviews with the workers; request information about the work population and about aspects of the workflow; identify requirements imposed on workers; and identify strategies and adaptations made by workers to keep the production process viable in the face of varying conditions. The situations identified are recorded through photo or video.

*4th stage—Data Consolidation.* We record and consolidate the data and information collected during technical visits in data analysis and reporting software. We organize the information using the EAMETA analysis tool [17, 18]. EAMETA is a Portuguese acronym for aspects evaluated in ergonomic analyses: Space; Environment; Furniture; Equipment; Task and Activity.

*5th stage—Restitution and Validation.* In this stage, we prepare and return the information obtained during the technical visits with suggestions for improvements. We invite the evaluated work team, its managers, and representatives of human resources to meet. This stage has an ethical function for all involved in the ergonomic action [6]. Here, we foster a space for collective construction and reflection on the work processes through the discussion, shared knowledge, recognition, and validation of the situations encountered.

*6th stage—Preparation and Delivery of the report.* The Diagnosis—with the information validated by the workers, we prepare a report that documents the suggestions for improvements of the work situations encountered. This report is an instrument to request and justify the implementation of work changes.

The involvement of workers in all stages of EAWA is an essential device to achieve and ensure its results [3, 6, 7, 13, 15, 18, 19]. To this end, the Social Construction must be present in all the stages. Ricart points out that "Social Construction aims to establish a good relationship between the Ergonomics Team and the different hierarchical levels of the institution in order to establish the commitment and involvement of these agents during all stages of ergonomic action" [16].

## 2.2   An Adapted Methodology

In the pandemic period, we are presented with new demands related to physical exhaustion in field work, complaints of pain while at the home office, and changes in the production process. These issues are generated by changes in the operating mode to meet new biosafety standards, the insertion of new technologies, and the centrality of technology in remote work.

To have access to work situations where on-site observation was impossible, we defined criteria for choosing analysis methods. First, we considered the dialogical action and the possible instruments to enable dialogue about the work. Second, we considered how the collective could produce new forms of work organization. Third, we considered how to get a depiction of the work situations.

Among the resources we researched, we chose the following as guides for action: the "paradigm of training in and by the analysis of work, to and by action" [3, 19, 20]; the Method of Collective Work Analysis (CWA) [21, 22]; and the Method of Workshop Photography [23]. We associated these with our previous methods: Ergonomic Analysis of Work Activity (EAWA) [7]. These practices align well with the methods and theory of the field of Workers' Health [11]. They are also in line with our pre-pandemic form and method of action.

Thus, we were able to compose a hybrid methodology that has in its scope: the elucidation of ergonomics needs; meetings with workers and with managers outside the workplace; photographic and video surveys, carried out by the workers themselves; dialogical action on work activity; identification of situations and construction of improvement proposals; restitution and validation of information for the collective of workers and for managers; and, finally, the preparation of a technical report. Through the whole process, educational actions and social construction are important transversal resources, taking place in virtual meetings by web conference.

We also highlight collective and/or individual strategies, developed over the period of social distancing: analysis of work situations prioritizing homogeneous groups; educational advances in expanded collectives; sensitization of managers to ergonomic issues; readaptation of instruments for identification of work situations that need intervention; the use of digital communication media for collective education in ergonomics; and also contribution in the multidisciplinary formulation of protocols for safe face-to-face work.

# 3 Results: The Practice in Action

## 3.1 First Action

We developed our first action with several teams of a department that develops vector control research. Here, we will present how we applied the new method with one of these teams. This ergonomic analysis looked at the activity of nine workers working in hybrid form (part in-person, part remote).

We note that their department was already familiar with the institution's ergonomic action. This intervention happened by solely virtual means. In the course of the analysis, we had to adjust the methodology.

In light of new methods, the first step was to strengthen the social construction that began pre-pandemic. We also reached out to Human Resources and department managers to obtain support for our action. In this stage, we used resources such as infographics or presentations in virtual meetings. Next, we structured a schedule for other virtual meetings.

In the first meeting with the workers, we briefly introduced the concepts of ergonomics and presented the proposed action. We then invited any adjustments to the schedule, as necessary.

In this first virtual meeting, we (ergonomists and workers) also established a verbal contract, with two basic criteria. First: the meetings would last a maximum of 2 h. Second: the workers' statements, during the meetings, would be presented as collective and non-individualized speech.

The first criterion serves to avoid the effects of zoom fatigue. For Wiederhold [24] it is important to limit the time of use of video conferencing technologies. He points out issues related to the potential for network connectivity generate a direct influence on the brain mechanism responsible for synchrony. The misalignment between the video's image and sound, even in milliseconds, generates an increase in cognitive load because there is an increase in brain effort to achieve the necessary adjustment.

The second criterion stems from respect for the premises of the fields of workers' health and ergonomics. It aims to promote the construction of knowledge about work in a dialogical, participative, and collective way. Seeking to foster the strengthening of the work collective, as well as the improvement of work processes.

According to the agreed schedule and the instructions presented, we divided the workers into two groups. Each group received the task to take 5 photos or short videos that illustrated health-promoting situations at work (positive) and another 5 of non-health-promoting situations (negative).

The workers themselves presented the photos and videos at virtual meetings. The material served as a source for understanding and discussion about depicted issues.

Through a process of knowledge construction, we sought to develop the topics that arose, while keeping focus on the situations demonstrated in the photos. We raised and discussed the issues related to the work process, started a process of reflection on the work, and drafted proposals for improvements.

Later, we returned our findings to the collective and validated them. To respect agreements, we held several meetings. This allowed the elaboration of proposals for improvements through a process of reflection and sharing knowledge about the work activity.

We made written records, which along with photos and videos, served as the basis for the action report.

The following Table 1 gives a summary of some general data from the analysis:

**Table 1.** Records/Situation/Proposal.

| Positive records | Negative records | Positive situations | Negative situations | Total of proposals |
|---|---|---|---|---|
| 11 | 10 | 15 | 22 | 41 |

The record shows that, despite the reduced number of photographs, they allowed for several topics to be worked on. The number of issues registered were 76% higher than initially listed by workers. As a result, the number of proposals was 95% higher than initial issues.

In terms of participation, 100% of the team fully participated in the process in 100% of the meetings.

## 3.2  Second Action

The second activity took place 100% online. Here, the stage of social construction was also completely online.

The proposal foresaw the following phases (see Fig. 1).

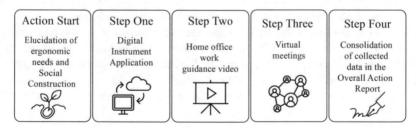

**Fig. 1.** Infographic proposal presented at the beginning of the action.

To present the proposal for action we held a videoconference with the workers. We also invited human resources, and management, to obtain support for the development ergonomic action. In this meeting, we briefly introduced the concepts of ergonomics and presented the proposed action.

Previously, the demand for ergonomic action was not clear. Thus, the virtual meeting also served to elucidate the needs for transformation perceived by the workers. About 30 out of 607 workers attended this meeting. Of these, two filled out the ergonomic needs survey form.

We carried out individual interventions with these two workers. Postural orientation and adjustment of their home office workplaces were made.

## 4  Discussion: Perceptions and Perspectives

The context presented brings to light the potential for adjustment to the variability imposed upon the work activity of both the ergonomist, and the workers. We all need to rebuild ways of working and relating to work and the work collective.

If, on the one hand, the new method allowed us to perform ergonomic action in different places, on the other, several difficulties can be identified. The SWOT Matrix below outlines this relationship (see Fig. 2).

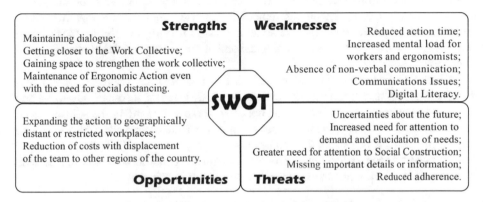

**Strengths**
Maintaining dialogue;
Getting closer to the Work Collective;
Gaining space to strengthen the work collective;
Maintenance of Ergonomic Action even
with the need for social distancing.

**Weaknesses**
Reduced action time;
Increased mental load for
workers and ergonomists;
Absence of non-verbal communication;
Communications Issues;
Digital Literacy.

**SWOT**

Expanding the action to geographically
distant or restricted workplaces;
Reduction of costs with displacement
of the team to other regions of the country.

**Opportunities**

Uncertainties about the future;
Increased need for attention to
demand and elucidation of needs;
Greater need for attention to Social Construction;
Missing important details or information;
Reduced adherence.

**Threats**

**Fig. 2.** SWOT Matrix analyzing the virtual action.

The issues related to social construction required even more effective care. Building the relationships of trust with the workers, to generate openness to work transformations, required greater commitment from the ergonomists. We observed that in workplaces where previous actions were carried out, and therefore, the social construction had already been carried out, the success of the activity was more evident.

Further study is needed to establish this correlation. However, our perception is that virtual action with smaller groups makes for more effective results than the large-group approach. This is important in respect to both the social construction, and the practice of EAWA itself.

With the advent of social distancing, much of the work activity began to adapt and to be executed through video conferencing, as did personal activities. The effects of brain synchronism, known as "zoom fatigue" [24] add to the cognitive demands of the task itself and characterize an increase in the mental workload.

The absence of face-to-face interaction does not allow for the perception of the gestures, looks and postures adopted by the participants [25]. Such expressions characterize nonverbal communication and are important during the development of work with groups. Often, they offer clues about information that could go unnoticed. However, in our first case with virtual group work, the participation of workers was verbally very active. The quantity and quality of issues raised and discussed was relevant. As ergonomists, our impression, in this case, was that the absence of nonverbal communications did not interfere in the final result of the action.

We noticed a larger volume of collected data. Its detail seemed to us to have depth at the level of the specificities of the work activity. For the ergonomic team, this volume of information generated more focus switching between data collection and the group of workers during the meetings. Thus, in this case, it became necessary to enlist another ergonomist as an observer/ rapporteur, in addition to those conducting the action.

A deeper understanding of the subject is necessary, but it is our perception that: in this remote modality, attention becomes a competence that the ergonomist must train. While on-site, we were immersed in the work situation. Different elements filled our senses: environment, furniture, equipment, temperature, noise, among others that crossed our perceptions. All of these were available for analysis. In remote conditions, the resources we used most were: attention to dialogical action; and visual attention, despite visual field restrictions.

Digital literacy concerns the capacities and potentialities related to interactions between people and technological resources [26–28]. It was also an issue to be considered in the processes of interaction between workers. Regarding the adjustments of ergonomists and workers, the pandemic situation demanded rapid adaptation to technological means. There was no time to develop training processes. This could have been another obstacle to the development of totally virtual ergonomic action. However, it did not constitute a hindrance in the experiences reported in this article.

## 5   Conclusions

Through the analysis of the ergonomic practices, we could access variability, adaptations, and different ways of developing work activity. Despite adverse conditions, the methodological composition could value dialogical and collective action.

We also observed inflection points in distance practice in several workplaces. We highlight the need for greater care in the stages of elucidation of ergonomics needs and social construction during this pandemic moment.

The sharing of experiences on the adaptations and innovations generated to enable the work in this scenario aims to contribute to the enrichment of the field of ergonomics. In addition, we could reflect on our practice, and provoke debate.

It is a fact that on-site observation is irreplaceable. However, in its impossibility, we were able to use the available resources to promote conversations about the work as well as, at some level, work transformations.

## References

1. Daniellou, F. (org): L'ergonomie en quête de ses principes: débats épistémologiques. Octarès éditions, France (2015)
2. Falzon, P.: Ergonomie. Presses Universitaires de France, Paris Cedex 14, France (2004)

3. Teiger, C., Lacomblez, M.: (Se) former pour transformer le travail: dynamiques de constructions d'une analyse critique du travail. Presses de l'Université Laval, Québec (2013)
4. Wisner, A.: Por dentro do trabalho ergonomia: métodos e técnicas. FTD, Brasil (1987)
5. Wisner, A.: A inteligência no trabalho: textos selecionados de Ergonomia. Fundacentro, Brasil (2003)
6. Vidal, M.C.: Guia para análise ergonômica do trabalho (AET) na empresa: uma metodologia realista, ordenada e sistemática. EVC, Rio de Janeiro, Brasil (2003)
7. Lacomblez, M., Bellemare, M., Chatigny, C., Delgoulet, C., Re, A., Trudel, L., Vasconcelos, R.: Ergonomic analysis of work activity and training: basic paradigm, evolutions and challenges. In: Pikaar, R.N., Koningsveld, E.A.P., Settels, P.J.M. (orgs.) International Ergonomics Association, Meeting Diversity in Ergonomics, pp. 129–142. Elsevier, Amsterdam, Boston (2007)
8. WEF, W.E.F.: The Future of Jobs Report. World Economic Forum. https://www.weforum.org/reports/the-future-of-jobs-report-2020. Accessed 15 Jan 2021
9. Viana, A.A., Pepe, C.C.C.A., da Gertner, S.R.C.B. (orgs): Guia de Orientação da Saúde do Trabalhador: convivência com a Covid-19 e atividades de trabalho, Brasil (2020)
10. Vasconcellos, L.C.F.: Saúde, trabalho e desenvolvimento sustentável: apontamentos para uma Política de Estado, Brasil (2007)
11. Minayo Gómez, C., Machado, J.M.H., Pena, P.G.L. (orgs): Saúde do trabalhador na sociedade brasileira contemporânea. Editora Fiocruz, Brasil (2011)
12. Minayo-Gomez, C., Thedim-Costa, S.: Incorporation of the social sciences in the production of knowledge about work and health. Ciência & Saúde Coletiva 8, 125–136 (2003). https://doi.org/10.1590/S1413-81232003000100010
13. Wisner, A.: A metodologia na ergonomia ontem e hoje. In: A inteligência no trabalho, p. 192. Fundacentro, Brasil (1994)
14. Guérin, F.: Comprendre le travail pour le transformer: la pratique de l'ergonomie. Agence nationale pour l'amélioration des conditions de travail, Montrouge, France (2001)
15. Ricart, S.L.S.I., Vidal, M.C.R., Bonfatti, R.J.: Evaluation and control of ergonomics actions in federal public service: the case of FIOCRUZ - RJ. Work 41, 532–538 (2012). https://doi.org/10.3233/WOR-2012-0208-532
16. Ricart, S.: Avaliação e Controle de Ações Ergonômicas no Serviço Público Federal: O Caso da FIOCRUZ – RJ, Brasil (2011)
17. Bonfatti, R.J., Vidal, M.C.: EAMETA: um método amigável de análise participativa de situações de trabalho. Ação Ergonômica 11, 1–16 (2017)
18. Jatobá, A., Bellas, H.C., Bonfatti, R., Burns, C.M., Vidal, M.C.R., de Carvalho, P.V.R.: Designing for patient risk assessment in primary health care: a case study for ergonomic work analysis. Cogn. Tech. Work. 18, 215–231 (2016). https://doi.org/10.1007/s10111-015-0355-x
19. Lacomblez, M., Teiger, C., Vasconcelos, R.: A ergonomia e o "paradigma da formação dos atores": uma parceria formadora com os protagonistas do trabalho. In: Métodos de pesquisa e intervenção em psicologia do trabalho: clínicas do trabalho, Atlas, Brasil, pp. 159–183 (2014)
20. Neves, M.Y.R., Alvarez, D., da Silva-Roosli, A.C.B., Moraes, T.D., Masson, L.P., de Oliveira, V.A.N., Neves, M.Y.R., Alvarez, D., da Silva-Roosli, A.C.B., Moraes, T.D., Masson, L.P., de Oliveira, V.A.N.: Action-training: a reading of the contributions of the Activity Ergonomics. Fractal: Revista de Psicologia 30, 112–120 (2018). https://doi.org/10.22409/1984-0292/v30i2/5872
21. Ferreira, L.: Análise Coletiva do Trabalho: quer ver? Escuta. Revista Ciências do Trabalho, Brasil, no. 4, pp. 125–137 (2015)
22. Ferreira, L.: L'analyse collective du travail et les syndicats. In: Teiger, C., Lacomblez, M. (orgs.) (Se) Former pour transformer le travail: dynamiques de constructions d'une analyse critique du travail, pp. 243–248. Presses de l'Université Laval, Québec (2013)

23. Osorio, C., Pacheco, A.B., de Barros, M.E.B.: Oficinas de fotos: experiências brasileiras em clínica da atividade. Cad. Psicol. Soc. Trab. **16**, 121 (2013). https://doi.org/10.11606/issn. 1981-0490.v16ispe1p121-131
24. Wiederhold, B.K.: Connecting through technology during the coronavirus disease 2019 pandemic: avoiding "Zoom Fatigue". Cyberpsychol. Behav. Soc. Netw. **23**, 437–438 (2020). https://doi.org/10.1089/cyber.2020.29188.bkw
25. Goffman, E.: Ritual de la interacción. Tiempo Contemporáneo, Argentina (1970)
26. Bawden, D.: Origins and concepts of digital literacy. In: Lankshear, C., Knobel, M. (orgs.) Digital Literacies: Concepts, Policies and Practices. Peter Lang, Switzerland (2008)
27. Belshaw, D.: What is "Digital Literacy"? A Pragmatic Investigation. Durham University, UK (2012). https://etheses.dur.ac.uk/3446/
28. Collard, A.-S., De Smedt, T., Dufrasne, M., Fastrez, P., Ligurgo, V., Patriarche, G., Philippette, T.: Digital media literacy in the workplace: a model combining compliance and inventivity. Ital. J. Sociol. Educ. **9**, 122–154 (2017). https://doi.org/10.14658/pupj-ijse-2017-1-7

# Overcoming the Challenges of Remote Home Office Assessments

Josie Blake[✉] and Carrie Taylor

Taylor'd Ergonomics Incorporated, Cambridge, Canada
josie@taylordergo.com

**Abstract.** COVID-19 required ergonomists to provide virtual office ergonomics assessments. We responded by developing an assessment process as close to our in-person assessment process as possible to ensure that the quality of the report and recommendations was not comprised. We have found success in using pre-recorded videos and video chat to capture key information about an employee's home office environment, make adjustments to the employee's workstation, and provide sound recommendations for improvement.

**Keywords:** Ergonomics · COVID-19 · Virtual assessment

## 1 Introduction and Problem

COVID-19 has changed the way ergonomists work and has required many office workers to work from home, temporarily at first, and now some permanently. Most home offices lack ergonomic furniture, which in turn has led to rampant discomfort for many home office workers. Employers who previously offered ergonomics support for employees were challenged to provide a thorough, effective remote assessment. Clients were unwilling to pay as much for a virtual assessment as they would have for an in-person assessment because they anticipated that the situation would be temporary. Some clients were reluctant to pay for furniture and accessories, preferring for employees to use materials at hand, or to purchase their own items. Ergonomists needed to find a way to provide sound advice for temporary, and now permanent, home office measures without visiting these employees in person. This paper outlines how we have overcome this challenge and discusses the cost-benefit and validity of this new approach compared to on-site ergonomics assessments.

## 2 Context

A full in-person office assessment involves a pre-assessment survey, interview, measurements of the employee and workplace, photographs, observations of the employee at work, immediate adjustments to the equipment and furniture, identification of work practices, repairs or purchases required, including vendor links to the appropriate products, completion of a report, review of a follow-up survey, and action on outstanding issues.

N. L. Black et al. (Eds.): IEA 2021, LNNS 221, pp. 13–20, 2021.
https://doi.org/10.1007/978-3-030-74608-7_2

When completing a virtual assessment, several of the steps required to provide objective advice and to be confident in recommending solutions that would reduce or eliminate discomfort present quite a challenge. In particular, these are difficult to conduct remotely: measurements of the employee and workplace, photographs, observations of the employee at work, adjustments, identifying work practices, and recommending repairs or purchases.

We needed to develop a way to "see" the employees in their work-from-home environment, to communicate effectively virtually, and to make effective recommendations, all without physically touching the workspace, using a tape measure, or making "live" observations of the employee's work habits. How could we be certain whether the employee can touch-type, or if the employee crosses the legs under the desk? How would we be able to confirm, objectively, that the employee's seated elbow height is aligned with the height of the work surface?

In our experience, one-on-one office ergonomics assessments are more effective than e-learning. How were we going to provide the same quality of assessment without physically visiting the employees in their workspaces?

## 3  Actions

### 3.1  Market Research

To develop an effective process, we completed some online market research, looking for virtual assessments that were already available in Canada. Based on what we found, we created an outline of what we thought our virtual office ergonomics assessment process might look like. We interviewed 6 clients to determine if we were on the right track. We asked the following questions:

1.  Do you have any experience with remote assessments? If so, what went well? Where were the challenges?
2.  We've done some market research and $250 seems like the going rate for a virtual assessment. Does that seem reasonable for an assessment of one person at one workstation?
3.  This price allows us considerably less time than an in-person assessment. What would you (as a customer) be hoping to achieve through the process? What would you hope to see in the report?
4.  What video conference options would work best for employees at your company, noting that we would be connecting from outside your company? (Facetime, Zoom, MS teams, Skype, Webex, Messenger, etc.)
5.  Would you have concerns regarding how much of the employee's time is required? We anticipate that 15–30 min will be required before the assessment, and an hour for the interview and adjustments. Is that reasonable?
6.  Right now, we are focusing on interventions that could be made with household items (e.g. books to be used as a footrest, a rolled towel for lumbar support). If the employee could benefit from purchased items (small equipment like footrests and lumbar supports, or bigger expenses such as desks and chairs),

    a.  Would you want us to assist with those? (Specifying furniture like chairs and desks can take more time than we have budgeted, and usually involves measurements, or requires the employee to visit a vendor… neither of these are possible right now. We can certainly suggest more specific smaller items, although without precise measurements it may be more of a "best guess".)

    b.  Would your company be willing to purchase equipment and/or furniture for home offices? (Do you currently have a process/budget for home office equipment and/or furnishings?)

7.  Our in-person assessment includes a follow-up survey and response. To keep within market-price, we will not be able to include this. How important is the follow-up? Should we increase the price to allow it? If we offer an optional follow-up, what do you think a reasonable price might be?

## 3.2   Develop Virtual Office Assessment Process

After completing market research and client interviews, we created a more robust outline of the virtual office assessment process.

First, we adapted our in-person pre-assessment discomfort survey to better describe the virtual assessment process to the employee. The surveys collected similar information, but the virtual assessment survey also asked about how long the employee has been working from home and asked the employee what equipment was available at their home office. For example, is an external keyboard, mouse, and/or monitor available? We also asked the employee to gather some "supplies", such as boxes or books to raise monitors or to use as a footrest, and a towel or scarf for temporary lumbar support, if required [1].

**Fig. 1.** A screen-shot showing the angle the "side" video is taken from.

**Fig. 2.** A screen-shot showing the angle the "behind and above" video is taken from.

As part of the pre-assessment survey, we asked employees to submit two 30-s videos of themselves working at their home office: one from the "side" to show heights of the workstation relative to the body, and forward reach to the keyboard, mouse, and other frequently used items (shown in Fig. 1), and one from behind and above to show lateral reaching distances and monitor position (shown Fig. 2). We created a short instructional video for employees to help ensure the videos would be of good quality for the ergonomist. We anticipated that this process would save time during the assessment interview as the ergonomist would be able to identify some issues from the videos and come up with ideas for solutions before the assessment interview [1].

We created the report template as a fillable form designed to be completed as the assessment was taking place to improve efficiency. We included all of our assessment criteria in the template to ensure all observations and suggestions were as consistent as possible between ergonomists. We also hoped to complete parts of the report *before* the assessment, while observing the videos. This process allowed us to "flag" specific questions for the employee, and to make note of potential solutions to trial during the assessment [1].

### 3.3    Trialed, Tested, and Put the Virtual Office Assessment to Market

To trial the assessment process, we ran a "test" run-through of a full assessment using our own employees. We made minor improvements to the report template and refined the process for making "live" observations through video chat.

After we had run a few internal trials, we offered to complete an assessment for a client in exchange for feedback on the process. We incorporated this feedback into our process and template and marketed the virtual assessment process through our website, email, and social media.

### 3.4    Complete Assessments and Refine the Process

We started completing assessments for our regular clients. We made continuous edits to the report template and process based on client feedback. We are still refining the virtual assessment process as the work-from-home situation appears to be a permanent reality for many employees. Clients are now asking for objective measurements to be taken to ensure allow objective recommendations, especially when more expensive solutions (e.g. new chair or desk) are required [1].

## 4    Outcomes

### 4.1    Market Research

During our market research, we found that the going rate for the few services that were available in Canada was around $250 (CAD). We could not find many details on how long the assessments took, whether or how the assessments included objective measurements, which virtual platforms they used to make "observations", and whether follow-up was included in that price. We only found one service that confirmed the use of a pre-assessment survey.

During our client interviews, we found that none had experience with virtual ergonomics assessments. Clients reported, on average, a perceived value for a virtual assessment of about 50% of the charge for an in-person assessment. Some expressed that they found $250 a bit high as, at the time of the interviews, they believed the work-from-home situation was only going to be temporary. For the same reason, most clients were only willing to spend the "minimum required" to help employees be comfortable and likely would not be making furniture purchases (i.e. chair and desk) for employee's home offices. Most clients were flexible on the platforms used to connect virtually with employees (e.g. Zoom, Microsoft Teams, etc.), but stated their internal preference. Finally, the consensus was that a follow-up should *not* be included in the price for the virtual assessment, and should be an optional add-on if the employee is still experiencing severe discomfort after the initial assessment.

### 4.2    The Virtual Office Assessment Process

As we developed the virtual assessment process, we concluded that we needed to allow ourselves to make more decisions based on observations and the employee interview, instead of measurements, and so our report template was designed to accommodate this approach.

We felt confident in our pre-assessment survey as this had not changed much from the in-person survey. We felt that the videos taken before the assessment would be challenging for the employee to take, especially if they live alone (no-one to take the video for them). However, we worked to provide the necessary resources and "tips" so that employees could provide us with good-quality videos that we could use to make observations. We found that most employees had challenges with space (for example, a very small home office), and taking the "behind and above" video (for example, no shelf or bookcase behind their desk, or no-one else to take the video). Many employees failed to follow the instructions in the video, and attempted to send their videos by email; the videos typically would not transmit through email, and a reminder to use a file-transfer site became a touchpoint in our communication before the assessment [1].

Developing a report format was challenging because we wanted it to be easy to fill out, and easy for employers to read. We made many revisions but eventually settled on a chart-style report with space for before and after photographs beside the relevant assessment criteria, adjustments made, and recommendations. We included ergonomist cues for observations, questions, and recommendations throughout the assessment in the "comments" feature (not visible to the employer in the final report)[1]. These criteria and cues have helped us to ensure consistency in report writing and recommendations between ergonomists.

Completing the assessment interview through video chat has been most successful when we can connect with the employee through a portable device such as a smartphone or tablet. The employee can position the device to allow the ergonomist to "see" the adjustments as they are made, to provide feedback to the employee, and to determine whether the furniture or equipment can be adjusted to fit. We have been able to coach the employee to use the supplies that they gathered, to "trial" footrests, monitor risers, and lumbar support as needed. We can take a screen-shot of the video call to include in the report as an "after" photograph, to show the employer the adjustments that were made and any outstanding issues[1]. Assessments completed with the employee using a built-in webcam on a laptop have resulted in lower confidence in making sound recommendations, as the ergonomist is unable to visually confirm if the adjustments were made, or whether the furniture could adjust to accommodate the employee's body size.

## 4.3  Completing Assessments and Refining the Process

We have completed many virtual assessments to date. Without measurements, we continue to be challenged to specify recommendations. For example, without seat pan width and anthropometric data, we may not be able to recommend an appropriate chair. We are learning to coach employees through the measurement process in these cases, to meet client requests for objective measurements, where employees expect to work from home more permanently [1].

Pre-COVID 19, we were concerned about privacy issues, and about the use of phones and tablets for video calls. However, employees are free to block, or not show, personal items in the background of their videos. The use of phones for workplace communication has become commonplace. We have not received any objections to using photos of employees working in their home offices to document workplace conditions, adjustments made, and outstanding problems.

Overall, our clients have been impressed by the amount of detail we have been able to capture in a virtual setting. In particular, they liked how we were able to include "before" and "after" photographs to show adjustments that we had made.

## 5 Discussion

Several challenges were encountered through the development and use of the virtual office assessment process.

Initially, when employees did not complete the survey and video before the assessment, the assessment could not be completed at the originally scheduled time. Therefore, we now schedule assessments in a three-step process:

1. Invite the employee to submit survey/video (and wait to receive),
2. Offer time slots (and wait for selection)
3. Confirm assessment, and request employee to invite ergonomist to video chat.

Unfortunately, while the assessment process takes less time compared to an in-person assessment, the administrative time is longer, for a remote assessment, which increases costs slightly.

The process involves considerable effort on the employee's part, which must be supported by the employer. The employee fills out a survey and creates two short videos. Employees who do not review the instructions have difficulty setting up the camera. Video files get "stuck" if they are not sent through the correct portal, and then the scheduling process breaks down (employee thinks video sent, meanwhile ergonomist is still waiting for video). However, in general, we have found that we have provided employees with enough resources to allow them to take good quality videos, and without exception, the videos have been critical to the effectiveness of the process.

We also often find that employees do not gather the supplies (boxes/books and towel/scarf) requested before the assessment. This makes it more challenging for us to "convince" employees that they need a footrest, for example. If the assessment is running on schedule, there may be time for the ergonomist to "wait" for the employee to find a suitable item to trial. However, this is an inefficient use of the ergonomist's time.

The flexibility to use the video-chat platform of the employee's choice is important since the employee generally needs to contact the ergonomist from a phone, rather than a computer. We have learned how to use multiple platforms, including Zoom, Microsoft Teams, Skype, Facebook Messenger, and Facetime to facilitate the assessments [1]. However, a poor internet connection on either end can make the assessment process awkward or frustrating.

During the development of the process, employers asserted that specific product recommendations were not required, a follow-up survey was not important, and dimensions were not necessary. However, employers are now asking for these items. We are never as confident in making purchase recommendations without measurements. When an employee requires a custom chair, we are always concerned that we might not be able to specify the appropriate features. Fortunately, we are seeing success in reducing employees' discomfort, and we are becoming more confident that our recommendations are valid. Coaching employees to obtain key measurements also provides the ergonomist, the employer, and the employee with more confidence in purchasing costly equipment [1]. However, this step takes additional time, which increases the cost of the assessment.

The validity of our assessments has been confirmed only through informal feedback from our clients and their employees, stating that the adjustments and recommendations have been successful in reducing discomfort and increasing the morale of work-from-home employees. Ideally, in the future when internal resources are available, more objective feedback should be collected and analyzed, including post-assessment discomfort surveys and productivity scores. In-person follow-up assessments should be completed for the same employees who received a virtual assessment to determine how reliable video chat is for making adjustments and recommending appropriate equipment.

## 6    Conclusion

Although we encountered challenges, we have found that employees and employers are generally grateful for remote office assessments. The provision of this service allows us to complete assessments in geographical areas that would previously have been infeasible. We are fortunate to be able to support home office workers during a difficult time, and we are grateful to have work to do when our other clients could not permit us access to the workplace.

## Reference

1.  Taylor'd Ergonomics Inc.: Virtual Office Ergonomics Assessment Process (2020)

# Does a 12-hour Shift Affect Brazilian Workers' Mental and Physical Health?

Flávia Helen Moreira da Silva[✉] and Marina Greghi Sticca

University of São Paulo, Ribeirão Preto, Brazil
flavia.helen.silva@usp.br, marinagreghi@ffclrp.usp.br

**Abstract.** This study aims to analyze the impact of the 12-hour work shift on the indices of physical and mental health, sleep, and work-family conflict of Brazilian road traffic inspectors. This project was run in a Brazilian highway concession company, based on developing a previous organizational diagnosis focused on Quality of Life at Work, which pointed out potential illness risk-carrying work organization aspects. Among them, the work shift was the target of dissatisfaction among operational workers. The project was carried out in three stages: stage 1: demand identification; stage 2: a survey was carried out with workers, based on the application of the Pittsburgh Sleep Quality Index; Physical Health Questionnaire; Work-Related Damage Assessment Scale (WRDAS), and Work-Family Conflict Scale (WAFCS); stage 3: results, diagnoses, and actions presentation. The survey counted on the participation of 42 road traffic inspectors in the company, representing a participation rate of 87.5% of the staff holding this position. All the participants were men, mostly aged 28–37 years (57%), with high school education (55%), married (71%), and with children (67%). As for the variables evaluated by the instruments, a high incidence of poor sleep quality (40%) was observed, while most had a good quality of sleep (57%). As for the variables related to physical, mental health, and social work-life relationship, the tools employed did not show negative impacts. The results obtained with this research were used to suggest preventive actions.

**Keywords:** 12-hour work shift · Mental · Health · Physical

## 1 Introduction

This project was run in a Brazilian highway concession company, based on developing a previous organizational diagnosis focused on Quality of Life at Work, which pointed out potential illness risk-carrying work organization aspects. Among them, the work shift was the target of dissatisfaction among operational workers. The company also presented the possibility of changing the shift to a 12 × 36-hour work/rest shift as a financial strategy. Before the change, traffic inspectors' work schedule was 6 × 2 workdays/rest, with three shifts (morning - from 6 am to 2 pm; afternoon - from 2 pm to 10 pm; night - from 10 pm to 6 am). The new 12 × 36 work/rest shift was implemented in the COVID-19 pandemic, and the project aimed to assess its impacts on workers after a month of change to support organizational decisions and actions.

© The Author(s), under exclusive license to Springer Nature Switzerland AG 2021
N. L. Black et al. (Eds.): IEA 2021, LNNS 221, pp. 21–27, 2021.
https://doi.org/10.1007/978-3-030-74608-7_3

This work aims to analyze the impact of the 12-hour work shift on the indices of physical and mental health, sleep, and work-family conflict of Brazilian road traffic inspectors.

### 1.1  Impact of 12-hour Work Shift on Workers' Health

The literature points out that long work shifts affect workers, leading to sleep (Ferreira et al. 2017; Wickwire et al. 2017) and circadian cycle imbalance, fatigue (Dorrian et al. 2011; Motamedzadeh et al. 2016), gastrointestinal (Choobineh et al. 2012) and cardiovascular symptoms (Marqueze et al. 2013; Skogstad et al. 2019), work-family relationship disruption (Estryn-Béhar and Van Der Heijden 2012), and other psychological disorders (Bazazan et al. 2014).

## 2  Methodology

### 2.1  Participants

The survey counted on the participation of 42 road traffic inspectors in the company, representing a participation rate of 87.5% of the staff holding this position. All the participants were men, mostly aged 28–37 years (57%), with high school education (55%), married (71%), and with children (67%). Table 1 shows the occupational data of participants.

**Table 1.**  Occupational data of participants.

| PREVIOUS WORKING HOURS | | | CURRENT WORKING HOURS | | |
|---|---|---|---|---|---|
| | f | % | | f | % |
| 06h to 14h | 14 | 33% | 06h to 18h | 19 | 45% |
| 14h to 22h | 11 | 26% | 18h to 6h | 23 | 55% |
| 22h to 06h | 12 | 29% | | | |
| Vacation relief worker | 5 | 12% | | | |

| | WORK SENIORITY | | | | |
|---|---|---|---|---|---|
| | f | % | | f | % |
| 0 to 6 months | 13 | 31% | 21 to 26 months | 4 | 10% |
| 7 to 13 months | 4 | 10% | 27 to 33 months | 6 | 14% |
| 14 to 20 months | 5 | 12% | 34 months and over | 10 | 24% |

### 2.2  Procedures

The project was carried out in three stages: In stage 1, demand was identified from meetings with the Board and Human Resources to define the project's scope. In step

2, a survey was carried out with workers, based on the application of the Pittsburgh Sleep Quality Index, to assess possible sleep pattern changes; the Physical Health Questionnaire, derived from the Standard Shiftwork Index (SSI) instrument, to identify the presence of cardiovascular and gastrointestinal symptoms; the Work-Related Damage Assessment Scale (WRDAS), to assess impacts on mental health; and, finally, the Work-Family Conflict Scale (WAFCS). Simultaneously, a systematic review of the literature was carried out to map studies that reported impacts on workers' health due to long work shifts. In step 3, we presented the results, diagnoses, and actions suggested to the Board in meetings to think together which strategies would be relevant to maintain productivity and act preventively.

### 2.3 Instruments

The following instruments were used in step 2: i) The Pittsburgh Sleep Quality Index (PSQI); ii) The Physical Health Questionnaire, derived from the Standard Shiftwork Index (SSI) instrument; iii) The Work-Related Damage Assessment Scale (WRDAS); and iv) The Work-Family Conflict Scale (WAFCS).

## 3  Results

### 3.1  Sleep Assessment

Table 2 shows the frequency of participants according to the assessment of sleep quality obtained with the PSQI instrument scores.

**Table 2.**  Frequency of participants according to the score obtained in the PSQI

| Score | f | % |
|---|---|---|
| Good Sleep Quality | 24 | 57% |
| Poor Sleep Quality | 17 | 40% |
| Sleep Disorder | 1 | 2% |

The results indicate that most workers (57%) have a good sleep quality. However, a high incidence of poor sleep quality (40%) has been observed. A Student t-test was performed to test the hypothesis of possible differences between shifts (day and night) regarding sleep quality, which did not allow inferring statistically significant differences between the two groups of workers. Therefore, we could not conclude that the different levels of sleep quality of the group of inspectors may be related to the work shift.

### 3.2  Physical Health Assessment

Regarding the results obtained with the Physical Health Questionnaire application, the percentages of responses by category of the frequency of digestive and cardiac symptoms are shown in Table 3.

**Table 3.** Frequency of responses regarding gastrointestinal and cardiovascular symptoms

| Gastrointestinal symptoms | Never | Rarely | Sometimes | Often | Always |
|---|---|---|---|---|---|
| Has your appetite been disturbed? | 83% | 17% | 0% | 0% | 0% |
| Are you careful with what you eat to avoid stomach problems? | 48% | 19% | 14% | 7% | 0% |
| Do you feel like vomiting? | 95% | 2% | 2% | 0% | 0% |
| Do you suffer from heartburn or stomach pain? | 74% | 14% | 12% | 0% | 0% |
| Do you complain about digestion problems? | 86% | 10% | 5% | 0% | 0% |
| Do you complain about bloating or gas in your stomach? | 76% | 14% | 10% | 0% | 0% |
| Do you complain about stomach pains? | 83% | 17% | 0% | 0% | 0% |
| Do you suffer from diarrhea or constipation? | 88% | 10% | 2% | 0% | 0% |
| Cardiovascular symptoms | Never | Rarely | Sometimes | Often | Always |
| Do you feel your heart beating fast? | 88% | 12% | 0% | 0% | 0% |
| Do you have chest pain and malaise? | 93% | 7% | 0% | 0% | 0% |
| Do you feel dizzy? | 88% | 10% | 2% | 0% | 0% |
| Do you feel your blood suddenly rising to your head? | 95% | 5% | 0% | 0% | 0% |
| Do you have difficulty breathing when climbing stairs? | 88% | 12% | 0% | 0% | 0% |
| Do you have high blood pressure? | 88% | 7% | 5% | 0% | 0% |
| Did you feel that your heart was beating irregularly? | 88% | 10% | 0% | 2% | 0% |
| Do you suffer from swollen feet? | 98% | 0% | 2% | 0% | 0% |
| Do you feel a "tightness" in your chest? | 93% | 7% | 0% | 0% | 0% |

We can observe that, in general, most of the participants reported not feeling these symptoms, except for the question "*Are you careful with what you eat to avoid stomach problems?*", Which had less than half (48%) of the respondents who pointed out that the symptom never occurred.

### 3.3 Mental Health Assessment

The reference values and interpretations shown in Table 4 are used to assess the scores obtained with the Work-Related Damage Assessment Scale (WRDAS).

**Table 4.** Interpretation of WRDAS scores

| Score interpretation | | |
|---|---|---|
| 1-2.2: Low-Risk | 2.3-3.6: Medium-Risk | 3.7-5: High-Risk |
| A positive result. Represents low psychosocial risks. | A median result. Represents a state of alert/borderline situation for psychosocial risks at work. Demands short- and medium-term interventions | Negative result. Represents high psychosocial risks. It requires immediate interventions in the causes to eliminate or mitigate them. |

The mean score obtained for the Inspection group was X = 1.24, with standard deviation SD = 0.28, with a frequency of 100% of participants with scores covered in the LOW-RISK category, indicating, therefore, that there are low psychosocial risks for the work-related psychological damage factor. In general, the participants indicated they never had the problems (more than 90% for all items), except for the item related to bad mood.

## 3.4   Assessing the Perception of Work-Family Conflict

Table 5 presents the range of values for interpreting the scores obtained with the application of the Work-Family Conflict Scale (WAFCS), Table 6 presents the results of the scores. The results indicate that, in general, most workers (90%) perceive no or low work interference with their family life. The mean obtained for the group was **X = 1.47**, with a standard deviation of **SD − 0.9**, which reinforces a homogeneous group perception.

**Table 5.** Interpretation of WAFCS scores.

| Score interpretation |
|---|
| 1-2.5: **no or low** work interference with the family |
| 2.6-4.5: **moderate** work interference with the family |
| Above 4.6: **high** work interference with family |

**Table 6.** Frequency of scores regarding the perceived work-family conflict

| Score | Frequency | % |
|---|---|---|
| No or low interference | 38 | 90% |
| Moderate interference | 3 | 7% |
| High interference | 1 | 2% |

## 3.5  Work Shift Satisfaction

In the opinion survey, 90% of workers stated that they felt satisfied with the 12 × 36 work schedule, and 38% pointed out that work breaks were not enough for their rest.

## 4  Discussion

The results obtained from the workers' perception did not indicate impacts on the investigated physical, mental health, and family life domains. However, in the sleep domain, we found that 40% of respondents have poor sleep quality, which can worsen if preventive and restoration measures are not taken. It was also shown that most respondents are satisfied with the new 12 × 36 work schedule, but short rest breaks in the working day are perceived.

Preventive actions have been suggested from these findings, such as i) breaks during the working day with greater frequency and duration, especially after the eighth hour of work, when the fatigue increases; ii) promoting guidance on nutrition, based on difficulties related to the lack of care in choosing food that can cause stomach problems; iii) reorganizing working hours, revising the entry-exit hours to avoid operational peak times at the end of the shift, and prevent workers from having to wake up too early, which can interfere with the quality and quantity of sleep; iv) identify tasks with higher cognitive demands that could be redistributed throughout the journey, such as the need to drive vehicles to carry out inspection and suggestion to avoid driving after 8 h of the shift; v) carry out socio-educational actions to raise awareness on the importance of a balanced sleep routine.

The results obtained with this research have limitations in their interpretations concerning sleep and health indices, which must be considered when planning actions to maintain health and quality of life at work. The instruments used to measure health and sleep indices are self-applicable and may suffer from biases in the participants' subjective tendencies to underestimate their symptoms in favor of what they deem to be a more favorable situation. The fact that 90% of the participants were satisfied with the 12 × 36 shift can also be explained by the short time they are submitted to this shift, and the symptoms of fatigue, stress, and impacts on physical health, may appear after a period of exposure to such conditions.

# 5 Conclusion

Organizational strategies to monitor service effectiveness indicators (such as service speed, number of errors), accidents, absenteeism, and assessments of employees' performance are suggested to reduce the effect of subjective biases from the instruments adopted. Another survey was also recommended three months after the first collection and regularly after that to compare the rates over time and detect possible changes that may affect employees' health and performance. Index monitoring is a strategy for preventing illness, along with organizational actions that can be adopted preventively.

# References

Ferreira, T.S., Moreira, C.Z., Guo, J., Noce, F.: Effects of a 12-hour shift on mood states and sleepiness of neonatal intensive care unit nurses. Revista Da Escola de Enfermagem **51**(1) (2017). https://doi.org/10.1590/S1980-220X2016033203202

Wickwire, E.M., Geiger-Brown, J., Scharf, S.M., Drake, C.L.: Shift work and shift work sleep disorder: clinical and organizational perspectives. Chest **151**(5), 1156–1172 (2017). https://doi.org/10.1016/j.chest.2016.12.007

Dorrian, J., Baulk, S.D., Dawson, D.: Work hours, workload, sleep and fatigue in Australian Rail Industry employees. Appl. Ergon. **42**(2), 202–209 (2011). https://doi.org/10.1016/j.apergo.2010.06.009

Motamedzadeh, M., Kazemi, R., Haidarimoghadam, R., Golmohamadi, R., Soltanian, A., Zoghipaydar, M.R.: Effects of shift work on cognitive performance, sleep quality, and sleepiness among petrochemical control room operators. J. Circadian Rhythms **14**(1), 1–8 (2016). https://doi.org/10.5334/jcr.134

Choobineh, A., Soltanzadeh, A., Tabatabaee, H., Jahangiri, M., Khavaji, S.: Health effects associated with shift work in 12-hour shift schedule among Iranian petrochemical employees. Int. J. Occup. Saf. Ergon. **18**(3), 419–427 (2012). https://doi.org/10.1080/10803548.2012.11076937

Marqueze, E.C., Ulhôa, M.A., Moreno, C.R.D.C.: Effects of irregular-shift work and physical activity on cardiovascular risk factors in truck drivers. Rev. Saúde Pública **47**(3), 497–505 (2013). https://doi.org/10.1590/S0034-8910.2013047004510

Skogstad, M., Mamen, A., Lunde, L.K., Ulvestad, B., Matre, D., Aass, H.C.D., Øvstebø, R., Nielsen, P., Samuelsen, K.N., Skare, Ø., Sirnes, P.A.: Shift work including night work and long working hours in industrial plants increases the risk of atherosclerosis. Int. J. Environ. Res. Public Health **16**(3), 521 (2019). https://doi.org/10.3390/ijerph16030521

Estryn-Béhar, M., Van Der Heijden, B.I.J.M.: Effects of extended work shifts on employee fatigue, health, satisfaction, work/family balance, and patient safety. Work **41**(Suppl. 1), 4283–4290 (2012). https://doi.org/10.3233/WOR-2012-0724-4283

Bazazan, A., Rasoulzadeh, Y., Dianat, I., Safaiyan, A., Mombeini, Z., Shiravand, E.: Demographic factors and their relation to fatigue and mental disorders in 12-hour petrochemical shift workers. Health Promot. Perspect. **4**(2), 165–172 (2014). https://doi.org/10.5681/hpp.2014.022

# Evaluating Physical Work Load and Posture During Testing of Welding Points – Case Study

Hermien Matthys[1,2]([⊠])

[1] Securex, Ghent, Belgium
hermien.matthys@securex.be
[2] External Service for Health and Safety at Work, Ghent, Belgium

**Abstract.** When manufacturing a car, robots are used for welding. To check if the welding points comply with the quality requirements, ultrasonic measurements are carried out. In the current situation, there are 29 measurement plans divided over 10 workstations, spread over the welding department. During his entire shift, a worker carries out one measurement plan on a certain workstation and then proceeds to another workstation. It happens that during the same shift a worker returns to a workstation, he visited earlier, to test another measurement plan. To reduce the travel time between workstation, the company decided to concentrate the different measurement plans on 6 workstations. In the future workers will spent more time testing welding points. In the present situation, more than 50% of the workers experienced shoulder and low back problems. To evaluate if the future situation is ergonomically acceptable, Key Indicator Method (KIM) was used. Reduction of workstations lead to a reduction in risk score of body movement (KIM-BM) and awkward body postures (KIM-ABP), but the intensity of the physical load stayed the same. To reduce the intensity of the physical load and the time spent in awkward body postures adjustments of the selected workstations were needed.

**Keywords:** Ergonomics · Physical load · Postures · Workstation · Automotive · Key Indicator Method

## 1 Background

### 1.1 Musculoskeletal Disorders

Musculoskeletal disorders (MSD) account for about 60% of work-related health problems [3]. This percentage has changed little or nothing in the last ten years. However, in Belgium, there is an increasing trend among young people (15–34 y) [5]. Of these problems, 43% are related to low back pain, 41% to upper limb pain and about 29% to lower limb pain [3]. MSD also account for about 60% of short and long-term absences [5].

The most common risk factors are prolonged standing, walking, repetitive movements, tiring postures and carrying and lifting loads [5].

## 1.2   Work Situation

In a large car assembly factory in Belgium, robots are used for welding. To check if the welding points comply with the quality requirements, ultrasonic measurements are carried out. The welding points are tested according to a measurement plan. There are 29 measurement plans divided over ten workstations, spread over the welding plant. The number of measurement plans per workstation differ from one to eleven. During his entire shift, a worker carries out one measurement plan on a certain workstation and then proceeds to another workstation. It happens that during the same shift a worker returns to a workstation, he visited earlier, to test another measurement plan.

The number of welding points to be measured varies from 23 to 343 per plan and takes 4 to 68 min. For 69% of the measurement plans the workers spent between 30 and 60 min (Table 1).

**Table 1.**  Overview measuring time of the measuring plans

| Measuring time | Number of measurement plans | % measurements plans |
| --- | --- | --- |
| $\leq$15 min | 6 | 20.69% |
| 16–$\leq$30 min | 2 | 6.90% |
| 31–$\leq$45 min | 11 | 37.93% |
| 46–$\leq$60 min | 9 | 31.03% |
| >60 | 1 | 3.45% |

To do the measurements each worker has a laptop connected to an ultrasonic measuring instrument. With two fingers the measurement unit is placed on the welding point. On the laptop the worker can see whether the welding point is good or not. To confirm the measurement results, the worker needs to press a few digits on a small numeric keypad.

Each worker has a step with a box to ride from one workstation to another. During the rides between workstations laptop and measurement instruments are in the box.

The different work stations are spread over the welding plant so that the welding points are tested close to the location where the robots weld them. When an error is found, it's easier to repair the default. On the other hand, a of lot of time is lost during a shift because of travelling between work stations.

The company decided to concentrate the testing of the welding points on six workstations, that were designed as ergonomic workstations, to reduce travel time. Three of the selected workstations can be tilted and one is in height adjustable.

Because already more than 50% of the workers experienced shoulder and low back problems, the question was raised if reducing the number of workstations would be ergonomically acceptable, and if not, what additional preventive measures should be taken.

## 2 Objective

The objective of this study was to evaluate if grouping of the measurements by a reduction of workstations is ergonomically acceptable and/or if additional preventive measures should be taken.

## 3 Methodology

Both for the present and the future situation, physical workload was evaluated by observation and video recording. For the present situation a worker was observed and filmed during a normal working day. The future situation was divided in two day schedules, as would be performed in the future. Five different workstations were done in schedule 1 and four workstation in schedule 2. Each schedule was carried out by a worker, who was observed and filmed.

Based on the information we received during the observation and of the videos, different Key Indicators Methods (KIM) were used [2]. KIM is developed by BAuA, the German Federal Institute for Occupational Safety and Health and was renewed in 2019 and expanded to six tools: lifting, holding and carrying (KIM-LHC), pulling and pushing (KIM-PP), manual work processes (KIM-MHO), whole-body forces (KIM-BF), body movement (KIM-BM) and forced body postures (KIM-ABP). They are quick user-friendly tools that can be applied at the workplace itself. The result of a KIM-tool is a risk score that can be used as an evaluation of the intensity of the load, the probability of the physical overload and the possible health consequences [2] (Table 2).

To evaluate the measuring of the welding point with ultrasonic testing, KIM-MHO was used. KIM-BM was filled in for the movement with the step between workstations. Per workstation KIM-ABP was used to evaluate the body posture during measuring. This means that per observed working day several KIM-ABP, one KIM-MHO and one KIM-BM were filled in.

**Table 2.** Relationship between KIM-risk score, intensity of the load and physical overload

| Risk score | Intensity of load | Probability of physical overload |
|---|---|---|
| <20 | Low | Unlikely |
| 20–<50 | Slightly increased | Possible for less resilient persons |
| 50–<100 | Substantially increased | Possible for normally resilient persons |
| >100 | High | Physical overload likely |

The results of all the KIM-methods per working day where imported in the Multi-KIM form (LMM-Multi-E). The LMM-Multi-E combines the assessment results of different sub-activities of a typical working day to determine the daily load [1]. Only the results of the different sub-activities of the same risk and evaluated by the same tool are combined [1].

In this case study LMM-Multi-E combined per working day (present, future schedule 1 and future schedule 2) the different KIM-APB to determine the daily work load. For KIM-BM and KIM-MHO only one tool was filled in which means that the risk score of the tool is the same as the risk score of the daily load.

During the observation workers were asked what they experienced as heavy and why.

## 4  Results

Comparing (Table 3) the scores of the LMM-Multi-E in the different situations future schedule 2 has the lowest scores for KIM-ABP and KIM-BM but has the highest score for KIM-MHO. Future schedule 1 has the lowest score for KIM-MHO but scores in the middle for KIM-BM and KIM-ABP between present and future -schedule 2. Although the scores for KIM-BM and KIM-ABP are in the future schedule 1 and 2 lower than the present, the risk score stays in the same category of load intensity: 20–<50: slightly increased, 50–<100: substantially increased and >100: high. With KIM-MHO the score of future -schedule 1 is in load intensity 3 while for the other situations the load intensity is 4.

By concentrating the testing of the welding points on six work stations, there is improvement score-wise for KIM-BM and KIM-ABP between the present and the future and for KIM-MHO between the present and future schedule 1 (Table 3).

**Table 3.** Results risk score LMM-Multi-E for current and future situation

| Situation | KIM-MHO | KIM-BM | KIM-ABP |
|---|---|---|---|
| Present | 101.8 | 48.1 | 145.2 |
| Future schedule 1 | 96.6 | 38.9 | 137.9 |
| Future schedule 2 | 109.8 | 33.1 | 101.9 |

The answer on the question what workers perceived as heavy was regular standing in awkward positions during measuring: back bent forward more than 20°, twisting and/or lateral inclination of the trunk and reaching far with the arms.

## 5  Discussion

As the results show in Table 3, the risk scores for measuring the welding points didn't vary a lot between the present and future situation, because the way of measuring remained the same. Only with future schedule 1 the risk score is a little lower then the rest because the total measuring time is less than the other situations. Therefore, to reduce the intensity of the load it is advisable to change the way welding points are measured and/or to reduce the measuring time. The latter is only possible when the time spent measuring is reduced by at least 50%. This means job rotation with another task where there is no risk for repetitive work. This is in contradiction with what the workers perceive. They didn't see the need of changing the measuring method and tools.

The risk scores for KIM-BM for the current and future situations were less than 50, indicating that the intensity of the load was slightly increased and physical overload is possible for less resilient persons. According to the workers, moving from one work station to another was a welcome change with regard to the awkward positions they had to work in when carrying out certain measurements.

Because already more than 50% of the workers experienced low back and shoulder problems improving the body postures during measuring was the most important measure to be taken. To reduce the combined risk score of KIM-ABP it is necessary to adapt the working stations.

Two of the six workstations had rotating fixtures so that the testing piece can be adjusted in such a way that the worker can perform the testing in acceptable postures for the different joints (low back, neck, shoulders, elbow, wrists) as mentioned in the European norm EN 1005-4 [4]. At another work station the part to be measured could be turned around its axis but was still too high. For this workstation it was advised to provide an in height adjustable work platform for the workers. Another work station was adjustable in height, but the degree of adjustability was too limited in relation to the plans to be measured. Here it was advised to expand the adjustability of the workstation or to provide an in height adjustable work platform. The other workstations were not adjustable. To reduce the time that workers worked in awkward body postures [4] it was advised that these workstations can be turned around.

## 6  Conclusion

When comparing the results of LMM-Multi-E for the present and future situations with the perception of the workers, there is a difference. improving the working postures was the most important measure for the workers. While the LMM-Multi-E indicated that measuring instruments and work postures needed additional preventive measures to lower the intensity of the work load during measuring.

**Acknowledgments.** The author wish to acknowledge Mr. Philippe Kiss for his useful linguistic advice. She extends special thanks to André Kruse, MD, Director of Securex, for the support to realize this study.

## References

1. BAuA. Hinweise zur Nutzung des PDF-Formulars zur belastungsartspezifischen Zusammen-fassung der Beurteilungen mit den Leitmerkmalmethoden über verschiedene Teil-Tätigkeiten eines Arbeitstages (LMM-Multi-E) (2020)
2. BAuA. https://www.baua.de/EN/Topics/Work-design/Physical-workload/Key-indicator-met hod/Key-indicator-method_node.html. Accessed 04 Feb 2021
3. European Agency for Safety and Health at Work. Work-related musculoskeletal disorders: prevalence, costs and demographics in the EU, European Risk Observatory, Publications Office of the European Union, Luxembourg (2019). https://doi.org/10.2802/66947

4. European Committee for standardisation. NBN EN 1005-4 A Safety of machinery - Human physical performance - Part 4: Evaluation of working postures and movements in relation to machinery (2008)
5. Eurostat, the statistical office of the European Union, Accidents at work and other work-related health problems (source LFS), Updated 10 February 2015

# Application of Participative Ergonomics in a Manufacturing Plant in the Health Area in Brazil

Fernanda Oliveira Petry[1], Cláudia Ferreira Mazzoni[1,2(✉)],
and Mônica Campos Garcia[1]

[1] ARBEIT, Belo Horizonte, Brazil
consultoria@arbeitergonomia.com
[2] FUMEC University, Belo Horizonte, Brazil
claudiam@fumec.br

**Abstract.** The applications of ergonomics have been commonly unidirectional, superficial and with interventions that are not very close to the reality of processes and people's commitment. The objective of this study is to report on the development and implementation of participatory method aimed at understanding production process, recognizing risks linked to ergonomic factors and developing an action plan in the manufacture of heart valves. Participatory ergonomics can be understood as the involvement of people in the planning and control of a significant amount of their own activities, with sufficient knowledge and power to influence both processes and results in order to achieve desirable objectives. Four methods were developed and applied that allowed the awareness, engagement and effective participation of the different hierarchical and technical levels of the company. The work carried out resulted in 132 items in the action plan, 25% of which were solved even before the end of all analyzes. This advance was possible due to the participatory approach that allowed knowledge, involvement and empowerment of people to implement the required actions.

**Keywords:** Participatory ergonomics · Participatory methods · Prevention · Manufacturing · Heart valves

## 1 Introduction

The application of ergonomics have been commonly unidirectional, superficial and with interventions that are not very close to the reality of processes and people's commitment. This reality is reflected in the inefficient results of ergonomic analysis both for understanding the risks and for proposing solutions. This difficult can be explained, at least partially, by the low involvement of people from organization in the analysis and intervention processes. In order to remedy or reduce this inefficiency, the participatory approach has been proposed.

Participatory ergonomics "is the involvement of people in the planning and control of a significant amount of their own work activities, with sufficient knowledge and power

N. L. Black et al. (Eds.): IEA 2021, LNNS 221, pp. 34–41, 2021.
https://doi.org/10.1007/978-3-030-74608-7_5

to influence both processes and results in order to achieve desirable objectives." For an iterative process to occur, it is essential to seek the active engagement of all stakeholders, managers and operators, contributing to the application in a strategic way [1].

Against the participatory approach, people's perception of the time of involvement weights, the efforts to transform interventions into programs of continuous improvement and the maintenance of the motivation of the participants [2].

However, promoting the participatory approach provides improved design solutions with systemic results of value for both organizations and individuals [3]. Higher returns on investments were produced by companies that place workers at the center of their strategies, obtaining a increase in products per individual, a reduction in delivery times and a reduction in the work area [4]. When working with the concept of comfort, the participatory approach is also fundamental, since it is a subjective concept and only the user of the work environment is able to assess the level of his presence, because he has an unique view of your task, work or activity [3].

The participatory ergonomics approach has 9 dimensions that must be considered depending on the characteristics o the participatory project. They are: 1) permanence of the initiative, that is, the participatory approach can be temporary or continuous; 2) employee involvement, which can be directly or through representation; 3) scope, that is, the project can be applied in a specific sector or in the entire organization; 4) decision-making power, refers to the definition of who has consultative participation and who has delegative participation; 5) composition, refers to occupational groups involved in participatory processes; 6) requirement, participation can be voluntary or mandatory; 7) focus, specify activity, equipment or work organization; 8) attributions of the participants, who may be involved in the development of the process, in the identification of the problem, in the generation of the solution, in the evaluation of the solution, in the implementation of the solution or in the maintenance of the process; and 9) the role of the ergonomics specialist, who can develop different roles, such as starting and guiding the process, acting as a team member, training participants or being available for consultation [2].

In practice, participatory ergonomics must be understood as an approach resulting from the participation of society, the organization of production based on sociotechnical principles and the development of ergonomics from the "micro" view to the "macro" view. Participation is not limited to "work participation" or formal representative participation. In principle, it covers all levels of the hierarchy, inviting those who have experience with the problem in question and who are necessary to solve the problem [5].

This article aims to present the development of methods that allowed the application of participatory ergonomics in a company that manufactures heart valves in the state of Minas Gerais, in Brazil.

## 2 Participatory Methodology

Participatory processes can and should be used in the design and planning of completely new facilities, but they are still more often used to find solutions to an existing problem. The methodology in participatory ergonomics does not have a solid body of knowledge based on a theoretical construction. It is a collection of structures and approaches that show its usefulness in the hands of an expert in ergonomics competent to apply tools and participatory means which must be used with honesty, diplomacy and tact, supported by knowledge of all complexity that is configures to organization. Therefore, many of these tools and technical means seem easy to apply, but they almost always require experience and understanding of the basic processes of participation. Kuorinka (1997) [5] warns that it must be borne in mind that participatory processes can create expectations and social forces that, if not properly controlled, can backfire.

## 2.1 The Company

It is a manufacture of heart valve, headquartered in the state of Minas Gerais Brazil, with about 500 employees, in the predominant age group of up to 39 years, 85% of whom are female. It presents resilient characteristics, which contributed to the application of the participatory approach.

Participatory methods aimed at understanding work processes, cognitive demands and interrelationships between sector. They were developed and applied in order to understand the difficulties and risks as well as the possibilities for improvements in 13 sectors of the company, including administrative and productive sectors.

## 2.2 Participatory Methods

**Perception Map** - aimed to engage participants in the description of the activities developed by them, in the presentation of demands and in the search for solutions valuing everyone's "speech". Group of workers were organized according to the work process and everyone was motivated to present their perceptions according to the guidelines given by the process coordinating ergonomist. The information was synthesized and categorized by domain of ergonomics, that is, physical, cognitive or organizational. In addition, proposals for improvement were also counted. (Figs. 1a and 1b).

**(a)**                                              **(b)**

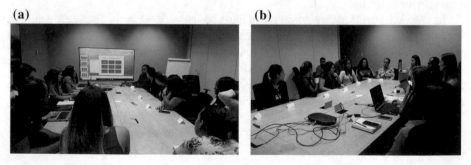

**Fig. 1.** (a) and (b) Moments of application of the "Perception Map".

**Operational Sprint** - raised the aspects and the cognitive demands of the activities of the productive and administrative sectors. Groups of workers were organized by sector and encouraged to give their opinion, at first, individually, responding to the following items: which situations demand attention, which factors favor error, which are the consequences of errors and which suggestions for improvements. After learning about the considerations of the entire group, each worker voted for the opinion that they considered most representative of their work situation. The most voted opinions were organized in information for the direct managers and supported the interactive meeting with the leadership. (Figs. 2a and 2b).

(a)                                                                (b)

**Fig. 2.** (a) and (b) Moments of application of the "Operational Sprint".

**Leadership Sprint** - the leaders formed a single group so that each one could describe situations of difficulties, whose improvement depended on decision-making and inter-action with other sectors. Each leader took time to understand the questions presented to their sector and then had the opportunity to make their considerations by defining items for the action plan. Thus, the method applied allowed integration among leaders and make it possible to outline an action plan that would respond to the demands presented, obtain information for decision-making, prioritize the demands, define the required competencies and the division of responsibilities in the situations that involved more than one sector. The results of previous sprints were also considered for the action plan. (Figs. 3a and 3b).

(a)                                                                (b)

**Fig. 3.** (a) and (b) Moments of application of the "Leadership Sprint".

**Action Sprint** - a spreadsheet with a conventional action plan model was used, but adapted to include the information resulting from previous sprints. The completion of the action plan was developed jointly with representatives of each sector through the facilitation and technical considerations of ergonomists.

# 3  Results

The application of the "Map of Perceptions" method resulted in a general knowledge of the employees' perception regarding the positive aspects, difficulties and suggestions for improvements related to the activities carried out. The perceptions obtained were classified according to the physical, cognitive and organizational domains of ergonomics. A legend was created to group perceptions in each domain: blue for positive aspects, red for the negative aspects and green for the improvement aspects. Table 1 shows the partial results obtained in the Training Center sector.

**Table 1.** "Map of Perceptions" result example.

| Training Center | | |
|---|---|---|
| Physical aspects | Organizational aspects | Cognitive aspects |
| Table with enough space | Respect and care for the employee | Noise outside the room disturbing concentration |
| Sitting posture for long periods | Psychology Service | Change the location to clock in to decrease external noise |
| Absence of footrest | Absence of breaks | |
| Necessity of more shelves | Deploy breaks | |

The application of the "Operational Sprint" method resulted in a survey of factors that affected cognitive and decision-making abilities. The results were computed insector -specific tables. Table 2 illustrates the partial data obtained by applying the method in the Assembly sector.

**Table 2.** "Operational Sprint" result example.

| Assembly sector | | | | |
|---|---|---|---|---|
| What is critical in my work? | What is the most difficult decision-making? | What makes me wrong? | What are the consequences of my mistake? | Improvements suggestions |
| Know how to deal with biological material of different thicknesses | Prioritize activities | Need to release large volumes | Putting the patient's life at risk | Encouraging quality rather than quantity |
| Batch control and validity | To know if there is a way to continue a valve with a problem or not | Emotional state, physical and psychological tiredness | Other people's low performance and productivity | Layout according to the need of the process |

The application of the "Leadership Sprint" method resulted in the presentation by the leaders of the aspects that affect the efficiency of their respective sectors and whose solution or part of it depends on changes or decision making by other sectors. After being aware of requests from other sectors, each leader answered the following question for each difficult posed by colleagues: "HOW CAN I COLLABORATE WITH THE FACT OF…?" For example, the "supplies" sector responding to the "materials preparation" sector: How can I collaborate with the fact that I receive materials after the deadline?" Table 3 exemplifies the difficulties of the "Material Preparation" sector in relation to the actions of the "Supplies" sector.

**Table 3.** "Leadership Sprint" result example.

| How can the SUPPLIES sector collaborate with the "MATERIAL PREPARATION" sector? |
|---|
| Deliver materials on time |
| Ensure supplies for the execution of activities |
| Plan the stock of sterile material |
| Organize "fixed" demand in the delivery of materials that we have to deliver sterile according to what we receive to process |

The application of the "Sprint Action" method resulted in the development of an action plan developed from the results of previous sprints. Thus, it contemplates the participation of managers, employees of the administrative and operational sectors. The required actions were organized according to the risks raised. From the data consolidation by the ergonomists, each action plan spreadsheet was validated by a specific team from each sector. Figure 4 illustrates the action plan worksheet header.

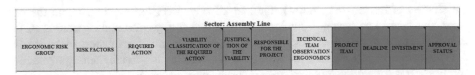

**Fig. 4.** Action Plan worksheet header.

The application of participatory methods resulted in gains, but also presented some difficulties. The main gains observed were:

– ease of understanding factors that affect processes
– high level of information quality
– naturalness in obtaining the data
– greater credibility at all levels of the organization
– less unforeseen and obstacles coming from top management
– greater acceptance and understanding of the contributions proposed by the ergonomist
– favoring integration between the different areas of the company and ergonomics

- sustainability of changes
- dissemination of knowledge to those involved
- greater sense of responsibility and demand for improvements

Regarding the difficulties, challenges were observed in the organization of the teams, in the planning for the interactive meetings and in the availability of time. However, this experience was facilitated by the resilient manufacturing culture, the real concern for improving working conditions and the ease relationship between people, including between different hierarchies. Besides, the experience and participation of workers at all levels were essential for understanding problems and proposing solutions.

The ergonomist had a different role, demanding the capacity and knowledge to extract the necessary information, skills for people management, conflict resolution, time management and analysis of results.

The work carried out resulted in 132 items in the action plan, 25% of which were solved even before the end of all analyses. This advance was possible due to the participatory approach that allowed knowledge, involvement and empowerment of people to implement the required actions.

It is noteworthy that the information in quantity and quality was obtained on the factors of the cognitive and organizational domains, which is not common when traditional methods are applied.

Future experiences, the use of the technological resources is already considered to favor the time management and enable a greater number of participants and the cost-benefit analyses in a longitudinal study should be implemented.

## 4 Conclusion

This experience reaffirmed the importance of acting considering the precepts of macroergonomy. The application of participatory methods, a premise for this approach, allowed the sharing of information, knowledge and effective decision-making. If, on the one hand, the time spent was a difficulty, on the other hand, wealth and deepening of the information was obtained with consequent assertiveness and effectiveness in the results. A fundamental aspect was the knowledge of the ergonomists in conducting interactive activities. It is concluded that the participatory methods contributed to the incorporation of ergonomics in the organizational culture of the company.

## References

1. Wilson, J.R.: Solution ownership in participative work redesign: the case of a crane control rool. Int. J. Ind. Ergon. **15**, 329–344 (1995)
2. Haines, H., Wilson, J.R., Vink, P., Koningsveld, E.: Validating a framework for participatory ergonomics (the PEF). Ergonomics **45**(4), 309–327 (2002)
3. Wilson, J.R., Haines, H.M.: Participatory ergonomics. In: Salvendy, G. (ed.) Handbook of Human Factors and Ergonomics, 2nd edn, pp. 490–513. Wiley, New York (1997)

4. Rhijn, J.W., Loose, M.P., Groenesteijn, L., Hagedoorn-de Groot, M.D., Vink, P., Tuinzaad, G.H.: Productivity and discomfort in manual assembly operations. In: Vink, P. (ed.) Comfort and Design: Principles and Good Practice, pp. 111–128. CRC Press, Boca Raton (2005)
5. Kuorinka, I.: Tools and means of implementing of participatory ergonomics. Int. J. Ind. Ergon. **19**, 267–270 (1997)

# Cases of Human Factors Engineering in Oil & Gas

Ruud N. Pikaar[✉], Niels de Groot, Erik Mulder, and Renske Landman

ErgoS Human Factors Engineering, Enschede, The Netherlands
ruud.pikaar@ergos.nl

**Abstract.** "Researchers and Practitioners: do we understand each other?" This is a major question for the Human Factors (HF) community. For scientists, it is time to accept structured Practitioner cases as a contribution to science. Practitioners: it is time to share your experiences. One way to share experiences is to publish real-world HF projects. For this paper, seven cases of Control Room (CR) design projects have been reviewed. The focus is not only on the product -the actual control room design result- but also on the roles of stakeholders, HF Consultants, as well as on HF methods and their effectiveness.

**Keywords:** Human factors engineering · Project ergonomics · Case study · Control center · Control room · Oil & gas · Engineering procurement contractor

## 1 Problem

### 1.1 The Value of Case Studies

Human Factors/Ergonomics (HF/E) has a unique combination of three fundamental characteristics: 1) it takes a systems approach (as shown in Fig. 1), 2) it is design driven, and 3) it focuses on two related outcomes: performance and well-being [1].

A practitioner case study is about an actual design and implementation of a work system [2]. Activities of HF Professionals are only a small part of such projects. Many other disciplines are involved, and usually leading. Case studies include a real-world intervention: a new production system is designed and implemented.

There are few case studies found in literature [2]. Also, the number of practitioner case studies submitted at the IEA Congresses decreased since 2012 [2]. A gap between science and practice can be noted. A real-world application is not an experiment and cannot be controlled the same way as scientific research. Each case is unique (sample size N = 1). No project is carried out twice for scientific comparison reasons. However, real-world projects can be observed and reviewed, which is what the authors of this article tried to do.

Scientists are experts in one or two HF areas, such as biomechanics, behavioral sciences, or cognitive sciences. The HF Practitioner applies research outputs, often for the design of complex production systems. Feedback from practice to research is limited: it is not in their scope of work. Scientists depend on publications for research funding. Usually, they do not ask for practitioners' feedback on their products.

© The Author(s), under exclusive license to Springer Nature Switzerland AG 2021
N. L. Black et al. (Eds.): IEA 2021, LNNS 221, pp. 42–49, 2021.
https://doi.org/10.1007/978-3-030-74608-7_6

## 1.2 Content of Case Studies

In the 80's, Prof. Rijnsdorp [3] and his co-workers at the Twente University Ergonomics Group implemented a systems ergonomics approach for large scale industrial projects, in line with Singleton's [4] generally accepted ideas. In a real-world project at the Esso Rotterdam Refinery, the systems approach (Fig. 1) was tested [5] for a large Control Center (CC). Phase 1 concerns the organization of the project and defining the HF goals and activities for the project. Getting a good insight in system tasks, is the next step (situation analysis), which is followed by a task allocation phase.

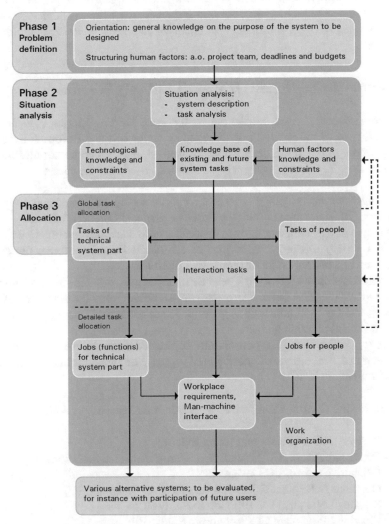

**Fig. 1.** System ergonomics approach (adapted from [4]).

There is evidence from reported case studies that (quote; [2]):

- *Professional ergonomics is not about additional efforts or higher project costs, probably on the contrary. HF contributions have a short return on investment.*
- *Stick to the systems ergonomics approach including a thorough situation analysis. It works well and is understood by the engineering community.*
- *Once a project manager has had the pleasure of working with ergonomists, he will do so in new projects. In particular he will remember the systematic design process, including effective tools to tackle HF and user participation.*
- *Job load assessment, and job & work organization design are HF issues, though not always accepted as such by projects. In this domain, useful and validated design tools are very difficult to use, or not very practical for relatively small organizations.* [end of quote]

## 2   Actions - To Be Honest, It Wasn't Entirely Scientific!

The authors selected 7 cases carried out by the same HF Engineering company. Each case, at least one of the authors was involved as senior certified European Ergonomist with experience in HF of CC design. One consultant has been co-authoring ISO 11064 *Ergonomic design of control centers* [6]. Selection criteria for the cases:

- Availability of archived project material (reports, documents, drawings), Request for Quotation (RfQ) documents, and the Purchase Order (PO)/Scope of Work.
- Application of a system ergonomics approach, or at least the intention to do so.
- Recent (>2010) CC projects, as part of an international investment project (i.e., realization of a process plant or production platform).
- One industrial domain (oil & gas), because operator jobs, process size and complexity, etc. are more or less the same. More cases are available from Maritime area, Off-shore industry, and Process Industries in general. These cases could not (yet) be included, due to a limited research budget.
- Different position of the HF consultants: contracted either by the project owner, an Engineering & Procurement Contractor (EPC), or Instrumentation and Control System (sub) Contractor (ICSC).

The following Control Center cases were selected (between brackets: contractor):

Case 1 - Refinery CC refurbishment (oil company)
Case 2 - Offshore platform CC Validation & Verification study (oil company)
Case 3 - Offshore platform CC Design (EPC)
Case 4 - On-shore LNG plant CC review and detailed design (ICSC)
Case 5 - Floating LNG plant CC Ergonomic Study (ICSC)
Case 6 - Floating FPSO plant CC Ergonomic Study (EPC)
Case 7 - Refinery CC and off-sites CC validation studies (building subcontractor).

The typical project investment was >200 million Euro. The HF contribution was between 60 - 120 days of work. In the first three cases, the explicit aim of the project was to optimize HF. The cases 4–6 concerned LNG processing plants (Liquified Natural Gas; on-shore or floating). These projects were handled by the same EPC. Contrary to the first 3 cases, the main drive for the EPC to hire ergonomists, was to achieve conformity with mandatory minimum HF requirements.

The research consisted of a document study and interviews with the HF Professionals to discuss their practical experiences and personal observations of the engineering process. An overview of documents, activities, findings, and highlights was compiled for each case. Central research question: what can be learnt from practitioners' experiences? This has two directions: 1) HF content (CC design), and 2) HF project management. The research should give feedback to HF scientists regarding HF content (usability of scientific guidance) and methods (usability of methods), or the lack of guidance and useful methods.

## 3   Outcomes

### 3.1   Content for Control Center Design

ISO-11064 [6] is the leading CC ergonomic design standard for process industries. Unlike standards based on consensus between stakeholders, which is not necessarily good ergonomics, ISO-11064 has been developed by HF Professionals. At the same time, the International Instrument Users' Associations published a study "Ergonomics in Process Control Rooms" consisting of three parts:

1. Engineering Guideline (HF project management, based on a system ergonomics approach [7]);
2. Design Guideline (the actual design guidelines [8]);
3. The Analyses (an overview of standards & regulations, and 6 case studies [9]).

Projects may request for an *ergonomic study*. Unfortunately, there are no clear definitions for terms such as *ergonomic study*, *good ergonomics* or *best HF practices*. Projects expect to get a CC layout, workplace drawings, and specifications of the physical work environment. Discussions on job and work organization design are not expected. HMI (Human Machine Interaction) and Alarm management may not be a part of the requested ergonomic study. Both topics are often claimed by the ICSC vendor and handled by process control engineers. Of course, HF Professionals could contribute as shown in 2 case studies [10].

For all cases, the same type of HF content related issues came up. Some examples are given below, including suggestions for further scientific research need.

- Designing a CC layout starts with determining the number and approximate size of operator workplaces. Obviously, we need to know the number of operator positions and possible variations due to off-normal process conditions. It requires task related knowledge, either handed to the HF Consultant, or to be established by doing a task analysis and task allocation (see Fig. 1). In case 1 a task analysis was carried out by the

HF consultant. For case 2 and 3, the projects relied on the job design of an old platform. For the cases 4–7, the HF consultants had limited resources, i.e., gathering data in a meeting with customer representatives. The assessment of (an acceptable) operator workload is difficult, in particular for greenfield projects. Process control engineers estimate workload by the number of controlled process variables. However, there is more to include to get a valid estimate, such as the amount of communication between CC operators and field technicians [5]. Research on operator workload indicators is needed!

- A CR layout should be based on communication requirements, routing and entrances, visual field (what should be visible from each work position), and avoiding distraction. Except case 5, engineering came up with a traditional layout, where operators are sitting back-to-back in a circle (Fig. 2). Alternative layout proposals proved to be eye-openers in most projects. For example, for easy communication, colleagues could be sitting opposite each other, or at least within the secondary field of view (Fig. 3).

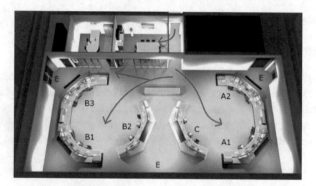

**Fig. 2.** Traditional CC layout example.

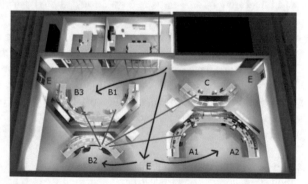

**Fig. 3.** CC layout based on lines of frequent communication (green lines), and creating quiet work areas by organizing the routing in the CC (blue arrows).

- The number of screens on the operator desk determines workplace measurements and viewing distances. In order to design process graphics, we need to know about acceptable viewing distances. Legibility of important text is guaranteed at a maximum of

200 × character height. For secondary text this may be 250 × character height. However, this guideline is based on old display technology. Nowadays, 4K high resolution screens might allow for larger viewing distances or smaller character sizes. Research (experiments) are needed.

- In process industries there are two points of view on workplace design. In the HF view, 4–5 displays positioned in one slightly curved row, display process schematics with typical viewing distances up to 1000 mm. These process graphics only show task related information needed by the operator for monitoring or particular process conditions. This leads to few graphics and thus simplified and quick navigation.

  The other view, is to present all available process information, rather a digital presentation of piping & instrumentation diagrams. Because of the detailed information, this view assumes working with one or two screens at a time, at viewing distances <600 mm, while frequently moving from one screen to another. Leading instrumentation vendors provide standard small character sizes (maximum viewing distance 600 mm), which is difficult to change. There is more to say about this topic [11]. Scientific research on this, including independent feedback on commercial/ICSC funded research, would be most welcome.

- An oil & gas CC, often includes an Emergency Center next to the CR. All cases (except case 5) favor a direct connection (open access, glass wall) to enable quick face-to-face communication, and seeing what is going on in the CR. In case 5, the EPC did not accept this best practice and dictated a corridor and windowless walls between EC and CC.

## 3.2 Management of HF Activities

A purchaser asks for an ergonomic study, because of a customer requirement to apply ISO-11064. Knowledge of the content of ISO-11064 varied from good to a limited notion of one topic: the operator workstation. Within EPC managed projects, an approved RfQ cannot be changed, only clarified. Hence, one needs to comply. At case 1, the oil company contracted HF for the full system ergonomics approach. Detailed design and implementation by an EPC, was verified by the same HF consultants. For all other cases, the EPC or ICSC, contracted the consultants. HF gets less emphasis, and is less effective, although the HF Professionals were highly experienced in coping with "difficult" project settings. Summarizing, project organization influences the HF quality of the CR design, as shown below in some observations.

- HF milestones for a control room project are:

  - Kick-off and explain what HF is about, including a task related approach.
  - Task analysis; availability of customer representatives may be limited; a field study may not be possible. There is a need for quick and valid task analysis methods.
  - Review initial (technical engineering) design proposals.
  - Disappointment phase: the review usually shows HF short comings, which is logical if the engineering is not done by ergonomists. However, this may not be liked very much by engineering.
  - Happy phase: HF based improved design, presented in 3D and Virtual Reality.

– Wrapping-up documents, eventually leading to an approved close-out.

• High customer HF-standards and understanding lead to good HF (Case 1–3). Otherwise, good results can only be obtained with additional efforts of the HF consultant (i.e., provide prove for the validity of guidelines/standards). This is a challenge within a fixed price contract. Anyhow, all cases resulted in significant design changes, such as altered CC layout and workstation design. To explain HF issues, availability of a quick visualization of ideas and solutions, is very useful.
• The HF Consultants encountered little collaboration, and in some cases unacceptable design results, as well as cases with an easy communication and satisfactory results. Differences can be explained by weak project lead, difficult communication due to travelling distances and different cultures (Europe, Asia, Middle East). Again, visualization tools, such as VR, are useful tools.

## 4   Discussion

The cases are representative for large industrial projects in oil & gas, off-shore (maritime), and process industries. Sometimes we wondered why HF Consultants were hired: there was no intention to change initial designs. To achieve good HF results, HF should be contracted by the Customer and/or high-quality HF standards should be followed, such as ISO-11064 (all parts), or a V&V method such as CRIOP [12].

The aim of this article has been to identify research needs of HF Practitioners. Oil & Gas is a traditional industry; EPC's are rather conventional. The HF consultant could be leading in innovation, but may need research support.

• There is a need to determine the right mix of in-person meetings, workshops, and videoconferencing enabling an efficient project. Virtual Reality (VR) could be helpful, and reduce costs, but VR techniques need a further development.
• There is a need to develop techniques to improve the management of stakeholder expectations. For example, how to cope with interventions that are not compliant with HF best practices.
• Practitioners need quick, but also validated tools for task analyses. The Scenario approach of the CRIOP-method [12] provides one way of doing this, but it is limited to off-normal situations and it is time consuming.
• A key issue is to establish or validate the number of operators in a CR. Workload not only depends on operator control and supervision tasks, but also on information presentation, decision support, etc. Practitioners need methods to estimate operator workload (for complex cognitive tasks).
• There are several operator console design issues (see Sect. 3.1) that need to be investigated in the context of technological innovation, such as the number of screens, large screen displays, viewing distances, HMI & navigation.

## 5   Conclusion

This article is based on case material of industrial HF Engineering projects. Each case deserves a full paper to share experiences, design solutions, and lessons learnt. For several reasons, as discussed in the introduction, this will not happen. Nevertheless, the authors recommend academics to take notice of practical experiences. Lessons can be learnt and in particular the limitations or shortcomings of projects can be most informative. HF Professionals need to publish their experiences, and a collaboration between science and practitioners should be stimulated.

There is clearly a need to better understand how investment projects are contracted, managed, and engineered. It is also clear that the HF community should do more to sell to industry, what HF in practice is really about, and what the benefits of a HF based approach could be.

For HF Professionals, the difficulty lies in the integration of all related factors in one production system. We are keen to system integration.

# References

1. Dul, J., et al.: A strategy for human factors/ergonomics: developing the discipline and profession. Ergonomics **55**(4), 377–395 (2012)
2. Pikaar, R.N.: Case studies – human factors in engineering projects. In: IEA2015 Congress Proceedings, Melbourne (2015)
3. Rijnsdorp, J.E.: Integrated Process Control and Automation. Elsevier, Amsterdam (1991)
4. Singleton, W.T.: Ergonomics in systems design. Ergonomics **10**, 541 (1967)
5. Pikaar, R.N., Thomassen, P.A.J., Degeling, P., Van Andel, H.: Ergonomics in control room design. Ergonomics **1990**, 589–600 (1990)
6. ISO 11064: Ergonomic Design of Control Centres – multi part standard. Geneva, International Organization for Standardization (1998–2007)
7. Pikaar, R.N., et al.: Ergonomics in Process Control Rooms, Part 2: Design Guideline. The Hague, WIB International Users' Association (1998)
8. Pikaar, R.N., et al.: Ergonomics in Process Control Rooms, Part 1: Engineering Guideline. The Hague, WIB International Users' Association (1998)
9. Pikaar, R.N., et al.: Ergonomics in Process Control Rooms, Part 3: The Analyses. The Hague, WIB International Users' Association (1997)
10. Pikaar, R.N., DeGroot, N., Mulder, E., Remijn, S.L.M.: Human factors in control room design & effective operator participation. In: Proceedings SPE Intelligent Energy International Conference and Exhibition. Society of Petroleum Engineers, Aberdeen (2016)
11. Pikaar, R.N.: HMI conventions for process control graphics. Work **41** (2012). https://doi.org/10.3233/WOR.2012.0533.2845
12. Johnsen, S.O., et al.: CRIOP: a scenario method for Crisis Intervention and Operability analysis. Sintef report A4312. Trondheim (2016). https://www.criop.sintef.no/theCRIOPreport/CRIOPreport.doc

# HFE in Ever-Changing Industrial Scenario

Era Poddar[(✉)]

Manufacturing Safety Alliance of BC, Chilliwack, BC V2R 07, Canada
e.poddar@safetyalliancebc.ca

**Abstract.** It is well recognized that inclusion of Human Factors and Ergonomics (HFE) in early design phase not only reduces overall cost, but also improves operational safety and operator well-being. However, in industry, particularly in manufacturing, majority of the time, active inclusion of HFE principles or involving ergonomics experts happens in much later stages (after reported incidents-reactive approach). Hence, it becomes challenging to control the problem at the root level. The aim of this paper is to re-emphasize the importance of HFE and its inclusion at early design phase, especially when manufacturing facilities are being set up, in order to optimize system safety focusing into human needs. Through real-world case scenarios the relevance of the scope was presented.

**Keywords:** Ergonomics in manufacturing · Human factors · Work Related-Musculoskeletal Disorders (WMSD) · Musculo-Skeletal Injuries (MSI) · Ergonomics program · Ergonomics in design

## 1 Introduction

### 1.1 Problem Statement

Since the beginning of the last century, Human Factors and Ergonomics (HFE) is always considered and practiced as a system level subject with the aim of improving human performance and reducing system errors. The International Ergonomics Association (IEA) [1] defines Ergonomics (or Human Factors) as a science concerned with the understanding of interactions among humans and other elements of a system...to design in order to optimize human well-being and overall system performance. It has always been recommended to include HFE considerations at an early design stage (proactive approach). Several research has successfully shown the effectivity of HFE in reducing overall costs, improving operational safety and operator well-being [2] if included in the early design phase. This HFE approach is not only an approved method in many industrial engineering projects, but also yields several positive results [3–5]. However, in industry practice, especially in manufacturing, things often remain rather reactive. In sectors, where manual handling to high-end automated system run side by side, situations are far more complex. With 24 × 7 operations, automation, aging workforce, and altering production rate, continuous consideration of HFE at system level appears to be an obvious choice, in theory. However, still in majority of the cases, inclusion of HFE principles or involving HFE professionals happens much later, often after incidents were

N. L. Black et al. (Eds.): IEA 2021, LNNS 221, pp. 50–58, 2021.
https://doi.org/10.1007/978-3-030-74608-7_7

reported or some regulatory order has been issued. As a result, it becomes challenging to control the risks at source, at the same time provide economically viable solutions and avoid retrofitting. At the end of the day, HFE is projected as an added task at additional costs to the company, which forfeits the aim of the discipline.

## 1.2  Objective

The main aim of this paper is to re-emphasize the need of including HFE at the time when a manufacturing facility is being set up to improve system safety focusing into human needs. To demonstrate the relevance, real world case scenarios of two very different manufacturing companies based in British Columbia (BC), Canada was presented. It is believed that there is still scope for regulatory bodies, to influence industry stakeholders and HFE practitioners to come together and continue discussion on using a broad potential of HFE to derive a sustainable solution.

## 2  Approach and Method

In the present paper, real-life case scenarios of two manufacturing companies (Company-A and Company-B) are shared. Both companies were distinctively different from one another with respect to the nature of products they produced, size and method of operation. 'Company-A' is a global large manufacturing facility producing insulated panel and structure while 'Company-B' is a local food processing (meat cutting and processing) company. In both cases, management chose to adopt a reactive approach and decided to consider involving HFE professionals after reporting some type of MSD (musculoskeletal disorder) or injury. Although, the management approach and awareness about HFE and company culture varied, both companies associated HFE activities with the prevention of the WMSD (work related musculoskeletal disorders).

Company A and Company-B both involved Manufacturing Safety Alliance of BC (MSABC) to perform ergonomic assessments of workstations at their facility to find out about risks employees may have while performing their job tasks. MSABC adopted a participatory ergonomics approach; employees and management were interviewed to gain understanding of the work system and the jobs in the specified work section. Employees were encouraged to share their problems/concerns freely. Observational studies and task analyses were performed and supported by taking photograph and video, to record jobs and activities around the facility when work was being performed. Various measurements of existing workstations were taken to investigate potential mismatches between users and workstation components. Assessments were carried out during the regular day shift at both facilities. A brief description of the approach adopted is included in Table 1.

**Table 1.** Brief description of ergonomic approach adopted.

| Ergonomic approach adopted |
| --- |
| 1. **Problem identification**: Problem definition (system goal, general constraints), Recording of existing scenario (expectations, management & employee feedback, interviews), Exploration (system limitations, viability of ergonomics input) |
| 2. **Analysis:**<br>- Analyzing existing situation (Observation studies, Task analyses, System description)<br>- Postural analyses (REBA) |
| 3. **Recommendation:**<br>- Providing report with recommendations<br>- Providing possible MSD control solutions |

## 3   Results and Outcomes

As indicated, Company-A and Company-B produced different products, naturally the operation processes were completely different from each other. However, in both cases the jobs were physically demanding and highly paced.

### 3.1   Operation Lines Under Assessment

**Company-A:** A global large manufacturing facility producing insulated panel where high end automated systems and manual activities ran side by side. Workstation analyses were accomplished on three identified operation lines (Table 2, Fig. 1). Observations and task analyses were performed on those job areas.

**Company-B:** A local food processing (meat cutting and processing) company, where heavy manual activities along with fewer automated functions ran simultaneously. Workstation analyses were conducted on four identified operation lines (Table 2, Fig. 2). Observations and task analyses were completed on those job areas.

An initial assessment of musculoskeletal risk factors was conducted throughout the facility focusing into identified jobs to understand existing task-specific and postural challenges. In both cases, based on the input provided by the management as well as the employees, it was identified that frequent MSD incidents and complaints were reported regularly in certain job areas. Therefore, detailed analysis of posture (using Rapid Entire Body Assessment, REBA) was conducted on those specific jobs.

In Company-A, Blue line jobs were reported as at high risk; hence REBA was performed on all four tasks of that operation line (Table 2, Fig. 1b). In Company-B, REBA was performed on almost all jobs, because almost all were reported as risky (Table 2, Fig. 2). Several workstation design-issues and risk factors were identified in both cases. A report with possible recommendation was presented to both companies.

**Table 2.** Operation lines under assessment

| Operation Lines | |
| --- | --- |
| **Company-A** | **Company-B** |
| 1.  Trimline work | 1.  Meat Processing (MP) |
| 2.  Blue line work | |
| *Lamella Flipper (LF), Blue line Mill (BM), Glue station (GS), Scrap Removal & Packaging (SRP)* | 2.  Meat cutting (MC) |
| 3.  Green line work | 3.  Packaging (P) |
| | 4.  Loading Dock (LD) |

**Fig. 1.** Operation lines under assessment at Company-A (1.a Trimline, 1.b Blue line, 1.c Green line work)

## 3.2  Outcome

**Company-A:** After considering various inputs and analyzing the data, it was confirmed that there were potential MSD risks associated with all three production lines (Trimline, Blueline and Greenline work) (Table 2, Fig. 1). However, the Blueline work was found to have potentially higher MSD risks (Table 3) than others. This may be because of complex operation processes at workstations, where combination of manual and automated tasks ran concurrently. Higher number of incidents and claims were also reported from this section of operation compared to others. It was indicated by the management that system level modifications of the Blueline work will be considered and will be based on the outcome of the present analysis.

*General Issues Identified:* Several workstation design limitations were identified, like anthropometric mismatch, inadequate space allocation, poorly designed assembly components to name but a few, which led to poor posture and work methods. Static posture

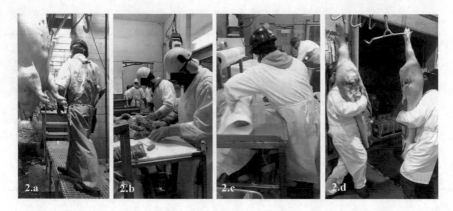

**Fig. 2.** Operation lines under assessment at Company-B (2.a MP, 2.b MC, 2.c P, 2.d LD)

with twisting, bending (both upper and lower body), forceful exertion of various body parts was common throughout. Workers were required to move fast (semiautomated system) within inadequate space which was a potential risk of other accidents.

**Company-B:** Musculoskeletal injuries (MSIs) especially cumulative trauma disorders (CTDs) are particularly prevalent in the meatpacking industry. Our findings were no different than that. All four analyzed job functions (meat preparation, meat cutting, packaging, and docking station) (Table 2, Fig. 2) were found to be having high to very high MSD risk (Table 3). The local regulatory authority, WSBC (Worksafe BC), had already identified this workplace as potentially at high risk (OHS 4.48 and OHS 4.50) [6]. It was mentioned that Company-B had to work on a MSI control plan.

**Table 3.** Level of MSD Risk (REBA score).

|  | Company-A (Blue line jobs) | Company-B (All jobs) |
|---|---|---|
| **Level of MSD Risk (REBA score)** | | |
| Low risk (2-3) | | |
| Medium risk (4-7) | LF | |
| High risk (8-10) | BM, SRP | MC, P |
| Very high risk (11+) | GS | MP, LD |

*General Issues Identified:* During observational analyses in all four job areas (Table 2, Fig. 2), primary postural risk factors observed were repetitive motion of hand-arm-wrist, static body posture with twisting, forward bending, trunk flexion and rotation, reaching overhead (shoulder abduction and adduction), neck flexion, wrist flexion, extension, pinching, and gripping. More than a few of those postures were adopted while handling loads (at times >120 lb) (Fig. 2d). These postural risk factors were known to cause debilitating back, shoulder and wrist injuries. Various system design and workstation design issues (like poorly designed assembly components, badly arranged workstation components, inadequate space allocation and poor anthropometric considerations etc.) were identified which may have forced the workers adopting poor postures.

## 3.3 Recommendations

For both companies, recommendations were proposed for each job that was classified risky and information was incorporated in the respective reports. Improvement strategies were outlined to reduce musculoskeletal risk factors and to enhance employee well-being. A summary of recommendations is included in Table 4.

**Table 4.** Summary of recommendations made for Company-A and Company-B.

| Recommendations | Company |
|---|---|
| 1. Establish ergonomics program as a part of company goal to proactively control MSI risks & reduce claim costs | Company-A & B |
| 2. Designing out risks when possible through implementation of engineering & administrative controls | Company-A & B |
| 3. Redesign/ install adjustable workstations; position work/workstation to reduce awkward postures & promote neutral postures | Company-A & B |
| 4. Consider engineering changes for Blueline (Fig. 1b) (work envelop, anthropometry & optimal space allocations). Involve HFE professional | Company-A |
| 5. Consider engineering changes that make carcass movement automatic (Fig. 2, 3) to control potential upper body MSD risks. Involve HFE professional | Company-B |
| 6. Opt for height adjustable carts for scrap removal to avoid awkward hand/body movement. Get floor clutter free & provide stable/adjustable step stools to control reaching above shoulder | Company-A |
| 7. Reduce work surface depth (consider work envelop) to avoid excessive leaning/reaching (especially when materials reaching through conveyors) | Company-B |
| 8. Introduce ergonomic height adjustable lift tables/arrange materials to arrive on pallets. Keep/store materials (at standing elbow height) on scissor lift tables during loading/unloading. Use mechanical devices (e.g., lifts, hoists) whenever possible (Fig. 3) | Company-B |
| 9. Providing handheld ergonomic tools to supports neutral hand/wrist position while cutting meat. Implement knife-sharpening program | Company-B |
| 10. Establish systems to rotate workers between tasks to minimize effects of continuous exertion, repetitive motion, and/or awkward postures | Company-A |
| 11. As meat cutting job is extremely repetitive/time bound incorporate stretching session /micro breaks. Establish systems to rotate workers (consider adding more trained meat cutters) between tasks | Company-B |
| 12. MSD-RTW* program: Additional care & strategy is required to accommodate worker suffered from past MSD injuries. Establish early MSD symptoms reporting system | Company-A &B |
| 13. Involve employees throughout change process to minimize resistance & improve acceptance | Company-A &B |
| 14. Establish ergonomics training that is specific to the job to make workers aware of MSD hazards and ways to control them | Company-A &B |
| 15. Train workers on biological hazards (symptoms/PPE/ hand hygiene) | Company-B |

*RTW = Return to Work*

It was proposed to both the companies that for future space planning and system improvement projects, a HFE professional should be consulted to ensure that space planning, storage area and the equipment will be appropriate for the workstation design and tasks being accomplished in the space. It was also emphasized that it is beneficial to involve experienced employees along the change process.

**Fig. 3.** Loading Dock (LD) activities at Company-B

## 4   Discussion

Company-A being a global company, their approach was to utilize the report (recommendations) as supporting document to justify the modification of workstation design. The management of Company-A was willing to go over the recommended engineering changes for Blueline operations. The report with the recommendations was helpful for them to substantiate and allocate the budget. On the other hand, Company-B was trying to comply with the local regulatory authority's (WSBC) order (OHS 4.48 and OHS 4.50) [6]. Under those orders, the employer must ensure that the MSI risk to workers is assessed and that they will (the employer) take actions to eliminate or minimize the identified MSI risks by creating control mechanisms for the risk factors found during the risk assessment [6]. During the site visit it was noticed and reported that the employer had already invested and procured machinery envisioning systems improvement. However, the investment decisions were made without proper consideration of the present job process or risk assessment. Neither the employee's (including safety manager) nor the HFES professional were involved or consulted on this. It was commonly observed that management strategies have often focused on one factor at a time, for example, improving productivity, through automation, or through employee motivation. However, more holistic approaches are more successful than one-dimensional approaches [7, 8].

It was conveyed to the management of both the companies through the report and recommendation that inclusion of HFE at an early stage of design will help them saving more and getting better ROI (return on investment). Additionally, it was reasoned that this would not only improve productivity, but system safety will also be improved. However, in neither case we as practitioners had much influence on the next step, organization policy or how the report would be utilized further. Especially when HFE is closely linked to occupational health and safety regulations [6, 9], companies experience ergonomics as additional component, and not as part of their own strategy, business goals and planning [10]. It is a well-recognized fact that the focus on WMSDs has been a contributing cause of the underuse of ergonomists and ergonomics expertise within industry besides several other reasons. In majority, ergonomics is supported as part of health and safety initiatives. As a result, the broader advantages of a comprehensive ergonomics program are not recognized that well [11]. This could only be addressed by engaging top management, shareholders, regulatory authorities, business functions and other stakeholders so that HFE considerations are included within the strategy to ensure internalization of HFE in organizations [10]. Then, it would be automatically considered as part of the early design phase and become part of the company culture. Despite several success stories reported throughout the world stating that inclusion of HFE at the architectural design phase were particularly helpful [5, 12], yet there is lot to be done locally, especially in the manufacturing sector, to ensure human well-being and system safety.

## 5    Conclusion

This paper re-emphasizes the importance of considering HFE at the design stage in the manufacturing sector in order to foster human well-being for ensuring system safety. Through two real world industry cases, it was presented that industry responses are still often reactive when it comes to the control of MSD risks. HFE as a profession has lot to offer beyond risk assessment; by addressing major business and societal challenges regarding work and product/service systems. Hence, it is only practical that regulatory bodies, HFE practitioners and industry stakeholders come together and continue the discussion to have sustainable results on integrating human needs while enhancing system safety.

## References

1. International Ergonomics Association. What is ergonomics (2000). https://iea.cc/what-is-erg onomics/
2. Golabchi, A., Han, S., Seo, J., Han, S., Lee, S., Al-Hussein, M.: An automated biomechanical simulation approach to ergonomic job analysis for workplace design. J. Constr. Eng. Manag. 141(8) (2015)
3. Engström, T., Bergqvist, L.G., Gasslander, J.: Linkage of user demands to the building facility. In: 1st HCTM Hospital of the Future Conference, Enschede, The Netherlands (2001)
4. Villeneuve, J.: The contribution of ergonomics to the design of hospital architecture. In: Proceedings of the 15th World Congress of International Ergonomics Association, Ergonomics for the new millennium, San Diego, CA (2000). ISBN 0945289138
5. Remijn, S.L.M.: Integrating ergonomics into the architectural design processes: tools for user participation in hospital design. In: Proceedings of the 16th World Congress of the International Ergonomics Association. Elsevier Science, Maastricht (2006). https://www.semanticscholar.org/paper/Integrating-ergonomics-into-the-archit ectural-%3A-for-Remijn/e562e176259760ea140272753b17aaa6ebe6377c?p2df

6. WorksafeBC: Occupational Health Safety Regulations, Part 4, Section 4.46-4.53 (2006). https://www.worksafebc.com/en/law-policy/occupational-health-safety/searchable-ohs-regulation/ohs-regulation/part-04-general-conditions. Accessed 02 Feb 2021
7. Shiba, S., Graham, A., Walden, D.: A New American TQM. Productivity Press, Portland (1993)
8. Eklund, J.: Ergonomics and quality management—humans in interaction with technology, work environment, and organization. Int. J. Occup. Saf. Ergon. **5**(2), 143–160 (1999)
9. Occupational Safety and Health Administration (OSHA), Ergonomics Program Standard, Federal Register 1910.900 (2000)
10. Dula, J., Neumann, P.: Ergonomics contributions to company strategies. Appl. Ergon. **41**, 745–752 (2009)
11. Larson, N.L.J.: Corporate ergonomics: it's musculoskeletal disorder management and system optimization. Ergon. Des. 29–33 (2012)
12. Eilouti, B.: A framework for integrating ergonomics into architectural design. Ergon. Des. 1–9 (2021). https://doi.org/10.1177/1064804620983672

# Teller's Workstation Design Project - Health and Wellbeing through Ergonomics

Rosa Ana Rizzo[1][✉] and Luciano Gabriel Adatto[2]

[1] Postgraduate School of Ergonomics, Universidad Tecnológica Nacional, Castro Barros 91, Buenos Aires, Argentina
rosanarizzo@frba.utn.edu.ar
[2] Ergohuman Consulting Designer, E. Conesa 3970, Buenos Aires, Argentina
lucianoadatto@ergohuman.com.ar

**Abstract.** A workstation design and implementation project can be poured with infinite decisions. An ergonomic approach to industrial design aimed at improving health and comfort to a large workforce has the potential to materialize many ergonomic concepts and ideas and turn them tangible. A new workstation demand from a multinational company will be the project's setting, and the opportunity to wield knowledge, gathered and learned, from multiple disciplines; and to learn from our mistakes regarding the project' process. This paper will illustrate the process from demand to implementation going through the methodology, decisions and challenges.

**Keywords:** Design project · Activity-centered ergonomics · Participative ergonomics · Workstation design

## 1 Main Message

The inquiry of a money exchange multinational company to design a teller's desk prototype to be implemented countrywide aimed at improving 800 job positions, sparked this project.

The goal: To design and manufacture a workstation including the actual desk, the device's layout and accessories and to promote healthier work habits, to be carried out within time, budget, space and industrial production limitations.

A multidisciplinary team composed of an ergonomist, an architect, a production expert and an industrial designer was set up.

The team's approach was based on activity-centered ergonomics (ACE) [1–3]. A deep analysis of teller activity, historical musculoskeletal disorders (MSD) data recollection, personal interviews with the workers and applying ergonomic methodologies was essential to support future design decisions.

Calm waters and smooth sailing during the design process transformed into a thunderstorm as the transition was made from paper to reality. Every line, so deceptively easy to draw on the screen, resisted to be uplifted to the physical world.

The outcome of the project reflects the knowledge and creativity poured into the design, as well as the hardships of production and real life implementation.

© The Author(s), under exclusive license to Springer Nature Switzerland AG 2021
N. L. Black et al. (Eds.): IEA 2021, LNNS 221, pp. 59–67, 2021.
https://doi.org/10.1007/978-3-030-74608-7_8

## 2   Context

The client's demand emanated from the desire to "improve the working conditions and productivity of their 800 tellers throughout the country through a new workstation", they'd had two previous attempts at redesigning the desk, and both failed to meet their expectations.

As for this third attempt, the company decided to hire an ergonomist to assemble and lead the entire design team, they bet for ergonomics to be up to the task and finally have a positive impact on their employees and their own bottom line.

The project was undertaken with the intent to use this mission as a lever to implement ergonomic knowledge as an essential factor in improving workers quality of life while increasing productivity.

## 3   Actions

Statistical data about teller's occupational diseases (OD) was collected, as Fig. 1a shows there is a growing trend of musculoskeletal disorders (MDS) over other OD. Figure 1b shows most OD are related to the spine and hands.

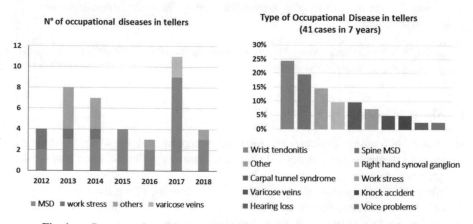

**Fig. 1.** a. 7 years series of Occupational Diseases; b. Percentages of OD in tellers

The Corlett Bishop physical discomfort test [4] was applied, see Fig. 2a, which revealed most tellers were suffering work related pain, mainly in the neck and lumbar area.

The HAL (Hand Activity Level) Method [5] applied to measure the risk of MSD in distal upper limb due to repetitive tasks. Figure 2b shows the results regarding two typical tasks analyzed at two different branches.

The results show that the right HAL is closer to the control zone than the left HAL; as the dominant hand in most cases, it's used more often regarding several tasks (mouse, keyboard, stapler, handling drawers, counting and sorting money, scanning barcodes, etc.).

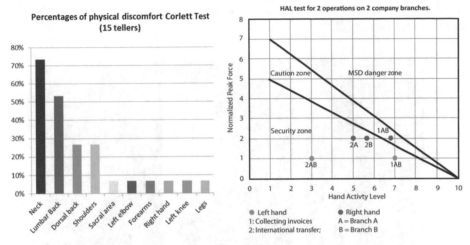

**Fig. 2.** a. Results of Corlett Test; b. Results of HAL Method

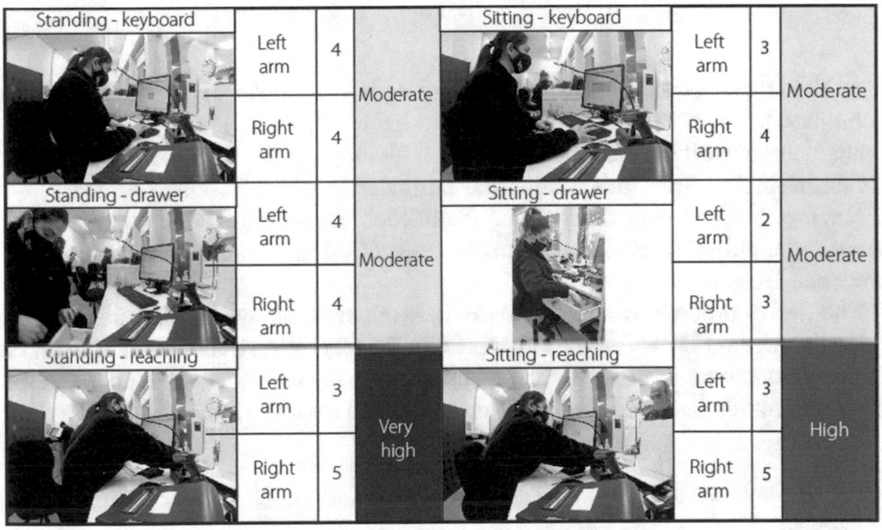

| Standing - keyboard | Left arm | 4 | Moderate | Sitting - keyboard | Left arm | 3 | Moderate |
|---|---|---|---|---|---|---|---|
| | Right arm | 4 | | | Right arm | 4 | |
| Standing - drawer | Left arm | 4 | Moderate | Sitting - drawer | Left arm | 2 | Moderate |
| | Right arm | 4 | | | Right arm | 3 | |
| Standing - reaching | Left arm | 3 | Very high | Sitting - reaching | Left arm | 3 | High |
| | Right arm | 5 | | | Right arm | 5 | |

**Fig. 3.** Results of RULA Method in standing and sitting postures before changes

The RULA Method (Rapid Upper Limb Assessment) [6] was applied.

Figure 3 shows that some of the typical postures of tellers' work go from moderate to high or very high risk due to spinal bends outside of comfort angles, arm bends greater than 90° when they reach the customer service window, almost permanent cervical bends due to the monitor being below the horizontal line of sight.

In Fig. 4 the tellers use a soft ergonomic chair, with height adjustment and comfortable lumbar support on the backrest but the legs were kept bent, due to lack of footrest and the knees collided with a ledge, causing contact stress. All this may result in varicose veins and leg fatigue [7].

**Fig. 4.** Lack of footrest causes poor leg posture

At the request of the client a productivity study was conducted [8] to have the data to compare the current situation to post redesign productivity levels. We were able to conclude that overall productivity decreased 25% compared to pre COVID-19 quarantine restrictions in Argentina, this decline was attributed to a 50% customer decrease.

Having finalized the primary data recollection phase, ergonomic observation and analysis, the old workstation problems were detected and appropriate solutions were stated, see Table 1.

The design process was aligned with the work systems' design systemic approach [2, 9, 10] based on E/FH and the PDCA (Plan, Do, Check, Act) model [2]. The process was iterative, having several presentation instances to management, their input was taken into consideration and made integral part of the final result. (Fig. 5).

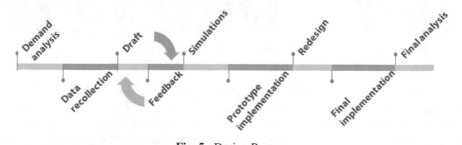

**Fig. 5.** Design Process

Simulations through virtual and physical models were used to test out design ideas, for example, a 1:2 wooden model of the height regulation mechanism for the footrest, several 1:1 shelves models to be attached to the desk, a full 3d virtual model of the workstation, among others. Supervisors and tellers participated in these simulations, contributing their experience and opinions [1, 9, 10].

After a prototype model was finally approved, one was manufactured and installed at the main branch on Oct 7th of 2020.

**Table 1.** Issues and proposed solution

| Problems found and analyzed | Design solutions |
| --- | --- |
| Lack of leg support | Height adjustable footrest |
| Contact stress on knees | Shorter tray redesign |
| Too much distance from the teller to the window | Desk depth shortening |
| Repetitive scanner use | New location and scanner's operation mode |
| Poor neck posture due to monitor height | Monitor lift module |
| Suboptimal device layout | Layout optimization and adding shelves |
| Lack of legroom | legroom widening |
| Poor cable management | Tray and cable channel standardization |

The prototype was tested by the company branch population for a month, after this period, the company's production manager gave us the feedback they had collected from the tellers and some of the company's chiefs.

The results were good but some minor adjustments were necessary, mainly, there were concerns about the device layout.

All the data we'd collected wasn't enough to yield an optimal device layout design. Even though we asked tellers about their opinions on the proposed new layout, and their answers were overwhelmingly positive, the contrary could be said about their input after they tested the prototype on real conditions.

Taking into account this feedback, we presented the final workstation version to management, the main differences being, new hanging shelves, for the bill counting machine and general office supplies, freeing up more space on the desk's work plane, addressing the staff's major concern about the first prototype.

Fourteen units of the final design were commissioned to us by our client, to be installed on different branches, the central one, where the prototype was tested and a second one with certain particularities, which would force us to customize each of the five desks intended for those premises.

This request was issued on Dec. 3rd and every workstation was expected to be installed and fully operational by Dec. 30th of 2020.

In spite of the constrained time frame and the new necessary customizations, the commission was accepted.

The workstations were delivered on time, and the installation began on schedule, unfortunately, there were several production errors: Some pieces were not as designed (the height of the portable iron brackets to support the shelves), carpenters had to work at night, as not to disturb daily operations, just one day before the holidays. (See Fig. 6 and 7).

Several more visits to the aforementioned branches had to be made to correct several production and installation errors (drawer locks; footrests did not slide well, portable shelves).

(a)                                                    (b)

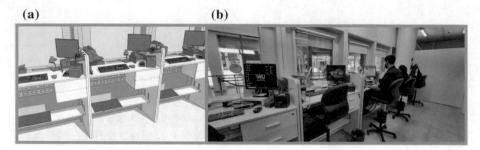

**Fig. 6.** a. Final design; b. Real installation

(a)                                                    (b)

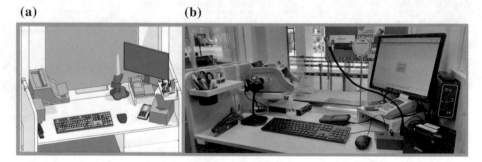

**Fig. 7.** a. Layout design; b. Real layout

## 4 Outcomes

As seen in Fig. 8 the legroom depth was extended, which lets arms to be partly supported by the desk and to get closer to the customer service window, which improves back and arm posture. The lift module raising the height of the monitor, minimizes neck tension and space on the work surface was gained thanks to portable shelves.

After installation, a survey was conducted among tellers and 100% agreed that the new furniture was very comfortable, the layout made their job much easier (43%) and that it moderately improved work (57%). 86% found it easy to adjust the height of the footrest. Regarding the discomfort that they currently felt, the answers were those shown in Fig. 9.

**Fig. 8.** Sitting and standing postures using the new design

The RULA method was also applied [6] to the post-installation situations. The results show that the risk indexes of postures out of comfort angles were substantially reduced in the characteristic postures of the activity (Fig. 10).

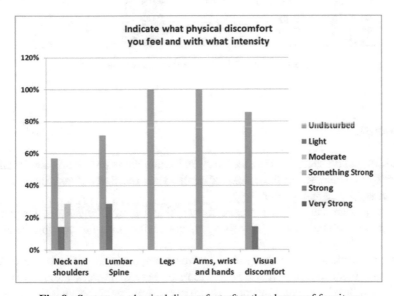

**Fig. 9.** Survey on physical discomfort after the change of furniture

Post installation productivity study showed there was no significant improvement despite rearranging devices to be more accessible. In any case, it would be convenient to have a broader post pandemic study.

The new design had a strong positive impact on the teller's comfort and in several ergonomic variables, and thus, this aspect of the project is considered a success by our team and the company. However, while the desks were delivered and installed on time, and were serviceable enough as to be operational and allow the company to not pause regular operations, the workstations had to be tweaked for several days after, until they presented no issues and were 100% finished and faithful to the blueprints. Therefore, the project did not meet the stipulated installation and implementation time frames.

| Charateristic postures | Arm | Risk level | Characteristic postures | Arm | Risk level |
|---|---|---|---|---|---|
| Standing - keyboard | | | Sitting - keyboard | | |
| | Left arm | 2 | | Left arm | 2 |
| | | | Low | | | Low |
| | Right arm | 2 | | Right arm | 2 |
| Standing - drawer | | | Sitting - drawer | | |
| | Left arm | 3 | | Left arm | 2 |
| | | | Moderate | | | Moderate |
| | Right arm | 3 | | Right arm | 3 |
| Standing - reaching | | | Sitting - reaching | | |
| | Left arm | 2 | | Left arm | 2 |
| | | | Moderate | | | Moderate |
| | Right arm | 3 | | Right arm | 3 |

**Fig. 10.** Result of RULA method, post-installation

## 5   Discussion

The most important success factor according to the client was production and installation within budget, which was fulfilled, and the quality and impact of the desk and accessories design on employee satisfaction.

For the project team this experience showed that the ergonomists and designers can work together in all the stages of a design project with the goal of improving the working conditions of the people [1, 9, 10].

Several mistakes were made by our team regarding production and implementation:

The outsourced furniture factory hired to manufacture the workstations was located in a different province than our team, this made it impossible to visit the factory for quality control before the implementation. Hiring a local factory would have allowed us to avoid many production mistakes.

This company is used to working on construction sites, therefore, their workers' presentation and attitude (image) was out of place inside operating commercial premises full of customers and employees (they were asked to fix desks issues during working hours). Choosing a provider with the right experience would have avoided certain complaints from the client regarding this issue.

Finally, eager to embark on this project, we reluctantly accepted a small timeframe to deliver results, this implied working frantically to reach the deadline, which precipitated many errors. Being honest with ourselves and analyzing our experience and capacity to determine how much it would take to properly finish this project would have made the experience much more enjoyable.

Regarding the RULA method, we noted it only classifies stable posture and unstable posture for lower limbs. In this case the legs were supported by a pipe as a foot rest below the chair, which provided a stable but uncomfortable posture. The method could be improved by adding a 3rd. classification: Supported but uncomfortable posture.

## 6 Conclusion

We believe our experience is a prime example of the importance of data gathering and analysis as the foundations of any ergonomic design project. It's also an example of the importance of thinking outside theoretical ideas, and considering practical aspects such as logistics, production technology and giving yourself the margin to correct mistakes.

Dealing with a big multinational company implies dealing with bureaucracy, which means you need to communicate to your client very precise information regarding what you need from them and what you can and will deliver, since they lack the flexibility a smaller company would have to adapt to unforeseen issues you, as a provider, could have during your workflow.

As a final conclusion, a well-designed product was delivered, that met the conceptual objective of the project and that could kick start an improvement process regarding ergonomics and worker wellbeing within the company.

## References

1. Daniellou, F., et al.: Comprender el trabajo para transformarlo, edición digital, colección Homo Faber, Ergotec, España (2010)
2. Mosier, K.L., Niu, S.: Principles and Guidelines for Human Factors/Ergonomics (HF/E) Design and Management of Work System, IEA-ILO (2020)
3. Leplat, J., Cuny, X.: Introduction à la psychologie du travail. PUF, Paris (1977)
4. Corlett, E., Bishop, R.: A technique for assessing postural discomfort. Ergonomics **19**(2), 175–182 (1976)
5. American Conference of Governmental Industrial Hygienists (ACGIH). Threshold Limit Values for chemical substances and physical agents & Biological Exposure Indices; Cincinnati, OH, USA: ACGIH (2001)
6. McAtamney, L., Corlett, E.N.: RULA: a survey method for the investigation of work related upper limb disorders. Applied Ergonomics (1993)
7. Messing, K., et al.: Distal Lower-Extremity Pain and Work Postures in the Quebec Population, p. 1, Table 3 (2011). https://ajph.aphapublications.org/author/Messing%2C+Karen
8. Kanawaty, G.: Introduction to the Study of Work. Fourth revised edition, Editorial LIMUSA, Geneva (1996)
9. Falzon, P.: Manual de Ergonomía, Colección Homo Faber, Modus Laborandi, Madrid (2010)
10. Nouviale, L.: Ergonomía Argentina Historia, Miradas y Aplicaciones, Cap. 2, AdEA, Buenos Aires (2019)

# Ergonomic Intervention in a Colombian Manufacturing Company: Successes and Failures

Yordán Rodríguez[1]([⊠]) [iD] and Elizabeth Pérez[2] [iD]

[1] National School of Public Health, Universidad de Antioquia, Medellín, Colombia
yordan.rodriguez@udea.edu.co
[2] School of Industrial Engineering, Universidad Pontificia Bolivariana, Medellín, Colombia
elizabeth.perezme@upb.edu.co

**Abstract.** The aim of this study was to present the results of an ergonomic intervention in a Colombian manufacturing company. The intervention process was carried out in five stages: (1) identify problems in the workstation, (2) ergonomic evaluation of workstations, (3) proposals for ergonomic intervention, (4) evaluation of the proposals, and (5) implementation and follow-up. As a result, several proposals for the physical and organizational redesign were projected. These proposals were elaborated and discussed with the workers involved in the intervened workstations and presented to the company's management. This work shows the benefits that can be obtained by employing a participatory approach in the ergonomic design of work systems. However, it should be mentioned that the implementation of the proposed redesigns was partial and focused mainly on the physical redesign, since barriers were generated that prevented its implementation. We believe that lessons learned (successes and failures) can serve as a reference for ergonomics practitioners in similar contexts.

**Keywords:** Participatory ergonomics · Workstation design · Musculoskeletal disorders · Ergonomic design

## 1 Introduction

According to statistics, work-related musculoskeletal disorders (WMSDs) are an important occupational problem in Colombia [1, 2]. For instance, 88% of the occupational diseases reported in Colombia between 2009 and 2013 were WMSDs [3]. Furthermore, it was estimated that WMSDs had a negative impact on productivity in Colombia in 2005 of US\$171.7 million, equivalent to 0.2% of the gross domestic product that year [1].

One strategy used to prevent WMSDs effectively is through ergonomic interventions of work systems [4, 5]. Participatory ergonomics is an approach used widely in ergonomic interventions in both developed and developing countries [6, 7]. This approach has been named in different terms, such as worker participation and participatory management [8].

Participatory ergonomics has been addressed from different perspectives, resulting in a variety of definitions [9, 10]. For instance, Wilson (1995) defined participatory ergonomics as: 'the involvement of people in planning and controlling a significant amount of their own work activities, with sufficient knowledge and power to influence both processes and outcomes in order to achieve desirable goals' [11].

Instead of a precise definition, it should be emphasized that the participatory ergonomics approach aims to take advantage of the knowledge and experience that workers have accumulated during the performance of their work and apply it to improve their working conditions.

This study aims to present the results of an ergonomic intervention in two workstations in a Colombian manufacturing company. A participatory ergonomics approach was used to carry out the intervention. Both workstations are considered critical due to the high number of WMSDs and worker complaints reported.

## 2 Methods

The intervention process was carried out in five stages [12]:

- Stage 1: Identify problems in the workstation. Two workstations in the company were analyzed: "sacks basting" and "sacks closing" (see Fig. 1), which are classified by the company as "critical" due to the number of WMSDs presented. The "sacks basting" workstation consists of sealing the sacks' side edges with a seam to not fray. The "sacks closing" workstation consists of shaping the sack by closing it from the sides.

**Fig. 1.** a shows the sacks basting workstation, and b shows the sacks closing workstation.

- Stage 2: Ergonomic evaluation of workstations. A musculoskeletal symptom questionnaire was administered to a total of forty-one workers in the area (36 men and 5 women) who performed the same tasks, ranging in age from 21 to 60 years (mean

39.3 years). The workers pointed out the parts of the body with pain through a body map. The intensity of musculoskeletal pain was assessed using a numerical scale with values from 0 (no pain) to 10 (maximum pain). Both workstations were evaluated with the Individual Risk Assessment (ERIN) ergonomic tool [13, 14].

- Stage 3: Proposals for ergonomic intervention. The anthropometric dimensions of the Colombian population were considered [15].
- Stage 4: Evaluation of the proposals.
- Stage 5: Implementation and follow-up.

The intervention process was carried out under a participatory approach; workers and managers were involved from the beginning.

## 3  Results

The main problems detected in the studied workstations were inadequate workspace layout (e.g., table and chair), causing the adoption of asymmetrical and unstable postures by the workers, very high work pace, poorly designed hand tools (e.g., scissors), and the lack of adequate recovery periods. As a result, many workers complained of pain in different regions of the body.

The musculoskeletal symptom questionnaire showed that 78% of the workers surveyed reported musculoskeletal pain. The most affected parts were the left shoulder (56%), left-hand wrist (44%) and right hand (44%), hip (42%), neck (39%), right shoulder (39%), lower back (39%) and upper back (34%). These results show that the pain is localized in the upper body, which corresponds to the activities performed. The body regions reported with the greatest intensity of pain were the left shoulder, the left wrist, and the right wrist.

Because the activities performed within the duty cycle of the sacks basting and sacks closing tasks are similar, the ERIN assessment results were also similar. This assessment indicated a very high-risk level (total risk = 40) for both tasks. The wrist, shoulder/arm, and neck were the most critical variables (interaction between posture and movement frequency). These results are consistent with those obtained with the musculoskeletal symptoms questionnaire. Work pace was also among the most critical variables (effective task duration and work speed).

Stages 3 and 4 were carried out simultaneously. The ergonomic intervention focused on minimizing exposure to risk factors for WMSDs. For this purpose, two 3D prototypes of the workstations were designed. The proposals were presented and discussed with the workers to select the prototype that would be built and tested in real working conditions. When testing these prototypes in practice, we noticed that the work surface of the sacks basting workstation needed to be wider to facilitate the sacks' handling. Finally, a third prototype was designed and selected considering the technical aspects and the workers' observations. Figure 2 shows the three prototypes designed and built.

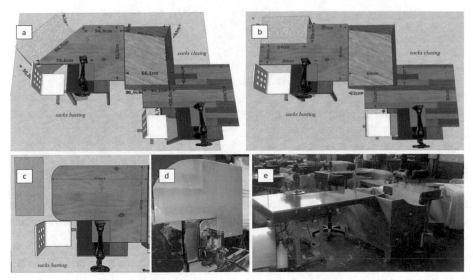

**Fig. 2.** a and b show the first two prototype workstations designed. c shows the selected prototype. In the prototypes, the workstations are connected by a channel that receives the bags and is located within the worker's reach. d and e show the prototypes built during the intervention process.

Besides, recommendations were made for the scissors, footrest and auxiliary table used. Figure 3 and Fig. 4 show these proposals.

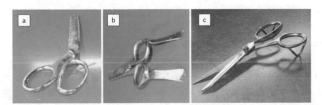

**Fig. 3.** a, b, and c show the different scissors used by de workers. In observing the workers, we noticed that scissors a were challenging to grip quickly. One initiative of the workers to solve this problem was to incorporate feet into the finger rings of scissors b and c. We also noticed that the legs on scissors b were getting tangled with the sacks, so it was proposed to extend the c scissors proposal throughout the area.

The acquisition of scissors lift tables with a minimum capacity of 500 kg was proposed to replace the auxiliary table. This new auxiliary table would allow workers to pick up the sacks at the same height as the work surface, thus reducing effort and awkward postures of the trunk, neck, and upper extremities.

The improvements focused on the workstations' physical redesign due to the company minimizing the importance of the proposed organizational changes. It should be noted that, up to stage 4, progress was gradual. Despite this, it was not possible to implement all the projected measures.

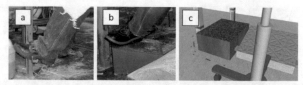

**Fig. 4.** a and b show examples of the different footrests used by the workers. c shows the proposal made together with the workers for the use of footrests. Aspects such as stability, dimensions, and location in the workplace were considered.

## 4  Discussions

As a result of this intervention process, a set of "successes" and "failures/barriers" can be mentioned, which could be valuable for other interventions carried out in similar contexts.

Main successes:

- Build the initial proposals with the participation of the workers involved.
- Discuss the initial proposals with workers and managers in economic, productive, and health terms. This discussion allowed the company to authorize the interventions.
- Build the proposals in 3D to facilitate the discussion with the workers involved and make modifications to the initial prototypes.
- Support from the professionals of the labor risk insurance company.
- A high commitment of the staff in charge of occupational health and safety in the company.
- Easy access to facilities and relevant information.

Main failures/barriers:

- The company did not consider it essential to work on improving macroergonomic factors. The intervention focused primarily on the physical aspects of the job, dismissing organizational and environmental factors.
- Intermittence in the intervention process. Sometimes activities were interrupted, contributing to workers losing confidence and associating what happened with previous interventions that did not materialize.
- Skeptical and change-resistant workers. Workers were not previously trained on the importance of ergonomically redesigning their working conditions. This caused notable differences among the workers in terms of their motivation to collaborate during the intervention process.
- Lack of integration of the stakeholders' interests: occupational risk insurance company, the company, and the ergonomics consultant.
- Limited resources.
- Non-integrated workplace analysis. For instance, the chair was not included in the intervention since it had recently been renovated, but without considering the worker's interaction with the elements that make up the workstation (e.g., worktable, work time, work speed, materials used).

- Lack of internal personnel trained in ergonomics issues.
- Lack of specialized personnel in the construction of the projected prototypes. This caused the designs not to be carried out according to the plans provided, resulting in the construction of inoperative prototypes and affecting the workers' credibility about the intervention's effectiveness.
- A reactive approach in the company to solve ergonomics problems. The statistics of WMSDs drove this intervention.
- Lack of standardization in work methods, causing each worker to perform the task according to his experience and judgment, but not according to an optimized and proven method.
- Lack of a cost-benefit analysis that would demonstrate the importance of preventing musculoskeletal diseases in the workstations studied.

## 5 Conclusions

Many intervention cases have been published showing successful examples of participatory ergonomics. However, there are few examples where the negative experiences, barriers, mistakes, and characteristics of the context (internal and external to the organization) that hinder the intervention are presented. This work's primary value consists of mentioning the success and failures that could occur during an ergonomic intervention project. These experiences can be useful for practitioners of ergonomics in similar contexts.

In the intervention cases presented (sacks basting and sacks closing), efforts were mainly focused on the physical redesign to reduce exposure to physical risk factors of WMSDs in the workstations. However, the importance of organizational factors in the emergence of these diseases should be noted, which should be analyzed and intervened, since physical redesign alone does not guarantee that all risk factors will be controlled. Finally, the benefits of projecting the redesigns using 3D modeling tools should be highlighted since facilitating the participation process of the workers involved.

## References

1. Piedrahita, H.: Costs of work-related musculoskeletal disorders (MSDs) in developing countries: Colombia case. Int. J. Occup. Saf. Ergon. **12**, 379–386 (2006)
2. Castillo, S.P., Bravo, G.P.: Comportamiento de la enfermedad laboral en Colombia 2015–2017. Revista Fasecolda, pp. 48–55 (2019)
3. MINTRABAJO: II Encuesta Nacional de Condiciones de Seguridad y Salud en el Trabajo en el Sistema de Riesgos Laborales de Colombia. Bogotá, Colombia (2013)
4. Dempsey, P.G.: Effectiveness of ergonomics interventions to prevent musculoskeletal disorders: beware of what you ask. Int. J. Ind. Ergon. **37**, 169–173 (2007)
5. Silverstein, B., Clark, R.: Interventions to reduce work-related musculoskeletal disorders. J. Electromyogr. Kinesiol. **14**, 135–152 (2004)
6. Torres, Y., Rodríguez, Y.: Ergonomic intervention for reducing the exposure to musculoskeletal disorders risk factors in pharmaceutical production centre. Ergonomics SA **24**, 58–75 (2012)

7. Kogi, K.: Participatory methods effective for ergonomic workplace improvement. Appl. Ergon. **37**, 547–554 (2006)
8. Brown, O.: Participatory ergonomics, Chap. 81. In: Stanton, N.A., Hedge, A., Brookhuis, K., Salas, E., Hendrick, H.W. (eds.) Handbook of Human Factors and Ergonomics Methods, pp. 81-1–81-6. CRC Press, Boca Raton (2005)
9. Hignett, S., Wilson, J.R., Morris, W.: Finding ergonomic solutions—participatory approaches. Occupat. Med. **55**, 200–207 (2005)
10. Burgess-Limerick, R.: Participatory ergonomics: evidence and implementation lessons. Appl. Ergon. **68**, 289–293 (2018)
11. Wilson, J.R.: Ergonomics and participation. In: Wilson, J.R., Corlett, E.N. (eds.) Evaluation of Human Work: A Practical Ergonomics Methodology, pp. 1071–1096. Taylor & Francis, London (1995)
12. Rodríguez Ruíz, Y., Pérez Mergarejo, E.: Procedimiento ergonómico para la prevención de enfermedades en el contexto ocupacional. Rev Cub Salud Pública **40**, 279–285 (2014)
13. Rodríguez, Y., Viña, S., Montero, R.: A Method for non-experts in assessing exposure to risk factors for work-related musculoskeletal disorders-ERIN. Ind. Health **51**, 622–626 (2013)
14. Rodríguez, Y., Viña, S., Montero, R.: ERIN: a practical tool for assessing work-related musculoskeletal disorders. Occup. Ergon. **11**, 59–73 (2013)
15. Estrada, J., Camacho, J., Restrepo, M., Parra, C.: Parámetros antropométricos de la población laboral colombiana-Acopla-95 (1995)

# Using SELR
# (Simplify-Enable-Leverage-Resource)
# to Develop Solutions to Identified Opportunities

Lawrence J. H. Schulze[✉]

Department of Industrial Engineering, Cullen College of Engineering, University of Houston, Building 2, 4722 Calhoun Road, Room E206, Houston, TX 77204-4008, USA
ljhs@uh.edu

**Abstract.** The SELR approach was introduced by the U. S. Navy Reserve Force in 2018 to make its associated operations more efficient and responsive to an ever-changing environment. Such an approach is exactly the focus of such programs as $6\sum$, Lean, Continuous Process Improvement, etc. SELR is defined by the following. **Simplify** the way business is conducted by streamlining activities, programs, to make them more efficient. **Enable** personnel to more effectively provide required capabilities and supportive policies. **Leverage** personnel skills and relationships to further enhance their contributions to the organization. **Resource** delivering more responsive personnel capabilities to the organization. This approach is applied to ergonomic intervention development and illustrated through case studies.

**Keywords:** Ergonomics · Simplify · Enable · Leverage · Resource · Intervention development

## 1 Introduction

Simplify: This has been the tradition way business has been improved by streamlining activities, programs and policies to make them more efficient. Organizations must have simplified processes to compete in time to meet the needs of changing demands. Simplify here is related to the solutions developed for identified opportunities. Solutions should be simple to develop, simple to implement, simple to understand by the workforce.

Enable: Traditionally, this approach has focused to more effectively delivering the required capabilities through innovative technology and support policies. Our staff is the "heart" of the support role and experience we bring to the organization. In this application, enabling refers to creating a winning organization that recognizes staff skills and allows a smoother transition between a specific position within an organization to a project team and supports decision making at the lowest level.

Leverage: Organizations have traditionally leveraged the skills and relationships of staff within an industry to support, champion and further improve their contributions to the organization. An organization's associations with industry and academia have

N. L. Black et al. (Eds.): IEA 2021, LNNS 221, pp. 75–81, 2021.
https://doi.org/10.1007/978-3-030-74608-7_10

created a powerful force multiplier for organizational success. Here, personnel are seen as talent assets and the face of the organization in their local communities, where key relationships are ideal to harness the power of trust, honesty and integrity with the community in which the organization operates. Organizations need to better utilize that unique combination of personnel skills that will give the organization a competitive advantage and allow individual talents to be leveraged to help the organization develop interventions to identified improvement opportunities.

Resource: Resourcing has traditionally focused on ensuring that funds are provided for skill improvement, training and equipment so staffing capabilities are more responsive to the organization. In this application, to create a path to success, organizations must have innovative processes that have the right tools for the job. Therefore, resourcing ensure that funds are dedicated to opportunity identification and intervention development and implementation.

## 2 Background

Several sources were evaluated to determine the impact of each of the SELR variables (Simplify, Enable, Leverage, Disqualify). One of the main resources was the Deloitte 2015 report entitled: Global Human Capital Trends 2015: Leading in the New World of Work [1]. Additional resources were consulted to provide additional information related to each SELR variable.

In this report, the authors found different levels of capacity gaps to simplify work for several countries around the world. The most significant gaps were in the application of work simplification efforts, despite the amount of work simplification certifications that are available to companies within these countries.

In addition, respondents to the Deloitte 2015 survey indicated that little more than 50% of the respondents had some level of a work simplification program and only 10% had a main program. The reason for these gaps may be related to the perceived complexity of the work. Agarwal, van Berkel and Rea [2], indicated that the following were contributors to their perception of the complexity of work: (A) Generalized technology and connectivity; (B) complexity in technology; (C) globalization; (D) increase administrative and compliance demands; and (E) too complex business processes and systems.

Administrative processes that are too complex, leads to a difficulty in finding simple solutions to identified ergonomic opportunities. Why? Because personnel see the system as complex, therefore, the solutions must be complex.

Companies must allow staff to make decisions and develop solutions to identified opportunities. Organizations should also take advantage of the skills and desires of their staff to develop and manufacture solutions to the identified opportunities. Personnel can be hired to perform a specific task within a company. However, it is their unique skills and talents that simplify the work, improve methods, develop solutions to identified ergonomic opportunities. Leveraging these skills and talents should also be used to help design and manufacture interventions.

Programs such as FastWorks [3] as illustrated in GE Beliefs [4] have led to better solutions requiring a focus on the following: (A) customers determine the company's success; (B) stay slim to go fast; (C) learn to adapt to win; (D) empower and inspire each other (enable and leverage staff resources); and (E) deliver results in an uncertain world.

Allowing personnel to improve the effectiveness of work methods, the work processes, tools and equipment used to provide goods and services allows the internal development and implementation of interventions. Leveraging the skills, talents and desires of personnel, together with the lowest level decision-making, reinforces the focus and effect of the Lean concept. Lean must not only be used in business processes, but also used in the identification of ergonomic opportunities, as well as the development and implementation of interventions.

The provision of resources must be a priority in order to identify opportunities and both develop and implement interventions. These resources must be a budget priority.

What happens without SELR?

- Workers may not report injuries and work with injuries because they are afraid of losing the jobs(s).
- Unreported injuries will manifest in long-term harm and reduced work capacity (productivity).
- Other works become aware of injurious conditions and focus on these conditions, not on work resulting in increased injuries, decreased productivity, and potential product and equipment damage.
- The community will become aware of such an injurious environment and talent acquisition will become difficult.
- Absenteeism will increase and personnel will depart to work in less injurious organizations
- Failure to address the work-related opportunities will undermine you Lean, $6\sum$, and related programs and reduce competitiveness.

## 3 Results

An ergonomic evaluation of the operations in a utility company (generation and transmission of energy and natural gas service, potable and waste water) was conducted. The SELR approach was applied to each area evaluated to develop solutions to identified ergonomic opportunities. The utility had implemented some work simplifications programs but had not yet see their benefit. Most of their simplification efforts had been applied to administrative processes rather than production, service and or maintenance operations.

Service technicians perform inspection and service of natural gas installations at residences and businesses requiring personnel to spend a significant amount of time in their assigned vehicles (trucks); driving, completing paperwork, eating, etc. They fill out service forms (paperwork) provided to customers and then complete their reports on company-provided laptops. Most often, these personnel use the console between the 2 front seats as a worksurface on which they complete the paperwork and use their laptops. This requires personnel to twist and sustain a static exertion of back muscles in a twisted posture to use the console. In addition, personnel have a wide range of individual anthropometric dimensions that makes posture requirements more difficult than for others.

As a result of the ergonomics analyses and interviews with personnel, static postures and back discomfort were identified as the leading issues among the personnel performing these job tasks. Therefore, sustained static twisted postures and reports of significant back discomfort were the focus of developing ergonomic interventions to eliminate / reduce both back discomfort and awkward postures required withing the truck cabin environment.

At first, a stand with a moveable arm was recommended to support the laptop. The stand that was recommended is similar to those used in police cars in the United States. See Fig. 1 for the universal laptop mount considered and Fig. 2 for an example of a typical body posture assumed by a police officer using a similar laptop support. As can be seen from a revies of Figs. 1 and 2, the issue of a sustained twisted body posture would not be addressed, typing posture would be awkward and there would not be a worksurface on which to complete paperwork unless the laptop was in a closed position.

**Fig. 1.** Universal laptop support.

**Fig. 2.** Posture assumed police officer using universal laptop support.

A second idea was to use a table similar to that found in a commercial plane. Personnel could lift the table and fold it on their lap. This would provide a surface between the worker and the steering wheel. However, there is a safety concern that was not immediately apparent; staff could still drive their vehicle while the table was in position for use. It is possible to provide an interlock to prevent movement of the vehicle. However, interlocks can be overridden. Figures 3a and 3b present the Executive Desk considered.

**Fig. 3.** a and b. Executive car desk and executive car desk with surface extended, respectively.

One of the personnel working in this job function recommended the final solution recommended and adopted (Simplify, Enable and Leverage). They found a table that attached to the steering wheel of the vehicle and provided two different worksurfaces on opposite sides (simplify); one surface was flat for writing and laptop support and the other provided compartments for food and drinks. While the worksurface is connected to the steering wheel, vehicle operation is prevented.

Additionally, the table is available on Amazon for $11.99 USD. Further exemplifying 'Simplify' as readily available off-the-shelf intervention. The company enabled this individual to manage the field evaluation of the table, leveraging their desire to improve worker health, decrease discomfort and improve operational effectiveness; addressing the back discomfort suffered by this worker and their colleagues.

The selected and implemented intervention is presented in Figs. 4a, 4b, 4c and 4d. The impact of implementing this simple solution is detailed below.

- The solution had an easy and instantaneous implementation
- The average direct cost of back pain per person in this organization was $2,500 USD.
- There were an average 38 reports of back pain within this of task group per year resulting in a cost of $95,000 USD per year (38 × $2500 USD).
- The cost of implementation was $599 USD (50 trucks × $11.99 USD)
- The SELR interventions was 0.53% of one year's costs of back pain in this job classification.

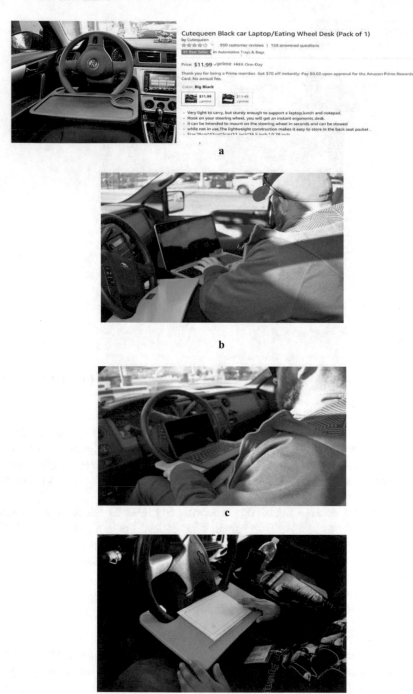

**Fig. 4.** a. Desk selected for implementation [5]. b. Desk selected for implementation with worker in original posture. c. Laptop positioned on implemented intervention. d. Completing paperwork on implemented intervention.

## 4 Discussion

The SELR approach was first used to identify feasible and implementable interventions and focused on the simplest solutions to identify, obtain, implement and use by the target user population. Enabling was used through encouraging workers to participate in the intervention identification managing the intervention evaluation process. Leveraging included encouraging personnel to use individual talents to identify, evaluate and implement interventions that affect their and their colleague's health and comfort on the job. Resourcing was used by demonstrating to management that funds should be budgetarily allocated to these types of activities based on their impact on worker health, worker wellbeing, and return-on-investment (ROI) through demonstrated benefits/costs analysis.

As can be seen, the application of SELR in concert with participative ergonomics, results in benefits to personnel that are measurable and more readily acceptable to the user population. SELR must be applied in organizations as we move forward during and after SAR-COV-19 to ensure that we are maximizing personnel talents to effectively address worker health and well-being. SELR is a viable and powerful methodology to identify simple interventions to complex issues leading to more resourcing by the organization to support such efforts.

## References

1. Schatsky, D., Schwartz, J.: Global Human Capital Trends 2015: Leading in the New World of Work. Deloitte University Press (2015). https://www2.deloitte.com/content/dam/insights/us/articles/work-simplification-human-capital-trends-2015/DUP_GlobalHumanCapitalTrends2015.pdf
2. Agarwal, D., van Berkel, A., Rea, B.: Simplification of Work: The Coming Revolution. Deloitte Insights (2015). https://www2.deloitte.com/us/en/insights/focus/human-capital-trends/2015/work-simplification-human-capital-trends-2015.html
3. Ries, E.: The Lean Startup: How Today's Entrepreneurs Use Continuous Innovation to Create Radically Successful Businesses. The Crown Publishing Group, The Random House (2011)
4. Krishnamoorthy, R.: GE's Culture Change after Welch and Immelt. Managing Organizations, 26 January 2015. https://hbr.org/2015/01/ges-culture-challenge-after-welch-and-immelt
5. Amazon: Amazon.com: Cutequeen Trading car Eating/Laptop Steering Wheel Desk (Black, 16.5″ × 11″ × 0.79″): Automotive (2021)

# The Immersion in Virtual Reality of Control Room Activity

Elaine C. Silva$^{(\boxtimes)}$ ⓘ, Carla A. G. Sirqueira ⓘ, and Fernanda G. S. Pinto ⓘ

Innovation Center in Ergonomics – SESI/FIEMG, Belo Horizonte, Brazil

**Abstract.** The mental burden associated with the activity of the control room operator has been the subject of study for ergonomics, which is interested in the strategies used during work situations. Aiming to support traditional training of control room operation activities in an innovative fashion, the Innovation Center in Ergonomics proposed to include immersive technology in a virtual environment as an integral part of the workers' learning process, aiming to facilitate and enhance responses to stimuli, provide a positive experience in the learning process and avoid possible accidents. For immersion in a 3D virtual environment, HTC VIVEPORT virtual reality glasses and gamification elements were used. For such, a company in the logistics industry was chosen, which manages part of the rail network in Brazil. The control room modeling process was carried out from the understanding of the activity through observation, activity analysis and semi-structured questionnaire. From this, it was possible to identify the operator's work requirements both in the physical, cognitive and organizational aspects. After modeling the game, the first pilot test allowed the identification of some items to be adjusted for a better understanding of the process. The second pilot test, carried out at the company, showed that most experiences were positive, based on the operators' perceptions. The development of educational projects using interactive technological resources of virtual simulation, can be very efficient in the work environment, making it easier the perception of risk and accelerating the knowledge curve of the control room operators.

**Keywords:** Control room · Mental burden · Ergonomics · Training · Virtual reality

## 1 Introduction

The desire to control industrial processes has accompanied humans since the creation of the first machines. In this context of industrial revolution, new technologies associated with the internet are being incorporated into control systems, in order to make it increasingly automatic [1]. Among the different sectors of a company, however, the control room still stands out for its complexity and for its mental requirements related to the content of the work, the perception, the treatment of information and decision making [2].

The control room operator's activity also depends on the degree and method of automation. Even so, when irregular situations occur, workers are indispensable to ensure

© The Author(s), under exclusive license to Springer Nature Switzerland AG 2021
N. L. Black et al. (Eds.): IEA 2021, LNNS 221, pp. 82–88, 2021.
https://doi.org/10.1007/978-3-030-74608-7_11

decision-making tasks. This action can be compromised, if the operator has not experienced proper training or if the system does not provide enough information to act when required [3].

Therefore, the processing of information occurring over time and dynamically in the control rooms, compose a system of interactions between people and technology, which needs to be well engaged or the number of incidents tends to increase due to the exchange of inefficient information or poor connection [4, 5].

Training is one of the methods used by companies for the operator to acquire a qualified interaction with the system and consequent competence.

The competences operationalize the knowledge and skills of the worker that are concretized in actions in a given work situation [6]. Currently, practical control room training is carried out with a more experienced professional. The lack of practical knowledge of the worker, however, can still be a reason for accidents and cognitive overload until he/she acquires competence to perform the function.

The search for companies for increasingly quick solutions to solve their problems has been essential to achieve success and stand out in the competitive market. They have been looking for ways to reduce risk, reduce costs and be more agile in their processes. As a result, it becomes increasingly necessary for workers to be able to develop their activities quickly, conveniently and safely.

Ergonomics considers operating strategies, the interaction between operators and between operators and the system [7]. This interaction occurs through mental processes representing a work situation and are manifested through attention, memory and reasoning [2].

One of the strategies used to make the learning of workers easier, to decrease time and cost, to provide security, in addition to enhancing the retention of knowledge, is the use of virtual simulators to conduct training. This practice allows workers to be inserted in a situation very close to reality and can experience rare risk situations in the production process, as in the case of the control room.

Faced with this complex activity, the need to update the way training is proposed becomes even more important, because from incorporated practical experiences that workers develop expertise that can positively contribute to regulate the cognitive workload, avoid accidents and improve productivity.

Bringing this reasoning to the needs of workers and industry, the Innovation Center in Ergonomics has developed a project able to enrich training for the activity of operating in the control room, focusing on the cognitive requirements of work, in addition to preventing possible accidents. It was proposed, as part of the training, before the practical experience in the control room, the experience of work situation from immersion in virtual reality. Immersion in the virtual environment is a strategy used to experience a real situation, but in a simulated way.

## 2  Methods

The Innovation Center in Ergonomics developed a project to enrich the training of operating activity in the control room, focusing on the cognitive demands of the job. It was proposed, as part of the training, before the practical experience in the control room, the experience of work situation from immersion in virtual reality.

A case study was carried out in a company in the logistics industry, which manages a railway network of more than 1,500 km in length in Brazil.

The qualitative research approach was used insofar it also emphasizes the perspective of the individual who is part of the study, considering it as an integral part of the research process [8].

For data collection, from on-site visits, an analysis of the control room operator's activity was performed, as an assumption of the Ergonomic Work Analysis method [9]. For analysis, information was collected from workers and supervisors in the area, in addition to systematic observations, filming and photographs.

A structured questionnaire with 9 questions was also used to understand the perceptions of control room operators, after immersion in virtual reality.

For the virtual modeling of the control room scenario, a detailed description of the environment, movements (biomechanics) and requirements based on the analysis of the activity was carried out, aiming to approximate the reality of the work.

This modeling was built in a 3D virtual environment with immersion through HTC VIVEPORT virtual reality glasses. In this simulation, some elements of gamification were used in order to make the learning easier, based on playfulness.

Pilot tests were initially carried out at the Innovation Center in Ergonomics with people who were unaware of the activity (analysts and manager), before conducting them at the company.

The study population at the company was composed of 2 control room operation technicians and 1 control room supervisor, who did the initial test (pilot) at the company. Due to the time of the pandemic, part of the workers were in home office, which made it impossible for more people to perform the test.

Before the test, the operators were informed about the purposes and were free to give up if they wanted to. For the experiment, 70% alcohol was used in all objects (glasses, levers, pen), a mask for the glasses and a mask for the nose and mouth region were used in order to take care of everyone's health.

One of the technicians in the control room operation is female and has worked at the company for 7 years, in the same activity, and will be called operator 1 in the results of the study. The other operation technician is male and has worked at the company for 1 year and will be called operator 2. The control room supervisor has worked in the industry for 25 years and will be called operator 3.

The activity observation site was the company's control room and the pilot's test site was a meeting room, in which the computer with the HTC VIVEPORT software and virtual reality goggles was installed.

## 3   Results

At first, a systematic observation of the control room was performed to learn about the activities related to the control room operator. After collecting the data, these were analyzed and, together with a Startup, a virtual environment was built with gamification elements, approaching situations in the reality of the control room operator's work.

The reality of the control room and the stimuli to which the operator is exposed, showed that this activity has a high cognitive demand, since it requires a high level of attention, concentration, reasoning, memory and decision making during the workday.

In the context of the studied control room, the operator sits in front of 6 monitors, wearing a headset and communicating with the drivers and those responsible for maintaining the railway network. His/her task has as its starting point the task of the programmer, who makes the licenses for the movement of trains, which keeps them in communication throughout the process.

The identification of the railway network in the control panels is carried out by different colors representing the licenses for the composition (train) in real time. Therefore, his/her activities in the control room require his/her senses (vision, hearing, mainly) to be able and in proper conditions to respond quickly during the process.

The result of the experience from the simulation in a pilot test with the team from the Innovation Center in Ergonomics allowed to identify the need for a more detailed explanation about the game process. This was necessary due to the demanding level of the task and also due to the fact that they did not know the activity of the control room operator.

Based on their perceptions, it was necessary to: increase the letters for easier and faster direction; increase the time for the learning operator to think and memorize; increase the focus on the main points of attention in the game.

These initial results allowed the game to be improved for further pilot testing at the company.

In the company, the pilot test allowed the experience of the work situation in a virtual environment (Fig. 1) and a maximum of 3 game attempts was established, since there is the possibility of feeling dizzy while wearing the 3D glasses. The game is restarted when the operator misses at some point. Therefore, operators 1, 2 and 3 played 3 times to reach the end of the game, as the level of demand increases as the same happens. Each play lasts for about 8 min, so each player played for about 20 min.

**Fig. 1.** Immersion in virtual reality of the operation activity of a railway network's control room.

Operator 1 reported feeling nauseated from the second move and operator 2 said he felt dizzy when removing his glasses at the end of the game. Player 3 reported not feeling dizzy at the end of the game's three attempts.

After playing, the players reported satisfaction with the experience, highlighting that this experience was very interesting and will be important for those who are in the training phase.

According to operator 2, dealing with the unexpected in the game was interesting and is something necessary in training, since it brings the perspective of the reality of the control room, in which the day-to-day variability is experienced.

Responding to the questionnaire:

In question 1, the three operators reported that the virtual environment is close to the reality of the control room (with regard to the environment).

In question 2, operators 1 and 2 pointed out that the use of glasses was not comfortable, because of the need to use the mask concurrently (pandemic) and because of dizziness and nausea. Operator 3, in turn, considered wearing glasses comfortable.

In question 3, the three operators found the use of the control (lever) easy.

In question 4, operators 2 and 3 considered that the stages of the games were clear, while operator 1 considered the last stage to be complex.

In question 5, the three operators considered that the time was sufficient to think and do the task.

In question 6, the three operators considered that what was accomplished in the game is part of the theory and practice of the control room operation.

In question 7, the three operators considered that the level of demand is similar to the reality of operation in the control room, with regard to the level of attention, time and decision making.

In question 8, the three operators considered that this experience is important after the theory and before the practical activity in the control room, since it puts the operator in contact with reality, but with greater security.

In the last question, a blank space was given for them to make some observation about this experience. Players 1 and 3 made some technical suggestions that are part of the day-to-day to be introduced, as they can help the control room operators in training to acquire greater knowledge and skill.

Although the operators did not comment, it was noticed the difficulty of fitting her glasses to the virtual glasses, which led operator 1 to remove the them for the experience, which compromised the sharpness, according to her.

The time for the responses to the stages of the game was considered important and sufficient, since the operator needs this period for memorization and reasoning, in order to be able to respond safely. According to the experienced operators, the time was adequate to the work reality.

## 4  Discussions

The technological expansion associated with the internet, called digital transformation, is the reason for the digital inclusion [10] of thousands of people and has been used as an educational tool to meet current demands. An example of demand is the training of company workers, who develop training aimed at teaching the practice of different jobs.

In this study, the proposal to include virtual reality in control room operation training, before practical training, enhanced the stimuli, through immersion in the simulated work situation in a 3D environment.

Recent studies prove the efficiency of the use of virtual reality in education, from the creation of didactic material (software). The use of web-based applications is common today, and student participation in interactive games generates new high-level media, visual and digital literacy skills [11, 12]. This has made the participation of these subjects easier in simulated environments.

The pilot's test with the competent operators for the control room activities brought positive results regarding the lived experience, from the immersion in a virtual environment. Its competencies operationalize knowledge and skills [6], giving the system greater reliability. Furthermore, they also made some suggestions that could enrich the game.

Players 1 and 2 presented complaints related to dizziness and nausea, which confirms the possible occurrence of side effects of immersion in virtual reality, after a period of 10 min of immersion [13], with most people.

The understanding of the control room operator's work activity was of great importance for the assertiveness in the conception of this virtual reality. As stressed by Gasperini (2010) [14], ergonomics and simulation are interconnected when it comes to solving a work-related problem.

## 5 Conclusions

The analysis of the activity allowed the understanding of different variability of the work situation in the control room, which allowed to identify important aspects to include in the virtual reality. The initial pilot test, carried out at the Innovation Center in Ergonomics, proved to be important for the identification of flaws in the simulation, which from adjustments could bring the virtual environment closer to the work reality, with the necessary requirements for the construction of worker knowledge that is in the learning process.

In the company, the feedback from competent workers (operators 1, 2, and 3) was positive and brought an important contribution to the final adjustments of the virtual training.

The development of educational projects teaching and simulating the use of systems and applications in an interactive fashion can be very efficient in the work environment, especially for activities involving risk of life and productivity.

Thus, in view of current events and technological developments, the resources used in this practice can collaborate to avoid mental overload, facilitate the perception of risks and decision making, in addition to enhancing the learning of workers.

This experience can be one of the ways to avoid possible accidents, illnesses and to improve productivity.

# References

1. Gutierrez, R.M.V., Pan, S.S.K.: Complexoeletrônico: automação do controle industrial. BNDES Setorial, Rio de Janeiro, no. 28 , pp. 189–231 (2008). https://bndes.gov.br/biblio tecadigital. Accessed 05 Jan 2021
2. Soares, F., Vidal, M.: Ergonomia: Trabalho adequado e eficiente. Elsevier Editora Ltda **1**, 124–128 (2011)
3. Carvalho, P.V.R., Vidal, M.C.: Modelagem de acidentes: uma discussão conceitual no plano cognitivo. In: X Congresso Brasileiro de Ergonomia, ABERGO, Rio de Janeiro (2000)
4. Stanton, et al.: Human Factors and the Design and Evaluation of Central Control Room Operations. Taylor & Francis, Boca Raton (2009)
5. Rooney, J.J., et al.: Reduce human error. Qual. Progress **35**(9), 27–36 (2002)
6. Abrahão, J., et al.: Introdução à Ergonomia. In: Abrahão, J., et al. (eds.) Cognição no Trabalho, pp. 147–175. Blucher, São Paulo (2009)
7. Iida, I., Buarque, L.: Ergonomia: Projeto e Produção. 3rd edn. Blucher, São Paulo (2016)
8. Michel, P.A.C.: Metodologia de pesquisa em engenharia de produção e gestão de operações. Elsevier (2012)
9. Guérin, F., et al.: Compreender o Trabalho para Transformá-lo – A Prática da Ergonomia. Edgard Blucher, São Paulo (2001)
10. Cooper, M.: The challenge of practical work in a university - real, virtual and remote experiments. In: Proceedings of the Information Society Technologies Conference (2000)
11. Sampaio, A., Martins, O.: The application of virtual reality technology in the construction of bridge: the cantilever and incremental launching methods. Automation in Construction, Technical University of Lisbon, Department of Civil Engineering and Architecture (2013)
12. Sousa, R.P., Moita, F.M.C.S.C., Carvalho, A.B.G.: Tecnologias Digitais na Educação. Editora da Universidade Estadual da Paraíba, Paraíba (2011)
13. Regan, C.: An investigation into nausea and other side-effects of head-coupled immersive virtual reality. Virtual Reality **1**, 17–31 (1995). https://doi.org/10.1007/BF02009710
14. Gasperini, R.: Realidade virtual aplicada à ergonomia por meio do design participativo. Dissertação de mestrado. Programa de Pós-Graduação em Desing da Universidade Estadual Paulista "Júlio de Mesquita Filho". UNESP. Bauru (2010)

# Ergonomics is Profitable – Experiences from a Holistic Manufacturing Plant Level Development Process

Teemu Suokko[1,2](✉) ⓘ and Arto Reiman[3] ⓘ

[1] MSK Group Oy, Kauhava, Finland
teemu.suokko@msk.fi
[2] School of Medicine, University of Eastern Finland, Kuopio, Finland
[3] Industrial Engineer and Management, University of Oulu, Oulu, Finland

**Abstract.** In industry, to enhance the operating conditions of companies, development measures are required for work, work environment, technologies and products. Development of the work affects the quality of working life, which is one of the factors that make it possible to experience well-being at work. The goal of ergonomics is to organize the work and the working environment so that the changes benefit both the company and its staff. Thus, it is important to look at ergonomic work and work-environment development at the same time as productivity and well-being at work. This study examines an ergonomics development process in one manufacturing plant in Finland. The aim of this process was to improve productivity and promote well-being at work by improving production capacity, reducing non-productive work, and optimizing material flows. The project was facilitated through a participatory ergonomics process. As a result of the process, the plant's total productivity increased by 5 percent, meaning an annual increase of 250 products in manufacturing capacity. The process also contributed significantly to health and safety, with decreased sick leave and occupational accidents and with increased perceptions of well-being at work. The company's total cost saving in two years was €210,700.

**Keywords:** Ergonomics · Participatory · Manufacturing

## 1 Ergonomics: A Driver of Development

### 1.1 Ergonomics as a System Perspective

As a discipline, ergonomics examines the interactions between people and other parts of an operating system and applies the theoretical principles, data, and methods of ergonomics to optimize human well-being and the efficiency of the operating system [1, 2]. In this review, the operating system is a multidimensional concept. It can be viewed microergonomically, focusing on an individual's work system, or it can be viewed macroergonomically, for example from the perspectives of the work community, organization, or organizational networks [2]. The concept of the operating system can also

N. L. Black et al. (Eds.): IEA 2021, LNNS 221, pp. 89–95, 2021.
https://doi.org/10.1007/978-3-030-74608-7_12

be extended to influence, for example, global challenges of sustainable development [3]. At its simplest, ergonomics looks at individual employees and their work environment. However, this perspective limits the development activities of several employees and can lead to sub-optimization at the expense of other parts of the larger system [2]. The fourth industrial revolution challenges companies to explore and develop the interaction between technological and social systems for a larger perspective [4].

A work system and the humans who use it are in constant interaction. Disruptions between work and health can pose a complex challenge to an organization. Problems at work can be reflected in workers through various psychosocial and organizational processes [5, 6]. Changing and developing the operating system serve as a functional guideline for ergonomics. Ergonomics can be used to find solutions for the system, which at best appear in terms of operational flow, organizational productivity, and staff well-being and health [2].

Ergonomics, by its nature, is a multidisciplinary field that provides tools for understanding and developing both microergonomic and broader macroergonomic entities. Managing and developing this requires the consideration of different actors and stakeholders. Participation and participatory planning are central to ergonomics. Participation within a company can take place in many ways, but it often means the involvement and commitment of all relevant employee groups and management [7, 8]. Participatory ergonomics uses staff skills to make working conditions healthier, safer, and more efficient [9, 10]. There are indicators that ergonomics can be effective to the companies [11, 12]. On the other hand, there are also challenges in efficacy research, such as the difficulty of conducting randomized controlled trials and of comparing cost–benefit calculation results between countries [11, 13].

The smooth implementation of demanding and large-scale development projects in the workplace requires cooperation with different levels of the organization. Thus, the development of ergonomics is best realized when it integrates the skills, experience, and solution ideas of the entire staff. Involving users of the operating system in planning the work means modifying their own activities, environment, and tools as appropriate. Incorporating employees' practical knowledge into a broader development package increases the chances of successful project implementation [14].

## 1.2 Promoting Ergonomics

As the ergonomics literature shows, the development of work conditions, community, and environment can be impactful, improving well-being and efficiency at work and eventually contributing to productive work [11, 12]. To contribute to this discussion, we describe in this paper a systematic, ergonomic change process in one small manufacturing plant in Finland. The company is part of a larger, Finnish-owned industrial group, MSK Group, which has six production units located in Finland, Germany, and Slovakia. The company operates as its own production unit, producing trailers and boat trailers to Scandinavian markets.

At the start of the development process, the production unit had fourteen blue-collar and four white-collar workers. The employees mainly did manual assembly work, divided into subassembly and trailer assembly sections. The production facilities also had a paint shop and a proto department, and included sheet metal machinery for part production, a sheet metal cutter, and two edging machines.

In this study we describe the development process and analyze its impacts on productivity and well-being at work. As an indicator describing productivity, we use product manufacturing capacity before and after the change. As indicators describing well-being, we use annual accident frequency (accidents at work per million working hours) and number of sick-leave days. As an indicator describing well-being at work, we use daily "Happy or not" measurements, whereby staff have the opportunity to comment daily on their current state of well-being, on a four-point scale from "very negative" to "very positive". Commenting is made on a terminal located outside social facilities. We also use notes from interviews conducted between the staff, the occupational safety and health manager (1st author), and the production manager at the start of the development process. In addition, we use workstation-specific workload measurements taken at the start of the process.

## 1.3    The Development Process of Production Facilities

This study focuses on a development process in a manufacturing plant. The available workspace in the plant assembly area posed challenges for efficient manufacturing. This led to a lot of unproductive work in the form of in-house logistics and moving of goods, for instance. Staff faced constant interruptions. Several tasks required heavy manual work. Well-being was not at a satisfactory level, and the amount of sick leave was high. A change process was therefore launched, with the goals of promoting productivity, improving well-being, reducing indirect work, and streamlining material flows.

The company's production manager started a development project. The aim was to improve competitiveness and well-being at work by involving staff. Before the change process began in 2018, physical load measurements were conducted with the workers to understand better the proportion of harmful working postures during the workday. Measurements were taken in a group consisting of the occupational health and safety (OSH) manager and the occupational physiotherapist. The production manager had overall responsibility for the change process and staff involvement.

At the start of the process, the production manager determined the workers' needs through individual interviews. Productivity metrics related to competitiveness were gathered in the company's HR accounts. The OSH manager acted as ergonomics expert throughout to ensure a human-centric approach to design. Weekly meetings were held in order to systematize worker participation. At these meetings, the change process and practical implementation issues were discussed openly and systematically, and design documents were openly shared. The production manager went through past and future changes and the Happy-or-not measurement situation. Workers had the opportunity to bring development proposals to the attention of the production manager.

During the change process in late 2018 and the first half of 2019, the production facilities were reorganized. The subassembly workstations were relocated and reorganized into areas with enough space to perform the work based on ergonomic principles. The trailer assembly was changed to a line model, allowing parts to be brought into truck racks without interrupting assembly work. The end-product logistics were improved.

Working hours were harmonized among the workers. The Enterprise Resource Planning (ERP) process and tools were updated to meet new production requirements.

## 2    Results

The aim of the change process was to improve production capacity, decrease non-productive work, optimize material flows, and promote well-being and productivity. The company invested €50,700 altogether in this change process, as calculated from the project bookkeeping. The investments in the plant operating system made it possible to reduce unproductive work and thus transfer resources to productive work. As a result of the change process, the plant's total productivity increased by 5 percent. This means an annual increase of 250 products in manufacturing capacity.

The change process led to clear cost savings, with a reduction in the number of sick days. Sick days were also affected by the improved possibilities of occupational health care to target suitable work at workers with temporary limitations in ability, because the work-related load was known more accurately from the load measurements (Fig. 1). In 2018, the production unit had 399 days of sick leave, while in 2020 there were 100 days. In addition, 34 days of replacement work were done in 2018–2020.

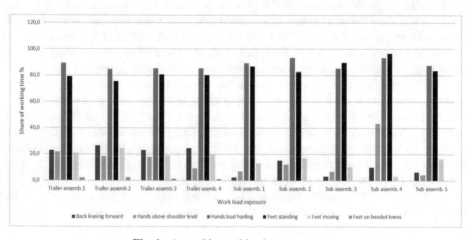

**Fig. 1.**  Assembly workload measurements.

The reduction in sick leave for 2020 compared to 2018 resulted in a cost saving of €198,800, plus €11,900 due to increased replacement work, for a total cost saving of €210,700 related to sick leave, compared to the situation in 2018 (Fig. 2).

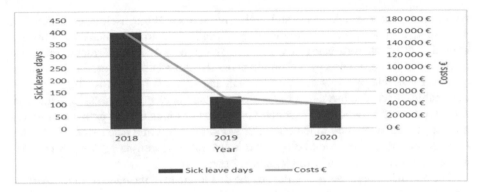

**Fig. 2.** Annual sick leave days and costs.

The frequency of accidents at work fell to zero in the second half of 2019 and remained at zero at the end of 2020. Workers' daily experiences of well-being at work improved significantly during the process (Fig. 3). The company stopped measuring well-being at work at the end of 2019.

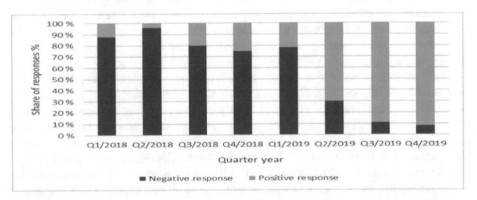

**Fig. 3.** Response distribution of Happy-or-not monthly measurements of employee well-being. In the figure, the negative experience describes the options "very negative" and "negative", and the positive experience describes the options "very positive" and "positive".

## 3   Discussion

It is important to identify what needs to be developed at work, so the resources can be used effectively. Promoting ergonomics is based not on emotion but on knowledge of the interaction between work and staff. This requires the application of information to practice, from a variety of sources. There are countless ways to develop work using different methods, limited only by the creativity of staff and the number of insights available. The ability to perceive the entire operating system and to understand the synergy in maximizing the use of technology and workers' ability is a key factor in maintaining a successful business and well-being at work. While useless, irrelevant, and unproductive work decreased, the meaning of work seems to have increased. This had a positive effect on well-being at work. The smoothness and uninterrupted operation of work was also promoted by the simultaneous development of the production control system. By developing this system, the planning of work became more logical and predictable, which also made the planning of work and work processes easier to manage. Thus, well-being at work and productivity in organizations can be promoted through practical solutions applied to the nature of work. Meetings and discussions alone may not be enough to improve well-being at work. It seems that well-being does not increase until changes are successfully implemented in practice.

The goal of ergonomics is to influence the development of the operating environment through two simultaneous approaches: to promote organizational performance and to improve workers' well-being [2]. This means investing in the continuous development of work, the work environment, products, systems, and methods. Work needs to be adapted to meet people's characteristics and needs. It is important to realize that constant change is not a threat but an excellent opportunity to improve one's well-being and ability at work and the competitiveness of one's company. What happens to companies that don't strive to change and develop their own practices? The fourth industrial revolution is forcing companies and managers to consider more social and technical system cooperation [4]. In industry, optimizing the operating system to achieve positive results requires understanding the capabilities of the social system and coordinating the growing potential of technology. Implementing change offers companies the opportunity to succeed in global competition, which is likely to be a common goal from a societal perspective.

An inclusive, collaborative change process offered employees a tangible opportunity to make an impact. Applying ergonomics and implementing changes requires the expertise of all staff, and the key word is *cooperation*. Knowing the practical work of supervisors and employees, combined with knowledge management and solid engineering skills, produces health and well-being for both company and staff. This is work ability management at its best. The outputs generated by the development are reflected in companies' business indicators. Productivity and well-being at work arise from understanding and adapting the social and technical system to smooth cooperation using ergonomic methods.

## 4  Conclusion

Ergonomists strive to improve well-being at work and productivity simultaneously. The rapid development of working life and technologies will make this synergistic development even more complex yet also even more desirable. The key element is that investments should be directed at developing the operating system in accordance with the principles of ergonomics. Settling on goals for the development of operating systems is the focus for modern and healthy organizations that seek to increase their competitiveness. No one will donate competitiveness or well-being at work to companies that operate in the global markets. Companies must be able to do this themselves. In practical work, this requires that companies consider ergonomics in development activities. The key question is, who can facilitate such a development process at company level?

The development process leader must be able to combine the technological and social systems from a practical point of view.

Ergonomics can improve well-being at work and can enable more efficient and productive work through the development of working conditions and environments. Changes and improvements are more readily accepted if workers feel valued and consulted. While discussion and consultation with staff are important, productivity and well-being at work appear to increase only after practical measures have been taken. It is essential to plan the work so that both company and staff can benefit from the work. When unnecessary, burdensome, and unproductive work is eliminated, the meaning of the work increases, and the effect is reflected positively in workers' performance. The success of planning, development, leadership, and collaboration is reflected in how easy and smooth the work is ultimately. We argue that ergonomics and ergonomists have not succeeded in finding their place in company-level development processes.

## References

1. Karwowski, W.: Ergonomics and human factors: the paradigms for science, engineering, design, technology and management of human-compatible systems. Ergonomics **48**(5), 436–463 (2005)
2. Dul, J., Bruder, R., Buckle, P., Carayon, P., Falzon, P., Marras, W.S., Wilson, J.R., van der Doelen, B.: A strategy for human factors/ergonomics: developing the discipline and profession. Ergonomics **55**(4), 377–395 (2012)
3. Thatcher, A., Waterson, P., Todd, A., Moray, N.: State of science: ergonomics and global issues. Ergonomics **61**(2), 197–213 (2018)
4. Neumann, W.P., Winkelhaus, S., Grosse, E.H., Glock, C.H.: Industry 4.0 and the human factor: a systems framework and analysis methodology for successful development. Int. J. Prod. Econ. **233**, 107992 (2021)
5. Neumann, W.P., Ekman, M., Winkel, J.: Integrating ergonomics into production system development: the Volvo powertrain case. Appl. Ergon. **40**, 527–537 (2009)
6. Wilson, J.: Fundamentals of system ergonomics/Human factors. Appl. Ergon. **45**, 5–13 (2014)
7. Vink, P., Imada, A.S., Zink, K.J.: Defining stakeholder involvement in participatory design processes. Appl. Ergon. **39**(4), 519–526 (2008)
8. Burgess-Limerick, R.: Participatory ergonomics: evidence and implementation lessons. Appl. Ergon. **68**(April), 289–293 (2018)
9. Van Eerd, D., King, T., Keown, K., Slack, T., Cole, D., Irvin, E., Amick lll, B., Bigelow, P.: Dissemination and use of participatory ergonomics guide for workplaces. Ergonomics **59**(6), 851–858 (2016)
10. Russ, A., Fairbanks, R., Karsh, B.-T., Militello, L., Saleem, J., Wears, R.: The science of human factors: separating fact from fiction. BMJ Qual. Saf. **22**, 802–808 (2013)
11. Driessen, M.T., Proper, K.I., van Tulder, M.W., Anema, J.R., Bongers, P.M., van der Beek, A.J.: The effectiveness of physical and organisational ergonomic interventions on low back pain and neck pain: a systematic review. Occup. Environ. Med. **67**(4), 277–285 (2010)
12. Westgaard, R.H., Winkel, J.: Occupational musculoskeletal and mental health: significance of rationalization and opportunities to create sustainable production systems – a systematic review. Appl. Ergon. **42**(2), 261–296 (2011)
13. Dempsey, P.G.: Effectiveness of ergonomics interventions to prevent musculoskeletal disorders: beware of what you ask. Int. J. Ind. Ergon. **3**(2), 169–173 (2007)
14. Van Eerd, D., Cole, D., Irving, E., Mahood, Q., Keown, K., Theberge, N., Village, J., St. Vincent, M., Cullen, K.: Process and implementation of participatory ergonomic interventions: a systematic review. Ergonomics **53**, 1153–1166 (2010)

# Using Knowledge Work Intensity Assessment to Improve the Effectiveness of Quality Assurance in New Drug Development

Silvio Viña-Brito[1]([⊠]) [iD], Aida G. Rodríguez-Hernández[1] [iD], Lisel Viña-Rodríguez[2] [iD], and Yordán Rodríguez[3] [iD]

[1] Industrial Engineering Faculty, Universidad Tecnológica de La Habana "José Antonio Echeverría", Havana, Cuba
{silviovi,aida}@ind.cujae.edu.cu
[2] Quality Department for Product Development, Centro de Inmunología Molecular, Havana, Cuba
[3] National School of Public Health, Universidad de Antioquia, Medellín, Colombia

**Abstract.** Research and development of new pharmaceutical products are very knowledge-intensive activities, which require an efficient quality assurance process. The trade-off between quality and time to market is increasingly critical, which generates stress in the face of the risks associated with delays in quality assurance or even longer delays if the regulatory agency rejects the proposal. To help resolve this dilemma in a company involved in the research, production and marketing of biopharmaceuticals, we assessed the knowledge intensity required for quality assurance. This was achieved by breaking down the quality assurance process into tasks and evaluating each of these tasks according to the dimensions of required qualification, autonomy, innovation, information intensity, interdependencies and decision variability. The most demanding dimensions founded in the study were information intensity and innovation, while level of autonomy was low. A content analysis technique was incorporated to uncover the knowledge present in the many documents of past technical reviews. This revealed the main sources of delays in past quality assurance processes and support findings proactive decisions. The working system was redesigned to facilitate the harmonisation of criteria and the presentation of the scientific basis of the results, thereby strengthening interdependencies, information analysis, innovation capacity and qualification.

**Keywords:** Knowledge work · Quality assurance · New drug development · Content analysis

## 1 Introduction

A truly responsible pharmaceutical industry needs to ensure its ability to detect any potential threat to the quality of the products it offers. Unfortunately, numerous products have had to be withdrawn from market a considerable time later after they were approved

© The Author(s), under exclusive license to Springer Nature Switzerland AG 2021
N. L. Black et al. (Eds.): IEA 2021, LNNS 221, pp. 96–101, 2021.
https://doi.org/10.1007/978-3-030-74608-7_13

and distributed due to the detection of adverse properties [1–4]. This is because the high level of cognitive complexity faced by researchers who develops these products. In contrast, there is a widespread belief that the occupation of quality assurance specialist demands instead a considerable amount of discipline, meticulousness and good memory, and requires virtually no creativity or ability to deal with new problems. This belief seems to be present among some specialists and managers in the biopharmaceutical industry based on the idea that what quality assurance specialists have to do is merely to check every aspect of the rules and regulations. However, the requirements for the development process of new medications are not limited to fulfilling predefined conditions, nor are the verification methods based on simple rules. In line with Quality by Design (QbD) trends, increasingly, the rationale for each design decision must be scientifically substantiated when submitted to regulatory agencies [5, 6] and, as a result, the review work of quality assurance staff has grown in complexity.

In this context, the question of how intensive the quality assurance work is, from a knowledge perspective, needs to be addressed. All jobs require some knowledge intensity, even the simplest; as society has evolved and become more technologically advanced, this intensity tends to increase, pursuing productivity gains, either in quantity or quality, or both. This is a progressive process; work will continue to become increasingly complex, governed by the pressures on organisations to respond to development and competitiveness demands. As Peter Drucker pointed out, a major challenge of the 21st century is how to achieve high productivities in knowledge-intensive jobs; these are not jobs whose productivity can even be measured by conventional methods of quantity and quality over defined periods of time, so it is complex to identify whether or not an increase in productivity has been achieved over a given period of time. [7].

In developing new pharmaceutical products, the trade-off between quality and time to market has become increasingly critical, creating stress over the risks of excessive delays in quality review or further delays if the regulatory agency rejects the proposal. In either case, the work skills of quality assurance specialists will be called into question.

Restructuring the work system to address these difficulties requires first to improves the understanding of the knowledge work intensity of quality assurances specialists. Ramirez and Steudel provided a conceptual and mathematical model that quantifies knowledge work on a continuous scale from 0 to 100. The level of knowledge work for each of the tasks the worker performs is assessed along 8 dimensions. Each task's dimension is assigned an integer value on a scale of 1 to 5, where 1 means "very low intensity" and 5 means "very high intensity". The total work intensity is obtained from the tasks' work intensity, weighted by the proportion of time spent on each task. In this model, the score of some of the dimensions does not increase but decreases the final result, as is the case for the dimension "physical effort" [8]. Therefore, for example, the knowledge intensity of long and complex orthopedic surgeries would be diminished by the magnitude of the physical work involved, despite the fact that simultaneously the surgeon and his entire team have to be jointly assessing multiple aspects and making decisions. Considering this shortcoming, Rodriguez, Casares and Viña modified the model. They kept the structuring into dimensions and tasks, assigning values and the concept that knowledge work intensity is a continuum. The changes included the readjustment of the selection and conceptual definition of six dimensions and the creation of specific metrics to evaluate each dimension to facilitate consistency of criteria in the application. The dimensions are: Minimum qualification required for the activity (regardless of the route by which it is acquired), Autonomy required (possibility to decide on methods, tools, breaks, schedules, objectives, standards), Innovation (to what extent the work requires simple or complex changes to maintain or increase competitiveness), Information intensity (required to connect large sets of dispersed information, producing continuous learning), Interdependencies (time and effort to coordinate activities, interactions with others, with continuous learning) and Variability and decisiveness (includes the complexity of decisions identifying and solving new problems and is opposed to repetitiveness). The metrics provide verbal descriptions of each scale. [9]. Final scores close to 100 are obtained for high-tech innovation jobs. This second version of the model has been used in the evaluation of jobs in software development, industrial and telecommunications operations, health and safety management, and others. [10–12] and has been used to design specific computer aids for ergonomic studies of human error at workplaces in the biopharmaceutical industry [13].

This paper aims to help increase the efficiency of quality assurance work and reduce their stress. The first question to be resolved in the analysis of these quality assurance tasks is to evaluate the intensity of the knowledge work required. This can help determine which aspects are causing greater cognitive demands and, consequently, propose support to facilitate the redesign of the work to make better use of human capacities and contribute to reducing stress and increasing productivity.

## 2   Materials and Methods

The study was conducted in the specific context of a Cuban company founded 25 years ago, dedicated to the research, production, and commercialization of biopharmaceutical products for national consumption and export, with innovations that have a notable impact on the health system and the economy.

The assessment of the knowledge intensity of the quality assurance specialists was done using the modified model discussed in the previous section. This was done jointly by one of the authors of this article and the head of the Product Quality in Development Department, with consultations with two quality assurance specialists. All of the participating subjects were university professionals, specialized with postgraduate studies, including one engineer with a Ph.D. degree and two masters, in biochemical sciences and biopharmaceutical sciences.

The evaluation included identifying the main tasks, estimation of the proportion of time spent on average on each task, assignment of value to each dimension of each task using corresponding metrics, calculations and comparisons of the contribution of each task and each dimension. For the proposal of cognitive support and restructuring of the work system, the contradictory aspects in the dimensions were taken into account, as well as the possibilities for improvement based on the benefits of cognitive strategies based on collective reflective practices, according to Jacobs [14] and with Pierre Falzon [15],

# 3 Results

Three main tasks were identified, for which the respective knowledge work intensities were calculated:

- Supervise the quality of the work done in elaborating the documentation of the dossiers for the proposal of new products. 78%.
- Auditing of good laboratory, production and clinical practices in new product development processes. 55%.
- Elaboration of procedures and programs to improve the quality assurance of new product development, including seminars for their implementation. 85%.

The total score for knowledge work intensity was 78%. The highest assessed dimension was information intensity, with 95%, as all three tasks require keeping up to date considerable volumes of information to be captured from various internal and external sources. This is followed by innovation, with a maximum score in the third task, which requires much creativity in form and content, more moderate in the first task and low in the second task where changes are infrequent.

The dimension with the lowest score was autonomy, with 51%. This is particularly true for the first task, in which the worker has no options to decide on deadlines and rules to be applied. In contrast, the third task has the highest score, as the worker plans his work within the team and selects methods, mainly in tasks that require a high level of skill. The complexity in the first task is critical because its low autonomy, with a very tight schedule, hinders the use of abundant and novel information. Supervisory decisions are made.

# 4 Discussion

The results confirm that this occupation requires a high intensity of knowledge but that its insufficient autonomy favours the appearance of anxiety and discouragement. The solution cannot be to give freedom to extend the deadlines for analyses and decisions, because this would imply delaying the already long time needed to make new products available to patients; on the contrary, what is needed is to shorten them. The solution is to design tools for collective reflective practices, facilitating and stimulating timely exchanges that make quality assurance more proactive and work more efficiently.

To achieve this, the specialists devised two strategies: first, the incorporation of a content analysis technique that structures the knowledge present in the many documents of past technical reviews, which carry comments and questions raised in past submissions of product proposal dossiers, to uncover the main issues that have delayed past processes and the sources that gave rise to them, and thus facilitate reflective practices by focusing attention on prevention. The first result of the application of this technique was to identify that the main failure was related to the weakness and insufficient structuring of the scientific basis for the design of quality specifications.

The second strategy undertaken collectively to strengthen the demands of knowledge intensity was also derived from these results. This strategy focused on redesigning the work system to strengthen interrelationships at the right moments and facilitate collective reflective practices, identifying the contributions corresponding to each member of the collective, establishing how to harmonise the criteria, and present the scientific bases of the results.

## 5   Conclusions

Assessing the knowledge work intensity of quality assurance of new pharmaceutical products can be very useful in revealing contradictions in these jobs' cognitive demands. This can inform the design of interventions to improve worker productivity and well-being.

## References

1. Qureshi, Z.P., Seoane-Vazquez, E., Rodriguez-Monguio, R., Stevenson, K.B., Szeinbach, S.L.: Market withdrawal of new molecular entities approved in the United States from 1980 to 2009. Pharmacoe R. Pidemiol. Drug Saf. **20**(7), 772–777 (2011). https://doi.org/10.1002/pds.2155
2. Siramshetty, V.B., Nickel, J., Omieczynski, C., Gohlke, B.O., Drwal, M.N., Preissner, R.: WITHDRAWN—a resource for withdrawn and discontinued drugs. Nucleic Acids Res. **44** (2016). https://doi.org/10.1093/nar/gkv1192
3. Nagaich, U., Sadhna, D.: Drug recall: an incubus for pharmaceutical companies and most serious drug recall of history. Int. J. Pharm. Investig. **5**(1), 13–19 (2015)
4. Suja, C., Manoj, N., Shuhaib, B., Rishana, K.V., Nidina, P., Ashfaque, M.: A Review on drug disaster in the history of medicine. Res. J. Pharm. Technol. **8**(4), 481 (2015). https://doi.org/10.5958/0974-360X.2015.00080.3
5. ICH. Q8(R2). Pharmaceutical Development (2009)
6. Zurdo, J.: Toward a two-tier process-development paradigm: prototype versus commercial biomanufacturing. Pharm. Bioprocess **3**(3), 179–183 (2015)
7. Drucker, P.F.: Knowledge-worker productivity: the biggest challenge. California Manag. Rev. **XLI**(2), 79–94 (1999)
8. Ramírez, Y., Steudel, H.J.: Measuring knowledge work: the knowledge work quantification framework. J. Intellect. Capital **9**(4), 564–584 (2008). www.emeraldinsight.com/1469-1930.htm
9. Rodríguez Hernández, A.G., Casares Li, R., Viña Brito, S.: La evaluación de la intensidad de trabajo de conocimiento en la ingeniería industrial. In: Memorias del VII Simposio de Ingeniería Industrial y Afines. La Habana: ISPJAE (2012)
10. Rodríguez-Hernández, A.G., Casares-Li, R., Viña-Brito, S.J., Rodríguez-Abril, O.: Diseño de ayudas al trabajador del conocimiento. Ingeniería Ind. **36**(2) (2015)
11. Echevarría Molina, C., Hernández Apaulaza, R., Garza Ríos, R.: Statistical analysis in the evaluation of intensity of knowledge work. In: 11th International Workshop on Operations Research, Universidad de La Habana, Havana, 10th–13th March (2015)
12. Casares-Li, R., Rodríguez-Hernández, A.G., Viña-Brito, S.: Análisis de errores humanos mediante la tecnología TEREH: experiencias en su aplicación. Ingeniería Ind. **37**(1) (2016)
13. Casares-Li, R., Rodríguez-Hernández, A.G., Viña-Brito, S.: Knowledge patterns to support ergonomic treatment of human error: technology TErEH. In: Boring, R.L. (ed.) Advances in Human Error, Reliability, Resilience, and Performance, pp. 88–98. Springer, Switzerland (2019)

14. Jacobs, R.L.: Knowledge work and human resource development. Hum. Resour. Dev. Rev. **16**(2), 176–202 (2017)
15. Falzon, P.: Ergonomics, knowledge development and the design of enabling environments. In: Proceedings of the Humanizing Work and Work Environment HWWE 2005 Conference, Guwahati, India, 10–12 December, pp. 1–8 (2005)

# Methods of Using the Lifting Fatigue Failure Tool (LiFFT) as an Ergonomic Assessment Tool in the Commercial Production of Turkey Eggs

Jack Y. Wang[1,2](✉), Chris M. Loma[1], Mitch K. Carswell[2], and Allison Stephens[1]

[1] Fanshawe College, London, ON, Canada
[2] Sandalwood Engineering and Ergonomics, Livonia, MI, USA

**Abstract.** Several manual lifting evaluation tools are currently available to analyze mono-task jobs, yet most jobs involve multiple varying tasks. Therefore, a summation of mono-task analysis may not be an accurate representation of the degree of compressive forces and stress placed on the spine. The Lifting Fatigue Failure Tool (LiFFT) has been adapted from the fatigue failure theory (FFT) and is capable of both mono-task and cumulative task evaluation. The FFT details cumulative damage of the applied stress and the number of cycles to failure, therefore calculating a representative spinal compression is important in applying the corresponding limits. The original Gallagher method only requires three variables to use the LiFFT: the weight of the load, horizontal distance, and repetition per day. Other methods of applying the tool have emerged to achieve a more accurate calculation of spinal compression. The Potvin method includes a vertical height of the load and the 3DSSPP method uses digital human modeling (DHM) to calculate spine compression. The objective of this study was to compare the different methods of calculating spine compression for entry into the LiFFT to determine the variance in outputs. The results showed that the Gallagher method is best suited for lifts that do not require significant vertical postural changes whereas the Potvin and 3DSSPP methods are able to assess more complex lifts. Although DHM is the gold standard, the Potvin method is preferred for practitioners due to its ease of use. Overall, the LiFFT is a practical, effective, and practitioner friendly tool capable of predicting the risk about the low back in simple and complex manual lift evaluations.

**Keywords:** Ergonomics · Evaluation methods · Digital human modeling · Cumulative loading · Low back compression · Fatigue failure theory

## 1 Introduction

In the agricultural field, the most common (47%) injuries reported were sprains and strains related to the back, with a large proportion (45%) coming from livestock production [1]. When taking a closer look at back pain, manual lifting tasks from the ground level were found to be a significant factor [1]. Similarly, turkey egg production is a physically demanding industry that requires a significant amount of varied manual lifting on the job. Workers may be exposed to a higher risk of developing musculoskeletal disorders (MSDs), prompting the partnership to conduct the task analyses.

There are several manual lifting evaluation tools currently available, each with their own strengths and limitations. Some of the most widely used tools include the NIOSH lifting equation, Liberty Mutual Manual Materials Handling Tables (Snook Tables), Mital Tables, and the ACGIH-TLV for lifting. These well-known tools are able to analyze single lift and mono-task jobs, yet most jobs involve multiple varying lifting tasks. Therefore, a summation of mono-task analysis using the traditional tools may not be an accurate representation of the degree of compressive forces physical stress placed on the spine during the entirety of a workday.

The Lifting Fatigue Failure Tool (LiFFT) is capable of both mono-task and cumulative evaluation of varied lifts throughout a job [2]. It has been adapted from the Fatigue Failure Theory (FFT) which focuses on the interdependence of force and repetition leading to the effects they have on tissues – specifically with regards to the low back [3]. It has long been recognized that materials experience failure through either: 1) application of a one-cycle high magnitude stress (at the so-called 'ultimate stress' of the material or 2) repeated application of loads at some percentage of the material's ultimate stress [4]. The rate of damage propagation in a material is a function of several loading characteristics and the number of cycles experienced at various loads.

The relationship between applied stress and the number of cycles to failure is exponential in nature and is typically described in an $S$-$N$ diagram, which depicts the way the number of cycles to failure ($N$) varies with respect to a constant cyclic stress ($S$) [5]. The FFT describes how materials undergo cumulative damage (CD) when they experience repetitive stress and applies this to the human body for low back injuries. With an understanding of the CD experienced by a worker over the course of a day, the probability of low back disorders can be estimated and used to improve the workplace conditions. The LiFFT is a new tool able to calculate risk of low back disorders and has been validated for use from a US automotive manufacturer database for variable tasks [2] and the Lumbar Motion Monitor (LMM) database for mono-task [6].

The LiFFT provides quantitative outputs detailing the cumulative damage, % total damage, total cumulative damage, as well as % probability of high-risk job/low back disorder. To use the LiFFT, repetition and a back compression force must be calculated. The original Gallagher method of using the LiFFT only requires three variables: weight of the load and horizontal distance from spine to load to estimate spine compression, and the number of repetitions per day [2]. The basis of the FFT is reliant on the accurate calculation of spine compression, therefore other methods of applying the tool have emerged to determine the percent risk more precisely.

One method from Potvin introduces the addition of a vertical height of the load at the origin and another method uses 3D Static Strength Prediction Program (3DSSPP) Digital Human Modeling (DHM) [7]. The Potvin method uses a regression equation from the NIOSH lifting equation to estimate L5/S1 compression [7]. This model was validated in a lab setting by comparing an assessment of the lifting task to a 3D dynamic model and was found to be statistically significant [8]. Another method is using 3DSSPP which provides an accurate estimation of back compression as the posture of the worker is modelled and an estimate of back compression can be input into the LiFFT.

The LiFFT was used in conjunction with traditional ergonomic assessments to help evaluate the risk of MSDs at a commercial turkey egg production facility. Being a relatively new tool, there is currently very limited literature documenting real-world cases and the application of this tool. Therefore, the purpose of this study was to evaluate the 3 methods of using the LiFFT (Gallagher, Potvin, 3DSSPP) to assess identified jobs and determine if the different methods of assessing varied cumulative lifting tasks are aligned with one another.

## 2 Methods

The company that participated in the assessments is a global leader in producing, packaging and delivering commercial turkey eggs and poults around the world. Multiple facilities exist to meet demands in artificial insemination, hatching eggs, picking eggs, as well as packing the eggs for transport. The company partnered with Fanshawe College to conduct this research and evaluate job specific tasks at their various sites. Jobs were assessed between March 3rd and March 12th, 2020 on site at three of the company's farm facility locations. The LiFFT tool was used in 2 jobs: *Egg Gathering* and *Egg Packing*. The first job of egg gathering was broken down into 1) pick up floor eggs 2) pick up nest eggs and 3) pick up collection box. The second job of egg packing was broken down into 1) lift eggs from shelves 2) pack boxes onto pallet and 3) lift stacks of eggs from table. * Note: frequencies vary greatly between seasons given the nature of agricultural work.

### 2.1 Task Descriptions

*Egg Gathering*: a turkey egg can range from 75 to 100 grams. Task 1: Pick up floor eggs: the worker manually collects the eggs on the floor of the pen and the number of floor eggs varies depending on the pick. Collections ranged from 11-25 eggs per walk. There are two walks per pick and 11 picks over an 8-hour shift for a total of around 75-500 eggs in total per day. Task 2: Pick up nest eggs: the worker picks eggs from the side nests that do not feed into the collection box. The nests are located at a height of 22cm forcing the worker to bend over to collect them. The worker was observed collecting about 19 eggs in total from both side nests. The worker will collect around 210 eggs in total per day. Task 3: Pick up collection box eggs: eggs laid in the center nests will roll onto a conveyor belt and deposits them into a collection box at the end of the two pens. The collection box is located 21cm off the ground, resulting in the worker bending over to collect the eggs. The worker collects around 200 eggs per pick, for 11 picks over an 8-hour shift totaling around 2200 eggs collected.

*Egg Packing*: task 1 and 2 are only performed once daily and task 3 is performed throughout the day. Task 1: Lift eggs from shelves the worker loads 2 stacks of eggs into each box by lifting each stack which weighs roughly 9.8kg off the shelf at four different heights (22cm, 68cm, 113cm, and 159cm). The average number of egg stacks was 92, split into 23 stacks per shelf height. Task 2: Pack boxes onto pallet once each box is packed and sealed, the worker lifts each box from the ground measured at 30cm and loads them onto a pallet. On average, there are 45 boxes to be loaded, each weighing around 19.9kg. Task 3: Lift stacks of eggs from table once the stack of eggs is fully loaded, the worker lifts the egg stack off of a table with a vertical height of 104cm and stores it in the fridge room. This occurs around 92 times a day.

## 2.2 Analysis

Three methods to calculate spine compression for entry into the LiFFT were used (Gallagher, Potvin, 3DSSPP) to determine total cumulative damage and probability of high-risk job/low back disorder. Horizontal distance, load mass, and repetition were used in the Gallagher method. Horizontal distance, vertical height, load mass and frequency were used in the Potvin method. Spine compression forces were calculated in a biomechanical DHM and used in the 3DSSPP method. Postures matched to photos taken while the task was performed, along with forces and vector direction were used to calculate the compression forces in 3DSSPP.

# 3   Results

Complete results for egg gathering and egg packing are summarized in Table 1 and Table 2 respectively. For both jobs, the Gallagher method yielded significantly lower outputs compared to the other methods. Conversely, the Potvin method and 3DSSPP method had comparable results for both jobs.

In the egg gathering job, the Gallagher method did not have valid results and failed to calculate the outputs, simply stating the total cumulative damage as 0 and % probability of risk as 0%. When comparing the Potvin method and the 3DSSPP method, a difference of 0.919 can be seen in the total cumulative damage, 369N in the peak compression and 5.0% in the probability of risk.

**Table 1.** A comparison of LiFFT input and output values for the egg gathering job

| Egg Gathering | | LiFFT Method | | |
|---|---|---|---|---|
| | | Gallagher | Potvin | 3DSSPP |
| Task 1: Pick up eggs from floor | *Compression Force (N)* | N/A | 1891 | 2085 |
| | *Individual Damage* | 0.0 | 0.1006 | 0.1698 |
| | *% Total Damage* | 0% | 17% | 11% |
| Task 2: Pick up eggs from nests | *Compression Force (N)* | N/A | 1917 | 2340 |
| | *Individual Damage* | 0.0 | 0.0411 | 0.1290 |
| | *% Total Damage* | 0% | 7% | 9% |
| Task 3: Pick up eggs in collection box | *Compression Force (N)* | N/A | 1971 | 2336 |
| | *Individual Damage* | 0.0 | 0.4535 | 1.2156 |
| | *% Total Damage* | 0% | 76% | 80% |
| **Total Cumulative Damage** | | 0.0 | 0.595 | 1.514 |
| **Peak Compression (N)** | | N/A | 1971 | 2340 |
| **% Probability of Risk** | | **0.0%** | **71.1%** | **76.1%** |

In the egg packing job, the Gallagher method had valid outputs. When compared to the other methods, the distribution of % total damage was similar, and it yielded significantly lower total cumulative damage and probability of risk. Both the Potvin method and 3DSSPP method produced very similar results with a difference of 0.207 in total cumulative damage, 28N in peak compression and 0.5% in the probability of risk.

**Table 2.** A comparison of LiFFT input and output values for the egg packing job

| Egg Packing | | LiFFT Method | | |
|---|---|---|---|---|
| | | Gallagher | Potvin | 3DSSPP |
| **Task 1a: Lift eggs from shelves** | *Compression Force (N)* | N/A | 2841 | 3199 |
| | *Individual Damage* | 0.0001 | 0.0547 | 0.1437 |
| | *% Total Damage* | 2.8% | 3% | 8% |
| **Task 1b: Lift eggs from shelves** | *Compression Force (N)* | N/A | 2405 | 2399 |
| | *Individual Damage* | 0.0001 | 0.0169 | 0.0166 |
| | *% Total Damage* | 2.8% | 1% | 1% |
| **Task 1c: Lift eggs from shelves** | *Compression Force (N)* | N/A | 1664 | 1645 |
| | *Individual Damage* | 0.0001 | 0.0023 | 0.0022 |
| | *% Total Damage* | 2.8% | 0% | 0% |
| **Task 1d: Lift eggs from shelves** | *Compression Force (N)* | N/A | 1108 | 1326 |
| | *Individual Damage* | 0.0001 | 0.0005 | 0.0009 |
| | *% Total Damage* | 2.8% | 0% | 0% |
| **Task 2: Pack boxes onto pallet** | *Compression Force (N)* | N/A | 3840 | 3868 |
| | *Individual Damage* | 0.003 | 1.5860 | 1.7116 |
| | *% Total Damage* | 83.3% | 95% | 91% |
| **Task 3: Lift stacks of eggs from table** | *Compression Force (N)* | N/A | 1641 | 711 |
| | *Individual Damage* | 0.0002 | 0.0086 | 0.0007 |
| | *% Total Damage* | 5.6% | 1% | 0% |
| **Total Cumulative Damage** | | 0.0036 | 1.669 | 1.876 |
| **Peak Compression (N)** | | N/A | 3840 | 3868 |
| **% Probability of Risk** | | 31.4% | 76.5% | 77.0% |

# 4   Discussion

The objectives of this study were to use the LiFFT to help evaluate the risk of MSDs in commercial turkey egg production and to compare methods of using the tool (Gallagher, Potvin, 3DSSPP method). The LiFFT was used to assess identified jobs and determine if the different methods of assessing varied cumulative lifting tasks are aligned with one another with respect to their outputs. The main findings of this study demonstrated evidence that gaps exist in the original Gallagher method of using the LiFFT.

In the egg gathering task, the hand load of 0.1kg was not enough to properly estimate a compression force, and therefore no valid outputs were generated using the Gallagher method. Although the low weight of the load may not contribute significantly to compression forces, the L5/S1 spine still experiences higher forces due to the posture adopted in order to pick-up the eggs. This is demonstrated in the Potvin method by introducing a vertical origin height of the load, and further demonstrated in the 3DSSPP method where a compression force was generated to reflect the stress to support the upper body in the posture that the worker has adopted.

In the egg packing task, similar trends were seen when compared to the egg gathering task. In this task, the hand loads were enough to generate valid outputs for the Gallagher method. Although the distribution of % total damage for the Gallagher method was similar to the other 2 methods, the results showed a significantly lower total cumulative damage and probability of risk. The majority of tasks assessed in this study looked at loads close to the ground and the Gallagher method only uses a horizontal distance and is unable to account for the vertical height. Evidence of this can be seen in task 1d or task 3 compared to task 2 where individual damage seem to be similar because load location of 1d and 3 are further from the ground. However, task 2 sees major differences in individual damage when the load is located on the ground.

When comparing between the Potvin and 3DSSPP methods, parallels are seen in the results. Despite the gold standard of using DHM 3DSSPP, the Potvin method was able to consistently estimate compression forces similar to 3DSSPP with the addition of vertical height from the original Gallagher method. As well, the Potvin method is easy to use and only requires four simple variables rather than a full DHM, making the Potvin method the preferred method for practitioners. Some of the limitations for the Potvin method may include when the task involves substantial twisting and/or lateral bending. The DHM is better equipped to account for these variables and this may help explain some of the differences that were observed in the results of both the egg gathering and egg packing jobs assessed.

## 5   Conclusion

The LiFFT is a valid ergonomic risk assessment tool adapted from the FFT requiring only basic inputs to be used. It is an easy to use, effective, and practitioner friendly tool capable of calculating risk of low back disorders in mono-task as well as cumulative risk evaluations. The original Gallagher method is best suited for lifts that do not require significant vertical postural changes or if the horizontal distance is the major contributor to spine compression whereas the Potvin and 3DSSPP method is able to assess more complex lifts. Strong evidence shows the addition of a vertical origin of load when using LiFFT is comparable with 3DSSPP results. Although the DHM 3DSSPP method is the gold standard, the Potvin method is preferred for practitioners due to its ease of use with minimal required variables.

**Acknowledgements.** The authors would like to thank the commercial turkey egg production company for inviting us to their facilities, Fanshawe College for their support and resources, London Ergonomics Inc for the collaboration opportunity, and Sandalwood Engineering and Ergonomics for their input.

## References

1. Bobick, T.G., Myers, J.R.: Back injuries in agriculture: operations affected. In: Agricultural Health and Safety – Workplace, Environment, Sustainability, pp. 325–332. Lewis Publishers (1995). https://books.google.ca/books
2. Gallagher, S., Sesek, R.F., Schall, M.C., Huangfu, R.: Development and validation of an easy-to-use risk assessment tool for cumulative low back loading: the Lifting Fatigue Failure Tool (LiFFT). Appl. Ergon. **63**, 142–150 (2017)

3. Gallagher, S., Heberger, J.R.: Examining the interaction of force and repetition on musculoskeletal disorder risk: a systematic literature review. Hum. Factors **55**(1), 108–24 (2013)
4. Peterson, R.E.: Discussion of a century ago concerning the nature of fatigue, and review of some of the recent researches concerning the mechanism of fatigue. ASTM Bull. **164**, 50–56 (1950)
5. Gallagher, S., Schall, M.C., Jr.: Musculoskeletal disorders as a fatigue failure process: evidence, implications and research needs. Ergonomics **60**, 255–269 (2017)
6. Marras, W.S., Lavender, S.A., Leurgans, S.E., Rajulu, S.L., Allread, W.G., Fathallah, F.A., Ferguson, S.A.: The role of dynamic three-dimensional trunk motion in occupationally related low back disorders: the effects of workplace factors, trunk position, and trunk motion characteristics on risk of injury. Spine **18**(5), 617–628 (1993)
7. Potvin, J.R.: Use of NIOSH equation inputs to calculate lumbrosacral compression forces. Ergonomics **40**(7), 691–707 (1997)
8. Kuijer, P.P., Faber, G.S., Van der Molen, H.F., Loos, R.C., Van Dieen J., Frings-Dresen, M.H.: Can peak compression forces at the low back be assessed in practice. Premus (2007). https://www.researchgate.net/publication/271514632

# Designing the BrainTagger Researcher Platform to Automate Development of Customized Cognitive Games

Bella (Yigong) Zhang[✉] and Mark Chignell

University of Toronto, Toronto, Canada
yigong.zhang@mail.utoronto.ca, chignell@mie.utoronto.ca

**Abstract.** Serious games have grown significantly in popularity, but proving their scientific validity through research studies is a common hurdle for researchers and game developers. To scale up capacity to collaborate with different groups of researchers, Centivizer Inc. (a University of Toronto spinoff company) has employed a user-centered design process to design a BrainTagger Research Platform (BRP) that will largely automate the development process of its customizable serious games for cognitive assessment. This new development will increase the capacity to gather research data needed to improve game mechanisms and demonstrate game validity.

**Keywords:** Human factors engineering · Serious games · Cognitive assessment · User interface design · Usability evaluation

## 1 Introduction

The serious games market has grown rapidly since around 2010. It has wide applications in healthcare, education, aerospace, government, retail, media, and entertainment industries. Serious games are defined as games that are created and used beyond entertainment purposes [1]. Compared with traditional cognitive interventions, serious games provide a sense of positivity and playfulness, which can be a good motivational factor when engaging with patients in clinical settings [2]. Cognitive testing, in particular, has been reported to be stressful and cause anxiety, which may impact the accuracy of assessments [3]. Serious games offer a way to carry out cognitive assessment more easily with the gameplay, not only making assessment more fun for the person being assessed but also introducing randomization elements that reduce the possibility of learning effects. This creates opportunities for using the same test repeatedly on the same person without losing validity.

Cognitive tests through serious games have four key advantages over those done in a paper-and-pencil format. Firstly, when a person is engaged with a cognitive assessment in a serious game format, the sense of "being tested" is less apparent. Paper-and-pencil tests can cause anxiety and be stressful, which may impact the accuracy of assessments [3]. Secondly, automated data collection done by software applications is more efficient, effective, and reliable than human transcribed data. This makes it possible to track detailed cognitive changes over time, allowing the game to serve as a health monitoring tool [4]. Thirdly, the use of software makes it possible for individuals to access cognitive testing in remote and rural areas and allowing health systems to be more proactive in implementing interventions where they are needed. Lastly, the labor costs of paper-and-pencil testing are greatly reduced.

## 1.1 Problem

Centivizer Inc. (www.centivizer.com) has developed BrainTagger, a suite of 8 (as of this writing) Target Acquisition Games for Measurement and Evaluation (TAG-ME), to assess a person's cognitive abilities. Braintagger began as a design concept [5], which was then implemented as a game for screening for delirium in emergency patients [6] and has seen a succession of games being added to the suite and validated (e.g., [7]). In 2019, Centivizer Inc. made the BrainTagger product freely available to different research groups for research use. As more and more researchers requested using our games in their research studies, a capacity bottleneck was reached, and thus the software development process became repetitive and hard to manage. This bottleneck led to increasing problems with labor costs and inefficiency. There was also a higher probability of human errors as administrators and developers had to manage multiple versions of the games simultaneously and manually. To create a long-term solution to this challenge, we reimplemented the games in the REACT framework to make the software more maintainable, and we created the Braintagger Researcher Platform (BRP) so that researchers could customize games for their research studies without having to have coding skills.

The development of online experimental platforms is still at an early stage and is fast evolving. At the time of this writing, the social distancing requirements of the COVID-19 pandemic have led to many in-person research projects being postponed, canceled, or changed to online experiments. The deployment of online experimental tools is beneficial, and not only in pandemics, because online delivery makes it possible for researchers to continue conducting research online with remote participants, and not just in times of pandemic. A significant advantage of running experiments online is that more diverse groups of participants can be run, including those in remote geographical locations and those with physical and other disabilities. In the long term, the trend of employing online experimental tools in social and behavioral sciences will likely continue to grow, benefiting from the rapid technological advances in big data, software development, and machine learning.

## 2   Objective

This research project's primary goal is to generate a usable and effective high-fidelity BRP prototype that will serve to scale up the usage of our proprietary games in different research studies. It will eventually contribute to the success of our game design, and we plan to make the games intelligent enough to diagnose brain abnormalities and detect cognitive decline among older adults. This is also an online behavior experiment tool that can be used not only for older adults but also for people of different age groups. The games can be applied for behavioral experiments with other purposes, such as tracking cognitive development in children, assessing distraction, or detecting symptoms of autism. These games have a high potential to advance future cognitive assessment so that it is more reliable, cheap, fun, and ubiquitous.

## 3   Method

As BRP is a new product, we approached the design process with a minimal viable product (MVP) mindset. We were not seeking to address all the possible user needs; instead, this prototype aims to visualize a product with the highest customer-valued features by engaging potential users throughout the design cycle. This design project followed the iterative cycle of the human-centered design process: Understand, Create, and Evaluate [8]. In the Understand stage, we first analyzed the game requirements for eight different ongoing research studies and conducted a requirements analysis to understand the common game parameters that needed to be customized (based on the underlying researchers' needs) through emails and interviews. Then we developed personas for three user groups (principal investigators, graduate research students, and undergraduate students) and envisioned common usage scenarios for the new platform. A series of paper wireframes (Fig. 1), mockups, and Figma (https://www.figma.com) prototypes (Figs. 2, 3 and 4) were created and iterated based on ongoing user feedback in the Create stage. In the Evaluate stage, two rounds of high-fidelity prototype usability evaluation were conducted remotely over videoconferences: 5 participants in the 1st round evaluation (October 2020) and 13 participants in the 2nd round evaluation (January 2021). The prototype was redesigned at the end of each round of usability evaluation based on the findings. The two rounds of usability evaluation were similar in format, each comprising three stages: pre-study questionnaire, scenario walkthrough, and post-study

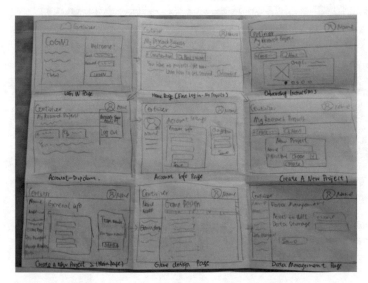

**Fig. 1.**  A sample of the initial paper wireframes

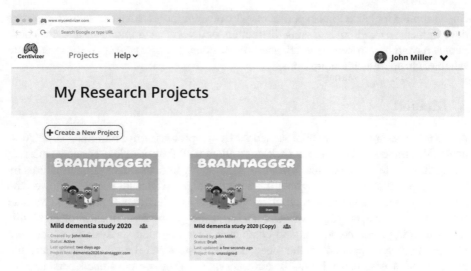

**Fig. 2.** Screenshot of BrainTagger Research Platform- Project Page

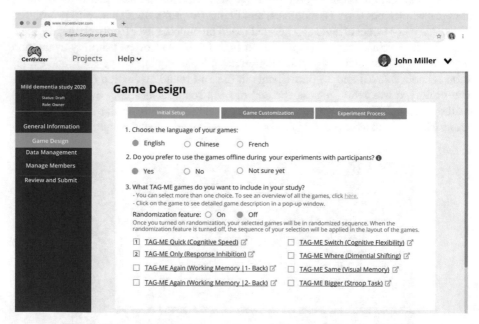

**Fig. 3.** Screenshot of BrainTagger Research Platform- Game Design Page

questionnaire with a focus on gathering quantitative usability feedback that included system usability scale (SUS) evaluative ratings.

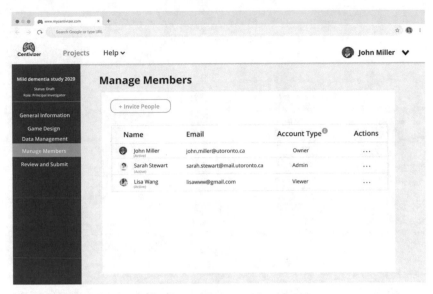

**Fig. 4.** Screenshot of BrainTagger Research Platform-Management Member Page

## 4 Results

In both rounds of usability evaluation, all participants commented favorably on the design. When asked about how well the design met their needs as a researcher, the average rating increased from 4.2/5 in the 1st round testing to 4.92/5 in the 2nd round (where 5 is excellent and 1 was poor). All researchers agreed that the researcher platform added high potential value to the TAG-ME games. They described the prototype as "very effective" and "very clean and thoughtful" and expressed their willingness to use it in their future studies. One participant said, "This was my first time viewing the prototype, and I think it is absolutely amazing. It looks very close to being ready for implementation, and I think it is an awesome tool for researchers. I cannot wait to use it!".

The quantitative findings also demonstrated that the prototypes' usability and effectiveness improved greatly between the two rounds of testing. The average SUS scores from both rounds of usability testing were well above the mean of 68 that was obtained over a large number of studies [9]. The average SUS score of the prototype increase from 82.5/100 in the 1st round testing to 87.3/100 in the 2nd round testing. The rating for almost all statements within the SUS scale improved between the two rounds of testing, i.e., the ratings for positive statements increased (Fig. 5) while the ratings for negative statements decreased (Fig. 6).

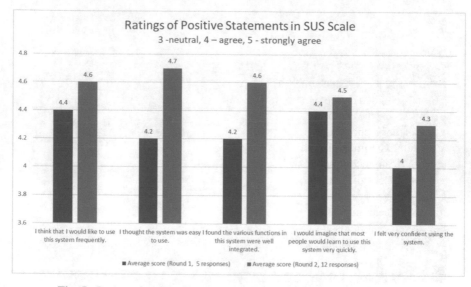

**Fig. 5.** Rating of positive SUS statements in two rounds of usability testing

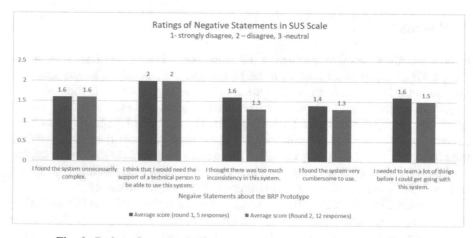

**Fig. 6.** Rating of negative SUS statements in two rounds of usability testing

## 5    Discussion

The design of the BRP was successful based on the favorable evaluation feedback received, and the resulting design has been handed to the software team as a specification for development. When completed, the BRP will automate the software development process for customizing those features of most interest to researchers. It will also include collaborative functionalities to facilitate teamwork and communication. As a result, the BrainTagger team will be freed up to work on more complex, special requests from researchers. Meanwhile, the researchers will be empowered to build projects on their own and will have to spend less time communicating their requirements and waiting for the BrainTagger team to respond to their requests.

We learned from the study that the researchers desire to have more autonomy and flexibility in designing and customizing the online experimental tool without resorting to the development team. Thus, it is important to allow them to make decisions based on the information provided on the interface without having to contact the service provider. It is also important for the user interface to be more informative and explain the functionality and how to make choices wherever possible. Researchers should have the power to generate their experimental tool in real time. Researchers also highly valued the system's ability to generate recommended parameters based on their target participant group and desired assessment difficulty. Data storage security and sharing agreements are also important concerns when reaching an agreement between the service providers and researchers. Researchers also desire opportunities to collaborate with other researchers working in relevant fields and learn from other people's experiment setups. In our final design, we have incorporated the option to make the project setup public and a page to view the public projects.

In future versions, we will consider increasing the customization ability of the games. For the first version of BPR, the design only allows researchers to choose each game once and, when chosen to prefill, all game parameters are generated with the same level of difficulty. One participant expressed a desire to have: "The option to repeat the same game more than once (for example, to have participants to complete the TAG-Me Only task twice - once with "easier" settings and once with "harder" settings)." An advanced customization feature we could include in the future is to allow researchers to customize each game with a different level of difficulty within their research project.

## 6 Conclusion

To establish a new, credible research tool requires rigorous efforts to build scientific evidence. The ability to automate software development creates possibilities to promote effective collaboration and scale up capacity to meet researchers' needs. Continuous user engagement coupled with the MVP mindset helped identify and prioritize the most valued features in the product's first iteration. In this product development cycle, we have chosen the waterfall model. The design was finalized before software implementation because there was a lack of software resources during this design process.

This is an ongoing project that aims to not only support ubiquitous cognitive assessment for researchers and others but also to gamify experiments in general, in an approach that we refer to as "Gamified Psychometrics." People who would like to use BrainTagger in their research should contact Mark Chignell (chignell@mie.utoronto.ca).

## References

1. Mestadi, W., Nafil, K., Touahni, R., Messoussi, R.: An assessment of serious games technology: toward an architecture for serious games design. Int. J. Comput. Games Technol. **2018** (2018)
2. Robert, P.H.P.H., et al.: Recommendations for the use of Serious Games in people with Alzheimer's Disease, related disorders and frailty. Front. Aging Neurosci. **6**(MAR) 54 (2014)

3. Cassady, J.C., Johnson, R.E.: Cognitive test anxiety and academic performance. Contemp. Educ. Psychol. (2002)
4. Wilkinson, A., Tong, T., Zare, A., Kanik, M., Chignell, M.: Monitoring health status in long term care through the use of ambient technologies and serious games. IEEE J. Biomed. Heal. Inform. **22**(6), 1807–1813 (2018)
5. Tong, T., Chignell, M., Lam, P., Tierney, M.C., Lee, J.: Designing serious games for cognitive assessment of the elderly. In: Proceedings of the International Symposium Human Factors Ergonomics in Health Care (2014)
6. Tong, T., Chignell, M., Tierney, M.C., Lee, J.: A serious game for clinical assessment of cognitive status: validation study. JMIR Serious Games **4**(1), e7 (2016)
7. Tong, T., Chignell, M., DeGuzman, C.A.: Using a serious game to measure executive functioning: response inhibition ability. Appl. Neuropsychol. (2019)
8. Lee, J.D., Wickens, C.D., Liu, Y., Boyle, L.N.: Designing for people: an introduction to human factors engineering. CreateSpace (2017)
9. Lewis, J.R., Sauro, J.: Item benchmarks for the system usability scale. J. Usability Stud. (2018)

# Part II: Aerospace (Edited by Guy André Boy)

# Heart Rate, Heart Rate Variability and Subjective Workload of Commercial Pilots During Jet Airplane Handling Maneuvers

Samuel Clément-Coulson[1]([✉]), Alaa Boutelaa[1,2], Ramiya Veluppillai[1,2], and Aaron P. Johnson[1,2]

[1] Concordia University, Montreal, Canada
{sam.coulson,aaron.johnson}@concordia.ca
[2] Québec Vision Research Network, Montreal, Canada

**Abstract.** Cardiac function (measured by heart rate and heart rate variability) have been investigated as objective measures of pilot workload, by comparing cardiac function between different flight manoeuvres. However, no study has investigated whether cardiac function measures can detect workload changes between manoeuvres of the same type, but different levels of difficulty (e.g., normal turns and steep turns). Commercial pilots (n = 14) flew a short scenario in a narrow-body jet simulator, which consisted of a normal turn, simple stall, steep turn, and complex stall. Heart rate, heart rate variability, NASA-TLX and flight path deviations were recorded. We found that heart rate and heart rate variability patterns were stable between participants and show clear differences between manoeuvre types. However, we did not observe any change due to manoeuvre difficulty. NASA-TLX ratings highlighted differences between manoeuvre difficulty, but not manoeuvre type. Our findings suggest that a combination of cardiac measures and subjective measures is best to understand workload. Additional research is required to establish guidelines for use of cardiac function as an indicator of workload.

**Keywords:** Workload · Aviation · Heart rate · Heart rate variability · NASA-TLX · Simulator

## 1 Introduction

Extensive research in human performance has investigated the association between operator states and performance. As pilots' primary role in flight operations is to perceive, process and act upon information from their environment, flight operations rely on the human operator's cognitive resources to accomplish this task (Endsley 1995; Rolfe and Lindsay 1973). A cognitive resource frequently discussed in aviation is workload. Workload arises when a human operator must dedicate physical and psychological resources towards performance on a task (Hart and Staveland 1988; Young et al. 2015). The association between operator workload and operator task performance is well established and can be described by an inverted U-shape: operator performance is poor when workload is either too low or too high (Young et al. 2015). As such, considerable efforts have

© The Author(s), under exclusive license to Springer Nature Switzerland AG 2021
N. L. Black et al. (Eds.): IEA 2021, LNNS 221, pp. 119–127, 2021.
https://doi.org/10.1007/978-3-030-74608-7_16

been dedicated by researchers to measuring workload. One of these approaches aims to infer operator workload from psychophysiological measures. Proponents of this approach highlight that, in addition to being objective measures, they are not intrusive to the primary task, allowing workload measurement in a naturalistic environment (Cain 2007; Lehrer et al. 2010). However, interpreting physiological measures in relation to flying tasks is difficult as these measures are a result of overall psychophysiological activity.

Of the various psychophysiological measures of workload, a large body of research has investigated cardiac function through electrocardiography (ECG; reviewed in Roscoe 1992). In aviation, this is commonly done by measuring heart rate and heart rate variability (HRV) across different phases of flight. Heart rate is higher in phases with increased workload such as take-off and landing, across different pilots and airplanes (Causse et al. 2012; Roscoe 1993). Even in trained fighter pilots, progressive increases in heart rate have been observed (Mansikka et al. 2015, 2016). Abnormal situations such as in-flight emergencies have also been shown to increase heart rate (Kinney and O'Hare 2020). Investigating HRV (i.e., the variation in the duration of the R-R interval), De Rivecourt et al. (2008) conducted a study of pilot candidates in an instrument flying simulator. Decreases in HRV from baseline, indicative of increased parasympathetic activation, were observed during manoeuvres considered to impose higher workload (Mansikka et al. 2015, 2019). Together, these experiments provide ample evidence that heart rate and HRV change across phases of flight.

While this research shows that cardiac function differs between separate phases of a flight, it remains difficult to establish that these changes are a direct function of differences in workload. It is conceivable that these changes are a result of other task-related factors (e.g., stress, attention). Roscoe (1978) reviewed early studies of cardiac response of two-crew operations (i.e.: one flying and one nonflying pilot). Because both pilots are exposed to the same psychological stressors, only workload is different between pilots. He suggested that cardiac responses changed consistently for the pilot flying, but nonflying pilot responses varied based on the degree of task involvement, supporting its use as an indicator of workload. Furthering the association between cardiac function and workload, cardiac function also correlates with subjective workload across different phases of flight (Lee and Liu 2003; Mansikka et al. 2019). Together, these studies provide further evidence that cardiac function changes in response to the workload imposed by flight. However, most of this research employs an experimental design where workload is compared between different types of flying tasks (e.g.: different phases of flight or different manoeuvres). Therefore, it is unknown whether heart rate and HRV are sensitive to workload changes between similar flight tasks, where workload is manipulated by increasing the task difficulty.

In sum, research in aviation and similar domains suggest that heart rate and HRV are reflecting the demands of flight on pilots. However, the majority of this research investigates workload by comparing measurements between manoeuvres, phases of flight, or pilots' task. To the authors knowledge, heart rate and HRV have seldom been used to measure workload across different variants of the same manoeuvre. Thus, the present study aims to investigate the use of ECG as a measure of workload through a different aviation paradigm where workload is induced by increasing the difficulty of a manoeuvre.

# 2  Method

The sample included commercial (n = 5) and airline (n = 9) pilots (males n = 12, $Age_{Range}$ 23–42, Median = 26.5). All pilots held a valid medical certificate, multi-engine qualification, and instrument flying rating. Participants flew an Ascent XJ flight training device (Mechtronix, Montréal, Canada); a fixed base simulator configured as a narrow body transport jet. Participants acted as pilot flying, while a qualified pilot researcher acted as pilot monitoring.

Electrocardiogram data were collected using a Polar H10 heart rate monitor (Polar Electro, Kempele, Finland) sampling at 1000 Hz. The Elite HRV app (Polar Electro, Kempele, Finland; Elite HRV LLC, Asheville, USA) exported the sequential R-R interval durations in milliseconds. Subjective workload was measured with the NASA-TLX (Hart and Staveland 1988) application on an Apple iPad Pro (Apple, Cupertino, USA).

## 2.1  Procedure

Study objectives, procedures, and simulator handling characteristics were briefed, along with informed consent. Then, pilots completed two flights. The first flight familiarized participants with the simulator's handling characteristics and ensure harmony between the pilot flying and pilot monitoring. The second flight was the experiment flight. Take-off and landing were conducted for ecological validity but were not evaluated. Table 1 describes the manoeuvre sequence for both flights. Pilots completed the NASA-TLX between manoeuvres.

**Table 1.** Manoeuvre sequence for practice and experimental flight.

| Seq | Practice flight | Experiment flight | Details |
|-----|-----------------|-------------------|---------|
| 0 | Take off | Take off | |
| 1 | Normal Turn (NT) | Normal Turn (NT) | 30° Bank Turn |
| 2 | Simple Approach to Stall (SAS) | Simple Approach to Stall (SAS) | Approach to Stall – Clean Configuration |
| 3 | Landing | Steep Turn (ST) | 45° Bank Turn |
| 4 | | Complex Approach to Stall (CAS) | Approach to Stall – Landing Configuration |
| 5 | | Landing | |

## 2.2  Data Handling

Due to the small participant sample size, missing data were excluded as interpolation or mean substitution would be unreliable. ECG data was missing for one participant. NASA-TLX subjective workload ratings were missing for two participants. Interbeat interval data were analyzed in Kubios HRV 3.3.1 (Kubios, Kuopio, Finland). Heart rate and heart rate variability (SDNN) were calculated for time windows corresponding to each manoeuvre. The simulator data was extracted via video recording of a screen displaying simulator parameters via optical character recognition using a custom R program implementing Google's Tesseract OCR engine (Google, Mountain View, USA). Flight path deviations were calculated as an objective performance measure for each manoeuvre. For turns, this refers to the time, in seconds, spent outside acceptable airspeed (240 knots – 260 knots) and altitude (4900 feet – 5100 feet) (Transport Canada 2017). For stalls, this refers to the interval between the stall warning onset and the point when safe airspeed (200 knots) and altitude (4800 feet) were attained.

## 3   Results

Descriptive statistics and distributions plots were calculated for flight path deviations to ensure the complex manoeuvres were more difficult, showed by increased deviations. Mean flight path deviations were higher during steep turns (M = 13.29, SD = 18.47) than during normal turns (M = 6.50, SD = 12.60, $t = -1.57$). Mean recovery time for the complex approach to stall was higher (M = 43.50, SD = 11.95) than for the simple approach to stall (M = 17.50, SD = 5.37; $t = -8.19$). The distribution plots suggest that greater range in performance between participants was greater for the complex variants. Altogether, these data suggest that the complex manoeuvres were more difficult than their simple counterparts.

**Table 2.** Descriptive Statistics for heart rate, heart rate variability (SDNN), flight path deviations and NASA-TLX

| | Heart rate (BPM) | | | | SDNN | | | |
|---|---|---|---|---|---|---|---|---|
| | CAS | NT | SAS | ST | CAS | NT | SAS | ST |
| $n$ | 13 | 13 | 13 | 13 | 13 | 13 | 13 | 13 |
| $M$ | 81.21 | 82.70 | 79.20 | 84.47 | 40.15 | 30.62 | 37.96 | 29.98 |
| $SD$ | 7.03 | 7.52 | 7.34 | 7.63 | 6.30 | 10.59 | 9.59 | 9.04 |
| Min. | 65.18 | 65.12 | 63.86 | 64.06 | 29.63 | 17.47 | 25.88 | 15.89 |
| Max. | 89.35 | 94.85 | 89.70 | 93.37 | 52.01 | 44.35 | 59.27 | 42.28 |
| | Flight path deviations | | | | NASA-TLX | | | |
| | CAS | NT | SAS | ST | CAS | NT | SAS | ST |
| $n$ | 14 | 14 | 14 | 14 | 12 | 12 | 12 | 12 |
| $M$ | 43.50 | 6.50 | 17.50 | 13.29 | 50.49 | 40.56 | 37.99 | 49.58 |
| $SD$ | 11.95 | 12.60 | 5.37 | 18.47 | 16.26 | 14.69 | 13.33 | 16.39 |
| Min. | 32.00 | 0.00 | 12.00 | 0.00 | 9.17 | 16.67 | 15.83 | 11.67 |
| Max. | 67.00 | 39.00 | 33.00 | 68.00 | 66.67 | 67.50 | 55.00 | 70.83 |

*Note.* CAS: complex approach to stall, NT: normal turn, SAS: simple approach to stall, ST: steep turn.

Descriptive statistics and distributions plots were calculated for heart rate, heart rate variability, and NASA-TLX ratings (see Table 2 & Fig. 1). Qualitative observation of the graphs suggests that heart rate and heart rate variability are different between manoeuvre types, but not between the levels of difficulty.

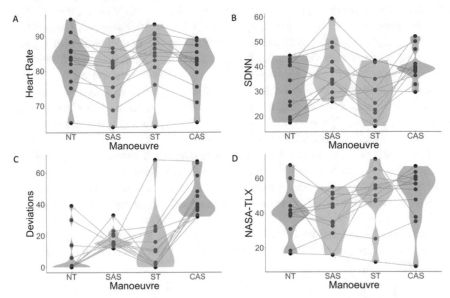

**Fig. 1.** Distribution plots for each manoeuvre. Each dot represents a single participant, and lines connect within-subject observations. (A) Heart rate in beats per minute (B) Heart rate variability (SDNN) in milliseconds (C) Time outside ideal flight path, in seconds. (D) Compound NASA-TLX subjective workload ratings, in percentage. *Note*: NT: normal turn, SAS: simple approach to stall (clean configuration), ST: steep turn, CAS: complex approach to stall (landing configuration).

Repeated-measures analyses of variance (ANOVA) were conducted to investigate between-manoeuvre differences in cardiac function, and NASA-TLX ratings. Planned post-hoc, uncorrected, dependent samples t-tests are reported to compare manoeuvre pairs, contrasting the turns (i.e., normal vs. steep turn) and approaches to stall (i.e., simple vs. complex). Effect sizes, Bayes Factors and confidence intervals will be reported, but not p-values. Interpretations of Bayes Factors follow general guidelines (Wetzels et al. 2011). Due to the sample size, these statistical tests are considered exploratory and should be interpreted with caution.

First, an ANOVA was conducted to investigate overall heart rate differences between manoeuvres, which suggests an effect of manoeuvre on heart rate, $F(3,36) = 9.97$, $\eta^2 = .45$, with decisive evidence for the research hypothesis ($BF_M = 324.58$). Pairwise comparisons found anecdotal evidence suggesting a medium increase in heart rate between normal and steep turns ($BF_{10} = 1.15$, $t = 1.92$, $d = .53$, 95% CI [$-.06$, 1.11]) and between the simple and complex approaches to stall ($BF_{10} = 1.09$, $t = 1.88$, $d = .52$, 95% CI [$-.07.$, 1.09]). However, the Bayes Factors and qualitative observation of the descriptives plot suggests these differences are not large enough to be meaningful.

Second, an ANOVA was conducted to investigate overall differences in SDNN between manoeuvres, which suggests a moderate effect of manoeuvre on SDNN ($F$(3,36) = 8.70, $\eta^2$ = .42) with decisive evidence for the research hypothesis ($BF_M$ = 164.82). Two non-directional, dependent sample t-tests were conducted compare simple and complex manoeuvre variants. Anecdotal evidence was found suggesting no difference in SDNN between normal and steep turns ($BF_{10}$ = .30, $t$ = .39, $d$ = .11, 95% CI [−.44, .65]) and between the complex and simple stalls ($BF_{10}$ = .38, $t$ = −.87, $d$ = −.44, 95% CI [−.79., .32]). However, qualitative observation of the descriptives plot suggested differences between manoeuvre types (Fig. 1). Dependent, non-directional t-tests were therefore conducted contrasting the normal turn with the simple approach to stall, and the steep turn with complex approach to stall. Substantial evidence was found suggesting that the SDNN was lower during the turns than during the stalls (for simple variants: $BF_{10}$ = 9.22, $t$ = −.36, $d$ = −.93, 95% CI [−1.58, .26]; for complex variants: $BF_{10}$ = 9.91, $t$ = −3.41, $d$ = −.95, 95% CI [−1.59, −.27]).

Last, an ANOVA was conducted to investigate overall differences in subjective workload, which found substantial evidence supporting differences in subjective workload between manoeuvres ($F$(3, 33) = 5.24, $\eta^2$ = .32, $BF_M$ = 9.78). Two non-directional, dependent sample t-tests were conducted to compare simple and complex manoeuvre variants. Substantial evidence was found suggesting a difference in subjective workload between normal and steep turns ($BF_{10}$ = 4.22, $t$ = 2.88, $d$ = .83, 95% CI [.15, 1.48]) and between the complex and simple stalls ($BF_{10}$ = 9.24, $t$ = 3.41, $d$ = .99, 95% CI [.27, 1.67]).

## 4 Discussion

Here we aimed to investigate the usability of heart rate and HRV to detect workload changes between maneuvers of varying complexity. We hypothesized that heart rate, HRV and NASA-TLX would be able to differentiate between high and low workload manoeuvres, and between manoeuvre types. Our results provide partial support for our hypothesis. Heart rate and HRV were different between turns and stalls, but did not vary meaningfully between the simple and complex variants. On the other hand, NASA-TLX scores were different between the simple and complex variants, but not between manoeuvre types.

Increases in heart rate and decrease in HRV (measured by SDNN) are associated with increased arousal and workload (Jorna 1993; Luque-Casado et al. 2016). Therefore, we expected to observe an increase in heart rate and a decrease in HRV in the complex exercises. However, we observed clear differences between manoeuvre types (i.e., turn vs stall), but little difference was found between the complex and simple variants of each manoeuvre. Pilots' heart rate was higher during the turns than during the approaches to stall, and HRV was lower during turns. When contrasting the complex manoeuvres to their simple variant, heart rate and HRV were similar. Given the limited sample size, we were unable to conduct traditional parametric statistical tests on these between-condition differences. Nevertheless, the general pattern of the results suggests cardiac function was different between manoeuvre types (i.e., turns vs. approaches to stall), but not between different difficulties of the same manoeuvre type.

These results do replicate the findings reported in similar studies (Causse et al. 2012; Hankins and Wilson 1998; Kinney and O'Hare 2020). Taken together with the results of the present experiment, heart rate appears to change predictably due to workload induced by different manoeuvre types, but not vary as a function of workload changes due to manoeuvre difficulty. It is probable that the manipulation of difficulty may not have been sufficient to create a significant change in heart rate (see workload and performance limitations later). Additional research is required to define contexts where psychophysiological measures are most appropriate measurements of workload in human factors research. For example, the changes in cardiac function related to workload imposed by basic processes required to complete a task, regardless of its difficulty level. One could hypothesize that the patterns of between-manoeuvre changes in heart rate and HRV are caused by the inherent differences in pilot resources required for completing each manoeuvre. Turns require sustained attention, and consistently require updating a model in working memory with multiple parameters (i.e., bank angle, altitude, airspeed, engine thrust) and precision. Conversely, stalls require the prompt application of a trained rehearsed recovery procedure, with an emphasis placed on quickly and successfully exiting the situation, and not on the precision of flying inputs. Changes in psychophysiological measures may occur due to these different types of task demands.

Conversely, subjective workload evaluations are biased by previous exposure to similar manoeuvre and performance (Moore and Picou 2018). In the present experiment, pilots reported differences in workload between the simple and complex manoeuvres, but not between manoeuvre types. It is possible that pilots' workload estimates were derived from previous exposure to similar situations, not as a function of the resources required. This may explain subjective workload scores' ability to differentiate between manoeuvre difficulty levels, as flight path deviations were generally higher during the difficult manoeuvre, but not manoeuvre type.

This study does have limitations. We were unable to attain the planned sample size due to the COVID-19 pandemic. As such, the statistical tests included are considered exploratory. However, our sample size remains similar to that of aviation psychophysiological research (e.g.: Hankins and Wilson 1998; Hidalgo-Muñoz et al. 2018; Lee and Liu 2003; Mansikka et al. 2019). This study retains the limitations associated with the use of heart rate and HRV as objective workload indicators. Cardiac function is the result of multiple physiological processes occurring simultaneously, so its use as a workload metric remains confounded by external physiological factors. This renders interpretation of heart rate and HRV difficult in the aviation environment. Further research is required to identify guidelines for use of cardiac function as a workload indicator.

The present results add to the literature supporting the strategic use of cardiac function as an objective workload measure to compare aviation situations likely to require different types of cognitive and physiological resources on behalf of the pilot. The present study suggests that heart rate and HRV are limited indicators of workload in the cockpit, especially when different variants of the same manoeuvre are being studied. Nonetheless, cardiac function can complement subjective measures to better understand workload in the cockpit.

**Acknowledgements.** The authors would like to thank the Centre Québecois de Formation Aéronautique for their expertise and simulator access, without which this experiment would not have been possible.

# References

Cain, B.: A review of the mental workload literature (2007). https://apps.dtic.mil/dtic/tr/fulltext/u2/a474193.pdf

Causse, M., Dehais, F., Faaland, P.-O., Cauchard, F.: An analysis of mental workload and psychological stress in pilots during actual flight using heart rate and subjective measurements. In: Proceedings of the 5th International Conference on Research in Air Transportation (ICRAT 2012) (2012)

De Rivecourt, M., Kuperus, M.N., Post, W.J., Mulder, L.J.M.: Cardiovascular and eye activity measures as indices for momentary changes in mental effort during simulated flight. Ergonomics **51**(9), 1295–1319 (2008). https://doi.org/10.1080/00140130802120267

Endsley, M.R.: Toward a theory of situation awareness in dynamic systems. Hum. Factors: J. Hum. Factors Ergon. Soc. **37**(1), 32–64 (1995). https://doi.org/10.1518/001872095779049543

Hankins, T.C., Wilson, G.F.: A comparison of heart rate, eye activity, EEC and subjective measures of pilot mental workload during flight. Aviat. Space Environ. Med. **69**(4), 360–367 (1998)

Hart, S.G., Staveland, L.E.: Development of NASA-TLX (task load index): results of empirical and theoretical research. In Hancock, P.A., Meshkati, N. (eds.) Advances in Psychology, no. 52, pp. 139–183. Elsevier Science Publishers (1988)

Hidalgo-Muñoz, A.R., Mouratille, D., Matton, N., Causse, M., Rouillard, Y., El-Yagoubi, R.: Cardiovascular correlates of emotional state, cognitive workload and time-on-task effect during a realistic flight simulation. Int. J. Psychophysiol. **128**, 62–69 (2018). https://doi.org/10.1016/J.IJPSYCHO.2018.04.002

Jorna, P.G.A.M.: Heart rate and workload variations in actual and simulated flight. Ergonomics **36**(9), 1043–1054 (1993). https://doi.org/10.1080/00140139308967976

Kinney, L., O'Hare, D.: Responding to an unexpected in-flight event: physiological arousal, information processing, and performance. Hum. Factors **62**(5), 737–750 (2020). https://doi.org/10.1177/0018720819854830

Lee, Y.H., Liu, B.S.: Inflight workload assessment: comparison of subjective and physiological measurements. Aviat. Space Environ. Med. **74**(10), 1078–1084 (2003)

Lehrer, P., Karavidas, M., Lu, S., Vaschillo, E., Vaschillo, B., Cheng, A.: Cardiac data increase association between self-report and both expert ratings of task load and task performance in flight simulator tasks: an exploratory study. Int. J. Psychophysiol. **76**(2), 80–87 (2010). https://doi.org/10.1016/j.ijpsycho.2010.02.006

Luque-Casado, A., Perales, J.C., Cárdenas, D., Sanabria, D.: Heart rate variability and cognitive processing: the autonomic response to task demands. Biol. Psychol (2016). https://doi.org/10.1016/j.biopsycho.2015.11.013

Mansikka, H., Simola, P., Virtanen, K., Harris, D., Oksama, L.: Fighter pilots' heart rate, heart rate variation and performance during instrument approaches. Ergonomics **59**(10), 1344–1352 (2016). https://doi.org/10.1080/00140139.2015.1136699

Mansikka, H., Virtanen, K., Harris, D.: Comparison of NASA-TLX scale, modified Cooper-Harper scale and mean inter-beat interval as measures of pilot mental workload during simulated flight tasks. Ergonomics **62**(2), 246–254 (2019). https://doi.org/10.1080/00140139.2018.1471159

Mansikka, H., Virtanen, K., Harris, D., Simola, P.: Fighter pilots' heart rate, heart rate variation and performance during an instrument flight rules proficiency test. Appl. Ergon. **56**, 213–219 (2015). https://doi.org/10.1016/j.apergo.2016.04.006

Moore, T.M., Picou, E.M.: A potential bias in subjective ratings of mental effort. J. Speech Lang. Hear. Res. **61**(9), 2405–2421 (2018). https://doi.org/10.1044/2018_JSLHR-H-17-0451

Rolfe, J.M., Lindsay, S.J.E.: Flight deck environment and pilot workload: biological measures of workload. In: Applied Ergonomics (1973). https://pdf.sciencedirectassets.com/271441/1-s2. 0-S0003687000X01391/1-s2.0-0003687073902159/main.pdf?x-amz-security-token=AgoJb3 JpZ2luX2VjECUaCXVzLWVhc3QtMSJHMEUCIE8HuUlP70id%2BofcCfxdRRcptOGEF sZxbs042ATeX70zAiEA1OOTw1EExc%2B%2BpX53gjbtSX3qgMHmKLor6gFrHdQ

Roscoe, A.H.: Stress and workload in pilots. Aviat. Space Environ. Med. **49**(4), 630–636 (1978)

Roscoe, A.H.: Assessing pilot workload. Why measure heart rate, HRV and respiration? Biol. Psychol. **34**(2–3), 259–287 (1992). https://doi.org/10.1016/0301-0511(92)90018-P

Roscoe, A.H.: Heart rate as a psychophysiological measure for in-flight workload assessment. Ergonomics **36**(9), 1055–1062 (1993). https://doi.org/10.1080/00140139308967977

Transport Canada: Pilot proficiency check and aircraft type rating flight test guide (Aeroplanes) (Issue First Edition (Revision 1)). Government of Canada (2017). https://www.tc.gc.ca/eng/civ ilaviation/publications/tp14727-menu-2709.htm

Wetzels, R., Matzke, D., Lee, M.D., Rouder, J.N., Iverson, G.J., Wagenmakers, E.: Statistical evidence in experimental psychology: an empirical comparison using 855 t tests. Perspect. Psychol. Sci. **6**(3), 291–298 (2011). https://doi.org/10.1177/1745691611406923

Young, M.S., Brookhuis, K.A., Wickens, C.D., Hancock, P.A.: State of science: mental workload in ergonomics. Ergonomics **58**(1), 1–17 (2015). https://doi.org/10.1080/00140139.2014.956151

# Fatigue-Indicator in Operational Settings: Vocal Changes

Heike Diepeveen[1,2], Maykel van Miltenburg[2(✉)], Alwin van Drongelen[2],
Floris van den Oever[2], and Henk van Dijk[2]

[1] Faculty of Social and Behavioural Sciences, Utrecht University,
3584 CS Utrecht, The Netherlands
[2] Royal Netherlands Aerospace Centre - NLR, 1059 CM Amsterdam, The Netherlands
maykel.van.miltenburg@nlr.nl

**Abstract.** Fatigue is an important factor in aviation accidents and incidents. Since fatigue cannot always be prevented, it needs to be detected in real time so that countermeasures can be taken. This study researches whether vocal changes (in vocal intensity and fundamental frequency) can be used as a measure for fatigue in an operational aviation setting. Sixteen participants were measured two times. Before the first test moment, they were asked to sleep eight hours or more and before the second test moment six hours or less. During each test moment, they performed a PVT, filled in the KSS, and did two speech tasks. One task was aimed at free speech and one task was aimed at procedural speech. Pre-processing included segmentation of the speech into words and extracting fundamental frequency (f0) and intensity values. An overall mean of both variables was calculated for both free and procedural speech. Speech, PVT reaction time, PVT lapses and KSS scores were analyzed in SPSS using Paired Samples t-Tests and Wilcoxon Signed Ranks Tests. Participants slept significantly less during the night before the second test moment and scored significantly higher on the KSS. For the PVT, no differences in both reaction time and lapses were found. No significant differences in average f0 and intensity for both free and procedural speech were found either. The results did not show a significant relationship between fundamental frequency, intensity and fatigue. Further research is needed to examine if vocal changes can be used as a reliable fatigue measure.

**Keywords:** Fatigue · Fundamental frequency · F0 · Vocal intensity · Fatigue detection · Real-time · Non-invasive · Operational setting · Aviation

## 1 Introduction

Fatigue, defined as a state of performance impairment as a result of sleep loss, extended wakefulness, circadian phase and workload [1, 2], plays an important role in aviation accidents and incidents [3]. Attention, a fast reaction time, decision making and memory retention are critical for aviation personnel to perform their job in a safe and effective manner [4]. Fatigue significantly impairs these types of cognitive and executive functions. A fatigued individual can experience difficulty suppressing task-irrelevant stimuli,

N. L. Black et al. (Eds.): IEA 2021, LNNS 221, pp. 128–135, 2021.
https://doi.org/10.1007/978-3-030-74608-7_17

a reduced ability to correct behavior after a mistake, impaired vigilance, and a slower reaction time [4–7].

To prevent accidents it is important to be able to detect fatigue in real time, so that direct countermeasures can be taken. Examples of objective measures for fatigue include electroencephalogram (EEG) and the psychomotor vigilance task (PVT). These measures have proven themselves to be effective [8, 9], but are not practical to apply in an operational setting in their current form, due to their invasiveness and/or disruptiveness. On top of that, the PVT in particular does not provide a constant and real-time assessment of a person's fatigue level.

A subjective measure is the Karolinska Sleepiness Scale (KSS). This is a quick method to determine subjective sleepiness at a certain moment in time. Even though this measure is less invasive and disruptive, it does not provide a real-time representation of fatigue either.

A measure that has not been thoroughly researched yet, but that could circumvent the issues mentioned above, is the vocal change as a result of fatigue. In particular, changes in intensity and fundamental frequency (f0). In a number of papers, these concepts are referred to as volume and pitch, but since the current research focuses on the analysis of voice rather than the human perception of voice the terms intensity and f0 will be used. Intensity is defined as the average amplitude of the speech signals in Decibel. Fundamental frequency is defined as the rate of vocal fold vibration in Hertz [10, 11].

Previous studies found a reduction in both f0 and intensity when individuals were fatigued versus non-fatigued [1, 2, 12–14] This could indicate that voice is indeed a good measure for fatigue and could be used in an operational setting. However, because the studies were performed with small samples, the relationship between voice and fatigue needs to be studied further. In addition, it has been found that an increase in fundamental frequency is positively correlated with higher emotional stress [15]. This could mean that f0 may not reflect the level of fatigue when combined with a high stress work environment, and the results could give a distorted image.

The objective of this study was to find out if vocal intensity and f0 are good potential measures for fatigue in an operational setting. Previous studies focused on speech while driving a car [13, 14], speech of a pilot during a flight [2] and free speech measured by answering "would you rather" dilemmas [1]. The present study contributes to the current body of knowledge by integrating free and procedural speech, as seen in a normal work setting, and focusing specifically on procedural speech used in aviation. The effect of fatigue on f0 and vocal intensity in both procedural and free speech was studied. Based on the research described earlier [1, 2, 12–14], it was expected that fatigue decreases f0 and vocal intensity during both types of speech.

Due to the covid-19 pandemic, the experiment could not take place in a laboratory setting, as was originally planned. For this reason, the study was performed online, during which participants carried out tasks from home. This has not been done in previous studies, for which this study could give insight in the feasibility and effectivity of such a method as well.

## 2  Methods

A power analysis was performed to determine the minimum amount of participants necessary for a power of 0.8. For this, effect sizes found in the literature were used [13, 14]. An r-value of $-.44$ was found for intensity and a value of $-.42$ was found for fundamental frequency. These values were converted to d-values with the Eq. (1):

$$d = \frac{2r}{\sqrt{1 - r^2}} \tag{1}$$

Based on the analysis, a minimum of 12 participants was determined. A total of 16 participants were recruited through Sona Systems (an online researcher and participant platform used by universities), social media and snowball sampling. One participant was excluded from further analysis, because the audio recordings contained loud and consistent background noises, making a reliable analysis impossible. The resulting subject group consisted of 9 females and 6 males between the ages 19 and 55 (M = 28.73, SD = 9.94). The subjects were of Dutch, Filipino, German, Greek and Romanian descent.

The study had a total duration of six days with online measurements at two time points. The three nights before the first measurement, participants were instructed to sleep 8 h or more, while they had to track their sleep by means of a digital sleep diary. The two nights before the second measurement, participants were requested to sleep 6 h or less. This methodological choice was based on the assumption that 5 to 7 h of sleep per night, for a period of at least two days, can lead to cognitive impairments as a result of sleep debt [16].

In addition to the sleep protocol, participants were instructed to abstain from any alcohol and fatigue inducing medicine during the six days of the experiment and to avoid caffeine containing beverages two hours before sleep during the full six days of the experiment.

The measurement procedure was identical on both test days. The participants first performed a PVT on their mobile phone, followed by two speech tasks on their computer. Before, between and after the two speech tasks participants filled in the KSS questionnaire.

The PVT consisted of a 3-min simple reaction time task that was integrated in a mobile app called Psych Lab 101 [17]. The task comprised 75 trials in which a red square appeared, with an inter-stimulus interval range of 1000 to 2000 ms. The participants had to respond to this by tapping the screen as fast as possible. If the participant did not touch the screen before the next trial appeared, this was registered as a miss. Misses and reactions times above 500 ms were counted as lapses [18].

Two types of speech tasks were applied. The first speech task consisted of answering fifteen "would you rather" dilemmas (e.g. Would you rather lose the ability to read or the ability to speak?). The second task involved answering radio commands taken from the Multi-Attribute Task Battery II (MATB-II) [19] to which the participants had to respond verbally by saying: "*Roger, turning radio to frequency [...]*". The task consisted of fifteen radio commands with the call sign NASA504 and ten radio commands with a different call sign. The participants were instructed to only answer commands with the call sign NASA504. The task-order was counterbalanced between participants, and the order did not change within-subjects. The commands and dilemmas were different between test days to avoid that speech was influenced by the participants recognizing the dilemmas and commands, and therefore being able to answer them more fluently. Participants were instructed to make use of their own microphone and the standard Apple or Windows recorder on their computer.

The Karolinska Sleepiness Scale (KSS) [20] was used to measure the subjective level of sleepiness during the measurements. The KSS version used had a ten-point Likert scale [20], where 1 is defined as being "extremely alert" and 10 represents being "extremely sleepy, can't stay awake".

The pre-processing and analysis of vocal intensity and fundamental frequency were done using PRAAT [21], which is an open source software tool for speech analysis. Firstly, all speech was segmented into phrases and words. Outliers caused by background noise were excluded from segmentation. After this, f0 and intensity values were extracted for each word using a pitch range of 75–300 Hz for males and 75–500 Hz for females. These ranges were determined based on the speech range of the participant sample [11]. The intensity values were extracted manually by selecting each word segment, letting PRAAT calculate the value, and logging the value. The f0 values were extracted using a TextGrid script [22]. Finally, the average pitch and intensity of all the extracted values per speech sample was calculated [23], resulting in four values per participant for both the well-rested and sleep deprived condition: average f0 for commands, average f0 for dilemmas, average intensity for commands, and average intensity for dilemmas.

## 3   Results

The Paired Samples t-Test showed a significant difference between the average sleep duration before the first measurement and the second measurement ($t = 15.17, p < 0.01$). The subjects slept 8 h and 39 min (SD = 0.72) the days before the first measurement, and on average 5 h and 55 min (SD = 0.23) before the second measurement. Table 1 shows the mean (M) and standard deviations (SD) of the following measured variables.

A significant difference was found for the average KSS score ($t = -2.69, p < 0.05$) (measured before, between and after the two speech tasks) of the two measurement days. The Wilcoxon Signed Rank Test showed no significant difference in reaction time ($Z = -1.08, p = 0.28$) and the number of lapses ($Z = -0.89, p = 0.37$) between the test days.

No significant differences were found for the voice measures either. The Wilcoxon Signed Rank Test showed no significant difference in average f0 between the two conditions for both the radio commands ($Z = -0.23, p = 0.82$) and the dilemmas ($Z = -1.08, p = 0.28$). This is shown in Fig. 1a. No significant differences were found with the Paired Samples T-tests between the two conditions for the intensity of the commands ($t = -0.99, p = 0.34$) and dilemmas ($t = -1.43, p = 0.17$). This is shown in Fig. 1b. Based on the observed trend between the commands and dilemmas, post-hoc analyses were performed to study the differences between the two speech tasks during the test days. A Wilcoxon Signed Ranks Test showed a significant difference between the average f0 of the dilemmas and the commands task during the first test moment ($Z = -3.07, p < 0.01$), and during the second test moment ($Z = -3.41, p < 0.01$). In addition, a Paired Samples T-test showed a significant difference between the intensity of the dilemmas and commands tasks during the first test moment ($t = 4.88, p < 0.01$), and the second test moment ($t = 4.70, p < 0.01$).

**Table 1.** Mean (M) and standard deviations (SD) of the measured variables.

| Variable | $M_{test\ 1}$ | $SD_{test\ 1}$ | $M_{test\ 2}$ | $SD_{test\ 2}$ |
|---|---|---|---|---|
| KSS score | 3.4 | 1.5 | 4.5 | 2.3 |
| Reaction time (in ms) | 259.6 | 32.9 | 253.7 | 25.5 |
| Lapses | 0.9 | 1.3 | 1.9 | 3.3 |
| f0 commands (in Hz) | 178.9 | 48.5 | 179.8 | 48.8 |
| f0 dilemmas (in Hz) | 161.1 | 37.0 | 159.3 | 38.8 |
| Intensity commands (in dB) | 59.8 | 9.7 | 60.7 | 8.9 |
| Intensity dilemmas (in dB) | 55.3 | 8.8 | 57.1 | 9.3 |

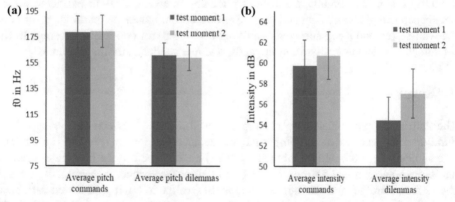

**Fig. 1.** (a) shows the mean pitch on both test moments for both the radio comments and dilemmas with error bars (SD). (b) shows the mean intensity on both test moments for both the radio commands and dilemmas, with error bars (SD).

## 4 Discussion

The purpose of this study was to explore whether changes in vocal intensity and fundamental frequency (f0) can be used as measures for fatigue detection in an operational setting. The outcomes of previous studies suggest that fatigue can lead to a reduction in both vocal intensity and f0 [1, 2, 12–14]. This relationship needed to be studied further, since only few studies have addressed this topic. The objective of the current study was to contribute to the available body of knowledge, while also including an operational element, namely different types of speech. Due to time constraints, the sample size was rather small, although the power analysis showed that a minimum of twelve participants should be sufficient to find a significant difference on vocal changes. A distinction was made between free and procedural speech by means of two different speech tasks, and the vocal measures were compared using two fatigue conditions. In the first, well-rested condition, participants were asked to sleep 8 h or more. In the second condition, participants were asked to sleep 6 h or less during the two days before the test day. It was assumed that the latter led to sleep-deprivation and a subsequent impaired alertness during the second test day. This was confirmed by the findings, where the KSS ratings during the sleep-deprived condition were significantly higher. The analyses on the vocal measures however showed no significant difference in vocal intensity and f0 between the two test days for both speech tasks. We could therefore not conclude that fatigue can be detected by measuring vocal changes. These results might be explained by a number of factors.

Firstly, it could be that the participants were not fatigued to the extent that it affected vocal intensity and f0. Even though the participants slept significantly less and scored significantly higher on the KSS, the average scores represented a limited degree of fatigue, ranging between "rather alert" and "neither alert, nor sleepy". In comparison, another study looking at fatigue and vocal changes, found a mean KSS score of 7.47 (on a scale from 1 to 10) as a result of sleep deprivation, which is a degree of fatigue in between "sleepy, but no effort to stay awake" and "sleepy, but some effort to stay awake" [14]. It could therefore be that changes in voice measures only occur when sleepiness reaches these type of levels. On top of this, no significant differences were found for the PVT measures reaction time and lapses in the current study, which could indicate that the participants experienced little cognitive impairment as a result of sleep deprivation.

The task difficulty may have played a role as well. Two studies that did find vocal changes as a result of fatigue, used a more cognitively demanding task, namely driving a car [13, 14]. In the current study the participants only had to focus on one task at a time (listening to and answering radio commands and answering dilemmas), presumably resulting in lower workload. Higher perceived workload might lead to higher subjective ratings of fatigue. On the other hand, a higher workload might also lead to a higher level of perceived stress, which might have resulted in the vocal changes found in the previous studies.

Stress could also have influenced the results of the current study if participants felt more stressed during the second measurement, resulting in an increase in voice pitch [15], and a mitigating effect on the outcome measures. According to the literature, sleep deprivation leads to a higher sensitivity to emotional and stressful stimuli [24]. The speech tasks and other external factors (i.e. covid-19) might have been possible stressors for participants after a period of reduced sleep. Stress could also explain the differences found in f0 and intensity between the speech tasks. Moreover, many subjects mentioned that they experienced stress during the radio commands task when asked to answer as rapidly and accurately possible.

Another, more methodological factor that might have played a role is the participants distance to the microphone during the experiment. According to the guidelines for voice production research [25] the intensity level decreases by approximately 6 dB when the mouth-to-microphone distance is doubled. This may have slightly affected the average intensity values of the participants. In future studies, participants can be asked to play a certain sound on both test days so a possible difference in loudness can be determined beforehand, and taken into account during the analysis.

Since the results of the current study do not confirm the findings of earlier studies, further research is needed. A better controlled, lab based study with more participants, would be preferable, since more objective control measures can be used in a lab setting (e.g. EEG) and there is more surveillance on how participants are performing the tasks. However, an online method as in the current study could also be used again, although a few factors should be considered. Firstly, a more severe sleep restriction should be applied in order to induce a higher level of sleepiness. A more effective protocol could be to ask participants to sleep 4 h for a consecutive period of 5 nights [16]. Sleep wearables or actigraphs could be used to objectively assess sleep duration. Secondly, possible confounding factors such as stress, should be measured (either objectively or subjectively) and controlled for. Furthermore, a task with a higher workload might be added to the measurement procedure (e.g. a difficult version of the MATB-II). Lastly, to control for microphone distance on both test days participants should be asked to hold their phone close to their mouth while playing a sound at maximum volume, while the laptop records the sound. This way a potential difference in sound intensity could be determined and controlled for.

Another possible study idea is to analyse voice recordings of pilots and air traffic controllers. A group of pilots and air traffic controllers can be asked to fill in the KSS questionnaire every hour during their normal duties. Afterwards, voice recordings during duty hours with low levels of fatigue could be compared to voice recordings during duty hours with high levels of fatigue. On top of that, other voice measures, such as disfluency, can be explored to determine if a combination of voice measures leads to a more accurate detection of fatigue.

## 5  Conclusion

In the current study no difference was found for vocal intensity and fundamental frequency (f0) between a well-rested and a sleep-restricted condition. The results of this study suggest that sleep restriction does not have an effect on f0 and vocal intensity. However, these findings do not have to imply that speech is an ineffective measure for fatigue detection altogether. Based on previous studies, it might still be possible that higher levels of fatigue do provoke an effect on voice measures. Since people working in the aviation sector often deal with a high workload, time zone shifts and night shifts, higher levels of fatigue are likely to occur. Additional research is needed to better understand the relationship between vocal changes and fatigue, taking into account the suggestions described earlier.

## References

1. Roelen, A.L.C., Stuut, R.: Association of sleep deprivation with speech volume and pitch. In: Ergonomics & Human Factors 2016, Daventry, United Kingdom, pp. 19–21 (2016)
2. de Vasconcelos, C.A., Vieira, M.N., Kecklund, G., Yehia, H.C.: Speech analysis for fatigue and sleepiness detection of a pilot. Aerosp. Med. Hum. Perform. **90**(4), 415–418 (2019)

3. Caldwell, J.A.: Fatigue in aviation. Travel Med. Infect. Dis. **3**(2), 85–96 (2005)
4. Ruudin-Brown, C., Rosberg, A., Krukowski, D.: If we'd only listen! What can tell us about aircrew fatigue. In: 20th International Symposium on Aviation Psychology, pp. 319–324 (2019)
5. Boksem, M.A.S., Meijman, T.F., Lorist, M.M.: Effects of mental fatigue on attention: An ERP study. Cogn. Brain Res. **25**(1), 107–116 (2005)
6. van der Linden, D., Frese, M., Meijman, T.F.: Mental fatigue and the control of cognitive processes: effects on perseveration and planning. Acta Psychol. **113**(1), 45–65 (2003)
7. Lorist, M.M., Boksem, M.A.S., Ridderinkhof, K.R.: Impaired cognitive control and reduced cingulate activity during mental fatigue. Cogn. Brain Res. **24**(2), 199–205 (2005)
8. Lee, I., Bardwell, W.A., Ancoli-Israel, S., Dimsdale, J.E.: Number of lapses during the psychomotor vigilance task as an objective measure of fatigue. J. Clin. Sleep Med. **6**(2), 163–168 (2010)
9. Zhang, C., Yu, X.: Estimating mental fatigue based on electroencephalogram and heart rate variability. Pol. J. Med. Phys. Eng. **16**(2), 67–84 (2010)
10. Aalto University Wiki: Fundamental frequency (F0) - Introduction to Speech Processing, https://wiki.aalto.fi/display/ITSP/Introduction+to+Speech+Processing. Accessed 2019
11. Intro 4.2. Configuring the pitch contour. https://www.fon.hum.uva.nl/praat/manual/Intro_4_2__Configuring_the_pitch_contour.html. Accessed 2019
12. Baykaner, K., Huckvale, M., Whiteley, I., Ryumin, O., Andreeva, S.: The prediction of fatigue using speech as a biosignal. In: Dediu, A.H., Martín-Vide, C., Vicsi, K. (eds.) Statistical Language and Speech Processing. SLSP. Lecture Notes in Computer Science, vol. 9449, pp. 8–17. Springer, Cham (2015)
13. Krajewski, J., Batliner, A., Golz, M.: Acoustic sleepiness detection: framework and validation of a speech-adapted pattern recognition approach. Behav. Res. Methods **41**(3), 795–804 (2009)
14. Krajewski, J., Trutschel, U., Golz, M., Sommer, D., Edwards, D.: Estimating fatigue from predetermined speech samples transmitted by operator communication systems. In: Proceedings of the 5th International Driving Symposium on Human Factors in Driver Assessment, Training, and Vehicle Design : Driving Assessment 2009, pp. 468–474 (2009)
15. Ruiz, R., Legros, C., Guell, A.: Voice analysis to predict the psychological or physical state of a speaker. Aviat. Space Environ. Med. **61**, 266–271 (1990)
16. Alhola, P., Polo-Kantola, P.: Sleep deprivation: Impact on cognitive performance. Neuropsychiatric Dis. Treat. **3**(5), 553–567 (2007)
17. Psychlab 101 (Version 2.1.0) [Software]: Neurobehavioral Systems. https://www.neurobs.com. Accessed 2020
18. Anderson, C., Wales, A.W.J., Home, J.A.: PVT lapses differ according to eyes open, closed, or looking away. Sleep **33**(2), 197–204 (2010)
19. NASA: The Multi-Attribute Task Battery II (MATB-II) software for human performance and workload research: a user's guide (NASA/TM–2011–217164) (2011)
20. Shahid, A., Wilkinson, K., Marcu, S., Shapiro, C.M.: Karolinska sleepiness scale (KSS). In: STOP, THAT and One Hundred Other Sleep Scales, pp. 209–210. Springer (2012)
21. Boersma, P., Weenink, D.: Praat (Version 6.1.08): doing phonetics by computer [Computer program]. https://www.praat.org/. Accessed 2019
22. Script for analysing pitch with a TextGrid. (2014). https://www.fon.hum.uva.nl/praat/manual/Script_for_analysing_pitch_with_a_TextGrid.html
23. Microsoft Corporation: Microsoft Excel (2018)
24. Vandekerckhove, M., Cluydts, R.: The emotional brain and sleep: an intimate relationship. Sleep Med. Rev. **14**(4), 219–226 (2010)
25. Švec, J.G., Granqvist, S.: Guidelines for selecting microphones for human voice production research. Am. J. Speech-Lang. Pathol. **19**(4), 356–368 (2010)

# Fatigue Assessment Methods Applied to Air Traffic Control – A Bibliometric Analysis

Larissa Maria Gomes de Carvalho⬤, Sarah Francisca de Souza Borges⬤, and Moacyr Machado Cardoso Júnior$^{(\boxtimes)}$ ⬤

Technological Institute of Aeronautics SJC, São José dos Campos 12228-900, Brazil
{larissalmgc,sarah,Moacyr}@ita.br

**Abstract.** The International Civil Aviation Organization (ICAO), which supervises the activities and provision of air services, as well as Brazil which is a signatory, issued a formal recommendation pointing fatigue as a criterion of high impact on aeronautical activities and in maintaining the safety of aircraft operations. The proposing management of human fatigue following scientific principles in two approaches: one prescriptive, which stipulates regulatory prescriptive limits, and the other, not mandatory, for data monitoring through a system called FRMS (Fatigue Risk Management System). This article is a bibliometric study on the scientific production in fatigue applied to air traffic control. A bibliometric survey was conducted on three databases "SCOPUS", "ENGINEERING VILLAGE", and "WEB OF SCIENCE", resulting in only 7 documents. Though a survey in other web sources, books, and international regulations was conducted, resulting in 13 methods. Among the subjective methods are: Sleep diaries; Visual Analogue Scale to Evaluate Fatigue Severity (VAS-F); Karolinska Sleepiness Scale (KSS); Samn Perelli Scale (SPS); Epiworth Sleepiness Scale; Stanford Sleepiness Scale. By the results, subjective methods have advantages, such as speed and ease of administration, application on paper or computer, the minimal interruption to the crew, many studies have used SPS and KSS and provide data for comparison. And, disadvantages, such as: relatively easy to cheat, may not have face validity. Until this moment, prescription limits have been adopted in Brazil following regulations, but the fatigue assessment and monitoring phase are still in the study and implementation strategy phase.

**Keywords:** Bibliometric study · Fatigue · Assessment methods · Air traffic control

## 1 Introduction

### 1.1 Problem Statement

The International Civil Aviation Organization (ICAO), which governs and supervises the activities and provision of air services, as well as Brazil which is an ICAO's signatory, issued a recommendation that formally points out fatigue as a criterion of high impact on aeronautical activities and in maintaining the safety of aircraft operations. The proposing

N. L. Black et al. (Eds.): IEA 2021, LNNS 221, pp. 136–142, 2021.
https://doi.org/10.1007/978-3-030-74608-7_18

management of human fatigue follow scientific principles in two approaches: one prescriptive, which stipulates regulatory prescriptive limits, and the other, not mandatory, for data monitoring through a system called FRMS (Fatigue Risk Management System).

According to the ICAO, fatigue is a physiological state of reduced capacity for mental or physical performance resulting from loss of sleep or prolonged wakefulness, circadian phase, or workload (mental and/or physical activity) that can impair alertness and ability of a crew member to safely operate an aircraft or perform safety-related tasks.

Nevertheless, the contributions of factors related to fatigue at work vary considerably between individuals and can be influenced by aspects of the tasks performed, the scheduling of work shifts, the routine, predictability, and planning of the work performed [1].

Among the activities carried out by the air traffic controller are: ensuring that aircraft fly safely, maintaining minimum regulatory separation; following complex operational procedures that are constantly changing (routes, levels, meteorological changes, availability of airport for landing, emergency declarations by aircraft, traffic prioritization, among others) and perform the control of aerodromes (TWR), of approach to terminal areas (APP), area control centers (ACC) and also air defense (CoPM). The controller is the one who makes the final decisions and in a limited time [2].

Also, it must consider that the responsibility for the effectiveness and success of a fatigue management program is shared by the organization and its employees. Therefore, among the measures adopted in an ATC fatigue risk management are reliable and qualified reports with details of sources of hazards; adopt a management committee; commitment of employees with senior management; continuous monitoring; adherence to a reactive investigation process to safety events and, consequently, compliance with safety recommendations, specifically the dissemination of best practices and information; adoption of a training and awareness program; and, effective application of standardized procedures and commitment to continuous improvement [3, 4].

In the study carried out and documented in this article, it was possible to verify few referring works in the field of ATC fatigue management. Among the methods, there are also different approaches, and it is necessary a method that better integrates human factors and is officially recognized for fatigue analysis.

Although scientific methods of fatigue management are already widely recognized in the field of aviation, it was found that this reality is not the same for the control of air traffic, given the few articles found.

Thus, it was possible to verify that there is still a research field for measuring the fatigue of air traffic control operators in Brazil and worldwide, about the scientific principles that must be considered when talking about a fatigue risk management program human.

## 1.2 Objective/Question

ICAO edited the Fatigue Management Guide for Air Traffic Services Providers [3], or Annex 11, noting that signatory countries should carry out these regulations as of 05/Nov 2020.

In this scenario, this article proposes a bibliometric study on the scientific production in fatigue applied to air traffic control.

At the end pointing out several methods, which most consider aspects of sleep loss and recovery, the biological circadian clock, as well as the impact of the activity and its workload.

### 1.3 Methodology

In the study of methods for fatigue analysis, bibliometric research was initially used, classified as a quantitative technique, which uses mathematical and statistical methods to quantify the production, dissemination, and use of previously registered information [5].

Bibliometrics consists of a set of laws and empirical principles that contribute to establishing the theoretical foundations of Information Science, a term used for the first time in 1922 by E. WyndhamHulme [6].

A bibliometric search was carried out to verify which assessment methods could be used to manage the fatigue applied to air traffic controllers.

In this way, the search scope was limited to three databases "SCOPUS" (7 documents), "ENGINEERING VILLAGE" (5 documents), and "WEB OF SCIENCE" (no document). The terms used were ("fatigue management" AND "ATC") OR ("fatigue management" AND "Air Traffic Control") OR ("fatigue management" AND "ATM"), resulting in only 7 documents, revealing the need for a more comprehensive search.

The 7 articles found covered subjects such as Samn Perelli Scale (SPS); FRMS as a monitoring tool; fatigue monitoring technologies with methods of assessing working hours, fatigue symptoms and real sleep time; human voice analysis system, which confirmed to measure the degree of activity fatigue.

Thus, through other web sources, books, and international regulations, 13 methods were found, and as described in this article.

## 2    Results

### 2.1    Identified Methods

There are different ways to measure fatigue, either in the laboratory or in an operational context, with methods:

Objectives, such as Temperature Measurement; Biological tests; Actigraphy, which is a simple test to detect changes in sleep and circadian rhythm [7]; Polysomnography, which is a non-invasive exam to measure respiratory, muscle and brain activity, in addition to other parameters, during sleep [8, 9]; Simple mental tasks; Complex behaviors.

Moreover, the following subjective methods:

- Sleep diaries analysis, which are records of sleep and waking periods, over a period of days and even weeks [10].
- Visual analog scale to assess fatigue severity (Visual Analogue Scale to Evaluate Fatigue Severity, VAS-F), which uses a scale composed of 18 items related to fatigue and energy, with simple instructions, minimal time and effort. In addition, it compares favorably with the Stanford Sleepiness Scale Standard and the Profile of MoodStates [11].

- Karolinska Sleepiness Scale (Karolinska Sleepiness Scale, KSS) is often used to study sleepiness in various contexts [12].
- Samn-Perelli Scale (Samn Perelli Scale, SPS) classification of the level of attention at seven points before a period of sleep (pre-sleep) and after (post-sleep). Considering: 1. Totally alert, wide awake; 2. Very excited, receptive, but not at the peak; 3. Okay, but little rest; 4. A little tired; 5. Moderately tired, disappointed; 6. Extremely tired, very difficult to concentrate; 7. Completely depleted, unable to function effectively.
- The Epworth Sleepiness Scale (ESE) is a questionnaire completed by the patient himself, whose objective is to determine a general measure of the degree of day-time sleepiness in adults. The subject provides a score, quantifying his sleepiness in monotonous situations of daily life. The main superiority of ESE is its simple, fast application, enabling its use in extensive population studies.
- The Stanford Sleepiness Scale (Stanford Sleepiness Scale), developed by Dement and colleagues in 1972, is a self-report questionnaire that measures sleepiness levels throughout the day. The scale, which can be administered for 1 to 2 min, is generally used to track general attention at each hour of the day.
- The Psychomotor Vigilance Test is a task with sustained attention and reaction time that measures the speed with which individuals respond to a visual stimulus. Research indicates that increased debt or sleep deficit correlates with impaired attention, slower problem solving, decreased psychomotor skills, and an increased rate of false responses. The PVT was developed by David F. Dinges and popularized for its easy scoring, simple metrics, and convergent validity.
- Fatigue Audit InterDyne Biomathematic Model (FAID), software for implementing Fatigue Management through quantification that relates the scheduling of tasks and the hours worked (that is, the start or end time of work periods).
- Biomathematic Model Sleep, Activity, Fatigue and Task Effectiveness (SAFTE) is a computer model that predicts changes in cognitive performance, based on sleep or wake time and the body's internal clock. It contains a circadian process, a circadian propensity to sleep process, an asleep fragmentation process, and a phase adjustment feature for time zone changes.
- Commercial Model System for Aircrew Fatigue Evaluation (SAFE), is an acronym for the Air Crew Fatigue Assessment System: a computer program that includes a set of algorithms that allows evaluating a series of factors that influence the alertness in the crew.
- Commercial Model Aviation Fatigue Risk Model (CAS-5) is a fatigue management software specially optimized for planning the scale of the crew of airlines.
- Circadian Performance Simulation Software (CPSS) business model is designed to predict the effects of sleep or wake times and exposure to light on the human circadian cycle, and the combined effects of the circadian phase and homeostatic sleep pressure on cognitive performance and subjective alert.
- Health and Safety Executive (HSE) model, supported by fatigue management software, constitutes a mathematical basis for assessing the level of fatigue using the analysis of the shifts of the scales, it serves to analyze engineering jobs, in aviation and other professions that deal with complex performance and safety systems, scale routines and fatigue management.

In addition to the methods, it is important to relate the risk analysis of the operation. Table 1 provides some examples of mitigations at the organizational level to manage fatigue risks, giving scope for further studies, as this is not an exhaustive list.

**Table 1.** Examples of fatigue hazards and operational controls for mitigation [3].

| Hazards of fatigue | Controls | Mitigations |
| --- | --- | --- |
| Many hours of service | Limit the number of hours of operational service | Have restrictions on operational procedures with minimal opportunity for deviation |
| Few hours between shifts | Have minimum time requirements between the shift and the start time of the next shift | Programming software programmed to prevent shift assignment with less than the required free time |
| Many shifts in the week of 7 days | Limit the number of shifts eligible for work in a work week | Ensure that employees have time to replenish the sleep facility, essential for the job |
| Position during low circadian times | Allow employees the opportunity to sleep restfully before and/or after likely circadian casualties | Ensure that ATCs have ample opportunities for break during shifts and ample sleep opportunities between scheduled shifts |
| Sleep opportunities after the night shift | Ensure minimum clearance after the night shift | Have limits on shift assignment after the night shift, that is, another night shift or day off the next day |

## 2.2  Discussion

In accordance with the results, subjective methods have advantages, such as speed and ease of administration, application on paper or computer, the minimal interruption to the crew, many studies have used Samn Perelli Scale - SPS and Karolinska Sleepness Scale - KSS and provide data for comparison. And, disadvantages, such as: relatively easy to cheat, may not have face validity, they do not always reliably reflect objective performance measures [13].

Fatigue needs to be assessed as part of a program to identify the level of risk, effective monitoring, and relevant mitigation measures. According to ICAO, it means having a data-driven means to continuously monitor and maintain safety risks related to fatigue, based on scientific principles and knowledge, as well as operational experience that aims to ensure that professionals are performing tasks at appropriate levels of alert [3]. In line with the research, the importance of considering operational aspects related to the execution of the control activity in the operational environment, as well as the organizational aspects, became evident.

# 3 Conclusions

The issue of implementing a Fatigue Management System is under discussion in several countries and the objective of this article is to concentrate on identify which assessment methods would be effective considering that the concept of fatigue covers several aspects (circadian cycle, sleep-wake cycle, and workload). In this way, a more reliable accurate assessment, encompassing several methods, as presented, the different instruments can only assess specific aspects.

Another important point to be discussed concerns the workload aspect. According to the regulatory documents covered, the workload covers three important aspects that influence the performance of the controller: the nature and amount of work to be done (including time on the task, difficulty, and complexity of the task and intensity); time constraints (including whether the time is driven by task demands, external factors or the individual); and, factors related to individual performance capacity (experience, skill level, effort, sleep history and characteristics of the circadian cycle).

When this article was written, there was still no valid regulation on Risk Management for fatigue in Brazil. In November 2020, the Airspace Control Department (DECEA) published the standardization through a CIRCEA 100-89 that provides for mandatory prescriptive limits for fatigue management in ATC; as well as MCA 81-1 which aims to establish the procedures and processes related to Fatigue Risk Management in the ATC bodies, structured by each operational body according to its complexity and must undergo prior authorization.

This bibliometric study was efficient in that it was able to identify the most applied fatigue assessment methods. Moreover, it is important to highlight that the measurement of fatigue in the context of air traffic control must comply with a management system in order to identify the level of related risk, the monitoring, and the relevant mitigation.

Until this moment, prescriptive limits in accordance with regulations have been adopted in Brazil, but the fatigue assessment and monitoring phase are still under study and implementation strategy. There is still no experimental research to answer this question, as it is still being studied.

Therefore, its effectiveness can only be verified if all the agents involved share responsibilities (regulators, Air Navigation Service Providers, and controllers) and are involved in the management processes in order to contribute to occupational health, quality of life, and maintenance of adequate levels of safety.

# References

1. Mello, M.T.: Trabalhador em Turno: Fadiga. 1st edn. Atheneu, São Paulo (2013)
2. Ministério da Defesa, PORTARIA DECEA N o. 227/DGCEA, DE 17 DE OUTUBRO DE 2016. https://paraserpiloto.com/wp-content/uploads/2016/11/ICA-100-12-Regras-do-Ar.pdf. Accessed 10 May 2020
3. CANSO/ICAO/IFATCA: Fatigue Management Guide for Air Traffic Service Providers. 1st edn. ICAO, Brasília (2016)
4. Chang, Y.H., Yang, H.H., Hsu, W.J.: Effects of work shifts on fatigue levels of air traffic controllers. J. Air Transp. Manage. **76**(1), 1–9 (2019)

 5. Tissot, P.B., Tondolo, V.A.G., Espíndola, A., Longaray, A.A., Camargo, E.M.: Bibliometric analysis of publications related to the term 'servitization' in operations management. Gestão Prod. Oper. Sist. **3**(1), 1–24 (2017)
 6. Guedes, V.L.S., Borschiver, S.: Bibliometria: Uma ferramenta estatística para a Gestão da Informação e do Conhecimento, em Sistemas de Informação, de Comunicação e de Avaliação científica e tecnológica. Encontro Nacional Ciência Inf. **6**(2), 1–18 (2005)
 7. Telles, S.C.L., Corrêa, É.A., Caversan, B.L., Mattos, J.M., Alves, R.S.C.: Significado clínico da actigrafia. Rev. Neurociências **19**(1), 153–161 (2011)
 8. Guimarães, G.M.: Diagnóstico Polissonográfico. Rev. SOPTERJ – Soc. Pneumol. Tisiol. Estado do Rio de Janeiro **19**(3–4), 88–92 (2010)
 9. de Menezes Duarte, R.L., Silva, R.Z.M., Silveira, F.J.M.: Métodos Resumidos no Diagnóstico da Apnéia do Sono. Rev. SOPTERJ – Soc. Pneumol. Tisiol. Estado do Rio de Janeiro **19**(3–4), 78–82 (2010)
10. Văcăreţu, T., Batalas, N., Erten-Uyumaz, B., Gilst, M.V., Overeem, S., Markopoulos, P.: Subjective sleep quality monitoring with the hypnos digital sleep diary: evaluation of usability and user experience. In: Proceedings of the 12th International Joint Conference on Biomedical Engineering Systems and Technologies, pp. 113–122. HEALTHINF, Prague (2019)
11. Lee, K., Hicks, G., Nino-Murcia, G.: Validity and reliability of a scale to assess fatigue. Psychiatry Res. **36**(1), 291–298 (1991)
12. Miley, A.Å., Kecklund, G., Åkerstedt, T.: Comparing two versions of the Karolinska Sleepiness Scale (KSS). Sleep Biol. Rhythms **14**(3), 257–260 (2016)
13. Stokes, E.K.: Measuring fatigue. In: Rehabilitation Outcome Measures, pp. 83–92. Churchill Livingstone, New York (2011)

# Comfort in the Regional Aircraft Cabin: Passenger Priorities

Neil Mansfield[(✉)], Anna West, Frederique Vanheusden, and Steve Faulkner

Department of Engineering, Nottingham Trent University, Nottingham, UK
neil.mansfield@ntu.ac.uk

**Abstract.** Regional turboprop passenger aircraft are more fuel efficient than equivalent regional turbofan jets. Aerodynamic interaction between the propeller and the aircraft wing and body cause higher noise and vibration in the turboprop cabin than in jets; to improve the passenger cabin of turboprops, an improve comfort model is required to enable design optimization. Three age-stratified focus groups were conducted with the aim of eliciting passenger priorities for comfort in aircraft cabins. Participants discussed view elicited in response to images of different aircraft, and aircraft interiors. Transcriptions of the focus groups were coded using NVivo and the most common thematic areas identified for each age group. Physical comfort (space and seat design), the physical environment (noise, air quality, vibration, thermal), safety and hygiene were the most commonly coded thematic areas. The oldest group (50–70) rated the thermal environment as more important than younger groups. Turboprop aircraft were considered noisy and to be less comfortable than turbojets. However, noise and vibration were considered to be outside of the passenger's control and therefore accepted.

**Keywords:** Comfort · Aircraft · Passenger · Turboprop · ComfDemo

## 1 Introduction

Passenger aircraft contribute to climate change due to emissions from fossil fuels and the formation of clouds [1]. Long term hybrid and full electrification in aviation will require a move from jet propulsion to propeller aircraft [2]. Even existing turboprop aircraft are generally 10–60% more fuel efficient than equivalent jet turbofan aircraft based on point-to-point analysis [3]. Whilst turboprop aircraft have environmental credentials, their cabin environment is generally considered inferior. This is due to the tonal nature of the noise and vibration, comprising harmonic components due to the interaction of the propeller blade pass and the aircraft wing and body [4].

To optimize the design of future propeller aircraft, an improved understanding of passenger perceptions of aircraft comfort is necessary. This process requires developing a predictive model of overall comfort in the aircraft cabin that is applicable to turboprop designs, and can be used as a starting point for improving turboprop design without the need for real-life test model. A digital twin of the aircraft-passenger system will be developed through the EU ComfDemo project of which this study forms a part.

N. L. Black et al. (Eds.): IEA 2021, LNNS 221, pp. 143–149, 2021.
https://doi.org/10.1007/978-3-030-74608-7_19

This study aimed to gain insight of passenger opinions on turboprops in comparison to jet aircraft and to understand passenger priorities in terms of cabin comfort in regional aircraft.

## 2  Methodology

Three focus groups were conducted with participants recruited into one of three age groups: 18–24 (n = 4), 35–49 (n = 5), 50–70 (n = 5) years old. Each group included male and female subjects. Focus groups were conducted over video conference due to social distancing restrictions during the COVID-19 pandemic. Audio was recorded and transcribed using NVivo, and then coded for analysis.

The focus groups were structured into 4 sections. In Sect. 1, participants were asked to '*write down your initial thoughts, words and associations which come to mind when looking at this image…*'. They were presented with an anonymized black and white image of a Bombardier Dash-8 turboprop aircraft (Fig. 1a). A group discussion led by a facilitator then followed to draw out common themes.

**Fig. 1.** Images of a turboprop aircraft (a) and turbojet aircraft (b) presented in Sects. 1 and 2 of the focus groups. Images were anonymized and presented in black and white.

In Sect. 2, participants were asked the same question as in Sect. 1, but presented with an image of an anonymized black and white image of an Embraer 190 turbojet aircraft (Fig. 1b). A group discussion led by a facilitator then followed to draw out common themes. Participants were given the opportunity to compare their views of both aircraft and able to view both images simultaneously.

In Sect. 3, participants were asked the same question as in Sect. 1/2, but presented with an image of the passenger cabin of a regional aircraft. In the group discussion, they were asked to state what aspects of the cabin environment were important, and what priority needs were in the space.

Section 4 presented 16 attributes previously associated with passenger experience in airline cabins (Table 1). Participants were asked to explain what was particularly important to them in relation to these attributes, and asked which, in their opinion, were the most important and least important attributes.

**Table 1.** Sixteen attributes relating to aircraft cabin comfort presented to participants in Sect. 4 of the focus groups.

| In-flight entertainment | Cabin crew |
| --- | --- |
| Cabin layout | Food and beverages |
| Seat design | Information and communication |
| Seat spacing | Air quality |
| Luggage storage | Climate |
| Safety | Light |
| Cleanliness | Noise |
| Personal factors | Vibration |

Audio from the focus groups was transcribed and coded to thematic nodes by a single investigator.

The study design was approved by Nottingham Trent University ethical advisory committee.

# 3   Results

From discussions comparing turboprop and jet aircraft, it became apparent that knowledge and experience of turboprop aircraft was not universal amongst groups. There were several comments stating that the turboprop in the image looked older than the turbojet aircraft. Participants across all groups recognized that turboprop aircraft were noisier than jet aircraft, although opinions were broad.

During the thematic analysis on in-cabin comfort, twenty-nine nodes were generated (Table 2). Group 18–35 generated 373 case classifications, 35–49 generated 115, 50–70 generated 492. To give equal weight to each age group, coding counts were normalized by the total number of coded statements within each focus group. Therefore, results were analyzed in terms of the percentage of statements within each of the three age-stratified focus groups.

**Table 2.** 29 nodes generated during thematic analysis of the three focus groups.

| Air quality | Cabin layout | Efficiency | Propulsion – jet | Toilets |
|---|---|---|---|---|
| Aircraft age | Children | Food drink | Propulsion – propellors | Vibration |
| Aircraft appearance | Comfort – experience | Hygiene | Safety | Vision |
| Aircraft range | Comfort – seat design | In flight entertainment | Sleep | WiFi |
| Aircraft speed | Comfort – space | Ingress egress | Storage/luggage | Windows |
| Body size | Crew | Noise | Thermal | |

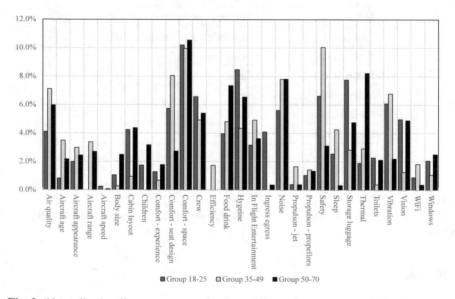

**Fig. 2.** Normalized coding count across the three different focus groups, showing the topics that were most often mentioned during the discussion.

The most commonly coded nodes for the three groups are shown in Table 3. Each node included in the table was ranked in the top 10 for at least one of the focus groups.

The most commonly coded themes were comfort (space), noise and safety. Opinions on space were consistently related to lack of space for the passenger, and the impact of other users' behavior/anthropometry on the subject's personal space (Fig. 2).

Regarding noise, the 18–25 group noted noise from children as a problem; this was not mentioned by other groups. Some participants in the 35–49 group stated that they used noise-cancelling headphones to resolve issues related to cabin noise.

Safety was the most coded theme for the 35–49 group. Despite participants being experienced travelers, many, but not all, expressed ongoing anxiety with safety. This was considered more acute for turboprop aircraft. The theme was ranked 4th for 18–25 and outside the top 10 for 50–70 group.

Whilst hygiene was considered important, many comments were related to the ongoing COVID-19 pandemic and therefore difficult to separate into short-term and established opinions. However, participants expressed concern over perceived effectiveness of cleaning, and hygiene of headrests and edges of seats used as handholds on either side of the aisle.

**Table 3.** Ranking of most common thematic areas for each of the three focus groups. 1 = the most coded theme. Each theme is ranked in the top 10 for at least one of the three groups.

| Thematic area | Group 18–25 | Group 35–49 | Group 50–70 |
|---|---|---|---|
| Comfort – space | 1 | 2 | 1 |
| Noise | 8 | 4 | 3 |
| Safety | 4 | 1 | 13 |
| Hygiene | 2 | 10 | 5 |
| Air quality | 11 | 5 | 6 |
| Crew | 5 | 8 | 7 |
| Comfort - seat design | 7 | 3 | 14 |
| Food drink | 13 | 9 | 4 |
| Storage luggage | 3 | 16 | 9 |
| Vibration | 6 | 6 | 19 |
| Thermal | 19 | 15 | 2 |
| In flight entertainment | 14 | 7 | 11 |
| Vision | 9 | 21 | 8 |
| Cabin layout | 10 | 23 | 10 |

A range of issues were highlighted under air quality. Several participants discussed issues related to personal hygiene (i.e. odors from other passengers), galley-related odors, toilet smells, and the smell of the apron and jet fuel.

Vibration was discussed in two contexts: aircraft-induced vibration (e.g. from engines and hydraulics) and aerodynamic-induced (e.g. turbulence). Vibration of the aircraft was considered as unavoidable and accepted as part of the flight experience. However, it was still considered as an important contributor to discomfort felt in aircraft.

Thermal issues were frequently coded (ranked 2) for the 50–70 group but were not so often discussed in the other groups. Comments were consistent, that passengers associated in-cabin experiences with getting cold, and that they would take additional clothing for a flight.

## 4  Discussion

The results support and expand on several previous studies. The top listed items here parallel those identified as general priorities for aircraft comfort [5]. Bouwens et al. developed a hierarchy of environmental factors for aircraft comprising, in order, anthropometrics, noise, smell, climate, vibrations, light. The priorities parallel with the order in which the items appeared in this study (Table 3).

Vanacore et al. has previously shown that there are differences in perceived aircraft seating comfort with age [6]. This study indicated that some factors (e.g. thermal) are more important for older passengers, and others are less important (e.g. safety). With an ageing population it is therefore necessary to consider the needs of older travelers in climate design.

Studies on scent in aircraft [7] have shown that addition of odors designed to improve the passenger environment have a complex association with comfort; the importance of unpleasant smells is illustrated in this study as being high. It appears that there is scope to design aircraft-specific masking scents to improve the perceived cabin environment.

Turboprop aircraft were considered noisy and to be less comfortable than turbojet aircraft. The priorities related to cabin environments reinforced the priorities in designing turboprop aircraft cabin environments, and highlighted that there is a need to prioritize the physical ergonomics including the space and seat design, and the environmental features including noise, vibration and thermal elements. As the noise and vibration environment in turboprop aircraft is different to that experience in turbojets [4], there is a need for specific research to understand the human response to the multi-factorial environmental attributes.

## 5  Conclusion

The study investigated passenger travel comfort opinions in turboprop and jet aircraft. Individual space was the most commonly coded theme during the focus groups. The 50–70 group spoke more about the thermal environment than other groups; 35–49 spoke more about safety than other groups. Noise and vibration were both considered important but somewhat out of the passengers' control and accepted.

**Acknowledgement.** Supported by EU CleanSky ComfDemo—H2020-CS2-CFP08–2018-01.

## References

1. Moore, R.H., Thornhill, K.L., Weinzierl, B., Sauer, D., D'Ascoli, E., Kim, J., Lichtenstern, M., Scheibe, M., Beaton, B., Beyersdorf, A.J., Barrick, J.: Biofuel blending reduces particle emissions from aircraft engines at cruise conditions. Nature **543**(7645), 411–415 (2017)
2. Schäfer, A.W., Barrett, S.R., Doyme, K., Dray, L.M., Gnadt, A.R., Self, R., O'Sullivan, A., Synodinos, A.P., Torija, A.J.: Technological, economic and environmental prospects of all-electric aircraft. Nat. Energy **4**(2), 160–166 (2019)

3. Babikian, R., Lukachko, S.P., Waitz, I.A.: The historical fuel efficiency characteristics of regional aircraft from technological, operational, and cost perspectives. J. Air Transp. Manage. **8**(6), 389–400 (2002)
4. Bellmann, M.A., Remmers, H.: Evaluation of vibration perception in passenger cabin. Fortschritte der Akustik–DAGA 2004 (2004)
5. Bouwens, J., Hiemstra-van Mastrigt, S., Vink, P.: Ranking of human senses in relation to different in-flight activities contributing to the comfort experience of airplane passengers. Int. J. Aviat. Aeronaut. Aerosp. **5**(2), 9 (2018)
6. Vanacore, A., Lanzotti, A., Percuoco, C., Capasso, A., Vitolo, B.: A model-based approach for the analysis of aircraft seating comfort. Work **68**(s1) (2020)
7. Yao, X., Song, Y., Vink, P.: Effect of scent on comfort of aircraft passengers. Work **68**(s1) (2020)

# Estimation of a Pilot's Workload In-Flight Using External Fluctuation Factors: An Experimental Approach Using a Flight Simulator

Yuki Mekata[✉], Kenta Shiina, Ayumu Osawa, and Miwa Nakanishi

Keio University, Yokohama, Kanagawa 223-8522, Japan

**Abstract.** Pilots must manage their workload correctly to achieve a safe operation. However, few studies have attempted to estimate a pilot's workload in real-time, and there are no established methods of doing so. To provide more direct support for a pilot's workload management, we attempted to construct a model that estimates the pilot's future workload using data on various flight-related parameters that can be acquired in real-time. Participants conducted simulated flights using the flight simulator. Based on the data obtained from these simulations, we used machine learning to construct a model to estimate the workload level 30 s later on a five-point scale. This model correctly estimated 32.0% of the test data, and in 72.3% of the test data, the deviation between the subjective value and the estimated value was within one workload level. We implemented a system that presents the estimated workload level to the pilot in real-time, and from the review of a license holder who conducted simulated flights using the proposed system, we confirmed that the system is effective for workload management.

**Keywords:** Workload management · Machine learning · Flight data · Pilot's workload level · Aircraft

## 1 Introduction

In general aviation, pilots must be able to manage their workload correctly to achieve a safe operation. Currently, pilots must anticipate their workload during flight and manage it appropriately to prevent accidents and workload-induced incidents. However, proper workload management is not easy to achieve, especially if the pilot is flying alone. It is even more difficult if the pilot is flying into an unfamiliar location or navigating hazardous weather. Therefore, it is necessary to help pilots support their workload management to be better prepared for flights.

It has become possible to acquire data related to various flight-related parameters in real time in recent years. As a result, the research and development of support methods that use those data for pilot workload management are progressing. Various suggestions include a system that provides the pilot with information on the airflow state of the route ahead [1] and a system that displays the timing of speed change to optimize the interval of aircrafts [2]. However, few studies have attempted to estimate a pilot's workload in

N. L. Black et al. (Eds.): IEA 2021, LNNS 221, pp. 150–158, 2021.
https://doi.org/10.1007/978-3-030-74608-7_20

real-time, and there are no established methods to do so. Therefore, we aim to construct a model that estimates a pilot's future workload using data on various flight-related parameters that can be acquired in real-time. This is expected to result in more direct support for the pilot's workload management.

## 2 Collecting Data Through Experiments

### 2.1 Identifying Factors that Increase the In-Flight Workload of the Pilot

From the Japan Transport Safety Board's accident investigation reports for the period of 2001–2019 (101 accidents involving small aircraft) [3], we determined the recognized factors of a pilot's workload during a typical flight. These workload factors were broadly classified into weather-related, airframe-related, and flight phase-related factors. Weather-related factors include bad weather, poor visibility at night, and strong winds; airframe-related factors include overload and lack of fuel; and flight phase-related factors include flight area (e.g., flight in mountainous areas), takeoff, and landing. The flight data affected by these factors were used as parameters for a model to estimate a pilot's workload in real-time.

### 2.2 Acquisition of Learning Data

#### 2.2.1 Experimental Outline

To construct a workload estimation model, we obtained experimental data of flight-related parameters and physiological indices corresponding to the workload at current time. We obtained the data using a flight simulator and, based on this data, we will clarify the relationship between flight-related parameters and workload.

#### 2.2.2 Experimental Task

The participants were tasked with piloting a small aircraft from takeoff to landing using a flight simulator. Before the start of the experiment, they were instructed on using the equipment and flying the Cessna 172SP. They were trained to become proficient in the aircraft's operation while following the experimental route. Twenty different flight patterns were set up based on the workload factors mentioned previously, each with random combinations of wind volume, wind direction, time of day, month, weather, visibility level, and flight route. The participants included one license holder (private pilot license) aged 21 years and three unlicensed men aged 21–24 years. The license holder made 10 flights, and the unlicensed participants made five flights each.

#### 2.2.3 Experimental System

The participants were seated facing a desk with two 34-inch curved displays and a flight simulator. The flight simulator was constructed using the Pro Flight Yoke System, the Pro Flight USB Throttle Quadrant, the Pro Flight Rudder Pedals, the Pro Flight Multi Panel, the Pro Flight Switch Panel, the Pro Flight Radio Panel, and the Pro Flight Instrument

Panel (all from Saitek); the display software was X-Plane 10 (from Laminar Research). The viewing distance from the display was set to 0.9 m. The participants were seated so that their line of sight was 1.2 m off the floor. Figure 1 shows the experimental environment.

**Fig. 1.** Experimental environment

### 2.2.4 Measurements

Experiments were conducted for two patterns with different measurement items.

In Experiment 1, flight data, physiological indices, and the subjective assessment of the workload level were obtained. For the flight data, 28 parameters output were obtained from X-Plane 10. The physiological indices were electrocardiogram, respiration, pulse wave, skin temperature, electroencephalogram, and cerebral blood volume change, which are considered to be related to workload and stress and can be measured while flying the flight simulator. ECG100C, RSP100C, PPG100C, SKT100C, EEG100C, and OEG-16 were used to measure the results. To subjectively evaluate the in-flight workload, the participants were asked to verbally respond to their current workload level every 30 s on a five-point scale (one being the lowest workload level and five being the highest workload level).

In Experiment 1, since the workload level was answered verbally, there was a concern that the measurement results of the physiological indices would include noise associated with speech. Therefore, in Experiment 2, only flight data and physiological indices were obtained.

### 2.2.5 Experimental Procedure

The measurement device was installed. After the participants received an explanation of the procedure, they rested with their eyes closed for two minutes. Next, they flew under randomly selected conditions from the flight patterns mentioned above. Flights with different settings were repeated, and each participant had a two-minute rest (eyes closed) before each flight. The flights in Experiments 1 and 2 were conducted on separate schedules. The Research Ethics Review Committee of Keio University Faculty of Science and Technology approved the study.

# 3    Construction of Estimation Model

## 3.1    Processing of Collected Data

Since the sampling rate of the OEG-16 recording of changes in cerebral blood volume is the lowest, and the acquisition interval is 0.65 s, the other physiological index data recorded at 2 kHz were also acquired at 0.65-s intervals. The flight data recorded at 10 Hz was also linearly interpolated to 0.65-s intervals. The analysis interval began at the start of takeoff (when the engine starts) and end after the landing is complete (when the engine stops). Other intervals were excluded from the analysis.

In Experiment 1, the participants verbally indicated their workload level every 30 s on a five-point scale, and the scale numbers tended to be smaller for higher workload levels. In constructing the estimation model, the number of data included in each workload level was aligned to reduce data bias. For the workload levels with a large number of data, the data corresponding to the workload level was defined as the five-second period immediately before the time of response. In contrast, for the workload levels with a small number of data, the data corresponding to the workload level was defined as the 10-s period immediately before the time of response. In this way, the number of samples was increased, and the number of datasets for each score was aligned.

## 3.2    Model 1: Estimating Future Flight Data from Current Flight Data

We constructed a model to estimate the flight data 30 s later time t + 30 (FD[t + 30]) using the flight data at time t (FD[t]). We performed machine learning using each parameter of the flight data obtained in Experiment 1 as a feature and the flight data 30 s later as an objective variable. The 28 parameters (Table 1) obtained in real-time from the experiment's flight data were used as the estimation parameters.

**Table 1.**  Flight-related parameters obtained in real-time from the flight data in the experiment

| Flight data | | | | | |
| --- | --- | --- | --- | --- | --- |
| Time | Elevator input | Flap | Roll angle | Throttle | Vertical force |
| Airspeed | Aileron input | Pitch velocity | Yaw angle | Fuel weight | Wing lift force |
| Vertical speed | Ladder input | Roll velocity | Attack angle | Weight | Wing drag |
| Wind speed | Elevator trim | Yaw velocity | Side slip angle | Lift force | |
| Wind direction | Aileron trim | Pitch angle | Altitude | Drag | |

The parameters were trained using a neural network. We used 70% of the total 1,705 data as training data and the remaining 30% as test data. We applied MLPRegressor from scikit-learn, a Python machine learning library, to the training data.

The constructed model was used to perform each parameter regression of the flight data 30 s later. The correlation coefficients between the actual values and the estimated values were calculated for each parameter. The estimation results regarding the training data show a high correlation for all parameters, but the test data's estimation results show a high correlation for only some parameters. Table 2 shows the parameters with large correlation coefficients in the test data. The number of parameters with correlation coefficients higher than 0.7 in the test data was 22 for the model using a neural network. Therefore, in the estimation using Model 1, the model with a neural network was used to output the 22 parameters whose correlation coefficients exceeded 0.7 in the estimation results of the test data based on the input of 28 parameters; only these 22 parameters were used when constructing the subsequent model.

**Table 2.** Parameters with correlation coefficients between the actual and estimated value $>0.7$ in the test data using the model with a neural network.

| Flight data | | | | | |
|---|---|---|---|---|---|
| Time | Elevator input | Flap | Roll angle | Throttle | Vertical force |
| Airspeed | Aileron input | Pitch velocity | Yaw angle | Fuel weight | Wing lift force |
| Vertical speed | Ladder input | Roll velocity | Attack angle | Weight | Wing drag |
| Wind speed | Elevator trim | Yaw velocity | Side slip angle | Lift force | |
| Wind direction | Aileron trim | Pitch angle | Altitude | Drag | |

### 3.3   Model 2: Estimating Workload Level from Physiological Indices

We constructed a model to estimate the workload level at a time t (WL[t]) using the physiological indices at a time t (PI[t]). We performed machine learning using each parameter of the physiological indices obtained in Experiment 1 as a feature and the five-scale workload levels that were verbally indicated in Experiment 1 as an objective variable.

The parameters used for training were calculated from the measurement results: heart rate; respiratory sinus arrhythmia (RSA) component of heart rate variability; pulse wave amplitude; the absolute value of nasal skin temperature; content of alpha, beta, and theta waves in electroencephalogram; and the changes of oxygenated hemoglobin in the dorsolateral prefrontal cortex (DLPFC), medial prefrontal cortex (MPFC), ventrolateral prefrontal cortex (VLPFC), and orbitofrontal cortex (OFC). These indices were categorized according to the workload level, and the trend of the change in values was checked. With the exception of the parameters related to electroencephalogram, a certain trend could be found in the change of workload level and the change in each parameter. However, because the variation in each workload level was so large that we could not confirm the relationship with the workload, parameters related to electroencephalogram were excluded from the analysis.

The above nine parameters were trained using neural networks and random forests. We used 70% of the total 923 data as training data and 30% as test data and applied MLPRegressor and RandomForestRegressor from scikit-learn, a Python machine learning library, to the training data.

The constructed models were used to estimate the workload level. The model's accuracy with a neural network was 96.6% for the training data and 67.6% for the test data. The model's accuracy with a random forest was 93.5% for the training data and 72.2% for the test data. The accuracy of the estimation tended to be high for both models. Therefore, to construct the next model, we applied these models to the 22,388 physiological indices data obtained in Experiment 2 to estimate the workload level. Table 3 shows the results of both models' estimates. In the model using a random forest, there were no cases where the workload was estimated to be five, and the estimation results were highly biased. Since the estimation results of the model using a random forest differed greatly from the percentage of workload level obtained from the subjective assessment in Experiment 1, we decided to use the estimation results of the model with a neural network, the workload level estimation results of which have a relatively small bias.

**Table 3.** Breakdown of the workload levels for the subjective assessment in Experiment 1 and estimation by Model 2

|  | Workload level | | | | |
| --- | --- | --- | --- | --- | --- |
|  | 1 | 2 | 3 | 4 | 5 |
| **Subjective value in experiment 1** | 99 | 88 | 57 | 35 | 23 |
| **Estimated by NN-model2** | 8450 | 4668 | 3234 | 2382 | 3653 |
| **Estimated by RF-model2** | 1402 | 10356 | 9825 | 804 | 0 |

### 3.4   Model 3: Estimating Workload Level from Flight Data

We constructed a model to estimate the workload level at a time t (WL[t]) using the flight data at a time t (FD[t]). We performed machine learning and used each parameter of the flight data obtained in Experiment 2 as a feature and the workload level from the five-scale estimate by Model 2 as an objective variable.

The 22 parameters estimated with high accuracy in Model 1 were used as flight data and were trained using neural networks and random forests. We used 70% of the total 22,388 data as training data and the remaining 30% as test data and applied MLPRegressor and RandomForestRegressor from scikit-learn, a Python machine learning library, to the training data.

The constructed models were used to estimate the workload level. The model's accuracy with a neural network was 70.4% for the training data and 66.8% for the test data. The model's accuracy with a random forest was 98.0% for the training data and 76.8% for the test data. The accuracy of the estimation tended to be relatively high for both models. So, we decided to use the more accurate random forest model.

## 4   Results

By combining Model 1, which used a neural network, and Model 3, which used a random forest, we were able to estimate the workload level 30 s later (WL[t + 30]) and the current flight data (FD[t]). The flight data that was not used to construct Model 1; the data of Experiment 1 were used as test data to estimate the workload level. The subjective value was subtracted from the estimated value, and this distribution is shown in Fig. 2. The results indicate that 32.0% of the data matched the subjective value and the estimated value. The deviation between the subjective value and the estimated value was <1 in 72.3% of the data, confirming that the probability of a large deviation in the estimation is small.

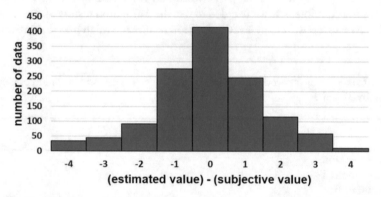

**Fig. 2.** Histogram of deviations between subjective value and estimated value

## 5   Verification of Proposed System

We implemented a system that presents the model's workload level in real-time and examined its effect on a pilot's workload management through an experiment using a flight simulator. The experimental environment and system were the same as those described in Sect. 2. The estimated workload level was presented on a screen located to the left of the instrument panel (Fig. 3).

**Fig. 3.** Example of workload level presentation during flight

The system presented the numerical value of the workload level, each of which had a distinct color (Fig. 4).

**Fig. 4.** Presentation images for each workload level in proposed system

After the participants completed the flight simulations, interviews were conducted. The license holder felt that the presentation of the estimated workload level was 60% or 70% accurate. However, the timing with which the level changed from two to three and three to four was sometimes uncomfortable. Regarding the safety of the proposed system, the license holder found that the presentation of the workload level did not significantly affect the aircraft's operation, although the number of checks was increased. He also suggested that the proposed system may help support a pilot's workload management. Specifically, he stated that the anticipation that the workload level would increase after 30 s could be useful when a pilot needs to determine when to start his checklists before landing.

## 6   Conclusion

Using current flight-related parameters, we constructed a model to estimate a pilot's workload level 30 s later. This model showed that presenting the pilot's estimated workload level during flight could effectively support workload management.

# References

1. Yoshikawa, E., Ushio, T.: Tactical decision-making support information for aircraft lightning avoidance: feasibility study in area of winter lightning. Bull. Am. Meteorol. Soc. **100**(8), 1443–1452 (2019)
2. Riedel, T., Takahashi, M., Tatsukawa, T., Itoh, E.: Evaluating applied flight-deck interval management using monte carlo simulations on the K-supercomputer. Trans. Jpn. Soc. Aeronaut. Space Sci. **62**(6), 299–309 (2019)
3. Japan Transport Safety Board, air accident statistics. https://jtsb.mlit.go.jp/jtsb/aircraft/air-accident-toukei.php. Accessed 26 Jan 2020

# Single Pilot Operations Along the Human-Centered Design Lifecycle: Reviewing the Dedicated Support Concept

Daniela Schmid$^{(\boxtimes)}$ (iD)

NA, Germany
daniela.schmid64@icloud.com

**Abstract.** Single pilot operations (SPO) for airliners represent the evolutionary cockpit crew development for future aviation. The present work replies to the call for a human-centered research agenda by providing a systematic review of the literature for one of the most-widely researched concepts of SPO: the *dedicated-support* concept, which is also known as harbor pilot concept. Accordingly, a remote-copilot supports a single-piloted aircraft to alleviate high workload that can occur during nominal, off-nominal, and emergency situations. All studies of a recently published systematic literature review on SPO [1] were coded according to the categories of type of article, concept of operation, and method. The studies on the concept under analysis were systematically reviewed further to evaluate their contribution to its current state in human-centered design according to ISO 9241-210. The theoretical foundations of such SPO are elaborated in detail in modeling studies and accident analyses whereas empirical evaluation of design solutions has been started only in a few studies. Nonetheless, workload seems consistently be able to be distributed in a comparable range as in nowadays flight operations. In the end, the *dedicated support* concept of SPO is at early stages in the human-centered design process.

**Keywords:** Reduced crew operations · Civil aviation · Human factors · Aerospace psychology · Crew development

## 1 Introduction

### 1.1 Single Pilot Operations for Civil Commercial Aircraft

Single pilot operations (SPO) represent the evolutionary approach to future cockpit crew development of an airliner in civil transport aviation [2]. Only one pilot on-board is foreseen to operate a civil transport category airplane. As such, SPO are often referred to synonymously as reduced (flight) crew operations (RCO) which include possible relief pilots on board for different flight durations [3]. 14 CFR Part 25 and CS-25 large aeroplane operations (including 10 or more passenger seats in case of a passenger transport

---

D. Schmid—Independent Researcher.

© The Author(s), under exclusive license to Springer Nature Switzerland AG 2021
N. L. Black et al. (Eds.): IEA 2021, LNNS 221, pp. 159–168, 2021.
https://doi.org/10.1007/978-3-030-74608-7_21

configuration) are currently limited to a minimum flight crew of at least two pilots whenever the applicable operating rule requires them for handling workload amongst other factors during pilot incapacitation [4, 5]. That does mean the second pilot must be able to land the aircraft safely on their own in this emergency. The copilot represents a back-up and redundancy measure against a loss of control of the Captain. Without a copilot, this measure is absent. A current modern airliner has consequently a minimum flight crew of two pilots to prevent an accident due to the incapacitation of one pilot. Pilot incapacitation is an emergency including its own emergency procedure [6], and the aircraft has to be landed at an adjacent airport as soon as possible.

Thus, when progressing to SPO, a single-pilot incapacitation represents the main hurdle and challenge on the way to operational practice of a proper concept of such operations. Workload and its associated tasks have to be newly distributed to single-pilot, aircraft automation, and a possible remote ground-based second operator to enable flight safety. In this way, the certifications requirements have to be either met or SPO/RCO have to demonstrate an at least equivalent level of safety to modern flight operations of large aeroplanes. The requirement for a human-centered design agenda for a single-piloted aircraft was proposed over a decade ago [7]. A ground-based workstation (the so-called *ground station* [GS]) for a remote operator, and the role of the pilot(s), aircraft automation, as well as the single-pilot cockpit have to be re-defined and re-conceptualized in order to ensure flight safety. Accordingly, different new concepts of operations (ConOps) for a reduced flight crew have been established and dominated academic research. Different types of them were investigated to varying extent during the last two decades [1]. The *dedicated-support* concept of SPO, also known as the harbor pilot concept, has been most-widely researched [8, 9]. It includes a remote-copilot as a specialist operator supporting a single-piloted aircraft.

### 1.2   The *Dedicated Support* Concept of Single Pilot Operations

The *dedicated-support* concept of SPO includes a remote-copilot as ground-based remote support who requires dedicated pilot skills [9, 10]. Their tasks are to support the single-pilot as pilot monitoring (PM) in flight planning and navigation or to take over control as pilot flying (PF) in case of need such as in an emergency. For example, a high-level function allocation contains support according to the characteristics of the standard flight phases. Here, the remote-copilot provides mandatory expertise support to a single-pilot aircraft during departure and arrival whereas cruise is supported only in case of need [11, 12]. In general, the *dedicated support* of an aircraft is conducted successively by a remote-copilot being assigned to one single-piloted aircraft at a time.

In normal and off-nominal situations, command and control remain with the Captain as single-pilot on-board except they command differently. This authority distribution allows overwriting a rogue pilot by the other pilot only in one direction [13]. In the present ConOps, the single-pilot is the ultimate authority. They can hand over control to the remote-copilot. Nonetheless, two advanced automation monitoring systems were suggested being able to switch control to the remote-copilot in case of a single-pilot incapacitation or a loss of control in terms of flight safety [11]. To do so, they would assess and evaluate physiological pilot health as well as aircraft system entries and their actual state on deviations from a safe norm.

The present work replies to the call for a human-centered design research agenda by providing a systematic review of the literature on the *dedicated support* concept of SPO. The studies are evaluated regarding their contribution to its human-centered design according to ISO 9241-210.

## 2 Method

### 2.1 Systematic Literature Review

The present study was conducted on base of a dataset of SPO studies that were collected in course of a systematic literature review in 2019 [1]. The dataset was updated to the state of 1 January 2021. Altogether $N = 83$ studies were retrieved on SPO and RCO. Of those, 4 studies stem from the area of business aircraft that are or can be currently certified for SPO. The search process and syntaxes are described in detail by Schmid and Stanton [1]. We analyzed the contents of these $N = 83$ studies further and focused on the publications that either solely contain research on the dedicated support ConOps or that compare it with other concepts of SPO or the current two-pilot crew concept.

### 2.2 Coding Categories and Data Analysis

I coded the $N = 83$ studies according to *type of article*, *ConOps*, and *method* referring to the superior class of the concerned Human Factors and Ergonomics (HF/E) method. The categories were clearly differentiated to keep coding as unambiguous as possible. The studies were coded according to them by asserting one specification per category:

- *Type of article*: Empirical study, modeling study, compilation, viewpoint, review.
- *ConOps*: Dedicated support concept, multi-aircraft support concept, single-pilot, two-pilot crew, several concepts, discussion.
- *Method*: Flight simulation, task analysis, accident analysis, computational model, systematic review, interview.

If no identifiable HF/E research method was applied the categories of (systematic) literature review or viewpoint was chosen. A viewpoint was indicated if the article merely presented a subjective commentary. If more than one reduced flight crew ConOps was investigated the category "several concepts" was chosen. If only one concept of RCO was compared to the two-pilot cockpit baseline the concerned RCO concept was assigned. The "discussion" category was only assigned if the authors had not focused on any ConOps. In this way, an unambiguous coding procedure was achieved. The details of the studies are listed by Schmid and Stanton [1].

### 2.3 Evaluation Regarding the Human-Centered Design ISO 9241-210

ISO 9241-210 (*Ergonomics of human-system interaction – Part 210: Human-centred design for interactive systems*) [14] was consulted to guide the literature review on the *dedicated support* ConOps of a reduced flight crew. In general, a standard facilitates international common agreement on industry and technical guidelines in different subject areas such as HF/E. Here, we focus on the human-centered design lifecycle of system development as shown in chapter 6 of ISO-9241-210 [14]. It represents an iterative process that starts with (1) *planning the human-centered design process* followed by (2) *understanding and specifying the context of use*, (3) *specifying the user requirements*, (4) *producing design solutions to meet user requirements*, (5) *evaluating the designs against user requirements*. The overall goal is that the designed solution meets the user requirements.

## 3   Results

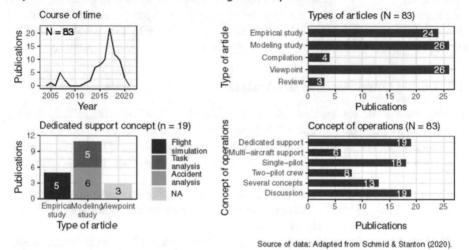

Systematic literature review on reduced flight crew operations

Source of data: Adapted from Schmid & Stanton (2020).

**Fig. 1.** An overview over the results of the systematic literature review. Altogether $n = 19$ studies dealt with research questions on the *dedicated support concept* of reduced flight crew operations.

The systematic literature review is summarized in Fig. 1. From around 2004 to 2014, SPO for commercial airliners were only discussed in research reports [15–18] and rarely in the academic literature [7, 10, 19]. *Planning the human-centered design process* of SPO was mainly worked out in these reports and conceptual discussions that lead to the next stage of research undertakings in the iterative human-centered design driven by following premise. Monitoring, surveillance, and checking activities of the copilot can be either automated or allocated to a remote operator.

In course of *understanding and specifying the context of use*, early studies profoundly ruled out the concept of SPO without a remote operator. It remains inferior in terms of flight safety when compared to alternatives that include a remote support. In a single-piloted aircraft with advanced automation, the single-pilot can become rapidly overloaded with information and data that are not mediated by ground-based assistance in an emergency (as shown in AcciMaps analyses comparisons of the Boeing 737–400 Kegworth accident [20]). Theoretical social network models of standard operations of the baseline two-pilot cockpit, different ConOps for SPO [21], and a data-link failure scenario for the *dedicated support* ConOps [22, 23] also showed a likely overload of the single-pilot as well as a decrease in network resilience against adverse events during flight. More information is required to be mediated, coordinated, and processed in course with more tasks to be conducted. A series of workload quantification studies considering human-in-the-loop flight simulations of six different technical failures scenarios confirmed overloading the single-pilot in emergencies [24]. Workload of the pilot(s) in the current cockpit crew configuration was compared when reducing the crew gradually to a single-pilot on the modern flight deck. Workload increased significantly. Hereinafter, we focus on the prominent *dedicated support* reduced flight crew ConOps which aims to distribute workload by including a remote-copilot.

Solely descriptive methods such as operational event sequence diagrams were used to map two-pilot operations as baseline and SPO in comparison [25–27]. A System-Theoretic Process Analyses (STPA) [28] based on the System-Theoretic Accident Modeling and Process (STAMP) [29] provided a detailed analysis of possible training concepts for such SPO [30]. Changes in pilot training are required to operate a single-piloted cockpit and the GS. Single-pilot and remote-copilot should rotate jobs to keep skills and knowledge continuously active. Concrete analyses of the worker competences will be required when research will have progressed to more detailed solutions for a single-pilot cockpit and GS. The *dedicated support* ConOps can be applied to different flight durations by adapting fatigue management mitigation strategies [3]. The core ideas to solve general context issues of SPO were specified further.

Further research efforts served *specifying user requirements* based on and extending the context-of-use analyses presented above. They simultaneously translated the user requirements to develop, analyze, and design SPO. The *dedicated support* ConOps was evaluated at each step of the analysis against its two-pilot baseline or different emergency situations. Thus, the iterative nature is included in most analyses. A high-level task analysis and function allocation was provided in a Cognitive Function Analysis [2], task analyses [31–33], and loosely derived from two-pilot studies [34, 35]. Cognitive Work Analyses (CWA) was combined with a social network analysis (SNA) to model the networks of interactions that possibly occur [12, 21]. It primarily achieved laying down a ConOps in detail, analyzing and allocating functions for normal situations, an emergency descent as well as during a data-link loss [23], a broad training needs analysis, and giving design advice. Workload and job design were only described and estimated broadly. In the end, the network resilience suffers without the remote-copilot being available as possible human back-up for off-nominal situations. Hence, a complete data-link loss as emergency requires a landing at an adjacent airport because the single-pilot is likely to get overloaded in not-anticipatable situations. The infrastructure required for data-link based SPO were specified in an STPA of a data-link outage scenario [22]. Technology challenges and limitations as well as cryptography issues are discussed elsewhere in detail [13]. The data-link technology has to evolve further to achieve a highly reliable and secure data-link.

In an STPA on single-pilot incapacitation(s), advanced automation tools were specified further [11, 36]. A pilot-health and aircraft-systems monitoring system provide a dual-graded alert in case of hazardous operations or a loss of control due to pilot incapacitation or technical failures. Consequently, the remote-copilot either assists as PM or resumes command and control as PF. Taking over control by the remote-copilot without a situation preview on interfaces showed no workload differences when compared to two-pilot operations for different off-nominal situation [37–39]. In normal situations, the remote-copilot can support 4–6 arrivals successively [8]. Collaboration tools making function allocation transparent improved collaboration of the distributed pilots [38, 40]. The situation awareness (SA) of the remote-copilot when being assigned to *dedicated support* of an aircraft can be established by providing its environmental and system data [39]. At this point, I have completely summarized the research regarding the *dedicated concept* SPO up to the current state of science.

## 4  Discussion

Now, to what extent do the designed solutions contribute to meeting the user requirements in the human-centered design lifecycle? *Planning the human-centered design process* has been concluded in detail including discussions and viewpoints [7, 10, 15–19]. Based on that, different reduced flight crew ConOps were established out of which the *dedicated support* concept of SPO has emerged. Its *context of use* was researched in depth in task analyses [31–34], descriptive methods [25–27], theoretical analyses of accidents [20, 36] and issues considered for SPO [3, 30], and in empirical human-in-the-loop flight simulation studies [24]. Normal situations as well as different off-nominal and emergency situations were considered to elaborate the context in depth. There is mostly common agreement that SPO require a human, remote, ground-based support to guarantee flight safety. The *dedicated support* concept of SPO follows this claim by including a remote-copilot to distribute workload in off-nominal or emergency situations.

In theoretical modeling studies, the *user requirements* of the *dedicated support* concept of SPO were further specified in CWA, SNA, STAMP and STPA for normal operations [21], pilot incapacitation [11, 36], data link outage [22], and rapid decompression [41]. They partially included specifying functions and tasks of advanced automation systems like a pilot health monitoring system, an aircraft system monitoring unit, as well as an *automated contingency management technology* and a *mission management system* to administer the data-link. Of these, the pilot health monitoring technology as well as the data-link technology exist but they are pre-mature and have to develop further to be practically relevant and applicable to manned cockpit applications such as to SPO [1]. Aircraft systems monitoring to detect hazardous entries into systems or security breaches is estimated as mature and can be easier adapted to applications in SPO from existent technologies [42–44].

In empirical modeling studies, mainly medium-fidelity mock-ups of a GS were used to simulate SPO for the remote-copilot. The single-pilot was either mocked-up or realized in a high-fidelity modern cockpit simulator. In *producing such design solutions*, user requirements were transferred to empirical evaluation of workload and rarely SA. An *evaluation of the designs against user requirements* was included in all studies by comparing SPO to the baseline of two-pilot flight operations. The evaluations of workload in SPO were consistent in several flight simulation studies with different types of a GS [37–39]. Copilot workload was comparable to the same of a two-pilot crew during normal flight, single-pilot incapacitation, and diverting the aircraft safely to another airport. Initial results point out that sufficient SA can be achieved when displaying environmental and system data of the specified aircraft [39]. However, one remote-copilot can only support 4–6 nominal arrivals successively [8]. Nonetheless, the GS was aggregated from elements of modern cockpit displays presented on monitor-based workstations being operated with mouse and keyboard. The pilot health monitoring alerts were mocked-up with voice commands whereas collaborations tools were integrated on-top of an existent interface. Nonetheless, these 4 flight simulations studies represent only the base for further empirical evaluations. The redesign of the single-pilot flight deck has not been considered in detail, although there is common agreement that it will undergo significant change. Hence, future research effort will need to go into detail in designing advanced automation systems, the interfaces for the ground-based workstation of the remote-copilot, as well as the flight deck of the single-pilot cockpit.

In sum, the *dedicated support* concept of SPO has been designed, analyzed and modeled in depth in theory but producing and empirically evaluating these design solutions has only been initially approached and conducted. Medium-fidelity prototypes of the GS for the remote-copilot were rarely evaluated empirically and if so, in a narrow problem-specific focus and situation. However, workload seems to be able to be kept in an acceptable range comparably to nowadays flight operations as well as pilot incapacitation seems manageable. The results on SA only give further design advice but cannot be generalized yet. In the end, the *dedicated support* ConOps seems a viable design solution for SPO whereas automation technologies need to mature, be integrated and be implemented in support of SPO. A reliable, fast and secure data-link appears to be a major limiting factor in realizing this concept. A new aircraft will need to be designed because retrofitting contemporary platforms will be not economically viable [13]. This is the reason why the *dedicated support* concept of SPO remains at early stages in the human-centered design lifecycle characterized by the iterative nature in research progress. Until the designed solution meets the user requirements of SPO, the issues presented in this article have to be investigated further and some technology has to be developed further.

# References

1. Schmid, D., Stanton, N.A.: Progressing toward airliners' reduced-crew operations: a systematic literature review. Int. J. Aerosp. Psychol. **30**(1–2), 1–24 (2020)
2. Boy, G.A.: Requirements for single pilot operations in commercial aviation: a first high-level cognitive function analysis. In: Boulanger, F., Korb, D., Morel, G., Roussel, J.-C. (eds.) Complex Systems Design & Management, pp. 227–234. Springer, Cham (2015)
3. Schmid, D., Stanton, N.A.: Considering single-piloted airliners for different flight durations: an issue of fatigue management. In: Stanton, N.A. (ed.) Advances in Human Factors of Transportation, pp. 683–694. Springer, Cham (2019)
4. European Aviation Safety Agency: Certification Specifications and Acceptable Means of Compliance for Large Aeroplanes: CS-25 Amendment 17. EASA, Cologne, Germany (2015)
5. Federal Aviation Administration: 14 CFR Part 25: Airworthiness Standards: Transport Category Airplanes. U.S. Department of Transportation (2011)

6. Airbus: A319/A320/A321 Flight crew operating manual. Airbus, Blagnac Cedex, France (2003)
7. Harris, D.: A human-centred design agenda for the development of single crew operated commercial aircraft. Aircr. Eng. Aerosp. Tech. **79**(5), 518–526 (2007)
8. Koltz, M.T., Roberts, Z.S., Sweet, J., Battiste, H., Cunningham, J., Battiste, V., Vu, K.-P.L., Strybel, T.Z.: An investigation of the harbor pilot concept for single pilot operations. Proc. Manuf. **3**, 2937–2944 (2015)
9. Lachter, J., Brandt, S.L., Battiste, V., Matessa, M., Johnson, W.W.: Enhanced ground support: lessons from work on reduced crew operations. Cogn. Tech. Work **19**(2–3), 279–288 (2017)
10. Bilimoria, K.D., Johnson, W.W., Schutte, P.C.: Conceptual framework for single pilot operations. In: Proceedings of the International Conference on Human-Computer Interaction in Aerospace. ACM, New York (2014)
11. Schmid, D., Stanton, N.A.: A future airliner's reduced-crew: modelling pilot incapacitation and homicide-suicide with systems theory. Hum.-Intell. Syst. Integr. **1**(1), 27–42 (2019)
12. Schmid, D., Korn, B., Stanton, N.A.: Evaluating the reduced flight deck crew concept using cognitive work analysis and social network analysis: comparing normal and data-link outage scenarios. Cogn. Tech. Work **22**, 109–124 (2020)
13. Driscoll, K., Roy, A., Ponchak, D.S., Downey, A.N.: Cyber safety and security for reduced crew operations (RCO). In: IEEE Conference on Aerospace, pp. 1–15. IEEE, Big Sky (2017)
14. International Organization for Standardization: Ergonomics of human-system interaction – Part 210: Human-centred design for interactive systems. ISO Standard, International Organization for Standardization (2019)
15. Deutsch, S., Pew, R.W.: Single pilot commercial aircraft operation. BBN Report. BBN Technologies, Cambridge, MA, USA (2005)
16. Norman, M.: Economic opportunities and technological challenges for reduced crew operations. Technical paper prepared for: Crew Vehicle Interface Element, NASA, Seattle, WA, USA (2007)
17. Schutte, P.C., Goodrich, K.H., Cox, D.E., Jackson, E.B., Palmer, M.T., Pope, A.T., Schlecht, R.W., Tedjojuwono, K.K., Trujillo, A.C., Williams, R.A., Kinney, J.B., Barry, J.S.: The naturalistic flight deck system: an integrated system concept for improved single-pilot operations. p. 63. NASA, Hampton (2007)
18. Comerford, D., Brandt, S.L., Lachter, J., Wu, S.-C., Mogford, R., Battiste, V., Johnson, W.W.: NASA's single-pilot operations technical interchange meeting: Proceedings and findings. p. 298. NASA, Moffett Field (2013)
19. Schutte, P.C.: How to make the most of your human: design considerations for single pilot operations. In: Harris, D. (ed.) Engineering Psychology and Cognitive Ergonomics, pp. 480–491. Springer, Cham (2015)
20. Harris, D.: Network re-analysis of Boeing 737 accident at Kegworth using different potential crewing configurations for a single pilot commercial aircraft. In: Harris, D. (ed.) Engineering Psychology and Cognitive Ergonomics, pp. 572–582. Springer, Cham (2018)
21. Stanton, N.A., Harris, D., Starr, A.: The future flight deck: modelling dual, single and distributed crewing options. Appl. Ergon. **53**, 331–342 (2016)
22. Schmid, D., Korn, B., Wies, M., Stanton, N.A.: Managing a data-link failure of a single-piloted airliner during flight: a system-theoretic process analysis. In: Proceedings of the Human Factors and Ergonomics Society Annual Meeting, vol. 63, pp. 106–110 (2019)
23. Schmid, D., Korn, B.: The operational issue of an airliner's reduced-crew caused by data-link break-up to remote support. In: Proceedings of the Human Factors and Ergonomics Society Annual Meeting, vol. 62, pp. 71–75 (2018)
24. Bailey, R.E., Kramer, L.J., Kennedy, K.D., Stephens, C.L., Etherington, T.J.: An assessment of reduced crew and single pilot operations in commercial transport aircraft operations. In: 36th Digital Avionics Systems Conference (DASC). IEEE (2017)

25. Huddlestone, J., Sears, R., Harris, D.: The use of operational event sequence diagrams and work domain analysis techniques for the specification of the crewing configuration of a single-pilot commercial aircraft. Cogn. Tech. Work **19**(2–3), 289–302 (2017)
26. Harris, D., Stanton, N.A., Starr, A.: Spot the difference: operational event sequence diagrams as a formal method for work allocation in the development of single-pilot operations for commercial aircraft. Ergonomics **58**(11), 1773–1791 (2015)
27. Revell, K.M., Stanton, N.A., Kelleher, G.: Exploring changes in pilot behaviour during distributed crewing. In: The Institute of Ergonomics and Human Factors Annual Conference, Daventry, UK (2016)
28. Leveson, N.G.: Engineering a Safer World: Systems Thinking Applied to Safety. MIT Press, Cambridge (2011)
29. Leveson, N.G.: A new accident model for engineering safer systems. Saf. Sci. **42**(4), 237–270 (2004)
30. Schmid, D., Stanton, N.A.: The training of operators in single pilot operations: an initial system theoretic consideration. In: 20th International Symposium on Aviation Psychology, Dayton, OH, USA (2019)
31. Gore, B.F., Wolter, C.A.: A task analytic process to define future concepts in aviation. In: Duffy, V.G. (ed.) Digital Human Modeling, pp. 236–246. Springer, Cham (2014)
32. Wolter, C.A., Gore, B.F.: A validated task analysis of the single pilot operations concept. NASA, Moffett Field (2015)
33. Huddlestone, J., Harris, D., Richards, D., Scott, S., Sears, R.: Dual pilot and single pilot operations – hierarchical task decomposition analysis of doing more with less. In: Harris, D. (ed.) Engineering Psychology and Cognitive Ergonomics, pp. 365–376. Springer International Publishing, Cham (2014)
34. Schutte, P.C.: Task analysis of two crew operations in the flight deck: investigating the feasibility of using single pilot. In: 19th International Symposium on Aviation Psychology, pp. 566–571 (2017)
35. Stanton, N.A., Plant, K.L., Revell, K.M.A., Griffin, T.G.C., Moffat, S., Stanton, M.J.: Distributed cognition in aviation operations: a gate-to-gate study with implications for distributed crewing. Ergonomics **62**(?), 138–155 (2019)
36. Schmid, D., Stanton, N.A.: How are laser attacks encountered in commercial aviation? A hazard analysis based on systems theory. Saf. Sci. **110**, 178–191 (2018)
37. Schmid, D., Stanton, N.A.: Exploring Bayesian analyses of a small-sample-size factorial design in human systems integration: the effects of pilot incapacitation. Hum.-Intell. Syst. Integr. **1**, 71–88 (2019)
38. Lachter, J., Brandt, S.L., Battiste, V., Ligda, S.V., Matessa, M., Johnson, W.W.: Toward single pilot operations: developing a ground station. In: Proceedings of the International Conference on Human-Computer Interaction in Aerospace. ACM, New York (2014)
39. Brandt, S.L., Lachter, J., Battiste, V., Johnson, W.: Pilot situation awareness and its implications for single pilot operations: analysis of a human-in-the-loop study. Proc. Manuf. **3**, 3017–3024 (2015)
40. Ligda, S.V., Fischer, U., Mosier, K., Matessa, M., Battiste, V., Johnson, W.W.: Effectiveness of advanced collaboration tools on crew communication in reduced crew operations. In: Harris, D. (ed.) Engineering Psychology and Cognitive Ergonomics, pp. 416–427. Springer, Cham (2015)
41. Revell, K.M., Allison, C., Sears, R., Stanton, N.A.: Modelling distributed crewing in commercial aircraft with STAMP for a rapid decompression hazard. Ergonomics **62**(2), 156–170 (2019)
42. Gaultier, D., SAFEE consortium: SAFEE (Security of Aircraft in the Future European Environment): final publishable report. (EC contract AIP3-CT-2003–503521) (2008)

43. Schmitt, D.-R., Többen, H., Philippens, H.: Passivation of misused aircraft to protect passengers, airports and infrastructure. In: Grant, I. (ed.) 27th Congress of the International Council of Aeronautical Sciences, pp. 1–3. Optimage, Edinburgh (2010)
44. Bueno, J., Herrería, J.A., Consortium, S.: SOFIA (safe automatic flight back and landing of aircraft): final publishable activity report. EC contract (2010)

# Some Major Human Issues in Aerospace Engineering: Review and Extension

Ephraim Suhir[1,2,3,4](✉)

[1] Portland State University, Portland, OR, USA
suhire@aol.com
[2] James Cook University, Townsville, QLD, Australia
[3] Technical University, Vienna, Austria
[4] ERS Co., Los Altos, CA, USA

**Abstract.** By employing quantifiable and measurable ways to assess the role of various uncertainties associated with the mental workload (MWL) and human capacity factor (HCF), and treating a human-in-the-loop (HITL) as a part, often the most critical part, of the complex man-instrumentation-equipment-vehicle-environment system, one can improve dramatically the human's performance, achieve the best human-system-integration (HSI) possible and predict, minimize and, when appropriate, even specify the probability of the occurrence of a casualty. The ultimate objective of the analysis is to develop effective predictive modelling techniques that would enable quantifying, on the probabilistic basis, the role of the human factor (HF) and improve his/hers HCF, so that he/she would be able to successfully cope, when necessary, with an elevated MWL and minimize the probability of an accident, when reliability of instrumentation and human performance contribute jointly to the outcome of an HSI related mission or an off-normal situation. It is concluded that the suggested MWL/HCF models and their possible modifications and generalizations can be helpful when developing guidelines for personnel selection and training; and/or when there is a need to decide, if the existing methods of reliability and ergonomics engineering are adequate in various off-normal situations, and if not, whether additional and/or more advanced and, perhaps, more expensive equipment or instrumentation should be developed, tested and installed to meet the safety requirements.

**Keywords:** Human-in-the-loop · Human-system-integration · Mission outcome · Mental workload · Human capacity factor

## Acronyms

AG = Automated Driving
BAZ = Boltzmann-Arrhenius-Zhurkov's (model)
DD = Driver Drowsiness
DEPDF = Double Exponential Probability Distribution Function
EVD = Extreme Value Distribution
FOAT = Failure Oriented Accelerated Testing
HALT = Highly Accelerated Life Testing

© The Author(s), under exclusive license to Springer Nature Switzerland AG 2021
N. L. Black et al. (Eds.): IEA 2021, LNNS 221, pp. 169–177, 2021.
https://doi.org/10.1007/978-3-030-74608-7_22

| HCF = | Human Capacity Factor |
| HE = | Human Error |
| HF = | Human Factor |
| HITL = | Human in the Loop |
| HnF = | Human non-Failure |
| HSI= | Human-System Integration |
| MTTE = | Mean Time to Error |
| MTTF = | Mean Time to Failure |
| MWL = | Mental Workload |
| PDfR = | Probabilistic Design for Reliability |
| PoF = | Probability of Failure |
| PPM = | Probabilistic Predictive Modelling |
| SA = | Sensitivity Analysis |
| SoH = | Symptom of Health |
| TTF = | Time to Failure |

# 1   Introduction

The state-of-the-art in aerospace ergonomics cannot be improved, if the outcomes of its critical missions or possible anticipated off-normal situations are not quantified in advance, and since nobody and nothing is perfect and the probabilities of failure (PoF) of a navigational device or a HITL or both are never zero, such quantification should be done on a probabilistic basis. Then the anticipated PoF and the corresponding times-to-failure (TTF) could be reviewed and, if possible, made adequate for a particular application. The PoF cannot be high, of course, but should not be lower than necessary either: it should be adequate for the particular instrumentation, mission and application. If the assessed operational PoF is very low, that could very well be an indication that the employed instrumentation is "over-engineered", i.e. is too robust and, most likely, too expensive for the given application, and/or that the HITL is overqualified for the given mission or an off-normal situation. A sensitivity analysis (SA) based on the developed methodologists and algorithms could be used, if necessary, to improve, the planned undertaking. The objective of the analyses that follow is to demonstrate how analytical ("mathematical") PPM can be fruitfully and effectively employed to predict the PoF of some more or less typical aerospace missions and extraordinary situations. Human error (HE) was addressed in numerous human psychology problems (see, e.g., [1]), including aerospace ergonomics (see, e.g., [2]), but it was done on a qualitative, rather than on a quantitative bases, not to mention using a probabilistic approach.

# 2   Review

An analytical convolution based PPM (see, e.g., [3]) was applied, to the authors' knowledge, for the first time in aerospace ergonomics engineering [4] in order to assess the roles of the decision making times of the two humans involved, the officer on the ship's board and the helicopter pilot, in making landing of a Navy helicopter on a ship deck successful and safe. Safe landing will take place, i.e., the helicopter undercarriage will not be damaged, if the probability that the random duration of the calm "widow" in the sea wave conditions exceeds appreciably the random sum of the two decision making times and the random time of actual landing is sufficiently large. Probabilistic assessment of the likelihood of a casualty if one of the two aircraft pilots becomes incapacitated [5] has indicated that the likelihood of a safe fulfillment of the aircraft mission might still be quite high, and will naturally depend on the duration of the flight and the moment of the mishap during the flight. The "quantitative aftermath" of the famous "miracle on the Hudson" event vs. infamous "UN shuttle" disaster has been undertaken in [6]. A way to evaluate the role of the Human-Capacity-Factor (HCF) vs. Mental-Workload (MWL) and its effect on the probability of the safe outcome of what seemed to be a "miracle" was suggested and it was argued that, in effect, the "miracle" was not that Captain Sullenberger managed to ditch his aircraft on Hudson river successfully, but because an individual with an exceptionally high hypothetical HCF/MWL ratio, like Captain "Sully", turned out to be in control, when the problem occurred. A methodology for the evaluation of the likelihood of a vehicular mission success and safety, based on a route segmentation model, was suggested [7] in application to an aircraft, with consideration of the roles of the reliability of the navigation equipment, human performance and most likely anticipated environmental conditions at each segment. The model is, generally speaking, applicable to any vehicular engineering field [8, 9], whether automotive, railway, maritime or even outer space. Several effective PPMs were developed in connection with the short- and long-term anticipation challenge in aeronautics [10]. It was shown [11] that a PPM based on the application of a double-exponential-probability-distribution function (DEPDF) can effectively quantify the role of the human factor (HF) in various HITL related tasks and problems. Several advanced probabilistic design-for-reliability (PDfR) techniques were addressed in [12–15] in application to the prediction, quantification and assurance of the reliability of aerospace electronics. Particularly, the suggested multi-parametric Boltzmann-Arrhenius-Zhurkov's (BAZ) kinetic constitutive model enabled developing methodologies for the evaluation of the PoF of an electronic device after the given time in operation at the given temperature and under the given (anticipated) stress (not necessarily mechanical). An Extreme Value Distribution (EVD) technique, which could be viewed as a special case of the DEPDF model, can be used to account for the number of repetitive loadings that eventually lead to the material/device failure by closing, in a step-wise fashion, the gap between its strength/capacity (characterized and quantified by its stress-free activation energy) and the applied stress/demand.

# 3 Extension

*Possible Role of Failure Oriented Accelerated Testing (FOAT) in Ergonomics*
Let us use as an example, aviation ergonomics [16, 17]. As is known, accelerated testing, such as highly accelerated life testing (HALT), is widely used in electronic and photonic engineering. It was shown [14–16] that highly focused and highly cost effective failure-oriented accelerated testing (FOAT) can often successfully and effectively complement

HALT in many reliability endeavors in electronics, photonics, MEMS and MOEMS, and that various FOAT means can be employed in high technologies, when failure-free operation is needed. Flight simulator could be employed as an appropriate FOAT vehicle to quantify, on the probabilistic basis, when fulfilling a particular mission, the required level $F$ of the HCF vs the expected MWL $G$.

The probability of non-failure of a HITL could be sought in such tests as, say, $P = \exp\left[-\gamma t I_* \exp\left(-\frac{F}{G}\right)\right]$. Here $I_*$ is the agreed upon high value of the continuously monitored, measured and recorded MWL characteristic $I$ (electro-cardiac activity, respiration, skin-based measures, blood pressure, ocular measurements, brain measures, etc.), $t$ is time and $\gamma$ is the sensitivity parameter. When flight simulator is used as an appropriate FOAT test vehicle, a group of more or less equally (preferably highly) qualified individuals should be tested. The HCF is a characteristic that remains more or less unchanged for these individuals during the relatively short time of the FOAT. The MWL, on the other hand, is a short-term characteristic that can be tailored, in many ways, depending on the anticipated MWL conditions. The above equation can be written as $-G \ln\left(\frac{n}{\gamma}\right) = F = Const$, where $n = -\frac{\ln P}{I_* t}$. Let the FOAT is conducted at two MWL levels, $G_1$ and $G_2$, and the criterion $I_*$ was observed and recorded at the times of $t_1$ and $t_2$ for the established percentages of $Q_1 = 1 - P_1$ and $Q_2 = 1 - P_2$ of failure, respectively. Then the parameter $\gamma$ can be evaluated as $\gamma = \exp\left(\dfrac{\ln n_2 - \frac{G_1}{G_2} \ln n_1}{1 - \frac{G_1}{G_2}}\right)$. The HCF of the individuals that underwent the accelerated testing can be determined as: $F = -G_1 \ln\left(\frac{n_1}{\gamma}\right) = -G_2 \ln\left(\frac{n_2}{\gamma}\right)$.

Let, e.g., the same group of individuals was tested at two different MWL levels, $G_1$ and $G_2$, until failure (whatever its definition and nature might be), and let the MWL ratio was, say, $\frac{G_2}{G_1} = 2$. Because of that the TTF was considerably shorter and the number of the failed individuals was considerably larger, for the same $I_*$ level (say, $I_* = 120$) in the second round of tests. Let the FOAT shows that $P_1 = 0.8$, $P_2 = 0.5$, $t_1 = 2.0$ h, and $t_2 = 1.5$ h. Then we obtain the following data: $n_1 = -\frac{\ln P_1}{t_1 I_*} = -\frac{\ln 0.8}{2 x 120} = 9.2976 x 10^{-4}$, $n_2 = -\frac{\ln P_2}{t_2 I_*} = -\frac{\ln 0.5}{1.5 x 120} = 38.5082 x 10^{-4}$,

$\gamma = \exp\left(\dfrac{\ln n_2 - \frac{G_1}{G_2} \ln n_1}{1 - \frac{G_1}{G_2}}\right) = \exp\left(\dfrac{\ln 38.5082 x 10^{-4} - 0.5 \ln 9.2976 x 10^{-4}}{1 - 0.5}\right) = 0.015948$, $\frac{F}{G_1} =$

$-\ln\left(\frac{n_1}{\gamma}\right) = \ln\left(\frac{9.2976 x 10^{-4}}{0.015948}\right) = 2.8422$, $\frac{F}{G_2} = -\ln\left(\frac{n_2}{\gamma}\right) = \ln\left(\frac{38.5082 x 10^{-4}}{0.015948}\right) = 1.4210$.

The calculated required HCF-to-MWL ratios $\frac{F}{G} = -\ln\left[62.7038\left(\frac{-\ln P}{t}\right)\right]$ for the given/required probabilities $P$ of non-failures are shown in the table:

| $P$ | 0.95 | 0.99 | 0.999 | 0.9999 | 0.99999 |
|------|------|------|-------|--------|---------|
| $t, h$ | $\times$ | $\times$ | $\times$ | $\times$ | $\times$ |
| 48 | 2.7030 | 4.3329 | 6.6400 | 8.9431 | 11.2457 |
| 240 | 4.3124 | 5.9424 | 8.2495 | 10.5525 | 12.8551 |
| 720 | 5.4110 | 7.0410 | 9.3481 | 11.8511 | 13.9537 |
| 8760 | 7.9097 | 9.5397 | 11.8468 | 14.1498 | 16.45424 |

As evident from the calculated data, the level of the HCF in this example should exceed considerably the level of the MWL, so that a high enough value of the probability of human-non-failure is achieved, especially for long operation times.

### Adequate Trust as an Important Part of the HCF and HSI

Since classical Shakespearian "love all, trust a few" and "don't trust the person who has broken faith once" and to the today's ladygaga's "trust is like a mirror, you can fix it if it's broken, but you can still see the crack in that mother f*cker's reflection", the importance of human-human trust was addressed by numerous writers, politicians and human psychologists. It was the 19th century South Dakota politician Frank Craine who seems to be the first one who indicated the importance of an *adequate trust* in human relationships: "You may be deceived if you trust too much, but you will live in torment unless you trust enough".

It is shown [18] that the entropy of the DEPDF distribution, when applied to the *trustee* (a human, a technology, a methodology, a concept, etc.), can be viewed as an appropriate quantitative characteristic of the propensity of a decision maker in a HSI situation to an under-trust or an over-trust judgment and, as a consequence of that, to the likelihood of making a mistake or an erroneous decision. The analysis that follows addresses some important aspects of a HITL problem for safety-critical missions and extraordinary situations. It is argued that the role and significance of trust can and should be quantified when preparing such missions. Certainly, it should be considered in any HSI activity, and the concept of an adequate trust should be included into an engineering technology, design methodology or a human activity, when there is a need to assure a successful and safe outcome of a particular engineering effort or an aerospace or a military mission.

A suitable modification of the DEPDF for the human non-failure, whether it is the performer (decision maker) or the trustee, is assumed here in the following simple form $P = \exp\left[-\gamma t \exp\left(-\frac{F}{G}\right)\right]$, where $P$ is the probability of non-failure, $t$ is time, $F$ is the HCF, $G$ is the MWL, and $\gamma$ is the sensitivity factor for the time. This expression makes physical sense. Indeed, the probability $P$ of human non-failure, when fulfilling a certain task, decreases with an increase in time and increases with an increase in the HCF/MWL ratio. At the initial moment of time ($t = 0$) the probability of non-failure is $P = 1$ and exponentially decreases with time, especially for low $F/G$ ratios. The above expression, depending on a particular task and application, could be applied either to the performer (the decision maker) or to the trustee, who could be a human, a technology, a concept, an existing best practice, etc.

The ergonomics underlying the above distribution could be seen from the time derivative $\frac{dP}{dt} = -\frac{H(P)}{t}$, where $H(P) = -P \ln P$ is the entropy of this distribution. Thus, the accepted distribution reflects an assumption that the time derivative of the probability $P$ is proportional to the entropy $H(P)$ of this distribution and decreases with an increase in time. This entropy, when applied to the distribution in question is the probability of non-failure of the trustee's performance, and is zero for both extreme values of this performance: when the probability of non-failure is zero, it should be interpreted as an extreme under-trust in someone else's authority or expertise, which is the case of a "not invented here (NIH)" attitude; when the probability of the trustee's non-failure is one, that means that there is an extreme over-trust in an NIH technology: as is known, "my neighbor's grass is always greener" and "no man is a prophet in his own land". The entropy $H(P)$ reaches its maximum value $H_{max} = e^{-1} = 0.3679$ for a rather moderate probability $P = e^{-1} = 0.3679$ of non-failure of the trustee. Note that in the well-known and still widely used Arrhenius equation $\tau = \tau_0 \exp\left(\frac{U_0}{kT}\right)$ MTTF $\tau$, the time $\tau$ is, in effect, the time $t$ needed, in accordance with the exponential law of reliability $P = \exp(-\lambda t)$, to reach the maximum entropy $H_{max}$ of the probability of the Arrhenius (actually, Boltzmann's) distribution. Indeed, by replacing the failure rate $\lambda$ in the exponential law of reliability with its reciprocal value $\frac{1}{\tau}$ the following expression for the entropy can be obtained: $H(P) = -P \ln P = \exp\left[-\frac{t}{\tau_0}\exp\left(-\frac{U_0}{kT}\right)\right]\left[-\frac{t}{\tau_0}\exp\left(-\frac{U_0}{kT}\right)\right] = \frac{t}{\tau}\exp\left(-\frac{t}{\tau}\right)$. The time $t$, when the entropy of the distribution $P = \exp(-\lambda t)$ reaches its maximum value $H_{max} = e^{-1}$, can be found from the equation $e^{-1} = \frac{t}{\tau}\exp\left(-\frac{t}{\tau}\right)$. This equation yields: $t = \tau$. Trust is an important HCF quality.

Captain "Sully", the hero of the miracle-on-the-Hudson event, did possess such a quality. He *"avoided over-trust"* in the ability of the first officer, who ran the aircraft when it took off La Guardia airport, to successfully cope with the emergency situation and took over the control, as well as in the possibility, with the help of the air traffic controllers at LaGuardia and at Teterboro, to land the aircraft safely at these airports. What is even more important, is that Captain "Sully" also *"avoided under-trust"*: 1)in his own skills, abilities and experience that would enable him to successfully cope with the situation (57-year-old Captain "Sully" was a former fighter pilot, a safety expert, an instructor and, most importantly, a glider pilot), and that was the case when "team work" was not the right thing to pursue (quite often, as is known, "too many cooks spoil the broth"); 2) in the aircraft structure that would be able to withstand the slam of the water during ditching and, in addition, would enable slow enough flooding after ditching; in the aircraft safety equipment that was carried in excess of that mandated for the flight; 3) in the outstanding cooperation and excellent cockpit resource management among the flight crew who *trusted* their captain and exhibited, after actual ditching, outstanding team work, when such work was needed during the rescue operation; 4) in the fast response from and effective help of the various ferry operators located near the USS Intrepid museum and in the ability of the rescue team to provide timely and effective help; and 5) in the exceptionally good visibility, an important contributing factor to the success of the accident.

Here is another indication on the role that the maximum entropy can be employed as a suitable quantitative criterion of the adequate trust. It has been determined [19] that the age groups of 20–25 and 65–70 years old are more prone, for the same driving time, to driver drowsiness (DD) than the 26–64 age group. Of course, this happened, first of all, because the middle-aged group possesses the best combination of experience and personal qualities, i.e., has, in general, a higher HCF. Fifty-four years old Captain "Sully" is a good example. The following human qualities have to do with age: ability to concentrate, to anticipate, to withstand fatigue (both physical and mental) for a long time (tolerance to stress), to act in cold blood in off-normal and even life-threatening situations, to make well substantiated decisions in the conditions of uncertainty, to operate the vehicle effectively under time pressure; situation awareness; self-control; mature (realistic) thinking; swiftness in reaction, when necessary; ability to maintain an optimum level of psychological arousal. All these qualities are naturally stronger in mature middle-aged individuals than in younger ones, not to mention elderly folks.

But what is much less obvious is that adequate trust in a system is equally important. The driver should definitely and first of all have adequate trust in himself/herself (again, Captain "Sully" is a good example), but, at the same time, have a reasonable, but a moderate, trust in the automated driving (AD) system. The system should be subjected FOAT for the most important anticipated missions and possible extraordinary situations, and the vehicle operator should be informed of these tests and their results for the given system. Such an information should be included into his/hers education as a driver of an automated driven vehicle and reflected in his/hers driver license. As to the human propensity to driver drowsiness (DD), we suggest, based on the study [19], that the area under the corresponding portion of the entropy curve is used as a suitable quantitative measure of the propensity of a particular age group to the DD "syndrome".

The entropy curve area located between two arbitrary probabilities is as follows:

$$A(P) = \int\limits_{P_1}^{P_2} H(P)dP = \int\limits_{P_2}^{P_1} P \ln P dP = \tfrac{1}{2}\left[P_1^2 \ln P_1 - P_2^2 \ln P_2 + \tfrac{1}{2}\left(P_2^2 - P_1^2\right)\right].$$ The area

under the entire entropy curve can be found by putting $P_1 = 0$ and $P_2 = 1$ in this expression and is $A_0 = A(1) = 0.25$. The age of drivers under test [19] ranged from 20 to 70, i.e., for 50 years, and since the total length of the probability axis is 1.0, each year corresponds therefore to the segment $1/50 = 0.02$ on the P axis. The lengths of the segments for the 20–25 "agers" and 65–70 "agers" are the same and are equal to $0.02 \times 5 = 0.1$. The 20–25, 65–70 and 26–64 areas under the H(P) curve are:

$$A_{65-70} = A(P_1 = 0.9; P_2 = 1) = \frac{1}{2}\left[-0.9^2\left(\ln 0.9 - \frac{1}{2}\right) + \frac{1}{2}\right] = 0.00483$$

$$A_{26-64} = A(P_1 = 0.1; P_2 = 0.9) = \frac{1}{2}\left[0.1^2 \ln 0.1 - 0.9^2 \ln 0.9 + \frac{1}{2}\left(0.9^2 - 0.1^2\right)\right]$$

$$= 0.23111$$

These data could be viewed as figures of merit for these three groups of people, as far as their ability to withstand DD is concerned. If one takes the performance of drivers in the 24–64 age group as 100%, the younger drivers are only 6.06% as good as the middle age people, and the older drivers are even worse – only 2.09%. These results should be attributed, first of all, to the belief that the level of the propensity to DD is lower, when the driver has more trust in himself/herself rather than in the system and because of that his/hers level of awareness is higher.

## 4 Conclusions

In any ergonomics effort of importance FOAT should be carried out beforehand to predict its outcome. Using several realistic examples, it was shown how significant should be the ratio HCF/MWL be to make the probability of the human failure low enough. Flight simulator can be employed as an appropriate and ergonomically meaningful test vehicle that could be used to quantify, on the probabilistic basis, the required HCF/MWL for the successful fulfilment of a particular aerospace mission or to successfully cope with an extraordinary situation Human trust is an important HCF quality and HSI feature and should be included into the list of such qualities for a particular HITL task in aerospace ergonomics. The entropy of the double exponential probability distribution function (DEPDF) for the random HCF can be viewed as an appropriate quantitative characteristic of the propensity of a human to an under-trust or an over-trust judgment and, as the consequence of that, to an erroneous decision making or to a performance error.

## References

1. Reason, J.T.: Human Error. Cambridge University Press, Cambridge, UK (1990)
2. Kern, A.T.: Controlling Pilot Error: Culture, Environment, and CRM (Crew Resource Management). McGraw-Hill, New York (2001)
3. Suhir, E.: Applied Probability for Engineers and Scientists. McGraw-Hill, New York (1997)
4. Suhir, E.: Helicopter-landing-ship: undercarriage strength and the role of the human factor. ASME Offshore Mech. Arctic Eng. J. **132**(1) (2009)
5. Suhir, E., Mogford, R.H.: "Two men in a cockpit": probabilistic assessment of the likelihood of a casualty if one of the two navigators becomes incapacitated. J. Aircr. **48**(4) (2011)
6. Suhir, E.: "Miracle-on-the-Hudson": quantified aftermath. Int. J. Hum. Factors Model. Simul. **4**(1), 35–62 (2012)
7. Suhir, E.: Likelihood of vehicular mission-success-and-safety. J. Aircr. **49**(1) (2012)
8. Suhir, E.: Human-in-the-loop (HITL): probabilistic predictive modeling of an aerospace mission/situation outcome. Aerospace **1**, 101–136 (2014)
9. Suhir, E.: Human-in-the-loop: probabilistic predictive modeling, its role, attributes, challenges and applications. Theor. Issues Ergon. Sci. (2014)
10. Suhir, E., Bey, C., Lini, S., Salotti, J.-M., Hourlier, S., Claverie B.: Anticipation in Aeronautics: Probabilistic Assessments. Theor. Issues Ergon. Sci. (2014)
11. Suhir, E.: Human-in-the-loop: application of the double exponential probability distribution function enables one to quantify the role of the human factor. Int. J. Hum. Factors Model. Simul. **5**(4), 354–377 (2017)
12. Suhir, E.: Aerospace electronics reliability prediction: application of two advanced probabilistic techniques. ZAMM **1**(16) (2017)
13. Suhir, E.: Aerospace mission outcome: predictive modeling, editorial, special issue "challenges in reliability analysis of aerospace electronics". Aerospace **5**(2) (2018)

14. Suhir, E.: What could and should be done differently: failure-oriented-accelerated-testing (FOAT) and its role in making an aerospace electronics device into a product. J. Mater. Sci.: Mater. Electron. **29**(4), 2939–2948 (2018)
15. Suhir, E.: Human-in-the-Loop: Probabilistic Modeling of an Aerospace Mission Outcome. CRC Press (2018)
16. Suhir, E.: Failure-oriented-accelerated-testing and its possible application in ergonomics. Ergon. Int. J. **3**(2) (2019)
17. Suhir, E.: Assessment of the required human capacity factor (HCF) using flight simulator as an appropriate accelerated test vehicle. Int. J. Hum. Factor Model. Simul. **7**(1), 71–74 (2019)
18. Suhir, E.: Adequate trust, human-capacity-factor, probability-distribution-function of human non-failure and its entropy. Int. J. Hum. Factor Model. Simul. **7**(1), 75–83 (2019)
19. Kundinger, T., Riener, A., Sofra, N., Weigl, K., Driver drowsiness in automated and manual driving: insights from a test track study. In: Proceedings of the 25th International Conference on Intelligent User Interfaces (IUI 2020). ACM (2020)

# Statistical Modelling of Comfort Preferences and Uncertainty in Subjective Evaluations of Aircraft Seat Comfort

Amalia Vanacore[1]([⊠]), Antonio Lanzotti[1], Chiara Percuoco[1], and Bonaventura Vitolo[2]

[1] Department of Industrial Engineering, University of Naples Federico II, Naples, Italy
amalia.vanacore@unina.it
[2] Geven Spa, Nola, Italy

**Abstract.** Aircraft seat is rated as the most unsatisfying aspect of flying; understanding the main factors impacting on passenger's evaluations can provide a concrete opportunity for airlines to improve seat comfort and thus enhance passenger satisfaction and loyalty. Although there is a great deal of interest, the research on effective assessment strategies for subjective comfort is still underdeveloped. In this study a model-based approach for the analysis of subjective comfort data is suggested. The model adopted can be interpreted as a parametric version of the psychological process generating comfort ratings. The proposed approach is exploited through a case study concerning comfort assessment of aircraft seats designed for regional flights.

**Keywords:** Aircraft seat comfort · Subjective data analysis · Laboratory experiments · Uncertainty

## 1 Introduction

The number of air passengers is growing and is expected to double to 8.2 billion in 2037 [1]. Contextually with this growth, there is also a growing attention towards passenger needs, service quality and comfort [2–4]. Specifically, seat comfort is an important factor for passenger satisfaction, it is related with the mode of travelling and passenger willingness to use it again. According to Hiemstra-van Mastrigt [5], "*comfortable seats can attract passengers*", since the seat is the interface of the passenger with the aircraft interior for most of the journey. For this reason, the airlines industry makes efforts to improve passenger comfort experience, in order to attract more passengers. Improving the sense of comfort associated with a trip, adopted as a measure of overall quality of the trip, results in an increase of proportion of passenger who wish to use the same airline on future occasions (*i.e.* passenger loyalty) [6, 7].

In their extensive literature review focusing on the relationships between comfort perception, anthropometry, seat characteristics and passengers activities, Hiemstra-van Mastrigt et al. [5] highlight that statistical evidence on these relationships is still lacking and emphasize the need of enhancing research on quantitative methods to properly

N. L. Black et al. (Eds.): IEA 2021, LNNS 221, pp. 178–183, 2021.
https://doi.org/10.1007/978-3-030-74608-7_23

investigate factors influencing passenger seating comfort so as to support seat designers and purchasers to make informed decisions.

In order to produce accurate and reliable findings, methods for the analysis of comfort data should take into account the complex nature of the subjective evaluation process. Comfort is defined as a pleasant state or relaxed feeling perceived by a human in reaction to an environment [8–10]. Comfort experiences are judged on the basis of a psychological mechanism where both preferences and uncertainty are always present and may be related to either the judge's characteristics and the environment or product features. As a consequence, the analysis of subjective comfort data should take into account both the judge's propensity for a meditated evaluation (*i.e.* based on the comfort feeling) as well as her/his propensity for a totally random one (*i.e.* uncertainty due to external circumstances such as individual comfort expectations, previous comfort experiences, state of mind). This logic characterizes the class of mixture models expressed as convex Combination of a Uniform and a shifted Binomial distribution [11–13], which have been adopted in this paper for the statistical analysis of subjective comfort evaluations of aircraft seats for economy class flights.

The remainder of the paper is organized as follows: in Sect. 2 an overview of experiments is reported; in Sect. 3 the results are fully described; in Sect. 4 a discussion of results is reported; finally, conclusions are summarized in Sect. 5.

## 2 Overview of Experiments

A total of 28 volunteers (14 females and 14 males; aged between 24 and 44 years) have been selected to participate in the aircraft seat comfort experiment using the following criteria:

(1) to be free from severe musculoskeletal disorders in the last year;
(2) to have taken at least 2 flights in the last year;
(3) to be economy class flyers.

Procedures for participant recruitment and data collection have been defined taking into account ethical considerations. Before providing the informed consent, participants have been briefed about type, number and duration (40 min) of each comfort trial, as well as on research aims and treatment of the collected data. The selected group of participants is representative of the anthropometric variability in the Italian adult population with respect to both weight and height [14]. The main anthropometric measures are listed in Table 1.

The comfort experiments took place in a laboratory environment equipped with two rows of aircraft double-seats. Each participant sat in a fixed posture in a seat of the second row with a pitch of 32 inches that realistically replicate legroom. Each participant was involved in 5 test sessions to evaluate the comfort of 3 aircraft seats. The seats differed in terms of weight, reclining, dimensions of seat pan and backrest. Specifically, participants assessed the comfort of 2 typical double-seats identified as "baseline configurations" (hereafter denoted seat A and seat B) and 1 lightweight double-seat (hereafter denoted C; confidential). Seat A, being not reclining, was tested only in upright position while

**Table 1.** Main anthropometric characteristics of the participants

|  | Num | Age [year] [min-max] | Weight [kg] [min-max] | Height [m] [min-max] | BMI [kg/m$^2$] [min-max] |
|---|---|---|---|---|---|
| Males | 14 | [27–41] | [69–100] | [1.60–1.90] | [22.8–34.7] |
| Mean (SD) |  | 36 (4.1) | 85.1 (10.10) | 1.78 (0.07) | 28.6 (3.29) |
| Females | 14 | [26–44] | [44.8–83] | [1.53–1.74] | [21.5–27.5] |
| Mean (SD) |  | 34 (5) | 67.2 (10.3) | 1.66 (0.06) | 24.8 (2.10) |

seat B and seat C were tested both in upright and reclined position. Each participant tested the 5 seats configurations following a crossover design in order to guarantee repeatable and homogeneous test conditions and minimize the impact of well-known noise factors like day of the week, testing order and inter-individual variability [15].

In each test session, a trained interviewer asked the participant to express her/his overall seat comfort perception as well as her/his perception related to the comfort of specific seat features.

## 2.1  Statistical Data Analysis

Seating comfort evaluation can be assumed as the result of a complex subjective decision influenced by two main components: the subject *feeling* towards the evaluated seat and the *uncertainty* surrounding the final choice due to external circumstances like the subject comfort expectations and her/his state of mind at the moment the evaluation is provided.

Starting from this premise, the collected subjective seat comfort evaluations have been modelled as a Combination of a Uniform distribution and a shifted Binomial distribution [11–13]. The Binomial distribution is intended to model the propensity to adhere to a meditated evaluation interpreted as the result of a counting process within a sequential selection among the $m$ ordered judgment categories, whereas the Uniform distribution is introduced as the most unpredictable case among all discrete alternatives to mimic a pure random choice. The adopted CUB model will be hereafter briefly described following the multi-product framework proposed in Capecchi et al. [16].

Let $\mathbf{x}_i^{(\pi)}$ and $\mathbf{x}_i^{(\xi)}$ be the covariate vectors explaining the uncertainty and feeling component, respectively, for subject $i$, with $i = 1,..,n$, and let H be the vector of measurements available for each product (*i.e.* seat) $k$, for $k = 1,...,K$.

A CUB model for the ordinal response $R$ is specified by:

$$\Pr\left(R = r \middle| \mathbf{x}_i^{(\pi)} ; \mathbf{x}_i^{(\xi)} ; \mathbf{z}_k\right) = \pi_{ik}\binom{m-1}{r-1}\xi_{ik}^{m-r}(1-\xi_{ik})^{r-1} + (1-\pi_{ik})\frac{1}{m} \quad (1)$$

for $r = 1,...,m$; $i = 1,..,n$; $k = 1,...,K$.

The subject and product covariates are linked to the CUB model parameters $(\pi, \xi)$ as follows:

$$\begin{cases} \pi_{ik} = \dfrac{1}{1+e^{(-\mathbf{x}_i^{(\pi)}\beta - \mathbf{z}_k\delta)}} \\ \xi_{ik} = \dfrac{1}{1+e^{(-\mathbf{x}_i^{(\xi)}\gamma - \mathbf{z}_k\eta)}} \end{cases} \quad (2)$$

for $i = 1,..,n$ and $k = 1,...,K$, being $(\boldsymbol{\beta}, \boldsymbol{\gamma})$ and $(\boldsymbol{\delta}, \boldsymbol{\eta})$ the parameter vectors measuring the impact of subject and product covariates on uncertainty and feeling components, respectively.

It should be noted that the intercepts $\beta_0$ and $\gamma_0$ in (2) represent the joint level effect of $i$-th subject and $k$-th product with regard to the CUB components.

## 3  Results

Coherently with the adopted framework for the analysis of subjective comfort responses, the seat comfort evaluations collected during the laboratory experiments have been arranged in the following three matrices:

- matrix R [5, 28] containing the subjective overall comfort ratings provided by the 28 participants for the 5 seat conditions under study;
- matrix X [28, 3] containing 3 anthropometrical characteristics for the 28 participants: age $(x_1)$, gender $(x_2)$ and BMI $(x_3)$;
- matrix Z [5, 15] including 8 physical attributes and 7 comfort attributes distinguishing the 5 aircraft seats. The physical attributes are height of seat $(z_1)$; height of seat pan $(z_2)$; depth of seat pan $(z_3)$; width of seat pan $(z_4)$; backrest configurations $(z_5)$; height of backrest $(z_6)$; width of backrest $(z_7)$ and backrest reclining $(z_8)$. The comfort attributes are comfort of seat pan padding $(z_9)$; comfort of seat pan at buttocks $(z_{10})$; comfort of seat pan at back of thighs $(z_{11})$; comfort of seat pan behind the knees $(z_{12})$; comfort of backrest padding $(z_{13})$; comfort of backrest support $(z_{14})$ and comfort of lumbar support $(z_{15})$.

The coefficient estimates for the CUB model fitted for aircraft seat comfort evaluations are reported in Table 2.

**Table 2.** Parameters estimates (standard errors) for the CUB model.

| $1 - \pi_{ik} = 1 - \pi$ | $\log it(1 - \xi_{ik}) = \gamma_0 - \eta_2 z_2 - \eta_{13} z_{13}$ | | |
|---|---|---|---|
| $1 - \pi$ | $\gamma_0$ | $\eta_2$ | $\eta_{15}$ |
| 0.121 | 3.645 | −0.715 | 0.374 |
| (0.053) | (0.850) | (0.144) | (0.083) |

The results provide evidence of low uncertainty in comfort responses $(1 - \pi_{ik} = 0.121)$; the comfort of lumbar support has a significant positive effect over the comfort responses $(\eta_{15} = 0.374)$ whereas the height of seat pan $(\eta_2 = -0.715)$ produces a negative effect.

## 4  Discussion

The estimated model shows that the uncertainty does not play an important role in the evaluation process, this result may be explained by the characteristics of the participants involved in the comfort experiments: they are all frequent flyers, fully engaged in the evaluation process and trained for the evaluation task.

The estimated model reveals that the seating comfort is positively influenced by the comfort of lumbar support and negatively influenced by the seat pan height.

As already emerged from previous research studies [17], the significance of the comfort of lumbar support draws attention to this seat parameter, which has been much investigated from the technical point of view but whose impact on subjective feeling of comfort is largely unknown [18, 19]. The lumbar support design is usually motivated by the idea that a seat to be comfortable should preserve the curve in the low back (*i.e.* low back lordosis). It is widely understood that lumbar lordosis decreases as the angle between the trunk and hip approaches 90%, as in an erect sitting posture [18]. However, a lumbar support designed in this way is not always perceived as comfortable as discussed in a recent study on office chairs that evidences a paradoxical behavior: the seat designed to ensure correct lumbar curvature recorded the highest level of discomfort and pain for the lower back by the evaluators who participated in the tests [19].

The seat pan height, measured as the distance between the top of the seat pan and the floor, is one of the most critical parameters for seat design [20] and a careful selection of this dimension is necessary in order to achieve an optimum trade-off between including people, increasing comfort experience and an efficient use of the space; it is the subject of several researches to derive the optimal value considering the dimensions of the popliteal height of the potential passenger [20]. It is clear that, depending on the amount of adjustability, it will be difficult to define dimensions that include the entire passenger population comfortably.

## 5  Conclusions

The strategy here proposed for analyzing comfort data seems helpful to produce evidence in order to identify critical factors to improve seat design. The main advantages of the proposed approach are the following: (1) it explicitly takes into account the subjective nature of comfort data; (2) it separates the role of expressed preferences from that of uncertainty; (3) it allows to study the effect of passenger and seat covariates on the liking patterns in a multi-product setting.

A critical issue of the study is the moderate sample size, it is likely that with a larger sample of potential passengers, more meaningful relationships could be derived. However, the investigated sample size is very common in laboratory experiments and the adopted approach revealed effective even in these conditions.

Finally, in future research, it would be interesting to investigate which physical seat factors significantly influence the overall discomfort perception and also to extend the investigation from a dynamic perspective, *e.g.* including the impact of aircraft vibration on passengers (dis-)comfort subjective analysis.

## References

1. IATA 20-Year Air Passenger Forecast. https://www.iata.org/en/pressroom/pr/2018-10-24-02. Accessed November 2020

2. Kokorikou, A., Vink, P., de Pauw, I.C., Braca, A.: Exploring the design of a lightweight, sustainable and comfortable aircraft seat. Work **54**(4), 941–54 (2016)
3. Brindisi, A., Concilio, A.: Passengers' comfort modeling inside aircraft. J. Aircr. - J AIRCRAFT **45**, 2001–2008 (2008). https://doi.org/10.2514/1.36305
4. Newson, C., Cairns, S.: Predict and decide: aviation, climate change and UK policy. Report of UK Environmental Change Institute (2008)
5. Hiemstra-van Mastrigt, S., Groenesteijn, L., Vink, P., Kuijt-Evers, L.F.: Predicting passenger seat comfort and discomfort on the basis of human, context and seat characteristics: a literature review. Ergonomics **60**(7), 889–911 (2017)
6. Vink, P., Franz, M., Kamp, I., Zenk, R.: Three experiments to support the design of lightweight comfortable vehicle seats. Work **41**(Suppl. 1), 1466–1470 (2012)
7. Dolnicar, S., Grabler, K., Grün, B., Kulnig, A.: Key drivers of airline loyalty. Tour. Manage. **32**(5), 1020–1026 (2011)
8. Vink, P., Hallbeck, S.: Comfort and discomfort studies demonstrate the need for a new model (2012)
9. De Looze, M.P., Kuijt-Evers, L.F., Van Dieen, J.A.A.P.: Sitting comfort and discomfort and the relationships with objective measures. Ergonomics **46**(10), 985–997 (2003)
10. Zhang, L., Helander, M.G., Drury, C.G.: Identifying factors of comfort and discomfort in sitting. Hum. Factors **38**(3), 377–389 (1997)
11. Kenett, R.S., Salini, S.: Modern analysis of customer satisfaction surveys: comparison of models and integrated analysis. In: Applied Stochastic Models in Business and Industry. Wiley (2012)
12. Piccolo, D.: Observed information matrix for MUB models. Quad. Stat. **8**, 33–78 (2006)
13. Piccolo, D., D'Elia, A.: A new approach for modelling consumers' preferences. Food Qual. Preference **19**(3), 247–259 (2008)
14. Tosi, F.: Design for Ergonomics. Springer, Cham (2020)
15. Bazley, C., Nugent, R., Vink, P.: Patterns of discomfort. Ergonomics **5**(1), 2015 (2015)
16. Capecchi, S., Endrizzi, I., Gasperi, F., Piccolo, D.: A multi-product approach for detecting subjects' and objects' covariates in consumer preferences. Br. Food J. **118**(3) (2016). https://doi.org/10.1108/BFJ-10-2015-0343
17. Vanacore, A., Lanzotti, A., Percuoco, C., Capasso, A., Vitolo, B.: A model-based approach for the analysis of aircraft seating comfort. Work **68**(1), S251–S255 (2021)
18. Vink, P.: Aircraft Interior Comfort and Design. CRC press (2016)
19. Santo, C.D., Araujo, R.C.: Assessment of changes in spine curvatures and the sensations caused in three different types of working seats. Motriz: Rev. Educacao Fisica **23**(3) (2017)
20. Hiemstra-van Mastrigt, S.: Comfortable passenger seats: Recommendations for design and research. TU Delft, Delft University of Technology (2015)

# A Staggered Seat is Beneficial for the Flying V Aircraft

Peter Vink[1](✉), Shabila Anjani[1], Chiara Percuoco[2], Roelof Vos[3], and Amalia Vanacore[2]

[1] Delft University of Technology, Landbergstraat 15, 2628 CE Delft, The Netherlands
P.Vink@tudelft.nl
[2] Department of Industrial Engineering, University of Naples Federico II, 80125 Naples, Italy
[3] Delft University of Technology, Kluyverweg 1, 2629 HS Delft, The Netherlands

**Abstract.** Staggered seats might be a solution for a V-shaped aircraft (the Flying V). The cabin longitudinal axis of this airplane has a 26° angle with respect to the direction of flight. When seats are positioned in the direction of flight, they consequently have an angle to the cabin and become staggered. It is unknown whether the comfort of this staggered seat is appreciated. In this study, 117 participants tested the comfort and the privacy experience in this staggered seat compared with a regular aircraft seat. The experiment showed that both comfort and privacy were significantly better in the staggered seats. However, the analysis is based on short-term evaluations, which means that long-term effects still need to be studied and also the effects of groups travelling together need to be investigated.

**Keywords:** Aircraft seat · Staggered · Comfort · Flying V · Leg room · Arm Rest

## 1 Introduction

### 1.1 A New Aircraft: The Flying V

Flying V is a new type of long-haul aircraft under development (Fig. 1), whose form will allow a reduction of 20% in energy consumption due to its unique shape (Vink et al. 2020). The Flying V does not consist of a traditionally configured circular fuselage with a set of wings, but the passenger cabin, cargo hold and fuel tanks are integrated in the wing structure of the Flying V. At the moment, the Flying V is designed to use traditional kerosene engines, but also carbon neutral ways of propulsion, like hydrogen or synthetic kerosene, are under study.

### 1.2 Staggered Seats

The wings of the Flying V have an angle of 26° with respect to the direction of flight, which means that the cabin (integrated in the wing structure) has this angle as well. As a consequence traditional seats placed in the direction of the cabin, would also have such an angle with respect to the direction of flight. Because of crashworthiness,

N. L. Black et al. (Eds.): IEA 2021, LNNS 221, pp. 184–190, 2021.
https://doi.org/10.1007/978-3-030-74608-7_24

**Fig. 1.** An impression of the Flying V that is under development.

safety regulations do not allow an angle of more than 18° from the direction of flight (Humm et al. 2016), for this reason, a staggered seat placed in the direction of flying was considered for the Flying V. This means that the seat has an angle of 26° with respect to the cabin and the adjacent seat closer to the center of the airplane is slightly set back (Fig. 2); the front of the seat can be flipped up to enable in- and egress (Fig. 3).

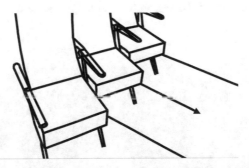

**Fig. 2.** Staggered seats of the Flying V. The arrow is the direction of the cabin in the wing and the seats are in the direction of flight and angled with respect to the cabin.

**Fig. 3.** To allow in- and egress and variation in posture the seat has the possibility of flipping up the front part of the seat.

The Rebel company had these seats available and adapted them for the Flying V. A 1:1 mock-up (6 m wide, 2.1 m high and 6 m long) of a cross section of the Flying V cabin was made and two rows of four staggered seats were placed in it.

Moving from the idea that the understanding of passenger comfort experience and its implications for the design of the aircraft interior is becoming a competitive edge in the aerospace industry, the research question is to investigate how Flying V staggered seats are perceived from potential passengers in terms of comfort. The comfort analysis includes also an investigation on the experience of privacy and control when potential passengers are seated in the aircraft, because this is an important factor in determining the overall comfort experience (Ahmadpour et al. 2016).

## 2   Overview of Comfort Study

An explorative study, involving 117 participants, was carried out to investigate the seating experience of new staggered seats (the Flying V seats) compared with regular aircraft seats, in terms of comfort and privacy. All participants tested in a random order both seats in the same conditions. In the first comfort test, each participant sat in the second row of the tested seats (regular or staggered); for the first 5 min the participant was free to choose to perform an activity (i.e. reading a magazine, talking to their neighbor or using his/her smart phone); in the last 5 min, he/she had to complete an online questionnaire with his/her mobile phone. The online questionnaire was accessible by scanning a QR code located at the back of the seat in front of the participant.

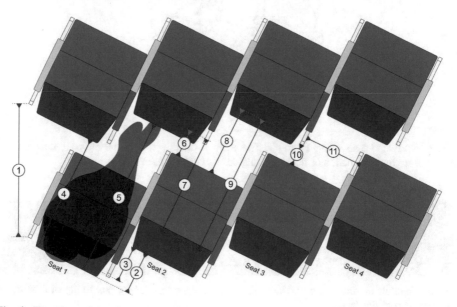

**Fig. 4.** Top view of the dimensions of the staggered seats. 1 = 79 cm (31″ pitch); 2 = 24 cm; 3 = 18 cm; 4 = 71 cm; 5 = 94 cm; 6 = 27 cm; 7 = 68 cm; 8 = 52 cm; 9 = 92 cm; 10 = 17 cm; 11 = 31 cm.

At the end of the first comfort test, participant moved to the other seat to be tested (e.g. the regular if he/she had tested the staggered and vice-versa), he/she repeated the comfort test, by performing the same activity and then completed the questionnaire.

The two seats analyzed were positioned at 31″ pitch, the regular aircraft seats were 18″ wide, the staggered ones were 17.8″ wide. It is worth pointing out that, the pitch of these seats is not comparable (Fig. 4 and Fig. 5) due to the 26° angle with respect to the flying direction of Flying V. Participants rated the overall seat comfort as well as the comfort of specific seat features using a 10-point Likert scale (1 = no comfort; 10 = extreme comfort) and the same scale was adopted to rate his/her privacy experience (1 = no privacy; 10 = extreme privacy).

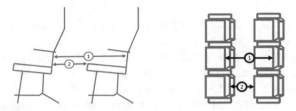

**Fig. 5.** Dimensions of the regular aircraft seat. 1 = 79 cm (31″ pitch); 2 = 35 cm.

### 2.1 Statistical Data Analysis

Data analysis was aimed at comparing the comfort and privacy experienced by participants when testing the regular seat and the staggered seat. The Wilcoxon signed rank test was applied to assess the significance of differences in perceived comfort between the two seats under study.

A cumulative logit model (CLM; McCullagh 1980) was applied in order to investigate whether differences in overall comfort ratings could be related to passenger characteristics and/or seat comfort features. The CLM is probably one of the most well-known regression models for ordinal data (Agresti 2010) and it can be properly adopted to model subjective comfort data that fall in an ordered finite set of categories.

## 3   Results

The main anthropometric characteristics of the 117 participants involved in the study are reported in Table 1.

For both staggered and regular seat, the median comfort score was 7 and the median absolute deviation (MAD) was 1. The Wilcoxon signed rank test did not show a significant difference in overall comfort between the staggered and regular seat, nevertheless the scores obtained by the staggered seat were significantly higher than the ones obtained by the regular seat for the comfort of the armrest ($pvalue = 5.33 \cdot 10^{-7}$), the comfort of the seat pan behind the knees ($pvalue = 0.013$) and the comfort at the upper part of the backrest ($pvalue = 0.012$). For the question 'do you have enough privacy?' (1 = no privacy; 10 = extreme privacy), the staggered seat obtained scores that were significantly

**Table 1.** Main anthropometric characteristics in terms of mean, (standard deviation), [min -max].

|        | Num | Age [years] | Height [cm] | Weight [kg] |
|--------|-----|-------------|-------------|-------------|
| Female | 58  | 30 (18.17) [11–70] | 166.4 (22.2) [153–184] | 65.4 (12.3) [36–94] |
| Male   | 59  | 33.7 (18.6) [11–71] | 180.5 (10.8) [146–205] | 75.3 (14.9) [38–116] |

higher (*pvalue* $= 0.0045$) than the regular seat with median scores equal to 6 (MAD $=$ 2) and 5 (MAD $= 2$), respectively.

The explanatory variables included in the two CLMs fitted to explain the overall comfort of the two seats under study are 4 anthropometrical descriptors (age, $x_1$; gender, $x_2$; height, $x_3$; weight, $x_4$) and 5 specific seat comfort features (comfort of the armrest, $x_5$; comfort of the backrest in the upper part, $x_6$; comfort of the backrest in the lower part, $x_7$; comfort of seat pan, $x_8$; comfort of seat pan behind the knees, $x_9$). In order to improve model interpretability, the 5 variables related to specific seat comfort features were transformed into dichotomous variables taking the value 7 as a cut-off point for assuming a good comfort perception. The estimates for the CLM parameters are reported in Table 2.

**Table 2.** Significant CLM parameters for staggered and regular seat.

| Staggered seat | | | | Regular seat | | | |
|----------|----------|-----------------|---------|-----------|----------|-----------------|---------|
| Parameter | Estimate | Standard error | p-value | Parameter | Estimate | Standard error | p-value |
| $\beta_2$ | 1.17 | 0.344 | 0.0006 | $\beta_6$ | 0.77 | 0.407 | 0.06 |
| $\beta_9$ | 0.659 | 0.339 | 0.052 | $\beta_7$ | 1.083 | 0.406 | 0.008 |

The significant variables are not the same in the two models: gender ($x_2$) and perceived comfort of the seat pan behind the knees ($x_9$) were significant for the staggered seat; whereas perceived comfort in the upper and lower part of the backrest ($x_6$, $x_7$) were significant for the regular seat.

Interpretation of the CLM parameter estimates by odds ratios provides interesting information. For the staggered seat, a high overall comfort evaluation is 3.2 times more likely for female participants than for males; participants with a good comfort perception of the seat pan behind knees are 1.9 times more likely to assign higher overall seat comfort score. For the regular seat, participants with a good comfort perception at the upper and lower part of the backrest are respectively 2.2 and 3 times more likely to assign a higher overall seat comfort score.

## 4    Discussion

The staggered aircraft seats of the Flying V that fulfill safety regulations seem promising. The comfort and privacy experience are both evaluated better. Probably the fact that each passenger has its own space on the armrest and the fact that there is more shoulder space because the shoulders are not exactly next to each other (Fig. 6) contributes to the positive comfort experience. This influence was affirmed in a previous study (Vink et al. 2020), though in that study participants mentioned more complaints like that the seat was hard and that the backrest angle should be more backwards. Some participants also mentioned that the arm rest is of hard plastic.

The comfort score for the regular seat in this study is comparable to the results of the study of Anjani et al. (2020), who reported around 6 for 30″ pitch and around 7 for a 32″ pitch. The comfort score for the staggered seats in this study was 7, while in another study it was 7.9 (Liu et al. 2021) with the same staggered seat. However, in that study there were not always neighbors, which might indicate the importance of privacy. Torkashvand et al. (2019) showed that in a conventional configuration, the middle seat is the least preferred one, because of the contact to neighbors, however, passengers that travel in groups like to have seats next to each other and they do not bother about the shoulder contact. So, probably for groups this seat might not be ideal, but this issue needs to be further investigated.

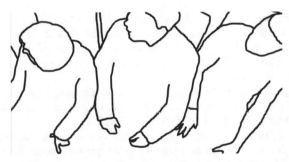

**Fig. 6.** In the staggered seat there is no shoulder contact and there is a separate space at the armrest.

An important limitation of this study and the previous study on staggered seats (Liu et al. 2021) is that the participants tested the seat for only 10 min. Smulders et al. (2016), Li et al. (2017) and Vanacore et al. (2019) show that discomfort increases over time. Therefore, long term tests are needed in order to confirm whether the observed effects hold for a 6–12 h flight.

## 5    Conclusion

A staggered seat was tested for a new aircraft configuration where passengers are positioned in the wing. The longitudinal axis of the cabin inside the wing has an angle of 26° with respect to the flight direction. The seats were placed in the direction of flight, which means that they had an angle towards the cabin and the adjacent seat closer to the middle of the airplane is slightly shifted backwards. This staggered position has the advantage that shoulders do not touch each other and arms have a separate spot at the arm rest. This study showed that the participants experiencing both this staggered seats and regular seats rated comfort for specific seat features and privacy of the staggered seats higher.

**Acknowledgement.** This work is part of a PhD research that is fully funded by Lembaga Pengelola Dana Pendidikan Republik Indonesia (Indonesian Endowment Fund for Education) under contract No. PRJ-7071/LPDP.3/2016 for Shabila Anjani. The authors would like to thank KLM for their support.

# References

Agresti, A.: Analysis of Ordinal Categorical Data, vol. 656. Wiley, Hoboken (2010)

Ahmadpour, N., Robert, J.M., Lindgaard, G.: Aircraft passenger comfort experience: underlying factors and differentiation from discomfort. Appl. Ergon. **52**, 301–8 (2016)

Anjani, S., Li, W., Ruiter, I.A., Vink, P.: The effect of aircraft seat pitch on comfort. Appl. Ergon. **88**, 103132 (2020)

McCullagh, P.: Regression models for ordinal data (with discussion). J. R. Stat. Soc. Ser. B **42**, 109–142 (1980)

Humm, J.R., Yoganandan, N., Pintar, F.A., Weese, R.L., Moorcroft, D.M., Taylor, A.M., Peterson, B.: Responses and injuries to PMHS in side-facing and oblique seats in horizontal longitudinal sled tests per FAA emergency landing conditions. Stapp Car Crash J. **60**, 135–63 (2016)

Liu, Z., Rotte, T., Anjani, S., Vink, P.: Seat pitch and comfort of a staggered seat configuration. Work (Preprint) 1–9 (2021)

Smulders, M., Berghman, K., Koenraads, M., Kane, J.A., Krishna, K., Carter, T.K., Schultheis, U.: Comfort and pressure distribution in a human contour shaped aircraft seat (developed with 3D scans of the human body). Work **54**(4), 925–940 (2016)

Torkashvand, G., Stephane, L., Vink, P.: Aircraft interior design and satisfaction for different activities: a new approach toward understanding passenger experience. Int. J. Aviat. Aeronaut. Aerosp. **6**(2), 1–14 (2019)

Vanacore, A., Lanzotti, A., Percuoco, C., Capasso, A., Vitolo, B.: Design and analysis of comparative experiments to assess the (dis-) comfort of aircraft seating. Appl. Ergon. **76**, 155–63 (2019)

Vink, P., Rotte, T., Anjani, S., Percuoco, C., Vos, R.: Towards a hybrid comfortable passenger cabin interior for the flying V aircraft. Int. J. Aviat. Aeronaut. Aerosp. **7**(1), 1 (2020)

Li, W., Yu, S., Yang, H., Pei, H., Zhao, C.: Effects of long-duration sitting with limited space on discomfort, body flexibility, and surface pressure. Int. J. Ind. Ergon. **58**, 12–24 (2017)

# Part III: Agriculture (Edited by Peter Lundqvist)

# Improvements of a Tractor Cab's Usability Based on Interaction Analysis and Ergonomics Adjustments

Teresita Bátiz-Flores, Andrea Perez, María Andrea Escoto-Aceves,
María Fernanda Martínez-López, and Pilar Hernández-Grageda[✉]

Facultad de Ingeniería, Prolongación, Universidad Panamericana, Calzada Circunvalación
Poniente 49, 45010 Zapopan, Jalisco, Mexico
{0215348,0216072,0214020,0215075,phernand}@up.edu.mx

**Abstract.** Being one of the main tools used in agriculture, tractors still cause physical fatigue in users and demand high cognitive processes. The main goal of this project is to detect interaction problems between the user and a chosen tractor cabin with the objective of applying ergonomic adjustments in order to improve the tractor's usability. As a result of applying ergonomic intervention strategies combined with design methods, a conceptual redesign for the main elements form the interior of a tractor cab: the front panel, the levers dashboard, and the seat was proposed.

**Keywords:** Tractor usability · Ergonomic intervention · Physical fatigue

## 1 Problem Statement

The Farm Journal Pulse conducted a study in 2013 in which 1,600 farmers, including tractor operators, reported how many hours a day they spend on their work. More than half of the respondents reported spending 10 to 14 h per day on their daily tasks [1].

Long working hour shifts can cause several damage to the tractor operators' mental and physical health. The impact on the operator's physical health can be caused by sitting with static muscle tension, stress on the blood-vascular system, a constant vibration movement, and musculoskeletal loads, especially on the neck, shoulder, back and knees area [2]. As stated by the article "Determination of comfortable position for tractor driver's hand based on dynamic load", the main body parts where fatigue is concentrated during long farming hours are: neck, eyes, wrists, and forearms [3]. While the need to focus on the field and multiple technical devices at the same time, constitutes a serious problem to the operators' mental health [2]. These health problems cause both cognitive and physiological fatigue.

The users' productivity when working with a tractor is compromised by its lack of comfort and, in consequence, by the his/her satisfaction when performing specific tasks. Different studies have demonstrated that operators become more productive when their work environment is designed for the greatest human performance [4]. Two main causes of low productivity are identified: when the user is not physically comfortable and when the interaction between the product and the user has not taken properly into account. According to Doucet et al. [5–7], disorder symptoms can be reduced through the use of an adjustable workstation on the basis of a driver's anthropometric characteristics. In order to improve the efficiency and effectiveness of all the mechanisms in a tractor, it is important to understand their function as well as their interaction with the user. A study conducted by the University College London [8] found that there is a relationship between the amount of information the user perceives and the responses they give to certain situations. The more information perceived, the harder it becomes to recognize other commands, potentially causing stress and frustration to the user. A proper association between controls and tasks, along with a logical grouping of controls, is essential in a human-machine system in order to be qualified as comfortable. Furthermore, controls need to be easy to use and intuitive, for instance, a lever indicates possibilities for action or movement in a direct way without requiring cognitive processing [9].

Maximizing comfort can increase the tractor operators' performance and satisfaction [10] while facilitating its use, providing safety and stimulating productivity [11].

## 2   Objective

The objective of this research is to analyze the main interaction issues detected among operators and the elements of a tractor's cabin that contains the most common elements in tractors used for agriculture, addressing these problems with ergonomic adaptations, mechanism's simplification and aesthetic arrangements with the goal of achieving a redesign of the tractor's cabin that reduces visual and physical fatigue providing a better user experience for the operator.

## 3   Methodology

With the aim to improve the tractor's cabin functionality, efficiency and a design that facilitates its use, an ergonomic approach was used supported by design methodologies for decision making. The SAME Dorado tractor cabin was taken as reference for the redesign process. A thorough literature research was carried out to identify the different components that make up the interior of a tractor cabin and the interaction problems between users and machinery. Three elements of the cabin's interior were selected for analyzing their interaction issues: front panel, levers dashboard and seat. The interaction issues detected when reviewing the literature could be biomechanical, cognitive, physiologic or anthropometric.

To solve these human-machine interaction issues, three methods were used. The *Reverse Brainstorming* tool [12] helped analyze critical points and prioritize ergonomic intervention strategies inside a tractor cabin to reduce mental and physical loads. Based on the findings of the first methodology, a *Procedures Analysis* was performed to focus on cognitive processes that users perform; the main focus was to ensure the highest level of efficiency, effectiveness, satisfaction and safety in the interaction between users and elements of the tractor cabin. Subsequently, a conceptual proposal was developed using the *Lightning Decision Jam* [13] tool with the intention of identifying improvement areas to have the greatest positive impact on the user experience.

# 4 Results

From the literature review, the main problems in the user-machine interaction were listed and classified, as some of them are shown in Table 1. The ergonomic intervention presents a redesign of three main elements: front instrumental panel, levers dashboard, and seat; resulting in a simplified and comfortable cabin.

**Table 1.** Main problems detected in the user-machine interaction

| Element of the cabin | Issue Detected | Type of risk |
|---|---|---|
| Front instrumental panel | Visual saturation due to signals in the display | Cognitive |
| Front instrumental panel | Visual fatigue due to the reflection of the sun on the display | Physiological |
| Levers dashboard | Uncomfortable position and movement of levers and buttons | Biomechanical |
| Levers dashboard | Excess of levers and buttons | Cognitive |
| Seat | Lack of suitable adaptability in the seat's range of movement | Anthropometric |

The proposal that takes into account improvements as a result of implementing various design and Ergonomics approaches, is shown in Fig. 1.

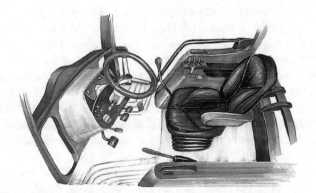

**Fig. 1.** Design proposal for the tractor cabin.

## 4.1 Redesign of the Front Instrumental Panel

The front instrumental panel that is shown in Fig. 2, has a cover (A) that allows its visualization by reducing the sun's reflection on the display. The hour (B) was integrated into the display. At both sides of where the hour is projected, two indicators are placed.

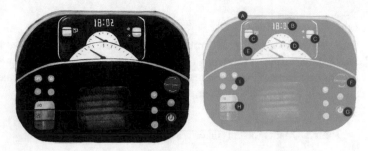

**Fig. 2.** Redesign of the front instrumental panel.

One shows the gasoline level (C) indicating with colors the amount of gasoline, green represents a full tank, while red represents an empty tank. The other indicator displays the motor's temperature (C) with the use of colors; blue color indicates a cold temperature, while red represents a hot temperature. Both indicators have a black pointer that moves along them to indicate their level. Between these elements, the speedometer (D) and the tachometer (D) are located. Both can be seen through the steering wheel while driving. Along the black display the warning sensors (E) are found. These sensors are classified by prevention importance, they only light up when a warning is presented. The warnings that need instant reaction light up in a red color, while the warnings that are just preventive light up in white. Below the display to the right, the emergency button (F) is set. It has a mechanism that works by turning the button and then pushing it when an emergency is presented. The ignition button (G) is positioned under the emergency button. When the key is put in the keyhole, this button lights up with a flashing light synchronized with an intermittent sound; once the button is pushed, it lights up in a green color indicating that the engine has started. Whenever the key is removed from the keyhole, the ignition button returns to its original position, so that it can be pressed again to start the engine next time the tractor is used. On the left side of the front instrumental panel there are 3 buttons for the different lights (H) on the tractor. The yellow button is for the front working lights, the light orange button is for the top lights and the dark orange button is for the rotating lamp. The color and symbols indicate which light will turn on when pressing it. The remaining buttons (I) were distributed around the panel, though there were no modifications to the original design presented on the SAME Dorado tractor cabin.

The steering column has a 45° angle from the floor. The frontal instrumental panel's shape is flat. Additionally, the black color creates contrast with the elements of the panel.

## 4.2   Redesign of the Levers Dashboard and Seat

The lifter command dashboard, shown in Fig. 3, is located on the right side of the cabin, and it was simplified and reorganized. In this new design, next to the user's seat there is a lever with a rotating mechanism along a circular axis with an orange handle (K) that controls the motor's power.

Beside this lever there is a joystick (L) that combines the functions of both rear lifter controllers. There is a new symbol on the lever to explain its movement with a

**Fig. 3.** Redesign of the levers dashboard.

green-yellow circle below the joystick. When the lever is moved forward and backward, the loader gets up and down (color green), and when it is moved right or left the angle of the load is adjusted (color yellow). The three buttons (M) were reorganized next to the joystick. At the right side of these buttons there are the blue valve levers (N), their base has an angle from the horizontal plane. These levers are located diagonally from the user's body. The lever's grip is adequate to the shape of the user's hand. In all the levers and buttons the color remained the same. This dashboard also includes an armrest (O) which serves as a storage compartment.

The seat's height and position are adjustable, allowing the user to move it forward, backward enabling it to come closer to the steering wheel. The seat's backrest allows the user to adjust its position and angle, and has a lumbar support. The seat pan has an inclination of 10°.

## 5 Discussion

The redesign of the cabin provides several advantages to satisfy the user's needs and experience while using it, with the integration of different methodologies that helped combine design functionality and aesthetics properly.

To address the improvement areas, several implementations were applied. Firstly, to manage visual fatigue, the design has a simplification and reorganization of certain elements, buttons and commands. The front panel was designed with a "Dark Mode" style which consists of the use of a dark background and light colored elements (such as buttons and symbols) that generates contrast, this with the purpose of reducing the visual strain and aiding the easy identification of the elements [14]. Additionally, the location of different light buttons help users differentiate each lamp due to their vertical organization and positioning; also the relocation of the emergency button enables its visualization and reach, allowing the user to stop the machine when needed [15].

Oversaturation caused by high load mental levels have an important effect on physiological indices and performance [16], to avoid this, the different levers and buttons on the lifter command dashboard were reorganized and their shape was redesigned considering the workplace design organization principles of "Shortest Distance" and "Using all Spaces" [17].

Addressing the physical fatigue presented by tractor operators', both anthropometric and biomechanical adaptations were implemented. According to the third principle of the Ergonomics for trainers program, the reach envelope is a semi-circle figure that the users' arms make when reaching something. Things that are frequently used should be within the reach envelope of the arm to reduce the fatigue in the upper limbs [18]. The blue valve levers are located at 581 mm from the seat, which is the reach envelope of men between 18 and 65 years old [19].

Conjointly, the 45° angle in the steering column provides a comfortable position for the tractor operator's back [20].

While it is suspected that forward inclination of the seat pan would lead to increased muscle activity in the lower body, studies have proved that the lumbar disk forces depend on the seat pan angle and the friction coefficient. At 10° these forces diminish the body's opportunity to press against the backrest thus approaching the conditions of a standing posture, and reducing the fatigue in the lower and upper back [21].

Moreover, several changes were implemented to provide a major usability. Both panels are designed with a smooth texture and with curved internal edges that prevents the accumulation of dust on its surface and simplifies the cleaning process. Additionally, the integration of a compartment in the right armrest allows the user to store any needed items. Furthermore, the emergency button's mechanism reduces the risk of pushing it accidentally, preventing an unintended engine stop.

Due to the global pandemic, there were some limitations and the design couldn't be tested by users. For this, further research should be undertaken to explore the user's feedback concerning the changes implemented. Owing to the fact that the methodologies implemented helped develop a design that combines several factors to address specific issues, this creates guidelines for future redesign processes to optimize their designs.

## 6   Conclusions

It can be concluded that the combination of several design methodologies, improved the design process by taking into consideration different aspects of the user experience. Each methodology provides specific approaches that help get a better understanding of what are the user's needs, interactions, and tasks in the given context; making them useful, effective, and constructive.

With the coming together of different elements and components as the simplification of mechanisms, the redistribution, and arrangement of controls and symbols, the tractor cabin redesign allows the user to understand its use, thus facilitating it, reducing mistakes and risks.

## References

1. Schafer, S.: Long hours (2014). https://d22t9forbost52.cloudfront.net/news/industry/long-hours
2. Vouri, K.: Tractor driver: are you aware of these six health risks? (2019). https://valtrateam.valtra.com/en/people/tractor-driver-are-you-aware-of-these-six-health-risks

3. Kuta, Ł., Stopa, R., Szyjewicz, D., Komarnicki, P.: Determination of comfortable position for tractor driver's hands based on dynamic load. Int. J. Ind. Ergon. **74**, 102866 (2018)
4. Gibson, J.: The theory of affordances. In: Perceiving, Acting and Knowing. Erlbaum, New Jersey (1977)
5. Doucet, T., Muller, F., Verdu-Esquer, C., Debelleix, X., Brochard, P.: Returning to work after a stroke: a retrospective study at the physical and rehabilitation medicine center La tour de Gassies. Ann. Phys. Rehabil. Med. **55**, 112–127 (2014)
6. Doucet, T., Muller, F., Verdun-Esquer, C., Debelleix, X., Brochard, P.: Returning to work after a stroke: a retrospective study at the physical and rehabilitation medicine center La tour de Gassies. Ann. Phys. Rehabil. Med. **55**, 112–127 (2012)
7. Johansen, U., Johren, A.: Personalekonomi Idag. Uppsala Publishing House (2002)
8. U. C. London: Cuando el cerebro se satura y se ciega por exceso de información (2012). https://www.intramed.net/contenidover.asp?contenidoid=76773
9. Ferrari, E., Cavallo, E.: Agricultural tractor cabin evaluation from users' perspective (2013)
10. Kujit-Evers, L., Krause, F., Vink, P.: Aspects to improve cabin comfort of wheel loaders and excavators according to operators. Appl. Ergon. **34**, 265–272 (2003)
11. Liaoa, M., Drury, C.: Posture, discomfort and performance in a VDT task. Ergonomics **43**, 345–359 (2000)
12. Evans, N.: Destroying collaboration and knowledge sharing in the workplace: a reverse brainstorming approach. Knowl. Manage. Res. Pract. **10**(2), 175–187 (2012)
13. Courtney, J.: Lightning design jams: the exercise that will solve all of your problems (2018)
14. Kim, K., Erickson, A., Lambert, A., Bruder, G., Welch, G.: Effects of dark mode on visual fatigue and acuity in optical see-through head-mounted displays. In: Symposium on Spatial User Interaction, p. 1 (2019)
15. Norman, D.: The Design of Everyday Things. Doubleday, New York (1990)
16. Hernandez-Arellano, J.L., Maldonado-Macias, A.A., Balderrama-Armendariz, C.O.: Physiological and subjective responses associated to physical and mental load in a simulated task. Rev. Cienc Salud **16**, 52–63 (2018)
17. Sangadji, K., Sangadji, L.: Employee performance improvement through workplace design. J. Ilmiah Wahana Pendidikan **5**(4), 105–109 (2020)
18. Lowell, U.O.M.: Ergoonomics for Trainers (2018). https://www.osha.gov/sites/default/files/2018-11/fy12_sh-23543-12_ErgoforTrainers-TTTProgram.pdf
19. Avila Chaurand, R., Prado Leon, L., Gonzalez Muñoz, E.: Dimensiones antropometricas de la poblacion lationamericana (2007). https://www.researchgate.net/publication/31722433
20. Zalewski, P.: Ergonomia Dla Mechanizatorów Rolnictwa. Wydawnictwo Rolnicze i Leśne **260** (1979)
21. Rasmussen, J., Torholm, S., de Zee, M.: Computational analysis of the influence of seat pan inclination and friction on muscle activity and spinal joint forces. Int. J. Inf. Ergon. **39**, 52–57 (2009)

# Agriculture in Transition: New Strategies for the Promotion of Occupational Health and Safety

Kari Anne Holte[1]([⊠]), Kari Kjestveit[1], Hilmar Rommetvedt[1], and Egil Petter Stræte[2]

[1] NORCE, Stavanger, Norway
kaho@norceresearch.no
[2] Ruralis, Trondheim, Norway

**Abstract.** It is well documented that farming is a high-risk industry in terms of fatalities and injuries, and with numerous risk factors associated with operating the farm. It has also proved difficult to find evidence for the effectiveness of interventions. Moreover, farming is in transition, with ongoing technological transformations as well as becoming increasingly more globalized. Thus, new perspectives that allow for more systemic understandings in the management and promotion of occupational health and safety (OHS) are needed. Our main objective is to present an integrated theoretical understanding of the farm as an enterprise and an integrated element in the political-economic agricultural system. The main question is how can farmers organize and manage the farm, in order to simultaneously improve efficiency, quality and OHS based on systemic models for OHS and a systemic understanding of the political-economical system of Norwegian agriculture? The framework is adapted to the Norwegian agricultural context, with ongoing transformations both technologically and organizationally, including visions and plans set by Norwegian agriculture itself. However, the framework can be applied irrespective of national context.

**Keywords:** Agriculture · Occupational health and safety · System theory · Technological change

## 1 Introduction

### 1.1 Agriculture – A Risk Prone Industry

It is well documented that farming is a high-risk industry in terms of fatalities and injuries [1, 2]. Numerous risk factors are associated with the operation of farms, and studies have shown that handling animals, tractors and other machinery are the most frequent causes of non-fatal injuries [3–9]. Other injury risk factors are gender, age, physical health and conditions of employment [8, 10, 11]. Moreover, studies of organizational aspects and OHS risks show that injury risk is correlated with being a full-time farmer and/or farm owner [1], the number of employees [12, 13], two-operators and operators with fellows [9], and cooperation with other farmers [5]. Correlations between injuries and

© The Author(s), under exclusive license to Springer Nature Switzerland AG 2021
N. L. Black et al. (Eds.): IEA 2021, LNNS 221, pp. 200–207, 2021.
https://doi.org/10.1007/978-3-030-74608-7_26

higher income levels, greater field size, and occupational health services membership is also found [10]. An increasingly more industrialized and competitive agriculture may therefore increase OHS risks. Despite a well-documented risk picture, it has proven difficult to find evidence for the effectiveness of interventions for the prevention of injuries, shown in several systematic reviews, when restricting the reviews to a rigid design [14, 15].

## 1.2 Agriculture in Transformation

Agriculture is in a state of transformation. Drivers for this include globalization, trade liberalization, population growth, urbanization, income increases, policy change, shifts in food consumption patterns, technological changes, and environmental changes [16]. Globalization is claimed to be one of the most significant drivers for this transformation due to a global market, lacking protectionist borders and trade across countries (ibid). In the case of Norway, farmers have become part of a globalized labor market, and dependent on labor supply across national borders [17] with an increasingly larger group of foreign, temporary, and seasonal workers [18]. Norwegian farmers face stronger competition in domestic markets, and increased interest from international capital [19]. Globalization represents complex and interconnected problems, thus calling for new management strategies at different levels [16].

Digitalization is another driver, and a central aspect of the so-called "fourth agricultural revolution" [20]. Various labels such as smart farming, digital farming, and agriculture 4.0 have been suggested, but the overall implication is that farm managers and organizations in the value chain can make more precise decisions based on different kinds of "big data" [21]. Data may be gathered by sensors, machines, drones and satellites monitoring animals, plants, water, and soils, as well as humans (ibid). The development has been characterized as a change from *process driven farming* combining past data, experience, and naked-eye observations, to *data driven farming* using "big data" and situational awareness [22]. Charatsari et al. argue that this shift from so-called physical-social systems to cyber-physical-social systems transforms farming regarding to both labor and related organizations [22].

Various OHS risk factors may be eliminated or reduced by new technologies. Norwegian dairy farmers who implemented automated milking systems (AMS) experienced reduced physical strain and more efficient production [23–25]. They were also more satisfied with safety and the working environment [26]. However, increased cognitive demands due to 24/7 system operation, including production of large amounts of data is requiring new competencies [25]. New technologies and smart farming may require new capabilities that potentially disrupt established ways of processing knowledge and thus contribute to the loss of tacit knowledge [20]. Moreover, social consequences may include new actors and alterations of power relations between different stakeholders in existing value chains [27]. In sum, the technological transformation changes both work practices and the management of the farm and expand the interplay with actors in the surroundings of the farm.

## 1.3 The Need for New Perspectives

Safety research has been criticized for focusing mainly on local failures and exposure of individual workers [28]. This critic has been repeated specifically for research in the construction industry, calling for the use of systemic approaches to understand hazards and OHS risks [29]. We believe this also holds for agriculture. A recent study among Norwegian farmers finds the most significant injury risk factors associated to workplace design, organization of work and production form, these risk factors highly interrelated in the work system and difficult to separate from each other [30]. The finding is novel and points to how we need to raise awareness regarding work system dynamics. Taking into consideration agriculture being globalized, even more connected through technology and smart farming, this underpins our point of organizational complexity calling for sociotechnical understanding.

Underpinning this point is critics raised for scientific evaluations and systematic reviews of OHS interventions, including interventions in agriculture [31]. The success or failure of interventions are suggested to be influenced by larger social systems in which interventions are embedded, including infrastructural (ex: politics, public support), institutional (ex: culture), interpersonal (ex: communication, learning environment, relationships) and individual factors [32]. Irrespective of studying OHS risk or OHS interventions, system perspectives increasing the understanding of the surroundings the farm and farmers are embedded within, and interplay of actors is therefore important.

We should therefore also pay attention to the political level. Due to "agricultural exceptionalism" [33], in most countries farming is more regulated by political authorities than other industries. Norway differ from other countries, were both regulations and economic support are settled through yearly corporatist negotiations between central government and the two Norwegian farmers associations. If the parties agree, the Parliament normally accepts the outcome of the negotiations. If they do not agree, the Parliament may play a more active role, depending on the parliamentary situation [34, 35].

Adding a practical perspective, we know that OHS is often seen as an "*occupational health and safety sidecar*" [36] associated with legislation [37], a finding echoed amongst Norwegian farmers [31]. Dul and Neumann [37] therefore suggest the integrating of OHS in overall management strategies. We believe this is a fruitful approach to reach farmers, hence trying to identify strategies that resonate well with how farmers manage the farm regarding production and income.

Based on this, the main objective is to present a systemic and integrated theoretical framework that can be further developed to improve our understandings of the organization of future agriculture in which OHS is embedded. This framework address' the farm and the farmer's role as a manager, while considering the structures surrounding the farm. Moreover, we seek to develop this framework in order to be used as a bottom-up practical action framework that can facilitate systemic learning and knowledge exchange between researchers, farmers and other actors and based on this develop new strategies and tools for the promotion of OHS.

# 2  An Integrated Framework for Understanding and Promoting Occupational Health and Safety in Agriculture

## 2.1  A Starting Point

Sociotechnical system theory is our point of departure. Several sociotechnical models are in use, serving different purposes [e.g., 38–40]. All of them acknowledge that organizations and work systems depend on the environment by which they are regulated and otherwise influenced [30]. We believe that the concentric circle model by Carayon et al. [28] is the most appropriate model for understanding the farm as an organization due to placing the worker in the center of the work system. The model consists of three circles, where the two inner layers are shown to the left in Fig. 1. The inner circle depicts the work system (the local context), where daily decisions are made and practical work is performed. Elements in the work system (technology, tasks, the individual, organization, and environment) are interdependent, so that changes in one of them will affect one or more of the others. However, the local context is embedded in a larger sociotechnical context, involving organizational structural elements (the second layer) and the external environment including regulatory regimes (the third layer) [28]. The work system is therefore not isolated from the world outside and decisions made in the farm enterprise are heavily influenced by constraints and policies made in the outer layers. In other industries, operators in the "sharp end" may have to work according to rigid procedures set by people far away in the organization. Much more influence is associated with being a worker in the center of the work system [28], which underscores the suitability of this model in agriculture, where a focus on day-to-day practice and the handling of unpredictability is essential.

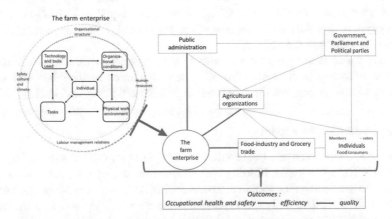

**Fig. 1.** Our framework based on Carayon et al. [28] and Rommetvedt [34]

The second layer in the circular model includes organizational structure elements, culture, etc. Agriculture in Norway and many other countries consists of small enterprises with few employees, often family members. Hence, the second layer points to organizational structures, which to a low degree is present in agriculture. An implication of this is that the third layer in the model, the external environment (regulation, market, industry standards) [28], directly impacts the local work system at the farm. In our framework (Fig. 1) this layer is replaced with the specified actors in the political-economical system of Norwegian agriculture [34], comprising the economic value chain (processing the food before it reaches the consumer) and the parliamentary chain of government where decisions on regulations are made politically and administratively. In addition, the framework includes organizations of which the farmers are members or involved in. Changing power relations and elections may change the political situation, thus influencing farmers [41], while the economic value chain may be influenced by global trends [42].

Dul and Neumann [37] suggest the integrating of OHS in overall management strategies, hence simultaneously improving efficiency, quality and OHS as a way forward to improve OHS. A Norwegian study found that farmers' high well-being and low level of stress was positively associated with animal welfare indicators [43]. Thus, correlations are indicated across several outcomes in agriculture, demonstrating the potential in simultaneous improvements across efficiency, quality and OHS.

## 2.2 Hypotheses Emerging from the Theoretical Approach

Based on the presented framework, three overall hypotheses are developed to guide future research on OHS:

- This framework stimulates for going beyond the individual and local causes for injuries, hence improving the understanding of latent conditions and work system dynamics' impact on farm injuries.
- This framework will reveal the system drivers for facilitating or inhibiting farm management across several outcomes: OHS, efficiency, and quality. This allows for identifying system conflicts and weaknesses that may entail dilemmas in managing and prioritizing efforts at the farm.
- Increased understanding of system conflicts and management dilemmas will improve our understanding of how we change system dynamics to stimulate and support farmers' efforts to improve OHS through improving efficiency and quality.

## 2.3 Application of the Model

To show the analytical and practical application of the framework we will use implementation of AMS as an example. Starting with the innermost circle, *the local work system* [28] was used as an analytical tool in a paper studying AMS and new occupational health and safety risks [25]. The study found AMS altering the whole dynamic within the local work system. AMS is completely changing the *physical work environment*, due to loose housing. Moreover, the *task design* also changes, reducing both physical demands and animal contact, while at the same time introducing new cognitive demands and data driven routines. In the *organizational domain*, AMS alters working hours because the robot operates 24/7. The loose housing entails new considerations regarding breed and affects strategic decisions, through the potential for utilizing the data produced by the robot. The study demonstrates that AMS changes the work system in a way that may expand the focus on management, organization, social life, and culture. Dairy production is embedded in the wider political-economic system illustrated by Fig. 1. To uphold scarcely populated districts, Norwegian agricultural policy restrains the size of farms by regulating the production volume through milk quotas. Investments in AMS requires higher income, hence also milk volume, which is solved by exploiting the marked for available milk quotas. From an economic and supply chain perspective, the farm is integrated both in terms of physical products and additional supporting relations, like advisory service and flow of data. In the example of AMS, utilization and access to data from the milking robot involve several actors (supplier, dairy company, advisors, accountants, etc.). These relations are examples of how the system is intertwined with farm management, also improving effectiveness and the quality of production, to increase competitiveness.

## 3 Conclusion

By combining sociotechnical system theory [28] and an established model of the political-economical system of Norwegian agriculture [34], we have established a framework opening for new approaches in agricultural research and in practice. System mechanisms' impact on farm management is essential, and higher levels of understanding may improve efficiency, quality and OHS.

## References

1. Jadhav, R., Achutan, C., Haynatzki, G., Rajaram, S., Rautiainen, R.: Risk factors for agricultural injury: a systematic review and meta-analysis. J. Agromed. 20(4), 434–449 (2015)
2. Jadhav, R., Achutan, C., Haynatzki, G., Rajaram, S., Rautiainen, R.: Review and meta-analysis of emerging risk factors for agricultural injury. J. Agromed. 21(3), 284–297 (2016)
3. McNamara, J., Kinsella, A., Osborne, A., Blake, C., Meredith, D., Kinsella, J.: Identifying farmer workplace injury factors in Ireland using farm accounts data. J. Agromed. (2020). https://doi.org/10.1080/1059924X.2020.1837704
4. Karttunen, J.P., Rautiainen, R.H.: Distribution and characteristics of occupational injuries and diseases among farmers: a retrospective analysis of workers' compensation claims. Am. J. Ind. Med. 56, 856–869 (2013)
5. Taattola, K., Rautiainen, R.H., Karttunen, J.P., Suutarinen, J., Viluksela, M.K., Louhelainen, K., Mäittälä, J.: Risk factors for occupational injuries among full-time farmers in Finland. J. Agric. Saf. Health 18(2), 83–93 (2012)
6. Day, L., Voaklander, D., Sim, M., Wolfe, R., Langley, J., Dosman, J., Hagel, L., Ozanne-Smith, J.: Risk factors for work related injury among male farmers. Occup. Environ. Med. 66, 312–318 (2009)
7. Erkal, S., Gerberich, S.G., Ryan, A.D., Renier, C.M., Alexander, B.H.: Animal-related injuries: a population-based study of a five-state region in the upper Midwest: Regional rural injury study. J. Saf. Res. 39, 351–363 (2008)
8. Virtanen, S.V., Notkola, V., Luukkonen, R., Eskola, E., Kurppa, K.: Work Injuries among finnish farmers: a national register linkage study 1996–1997. Am. J. Ind. Med. 43, 314–325 (2003)
9. Solomon, C.: Accidental injuries in agriculture in the UK. Occup. Med. 52(8), 461–466 (2002)

10. Rautiainen, R.H., Ledolter, J., Donham, K.J., Ohsfeldt, R.L., Zwerling, C.: Risk factors for serious injury in finnish agriculture. Am. J. Ind. Med. **52**, 419–428 (2009)
11. Sprince, N.L., Park, H., Zwerling, C., Lynch, C.F., Whitten, P.S., Thu, K., Burmeister, L.F., Gillette, P.P., Alavanja, M.C.R.: Risk factors for animal-related injury among iowa large-livestock farmers: a case-control study nested in the agricultural health study. J. Rural Health **19**(2), 165–173 (2003)
12. Van den Broucke, S., Colémont, A.: Behavioral and nonbehavioral risk factors for occupational injuries and health problems among Belgian farmers. J. Agromed. **16**(4), 299–310 (2011)
13. Jadhav, R., Achutan, C., Haynatzki, G., Rajaram, S., Rautiainen, R.: Injury risk factors to farm and ranch operators in the central United States. Am. J. Ind. Med. **60**, 889–899 (2017)
14. DeRoo, L.A., Rautiainen, R.H.: A systematic review of farm safety interventions. Am. J. Prevent. Med. **18**, 51–62 (2000)
15. Rautiainen, R.H., Lehtola, M.M., Day, L.M., Schonstein, E., Suutarinen, J., Salminen, S., Verbeek, J.: Interventions for preventing injuries in the agricultural industry. Cochrane Database Syst. Rev. (1), CD006398 (2008)
16. Borsellino, V., Schimmenti, E., El Bilali, H.: Agri-food markets towards sustainable patterns. Sustainability **12**(6), 2193 (2020)
17. Rye, J.F., Scott, S.: International labour migration and food production in rural Europe: a review of the evidence. Sociol. Ruralis **58**(4), 928–952 (2018)
18. Rye, J.F., Slettebakk, M.H., Bjørkhaug, H.: From family to domestic and global labour? A decade of proletarisation of labour in the norwegian horticulture industry. Eur. Countryside **10**(4), 528–542 (2018)
19. Bjørkhaug, H., Magnan, A., Lawrence, G.: The financialization of agri-food systems: contested transformations. In: Earthscan Food and Agriculture. Routledge, Oxon (2018)
20. Ingram, J., Maye, D.: What are the implications of digitalisation for agricultural knowledge? Front. Sustain. Food Syst. **4**, 66 (2020)
21. Klerkx, L., Jakku, E., Labarthe, P.: A review of social science on digital agriculture, smart farming and agriculture 4.0: new contributions and a future research agenda. NJAS-Wageningen J. Life Sci. **90**, 100315 (2019)
22. Charatsari, C., Lioutas, E.D., De Rosa, M., Papadaki-Klavdianou, A.: Extension and advisory organizations on the road to the digitalization of animal farming: an organizational learning perspective. Animals **10**(11), 2056 (2020)
23. Stræte, E.P., Vik, J., Hansen, B.G.: The social robot: a study of the social and political aspects of automatic milking systems. In: Proceedings in System Dynamics and Innovation in Food Networks (2017). https://doi.org/10.18461/pfsd.2017.1722
24. Hansen, B.G., Herje, H.O., Höva, J.: Profitability on dairy farms with automatic milking systems compared to farms with conventional milking systems. Int. Food Agribus. Manage. Rev. 1–14 (2018). https://doi.org/10.22434/ifamr2018.0028
25. Holte, K.A., Follo, G., Kjestveit, K., Stræte, E.P.: Agriculture into the future: new technology, new organisation and new occupational health and safety risks? In: Bagnara, S., Tartaglia, R., Albolino, S., Alexander, T., Fujita, Y. (eds.) Proceedings of the 20th Congress of the International Ergonomics Association (IEA 2018). Advances in Intelligent Systems and Computing, vol. 825. Springer, Cham (2019)
26. Hansen, B.G., Stræte, E.P.: Dairy farmer's job satisfaction and the influence of automatic milking systems. Wageningen J. Life Sci. **92**, 100328 (2020)
27. Wolfert, S., Ge, L., Verdouw, C., Bogaardt, M.J.: Big data in smart farming–a review. Agric. Syst. **153**, 69–80 (2017)
28. Carayon, P., Hancock, P., Leveson, N., Noy, I., Sznelwar, L., van Hootegem, G.: Advancing a sociotechnical systems approach to workplace safety—developing the conceptual framework. Ergonomics **58**(4), 548–564 (2015)

29. Harvey, E.J., Waterson, P., Dainty, A.R.: Beyond ConCA: rethinking causality and construction accidents. Appl. Ergon. **73**, 108–121 (2018)
30. Kjestveit, K., Holte, K.A., Aas, O.: Occupational injury rates among Nowegian farmers; a sociotechnical perspective. J. Saf. Res. (Accepted)
31. Holte, K.A., Follo, G.: Making occupational health and safety training relevant for farmers: evaluation of an introductory course in occupational health and safety in Norway. Saf. Sci. **109**, 368–376 (2018)
32. Pawson, R., Greenhalgh, T., Harvey, G., Walshe, K.: Realist review – a new method of systematic review designed for complex policy interventions. J. Health Serv. Res. Policy **10**, 21–34 (2005)
33. Daugbjerg, C., Swinbank, A.: Ideas, Institutions and Trade: The WTO and the Curious Role of EU Farm Policy in Trade Liberalization. Oxford University Press, Oxford (2009)
34. Rommetvedt, H.: Matsystemet – et politisk-økonomisk system i endring. In: Rommetvedt, H. (ed.) Matmakt. Politikk, forhandling, marked. Bergen: Fagbokforlaget, pp. 13–35 (2009)
35. Farsund, A.: Norway: agricultural exceptionalism and the quest for free trade. In: Langhelle, O. (ed.) International Trade Negotiations and Domestic Politics, pp. 148–173. Routledge, London (2014)
36. Greig, M.A., Village, J., Dixon, S.M., Salustri, F.A., Neumann, W.P.: Assessing human factors and ergonomics capability in organisations – human factors intregration toolset. Ergonomics. **62**(10), 1254–1272 (2019)
37. Dul, J., Neumann, W.P.: Ergonomics contributions to company strategies. Appl. Ergon. **40**(4), 745–752 (2009)
38. Carayon, P.: The balance theory and the work system model … twenty years later. Int. J. Hum.-Comput. Interact. **25**(5), 313–327 (2009)
39. Leveson, N.: A new accident model for engineering safer systems. Saf. Sci. **42**, 237–270 (2004)
40. Rasmussen, J.: Risk management in a dynamic society: a modelling problem. Saf. Sci. **27**(2), 183–213 (1997)
41. Rommetvedt, H., Veggeland, F.: Parliamentary government and corporatism at the crossroads. Principals and agents in Norwegian agricultural policymaking. Govern. Opposit. **54**(4), 661–685 (2019)
42. Stræte, E.P., Jacobsen, E.: Integrasjon og konkurranse. Strukturendringer i matvaresystemet. In: Rommetvedt (ed) Matmakt. Politikk, forhandling, marked. Fagbokforlaget Vigmostad og Bjørke, Bergen (2002)
43. Hansen, B.G., Østerås, O.: Farmers welfare and animal welfare – exploring the relationship between farmer's occupational well-being and stress, farm expansion and animal welfare. Prevent. Veterinary Med. **170**, 104741 (2019)

# Manual Handling Task of Bovine Quarters Among Delivery Operators in a Chilean Slaughterhouse Company: A Case Study with Ergonomic Approximation

Carlos Ibarra[✉] [iD] and Pamela Astudillo[iD]

Occupational Ergonomics Program, Kinesiology Department, Faculty of Health Sciences, Atacama University, 1533722 Copiapó, Chile
carlos.ibarra@uda.cl

**Abstract.** Few studies in the South American context, and none in Chile, have been carried out in bovine slaughterhouse workers. However, the little evidence available mainly in North America and Europe is consistent with our findings, regarding the demands at the lumbar level, upper limbs and physical workload and the determinants of work activity. **Objectives:** Identify and describe the risk factors for WMSDs associated with Manual Handling of meat products, as well as other risk, the demand for physical work and biomechanical load, in truck loading and unloading activities in a slaughterhouse company and the determinants of work activity for the intervention. **Material and Methods:** Case study, observational descriptive cross-sectional design with mixed approach, considers the analysis of lumbar force moment, kinematic analysis and measurement of cardic frequency to determine the physiological workload, verbalizations, perceptions and observation of work activity **Results:** The Manual Handling of meat products exceeds 3400N of disc compression in L4-L5 and L5-S1 level, the % HRR is over 40% and the activity is determined by the type of working day, the organization of the distribution and the lack of means support mechanics for loading and unloading trucks. **Conclusions.** Manual Handling tasks in this industry are physically very demanding and improving these working conditions represents a major challenge for prevention and ergonomics.

**Keywords:** Ergonomic assessments · Meat industry · Workload · WMSDs · Manual handling

## 1 Introduction

Currently, musculoskeletal disorders (MSD) represent a considerable disease and economic burden in the world; lumbar and neck pain being one of the main causes of disability in most countries [1]. In Chile, MSDs are the most prevalent group of diseases in the working population, in 2018 MSDs represented 43%, a total of 2,445 occupational diseases being recognized in this group and the most frequent diagnoses were

N. L. Black et al. (Eds.): IEA 2021, LNNS 221, pp. 208–216, 2021.
https://doi.org/10.1007/978-3-030-74608-7_27

lateral epicondylitis, syndrome of rotator cuff, carpal tunnel syndrome and other synovitis and tenosynovitis [2]. However, it is unknown how many complaints and disease qualifications correspond to back injuries, which reveals the underreporting and lack of recognition of this type of work injury, a phenomenon that has been described in numbers of studies [1].

Despite everything in Chile, there are no studies that show the risks to which workers who handle large animals are exposed. The objective of this study was to identify and describe the risk factors for MSD associated with Manual Handling of Loads (MHL), as well as other risk factors for MSD, the demand for physical work and the biomechanical load, in loading and unloading activities. of meat products for dispatch to butchers in the city in a slaughterhouse.

## 2 Methodology

**Study Design:** An ergonomic study was carried out focused on the analysis of the work activity of loading and unloading operators in the distribution of meat products to butchers in a city in a large animal slaughtering company in southern Chile. The case study it's a descriptive, cross-sectional observational type, with a mixed approach, based in ergonomic work activity analyses [3, 4].

**Participants.** 4 male employees work at the bovine dispatch. During the work activity, all workers who were between 30 and 46 years old (38 ± 7.3) were interviewed and observed, in addition they had 3.9 (± 1.3) years working in the company, their average weight was of 84.8 Kg (± 11.6), height 1.70 m (± 1.5) and BMI of 29.3 (± 3.7).

**Observations and Verbalizations:** Open and planned field observations of the work activity was made during the working day, in 3 full days, in which photographic and video records were taken to analyze the tasks with Captiv® Software v. 1. 2100, to determine the times involved in each activity and the type of risk exposure for each operation. Observations were made filming with 2 cameras Cannon VIXIA® model HFR800 to analyze the tasks, always obtaining 2 planes of each record.

**Biomechanical Workload:** Kinovea® software version 0.8.15 was used to determine the angular displacement of body segments of the workers during MHL operations and then the 3D Static Strength Prediction Program ™ Version 7.0.5 University of Michigan® to assess compression and shear forces in the low back, included in the intervertebral discs of the L4-L5 and L5-S1 levels. For the push and pulling of loads, a measurement was made with a SHIMPO® dynamometer, model FGV-XY 500, then the value obtained was compared with the reference value in the Liberty Mutual Tables [5] considering the displacement condition of 2.1 m, for 8 hours of work and a height of application of force of 144 cm for men and with protection criteria of 90% of the workers. The weight of the beef quarters, the lambs, the heads and the trays with viscera were quantified in a digital industrial scale model 14191-489F and with the dynamometer if necessary.

**Dynamic Physiological Workload:** A monitoring the working heart rate was carry out using two Polar® heart rate monitors Vantage-V model and their traces were obtained with PolarFlow® software, then we export the data to excel spreadsheets to getting the Percentage of Heart Rate Reserve (% HHR) as an indicator of de workload. The Eq. (1) define the %HRR.

$$\%HRR = (HRwork - HRrest)/(HRmax - HRrest) \times 100 \qquad (1)$$

The resting heart rate (HRrest) was obtained with the workers seated for 30 min at the beginning of the work day and the maximum heart rate (HRmax) was obtained with the Eq. (2) [6].

$$HRmax = 220\text{-age.} \qquad (2)$$

Perception of effort was also required through the modified 10-point Borg Scale. The SigmaPlot® Software version 12 was used for the descriptive statistical analysis.

**Ethical Aspects:** Each participant was informed about the purpose of the study, the procedures that would be carried out, the benefits of the research-intervention, the confidentiality of personal data, as well as the scope of the study of the job. Their voluntary participation was requested with oral and written consent, respecting the criteria of the Declaration of Helsinki, regarding the privacy and confidentiality of the data collected throughout the process.

## 3 Results

### 3.1 Description of the Work Activity Analysis

In both tasks, loading and unloading dispatch truck, both the loader operator and the driver perform manual handling of heavy loads (MHL) when transporting the Bovine Front Quarters (73 Kg), Rear Quarters (81 Kg); Heads (16Kg); Lambs (16 Kg), Boxes with viscera (60 Kg) and Hooks (3 Kg), among others, from the slaughterhouse storage area to the dispatch truck or from the truck to the butcher shop in the case of dispatch. Workers must manually manipulate the pieces of meat (Fig. 1A), pushing them along the rails and/or manually transporting them over one shoulder, in addition to cutting each half of the beef hanging on the rail, at the height of the ninth or tenth rib with a handsaw and a knife, while holding it with one arm and shoulder. To then mount with de load the ramp of approximately 3 m in length with a slope greater than 20°, until reaching the platform that is at the height of the dispatch truck where they deposit the beef quarter on a hook on the rail inside the truck. This on wet floors due to fluids and cleaning with water, for which a rubber mat is available on the ramp.

The second task evaluated is the unloading of the truck in the dispatch to the butchers, both workers must manually manipulate the meat pieces again (Fig. 1B). In this task, the roles of both operators are more differentiated. Regarding the bovine quarters, which is the most frequent activity, the driver pushes the meat pieces on the rails of the truck to bring them closer to the door where the loader operator is waiting. For this, the driver unhooks the piece from the rail and holds it manually with the hooks to gently deposit it on the worker shoulder (Fig. 1B). It is an important effort, which the worker qualifies

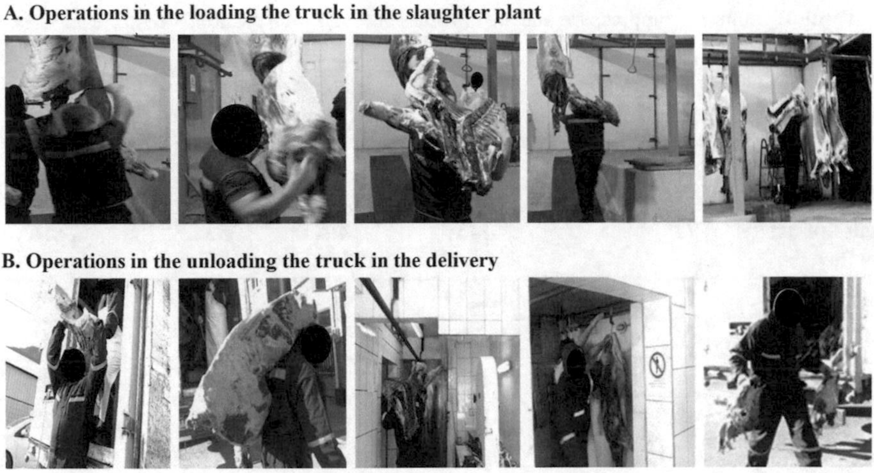

**A. Operations in the loading the truck in the slaughter plant**

**B. Operations in the unloading the truck in the delivery**

**Fig. 1.** Operations of manual handling of loads in activity of loading (A) and unloading (B) of the bovine quarters in the dispatch truck.

with 8 points on the Borg scale and involves a static muscular effort when holding the heavy load for a few seconds. The operator then manually lifts and transports the beef quarter from the truck to the unloading area of each butcher shop on the planned route. At this point the working context becomes extremely variable, since in each delivery point the conditions vary, considering the parking of the truck, the weather conditions, the presence of stray animals (dogs) and others obstacles during the manual transport holding the load on one of his shoulders, with the absence of mechanical assistance devices for loading and unloading the truck. On the other hand, the boxes with viscera weighing 60 kg are transported as a team by both workers, and the heads are transported by both, but individually (Fig. 1B). To this manual activity, the cognitive activity associated with controlling the dispatch order is added with respect to what is being delivered and in some cases the receipt of cash for pending payments.

### 3.2 Biomechanical Workload

The manual handling activities described in Table 1, in general, exceeds 3400N of disc compression [7], both in the loading phase at the slaughterhouse and in the unloading during delivery in the butcher shops in different places of the city. The operations that generate greater compression are the MHL of the Posterior Bovine Quarters (81 Kg) with 5,844 N for L4-L5 and 4,612 N for L5-S1; then the raising of 2 lambs simultaneously (30 Kg) with a compression of 4,557 N in L5-S1 and with 4,323 N in L4-L5 and the raising of the Anterior Bovine Quarters (76 Kg) with 4.143 N for L4-L5 and 4.041 N for L5-S1.

The results of the initial forces of push and pull allowed to show that the workers when pushing with both hands above the level of the head a half of a bovine hanging on the rail (160 Kg), is 51.2 Kg * f , exceeding 31 Kg * f which is the acceptable limit (25.26). In the pulling of the viscera box (60 kg) the initial force is 27.3 Kg * f, the limit

**Table 1.** Lumbar compression and shear forces at levels L4-L5 and L5-S1 for each Task

| Lifting tasks | Unit weight (Kg) | Compression force (N) | | Shear force (N) | |
|---|---|---|---|---|---|
| | | L4-L5 | L5-S1 | L4-L5 | L5-S1 |
| Posterior quarter bovine | 81 | 5844* | 4612* | 39 | 923 |
| Anterior quarter bovine | 73 | 4143* | 4041* | 253 | 816 |
| Lambs | 16 | 4323* | 4557* | 387 | 598 |
| Beef heads | 16 | 2687 | 2838 | 278 | 551 |
| Box with viscera | 60 | 3886* | 3988* | 137 | 499 |
| **Average** | **49,2** | **4176,6*** | **4007,2*** | **218,8** | **677,4** |
| **Standard deviation** | **±31,2** | **±1129,8** | **±713,5** | **±134,1** | **±182,8** |

\* Exceeds the NIOSH recommended compression limit of 3400 N

being 23 Kg \* f, therefore in both cases the maximum acceptable for a working day is exceeded.

The effort for each worker is important depending on the time the load must be fully supported during the MHL (Fig. 2). The time of each lifting operation is always longer when unloading at the butchers. Lifting each load lasts 1.86 s (± 0.53 s), manually carrying 11.17 s (± 2.08 s), lowering the load 2.68 s (± 1.29 s). While the operations of pushing 2,6 s (+-0,67 s) and pulling 2,2 s (± 0,9 s) loads are greater during the loading of the truck in the slaughter plant.

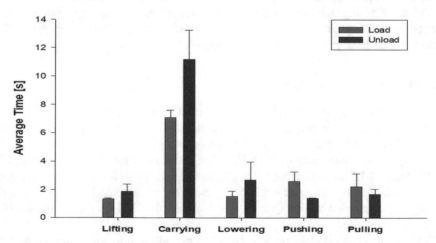

**Fig. 2.** Average time of MHL operations during the task of loading and unloading the dispatch truck, obtained with Captiv® program

### 3.3  Dynamic Physiological Workload

Regarding the analysis of %HRR (Fig. 3), the global average of the day (8 h) is 48.2% (±6.4%), means it's a heavy work. The highest values are presented during the loading of the truck 66.3% (±4.9%), one of the longest continuous phases of approximately 1 h and in several downloads in the delivery phase in the butcher shops, with higher values (66.8% ± 20.7%) in shorter cycles of 15 to 20 min.

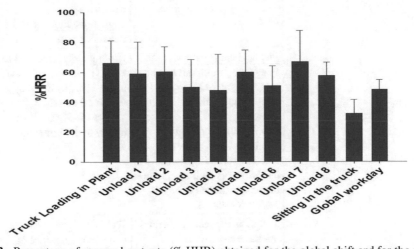

**Fig. 3.** Percentage of reserve heart rate (% HHR) obtained for the global shift and for the main tasks of loading and unloading the truck

### 3.4  Determinants of Work Activity

In Table 2 it shows the determinants of work activity in loading and unloading meat products from delivery trucks.

**Table 2.** Determinants of work activity in loading and unloading meat products

| Category determinants | Macro determinants | Micro determinants |
|---|---|---|
| The conditions offered by the workplace | Work organization: Teamwork of 2 people, in normal working hours, manual work Organization of training: There is no training in the MHL | Work rate: Very Intense 1h for the load. Reduced time in each discharge, with insufficient periods for rest. There is no established pause in city deliveries High unloading variability: No unloading parking on the street |
| | Physical environment at the Plant: Very cold, rail height, ramp height and length, slippery ground, distance to truck Physical environment in butchers: Cold, storage location variability, floor height, doors, entrance, ramps or steps, distance to travel, various obstacles | Raw material: Beef (73 to 81 kg.). The lamb loads relatively heavy (16Kg.) But they are handled 3 at a time. Box of viscera (60 Kg), without trolley to drag or push, regular grip |
| | Technical device: Truck does not have mechanical assistance devices such as hydraulic arm for unloading, joining of rails with loading areas | Technical device: Manual rail in the plant, absence of mechanical and / or automated aids, knife, handsaw, tray, short and long hooks, plastic box, difficult to grip, dimensions, weight and design |
| The social environment | Hierarchical relationships: Authoritarian Functional relationships: Adequate for the achievement of objectives | Relations with clients and users: variable contexts, cordial relationships, in some cases demanding |
| Tasks and demands | Task: Food safety policies determine the types of cuts of large animals | Procedure: Precision to insert the knife into the intercostal space (9th or 10th rib), cut, cross to the other side without reaching the vertebra. Insert the handsaw hard to make a hole for the truck rail hook to be inserted. Work physically demanding; Payment control |

# 4   Discussion

The study confirmed that MHL tasks in the meat processing industry are physically demanding, with the application of significant manual force, with very high biomechanical and physiological demands [8, 9]. Few studies in the South American context [10, 11], and in Chile none, have been carried out in bovine slaughterhouse workers, however, the little evidence available mainly in North America and Europe [8, 9] is consistent with the findings of this case study, regarding the demands at the lumbar level, upper extremities and the physical workload.

The results of the analysis of the% HRR showed that these activities can be categorized as heavy work, having globally in the working day values above the 30% limit of% HRR [12]. Current recommendations for maximum acceptable working hours suggest that an average worker in a physically demanding occupation can sustain 29, 31, 35 and 44% VO2max for 12, 10, 8 and 4 hours respectively [13, 14]. If the direct relationship between % VO2Max and % HRR [6] is considered, we can affirm that it is not advisable to sustain a full 8-hour shift at that level of demand.

The fact that much of the time, the load is sustained or manipulated at the level of the shoulders, is also important given that there is evidence that indicates that this increases the biomechanical risk and the physical workload [8, 10, 11]. This can be significantly reduced with mechanical aids and automation, such as mechanization or automation of rails, change of channels from tubular to bi-rail, a hydraulic truck loading arm, transport carts for cattle and lamb rooms for unloading, or even the use of exoskeletons, among others and by focusing ergonomic intervention on determinants of work organization such as work and rest cycles [8–10].

# 5   Conclusion

It is important to note that price competition and the continuous search for productivity gains that accompany this type of work have direct effects on working conditions and workers' health. The problem of MSDs in meat processing establishments is not new and risk prevention actions should be a priority, just as food safety conditions are surveyed today in this industry, working conditions should also be surveyed and particularly those of MHL associated with the production process.

Improving these working conditions and the regulation of these aspects at the time of authorizing the operation of butcher shops and slaughter plants represents a challenge for public health policy and for those who are dedicated to risk prevention, ergonomics and production.

# References

1. Vos, T., Allen, C., Arora, M., Barber, R.M., Brown, A., Carter, A., et al.: Global, regional, and national incidence, prevalence, and years lived with disability for 310 diseases and injuries, 1990–2015: a systematic analysis for the global burden of disease study 2015. Lancet. **388**, 1545–1602 (2016). https://doi.org/10.1016/S0140-6736(16)31678-6

2. Superintendencia de Seguridad Social de Chile. Informe Estadísticas de Accidentabilidad 2019. SUSESO (2020). https://www.suseso.cl/607/articles-595996_archivo_01.pdf. Accessed 09 Feb 2021
3. St-Vincent, M., Vézina, N., Bellemare, M., Denis, D., Ledoux, É., Imbeau, D.: Ergonomic intervention. Institut de recherche robert-sauvé en santé et en sécurité du travail (IRSST), Montréal (2014)
4. Guérin, F., Laville, T., Daniellou, F., Durrafourg, J., Kerguelen, A.: Comprendre le travail pour le transformer: la pratique de l'ergonomie. ANACT, Lyon (2006)
5. Snook, S.H., Ciriello, V.M.: The design of manual handling tasks: revised tables of maximum acceptable weights and forces. Ergonomics 34(9), 1197–213 (1991). https://doi.org/10.1080/00140139108964855
6. Robergs, R.A., Landwehr, R.: The surprising history of the "HRmax = 220-age" equation. J. Exerc. Physiol. Online 5(2), 1–10 (2002)
7. Waters, T.R., Putz-Anderson, V., Garg, A., Fine, L.J.: Revised NIOSH equation for the design and evaluation of manual lifting tasks. Ergonomics 36(7), 749–776 (1993)
8. Institute National de Recherche en Santé et Sécurité de France. Pour améliorer le transport et la livraison des carcasses de viande. INRS France (2016). https://www.inrs.fr/media.html?refINRS=ED%206252. Accessed 09 Feb 2021
9. Toulouse, G., Vézina, N., Geoffrion, L.: Étude descriptive des déterminants des facteurs de risque de LATR aux postes d'éviscération abdominale de deux abattoirs de porcs. IRSST Québec (1995). https://www.irsst.qc.ca/publications-et-outils/publication/i/470/n/etude-descriptive-des-determinants-des-facteurs-de-risque-de-latr-aux-postes-d-evisceration-abdominale-de-deux-abattoirs-de-porcs-r-108. Accessed 09 Dec 2021
10. Tirloni, A.S., dos Reis, D.C., Dias, N.F., Moro, A.R.P.: Ergonomic risk evaluation of the manual handling task of bovine quarters in a Brazilian slaughterhouse. In: Goonetilleke, R., Karwowski, W. (eds) Advances in Physical Ergonomics and Human Factors. AHFE 2019. AISC, vol. 967, pp. 57–69. Springer, Washington (2020). https://doi.org/10.1007/978-3-030-20142-5_6
11. Vergara, L.G.L., Pansera, T.R.: Ergonomics analysis of the activity of boning shoulder in a pig slaughter-house in the city of Ipiranga-SC. Work 41, 703–709 (2012). https://doi.org/10.3233/WOR-2012-0229-703
12. Ministerio del Trabajo y Previsión Social de Chile. Guía Técnica para la Evaluación del Trabajo Pesado. Superintendencia de Pensiones (2010). https://www.spensiones.cl/portal/institucional/594/articles-12791_guia_tecnica_evaluacion.pdf. Accessed 09 Feb 2021
13. Gupta, N., Jensen, B.S., Søgaard, K., Carneiro, I.G., Christiansen, C.S., Hanisch, C., Holtermann, A.: Face validity of the single work ability item: comparison with objectively measured heart rate reserve over several days. Int. J. Environ. Res. Public Health 11(5), 5333–5348 (2014). https://doi.org/10.3390/ijerph110505333
14. Wu, H.C., Wang, M.J.J.: Relationship between maximum acceptable work time and physical workload. Ergonomics 45(4), 280–289 (2002). https://doi.org/10.1080/00140130210123499

# Development of Underground Posture Assessment Tool (UPAT) for Underground Enclosed Spaces: The Algerian Foggara as an Example

Bouhafs Mebarki[1] ⓘ, Mohammed Mokdad[2](✉) ⓘ, Mourad Semmani[3] ⓘ, and Ibrahim Mokdad[4] ⓘ

[1] Laboratory of Ergonomics, University of Oran 2, Oran, Algeria
mebarki.bouhafs@univ-oran2.dz
[2] College of Arts, University of Bahrain, Sakhir, Bahrain
mmokdad@uob.edu.bh
[3] University of Adrar and Laboratory of Ergonomics and Risks Prevention, University of Oran 2, Adrar, Algeria
mouradsmpsy@univ-adrar.edu.dz
[4] Mohammed Shaikhedine Establishment, Manama, Bahrain

**Abstract.** The traditional irrigation system called Foggara is still used at a large scale in the western deserts of Algeria. In order for the Foggaras to survive, they must be maintained. Maintaining Foggara needs a lot of human work along the year, particularly in hot months when the water becomes vital for humans, animals and the palmary as a whole. Foggara maintenance work is usually done underground in wells, tunnels and shafts (confined areas).

This research aims to develop an ergonomics assessment tool for working postures in confined underground spaces. Research sample consisted of 13 male subjects working in the Foggara maintenance for many years. The development of the tool has gone through various stages.

Researchers were able to build the tool (UPAT) that fits the situation being researched. UPAT has been proven to be valid and reliable, not to be used in this research only, but to be accessible to other researchers to use in similar situations.

The use of the tool in the field, showed that Foggara maintenance workers, whether working in wells or in tunnel, adopt different working postures (standing, stooping, squatting, kneeling and crawling), for different time periods. The full picture of what is happening in the maintenance of the Foggara can be extrapolated from these partial results. Therefore, it can be comprehended that this type of work is hazardous, tiring and exhausting as it involves a lot of physical, mental and psychological stress.

**Keywords:** Foggara · Standing postures · Kneeling postures · Squatting postures · Crawling postures · Confined areas

N. L. Black et al. (Eds.): IEA 2021, LNNS 221, pp. 217–224, 2021.
https://doi.org/10.1007/978-3-030-74608-7_28

# 1   Introduction

The traditional irrigation system called Foggara is still used at a large scale in the western deserts of Algeria. Most of the palmary oasis relay on such irrigation system, without which life cannot exist in desert Sahara around palmary oasis [1].

It is necessary to maintain the Foggara to ensure the flow of water to the inhabitants and to the farms.

Maintaining Foggara irrigation system needs a lot of human work along the year, particularly in hot months when the water becomes vital for humans, animals and the palmary as a whole. Foggara maintenance work is usually done underground in wells, tunnels and shafts. This work space is a confined and underground space, characterized by poor physical working conditions, and carried out in wet floor over which water flows. So the work in this work space imposes awkward, non-conventional work postures on workers [2].

This research aims to develop an ergonomics assessment tool for working postures in confined underground spaces in which restricted movements are present. In addition it aims to evaluate work postures adopted by Foggara maintenance workers while performing the work.

# 2   Methods

## 2.1   Sample

It consisted of 13 male subjects working in the Foggara maintenance for many years. The average age was 33.84 years $\pm$ 8.84 (mean $\pm$ SD), the average mass was 71.7 kg $\pm$ 07.7, the average stature was 167.0 cm $\pm$ 8.4 and the average work experience was 08.38 years $\pm$ 04.64. The sample was chosen using convenience sampling method. All members agreed to be observed to record their working postures while inside the wells or the tunnel, taking gravel, stones, sand and dirt that impede the flow of water in the Foggara. Each of them has signed a consent form to participate in the research.

## 2.2   Data Collection Tool

The literature on methods of measuring working postures was examined. It turned out that a large number of methods exist such as OWAS [3], RULA [4], REBA [5].

All of these methods have been examined and found that they could not measure all the work postures that were observed during the maintenance of the Foggara. So, it was decided to build a new tool that would be able to measure the different work postures adopted by workers during the maintenance of the Foggara.

The development of the tool has gone through the following stages:

1. **Video recording of working postures during Foggara maintenance:** Two Foggara maintenance workers were observed and recorded at work by one researcher (S.M.). Maintenance work was done in Othman bin Issa's Foggara in Tasabit (Adrar governorate). Each worker was observed and recorded the length of time he worked, using a Canon camera (Canon PowerShot D30).

2. **Definition and classification of postures:** Two researchers (B.M. & M.M.) analyzed the videos at the University of Adrar (Algeria). The analysis was done on the monitor after the recording has been completed. It was found that Foggara maintenance workers adopt multiple postures while they work in the Foggara tunnel and wells. These postures are classified into five categories: (1) standing postures, (2) stooping postures, (3) kneeling postures, (4) squatting postures, and (5) crawling postures.
3. **Developing the tool:** The tool has three sections: explanatory instructions, demographic data, and posture drawings that include standing, stooping, kneeling, squatting and crawling postures (Fig. 1).
4. **Tool testing:** Under the supervision of the researcher (S.M.), two raters tested the tool with seven workers. This operation was completed in two days (July 27 & 28, 2020). It was found that the tool is appropriate for field use.
5. **Data collection:** For the data collection and storage a custom solution was developed by one of the researchers (I.M.) using Python and Flask web framework (for the business model. However, for the data storage, postgres database was used. Data collectors (under the supervision of S.M.) through their mobile phones and the custom solution would simply observe the worker and add the time for every posture the worker is adopting.

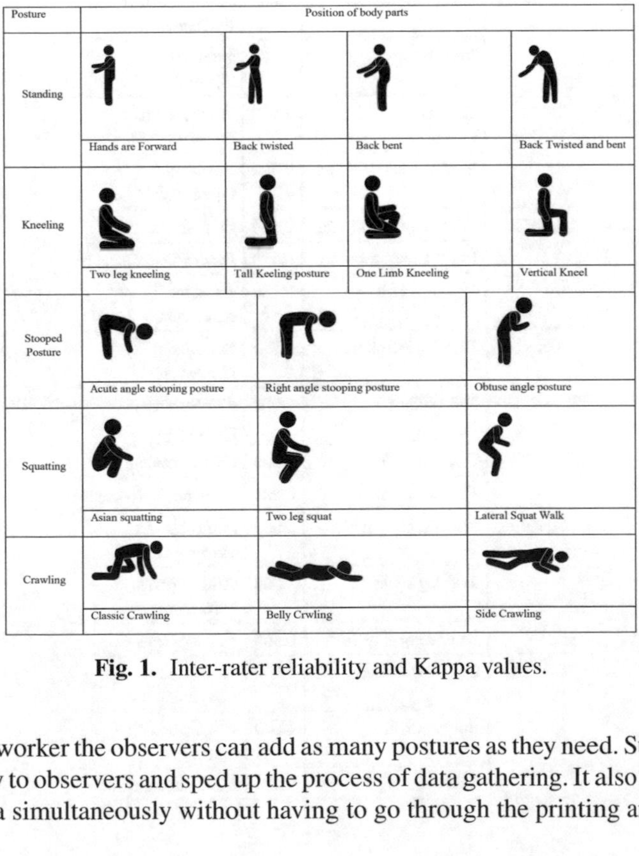

**Fig. 1.** Inter-rater reliability and Kappa values.

For each worker the observers can add as many postures as they need. Such a solution gave mobility to observers and sped up the process of data gathering. It also allowed them to gather data simultaneously without having to go through the printing and syncing of data.

# 3 Results

This research sought to achieve two goals:

## 3.1 First, the Development of an Ergonomics Assessment Tool for Working Postures in Confined Underground Spaces

A tool was developed. Researchers have confirmed both the validity and the reliability of the tool. As to the validity, researchers used the content validity. A group of four experts (one ergonomics practitioner, two Foggara workers and the director of the national observatory of Foggara in Adrar engineer Y.B.) assessed the content validity of the tool in terms of content, inclusivity and ease of use. The experts (100%) agreed that the tool measures working postures in the Foggara, is comprehensive and easy to use.

As to the reliability, researchers computed the inter-rater reliability (the extent of agreement among data collectors). According to Bao, et al. [6] inter-rater reliability is

**Table 1.** Inter-rater reliability and Kappa values.

| Posture | sub- posture | k | Interpretation |
|---------|--------------|-----|----------------|
| Standing | Hands are forward | 1.000 | Almost perfect agreement |
| | Back twisted | 0.700 | Substantial agreement |
| | Back bent | 1.000 | Almost perfect agreement |
| | Back twisted and bent | 0.700 | Substantial agreement |
| Stooped | Acute angle stooping | 0.300 | Fair agreement |
| | Right angle stooping | 0.588 | Moderate agreement |
| | Obtuse angle | 0.720 | Substantial agreement |
| Kneeling | Two-leg kneeling | 0.696 | Substantial agreement |
| | Tall keeling | 1.000 | Almost perfect agreement |
| | One limb kneeling | 0.300 | Fair agreement |
| | Vertical kneel | 0.588 | Moderate agreement |
| Squatting | Asian squatting | 1.000 | Almost perfect agreement |
| | Two-leg squat | 1.000 | Almost perfect agreement |
| | Lateral squat walk | 0.364 | Fair agreement |
| Crawling | Classic crawling | 1.000 | Almost perfect agreement |
| | Belly crawling | 1.000 | Almost perfect agreement |
| | Side crawling | 0.588 | Moderate agreement |

convenient to assess posture observations reliability. Two raters were asked to assess the posture of seven workers. Results are shown in Table 1.

The interpretation of the obtained results was done in light of the proposals presented by Landis and Koch [7].

It is noticed that reliability of each working position is good. Since the almost perfect agreement between the raters has occurred seven times at a percentage of (41)%, and the substantial agreement has occurred four times at a percentage of (24)%, and the moderate agreement has occurred twice at a rate of (24%), and the fair agreement has occurred four times at a rate of (24%), it can be said that the tool has a respectable level of reliability.

## 3.2   Second, the Evaluation of Work Postures Adopted by Foggara Maintenance Workers While Performing the Work

The data recorded was stored in a JavaScript Object Notation format. This allowed for easier grouping of postures for each individual. Some individuals performed the same posture several times for different durations. Those cases were combined and the mean was calculated generating a single number for every posture. Based on a predefined set of rules (The worker can perform the work in a bad posture for a short period, and if the work time in this posture increases, the worker may be able to do the work, but if the work continues in this posture for a longer period of time, the worker may not be able to do the work at all). The conclusions were easily made.

The custom solution would easily map those rules to the data recorded and that allows for the researchers to easily determine which posture is commonly performed by the sample and for each individual and how that can impact the respective individual.

**Table 2.** Working postures and time spent at Foggara work.

| Working site | Working posture | Sub-posture | % Time spent | Working time |
|---|---|---|---|---|
| Wells and shafts | Standing | Standing with hands forward | 74 | 120 m |
| | | Standing back twisted | 07 | |
| | | Standing back bent | 14 | |
| | | Standing back twisted and bent | 05 | |
| Foggara tunnel | Stooping | Acute angle stooping posture | 13 | 120 m |
| | | Right angle stooping posture | 7 | |
| | | Obtuse angle stooping posture | 7 | |
| | Kneeling | Two-leg kneeling | 28 | |
| | | Tall keeling | 6 | |
| | | One-limb kneeling | 5 | |
| | | Vertical kneel | 1 | |
| | Squatting | Asian squat | 16 | |
| | | Two-leg squat, | 3 | |
| | | Lateral squat walk | 1 | |
| | Crawling | Classic crawling | 5 | |
| | | Belly crawling | 1 | |
| | | Side crawling | 7 | |

As to the maintenance of wells and shafts, Table 2 illustrates that workers spend a lot of time doing the work in awkward working postures.

# 4  Discussion

Nowadays, researchers have a large number of postural observation techniques at work. Each technique has its own peculiarities and features that distinguish it. In this context, Kee & Karwowski, [8] stated that "each technique has its own strengths and weaknesses depending upon the industries or assumptions made". It is necessary for the researcher to be aware of these characteristics in order to be able to choose the tool that fits his research completely. The researcher may sometimes have to build the tool that fits the variables of the research he is conducting. In this way the current research proceeded. The researchers were able to build a tool (UPAT) that has been proven to be valid and reliable, not to be used in this research only, but to be accessible to other researchers to use in similar situations.

The application of the present ergonomics evaluation tool for Working Postures in Confined Underground Spaces (UPAT) in the maintenance of Foggara irrigation system demonstrated that UPAT is a reliable analysis and evaluation tool for the identification of working postures occurring in such tasks. Extrapolation and generalization of these findings to similar work conditions (confined underground spaces) should be considered with some reserve. The application of UPAT in these conditions is well justified to assert its utility for the evaluation of working postures in different confined underground space tasks like mining, sewerage network, underground electricity and telephone network, and the like.

With regard to the maintenance of the Foggara wells and shafts, it is known in Ergonomics that standing for long hours with the inability to move or walk causes many health problems for humans [9]. This is exactly what applies to those who work in the maintenance of Foggara, where the workplace is confined and does not allow movement or walking in the presence of water and mud.

Concerning the maintenance of the Foggara tunnel, it was found that the most common working postures adopted by workers are the two-leg kneeling posture, the Asian squatting posture, the acute-angle stooping posture, and the side crawling posture. As is evident, all of them are awkward postures (deviating from the neutral posture, whether in sitting or standing) to cause health problems for workers. Many researchers have warned of the danger of such postures [10].

It was found that working in the Foggara is tiresome and dangerous as well. What increases the risk of the work are other factors, including that it is carried out in a confined area, done underground, under very poor physical conditions (darkness and humidity), and done in water.

Ergonomics practitioners have shown that underground work is both strenuous and dangerous because it endangers workers' lives [11]. Risks in this type of work include heavy physical labor, chemical fumes, radon gas, hypoxia, suffocation, possibly falling roofs or caves. Sometimes this work has to be done in a pressurized environment. In addition to these risks, work in Foggara maintenance sometimes causes workers to drown. When the workers remove the stones, sand, and dirt that obstructed the flow of water, the water that collects at the site of the blockage will flow like a torrent, sweeping away whatever it finds in front of it.

Ergonomics practitioners have shown that the poor physical environment (noise, lighting, temperature, humidity, etc.,) influences employee's attitudes, behaviors, satisfaction, performance and productivity [12]. They believe that working in a workplace where the physical environment is supportive and good can effectively promote health and quality of workers [13]. One of the important physical conditions is lighting. Research shows that an adequate amount of light improves mood and energy levels, while poor lighting contributes to depression and other deficiencies in the body [14].

With regard to the Foggara, researchers using Light Meter (PCE-170 A) found that the level of lighting varies. It is slightly illuminated at the exit, and at the bottom of the well and ventilation shafts, but in the tunnel, especially in the area between the ventilation shafts, it is dark.

Foggara maintenance work includes doing the majority of activities in sandy-clay soil. Such soil encourages workers to do the work barefooted. Working in sandy-clay soil for a long period of time exposes workers to some health problems such as tropical immersion foot [15]. This is precisely what we noticed with some workers, especially the elderly with whom clear feet defects can be seen [16]. In addition to safety, sandy-clay soil affects human movement. When compared with dry soil, sandy-clay soil negatively affects the movement. Further it increases the risk of slips and falls [17].

## 5   Conclusion

UPAT results and the evaluations of both the experts and raters demonstrated that working postures in the maintenance of Foggara irrigation system are awkward, strenuous and dangerous.

Results were obtained from the work of workers in Foggara maintenance for two hours (in the well and shafts maintenance) and two hours (in tunnel maintenance). To have a complete picture, we must not forget that Foggara maintenance workers usually work for about four to five hours per day, especially in the hot months (May - September). Work usually starts at about (05) am in the morning and continues until about (10) am. The full picture of what is happening in the maintenance of the Foggara can be extrapolated from these partial results.

**Acknowledgements.** Special thanks go to the president and members of the association of the Foggara ( Mohamed Djelloul), particularly to: Mr. Djoudi Mohamed & Kina Abdelkader. In addition to the president and members of the association of the Foggara (Tagraf), particularly to: Reggani Hassane, Reggani M'Barek, Kessassi Djelloul & Bahki Mostapha.

## References

1. Ait-Saadi, M.A., Remini, B.: Water in the ksours: what genius? Case of Timimoun and Tiout (Algeria). J. Fundam. Appl. Sci. **12**(2), 525–537 (2020)

2. Mokdad, M., Mebarki, B., Mokdad, I., Bouabdallah, L.: Ergonomics of date palm irrigation work: Algerian Foggara as an example. In: International Conference on Applied Human Factors and Ergonomics, pp. 282–288. Springer, Cham (2020)
3. Karhu, O., Kansi, P., Kuorinka, I.: Correcting working postures in industry: a practical method for analysis. Appl. Ergon. **8**, 199–201 (1977)
4. McAtamney, L., Corlett, E.N.: RULA: a survey method for the investigation of work-related upper limb disorders. Appl. Ergon. **24**(2), 91–99 (1993)
5. Hignett, S., McAtamney, L.: Rapid entire body assessment (REBA). Appl. Ergon. **31**(2), 201–205 (2000)
6. Bao, S., Howard, N., Spielholz, P., Silverstein, B., Polissar, N.: Interrater reliability of posture observations. Hum. Factors **51**(3), 292–309 (2009)
7. Landis, J.R., Koch, G.G.: The measurement of observer agreement for categorical data. Biometrics **33**(1), 159–174 (1977)
8. Kee, D., Karwowski, W.: A comparison of three observational techniques for assessing postural loads in industry. Int. J. Occup. Saf. Ergon. **13**(1), 3–14 (2007)
9. Fewster, K.M., Gallagher, K.M., Howarth, S.H., Callaghan, J.P.: Low back pain development differentially influences centre of pressure regularity following prolonged standing. Gait Posture **78**, e1–e6 (2020)
10. Anagha, R., Xavier, A.S.: A review on ergonomic risk factors causing musculoskeletal disorders among construction workers. Int. J. Eng. Res. Technol. **9**(06), 1234–1236 (2020)
11. Kim, I.J.: ergonomic inputs for the improvement of safety and health exercises in the mining industry. J. Ergon. **8**(1), 1–3 (2018)
12. Katabaro, J.M., Yan, Y.: Effects of lighting quality on working efficiency of workers in office building in Tanzania. J. Environ. Public Health **2019**, 1–12 (2019)
13. Lee, S.Y., Chaudhury, H., Lee, S.J.: Effect of physical environment on the behaviors of residents with dementia: a comparison between a small-group unit and a traditional care unit. J. Civ. Eng. Archit. **8**, 1353–1363 (2014)
14. Kompier, M.E., Smolders, K.C., van MarkenLichtenbelt, W.D., de Kort, Y.A.: Effects of light transitions on measures of alertness, arousal and comfort. Physiol. Behav. **223**, 1–12 (2020)
15. Zani, M.L.C., Lazzarini, R., Silva-Junior, J.S.: Warm-water immersion foot among car wash workers. Rev. Brasileira Med. Trabalho **15**(3), 217 (2017)
16. Barbe, M.F., Barr, A.E.: Inflammation and the pathophysiology of work-related musculoskeletal disorders. Brain Behav. Immunity **20**(5), 423–429 (2006)
17. Moncalero, M., Signetti, S., Mazzanti, B., Bruzzi, P., Pugno, N.M., Colonna, M.: Effect of material elastic properties and surface roughness on grip performances of ski boot soles under wet and icy conditions. Int. J. Ind. Ergon. **61**, 62–70 (2017)

# Ergonomics Intervention Program to Train Water Measurers (Al-Kayyals) for Work at Foggara Irrigation System in Algeria

Bouhafs Mebarki[1] (iD), Mohammed Mokdad[2]([⊠]) (iD), Mourad Semmani[3] (iD), and Imane Mokdad[4] (iD)

[1] Laboratory of Ergonomics, University of Oran 2, Oran, Algeria
mebarki.bouhafs@univ-oran2.dz
[2] College of Arts, University of Bahrain, Sakhir, Bahrain
mmokdad@uob.edu.bh
[3] University of Adrar and Laboratory of Ergonomics and Risks Prevention, University of Oran 2, Adrar, Algeria
mouradsmpsy@univ-adrar.edu.dz
[4] 01Systems, Manama, Bahrain
imokdad@01systems.com

**Abstract.** The Foggara system consists of two main parts: The water obtaining part and the water distribution part. One of the main figures in the management of the Foggara system is the water measurer (Al-Kayyal). Among his work activities are monitoring the amount of water that flows from Foggara, and measuring the share of each beneficiary. Al-Kayyal should have basic knowledge of math, keep accurate records, be honest, intelligent, and have religious values.

Nowadays, most of Al-Kayyals are elderly. They are unable to fulfill the demands of water measuring job. As a result, many Foggaras have serious problems to stay functioning in the absence of Al-Kayyal. The aim of the present research is to introduce a training program to train interested young people to do the job of Al-Kayyal.

Researchers chose randomly five students who expressed a desire to learn the profession of Al-Kayyal. They are of approximate age (mean age was 22.40 and standard deviation of 1.14 years). The data collection tool was the ergonomics intervention program. The development of the program has gone through four successive phases: preparation, implementation, evaluation and follow-up phases. It consisted of (8) sessions as follows: an introductory session, (5) working sessions to cover both the theoretical and practical parts of the program, a closing session for evaluating the program and a final session for follow-up.

The evaluation of the program using both the quantitative (experimental), and the qualitative (Kirkpatrick model) approaches, and the follow-up test have confirmed the program effectiveness.

**Keywords:** Foggara · Al-Kayyal · Intervention program · Job competencies

N. L. Black et al. (Eds.): IEA 2021, LNNS 221, pp. 225–232, 2021.
https://doi.org/10.1007/978-3-030-74608-7_29

# 1    Introduction

Physically, the Foggara system consists of two main parts: First, the water obtaining part which consists of the main well, shafts used for maintenance and ventilation of the Foggara, and a tunnel of several kilometers in length, with a low slope that leads to the delivery of groundwater to the surface of the earth. Second, the water distribution part which consists of the Kasriya (the comb-shaped distributer of water to the beneficiaries participating in the water of the Foggara), the Saqiyah (channel that delivers water to beneficiaries), and the Majen (the basin in which the farmer collects the water carried by the channel for use when needed) [1].

The Kasriya is placed at the outlet of each Foggara. The intervals between its teeth are calculated so as to allow a certain amount of water to reach the beneficiary. The flow of the Foggara is constant in principle, so that each beneficiary receives the same amount of water at night as during the day. This amount is either used or stored in the Majen.

The Ministry of Culture in Algeria and the UNESCO are now keenly interested in the Foggara. In 2018, the job of Al-Kayyal was considered a great human heritage [2].

One of the main figures in the management of the Foggara system is the water measurer (Al-Kayyal). He is the person who calculates the amount of water that is given to any of the beneficiaries. Among his work activities are monitoring the amount of water that flows from Foggara, measuring the share of each beneficiary, designing the Kasriya, and checking the Saqiyah that transports water to beneficiaries as he makes sure that there is nothing obstructing the flow of water.

However, the job competencies (knowledge, skills, abilities, other things) that make Al-Kayyal successful on the job, are to have a basic knowledge of math, to maintain neat and accurate records, to be honest, sincere, intelligent, religious and ethical. If these competencies are available, Al-Kayyal does his job properly and efficiently accompanied by his assistant Al-Zammam (the book keeper).

Currently, most of the Al-Kayyals are elderly. They are hardly able to fulfill the demanding task of water measurement. For this reason, a number of Foggaras are having serious problems staying functioning in the absence of the Al-Kayyal, and finding replacement to fulfill his duties.

Researchers have warned of the shortage in the people doing the water measurement job. Remini, et al. [3] stated; "the scarcity of Al-Kayyal has become a thorny social problem". Slimani, et al. [4] commended the role of Al-Kayyal in the continuation of the Foggara life, and stressed its importance.

The aim of the present research is to develop, implement, evaluate and follow-up an ergonomics intervention program to train young people to acquire the job competencies that enable them to perform the activities of Al-Kayyal efficiently.

# 2    Methodology

## 2.1    Method

Researchers used the mixed approach because they realized that using one approach (i.e., quantitative or qualitative) does not enable them to reach an accurate conclusion about the effectiveness of the intervention program used. The quantitative approach alone can show that the program is effective, but if the qualitative approach confirms this result, then researchers are reassured about the program's effectiveness.

## 2.2 Sample

Due to the COVID-19 circumstances, and taking into consideration the principle of preventing large gatherings, researchers have chosen randomly five students who expressed
a desire to learn the profession of Al-Kayyal. They were of mean age of 22.40 and
standard deviation of 1.14 years. All belong to the department of socials sciences at
Adrar University (Algeria). Subjects possessed superficial information about Al-Kayyal
profession. None of them had previously practiced it.

## 2.3 Tool

The data collection tool used in this study was the ergonomics intervention program.
Researchers developed, implemented, evaluated and followed-up the program.

**First, the Development Phase.** To have a successful intervention program, researchers
identified the intervention needs, defined the intervention content, decided on the appropriate method for intervening and carried out the follow-up process. It is evident that an
ergonomics intervention program has a better chance of success when trainees needs are
identified, a good content is identified, and training methods are carefully selected [5].

*Identifying the Intervention Needs.* It was previously indicated that the sample subjects
had never experienced the water measure job. Also, it was found that they were eager to
learn this profession. To ascertain the existence of the need for training, the researcher
(B.M.) conducted an interview with the sample members, whose questions focused
on the profession of Al-Kayyal. The results indicated that the respondents lack water
measuring skills, and would like to learn them.

*Determining the Intervention Content.* Researchers included in the intervention content
a theoretical part, and a practical part.

The theoretical part consisted of information about the Foggara, its role in the Touat
community, major components of Foggara (Wells, shafts, tunnel, Kasriya, Saqiyah,
Majen), people necessary for the continuation of the course of the Foggara (Foggara
Chair, Al-Kayyal, Al-Zammam), the tools required for the distribution of Foggara water.

As for the practical part, it included real-world applications about practicing the
profession of Al-Kayyal. Initially, the applications took place in the lecture hall where
the theoretical part was presented. Then, the practical work was completed in three real
Foggaras, which are MataAllah Foggara, Abido Foggara, and Bukhari Foggara. All the
three Foggaras are located in the department of Reggane in the state of Adrar (Algeria).

*Deciding on the Appropriate Method for Intervening.* It was found that the trainees lack
theoretical and practical information about the Foggara and Al-Kayyal job. Therefore,
the apprentice training method was used. Apprenticeship training consists of theoretical
instructions and an on-the-job training at actual work place [6].The model of apprenticeship that was adopted in this research was the "young-person paradigm" according
to Gonon, et al. [7]. In order to make the apprenticeship training of a good quality, ILO
instructions were as much as possible followed [8].

After the program was developed, it had to be judged to see how good the development process was. To estimate the validity of the program, researchers used the content validation method. After completing its preparation, the program was handed over to a group of experts (Four engineers working in the National Observatory of Foggara in Adrar) to ensure the validity of the content. The four judges stated that the program content is consistent with what we know about the tasks that Al-Kayyal should normally perform. Accordingly, the program was considered valid. The validity rate has reached (100%). To assess the reliability of the program, **the inter-rater reliability method was used**. Two psychologists at the University of Adrar were requested to implement the program, at the same time, but in two different locations. At the end of the implementations, results were analyzed. It was found that rater (A) results confirm the results of rater (B), see Table 1.

**Table 1.** Inter-rater reliability.

| Applications | Conformity level between raters (A&B) | % of agreement | Cohen's k | Interpretation |
|---|---|---|---|---|
| 1st application in Tsabit (Algeria) | 73 points from 100 points (60 points for theory, 40 for practice) | 73 | 0.780 | Substantial agreement |
| 2nd application in Adrar (Algeria) | 82 points from 100 points (60 points for theory, 40 for practice) | 82 | 0.668 | Substantial agreement |

According to Landis, & Koch, [9], both results mean that agreement between the two raters is substantial. These results indicate that the program is sufficiently reliable.

**Second, the Implementation Phase.** First of all, it should be noted that the intervention program consisted of (08) sessions. Table 2 shows the sessions, the length and the content of each session.

**Third, the Evaluation Phase.** This phase consisted of one session with two types of evaluation. In the quantitative evaluation, researchers used the one-group method. Trainers are given a pre-exam, then training program, then a post-exam.

**Fourth, the Follow-Up Phase.** This phase consisted of one session. The follow-up session (the last session), took place after three weeks of closing the program. In this session the test that was used in the quantitative evaluation session was used.

**Table 2.** The session, the length and content of each session.

| Session number | Nature of session | Session length (minutes) | Session content |
|---|---|---|---|
| 1 | Introductory session | 90 | After acquaintance, trainees were given an introduction to the intervention, program objectives, number of sessions, content of each session, training methods |
| 2 | Working session | 90 | Trainees were given an introduction to the Foggara, the challenges facing it, the efforts made to preserve it, and job analysis of Foggara team (the head of the Foggara, the technician, Al-Kayyal, Al-Zammam). The focus was on the Al-Kayyal job analysis |
| 3 | Working session | 60 | The trainees were presented with the ergonomics of equipment used by Al-Kayyal such as the Kasriya and water measuring instrument (Hallafa) |
| 4 | Working session | 120 | A visit was made to MataAllah Foggara (Reggane). Trainees were accompanied by the trainer and Al-kayyal (S.A.), to demonstrate and practice the water measurement process. At the Q and A session, Al-Kayyal asked various questions to the trainees to see how well they understood what they had witnessed |
| 5 | Working session | 120 | A visit was made to Abido Foggara (Reggane). Trainees were accompanied by the trainer and Al-Kayyal (H.B.), to test what the trainees learned in the previous session in the Foggara of MataAllah. Al-Kayyal chose two of the trainees who wanted to practice, and asked them (one before the other) to perform the water measurement using only virtual data |
| 6 | Working session | 120 | A visit was made to Bukhari Foggara (Reggane). Trainees were accompanied by the trainers, and Al-Kayyal (B.A.). Its goal was for every trainee to practice the job as water measurer. Al-Kayyal provided accurate feedback to each trainee on his application. At the end, the floor was open for discussion |
| 7 | Evaluation and closing | 90 | The training was evaluated. Researchers used two types of evaluation. The quantitative evaluation and the qualitative evaluation |
| 8 | Follow-up | 60 | Follow-up evaluation |

# 3   Results

This research aimed at developing, implementing, evaluating and following-up an ergonomics intervention program to train young people to acquire the job competencies that enable them to do efficiently the work activities of Al-Kayyal.

In this part of the research, results related to the evaluation and follow-up of the program will be presented.

## 3.1   Results of the Evaluation of the Program

To identify the effectiveness of training, a quantitative comparison between the results of the pre-exam and the post-exam was carried out [10]. Results are depicted in Table 3.

In addition, researchers supported this with a qualitative approach represented in the Kirkpatrick model, which has four levels: (1) reaction, (2) learning, (3) behavior, and (4) results [11]. Results are depicted in Table 4.

## 3.2   Results of the Follow-Up of the Program

A comparison was made between the results of the quantitative evaluation (post-exam results) and the results of the follow-up evaluation. Results are tabulated in Table 5.

**Table 3.** Mann-Whitney results.

| Group | Sum of ranks | Mean of ranks | Standard deviation | Mann-Whitney U test value | P-value | Decision |
|---|---|---|---|---|---|---|
| Post-measurement | 15 | 3 | 1.58 | 0.00 | 0.01 | The critical value of U at $p < .01$ is 0. Therefore, the result is significant at $p < .01$ |
| Follow-up measurement | 40 | 8 | 1.54 | | | |

**Table 4.** Kirkpatrick model results.

| Model level | Results |
|---|---|
| Reaction | Trainees enjoyed the intervention |
| Learning | Trainees' knowledge, skills and attitudes towards water measurement have increased |
| Behavior | Trainees believe that their water measurement behavior has changed positively |
| Results | Trainees showed the intervention has impacted their personality, and society as a whole |

**Table 5.** Mann-Whitney results

| Group | Sum of ranks | Mean of ranks | Standard deviation | Mann-Whitney U test value | P-value | Decision |
|---|---|---|---|---|---|---|
| Post-measurement | 40 | 8 | 1.54 | 0.00 | 0.01 | The U-value is 11. The critical value of U at $p < .05$ is 2. Therefore, the result is not significant at $p < .05$ |
| Follow-up measurement | 26 | 5.2 | 3.17 | | | |

It can be seen from the results depicted in both Table 4 and 5 that the ergonomics intervention program is effective.

# 4   Discussion

After knowing that the ergonomics intervention program is effective, we can ask what led to its effectiveness. Here, we refer to some factors that we think are important.

First of all, the alignment of trainees and ergonomics intervention program goals [12]. According to Semler's systematic agreement theory of organizational alignment, if alignment between trainees and program goals is achieved, the organization can achieve greater individual and collective efficiency and effectiveness [13].

When it comes to the practical work, it has been found that having your trainees practice what they learn as much as possible, will lead to successful training program [14].

It was mentioned above that those selected to participate in the training process were students who wanted to learn the Al-Kayyal profession. Consequently, their enthusiasm and attendance of the training program sessions without delay or absence are indications that the trainees have positive attitudes towards training. The researchers indicated that positive attitudes towards training contribute to the success of training [15].

# 5   Conclusions

The field of work in the Foggara is in dire need of water measures. There are some Foggaras that do not have Al-Kayyal, which is a major issue to the beneficiaries. Consequently, the need to train new personnel to undertake the Al-Kayyal's task is becoming evident. In this case, the existence of Ergonomics Intervention Programs and competent trainers is necessary in order to achieve this goal. This research presented one of these interventions. The researchers built it and ensured its effectiveness.

**Acknowledgements.** Special thanks go to the president and members of the association of the Foggara (Mohamed Djelloul), particularly to: Mr. Djoudi Mohamed & Kina Abdelkader. In addition to the president and members of the association of the Foggara (Tagraf), particularly to: Reggani Hassane, Reggani M'Barek, Kessassi Djelloul & Bahki Mostapha.

# References

1. Mebarki, B., Mokdad, M., Semani, M., Mokdad, I.: Development of underground posture assessment tool (UPAT) for underground enclosed spaces: the Algerian Foggara as example. A Paper given to The 21st Triennial Congress of the International Ergonomics Association "HFE (Human Factors and Ergonomics) in a connected world", 13–18 June 2021
2. UNESCO's Convention for the Safeguarding of the Intangible Cultural Heritage: Knowledge and skills of the Al-Kayyals of the Foggaras or water bailiffs of Touat and Tidikelt (No. 01274), Paris (2018)
3. Remini, B., Achour, B., Albergel, J.: Timimoun's Foggara (Algeria): an heritage in danger. Arab. J. Geosci. **4**(3–4), 495–506 (2011)
4. Slimani, S., Benziada, S., Boutaoutaou, D., Kettab, A.: Study of the reliability of "Chekfa" in water distribution in the "Foggara" system: a case of Adrar region, Algeria. Alger. J. Environ. Sci. Technol. **6**(3), 1512–1515 (2020)

5. Martin, B.O., Kolomitro, K., Lam, T.C.: Training methods: a review and analysis. Hum. Resour. Dev. Rev. **13**(1), 11–35 (2014)
6. Hess, J.A., Kincl, L., Weeks, D.L., Vaughan, A., Anton, D.: Safety voice for ergonomics (SAVE): evaluation of a masonry apprenticeship training program. Appl. Ergon. **86**(103083), 1–8 (2020)
7. Gonon, P.: Apprenticeship as a model for the international architecture of TVET. In: Zhao, Z., Rauner, F., Hauschildt, U. (eds.) Assuring the Acquisition of Expertise: Apprenticeship in the Modern Economy, pp. 33–42. Foreign Language Teaching and Research Press, Beijing (2011)
8. ILO: Toolkit for Quality Apprenticeships, Volume I: Guide for Policy Makers. ILO, Geneva (2017)
9. Landis, J.R., Koch, G.G.: The measurement of observer agreement for categorical data. Biometrics **33**(1), 159–174 (1977)
10. Aamodt, M.: Industrial/Organizational Psychology: An Applied Approach, 8th edn. Nelson Education, Canada (2015)
11. Kirkpatrick, J.D., Kirkpatrick, W.K.: Kirkpatrick's four levels of intervention evaluation. Association for Talent Development, USA (2016)
12. Ayers, R.S.: Aligning individual and organizational performance: goal alignment in federal government agency performance appraisal interventions. Public Pers. Manage. **44**(2), 169–191 (2015)
13. Semler, S.W.: Systematic agreement: a theory of organizational alignment. Hum. Resour. Dev. Q. **8**(1), 23–40 (1997)
14. Kindrativ, E.O., Chuiko, N.Y., Huryk, Z.Y., Kostiuk, V.M., Rudiak, O.M., Vasylyk, V.M.: Practical training on "pathomorphology" as a way to form future doctor's professional competence. Art Med. **4**(2), 96–101 (2020)
15. Noe, R.A.: Trainees' attributes and attitudes: neglected influences on training effectiveness. Acad. Manage. Rev. **11**(4), 736–749 (1986)

# Smart Farming: Application of Internet of Things (IoT) Systems

Chander Prakash[1]([✉]), Lakhwinder Pal Singh[1], Ajay Gupta[1], and Amandeep Singh[2]

[1] Department of Industrial and Production Engineering, Dr B R Ambedkar National
Institute of Technology, Jalandhar 144011, Punjab, India
[2] Department of System Design Engineering, University of Waterloo, Waterloo, Canada

**Abstract.** IoT is a new trending technology that enables digitalization and modernization in every field. Things connected to the cloud makes the entire system smart. We have using the IoT system in every way of life: Smart city, Smart homes, Smart supply chain, Smart retail, Wearables, Connecting health, Smart grid, Smart industry, and smart farming. In the current scenario, the rapid population growth has increased the production demand and consequently, the pressure among farmers also increased to satisfy customer demand. Certainly, the automation and advanced machinery may lead to speed up the farm activities to increase productivity. The most important part of the IoT system is using sensor devices that collect cloud-based data which is interpreted to get the desired analysis. For the smart agriculture system, sensors play a major role collect data to measure NPK values, plant health, detect diseases and other soil properties. This paper is focused on the exploratory study in the agriculture sector to enhance smart technologies. This future research plan delivers a sample scope for future interdisciplinary science on smart farming, digital agriculture, precision farming, and agriculture 4.0.

**Keywords:** IoT · Smart farming · Agriculture

## 1 Introduction

The Agro-Industry has a vital role in the economy in terms of contribution to gross domestic product (GDP) as well as a source of employment in developing countries. More than 58% of the rural population is dependent on farming as a primary income source (IBEF 2014). The increasing demand for productivity and output are key contributors to agriculture farm mechanization. Emerging Internet of Things (IoT) technologies are a perfect novel solution and smarter application development in all aspects of the agricultural sector. In the current agricultural era, several concepts have been made for the digitalization and modernization in the agricultural automated steering systems, data-driven targeted application of fertilizers and pesticides, field robots and drones, soil analysis sensors, autonomous driving-digitization is advancing in agriculture as elsewhere (Giesler 2019). These include digital agriculture (Keogh and Henry 2016; Shepherd et al. 2020), Smart Farming (Blok and Gremmen 2018; Wolfert et al. 2017), Decision Agriculture (Leonard

N. L. Black et al. (Eds.): IEA 2021, LNNS 221, pp. 233–240, 2021.
https://doi.org/10.1007/978-3-030-74608-7_30

et al. 2017), Agriculture 4.0 (Rose and Chilvers 2018), Precision Agriculture or Precision Farming (Eastwood et al. 2017). However, Digitalization in agriculture indicates
that management of various tasks on-farm and off-farm focused on different kinds of
data (on location, prices, and economic information, weather behavior, phytosanitary
status, consumption, energy use, etc.), using drones, machines, sensors, and satellites to
monitor soil, water, animals, plants and humans. The data obtained is used to clarify the
past and predict the future, to make accurate decisions in a timely, through continuously
monitoring or specific big data science inquiries (Eastwood et al. 2017; Janssen et al.
2017; Wolfert et al. 2017).

Advancement in communication networks and protocols, From the last decade data
collection has been quite easy. The two types of protocol categories are followed by the
request/response model and publish/subscribe model. It can be also used in parts only
the IoT communication architecture system, an IoT application protocol can be used for
communication between the IoT devices and IoT gateway, cloud, and gateway or cloud
and the end-user illustrated in Fig. 1.

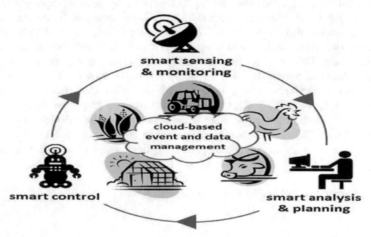

**Fig. 1.** Smart farming enhanced by cloud-based event and data management. Source "Wolfert
et al. 2014"

Whereas IoT in agriculture plays a major role in the center of smart farming research
efforts for several years, the majority of works is focused on the challenges and benefits
of IoT in agriculture (Elijah et al. 2018; Khanna et al. 2019) or IoT technologies, architectures and practices for smart agriculture (Ray 2017; Köksal and Tekinerdogan 2018),
focusing on IoT hardware, platforms, and wireless communication protocols (Tzounis
et al. 2017; Haider et al. 2017).

The aim of this paper is an analysis of enhanced smart farming and health monitoring
in the current agriculture domain. In particular, analysis in detail selected literature of
smart farming and health monitoring application. Thereby identifying the possible way
to face the current challenges and open issues in smart farming. Furthermore, Outline
the research trends and provide tips for future work. Some outline research questions
are define following based on these question literature has been analyzed.

Q1 - Adoption and uses of digital technologies on the farm.
Q2 - Various health assessments by using the IoT Application.

## 2  Methodology

The systematic relevant literature has been analyzed between 2010 to 2021 as shown in Fig. 2. Besides the period of publication, we refer to two inclusion criteria for the literature search: 1) Full manuscript publication; 2) Relevance to the outlined questions. Two exclusion criteria were used: 1) Full article publication rather than the English language; 2) Articles focusing only on technological design. The literature was collecting from the SCI (Science Citation Index), Scopus, Web of Science, Thomson Reuters, and other reputed sources. For collecting the relevant literature two databases were considered. The first database is considered smart farming and the second database was referred to as human health monitoring. From these two databases, 136 full published articles were retrieved. In the screening of literature, firstly search the paragraphs whether the keywords are present or not. After that, saw whether the outlined questions are covered in this paragraph. As the result, a total of 23 articles are most relevant and 113 relevant.

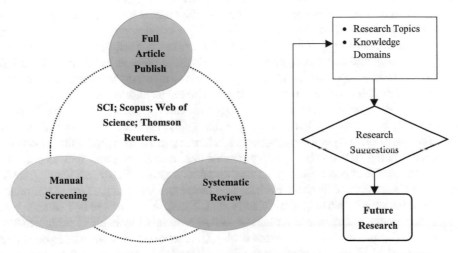

**Fig. 2.** A systematic overview of research methodology. Source "Yanes et al. 2020"

The remaining articles are not directly related to this study so excluded for further study and analysis purposes. There was very limited peer-reviewed literature was found due to a new concept of study as human health monitoring and smart farming.

## 3  Literature Review

This section discusses the IoT sensor healthcare system applications and assistance system. With the use of sensors with cloud bases systems, anything could be integrated into IoT domain.

Industry 4.0 (I4.0) is a new layer of this technology, among the numerous functions of IoT that is going to control most organizational activity (Lu 2017). The main function of I4.0 is collection information, data, detection, analysis, storing, and controlling the real-time activities, which led to decreased production cost and increase good service and quality of the product. The concept of I4.0 is directly related to the smart instrument installing and controlling the resources, In addition to enhancing versatility, as well as increasing performance. Also besides, the significant use of this smart cloud-based technology in agriculture, which could lead to forward.

Smart farming is directly related to the 3R- Right place, Right Product on Right time. Smart farming is all about the advancement in technology in a controlled and accurate manner. Pivoto et al. (2018) proposed communication technology into machinery equipment also various IoT sensors to use in the agricultural production system. Ullah et al. (2017) explained that precision farming collects various data, effectively analysis and integrated several technologies to improve production efficiency simultaneously minimize the cost. According to the survey, such techniques have been useful for smart farming such as GPS/GNSS, wearables, driverless vehicles, irrigation, Unmanned aerial vehicle, soil monitoring, weather condition etc. There are four major phases of smart farming data collection; analysis of data; managing decisions and farming. Khanna and Kaur (2019), proposed a systematic review on smart farming as the backbone IoT technology. Also derived the importance to the classification of precision farming. Aqeel-ur-Rehman et al. (2014) reviewed in detail the WSN technology and its application in different aspects of the agriculture domain. This author defined the successful use of wireless sensors and network systems in the agriculture domain. Hakkim et al. (2016) reduced the energy input and environmental impacts to increase the economic returns of agriculture through smart farming. Advancement in tool technology and equipment used were Global Positioning System (GPS), Geographic Information System (GIS), Sensors technologies, Soil mapping, Variable rate fertilizer (VRT) application, crop management, rate controller, soil and plant sensors, precision farming in the fruit production, precision livestock farming. Ultimately, it was concluded that the need to guide new technology found in the factor of precision agriculture depends (Pire et al. 2019). Sociodemographic variables, such as age, education level, in-field farm experience of the farmer is directly related to the activity participation (Kassie et al. 2013). As far as age and education is concerned, young and educated farmers can adopt new smart technology for increasing production (Barnes et al. 2019). Paxton et al. (2011) reported the concern of young age and high level of education among cotton farms in the USA are good preditors to accept WSN technology in the agriculture sector.

On the other side, there are much limited studies on health monitoring; only a few studies are performed on the animal health system. Besides, till now there is a still research gap in the literature to monitor human health especially farmer health. Diez-Olivan et al. (2019) formed a decision-support system based on environmental indicators, leg problems, and mortality rates. This is a data-driven process system that allows health monitoring, estimate growth, mortality parameters which are performed by the QRT method and basis on environmental deviations from optimal farm conditions.

Li et al. (2020) developed a wearable sensor to monitoring health systems of sports athletic using IoT. Describe the wearables devices for monitoring health assessment with minimizing the cost and stored in a cloud-based system. Huifeng et al. (2020) analyzed and monitoring the athlete sports player by using wearable sensor-based technology as well as optimizing and machine learning techniques are introduced. Ghosh et al. (2020) proposed real-time IoT-based health monitoring Wireless Body Sensor Nodes (WBSN) are frequently used for patients outside the hospital environment.

According to the different author's studies, healthcare applications could be enhanced by the using internet of things (IoT) because it collects real-time data in a cloud system and helpful for further analysis and future prediction. There are some foremost benefits and agriculture application of IoT technologies in smart farming (Table 1).

**Table 1.** IoT Technologies in Smart Farming (Boursianis et al. 2020)

| S. No | IoT technology | Agriculture application | Benefits |
|---|---|---|---|
| 1 | WSNs | Multiple sensors in a mesh network to collect the data | Easy to collect and manage the data |
| 2 | Cloud computing | Deliver and transfer various files from one place to another with the help of a Centralized system across the internet to data centers | Internet-based data computing and programs can be accessed easily from a centralized cloud system |
| 3 | Big data analysis | Refers as a collection of vast and complex data | Analysis to separate poor quality and high-quality data |
| 4 | Embedded systems | The system contains both hardware and software access | Provide flexibility and efficiency from collecting the data |
| 5 | Communication protocols | Exchange the data over the network | Easy to collect data from sensors and cloud computing systems |

Moreover, attaining the remote-control system or wireless sensor systems is very cheap and easy to use. It reduced the complication rate and easy to enhance the treatment procedure. However, for assistance rate should be further improved and increase accuracy with decrease complexity.

## 4  Results

The present study has been focused to address the application of IoT systems into various disciplines. During the literature survey, it has been found that the majority of studies were based upon the IoT application among multiple areas like manufacturing, service, medical and many more. However, there has been observed a small volume of studies targeting the role of IoT systems in the agricultural sector. Moreover, the application of IoT systems is well-thought-out a new concept that comes into existence mainly in the last five (5) years. In this study, the literature somewhere related to the application of IoT systems in various agricultural activities only taken into the account for the comprehensive review as mentioned in Sect. 3.

The reviewed studies were found to be focusing on the assessment, evaluation and analysis of various factors impacting agricultural activities. Mainly, the researchers prevalently stressed the role of humidity, temperature, plant health, soil contamination, NPK (Nitrogen-Phosphorus-Potassium), air contamination, irrigation, weather conditions, crop spray system (CPS). On the other hand, the research studies were found to barely focused on the human-machine interaction application like the tractor and its operated machinery. The increase in population has raised productivity demand which puts significant pressure on the farmers to fulfill the demand. Therefore, the use of human-driven agricultural mechanized machinery has been increased in the past decade. So the study of human-machine interaction systems is one of the important aspects to be considered in terms of assessing and monitoring the machine health and human health system using the IoT application. The machine health assessment may be based upon various impacting parameters like gearbox temperature, lubrication, tool position, machine vibration, etc., and on the other hand, the human health parameters may be assessed in terms of human vibration (i.e. transmission from the machine into the human body), fuel exhaust inhalation, noise, comfort and many more. Therefore, the present study highlights the future investigation to be carried out by considering machine and human health using required IoT systems.

## 5  Conclusion

From the above literature, It is clear that how smart farming is helpful in agriculture. It will be very soon adopted by the farmers and replace the traditional methods to enhance productivity. It has been already practiced in developed countries but India, China, and Africa are still unexplored in this area. If it has been corrected using in these countries it can easily put an end to world hunger. Modern technology in agriculture can make drastic development for a country like India in which 58% population directly depends as a primary source of income. It has been clear from the above literature how various types of sensors that work in cloud-based systems on general scientific principles are used in IoT. Sensor-based systems provide accurate information on factors affecting livestock, such as temperature, position, weather status, soil quality, and animal health status, and human health status measurements. The use of WNS sensors and data analysis focusing on real farm problems could lead to sustain the environment and also decrease wastes that fall harmful effect on soil property.

The focus of this paper was to explain the IoT systems which are developed by authors and useful in agriculture practices. The main objective of this paper is to explain the various types of sensors and which can be used for the agriculture practice purpose to enhance productivity and fulfill the customer demand in the farm.

## References

Khanna, A., Kaur, S.: Evolution of internet of things (IoT) and its significant impact in the field of Precision Agriculture. Comput. Electron. Agric. **157**, 218–231 (2019)

Tzounis, A., Katsoulas, N., Bartzanas, T., Kittas, C.: Internet of things in agriculture, recent advances and future challenges. Biosyst. Eng. **164**, 31–48 (2017)

Blok, V., Gremmen, B.: Agricultural technologies as living machines: toward a biomimetic conceptualization of smart farming technologies. Ethics Policy Environ. **21**(2), 246–263 (2018)

Eastwood, C., Klerkx, L., Nettle, R.: Dynamics and distribution of public and private research and extension roles for technological innovation and diffusion: case studies of the implementation and adaptation of precision farming technologies. J. Rural Stud. **49**, 1–12 (2017)

Giesler, S.: Digitization in agriculture-from precision farming to farming 4.0. (2019)

IBEF (2014). https://www.ibef.org/industry/agriculture-india.aspx

Janssen, S.J., Porter, C.H., Moore, A.D., Athanasiadis, I.N., Foster, I., Jones, J.W., Antle, J.M.: Towards a new generation of agricultural system data, models and knowledge products: information and communication technology. Agric. Syst. **155**, 200–212 (2017)

Keogh, M., Henry, M.: The implications of digital agriculture and big data for australian agriculture: April 2016. Australian Farm Institute (2016)

Leonard, E., Rainbow, R., Laurie, A., Lamb, D., Llewellyn, R., Perrett, E., Jakku, E.: Accelerating precision agriculture to decision agriculture: enabling digital agriculture in Australia (2017)

Elijah, O., Rahman, T.A., Orikumhi, I., Leow, C.Y., Hindia, M.N.: An overview of internet of things (IoT) and data analytics in agriculture: benefits and challenges. IEEE Internet Things J. **5**, 3758–3773 (2018)

Ray, P.P.: Internet of things for smart agriculture: technologies, practices and future direction. J. Amb. Intell. Smart Environ. **9**, 395–420 (2017)

Rose, D.C., Chilvers, J.: Agriculture 4.0: broadening responsible innovation in an era of smart farming. Front. Sustain. Food Syst. **2**, 87 (2018)

Shepherd, M., Turner, J.A., Small, B., Wheeler, D.: Priorities for science to overcome hurdles thwarting the full promise of the 'digital agriculture' revolution. J. Sci. Food Agric. **100**(14), 5083–5092 (2020)

Wolfert, S., Ge, L., Verdouw, C., Bogaardt, M.J.: Big data in smart farming–a review. Agric. Syst. **153**, 69–80 (2017)

Wolfert, S., Goense, D., Sørensen, C.A.G.: A future internet collaboration platform for safe and healthy food from farm to fork. In: 2014 Annual SRII Global Conference, pp. 266–273. IEEE (2014)

Yanes, A.R., Martinez, P., Ahmad, R.: Towards automated aquaponics: a review on monitoring, IoT, and smart systems. J. Clean. Prod. 121571 (2020)

Lu, Y.: Industry 4.0: a survey on technologies, applications and open research issues. J. Ind. Inf. Integr. **6**, 1–10 (2017)

Pivoto, D., Waquil, P.D., Talamini, E., Finocchio, C.P.S., Dalla Corte, V.F., de Vargas Mores, G.: Scientific development of smart farming technologies and their application in Brazil. Inf. Process. Agric. **5**(1), 21–32 (2018)

Ullah, A., Ahmad, J., Muhammad, K., Lee, M.Y.: A survey on precision agriculture: technologies and challenges. In: The 3rd International Conference on Next Generation Computing (ICNGC 2017b), pp. 1–3 (2017)

Aqeel-ur-Rehman, Abbasi, A.Z., Islam, N., Shaikh, Z.A.: A review of wireless sensors and networks' applications in agriculture. Comput. Stand. Interfaces **36**(2), 263–270 (2014)

Hakkim, V.M.A., Joseph, E.A., Gokul, A.J.A., Mufeedha, K.: Precision farming: the future of indian agriculture. J. Appl. Biol. Biotechnol. **4**(6), 068–072 (2016)

Pire, T., Mujica, M., Civera, J., Kofman, E.: The rosario dataset: multisensor data for localization and mapping in agricultural environments. Int. J. Robot. Res. 027836491984143 (2019)

Kassie, M., Jaleta, M., Shiferaw, B., Mmbando, F., Mekuria, M.: Adoption of interrelated sustainable agricultural practices in smallholder systems: evidence from rural Tanzania. Technol. Forecast. Soc. Chang. **80**, 525–540 (2013)

Barnes, A.P., Soto, I., Eory, V., Beck, B., Balafoutis, A., Sanchez, B., Vangeyte, J., Fountas, S., van der Wal, T., Gomez-Barbero, M.: Exploring the adoption of precision agricultural technologies: a cross regional study of EU farmers. Land Use Policy **80**, 163–174 (2019)

Paxton, K., Mishra, A., Chintawar, S., Roberts, R., Larson, J.A., English, B., Dayton, M.L., Marra, M.C., Larkin, S.L., Reeves, J.M., Martin, S.W.: Intensity of precision agriculture technology adoption by cotton producers. Agric. Resour. Econ. Rev. **40**(1), 133–144 (2011)

Li, S., Zhang, B., Fei, P., Shakeel, P.M., Samuel, R.D.J.: Computational efficient wearable sensor network health monitoring system for sports athletics using IoT. Aggress. Violent Behav. 101541 (2020)

Huifeng, W., Kadry, S.N., Raj, E.D.: Continuous health monitoring of sportsperson using IoT devices based wearable technology. Comput. Commun. **160**, 588–595 (2020)

Ghosh, A., Raha, A., Mukherjee, A.: Energy-efficient IoT-health monitoring system using approximate computing. Internet Things **9**, 100166 (2020)

Boursianis, A.D., Papadopoulou, M.S., Diamantoulakis, P., Liopa-Tsakalidi, A., Barouchas, P., Salahas, G., Goudos, S.K.: Internet of things (IoT) and agricultural unmanned aerial vehicles (UAVs) in smart farming: a comprehensive review. Internet Things 100187 (2020).

# Musculoskeletal Symptoms and Postural Analysis of Lettuce Farmers

Yogi Tri Prasetyo$^{(\boxtimes)}$ and Reginald Lance E. Dones

Mapúa University, 658 Muralla Street, Intramuros, 1002 Manila, Philippines
ytprasetyo@mapua.edu.ph, rledones@mymail.mapua.edu.ph

**Abstract.** This study identifies the musculoskeletal symptoms of agricultural workers, specifically lettuce farmers. Data was collected in a lettuce farm in Cavite, Philippines, questionnaire, and direct observation was used. There are 50 participants in the study, including twenty-two greenhouse workers, eleven soil mixing workers, nine nursery workers, and eight fermentation workers. Prevalence of musculoskeletal symptoms in the shoulder (80%), lower back (70%), neck (64%), and hand/wrist (73%) is high for all occupation groups. 92% of the participants were reported to have work interference due to musculoskeletal symptoms. The severity of musculoskeletal symptoms was typical for the lower back, upper back, shoulder, and neck. The overall mean of the farmer's Rapid Upper Limb Assessment (RULA) score was 6.4, which corresponds to RULA action level 3, highlighting that the current working posture of farmers must have a further investigation or needed change soon. Association between socio- demographic results and musculoskeletal symptoms are identified using logistic regression analyses.

**Keywords:** Musculoskeletal symptoms · Pain · Agricultural workers · Farmers · Rapid upper limb assessment

## 1 Introduction

The agricultural sector employs half of the world's labor force, which estimates around 1.3 billion laborers [1]. Agriculture farmers work every day, planting and harvesting crops. They spend their time either bending over or kneeling on the ground. With such movements, they are prone to have Musculoskeletal Disorder (MSD). Thus, making agricultural labor one of the most hazardous industries [2].

Farmers have a potential risk for musculoskeletal symptoms due to the arduous work. Thereby, osteoarthritis in the lower back, hips, knee, neck, and upper limb is common [3]. According to [4], musculoskeletal symptoms are currently the most common cause of chronic disability.

Some related studies about the prevalence of musculoskeletal symptoms are made among agricultural workers [5–13]. This paper will focus on a group of agricultural workers, specifically lettuce farmers. Emphasis will be given to what causes musculoskeletal symptoms in the work conditions of lettuce farmers. There are four main tasks in lettuce farming; nursery production, greenhouse farming, soil mixing, and fermentation. Gender differences, smoking status, and farm experience in Indian rice farmers were studied by some researchers [14]. Prolonged awkward working posture is a significant factor affecting musculoskeletal symptoms of farmers. Recent studies suggest that harvesting crops result in a distinct manner of how agriculture workers are exposed to musculoskeletal disorder [2].

This study evaluates the frequency, severity, and work interference of musculoskeletal symptoms among the different areas of lettuce farming, the linkage of socio-demographic factors with musculoskeletal symptoms among lettuce farmers, and to score RULA of farmers based on their specific work in lettuce farming.

## 2 Methodology

### 2.1 Study Design and Setting

This study was achieved in a local organic lettuce farm in Cavite, Philippines. The study population consisted of agricultural workers from the farm who mainly are doing greenhouse work (e.g., harvesting) and nursery cultivation (e.g., sowing). Farmers who have a least twelve months or one-year experience in the specific occupation were considered the target population. All farmers who participated in the study were given written consent before participating in the study.

### 2.2 Instruments

A questionnaire and close observation of the participants during the actual work process were used for data gathering. The questionnaire used was a Standardised Nordic questionnaire for the analysis of musculoskeletal symptoms [15]. The questionnaire consisted of information on demographics, job characteristics, and Musculoskeletal symptoms of farmers in the last twelve months. Observation of the farmers' working posture during their work was assessed using Rapid Upper Limb Assessment (RULA) method [16].

### 2.3 Data Collection

The questionnaire was administered by interviewing the participants, and items on demographic and job characteristics are included in the questionnaire. Socio-demographic details include farmer's age, gender, weight, height, if the participant is doing exercises (yes, no), and smoking habits (yes, no). Work-related items on the questionnaire include: occupation (greenhouse, nursery, soil mixing, fermentation), number of years worked as an agricultural worker, number of hours worked per day and number of hours per day working in a standing position. The frequency of musculoskeletal symptoms in the last twelve months in different body regions was assessed using a Standardised Nordic questionnaire to analyze musculoskeletal symptoms [15]. Work interference of musculoskeletal symptoms (e.g., disruption of work-related activities during musculoskeletal symptoms) was assessed in the study. Musculoskeletal symptoms within the last seven days were also evaluated, and the severity of musculoskeletal symptoms in different body regions was rated in the study using a scale (0–5, where 0 = no pain and 5 = very high pain). The time to complete the whole questionnaire was approximately 8 min. Working postures of the agricultural workers during working were assessed by using Rapid Upper Limb Assessment (RULA) method [16]. RULA method scores the analysis by combining table A (lower arm, upper arm, and wrist) and table B (neck, trunk, and leg) to get the final score. The work cycle was also identified for the process of lettuce farming, and the work cycle included the following work elements: nursery, soil mixing, greenhouse process, fermentation.

## 2.4  Statistical Analysis

Analysis ToolPak in Microsoft excel 2016, and IBM SPSS statistics 26 was used for data analysis. Descriptive analytics was used to assess the difference between each occupational group and body pain in different regions. ANOVA was used to compare the RULA score of each occupational group. Logistic regression analysis was used to assess the socio-demographic result and musculoskeletal symptoms in different body regions.

# 3  Results

## 3.1  Socio-demographic and Work-Related Details

The socio-demographic and job details of the studied farmers are presented in Table 1. Thirty-eight men (76%) and twelve women (24%) participated in the study. The age of farmers ranges from 23–47 years old (mean = 31.6 years old; standard deviation [SD] = 4.9 years). Weight of the farmers ranges from 55–79 kilos (mean = 66.0 kg; standard deviation [SD] = 5.8kg). The height of the farmers ranges from 4.11–5.9 feet (mean = 5.4ft; standard deviation [SD] = 0.3). Most of the farmers are a non smoker (64%) and is not involved in regular exercise or sports activity (72%). The study participants included 22 (14%) greenhouse workers, 11 (22%) soil mixing workers, 9 (18%) nursery workers, and 8 (16%) fermentation workers. The participants had been working as agriculture workers for 1.5–16 years (mean = 5.8; standard deviation [SD] = 3.1). Their mean time spent in a standing position is 3.9 h (standard deviation [SD] = 1.2 h).

**Table 1.** RULA scores by assigned area.

| Variables | Males (n = 38) | Females (n = 12) | Whole sample (n = 50) |
|---|---|---|---|
| Age (Years) | | | |
| Mean (SD) | 31.4 (5.2) | 30.5 (3.2 | 31.2 (4.9) |
| Range | 23–47 | 26–36 | 23–47 |
| Job tenure | | | |
| Mean (SD) | 6.1 (3.3) | 4.4 (2.1) | 5.8 (3.1) |
| Range | 1.5–16 | 2–8 | 1.5–16 |
| Working hrs/day | | | |
| Mean | 8 | 8 | 8 |
| Range | 8 | 8 | 8 |
| Number of hrs/day in a standing position | | | |
| Mean (SD) | 3.9 (1.2) | 3.8 (1.4) | 3.9 (1.2) |
| Range | 2–6 | 2–5 | 2–6 |
| Weight (kg) | | | |
| Mean (SD) | 67.4 (5.9) | 61.8 (4.4) | 66.0 (5.8) |
| Range | 57–79 | 55–68 | 55–79 |
| Height (ft) | | | |
| Mean (SD) | 5.5 (0.2) | 5.2 (0.4) | 5.4 (0.3) |
| Range | 5.1–5.9 | 4.11–5.5 | 4.11–5.9 |
| Smoking, n (%) | | | |
| No | 24 (63) | 8 (67) | 32 (64) |
| Yes | 14 (37) | 4 (33) | 18 (36) |
| Exercise/Sports, n (%) | | | |
| No | 26 (68) | 10 (83) | 36 (72) |
| Yes | 12 (32) | 2 (17) | 14 (28) |
| Assigned area, n (%) | | | |
| Nursery | 3 (8) | 6 (50) | 9 (18) |
| Soil mixing | 11 (29) | 0 | 11 (22) |
| Greenhouse | 16 (42) | 6 (50) | 22 (44) |
| Fermentation | 8 (21) | 0 | 8 (16) |

## 3.2 Musculoskeletal Outcomes

Tables 2, 3 and 4 presents the characteristics of musculoskeletal symptoms among agricultural workers. 49 out of 50 (98%) of the farmers experienced musculoskeletal symptoms in the last twelve months. Shoulder (80%), lower back (70%), neck (64%), and hand/wrist (54%) were the most common locations of pain discomforts. Prevalence of musculoskeletal symptoms in the shoulder (82%), lower back (82%), and neck (77%) is higher for greenhouse workers, and musculoskeletal symptoms for hand/wrist (73%) is higher for soil mixing workers. 92% (46) of the farmers were reported to have work interference due to musculoskeletal symptoms. This was mainly due to lower back (60%), neck (46%), hips/thigh (42%), and knee (40%) symptoms. The severity of muscle symptoms among farmers is between moderate to severe (3–4, on a scale of 1–5). Generally, lower back (mean = 2.9; standard deviation [SD] = 2.0), upper back (mean = 1.7; standard deviation [SD] = 1.7), shoulder (mean = 2.5; standard deviation [SD] = 1.5), and neck (mean = 2.0; standard deviation [SD] = 1.6) areas have the most severe cases between the four working groups.

**Table 2.** Prevalence of musculoskeletal symptoms of agricultural workers.

| Body region | Prevalence of MSS | | | | |
| --- | --- | --- | --- | --- | --- |
| | Nursery | Soil mixing | Greenhouse | Fermentation | All |
| | n(%) | n(%) | n(%) | n(%) | n(%) |
| Neck | 6 (67) | 5 (45) | 17 (77) | 4 (50) | 32 (64) |
| Shoulder | 7 (78) | 7 (64) | 18 (82) | 8 (100) | 40 (80) |
| Elbows | 6 (67) | 6 (55) | 7 (32) | 2 (25) | 21 (42) |
| Hand/Wrist | 4 (44) | 8 (73) | 12 (55) | 3 (38) | 27 (54) |
| Upper back | 5 (56) | 6 (55) | 12 (55) | 3 (38) | 26 (52) |
| Low back | 5 (56) | 8 (73) | 18 (82) | 4 (50) | 35 (70) |
| Hips/Thighs | 3 (33) | 6 (55) | 12 (55) | 4 (50) | 25 (50) |
| Knees | 1 (11) | 6 (55) | 15 (68) | 4 (50) | 26 (52) |
| Ankles/Feet | 4 ( 44) | 4 (36) | 12 (55) | 4 (50) | 24 (48) |

**Table 3.** Work interference of agricultural workers due to musculoskeletal symptoms.

| Body region | Work interference of MSS | | | | |
| --- | --- | --- | --- | --- | --- |
| | Nursery | Soil mixing | Greenhouse | Fermentation | All |
| | n(%) | n(%) | n(%) | n(%) | n(%) |
| Neck | 5 (55) | 4 (36) | 11 (50) | 3 (38) | 23 (46) |
| Shoulder | 2 (22) | 3 (27) | 9 (41) | 3 (38) | 17 (34) |
| Elbows | 3 (33) | 1 (9) | 4 (18) | 1 (13) | 9 (18) |
| Hand/Wrist | 2 (22) | 4 (36) | 6 (27) | 1 (13) | 13 (26) |
| Upper back | 3 (33) | 4 (36) | 4 (18) | 3 (38) | 14 (28) |
| Low back | 5 (55) | 6 (55) | 15 (68) | 4 (50) | 30 (60) |
| Hips/Thighs | 2 (22) | 6 (55) | 9 (41) | 4 (50) | 21 (42) |
| Knees | 1 (11) | 6 (55) | 11 (50) | 2 (25) | 20 (40) |
| Ankles/Feet | 2 (22) | 2 (18) | 8 (36) | 3 (38) | 15 (30) |

**Table 4.** The severity of musculoskeletal symptoms of agricultural workers.

| Body region | Severity of MSS (Scale 0–5) | | | | |
|---|---|---|---|---|---|
| | Nursery | Soil mixing | Greenhouse | Fermentation | All |
| | Mean (SD) | Mean (SD) | Mean (SD) | Mean (SD) | Mean (SD) |
| Neck | 2.1 (1.8) | 1.0 (1.3) | 2.5 (1.5) | 1.5 (1.7) | 2.0 (1.6) |
| Shoulder | 2.2 (1.5) | 2.0 (1.7) | 2.7 (1.6) | 2.8 (0.9) | 2.5 (1.5) |
| Elbows | 1.7 (1.3) | 1.2 (1.3) | 0.6 (1.0) | 0.6 (1.2) | 0.9 (1.2) |
| Hand/Wrist | 1.1 (1.4) | 1.3 (0.9) | 1.2 (1.2) | 0.6 (0.9) | 1.1 (1.1) |
| Upper back | 2.2 (2.2) | 1.7 (1.7) | 1.5 (1.5) | 1.4 (1.9) | 1.7 (1.7) |
| Low back | 2.2 (2.2) | 2.9 (2.0) | 3.4 (1.8) | 2.1 (2.4) | 2.9 (2.0) |
| Hips/Thighs | 0.9 (1.4) | 1.7 (1.7) | 1.7 (1.7) | 1.3 (1.4) | 1.5 (1.6) |
| Knees | 0.2 (0.7) | 1.9 (1.9) | 1.9 (1.4) | 1.5 (1.7) | 1.5 (1.6) |
| Ankles/Feet | 0.9 (1.2) | 0.9 (1.3) | 1.5 (1.5) | 1.0 (1.2) | 1.2 (1.3) |

## 3.3  RULA Analysis

RULA score by farmer's assigned area is shown in Table 5. The overall final RULA scores ranged from 4 to 7 (mean = 6.4; standard deviation [SD] = 0.9), which corresponds to a RULA action of level 3. RULA's final score was significantly higher than other groups (6.9, 6.8, 6.5, and 4.9, respectively, for greenhouse workers, fermentation workers, soil mixing workers, and nursery workers; $p < 0.05$). By assigned area, greenhouse workers received a higher table A (arm & wrist, and lower arm) score (6.5, 6.0, 5.9, and 5.0, respectively, for greenhouse workers, soil mixing workers, fermentation workers, and nursery workers; $p < 0.05$), and a higher table B (neck, trunk, and leg) score (6.5, 6.2, 6.0, and 4.0, respectively, for greenhouse workers, soil mixing workers, fermentation workers, and nursery workers; $p < 0.05$) than the other studied groups.

**Table 5.** RULA scores by farmer's assigned area

| Assigned area | RULA score A | | RULA score B | | RULA Final score | |
|---|---|---|---|---|---|---|
| | Min-Max | Mean (SD) | Min-Max | Mean (SD) | Min-Max | Mean (SD) |
| Nursery | 4–7 | 5.0 (1.0) | 3–5 | 4.0 (0.7) | 4–7 | 4.9 (1.2) |
| Soil mixing | 5–7 | 6.0 (0.8) | 5–7 | 6.2 (0.9) | 5–7 | 6.5 (0.8) |
| Greenhouse | 5–8 | 6.5 (0.9) | 5–8 | 6.5(1.0) | 6–7 | 6.9 (0.4) |
| Fermentation | 5–7 | 5.9 (1.0) | 5–7 | 6.0 (0.8) | 6–7 | 6.8 (0.5) |
| Whole sample | 4–7 | 6.0 (1.0) | 3–8 | 5.9 (1.3) | 4–7 | 6.4(0.9) |

## 3.4  Factors of Musculoskeletal Symptoms to Farmer's Socio-demographic

Using binary logistic regression analyses, the association of socio-demographic and work habits of agricultural workers was analyzed. For gender, females have a higher probability of experiencing lower back, upper back, and neck symptoms (75%, 58.3%, and 66.7%, respectively), while males have a higher probability of having shoulder pains than females (81.6%). Farmers aged 31 to 47 years old are more prone to have lower back, shoulder, and neck symptoms (82.6%, 91.3%, and 73.9%, respectively), while farmers 30 years old and below have a higher risk of having upper back symptoms (55.6%). Job tenure, working in standing position, weight, height, and smoking habits are also reported to have an association with musculoskeletal symptoms.

# 4 Discussion

Agricultural workers directly associate musculoskeletal symptoms due to the nature of their work, which corresponds to the results achieved in the study; this agrees with several previous studies [14]. 98% of the participants have experienced muscle pain in the last 12 months. The workers are divided into three groups: Nursery, Soil Mixers, Greenhouse, and Fermentation, and their activities and RULA analyses are follows: Nursery workers' job is to put seedlings in a tray and grow those seedlings before transplanting them in the greenhouse. They kneel in the ground to put soil in the seedling trays, sit in an upright position when planting seeds and carry a heavy watering can when watering the seedlings. With such activities, they have a high risk of having a shoulder (78%), neck (67%), and elbow (67%) pain (see Fig. 1, 2 and 3). Soil mixing happens when its time to transplant the grown seedlings inside the greenhouse, and repeated movements of mixing different kinds of soil and substrates gives the farmer a risk of having lower back (73%), hand/wrist (73%), and shoulder (64%) pains. Greenhouse workers are the ones who plant and harvest fully grown lettuce from the ground on a repeated cycle. They bend forward their lower back, head, and trunk. This group of farmers is the most likely to have musculoskeletal symptoms of the shoulder (82%), lower back (82%), and neck (77%) compared to the other groups (see Fig. 3). Fermentation is done to serve as a fertilizer for the lettuces; workers in this group get all the trimmings from the previous batch of harvest and mix it with molasses, fermentation workers are responsible in the watering of lettuce, and drenching the fermented fertilizer, they carry a heavy watering tool that they made (see Fig. 4), with such movements they have a high risk of having shoulder (100%), neck (50%), and lower back (50%) issues.

Work interference due to musculoskeletal symptoms and their degree of severity was also reported. A high number of farmers have difficulty working when they are experiencing lower back (60%), neck (46%), and hip/thigh (42%) pain. Severe musculoskeletal symptoms on the other hand are also reported as follows: lower back (mean = 2.9; standard deviation [SD] = 2.0); upper back (mean = 1.7; standard deviation [SD] = 1.7); shoulder (mean = 2.5; standard deviation [SD] = 1.5); and neck (mean = 2.0; standard deviation [SD] = 1.6) areas. The mean final Rapid Upper Limb Assessment (RULA) score of farmers, in general, is 6.4. Greenhouse workers, in particular, have the highest RULA score of 6.9. RULA, while the final score for nursery, soil mixing, and fermentation workers ranges from 4.9–6.8.

With high results of prevalence, work interference, severity, and RULA score, it is therefore, advisable to conduct an ergonomic intervention for the agricultural workers affected by musculoskeletal symptoms, or the effects may worsen over time.

Socio-demographic of the participants revealed that females are more likely to have musculoskeletal symptoms than males. Age, job tenure, working in standing position, weight, height, and smoking habits have associations to musculoskeletal symptoms. The older and longer the farmer worked for in the agriculture field, the higher risk the farmers have for musculoskeletal symptoms.

This study was solely based on a specific group of agricultural workers. The evaluation results in the different analyses may not be accurately perfect, but it gives a clear picture that intervention must be done the soonest to help the farmers have a better quality of performance and endurance in accomplishing their tasks. Advanced studies considering other fields of agriculture are recommended.

## 5 Conclusions

Participants needed a necessary ergonomic intervention to reduce musculoskeletal symptoms, particularly in common areas, shoulder, lower back, neck, and hand/wrist. Socio-demographic factors should be considered in doing ergonomic intervention. Results from the data may show high rates of musculoskeletal symptoms, although farmers still perform well in their specific occupation groups.

## References

1. International Labour Organization: Agriculture: a hazardous work (2009)
2. Fathallah, F.A.: Musculoskcletal disorders in labor-intensive agriculture. Appl. Ergon. **41**(6), 738–743 (2010)
3. Walker-Bone, K., Palmer, K.: Musculoskeletal disorders in farmers and farm workers. Occup. Med. **52**(8), 441–450 (2002)
4. Bihari, V., Kesavachandran, C., Pangtey, B., Srivastava, A., Mathur, N.: Musculoskeletal pain and its associated risk factors in residents of National Capital Region. Indian J. Occup. Environ. Med. **15**(2), 59 (2011)
5. López-Aragón, L., López-Liria, R., Callejón-Ferre, Á.-J., Pérez-Alonso, J.: Musculoskeletal disorders of agricultural workers in the greenhouses of Almería (Southeast Spain). Saf. Sci. **109**, 219–235 (2018)
6. Dianat, I., Afshari, D., Sarmasti, N., Sangdeh, M.S., Azaddel, R.: Work posture, working conditions and musculoskeletal outcomes in agricultural workers. Int. J. Ind. Ergon. **77**, 102941 (2020)
7. Hildebrandt, V.: Musculoskeletal symptoms and workload in 12 branches of Dutch agriculture. Ergonomics **38**(12), 2576–2587 (1995)
8. Kee, D., Haslam, R.: Prevalence of work-related musculoskeletal disorders in agriculture workers in Korea and preventative interventions. Work **64**(4), 763–775 (2019)
9. Sarker, A.H., Islam, M.S., Haque, M.M., Parveen, T.N.: Prevalence of musculoskeletal disorders among farmers. MOJ Orthop. Rheumatol. **4**(1), 1–4 (2016)
10. Osborne, A., Blake, C., McNamara, J., Meredith, D., Phelan, J., Cunningham, C.: Musculoskeletal disorders among Irish farmers. Occup. Med. **60**(8), 598–603 (2010)
11. Jain, R., Meena, M., Dangayach, G.: Prevalence and risk factors of musculoskeletal disorders among farmers involved in manual farm operations. Int. J. Occup. Environ. Health, 1–6 (2018)
12. Gadhavi, B., Shukla, Y.: Prevalence of work related musculoskeletal disorders in farmers of Gujarat. Ergonomics **6**(11) (2019)

13. Vyas, R.: Ergonomic assessment of prevalence of musculoskeletal disorders among Indian agricultural workers. J. Ergon. S **4**, 1–4 (2014)
14. Luangwilai, T., Norkaew, S., Siriwong, W.: Factors associated with musculoskeletal disorders among rice farmers: cross sectional study in Tarnlalord sub-district, Phimai district, Nakhonratchasima province, Thailand. J Health Res. **28**(Suppl.), 85–91 (2014)
15. Kuorinka, I., Jonsson, B., Kilbom, A., Vinterberg, H., Biering-Sørensen, F., Andersson, G., Jørgensen, K.: Standardised Nordic questionnaires for the analysis of musculoskeletal symptoms. Appl. Ergon. **18**(3), 233–237 (1987)
16. McAtamney, L., Corlett, E.N.: RULA: a survey method for the investigation of work-related upper limb disorders. Appl. Ergon. **24**(2), 91–99 (1993)

# Protection of Pineapple Crop Workers: Outline of Attributes and Technical Specifications for a Set of Personal Protective Equipment

Frederico Reinaldo Corrêa de Querioz[1] ⓘ, Roberto Funes Abrahão[1] ⓘ,
Mauro José Andrade Tereso[1] ⓘ, and Daniel Braatz[2](✉) ⓘ

[1] Faculty of Agricultural Engineering, UNICAMP, Campinas, Brazil
[2] Production Engineering Department, UFSCar, São Carlos, Brazil
braatz@ufscar.br

**Abstract.** Introduction: pineapple cultivation presents a series of risk factors that pose a serious challenge to the design of personal protective equipment (PPE) appropriate to the operations involved in the production process. Objective: to outline attributes and technical specifications for the design of a set of PPE that are efficient in controlling risk factors, and reach a level of comfort that does not generate rejections of use. Methods: general and systematic observations were made of the work performed by eight workers during the pineapple harvest stage, besides the application of semi-structured interviews and a questionnaire. The QFD (Quality Function Deployment) method was partially used to delineate the attributes and technical specifications of the PPE, based on the information obtained by the work analysis. Results: the deployment table and quality matrix for the development of PPE for pineapple harvesting operation were constructed. The main attributes pointed out by the workers were that the PPE does not cause thermal discomfort or disrupt the execution of the task. Conclusion: The methodological proposal presented in this paper is promising as a basis for the design and development of personal protective equipment suitable for agricultural work.

**Keywords:** Personal protective equipment · Agricultural work · Work analysis · Pineapple cultivation · Design methodology

## 1 Introduction

Agriculture, together with construction and mining, is considered one of the most dangerous productive sectors from the point of view of human work [1]. In Brazil, the Special Secretariat of Social Security and Labor of the Ministry of Economy recognizes agriculture as an activity of high risk for the safety and health of workers, classifying it, and all its sub-branches, in grade 3, on a scale of 1 to 4, with the exception of forestry, which is assigned grade 4 [2].

The Brazilian agricultural sector employs more than 18 million people, almost 20% of the workforce[2]. Fruit farming, in particular, is one of the sectors with the highest

N. L. Black et al. (Eds.): IEA 2021, LNNS 221, pp. 250–261, 2021.
https://doi.org/10.1007/978-3-030-74608-7_32

employment rate in Brazilian agribusiness. Brazil is the world's third largest fruit producer with about 45 million tons per year, of which 65% are consumed internally and 35% are destined for the external market [3]. It is evident the relevance of studies of the sector's risk factors and initiatives to protect rural workers.

Epidemiological studies have consistently associated rural work with the occurrence of various types of occupational diseases. Among the injuries associated with agricultural work, musculoskeletal disorders are the most common, with manual handling of loads, permanence in extreme postures, and repetitive movements of the hands as the main inducers [1].

The issue of wearing personal protective equipment (PPE) is emblematic of the difficulties faced by rural workers in their daily work. The production of PPE for rural work corresponds to a small market niche (less than 4% of the total PPE market), and there is no investment required in research and development to meet the specific needs of the agricultural worker. These workers are then left to use, to a large extent, the PPE designed for other work situations, generally in the mechanical or chemical industry, with all the consequent maladjustments and discomforts.

Some of the desirable characteristics of PPE designed for other work contexts and ensuring greater safety may introduce operational difficulties when used in other work situations, such as rural work [4].

The use of personal protective equipment is part of the daily routine of many workers. Many occupational health and safety projects contemplate the use of PPE since its conception, seeking to reduce and control risks to workers' health and safety.

The preventive measures are those that aim to eliminate or reduce the risks at their source. Prevention should have priority over protection measures; however, in most situations, protection seems to be more economical than prevention [5–7]. For this reason, it is necessary that legislation provide mechanisms that encourage prevention and collective protection measures by employers. However, especially in real agricultural situations, these measures are often not simply used, for numerous reasons, including the high cost and technical difficulties inherent to specific conditions in the agricultural sector.

Brazilian legislation is naive about PPE when it universally accepts that the use of these products eliminate or neutralize insalubrity, assuming that worker protection when using them is efficient [8]. Studies [9–11] show that, in some cases, PPE did not eliminate or neutralize insalubrity, as stated in the legislation, and even increased the probability of contamination of rural workers in some activities, such as the application of pesticides [6, 8].

In Brazilian agriculture, especially in small rural communities, it is common to encounter rural workers without mandatory PPEs during pesticide handling and application. This fact is attributed to the inadequacy of these equipments in relation to agricultural tasks and the thermal environment, generating a lot of discomfort and may lead, in extreme cases, to the thermal stress of the rural worker [6, 8].

The PPE certification process in effect in Brazil does not require field tests that take into account real work situations, considering all risk factors present and ignoring potential synergistic effects [12]. An example is the use of protective gloves in the manual cutting of sugarcane: it is not enough that the gloves protect the hands against abrasive, draining, cutting and perforating agents. There is also the need to consider peculiarities such as flexibility of finger and hand movements; ease of perspiration of the hand; and high grip of the hand on the knife.

In Brazil, this problem of PPE inadequacy for ergonomic and environmental conditions is particularly present in agriculture, where it is common to find rural workers who do not use mandatory PPE during handling and application of agricultural chemicals. One of the reasons given is that the use of PPE causes thermal discomfort, and in extreme cases can lead to heat stress [8].

Among the numerous crops in the agricultural sector, the production process of pineapple has deserved little attention from researchers regarding safety and ergonomic issues. In this context, three publications focused on occupational safety for this sector of activity stand out.

The first study [13] sought to identify the risks associated with the productive process of the pineapple culture. The authors used the technique of collective analysis of the work, complemented with semi-structured questionnaires, together with the social actors involved in its production in municipalities of the state of Paraíba. Direct observations of the work in real conditions of execution were made. The study pointed out risk factors in all phases of the productive process, especially in the preparation and application of pesticides, besides highlighting several social and economic problems, in particular the role of public and private social agents in the maintenance of unfavorable conditions for workers.

In the second study [14], the authors conducted a comprehensive analysis of the working conditions in the pineapple production process in the municipality of Guaraçaí, interior of São Paulo Estate. The initiative of this study was based on a demand from the Sindicate of Rural Workers for the analysis of PPE commonly used. However, it acknowledged that the labor problems were more comprehensive and a study was chosen to cover all stages of the harvest. The researchers also used the technique of collective work analysis, besides general and systematic observations. The work highlighted the accidents with venomous animals and the occurrence of sharp-leaf perforations in several bodly segments, mainly in the stages of cutting seedlings, planting seedlings and harvesting fruits. The inadequacy of PPE was highlighted, both in the effective protection of workers and as an element that made it difficult to perform the tasks. An inventory of the identified risk factors was presented, pointing out the suffering of the workers and the precariousness of the physical and social conditions associated with the work in the pineapple culture. The lack of appropriate technology to relieve the workload and protect workers was also highlighted.

The third study [15] sought to evaluate the effectiveness of a set of PPE, usually used by workers in pineapple cultivation, in protecting against snake attacks. The PPE approved in the real tests were evaluated in field condition with the workers. The main result pointed out the necessity of designing specific PPE for the tasks in pineapple cultivation.

Based on all the arguments presented above, the main objective of this work is to outline attributes and technical specifications for the conception of a set of PPE that are efficient in controlling the risk factors present in the operations of the pineapple production process, besides reaching a level of comfort that does not generate rejections to use. To this end, it was sought to carry out an analysis of the real work of one stage of the productive process - the harvest of the fruits - to generate data and feed a classic method of engineering design, the QFD [16] (Quality Function Deployment), which allows to incorporate in the development of the product (in this case, the PPE), the real needs of users.

# 2 Methods

## 2.1 Work Analysis

The method of Ergonomic Analysis of Work (EWA) [17] was partially used in the analysis of the work involved in harvesting pineapple. The EWA is presented in three macro steps - the analysis of demand, task and activity - and involves general and systematic observations of real work and verbal interactions with the actors of the work. Through observations and the application of semi-structured interviews, photos and filming, it was sought to understand the effective use made by workers of available PPE, including qualitative assessments of their effectiveness and convenience. A questionnaire containing 108 questions was also applied based on the modified Likert methodology. The subjects covered involved the working conditions observed in the experiment; the use of PPE; foot protection; leg protection; trunk protection; arm protection; hand protection; eye protection; respiratory protection; head protection; opinions and suggestions. The questions also sought to evaluate the PPE according to criteria of use, more specifically related to the effort (sensation of weight and forces needed in handling); comfort (physical, thermal, pos-tural and relative to contact with the equipment) and usability (ease, speed, adjustments, difficulties, limitations, aesthetics and satisfaction with the use).

Eight workers who harvested the fruit in plants of Aparecida de Minas, a sub-district of the city of Frutal, state of Minas Gerais, participated in the analysis. The study was approved by the Research Ethics Committee of the Faculty of Medical Sciences of the State University of Campinas.

## 2.2 Application of the QFD Method and Construction of the Quality Matrix

Through a set of matrices, the QFD method allowed the "unfolding" of the requirements exposed by customers transforming them into technical specifications of the product. Quality matrices or first "quality houses" [18] were elaborated, where the real qualities required by the users were systematized and correlated to the technical characteristics of the products to be developed. These matrices were built from priority hierarchy tables with the relative weights of the required qualities (needs and/or desires) and technical characteristics of the product's quality required for the development of PPE for the pineapple harvest operation.

This work reports the development of the deployment table and quality matrix that outline attributes and technical specifications of a product (PPE) for the protection of workers' upper limbs during the pineapple harvest.

# 3   Results and Discussion

## 3.1   Analysis of Pineapple Harvesting Work

The practices observed during the pineapple harvest included four operations: harvesting the fruit itself, selection with eventual disposal, transportation and packaging of the fruit in the truck. The eight workers observed and interviewed were between 19 and 33 years of age; they were all male; the seniority in the function ranged from 3 to 12 years; four of them had completed elementary school, two had completed high school and two had completed high school. Six of them worked on a contract basis while two were registered farm workers.

The workers begin to arrive at 5:00 a.m. in the shed of the company that intermediates the sale of pineapple, which is located on the highway at one of the entrances to the city of Frutal in Minas Gerais state.

Each worker brings his meal and fresh water in thermal canteens. There are no explicit rules regarding breaks, being at the worker's own discretion.

Their task will only be finished when the loading of the transport vehicle of the day is finished, which often occurs before the afternoon period, around 12:00. There is not a daily production goal, but the task of everyone is to follow the pattern of the harvest until the end of the load.

In the task of harvesting the pineapple, the main objective assigned by the contractor is that the workers should remove the fruit with stipulated size and weight in the sale, and load the full carriages to the place where the truck sent by the buyer of the fruit is located. The workers remove the bagging of the fruit, visually select it according to the demand of the day (size, without holes, diseases and standardized colors) and fill the carriages with the selected fruit, which are taken through the streets between the beds to the porters, where the trucks that will be loaded are located.

The pineapple, being a non-climate fruit, has to be harvested at the right time of its ripening in order to be marketed, thus not allowing a very long period between the harvest and the final destination for marketing. Thus the harvest is made directly at the time of loading the vehicles that transport the fruit to large distributors or supermarket chains. The product must reach the final customer within 10 days, which requires that the task is performed in large areas with short periods so that there is no loss of fruit still on the feet.

Pineapple plantations are very dense with many clumps and leaves with thorns; 33,000 seedlings are planted each hectare. There are streets of one meter wide and more than 150 m long, through which the workers transit to do the crop handling and harvest.

The pineapple plant has serrated and pointed leaves with cutting and perforating potential that easily exceed the height of 1.20 m, thus providing a very hostile working environment for workers, besides being a natural habitat for poisonous animals.

The pineapple sprouts in the middle of the clumps of leaves at an average height of 45 cm from its base in relation to the ground. The crown starts at 75 cm and ends at 85 cm from the ground, forcing the pineapple pickers to bend between the clumps, which generates the risk of cuts and perforations in the trunk, arms, face and eyes. Besides the danger of cuts and perforations, the pineapple picker performs several repetitive movements of torsion and bending of the trunk, upper limbs and wrist, during the breaking of the lower stem that supports the fruit. These joint movements and postural configurations are performed thousands of times during a working day, which also exposes them to biomechanical risks (Fig. 1).

The transport of the fruits by wheelbarrow requires a great physical effort from the worker, who faces difficulties moving the wheelbarrow loaded with pineapples. The workers faces irregular soils with danger of falling, twisting of the feet in holes and long distances to be traveled to the place of loading in the truck.

**Fig. 1.** Postural difficulties and risk of excoriations and perforations in the pineapple harvest

A usual composition observed in this case study was the use of a truck with capacity for 16 thousand fruits and a team of 12 workers: two freighters, two launchers and eight pickers. In this scenario, each picker picks approximately 2 thousand fruits per day, which weigh around 1.5 kg; each pitcher throws something like 8 thousand fruits. These numbers illustrate well the physiological demand of the pineapple harvesting work.

The workers' perception of the PPE used, captured by the questionnaire, was quite negative. The problems pointed out were the lack of adequate protection, discomfort, inadequacy for the task of harvesting and excessive heat. All the workers interviewed stated that they have already bought PPE with their own resources, because not all the necessary PPE are usually provided by the contractors, who justify themselves by claiming that the service is outsourced and temporary or even eventual. Six workers affirmed that they already had to improvise some kind of PPE, particularly for arm protection. Some verbalizations collected exemplify these difficulties: "…I receive PPE from the intermediary who buys the pineapple to resell…"; "…All the PPE I use was me who bought it…"; "…I made legs with the big bag because there is no PPE for the legs of my size…"; "…When the PPE needs replacement I buy it myself…".

### 3.2 Priority Hierarchy Tables and Quality Matrices

To illustrate the application of the method proposed by this work, which unites the analysis of the work inspired by the EWA method with the QFD product development tool, the unfolding table and the quality matrix developed with the attributes and technical specifications for the protection of the workers' arms during the pineapple harvest are presented.

Of the eight rural workers interviewed in the pineapple harvest, four used unconventional arm protection (Fig. 2) and four did not use any type of arm protection during harvest.

**Fig. 2.** Improvisation for arm protection during harvest.

When asked how they protected their arms during the harvest, some of the workers responded as follows: "*...Only two shirts with long sleeves...*"; "*...Very expensive to buy the arm protection, sometimes I do it with my jeans legs...*"; "*...I use only one thick shirt with long sleeves...*"; "*...The farm offers canvas arm protection, but I don't like...*"; "*... arm protection, made of soccer socks...*"; "*...I use two soccer socks...*".

Table 1 corresponds to the table of quality required for the product (EPI) of protection of the workers' arms during the pineapple harvest; Fig. 3 corresponds to the quality matrix designed to support the corresponding PPE project. While in the table, the factors related to quality (voice of the user) and the technical specifications of the product (voice of the expert) are only juxtaposed, in the quality matrix they are confronted, with the relative weights related to weighting and arbitration. For example, the numbers 1, 3 and 9 of the matrix indicate the intensity of correlation (1 - low; 3 - medium; 9 - high) between the required quality and the technical characteristic of PPE.

It should be noted that the assembly of the quality matrix for the development of the product "protection of the arms in the pineapple harvest" was made from the verbalizations of the workers, the observation and analysis of the actual work and the expertise of the technical team. In the matter of comfort, for example, the qualities required by the workers associated to a future PPE of protection of the arms during the harvest, it was highlighted: to have appropriate size, not to disturb the movement of the arms and not to cause thermal discomfort.

**Table 1.** Deployment of technical characteristics of quality as a function of the product qualities required for protection of arms in pineapple crop.

| Quality required (worker's voice) | | Elements of quality | Technical characteristics of product quality |
|---|---|---|---|
| Level 1 | Level 2 | | |
| Comfort | Appropriate size | Dimensions | Length |
| | | | Width |
| | | | Diameter |
| | Do not disturb movements | Raw material | Maleability |
| | | Dimension | Thickness |
| | Do not hurt | Raw material | Texture |
| | | Dimension | Thickness |
| | Do not heat | Raw material | Thermal Resistance |
| | | Dimension | Thickness |
| | | Color | Tonality |
| | Facilitating perspiration | Raw material | Porosity |
| | | | Leak |
| | Lightweight | Raw material | Density |
| | | Dimension | Thickness |
| | Antiallergic/Do not scratch | Raw material | Texture |
| | | | Composition/Treatment |
| | | | PH |
| Protection | Excoriation by serrated leaves | Raw material | Fibrousness |
| | | Dimension | Thickness |
| | Drilling by thorns | Raw material | Fibrousness |
| | | Dimension | Thickness |

(*continued*)

Table 1. (*continued*)

| Quality required (worker's voice) | | Elements of quality | Technical characteristics of product quality | |
|---|---|---|---|---|
| Level 1 | Level 2 | | | |
| | Bite by venomous animals | Raw material | Fibrousness | |
| | | Dimension | Thickness | |
| | Impermeable to fluids and dust | Raw material | Porosity | |
| | | | Leak | |
| Design | Arm protection | Model/Form | Tubular | Total |
| | | | | Forearm |
| | | Lining | Quantity | Fixed |
| | | | | Mobile |
| | | | Raw material | Texture |
| | | | | Thickness |
| | | | | Composition/Treatment |
| | Long sleeve shirt | Model /Form | Fair | |
| | | | Wide | |
| | | | Padded | Total |
| | | | | Arms |
| | | Lining | Quantity | Fixed |
| | | | | Mobile |
| | | | Raw material | Texture |
| | | | | Thickness |
| | | | | Composition/Treatment |

The matrix leads the project team to prioritize a long shirt type solution, present in the traditional work uniforms of other agricultural sectors, but also to review the requirements of traditional mangoes. In order for the project team to be able to incorporate the required qualities to the final product, it is necessary to prioritize the technical characteristics of the quality which are: fibrousness, composition and treatments of the raw material; thickness; composition and adequate treatments of the lining raw material, which must be able to be removed, at the user's discretion, in case of, for example, accentuated thermal discomfort.

The requirements that stood out concomitantly in the three activities of pineapple cultivation related to the protection of the arms were: not to cause thermal discomfort (attractive quality); design in long shirt or sleeve (linear quality); composition and appropriate treatments for the raw material; thickness (dimensions); mobile lining with composition and appropriate treatments. The requirements that need to be incorporated

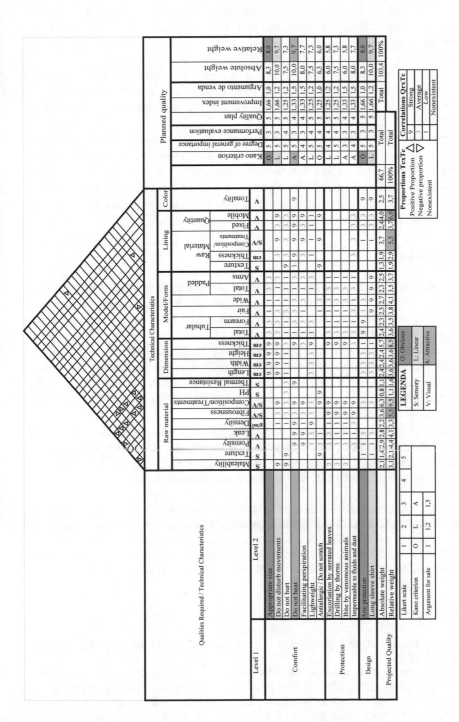

**Fig. 3.** Quality Matrix to design the product Arm Protection in the Pineapple Crop.

to the final product or be present in the form of device(s)/accessory(s) of regulation are: appropriate size (obvious quality); not to disturb movements, not to hurt, lightness and to resist the perforation by thorns (linear qualities); to facilitate the perspiration as attractive quality; porosity and fibrousness pertinent to the raw material.

The next step towards product development would be the search for pre-existing products that could serve as inspiration for PPE development. Another obvious source of inspiration are the adaptations and inventions developed by the workers themselves to protect their arms.

A first research for products available on the market revealed the availability of mangoes developed with several materials and with anatomical design to protect the arms and even the hands against abrasive, bracing, cutting and drillers agents. These products follow technical manufacturing standards and have the approval certificate. Some manufacturers claim that the mangoes they produce are more comfortable because the textile material used favors adequate skin perspiration.

## 4   Conclusion

It can be affirmed that the methodological proposal presented in this work has proved promising as a basis for the design and development of personal protective equipment suitable for agricultural work, i.e., PPE that are effective in protecting workers and are not uncomfortable and do not limit the execution of tasks.

The work analysis, inspired by EWA, including the application of semi-structured interviews and questionnaires, allowed the identification of workers' needs and expectations. This knowledge fed the deployment tables and quality matrices of the QFD method, generating a set of attributes and technical specifications that should guide the project teams in developing PPE.

Specifically regarding the protection of pineapple cultivation workers, the work of other pioneering researchers, who identified risk factors and difficulties in operations, in addition to analyzing the effectiveness and convenience of available PPE, served as inspiration and was of great value for the execution of this research.

**Acknowledgements.** The authors thank the workers involved in the research and the owners of the crops. To FAPESP, for the "Research Aid n° 2015/12907-6, Fundação de Amparo à Pesquisa do Estado de São Paulo (FAPESP)", as associate researcher. To CAPES, for the granting of the doctorate scholarship. "This work was carried out with the support of the Coordination for the Improvement of Higher Education Personnel - Brazil (CAPES) - Financing Code 001".

## References

1. Fathallah, F.: Musculoskeletal disorders in labor intensive agriculture. Appl. Ergon. **41**(6), 738–743 (2010)
2. Ferreira de Sousa, F.N., Santana, V.S.: Mortalidade por acidentes de trabalho entre trabalhadores da agropecuária no Brasil, 2000-2010. Cad. Saúde Pública, **32**(4), 1–13 (2016)
3. IAC – Instituto Agronômico de Campinas. Abacaxi IAC Gomo-de-mel. https://www.iac.sp.gov.br/cultivares/inicio/Folders%5CAbacaxi%5CcIACGomo-de-Mel.htm. Acesso em 30 de agosto de 2016

4.  Meirelles, L.A., Veiga, M.M., Duarte, F.J.C.M.: Efficiency of personal protective equipment used in agriculture. Work **41**(1), 14–18 (2012)
5.  Zhang, F., Yang, M., Liu, W.: Using integrated quality function deployment and theory of innovation problem solving approach for ergonomic product design. Comput. Ind. Eng. **76**, 60–74 (2014)
6.  Garrigou, A., Baldi, I., Dubuc, P.: Contributos da ergotoxicologia na avaliação da eficácia real dos EPI que devem proteger do risco fitossanitário: da análise da contaminação ao processo colectivo de alerta. Laboreal **4**(1), 92–103 (2008)
7.  Goutille, F., Galey, L., Rambaud, C., Pasquereau, P., Jackson Filho, J.M., Garrigou, A.: Prescrição e utilização de Equipamentos de Proteção Individual (EPI) em atividades com exposição a produtos químicos cancerígenos, mutagênicos e reprotóxicos (CMR): pesquisa-ação pluridisciplinar em uma fábrica francesa de decoração para móveis. Laboreal **12**(1), 23–38 (2016)
8.  Veiga, M.M., Duarte, F.J.C.M., Meirelles, L.A., Garrigou, A., Baldi, I.: A contaminação por agrotóxicos e os equipamentos de Proteção Individual (EPIs). Rev. Bras. Saúde Ocup. **32**(116), 57–68 (2007)
9.  Brouwer, D., Goede, H., Tijssen, S.: Introdução de ergonomia e conforto na seleção de equipamento de proteção individual (EPI); conceitos para uma nova abordagem. In: 8th International Symposium of ISSA Research Section, Athens, Greece. Proceedings (2003). https://www.elinyae.gr/en/lib_file_upload/FINAL%20TEXT%20186.1152876102435.pdf. Acesso em 19 de agosto de 2016
10. Akbar-Khanbzadeh, F., Bisesi, M.S.: Conforto equipamento de proteção individual. Appl. Ergon. **26**(3), 195–198 (1995)
11. Williams, G.L.: Improving fit through the integration of anthropometric data into a computer aided design and manufacture based design process. Doctoral thesis. Loughborough University (2015)
12. Abrahão, R.F., Gonzaga, M.C., Braunbeck, O.A.: Protective gloves on manual sugar cane are really effective? Work **41**(1), 4963–4966 (2012)
13. Adissi, P.J., Almeida, C.V.B.: Riscos na produção do abacaxi: o caso do baixo Paraíba/PB. XXII Encontro Nacional de engenharia de Produção, Curitiba-PR. Anais (2002). www.abepro.org.br/biblioteca/enegep2002_tr43_1257.pdf. Acesso em 28 de abril de 2015
14. Gonzaga, M.C.: Proteção dos trabalhadores durante o cultivo de abacaxi contra ataques de serpentes peçonhentas. Tese (Doutorado em Engenharia Agrícola). Faculdade de Engenharia Agrícola, Universidade Estadual de Campinas, Campinas (2017)
15. Gonzaga, M.C., Lima, C.Q.B.: Dificuldades e limitações das luvas de proteção usadas no corte manual da cana. Laboreal **12**(1), 77–87 (2016)
16. Cheng, L.C., Melo Filho, L.D.R.: QFD – Desdobramento da função qualidade na gestão de desenvolvimento de produtos, 2edn. Edgard Blücher, São Paulo (2010)
17. Guèrin, F., Lavile, A., Daniellou, F., Durafforg, J., Kerguelen, A.: Compreender o Trabalho para Transformá-lo: a prática da ergonomia. Blücher, São Paulo (2001)
18. Dedini, F.G.: QFD – Sistemática e Metodologia do Projeto. Faculdade de Engenharia Mecânica da UNICAMP, Campinas (2015)

# Leg Swelling Among Colombian Florists

Yordan Rodríguez[1]([✉]) [iD], Jonathan Osorio-Vasco[2] [iD], Ivonne Zuluaga[1] [iD],
and Ana Múnera[1] [iD]

[1] National School of Public Health, Universidad de Antioquia, Medellín, Colombia
yordan.rodriguez@udea.edu.co
[2] Centro Regional Aburrá Sur, Corporación Universitaria Minuto de Dios-UNIMINUTO,
Bello, Colombia
jvascoosori@uniminuto.edu.co

**Abstract.** This research aimed to analyze leg volume changes in a florists population—a cross-sectional study where lower leg circumference measurements were
taken at the beginning and end of an 8-h workday. Seventeen florists (8 women,
9 men) voluntarily participated; their legs' circumference was measured in 5 segments every 4 cm (20 cm in total) with the Gulick II tape measure to calculate the
lower legs' volume. The average volume in both legs increased (right leg 2.12%,
left leg 1.83%), with significant changes in both the right ($Z = -3.337$, $p = 0.001$)
and left ($Z = -2.769$, $p = 0.006$) legs between the start and end of the workday.
The left leg volume increased more in women (women: 11.63, men: 6.67, $p =
0.043$). This research shows a significant increase in leg volume in a population
of Colombian flower growers during an 8-h workday. These findings indicate the
need to pay more attention to standing work's effects to take preventive actions to
improve their working conditions from an ergonomic perspective.

**Keywords:** Floriculture · Agriculture · Leg swelling · Lower extremity

## 1  Introduction

Agricultural workers are exposed to high biomechanical loads [1], with the lower extremities being among the most affected body regions [2–4]. Floriculturists must remain for
long periods in a standing position during the development of their work activities,
which has been associated with the appearance of musculoskeletal symptoms in the
lower extremities [5].

One of the symptoms and problems reported with prolonged standing is increased
leg volume [6–11]. Leg volume increases due to reduced blood flow in the leg muscles, causing swelling of veins that may develop into varicose veins or chronic venous
insufficiency [7, 11, 12].

Increased leg volume and other lower extremity symptoms have been associated
with some risk factors such as flat shoes [13], a hard surface [14], standing time [9], and
some individual factors such as gender [12], weight, and height [14].

Colombia is the second-largest flower exporter in the world [15]. This sector generates about 130,000 jobs in the country [15], so improving working conditions in this

© The Author(s), under exclusive license to Springer Nature Switzerland AG 2021
N. L. Black et al. (Eds.): IEA 2021, LNNS 221, pp. 262–268, 2021.
https://doi.org/10.1007/978-3-030-74608-7_33

sector would significantly impact the Colombian labor force. However, few studies have been carried out in the flower-growing population to analyze the volume changes that occur in the legs related to their work activity.

This study aims to analyze the changes in leg volume in Colombian florists during a standard 8-h workday.

## 2 Materials and Methods

### 2.1 Type of Study and Population

In this study, the lower legs' circumference (right and left) was measured in 17 florists (8 females, 9 males). Measures were taken at the beginning and end of an 8-h workday. Nine different jobs were selected. The number of florists by job was distributed as follows: one in box assembly, one in the sprinkler, three in bouquet assembly, two in unbuttoning flower, one in cuttings transport, three in fumigation, three in hydration of flowers, two in irrigation of flowers and three in planting flowers. Figure 1 shows the workstations and some of the flower growers.

Participants were selected based on the number of florists assigned to each job. In jobs where between one and three florists were assigned, all were selected. In cases where there were more than three florists assigned to the job, the selection was random. To participate in the study, florists had to perform their activities in one of the selected jobs, be present on the day of data collection and express their voluntary participation in the study by signing an informed consent form.

A detailed observation of the workday activities was carried out to determine the florists' main postures. It was observed that florists remained between 80% and 100% of the working day in a standing position on a soil planting.

### 2.2 Leg Circumference Measurement

**Measuring Instrument**
To measure the circumference in both legs (right and left), we use the Gulick II tape measure [16]. The use of this tape reduces measurement error, according to several studies [14, 17, 18]. The tape measure proved reliable, with a reliability coefficient of 0.97 for the calf and 0.98 for the ankle [19]. Similarly, a high correlation (0.98) was found between leg measurements made with the Gulick II tape measure and a Pero-System optoelectronic [20].

**Measurement Procedure**
The work team consisted of two physiotherapists, one occupational health and safety professional, and one ergonomist. The two physiotherapists were in charge of collecting the information in the field and received prior training. The following is a description of the measurement protocol performed:

Measurements were taken in the area surrounding the workplace during the first and last hour of the workday. The florists were weighed, and their height and leg circumference were measured using the Gulick II tape measure. For left/right leg circumference

**Fig. 1.** Example of activities carried out by the population florists studied.

measurements, participants were asked to sit in a chair, remove their shoes, pull up their left/right leg pant boot, place it on a chair of similar height to the chair they were sitting in, and leave the left/right leg extended for measurements.

Circumference was measured at five points on the leg, each separated by 4 cm, starting from the lateral malleolus along the malleolus's longitudinal axis to the calf (20 cm). To facilitate and ensure the consistency of the measurements, the reference points were marked with permanent ink, and a wooden board was placed on the legs to make the reference marks. [14, 17, 21].

### 2.3   Calculation of Volume and Percentage of Change

Equation (1) (truncated cone formula) was used to calculate the legs' volume, based on the circumference records: [14, 17]:

$$V = \sum (X2 + Y2 + XY)/3\pi \qquad (1)$$

Where "V" is the volume of the leg, "X" is the lower circumference of the segment, and "Y" is the upper circumference of the segment 4 cm away from "X". Equation 1 was used to calculate the volume at the beginning of the working day (V1) and the volume at the end of the working day (V2). With Eq. (2), the percentages of volume variation were calculated [17]:

$$\Delta V\% = ((V2 - V1)/V1) \times 100 \qquad (2)$$

## 2.4 Statistical Processing

SPSS version 23 software (SPSS, Inc. 2012) was used for statistical analysis. A descriptive statistical analysis was performed for the socio-demographic characteristics. The average differences between the initial and final measurement of leg volume variation were calculated. The average percentage of leg volume change was calculated. The Wilcoxon signed-rank test was used to find significant differences in leg volume variation. For the analysis of the relationship between leg volume and sex, the U-Mann Whitney test was used.

## 3 Results

Twelve florists reported the right leg as the dominant leg, while only two florists reported the left leg. Age ranged from 20 to 45 years (mean 34.35 years), mean height was 165.4 cm (SD = 9.91); mean weight 71.82 kg (SD = 12.64).

The volume calculation showed that it increased at the end of the working day with significant differences in the right leg (Z = −3.337 p = 0.001) and left leg (Z = −2.769, p = 0.006). The right leg increased 0.29% more than the left leg (see Table 1).

**Table 1.** Average variation of volume in the legs, average difference, average percentage of variation, and Wilcoxon test. (N = 17, P < 0.05).

| Leg | Initial Volume $\overline{X}$ cm$^3$ | SD | Final Volume $\overline{X}$ cm$^3$ | SD | $\Delta \overline{X}$ cm$^3$ | $\Delta V \overline{X}\%$ | Wilcoxon test | |
| --- | --- | --- | --- | --- | --- | --- | --- | --- |
| | | | | | | | Z | P |
| Right | 1562.0453 | 228.45 | 1595.1947 | 221.15 | 33.14 | 2.12 | −3.337 | **0.001** |
| Left | 1579.8271 | 248.07 | 1608.8906 | 258.66 | 29.06 | 1.83 | −2.769 | **0.006** |

A significant association was found between sex and left leg volume changes, with females presenting a more significant leg volume increase (males: 6.67, females: 11.63, P = 0.043) (see Table 2).

**Table 2.** Relationship between sex and leg volume. $P < 0.05$.

| $\Delta \overline{X}$ | Bodyside | Sex | | |
|---|---|---|---|---|
| | | Men | Woman | P |
| Volume leg | Right | 8.11 | 10.00 | 0.441 |
| | Left | 6.67 | 11.63 | **0.043** |

# 4 Discussion

This study found that the floriculturists' legs' volume increased significantly between the beginning and the end of the workday. This symptom may be related to the appearance of varicose veins [12, 22].

On average, the left leg showed the greatest increase in volume between the beginning and the end of the workday (left leg 1608.8906 cm3 and right leg 1595.1947 cm$^3$). However, the right leg (2.12%) presented on average a higher percentage change in volume compared to the left leg (1.83%), which could be linked to the fact that the majority of florists (12) reported the right leg as the dominant leg.

Our study results are similar to that found by Zander et al. (2004), who found an increase in leg volume in 13 manufacturing florists over 8 h, with work on hard surfaces causing the greatest increase [14]. On the other hand, in our study, the florists remained on a considerably soft surface (planting soil). Besides, in our study, no variables were controlled, and two additional measurements (5 measurements every 4 cm) were performed in addition to those performed by Zander et al. (2004).

According to the results obtained in our study, the left leg volume was greater in women than in men (women: 11.63, men: 6.67, p = 0.043). It is possible that vascular symptoms or problems such as varicose veins appear more in women than in men, as Bahk et al. (2012) reported a higher prevalence of varicose veins in women than in men [22]. However, the occurrence in men of varicose veins in the lower extremities cannot be underestimated [12].

Future research should focus on analyzing what risk factors may be related to the occurrence of musculoskeletal pain and leg enlargement in flower growers.

# 5 Conclusions

This research shows a significant increase in leg volume in a population of Colombian flower growers during an 8-h workday. These findings indicate the need to pay more attention to standing work's effects to take preventive actions to improve their working conditions from an ergonomic perspective.

# References

1. Nguyen, T.H.Y., Bertin, M., Bodin, J., Fouquet, N., Bonvallot, N., Roquelaure, Y.: Multiple exposures and coexposures to occupational hazards among agricultural workers: a systematic review of observational studies. Saf. Health Work **9**, 239–48 (2018)

2. Jain, R., Meena, M.L., Dangayach, G.S., Bhardwaj, A.K.: Risk factors for musculoskeletal disorders in manual harvesting farmers of Rajasthan. Ind. Health **56**, 241–8 (2018)

3. Osborne, A., Blake, C., Fullen, B.M., Meredith, D., Phelan, J., Mcnamara, J., et al.: Risk factors for musculoskeletal disorders among farm owners and farm workers: a systematic review. Am. J. Ind. Med. **55**, 376–89 (2012)

4. Osborne, A., Blake, C., Fullen, B.M., Meredith, D., Phelan, J., McNamara, J., et al.: Prevalence of musculoskeletal disorders among farmers: a systematic review. Am. J. Ind. Med. **55**, 143–58 (2012)

5. Kong, Y.K., Lee, S.J., Lee, K.S., Kim, G.R., Kim, D.M.: Development of an ergonomics checklist for investigation of work-related whole-body disorders in farming - AWBA: agricultural whole-body assessment. J. Agric. Saf. Health **21**, 207–15 (2015)

6. Halim, I., Omar, A.R., Teknikal, U., Jaya, H.T.: A Review on health effects associated with prolonged. Int. J. Recent Res. Appl. Stud. **8**, 14–21 (2011)

7. Waters, T.R., Dick, R.B.: Evidence of health risks associated with prolonged standing at work and intervention effectiveness. Rehabil. Nurs. **40**, 148–65 (2015)

8. Coenen, P., Willenberg, L., Parry, S., Shi, J.W., Romero, L., Blackwood, D.M., et al.: Associations of occupational standing with musculoskeletal symptoms: a systematic review with meta-analysis. Br. J. Sports Med. **52**, 1–10 (2016)

9. Coenen, P., Parry, S., Willenberg, L., Shi, J.W., Romero, L., Blackwood, D.M., et al.: Associations of prolonged standing with musculoskeletal symptoms—A systematic review of laboratory studies. Gait Posture **58**, 310–8 (2017)

10. Chester, M.R., Rys, M.J., Konz, S.A.: Leg swelling, comfort and fatigue when sitting, standing, and sit/standing. Int. J. Ind. Ergon. **29**, 289–96 (2002)

11. Canadian Centre for Occupational Health and Safety. Working in a Standing Position – Basic. https://www.ccohs.ca/oshanswers/ergonomics/standing/standing_basic.html. Accessed 25 Jan 2021

12. Krijnen, R.M., de Boer, E.M., Ader, H.J., Bruynzeel, D.P.: Venous insufficiency in male workers with a standing profession. Part 1: epidemiology. Dermatology **194**, 111–20 (1997)

13. Sousa, A., Tavares, J.M.R.S., Macedo, R., Rodrigues, A.M., Santos, R.: Influence of wearing an unstable shoe on thigh and leg muscle activity and venous response in upright standing. Appl. Ergon. **43**, 933–9 (2012)

14. Zander, J.E., King, P.M., Ezenwa, B.N.: Influence of flooring conditions on lower leg volume following prolonged standing. Int. J. Ind. Ergon. **34**, 279–88 (2004)

15. Villamizar, F, Cruz F, Caceres N, Valero E. Desempeño Del Sector Floricultor Informe, https://www.supersociedades.gov.co/Noticias/Documents/2016/EE-Estudio sector Flores-2016 VI 13_Final.pdf, last accessed 2021/02/07.

16. Country Technology Inc. Gulick II Plus Tape Measure, (Model 67019). https://www.fitnessmart.com/collections/gulick-ii-tape-measures-calibrated-for-accuracy-and-repeatability/products/gulick-ii-plus-tape-measure?variant=291235270471999. Accessed 20 Jan 2021

17. Karimi, Z., Allahyari, T., Azghani, M.R., Khalkhali, H.: Influence of unstable footwear on lower leg muscle activity, volume change and subjective discomfort during prolonged standing. Appl. Ergon. **53**, 95–102 (2016)

18. Lin, Y.H., Chen, C.Y., Cho, M.H.: Influence of shoe/floor conditions on lower leg circumference and subjective discomfort during prolonged standing. Appl. Ergon. **43**, 965–70 (2012)

19. Labs, K.-H., Tschoepl, M., Gamba, G., Aschwanden, M., Jaeger, K.A.: The reliability of leg circumference assessment: A comparison of spring tape measurements and optoelectronic volumetry. Vasc Med **5**, 69–74 (2000)

20. Mayrovitz, H., Sims, N., Macdonald, J.: Assessment of limb volume by manual and automated methods in patients with limb edema or lymphedema. Adv Ski Wound Care **13**, 272–6 (2000)

21. Lin, Y.H., Chen, C.Y., Cho, M.H.: Effectiveness of leg movement in reducing leg swelling and discomfort in lower extremities. Appl Ergon **43**, 1033–7 (2012)
22. Bahk, J.W., Kim, H., Jung-Choi, K., Jung, M.C., Lee, I.: Relationship between prolonged standing and symptoms of varicose veins and nocturnal leg cramps among women and men. Ergonomics **55**, 133–9 (2012)

# Case Study: Ergonomic Analysis and Intervention of a Tractor Cabin: Improving Its Usability and Reducing the Risk of Physical Fatigue

Guillermina Dinora Suárez-Gómez[✉], Julieta Ramírez-Reynoso,
Lizbeth Arévalo González, María Fernanda Flores-Espinoza, Mariana Díaz-Pinal,
and Pilar Hernández-Grageda

Universidad Panamericana Campus Guadalajara, Calzada Circunvalación
Poniente N. 49 Ciudad Granja, 45010 Zapopan, Jalisco, México
{0215081,0216853,0215071,0214693,0215338,phernand}@up.edu.mx

**Abstract.** There is a lack of information regarding the ergonomic principles that should be followed when designing the interior of a tractor cabin in order for it to be comfortable, usable and safe. This design must take into account operator's characteristics such as his posture when driving, the forces that need to be applicated when manipulating the instruments panel or the cognitive processes implied when the operator is interacting with the interior of the cabin. Since an ergonomic cabin can not only ensure the safety of the driver, but it can also help him/her to be more efficient in their daily activities, the objective of this report is to propose ergonomic interventions through literature research, suggesting a conceptual design that could improve the usability of a tractor cabin. Some decision-making methodologies such as Reverse brainstorming and Lightning Decision Jam are applied along the design process in order to evaluate and delimit the attributes of the new design that could best impact the positive experience of the tractor's operators.

**Keywords:** Tractor users · Tractor ergonomics · Physical fatigue · Ergonomic intervention · Cognitive process · Operational Systems · Endurance · Usability · Efficiency

## 1 Problem Statement

Ergonomics are fundamental for the design of a tractor cabin, as they can improve their efficiency and safety. However, in-depth research on tractor driving posture is lacking and quality of work is affected when the driver is subjected to poor posture [1]. Occupational musculoskeletal injuries were identified as significant health problems among tractor operators. This could happen if the forces used to operate the tractor cabin exceed the muscular endurance of the driver [2]. For instance, exposure time and frequency can also increase the risk of injuries [3].

© The Author(s), under exclusive license to Springer Nature Switzerland AG 2021
N. L. Black et al. (Eds.): IEA 2021, LNNS 221, pp. 269–273, 2021.
https://doi.org/10.1007/978-3-030-74608-7_34

## 2  Objective

A tractor design that does not consider the characteristics and limitations of the driver can cause him/her interaction problems. According to a study made on adequate driving posture for tractor drivers, accurate working posture prediction for tractors must include an understanding of the operational state of both the agricultural vehicle and the implement pulled by the tractor [1]. The objective of this report is to identify and prioritize problems with the interaction between the driver and each component of a tractor cabin, with the purpose of planning ergonomic intervention strategies and to provide a new design proposal that can improve the usability of the interior of the cabin and the user experience.

## 3  Methodology

The first thing was to learn about the components of a tractor cabin and the problems with the interaction between the user and each component, so a commercial research and literature review were made. Then, in order to identify and prioritize ergonomic intervention strategies inside a generic tractor cabin, the *Reverse Brainstorming* tool was used [4]. Following that, we focused on the usability objectives to identify the highest possible level of effectiveness, efficiency, and safety in the interaction between users and the elements of the tractor cabin. Also, a *Procedures Analysis* was conducted to take into consideration the cognitive processes of the users to identify important points where we could step in to reduce the mental load during the interaction according to what we found in the literature review. Finally, a conceptual proposal including all the important points found in the first steps of our methodology was developed and analyzed by the *Lightning Decision Jam* [5], a tool used to identify improvement points and to prioritize solutions according to the greatest positive impact on the user experience.

## 4  Results

The interventions proposed for the tractor cabin follow the ASAE EP443 1 FEB04 Color Coding Hand Controls for buttons and levers and focus on four areas: front panel, lifter command dashboard, multi-purpose panel and seat.

Figures 1a, b, 2, 3 and 4, show the representation of how the ergonomic interventions were applied inside the tractor cabin. A paragraph is followed after each image to indicate how the interventions could work for each component.

The front panel is mainly made up of three parts which are the meters, the buttons, and the digital indicators. There are 2 different forms of meters: The first ones are meters with needle indicators (k), the speedometer, the tachometer and gasoline meter. These three meters should have visual aid apart from the needle, and a light rail that indicates along with the needle the position of the speed, the revolutions, and the amount of gasoline. The reason for this is that it would be easier to identify the measures without requiring any effort from the driver. The second meter is in linear form (f), which resemble a thermometer. These meters indicate the temperature, the maximum height of the attachment and minimum as well as its angle.

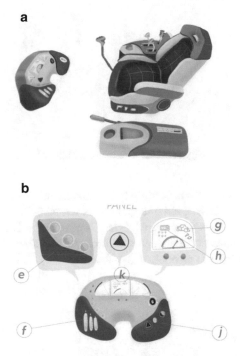

**Fig. 1.** **a** General view of the tractor's cabin with the ergonomic interventions **b** Front instrument's panel.

It is recommended that all the buttons are designed with a small ring of light as this is a very useful visual aid for the correct operation of the tractor. This way. can quickly see which attachments are activated or deactivated. To activate each button and deactivate it is only necessary to press it. It is proposed that the emergency button (i) is the only one that works differently to avoid activating it by mistake. A mechanism where it is necessary to keep the button pressed in order to turn it can be added. The distribution of the buttons should be based on anthropometric measurements as well as biomechanical. The most important buttons should be on the right side (j), as they are the most frequently used, the most important and those that require the most force (flashing, emergency, initiated, non-classic Front PTO). On the other hand, there are the buttons on the left side (e), which should be the less frequently used: front, rear and rotating lights, stand and steel, CPC.

The digital indicators are the icons that light up on the screen (h) to indicate the status of the tractor, these indicators should be only activated if it is necessary to report something about the tractor. The only visible indicator that should always be on, is the silhouette of the tractor (g). If a part of the tractor fails, the area of the tractor where the failure is located lights up.

The panel proposed consists of 9 levers and buttons that help the user be more precise in each task thanks to the location of each one, the ergonomic form and the security button. Each piece should be designed with anatomical adaptations to the form of the

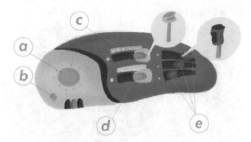

**Fig. 2.** Lifter command dashboard.

hand that makes it easier to use according to the movement needed. All the components of this dashboard should have a led line that blinks when the lever is being used to help the user identify which lever is activated. Each form must be different because it helps the user to make a connection between the form and function. (a)-Power. (b)-Engine Memory. (c&d)-Rear lifter controllers. (e)-Valve levers.

**Fig. 3.** Multipurpose panel

For the comfort of the driver, there could be 3 compartments in the multipurpose panel. The first is a cup holder for any type of drink (o), the second compartment (p) has a sliding door so that when the driver opens it, it does not take up any space. Inside this compartment, it could have a cooling system so that food or objects can be kept at an appropriate temperature. The third compartment (r) is at the back of the board to the side of the connection panel (q) so that the user could have a comfortable place to put their electronics.

The seat should be primarily based on the comfort and adjustability of the driver. It should be made up of three buttons placed at the bottom of the seat so that the user can adjust the seat according to their needs (raise or lower it (n) recline or straighten it (m) and move it closer or further away (o), all within the driver's reach and with easy handling.

The shape of the seat should be ergonomic so that the driver has a comfortable posture during his/her workday. Based on reach and posture, the design must have a curve for greater lumbar support (q), the head (p)must be focused so that it can be adjusted at different heights and based on clearance and strength. There should be armrests (l) for better support, and considering the safety of the driver, the seat belt.

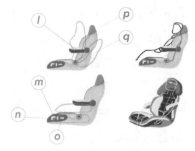

**Fig. 4.** Seat

## 5  Discussion

According to the literature research, analysis of ergonomic methodology and the results presented, it is important to consider that the design of the tractor must be focused on the driver to improve his/her experience in their work day and facilitating the operation of the tractor using color coding hand controls, visual aids and anatomically adapted forms. Consider as a limitation that the results presented are theoretical and not proved with real users because of the Covid-19, but the next step would be to design tests with real users to confirm the ergonomic interventions presented previously.

## 6  Conclusion

By following this methodology and the design recommendations, tractor drivers could be highly benefited. The aim of this design is not only to promote good posture and a safe working space, but also to help drivers become more efficient in their daily tasks. Besides, along with the color coding and ergonomic forms, drivers can identify more easily the function of each button and lever and reduce the number of incidents that could be caused by wrong recognition. Finally, safety could be better ensured for the driver, as they spent long working hours manipulating the tractor.

## References

1. Li, H.: Predictive model of tractor driving posture considering front and rear view. Biosyst. Eng. **189**(1), 64–75 (2019)
2. Zhang, Z., Way, K., Zhang, W., Ma, L., Chen, Z.: Muscular fatigue and maximun endurance time assesment for male and female industrial workers. Int. J. Ind. Ergon. **44**, 292–297 (2014)
3. Feyzi, M.: Ergonomically design based of tractor control tools. Int. J. Ind. Ergon. **72**, 298–307 (2019)
4. Evans, N.: Destroying collaboration and knowledge sharing in the workplace: a reverse brainstorming approach. Knowl. Manag. Res. Pract. **10**(2), 175–187 (2012)
5. Courtney, J.: Lightning design jams: the exercise that will solve all of your problems (2018). https://www.invisionapp.com/inside-design/lightning-design-jams/

# Safety in the Field: Assessing the Impact of Stress and Fatigue on Situation Awareness in Irish and British Farmers

Ilinca-Ruxandra Tone[✉] and Amy Irwin

Applied Psychology and Human Factors, Non-Technical Skills in Agriculture,
School of Psychology, University of Aberdeen, Aberdeen, UK
i.tone.19@abdn.ac.uk

**Abstract.** Situation awareness (SA) is a cognitive safety-critical skill, consisting of three levels – perception, comprehension, and anticipation. SA lapses have been associated with many incidents and accidents across high-risk industries. Stress and fatigue can negatively impact SA, leading to some of these lapses. More recently, the importance of SA has also been acknowledged in agriculture, the most dangerous industry in Ireland and the United Kingdom by injury and fatality rate. The current study aimed to explore SA lapses and the impact of stress and fatigue on SA in agriculture. Fifteen Irish and British farmers were interviewed using the critical incident technique followed by general questions on stress and fatigue in farming. In the critical incident section, interviewees were asked to verbally recall a recent negative farming experience, an error that occurred, or adverse conditions which they had to manage on the farm while feeling tired or stressed. Additional questions were asked to uncover implicit knowledge on SA lapses, stress, and fatigue. Interviews were analysed using qualitative content analysis. SA lapses were reportedly involved in all accidents and incidents. Many occurred at the perception level, as a failure to monitor or observe data, usually because of attentional narrowing. Several lapses also occurred at the comprehension level as an incomplete or an inaccurate mental model, usually in the context of a recent change in equipment or machinery. Stress and fatigue had a negative impact on SA through cognitive impairments. A twofold strategy is suggested, focused on strengthening SA and managing stress and fatigue.

**Keywords:** Situation awareness · Stress · Fatigue · Safety · Agriculture

## 1 Introduction

Situation awareness (SA) is a cognitive safety-critical skill, essential for reducing the likelihood of errors in high-risk industries. Conversely, failures in SA have been associated with major incidents and disasters such as Deepwater Horizon (Sneddon et al. 2013). A widely accepted definition of SA is "the perception of the elements in the environment within a volume of time and space, the comprehension of their meaning, and the projection of their status in the near future" (Endsley 1995a). The triadic model

N. L. Black et al. (Eds.): IEA 2021, LNNS 221, pp. 274–283, 2021.
https://doi.org/10.1007/978-3-030-74608-7_35

by Endsley (1995a) will hereby be adopted as theoretical background. Thus, Level 1 SA involves perceiving relevant aspects in the environment, whilst Level 2 SA relies on a synthesis of separate Level 1 data and encompasses a subsequent understanding of the situation by considering such patterns in the light of operator goals. Finally, Level 3 SA consists of the ability to predict the future state of the system and is founded on both Level 1 and Level 2 SA. Errors of SA can occur at all three levels and can be classified according to an SA error taxonomy developed in aviation (Endsley 1995b; Jones and Endsley 1995).

Stress represents one of the factors which can negatively affect SA (Endsley 1995a). Whilst a certain amount of stress may have a beneficial effect by directing attention to important aspects of the situation, a higher amount may impair SA by demanding a portion of limited attentional resources. The most common ways in which stressors can decrease SA are attentional narrowing and premature closure i.e., reaching a decision without considering all available information. These cognitive lapses can lead to Level 1 "failure to monitor or observe data" errors. In novel situations where a mental model does not exist, stress is also likely to lead to inaccurate or incomplete Level 2 SA through reductions in working memory capacity. Alongside stress, fatigue could also impair SA by reducing alertness levels (HSE 2006).

Research across high-risk industries using the original SA error taxonomy or an adapted version to analyse and quantify SA lapses has consistently shown that a large proportion of incidents and accidents are caused by failures in SA. In most studies, Level 1 lapses were identified most frequently, followed by Level 2 and Level 3 lapses, respectively. Nevertheless, since errors are typically coded at the lowest level, comprehension and projection lapses may have been underestimated. In studies which reported factors affecting SA at each of its three levels, the most common single type of error was failure to scan or observe data, typically due to attentional narrowing or distraction and low vigilance (e.g., Endsley 1995b; Sandhåland et al. 2015; Sneddon et al. 2006). Various sources of data were analysed, including accident reports in aviation and bridge operations (Endsley 1995b; Sandhåland et al. 2015); incident reports in anaesthesia and offshore drilling (Schulz et al. 2016; Sneddon et al. 2006); patient records in primary care (Singh et al. 2012); and closed malpractice claims in anaesthesia (Schulz et al. 2017). However, an acknowledged limitation of many of these narratives is the incomplete information available on SA. Consequently, some studies also employed semi-structured qualitative interviews with subject-matter experts to explore SA aspects further (Singh et al. 2012).

Specific factors leading to SA lapses have also been studied in offshore drilling, leading to mixed results. Thus, through interviews with oil and gas drilling personnel, Sneddon et al. (2006) found that stress and fatigue were amongst the largest contributory factors to decreased SA quality. A subsequent study investigated the impact of stress and fatigue on SA as measured through a self-report scale and the relationship with safety behaviour and accident involvement (Sneddon et al. 2013). Expectedly, higher levels of stress and fatigue were negatively associated with SA. Nevertheless, stress remained the sole significant predictor of poor SA after the regression analysis.

Agriculture is the most dangerous industry in Ireland and the United Kingdom, with a fatality and injury rate much higher than any other industrial sector (HSA 2020; HSE

2020). A recent series of studies has revealed that failures in SA, especially because of fatigue or stress, significantly contribute to agricultural accidents. In an initial interview study with British farmers, lack of SA was identified in many reported incidents and was frequently associated with impaired attention due to rushing or fatigue (Irwin and Poots 2015). Most participants also identified stress due to task pressure as a potential cause of accidents. Several farmers also acknowledged the importance of experience in developing mental models and enhancing their higher levels of SA. In a subsequent investigation of risk perception in tractor-based scenarios, most farmers decided not to proceed with the task when tired, expressing concern about the detrimental effects of fatigue on awareness (Irwin and Poots 2018). Finally, an analysis of error types and factors impacting SA in British and Irish agricultural machinery operators found that the most frequent lapse occurred at Level 1 due to information not being observed (Irwin et al. 2019), mirroring the results from other high-risk industries. This type of error was commonly linked with individual performance limitations or task-based pressures such as fatigue, distraction, rushing or stress. Level 2 errors were also reported, either in the form of a poor mental model in unfamiliar situations or of complacency and overconfidence.

Some studies conducted outside of the UK have also analysed the impact of stress and fatigue on farm safety. Thus, high levels of perceived stressors including financial issues and time pressure, stress symptoms and poor safety behaviours predicted farm accidents in a sample of Danish farmers (Glasscock et al. 2006). An interaction was observed, so that higher levels of stress symptoms and not performing safety checks increased the risk of injury. The authors argued that farmers with poor safety habits cannot manage risks when stressed, due to impaired attention and concentration. Hagel et al. (2013) also identified an association between economic worry and accident risk. Financial stress associated with conditions on Saskatchewan farms impacted safety indirectly through behavioural changes linked to fatigue. Long working hours and subsequent limited sleep duration as factors leading to fatigue have also been shown to increase the risk of workplace injury in farming (Choi et al. 2006; Day et al. 2009; Lilley et al. 2012; Sprince et al. 2003; Stallones et al. 2006).

In the light of the above, the current study was conducted to identify SA lapses and to determine the impact of stress and fatigue on SA and safety in agriculture, through a qualitative content analysis of semi-structured interviews with Irish and British farmers. Expanding our emergent knowledge of SA in agriculture and understanding underlying psychosocial causes of farm accidents can help inform future safety interventions.

## 2 Method

### 2.1 Participants

Farmers (N = 15; 1 female, 14 males; aged 25–59) were recruited from Ireland (n = 10) and the United Kingdom (n = 5) in February-March & June-August 2020. Participants worked on several types of farm: dairy (n = 7), animals and arable crops (n = 3), mixed animals (sheep & beef cattle) (n = 2), dairy & beef cattle (n = 1), sheep (n = 1), arable crops (n = 1). Recruitment criteria were farming as main occupation and age over 18.

## 2.2  Design

**Interview.** The critical incident technique (Flanagan 1954) was employed in the first part of each qualitative semi-structured interview. The method had been previously used to elicit detailed information from domain experts on non-technical skills (Irwin and Poots 2015), including SA.

In the critical incident section, participants (all but one who could not recall a critical incident) were asked to verbally recall from memory a recent negative farming experience, an error that occurred, or adverse conditions which they had to manage on the farm while feeling tired or stressed. The interviewees were asked to provide as many details as possible surrounding the critical incident, from the lead up to the consequences of the event. Participants were asked to describe their thoughts and behaviours, as well the actions of any other individuals present. Additional questions were asked to uncover implicit knowledge with a focus on SA lapses, stress, and fatigue. These questions were adapted from an interview schedule exploring critical incidents in helicopter pilots (Hamlet et al. 2018) and from SA literature.

In the second and third part of the interview, participants were asked more general questions on stress and fatigue in agriculture, including on the potential impact of these factors on SA. These were based on a literature review conducted on the topic.

**Demographic Survey.**  Farmers were asked to report their age, gender, role, work schedule, average number of hours worked, any off-farm employment, number of hours worked per week in off-farm employment, number of hours of sleep per 24h, and the type and size of current farm. This information was collected to describe the sample.

## 2.3  Data Collection

This research project was approved in January 2020 by the Psychology Ethics Committee, University of Aberdeen. Participants were recruited through an email invitation sent to contacts within agricultural organisations or from a farming background. Recruitment was also conducted online via Twitter and specialized farming forums. All participants from Ireland were recruited through two organisational contacts within Teagasc. Both the invitation letter and the information sheet offered potential participants information about the study and indicated the opportunity to ask additional questions before participation. Suitable dates and times were arranged for the interviews, either through organisational contacts or directly.

Informed consent was obtained prior to the interview. Consent forms were stored separately from interview transcripts to maintain anonymity. Audio recorded interviews lasting between 20 and 50 min (30 min on average) were conducted by the first author in March (13 interviews) & August (2 interviews) 2020. The interviews were conducted over the telephone, due to the remote geographical location of participants and COVID restrictions and were followed by the demographic survey. Due to the semi-structured nature of the interview schedule, existing questions were omitted or altered where relevant to accommodate information already provided by the participant. Similarly, additional questions were asked if necessary. Participants were fully debriefed at the end of the study. All interview recordings were transcribed verbatim by the first author and sub-sequently deleted. To maintain anonymity, personally identifiable details were removed from the interview transcripts.

An initial minimum sample size of 12 participants was established based on relevant literature (Guest et al. 2006) and similar studies (Irwin and Poots 2015). Since most participants in the initial sample had been recruited from Ireland ($n = 9$) and since data saturation had not yet been reached (i.e., the point where no new concepts or behaviours are identified), a second wave of data collection occurred in August 2020. After this stage, data saturation was reached.

### 2.4 Data Analysis

The interview transcripts were coded using qualitative content analysis (Hsieh and Shannon 2005). All coding and analysis were conducted using qualitative analysis software NVivo 12.

Stage 1 of coding involved the first author reading the transcripts and then coding using primarily manifest, descriptive coding, each code capturing what the interviewees had said. Latent coding was also used for certain codes where further interpretation was necessary. For example, fragments describing cognitive lapses were interpreted and coded according to SA theory (Endsley 1995a). The first three interviews coded were from British farmers; these were then compared to four of the interviews from Irish farmers to determine any differences between geographical regions. As similar patterns were observed and given the small number of British farmers, data from both locations was considered as a single sample. Stage 2 of coding required codes to be streamlined and then their meaning was checked for accuracy. The first seven interviews coded, alongside the codebook derived from this analysis were also checked by the second author to ensure the consistency of the coding strategy. Minor amendments to the code names and meanings were made. Codes were then grouped into broad categories and several levels of sub-categories, describing underlying trends within the data. Some of these sub-categories were informed by relevant models and theories, for instance the taxonomy of SA errors (Endsley 1995b).

Data from the two interviews collected later was analysed using the existing frame-work, whilst allowing for minor amendments to the structure. When preparing the current chapter, data from all interviews was reconsidered and recoded where necessary.

## 3 Results

### 3.1 Demographic Characteristics

Most participants ($n = 13$) were aged 40–59, with the remainder ($n = 2$) aged 25–29. All participants were farm owners, except for one farm tenant. All participants worked full-time, with one participant working part-time on their own farm and full-time in off-farm employment. Participants reported working a minimum of either 49h per week ($n = 8$) ($M = 64$) or 8.5h per day ($n = 7$) ($M = 10.6$). Two participants currently held off-farm employment, in which they spent 30-40h and 55-60h per week, respectively.

Typical reported sleep duration varied between 5.5 and 7.8h (M = 6.6). The size of the farms (n = 14) ranged between 79 and 800ac (M = 272), with one significant outlier of 2200ac.

## 3.2 Situation Awareness

SA lapses were reportedly involved in all accidents and incidents. These were broadly described as a general loss of concentration or focus. Some participants mentioned specific elements of which they lost awareness, such as own location, personal status, or safety aspects including risks and hazards. For example, the following interviewee reported a complete loss of spatial awareness leading up to the critical incident: *"I don't know where I am anymore." (P2).* Another participant reported a lack of self-awareness prior to the accident, especially of fatigue levels: *"I didn't know I was tired and rushing at all." (P4).* For some participants, the realisation of what was going on only occurred in hindsight: *"I did realize afterwards." (P6).* The general role of good SA as a protective factor and of poor SA as a contributing factor to errors, incidents and accidents was also mentioned by many participants who solely described adverse circumstances: *"Not as aware of your surroundings and obviously that can lead to accidents." (P8).*

Of the SA lapses which could be accurately classified, many occurred at Level 1 SA, as a failure to monitor or observe data which was otherwise readily available and discernible in the environment: *"I didn't see any risk at all." (P1).* For instance, one participant failed to notice that a shed door was not closed properly, which led to an incident involving cattle. In most of these instances, participants demonstrated attentional narrowing, whereby they focused excessively on one element whilst ignoring others: *"I was just totally focused on his nostrils." (P1).* Some interviewees also exhibited premature closure: *"I just saw the bucket and I reacted." (P4).* These cognitive failures were compounded by the addition of heavy workload and rushing.

Many SA lapses also occurred at Level 2 in the form of poor comprehension of perceived data in the light of operator goals. Most participants explicitly expressed an inability to understand the situation, either in the form of an incomplete or an inaccurate mental model: *"I didn't realize how serious the situation was" (P6).* Some interviewees also reported a recent change in equipment or machinery or over-familiarity with existing equipment. For instance, the following participant used an outdated mental model when operating a new tractor, formed through their experience with the old one: *"Possibly because of that I was not used to the operation of it." (P6).*

## 3.3 Stress and Fatigue

The contribution of fatigue to farm safety was widely acknowledged, both in general terms and as a causal factor in the context of critical incidents: *"Fatigue was the problem there." (P2).* Participants took more risks and shortcuts to complete tasks quicker when fatigued: *"You would definitely cut corners." (P12).* In most critical incidents, long working hours, high workload, and lack of sleep were the main contributory factors to this extreme tiredness. Many participants reported that fatigue led to decreased alertness, which in extreme cases meant that the operator was falling asleep on the job. In terms of cognitive lapses, fatigue caused impaired concentration and poor SA. For instance, several participants described their actions when fatigued as *"going through the motions"*, resulting in SA failures in both their perception and comprehension.

Similarly, stress was regarded as a contributory factor to errors, incidents and lapses on the farm. What is more, many participants also reported disregarding safety when stressed. At a cognitive level, stress led to impaired concentration and internal focus on worries and concerns, contributing to many of the previously outlined SA lapses: *"You're on the job, but your mind is not there, that's stress for me."* (P13).

# 4  Discussion

The results of the current study highlight the importance of SA within agriculture, adding to the existing literature in other high-risk industries and to more recent findings in farming (Irwin and Poots 2015; 2018; Irwin et al. 2019). Thus, general SA failures and lapses at Level 1 (perception) and Level 2 (comprehension) were present in all accidents and incidents reported. The data also indicated the potential negative impact of stress and fatigue on SA, both generally and in the context of critical incidents, mirroring previous results from offshore drilling (Sneddon et al. 2006; 2013) and farming (Irwin and Poots 2015; 2018; Irwin et al. 2019). Stress and fatigue were regarded as main contributory factors to errors, incidents, and accidents, in line with studies on accident and injury risk within agriculture (Choi et al. 2006; Day et al. 2009; Glasscock et al. 2006; Hagel et al. 2013; Lilley et al. 2012; Sprince et al. 2003; Stallones et al. 2006).

Many SA lapses which occurred in the reported accidents and incidents were Level 1 "failure to monitor or observe data" errors, which happened because of underlying attentional narrowing or premature closure. SA error analyses in aviation, offshore drilling, bridge operations and farming have frequently identified this single type of lapse, also occurring due to distraction or attentional narrowing (Endsley 1995b; Irwin et al. 2019; Sandhåland et al. 2015; Sneddon et al. 2006). This is an important issue for SA, as certain elements in the environment are attended at the expense of others which are often safety-critical, as it was also the case in the current study. For instance, airplane crashes have occurred due to an excessive focus on landing gear leading to a neglect of fuel usage, due to attentional narrowing on the flight direction indicator or due to a failure to check flap status (Endsley 1995a).

Many SA lapses also occurred at Level 2 as either an incomplete or an incorrect mental model, in the context of a recent change in equipment or machinery or over-familiarity with existing equipment. This would suggest that operators were using old mental models when dealing with new equipment. The same underlying factors have also been identified through a previous SA error analysis in farming (Irwin et al. 2019). Although these errors are typically less frequently identified in the literature than errors of perception, some studies in anaesthesia and primary care found Level 2 SA lapses to be equally prevalent (Schulz et al. 2016; Singh et al. 2012). It can be argued that like medicine, farming is an unstandardized industry in terms of training and work settings, as opposed to aviation (Schulz et al. 2016).

The current study extended the existing literature in aviation, offshore drilling and farming by exploring the specific impact of stress and fatigue on SA and safety in agriculture. Many participants reported that fatigue led to decreased alertness and to cognitive lapses, such as impaired concentration and poor SA. Stress also reportedly led to impaired concentration and internal focus on worries and concerns, contributing to many SA lapses. In other words, fatigue impacted SA through decreased vigilance, whereas stress demanded a portion of the limited attentional resources of the operator (Endsley 1995a).

A few limitations of the project should be noted. The current data is specific to a purposive sample of farmers from Ireland and the UK predominantly running animal farms. As such, generalizability of results is not advised to farmers outside these geographical regions or in different farm operations. The current study may be subject to self-selection bias, whereby the sample mostly consisted of participants with an interest in safety issues or who had previously sustained workplace accidents or injuries. Participant recruitment was mainly conducted during busy times of the year, namely calving and lambing season, which may also explain the reduced sample size. Despite taking measures to ensure rigor in the data analysis process, such as cross-checking of the coding structure by the second author and data saturation, qualitative analysis is founded on subjectivity and interpretation and multiple meanings are possible within the data. The causality between variables of interest warrants further investigation. What is more, self-reports are subject to individual and recall bias. Furthermore, although self-reports of critical incidents provide valuable insight into cognitive aspects otherwise not available in official accident and incident reports, SA lapses were sometimes not verbalised despite probing efforts. Importantly, lapses in the current study were coded at the lowest identified level, as per similar studies, which might explain the absence of Level 3 errors. Frequency was not reported within the results section as the number of accidents and incidents was too small for reliable statistical inferences. However, the participant quotes provided good descriptive illustrations of the types of SA lapses and contributory factors.

The identified connection between stress and fatigue and SA lapses flags the need for a twofold strategy in agriculture, focused on strengthening SA on the one hand and managing stress and fatigue on the other hand. This is based on the acknowledgement that certain levels of stress and fatigue are sometimes inevitable in the farming industry. Mental models which support higher levels of SA can be improved through training of both technical skills and SA. Furthermore, checklists which have recently been developed based on research with tractor operators can prompt users to complete procedural steps and can further support SA (Irwin et al. 2019).

# References

Sneddon, A., Mearns, K., Flin, R.: Stress, fatigue, situation awareness and safety in offshore drilling crews. Saf. Sci. **56**, 80–88 (2013)

Endsley, M.R.: Toward a theory of situation awareness in dynamic systems. Hum. Factors **37**(1), 32–64 (1995a)

Endsley, M.R.: A taxonomy of situation awareness errors. Hum. Factors Aviat. Oper. **3**(2), 287–292 (1995b)

Jones, D.G., Endsley, M.R.: Investigation of situation awareness errors. In: Proceedings of the 8th International Symposium on Aviation Psychology. The Ohio State University, Columbus, OH (1995)

HSE: The development of a fatigue/risk index for shiftworkers, RR446. HSE Books, Sudbury (2006)

Sandhåland, H., Oltedal, H., Eid, J.: Situation awareness in bridge operations–A study of collisions between attendant vessels and offshore facilities in the North Sea. Saf. Sci. **79**, 277–285 (2015)

Sneddon, A., Mearns, K., Flin, R.: Situation awareness and safety in offshore drill crews. Cogn. Technol. Work **8**(4), 255–267 (2006)

Schulz, C.M., Krautheim, V., Hackemann, A., Kreuzer, M., Kochs, E.F., Wagner, K.J.: Situation awareness errors in anesthesia and critical care in 200 cases of a critical incident reporting system. BMC Anesthesiol. **16**(1), 1–10 (2016)

Schulz, C.M., Burden, A., Posner, K.L., Mincer, S.L., Steadman, R., Wagner, K.J., Domino, K.B.: Frequency and type of situational awareness errors contributing to death and brain damage: a closed claims analysis. Anesthesiology **127**(2), 326–337 (2017)

Singh, H., Giardina, T.D., Petersen, L.A., Smith, M.W., Paul, L.W., Dismukes, K., Bhagwath, G., Thomas, E.J.: Exploring situational awareness in diagnostic errors in primary care. BMJ Qual. Saf. **21**(1), 30–38 (2012)

HSA: Fatal accidents (2020). https://www.hsa.ie/eng/Your_Industry/Agriculture_Forestry/Fur ther_Information/Fatal_Accidents/

HSE: Fatal injuries in agriculture, forestry and fishing in Great Britain 2018/19 (2020). https://www.hse.gov.uk/agriculture/resources/fatal.htm

Irwin, A., Poots, J.: The human factor in agriculture: an interview study to identify farmers' non-technical skills. Saf. Sci. **74**, 114–121 (2015)

Irwin, A., Poots, J.: Investigation of UK farmer go/no-go decisions in response to tractor-based risk scenarios. J. Agromed. **23**(2), 154–165 (2018)

Irwin, A., Caruso, L., Tone, I.: Thinking ahead of the tractor: driver safety and situation awareness. J. Agromed. **24**(3), 1–10 (2019)

Glasscock, D.J., Rasmussen, K., Carstensen, O., Hansen, O.N.: Psychosocial factors and safety behaviour as predictors of accidental work injuries in farming. Work Stress **20**(2), 173–189 (2006)

Hagel, L., Pahwa, P., Dosman, J.A., Pickett, W.: Economic worry and the presence of safety hazards on farms. Accid. Anal. Prev. **53**, 156–160 (2013)

Choi, S.W., Peek-Asa, C., Sprince, N.L., Rautiainen, R.H., Flamme, G.A., Whitten, P.S., Zwerling, C.: Sleep quantity and quality as a predictor of injuries in a rural population. Am. J. Emerg. Med. **24**(2), 189–196 (2006)

Day, L., Voaklander, D., Sim, M., Wolfe, R., Langley, J., Dosman, J., Hagel, L., Ozanne, J.: Risk factors for work related injury among male farmers. Occup. Environ. Med. **66**(5), 312–318 (2009)

Lilley, R., Day, L., Koehncke, N., Dosman, J., Hagel, L., William, P.: The relationship between fatigue-related factors and work-related injuries in the Saskatchewan Farm Injury Cohort Study. Am. J. Ind. Med. **55**(4), 367–375 (2012)

Sprince, N.L., Zwerling, C., Lynch, C.F., Whitten, P.S., Thu, K., Logsden-Sackett, N., Burmeister, L.F., Sandler, D.P., Alavanja, M.C.: Risk factors for agricultural injury: a case–control analysis of Iowa farmers in the agricultural health study. J. Agric. Saf. Health **9**(1), 5–18 (2003)

Stallones, L., Beseler, C., Chen, P.: Sleep patterns and risk of injury among adolescent farm residents. Am. J. Prev. Med. **30**(4), 300–304 (2006)

Flanagan, J.C.: The critical incident technique. Psychol. Bull. **51**(4), 327 (1954)

Hamlet, O., Irwin, A., McGregor, M.: Is it all about the mission? Comparing non-technical skills across offshore transport and search and rescue helicopter pilots. Int. J. Aviat. Psychol. **30**, 215–235 (2018)

Guest, G., Bunce, A., Johnson, L.: How many interviews are enough? An experiment with data saturation and variability. Field Methods **18**(1), 59–82 (2006)

Hsieh, H.F., Shannon, S.E.: Three approaches to qualitative content analysis. Qual. Health Res. **15**(9), 1277–1288 (2005)

# Interaction Analysis and Usability Adjustments in Conceptual Design of a Generic Tractor Cabin

Natalia Villalpando-Chávez[✉], Cristina Vázquez-Hernández,
María Fernanda Aldana-Castillo, and Pilar Hernández-Grageda

Universidad Panamericana Campus Guadalajara, Calzada Circunvalación Poniente N. 49,
Zapopan, México
{0215080,0213780,0215201,phernand}@up.edu.mx

**Abstract.** Considered to be the most used machinery in agriculture and forestry, and being the interior of a tractor's cabin the place where the user gets involved and develops most of the tasks every day at this industry, the design and construction of standard tractors cabins should contemplate ergonomic strategies and design principles in order to guaranty an improvement of the user's work efficiency, comfort, health, and safety based on tractor requirements standardized by SAE (Society of Automotive Engineers), ISO and safety range tests. The purpose of this job is to present a new proposal for the interior of a tractor's cabin based on a conceptual design, as a result of combining the findings of a literature review with design and decision-making methodologies, providing visual, biomechanics, posture, and tool simplification refinements in the frontal panel, multipurpose accessories' area, lever system, and the seat.

**Keywords:** Tractor cabin · User experience · Usability · Product ergonomics · Transportation design

## 1  Introduction

Tractors constitute one of the most used machinery in agriculture but are not designed for the user's comfort and safety, provoking musculoskeletal injuries and long-term health damage [1]. If a design is grounded in Ergonomics, the outcomes can optimize human well-being and overall system performance [2]. Ergonomics ease the analysis of user experience, being the driver in this case. The objective of this article is to implement a user-centered approach that considers usability testing, cognitive processes, and tasks hierarchization, for proposing specific ergonomic adjustments in order to combine physiological, anthropometric, and biomechanical improvements within a chosen tractor's cabin.

SAE (Society of Automotive Engineers) and ISO (International Organization for Standardization) identify standardized parameters when working with tractors, and safety ranges tests need to be implemented to maintain the driver inside the 30% of risk at the moment of tractor operation [3]. This way, the level of musculoskeletal injury exposure will reduce.

N. L. Black et al. (Eds.): IEA 2021, LNNS 221, pp. 284–290, 2021.
https://doi.org/10.1007/978-3-030-74608-7_36

Design and sizing of products should ensure accommodation, compatibility, operability, and maintainability by the user population. Generally, design limits are based on a range of the user population from the 5th percentile values for critical body dimensions, as appropriate. The use of this range will theoretically provide coverage for 90% of the user population for that dimension [4].

This work presents a redesign applied mainly to four zones of the tractor's cabin: frontal panel, multipurpose accessories area, lever system, and the seat; in a way that it decreases the number of components in the cabin, but increases its control, accessibility, and user performance. It applies ergonomic strategies focused on improving the user experience of the tractor's operator and proposes a conceptual design that combines physiological, anthropometric, and biomechanical adjustments inside the tractor's cabin, beneficiating the interaction between the operator and the elements of the cabin.

## 2   Method

### 2.1   Literature Review

Literature review and commercial research were made for detecting those elements involved in the interior of a tractor cabin and the possible matters in the interaction between operators and those elements. They were broken down into smaller sections for better understanding of the operations made by these parts. In addition, a reverse brainstorming method [5] was used to establish and prioritize ergonomic intervention strategies inside the cabin, based on the weaknesses spotted in each section previously detected. Finally, usability goals were used to assure how the new design would grant the highest achievable level of effectiveness, efficiency, and safety.

### 2.2   Procedures Analysis

Based on the findings from the literature review, a Procedures Analysis was performed to focus on the cognitive processes made by the users and to find the critical points in which we could intervene to minimize the mental load involved in certain points of the interaction. A conceptual proposal was made and analyzed using the Lightning decision jam tool [6] with the purpose of identifying opportunity areas for improvement and of prioritizing those solutions with the greatest positive impact on the user experience.

### 2.3   Conceptual Design

As mentioned before, general problems were detected and were refined into specific problems which were divided into detailed problems in order to aim for a solution. The next step was the directed conceptual design which consisted of proposing several solutions which can be viable or not. Later on, one of these solutions was chosen for the defined conceptual design; which lead the path for the final conceptual design. This stage was grounded on more creative viable ideas and ergonomic strategies applied into each zone previously described. Finally, the final conceptual design was sketched and approved by all the members of the team.

# 3   Results

Our redesign is focused in three main categories: tool simplification, ideal posture for the driver and user experience. These three categories can be applied in the four chosen sections of the tractor cabin., which are shown in Fig. 1 and will be described in the following sections.

**Fig. 1.** General views of the design proposal for the tractor's cabin interior with ergonomics adjustment in the driver's seat, multi-purpose accessory, joystick and frontal panel.

## 3.1   Driver's Seat

Literature review shows that tractor drivers lack good posture due to visibility matters, even though the main function of agriculture vehicles consists of moving forward and backward to an objective. The driving posture is affected by the cabin space arrangement, consequently increasing discomfort and injury risk (Haoyang, Dongwei, Xuechao, & Xiaoping, 2019). Being the main component in the cab, where the user takes most of its interaction, the backrest angles, percentiles, and pressure distribution provide a comfortable posture that allows the operator to perform tasks efficiently, maintaining a correct posture in which all joints must be between 90 to 120 degrees.

A seat is proposed quilted with uniformly flat medium type seat cushioning. It provides better stability and weight distribution through an extensive surface. It can reduce loads in the ischial tuberosity's that could lead to ischemia or interference in irrigation blood, causing pain and even numbness. It also proposes a 90 degrees' angle formed by the backrest and seat seeks to collect the spinal profile in the lower back, specifically the lumbar, to provide support in this section. Our proposal for the seat considers the user's movements involved: tilt movement, where its maximum angle of inclination is 30 degrees for the backrest, increasing the user's comfort, and vertical and horizontal, facilitating the user adjustments to accurate it with their measurements. It also contains an axis easing rotation inside the cabin 45 degrees on each side for a better reach to the other components. Besides, the two armrests can be moved up or down depending on user needs.

## 3.2   Multi-purpose Accessory

This space hosts comfort accessories to bring users more effectiveness while using them and working, aiming for an enjoyable laboring experience. It is commonly composed of five sections, and our proposal design considers all of them as it follows. The storage area opens with a sliding door mechanism allowing the user to open or close rapidly. The front hollow considers the handgrip thickness and width specified by men 5 percentile, allowing better access to the area and bringing fast maneuvering. Next, to avoid spilling, accidents, or even burns caused by liquids. The adjustable drink holder guarantees better maneuvering throughout working hours. It adapts to the maximum and minimum diameter for the drink container. As a consequence of cabins usually lacking space, a push-open GPS screen allows better visibility by adjusting the height and reach to maintain a correct posture while operating. And, to ensure differences between tractor functions and commodity functions, it works through a touch screen.

### 3.3 Joystick

Physical and mental fatigue, as well as stress, are imposed upon the driver while driving [7]. The appliance of anthropometric dimensions and biomechanical gestures on tool simplification for the lever system and adjustments controls provide an accurate operator accommodation. Granting better reach, avoiding Kumar's overextension, and enhancing drivers productivity, comfort, and safety. Anthropometry relates to physical and individual human dimensions and is only meaningful if the worker's activities are also analyzed, meaning that biomechanics are involved too. As mentioned before, the overextension theory involves continuous holds of contractions, increasing injury risks. The suggestion is to maintain activities on the preferred work level (PWL), meaning gross motor efforts are under 40 percent of Model View Controller (MVC) and overestimate efforts greater than that value, maintaining the job risk-neutral. Three different operations gathered into a multifunctional joystick can decrease wrists and forearms musculoskeletal injuries. Replacing overextension and continuously holds with a better handgrip by using just thumbs force. Moreover, the armrest can adjust its height to connect with the joystick, providing a 90-degree angle between the upper arm and the forearm, resting the elbow and the wrist in a neutral position. And, maintaining hands between waist and shoulder height [8].

Joystick design depends on the optimal cylinder grasping with minimal joint torques in the fingers. This configuration will relate to the diameter to freely move the thumb and the other four fingers wrapped around the stick. Previous experiments have shown that the smaller the radius is, the larger joint displacements are concerning the neutral hand gesture. Therefore the suggested radius for the middle finger is between 15–20 mm and for the other fingers, smaller than 15 mm [9].

A new joystick design is proposed based on the movements are applied deppending on the user's purpose. In this case, a 2-axis joystick allows forward, backward, left, and right. Tilting for velocity adjustments and changing direction. And the buttons, organized by color-coding: blue for hydraulics, orange for engine and gearbox, yellow for power take-off, and white for headlights. Rapid identification of functions and feedback about the correct application of the elements was accomplished by the use of visibility and feedback, principles from Don Norman´s Interaction Design [10] that are ment to help the user by using pictogram tags, color, lighting scheme, and constraints.

### 3.4  Frontal Panel

The main operating functions of a frontal panel are the indicators, engine receptor, movement levers, tachometer, among others. After applying ergonomic adjustments, a frontal panel is proposed where the fuel gauge and the brakes illuminate with a light scheme to ease visual contact with each level indicator (e.g. activated, deactivated), resulting in lessening distractions while driving. Two levers were simplified; the first one controls the basic movements; for example, drive, reverse, and neutral. The additional lever includes specific functions; as the 4X4, the Independent Power Take-off (IPT), and the Dependent Power Take-off (DPT). These functions are shown on the screen next to each lever to indicate the driver the selected operation. In addition, every time the screen lights on with a new warning it emits a sound to get the driver's attention. If the warning signal involves immediate danger to the driver (a flat tire, low gas, engine overheating, etc.) it should remain sparkling and emitting sound until the problem is attended to. Finally, the tachometer, the temperature gauge, and the symbols or pictograms on the dashboard are clear and visible.

## 4  Discussion

Attending ISO and SAE norms, the redesign was based on comfort, safety, and productivity for the user in a standard tractor cabin.

According to Norm ISO 26322-1, which specifies general safety requirements and their verification for the design and construction of standard tractors used in agriculture and forestry, these standard tractors have at least two axles for pneumatic-tired wheels, with the smallest track gauge of the rear axle exceeding 1 150 mm, or tracks instead of wheels, with their unballasted tractor mass being greater than 600 kg. In addition, this part of ISO 26322-1 specifies the type of information on safe working practices (including residual risks) to be provided by the manufacturer, as well as technical means for improving the degree of personal safety of the operator and others involved in a tractor's normal operation, maintenance and use. It is not applicable to vibration or braking [11].

Ergonomics takes an important place in this matter, by making all designs suitable to a major quantity of users, and reducing physical fatigue, as well as short or long term injuries. A requirement established in the norm ISO 4254-1, is to provide the driver a system that permits to simultaneously use two hands and a foot or two feet and one hand when boarding, or dismounting from, a machine [12]. This three-point contact support allows the user to be regarded as a part of a vibro-acoustic system coupled via the contact points steering wheel, seat, floor panel and pedals with the vehicle, a coupled person-machine system [13].

The reach is defined for hands by a sphere of 1 000 mm radius, centered on the seat centered, 60 mm in front of and 580 mm above the seat index point (SIP) as defined in ISO 5353 and for feet by a hemisphere of 800 mm radius, centered on the seat centered at the front edge of the cushion and extending downwards, with the seat in its central position (Fig. 2).

Anthropometry information percentile was taken into consideration, 5 and 95, even though cabin dimensions make a challenge to suit accessories and other elements due to

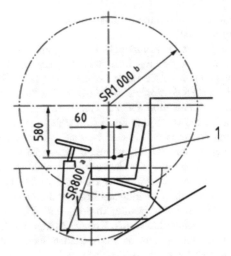

**Fig. 2.** Hand and foot reach defined in ISO 4254-1.

its small workspace. The cultural recognition and human factors involving the agriculture system were the basis to give users proper adaptation and good management of a tractor as their daily work tool.

A next step for complementing this project and validating the correct implementation of the adjustments we're proposing should be a usability test with real users, which couldn't be achieved in this first stage due to the COVID-19 Pandemic restrictions.

## 5   Conclusion

Tractor cabins should consider the variability of user needs and limitations regarding their safety and comfort to avoid musculoskeletal injuries and long-term health damage. The design is grounded in Ergonomics. Beneficiating the outcomes which optimize the drivers' well-being and overall system performance. The methodologies applied for recognizing the main interaction issues and for achieving a specific design proposal have been proved to make a positive impact on the tractor's usability and the operator's experience since they provide the new design with physiological, anthropometric, and biomechanical adjustments. While investigating actual proposals and ergonomic approaches to transportation design, problems were prioritized and analyzed in order to adapt our concept to the user's health and satisfaction. Using symbols and other culturally recognized elements, aside from regulated standards, the user can exercise better usability, faster interpretation, better use of tools, and performance in their work.

## References

1. Haoyang, L., Dongwei, Z., Xuechao, M., Xiaoping, J.: Predictive model of tractor driving posture considering front and rear view. Biosyst. Eng. **185**(1), 64–75 (2019)

2. International Ergonomics Association: Human Factors/Ergonomics for a better life for everyone (2020). https://iea.cc/
3. Kuta, L., Stopa, R., Szyjewicz, D., Komarnicki, P.: Determination of comfortable position for tractor driver's hands based on dynamic load. Int. J. Ind. Ergon. **74**, 102866 (2019)
4. Human Factors and Ergonomics: ACF Design Technology (2021). https://acfdesigntech.pbworks.com/w/file/fetch/103526039/Topic%201%20Overview%20Part%202.pdf
5. Evans, N.: Destroying collaboration and knowledge sharing in the workplace: a reverse brainstorming approach. Knowl. Manag. Res. Pract. **10**(2), 175–187 (2012)
6. Courtney, J.: Lightning design jams: the exercise that will solve all your problems (2018). https://www.invisionapp.com/inside-design/lighting-design-jams
7. Hegazy, R.: Ergonomic studies on controls layout, drivers anthropometric and noise exposure for Egyptian farm tractors. Farm Mach. Power **28**, 898–916 (2011)
8. Jaques, E., Grants, H.: Work simplification and Ergonomics can relieve pain (2020). https://www.verywellhealth.com/what-is-work-simplification-2564436
9. Peña-Pitarch, E., Yang, J., Abdel-Malek, K., Kim, J., Marler, R.: Joystick ergonomic study in material handling using virtual humans. In: American Society of Mechanical Engineers, Manufacturing Engineering Division, MED (2005)
10. Norman, D.A.: The Design of Everyday Things. Doubleday, New York (1990)
11. I.O.f.S. ISO: «Tractors for agriculture and forestry - Safety - Part 1: Standard tractors (ISO 26322-1)» (2008)
12. I.O.S. ISO: «Agricultural machinery - Safety - Part 1: General requirements (ISO 4254-1)» (2013)
13. Genuit, K.: «Vehicle interior noise: a combination of sound, vibration and interactivity», pp. 1025–1035 (2008)

# Part IV: Building and Construction (Edited by John Smallwood)

# Conscious Ergonomics in Architecture: Energy, Matter, and Form from Theory to Practice

María Araya León[1,2,3](✉) ⒾⒹ, Ricardo Guasch[2], Alberto T. Estévez[3] ⒾⒹ, and Javier Peña[2]

[1] University of Santiago of Chile (USACH), Santiago, Chile
maria.araya.l@usach.cl
[2] Elisava Barcelona School of Design and Engineering (ELISAVA), Barcelona, Spain
[3] Universitat Internacional de Catalunya (UIC), Barcelona, Spain

**Abstract.** Given the importance of how the built environment influences the well-being and health of people in a positive or negative way, in addition to the need of expanding this field of knowledge, this work teaches the model of "Conscious Ergonomics" in Architecture, which proposes a holistic and systemic view to contribute to integral well-being. Formed by the trinomial *energy, matter,* and *form* as articulators of perceived and unperceived information. For the above, a mixed method is developed comprising the state of scientific art and various empirical experiences. As results, the most representative parameters of each dimension –the built environment and the human being– are defined, which, depending on their level of relationships, respond better to this holistic vision. It is seen as an opportunity to strengthen the formal, energetic, and biophilic aspects, the exploration in commercial and industrial contexts, and the link with more objective studies on the human being and its biological responses. Finally, this research seeks to codify knowledge for new evidence-based architectural design strategies.

**Keywords:** Conscious ergonomics · Built environment · Health · Well-being

## 1 Introduction and Background

The built environment positively and/or negatively affects the physical and psychological well-being and health of the people who inhabit it [1]. Extensive scientific evidence supports this statement from various explanatory paradigms, such as ergonomics, psychology, chemistry, physics, among others. However, while critical issues are addressed, much negative impact of this environment on human beings continues to be found. Positive data and statistic findings should also be enhanced for application in specific projects, such as the effects of certain materials, for example [2].

Recurrent problems may be due, on the one hand, to the lack of correlation and systemic perspective between the built environment and users [3], because for environments

---

The original version of this chapter was inadvertently published with incorrect information. The correction has been amended. The correction to this chapter is available at
https://doi.org/10.1007/978-3-030-74608-7_105

to have healthy and comfortable characteristics, it is important to consider all the factors that interact among them [1]. On the other hand, the science-project gap opens a need to put knowledge into practice.

To globally and effectively understand this relationship between the built environment and human beings and how it affects people's health and well-being, the "Conscious Ergonomics" model is proposed as an application model, based on matter to demonstrate the influence of the environment on human beings. The model defines that *"the description of the relationships and interactions between the environment and the human being is based on the exchange of information, characterized as coherent energy that allows matter to organize and construct the known reality, made up of Energy, Matter, and Form* [4] (Fig. 1). Framed in a holistic vision that explores what is perceived –light, sound, temperature, and more– and what is not perceived in the environment –electromagnetic waves or VOCs, for example– [5]. What is conscious and unconscious in the human being –emotions, cognition, hormonal, and neuronal responses, among others– with the aim of contributing to their integral well-being.

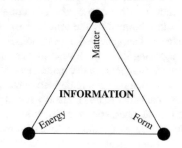

**Fig. 1.** Conscious Ergonomics Model [4].

## 2  Objective

The objective of this article is to show the theoretical and empirical results that respond to the model of "Conscious Ergonomics" in the field of Architecture. What seeks to strengthen traditional environmental and cognitive ergonomics with new relationship strategies between parameters of both the built environment and the human being. To open new avenues of exploration of evidence-based design –EBD–, in the architectural field.

## 3  Method

For the above, a mixed method is developed comprising the state of scientific art and various empirical experiences. This allows a dialectical approach between the documentary analysis and the data obtained in the application of the analyzed knowledge.

### 3.1 Scientific State-of-the-Art

A documentary research is carried out in the Web of Science (WOS) database for the period between 1998 and 2018. To guide the selection of articles to be analyzed with regard to the central theme of this research, several guiding questions, inclusion and exclusion criteria and the concepts drawn from the initial theoretical framework that respond to the hypothesis are stipulated. The guiding questions are:

1A. Which concepts and combinations respond most completely to this search?
1B. What parameters are classified to respond to the "Conscious Ergonomics" model from the built environment and human being dimensions? These parameters are the essential drivers for the development of theoretical and empirical research.
1C. What studies exist regarding these parameters, where they have been studied and how?
1D. What level of systemic vision has been applied in the research?

Inclusion criteria have been defined as: interior built environment, environmental ergonomics, well-being and health, and environmental and human assessment. And as exclusion criteria: urban and rural environment, virtual reality, social and economic environment, chronic diseases, and public policies.

Subsequently, the final concepts are defined, which are extracted from the analysis of point 1A and are combined in different engines that enable wider access to existing information.

Through the application of filters, the total number of articles to be analyzed is obtained in order to address the questions presented. This includes titles, summaries, impact, years, and holistic and systemic perspective, i.e., the articles that respond to more parameters according to the categorization of question 1B.

### 3.2 Empiric Experiences

Based on the findings of the scientific state-of-the-art, several empirical experiences are developed that allow to put into practice the analyzed in the theory (Table 1). Each one with the application of different research methodologies and tools. Experiences are based on:

2A. Academics: sensitive space projects and well-being in work environments. Of career programs in Design, specializing in space and engineering in design.
2B. Empirical: practical applications in the contexts: work, domestic and hotel.

The tools used for the built environment found include physical-environmental meters, project evaluation, apps, energy meters and materials evaluation software.

Those for human beings include psychological tests of perception, emotion, cognition and health, and physiological and neuronal measurement.

**Table 1.** Details of empirical experiences.

| 2 | Name | Participants | Procedure/Description |
|---|------|-------------|----------------------|
| A | 1. Percibo, Experimental Emotional and Sensory Module of the Environment [6] | ELISAVA University Students | Design of a sensitive space that allows to measure and interpret the emotions of university students through neuroscientific tools to transform them into restorative experiences[a] |
| | 2. Decoding Well-being in Workspaces | ELISAVA researchers and academics | Redesign of Elisava Research's spaces from the perspective of well-being and new working cultures |
| B | 1. Heterotopía Work [7] | 11 Volunteers from different territories | A study that explains the relationship between the domestic built environment and certain elements that shape it, the perception and emotional state of the users, and its efficiency, including types of activity and cognitive needs |
| | 2. Decoding Efficient Interiors (Interiors Living Lab) | 18 Volunteers visitors to the Interihotel trade fair | Study on the perception, emotion, and behavior of users within the hotel context through the correlation of existing evaluation and measurement methods for psychological, physiologic, and environmental aspects |

[a]A multidisciplinary project developed in collaboration with the SPECS research center, https://specs-lab.com/.

## 4    Results

### 4.1    Scientific State-of-the-art Results

Of a total of 11,997 articles found under the search criteria applying the first filters, 244 allow us to answer questions A, B and C. One last filter allows us to respond to question D, where the following is observed:

**1A. Concepts and Combinations:** Based on a matrix of common and logical concepts in the relationship between the built environment and the human being, around the comprehensive well-being of people. The popularity of the concepts has been analyzed and evaluated through different thesauri to guarantee a more complete search. As initial results, for the built environment, we obtain sick building syndrome, ambioma, natural environment, ergonomics, and environment planning. For human beings, it is obtained: perception, emotion, physiological response, health, and ergonomics.

Finally, from these results, the final concepts of *Built Environment, Health, Emotion, Ergonomics, Natural Environment,* and *Perception* are defined. The concepts are combined to generate the search engines to be applied in the database (Fig. 2):

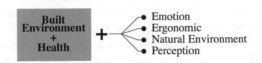

**Fig. 2.** Base order for the definition of search engines.

**1B. Parameters:** Based on the results obtained –articles– and the application of the first filters, the parameters that best represent "Conscious Ergonomics" in Architecture (Table 2), of the built environment and human beings are defined:

**Table 2.** Definition of parameters and sub-parameters of Conscious Ergonomics –CE–.

| Parameters | Sub-parameters | CE |
|---|---|---|
| Built Environment | | |
| Physical environmental | Artificial lighting -light intensity, brightness, blinding, lighting design-, environmental temperature, relative humidity, noise, color | E |
| Air quality | Volatile organic compounds, CO2, and odor | E |
| Biophilia | Nature in the space, natural analogs, and nature of space | M - F |
| Form | Size, composition, atmosphere, and style | F |
| Matter | Textures, patterns, surface temperature, reflectance, opacity, and color | M- E |
| Energy | Electromagnetic waves, ultrasound, infrasound, radioactivity, ozone | E |
| Human Being | | |
| Biological | Physiological and neuronal responses | E - M |
| Psychological | Self-report on perception, emotion, well-being, and health | E- F |

The parameters reflect perceived or unperceived characteristics for the case of the environment, and conscious and unconscious ones for the case of human beings.

**1C. Studies, where, and how:** It is observed how the investigations focus on air quality, thermal, and lighting [8, 9], followed by studies on materials and their toxicity levels

[10]. Less is found on energy [8], biophilia, and form [12]. The final two parameters are an opportunity to further advance in terms of well-being, as it is demonstrated that biophilic and formal characteristics positively influence well-being and health. On the other hand, matter and its sensory characteristics are another field of interest that must be reinforced in this framework.

The most studied contexts are work, domestic and educational environments, followed by sanitary, commercial, and industrial environments. It is a challenge to address these last contexts It is a challenge to delve further into the last context mentioned, in terms of labor perspective and permanency criteria.

With regard to human beings, more studies are found on the psychological response, through self-report [13, 14] and fewer, on biological responses, which respond largely to physiological responses [1] and little to neuronal responses [12]. It should be noted that many of the studies on the built environment and its impact on human well-being do not include human measurements.

Tools used for the case of a built environment include frequently repeated classic measurement tools such as sound meters, thermometers, anemometers, among others. For air quality and other energy characteristics, both methods and tools are of a higher level of complexity. On the other hand, there are many other parameters that require only observation. For human beings, there are many psychological methodologies and tests. In the case of biological tools, heart rate meters, galvanic skin response, urine studies, and electroencephalography for neuronal response studies are found.

**1D. Systemic/Holistic Vision:** After applying the last filter on articles that respond to three or more parameters of the built environment and at least one of human beings, 14 works of the total of 244 are classified (Fig. 3), allowing to understand the systemic/holístic perspective of these investigations.

| | Built environment parameters | | | | | | Human parameters | |
|---|---|---|---|---|---|---|---|---|
| | Physical-Environmental | Air quality | Biophilia | Form | Matter | Energy | Biological | Psychological |
| 1. [8] | • | • | | | | • | | • |
| 2. [9] | • | • | | | • | | | • |
| 3. [10] | • | • | | • | | | • | • |
| 4. [11] | • | • | • | • | • | • | • | • |
| 5. [12] | | | • | • | • | | • | |
| 6. [13] | • | • | | | • | | | • |
| 7. [14] | • | • | | • | • | | | • |
| 8. [15] | • | • | | | • | | | • |
| 9. [16] | • | • | | • | | | | • |
| 10. [17] | • | | • | | • | | | • |
| 11. [18] | • | • | | • | | | | • |
| 12. [19] | • | • | | • | • | | | • |
| 13. [20] | • | • | | | • | | | • |
| 14. [21] | • | • | | • | | | | • |

**Fig. 3.** The systemic/holistic approach of the 14 selected articles.

There is a low level of systemic vision and relation between parameters of both the built environment and the human being, i.e., many studies focus mainly on one or two parameters. Very few relate psychological and biological aspects.

## 4.2  Empirical Experiences Results

**2A.1 Percibo [6]:**  The result is the design of a sensory module that receives emotional information through neurological data of the users via EGG with the Emotiv Insight[1] tool, to cause a reaction –multi-sensory restorative experience– based on well-being. This consists of a system of stimuli between light, color, odor, and sound.

**2A.2 Decoding Well-being in Workspaces:**  Four projects are developed (2020), which seek to respond to new working cultures based on design and well-being, they are framed within the specific spaces of Elisava Research. These include:

- *Move*[2], proposes different workstations that allow you to choose different postures and a variety of environmental characteristics of light, materials, and acoustics.
- *Felt*[3], develops a product that allows for isolation and provides a restorative experience in the same workplace, through textures, smells, colors, and sounds linked to an app in the project. The product is portable and of single use.

**2B.1. Heterotopía Work (HW) [7]:**  A study that seeks to understand the relationship between home and telework, from a perspective of well-being and productivity. Periodic tests are applied for 7 days that relate information from the environment to perception, emotional states, comfort, and cognitive aspects. Environmental data is evaluated with light and noise measurement apps. On the one hand, increased empowerment of participants in terms of their well-being is observed. On the other hand, it is evident how wood is the material of preference and how the proximity to natural light marks part of the development of the activity.

**2B.2. Decoding Efficient Interiors (DEI):**  A toolkit is developed to measure and evaluate users' perceptions, emotions, and behavior in indoor hotel spaces. This kit is applied in four spaces with different design characteristics and objectives, called concept rooms located in interihotel 2019[4]. Through self-reports, which are subsequently linked to physiological and body motion measurements with Goli[5] and Empatica E4[6] for heart rate, galvanic skin response, etc.

Objective and qualitative data are related around stimuli such as materials, lighting colors, smells, among others. It is highlighted that, on the one hand, smells cause the opposite effect to that proposed. On the other hand, what is self-reported is not always related to what is being measured physiologically.

---

[1] https://www.emotiv.com/insight/.
[2] Student: Irene Menez, Elisava.
[3] Student: Otilia Benitez, Elisava.
[4] https://www.10decoracion.com/resumen-interihotel-bcn-2019/.
[5] https://golineuro.es/.
[6] https://www.empatica.com/research/e4/.

## 5  Discussion and Conclusions

The holistic and systemic view in the study of the influence of the built environment on people is seen as a complex but necessary challenge, since many of the studies that do relate parameters show how they influence each other, at perceptual and even biological levels. In the case of the visual environment, this included not only are the characteristics of artificial lighting [22], but also those of natural light, incoming light, their sizes, shapes, and direction. How these are linked to biophilic [23] and material aspects, either by reflective or thermal characteristics, which is combined with the effects this may have on the thermal environment. One study combines thermal perception with the color temperature of lighting. Another one studies material characteristics in combination with the acoustic ones, the levels of contamination [10], as well as their haptic characteristics. The above, in addition to other formal and energetic characteristics [11], constitute the habitable units that generate atmospheres and styles that also influence well-being.

Since the focus of this research is to contribute to ergonomics, it is important to highlight the scarcity of articles around this concept. Of a total of 11,997 articles, 30 have combinations that include "ergonomics," combined only with "built environment" and "health." Additionally, is important to mention the relevance of incorporating this discipline into the curricula of the academic program of Architecture, since it is an essential articulating factor, from the point of view of well-being and health for the design of conscious spaces.

On the other hand, there is a constant need to further strengthen the data on human responses to everything described above, both quantitatively and qualitatively. Self-reporting tests on perception, sensation, and even health, in combination with physi-ological and neuronal biological responses [12], enrich knowledge and provide more effective guidelines for the development of healthy spaces. These contributions include, for instance, materials that help balance blood pressure or influence faster recovery in a hospital room [24] and contribute to understanding the negative effects that certain materials or places have on health.

Understanding of this housing system in relation to health and well-being, in its appli-cation, facilitates exploring other pathways related to neuroarchitecture and responsive architecture, as in the case of PERCIBO. On the other hand, it allows combining the various phenomena to generate new data that contributes to evidence-based design, such as the cases of HW –2B.1.– and DEI –2B.2.–.

"Conscious Ergonomics" is a timely vein of work, especially in the current global context. The impact of the COVID-19 crisis on ways of living calls for rethinking spaces centered on human beings, their health and well-being, to contribute to issues of positive aging, smart cities, and healthy and healing environments.

As ways for the future, to make this work operational, it is proposed to systematize the information and results of the experiences through matrix coding. That facilitates the application of this knowledge through a friendly tool that reduces the gap between the scientific and operational world.

**Acknowledgments.** The authors would like to thank ELISAVA, Barcelona School of Design and Engineering, University of Santiago of Chile (USACH), and International University of Catalonia (UIC), for making this work possible.

# References

1. MacNaughton, P., et al.: The impact of working in a green certified building on cognitive function and health. Build. Environ. **114**, 178–186 (2017)
2. Demattè, M.L., Zucco, G.M., Roncato, S., Gatto, P., Paulon, E., Cavalli, R., Zanetti, M.: New insights into the psychological dimension of wood–human interaction. Eur. J. Wood Wood Prod. **76**(4), 1093–1100 (2018)
3. Durmisevic, S., Ciftcioglu, Ö.: Knowledge modeling tool for evidence-based design. HERD: Health Environ. Res. Design J. **3**(3), 101–123 (2010)
4. Elisava Research: Decoding Design Does. Elisava Escola Superior de Disseny i Enginyeria de Barcelona, pp. 27–35 (2018). https://www.elisava.net/en/research/publications/design-does. Accessed 25 Jan 2021
5. Son, Y.S., Lim, B.A., Park, H.J., Kim, J.C.: Characteristics of volatile organic compounds (VOCs) emitted from building materials to improve indoor air quality: focused on natural VOCs. Air Qual. Atmos. Health **6**(4), 737–746 (2013)
6. Araya, M.J., de Mura, A., Guasch, R., Estevez, A.T., Peña, J.: PERCIBO, experimental emotional and sensory module of the environment. In: ANFA 2020 (2020)
7. Araya, M.J., Abella, A., Guasch, R., Estévez, A.T., Peña, J.: HETEROTOPIA WORK: correlation between the domestic built environment and home offices during COVID-19 confinement. Strateg. Design Res. J. **13**(03), 614–631 (2020)
8. Claeson, A.S., Palmquist, E., Nordin, S.: Physical and chemical trigger factors in environmental intolerance. Int. J. Hyg. Environ. Health **221**(3), 586–592 (2018)
9. Dolan, P., Foy, C., Smith, S.: The SALIENT checklist: gathering up the ways in which built environments affect what we do and how we feel. Buildings **6**(1), 9 (2016)
10. Sahlberg, B., Gunnbjörnsdottir, M., Soon, A., Jogi, R., Gislason, T., Wieslander, G., Janson, C., Norback, D.: Airborne molds and bacteria, microbial volatile organic compounds (MVOC), plasticizers and formaldehyde in dwellings in three North European cities in relation to sick building syndrome (SBS). Sci. Total Environ. **444**, 433–440 (2013)
11. Barrett, P., Barrett, L., Davies, F.: Achieving a step change in the optimal sensory design of buildings for users at all life-stages. Build. Environ. **67**, 97–104 (2013)
12. Olszewska-Guizzo, A., Escoffier, N., Chan, J., Puay Yok, T.: Window view and the brain: effects of floor level and green cover on the alpha and beta rhythms in a passive exposure EEG experiment. Int. J. Environ. Res. Public Health **15**(11), 2358 (2018)
13. Zhang, X., Zhao, Z., Nordquist, T., Norback, D.: The prevalence and incidence of sick building syndrome in Chinese pupils in relation to the school environment: a two-year follow-up study. Indoor Air **21**(6), 462–471 (2011)
14. Dreyer, B.C., Coulombe, S., Whitney, S., Riemer, M., Labbé, D.: Beyond exposure to outdoor nature: exploration of the benefits of a green building's indoor environment on well being. Front. Psychol. **9**, 1583 (2018)
15. Shafaghat, A., Keyvanfar, A., Ferwati, M.S., Alizadeh, T.: Enhancing staff's satisfaction with comfort toward productivity by sustainable open plan office design. Sustain. Cities Soc. **19**, 151–164 (2015)
16. Nriagu, J., Smith, P., Socier, D.: A rating scale for housing-based health hazards. Sci. Total Environ. **409**(24), 5423–5431 (2011)
17. Adams, A., Theodore, D., Goldenberg, E., McLaren, C., McKeever, P.: Kids in the atrium: comparing architectural intentions and children's experiences in a pediatric hospital lobby. Soc. Sci. Med. **70**(5), 658–667 (2010)
18. Kishi, R., Saijo, Y., Kanazawa, A., Tanaka, M., Yoshimura, T., Chikara, H., Takigawa, T., Morimoto, K., Nakayama, K., Shibata, E.: Regional differences in residential environments and the association of dwellings and residential factors with the sick house syndrome: a nationwide cross-sectional questionnaire study in Japan. Indoor Air **19**(3), 243–254 (2009)

19. Newsham, G.R., Birt, B.J., Arsenault, C., Thompson, A.J., Veitch, J.A., Mancini, S., Galasiu, A.D., Gover, B.N., Macdonald, I.A., Burns, G.J.: Do 'green' buildings have better indoor environments? New evidence. Build. Res. Inf. **41**(4), 415–434 (2013)
20. Pejtersen, J., Allermann, L., Kristensen, T.S., Poulsen, O.M.: Indoor climate, psychosocial work environment and symptoms in open-plan offices. Indoor Air **16**(5), 392–401 (2006)
21. Wyon, D.P.: The effects of indoor air quality on performance and productivity. Indoor Air **14**, 92–101 (2004)
22. Gou, Z., Khoshbakht, M., Mahdoudi, B.: The impact of outdoor views on students' seat preference in learning environments. Buildings **8**(8), 96 (2018)
23. Ergan, S., Shi, Z., Yu, X.: Towards quantifying human experience in the built environment: a crowdsourcing based experiment to identify influential architectural design features. J. Build. Eng. **20**, 51–59 (2018)
24. Nyrud, A.Q., Bringslimark, T., Bysheim, K.: Benefits from wood interior in a hospital room: A preference study. Archit. Sci. Rev. **57**(2), 125–131 (2014)

# Incorporating Ergonomics into a Construction Safety Management System

Ann Marie Dale$^{(\boxtimes)}$ ⓘ, Marco Barrera, and Bradley A. Evanoff ⓘ

Washington University, St. Louis, MO 63110, USA
amdale@wustl.edu

**Abstract.** Ergonomics must be integrated into a construction safety program to reduce the risks associated with musculoskeletal disorders. There is little guidance available on how ergonomics may be added to safety programs nor on the effectiveness of the additional ergonomic activities to reducing risks related to ergonomic exposures over time. This study illustrated the programmatic change process of adapting ergonomic activities into an existing safety management system of a single contractor, and the change in leading indicators, worker awareness, and observed behaviors over a 1.5 year period after delivering the revised program. The results showed improvement in worker awareness and in the leading indicators for attendance and number of trainings, discussion about ergonomics in safety meetings, and the frequency of identification of ergonomic hazards and controls on worker assessments and on management audits. These leading indicators provided information at interim points in time to indicate the need for additional programmatic changes. During this study, there was little change in observed behaviors. Integrating ergonomics into safety programs requires time and resources and change in work exposures occurs gradually over time.

**Keywords:** Leading indicators · Safety programs · Injury prevention · Worker · Musculoskeletal disorders

## 1 Introduction

Construction is the most hazardous industry in the US, with the highest number of fatalities of any industry and high rates of nonfatal injuries (Anderson et al. 2013) Musculoskeletal disorders (MSDs) are a leading work-related health issue among construction workers (McCoy et al. 2013). The physically demanding nature of the work, including manual materials handling, awkward and static postures, vibration, and strenuous physical exertions, explain why MSDs account for the majority of all injuries resulting in days away from work (CPWR 2007). There are many task specific interventions to reduce MSD risk factors that are readily available through a variety of sources (CPWR 2009; NIOSH 2007). Despite the existence of practical, low cost solutions for reducing physical exposures, and efforts by NIOSH and other groups to disseminate these solutions, prevention efforts to reduce MSDs in construction have not been systematically incorporated in most safety programs (Choi 2012). Ergonomic training is often a one

© The Author(s), under exclusive license to Springer Nature Switzerland AG 2021
N. L. Black et al. (Eds.): IEA 2021, LNNS 221, pp. 303–308, 2021.
https://doi.org/10.1007/978-3-030-74608-7_38

time "add on" to safety programs, insufficient to bring about changes in work behaviors that are effective in preventing MSD. In contrast, efforts to reduce electrical, struck-by, caught in-between, and fall hazards in construction have been successful in part because of sustained attention at multiple organizational levels on these OSHA required "Focus Four" topics (US Department of Labor 2013).

A review of ergonomics programs in construction (Yazdani and Wells 2012) found that existing programs do not typically encompass the majority of elements required for an effective occupational health and safety management system. Ergonomic programs are usually project specific, not company-wide, and there is minimal description of resources, accountability, operational control, communication, management review, or incident reporting. This lack of adherence to many of the elements of an effective occupational health and safety management program is likely to reduce the effectiveness and sustainability of ergonomics programs. Adding MSD hazards to a "Focus Five" safety program would incorporate MSD prevention into existing multi-level safety assessment and training procedures and bring new, sustained attention to this important hazard.

## 1.1 Objective

The purpose of this paper was to describe a construction general contractor's process to systematically incorporate ergonomics into their existing safety management program and use leading indicators to drive the development and implementation process. We conducted a pre/post study to assess ergonomic leading indicators in the safety program at baseline, document the change of ergonomic activities into the safety program, and assess the change in ergonomic leading indicators at multiple points in time after delivering the revised ergonomic program. The research team used company documented leading indicators and collected independent measures of observations and worker surveys to record change in ergonomics.

## 2   Methodology

At baseline, we collected the documents related to ergonomics, practices and procedures of three construction projects between 07/01/2015 and 04/30/2016 from one construction general contractor. We surveyed workers to learn about their awareness of ergonomics in safety activities from project orientation, weekly toolbox talks, worksites postings, and in safety meetings. We also collected researcher observations on a sample of work tasks over the period, in each project to document hazards and controls related to manual material handling, overhead work and poor below knee work posture.

We reviewed the results of the baseline data with the contractor's safety team to identify the gaps in ergonomics. The safety team made changes to their documents, policies, procedures, and practices to incorporate ergonomics into all elements similar to the activities designed for the hazard and controls for fall risk. The revised program emphasized three ergonomic objectives that related to the most common cause of injuries for this company: a) overexertion from manual material handling b) working with hands overhead c) working below knee level in a forward bent back posture. The safety team delivered the new program.

After initiating the new program, the research team collected the leading indicator measures, worker surveys, and researcher observations on three new construction projects between 05/01/2017 and 11/30/2018. The leading indicators were collected from the company records including the following: 1) annual training on ergonomics for all workers of the general contractor, 2) topic of project weekly toolbox safety talks (ergonomics and falls), 3) Subcontractor weekly meetings 4) Worker daily hazard assessments (ergonomics and falls), and 5) Management worksite audits (ergonomics and falls). We conducted interim assessments at 9 months, 15 months, and 19 months after start of delivering the new program. At each of these assessments, we collected a sample of worker surveys and researcher observations from each of the three projects.

We reported the data for the leading indicators, worker surveys, and researcher observations at baseline (control projects) and at follow up (intervention projects). We computed the difference in worker awareness of ergonomic activities between the control and intervention projects using Fisher's exact, and Wilcoxon Rank Sum tests. We examined the change in hazards and controls from the researcher observations. We also matched these observations to the worker reported hazard and controls assessment on the day corresponding to the observation to determine if workers assessed hazards and controls similarly to the observations.

## 3   Results

We collected data on six construction projects, three control projects before program changes and three intervention projects after initiating the new program. From the company records, we collected the a number of leading indicators: percent of general contractor employees trained (n = 299), the number of toolbox talks (129 control, 125 intervention projects), number of manager completed worksite audits (673 control and 227 intervention projects) and a random sample from the daily hazard assessment forms (494 control and 517 intervention projects). We collected surveys on 608 workers (233 on control projects and 375 intervention projects). We collected 360 researcher observations (191 control projects and 169 intervention projects).

The results of the company leading indicators are shown in Table 1. There was no ergonomic information in the company annual training program at baseline but 94% of the general contractor employees were trained after delivering the intervention. The proportion of toolbox talks training that related to ergonomics increased from 5% to 15% (p = 0.023) while the focus on falls increased even more (from 12% to 43%). There was a large increase in having ergonomics covered in the subcontractor meeting agenda, changing from 5% to 93% (p < 0.001). Worker daily assessments showed the proportion of jobs that recognized one or more ergonomic risks. Hazard recognition increased from 44% to 86% (p < 0.001) and controls for the recognized hazards increased from 88% to 97% (p < 0.001). Management recognizing ergonomic hazards in worksite audits increased from 5% to 32% (p < 0.001) and appropriate ergonomic controls increased from 28% to 96% (see Table 1).

Worker surveys showed changes in awareness of ergonomics in general contractor weekly toolbox talks (p = 0.023) and management meetings with subcontractor foreman (p = 0.001). Workers also reported daily ergonomic hazards more often, increasing from 69% to 80% (p = 0.005) on hazard assessment forms (see Table 2).

**Table 1.** Leading indicators on control and intervention projects

| Organization level | Activity | Type | Leading indicators | Control projects | Intervention projects |
|---|---|---|---|---|---|
| Corporate | Annual training | Training | % trained (n=299) | 0% | 94% |
| Project | Weekly Toolbox Talks | Training | % Ergo vs Falls | Ergo: 5%<br>Falls: 12% | Ergo: 15%<br>Falls: 43% |
| Project | Subcontractor weekly meeting | Meetings | % with Ergo topic | 5% | 93% |
| Project | Worker daily hazard assessment | Planning | % with H/C of Ergo vs Falls | Ergo: H: 44%<br>C: 88%<br>Falls: H: 67%<br>C: 97% | Ergo: H: 86%<br>C: 97%<br>Falls: H: 89%<br>C: 98% |
| Project | Management worksite audits | Review | % audit of H/C of Ergo vs Falls | Ergo: H: 5%<br>C: 28%<br>Falls: H: 76%<br>C: 99% | Ergo: H: 32%<br>C: 96%<br>Falls: H: 66%<br>C: 95% |

Control period: 07/01/2015 to 04/30/2016; Intervention period: 05/01/2017 to 11/30/2018; Hazards/Control: H/C

Number of samples for each data element: Toolbox talks: control (n=129), intervention (n=125); Daily hazard forms: (randomly selected sample) control (n=494), intervention (n=517); Audits: control (n=673), intervention (n=227)

**Table 2.** Worker survey measures of awareness by study group

| Awareness of ergonomic in safety activities | n | Overall | Control | Intervention | p† |
|---|---|---|---|---|---|
| | | 608 | 233 | 375 | |
| Worksite orientation | n (%) | 494 (83.7) | 186 (80.5) | 308 (85.8) | 0.109 |
| Contractor weekly toolbox talks | n (%) | 495 (83.6) | 183 (79.2) | 312 (86.4) | 0.023 |
| Contractor Safety Work Rules | n (%) | 350 (60.7) | 98 (43.8) | 252 (71.4) | <0.001 |
| Worksite postings | n (%) | 415 (71.2) | 154 (67.2) | 261 (73.7) | 0.093 |
| Subcontractor meeting attendees, n | | 246 | 109 | 137 | |
| Subcontractor foreman meetings | n (%) | 105 (46.7) | 36 (34.3) | 69 (57.5) | 0.001 |
| Monthly Worker Safety meetings | n (%) | 171 (69.5) | 78 (67.8) | 93 (71.0) | 0.677 |
| Worker Daily Hazard Assessment | n (%) | 433 (75.4) | 159 (69.1) | 274 (79.7) | 0.005 |

†Fisher's exact test for dichotomous variables, Wilcoxon Rank Sum test for ordinal variables
‡dichotomous symptom variables derived from ordinal responses, where ordinal score 0="no discomfort" and scores 1-7="Any discomfort".

Research observations collected between control and intervention projects showed no difference in proportion of ergonomic hazards for MMH and working below knee (p = 0.559; p = 0.393) but slightly less often for overhead hazards (p = 0.027). There was no difference in proportion of controls for each recognized hazard of MMH (p = 0.176) and working overhead (p = 0.737) but significantly more controls were observed for below knee hazards (p < 0.001). We compared the observed ergonomic hazards to the worker daily assessment of ergonomic hazards (shown in Table 3).

Results showed much greater recognition of all ergonomic hazards after change in ergonomic program (p < 0.001) and greater recognition of appropriate controls for each hazard identified on the worker assessment form (p < 0.001 for MMH and working overhead controls, p = 0.005 for working below knee controls).

**Table 3.** Researcher observed hazards and controls of ergonomic exposures with hazards matched to worker reported daily assessment forms by study group

| Objectives | Hazards/ controls | Researcher Observed | | | Worker Reported Assessments* | | |
|---|---|---|---|---|---|---|---|
| | | Overall | Control | Intervention | Overall | Control | Intervention |
| Manual material handling (MMH) | n | 360 | 191 | 169 | 55 | 27 | 28 |
| | Hazards | 55 (15.3) | 27 (14.1) | 28 (16.6) | 41 (74.5) | 13 (48.1) | 28 (100.0) |
| | Controls | 32 (58.2) | 13 (48.1) | 19 (67.9) | 27 (65.9) | 4 (30.8) | 23 (82.1) |
| Working overhead | n | 360 | 191 | 169 | 163 | 97 | 66 |
| | Hazards | 163 (45.3) | 97 (50.8) | 66 (39.1) | 103 (63.2) | 38 (39.2) | 65 (98.5) |
| | Controls | 108 (66.3) | 63 (64.9) | 45 (68.2) | 9 (8.7) | 0 (0.0) | 9 (13.8) |
| Working below the knee | n | 360 | 191 | 169 | 191 | 97 | 94 |
| | Hazards | 191 (53.1) | 97 (50.8) | 94 (55.6) | 98 (51.3) | 6 (6.2) | 92 (97.9) |
| | Controls | 86 (45.0) | 27 (27.8) | 59 (62.8) | 57 (58.8) | 0 (0.0) | 57 (62.6) |

* cases matched to observed hazards (n=55 for MMH, n=163 for overhead; n=191 below knee)

# 4   Discussion

This construction contractor had a robust safety management system at the start of study as shown by the number of safety activities and high level of safety ratings for the "Falls" hazard and controls. From the three control projects, it was evident that ergonomic information was not present in the contractor's safety program. There was no annual training on ergonomics for the employees of the general contractor, and ergonomic information was rarely observed in toolbox talks, subcontractor weekly meetings, and management audits. Ergonomic hazards were more often observed on worker daily hazard assessment forms (44%). However, workers reported that ergonomics was discussed in the worksite orientation, mentioned in toolbox talks of the general contractor, discussed in foreman and safety meetings, and listed on daily hazard assessment forms. After the general contractor changed their program to incorporate ergonomics in all safety documents, procedures, and practices, the results showed significant changes in several leading indicators: the number of trained workers, discussion of ergonomics in safety meetings, and recognition of ergonomics on daily hazard assessments. There was much less improvement in recognition of ergonomic hazards on management audits but most ergonomic hazards had appropriate ergonomic controls (96%). Workers did not report much improvement in awareness of ergonomic information likely due to the high number of workers who perceived ergonomics was present in the program before changes were made. Researcher data collected independently from company leading indicators showed no significant change in the proportion of observations involving MMH hazards and controls. There was a lower proportion of cases with overhead work (51% down to 39%) but only 68% of these observations had adequate controls for the hazards. There was also a similar proportion of cases with the hazard of working below the knee but a much greater number of these cases had adequate controls in place ($p < 0.001$).

The process of integrating ergonomics into a safety program takes substantial time and knowledge. This contractor had already developed a robust safety management system that provided the framework to layer on the ergonomics program. The contractor regularly collected leading indicators which provided the framework to evaluate the presence of ergonomics at baseline and the leading indicators could be adapted to monitor the effectiveness of programmatic changes of the new ergonomic activities. A successful program requires a means to monitor the program status with ongoing measures and a process to review the findings. This study collected information at three points in time after delivering the ergonomics program. The company adapted the ergonomics program to respond to the results from each of those interim reviews. However, even after 1.5 years of delivering the program the observed findings showed good change in awareness and most indicators but little change in behaviors such as putting in controls for overhead exposures and no change to reduce the incidence of below knee and manual material handling risks.

The revised ergonomics program included changes in all aspects of the safety management system including training, meetings, written documentation, signage, and hazard assessment and controls. The ongoing attention to this topic within this safety management system is needed to eventually create change in behaviors (shown here in the observations) and health outcomes (i.e. injuries). This case study demonstrates the steps needed to implement an ergonomics program. If the program is integrated into the existing safety management system, it has a greater chance to be sustainable.

## 5 Conclusion

Ergonomics program may be mapped onto existing employer safety programs but it will take time and resources to develop materials, provide training, and communicate the program over time to achieve the desired results. Program awareness and change in worker behaviors take time.

## References

Anderson, N.J., Bonauto, D.K., Adams, D.: Prioritizing industries for occupational injury and illness prevention and research: washington state workers' compensation claims data, 2002–2010. Technical Report Number 64-1-2013. Washington State Department of Labor and Industries, Olympia, Washington (2013)

McCoy, A.J., Kucera, K.L., Schoenfisch, A.L., Silverstein, B.A., Lipscomb, H.J.: Twenty Year of work-related injury and illness among union carpenters in Washington State. Am. J. Ind. Med. 56(4), 381–388 (2013)

The Center for Construction Research and Training (CPWR): The Construction Chart Book: The US Construction Industry and Its Workers. Silver Spring, MD (2007)

The Center for Construction Research and Training (CPWR): Construction Solutions Database. Silver Spring, MD (2009)

National Institute for Occupational Safety and Health (NIOSH): Simple Solutions: Ergonomics for Construction Workers. U.S. Department of Health and Human Services, Public Health Service, Centers for Disease Control and Prevention, National Institute for Occupational Safety and Health. Cincinnati, OH (2007)

Choi, S.D.: A study of trade-specific occupational ergonomics considerations in the U.S. construction industry. Work J. Prev. Assess. Rehabil. 42(2), 215–222 (2012)

Yazdani, A., Wells, R.: Prevention of MSD within OHSMS/IMS: a systematic review of risk assessment strategies. Work J. Prev. Assess. Rehabil. 41, 2765–2767 (2012)

# Trends of Fatal Falls in the U.S. Construction Industry

Xiuwen Sue Dong[(✉)], Samantha Brown, and Raina D. Brooks

CPWR – The Center for Construction Research and Training, Silver Spring, MD, USA
sdong@cpwr.com

**Abstract.** Falls are a common cause of fatal and nonfatal occupational injuries in the U.S. construction industry, causing 5,701 deaths among construction workers from 2003 to 2018. The purpose of this study is to examine trends of fatal falls in the construction industry and analyze patterns of fatalities from falls to a lower level among U.S. construction workers from 2011 to 2019. Two large national datasets in the U.S. were analyzed, including the Census of Fatal Occupational Injuries and the Current Population Survey. Findings indicated that the number of fatal injuries in construction continued to increase, and reached 1,102 deaths in 2019, the highest level since 2011. The number of fatalities among Hispanic construction workers were particularly concerning, outpacing their employment growth during this period. Falls to a lower level were largely responsible for the increase in construction fatalities in 2019, as both the number and rate of fatal falls to a lower level increased in 2019 after reductions in 2017 and 2018. To prevent fatal fall injuries in construction, continued and enhanced fall protection efforts are needed.

**Keywords:** Construction workers · Fall to a lower level · Hispanic workers

## 1 Introduction

### 1.1 Problem Statement

Falls are a leading cause of fatalities in the construction industry. From 2003 to 2018, 5,701 construction workers died of fall injuries, responsible for more than one-third of the overall fatal injuries in this industry. While construction employment accounted for less than 7% of the U.S. workforce, more than half of the fatalities due to fall to a lower level occurred on construction worksites.

### 1.2 Objective/Question

The purpose of this study is to examine recent trends of fatal falls in the construction industry and analyze patterns of fatalities from falls to a lower level among U.S. construction workers.

© The Author(s), under exclusive license to Springer Nature Switzerland AG 2021
N. L. Black et al. (Eds.): IEA 2021, LNNS 221, pp. 309–313, 2021.
https://doi.org/10.1007/978-3-030-74608-7_39

## 2 Methodology

Two large national datasets in the U.S. were analyzed, including the Census of Fatal Occupational Injuries (CFOI) and the Current Population Survey (CPS). Both are data collections by the U.S. Bureau of Labor Statistics (BLS). The number of fatal injuries among construction workers was obtained from the CFOI, while construction employment was estimated from the CPS. Risk was measured by deaths per 100,000 full-time equivalent workers (FTEs). To calculate injury rates, employment was adjusted for the number of hours worked, assuming that full-time employees work 2,000 hours per year. SAS version 9.4 was used for all data analyses.

## 3 Results

Construction employment has increased steadily since 2011, reaching 11.4 million in 2019 (Fig. 1). Following the growth in employment, the total number of construction fatalities in 2019 climbed to 1,102, the highest level since 2011 (Fig. 2). The increase in fatalities was especially pronounced for Hispanic construction workers, surging by 89.8% from 2011 to 2019, outpacing their employment gains during this period.

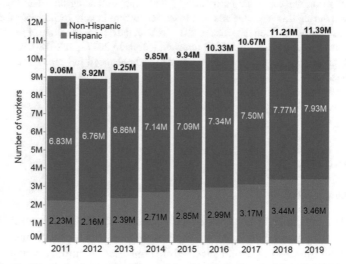

**Fig. 1.** Number of construction workers, by Hispanic ethnicity, 2011–2019

Fatalities from falls to a lower level among construction workers increased between 2011 and 2019 in general except for 2017 and 2018 (Fig. 3). In 2019, 401 fatal injuries were due to falls to a lower level, a 25% increase from 2018, accounting for 36% of all fatalities in construction. The rate of fatal falls to a lower level in construction also increased from 2.8 deaths to 3.5 deaths per 100,000 FTEs (Fig. 3).

Construction had the highest number of fatal falls among major industry sectors in the U.S. In 2019, the number of fatal falls in construction was nearly 10 times more than

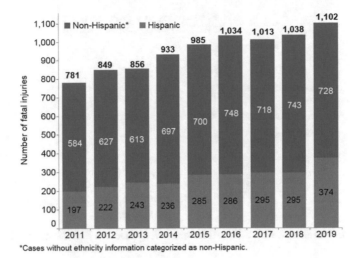

**Fig. 2.** Fatal injuries in construction, by Hispanic ethnicity, 2011–2019

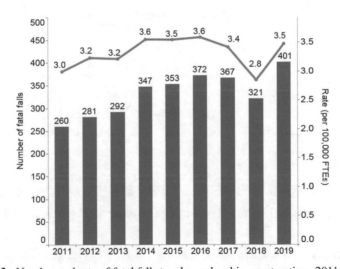

**Fig. 3.** Number and rate of fatal falls to a lower level in construction, 2011–2019

the number in manufacturing, which was ranked second in fatal falls, and even higher than the sum of the other major industry sectors combined (Fig. 4).

Roofs, ladders, and scaffolds are the three major sources of fatal falls in construction. Between 2011 and 2019, the number of construction fatalities for which roofs, ladders, or scaffolds were the primary source increased, consistent with the trend of increasing fatal falls to a lower level observed over these years. Roofs were involved in more construction fatalities than ladders or scaffolds during each year of the time period. Moreover, deaths involving roofs spiked in 2019 at 146, a 28.1% increase from 2018 (Fig. 5).

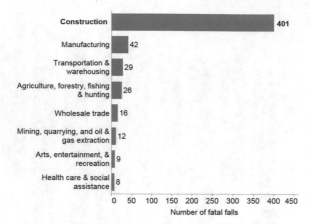

**Fig. 4.** Number of fatal falls to a lower level, by selected major industry, 2019

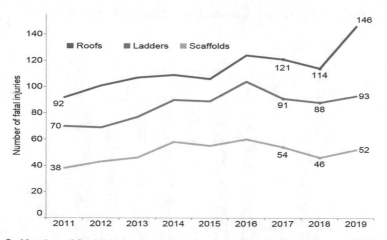

**Fig. 5.** Number of fatal injuries in construction, by selected primary source, 2011–2019

## 4  Discussion

The number of fatal injuries in construction has continued to increase, and reached the highest level since 2011. Fatalities among Hispanic construction workers are particularly concerning with the number of fatal injuries rising about 90% from 2011 to 2019, outpacing their employment growth in construction during the period.

Falls to a lower level were largely responsible for the increase in construction fatalities in 2019. Both the number and rate of fatalities from falls to a lower level increased in 2019, after reductions in 2017 and 2018. While this study is unable to analyze fatal falls by demographics due to data limitations, our previous research has found that Hispanic workers and older workers are more likely to suffer from fall injuries [1]. Given the growing Hispanic employment in the U.S. construction industry and increased fatalities in this worker group, employers should ensure that safety trainings can effectively reach Hispanic workers, especially young and new immigrants, by meeting their cultural and bilingual needs. Similarly, work redesign and retraining may be necessary for older construction workers to improve their safety and health statuses and sustain their employability so that their talents, knowledge, and experience can continue to benefit the construction industry.

## 5  Conclusions

These findings show that falls to a lower level remain fatal threats to construction workers. Construction is the industry with the largest number of fatal falls to a lower level among all major industry sectors in the U.S., and the number of fatal falls in the construction industry continues to grow. To prevent workers from fall injuries, continued and enhanced fall protection efforts are needed. Construction contractors should reduce fall hazards in construction sites, provide the right equipment to workers, and train workers to use the equipment safely [2–5].

## References

1. CPWR: The Center for Construction Research and Training, Trends of Fall Injuries and Prevention in the Construction Industry. https://www.cpwr.com/wp-content/uploads/publications/Quarter2-QDR-2019.pdf. Accessed 09 Feb 2021
2. CPWR: The Center for Construction Research and Training, Stop Construction Falls. https://stopconstructionfalls.com/about-the-campaign/. Accessed 09 Feb 2021
3. U.S. National Institute for Occupational Safety and Health, Construction Safety and Health: Directory of Construction Resources. https://www.cdc.gov/niosh/construction/default.html. Accessed 09 Feb 2021
4. Occupational Safety and Health Administration. Construction Focus Four Training. https://www.osha.gov/training/outreach/construction/focus-four. Accessed 09 Feb 2021
5. Occupational Safety and Health Administration. Recommended Practices for Safety & Health Programs in Construction. https://www.osha.gov/sites/default/files/OSHA3886.pdf. Accessed 19 Apr 2021

# Effect of Safety Culture on Safety Citizenship Behavior of Construction Personnel in China

Xiangcheng Meng[✉] (ID), Kapo Wong(ID), and Alan H. S. Chan(ID)

Department of Systems Engineering and Engineering Management, City University of Hong Kong, Kowloon, Hong Kong SAR
{xcmeng3-c,kpwong42-c}@my.cityu.edu.hk, alan.chan@cityu.edu.hk

**Abstract.** Personnel safety problems on the construction sites are still serious concerns, which need to be particularly emphasized and mitigated. In recent times, safety culture and safety citizenship behavior are considered influential to promote the safety of construction personnel. However, no study has focused on analyzing the correlation between safety culture and safety citizenship behavior of construction workers in a quantitative way, and the lack of relevant research can cause obstacles to the safety development of the construction industry. Therefore, this study was carried out to examine the correlation between safety culture and safety citizenship behavior among construction personnel working onsite by conducting a questionnaire survey with 140 respondents in China. The data were analyzed using statistical approaches, such as Pearson correlation analysis, structural equation modeling, and linear regression modeling, that the underlying mechanisms of the influence were verified. The findings provide both practical and theoretical contributions to the industrial field, which highlight the importance of effective relationship exchange and working culture promotion among organizations.

**Keywords:** Construction industry · Safety culture · Safety citizenship behavior · Structural equation modeling · Pearson correlation

## 1 Background Introduction

The personnel safety of China's construction industry is still unsatisfactory in view of the reported accident rates and casualties. The Ministry of Housing and Urban Rural Development of China [1] reported 3.32 injuries of every 100 construction personnel and 14.13 fatalities of every 100,000 construction personnel in China's overall construction industry in 2018. To improve the safety status of construction personnel, scholars support the use of proactive indicators, like safety culture (SCU), to evaluate and monitor the work safety of the employees, instead of focusing on the static injury rate [2]. In particular, SCU is negatively correlated with safety accidents in construction sites, because the act of construction workers will be positively shaped by the SCU through improving safety participation and safety compliance [3, 4]. As one example of the act of construction workers, safety citizenship behavior (SCB) is identified as compelling variable that play a significant role in organizational safety improvement [5]. However, no study has focused on revealing the quantitative correlation between SCU and SCB for construction workers at the present time, and the lack of relevant research will decelerate the safety development in the construction industry. Thus, this study was conducted with the aim of measuring SCU and SCB and their corresponding dimensions, as well as verifying the effect of SCU on SCB among construction personnel in China.

## 2  Literatures Review

### 2.1  Safety Constructs

SCU was defined as the product of personal and organizational behaviors and attitudes, which plays a determinative role for the style and commitment of an organization [6]. It also controls the personnel behavior of safety performance within the site environment of construction workers [2]. Five dimensions were classified for SCU of construction workers, namely: safety commitment of the manager (C1), personal safety attitude of the employees (C2), safety support of coworkers (C3), safety management system of the construction site (C4) and acceptability of work pressure (C5) [7].

SCB was identified by Conchie and Donald [8] as a specific kind of organizational citizenship behavior involving voluntary acts to ensure the safety of colleagues and group members. This particular behavior was also considered of importance for enhancing the work safety of organizations and promoting mutual assistance among colleagues with remarkable effectiveness at the organizational level [9]. Meng et al. [10] further classified SCB in four dimensions and designed corresponding scales for the measurement in terms of the construction context, namely, mutual aid (S1), self-control (S2), relationship between superiors and subordinates (S3), and participation in making suggestion (S4).

### 2.2  Hypotheses

SCU was identified as a group indicator of organizational values and beliefs about working safety [11]. A positive SCU was confirmed to foster strategies for risk mitigation and management by increasing the commitment and cooperation of workers for achieving safety in the organization with the outcome of better readiness of possible dangerous situations and contingencies [12]. Accordingly, this study hypothesized the possible relationship between SCU and SCB. Interrelationships among the dimensions of two constructs were postulated for in-depth understanding of the relevant theories. Ten hypotheses are listed in Table 1.

**Table 1.** Hypothesized correlations between SCU and SCB of construction personnel in China.

| No | Descriptions |
| --- | --- |
| H1 | SCU is positively correlated with SCB of construction workers |
| H2 | SCB is increased with the greater safety commitment of the management |
| H3 | SCB is increased with the greater personal attitude toward safety by employee |
| H4 | A stronger co-worker support will enhance the SCB of construction workers |
| H5 | Construction workers with greater acceptability of work pressure will exhibit better performance of SCB |
| H6 | The better the safety management system in a construction site, the better will be the performance of workers' SCB |
| H7 | The increased SCU can positively affect the workers' mutual assistance |
| H8 | An enhanced SCU can positively affect the relationship between subordinate and superior in the construction industry |
| H9 | An enhanced SCU will have positive effects on construction worker's willingness to participate in suggestion making |
| H10 | An enhanced SCU will enhance the self-control of construction works |

## 3   Methodology

### 3.1   Questionnaire Survey

A questionnaire survey was carried out on construction sites for measuring the SCU and SCB of workers in China and 140 respondents were recruited, which were all construction workers from different construction companies. The questionnaire consisted of two subscales, among which the SCB scale was designed with twelve items based on the previous research of Meng et al. [10]. The items were further classified into four parts in accordance with the corresponding dimensions of the SCB. SCU was measured using the 15-item scale developed in accordance with the research achievements of Alrehaili [7]. The scales were all verified with high reliability and validity by previous studies [7, 10]. After the questionnaires were completed by respondents, they were reviewed and checked for completeness, and questionnaires with unfinished and missing answers were abandoned. Finally, a total of 125 valid responses were gained.

### 3.2   Data Analysis

Pearson correlation was analyzed using SPSS 24 to test the influence of SCU on SCB, after which the structural equation modeling (SEM) was established using AMOS 24 to assess the hypothesized research model both quantitatively and graphically, so as to analyze the influence pathways among safety constructs and the corresponding dimensions. Moreover, linear regression with simple and multiple elements was applied for prediction of the possible outcomes of SCB by setting SCU as independent variable.

# 4  Results

## 4.1  Structural Equation Modeling

Structural equation modeling was conducted to analyze the influence of the pathways among safety constructs and their dimensions [13]. The framework of the research model is depicted in Fig. 1, including the path coefficients of the influence channels. The fitness indexes of the SEM are listed in Table 2, which verify the acceptability of the model fit to corresponding data since all the indexes met the standard of relevant criteria.

**Table 2.** Fitness indexes of SEM in terms of SCU and SCB.

|  | $\chi^2/df$ | SRMR | GFI | TLI | CFI | PGFI | RMSEA |
|---|---|---|---|---|---|---|---|
| Research model | 2.768 | 0.057 | 0.851 | 0.928 | 0.927 | 0.658 | 0.057 |
| Criteria | $\leq 5$ | $\leq 0.08$ | $\geq 0.5$ | $\geq 0.9$ | $\geq 0.9$ | $\geq 0.5$ | $\leq 0.08$ |

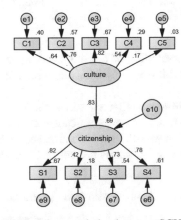

**Fig. 1.** SEM of the correlation between SCU and SCB.

The path coefficients of the SEM and their corresponding levels of significance are provided in Table 3. The correlation between SCU and SCB was 0.83, which reveals a significantly positive influence on SCB caused by SCU. Moreover, the path coefficient between SCU and its dimension C5 (acceptability of work pressure) was significant at 0.01 level, while the path influences between SCU and C4 (safety management system), as well as between SCB and S2 (self-control) were significant at the 0.005 level. Besides, the remaining path influences were verified to be significant at 0.001 level.

## 4.2  Pearson Correlation

In line with the findings of SEM, SCU and SCB were significantly and positively correlated at the 0.001 level and the corresponding pathway coefficient was 0.826. Accordingly, Pearson correlation was further analyzed for each dimension of SCU and SCB

**Table 3.** Path coefficients in SEM of the correlation between SCU and SCB.

| Path | | | Estimate | Significant (double tailed) |
|------|------|------|------|------|
| Citizenship | < --- | Culture | .830 | *** |
| C1 | < --- | Culture | .636 | *** |
| C2 | < --- | Culture | .756 | *** |
| C3 | < --- | Culture | .818 | *** |
| C4 | < --- | Culture | .536 | ** |
| C5 | < --- | Culture | .166 | * |
| S1 | < --- | SCB | .781 | *** |
| S3 | < --- | SCB | .733 | *** |
| S2 | < --- | SCB | .423 | ** |
| S4 | < --- | SCB | .816 | *** |

Note: ***At 0.001 level, the correlation is significant. **At 0.005 level, the correlation is significant. *At 0.01 level, the correlation is significant

to achieve an in-depth understanding of the influence mechanism by revealing which dimension of SCB is mostly influenced by SCU and which dimension of SCU is mostly influential towards SCB.

The results listed in Table 4 show that apart from the acceptability of work pressure, the remaining dimensions of SCU were significantly correlated with SCB at the 0.01 level. The strongest correlation with SCB was obtained at the SCU dimension of "safety support of co-worker", followed by "safety commitment of management".

**Table 4.** Pearson correlation between SCB and the dimensions of SCU.

| Safety construct | | Dimensions | | | | |
|------|------|------|------|------|------|------|
| | | C1 | C2 | C3 | C4 | C5 |
| SCB | Pearson correlation | .513** | .424** | .601** | .424** | .065 |
| | Significance (2-tailed) | .000 | .000 | .000 | .000 | .428 |
| | Number | 125 | 125 | 125 | 125 | 125 |

Note: **significant correlation at the 0.01 level (2 tailed)

Table 5 shows the correlation between SCU and each dimension of SCB, which indicates that all the dimensions of SCB were positively influenced by the SCU at 0.01 significance level other than "self-control", which shows insignificance of the influence. The most powerful relationship with SCU exists at the dimension of "mutual aid among workers", followed by "relationship between superior and subordinate".

**Table 5.** Pearson correlation between SCU and the dimensions of SCB.

| Safety construct | | Dimensions | | | |
|---|---|---|---|---|---|
| | | S1 | S2 | S3 | S4 |
| SCU | Pearson correlation | .603** | .126 | .478** | .531** |
| | Significance (2-tailed) | .000 | .123 | .000 | .000 |
| | Number | 125 | 125 | 125 | 125 |

Note: **significant correlation at the 0.01 level (2 tailed)

## 4.3 Linear Regression

Given the positive influence of SCU on SCB, the data were further processed for regression analysis to present the mathematical expression of the quantitative relationship between constructs [14]. Single linear regression was firstly simulated and the results is depicted in Fig. 2. The value of adjusted $R^2$ was 0.612, which verified the considerable degree of significant explanation of SCB by SCU. The mathematical equation of the single linear regression is expressed in Eq. (1) with the corresponding intercept (1.462) and slope (0.651).

$$Safety\ Citizenship\ Behavior = 0.651 \times Safety\ Culture + 1.462 \qquad (1)$$

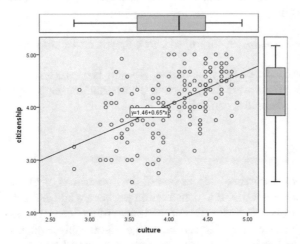

**Fig. 2.** Linear regression of the relationship between SCU and SCB (single element).

In addition, the independent variable of the regression model was further expanded from a single construct (SCU) to its five dimensions (C1-C5), so as to improve the effectiveness and scientificity of the research model, as well as obtain a greater precision for mathematical prediction. The simulation results of the multiple regression are showed in Table 6. No multiple collinear issue exists since the values of variance inflation factor

(VIF) were all less than 10. The adjusted $R^2$ went up to 0.681, which indicates the 68.1% of the SCB explanation by all of the five dimensions of SCU. Moreover, apart from C5 (acceptability of work pressure), the effects of C1, C2, C3 and C4 on SCB were verified to be significantly positive since the $p$ values of all of the corresponding estimates were lower than 0.05.

**Table 6.** Linear regression for the relationship between SCU and SCB (multiple elements).

| Estimate | Unstandardized coefficient | | Col-Linearity statistics | | $p$ value | $R^2$ |
|---|---|---|---|---|---|---|
| | B | Standard deviation | Tolerance | VIF | | |
| Constant | .679 | .343 | | | .041 | .681 |
| C4 | .293 | .057 | .642 | 1.558 | .008 | |
| C2 | .284 | .065 | .485 | 2.062 | .009 | |
| C3 | .397 | .071 | .532 | 1.880 | .000 | |
| C1 | .365 | .082 | .792 | 1.262 | .000 | |
| C5 | -.010 | .038 | .958 | 1.044 | .791 | |

The regression model with multiple elements is mathematically expressed in Eq. (2) with intercept (0.679) and the coefficients of corresponding variables (0.293 for C4, 0.284 for C2, 0.397 for C3, and 0.365 for C1) The insignificant variable (C5) was deleted accordingly.

$$Safety\ Citizenship\ Behavior = 0.679 + 0.293 \times C4 + 0.284 \times C2 + 0.397 \times C3 + 0.365 \times C1 \quad (2)$$

For the verification of the hypotheses, H5 and H10 were rejected since the corresponding correlations were insignificant. The remaining eight hypotheses were all verified with considerable acceptability.

## 5 Discussion

Safety support of co-workers (C3), as one of the dimensions of SCU, played the most powerful role in improving SCB of construction workers, while the second largest impact was found at the dimension of "safety commitment of the leaders (C1)". These findings are in line with the theories of social exchange relationship, which portray the organizational relationship interactions in both peer-to-peer and leader-to-member aspects [15]. A high quality of social exchange relationship with better leadership commitment and organizational cohesion is important to safety improvement of construction personnel, which leads to better participation in suggestion-making and mutual assistance [16]. Moreover, SCU has a positive influence on SCB among construction workers. Prior research has shown that SCU has positive effects on management commitment and colleague support, which facilitates the relationship exchange of members within the organization [5, 10].

# 6    Conclusion and Limitation

This study offers a unique opportunity to ascertain the influence of SCU on SCB of construction workers in China. A questionnaire survey with two scales measuring the SCU and SCB of construction workers was conducted. Pearson correlation was primarily verified to identify the relationship among safety constructs and their dimensions, and the results were further complemented by structural equation modeling. Linear regression was established for the mathematical simulation of the impact of SCU and its dimensions towards SCB. However, this research does have limitation. The cross-sectional data will fasten the research findings onto a static point of time instead of on the overall developing process, which may partially limit the interpretation of the influence mechanism of the SCU on the SCB. Future research is recommended to distribute and collect data over several periods of time, so as to eliminate the corresponding research limitation.

# References

1. Ministry of housing and urban rural development of China. https://www.mohurd.gov.cn/. Accessed 1 Dec 2020
2. Qayoom, A., Hadikusumo, B.H.W.: Multilevel safety culture affecting organization safety performance: a system dynamic approach. Eng. Constr. Architect. Manag. **26**(10), 2326–2346 (2019)
3. Osman, A., Khalid, K., AlFqeeh, F.M.: Exploring the role of safety culture factors towards safety behaviour in small-medium enterprise. Int. J. Entrep. **23**(3), 1–11 (2019)
4. Chen, W.T., Wang, C.W., Lu, S.T., Pan, N.H.: The impact of safety culture on safety performance-a case study of Taiwan's construction industry. Int. J. Organ. Innov. **11**(1), 1–15 (2018)
5. Meng, X., Chan, A.H.S.: Demographic influences on safety consciousness and safety citizenship behavior of construction workers. Saf. Sci. **129**, 104835 (2020)
6. Trinh, M.T., Feng, Y.: Impact of project complexity on construction safety performance: moderating role of resilient safety culture. J. Constr. Eng. Manag. **146**(2), 04019103 (2019)
7. Alrehaili, O.: Assessing safety culture among personnel in governmental construction sites at Saudi Arabia: a quantitative study approach. Electronic theses and Dissertations. 5261. University of Central Florida (2016)
8. Conchie, S.M., Donald, I.J.: The functions and development of safety-specific trust and distrust. Saf. Sci. **46**(1), 92–103 (2008)
9. Curcuruto, M., Conchie, S.M., Griffin, M.A.: Safety citizenship behavior (SCB) in the workplace: a stable construct? Analysis of psychometric invariance across four European countries. Accid. Anal. Prev. **129**, 190–201 (2019)
10. Meng, X., Zhai, H., Chan, A.H.S.: Development of scales to measure and analyse the relationship of safety consciousness and safety citizenship behaviour of construction workers: an empirical study in China. Int. J. Environ. Res. Public Health **16**(8), 1411 (2019)
11. Fang, D., Chen, Y., Wong, L.: Safety climate in construction industry: a case study in Hong Kong. J. Constr. Eng. Manag. **132**(6), 573–584 (2006)
12. Pidgeon, N.: Safety culture: key theoretical issues. Work Stress **12**(3), 202–216 (1998)
13. Hayes, A.F., Montoya, A.K., Rockwood, N.J.: The analysis of mechanisms and their contingencies: process versus structural equation modeling. Australas. Mark. J. **25**(1), 76–81 (2017)
14. Ober, P.B.: Introduction to linear regression analysis. J. Appl. Stat. **40**(12), 2775–2776 (2013)

15. Cropanzano, R., Dasborough, M.T., Weiss, H.M.: Affective events and the development of leader-member exchange. Acad. Manag. Rev. **42**(2), 233–258 (2017)
16. Hackett, R.D., Wang, A., Chen, Z., Cheng, B., Farh, J.: Transformational leadership and organisational citizenship behaviour: a moderated mediation model of leader-member-exchange and subordinates' gender. Appl. Psychol. **67**(4), 617–644 (2018)

# Concrete Casting – Construction Engineers' Attitudes and Knowledge About Work Environment, Risk Factors, Injuries and Self-compacting Concrete

Inga Mikhaltchouk[1,2(✉)] 🆔 and Mikael Forsman[1] 🆔

[1] School of Engineering Sciences in Chemistry, Biotechnology and Health, KTH Royal Institute of Technology, Stockholm, Sweden
inga.mikhaltchouk@ri.se

[2] Division Built Environment – Infrastructure and Concrete Construction, RISE Research Institutes of Sweden, Stockholm, Sweden

**Abstract.** The construction industry has one of the highest frequencies of sick leaves caused both by accidents and by work-related diseases. Casting is one example of a demanding task. After casting with regular concrete, the concrete mass needs to be manually vibrated to reduce the air and to fill the formwork properly. During this activity workers are exposed to forward bent postures, repeated heavy lifts, noise and hand-arm vibrations. Self-compacting concrete (SCC) is a fluid concrete and as such, does not need vibrations. In addition, one may expect economic benefits when using SCC. Despite the advantages of SCC its market share in Sweden is about 10%, and lower than in a neighboring country. There is yet no explanation for the low usage of SCC in Sweden. The aim of this study is to reach a deeper understanding of construction engineers' attitudes and knowledge concerning work health and work environments during concrete casting, and about SCC and its usage. One-hour-interviews were conducted with 6 male construction engineers. The results indicated that respondents were familiar with risks for accidents, but much less familiar with risks for musculoskeletal disorders, and with risks from hand-arm vibrations. The study also revealed low level of knowledge about SCC and other new methods and materials that could improve and streamline processes at a construction site.

**Keywords:** Construction workers · Musculoskeletal disorders · Hand-arm vibration · Self-compacting concrete · Qualitative

## 1 Introduction

The construction industry is one of the toughest and most hazardous industrial sectors. The sector has among of the highest frequencies of sick leaves caused both by accidents and by work-related diseases. In Sweden during 2017 and 2018, 52% of all diagnosed work-related diseases in the construction industry were various strain injuries, and 36% were vibration-related injuries [1].

N. L. Black et al. (Eds.): IEA 2021, LNNS 221, pp. 323–328, 2021.
https://doi.org/10.1007/978-3-030-74608-7_41

The total cost of construction industry work-related diseases in EU has been esti-mated to 0.5–2.0% of BNP [2]. In Sweden sick leaves in construction industry caused by strain and vibration injuries cost the society up to 120 million euros € per year [3].

While performing various work tasks at a construction site, a worker executes heavy lifts, subjects himself to strenuous awkward body postures, and needs to handle vibrating tools and machinery. One demanding task after casting with regular concrete is to use so-called vibration rods, and manually vibrate the concrete to reduce the air content and fill the formwork properly. This manual vibration is a laborious work activity: the workers are exposed to forward bent postures, repeated heavy lifts, noise and hand-arm vibrations.

Self-compacting concrete (SCC) was invented in Japan around 1990. It was used in Sweden for the first time in 1997. SCC is a fluid concrete and as such, does not need vibrations to fill a formwork, even if the formwork is of considerable complexity. It is also denser, has higher compressive strength and requires less post-production treatment [4]. As there is no need for vibrations when casting with SCC, this strenuous, noisy and potentially harmful task is eliminated. This may improve concrete workers' work environment, health and safety [5]. In addition, one may expect economic benefits when using SCC. Total cost of SCC casting has been estimated to be lower, since fewer workers are needed [6]. However, disadvantages such as of timing difficulties have been discussed. The market shares of SCC in concrete casting varies considerably among the Nordic countries. Denmark uses it in about 30% of its total casting occasions, Norway's use is about 4%, and Finland's – about 3% [7]. Despite the advantages of SCC, its market share in Sweden is about 10% [5]. There is yet no explanation for the low usage of SCC in Sweden.

The aim of this qualitative study was to reach a deeper understanding of construction engineers' attitudes and knowledge concerning good work environments during concrete casting, injuries related to concrete casting, the existence of SCC and its usage, and SCC's associated influence on efficacy and economy in the construction process.

## 2  Method

Deep semi-structured interviews (1 h) were conducted with 6 male construction engi-neers. Five of them were employed by various contractor firms: 2 design engineers working in-office with calculations, 3 managers from different construction compa-nies working in lower management positions at actual construction sites. There was also 1 recent graduate with no work experience, who was actively applying for jobs in construction industry at the time of the interview.

An interview guide was created. It covered questions concerning respondent's work experience, work culture and organization at the respondent's workplace; questions about respondent's reflections on health and safety of construction workers; questions around perceived possibilities for efficiency improvements in construction; question about respondent's reflections about various working methods and materials (SCC included) that would improve and streamline processes at a construction site.

*The qualitative manifest content analysis* [8] was used to analyze the interviews. The analysis was conducted in 5 steps: 1) Listening and reading the transcribed interviews several times. 2) Highlighting of meaning units which were related to research aim. 3) Condensing and coding meaning units. 4) Clustering of codes into sub-categories. 5) Creating 4 main categories.

# 3 Results

The replies from the different interviewees were similar to a high degree. The most important findings after analysis of the interviews in the four areas work environment – where accident prevention was mentioned – but hardly risks for strain injuries; work priorities – which mostly included balances between quality and costs; efficacy of construction processes – high importance of planning, materials and machinery and qualified workers, but nothing about working environment; and in SCC and other construction-related methodologies – there very low level interest about new methodologies that might decrease risks for work-related disorders.

## 3.1 Work Environment

When the work environment was discussed, it was almost exclusively associated with accident prevention and general safety measures at work. Only one interviewee had some thoughts on work-related illnesses and awareness on long-term health risks connected with concrete casting albeit without mentioning hand-arm vibrations. That person worked at a construction site as a foreman. He confirmed that "...concrete casting is bad for the workers' health. With time I see many wear and tear hands, legs and backs. Workers that operate heavy machinery get bad vibrations in the whole body".

Interviewees' attitudes towards work environment, injuries, accidents and their prevention as well as workers' health were highly associated with economic concerns of their companies and projects (sick leave costs, idle time because of injury or illness, prices for protective equipment). One interviewee who was a project leader with economic responsibilities mused: "...work environment is important for a project's budget. If more requirements are imposed, the project becomes more expensive. On the other hand, workers getting sick and injured also raises costs". Yet another one (a design engineer) mentioned that "...Injuries and accidents are bad for a company's reputation; also work gets halted. At the same time, a lot of rules and regulations impose higher costs; safety measures such as protective equipment and appropriate clothes are also expensive in the beginning but may help to lower costs in the long run". As the last part of the citation shows there were a few thoughts of improved economy with work environment investments, but they were indeed few.

## 3.2 Work Priorities

When asked about their or their firms' specific priorities to ensure best delivery, the interviewees' answers converged towards decreasing the costs, even when discussing time or quality aspects. They did not explicitly mention such priorities as personnel and workers' health. Several interviewees stated: "...order of priority is costs, quality and time. We always keep construction simple, to lower costs" or "...quality, costs and time are linked and impact each other". One construction engineer who worked at a construction site explained: "All too often we are forced to make our clients happy – and they always choose the cheapest option. Both when it comes to materials and ways of working. We make these choices for them at the expense of quality".

### 3.3 Efficacy of Construction Processes

The efficacy of construction processes was associated with better planning, better materials and machinery and raised qualification of workers, but not with better working environment, reduction of health risks or safer, less hazardous work procedures. This attitude was exemplified by such statements as "...right personnel on sight must have right knowledge and appropriate education", "...more machines and better materials for raising quality" or "optimize number of people to reduce idle time".

### 3.4 SCC and Other Construction-Related Methodologies

The interviewees expressed low level of knowledge and interest in learning about and implementing new construction-related methodologies and procedures that might lower the work-related illnesses. One respondent, with five years' experience as a project leader and a foreman generalized the branch attitudes as "...companies and project leaders want to work as they always did and not try anything new. They are concerned that something can go wrong. New products and technologies may lead to bad results and money loss".

The interviewees also displayed low level of knowledge and interest of learning about SCC and its benefits. One respondent, a design engineer working in-office conveyed: "I don't know anything about rolled reinforcement or SCC. I don't think I need this knowledge because I don't work with it". Only one respondent, a recent graduate mentioned learning about SCC in college and expressed his interest to learn more about it. He said: "I don't currently work with SCC but would like to learn more because an order might come, and I'd need the detailed knowledge for the budget calculation".

## 4    Discussion

For this study we have interviewed construction engineers, working in-office or on-site. The interviewees associated good work environment during concrete casting with prevention of accidents. The level of awareness about work-related injuries such as musculoskeletal disorders (MSDs) and hand-arm vibration syndrome (HAVS), seems to be low. This is not at all surprising as people generally maintain awareness of risks they have been previously exposed to [9], and if the construction engineers have not been construction workers themselves, they may not be familiar with the physical exposures. On the other hand, being aware about MSDs is natural for construction workers, who are engaged in physical labor [10]. It is however a distant problem for engineers and managers. Accidents on the other hand are visible to everybody and affect a whole company "here and now". Managing accidents and their consequences is part of our respondents' responsibilities and so, as engineers and managers they are highly aware of them. Overall understanding of risks concerning MSDs and HAVS has been found to be low in many Swedish companies, as shown in a report by the Swedish Work Environment Authority [11].

We have also observed that the main priority for planning and executing a construction project is money. This is entirely in line with other studies that confirm the construction industry's orientation towards immediate profit and disregard for long-term investments [12]. Consequently, we have one of many possible explanations for the respondents' lack of interest in the new methods and technologies and a reason for not mentioning anything related to long-term workers' health as either a priority or a method of raising construction process efficacy.

Construction industry is a complex system with many actors having different goals interests and problems. This study has barely scratched the surface and is a small part of a larger study. For this large study we plan to collect answers from a larger number of employees across a more varied selection of construction industry roles.

From such a study, with many respondents, one may be able to obtain generalizable, representative results, while in this study, one cannot generalize reliably. However, in this study several lines of answers were similar for all the interviewees and may therefore be thought of as representative for the occupational group.

## 5 Conclusions

This study indicates that construction engineers working in lower management positions on-site or as design engineers in-office often associate good work environment mostly with accident prevention. The awareness of risks for work-related diseases such as MSDs, HAVS seems low. The study also revealed a lack of interest and knowledge concerning SCC and its usage, as well as other new methods and materials that would improve and streamline processes at a construction site.

**Acknowledgements.** We like to thank Associate Professor Andrea Eriksson and Professor Jörgen Eklund for highly appreciated advices concerning this study, and the interviewees for their participation.

## References

1. BCA: Byggindustrins Centrala Arbetsmiljöråd. https://www.byggnads.se/siteassets/rapporter/arbetsskador/arbetsskador-i-byggverksamhet-2017.pdf. Accessed 05 Feb 2021
2. EU-OSHA: European Agency for Safety and Health at Work, Annual activity report. https://osha.europa.eu/sites/default/files/publications/documents/Annual_report_2017_0.pdf. Accessed 2021/02707
3. Rwamamara, R., Simonsson, P.: Self-compacting concrete use for construction work environment sustainability. J. Civ. Eng. Manag. 5(18), 724–734 (2012)
4. Cussigh, F.: SCC in practice: opportunities and bottlenecks. In: 5th International RILEM Symposium on SCC, Ghent, pp. 21–27 (2007)
5. Simonsson, P.: Buildability of concrete structures – processes, methods and material. Division of structural engineering of Luleå University of Technology, Luleå (2011)

6. Simonsson, J.A.: Självkompakterande betong, utveckling och uppföljning vid tunnellining i Stäket. Luleå Tekniska Universitet, Luleå (2000)
7. ERMCO: European Ready Mixed Concrete Association. Ready-mixed concrete industry statistics year 2015. https://www.anefhop.com/wpcontent/uploads/2019/02/ERMCO_Statis tics_2014_DdYHASuJ.pdf. Accessed 07 Feb 2021
8. Graneheim, U.H., Lundman, B.: Qualitative content analysis in nursing research: concepts, procedures and measures to achieve trustworthiness. Nurse Educ. Today 2(24), 105–112 (2004)
9. Slovic, P.: Understanding perceived risk: 1978–2015. Environ. Sci. Policy Sustain. Dev. 1(58), 25–29 (2016)
10. Village, J., Ostry, A.: Assessing attitudes, beliefs and readiness for musculoskeletal injury prevention in the construction industry. Appl. Ergon. 6(41), 771–778 (2010)
11. Arbetsmiljöverket. Hälsorelaterad arbetsmiljöövervakning: Kunskapssammanställning rapport 2014:1. https://www.av.se/globalassets/filer/publikationer/kunskapssammanstallni ngar/halsorelaterad-arbetsmiljoovervakning-kunskapssammanstallningar-rap-2014-1.pdf. Accessed 07 Feb 2021
12. Törner, M., Pousette, A.: Safety in construction – a comprehensive description of the characteristics of high safety standards in construction work, from the combined perspective of supervisors and experienced workers. J. Saf. Res. 6(40), 399–409 (2009)

# Social Housing and Working-From-Home: An Ergonomic Analysis of Brazilian Dwelling During the Covid-19 Pandemic

Thaisa Sampaio Sarmento[1], Polyanna Omena Santos[2], and Erminia Attaianese[3(✉)]

[1] Federal University of Alagoas, Maceió 57035-400, Brazil
thaisa.sampaio@fau.ufal.br
[2] Federal University of Alagoas, Maceió 57074-422, Brazil
[3] Universitàdi Napoli Frederico II, 80059 Naples, Italy
erminia.attaianese@unina.it

**Abstract.** In Brazil, covid-19 reached 5 million infected people, with more than 200 thousand deaths. It is the 3rd country in the global contamination ranking, behind only the USA and India. Studies have shown that the covid-19 pandemic lethally reached the poorest in the world, those who could not stop working during the social isolation. In Brazil, Valente (2020) published that 20% poorest had twice the chance to be infected than the 20% of the wealthiest people. The study relates living conditions in popular homes during the pandemic and focuses on working-from-home and occupants' new needs from an ergonomics perspective. This research evaluated the ergonomic conditions in a social house dwelling in Brazil. Its users are a young couple and one child, who remained in social isolation for 03 months - from March to June 2020. The analysis included the environmental conditions as comfort, accessibility, habitability, functionality, privacy, and ergonomics. Results highlighted the provisional workstations inside minimal housing and the problems of sharing these workstations between the different users' profiles. Interior dimensions and furniture were not prepared to accommodate working activities for such a long time and simultaneously for the whole family.

**Keywords:** Social housing · Working-from-home · Covid-19 · Ergonomics of the built environment

## 1   Introduction

During 2020, the covid-19 pandemic isolation highlighted a lot of unexpected problems of Brazilian popular housing. This article analyzes the improvised situation of a family of three people during the quarantine period inside a popular housing model of the Brazilian government program Minha CasaMinha Vida (MCMV) (translated as My house, my life). The aim is to verify the ergonomic conditions of not planned working/studying activities inside their minimum residential space. The analysis method is based on demand analysis techniques, task analysis, and elaboration of ergonomic diagnosis.

According to NBR 15575:1(ABNT 2013), the house project should plan environments according to the essential family activities in a minimal housing program. Longsdon et al. (2019) and Villarouco (2011) agree that the quality of the housing is related to the adequacy of their functional characteristics to users' needs. These aspects include comprehensive accessibility, flexibility, efficient and understandable arrangement, and adequate physical space for promoting users' safety, health, and well-being (Attaianese 2016, 2017).

For work/study activities done at home, it is necessary to accommodate minimal furniture and equipment that allow the execution of activities – reading, writing, computer use, telephone, and peripheral devices. The user should arrange his/her work tasks in a place that allows physical comfort and concentration, as recommended by Costa (2016).The individual desk must allow:

- Handling papers during work,
- Supporting the upper limbs (forearm and wrist),
- Accommodate printed materials, while read or used as writing support,
- Accommodate a computer on the table (depth of 75 cm),
- Storage papers and other work materials in a minimum drawer 40 cm wide, below the table,
- Comfortably accommodate the user's legs while sitting,
- A functional working dimension of 3.02 m$^2$ (200 cm $\times$ 151 cm).

Sarmento et al. (2020) recommend the following arrangements for digital study activities at school in hybrid study situations.These may be positive for studying at home:

- Arrangement of sockets, allowing to connect mobile and laptop chargers on the tables (Littlefield 2011), at a height accessible to the user (from 65 to 75 cm of the finished floor),
- Dynamic general lighting that alternates daylight, related to color temperature, varying by activity, without obfuscation for comfortable use of computers and tablets,
- For precision tasks at desks, it should exista direct white light withan average flow between 300 and 500 lux (Sleegers et al. 2013) and lamps with IRC > 80,
- Adjustable table-chair system management to each user's needs (size, age, duration of activity),
- The backrest should tilt back and forth with an adjustable backrest, forming an obtuse angle (95–110°) between the seat and the backrest; it should support the lumbar spine, both in the straight position and when tilted forward or backward (CEN 1729, 2015). The seat should be soft to absorb noise, so it should not press the thighs on the curvature of the knee,
- Surface writing desk with non-slip coatings; and sufficient widthto support both forearms and elbows. The individual workspace should accommodate computers, tablets, and smartphones and offer space to write and read on papers and notebooks.

## 2  Obtained Data from the Environment and the Workplace

The research analyzed a standard popular housing with two bedrooms (50.43 m²) for three months long. This housing type features a family room, with space for living and dining, a kitchen, an external laundry (in the backyard), a bathroom, and two bedrooms.

During covid-19 isolation, the authors conducted an internet-applied survey with a semi-structured questionnaire. They obtained feedback from 163 people from different professions who were working from home in Brazil during the covid-19 pandemic. Primary data are: 69% of respondents were women, 43.6% spent 4 to 7 h working at the computer, and 35% spent more than 8 h working at the computer; 49.3% of them had to adapt a space to perform work activities at home, 25.3% used their bedroom environment, 11% used their children's bedroom to complete a working activity. 64.4% of them said that while working at home, they need to take care (even occasionally) of children, spouses, parents, grandparents, etc. This parallel activity interferes with the income of work home. The work tools most pointed out were internet (98%), printer (90%), mobile phone and headphones (88%), laptop (86%), office desk (80%), mouse (78%), air conditioner (77%), webcam (72%), swivel chair, pens, or pencil (71%). Among the total respondents, 26.9% stated that they were dissatisfied with the working conditions adapted at home. That dissatisfaction may also be associated with the furniture's features, the physical environment, the internal temperature/lighting conditions, and the coexistence with other people that can hinder the work's effectiveness.

Table 1 demonstrates how the analyzed dwelling's dimensioning condition disagreed with the specific literature. Noteworthy are the dimensional divergences found in the bathroom, bedrooms, and laundry, with functional areas up to 75% smaller than the minimum recommended.

**Table 1.** Comparative analysis of the functional areas of the analyzed housing environments and the references found in the literature. The dimensions with more extraordinary nonconformity stand out in yellow.

| Useful area (m²) | Living | Dinner | Hall | BWC | Kitchen | Laundry | Bedroom1 | Bedroom 2 |
|---|---|---|---|---|---|---|---|---|
| House template | 7,58 | 6,08 | 3,10 | 2,40 | 6,40 | 1,36 | 8,30 | 6,60 |
| Boueri Filho (2008) | 15,00 | | – | 4,20 | 7,20 | 5,40 | 14,00 | 8,00 |
| Pedro (2001) | 12,00 | | – | 3,50 | 6,00 | – | 10,50 | 6,50 |
| NBR 15.575* (ABNT 2013) | 2,40* | | – | 1,10* | 1,5* | – | – | – |

Note: (*) NBR 15575 (2013) establishes only minimum widths for rooms and not minimum areas, leaving the designer the competence of minimum housing formation, according to state and municipal laws. Source: The authors

Figure 1 simulates layout adaptations to accommodate ergonomic workstation furniture and personal work dimensions space inside the house. The authors show that it is impossible to adjust this extra workstation inside the living room, kitchen, and bedrooms without discomforting the whole family. Occupants described that decided to accommodate a simple workstation inside the 2nd bedroom for use as a working/studying desk, which triggered conflicts, mainly due to time of work and concentration needs against child sleeping time, users' physical discomfort and pain, and furniture overlaps.

**Fig. 1.** Change layout possibilities are due to accommodate study/work furniture in the analyzed house— source: the authors.

## 2.1 Analysis of the Demand

Do work activities from home implies environments' improvisation arrangements to allow occupants to carry out. A workstation set (desk, chair, and devices) should be prepared for many hours of work, supporting tasks as read, type at a computer device, and participate in video calls and on-line classes. These tasks require papers, notebooks, pens, cellphones, wi-fi access, print, tablet, and energy supply near the desk. The available furniture was not suitable for the quarantine performance of all user's routine activities (Fig. 2), resulting in body discomforts and task conflicts.

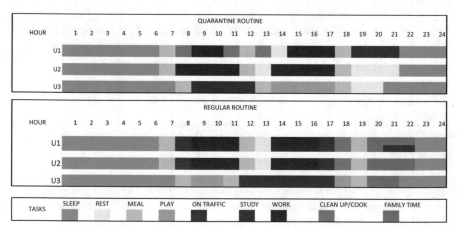

**Fig. 2.** Family routines comparison at the quarantine and a regular period. U1 – Woman, U2 – Man, U3 – Child. Work and study tasks are in black and purple colors— source: the authors.

## 2.2 Activity Analysis

Table 2 shows users' profiles that live together as a 03 people family: a woman, a man, and a child. All of them used the same workstation during the quarantine period for working or studying activities.

**Table 2.** Users' profiles at analyzed family

| Users' profile | U1 woman | U2 man | U3 child |
|---|---|---|---|
| Age | 30 | 32 | 10 |
| Body conditions | She is 1,62m, good health, and rightsleep conditions, light-activities performance | He is 1,83m, good health, and light-activities performance | She is 1,45m, good health, average activity level for her age, andloves digital games |
| Described work conditions at home | Because of working-from-home activities, she spent 06–08 h seated at the computer desk (Fig. 2b), even at weekends. She complained of body pain atthe wrists, lower back, neck, and buttocks. Itdemonstrates that the work duration at an improvised workstation is ergonomically harmful | Regular five working days routine He spent 06–08 h seated at the computer desk, but not at weekends. He complained of little space at the workstation and difficulties accommodating arms and wrists during computer use and described body pain at upper joints | She spent 04 h per day seated at the computer desk or tablet device, having classes. She did not describe body pain, but after three months of quarantine,her parents related a lack of attention to the on-line courses |

Source: The authors

- Workstation (Fig. 3): The furniture set is a tiny desk dimension (60 x 45 cm) and an uncomfortable chair. These elements for such long hours caused lower back, neck, shoulders, arms, wrist, and legs pain among adult users. The task duration is the main perceived problem among parents. The furniture used to perform the work/study activities is not suitable for the demand. It is insufficient dimensioned to accommodate upper body segments during tasks. The chair is hugely uncomfortable without adjustment of seat, backrest, armrest, or lumbar support. The sun lighting goes inside through a window sufficiently dimensioned to support these activities during the daytime.

The environment's minimal layout prevents the users from seeing outside landscape from the workstation, which could be a relief during long journeys. Thermal comfort is in good perception because natural ventilation keeps the interior environment airy

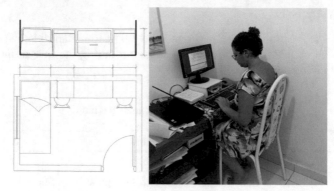

**Fig. 3.** The adapted workstation inside the 2<sup>nd</sup> room (child bedroom) (a). User 1 - Woman during her working activities at the workstation (b). Source: the authors.

and fresh. Unwanted noise around the house, which could hinder the concentration at work/study, was not reported.

- RULA analysis: the RULA method evaluated postures, strength, and muscle activities that contributed to the appearance of pain and upper limb injuries (Table 3). Users complained of physical and mental fatigue during the execution of their tasks and body pain that they tell to do not to perceive on a regular journey outside the home.

**Table 3.** Users' postural analysis with the RULA method.

| Group A | Situation | Score U1 woman | Score U2 man | Score U3 child |
|---|---|---|---|---|
| Arms | Arms above 90° | 4 | 4 | 4 |
| Forearms | Forearm above 100° | 2 | 2 | 2 |
| Fists | Upward inclined handle | 2 | 2 | 2 |
| Framework 1 | Fundamentally dynamic posture (static posture less than 1min) and non-repetitive | 0 | 0 | 0 |
| Framework 2 | Less than 2 kg | 0 | 0 | 0 |
| Total | | 8 | 8 | 8 |
| Group B | Situation | Score U1 woman | Score U2 man | Score U3 child |
| Neck | Slight tilt down | 2 | 2 | 0 |
| Neck | Slight tilt up | – | – | 3 |
| Upper body | Slight forward tilt | 2 | 1 | 3 |
| Legs and Feet | Legs and feet supported | 1 | 1 | 2 |
| Framework 1 | Prolonged static posture for more than 1 min | 1 | 1 | 1 |
| Framework 2 | Less than 2 kg | 0 | 0 | 0 |
| Total | | 6 | 5 | 9 |

Source: the authors

Groups A and B analysis indicate postures that need to be investigated and changed rapidly. The child's situation is a particular focus since his body is under development, and no mentions of pain or body discomfort have been reported.

### 2.3 Ergonomic Diagnosis and Recommendations

The main problems found are inadequate workstation dimensions (1), lack of visibility outside from the workstation desk (2) that could minimize discomfort perception, conflict of activities among users (3), complaints of pain (4), physiologic stress among adults (5), and severe risks to the child's body health (6). Expert suggestions involve reducing the exposure duration to these working conditions (1), take frequent rest breaks during the journey (2), take days off to do some leisure activities together (3). These actions could reduce mental and physical stress.

The Brazilian government should take public measures to minimize damage caused to users' health during the covid-19 pandemic. It is necessary to go beyond hygiene guidelines and vaccination because poor ergonomic conditions will be longer than covid-19. Some urgent actions should involve stricter technical norms to the furniture industry, reducing the tax on purchasing products (furniture and digital equipment) to vulnerable workers and students that improve their work-from-home arrangement in the post-pandemic future. A longer measure should provide at-home preventive health assistance by assessing both the physical and the mental risks of this new work tendency.

## 3 Final Considerations

This research described a worsening condition of dimensional restriction to which Brazilian families are exposed. Social isolation impacts and working-from-home bad conditions both accentuated the physical and psychological discomfort. During meals, leisure, and rest moments, the conflicts of use against work and hygiene tasks increased the perception of despair because people may be performing divergent activities in the same minimal spaces. If this family needed to accommodate a sick relative in their home or one of the residents themselves would affect by covid-19, the conflicts of use arising from emerging needs further aggravate the perception that they are cohabiting in insufficient and uncomfortable spaces.

This research highlighted the impact of the improvisation of working-from-home conditions for a regular Brazilian family and how a poorly designed house (and furniture) cannot offer the flexibility, habitability, and personalization conditions for dwellers, aggravating vulnerability conditions.

## References

Attaianese, E.: Ergonomic design of built environment. In: Anais do VI Encontro Nacional de Ergonomia do AmbienteConstruído & VII SeminárioBrasileiro de Acessibilidade Integral, Blucher Design Proceedings, Blucher, São Paulo, vol. 2, no. 7 (2016)

Attaianese, E.: Ergonomics of built environment ie how environmental design can improve human performance and well-being in a framework of sustainability. Ergon. Int. J. 1(1), 1–8 (2017)

Associação Brasileira de Normas Técnicas: NBR 15575-1: Edificações Habitacionais, Desempenho Parte 1: Requisitos gerais. ABNT, Rio de Janeiro (2013)

Boueri Filho, J.J.: Projeto e dimensionamento dos espaços da habitação – Espaço de Atividades. Estação das Letras e Cores, São Paulo (2008)

Costa, A.P.L.: Contribuições da ergonomia para a composição de mobiliário e espaços de trabalho em escritório. Doctorate thesis, Universidade Federal de Pernambuco. Recife (2016)

European Committee for Standardization. CEN EN 1729-1, Furniture – Chairs and tables for educational institutes. Part 1: Functional dimensions (2015)

Littlefield, D.: Manual do Arquiteto - Planejamento, dimensionamento e projeto. Bookman, Porto Alegre (2011)

Longsdon, L., et al.: Funcionalidade e mobiliário da habitação: contribuições para o projeto de moradias sociais. Arquitetura Revista São Leopoldo 15(2), 212–237 (2019)

Pedro, J.B.: Programa Habitacional: Habitação, 4th edn. LNEC, Lisbon (2001)

Sarmento, T.S., Villarouco, V., Gomes, A.S.: Arranjos espaciais e especificações técnicas para ambientes de aprendizagem adequados a práticas educacionais com blendedlearning. Ambiente Construído 20(1), 365–390 (2020)

Sleegers, P., et al.: Lighting affect students' concentration positively: Findings from three dutch studies. Lighting Res. Technol. 45(2), 159–75 (2013)

Valente, J.: Conheça o resultado sobre o maior estudo no Brasil sobre covid-19. Agência Brasil, Empresa Brasileira de Comunicação. https://agenciabrasil.ebc.com.br/saude/noticia/2020-07/conheca-resultado-maior-estudo-sobre-covid-19-no-brasil. Accessed 03 Nov 2020

Villarouco, V.: Tratando de ambientes ergonomicamente adequados: seriam ergoambientes? In: Mont'alvão, C., Villarouco, V. (eds.) Um Novo Olhar Para o Projeto: a Ergonomia no Ambiente Construído. 2AB, Teresópolis (2011)

# Construction Ergonomics: Can the Challenges Be Overcome?

John Smallwood[(⊠)] and Chris Allen

Nelson Mandela University, Port Elizabeth 6031, South Africa
john.smallwood@mandela.ac.za

**Abstract.** Historical H&S challenges, in terms of a range of issues, continue to be experienced, namely not following procedures, unsafe acts, unsafe conditions, non-compliance, untrained workers undertaking work, commencement of activities without conducting hazard identification and risk assessment (HIRA), data gathering and recording, monitoring, and ultimately the experience of injuries. Given the abovementioned, and the advent of Industry 4.0, an exploratory quantitative study, which entailed a self-administered questionnaire, was conducted among registered professional (Pr) Construction H&S Agents to determine the H&S challenges experienced, H&S performance, and the potential of Industry 4.0 to contribute to resolving the former cited challenges. The findings indicate that a range of historical challenges, which negatively impact H&S performance, continue to be experienced in construction, and that Industry 4.0 technologies can contribute to resolving the H&S challenges experienced in construction. Conclusions include that Industry 4.0 technologies have the potential to contribute to resolving the H&S challenges experienced in construction. Recommendations include: employer associations, professional associations, and statutory councils should raise the level of awareness relative to the potential implementation of Industry 4.0 relative to H&S in construction; case studies should be documented and shared; tertiary construction management education programmes should integrate Industry 4.0 into all possible modules, especially H&S-related modules, and continuing professional development (CPD) H&S should address Industry 4.0.

**Keywords:** Construction · Health and safety · Industry 4.0 · Performance

## 1 Introduction

The considerable number of accidents, fatalities, and other injuries that occur in the South African construction industry were highlighted in the Construction Industry Development Board (cidb) report 'Construction Health & Safety Status & Recommendations' [1]. The disabling injury incidence rate (DIIR) of 0.98, which equates to 0.98 disabling injuries per 100 workers, the all-industry average being 0.78, is also noted in the report. The unfavourable DIIR is underscored by a fatality rate (FR) of 25.5 per 100 000 workers, which does not compare favourably with international rates, the Australian construction industry FR for 2019 was 2.2 [2], and for the United Kingdom (UK), was 1.74 in 2019/2020 [3]. Furthermore, based upon the value of construction work completed in

South Africa, the total cost of accidents (COA) could have been between 4.3% and 5.4% [1].

The cidb [1] contends the high-level of non-compliance with H&S legislative requirements is indicative of a deficiency of effective management and supervision of H&S on construction sites, as well as planning from the inception/conception of projects within the context of project management. However, the contention that the traditional approach to monitoring and measuring H&S-related issues is largely manual in nature, which has its limitations, whereas automated H&S monitoring is considered one of the most promising methods for accurate and continuous monitoring of H&S performance on construction sites, provides insight in terms of a likely response [4]. The contention is underscored by Nath et al. [5] that construction work is physically demanding, and workers can exceed their physical capacity, the challenge being to mitigate same i.e. the ability to monitor activities that entail such exposure.

According to Autodesk & the Chartered Institute of Building (CIOB) [6], digital technologies are transforming every industry, and construction is no exception. Infinite computing, robotics, machine learning, drones, the IoT, augmented reality, gaming engines, and reality capture, to name just a few, are innovating the design, build, and operation of buildings and infrastructure. Considering the numerous challenges experienced in construction, especially H&S, Industry 4.0 technologies should be considered in terms of responding to and mitigating these.

Given the continuing poor H&S performance in South African construction, and the cited benefits of implementing Industry 4.0 technologies, an exploratory study was conducted to determine the:

- Frequency that phenomena are experienced on projects;
- Extent of the need for performance improvement on projects, and
- Potential of Industry 4.0 technologies to reduce the occurrence of phenomena.

## 2   Review of the Literature

Gheisari and Esmaeili [7] state that using unmanned aerial systems (UASs) commonly referred to as 'drones', provide an effective solution to carry out real-time monitoring and improve H&S monitoring and control practices on site. Furthermore, UAS technology can enable H&S managers to identify hazards at different stages of the project and develop suitable mitigation strategies [8].

During recent years visualisation technologies such as virtual reality (VR) and augmented reality (AR) have been evolved and used to improve construction productivity, H&S, and quality [9]. Both AR and VR have the potential to improve on site construction processes [9]. According to Park et al., AR based applications and systems have been developed to improve on-site tasks such as data visualisation, work inspection, and checking for omissions. These systems have improved on-site H&S performance to some extent [10].

According to the Health & Safety Executive (HSE) [11], there is growing evidence that wearable devices can significantly benefit H&S in the workplace through positioning and sensor technologies. Cousins [12] in turn highlights that wearable devices can detect fatigue risk, high heart rates, and stress. A study conducted by Nath et al. [5] determined that wearable technology was able to prevent work related injuries and fatalities by ergonomically designing the work environment based on previous data collected.

# 3  Research

A 14-question questionnaire was administered to delegates attending a two-day construction H&S summit in Durban, South Africa, prior to the commencement of the proceedings to avoid influencing the delegates' responses through any presentations as the theme of the summit was 'The role of Industry 4.0 in construction H&S'. The sample is best described as a convenience sample. Seven of the questions were demographic related, six were closed-ended and Likert Scale type questions, and one was open-ended. 28 Responses were included in the analysis of the data, which entailed the computation of frequencies, and a measure of central tendency in the form of a mean score (MS).

Table 1 indicates the frequency at which nineteen phenomena are experienced on projects in terms of percentage responses to a scale of never to constantly, and MSs ranging between 1.00 and 5.00.

It is notable that 17/19 (89.5%) of the MSs are above the midpoint of 3.00, which indicates that in general the respondents can be deemed to perceive the phenomena to be experienced on projects.

It is notable that no phenomena are experienced between often to constantly/constantly (MSs > 4.20 ≤ 5.00).

16/19 (84.2%) of the MSs are > 3.40 ≤ 4.20, which indicates the frequency is between sometimes to often/often. The MSs of non-compliance similar or alike errors are repeated, late information, data/statistics is/are not available, fatigue among workers, underpricing, and inadequate coordination of subcontractors are > 3.80 ≤ 4.20 – the upper part of the range. The remaining 9/16 (56.3%) MSs are > 3.40 ≤ 3.80 - materials containing hazardous chemical substances, information anomalies/ambiguities, unhealthy/unsafe plant and equipment, difficulty monitoring the process and activities of construction (in terms of H&S), sprains and strains among workers, management information is not available, heat stress among workers, unauthorised people fulfil functions, and injuries.

2/19 (10.5%) MSs are > 2.60 ≤ 3.40, which indicates the frequency is between rarely to sometimes/sometimes – accidents, and fatalities. The MS of the last ranked phenomenon, namely occupational disease, is > 1.80 ≤ 2.60, which indicates it is experienced between never to rarely/rarely.

Many of these phenomena are frequently referred to in the literature [6; 11], and furthermore, Industry 4.0 technologies have been identified as being able to reduce the occurrence of phenomena as per the literature [6].

**Table 1.** Frequency at which nineteen phenomena are experienced on projects.

| Phenomenon | Response (%) | | | | | | MS | Rank |
|---|---|---|---|---|---|---|---|---|
| | Unsure | Never | Rarely | Sometimes | Often | Always | | |
| Non-compliance | 0.0 | 0.0 | 0.0 | 21.4 | 46.4 | 32.1 | 4.11 | 1 |
| Similar or alike errors are repeated | 3.7 | 0.0 | 0.0 | 25.0 | 39.3 | 32.1 | 4.07 | 2 |
| Late information | 0.0 | 0.0 | 0.0 | 18.5 | 55.6 | 25.9 | 4.07 | 3 |
| Data/Statistics is/are not available | 0.0 | 0.0 | 0.0 | 25.9 | 51.9 | 22.2 | 3.96 | 4 |
| Fatigue among workers | 0.0 | 0.0 | 3.7 | 25.9 | 40.7 | 29.6 | 3.96 | 5 |
| Underpricing | 12.5 | 3.7 | 0.0 | 14.8 | 51.9 | 18.5 | 3.92 | 6 |
| Inadequate coordination of subcontractors | 0.0 | 0.0 | 0.0 | 33.3 | 51.9 | 14.8 | 3.81 | 7 |
| Materials containing hazardous chemical substances | 0.0 | 0.0 | 7.4 | 33.3 | 33.3 | 25.9 | 3.78 | 8 |
| Information anomalies/ambiguities | 3.8 | 0.0 | 0.0 | 33.3 | 55.6 | 7.4 | 3.73 | 9 |
| Unhealthy/Unsafe plant and equipment | 0.0 | 0.0 | 11.1 | 25.9 | 48.1 | 14.8 | 3.67 | 10 |
| Difficulty monitoring the process and activities of construction (in terms of H&S) | 0.0 | 3.7 | 11.1 | 25.9 | 37.0 | 22.2 | 3.63 | 11 |
| Sprains and strains among workers | 0.0 | 0.0 | 11.1 | 33.3 | 40.7 | 14.8 | 3.59 | 12 |
| Management information is not available | 0.0 | 0.0 | 10.7 | 35.7 | 39.3 | 14.3 | 3.57 | 13 |
| Heat stress among workers | 0.0 | 0.0 | 7.4 | 48.1 | 25.9 | 18.5 | 3.56 | 14 |
| Unauthorised people fulfill functions | 0.0 | 3.7 | 3.7 | 40.7 | 37.0 | 14.8 | 3.56 | 15 |
| Injuries | 0.0 | 0.0 | 11.1 | 44.4 | 33.3 | 11.1 | 3.44 | 16 |
| Accidents | 0.0 | 0.0 | 18.5 | 44.4 | 33.3 | 3.7 | 3.22 | 17 |
| Fatalities | 0.0 | 11.1 | 33.3 | 37.0 | 18.5 | 0.0 | 2.63 | 18 |
| Occupational disease | 3.8 | 0.0 | 48.1 | 40.7 | 7.4 | 0.0 | 2.58 | 19 |

Table 2 indicates the extent of the need for performance improvement on projects in terms of percentage responses to a scale of 1 (minor) to 5 (major), and MSs ranging between 1.00 and 5.00. It is notable that all the MSs are above the midpoint of 3.00, which indicates that in general the respondents can be deemed to perceive the need for improvements to be major as opposed to minor.

It is notable that 10/17 (58.8%) MSs are > 4.20 ≤ 5.00, which indicates the respondents perceive the need for improvement to be between near major to major/major - integration of information (design), link processes across the stages of projects, integration of information (procurement), healthier and safer plant and equipment, workers with technical skills, improved communication, integration of information (construction), improved planning & control of activities on site, identification of hazardous materials, and workers with technology skills.

The seven (41.2%) needs ranked eleventh to seventeenth have MSs > 3.40 ≤ 4.20, which indicates the respondents perceive the need to be between some improvement to a near major/near major improvement - deployment of technology, improved security, digitalisation of information, improved materials management, simulation of activities, automation of activities on site, and workers with IT skills. It should be noted that deployment of technology, and improved security have MSs of 4.19, which means they fall below the upper range by 0.02.

These needs are varied, however, the empirical findings reflect the findings of the literature in terms of the implied need for performance improvement [6]. Furthermore, they can be responded to by Industry 4.0 technologies [6].

**Table 2.** Extent of the need for performance improvement on projects.

| Need | Response (%) | | | | | | MS | R |
|------|-------|-------|-----|-----|-----|-----|------|---|
| | Unsure | Minor.....................Major | | | | | | |
| | | 1 | 2 | 3 | 4 | 5 | | |
| Integration of information (design) | 3.8 | 0.0 | 0.0 | 11.1 | 22.2 | 63.0 | 4.54 | 1 |
| Link processes across the stages of projects | 0.0 | 0.0 | 0.0 | 3.8 | 42.3 | 53.8 | 4.50 | 2 |
| Integration of information (procurement) | 4.0 | 0.0 | 0.0 | 7.7 | 34.6 | 53.8 | 4.48 | 3 |
| Healthier and safer plant and equipment | 0.0 | 0.0 | 0.0 | 11.1 | 33.3 | 55.6 | 4.44 | 4 |
| Workers with technical skills | 0.0 | 0.0 | 0.0 | 11.1 | 33.3 | 55.6 | 4.44 | 5 |
| Improved communication | 0.0 | 0.0 | 0.0 | 11.1 | 40.7 | 48.1 | 4.37 | 6 |
| Integration of information (construction) | 0.0 | 0.0 | 3.7 | 11.1 | 33.3 | 51.9 | 4.33 | 7 |
| Improved planning & control of activities on site | 0.0 | 0.0 | 0.0 | 18.5 | 33.3 | 48.1 | 4.30 | 8 |
| Identification of hazardous materials | 0.0 | 0.0 | 0.0 | 18.5 | 33.3 | 48.1 | 4.30 | 9 |
| Workers with technology skills | 0.0 | 0.0 | 3.7 | 11.1 | 40.7 | 44.4 | 4.26 | 10 |
| Deployment of technology | 0.0 | 0.0 | 3.8 | 19.2 | 30.8 | 46.2 | 4.19 | 11 |
| Improved security | 0.0 | 0.0 | 0.0 | 22.2 | 37.0 | 40.7 | 4.19 | 12 |
| Digitalisation of information | 0.0 | 0.0 | 0.0 | 33.3 | 25.9 | 40.7 | 4.07 | 13 |
| Improved materials management | 0.0 | 0.0 | 0.0 | 23.1 | 50.0 | 26.9 | 4.04 | 14 |
| Simulation of activities | 4.0 | 0.0 | 3.8 | 26.9 | 30.8 | 34.6 | 4.00 | 15 |
| Automation of activities on site | 0.0 | 0.0 | 7.4 | 29.6 | 40.7 | 22.2 | 3.78 | 16 |
| Workers with IT skills | 0.0 | 0.0 | 7.4 | 37.0 | 33.3 | 22.2 | 3.70 | 17 |

Table 3 indicates the potential of Industry 4.0 technologies to reduce the occurrence of nineteen phenomena in terms of percentage responses to a scale of 1 (minor) to 5 (major), and MSs ranging between 1.00 and 5.00.

It is notable that all the MSs are above the midpoint of 3.00, which indicates that in general the respondents can be deemed to perceive the potential to be above average.

It is notable that no MS is > 4.20 ≤ 5.00 – near major to major/major potential.

17/19 (89.5%) MSs are > 3.40 ≤ 4.20, which indicates between potential to near major/near major potential – the MSs of data/statistics is/are not available, late information, and similar or alike errors are repeated fall within the upper half of this range, namely

**Table 3.** Potential of Industry 4.0 technologies to reduce the occurrence of phenomena.

| Phenomenon | Response (%) | | | | | | MS | R |
|---|---|---|---|---|---|---|---|---|
| | Unsure | Minor....................Major | | | | | | |
| | | 1 | 2 | 3 | 4 | 5 | | |
| Data / Statistics is / are not available | 0.0 | 0.0 | 3.6 | 28.6 | 35.7 | 28.6 | 3.93 | 1 |
| Late information | 0.0 | 0.0 | 3.8 | 26.9 | 42.3 | 26.9 | 3.92 | 2 |
| Similar or alike errors are repeated | 0.0 | 0.0 | 3.8 | 34.6 | 34.6 | 26.9 | 3.85 | 3 |
| Non-compliance | 0.0 | 0.0 | 11.1 | 22.2 | 44.4 | 22.2 | 3.78 | 4 |
| Unhealthy / Unsafe plant and equipment | 3.7 | 3.7 | 7.4 | 18.5 | 51.9 | 18.5 | 3.74 | 5 |
| Management information is not available | 3.8 | 3.7 | 3.7 | 29.6 | 37.0 | 22.2 | 3.73 | 6 |
| Accidents | 0.0 | 0.0 | 7.4 | 25.9 | 55.6 | 11.1 | 3.70 | 7 |
| Information anomalies / ambiguities | 0.0 | 0.0 | 3.7 | 40.7 | 37.0 | 18.5 | 3.70 | 8 |
| Materials containing hazardous chemical substances | 0.0 | 0.0 | 14.8 | 22.2 | 48.1 | 14.8 | 3.63 | 9 |
| Difficulty monitoring the process and activities of construction (in terms of H&S) | 0.0 | 0.0 | 14.8 | 29.6 | 33.3 | 22.2 | 3.63 | 10 |
| Inadequate coordination of subcontractors | 3.7 | 3.7 | 7.4 | 29.6 | 40.7 | 18.5 | 3.63 | 11 |
| Injuries | 0.0 | 0.0 | 10.7 | 35.7 | 35.7 | 17.9 | 3.61 | 12 |
| Fatigue among workers | 0.0 | 0.0 | 14.8 | 40.7 | 22.2 | 22.2 | 3.52 | 13 |
| Heat stress among workers | 3.7 | 3.7 | 11.1 | 37.0 | 29.6 | 18.5 | 3.48 | 14 |
| Sprains and strains among workers | 3.7 | 3.7 | 14.8 | 33.3 | 25.9 | 22.2 | 3.48 | 15 |
| Fatalities | 3.6 | 3.6 | 10.7 | 32.1 | 42.9 | 10.7 | 3.46 | 16 |
| Underpricing | 3.7 | 3.6 | 17.9 | 25.0 | 32.1 | 17.9 | 3.44 | 17 |
| Occupational disease | 3.8 | 3.7 | 7.4 | 48.1 | 25.9 | 11.1 | 3.35 | 18 |
| Unauthorised people fulfill functions | 7.7 | 7.4 | 3.7 | 44.4 | 29.6 | 11.1 | 3.35 | 19 |

> 3.80 ≤ 4.20. The phenomena whose MSs are > 3.40 ≤ 3.80 include non-compliance, unhealthy/unsafe plant and equipment, management information is not available, accidents, information anomalies/ambiguities, materials containing hazardous chemical substances, difficulty monitoring the process and activities of construction (in terms of H&S), inadequate coordination of subcontractors, injuries, fatigue among workers, heat stress among workers, sprains and strains among workers, fatalities, and underpricing.

Only 2/19 (10.5%) of the MSs are > 2.60 ≤ 3.40, which indicates between near minor potential to potential/potential - occupational disease, and unauthorised people fulfill functions.

The empirical findings reflect the findings of the literature in terms of the potential of Industry 4.0 technologies to reduce the occurrence of the phenomena as per the literature [6].

## 4   Conclusions

Given the frequency that phenomena are experienced on projects, it can be concluded that the respondents' H&S perceptions reflect the general research findings relative to H&S performance in South African construction, and that there is a need for improvement, potential to improve, and a need for the implementation of Industry 4.0 technologies.

Given the extent of the need for performance improvement on projects, it can be concluded that the respondents' perceptions reflect the general research findings relative to H&S performance in South African construction, and that there is a need for the implementation of Industry 4.0 technologies.

Given the potential of Industry 4.0 technologies to reduce the occurrence of nineteen construction resource-related H&S phenomena, the need for the implementation of Industry 4.0 in construction is amplified.

## 5   Recommendations

Construction management, and construction H&S-related tertiary education, and construction H&S-related training must include, or rather embed Industry 4.0 in their programmes.

Construction employer associations, and built environment associations and statutory councils must promote, and preferably provide Industry 4.0-related H&S continuing professional development (CPD) and evolve related guidelines and practice notes.

The Construction Industry Development Board (cidb) should evolve a position paper relative to Industry 4.0 in construction, and deliberate the development of a related industry standard.

## References

1. Construction Industry Development Board (cidb): Construction health & safety in South Africa status & recommendations. CIDB, Pretoria (2009)
2. Safe Work Australia (SWA): Work-related Traumatic Injury Fatalities, Australia 2019. SWA, Canberra (2020)

3. Health & Safety Executive (HSE): Workplace fatal injuries in Great Britain, 2020. HSE (2020)
4. Awolusi, I., Marks, E., Hallowell, M.: Wearable technology for personalized construction safety monitoring and trending: review of applicable devices. Autom. Constr. **85**, 96–106 (2018)
5. Nath, N.D., Akhavian, R., Behzadan, A.H.: Ergonomic analysis of construction worker's body postures using wearable mobile sensors. Appl. Ergon. **62**, 107–117 (2017)
6. Autodesk and Chartered Institute of Building (CIOB): discussion paper reimagining construction: the vision for digital transformation, and a roadmap for how to get there. CIOB, London (2019)
7. Gheisari, M., Esmaeili, B.: Unmanned aerial systems (UAS) for construction safety applications. In: Construction Research Congress 2016: Old and New Construction Technologies Converge in Historic San Juan, pp. 2642–2650. American Society of Civil Engineers (ASCE). San Juan (2016)
8. Alizadehsalehi, S., Asnafi, M., Yitmen, I., Celik, T.: UAS-BIM based real-time hazard identification and safety monitoring of construction projects. In: 9th Nordic Conference on Construction Economics and Organization, pp. 22–32. Polyteknisk Forlag, Lyngby (2017)
9. Le, Q.T., Pedro, A., Lim, C.R., Park, H.T., Park, C.S., Kim, H.K.: A framework for using mobile based virtual reality and augmented reality for experiential construction safety education. Int. J. Eng. Educ. **31**, 713–725 (2015)
10. Park, C.S., Lee, D.Y., Kwon, O.S., Wang, X.: A framework for proactive construction defect management using BIM, augmented reality and ontology-based data collection template. Autom. Constr. **33**, 61–71 (2013)
11. Health & Safety Executive (HSE): Shared Research Project Wearables in the Workplace. HSE, London (2019)
12. Cousins, S.: Workplace monitoring: Orwell's world of work (2018). https://www.healthand safetyatwork.com/feature/orwells-world-of-work

# Part V: Ergonomics in Manufacturing
## (Edited by Jim R. Potvin)

# Knowledge and Expertise Sharing – Designing an AR-Mediated Cyber-Physical Production System for Industrial Set-Up Processes

Nils Darwin Abele[1]([⊠]) , Sven Hoffmann[2] ,
Aparecido Fabiano Pinatti De Carvalho[2] , Marcus Schweitzer[3] , Volker Wulf[2] ,
and Karsten Kluth[1]

[1] Ergonomics Division, University of Siegen, Siegen, Germany
`darwin.abele@uni-siegen.de`
[2] Institute of Information Systems and New Media, University of Siegen, Siegen, Germany
[3] Chair of Technology Management, University of Siegen, Siegen, Germany

**Abstract.** Cyber-Physical Production Systems (CPPS) are receiving a lot of attention in the context of the fourth industrial revolution, especially in terms of complex
architectures for data exchange among intelligent machines. However, the present
elaboration is rather based on the question of what support such systems can provide for the exchange and appropriation of knowledge-intensive human practices
in industrial surroundings. This paper presents the method and conceptual foundations of an Augmented Reality (AR) and sensor technology based CPPS for
manual set-up processes on modern production machines. In the present context,
both the recording of physical movements and the representation of local knowledge are potentially relevant. The basis is formed by design implications identified
in the course of an extensive ethnographic study through the implementation of
which a new methodological approach to the capture and transfer of (technical)
knowledge embedded in embodied actions could be realized.

**Keywords:** Augmented reality · Cyber-physical production systems · Design
case study · Human-computer interaction · Industrial set-up · Knowledge and
expertise sharing

## 1 Introduction

Within the industrial production environment, the growing demand for customized products leads to an increase in set-up operations on machines, which are often performed
manually, especially in small and medium-sized enterprises (SMEs) [1]. In this context, the complexity of the individual set-up steps increases and influences both the time
required and the quality of the process [2]. In order to provide inexperienced machine
setters or those to be trained with the necessary specific knowledge based on theory,
state of the art and, above all, expertise, digital solutions are increasingly being used.
The approaches of lean production and the Industrial Internet of Things (IIoT) open up

N. L. Black et al. (Eds.): IEA 2021, LNNS 221, pp. 347–354, 2021.
https://doi.org/10.1007/978-3-030-74608-7_44

possibilities for physical process design. AR is a new type of visualization that can transmit location-based information quickly and easily. However, research on the practical application of AR-based tools in the form of data glasses or Head-Mounted Displays (HMDs) has been considered underrepresented. At the same time, it shows their potential [3]. Due to the relatively early stage of development, some of them have e.g. ergonomic or interactive limitations that inevitably affect user acceptance. Therefore, it is crucial to define essential design implications for such a CPPS.

Industrial set-up is a process that involves a series of preparatory actions on a machine or tool before the start of a production cycle. It takes place between the end of series production of one article and the start of series production of another article. From an economic point of view, this is a central and time-critical process: without set-up, there could be no production [4]. Depending on the complexity of the set-up procedure and the size of the machine, set-up can be time-consuming and can also be performed by several operators.

The knowledge-intensive process of setting up with process-relevant and codified information about a machine as well as about tool and material properties and suitable sensory input values is now to be supported by AR technology. Archiving of (technical) knowledge and its context-specific processing are indispensable in this regard. In this way, both set-up time minimization and access barriers to this technology are to be reduced. This motivation was taken up in the research project 'Cyberrüsten 4.0' [5] and pursued by means of the mixed reality data glasses 'HoloLens' from Microsoft and the prototype application 'Expert to Go'.

## 2 Related Work

Studies on knowledge and experience sharing largely acknowledge the importance of knowledge management as a strategic resource in favor of potential competitive advantages for companies [6]. However, none of these studies examine the role of sharing knowledge-intensive practices, expertise, and knowledge transfer in industrial set-up processes. Rather, the focus is often on elaborating models related to organizational knowledge creation [7] or motivational aspects to realize successful knowledge transfer. In this context, Ackerman & Halverson [8] point out the importance of acquiring a detailed empirically based understanding of the practices associated with knowledge transfer.

Practices are regarded as 'ways of doing' and mostly presuppose context-dependent knowledge [9]. However, non-propositional knowledge, e.g. in the form of embodied or non-verbalizable actions, also plays an important role [10].

AR technologies can help to record and visualize the knowledge embedded in embodied actions. In knowledge-intensive environments the fast, unrestricted, and context-specific access to information is a promising means to support learning processes [11]. Findings from the literature also suggest that AR tools can improve users' skills and perceptions by potentially improving work processes, such as assembly processes [12], in a sustainable way.

Despite the work of Tang et al. [13], that investigated the role of embodiment in relation to group effects considering mixed presence, there is no evidence in the literature of knowledge-based use of AR systems in relation to captured embodied actions. Furthermore, little attention has been paid to asynchronous collaboration.

AR and sensor technologies can potentially support and facilitate numerous different processes when used in a socio-technical context. In this regard, Cyber-Physical Systems (CPS) or the Internet of Things (IoT), also referred to as CPPS or IIoT in the industrial environment, are approaches for the innovative handling of knowledge-intensive processes in favor of efficient work practices [14]. They represent systems of tightly coupled physical and virtual or digital components that integrate software, hardware, sensors, and actuators [15]. Interaction with such systems occurs through a human-machine interface, which can be implemented through conventional PC interfaces, touchscreens, or AR-based technologies. To date, there has been no known investigation of the extent to which such systems could support knowledge and expertise sharing by collecting knowledge embedded in embodied actions.

Despite the described aspects' potential identified in the literature, only few findings regarding the needs and requirements of the users have been published. The research work in the context of 'Cyberrüsten 4.0' started from this in order to design a promising tool for the exchange of knowledge and experience in industrial set-up processes and, at the same time, to answer the question of how knowledge manifests itself in actions in this particular context of embodiment.

## 3  Methodology

The research effort was focused on designing an AR-based CPPS that can help machine setters share and equally consume knowledge and expertise about context-specific set-up processes in an effective, performance-enhancing, and stress-minimizing manner.

For this purpose, a design case study [16] was conducted in order to be able to follow a user-centered design approach of an IIoT tool. Based on an empirical analysis of the field of action, which consisted of expert interviews, eye-tracking recordings, process observations as well as document analyses, a design process was carried out on the basis of the evaluated data. An ethnographic approach was chosen to understand the practices and social context of machine setters as well as their possible impact on the design of new technologies.

Ethnographic research aims primarily to 'make the invisible visible' [17] by describing the implicit, social, and cultural organization that characterizes participants' activities. In the course of the analysis, an 'Interaction Analytic' view was adopted that emphasizes the sequential organization of activities and the thought processes of those who perform them and others who seek to understand them. In this view, actors often perform activities through their collaborative work that are closely interrelated without explicitly discussing their actions [18].

In the field of workplace studies there is a growing interest in different ways of representing visible behavior, conversations, and other possible behaviors to analyze the interactive organization of activities, e.g. in offices and call centers, in operating rooms, or in medical consultations. Much of this work included a careful analysis of Knoblauch et al. [19].

For a very close-meshed analysis of a complex set-up process, as in the case of 'Cyberrüsten 4.0', detailed video recordings, e.g. with the aid of eye-tracking technology, were required in addition to so-called 'Shadowing' sessions [20] for the collection of in-situ data on work practices and social interaction. Eye-tracking helps to build up an intensive understanding of performed actions as well as used tools and assembly aids in the context of the set-up processes by means of heat map analyses. In addition, participants were asked to follow the 'Think Aloud' principle during the recording to gather information about their reflections during the set-up process. Together with the transcribed comments of the participants, even complex process steps could thus be captured and evaluated in their entirety. In-depth interviews [21] were conducted to examine knowledge transfer practices in detail. These were also recorded and transcribed.

A total of 14 shadowing sessions were conducted with accompanying eye-tracking recordings. Field notes were used to document interactions before, during, and after the sessions. Twenty-four interviews were conducted, ranging in duration from 45 to 120 min. Transcription was done using the 'Intelligent Verbatim' method. A total of 24 workers from 4 different SMEs, aged between 20 and 60 years, participated. All companies produced cold formed parts via bending or deep drawing processes. The participants held different positions in the company (e.g. machine setter, production engineer, foreman, etc.), came from different educational backgrounds (apprenticeship, graduated or master school) and had different career histories (10 employees under and 14 employees over ten years of job tenure). Thus, a differentiated investigation on the design of technologies for a wide range of end users could be realized.

The interview transcripts, field notes, eye-tracking recordings, and internal company documents relevant to the process were subjected to thematic analysis, which involves a series of well-established steps that include open coding of media excerpts, systematic revision of coded segments, and identification of code families and their relationships [22]. This enables the elicitation of a deep contexts' and phenomena's understanding. Findings from different data artifacts were triangulated to ensure their trustworthiness as a quality criterion for qualitative research [23].

In order to be able to verify or falsify and ultimately extend the qualitative findings obtained, sub-studies were conducted that also included quantitative components [24, 25]. The 'Sequential Exploratory Design' [26] is a mixed-methods approach based on the analysis of mainly qualitative, but also quantitative data, which were sequentially collected, prioritized and integrated into one or more phases of the research process. In the context of this elaboration, the primary objective is to present to the reader how existing practices have been carried out and what implications this might have for the design of new technologies.

## 4   Results

In combination with suitable sensory input values and process-relevant and codified information about a machine as well as about tool and material properties, an AR technology can be implemented in a process-safe manner. Design implications for conceptualizing an appropriate support system should cover at least three key aspects. First, due to the lack of 'expert knowledge' and the error-intolerant production environment, any solution should provide relevant information in a timely manner with minimal errors to ultimately keep production costs low. Second, the process-relevant data material must be visualized appropriately. Both the step-by-step acquisition and the playback of instructions or instructional material in the form of text, auditory comments, and image- and video-based content should be realized from the first-person perspective, e.g., with the help of HMDs, to ensure the use of both hands for the working persons. In addition, appropriate sensor technology helps to reduce user uncertainty by monitoring the workspace. This increases the efficiency of instruction by avoiding errors and reducing stress. The step-by-step recording of the set-up steps, in combination with the recording of path distances, also helps to achieve rolling possible optimization measures of the entire set-up process.

The implementation's result of the design implications is the prototype set-up application 'Expert to Go' for the AR data glasses Microsoft 'HoloLens'. The basic functions of the IIoT tool can be divided into a recording mode ('Writing Mode') and a playback mode ('Reading Mode') for the benefit of effective knowledge and experience exchange. The AR aspects of the technology can be used to ensure appropriate contextualization of the information. 'Writing' allows the expert to record content relevant to the process. Using 'Reading mode', set-up instructions are visualized in a context-specific and step-by-step manner and enriched with internal and external sensor data and simulations. For example, a 3D camera mounted above the assembly area helps to check the positioning of tools and machine components regardless of light and dirt conditions.

Figure 1 shows the model for knowledge and experience exchange that was created on the basis of the described aspects. The model itself was constructed to support the design and implementation of new and innovative technologies that respond to the identified

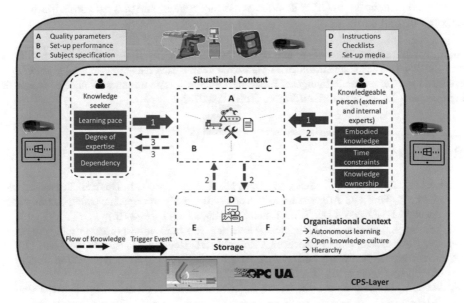

**Fig. 1.** Knowledge transfer model as part of the 'Cyberrüsten 4.0' research project.

problems. It represents the realized design implications or performed design activities in the situational and organizational context.

Specific content that is not presented in full in this paper for presentability reasons can be found especially in the elaboration of De Carvalho et al. [27] and in Abele [24] as well as Abele & Kluth [25].

## 5   Discussion and Conclusion

The elaborations show the complexity of knowledge. It is not sufficient to distinguish only between tacit and explicit knowledge or 'Know-how' and 'Know-why'. The research approach was to share supposedly irrelevant, self-evident and banal knowledge with other or inexperienced employees, as this is where the knowledge embedded in expert work is hidden. This is also accompanied by the difficulty of making available (expert) knowledge that has been intentionally withheld.

Therefore, the benefits of the technology should be used and applied as part of a knowledge sharing system. In addition, the 'Expert to Go' can be seen as a lean or set-up optimization tool that supports, among other things, the widely used 'Single Minute Exchange of Die' (SMED) approach [28].

The results provide a detailed representation of the machine setters' practices for set-up operations on bending or forming machines. The approach and design were chosen in such a way that the CPPS has to be specifically adapted to the respective work process, but can also be transferred and applied to other knowledge areas.

In the future, the exchange of knowledge and expertise will remain a relevant and always topical issue. Research will have to address both the potentials and the challenges associated with the use of CPPS in terms of user acceptance and the ergonomic limitations of software and hardware.

**Acknowledgements.** The findings in this paper originate from the research project 'Cyberrüsten 4.0: Cyber-physische Unterstützung des Menschen beim Rüstvorgang am Beispiel eines Biege-prozesses zur Kleinserienfertigung auf Basis eines Wissenstransferansatzes', funded by a grant of the European Union and EFRE.NRW (No. EFRE-0800263).

## References

1. Ludwig, T., Kotthaus, C., Stein, M., Durt, H., Kurz, C., Wenz, J., Doublet, T., Becker, M., Pipek, V., Wulf, V.: Arbeiten im Mittelstand 4.0 – KMU im Spannungsfeld des digitalen Wandels. HMD Praxis Der Wirtschaftsinformatik, **53**(1), 1–16 (2016)
2. Janssen, S.: Möller, K: Erfolgreiche Steuerung von Innovationsprozessen und -projekten – Ergebnisse einer empirischen Studie. Zeitschrift für Controll. Manag. **55**(2), 97–104 (2011)
3. Bhattacharya, B., Winer, E.H.: Augmented reality via expert demonstration authoring (AREDA). Comput. Ind. **105**, 61–79 (2019)
4. Voigt, K.-I.: Rüstprozesse. In: Winter, E. (eds.) Gabler Wirtschaftslexikon. Springer Gabler (2016)

5. Abele, N.D., Hoffmann, S., Kuhnhen, C., Ludwig, T., Schäfer, W., Schweitzer, M., Wulf, V.: Supporting the set-up processes by cyber elements based on the example of tube bending. In: Mayr, H.C., Pinzger, M. (eds.) Informatik 2016 – Informatik von Menschen für Menschen. GI-Edition-Lecture Notes in Informatics (LNI), Klagenfurt, pp. 1627–1637 (2016)
6. Watson, S., Hewett, K.: A multi-theoretical model of knowledge transfer in organizations: determinants of knowledge contribution and knowledge reuse. J. Manag. Stud. **43**(2), 141–173 (2006)
7. Nonaka, I., Toyama, R., Konno, N.: SECI, Ba and leadership: a unified model of dynamic knowledge creation. Longe Range Plan. **33**(1), 5–34 (2000)
8. Ackerman, M.S., Halverson, C.: Sharing expertise: the next step for knowledge management. In: Huysman, M., Wulf, V. (eds.) Social Capital and Information Technology, pp. 273–299. MIT Press, London (2004)
9. Schmidt, K.: The concept of 'practice': what's the point? In: Rossitto, C., Ciolfi, L., Martin, D., Conein, B. (eds.) COOP 2014. Proceedings of the 11th International Conference on the Design of Cooperative Systems, pp. 427–444. Springer, Nice (2014)
10. Gallagher, S.: Merleau-Ponty's phenomenology of perception. TOPOI **29**(2), 183–185 (2010)
11. Klopfer, E., Perry, J., Squire, K., Jan, M.: Collaborative learning through augmented reality role playing. In: Proceedings of the 2005 Conference on Computer Support for Collaborative Learning: Learning 2005: the Next 10 years!. International Society of the Learning Sciences, pp. 311–315 (2005)
12. Ong, S.K., Yuan, M.L., Nee, A.Y.C.: Augmented reality applications in manufacturing: a survey. Int. J. Prod. Res. **46**(10), 2707–2742 (2008)
13. Tang, A., Neustaedter, C., Greenberg, S.: Videoarms: embodiments for mixed presence group-ware. In: Bryan-Kinns, N., Blanford, A., Curzon, P., Nigay, L. (eds.) People and Computers XX – Engage, pp. 85–102. Springer, London (2007)
14. Paelke, V., Röcker, C.: User Interfaces for Cyber-Physical System: Challenges and Possible Approaches. Springer, Cham (2015)
15. Lee, J., Bagheri, B., Kao, H.A.: A cyber-physical systems architecture for Industry 4.0-based manufacturing systems. Manuf. Lett. **3**, 18–23 (2015)
16. Wulf, V., Rohde, M., Pipek, V., Stevens, G.: Engaging with practices: design case studies as a research framework in CSCW. In: Proceedings of CSCW 2011, pp. 505–512 (2011)
17. Goodwin, C.: Professional Vision. American Anthropologist (1994)
18. Heath, C., Luff, P.: Disembodied Conduct: communication through video in a multi-media office environment. In: CHI 1999 – Proceedings of the SIGCHI Conference on Human Factors in Computing Systems, pp. 99–103. ACM, New York (1991)
19. Knoblauch, H., Baer, A., Laurier, E., Petschke, S., Schnettler, B.: Visual analysis. New developments in the interpretative analysis of video and photography. In: Forum: Qualitative Social Research (2008)
20. Czarniawska, B.: Shadowing, and Other Techniques for Doing Fieldwork in Modern Societies. Copenhagen Business School Press, Herndon (2007)
21. Hermanowicz, J.C.: The great interview: 25 strategies for studying people in bed. Qual. Sociol. **25**(4), 479–499 (2002)
22. Braun, V., Clarke, V.: Thematic analysis. In: Cooper, H., Camic, P.M., Long, D.L., Panter, A.T., Rindskopf, D., Sher, K.J. (eds.) APA Handbook of Research Methods in Psychology, vol. 2, pp. 57–71. American Psychological Association, Washington DC (2012)
23. Bryman, A.: Social Research Methods. Oxford University Press, New York (2008)
24. Abele, N.D.: Cyber-physische Rüstunterstützung – Ergonomische Untersuchung zur Evaluierung physischer und kognitiver Beanspruchung des Menschen bei der Nutzung eines Head-Mounted Display (HMD). In: Arbeit interdisziplinär analysieren – bewerten – gestalten, Proceedings des 65. Frühjahrskongresses der Gesellschaft für Arbeitswissenschaft. GfA-Press, Dortmund (2019)

25. Abele, N.D., Kluth, K.: Beanspruchungsbezogene Evaluierung AR-basierter versus papierunterstützter Rüstinstruktionen zur Einrichtung von Industriemaschinen. In: Digitale Arbeit, digitaler Wandel, digitaler Mensch? Proceedings des 66. Frühjahrskongresses der Gesellschaft für Arbeitswissenschaft. GfA-Press, Dortmund (2020)
26. Creswell, J.W., Clark, V.L.P., Gutmann, M., Hanson, W.E.: Advanced mixed methods research designs. In: Tashakkori, A., Teddlie, C. (eds.) Handbook of Mixed Methods in Social and Behavioral Research, pp. 209–240. Sage, Thousand Oaks (2003)
27. De Carvalho, A.F.P., Hoffmann, S., Abele, N.D., Schweitzer, M., Tolmie, P., Randall, D., Wulf, V.: Of embodied action and sensors. Knowledge and expertise sharing in industrial set-up. Comput. Supp. Coop. Work **27**(3–6), 875–916 (2018)
28. Shingo, S.: A Revolution in Manufacturing: The SMED System. CRC Press, Boca Raton (1985)

# Strain-Related Evaluation of an AR-Based Cyber-Physical Production System for Setting up Industrial Machines

Nils Darwin Abele(✉) ⓘ and Karsten Kluth ⓘ

Ergonomics Division, University of Siegen, Siegen, Germany
darwin.abele@uni-siegen.de

**Abstract.** Fast and efficient learning is a necessary requirement for modern workplaces in response to dynamic markets and constantly changing work practices. Sharing knowledge and experience is an essential part of this. Computer technologies, such as Cyber-Physical Production Systems (CPPS) built according to the concept of Augmented Reality (AR), are used in this context. In a research project, such a system was developed to support machine setters for set-up processes on industrial machines. This paper evaluates the tool with respect to selected parameters relevant to strain and performance. The findings provide information on the extent to which an AR-based tool can be used in an industrial context from a physiological and psychological perspective as well as from an entrepreneurial point of view.

**Keywords:** Augmented Reality · Cognitive load · Cyber-Physical Production System · Head-mounted display · Industrial set-up · Surface electromyography

## 1 Introduction

In the industrial environment, the number of set-up processes on machines, which are often still carried out manually, is increasing as a result of the growing demand for customized products. The complexity of individual set-up steps is growing and influencing the time required as well as the quality of the set-up process [1]. Digital solutions are increasingly being used to provide inexperienced machine setters or those in need of training with necessary set-up-specific knowledge as efficiently and ergonomically as possible. AR is a new type of visualization that can transmit location-based information quickly and easily.

In the course of the research project 'Cyberrüsten 4.0', a prototype application for the mixed reality technology Microsoft 'HoloLens' (HL) was developed using the example of industrial set-up processes on forming and bending machines [2]. With the help of that Head-Mounted Display (HMD), process-relevant information can be projected holographically and context-specifically into the user's real field of view via the so-called 'Expert to Go'. In combination with process-relevant and codified information about the machine, tool and material properties, suitable sensory input values as well as simulations, AR technology can help to implement the system in a process-safe manner and to strive for set-up time minimization. Against this background, several experimental studies were conducted with the research objective of identifying possible factors influencing the physical and mental workload as well as the performance of a machine setter through the use of such a tool.

## 2   Related Work

To improve competitiveness industrial companies have been pursuing lean philosophy since the 1980s to continuously search for improvements and elimination of waste [3]. Examples are mainly just-in-time practices, such as the 'Single Minute Exchange of Die' (SMED) approach to reduce set-up times. Shingo [4] recognized the importance of the machine setters' role in addition to economic, design and technical improvements, especially with regard to their qualification or knowledge level. Currently, the Human-Computer Interaction (HCI) research area is considering this issue in terms of designing digital visualization technologies for knowledge transfer [5]. Cyber-Physical Systems (CPS) or the Internet of Things (IoT), which are also referred to as CPPS or Industrial IoT (IIoT) in the industrial environment, are approaches for the innovative handling of knowledge-intensive processes in favor of efficient work practices [6].

In this context, AR is considered a pioneer of the modern workplace. Looking at AR technology in learning processes in an industrial work environment, a large number of studies are available in the field of assembly support [7]. It was found that a lower interaction effort is accompanied by improved task performance and a decrease in cognitive load. However, handling AR tools, especially in the form of HMD, can also lead to increased psychological or cognitive strain [8] as well as increased physiological strain in the user's shoulder-neck region [9–11]. There is still a need for ergonomic studies based on both quantitative and qualitative data with regard to industrial activities and binocular as well as gesture-controlled AR systems.

## 3   Methodology

The research work was based on a user-centered design approach of an IIoT tool to support machine operators during set-up processes of bending machines. For this purpose, a design case study was conducted. Based on an empirical analysis of the action's field, a design process was carried out using the evaluated data to develop a technical solution that would adequately support users in their daily work. An ethnographic approach was chosen to understand the practices and social context of the machine setters. For reasons of redundancy, specific contents and methods of 'Cyberrüsten 4.0' can be taken from the explanations of Abele et al. [2], Abele [9], Abele & Kluth [10] and De Carvalho et al. [12].

In order to be able to verify or falsify and ultimately extend the qualitative findings obtained, sub-studies were conducted that also included quantitative components. As a mixed-methods approach, the 'Sequential Exploratory Design' is based on the analysis of mainly qualitative but also quantitative data which are sequentially collected, prioritized and integrated into one or more phases of the research process.

A first sub-research project included an ergonomic study to investigate possible stresses and strains as a result of handling an HMD during simple assembly activities and static gaze positioning [11]. In order to also evaluate dynamic and realistic motion sequences, the task in a further study consisted of a mechanical rotary draw bending machine's set-up. The test design comprised three set-up processes, which were carried out in two test sections. Four of a total of six set-up processes were performed using the 'HoloLens' or the 'Expert to Go' set-up application as the object of investigation. It visualized the assembly instructions in the form of text-, image- and video-based as well as holographic content. The HL application is divided into two modes: performing the set-up process with HL in fixed window mode, i.e., the instructions are localized or fixed to one position (1), and performing the set-up process with HL in variable window mode, i.e., the instructions follow the user's field of view (2). The user interacts with the HL or the application in a gesture-controlled manner. The two remaining set-ups were based on a localized paper instruction (PI) without using the HL, which, except for the holographic visualizations, has the same information content as the AR-based support system. To exclude interactions in the variants' sequence among each other, defined patterns in the sequence were randomized for each test subject, i.e. the start of the experiment with or without HL. Moreover, recovery breaks were arranged between the runs in order not to provoke fatigue.

12 work steps were carried out per set-up process. These included a logistics step for providing the tools and 11 set-up steps of varying complexity for assembling the tools, i.e. by screw or plug-in connections. Figure 1 shows a setting's section during the test execution.

**Fig. 1.** The figure shows test subjects during the execution with the help of a PI (left) and when using the HL (middle and right).

A total of 24 male subjects (age: $26.2 \pm 3.63$ years; body size: $182 \pm 5.60$ cm; body mass: $83.33 \pm 12.02$ kg; sport activity: $4.63 \pm 3.03$ h/week) with a predominantly technically oriented professional background (including mechatronics engineers, machine and plant operators, mechanical engineering students, etc.) were studied for a population that reflects the present application scenario in the best possible way. None of the subjects had prior experience with the set-up process of the rotary draw bending machine used in this study. Only 12.5% of the test subjects have used data glasses on a small scale or for testing purposes so far.

The objective measurement data were based on the recording of electromyographic activities (EA) of the shoulder-neck region (m. trapezius pars descendens and m. sternocleidomastoid), which were measured bilateral via electrodes and corresponding measuring devices (Noraxon 'TeleMyo 2400T G2') on the skin surface. The measurement system is called surface electromyography [13]. The incoming analog signals were processed, filtered and finally converted into digital signals by transformation from time to frequency domain. To normalize the derived rectified and smoothed activity, a measurement of resting activity $EA_0$ is first taken for each muscle at the beginning of the experiment. Using isometric maximum voluntary contraction, the muscle-specific maximum $EA_{max}$ is measured. The standardized EA (sEA) can then be calculated for all work phases. Furthermore, thermographic images of the head area were recorded. In addition, the assembly time and any process errors were recorded.

Subjective experience of stress was conducted through both standardized surveys, i.e. physiological sensation questionnaires (scaling from 0 'no stress' over 1 'moderate stress' to 4 'unbearable stress'), the 'NASA Task Load Index' (NASA-TLX), the 'Visual Fatigue Questionnaire' (VFQ) and the 'Rating Scale of Mental Effort' (RSME), and a semi-structured interview. The latter was based on a mixture of open and closed questions using an ordinal scale from −4 (strongly disagree) to +4 (strongly agree).

The quantitative data were analyzed both descriptively and inferentially. In the present study, the same measurements were repeated with a differing parameter: the HL. Therefore, the two-sided t-test for dependent samples was applied. Unless t-test requirements were met, the nonparametric Wilcoxon signed-rank test was used. Finally, with the help of the 'Intelligent Verbatim' method, the qualitative data could be transcribed and finally coded and analyzed.

## 4   Working Hypotheses

For reasons of presentability, only the working hypotheses listed in Table 1 are referred to in this paper. The data for the HL's different execution modes were averaged and compared to the implementation with the PI.

**Table 1.** Selection of the study's working hypotheses.

| Hypothesis | Description |
| --- | --- |
| H1 | The use of the HL influences the objective muscle strain in the shoulder-neck area. |
| H2 | The use of the HL influences the subjectively perceived muscle strain. |
| H3 | Cognitive load differs when using the HL compared to performing with the PI … |
| H3a | … measured by RSME. |
| H3b | … measured by NASA-TLX. |
| H4 | The cognitive load during the HL's use changes as the duration of the experiment progresses. |
| H5 | The HL's use influences the time duration of a set-up process compared to performing it with the PI. |
| H6 | With the help of HL, the test subjects cause fewer errors than without using HL. |

# 5   Results

The results from the overall study published here partly show a discrepancy between objective and subjective data. While the data on comfort impairment in the head area are consistent, the subjects do feel an increased muscular as well as cognitive strain when using the HL. However, Fig. 2 shows that the objective muscle activation of the m. trapezius pars descendens and the m. sternocleidomastoideus is lower when using the HMD than when performing without data glasses ($M_{sEA,HL} = 4,31 \pm 3,14\%$, $M_{sEA,PI} = 4,89 \pm 3,33\%$, $t = -3.54$, $p = .001$, $n = 24$) – with one exception. Only the lower right part of the trapezius pars descendens muscle shows increased physiological costs ($M_{sEA,HL} = 5,83 \pm 4,87\%$, $M_{sEA,PI} = 4,48 \pm 3,66\%$). Accordingly, all muscle groups show a significant difference when comparing the performance with HL and with PI.

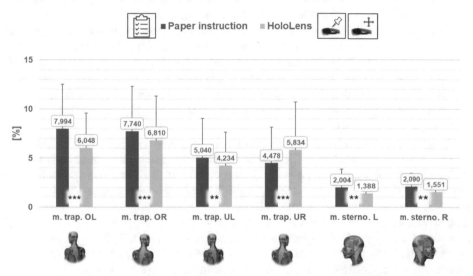

**Fig. 2.** Standardized electromyographic activity's [%] visual representation of the individual muscle sites across all set-up procedures to compare the application without and with the use of HL.

While the subjectively perceived strain (PS) of the shoulder-neck musculature (-M) did not exceed a moderate level ($M_{PS-M,HL} = 0.5 \pm 0,45$, $M_{PS-M,PI} = 0.25 \pm 0,32$, $z = -4.020$, $p < .001$, $n = 24$), the subjects experienced more severe heat and pressure points when using HL, especially in the head area (-H), i.e. nose ($M_{PS-H,Nose,HL} = 0,9 \pm 0,48$, $M_{PS-H,Nose,PI} = 0.134 \pm 0,26$) and forehead ($M_{PS-H,Forehead,HL} = 1,04 \pm 0,52$, $M_{PS-H,Forehead,PI} = 0.28 \pm 0,39$). However, they were also classified as only 'moderate' ($M_{PS-H,HL} = 0,69 \pm 0,3$, $M_{PS-H,PI} = 0,16 \pm 0,22$, $t = 7,72$, $p < .001$, $n = 24$). These findings were also supported by qualitative statements from the test subjects. A test person noted: 'Overall, the HoloLens is a bit too heavy. As a result, you quickly get pressure marks on your nose and forehead.'

Results analysis further shows that, as measured by the RSME, the HL use increases user cognitive load ($M_{RSME,HL} = 30,53 \pm 17,26$) compared to the use with the PI

($M_{RSME,PI} = 27,33 \pm 17,83$, $t = -2.43$, $p < .05$, $n = 24$). In addition, the subjects show a lower cognitive load with a simultaneous reduction of errors and set-up time in the second experimental section ($z = -2.95$, $p < .01$, $n = 24$).

Evaluation of the multidimensional NASA-TLX questionnaire suggested that the subjects' overall strain was slightly higher when using the 'Expert to Go' ($M_{NASA,HL} = 35,39 \pm 9,70$) compared to the PI usage ($M_{NASA,PI} = 32,85 \pm 11,24$). Due to an interaction with the HMD required in addition to the work task, the mental demand (-MD) increased ($M_{NASA-MD,HL} = 22,03 \pm 14,66$; $M_{NASA-MD,PI} = 19,58 \pm 13,94$). On the other hand, there was an increased performance (-P) ($M_{NASA-P,HL} = 77,03 \pm 19,32$; $M_{NASA-P,PI} = 69,90 \pm 27,25$), which could be realized with the help of the support system and objectively proven by a reduced failure rate. The findings described were also confirmed by the test persons during the interviews, as one test subject made clear: 'After a certain amount of familiarization, I got along quite well with the glasses [HoloLens, note]. You do have to concentrate to get everything right, though.'

The use of the HL has significant effects on the time duration of the set-up process ($t = -3.054$, $p < .01$, $n = 24$). The average set-up time with the PI was 10.38 min ($SD_{t,PI} = 2.36$ min). With the aid of the support system, subjects required an average set-up time of 12.16 min ($SD_{t,HL} = 2.49$ min). However, a comparison of the two test sections (TS) showed that the set-up times decreased both without and with the use of the HL ($M_{t,TS-1,HL} = 14:44 \pm 3:36$, $M_{t,TS-1,PI} = 12:21 \pm 2:49$, $M_{tTS-2,HL} = 9:48 \pm 2:02$, $M_{tTS-2,PI} = 8:55 \pm 2:24$).

While in the first test run about two errors per subject ($M_{ERROR} = 2,21 \pm 1,4$) were caused, the number of errors in the second test run was significantly lower ($M_{ERROR} = 0,43 \pm 0,63$, $t = 8.91$, $p < .01$, $n = 24$). In this context, it also became clear that the use of the HMD did not have a statistically significant effect on error causation ($t = 0.98$, $p > .05$, $n = 24$). It is true that the subjects required on average 13.03% more set-up time with data glasses. However, with the help of the HL support, a significant error reduction ($\Delta_{ERROR} = 35.63\%$) was realized compared to the PI. With regard to the two test sections, the number of errors was reduced by 87.43% (PI: 75.59%) and the set-up time decreased by 33.38% (PI: 27.94%) when using the 'Expert to Go'.

Thus, all hypotheses except for hypothesis H6 could be confirmed inferentially.

## 6 Discussion and Conclusion

The HL's high weight of around 580 g and the unfavorable weight distribution on the face are its strongest ergonomic limitations. These limitations cause pressure points in the head area, which lead to circulatory problems and ultimately to pain. The material properties and the necessary shifting of the HMD's seat for spectacle wearers (25% of the subjective collective) intensify the resulting compressive stress.

Abele [9] has shown that static gaze positioning and uncomfortable positioning of holograms result in significantly higher muscle activity compared to a paper-based or analog display of the corresponding information. In the case of dynamic activities, such as the set-up process of a bending machine, this effect is not necessary. In this case, the natural movements of the test person result in constant contraction and relaxation of the muscles, which are thus less stressed than in the case of a purely static muscle load. However, the stationary nature of the PI means that the subject is subjected to extra strain by grasping the instruction. On the other hand, the holograms of the HL follow the user's field of view, resulting in a spatial overlapping of the instructions with the subject's operative field of activity. The results are reduced head movements and deflections of the upper body. This can be demonstrated by the reduced activation of the trapezius and sternocleidomastoid muscles. Only the lower right part of the trapezius pars descendens muscle is more stressed when using the HMD. This is due to the need for interaction with the HL in the form of gesture control, whereby the subject extending the right arm cranial-ventrally at face level. 19 of 24 subjects were right-handed and accordingly used their 'strong' hand for interaction. When using the HL, the subjectively perceived additional muscular effort results from the perceived conclusion of the subjects that the comfort impairments in the head area are accompanied by a higher muscular stress in the shoulder-neck area. Overall, it should be noted that both the objective and subjective strain data do not exceed a moderate level during the set-up process. Furthermore, the differences of the OEMG data with and without the use of the HL are small. Thus, the interpretability of the objective results is only possible to a limited extent with a simultaneously prevailing very low degree of stress. Accordingly, fatigue symptoms are only likely to occur during repetitive execution without observing breaks.

By repeating the tasks several times, i.e. the set-up process as well as the interaction with the respective instructions, the subjects experience a reduced cognitive load and also produce fewer errors. The visualized holographic content compared to a paper-based instruction enables the subjects to perform the process more efficiently. Furthermore, the AR support prevents the onset of concentration lapses.

Due to the intuitive operation as well as the intensive and concentrated involvement with the support system, a learning effect quickly sets in both with regard to the set-up process and with regard to the handling of the data glasses and the application. In practice, this connection plays an important role, since the system supports inexperienced machine setters or those who need to be trained in a reliable and error-minimized set-up process. The familiarization with the system as well as expected optimization measures of the HMD and the application will also lead to further minimization of set-up times in the future. The extent to which AR systems are actually practicable in everyday practice from an ergonomic and economic point of view must be shown by further investigations.

**Acknowledgements.** The findings in this paper originate from the research project 'Cyberrüsten 4.0: Cyber-physische Unterstützung des Menschen beim Rüstvorgang am Beispiel eines Biege-prozesses zur Kleinserienfertigung auf Basis eines Wissenstransferansatzes', funded by a grant of the European Union and EFRE.NRW (No. EFRE-0800263).

# References

1. Janssen, S., Möller, K.: Erfolgreiche Steuerung von Innovationsprozessen und -projekten – Ergebnisse einer empirischen Studie. Zeitschrift für Controll. Manag. **55**(2), 97–104 (2011)
2. Abele, N.D., Hoffmann, S., Kuhnhen, C., Ludwig, T., Schäfer, W., Schweitzer, M., Wulf, V.: Supporting the set-up processes by cyber elements based on the example of tube bending. In: Mayr, H.C., Pinzger, M. (eds.) Informatik 2016 – Informatik von Menschen für Menschen, GI-Edition-Lecture Notes in Informatics (LNI), Klagenfurt, pp. 1627–1637 (2016)

3. Miina, A.: Lean problem: why companies fail with lean implementation? Management **2**(5), 232–250 (2012)
4. Shingo, S.: A Revolution in Manufacturing: The SMED System. CRC Press, Boca Raton (1985)
5. Tergan, S.O., Keller, T.: Knowledge and Information Visualization: Searching Synergies. Springer, Heidelberg (2005)
6. Paelke, V., Röcker, C.: User Interfaces for Cyber-Physical System: Challenges and Possible Approaches. Springer, Cham (2015)
7. Tang, A., Owen, C., Biocca, F., Mou, W.: Comparative effectiveness of augmented reality in object assembly. In: CHI '03: Proceedings of the SIGCHI Conference on Human Factors in Computing Systems, pp. 73–80 (2003)
8. Theis, S., Pfendler, C., Alexander, T., Mertens, A., Brandl, C., Schlick, C.M.: Head-Mounted Displays - Bedingungen des sicheren und beanspruchungsoptimalen Einsatzes: Physische Beanspruchung beim Einsatz von HMDs. Bundesanstalt für Arbeitsschutz und Arbeitsmedizin, Dortmund (2016)
9. Abele, N.D.: Cyber-physische Rüstunterstützung – Ergonomische Untersuchung zur Evaluierung physischer und kognitiver Beanspruchung des Menschen bei der Nutzung eines Head-Mounted Display (HMD). In: Arbeit interdisziplinär analysieren – bewerten – gestalten, Proceedings des 65. Frühjahrskongresses der Gesellschaft für Arbeitswissenschaft. GfA-Press, Dortmund (2019)
10. Abele, N.D., Kluth, K.: Beanspruchungsbezogene Evaluierung AR-basierter versus papierunterstützter Rüstinstruktionen zur Einrichtung von Industriemaschinen. In: Digitale Arbeit, digitaler Wandel, digitaler Mensch? Proceedings des 66. Frühjahrskongresses der Gesellschaft für Arbeitswissenschaft. GfA-Press, Dortmund (2020)
11. Cometti, C., Païzis, C., Casteleira, A., Pons, G., Babault, N.: Effects of mixed reality head-mounted glasses during 90 minutes of mental and manual tasks on cognitive and physiological functions. Peerj (2018)
12. De Carvalho, A.F.P., Hoffmann, S., Abele, N.D., Schweitzer, M., Tolmie, P., Randall, D., Wulf, V.: Of embodied action and sensors knowledge and expertise sharing in industrial set-up. Comput. Supp. Coop. Work **27**(3–6), 875–916 (2018)
13. Steinhilber, B., Anders, C., Jäger, M., Läubli, T., Luttmann, A., Rieger, M.A., Scholle, H.C., Schumann, N.P., Seibt, R., Strasser, H., Kluth, K.: S2k-Leitlinie zur Oberflächen-Elektromyographie in der Arbeitsmedizin, Arbeitsphysiologie und Arbeitswissenschaft. ZEITSCHRIFT FÜR ARBEITSWISSENSCHAFT, vol. 67, pp. 113–128. Springer, Heidelberg (2013)

# Derivation of MTM-HWD® Analyses from Digital Human Motion Data

Martin Benter[✉] and Peter Kuhlang

MTM ASSOCIATION e. V., 15738 Zeuthen, Germany
martin.benter@mtm.org

**Abstract.** Productively and ergonomically designed work is a key factor for the competitiveness of industrial companies. MTM-HWD® is a method to describe human work that allows an integrated analysis of both productive and ergonomic aspects. Although it considers these aspects in a single process, the method still requires a considerable amount of effort [1]. One possibility to reduce this effort is the utilization of digital human motion data from human simulation tools.

This paper presents an approach that can use this motion data to derive a HWD analysis in a semi-automated way. The implementation of this approach is illustrated using the simulation software imk ema [2].

**Keywords:** Human motion data · Human simulation · MTM-HWD · Production planning

## 1 The MTM-HWD® Process Building Block System

Goal of the MTM process building block system MTM-HWD® (Methods-Time Measurement-Human Work Design, short: HWD) is the combined productive and ergonomic evaluation of human work [1]. To achieve this goal, the user records the performed actions and their productive and ergonomic influencing variables. To simplify and systematize the recording, these variables are classified according to human body parts [1].

Due to its objective description of human movements, it also represents a suitable basis for the digitization of the planning and design of human work [3, 4]. Digitally recorded work sequences can be complemented with feasible times. Moreover, it can be ensured that these sequences are ergonomically harmless for the involved workers [1]. It is thus a key for the meaningful application of digital planning tools [4].

## 2 Application of MTM-HWD®

In order to use HWD successfully, it is necessary to correctly assess the HWD building blocks and their influencing variables. Figure 1 shows an overview of the necessary information [5]. The central components are the building block elements that describe the work sequence (Fig. 1, left). The influencing factors (Fig. 1, right) must then be determined for each building block in order to evaluate the sequence in terms of time and ergonomics.

**building block description**  **influencing factors**

| building block elements | description segment | name | description segment | name |
|---|---|---|---|---|
| object | | path | | upper arm posture |
| action | | floor conditions | | hand position |
| active limb | lower limbs | stability | | arm extension |
| passive limb | | basic position | | wrist posture |
| | | leg posture | | weight |
| | | trunk flexion | | force |
| | trunk | trunk rotation | | direction of force |
| | | trunk inclination | upper limbs | distance class |
| | head/ neck | head posture | | supply |
| | | eye travel | | place accuracy |
| | | | | assembly position |
| | | | | positioning conditions |
| | | | | grasp motion |
| | | | | type of grasp |
| | | | | vibration |

**Fig. 1.** HWD building block elements and influencing factors

## 2.1 Building Block Elements

The most important building block element is the action that the worker performs, i.e. whether he picks an object up or moves it. The building block description also includes the type of object with which the worker interacts (e.g. actuator or tool). Other elements capture information about which limb is active during the action and what the passive limb is doing meanwhile [1].

In addition to the building block elements, the user records the relevant influencing variables for the action. These variables are briefly explained below [1, 4, 6].

## 2.2 Influencing Factors - Lower Limbs

The assessment of influencing variables starts with the lower limbs. The path is the distance an employee covers during an action. HWD distinguishes between walking, climbing steps/ladders and crawling. The floor conditions describe if the floor is uneven or if obstacles may block the path and thus, an increased amount of control is required while walking. The basic position depicts the position of the body at the end of the action. A distinction is made between standing, sitting, kneeling, crouching or lying down. The influencing factor leg posture indicates whether the employee extends or bends the legs, and the variable stability describes whether the posture of the lower extremities allows a secure stand.

## 2.3 Influencing Factors - Trunk and Head/Neck

The next influencing factors describe the posture of the employee's trunk and head. Trunk flexion, rotation and tilt reflect the posture of the upper body. The flexion shows the forward/ backward bending of the torso, the tilt the deflection to the side and the rotation how much the shoulders are twisted in relation to the hips. Head posture analogously represents whether the head is deflected in one of the three directions or if it has a normal posture. Finally, the factor eye travel describes whether time relevant eye movements are necessary.

## 2.4  Influencing Factors - Upper Limbs

The posture of the arms, the necessary forces as well as the required control effort of the actions are described in the segment upper limbs. The upper arm posture reflects the deflection of the arms to the front, back and side. The hand position describes the height of the hand in relation to the shoulder joints. Arm extension indicates the distance between the hand and the shoulder. The influencing factor wrist posture represents the bending, inclination or rotation of the wrist similar to the trunk posture.

With the influence factors weight, force and direction of force, the user records the load of moved objects as well as necessary forces.

The influencing factors for describing the control effort have a high time relevance. They include the distance class, which describes the distance covered by the hand. The influence factor supply reflects the position of the objects that have to be obtained. Place accuracy, assembly position and positioning conditions describe the accuracy with which the employee must place objects. Grasp motion and type of grasp describe the required position of the fingers so that the employee can control or hold the object. The final factor is vibration, which indicates whether potentially harmful vibrations occur during the work.

Once all the building block elements and influencing factors have been assessed, the required time and the ergonomic load of the work task can be determined. This provides the basis for a target oriented design of the workplace.

## 3  Categorization of the Influencing Variables

The derivation of a HWD analysis from a human simulation tool requires the correct assessment of all building block elements and influencing factors. The central question is therefore, which information can be determined automatically and which information has to be put in manually.

To answer this question systematically, it is helpful to classify the influencing factors of HWD into categories first [5]. Figure 2 shows a possible categorization of the factors.

One essential property to distinguish the influence factors is the building block specificity. An influence factor is building block specific if it can be assigned to an action. An example of this is the supply. It is only relevant for one of the possible actions and it has to be assessed for each occurrence of that action.

Overarching influencing factors, on the other hand, are not limited to specific actions. Moreover, they can apply to several successive actions. Additionally, they are not limited to HWD, but are also used in other methods. An example is the basic position. It can remain the same for several actions or entire work sequences and is also relevant for ergonomic methods such as EAWS [7].

| description segment | influencing factor | category building block specific | | category overarching | |
|---|---|---|---|---|---|
| | | accuracies | distances | postures | forces |
| lower limbs | path | | x | | |
| | floor conditions | x | | | |
| | stability | | | x | |
| | basic position | | | x | |
| | leg posture | | | x | |
| trunk | trunk flexion | | | x | |
| | trunk rotation | | | x | |
| | trunk inclination | | | x | |
| head/ neck | head posture | | | x | |
| | eye travel | | x | | |
| upper limbs | upper arm posture | | | x | |
| | hand position | | | x | |
| | arm extension | | | x | |
| | wrist posture | | | x | |
| | weight | | | | x |
| | force | | | | x |
| | direction of force | | | | x |
| | distance class | | | | x |
| | supply | | x | | |
| | place accuracy | x | | | |
| | assembly position | x | | | |
| | positioning conditions | x | | | |
| | grasp motion | x | | | |
| | type of grasp | x | | | |
| | vibration | x | | | |
| | upper arm posture | | | | x |

**Fig. 2.** Categorization of HWD influencing factors

The specific influence factors can be subdivided into accuracies and distances. Accuracies describe the required control effort and include, among others, the place accuracy and the positioning conditions. They depend above all on the used objects. For example, a screwdriver requires a greater accuracy than a file.

Distances, on the other hand, indicate the necessary movement lengths of the actions. They are mainly determined by the workstation layout. Thus, a better layout leads to shorter distances.

The overarching influencing factors are the postures and the forces. Postures describe the position of human body parts. Their correct recording is the basis for the ergonomic evaluation of the work process. Like distances, they mainly depend on the layout. A poorly designed workplace thus leads to an increased ergonomic load.

The last group is the applied forces. They include weights or necessary finger-hand forces. Like postures, they play an important ergonomic role. Unlike these, however, they depend primarily on the used objects. The heavier the used tools, the higher the required forces.

This categorization of influencing factors can also be applied to other methods for assessing human work. For example, the MTM-UAS method [8] mainly uses accuracies and distances for the time evaluation of work processes. The EAWS method [7], on the other hand, relies on postures and forces for ergonomic evaluation.

## 4   Determining the Information Through Human Simulations

The building block elements as well as the categories of influencing factors are now examined to determine to what extent human simulations are capable of providing the required information for a HWD analysis. The focus in this article are the possibilities of the tool imk ema [2]. In case of missing information, the article addresses how the data can be added. Figure 3 shows the result of the examination.

| HWD information | | determination of information | necessity of additional user activity |
|---|---|---|---|
| building block elements | object | necessary input | no |
| | action | assignment of action sequences | yes (verification) |
| | limbs | necessary input | no |
| influencing factors | accuracies | additional input | yes (manual input) |
| | distances | automatic determination | no |
| | postures | automatic determination | no |
| | Forces | necessary/ additional input | partial (manual input) |

**Fig. 3.** Determination of HWD information using human simulations

### 4.1   Building Block Elements

Simulation tools such as imk ema digitally depict human work processes. When modelling the processes, the necessary information and parameters are similar to the required data when creating a HWD analysis. The similar information includes the used objects and with which extremity they are handled. Thus, an important part of the building block elements is already present in the simulation. The actions, however, cannot be trivially derived from the simulation input, but they represent an important part of a correct HWD application. To meet this challenge, frequently used objects have been identified and the corresponding relevant action sequences have been defined. For example, the necessary actions for handling a cordless screwdriver have been specified.

With this approach, a determination of the building block elements can be ensured for a large number of use cases. However, a correct derivation in all cases cannot be guaranteed. Therefore, it is necessary that the HWD user verifies the results and corrects them if necessary.

## 4.2 Influencing Factors - Accuracies

The determination of the accuracies is as difficult as the determination of the actions. They cannot be derived directly from the simulation input. In order to be able to assess them, they are integrated as additional manual inputs during the creation of the simulation model. Thus, for example, the influence factor supply is collected when the simulation objects are entered. Similar to the actions, an experienced HWD user should enter the inputs or verify the simulation results.

## 4.3 Influencing Factors - Distances

A simulation tool calculates and visualizes human movements using a digital human model. The generated motion data contains, among other things, the coordinates of the body parts during the work process. The distances can be derived very well from this data. This way of determination might even be more accurate than manual recording by a HWD user, since measurement errors and estimates are avoided. However, an incorrect model of the workplace or unrealistically simulated movements can lead to the fact that the determined distances do not exist in reality.

## 4.4 Influencing Factors - Postures

Analogous to the distances, the postures can be derived well from the motion data of the human simulation. However, the existing posture definitions had been intended for manual evaluation. Therefore, the existing definitions have been specified for the digital application. For example, it was not clearly defined at which body angles an employee lies or sits.

## 4.5 Influencing Factors - Forces

The forces cannot be derived directly from the data of the digital human model, but are part of the possible inputs when modelling the simulation. For example, the weights of the used objects can be entered. Other occurring forces have to be added manually so that the information for the HWD analysis is complete. Thus, the input or verification by an experienced user is necessary here as well.

## 5  Implementation with the imk ema Simulation Tool

In a joint project of the MTM ASSOCIATION e. V. and the imk automotive GmbH, a solution for the automated derivation of HWD analyses from human simulation tools has been implemented. In this solution the explained necessary additions and adaptations were made.

After creating the simulation model with the additional data and simulating the work process, the generated data is transferred to the MTM software TiCon via a jointly developed interface. TiCon then checks the transferred data and the HWD rules. After this, TiCon assigns the appropriate MTM times. In addition, the ergonomic evaluation of the work task is performed. The result is a simulation analysis that provides a reliable planning time and enables a meaningful ergonomic evaluation.

This simulation analysis describes the work process that took place in the simulation tool. Thus, the analysis would also reflect incorrect or humanly impossible workflows if the simulation was not created correctly.

This solution for an automated derivation of a HWD analysis is currently being tested extensively in a joint validation project. An example used in this validation is shown in Fig. 4. It depicts the user interface of the imk ema software.

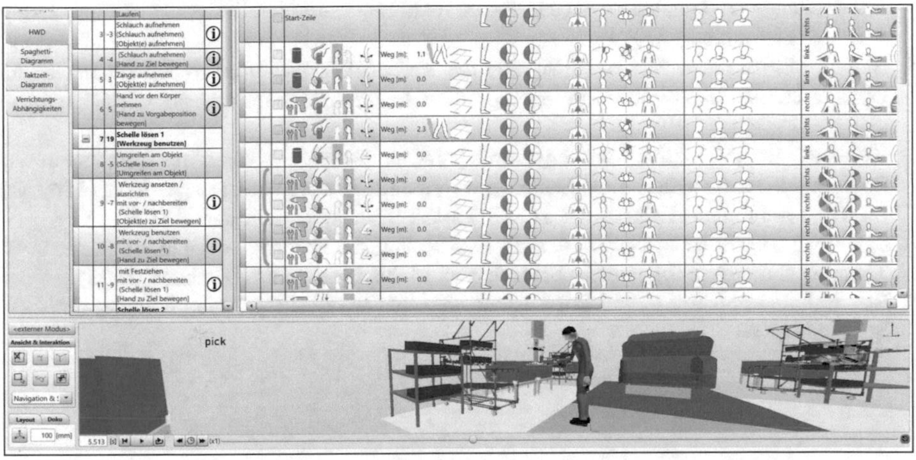

**Fig. 4.** Illustration of a derived HWD analysis in imk ema

The bottom of the figure shows the workstation layout as well as the simulated human performing the work task. In this case, the task is the assembly of a hose on a passenger car.

In the upper area, a section of the corresponding correct HWD analysis can be seen. With the functionalities of the ema the user can jump to certain actions in the sequence and see the corresponding part of the simulation.

# 6 Conclusion

This paper described how a MTM-HWD analysis can be created using human simulation tools. It showed that a large part of the information is entered or generated anyway when creating a simulation model. The remaining information has to be added manually by a HWD user. The result is a simulation analysis that contains both, time and ergonomic evaluation of the simulated work process.

The article clarifies that deriving HWD analyses from digital motion data is possible and useful. This is of high importance for a productive and ergonomic design of human work in the increasingly digitalized production.

# References

1. Finsterbusch, T.: Entwicklung einer Methodik zur Bildung von Bausteinsystemen für die Gestaltung menschlicher Arbeit. Techn. Univ, Dresden (2016)
2. Leidholdt, W., Fritzsche, L., Bauer, S.: Editor menschlicher Arbeit (ema). In: Homo Sapiens Digitalis - Virtuelle Ergonomie und digitale Menschmodelle. Springer Vieweg, Berlin (2016)
3. Finsterbusch, T., Kuhlang, P.: A new methodology for modelling human work – evolution of the process language MTM towards the description and evaluation of productive and ergonomic work processes. In: Proceedings of 19th Triennial Congress of the IEA, Melbourne (2015)
4. Kuhlang, P.: Positionen der Deutschen MTM-Vereinigung e. V. zu Assistenzsystemen und zur Verarbeitung von digitalen Bewegungsdaten. In: MTM-Schriftenreihe Industrial Engineering, Ausgabe 12, Hamburg (2019)
5. Benter, M., Kuhlang, P.: Kategorisierung der MTM-HWD®-Einflussgrößen zur Bewertung der Ableitbarkeit aus digitalen Bewegungsdaten. In: GfA, Tagungsband der Herbstkonferenz (2019)
6. Kuhlang, P.: Produktive und ergonomiegerechte Arbeit – Von Grundsätzlichem zur Prozesssprache MTM über die Ergonomiebewertung zu Human Work Design (MTM-HWD®). In: ifaa, Leistung und Entgelt. Joh. Heider Verlag, Düsseldorf, Ausgabe 2/2018
7. Schaub, K., Caragnano, G., Britzke, B., Bruder, R.: The European assembly worksheet. In: Theoretical Issues in Ergonomics Science, vol. 14. Taylor & Francis, London (2012)
8. Bokranz, R., Landau, K.: Produktivitätsmanagement von Arbeitssystemen. Schäffer-Poeschel, Stuttgart (2006)

# A Systemic Overview of Factors Affecting the Cognitive Performance of Industrial Manual Assembly Workers

Cecilia Berlin[1][✉] [ID], Matilda Wollter Bergman[1], Maral Babapour Chafi[1,2] [ID],
Ann-Christine Falck[3], and Roland Örtengren[3]

[1] Department of Industrial and Materials Science, Division of Design and Human Factors,
Chalmers University of Technology, Gothenburg, Sweden
cecilia.berlin@chalmers.se
[2] Institute of Stress Medicine, Region Västra Götaland, Gothenburg, Sweden
[3] Department of Industrial and Materials Science, Division of Production Systems, Chalmers
University of Technology, Gothenburg, Sweden

**Abstract.** In paced assembly lines, cognitive processing is required from assembly workers to perform correct and timely assembly of complex products with varying specifications. This interview study involving 75 industrial assemblers, design- and manufacturing engineers explores how assemblers' cognitive performance is influenced by multiple factors within the contexts of product design, production setup and assembly. Our results indicate that both positive and negative effects on assemblers' cognitive performance can stem from task design, timing, physical loading demands, extrinsic motivation factors, teamwork and the assembly "interface" design. Among design- and manufacturing engineers, two mindsets emerged: (i) a product-centred mindset relying on assemblers having sufficient experience, knowledge, and assembly instructions, (ii) an assembler-focused mindset characterised by an iterative and collaborative development process to ensure easy-to-assemble solutions, and avoid errors, delays and costly re-work. Despite organizational differences and conditions between the companies that took part in the study, the results are largely consistent.

**Keywords:** Cognitive ergonomics · Mental workload · Manual assembly · Work environment · Cognitive performance

## 1 Introduction

Achieving consistent, timely and high-quality assembly of complex products is paramount for manufacturers to ship value to customers. Although a well-established part of the threat to quality is attributable to high physical loading [1–4], *cognitive* over- as well as underloading [5] may result in lowered task performance, possibly leading to increases in costly assembly errors, time consumption and frustration. Working conditions that can distract, confuse, overload or even bore assembly workers throughout a full working day may threaten successful assembly, as well as the well-being of the

© The Author(s), under exclusive license to Springer Nature Switzerland AG 2021
N. L. Black et al. (Eds.): IEA 2021, LNNS 221, pp. 371–381, 2021.
https://doi.org/10.1007/978-3-030-74608-7_47

assembly workers and their willingness to remain in the profession. In the long run, keeping assemblers motivated to stay in the workplace over time is desirable for companies in order to build up expertise, experience, routine and a sense of confidence and pride in the craftsmanship of assembling correctly. Assemblers who achieve these characteristics often provide great value by being able to spot potential errors, instruct junior colleagues, and suggest process improvements.

In the long run, keeping assemblers motivated to stay in the workplace over time is desirable for companies in order to build up expertise, experience, routine and a sense of confidence and pride in the craftsmanship of assembling complex products. Assemblers who achieve these characteristics often provide great value by being able to spot potential errors, instruct and advise junior colleagues, and suggest process improvements. Still, not much of assembly ergonomics literature concerns itself with cognitive aspects of purely manual assembly. Much of the recent research regards cognitive aspects of technological and automation innovations, such as those of the Industry 4.0-paradigm, automated solutions, assembly instructions using Virtual and Augmented reality, etc. [6, 7].

*Cognitive performance* in assembly work is defined in this study as the degree to which individual workers are able to perceive relevant signals from the assembly situation; recognize, process and interpret them; and finally, make decisions that lead to actions contributing to correct component assembly. Cognitive performance may vary depending on prerequisites like experience levels, training, available instructions, relations with colleagues and supervisors, disturbances, and on mental loading factors like emotional state, frustration levels and even the time of day. Needing to complete assembly tasks within a limited amount of time may also add an aspect of pressure and stress, where part of the individual's cognitive resources are spent on awareness of time running low, and not just on the task itself. The literature also makes a distinction between cognitive and mental workload [8, 9]. although the two concepts overlap, a rough distinction can be made, where *cognitive workload* concerns the process of taking in sensory signals, interpreting them and deciding on a course of action based on that process; while *mental workload* appears to include a broader range of performance-affecting factors apart from cognition, including affective state, fatigue, social aspects, teamwork and the worker's own perception of and satisfaction with their performance.

A *sustainable* cognitive performance is defined in this study as an ideal level of mental workload that keeps assemblers alert and engaged with their cognitive work tasks, matching their skill level and maintaining a sense of control, without causing too-high or too-low degrees of mental strain that either overwhelm or cause lack of focus or distraction (as illustrated by Van Acker et al. [9]). Thus, a holistic understanding of working conditions that can support or threaten a sustainable cognitive performance within the assembly context constitutes knowledge that should enable design- and manufacturing engineers, as well as companies as a whole, to provide optimal working conditions for assembly workers.

Early phases of product and production design, where design- and manufacturing engineers are involved, are the most optimal development stages for proactive ergonomics action [2]. At the same time, early intervention is a very cost-effective way to ensure good working conditions for the workers. However, proactive interventions in production have most often been considered from a physical perspective, and less so from a cognitive/mental loading perspective.

This interview study aims at exploring how assembly workers' cognitive performance is influenced by multiple factors within the assembly context and stemming from the design of the product as well as the production setup. Two research questions are addressed in this paper: (RQ1) *which working conditions support and/or hinder a sustainable cognitive performance throughout a work shift?* And (RQ2) *how can design and manufacturing engineers support sustainable cognitive loading for assemblers?* Since space is limited in this paper, we limit the results to cognitive, rather than physical, ergonomics aspects.

## 2  Methodology

The main part of this study consists of semi-structured interviews with 50 individual manual assembly workers and 25 design- and/or manufacturing engineers at three Swedish industrial manufacturing companies. Interviews were carried out individually, either on-site at the companies or via telephone. Interviewees were recruited via an initial contact person (CP) near the production organization at each of the companies. The CP organized a sample of assemblers who were permitted to take time out of their working day to participate in a scheduled interview on-site, allocating approximately 30–40 min for each interview. Table 1 shows the overall demographics of our sample.

**Table 1.** Demographic information about participants (total N = 75)

| Company | Roles (M = male, F = female) | Assemblers' age span/Work experience |
|---|---|---|
| A (vehicle manufacturer), N = 22 | Assemblers (10M, 5F); Design Engineers (3M); Manufacturing Engineers (3M, 1F) | 22–54 yrs/ 10 mo–32 yrs |
| B (vehicle manufacturer) N = 33 | Assemblers (16M, 6F); Design Engineers (5M, 3F); Manufacturing Engineers (3M) | 20–56 yrs/ 5 mo–39 yrs |
| C (automotive component manufacturer), N = 20 | Assemblers (5M, 8F); Design Engineers (7M) | 19–60 yrs/ 6 mo–30 yrs |

In order to disrupt the assembly work as little as possible, the research team agreed to comply with the company's selection of participants and the requirement to complete all interviews during the same day or consecutive two days. As a rule, assemblers were selected by the CP to fulfil the research team's request to represent a wide range of work experience and age, as well as on the merits of being able to speak Swedish. In contrast, the design- and manufacturing engineers were recruited via outreach in the company's internal network and a "snowball" approach [10], as the CP was rarely affiliated with the departments where those engineers worked. They were contacted individually by the researchers, and participated on a voluntary basis.

Each interview was semi-structured, using an interview guide with an introduction script followed by a set of questions adapted to each of the roles Assembler, Design engineer or Manufacturing engineer. The questions explored how each person carried out their work, what they perceived as enabling or hindering their work, and how the product or production work tasks and environment affected assemblers' ability to perceive signals, recall from memory, solve problems and make decisions. All interviews were audio-recorded and afterwards transcribed verbatim. A qualitative analysis followed, involving a combination of top-down as well as thematic analysis [11]. Figure 1 shows examples of the interview questions and illustrates the procedure for the analysis of the interviews.

The qualitative analysis resulted in a wide range of codes, segmented by roles (Assemblers vs. Design or Manufacturing Engineers) to clarify the interviewees' respective involvement with the operative phase vs. the design and planning phases of production. To provide an overview of themes identified in the analysis, a (selective) "coding tree" is shown in Fig. 2, indicating the first two analysis steps in Fig. 1. Due to the limited space in this paper, we can only elaborate on the contents of a limited selection

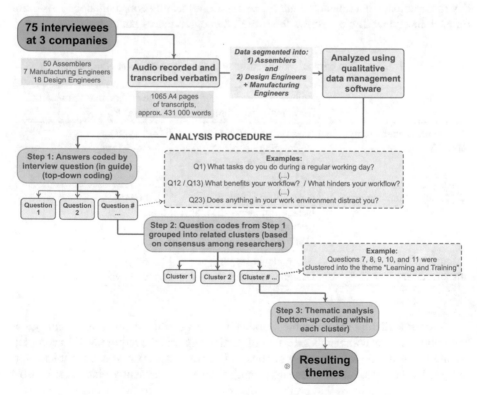

**Fig. 1.** The data processing and analysis procedure for the interviews, with examples

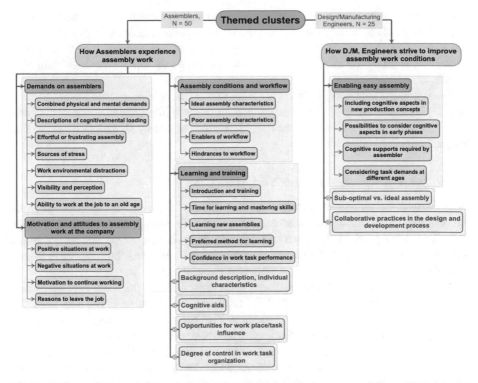

**Fig. 2.** Excerpt of the overall top-down "coding tree" - green clusters are elaborated upon in this paper. Each cluster was coded thematically (bottom-up) in the third analysis step.

of themes; the bottom-up thematic analysis is elaborated for the clusters marked green in Fig. 2.

## 3 Results

Assemblers chiefly spoke about on-site work conditions, teamwork and experiences of dealing with assembly under time pressure, while the engineers provided perspectives on workflow in the earlier phases and whether they perceived opportunities to introduce assembly-facilitating design solutions to decrease the risk of mistakes or confusion. In this paper we concentrate on the cognitive aspects reported, however most assemblers characterized the workload as more physical than mental in nature, due to the intense tempo, component handling and sometimes heavy lifting.

The assembly complexity handled by the assemblers varied, mostly due to the fact that both vehicle manufacturers produce largely customized vehicles with specific instructions and component setups for each individual vehicle on the line. The component manufacturer made batches with mostly identical assembly steps and components, but still with a high degree of manual assembly. Furthermore, the assemblers worked at different factory line segments within vehicle assembly, for instance engine, gearbox, axles, frame, chassis, brakes etc., and some were also team leaders. Some inexperienced assemblers worked at only one station performing repetitive manual assembly work like entering screws, while more experienced assemblers performed a wide variety of work tasks such as assembling special customization solutions in vehicles with high complexity.

Quotes in the following sections are traceable to interviewees using the code [company][role][serial number]; for example, *AA-5* is the fifth interviewed assembler at company A, *BM-2* the second manufacturing engineer at company B, and *CD-1* is the first design engineer at company C.

### 3.1    Physical and Mental Demands on Assemblers

Many assemblers tended to associate the mention of *"ergonomics"* to physical strain and provided many telling examples of heavy, physically tiring, strenuous, cumbersome and pain-inducing workload, often with high loads on hands, wrists and backs. Many vehicle assemblies involved far reaches, challenging gripping positions and heavy lifting, depending on the component size, weight and placement.

All assemblers reported working under some degree of time pressure. For new assemblers, the countdown of the station cycle time added a sense of stress until they felt habituated to the tasks. Cycle times at paced workstations varied between approximately one and a half to seven minutes (indicating varied degrees of repetitiveness) although some specialist assemblers worked on customized installations that involved a lot more problem-solving and decision-making, and could take up to several weeks to complete. Other taxing time aspects included long days, additional mental strain when working overtime, and often needing to be *"quick-thinking" (AA-1)*. Sources of stress mentioned included *"When somebody is unfocused and causes stoppage time" (AA-4)*, i.e. a team member making mistakes, or when unusual product variants had a large impact on the remaining time on the cycle time. In contrast, some assemblers stated that the ideal was to be in control and work calmly, following a standardized work procedure. Some "older" longtime workers at one company served as good examples to their younger colleagues, by working *"calmly and methodically" (AM-5)*.

Regarding complexity, the sequence of vehicles could be both over- and under-stimulating. The former situation involved *"A lot to keep track of" (AA-12)*, and many attributed high mental effort to whenever there was great variation between vehicles in a sequence. *"You always need to stay one vehicle ahead, in your mind"* said assembler *BA-11*, and three others explained how much there was to take in as a new employee. Whenever mistakes occurred, additional handling could lead to heavier physical loading, particularly when undoing tightened assemblies. Small components with high precision demands and tight tolerances were seen as challenging to deal with, as were complicated and fragile sub-assemblies. Experienced vehicle assemblers felt that having a holistic knowledge of the product was a valuable resource that benefited their craftsmanship: *"Those who have been in the main-line flow and have seen how they build (...) have a better understanding for why we do things in certain ways (...) in particular, you can tell when the specifications are wrong." (BA-14)*.

Receiving incorrect assemblies from earlier stations in the line or having a lack of materials were sources of frustration, as well as when a vehicle needed to be taken out of the production sequence to be dealt with and then reintroduced out of order. A recurring explanation for mistakes was that the time pressure and some over-balanced stations led to rushed, careless work and letting mistakes go unadjusted: *"When you're behind (...) the mistakes come. Because you more or less throw in the screws and washers. Whether it's the wrong way round or not (...) I have to hurry on to the next one."* (BA-12) One assembler reflected that just knowing or expecting that a coming vehicle would be difficult could cause feelings of reluctance, disturbing concentration.

Some vehicle assemblers mentioned incorrect or incomplete instructions and dealing with missing components as disturbance situations that could cause insecurity, particularly if no help was available from local technician teams. Sometimes changes were introduced with short notice without changes being made to the specifications. Sounds, noises and blinking lights from machines, Andon systems and materials in the production line added to the distraction and mental strain.

## 3.2 Assemblers' Motivation and Attitudes Towards the Work

The assemblers reported different factors motivating them to continue working or wanting to move onward in their career. These factors were further divided into intrinsic and extrinsic factors [12]. The intrinsic factors included the possibility for further self-development, being driven to learn new things, having the ability to focus on tasks during working hours, collegial interaction, having good group dynamics and friendly work colleagues. Dysfunctional collegial interaction could however lead to decreased motivation. One significant intrinsic factor that emerged was professional pride, which involved feeling enjoyment from the work tasks, working with high quality and having the sense of performing good work. Regarding the extrinsic factors there are two that motivate assemblers to continue working: a good salary and good working hours. Assemblers also described that high physical workload and poor ergonomic conditions decrease their motivation to continue on the job.

Moreover, the assemblers' attitude towards their work also influenced motivation to continue working or wanting to change career tracks. Some described how lack of collegial cohesion had a negative effect on their work attitude. It therefore appears important to support collegial well-being and collegial interaction to sustain assemblers' interest in continuing working. Assemblers also described how feeling positive emotions, satisfaction with the work tasks and experiencing variation within the work tasks is a fundamental basis for a positive attitude towards the assembly work. Furthermore, inner calm, good ergonomic conditions and having a complete overall picture were factors that contributed positively to their wanting to remain as assemblers. In contrast, they highlighted that having limitations within the work tasks, lack of support and lack of development possibilities decreased their positive attitude towards the work and created a feeling of wanting to do other tasks, either within their present employment or with a different employer.

### 3.3 Assembly Conditions and Work-Related Flow

According to the participants a good "flow" in their work meant having good conditions to assemble correctly, being in step with the assembly sequence, having a smooth collegial interaction between assemblers, and feeling content at the workplace. The analysis revealed three main factors affecting the assembler's ability to achieve flow in assembly work. First, the individual characteristics that varied among assemblers in terms of level of prior experience, daily form, the ability to concentrate (especially on quality) in order to reduce the number of adjustments, and committing to follow a standardized way of working (e.g., the principle of 5S, a common methodology within Lean management for keeping good workplace order, abbreviating: Sort, Set in order, Standardize, Shine and Safety [13]). Second, organizational factors that influenced assemblers' work-related flow were: adequate staffing; as little process disturbance as possible; manageable product variability and precision-demanding tasks; the possibility to influence the work conditions; well-balanced and planned workstations that enable the feeling of calm and having time to perform the work task; and having had adequate training for new work tasks. According to one vehicle assembler, *"Everything beyond the standard [way of working] takes extra time and contributes to more stress" (AA-14).* Overbalanced workstations (i.e., with a high task-to-time ratio) could create stress, forcing assemblers to take shortcuts potentially leading to personal injury and improper assembly that deteriorated the quality. Third, design-related aspects of the work environment that influenced the work-related flow were: easy-to-read instructions, frequent work rotation, having necessary functional equipment at the assembly station without unnecessary clutter, structured materials delivery and functional placement to avoid time losses, and forgiving tolerances for the components, to avoid incomplete assembly.

### 3.4 Learning and Training

Several factors regarding the learning method have in our results proved to be important for correct execution of the work. Having a uniform, systematic learning method enables the assembly supervisor to teach methods that facilitate the assembly work. Assemblers also stated that the introduction needs to be accurate and clear to avoid causing stress. Additionally, it was considered important to introduce correct movements and routines from the beginning. To avoid creating overload when learning, assemblers needed to learn the work one step at a time and the introduction time needed to be long enough to avoid the feeling of being left alone too soon. One vehicle assembler stated: *"I believe the most important thing is to have enough time to learn. (…) I don't know if there are any shortcuts to learning faster, but during this particular time you shouldn't have to be feeling stress, just doing it at your own pace, letting it take time" (BA-19).*

The assemblers had different opinions regarding the number of supervisors who should be involved during the introduction. Some argued that it was important to be taught by the same supervisor to ensure continuity, while others wanted to have different supervisors during the introduction to get exposed to different individuals' working methods. According to the assemblers the supervisor needed to have patience and provide the opportunity to ask follow-up questions to support the assemblers in their learning process. Furthermore, the analysis showed that the assemblers needed an overall picture of the product and a general background understanding of the execution of the work steps. Regarding work instructions, it was found that present work instructions were not successful at conveying visual angles and "tricks", making it harder to learn how to assemble correctly and efficiently. In addition, having consistently updated work instructions facilitated the learning process.

### 3.5 Design- and Manufacturing Engineers' Perspectives on How to Contribute to Sustainable Cognitive Performance

According to the 25 interviewed design- and manufacturing engineers, the focus of their development process was generally on ensuring good quality of product components and minimising the risk of errors. When considering easy assembly, the focus was mainly on addressing physical ergonomics aspects, such as lifting or reaches. Nonetheless, two distinct mindsets were identified among the interviewees, when asked how they contribute to an easy assembly during the design process.

The first mindset can be described as a product-centred mindset, characterised by prioritising the optimisation of the product's functionality and quality over making easy-to-assemble solutions. According to design- and manufacturing engineers with this mindset, assembly experience and knowledge among assemblers is a prerequisite for avoiding errors. There appeared to be a general absence of strategies and measures to address cognitive aspects of assembly. Sufficiently good assembly instructions were therefore considered the main measure to ensure accurate assembly.

The second mindset was *assembler-centred*, characterised as an iterative and collaborative process. These interviewees spoke of using early-phase prototyping and engagement of assembly representatives and ergonomists throughout the process to ensure easier component assembly. The mindset is called assembler-centred due to a focus on designing solutions that rely less on prior experience: *"There is so much [employee] rotation here that it becomes very important to have solutions that can be understood by anyone"* said design engineer *BD-3*. In addition, the design- and manufacturing engineers with this mindset emphasized the importance of learning from evaluating existing production lines for further improvements.

Both mindsets were identified on an individual level, appearing at each organisation. Regardless of their mindsets, the design- and manufacturing engineers mentioned limitations in the design process that hinder and complicate achieving easy-to-assemble solutions. For example, collaboration difficulties between design engineering and production in early phases and limited feedback on early concept drawings were raised as impediments. Limited time and resources, and conflicting requirements (such as spatial limitations within the component design) were also commonly mentioned.

## 4   Discussion

This study identifies a variety of factors that can impact assemblers' cognitive performance, many of which could be possible to consider (but are currently not fully) in early design phases. A preliminary analysis indicates that task design, assembly timing, physical loading demands, extrinsic motivation factors, teamwork and the assembly "interface" design all have both positive and negative potential to affect workers' cognitive performance. Despite organizational differences and conditions between the companies that took part in the study, these factors are largely consistent. Our results point to the influence of social interaction on the mental workload. Our results indicate that good teamwork is a valuable resource to achieve sustainable cognitive loading.

Our study has not carried out measurements of quality outcomes related to cognitive load factors, which is something that could be elaborated in future studies. This could be useful to clarify the business rationale of developing better proactive guidelines for prevention of cognitive over- or underload. These interviews were conducted mainly in the automotive industry, but the results may contain applicable lessons-learned for other manufacturing sectors that are also characterized by highly customized and timed manual assembly.

Our results show a general absence of strategies and methods for engineers to address cognitive ergonomics during the product and production development process. A future goal is to convert the (more detailed) results of this analysis into a system model of cognitive aspects that can be associated with work task properties and demands; cognitive resources available at individual, group and organization levels; and desired vs. undesired outcomes.

## 5  Conclusions

Regarding assemblers' work conditions, we have found that factors related to product design, workplace culture, social support, workstation design, training, experience, standardized work, participation and motivation and attitudes all contribute profoundly to either benefiting or hindering cognitive performance when coping with day-to-day complexity in manual assembly.

Regarding design- and manufacturing engineers' role in ensuring an easy assembly of complex products, two mindsets were identified: (i) a product-centred mindset relying on assemblers having sufficient experience, knowledge, and assembly instructions, (ii) an assembler-focused mindset characterised by an iterative and collaborative development process to ensure easy-to-assemble solutions, and avoid errors, delays and costly re-work. The latter mindset should be encouraged among assembly workplace designers and product developers to increase their facilitation of good cognitive working conditions for assemblers.

## References

1. Falck, A.C., Rosenqvist, M.: A model for calculation of the costs of poor assembly ergonomics (part 1). Int. J. Ind. Ergon. **44**(1), 140–147 (2014)
2. Falck, A.C., Örtengren, R., Högberg, D.: The impact of poor assembly ergonomics on product quality: a cost–benefit analysis in car manufacturing. Hum. Factors Ergon. Manuf. Serv. Ind. **20**(1), 24–41 (2010)
3. Falck, A.C., Örtengren, R., Rosenqvist, M.: Assembly failures and action cost in relation to complexity level and assembly ergonomics in manual assembly (part 2). Int. J. Ind. Ergon. **44**(3), 455–459 (2014)

4. Zare, M., Croq, M., Hossein-Arabi, F., Brunet, R., Roquelaure, Y.: Does ergonomics improve product quality and reduce costs? A review article. Hum. Factors Ergon. Manuf. Serv. Ind. **26**(2), 205–223 (2016)
5. Young, M.S., Brookhuis, K.A., Wickens, C.D., Hancock, P.A.: State of science: mental workload in ergonomics. Ergonomics **58**, 1–17 (2015)
6. Öztemel, E., Gursev, S.: Literature review of Industry 4.0 and related technologies. J. Intell. Manuf. **31**(1), 127–182 (2020)
7. Frank, A.G., Dalenogare, L.S., Ayala, N.F.: Industry 4.0 technologies: implementation patterns in manufacturing companies. Int. J. Prod. Econ. **210**, 15–26 (2019)
8. Galy, E., Cariou, M., Mélan, C.: What is the relationship between mental workload factors and cognitive load types? Int. J. Psychophysiol. **83**(3), 269–275 (2012)
9. Van Acker, B.B., Parmentier, D.D., Vlerick, P., Saldien, J.: Understanding mental workload: from a clarifying concept analysis toward an implementable framework. Cogn. Technol. Work **20**(3), 351–365 (2018)
10. Patton, M.Q.: Qualitative research and evaluation methods (2002)
11. Braun, V., Clarke, V.: Using thematic analysis in psychology. Qual. Res. Psychol. **3**(2), 77–101 (2006)
12. Ryan, R.M., Deci, E.L.: Intrinsic and extrinsic motivations: classic definitions and new directions. Contemp. Educ. Psychol. **25**(1), 54–67 (2000)
13. Womack, J.P., Jones, D., Roos, D.: The Machine that Changed the World. The Story of Lean Production. Rawson Associates, New York (1990, republished 2007)

# Ergo4All: An Ergonomic Guidance Tool for Non-ergonomist

Quentin Bourret[1], Julie Charland[1(✉)], Daniel Imbeau[2], David Brouillette[1], and Jean-Baptist Djire[2]

[1] Dassault Systèmes, 393 Rue Saint-Jacques #300, Montréal, QC H2Y 1N9, Canada
quentin.bourret@3ds.com
[2] Department of Mathematics and Industrial Engineering,
Polytechnique Montreal, Montreal, Canada

**Abstract.** Occupational Ergonomics related aspects have a significant impact in the manufacturing world, from Musculoskeletal Disorders (MSD) to quality issues; it is an important knowledge domain in manufacturing organizations.

This paper presents a new decision tree called Ergo4All™ aimed at giving ergonomic guidance to manufacturing engineers while designing workstations in 3D. Combined with the Smart Posturing Engine™ (SPE™) technology, which generates posture automatically in a 3D environment, Ergo4All™ analyses the potential risk of developing MSD by workers. It then provides guidance to the user on changes to the workstation that will lower the ergonomics risks.

The goal of this decision tree is to provide simple ergonomic guidance to engineer that do not have training in ergonomics.

The Ergo4All™ decision tree was designed as a rapid assessment tool for people designing workstations early in the virtual design process. This by no means replaces the expertise of a certified ergonomist.

**Keywords:** DHM · Ergonomic assessment · 3D · Manufacturing · MSD

## 1 Introduction

### 1.1 Problem Statement

Currently, Digital Human Model (DHM) offers a unique possibility to evaluate risks for a worker before a production line is build. However, to achieve this goal with current DHM softwares, ergonomics knowledge is required to interpret the results of the ergonomics methods available in these softwares. DHM software are also complex to use for engineers while they are designing workstations, especially when posturing the manikins [1].

### 1.2 DHM for Manufacturing Engineers

As Stephens and Jones [1] explained: "DHM have increased the ability to determine risk and acceptability of design very early in the product development cycle." The main advantages of DHM are the important number of biomechanical and anthropometrical data available. They allow the comparison of different scenarios in a measurable way. Several applications allow the use of DHM in an 3D manufacturing context: Santos [2], Jack (Siemens) [3], DELMIA Ergonomics (Dassault Systemes) [4].

Stephens [1] highlighted that one of the challenges of DHM applications lies in their low efficiency in the process of placing a manikin in a 3D environment, which comes from the fact that the user has to posture the manikin manually by moving each joint separately. This process is very time consuming.

Recently, Jack [5] and IPS IMMA [6] have published some work that shows posture automation inside their software. The posture generation is not yet fully automatic as there is still the need to place a manikin close to the object, but it is a step forward in shortening the manikin posturing duration.

When the posture is generated, a number of methods are available to evaluate the simulated work situation: RULA (Rapid Upper Limb Assessment) [7], REBA Rapid Entire Body Assessment [8], revised NIOSH lifting equation [9], etc. However, Chaffin [10] showed in a survey that less than 10% of engineers could show at least one complete course in human factor and ergonomics in their background. This means that even if the posture is easily generated with a DHM, the user likely does not know which method to use to assess the simulated work situation, nor how to interpret its results.

This is the problem the Ergo4All™ is contributing to solve. It is integrated inside an application called Ergonomic Workplace Design (EWD) [4]. This application is aimed at manufacturing engineers and it reuses their process planning data. Using EWD, they can represent worker tasks in 3D. Thanks to the SPE™, the manikin posture is generated fully automatically in the 3D environment [11–13]. Then, Ergo4All™ analyses the work situation, that is, a mannikin performing an action in a 3D environment. It identifies the MSD risk level, as well as its type and body area at risk. It then provides suggestions to improve the workstation design to lower the MSD-related risk for the worker. EWD provides manufacturing engineers with ergonomics basis that they often lack. They need to perform rapid assessments while designing workstations early in the virtual design process.

### 1.3 Objective

The objective of this paper is to present the Ergo4All™ technology. It takes the form of a decision tree that was developed to assess the risk of developing MSDs in a 3D simulation of a work situation (e.g., workstation along a production line). It performs an MSD risk evaluation on the simulation and provides suggestions to the engineer on ways to improve the design.

## 2 Methodology

### 2.1 Ergo4All™ Integration

The Ergo4All™ decision tree is integrated within an application called Ergonomic Workplace Design (EWD) [4]. EWD uses the process planning data as a starting point. This contains all information related to the product assembly at the workstation, from the 3D environment to the assembly process. Using EWD, the engineer can generate worker tasks in 3D, by first indicating a worker action in the form of a sentence that specifies which hand should grasp which object (Fig. 1).

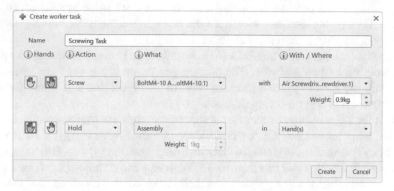

**Fig. 1.** EWD panel indicating the action to be performed by the worker

From there, a posture is automatically generated by the Smart Posturing Engine™ for 4 manikins of different anthropometries (5%ile female, 50%ile male and female, 95%ile male respecting the stature of an American population [14, 15]). Then Ergo4All™ analyses the combination of posture and force application, indicates the potential risks, and provides suggestions on how to help lowering those risks.

## 2.2 The Decision Tree Structure

The decision tree is divided in 4 sections that asses different risk types.

**Section 1:** The object weight is compared to EN1005-2 [16] which is based on the Revised NIOSH lifting equation, and the work from Mital and his colleagues [17] to ensure it is not too heavy.
**Section 2:** The hand position relative to the pelvis is evaluated using ISO 14738 [18]. The objective is to determine if the hand is too high, too low, too far,…
**Section 3:** The joint loads are evaluated using 3D static biomechanical model, and then the MSD risk score is assessed using EN 1005-3 [19].
**Section 4:** The body joint angles are evaluated using EN 1005-4 [20], ISO 11226 [21] and ISO 11228-3 [22].

Within the four sections of the tree, the risk is prioritized and then presented to the engineer instantaneously during the design process. The objective is to present the worst and most critical risks first before any low impact risks. For instance, if an object weights 40 kg, there is no need to proceed to a joint load analysis since the object is simply too heavy for the task to be deemed safe and should be the first risk to be presented and addressed.

## 2.3 Ergo4All™ Output

If a risk is detected at section 1, 3 or 4 of the decision tree, the tree ends and the following are presented (Fig. 2):

- The risk type (object too heavy, joint load, joint angle)
- The risk location (which joint is at risk: shoulder, back, wrist, neck, elbow)
- The risk level (high = red, mid = yellow, low risk = green)
- Suggestions to improve workstation design

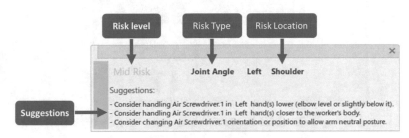

**Fig. 2.** Output example for Ergo4All™ as presented to the engineer

To provide the best ergonomic guidance possible to the engineer, only one risk (level, type and location) is displayed at a time for a given work situation. Ergo4All™ as been designed to flag the worst risk for the simulated worker. On the other hand, there can be several suggestions to improve workstation design and lower the associated risks.

## 2.4 Inside Ergo4All™

### Section 1: Object Weight
The first element checked by the decision tree is the object weight. First, it determines if one object is grasped with both hands or if each hand is grasping a separate object. The acceptable weight limit is 27 kg for males and 20 kg for women [17]. If only one object is grasped with one hand then the weight limit is 60% of the weight limit of an object grasped with two hands [16]. If the object weight is higher than the limits, it is considered a high risk and the set of suggestions displays "Lighten the object" (Fig. 3). If the object weight is below the limits, the tree checks continue to section 2.

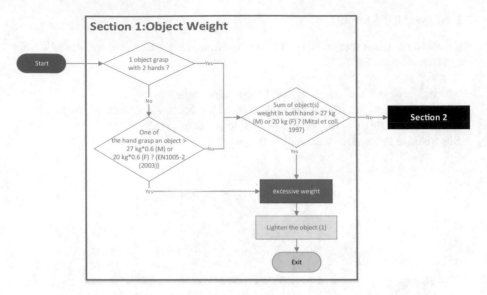

**Fig. 3.** Decision tree section 1 check the object weight

## Section 2: Hand Position

The second section of the decision tree checks for the hands' position relative to the pelvis (Figs. 4). Following ISO 14738 [18], it checks if the hand is not too: high/low, on the right/left, far/close to the body. No risk is associated with this evaluation. Only suggestions will be given to the engineer.

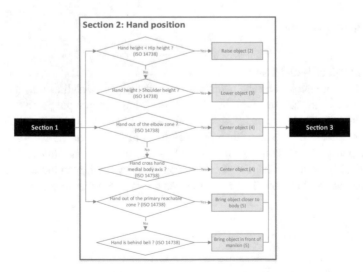

**Fig. 4.** Decision tree section 2 checks the hands' position relative to the body.

## Section 3: Join Load

The third section of the decision tree checks the internal load of the back, shoulder and elbow joints (Fig. 5). The load is the internal static moment in the different planes at the joint location. It can be easily calculated thanks to the object weight and manikin joint location in 3D. This load is then modulated using the multiplying factors from EN 1005-3 [19], taking into account the task frequency, duration over the workshift, action duration and velocity. The result is a score between 0 and 1 that represents the percentage of actual joint load compared to the maximum acceptable load. If a joint has a score higher then 0.7 then the risk is considered high. A score between 0.5 and 0.7 is considered medium risk. Below 0.5, the risk is considered low.

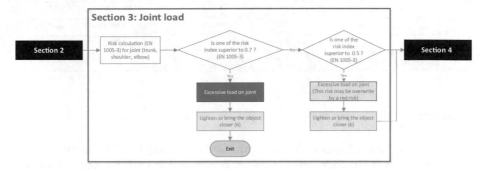

**Fig. 5.**  Decision tree section 3 checks for back, shoulder and elbow joint loads

## Section 4: Joint Angle

The last section of the decision tree checks the angles of the following joints: shoulder, back, neck, wrist. Following European and International standards [9–12]. Depending on the task frequency, joint angles are categorized into 3 categories: acceptable, acceptable under condition and unacceptable. These categories are the equivalent of the three risk levels defined in the Ergo4All™: low, mid and high. As a reminder, only one risk is displayed for each posture. So, if one posture has several unacceptable joint angles, then a decision needs to be made on which risk to display for a specific posture.

The order of risk to display is the following:

– First: Unacceptable risks to shoulder, trunk and neck.
– Second: Acceptable risks under condition to shoulder, trunk, wrist, forearm and neck.

If all joints angles are acceptable then the posture is considered low risk because it means that all the previous checks (object weight and joint load) were acceptable.

## Suggestions

The suggestions are derived from the "Ergonomic Checkpoints" book from ILO [23]. When a risk is found by the decision tree, at least one suggestion group is displayed. This suggestion group contains at least one suggestion. Suggestions are numbered from 1 to 12 and are all different (Table 1).

**Table 1.** Table containing all the suggestions that are displayed to the process engineer.

| Section | Suggestion Group | Suggestion number | Text displayed |
|---|---|---|---|
| Part 1:<br>Object<br>Weight | Lighten the object (1) | (1) | - Consider lightening [*name of the object*] weight (less than [*maximum weight*] kg) :<br>  - Use **lifting device** or balancer for handling<br>  - Divide into **lighter packages**<br>  - Use **lighter material** |
| Part 2:<br>Hand<br>position | Bring closer to body (5) | (5) | - Consider handling [*name of the object*] in [*hand side*] hand [*s*] **closer to** the worker body |
| | Lower (3) | (3) | - Consider handling [*name of the object*] in [*hand side*] hand [*s*] **lower** (elbow level or slightly below it) |
| | Raise (2) | (2) | - Consider handling [*name of the object*] in [*hand side*] hand [*s*] **higher** (hip level or slightly over it) |
| | Center (4) | (4) | - Consider handling [*name of the object*] in [*hand side*] hand [*s*] **in front** of the worker |
| Part 3:<br>Joint load | Lighten or bring the object<br>closer (6) | (5) | - Consider handling [*name of the object*] **closer to** the worker body |
| | | (6) | - Consider Lighten [name of the object] weight:<br>  - Use a **lifting device** for handling<br>  - Divide [name of the object] into **lighter packages**<br>  - Use **lighter material** |
| | | (7) | - Consider changing Task Specifications to reduce Task Frequency, Task Time, Speed and/or Work Hours per day |
| Part 4:<br>Joint angle | Change grasp access spine (7) | (8) | - Consider changing [*name of the object*] orientation or position allow spine neutral posture |
| | | (12) | - Consider reducing Task **Frequency** (in Task Specifications) |
| | Change grasp access arm (8) | (9) | - Consider changing [*name of the object*] **orientation or position** to allow arm neutral posture |
| | | (12 | - Consider reducing Task **Frequency** (in Task Specifications) |
| | Change grasp access neck (9) | (10) | - Consider changing [*name of the object*] **orientation and/or position** to allow neck neutral posture |
| | | (12) | - Consider reducing Task **Frequency** (in Task Specifications) |
| | Change grasp access wrist (10) | (11) | - Consider changing [*name of the object*] **orientation and/or position** to allow wrist neutral posture |
| | | (12) | - Consider reducing Task **Frequency** (in Task Specifications) |

## 3 Result

Figure 6 shows an example of a posture generated automatically with the SPE™ technology and analysed by Ergo4All™ module. A yellow dot is displayed at the manikin shoulder with a warning sign. This means that there is medium risk on the left shoulder. There are also details about the risk assessment and suggestions on the bottom left panel.

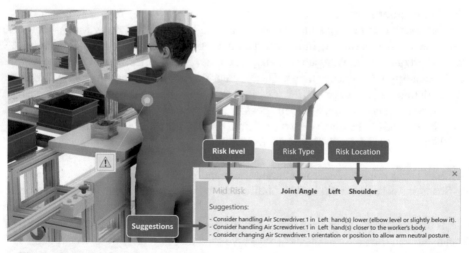

**Fig. 6.** Example of a risk assessment for a posture with suggestions to enhance the design

# 4 Discussion

The Ergo4All™ decision tree implements existing standards, which are based on ergonomics methods published in scientific journals over the years, to evaluate the posture and force combination of a manikin performing an action in a 3D environment. The challenge was to organise and order the checks made to provide coherent information to the engineer while designing work situations.

A number of different standards had to be used because no unique ergonomics standard considered all aspects needed to analyse the manikin posture in relation to the work situation: object weigh, hand location, joint load and angle.

This is the first version of the Ergo4All™ decision tree. In the version presented in this paper, the decision tree considers only individual static postures. This means that postures are considered without taking into account the previous tasks. In the future, we intend to consider group or sequences of tasks performed in time by a worker. This could be achieved for instance, through the use of an ergonomic assessment worksheet (EAWS) linked to a Predetermined Motion Time System (PMTS) such as MTM, MOST, or Modapts. This would allow the engineer to gain insight on his design through ergonomics evaluations that can span over different periods of time (e.g., part of a workday, whole workshifts).

# 5 Conclusion

This "Ergo4All™" decision tree was built to help manufacturing engineers to design safe workplaces. It is linked to the Smart Posturing Engine™ technology that automatically generates manikin postures in 3D. This combination (Ergo4All and SPE) provides very quick assessments of 3D simulated work situations. It is meant to serve as a first assessment tool for large scale evaluation.

One of the limitations of this risk assessment tool in its current iteration, is that it only considers static postures individually. No cumulative effect or risk is assessed.

In the future, we intend to fully consider cumulative effects such as fatigue over a work period of variable duration, to have a more precise and realistic risk assessment.

We also plan to conduct a validation study, which will compare the Ergo4All versus certified ergonomists analysis.

# References

1. Stephens, A., Jones, M.: Workplace methods and use of digital human models. In: Handbook of Digital Human Modeling, pp. 6.1–6.11. Taylor and Francis, USA (2009)
2. Santos Human. https://www.santoshumaninc.com/. Accessed 22 Jan 2021
3. Blanchonette, P.: Jack human modelling tool: a review. Air Operations Division Defence Science and Technology Organisation (2010)
4. Ergonomics at Dassault Systèmes. https://www.3ds.com/products-services/delmia/disciplines/industrial-engineering/tag/88-1007/. Accessed 22 Jan 2021
5. Cort, J.A., Devries, D.: Accuracy of postures predicted using a digital human model during four manual exertion tasks, and implications for ergonomic assessments. IISE Trans. Occup. Ergon. Hum. Factors 7(1), 43–58 (2019)

6. Hanson, L., Högberg, D., Carlson, J.S., Bohlin, R., Brolin, E., Delfs, N., et al.: IMMA–Intelligently moving manikins in automotive applications. In: Third International Summit on Human Simulation (ISHS 2014) (2014)

7. McAtamney, L., Corlett, E.N.: RULA: a survey method for the investigation of work-related upper limb disorders. Appl. Ergon. **24**(2), 91–99 (1993)

8. Hignett, S., McAtamney, L.: Rapid entire body assessment (REBA). Appl. Ergon. **31**(2), 201–205 (2000)

9. Waters, T.R., Putz-Anderson, V., Garg, A., Fine, L.J.: Revised NIOSH equation for the design and evaluation of manual lifting tasks. Ergonomics **36**(7), 749–776 (1993)

10. Chaffin, D.: Engineers with HFE education—Survey results. HFES–ETG News Lett. **3**, 2–3 (2005)

11. Lemieux, P.-O., Barré, A., Hagemeister, N., Aissaoui, R.: Degrees of freedom coupling adapted to the upper limb of a digital human model. Int. J. Hum. Factors Model. Simul. **5**(4), 314–337 (2017)

12. Lemieux, P., Cauffiez, M., Barré, A., Hagemeister, N., Aissaoui, R.: A visual acuity constraint for digital human modeling. In: 4th Conference proceedings (2016)

13. Zeighami, A., Lemieux, P., Charland, J., Hagemeister, N., Aissaoui, A.: Stepping behavior for stability control of a digital human model. ISB/ASB (2019)

14. Reed, M.P., Raschke, U., Tirumali, R., Parkinson, M.B.: Developing and implementing parametric human body shape models in ergonomics software. In: Proceedings of the 3rd International Digital Human Modeling Conference, Tokyo (2014).

15. Parkinson, M.B., Reed, M.P.: Creating virtual user populations by analysis of anthropometric data. Int. J. Ind. Ergon. **40**(1), 106–111 (2010)

16. EN 1005-2. Safety of machinery—Human physical performance. Part 2: Manual handling of machinery and component parts of machinery. Brussels, European Committee for Standardization (2003)

17. Mital, A.: Guide to Manual Materials Handling. CRC Press, Boca Raton (1997)

18. ISO 14738: Sécurité des machines-Prescriptions anthropométriques relatives à la conception des postes de travail sur les machines. Geneva: International Organization for Standardization (2003). (in French)

19. EN 1005-3. Safety of machinery—Human physical performance. Part 3: Recommended force limits for machinery operation. Brussels, European Committee for Standardization (2003)

20. EN 1005-4. Safety of machinery—Human physical performance. Part 4: Evaluation of Working Postures and Movements in Relation to Machinery. Brussels, European Committee for Standardization (2003)

21. ISO 11226. Ergonomics - Evaluation of static postures. Geneva: International Organization for Standardization (2000)

22. ISO 11228-3. Ergonomics. Manual handling: Part 3: Handling of low loads at high frequency. Geneva: International Organization for Standardization (2010)

23. International Labour Office and International Ergonomics Association: Ergonomic Checkpoints: Practical and Easy-to-Implement Solutions for Improving Safety, Health and Working Conditions. International Labour Organization, Geneva (1996)

# Development of Cooperative Artificial Intelligence (AI) Applications to Support Human Work in Manufacturing

Ralph Bruder, Christopher Stockinger[✉], Deborah Petrat, and Ilka Subtil

Institute of Human Factors and Ergonomics, Technical
University of Darmstadt, Darmstadt, Germany
{bruder,c.stockinger}@iad.tu-darmstadt.de

**Abstract.** A competence center for work and AI, funded by the German Federal Ministry of Education and Research for five years, is intended to strengthen the humane use of AI applications in manufacturing. The cooperation between specialists from human factors and ergonomics (HFE), AI development and engineering is the core of the competence center. In this paper its main research topics and structure is presented and illustrated using the example of the development of manufacturing assistance systems .

**Keywords:** Cooperative Artificial Intelligence · Worker assistance systems · Competence center · Human factors · Research project

## 1   Problem Statement/Introduction

It is a well-known dilemma in Human Factors & Ergonomics (HFE) research that it mostly deals with technical development and its impact on the world of work in a subsequent phase. As a rule, the possibilities of a new technology are first tapped by developing it to market maturity and bringing it into applications. The discussion about the possible effects of a technical development on the world of work then takes place with a clear time lag; for example, when employees are already using it or its use is imminent.

This time lag between technical development and the Human Factors & Ergonomics perspective can currently also be observed in connection with developments under the collective term "Artificial Intelligence" (AI) (Bughin et al. 2017; Marr 2019). In this context a close interlinking of AI development and Human Factors & Ergonomics is necessary, as various AI approaches have the potential to change wide areas of society and the economy and thus further accelerate the debate on the transformation of the world of work and Work 4.0 (Fountaine et al. 2019).

However, it is important to emphasize that the situation in Germany is such that many companies currently have only little experience with the integration of AI approaches into their processes and employees usually lack the skills to deal with AI-based systems

© The Author(s), under exclusive license to Springer Nature Switzerland AG 2021
N. L. Black et al. (Eds.): IEA 2021, LNNS 221, pp. 391–397, 2021.
https://doi.org/10.1007/978-3-030-74608-7_49

(VDI 2018; Balakrishnan et al. 2020). In addition, there are often reservations about the new technical possibilities.

Especially for Human Factors & Ergonomics research, the use of AI-applications in manufacturing raises various questions that can be summarized into three research topics:

- Requirements and potentials for AI-based applications: Where does the use of an AI-based application make sense from the perspective of humane work design? What requirements does such an AI application have to meet?
- Development of employee-friendly, simple and transparent AI applications: How should an AI application be designed so that users in companies understand it well and can use it easily? What would be a suitable approach for the design of AI-based applications in order to achieve the best possible acceptance among employees?
- Analysis and evaluation of AI-supported work systems: How does the use of AI affect the employees in the work system? Are there any additional burdens? What skills do these employees need? How can qualification programs be designed? How do you have to prepare employees for the use of AI?

## 2    KompAKI - Competence Center for Work and AI

KompAKI the Competence Center for Work and AI addresses these questions mentioned above. It is a joint project funded by the German Federal Ministry of Education and Research for five years, in which an interdisciplinary team is researching the implementation, design and effects of AI-based applications in the world of work. KompAKI thus offers a space for interdisciplinary cooperation between AI development, Human Factors & Ergonomics and domain sciences, especially production research and engineering. It also combines basic research with development of concrete applications in partner companies, including the transfer of results and training formats.

In terms of content, KompAKI pursues three main goals that are very closely linked to the research topics described in the first section (see Fig. 1):

1. Research and development of new applications and application potentials for AI-based systems

The first main objective in terms of content relates to the analysis of requirements and potentials of AI systems. KompAKI aims to gain comprehensive insights into when the use of an AI-based system is useful and what potential such a system offers. However, insights will also be gained into the requirements that the use of AI systems places on the conditions in companies, such as the data structure and the integration into existing IT systems. The same applies to the requirements to be placed on the AI system. This is based in particular on the needs of the employees, their qualifications and workload situation (Hirsch-Kreinsen and Karacic 2019). A fundamental prerequisite for bringing AI systems into new applications is, in addition to the requirements and potentials, the willingness of users to pay for it. Respectively in KompAKI insights into suitable business models are developed (Buxmann and Schmidt 2019). This applies even more to

AI systems that are based on the approaches of cooperative AI (next section) (Winfield and Jirotka 2018; Tauchert and Mesbah 2019; Mesbah et al. 2019). For this reason, KompAKI aims to gain insights from the user perspective on how the cooperative aspect of AI, such as transparency and explainability, changes the willingness to pay. From the provider perspective, insights into possible business models will emerge, especially for cooperative AI systems.

2. Development of new methods for a cooperative AI, which can be easily trained by users, which are self-explanatory and which can adapt to the users.

The second main objective is based on the question how a suitable human-machine interaction between AI systems and end users can be designed. In the future, there will be more AI scenarios with continuous interaction between humans and machines and therefore more complex interaction processes. The employees who operate these AI systems today are highly qualified specialists. However, for practical and humane use in the broad world of work, it is essential to develop forms of AI that can be operated and understood by non-experts. For this purpose, forms of cooperative artificial intelligence are part of the research program atKompAKI, which can be characterised by three essential features:

a) Cooperative AI should be able to be trained by end users without knowledge in the field of artificial intelligence in such a way that they can use it in work processes ("Automated AI"). This enables practice-oriented use in different areas and also for small and medium sized companies without the corresponding know-how (Shang et al. 2019; Binnig et al. 2018).
b) Cooperative AI should be able to explain itself ("Explainable AI"). This is important, since humans will surely have the function of control in an interaction with automated AI systems. It must be possible to transparently understand the decisions of the AI in a way that is comprehensible to end users (Kersting and De Raedt 2001; Samek and Müller 2019).
c) Furthermore, it is important that AI can adapt to humans through interaction with employees ("Interactive AI") (Fails and Olsen 2003; Holzinger 2016; Amershi et al. 2014).

These three features of cooperative AI will make it possible for learning systems to emerge dynamically depending on the activity and profile of the employees, in order to optimally support the individual employee in his or her activity. Thus, these approaches should contribute to increasing employees' trust in AI and thus to strengthening the acceptance of AI in companies.

3. Evaluation and prediction of consequences for work in AI-supported work systems.

The third main objective relates to the development of methods for assessing the consequences of the use of AI. On the one hand, this relates to the level of employment, i.e. how many employees are needed in AI-supported work systems and how efficient these systems are. In addition, findings have to be generated on questions of qualification, such as which competences the use of AI requires and how employees can be qualified accordingly. Furthermore, assessment methods are being developed in KompAKI that systematically record the stress situation in AI-supported work systems.

On the other hand, the goal of AI use is also to enable a form of cooperation that is accepted by employees. In KompAKI, extensive findings on the acceptance of AI-based systems will be generated. In particular, it will be investigated how acceptance can be influenced and how AI systems, their interfaces and the application of these should be designed so that they experience the highest possible employee acceptance (Davis 1989; Kim and Hinds 2006).

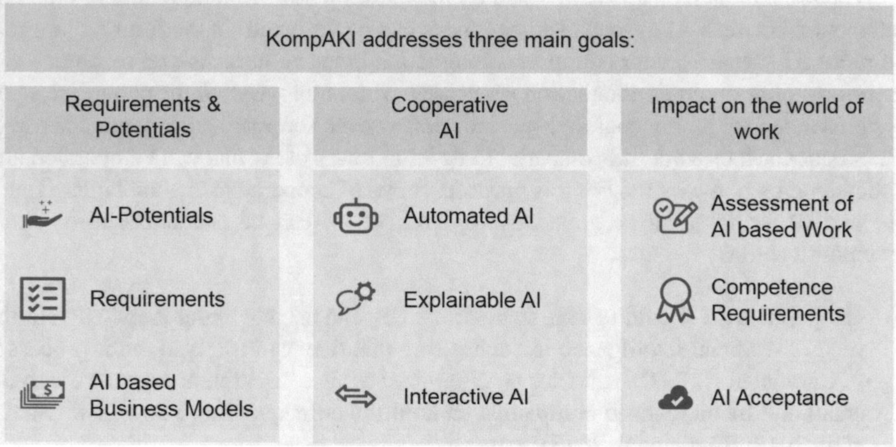

**Fig. 1.** Summary of the three main goals of KompAKI

In order to achieve these three main goals, the activities in KompAKI are divided into three areas:

The activities of basic research are bundled in so-called development projects, such as the development of AI methods or the development of evaluation procedures for AI-supported work systems.

Pilot projects describe the application-oriented research and development that in KompAKI always takes place in and with the strong involvement of corporate partners and from which concrete AI-based applications in the area of production emerge.

All results of the development and pilot projects are also made available to the public. For this purpose, KompAKI also includes a transfer division in which these results are processed and made available to companies and employees through advisory talks or training formats. In this way, the actual competence center is being built up, which in the medium term should establish itself as a recognisable point of contact for questions of AI-based work design in the region.

As mentioned above, these research foci are dealt with in an interdisciplinary manner in KompAKI, in which both AI developers and HFE as well as domain researchers conduct research together. The scientific part of the consortium is made up of partners from the Technical University of Darmstadt (Centre for Cognitive Science, Data

Management Lab, Chair for Marketing and Human Resource Management, Software & Digital Business Group, Artificial Intelligence and Machine Learning Lab, Institute for Production Management, Technology and Machine Tools, Institute for Human Factors and Ergonomics) and the University of Applied Sciences Darmstadt (professorship of Applied AI, professorship of Industry 4.0, professorship of control and instrumentation, professorship of process and product innovation). In addition, eight corporate partners are involved: metaphacts GmbH, Serviceware SE, Gebr. Heller Maschinenfabrik GmbH, SimPlan AG, Software AG, STAUFEN. Quality Engineers GmbH, TRILUX GmbH & Co. KG, WIKA Alexander Wiegand SE & Co. KG The consortium is complemented by Chamber of Industry and Commerce Darmstadt, Hessian Association of Metal and Electrical Companies, IG Metall, Hessian Ministry for Social Affairs and Integration, Hessian Ministry of Digital Strategy and Development and Hessian RKW.

# 3   Use Case

A total of five pilot projects are being carried out in KompAKI, which transfer basic research into concrete applications and thus represent practical use cases. One pilot project is concerned with the development of AI-based assistance systems for assembly. In general, the use of digital assistance in assembly is of great relevance, especially for companies with a high product variance. Through the digital and thus also dynamic, context- and product-adapted provision of assembly information, employees are supported more specifically than through paper-based assembly instructions. In this context, AI can be used in two areas, both of which are addressed in the pilot project:

On the one hand, AI can be used to generate the relevant assembly information in the first place. This is particularly relevant for the assembly of a large number of product variants and can significantly relieve the work preparation department, which usually compiles this information manually. The focus of this part is then particularly on the question of the data basis for AI and how various information systems in companies can be used in this regard.

On the other hand, and more strongly related to the end user, AI can be used to design digital assistance systems in the way of adaptive assistance systems. For example, current research results show that different approaches for digital assistance have an effect on assembly performance and user experience for different combinations of employee competence and product complexity (Keller et al. 2020). The aim of the pilot project is therefore also to equip digital assistance systems with AI in such a way that they support the individual employee by optimally presenting the information.

The procedure in both parts is based on the human-centered design process according to ISO 9241-210 (2020), in which the analysis of the context of use focuses in particular on the goals, wishes and habits of the users. In the phase of requirements determination, the focus is then on the analysis of data structures in the companies by also considering which information systems must be integrated and how autonomously the assistance system can be designed. The developed design solutions are evaluated in several user studies, with a focus on the acceptance of the users.

## 4 Discussion

The core of KompAKI is interdisciplinary collaboration. In addition to the application in domains, this particularly concerns the collaboration of AI development and Human Factors & Ergonomics. KompAKI offers a suitable framework for this, even as a pilot project for five years. According to this view, the great potential of KompAKI lies in overcoming the technology-oriented view of AI. However, this still prevails today, especially in practice, in that the technical feasibility and the economic consequences are first and foremost questioned. How the employees must now adapt to these new processes is mainly discussed downstream. The early, interdisciplinary cooperation in KompAKI between AI development, engineering and Human Factors & Ergonomics, can succeed in developing a socio-technical view of AI design that starts from both technical feasibility and economic aspects as well as from the needs of people: Where does the value of AI lie for employees? How can AI concretely support employees and thus improve working conditions? How can AI systems be designed so that acceptance is achieved and employees enjoy working with them? At the same time and from the very beginning, the consequences for AI-supported work systems are also considered: How does AI change human work? How will the situation of stress and strain change as a result? Are there qualification programs that should accompany the technical development? The change to a socio-technical view of AI use, as it can arise in KompAKI, is a decisive prerequisite for the humane use of AI methods in the world of work.

## 5 Conclusion and Outlook

This article presented the Competence Center for Work and Artificial Intelligence (KompAKI) in detail, focusing on the three main topics and its structure. With the case study of assistance systems, a type of application of AI in the world of work that will be developed in KompAKI was presented in more detail, which has the potential to support employees and improve working conditions. The procedure and the planned work in KompAKI were shown in more detail here.

The expected results in KompAKI can be divided into two types: On the one hand, fundamental findings and methods are being developed, for example on cooperative AI, possible business models or evaluation methods for AI-supported work. On the other hand, concrete applications are developed, such as the AI-based assistance systems described. All results are made accessible to the public so that they are available to the world of work and KompAKI establishes itself as an actual center of competence.

## References

Amershi, S., Cakmak, M., Knox, W.B., Kulesza, T.: Power to the people: the role of humans in interactive machine learning. AI Mag. **35**(4), 105–120 (2014)

Balakrishnan, T., Chui, M., Hall, B., Henke, N.: The State of AI in 2020. McKinsey Global Institute (2020)

Binnig, C., Kersting, K., Molina, A., Zgraggen, E.: DeepVizdom: deep inter-active data exploration. In: Proceedings of the Inaugural Systems and Machine Learning Conference (SysML) (2018)

Buxmann, P., Schmidt, H.: Künstliche Intelligenz. Mit Algorithmen zum wirt-schaftlichen Erfolg. Springer Gabler, Berlin (2019)

Bughin, J., Hazan, E., Ramaswamy, S., Chui, M., Allas, T., Dahlström, P., Trench, M: Artificial Intelligence—The Next Digital Frontier? McKinsey Global Institute (2017)

Davis, F.D.: Perceived usefulness, perceived ease of use, and user acceptance of information technology. MIS Q. **13**(3), 319–340 (1989)

Fails, J.A., Olsen Jr, D.R.: Interactive machine learning. In: Proceedings of the 8th International Conference on Intelligent User Interfaces, pp. 39–45. Association for Computing Machinery, New York (2003)

Fountaine, T., McCarthy, B., Saleh, T.: Building the AI-Powered Organization. Harvard Business Review, New York (2020)

Hirsch-Kreinsen, H., Karacic, A.: Autonome Systeme und Arbeit: Perspektiven, Herausforderungen und Grenzen der Künstlichen Intelligenz in der Arbeitswelt. Transcript Verlag, Bielefeld (2019)

Holzinger, A.: Interactive machine learning for health informatics: when do we need the human-in-the-loop? Brain Inform. **3**(2), 119–131 (2016)

International Organization for Standardization: Ergonomics of human-system interaction – Part 210: Human-centred design for interactive systems (ISO Standard No. 9241-210:2019) (2020)

Keller, T., Behling, M., Stockinger, C., Metternich, J., Schützer, K.: Analysis of the influence of process complexity and employee competence on the effect of digital assistance in industrial assembly. Prod. Eng. **15**, 1–8 (2020)

Kersting, K., De Raedt, L.: Towards combining inductive logic programming with Bayesian networks. In: Inductive Logic Programming. LNAI, pp. 118–131. Springer (2001)

Kim, T., Hinds, P.: Who should I blame? Effects of autonomy and transparency on attributions in human-robot interactions. In: Proceedings of the 15th International Symposium on Robot and Human Interactive Communication, Hatfield, UK, pp. 80–85 (2006)

Marr, B.: The 10 Best Examples of How AI is Already Used in Our Everyday Life. Forbes (2019)

Mesbah, N., Tauchert, C., Olt, C.M., Buxmann, P.: Promoting trust in AI-based expert systems. In: Americas Conference on Information Systems - AMCIS 2019, Cancun, Mexico (2019)

Samek, W., Müller, K.-R.: Towards explainable artificial intelligence. In: Samek et al. (Hrsg.) Explainable AI: Interpreting, Explaining and Visualizing Deep Learning. Lecture Notes in Computer Science, vol. 11700, pp. 5–22. Springer (2019)

Shang, Z., Zgraggen, E., Buratti, B., Chung, Y., Eichmann, P., Binnig, C., Upfal, E., Kraska, T.: Democratizing data science through interactive curation of ML pipelines. SIGMOD (2019)

Tauchert, C., Mesbah, N.: Following the robot? Investigating users' utilization of advice from robo-advisors. In: International Conference on Information Systems (ICIS) 2019 Conference, Munich, Germany (2019)

VDI: VDI-Statusreport Künstliche Intelligenz (2018)

Winfield, A.F., Jirotka, M.: Ethical governance is essential to building trust in robotics and artificial intelligence systems. Philos. Trans. Roy. Soc. A: Math. Phys. Eng. Sci. **376**(2133), 20180085 (2018)

# Exoskeletons in Automotive Industry: Investigation into the Applicability Across Regions

Chiara Carnazzo[1]($\boxtimes$), Stefania Spada[1], Lidia Ghibaudo[1], Lynn Eaton[2],
Izonel Fajardo[3], Shi Zhu[4], and Maria Pia Cavatorta[5] ⓘ

[1] FCA Italy S.p.A – Manufacturing Planning and Control – Direct Manpower Analysis and Ergonomics, Turin, Italy
chiara.carnazzo@stellantis.com

[2] FCA US LLC – Manufacturing Planning and Control – Ergonomics, Auburn Hills, Michigan, USA

[3] FCA South America – Manufacturing – EHS / Ergonomics, Betim, Brazil

[4] FCA Asia Pacific Investment Co. Ltd. – Manufacturing Planning and Control – Industrial Engineering, Shanghai, China

[5] Department of Mechanical and Aerospace Engineering, Politecnico di Torino, Turin, Italy

**Abstract.** In the present day, manufacturing companies are constantly facing new challenges, mostly deriving from the possibilities offered to industry by the fourth industrial revolution. New capabilities and services are available for customers and companies by advanced technologies and interconnections, changing the way we live, work and relate to one another. A promising example of Human-Robot Collaboration is the exoskeleton, a wearable device that interacts with the users to reduce the strain associated to the repetitive tasks present in the manufacturing environment. Fiat Chrysler Automobiles (FCA) (The company merged with PSA creating Stellantis N.V. in January 2021. Abstract was submitted at an earlier stage.), a multinational corporation operating into four (4) Regions: EMEA, North America, LATAM and APAC, had the opportunity to benchmark and test exoskeletons in the different Regions. The focus of the present paper is to present a collaborative approach within Regions on exoskeletons application and feasibility studies including experimental tests, key performance indicators and legal requirements. Main aspects and results are presented together with the open questions.

**Keywords:** Exoskeletons · Ergonomics · Automotive · Industrial exoskeletons · Musculoskeletal disorders · Industrial ergonomics

## 1 Introduction

The automotive manufacturing industry is characterized by manual tasks of high precision and complexity that can be repetitive in nature. It is therefore one of the priorities for automotive manufacturers to design and optimize workstations in order to improve

N. L. Black et al. (Eds.): IEA 2021, LNNS 221, pp. 398–406, 2021.
https://doi.org/10.1007/978-3-030-74608-7_50

the ergonomics conditions of the workplace. In recent years, the flexibility of the work-station has become more and more important to accommodate the dynamic nature of the production scenario. In this context, the use of an exoskeleton, to assist the operator during assembly work task, may represent a feasible option for improving the ergonomics of the workplace while complying with industrial constraints.

The use of exoskeletons in the industrial sector is expected to become more common-place in the future, as prototypes have proven beneficial in areas such as rehabilitation [1]. In particular, tasks that require postures with elevated arms or overhead works are potential target applications for passive exoskeletons in manufacturing. The principle that technological devices may be of help in assisting humans in difficult or unsafe tasks is embraced by Industry 4.0 [2], although it is necessary for these technologies to demonstrate their efficacy and safety to support the uptake in industry [3].

Very few studies investigate the effectiveness, usability, comfort, as well as the draw-backs and biomechanical strain associated to the use of passive exoskeletons in manu-facturing tasks. Studies have been conducted mainly in the laboratory, without extended longitudinal tests in a manufacturing production line environment. An evaluation of the biomechanical strain is generally performed through electromyography on target mus-cles [4–6], although often the analysis is carried out on very simple tasks, executed with prototypes that are not yet suited for industrial application.

To investigate further the effectiveness, usability, comfort, and possible drawbacks of passive exoskeletons application in the automotive industry, the company has been conducting dedicated experimental campaigns across Regions with a focus on production line short-term implementation trials. In this paper, an overview of the trials conducted in each Region is presented, together with common findings, challenges and future perspectives.

## 2  Experimental Usage Across Regions

Focus in the **EMEA Region** has been centered on the activities coordinated by the ErgoLab Team (Turin, Italy). After an initial benchmark activity, a series of experimental campaigns involving workers was started on the Levitate exoskeleton for the upper-limbs in 2016 [7, 8] and soon after on MATE, the passive upper limb exoskeleton designed by COMAU to assist workers when performing overhead activity [9].

Test campaigns have been structured into two phases:

1. Laboratory Phase: tests were designed to mimic manufacturing tasks and were aimed at assessing both the performance variation deriving from the exoskeleton usage (time of execution, ease of execution, precision, fatigue) and the fraction of users positively affected by the use of exoskeleton. In the case of MATE, these tests were also part of a co-design process and findings were analyzed with the exoskeleton manufacturer, who released new updated versions of the device [10].
2. Plant Phase: workers performed tests directly in the assembly workstation. Tests aimed to investigate usability and acceptability aspects, to assess the interaction between workers and the exoskeleton device and between the exoskeleton device and the workstation, and to investigate on practical aspects that may emerge in the long-term (i.e. hygiene, storage, duration of settings).

Initial investigations indicated that effectiveness, usability and comfort are strongly dependent on the exoskeleton design and on the type of tasks workers are required to perform. For this reason, some "target workstations" were selected for the test campaign: i.e. belly pans application or brake underbody installation, or any other workstation that requires overhead or shoulder level work (Fig. 1).

Both in the Laboratory and in the Plant Phase, the participation of workers was voluntary. In particular, all participants were informed about the nature of the study and signed an informed consent. Workers were free to interrupt the tests at any moment, and for any reason. Furthermore, only participants without pre-existing injuries or limitations defined by the Medical team were accepted for the trials. To avoid bias, a minimum period of six months was required on current job.

**Fig. 1.** Example of target application in EMEA Plant (Turin)

For the MATE exoskeleton, the Plant Phase was divided into two (2) steps:

Step 1, which involved 21 male workers and the pre-production prototype of MATE. This initial step aimed at verifying compliance of the prototype with the design requirements and at investigating usability and acceptability aspects.

Step 2, which involved 135 workers and the first final release of MATE. This step aimed at understanding further usability and acceptability and at investigating the workstation characteristics of the "optimal target application". In total, within Step 2, 135 operators from six(6) Italy plants (84 workstations in total) participated in the testing campaign, collecting 805 h of usage.

General Protocol/methodology for Step 2 includes four main phases:

*Onboarding session:* dedicated to each Plant in order to communicate effectively the exoskeleton to workers. During the on boarding session, operators may decide to voluntary "subscribe" for their inclusion in the tests.

*Training session:* at the beginning of each trial, a one-to-one training session was held. Focus is on explanation of exoskeleton functioning and practical information (i.e. plant contact/reference person in case of questions/issues during the usage).

*Pilot usage:* volunteer workers try the device, performing their usual working activity in the production line, with the incremental plan presented in Table 1.

**Table 1.** Plant Phase Step2: EMEA incremental usage plan

|                                      | Day1 | Day2 | Day3 | Day4 | Day5 |
|--------------------------------------|------|------|------|------|------|
| Working hours with exoskeleton [h]   | 2    | 4    | 8    | 8    | 8    |
| % over full shift                    | 25%  | 50%  | 100% | 100% | 100% |

*Follow up:* an ergonomics specialist administrated usability and acceptability questionnaire at the end of each trial. In addition, qualitative data, results and suggestions for device improvement were collected. Usability and acceptability questionnaires were built specifically for the purpose, thanks to the partnership with a cognitive ergonomics specialist team [11]. Operators were asked to provide their opinion regarding specific items, by using a 7 points scale. Topics investigated in the interview are: perceived usefulness, voluntariness, experience, image, job relevance, output quality, results demonstrability, perceived ease of use and control, intention of use, suitability of the device for the workstation and for the task, comfort, reliability, freedom of movement, interference with workstation equipment, training efforts and requirement.

As result of the trials, the characteristics of the "target workstation" were defined. As exclusion criteria, a workstation was defined "not in target" when: dangerous interference of the exoskeleton with the car body or wheels is possible; there is high variability of actions within the cycle; the percentage of time impacted by awkward posture of the upper arm is below 20% of the cycle time.

Focus in the **North America region** has been on benchmarking and short-term trials to better understand functionality, applicability, benefits, and general protocol for potential future implementation. The initial evaluation consisted of obtaining qualitative feedback on the feasibility and practicality of passive device exoskeleton usage in work stations where static or upper limb postures are present for >50% of the job cycle. Working collaboratively with Safety, Plant Medical, Plant Management/Production teams and regional/local union representatives, this experimental phase of activity consisted of literature reviews, benchmarking (internal/external), supplier demonstrations, short-term plant trials and subjective assessment.

General Protocol/methodology:

*Plant Overview/Onboarding:* Testing methodology/protocol reviewed with plant teams. Key participants included: Plant Management, Production teams, volunteer workers, local union, Safety, Ergonomics, Plant Medical and Supplier.

*Supplier Demonstration/Training:* Operators complete training (1–2 days) prior to involvement in trial in the workstation. Training provided onsite with supplier and plant teams. Focus included device fit, functionality, and hands on demonstration.

*Station Walkthrough* of plant to identify workstations collaboratively with Plant medical, Plant Management, team leaders, Safety and Ergonomic representatives to determine work elements that meet overhead >50% threshold and were free of safety concerns. Plant teams identified overhead workstations along with ergonomic team and participants (volunteers). Volunteers identified with no preexisting injuries and minimum working duration in the workstation.

*Pilot usage:* volunteer workers trial the device, performing their usual working activity in the production line, with the incremental plan presented in Table 2.

*Follow up:* volunteers completed initial questionnaire with Medical team, assess pre-existing conditions. General comfort, usability and MSD questionnaire completed by participants at trial intervals.

Three (3) passive exoskeleton devices were identified (Levitate, MATE, EksoBionics) through internal/external benchmarking and supplier demonstrations. Ultimately, for the initial trial two (2) devices were trialed at two (2) assembly locations with 37 participants total in 10 workstations. For each of the trials, the general protocol and initial usage was based on a 3-week trial (15-day use) timeframe with incremental usage (2–8 h) to acclimate operator to device. Overall, general protocol followed the incremental duration. However, plant shift schedules and participant willingness to volunteer were factors that affected the duration of usage at each assembly plant location.

**Table 2.** North America incremental usage plan

|  | Day 1 to 2 | Day 3 to 4 | Day 4 to 15 |
|---|---|---|---|
| Working hours with exoskeleton [h] | 2 to 4 | 4 | 8 |
| % over full shift | 25 to 50% | 50% | 100% |

During the trial, participants used the device on workstation tasks identified during an initial workstation walkthrough. Volunteer participants utilized the device and completed the associated questionnaires with the Medical team. Subjective feedback was obtained from the operators using a quantitative questionnaire initiated at the beginning of the trial and at subsequent intervals using a scale (1–10) rating usability and functionality.

Focus in the **LATAM Region** began with a benchmark activity of upper arms passive exoskeletons. The trials involved the majority of exoskeletons for industrial purpose available on the market, including MATE, Skelex, ShoulderX [9, 12, 13]. Tests were performed directly in the plant to assess the actual conditions of the equipment and its effectiveness. In total, 400 h of usage have been completed with MATE, 720 with Skelex and 765 h with ShoulderX.

Similar to the common approach with others Regions, participation of workers was voluntary; workers had no pre-existing injuries or limitations defined by the ergonomics team (i.e. pre-disposition of injury, muscle dominance syndrome or ligament laxity); furthermore, the condition of "minimum working period" on the specific workstations of six months was verified.

A dedicated team identified overhead workstations suitable for the trials. This includes workstations having height above 1800 mm from the ground (i.e. body-to-chassis marriage in the assembly shop; sealing application in the paint shop). The analyzed workstations require the operator to work with an awkward posture of the upper limb for a certain percentage of cycle time, introducing a biomechanical overload at the shoulder level. The team observed that the efficacy of the exoskeleton could be evaluated positively in workstations in which the percentage of time in awkward posture is greater than 10% of cycle time.

The Plant Phase was structured into two (2) steps:

Step1 – trials in the current workstation for 3 days (2 h/day) included six workers.

Step 2 – trials in the current workstation for 15 days for the full shift. Volunteers in this step were included only with a positive experience in Step 1 and interest in continuing in the mid-term trial: 4 workers were involved. During trials a questionnaire was administered. In particular, a "discomfort assessment" was conducted during Step 2, at the beginning, in the middle and at the end of the trial (Table 3).

**Table 3.** LATAM incremental usage plan

|  | STEP 1 | | | STEP 2 |
| --- | --- | --- | --- | --- |
|  | Day1 | Day2 | Day3 | Day 1 to 15 |
| Working hours with exoskeleton [h] | 2 | 2 | 2 | 8 |
| % over full shift | 25% | 25% | 25% | 100% |

Focus in the **APAC Region** included benchmarking and leveraging lessons learned from the other Regions trial phases and shared approach (protocol and methodology) to initiate in plant trials at the end of 2020. One week-trials, focused on MATE exoskeleton, have been conducted in 6 workstations in engine production line and in 11 workstations in the vehicle chassis line.

## 3 Findings Across Regions: Common Approach, Outcomes and Challenges

Common approach within Regions is based on a shared roadmap defining steps from the benchmarking towards the implementation phase.

Key points of the common methodology adopted within Regions are defined and grouped into four (4) macro-areas (Fig. 2):

1. *Common goals:* improve the life quality of assembly operators, enhance safety, reduce fatigue and injury in repetitive overhead tasks; quantify benefits on productivity and quality in the product/process; reduce the risks of absenteeism;
2. *Basic assumptions:* usage on volunteer basis (on current job 6 months or more); volunteers with no pre-existing injuries (the device is not intended for rehabilitation); device not intended as a design solution nor as a lift assist; fit to individual operator (personal device); device not to impede work flow.

3. *General protocol:* research (supplier meetings and demonstrations, internal/external benchmarking); investigation (key stakeholder overview, protocol development and lab tests); feasibility (trials in the production line, subjective data questionnaire data collection); application
4. *Key participants in the process/Team*: Plant Management, Production Teams, Local union, Corporate/Plant Safety, Corporate Ergonomics, Plant Medical Staff

**Fig. 2.** Common approach/methodology

Common outcomes resulting from the experimental campaign highlighted the importance of testing with workers in the manufacturing workstation environment; the role of training and adjustment period to acclimate to wearing the device; the importance of taking part in the co-design process of the device; the necessity of appropriate selection of the target workstations for each type of exoskeletons device.

Across Regions the feedback from the in plant passive upper limbs exoskeletons trials indicate mixed feedback on usage, functionality and acceptability. Positive feedback show device support when working with arms above shoulder and less fatigue at the end of the day. Discomfort, size of device (fit), weight of device, restricted mobility and donning and doffing procedures were initial reasons operators choose to discontinue wearing the devices. Tests performed during the spring and summer months highlighted the need of using fabric with higher breathability. The encumbrance of the device along the arm introduces the risk of damaging the equipment or the product. This leads the operator to worry about the possible interference with other objects and, consequently, to not feel comfortable in the usage.

In general, the benefit of the exoskeleton is perceived as much as the device is perfectly set on the worker's body. In observing long-term usage, it happened that initial settings were not maintained over time, and consequently further adjustment was needed.

Defining a common approach includes the challenge that derives from the different regional boundary conditions. This includes local/federal regulations, legal requirements and potential cultural differences between Regions. Nevertheless, some refinements and further alignment in the protocol can be adopted in order to increase the "comparison criteria" of multi-located trials. These include the questionnaire to investigate usability, acceptability, practical suggestions and discomfort information.

## 4   Conclusions and Future Perspectives

Wearable technologies have been rapidly evolving in the manufacturing automotive sector. Across plants within the company a collaborative approach was initiated to leverage benchmarking and device investigation across Regions and shared knowledge for potential future implementation. Common goals related to perceived benefits to improve safety, quality of life and reduce the risk of injury are shared across Regions. Initial benchmarking and experimental trials both in labs and in the assembly plant have allowed Regions to develop experimental methodology and usage protocols, share information related to usability/functionality and identify future opportunities for application: volunteer workers tried the exoskeleton while executing their standard tasks. The campaign seeks for a holistic evaluation of the device considering long-term trials. It also investigates how the presence of other workers, equipment, limited spaces may interfere with the exoskeleton adoption.

Targeted trials within the assembly plant workstation provide insight into the biomechanics of the devices, alternative risk reduction and potential overhead work stations application. Initial qualitative data and findings indicate mixed feedback on usage, functionality and acceptability. While workers generally recognized a potential benefit of the exoskeletons when working with arms above the shoulder, they also pointed out size fit, ease of use, freedom of movement and wearing comfort as essential elements for adoption. Utilizing the workers' feedback to support the co-design process and the supplier feedback is valuable in identifying the device that aligns with the needs and expectations of the operators in an assembly workstation. In addition, legal requirements and the development of product related standards associated with exoskeleton usage and application in the automotive manufacturing will be a factor of consideration regarding future implementation and application. Although, methodology and protocol may be common across Regions, there still may be legal regulatory and/or local standards to consider that can affect the implementation on a regional basis.

The dynamic nature of manufacturing, the level of complexity in the workstation and the evolving technologies continue to challenge the practitioner in seeking alternative solutions to address the biomechanical risk factors and to maintain a safe workspace for the operator. These challenges are shared across Regions, pursuing a collaborative approach is key to leveraging experience and potential exoskeleton application across Regions.

# References

1. Peters, M., Wischniewski, S.: The impact of using exoskeletons on occupational safety and health EU-OSHA Discussion Paper (2019)
2. Romero, D., Stahre, J., Wuest, T., Noran, O., Bernus, P., Fast-Berglund, Å., Gorecky, D.: Towards an operator 4.0 typology: a human-centric perspective on the fourth industrial revolution technologies. In: CIE 2016: 46th International Conferences on Computers and Industrial Engineering (2016)
3. de Looze, M.P., Bosch, T., Krause, F., Stadler, K.S., O'Sullivan, L.W.: Exoskeletons for industrial application and their potential effects on physical work load. Ergonomics **59**, 671–681 (2016)
4. Kim, S., Nussbaum, M.A., Mokhlespour Esfahani, M.I., Alemi, M.M., Alabdulkarim, S., Rashedi, E.: Assessing the influence of a passive, upper extremity exoskeletal vest for tasks requiring arm elevation: part I – "Expected" effects on discomfort, shoulder muscle activity, and work task performance. Appl. Ergon. **70**, 315–322 (2018)

5. Kim, S., Nussbaum, M.A., Mokhlespour Esfahani, M.I., Alemi, M.M., Jia, B., Rashedi, E.: Assessing the influence of a passive, upper extremity exoskeletal vest for tasks requiring arm elevation: part II – "Unexpected" effects on shoulder motion, balance, and spine loading. Appl. Ergon. **70**, 323–330 (2018)
6. Huysamen, K., Bosch, T., de Looze, M., Stadler, K.S., Graf, E., O'Sullivan, L.W.: Evaluation of a passive exoskeleton for static upper limb activities. Appl. Ergon. **70**, 148–155 (2018)
7. Spada, S., Ghibaudo, L., Gilotta, S., Gastaldi, L., Cavatorta, M.P.: Investigation into the applicability of a passive upper-limb exoskeleton in automotive industry. Proc. Manuf. **11**, 1255–1262 (2017)
8. Spada, S., Ghibaudo, L., Gilotta, S., Gastaldi, L., Cavatorta, M.P.: Analysis of exoskeleton introduction in industrial reality: main issues and EAWS risk assessment. In: International Conference on Applied Human Factors and Ergonomics. AHFE 2017: Advances in Physical Ergonomics and Human Factors (2017)
9. MATE – COMAU. https://mate.comau.com. Accessed 30 Oct 2020
10. Spada, S., Ghibaudo, L., Carnazzo, C., Gastaldi, L., Cavatorta, M.P.: Passive upper limb exoskeletons: an experimental campaign with workers. In: Proceedings of the 20th Congress of the International Ergonomics Association, pp. 230–239 (2018)
11. Gilotta, S., Spada, S., Ghibaudo, L., Isoardi, M., Mosso, C.O.: Acceptability beyond usability: a manufacturing case study. In: Proceedings of the 20th Congress of the International Ergonomics Association, pp. 922–934 (2018)
12. Skelex. https://www.skelex.com. Accessed 30 Oct 2020
13. ShoulderX - SuitX. https://www.suitx.com/shoulderx. Accessed 30 Oct 2020

# The Impact of a Customized, Job-Specific Stretching Program in Manufacturing: A Pilot Study

Tara L. Diesbourg$^{(\boxtimes)}$ ⓘ and Kathryn M. Rougeau ⓘ

Public and Environmental Wellness Department, Oakland University, Rochester, MI, USA
tdiesbourg@oakland.edu

**Abstract.** The goal of the current study was to mitigate employee discomfort and fatigue and improve emotional well-being through a job-specific stretching program at a local manufacturing facility. While preliminary analyses suggest that this program may have the desired impact on flexibility, fitness, and affect, it is only as good as its buy-in from the company. While the company seemed eager to adopt such a program at the initial planning-stages, large-scale implementation strategies were met with resistance. Some departments encouraged their employees to stretch together before starting the shift but did not promote the mid-shift or post-shift stretching to the same degree, while other departments were not as supportive of the program and did not complete any stretches as a group. Some employees in these departments noted that they wanted to take part independently. However, while completing the stretches on their own at their workstation, nearby coworkers led them to feel self-conscious. Employees noted that they would try to find an isolated place to do their stretches but that they were frequently "caught," which led them to stop participating. Further investigation is underway after having addressed some of the identified issues with the initial launch. Based on the researchers' feedback, the company has established a wellness committee to support engagement and lead group stretches. The safety and management teams have been actively engaged with promoting the program, leading to overall positive feelings towards the relaunch on the part of employees. Further data collection is underway.

**Keywords:** Dynamic warm-up · Yoga cool-down · Static stretching · Physical demands · Affect · Discomfort · Engagement

## 1 Introduction

### 1.1 Description of the Problem

The management team at a local manufacturing facility noted that many employees were completing stretches together before their shift, but the stretching routine was informal and not rooted in any stretching theory. Management was concerned that the employees would injure themselves through improper stretching practices and invited the researchers to develop a formalized stretching program for the employees according to published best practices.

N. L. Black et al. (Eds.): IEA 2021, LNNS 221, pp. 407–416, 2021.
https://doi.org/10.1007/978-3-030-74608-7_51

## 1.2  Background Information

While there are several theories associated with stretching pre-and post-exercise, proper exercise protocol dictates that individuals should warm-up before and cool-down following exercise [1–3]. Static stretching is the most common stretching technique. However, static stretching may not provide the best opportunity for injury reduction and consequently, support for dynamic warm-ups has increased in popularity [4, 5]. Dynamic stretching has been shown to incorporate functional, task-specific movements into warm-ups, increasing body temperature and enhancing activity-related flexibility [2].

Occupational stretching programs have been associated with increased range of motion and flexibility and decreased discomfort ratings [6–9]. These occupational stretching programs have also been shown to significantly reduce the effect of work-related psychosocial risk factors such as stress and low job satisfaction and increase a person's feeling of self-worth, self-efficacy, and personal attractiveness [7, 8, 10].

Despite the proven benefits stretching on injury prevention with physical activity and the notable impact of such programs in the workplace, they are often difficult to implement and are met with resistance on the part of employees and management alike [11–13].

## 1.3  Purpose/Research Question

The purpose of the current investigation was to determine whether a facility-wide stretching program would increase employee outlook, psychological well-being, job satisfaction, reduce recordable injuries and discomfort, and improve quality of life outside the workplace, and to assess the feasibility of implementing such a large-scale intervention facility-wide.

# 2  Materials and Methods

## 2.1  Context

The data collection schedule was planned for 180 days with in-person fitness collections and virtual surveys on days 0, 30, 60, 90, and 180. Unfortunately, the Coronavirus Disease 2019 (COVID-19) pandemic resulted in a full shut-down of the facility after day 90, and as such, the data collection process was halted prematurely.

## 2.2  Participant Description

Employees from a local manufacturing facility were recruited from all departments including administrative offices, laboratory, research and development, manufacturing, and shipping and receiving. To focus on program development and troubleshoot ways of increasing employee engagement and participation only the first shift (day-shift) employees were enrolled in the stretching program. The second and third shift employees served as waitlist control subjects (to be enrolled in the stretching program at a later date). A sample of first-shift employees also volunteered to participate in further data collections to monitor flexibility and cardiovascular fitness throughout the program. The 31 participants who volunteered for the additional data collections consisted of males and females of all ages and represented each of the facility's departments.

## 2.3 Stretching Program Development and Implementation

For this investigation, a typical shift was defined as the employees' "exercise," and a pre-shift dynamic warm-up program and post-shift yoga-based cool-down routine were developed. These were low-impact, standing routines that would be easy to complete in the space confines of the facility (generally, in the break rooms or the area surrounding the punch-clock) and that would target most of the large muscle groups and joints of the body. Modifications were provided for exercises that proved painful or difficult for some employees. These programs were provided as "exercise videos" that the employees could follow along with. They were stored on shared computers within the facility, and paper-based versions were posted to walls in common-areas and near the punch clock.

A task-specific mid-shift static stretching program was also developed to mitigate progressive muscle fatigue and discomfort throughout the day. The mid-shift stretching program was presented to the organization as a "menu" of static stretches, where stretches were categorized based on their appropriateness for specific physical demands. These mid-shift stretches could be completed during a lunch break or at their workstation. Because the static stretch program consisted of three 5-s repetitions of 10–12 individual stretches, the employees were instructed that they could also complete one repetition between machine cycles at their workstation if the machine's pacing allowed. A program card with pictures of each stretch was placed near each workstation so employees could refer to them as needed. These cards were posted on walls and pillars in the immediate vicinity but were not posted at each workstation following concerns voiced by the management team. Each employee was instructed to complete the 10–12 stretches at least once throughout the day at their convenience.

## 2.4 Survey Development and Distribution

Surveys were used to assess the employees' health and injury history, affect, fatigue, opinions regarding the stretching program, physical and mental fatigue, and physical discomfort. These were presented at various times throughout the intervention to allow for longitudinal monitoring of this program's impact.

**Initial Health Assessment Survey.** An initial survey sent to all employees in the facility, across all three shifts was used to collect information about employee demographics, work history, injury history, job satisfaction, physical discomfort (via pain mapping), physical and mental fatigue, perceived health status (physical and emotional), affect (energy, tiredness, calmness, tension) and limitations to daily activities and social activities as a result of health status. This survey was sent as an anonymous link via email one week before the stretching program was implemented. This survey was also intended to be administered at the end of the intervention but was not due to COVID-19.

**Pre-, Mid-, and Post-Shift Surveys.** These surveys were used to monitor changes throughout the day as a result of their participation in the stretching program by focusing on discomfort, affect, physical and mental fatigue, and physical activity enjoyment. On Days 0, 30, 60, and 90 three separate links were sent to all employees across all shifts to complete at the start of their shift, mid-shift, and at the end of their shift. Respondents who indicated that they worked the second or third shift did not receive the questions about their opinion regarding the effectiveness of the stretching program questionnaire.

## 2.5  Fitness Testing

On Days 0, 30, 60, and 90, the researchers attended the facility to complete the fitness testing protocol. The safety intern at the facility scheduled each person's appointment for testing to ensure that they would have a replacement to cover the employee's workstation at that time. Management and the safety team were not otherwise involved in this collection. The fitness tests were completed in a private room within the facility. However, it should be noted that this room is on the second floor, and some participants arrived to complete their tests with an increased heart and respiration rate. Employees were given some time to allow their heart rate to return to its resting level before beginning their fitness testing. However, time was limited, and their heart rate may not have been able to completely return to baseline levels.

**Flexibility & Range of Motion.** As the impacts of stretching on flexibility are well-documented, flexibility and range of motion were used to indicate participation and adherence to the program. Flexibility measures used in the current analysis include the Sit and Reach Test, the Seated Trunk Rotation Test, and the Back Scratch Test.

**Cardiovascular Fitness.** The dynamic warm-up stretches and the expected outcome of feeling better overall was expected to be reflected in the participants' cardiovascular fitness measures. Resting heart rate and blood pressure were used to monitor changes in cardiovascular fitness throughout the intervention.

## 2.6  Ergonomic Injury Data

Following intervention completion, the safety team at the facility extracted data from their injury and incident recording software to monitor the effect of the stretching program on recordable ergonomic injuries for 2019 and 2020. Variables examined included: Affected body region, Nature of injury, and Shift. These results were only provided to the research team as counts, and due to the low number of injuries recorded by the facility, only anecdotal observations could be drawn from the provided data.

## 2.7  Data Analysis

Due to the low response rate and the small number of participants, statistical power could not be achieved in this analysis. As such, the data analysis consisted of trend-analyses. These trends are thought only to suggest areas for future investigation in subsequent offerings of this intervention, but definitive conclusions cannot be drawn from this analysis method. To generate the trends for this analysis, each participant's responses and test scores were plotted either over time (Days 0, 30, 60, and 90), or over the course of the shift (pre-, mid-, post-shift). The slope of the linear trendline connecting these points was used as the outcome for each variable, where a negative slope suggested a decrease in the score, while a positive slope represented an increase in the score. Trendlines that appeared horizontal on the graphs were classified as "no change" regardless of the actual sign of the slope in question.

# 3  Results

Due to the premature suspension of the study, the data is incomplete, and the result of participation cannot be determined. The researchers attempted to identify trends in the data during the three months that were completed, however due to low response rates to the surveys and missed fitness testing sessions by most of the participants ($n = 31$), only the data from those people who participated in at least 75% of datasets ($n \leq 8$) could be analyzed. To increase the number of data points whenever possible, data from the same person may have been used as individual responses for different days.

## 3.1  Physical Fitness Outcomes

**Resting Heart Rate.** On average, resting heart rate decreased in four employees and remained the same in two employees (Fig. 1). Two employees did see an increase in heart rate over time, but this could also be due to testing effects and the need to rush to their testing session on some days and not others.

**Sit and Reach.** On average, Sit and Reach flexibility either increased slightly ($n = 3$) or stayed roughly the same ($n = 3$) (Fig. 2).

**Spine Range of Motion/Rotational Stiffness.** Spine rotational stiffness was assessed by measuring bilateral trunk rotation. Spine range of motion also appeared to increase on average over the course of the intervention ($n = 4$) (Fig. 3).

## 3.2  Perceived Discomfort Outcomes

Discomfort, for the most part, decreased or stayed the same for those involved in the stretching program during the day when compared to those who did not participate in the intervention, except for head and neck discomfort. The same question was presented each month to track longitudinal changes in discomfort for the nine body regions. Very little change in discomfort was observed over time.

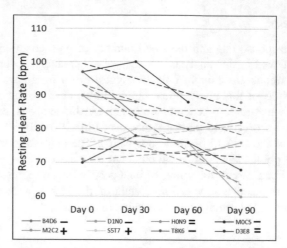

**Fig. 1.** Changes in resting heart rate over time for 8 participants who completed at least 3 out of 4 testing sessions. Identified trends are derived from the slope of the trendline for each participant (dashed lines) and are described next to the participant ID in the legend: " +" suggests an increase in resting heart rate over time, "−" suggests a decrease in resting heart rate over time, and " = " represents no detected change in resting heart rate over time.

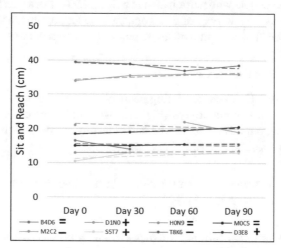

**Fig. 2.** Changes in sit and reach flexibility over time for 8 participants who completed at least 3 out of 4 testing sessions. Identified trends are derived from the slope of the trendline for each participant (dashed lines) and are described next to the participant ID in the legend: "+" suggests an increase in flexibility over time, "−" suggests a decrease in flexibility over time, and "= " represents no detected change in sit-and-reach flexibility over time.

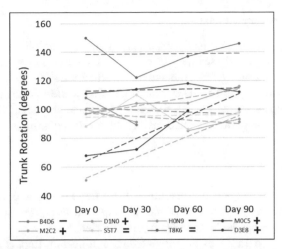

**Fig. 3.** Changes in spine rotational flexibility over time for 8 participants who completed at least 3 out of 4 testing sessions. Identified trends are derived from the slope of the trendline for each participant (dashed lines) and are described next to the participant ID in the legend: " +" suggests an increase in flexibility over time, "−" suggests a decrease in flexibility over time, and " = " represents no detected change in flexibility over time.

## 3.3  Affective Outcomes

Due to the nature of the affect survey and its interpretation, only responses with full datasets (pre-, mid-, post-shift) could be analyzed (n = 6). The results demonstrate trends as expected with this type of intervention (Fig. 4).

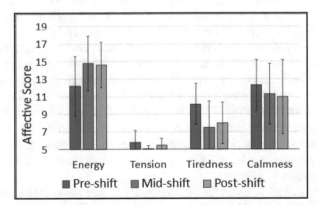

**Fig. 4.** Changes in the four affective variables (Energy, Tension, Tiredness, and Calmness) throughout the day. The y-axis represents the average "Affective Score" across all responses, calculated using the protocol for the Activation/Deactivation Checklist (ADACL). Error bars represent the standard deviations.

## 3.4  Ergonomic Injury Reporting

While this facility does not typically experience many ergonomic injuries each month, they did report a change in these injury trends while the stretching program was in effect. Compared to the previous year at the same time, they reported 50% fewer ergonomic injuries among their employees. They also noted that while injuries typically affected large muscle groups such as those in the back, neck, and shoulders, injuries sustained during the intervention period affected mainly the hands and arms.

# 4  Discussion

While the ability to interpret the responses from the surveys and the fitness testing was limited due to the poor response and participation rates, the observed trends are promising, and much can be learned from this experience.

The stretching program was not expected to significantly impact resting heart rate as the exercises were not intense enough for marked improvements in cardiovascular health. However, heart rate was shown to have improved for half of the participants. While the role of the dynamic warm-up is to prepare the body's cardiovascular and muscular systems for the upcoming demands [14], it is unlikely due to the dynamic warm-up at the beginning of the shift.

While flexibility and spine range of motion were expected to show marked improvements as a result of the intervention, the effects were variable. Sit and reach testing did not show the improvements that were expected with the intervention. The lack of improvement may have been partly because the stretches provided were functional in nature and did not directly target hamstring flexibility. However, the lack of participation and engagement in the program are also likely contributing factors. On average, participants did show an improvement in spine rotational range of motion. This suggests that employees' rotational stiffness decreased slightly, although this did not appear to translate to discomfort scores as the researchers had expected [15].

Discomfort stayed the same on average throughout the shift and over the 90-day intervention period, except for head and neck discomfort which increased throughout the day. Head pain/headaches is not easily remedied through stretching and is often a result of ambient conditions such as noise and light, and psychosocial conditions such as stress and job satisfaction [16–18]. While ambient conditions were not expected to change throughout the intervention, the psychosocial factors could have been positively influenced by the stretching program through an overall increased sense of wellbeing. However, the bullying behavior exhibited towards the people stretching may have negated some of these positive feelings.

Affect as described by energy, tension, tiredness, and calmness has been shown to improve with both acute and chronic physical activity [19]. Physical activity tends to increase energy and decrease tiredness. While tension did not change markedly over time (possibly due to a floor-effect), energy increased and calmness and tiredness decreased, as anticipated at the start of the shift. Following the mid-shift stretching protocol, there was an increase in energy and a decrease in calmness. While the researchers would like to attribute this to the stretching protocol, this could also be a 'time-out effect' from returning to work following their mid-shift break [20, 21]. By the end of a shift, data showed that participants were less energetic, as expected due to the onset of end-of-day fatigue.

The most significant findings from this analysis revolved around the engagement and participation in the stretching program. When the protocol was initially presented and demonstrated to the employees, the overall enthusiasm and energy were extremely high. However, as the program progressed, they became disengaged. Soliciting feedback and implementing appropriate changes were met with resistance from management who were unwilling to implement the changes requested by the employees (i.e. exercise cards at the individual workstations, televisions in break rooms and near punch clocks to display stretching videos, audible cues to remind of times to stretch…). Management was also not setting a good example for employees as they were disengaged and not completing their stretches.

## 5  Conclusions

While the company seemed eager to adopt such a program at the initial planning-stages, large-scale implementation strategies were met with resistance. The departments that bought-in fully and actively participated in the program commented on feeling better overall, sleeping better, and feeling less physically exhausted after their shift, which was the expected findings from such an intervention. However, without 100% participation throughout the facility, these improvements will never be systemic and will be reserved for the select few who prioritize their health. Further investigation is currently underway after having addressed some of the identified issues with the initial launch. Based on the researchers' feedback, the company has established a wellness committee to support engagement and lead group stretches. The safety and management teams have also been much more actively engaged in promoting the program and educating about the benefits of stretching the workplace. They have also enlisted the cooperation of the health insurance provider to potentially incentivize participation at a later date. Further data collection is underway, but the future looks bright!

## References

1. Smith, C.A.: The warm-up procedure: to stretch or not to stretch. A brief review. J. Orthop. Sports Phys. Ther. **19**(1), 12–17 (1994)
2. Liguori, G. and American College of Sports Medicine: ACSM's Guidelines for Exercise Testing and Prescription. Lippincott Williams & Wilkins, Philadelphia (2020)
3. Behm, D., Button, D., Butt, J.: Factors affecting force loss with prolonged stretching. Can. J. Appl. Physiol. **26**, 262–272 (2001)
4. da Costa, B.R., Vieira, E.R.: Risk factors for work-related musculoskeletal disorders: a systematic review of recent longitudinal studies. Am. J. Ind. Med. **53**(3), 285–323 (2010)
5. McMillian, D.J., Moore, J.H., Hatler, B.S., Taylor, D.C.: Dynamic vs static-stretching warm-up: the effect on power and agility performance. J. Strength Cond. Res. **20**(3), 492–499 (2006)
6. Szeto, G.P.Y., Wong, T.K.T., Law, R.K.Y., Lee, E.W.C., Lau, T., So, B.C.L., Law, S.W.: The impact of a multifaceted ergonomic intervention program on promoting occupational health in community nurses. Appl. Ergon. **44**(3), 414–422 (2013)

7. Lee, H., Chae, D., Wilbur, J., Miller, A., Lee, K., Jin, H.: Effects of a 12-week self-managed stretching program among Korean-Chinese female migrant workers in Korea: a randomized trial. Jpn. J. Nurs. Sci. **11**(2), 121–134 (2014)
8. Gasibat, Q., Simbak, N.B., Aziz, A.A.: Stretching exercises to prevent work-related musculoskeletal disorders – a review article. Am. J. Sports Sci. Med. **5**(2), 27–37 (2017)
9. Shariat, A., Cleland, J.A., Danaee, M., Kargarfard, M., Sangelaji, B., Tamrin, S.B.M.: Effects of stretching exercise training and ergonomic modifications on musculoskeletal discomforts of office workers: a randomized controlled trial. Braz. J. Phys. Ther. **22**(2), 144–153 (2018)
10. Moore, T.M.: A workplace stretching program: physiologic and perception measurements before and after participation. AAOHN J. Workplace Health Saf. **46**(12), 563–568 (1998)
11. Thompson, B.K.: Employee participation in an on-site stretching program: a case study in a central Wisconsin manufacturing company. https://minds.wisconsin.edu/bitstream/handle/1793/39741/2000thompsonb.pdf?sequence=1. Accessed 03 Feb 2021
12. Lowe, J.: Do workplace stretching programs work? Prof. Case Manag. **12**(5), 300–302 (2007)
13. Choi, S., Woletz, T.: Do stretching programs prevent work-related musculoskeletal disorders? J. Saf. Health Environ. Res. **6**(3), 1–19 (2010)
14. Rutledge, I., Faccioni, A.: Dynamic warm-ups. Sports Coach **24**, 20–22 (2001)
15. Lee, H., Nicholson, L.L., Adams, R.D.: Cervical range of motion associations with subclinical neck pain. Spine **29**(1), 33–40 (2004)
16. Schwartz, B.S., Stewart, W.F., Lipton, R.B.: Lost workdays and decreased work effectiveness associated with headache in the workplace. J. Occup. Environ. Med. **39**(4), 320–327 (1997)
17. Parkes, K.R.: Shiftwork, job type, and the work environment as joint predictors of health-related outcomes. J. Occup. Health Psychol. **4**(3), 256–268 (1999)
18. Holroyd, K.A., Stensland, M., Lipchick, G.L., Hill, K.R., O'Donnell, F.S., Cordingley, G.: Psychosocial correlates and impact of chronic tension-type headaches. Headache: J. Head Face Pain **40**(1), 3–16 (2001)
19. Petruzzello, S.J., Landers, D.M., Hatfield, B.D., Kubitz, K.A., Salazar, W.: A meta-analysis on the anxiety-reducing effects of acute and chronic exercise. Sports Med. **11S**(3), 143–182 (1991)
20. Bahrke, M.S., Morgan, W.P.: Anxiety reduction following exercise and meditation. Cogn. Ther. Res. **2**(4), 323–333 (1978)
21. Breus, M., O'Connor, P.: Exercise-induced anxiolysis: a test of the "time out" hypothesis in high anxious females. Med. Sci. Sports Exerc. **30**(7), 1107–1112 (1998)

# Multidisciplinary Approach Ergonomics and Lean: Articulation Between Performance, Health and Safety

Valentin Lamarque[1,2](✉), Estelle Chin[3], Julie Queheille[3], and Olivier Buttelli[4]

[1] CRTD Laboratory CNAM, Paris, France
valentin.lamarque@lecnam.net
[2] EPICENE Team BPH, Bordeaux, France
[3] Safran Landing Systems, Bidos, France
[4] Prisme Laboratory University of Orleans, Orléans, France

**Abstract.** In recent years, important changes in work have appeared in the industrial landscape. However, there is still work to be done, and we need to go further and faster, which is why we, at Safran Landing Systems, thought of combining ergonomics with continuous improvement, or Lean management. So through the One Safran Lean workshops, Ergonomics has shown that it is possible to transform this "top-down" approach into a participative "bottom-up" approach built jointly with operators, taking into account the actual work, to adapt prescriptions and better control the WAI (work as imagine)/WAD (work as done) gap. This approach, focused on the workers and the work as they actually do it, allowed us to take into account their professional culture, to collectively build their own rules regarding health and safety issues, while contributing to the overall performance of the work unit.

**Keywords:** Ergonomics · Lean articulation · Safety · Professional culture

## 1 Introduction

In the industry, there is no need to prove the benefits of Lean management anymore nor, to talk about its limitations on worker health and safety (Bellies and Buchman 2011; Bourgeois 2012; Morais and Aubineau 2012). It is also not necessary to prove the benefits of the complementary nature of Ergonomics and Lean (op cit.). However, it must be noted that these Lean sites, located in a limited space and time and focused on industrial performance, still pay too little attention to issues of operator health and safety. Indeed, the link between working conditions and occupational risks on one hand, and the search for added value on the other, is not always analyzed and highlighted, while healthy operators working in safe conditions will be able to find and organize better the most efficient operating procedures, provided they have sufficient resources to cope with the constraints.

So, as part of a 12-week Lean "One Safran" workshop, this text provides feedback on one of the possible links between Lean and Ergonomics, between performance and

© The Author(s), under exclusive license to Springer Nature Switzerland AG 2021
N. L. Black et al. (Eds.): IEA 2021, LNNS 221, pp. 417–422, 2021.
https://doi.org/10.1007/978-3-030-74608-7_52

health in the workplace. This opportunity, which must be seized, is an opportunity to put back at the heart of the search for industrial performance, health and safety issues as well as professional culture, a guarantee of a successful and favorable intervention for workers.

## 2    A Necessary Collaboration

Ergonomists agree on the link between activity and culture (Wisner 1985; Rabardel 1995; Béguin 2010). So, faced with a change of an organizational or technical nature "there is a need for appropriation and development of the activity" (Béguin 2010), for the preservation of the vital resources of the profession (Clot 2010). Taking into account the "professional culture" as a provisional but stable set of what is publicly shared (knowledge, know-how, judgments, meanings and ways of thinking)" (Nascimento 2020) thus becomes essential in the face of a Lean approach that is still too top-down.

On the other hand, over time, the understanding of the gap between what is to be done (WAI), directed by rules, prescribers, and how it is done (WAD), in relation to experience, knowledge and know-how, has become more refined and diversified in French-speaking works to transform work situations (Cuvelier and Woods 2019). Nevertheless, the participatory nature of workers is essential and promotes, within acceptable limits, the control of the WAI (Work As Imagine)/WAD (Work As Done) gap (Cuvelier and Woods 2019).

To do this, the ergonomic intervention has focused on a triple positioning - skills, instruments and collective - that will make it possible to control the WAI/WAD gap and to "manage it in a conscious and reasoned way" (Mollo and Nascimento 2013, p. 218), between the need for Lean rationalization and the will of Ergonomics to adapt work to Man, and to understand it in order to transform it.

Indeed, studies show (Bellies and Buchman 2011; Bourgeois 2012; Morais and Aubineau 2012) that work prescribed too much leads the operator towards constraints not thought of by management. A discussion must then be built around the characteristic notions of Lean (the role of standards, waste management, the "one best way, etc.), which beyond the effective time saving can contribute to a reduction of important "marge de manoeuvre" (Coutarel et al. 2015) and transform a resource into a constraint.

However, acting together with different methodologies and knowledge, makes it necessary to build a common and shared repository. Thus, the use of a plan of the workspace (or the use of rating grids) as an intermediate object (Vinck 2009), facilitates the collective construction of future work situations, also based on the simulation of future activity. The meeting of this plurality of actors around a common object, makes possible the crossing of the experience of each one, between knowledge, and know-how, procedures and regulations (respectively WAI and WAD). Moreover, it is through the intervention of "immersed agents" in future simulated work situations that it is possible to anticipate future risks and benefits, based on the needs and constraints of existing work (Van Belleghem et al. 2018).

This approach is also a means of supporting the players towards acceptance of change, by acting on the prescriptive system (Van Belleghem 2018), while rediscussing the trade-offs between quality, efficiency and safety, all of which is bathed in their professional culture.

# 3   Methodology

The ergonomic intervention took place in a cell of 2 machines which carry out the roughing of the raw parts, the first phase of the manufacture of the landing gear; as well as a maintenance station for the cutting tools. 7 operators divided into 2 shifts are assigned to the different workstations.

First of all, the analysis of work situations (4 weeks) allowed to collect the real operating modes of each operator (manual handling, machine piloting, control and taking dimensions…) and to identify the professional risks associated with health, safety and work organization among the risks already identified, which could be treated and reduced during the Lean worksite. Occupational risks are of 3 categories: related either to general safety, chemical risk or ergonomics. Risks are evaluated and prioritized according to 4 levels of Criticality represented by colors (1/Red: Major, 2/Yellow: Significant, 3/Green: Medium, 4/Blue: Minor). Assessments are performed by trained workers, using a rating grid developed for the Safran Group. For example, general risks are assessed by calculating criticality by taking into account the frequency of exposure to the hazard, the severity of the foreseeable damage and the level of control of the risk. For ergonomics, 3 dimensions are rated: posture (rating based on the NF EN 1005-4 standard); load handling based on the ISO 11228, NF EN 1005-2 and NIOSH lifting equation standards; repeatability based on the European standard NF EN 1005-5. The ergonomic analysis was based on an alternation of open and systematic observation methods (to understand the work activity, the interactions between operators/teams, the general organization of the cell, the operating strategies…), and informal interviews (to discuss in situation the intention, the reasons of these acts). In a second phase, 3 work sessions took place in multidisciplinary groups, which allowed to deepen the analysis of the work situations, as well as to find ways of improvement in a collective way. Discussions were conducted on the basis of a plan of the cell, representing the tools, furniture, parts and tool storage areas, as well as the flow of people and parts. The participatory work made it possible to define and set up a new implantation of the unit, as well as an action plan to reduce occupational risks. Some actions that were implemented during the Lean workshop were tested and verified in real working conditions, taking into account the variability of production conditions (hazards such as missing parts, urgent touch-ups, absence of colleagues…).

# 4   Working Together and Moving Towards Major Improvements in Working Conditions and Performance

The 12-week Lean workshop led to a reorganization of the initial space with the creation of dedicated areas and new work areas (activities not prescribed, but actually carried out), but also to an increase in workspace ($+17$ m$^2$) thanks to a rearrangement of the areas annexed to the two machines. In addition, the restructuring of space and traffic flows has made it possible to reduce operations without added value (manual handling and unnecessary travel), and to reorganize work without reducing the operator's resources needed to maintain his activity, helping to reduce professional risks (30% reduction in the risks of co-activity, falls, shocks, postures, load handling).

In fact, observations have shown that there was no distinction between the entry and exit of the part, thus generating a significant congestion of the work areas and the presence of cross-flows. The latter lead to a permanent co-activity between the operators, source of risks of shock, fall and unnecessary handling (risks that have so far been controlled by the workers thanks to a constant interaction during the transport of parts). These new traffic flows have been co-constructed with the operators, with the compromise between, on the one hand, clarifying procedures, reducing "lost time" and cross-flows and, on the other hand, taking into account the spatio-temporal needs and constraints of the different activities, by integrating the knowledge, know-how, but also the protection strategies, which they have already put in place.

We will take here as an example of these strategies, an off-machine operation to turn a landing gear leg, which requires the installation of bulky machining tools, where the clamps are difficult to access. The operation prescribed to be done in the machine is then performed by the operators, off-machine on the storage carriage in the middle of the two machines. The creation of a dedicated area for the operation (close to the machine but far from the co-activity zone), has made it possible to reduce the risk related to the activity, while taking into account the protection strategies built individually at the beginning and then shared within the collective.

Finally, in addition to the installation, many improvements concerning storage and tools were identified through action plans, some of which were carried out during the Lean workshop. Indeed, we were able to notice during our analysis that the operators of this work unit need a certain number of tools. They pace their activities: using slings to transport parts before and after machining, numerous measuring tools to accurately check all parts, clamping and cleaning tools throughout the machining phase. Special attention has therefore been paid to them to limit the risks during their use (adequate height, storage positioned according to the actual activity, restoration of their storage).

## 5   Contribution of the Ergonomic Approach

The gains identified at the end of the workshop showed an improvement in the overall performance of the work unit, while reducing the professional risks to which the operators were exposed.

In addition to these benefits which have been objectified, the implementation of a participative approach with the whole team, operators and managers, focused on the real work has led to collectively accepted transformations.

More precisely, the ergonomic intervention in the Lean workshop showed the importance of taking into account the real work and the involvement of the operators as actors in the construction of their own health and safety, themselves linked to the performance of the work unit. In fact, performance is built collectively, and health and safety then becomes a lever for developing it. Then, the integration of all the actors has allowed to understand the activities as they are really carried out, and to valorize them in their professional culture.

By taking the example of the circulation flow of coins we could see that a participative approach allows to control the gap between WAI/WAD, favouring its adaptation by taking into account the work and the needs of the workers. Thus, it is no longer a question of seeing only a "maximum" time saving, but an "optimized" time saving according to the situations allowing the operator to have sufficient resources to intervene and react to the production hazards. In this workshop, the creation of dedicated areas throughout the circulation flow of the part protects the workers, limits risks (linked to co-activity, transport of parts, etc.) and it is all these gains that contribute to a better general organization of the unit.

Moreover, apart from the term "protection" commonly understood in the sense of "protective equipment" or "activity prescription" in risky situations, we have seen that the notion of protection refers to a dynamic individual and collective process, where it is readapted, "tamed" by the worker and put in his "hand", contributing to the importance of the WAD valorization. Indeed, rules are always at least interpreted, adjusted or appropriate to deal with the unexpected (Cuvelier and Caroly 2009), so it is essential to observe and adapt the prescriptions as they fit into the professional culture. The analysis of the knowledge, know-how and ways of thinking of the business lines has enabled us to promote this culture and to encourage the involvement of the players in this approach. It was also an opportunity for ergonomics to intervene directly in the design, thus limiting the risk of major modifications afterwards.

## 6 Conclusion

The operator constantly acts within a framework of resources and constraints, which he regulates in order to carry out an efficient action, at a lower mental and physical cost for him. In this sense, the will of Lean to increase the industrial performance, which in fact engages the activity of the first level workers, must take into account their experiences, knowledge and know-how in the field in order not to constrain the activity for a higher performance. Here, thanks to the analysis of the activity, in addition to being able to get closer to the real needs of the operators, we apprehend the professional culture in which it is inscribed.

So, by immersing ourselves in the real activities developed *in situ*, we have targeted the reality of the work, such as a management of quality/performance/health/safety compromises, integrated into the professional culture, favouring the coherence of the new organisations, the capitalisation of new business rules. We then discussed this set of compromises, thus becoming a performance lever that could be justified in terms of health and safety. Indeed, beyond the simple control of the gap between WAI and WAD and the consideration of the professional culture, what was important to question in this lean workshop were the links between health, safety and performance at work. Indeed, we think that beyond an isolated intervention, this collaboration between Lean and Ergonomics should be generalized given the advantages of these two intervention methodologies.

## References

Béguin, P.: Conduite de projet et fabrication collective du travail (Habilitation à diriger des recherches). Université Victor Segalen Bordeaux 2, Bordeaux (2010)

Bellies, L., Buchmann, W.: Le Lean et les Lean: Marges de manoeuvre de l'ergonome et conséquences sur les conditions de travail des opérateurs. In: Actes des Journées de Bordeaux sur la pratique de l'ergonomie, Bordeaux, France, Mars (2011)

Bourgeois, F.: Que fait l'ergonomie que le lean ne sait/ne veut pas voir? Activités **9**(2), 138–147 (2012)

Clot, Y.: Le travail à cœur: pour en finir avec les risques psycho-sociaux. La Découverte, Paris, France (2010)

Cuvelier, L., Woods, D.D.: Sécurité réglée et/ou sécurité gérée: quand l'ingénierie de la résilience réinterroge l'ergonomie de l'activité. Le travail humain **82**(1), 41–66 (2019)

Cuvelier, L., Caroly, S.: Appropriation d'une stratégie opératoire: un enjeu du collectif de travail. Activités **6**(2), 61–82 (2009)

Coutarel, F., Caroly, S., Vézina, N., Daniellou, F.: Marge de manœuvre situationnelle et pouvoir d'agir: des concepts à l'intervention ergonomique. Le travail humain **78**(1), 9–29 (2015)

Mollo, V., Nascimento, A.: Pratiques réflexives et développement des individus, des collectifs et des organisations. In: Falzon, P. (ed.) Ergonomie Constructive, 1st edn., pp. 207–221. PUF, France (2013)

Morais, A., Aubineau, R.: Articulation entre l'ergonomie et le lean manufacturing chez PSA. Activités **9**(2), 179–197 (2012)

Nascimento, A.: Changement organisationnel, changement culturel? Repères pour l'intervention ergonomique. Le travail humain **83**(2), 161–177 (2020)

Rabardel, P.: Les hommes et les technologies. Une approche instrumentale des technologies contemporaines. Armand Colin, Paris, France (1995)

Van Belleghem, L.: La simulation de l'activité en conception ergonomique: acquis et perspectives. Activités **15**(1), 1–22 (2018)

Van Belleghem, L., De Gasparo, S., Demas, B., Soulard, P., Samson, M.: Simuler le métier: accompagner l'évolution des pratiques professionnelles. In: Actes complet 53ème congrès international Société d'Ergonomie de Langue Française, pp. 1105–1111 (2018)

Vinck, D.: From intermediary object towards boundary-object. Revue d'anthropologie des connaissances **3**(1), 51–72 (2009)

Wisner, A.: Quand voyagent les usines: essai d'anthropotechnologie. Syros, Paris, France (1985)

# Reaction Force Exposure for Tightening Tool Users: An Experimental Study on Nutrunners

Ava Mazaheri[1,2](✉) ⓘ, Mikael Forsman[1] ⓘ, Romain Haettel[2], and Linda Rose[1] ⓘ

[1] KTH Royal Institute of Technology, Stockholm, Sweden
mazaheri@kth.se
[2] Atlas Copco Industrial Technique, Nacka, Sweden

**Abstract.** Assembly workers within for example the motor vehicle industry, are subject to physically demanding work tasks. One common type of load exposure for assembly workers, are reaction forces generated by tightening tools, such as nutrunners. The tool users counteract these forces through repetitive muscular force exertions, which in the long-term can pave the way for musculoskeletal disorders. As with other well-acknowledged load exposures commonly occurring in the assembly line environment, such as vibrations from tools, or adverse postures, reaction loads generated by nutrunners need thoroughly founded recommendations regarding acceptable exposure, in order to enable sustainable physical workloads for the tool users. The aim of this study was to lay a foundation for such recommendations. An experimental study was carried out in a simulated workstation, where assembly workers performed tightenings with an electric angle nutrunner, at different tool settings, joint stiffnesses and work-paces. Through a psychophysical approach, the participants judged the maximum amount of reaction load exposure which they perceived would enable a sustainable workload. The highly dynamic tool setting resulted in the highest chosen tightening torque levels, i.e. 35.0 and 37.7 Nm at five and eight tightenings per minute, respectively. This corresponded to a peak reaction force exposure of 71.6 and 69.8 N, respectively. Despite the statistically significant differences in impulse between the highly dynamic tightenings on hard joints and continuous drive tightenings on medium joints, no statistically significant difference between the chosen torque levels was found, suggesting that additional factors may contribute to the experience of reaction load exposure.

**Keywords:** Assembly work · Torque tools · Musculoskeletal disorders

## 1 Introduction

Industrial handheld power tools greatly contribute to the productivity of assembly lines. These tools may however expose the users to various physical loads such as forces and vibrations [1]. One type of such tools commonly used by assembly workers are nutrunners, i.e. tools used for tightening joints such as screws, nuts and bolts, within e.g. the motor vehicle industry. As these tools are externally powered, i.e. by electric, pneumatic or hydraulic means, they can tighten joints to torque levels far beyond those which manual tools can. Conversely, handheld tightening tools can generate reaction

N. L. Black et al. (Eds.): IEA 2021, LNNS 221, pp. 423–431, 2021.
https://doi.org/10.1007/978-3-030-74608-7_53

forces, which in turn need to be counteracted by the tool user through exertion of muscular effort. It is acknowledged that repetitive exposure to physical loads, which assembly work indeed entails, over time may cause musculoskeletal disorders (MSDs) [2].

At one of Sweden's largest motor vehicle manufacturers, with around 3000 employed assembly workers, it is estimated that nearly all assembly workers use powered tightening tools as a part of their daily job (J. Sandblad, personal communication, September 10, 2020). Along with the technical advancement of electric tools, torque buildup curves can be controlled more precisely, thus requiring thorough knowledge about the implications for the user.

Tool manufacturers today continuously receive requests for information and guidance from customers regarding reaction force exposure, but only have a limited number of recommendations or benchmarks to refer to. In order to enable sustainable workloads for assembly workers, commonly occurring loads, such as reaction forces, need to be monitored and controlled, and therefore, recommendations are necessary. Further, as investigated by Mazaheri and Rose [3], a few research-based suggestions for acceptable reaction load exposure are available, but may not capture all relevant aspects. For instance, exposure limits for pneumatic angle tools proposed by Kihlberg et al. [4], are expressed in terms of tool handle displacement – a physical quantity which may not fully reflect the load on the operator. In addition, values recommended for pneumatic tools may not analogously apply to the increasingly used electric tools.

In order to address the knowledge-gap regarding appropriate reaction load exposure from nutrunners, a research project was initiated by a tool manufacturer in collaboration with a university. The aim of the study was to lay a foundation for establishing recommendations for reaction force exposure resulting from electric nutrunner use, with respect to human operators' physical abilities. This to provide tool manufacturers and occupational safety and health (OSH) practitioners within assembly industries, with benchmarking values and ergonomics requirements for reaction force exposure.

## 2 Methods

### 2.1 Experimental Procedure

Eighteen assembly workers, both women (n = 8) and men (n = 10), with in average 13 years of experience in the job, participated in the study. They performed tightenings with an electric right-angle nutrunner in a simulated workstation, with combinations of the following independent variables: two different work paces (five and eight tightenings per minute), two joint types (with medium and hard stiffness) [5], and two different types of tool settings. The first setting, Turbo Tight (TT), is a highly dynamic tightening strategy which utilizes very high tool speed, thereby taking advantage of the tool inertia, which leads to the reaction force being absorbed by the tool to a large extent. This results in a reduced impulse exposure for the operator. The second setting, Quick Step (QS), is a conventional continuous drive tightening strategy, which shifts from a high to a low tool speed when approaching finalization of the tightening procedure. The TT strategy was not used on medium joints, as it mainly is intended for hard joints.

The participants were randomly assigned to four of the six experimental conditions. For each condition, tightenings were performed during three time intervals, each eight minutes long, with two minutes of rest allocated in between each interval. The same study protocol was used for all experimental conditions. The participants worked with the tool in a horizontal position, as seen in Fig. 1.

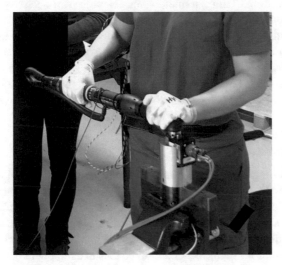

**Fig. 1.** Working position of study participants.

## 2.2 Psychophysics Approach

A psychophysics approach [6] was utilized to gain understanding of the participants' perception of the reaction load exposure resulting from tool use. The task for the participants was to converge towards a reaction load level which they individually judged to be a sustainable physical workload during a whole workday.

For each experimental condition, the participants started at a baseline tightening torque level, 30 Nm, and performed tightenings at the given work pace. While being exposed to the reaction loads resulting from the tool, they assessed the exposure magnitude with respect sustainable physical workload. This concept was explained thoroughly in the instructions given to the participants prior to the experiments. The participants were instructed to articulate whether they wanted an increase or a decrease of the load based on their perception of the load magnitude.

After each interval of tightenings, the research leader increased or decreased the tightening torque, at a magnitude and direction unknown to the participant. This way, the participants' most recent experience of load magnitude was interrupted, and thus allowed for investigation of consistency in accepted load levels. The participants were blinded to all tightening torque levels, as well as to the amount of torque increase or decrease.

Based on the impulse reduction when using TT, as well as findings from a study conducted by Valencia [7], it was anticipated that the TT conditions would be experienced as less physically demanding than the QS on medium joints, and thus result in higher chosen tightening torque levels.

### 2.3  Measured Parameters

Dependent variables were tightening torque (measured in the joint), reaction force and displacement (both measured at the tool handle), and reaction impulse (calculated based on the force). Additional joint parameters and reaction parameters were measured and calculated, but are not reported in this paper.

Upon finalization of each experimental condition, the participants rated their perceived discomfort on a modified body map based on the Nordic Musculoskeletal Questionnaire [8] with six upper body regions, using Borg's CR10 scale [9]. The six body regions were wrists and hands (grouped as one region), neck, shoulders, upper part of the back, lower part of the back, and elbows. They also rated the overall sensation of discomfort, i.e. not tied to any specific body region.

### 2.4  Measurement Equipment

Reaction load resulting from the tool during tightenings was measured with two different types of equipment. For the QS conditions, an external simulated tool handle was attached to the tool, equipped with a six-degree-of-freedom force and torque transducer (Mini45 F/T Transducer, ATI Industrial Automation, Apex, North Carolina, USA). The force vector corresponding to the force in the transversal plane was utilized for data analysis.

For the TT conditions on the other hand, the inertia component becomes highly relevant, and therefore a light-weight measurement equipment was essential. The simulated tool handle used for QS, greatly affects the dynamics of the system with its weight of 1.2 kg, thus contributing to increased system inertia. Instead, a linear accelerometer with negligible weight (Piezoelectric CCLD Accelerometer, Type 4508, Brüel & Kjaer, Naerum, Denmark), was used for the TT conditions, to calculate the resulting reaction force. It should be noted that the peak reaction forces measured during the TT conditions are expected to be overestimated by the measurement system, i.e. a lower peak force is highly probable in reality.

Joint tightening parameters such as torque and angle were measured with a torque transducer (IRTT-B 180A-13, Atlas Copco BLM, Paderno Dugnano, Italy).

### 2.5  Data Analysis

Based on the psychophysics approach, the dependent variables corresponding to the chosen tightening torque levels were extracted and analyzed. Statistical analysis was performed using a one-way ANOVA ($\alpha = 0.05$), comparing differences in means between the six experimental conditions, as well as investigating any main effects and interactions of the independent variables. Data from one of the participants was excluded from the data analysis, since that person's chosen tightening torque values heavily exceeded reasonable amounts of physical load.

## 3  Results

### 3.1  Chosen Tightening Torques and Corresponding Reaction Load Levels

Based on the psychophysical approach, the average tightening torques presented in Table 1, were perceived by the participants (n = 17) as acceptable to work with during a whole workday, meaning that these loads were assessed by the participants to allow for a sustainable physical workload. The corresponding reaction load exposures, expressed as peak reaction force, tool handle impulse and tool handle displacement, are also listed in Table 1.

**Table 1.** Average of chosen tightening torques for the six experimental conditions, and the corresponding physical quantities of the reaction load. Standard deviations are presented in parenthesis. HJ = Hard Joint, MJ = Medium Joint.

| Experimental condition | Tightening torque [Nm] | Peak reaction force [N] | Impulse [Ns] | Displacement [cm] |
|---|---|---|---|---|
| TT-HJ-5/min* | 35.0 (12.6) | 71.6 (21.7) | 3.9 (0.8) | 3.1 (1.0) |
| TT-HJ-8/min* | 37.7 (12.7) | 69.8 (14.5) | 3.6 (0.7) | 3.7 (2.0) |
| QS-HJ-5/min | 30.9 (3.8) | 61.6 (22.3) | 11.4 (6.6) | 3.6 (0.0) |
| QS-HJ-8/min | 31.5 (5.5) | 64.3 (30.6) | 12.5 (10.6) | 3.8 (1.0) |
| QS-MJ-5/min | 30.5 (15.4) | 66.8 (34.1) | 14.1 (9.8) | 3.6 (1.0) |
| QS-MJ-8/min | 33.1 (13.9) | 80.2 (40.8) | 17.3 (14.3) | 3.1 (0.0) |

*Due to uncertainties in the measurement method used for TT, peak reaction force and impulse values for the TT conditions are expected to be overestimated, meaning that they likely are lower in reality.

As seen in Table 1, the TT conditions resulted in the highest accepted tightening torques. The differences between the chosen tightening torques among the six conditions, were however not statistically significant, and no main effect or interaction was found.

TT resulted in a higher mean peak reaction force (70.7 N) than QS (68.2 N). No main effect or interaction between the independent variables was found for the accepted peak reaction force levels.

Working with the TT strategy resulted in lower impulse exposure for the operators, compared to the QS strategy. Further, hard joints resulted in lower impulse exposure compared to medium joints. A statistically significant difference in impulse was found between the TT on hard joint conditions and the QS on medium joint conditions. A main effect of tightening strategy was found ($p < 0.05$), with QS resulting in a higher mean impulse (13.8 Ns) than TT (3.8 Ns). A main effect of joint stiffness was also found ($p < 0.05$), with medium joints resulting in a higher mean impulse (15.7 Ns) than hard joints (7.9 Ns). No interaction between the independent variables was found for the accepted impulse levels.

The mean tool handle displacements corresponding to the chosen tightening torques ranged from 3.1 cm to 3.8 cm between the six conditions, although the differences were not statistically significant.

### 3.2 Subjective Ratings of Discomfort

The differences in subjective ratings of overall discomfort across the experimental conditions were small (range: 2.1–2.8), and not statistically significant. However, comparisons among the six subjectively rated body regions were notable (range: 1.4–2.5). The mean ratings for all six body regions are presented in Fig. 2.

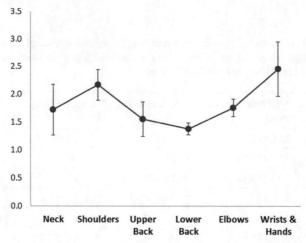

**Fig. 2.** Average subjective ratings of discomfort on Borg's CR10 scale, for the six defined body regions, with standard deviation bars.

Out of the six body regions subjectively rated using Borg's CR10 scale, wrists and hands (grouped as one body region) received the highest ratings of discomfort (average rating of 2.5) for all experimental conditions, followed by the shoulder area (average rating of 2.2), whereas the lower back region received the lowest ratings of discomfort (average rating of 1.4).

Working at the higher pace (i.e. 8 tightenings per minute) resulted in higher discomfort ratings in the wrists and hands, neck, shoulders and elbows, compared to working at the lower pace conditions (i.e. 5 tightenings per minute). This difference was, however, not statistically significant.

## 4   Discussion

### 4.1   Discussion of Results

The present study was conducted in order to lay the foundation for recommendations for reaction load exposure resulting from tightening tool use, with respect to sustainable physical workload. The effect of joint stiffness, tightening strategy and work pace on acceptable reactions loads was assessed. In this paper, a few of the measured physical quantities are presented, while others will be reported elsewhere.

As shown in Table 1, chosen tightening torques across the six experimental conditions ranged between 30.5 Nm and 37.7 Nm. Despite the anticipation that TT would result in noteworthy higher chosen torque levels than QS, this was not observed in this study. Instead, some participants verbally expressed that the tightenings conducted with TT were perceived as too rapid and 'jerky', and for that reason, uncomfortable. Although

TT resulted in statistically significant less reaction impulse than QS, it did not lead to significantly higher chosen tightening torque levels. Therefore, using the impulse metric as an ergonomics indicator may not provide full insight into the experience of the reaction load for the operator. For instance, the impulse metric may not account for the time needed to adjust muscle tension, which could reflect the sensation of muscle control as well as comfort [10]. Physical properties of the reaction load which account for the motion changes of the tool handle, e.g. jerk expressed in $m/s^3$, could complement the impulse and peak force metrics, and should be investigated in future work.

The findings regarding subjective ratings of discomfort did not differ much between the six experimental conditions, but suggest the different body regions were involved to varying extent, when working with the tool. The subjective ratings need to be evaluated with respect to the working posture of the participants during the experiments, as well as the orientation of the tool and joint. In this study, the participants performed tightenings on a horizontal workspace, with the tool handle positioned parallel to the floor, as seen in Fig. 1. Working in this particular posture resulted in higher perceived discomfort in the wrists and hands, shoulders and elbows, than in the upper and lower part of the back and the neck. It is plausible that other working postures would yield different subjective ratings of discomfort, as other body regions or muscles come into play. In addition, as the QS conditions where measured using a simulated tool handle with an integrated force sensor, it is plausible that this has affected the true experience of working with the tool. The simulated tool handle added an extra 1.2 kg of weight on to the tool, which likely increased the demand as it required the participants to balance it in on order to keep the tool handle parallel to the floor. This likely contributed to the discomfort sensation in the hands and arms.

As previously mentioned, additional parameters, not reported in this paper, will be reported in upcoming work. Their respective relevance as ergonomics indicators needs to be carefully assessed in order to ensure recommendations which appropriately reflect the tool use experience for the operators, and the risk of developing MSDs.

## 4.2 Discussion of Methods

The psychophysics approach used in this study was suitable for investigating the relationship between reaction loads from tightening tools and accepted load levels with respect to sustainable physical workload. However, although hypothesized that a higher work pace would result in a lower accepted load exposure, work pace did not show a significant difference in acceptability of load magnitude. This could potentially be explained by the inherent shortcomings of the psychophysics approach, inducing difficulties for the participants to discriminate between the experience when working at five and eight tightenings per minute, respectively. It should be kept in mind that the limited experimental time (30 min per condition) may not have been sufficient for the experience of working at different work paces to manifest. By increasing the experimental time and allowing for greater contrast between the work paces, such an effect may be observed.

Further, as experienced assembly workers were included in the study, the developed recommendations for reaction loads stem from a sample representing the tool user population, as opposed to studies utilizing study samples from an alternative background, e.g. students, as in the Valencia study [7].

The fact that the simulated tool handle increases the system inertia, and modifies the experience of working with the tool, motivates the need for a more appropriate measurement method to determine angle tool reaction forces, hence the ongoing development of the accelerometer method described in Sect. 2.4.

# 5  Conclusion

This study investigated reaction load exposures from tightening tool use, assessed by experienced assembly workers. The accepted load magnitudes which were perceived to enable a sustainable physical workload throughout the participants' workdays, were expressed both in terms of joint parameters, as well as parameters of the reaction load. Despite statistically significant differences in impulse exposure between the TT on hard joints and QS on medium joints, the chosen tightening torques did not significantly differ between the conditions. This suggests that other physical quantities of the reaction load generated by the tool, may contribute to the experience of reaction load exposure, and thus need further investigation. The results presented in this paper are intended to form part of a basis for recommendations for sustainable reaction load exposure from tightening tools, and continued analysis is anticipated to complement the results presented in this paper.

**Acknowledgements.** The participation of the assembly workers and their organization is greatly acknowledged, as well as the support from the research assistant, Lina Kluy, throughout the experiments. We would like to pay gratitude to the valuable contributions from other researchers, and in particular Dr. Joel Cort from University of Windsor, for continuous input.

# References

1. Potvin, J., Agnew, M., Ver Woert, C.: An ergonomic comparison of pneumatic and electrical pistol grip hand tools. Int. J. Ind. Ergon. **34**(6), 467–478 (2004)
2. Putz-Anderson, V.: Cumulative Trauma Disorders, 1st edn. Taylor & Francis Group, London (1988)
3. Mazaheri, A., Rose, L.: Reaction load exposure from handheld powered tightening tools: a scoping review. Int. J. Ind. Ergon. **81**, 103061 (2021)
4. Kihlberg, S., Kjellberg, A., Lindbeck, L.: Discomfort from pneumatic tool torque reaction: acceptability limits. Int. J. Ind. Ergon. **15**(6), 417–426 (1995)
5. Radwin, R., Chourasia, A., Fronczak, F., Subedi, Y., Howery, R., Yen, T., Sesto, M., Irwin, C.: Predicting tool operator capacity to react against torque within acceptable handle deflection limits in automotive assembly. Appl. Ergon. **54**, 205–211 (2016)
6. Snook, S., Irvine, C.: Maximum acceptable weight of lift. Am. Ind. Hygiene Assoc. J. **28**(4), 322–329 (1967)
7. Valencia, J.: Ergonomic determination of physical capability limits while using right angle power tools. https://scholar.uwindsor.ca/etd/7483. Accessed 16 Dec 2020
8. Kuorinka, I., Jonsson, B., Kilbom, A., Vinterberg, H., Biering-Sørensen, F., Andersson, G., Jørgensen, K.: Standardised Nordic questionnaires for the analysis of musculoskeletal symptoms. Appl. Ergon. **18**(3), 233–237 (1987)

 9. Borg, G.: Psychophysical scaling with applications in physical work and the perception of exertion. Scand. J. Work Environ. Health **16**(1), 55–58 (1990)
10. Zhang, L., Diraneyya, M., Ryu, J., Haas, C., Abdel-Rahman, E.: Jerk as an indicator of physical exertion and fatigue. Autom. Constr. **104**, 120–128 (2019)

# The European Machinery Directive:
# A Challenge for Manufacturers and Users

Pascal Etienne[1], Aleksandar Zunjic[2], Pedro Ferreira[3], Bernard Michez[4(✉)],
and Gyula Szabó[5]

[1] Federation of the European Ergonomic Societies, Toulouse, France
[2] Faculty of Mechanical Engineering, University of Belgrade, 11000 Belgrade, Serbia
[3] CENTEC - Centre for Marine Technology and Ocean Engineering, IST, University of Lisbon,
Lisbon, Portugal
[4] Ergotec Company, 213 Av de Muret, 31300 Toulouse, France
bernard.michez@ergotec.fr
[5] Donát Bánki Faculty of Mechanical and Safety Engineering, Óbuda University,
Budapest, Hungary

**Abstract.** The objective of the European "machinery" directive (EC/2006/42
directive) is the free movement of products in the 27 member states of the European
Union, provided that they comply with the minimum health and safety requirements for the users of these machines. All equipment imported into Europe must
meet these requirements.

Ergonomics and human factors are at the core this directive, as an increasing
number of design and operation factors are considered. For instance, a condition
to satisfy is the "reasonably forecastable misuse". Once it is explained, it becomes
very clear, and it is a condition for any product to be sold in Europe.

Ergonomics 4.0 have many strong points to valorize about this directive, and
all machine builder has to deal with this directive in order to be successful in
Europe. The industrial and commercial implications of the Directive are therefore,
increasingly meaningful for both manufacturers within and outside Europe.

This paper summaries the workshop on the EU machinery directive organized
by FEES representatives in the frame of the IEA 2021 Congress.

**Keywords:** Machinery directive · Ergonomics/human factors · Machinery
safety · Artificial intelligence · Resilience · Risk concept

## 1 Introduction

The European "machinery" directive (EC/2006/42 directive), implemented in Europe
for several decades, is an opportunity for the machines designers, the manufacturers, the
users and the ergonomists in the design and use of such products an how this work is
being transformed in a new technical, social and legal context.

The machinery directive which set up the legal frame in Europe for the machines
design presents in its Annex I the principles of safety integration (point 1.1.2 (a) and the
ergonomic principles (point 1.1.6 – Ergonomics). These principles have been usefully

N. L. Black et al. (Eds.): IEA 2021, LNNS 221, pp. 432–438, 2021.
https://doi.org/10.1007/978-3-030-74608-7_54

transposed in the specifications of the European harmonized standards, which have been adopted with the implementation of the directive and in the design of the products put on the European market, with a significant contribution of the ergonomists and the end users that will be developed later in the present paper.

In addition to the general requirements set out in section 1.1.6, the ergonomic principles must also be taken into account when applying the essential health and safety requirements (EHSRs) set out in a number of other sections of the Annex I [Guide to application for the Machinery Directive, 2006/42/EC]. So several EHSRs include important ergonomic aspects: EHSRs applicable to lighting (section 1.1.4), to handling of machinery (section 1.1.5), to operating positions (sections 1.1.7 and 1.1.8), to control devices (section 1.2.2), to emissions of hazardous materials and substances (section 1.5.13), to information (section 1.7), and so on. Such requirements are broadly understood and implemented, as we will show.

But the technological and social changes in the 2020's, (such as the digitisation of the economy, the industry 4.0, the development of the Artificial Intelligence (AI), the "uberisation", the telework, …) put on the agenda new issues. One of the aims of the present workshop is to inventory these issues and to put it on the debate.

Since the discussion and the adoption of the machinery directive in the 1980's [the first version of the «machinery» directive being the directive adopted in 1989 (/89/392/EEC), in parallel with the so called «framework» health and safety directive (89/391/EEC), several technical and social issues appeared which shape the machines design or the working conditions of its users. The present stakes may be sum up as follows:

- The industry 4.0 leans on automatization and data exchanges between specific machines with European standards. Adaptations of the legal and standard requirements are therefore on the agenda.
- Also, from the machines users' standpoint, the new company management and organization methods have significant consequences on the product and work quality, with especially the increase of psycho-social and musculo-squeletal disorders.
- In the end, machines sector is crucial at industrial at global scale with regard to the competitivity of the different economies. The upkeeping of a performing industry is based on innovation, safety of the equipment put on the market, its ability to integrate the regulatory principles and requirements. High level standards allow to protect the concerned users and economies against a low costs competition from manufacturers which do not comply with the same requirements concerning the social, safety or environmental issues.

## 2    The Impact Study Presented by the European Commission

In such a context, the impact study presented by the European Commission during the year 2020 aims to challenge the new stakes in front of the technological developments, adapting the Essential Health and Safety Requirements (ESR) of the machinery directive: addressing the challenges posed by innovation in digitization through self-regulation by market participants is not sufficient because it could create a risk of increased diverging situations, some industry stakeholders implementing stricter requirements for their products than others.

In the frame of the impact study several ongoing issues have been analyzed: the networking machines and the risks due to the connectivity defaults, the collaborative robots, the Artificial Intelligence (AI) and Machine Learning (ML), the software updating, the cybersecurity (which is beyond the machines sector). The legislation on cybersecurity is also mentioned as a good start for a further regulatory development if the legal requirements become compulsory [1].

The proposals of the impact study aim to address the problems identified during the evaluation of the Machinery Directive, such as the need of an alignment to the European New Legislative Framework (NLF) due to the harmonization of the market surveillance process and a decreasing of the non-compliant products, the adaptation/clarification of the list of the products excluded from the machinery directive, such as those covered by the "Low Voltage" directive, the improvement of the definition of "partly completed machinery", the possibility for the manufacturers to allow to end users digital formats for documentation (and a printed documentation on demand with minimal requirements in this case).

The impact study aims also to suppress the internal checks for the products listed in Annex IV of the current MD, which includes types of high-risk machinery that is to be assessed through internal checks, only if the machinery is manufactured in full accordance with harmonized standards. For the manufacturers of annex IV machines, it could mean higher costs for the conformity assessment due to the conformity assessment costs by a third party for each of the product listed in this Annex. However, the study concludes that the stakeholders consider that internal checks of the Annex IV machines engender safety problems.

All these issues are being discussed in the frame of the experts group set up by the European Commission and should be arbitrated at the beginning of the year 2021.

## 3   The Proposals Mentioned in the European Commission Projects

The IEA workshop has given the opportunity to present and evaluate, according to the ergonomics knowledge and requirements, the proposal issued by the European Commission, under discussion in the frame of the above-mentioned Expert Group, that FEES attends (and which is made of the main concerned stakeholders).

In the proposal, the Commission leans on the "White Paper" on AI (February 2020) which outlined the objective of the Commission to propose a new legislation covering safety and fundamental requirements for AI systems.

The main aims of the revision are to cover new risks related to digital emerging technologies (AI, IoT, robotics) and to update the essential health and safety requirements, especially the ergonomics requirements, to ensure a coherent interpretation of the directive scope throughout the different European Union countries, to reassess the machines considered as high risk and the related conformity assessment procedure, to reduce paper-based requirements for documentation, to ensure coherence with the so called NLF legislation (the New Legislative Framework concerning the market surveillance of the products).

A proposition of the machinery Directive modification is announced during the year 2021.

## 4  The Stakes for the Designers and the Buyers

The global stake for the equipment designers/manufacturers and the purchasers is about competitiveness, but not only. One may identify three main fields:

- Health/Safety/Security: the key word to define the situations in which the machines are used is "Variability". Experience shows that the operators adapt themselves to these situations, but sometimes with consequences for health, safety and security. That is the aim of the "reasonably foreseeable misuse" clause, specified by the European directive: to take variability into account. Methods exist that ensure the identification of the variabilities, in order to integrate them in the design and the use of the machines.
- Productivity/Quality: to define achievable aims and shape the installation in line with it. The returns of experience show that the investment returns are not always met as expected. Along with the issue of the compliance with the design requirements comes the adequacy of the machines with the needs related with a given production or service. With that aim also, methods can provide answers.
- Liability: the industrial accident is nowadays unacceptable, for the public control bodies, and for the population where the installations are located. Even though the risk can never be completely avoided, the present methods allow to eliminate a range of co-factors, in the core design of the installation. This reassures the buyer of the installation, who plans to use it for a long time. With the purchase of the equipment, a transfer of responsibility is declared between the supplier and the purchaser. In the event of an accident, compliance of use with the specifications will be sought, and the responsibility of the user is involved most of the time.

The production or the sale of machines (from the simplest one to the nuclear power plants) does not represent the end of obligations for producers or sellers. For most of the machines, producers or sellers maintain relationships with the buyers for service, maintenance, or repair, for example. In addition, in all cases, producers and sellers are responsible to the customers in accordance with the notion of product liability. In the United States, the issue of product liability has taken on increasing importance, to the point that producers and sellers must give advance attention to such liability in designing, producing, as well as selling products [1]. The liability issue applies equally to products that are used in industry (machines, tools, etc.), as well as to devices purchased by consumers (household appliances, etc.).

In essence, cases of product liability are usually tried under one of the next bodies of law [2]: (a) negligence, which tests the conduct of the defendant; (b) strict liability, which tests the quality of the product; (c) implied warranty, which also tests the quality of the product; and (d) express warranty and misrepresentation, which tests the performance of a product against the explicit representations made about it by the manufacturer or sellers. Three types of defects that are usually involved in product liability cases are: design defects, manufacturing defects, and warning defects [3–5].

Although sellers are mostly liable for express warranty and misrepresentation, here does not ends their responsibility. Before they sell machines, they should check, from their side, the compliance of a machine with the Machinery Directive. It should be done at least on the global level. Such approach will additionally minimize the possibility of appearance of product liability cases.

## 5   Dealing with the Changing Nature of Risk

Beyond the rules established in the European machinery directive, it is necessary to integrate the technological revolutions underway. These very significant changes require rethinking the role of operators in the facilities, as well as the means given to them.

The concept of industry 4.0 leans on automation and data exchanges between specific machines. Adaptations of the legal and standard requirements are therefore on the agenda and this is the remit of the ongoing review of the EU Machine Directive. However, this cannot possibly addressed without considering the wider implications of technological and social changes, namely those resulting from the broader digitisation of the economy, the fast development of Artificial Intelligence (AI), and the teleworking phenomena that has so rapidly come to be in the centre of so many workers worldwide [6]. To a great extent, these are already ongoing transformations, but are expected to further accelerate within the upcoming years, and the way they may come to shape remains significantly unclear.

All aspects of economic and social life are becoming increasingly interconnected and tightly coupled. This is undoubtedly at the source of many widespread, profound and unexpected impacts across entire supply chains and even industry sectors. This has motivated important discussions around new safety perspectives and practices. An example of this can be found under the scope of "Safety II [7], which has registered significant conceptual and industry applied developments. At the core of the Safety II notion is the need to better understand the variability of "real work" in order to develop the ability to successfully adjust to continuously changing operational conditions.

Despite progress, the pace at which technology is transforming societies and their economies, clearly outweighs the capacity to mature new safety and risk thinking, transform industry-based practices, and update normative and legal references. This is recognised in different ways within the scope of the Machine Directive, namely through the provision of the "reasonably foreseeable misuse" clause. The aim is to enhance the way which variability and unpredictability are contemplated in the design and use of machines.

The idea of "resilience by design" aims to tackle similar challenges, although this has been mainly applied in the scope of societal change and disaster related risk [8]. The challenge here is not only the design and use of technology but often, also the design of large-scale infrastructure that must withstand several decades of operation under increasingly unpredictable and dynamic social and environmental conditions [9, 10]. Machinery and technology in general remain critical, as such large-scale infrastructures are increasingly reliant on remote assets, whose operation is centrally monitored and controlled through automation and high output communication technologies.

Keeping pace with high dynamics and increasingly unpredictable systems cannot singly rely on human's ability to adjust performance. Technology must integrate enhanced degrees of adaptability, so that it may effectively (and cost efficiently) be adjusted to ever changing operational conditions and demands. Integrating such adaptive capacities in technological systems must therefore be at the core of "resilience by design" [8]. Some progress is noticeable and the inclusion of thinking forward provisions, namely the "reasonably foreseeable misuse" clause, can steer further meaningful improvements. However, the path towards applying the principles of "reasonability" and "foreseeable misuse" in a meaningful and effective way remains as unknown as the challenges ahead of Industry 4.0.

### 5.1 Machinery Safety at Workplaces

The national regulations implementing the provisions of the EU Directives relating to health and safety at work are based on the articles relating to the protection of workers' health and safety. They set out minimum requirements, which means that Member States remain free to maintain or adopt more stringent requirements if they see fit. The most important Directives relating to the use of machinery are: the Council Directive 89/391/EEC of 12 June 1989 on the safety and health of workers at work and Directive 2009/104/EC125 on the use of work equipment by workers at work. This is the second individual Directive adopted under the "Framework" Directive.

Although the concept of work equipment is broader than that of machinery, machinery for professional use constitutes an important category of work equipment. Directive 2009/104/EC can be considered as a measure complementary to the Machinery Directive: employers are required to make available to workers work equipment that is suitable for the work to be carried out and which complies with the provisions of any relevant EU Directive which is applicable to it.

Consequently, all new machinery made available to workers must comply with the Machinery Directive and any other EU Directives that may be applicable. During the lifetime of the machinery, the employer must take the measures necessary to ensure that machinery in service is kept, by means of adequate maintenance, at a level such that it complies with the provisions that were applicable when it was first made available in the undertaking or establishment. This does not mean that the machinery must be maintained in an "as new" condition, since it is subject to wear. But the necessary maintenance must be carried out to ensure that it continues to comply with the applicable health and safety requirements. To do so, the employer must follow in particular the manufacturer's instructions (cf section 1.7.4.2 (r) of Annex I).

## 6 Conclusion

The European Machinery Directive is one of the tools to improve the safety, security and productivity of equipment as well as the health of operators. It is part of a network of standards which take into account the knowledge acquired to date. Compliance with this directive is a condition for the marketing of machines, and it is a stake for manufacturers. It is also a stake for buyers, who must ensure the conformity of the machines when they are received. This will result in the presence of human factors specialists as much among designers as among buyers.

# References

1. Szabó, G.: Usability of machinery. In: Advances in Intelligent Systems and Computing, vol. 604, pp. 161–168, 8 p. (2018). https://doi.org/10.1007/978-3-319-60525-8_17. ISBN 9783319605241
2. Sanders, M.S., McCormick, E.J.: Human Factors in Engineering and Design, 7th edn. McGRAW-HILL, INC., Singapore (1993)
3. Lawson, B.D., Graeber, D.A., Mead, A.M., Muth, E.R.: Signs and symptoms of human syndromes associated with synthetic experiences. In: Stanney, K.M. (ed.) Handbook of Virtual Environments – Design, Implementation, and Applications, pp. 589–618. Lawrence Erlbaum Associates Inc., Mahwah (2002)
4. Wann, J.P., Mon-Williams, M.: Measurement of visual aftereffects following virtual environment exposure. In: Stanney, K.M. (ed.) Handbook of Virtual Environments – Design, Implementation, and Applications, pp. 731–750. Lawrence Erlbaum Associates Inc., Mahwah (2002)
5. May, J.G., Badcock, D.R.: Vision and virtual environments. In: Stanney, K.M. (ed.) Handbook of Virtual Environments – Design, Implementation, and Applications, pp. 29–64. Lawrence Erlbaum Associates Inc., Mahwah (2002)
6. Kennedy, R.S., Kennedy, K.E., Bartlett, K.M.: Virtual environments and product liability. In: Stanney, K.M. (ed.) Handbook of Virtual Environments – Design, Implementation, and Applications, pp. 543–554. Lawrence Erlbaum Associates Inc., Mahwah (2002)
7. Hollnagel, E.: Safety-I and Safety-II: The Past and Future of Safety Management. Ashgate, Aldershot (2014)
8. Brown, C., Boltz, F., Freeman, S., Tront, J., Rodriguez, D.: Resilience by design: a deep uncertainty approach for water systems in a changing world. Water Secur. 9, 100051 (2020)
9. CEN/TR 16710-1:2015 Ergonomics methods - Part 1: Feedback method - A method to understand how end users perform their work with machines (2015)
10. Strambi, F., Bartalini, M., Boy, S., Gauthy, R., Landozzi, R., Novelli, D., Stanzani, C.: End users "feedback" to improve ergonomic design of machinery. Work 41(SUPPL.1), 1212–1220 (2012). https://doi.org/10.3233/WOR-2012-0305-1212

# Reduced Work Pace in a Poultry Slaughterhouse

Diogo Cunha dos Reis[1][(⊠)] ⓘ, Adriana Seara Tirloni[2] ⓘ,
and Antônio Renato Pereira Moro[1,2] ⓘ

[1] Biomechanics Laboratory, Federal University of Santa Catarina, Florianópolis, SC, Brazil
[2] Technological Center, CDS, Federal University of Santa Catarina, Florianópolis, SC, Brazil

**Abstract.** Slaughterhouse workers are often exposed to many biomechanical risk factors that contribute to the development of upper-limb work-related musculoskeletal disorders (UL-WMSD). Therefore, the aim of this study was to evaluate the risks in relation to repetitive movements of the upper limbs in a poultry slaughterhouse, as well as analyze the effects of a reduced work pace on the risk levels. The study was conducted in a slaughterhouse with 1,500 workers, who were divided into two shifts, where 150,000 chickens were slaughtered daily. The OCRA checklist was implemented to assess 10% of the total workforce. The Student t-test was applied to examine the difference between the risks of both sides of the body ($p \leq 0.05$). The 14 analyzed work tasks were from the sectors: cutting (8), packing (5) and reception (1). The workers performed $72.8 \pm 15.3$ actions per minute (10/10 points on the OCRA scale). The average score of the OCRA checklist was $23.4 \pm 4.4$ (high risk). The scores for the right upper limb ($23.1 \pm 4.8$ - high risk) were not significantly different ($p = 0.175$) than the left ($21.8 \pm 5.2$ - moderate risk). Considering the five risk categories of the OCRA method, 10 tasks were deemed high risk (71%) and 4 presented moderate risk (29%). By conducting simulations, it was possible to reduce the risk to a very low level in 13 of the 14 tasks by only decreasing the work pace ($-56.9 \pm 10.4\%$). In this way, simulations of a reduced work pace showed the effectiveness of this organizational measure in lowering the risk of UL-WMSD.

**Keywords:** Risk assessment · WMSD · OCRA · Slaughterhouse · Ergonomics

## 1 Introduction

The organization of work in meat processing companies still follows the assumptions of the Taylorist-Fordist system, centered on production goals, without respecting the employees' psychophysiological characteristics or more rational methods aimed at reducing the risks inherent to work. In this production model, the prevalence of health problems considers an accelerated work pace as one of the main aggravating factors [1]. As Brazil is one of the world's leaders in meat production and exportation [2] it further exacerbates this situation, due to the large product volume that is processed manually (cuts).

In this context, the OCRA method resulted from a consensus document established by the Technical Committee on Musculoskeletal Disorders of the International Ergonomics

N. L. Black et al. (Eds.): IEA 2021, LNNS 221, pp. 439–444, 2021.
https://doi.org/10.1007/978-3-030-74608-7_55

Association (IEA) endorsed by the International Commission on Occupational Health (ICOH) [3]. This method was developed to evaluate workers' exposure to tasks featuring many upper-limb injury risk factors (repetitiveness, lack of recovery periods, force requirement, awkward postures and movements, and 'additional factors') [4].

Several recent studies have examined the work-related musculoskeletal disorders (WMSD) risks in poultry slaughterhouse workers [5–13], using the OCRA method. This sequence of studies is justified since each slaughterhouse has its particularities, producing different types of products/cuts, which require diverse work activities, and consequently, expose workers to various occupational risks.

For that reason, the aim of this study was to assess the risks in relation to repetitive movements of the upper limbs in a poultry slaughterhouse, as well as analyze the effects of a reduced work pace on the risk levels.

## 2 Method

In accordance with the Declaration of Helsinki, the local Human Research Ethics Committee approved the procedures for this study.

The analysis was conducted in a Brazilian slaughterhouse with 1,500 workers, where 150,000 chickens were slaughtered daily, divided into two work shifts. In order to evaluate the risks related with repetitive movements of the upper limbs, 10% of the workforce was assessed while carrying out their work tasks, by means of the OCRA checklist [4]. The evaluated tasks were considered individually, regardless of whether they were part of job rotation schemes. A sampling of 10 cycles for each activity was recorded with a Sony® HDR-XR160 camera.

Based on the results of the evaluation using the OCRA checklist, simulated interventions were made to achieve borderline risk levels by reducing the work pace for each of the investigated activities. The scores for each risk factor were weighted in proportion to the proposed work pace reductions.

Descriptive statistics were used (mean, standard deviation and percentage), as well as the Student t-test, in order to compare the risk between both sides of the workers' body (SPSS 17.0; $p \leq 0.05$).

## 3 Results and Discussion

The 14 analyzed work activities were from the following sectors: cutting (8), packing (5) and reception (1) (Table 1).

Each work shift totaled 08 h 48 min, including six rest breaks of 10 min each, thus, the net repetitive work time was classified in the range of 421 to 480 min ('duration' multiplier 1). For the risk factor 'recovery', the multiplier 1.05 was assigned for all tasks examined. In order to achieve the ideal multiplier (1.0) associated with the 'recovery' factor (5:1 ratio work time to recovery time), it would be necessary to allocate at least one more rest break. Insufficient rest breaks for the recovery of fatigue caused by repetitive work in the industry can lead to muscle injuries [14]. In a study testing the inclusion of extra rest breaks in a meat processing plant, Dababneh et al. [15] established that taking

**Table 1.** The OCRA Checklist risk assessment and simulations to reduce the risk by decreasing the work pace.

| Tasks | Current situation | | | | Simulations for risk reduction | | | |
|---|---|---|---|---|---|---|---|---|
| | Units /min | TA/ min | OCRA score | Risk level | Units /min | TA/ min | OCRA score | Risk level |
| Sealing packages | 1.5 | 72.0 | 37.0 | 5 | # | # | # | # |
| Packing boneless leg | 4.8 | 76.8 | 25.0 | 5 | 2.5 | 25.0 | 11.0 | 2 |
| Re-hanging chicken – A | 25.0 | 75.0 | 25.0 | 5 | 15.0 | 30.0 | 11.0 | 2 |
| Re-hanging chicken – B | 35.3 | 70.6 | 25.0 | 5 | 15.0 | 30.0 | 11.0 | 2 |
| Slitting legs – cone | 17.1 | 85.7 | 23.0 | 5 | 6.0 | 30.0 | 11.0 | 2 |
| Weighing boneless leg | 50.0 | 100.0 | 23.0 | 5 | 17.0 | 35.0 | 11.0 | 2 |
| Trimming breast | 7.0 | 76.7 | 23.0 | 5 | 2.7 | 30.0 | 11.0 | 2 |
| Removing sassami | 17.1 | 85.7 | 23.0 | 5 | 6.0 | 30.0 | 11.0 | 2 |
| Packing breast – trays | 1.7 | 72.0 | 23.0 | 5 | 0.7 | 30.0 | 11.0 | 2 |
| Boning leg | 3.8 | 90.0 | 23.0 | 5 | 1.3 | 30.0 | 11.0 | 2 |
| Labeling packages | 31.6 | 63.2 | 20.0 | 4 | 15.8 | 30.0 | 11.0 | 2 |
| Hanging live chickens | 16.0 | 48.0 | 20.0 | 4 | 10.0 | 30.0 | 11.0 | 2 |
| Removing breast and wing | 17.1 | 51.4 | 19.0 | 4 | 10.0 | 30.0 | 11.0 | 2 |
| Removing leg | 17.1 | 51.4 | 19.0 | 4 | 10.0 | 30.0 | 11.0 | 2 |
| Average | 17.5 | 72.8 | 23.4 | 5 | 8.6 | 30.0 | 11.0 | 2 |
| Standard-deviation | 14.1 | 15.3 | 4.4 | – | 5.9 | 2.0 | 0,0 | – |

Risks: 5-high; 4-medium; 3-low; 2-very low; 1-acceptable; TA-technical actions; # The task needs to be restructured due to the high force requirement.

hourly rest breaks does not compromise production and are beneficial to the workers' well-being.

The scores of the other risk factors considered by the OCRA checklist (frequency of technical actions, posture with stereotyped movements, force, and 'additional factors') were assigned according to the features of each task and the technique adopted by each worker.

The occupational repetitive actions performed by workers were 72.8 ± 15.3 per minute, representing 10 points on the OCRA scale (0- to10-point scale). (Table 1). Many studies have also shown a high frequency of technical actions in poultry slaughterhouses, with averages between 63.7 and 79.8 [6, 8–11, 13, 16]. As recommended by Kilbom

[14], workers must not exceed 25–33 actions/min. to prevent tendon injuries, since higher rates offer insufficient time to recover from fatigue between muscle contractions (micropauses).

The work in chicken processing industries is repetitive, strenuous and exposes workers to overuse injuries [17]. Upon arrival to the slaughterhouse, the live chickens are received and subsequently introduced to a production line that requires workers to hang, slaughter, pluck, clean, eviscerate, cut, pack and box chicken parts at a fast pace. In addition, the workers clean and repair equipment, assemble boxes and move packaged chicken pallets.

The average OCRA checklist score was $23.4 \pm 4.4$ (high risk), and there was no significant difference (p $= 0.175$) between the scores on the right upper limb ($23.1 \pm 4.8$ – high risk) and left upper limb ($21.8 \pm 5.2$ – moderate risk). Reis et al. [8] analyzed 30 poultry slaughterhouse tasks and found similar results ($22.8 \pm 5.6$ points – high risk). On the other hand, most studies in Brazilian slaughterhouses have obtained a moderate risk level [5–7, 9, 10, 12, 13]. In an Italian poultry slaughterhouse, Colombini and Occhipinti [4] discovered that 22.4% of workers exposed to moderate risk tasks (an average of 20 points on the OCRA Checklist) were diagnosed with UL-WMSD (based on clinical evaluations and complementary medical examinations).

Although the OCRA method classifies the WMSD risk in 5 categories, in the analyzed slaughterhouse, only two levels were detected, high (10 tasks) and moderate (4 tasks). Even though some studies have found that high-risk activities prevail in slaughterhouses in Brazil (56.5%, 55%, respectively) [5, 11], Italy (90%) [16] and Iran (67%) [18], many recent studies indicate that moderate-risk activities predominate in Brazilian slaughterhouses [6–10]. These studies speculated that the reduction of high-risk activities may be interrelated to the promulgation of the Brazilian Regulatory Standard n° 36 (NR-36) [19]. This standard establishes parameters for the assessment, monitoring and controlling occupational risks in meat processing industries [19]. Among the parameters defined by NR-36, the mandatory inclusion of rest break periods directly influences the results of the OCRA checklist [19]. When meeting these parameters, the exposure time to repetitive work was reduced throughout the Brazilian meat processing industry. According to the analyses using the OCRA checklist, the 'recovery' score is reduced, and consequently, the UL-WMSD risk decreases as well.

The creators of the OCRA method [4], based on epidemiological data, developed hypotheses of WMSD disease prevalence according to the occupational conditions [4]. Specific percentages were determined for each level of WMSD incidence. As an example of precursor studies of the method, Colombini and Occhipinti [4] found an incidence of 47.7% of WMSD in meat deboning workers, who were classified with a high risk (28 points) on the OCRA checklist. In that same sense, most workers assessed in the present study had a probability of developing WMSD greater than 21.51% (high-risk tasks).

Considering that repetitive movements of the upper limbs are prevalent in poultry slaughterhouses [5, 6, 8–11, 20], studies have suggested that a reduced work pace decreases the WMSD risk in chicken slaughterhouses [5, 6, 8–11]. Thus, simulated interventions were executed, reducing the work pace to reach very low risk levels on the OCRA checklist. By conducting these simulated interventions, it was possible to reduce the UL-WMSD risk to very low levels in 13 of the 14 tasks by only decreasing the work pace ($-56.9 \pm 10.4\%$). One of the tasks ('sealing the packages') was unachievable because of the high demand for strength required to perform this task. Likewise, previous studies also carried out simulated interventions to lower the risk by reducing the work pace ($-42.1 \pm 14.5\%$; $-44.9 \pm 13.7\%$; $-48.5 \pm 11.8\%$; $-38.8 \pm 4.8\%$ and $-50.4 \pm 7.7\%$, respectively) and were effective in most cases (24/26, 28/30, 15/15, 33/35 and 46/47 tasks, respectively), except for those activities with excessive demand for strength. [6, 8–11].

## 4 Conclusion

Given the results of this study, it is possible to conclude that:

- Most of the work activities analyzed were classified as high risk, predisposing the workforce to a WMSD incidence greater than 21.51%;
- The risk of developing WMSD is similar for both sides of the body;
- Simulated interventions that reduce the work pace demonstrated the effectiveness of this organizational measure to reduce the WMSD risk in most of the analyzed tasks.

Finally, it is suggested that several organizational measures should be considered to decrease the WMSD risk: increase the workforce in each task, reduce the work pace, take rest breaks every hour, implement efficient job rotation (between activities with different biomechanical demands), keep knives sharp (avoid unnecessary effort), and monitor the risk level of work tasks using quantitative tools, such as the OCRA checklist.

## References

1. Sardá, S., Ruiz, R.C., Kirtschig, G.: Juridical tutelage concerning the health of meat packing workers: public service considerations. Acta Fisiatrica 16, 59–65 (2009)
2. Brazilian Association of Animal Protein: Annual Report 2020. https://www.abpa-br.org/rel atorios. Accessed 08 Dec 2020
3. Colombini, D., Occhipinti, E., Delleman, D., Fallentin, N., Kilbom, A., Grieco, A.: Exposure assessment of upper limb repetitive movements: a consensus document. In: Karwowski, W. (ed.) International Encyclopedia of Ergonomics and Human Factors, Taylor & Francis, New York (2001)
4. Colombini, D., Occhipinti, E.: Risk Analysis and Management of Repetitive Actions: A Guide for Applying the OCRA System. CRC Press, New York (2016)
5. Reis, D.C., Reis, P.F., Moro, A.R.P.: Assessment of risk factors of musculoskeletal disorders in poultry slaughterhouse. In: Azeres, P., Baptista, J.S., Barroso, M.P., Carneiro, P., Cordeiro, P., Costa, N., Melo, R., Miguel, A.S., Perestrelo, G. (Org.) SHO 2015, 1st edn., vol. 1, pp. 294–296. SPOSHO, Guimarães - Portugal (2015)
6. Reis, D.C., Ramos, E., Reis, P.F., Hembecker, P.K., Gontijo, L.A., Moro, A.R.P.: Assessment of risk factors of upper-limb musculoskeletal disorders in poultry slaughterhouse. Proc. Manuf. 3, 4309–4314 (2015)
7. Reis, D.C., Moro, A.R.P., Ramos, E., Reis, P.F.: Upper limbs exposure to biomechanical overload: occupational risk assessment in a poultry slaughterhouse. In: Goonetilleke, R., Karwowski, W. (eds.) Advances in Physical Ergonomics and Human Factors, vol. 489, pp. 275–282. Springer, Cham (2016)

8. Reis, D.C., Tirloni, A.S., Ramos, E., Moro, A.R.P.: Assessment of risk factors of upper-limb musculoskeletal disorders in a chicken slaughterhouse. Jpn. J. Ergon. **53**, 458–461 (2017)
9. Reis, D.C., Tirloni, A.S., Ramos, E., Dias, N.F., Moro, A.R.P.: Risk assessment of repetitive movements of the upper limbs in a chicken slaughterhouse. In: Bagnara, S., Tartaglia, R., Albolino, S., Alexander, T., Fujita, Y. (eds.) Proceedings of the 20th Congress of the International Ergonomics Association (IEA 2018). Advances in Intelligent Systems and Computing, vol. 825, pp. 323–329. Springer, Cham (2019)
10. Reis, D.C., Tirloni, A.S., Moro, A.R.P.: Risk assessment of upper limb musculoskeletal disorders in a poultry slaughterhouse. In: Arezes, P. (ed.) Advances in Safety Management and Human Factors. AHFE 2019. Advances in Intelligent Systems and Computing, vol. 969, pp. 265–272. Springer, Cham (2020)
11. Reis, D.C., Tirloni, A.S., Moro, A.R.P.: Effects of reduced work pace on the risk of developing upper-limb musculoskeletal disorders in a poultry slaughterhouse. In: Karwowski, W., Goonetilleke, R., Xiong, S., Goossens, R., Murata, A. (eds.) Advances in Physical, Social & Occupational Ergonomics. AHFE 2020. Advances in Intelligent Systems and Computing, vol. 1215, pp. 87–94. Springer, Cham (2020)
12. Dias, N.F., Tirloni, A.S., Reis, D.C., Moro, A.R.P.: Effect of job rotation on the risk of developing UI-WMSDS in poultry slaughterhouse workers. Braz. J. Poultry Sci. **21**(2), 1–12 (2019). eRBCA-2018-0843
13. Dias, N.F., Tirloni, A.S., Reis, D.C., Moro, A.R.P.: Risk of slaughterhouse workers developing work-related musculoskeletal disorders in different organizational working conditions. Int. J. Ind. Ergon. **76**, 102929 (2020)
14. Kilbom, A.: Repetitive work of the upper extremity: part II—the scientific basis (knowledge-base) for the guide. Int. J. Ind. Ergon. **14**, 59–86 (1994)
15. Dababneh, A.J., Swanson, N., Shell, R.L.: Impact of added rest breaks on the productivity and well-being of workers. Ergonomics **44**(2), 164–174 (2001)
16. Colombini, D., Occhipinti, E.: Results of risk and impairment assessment in groups of workers exposed to repetitive strain and movement of the upper limbs in various sectors of industry. La Medicina del Lavoro **95**, 233–246 (2004)
17. Cartwright, M.S., Walker, F.O., Blocker, J.N., Schulz, M.R., Arcury, T.A., Grzywacz, J.G., Mora, D., Chen, H., Marín, A.J., Quandt, S.A.: The prevalence of carpal tunnel syndrome in Latino poultry processing workers and other Latino manual workers. J. Occup. Environ. Med. **54**(2), 198–201 (2012)
18. Mohammadi, G.: Risk factors for the prevalence of the upper limb and neck work-related musculoskeletal disorders among poultry slaughter workers. J. Musculoskelet. Res. **15**, 1250005 (2012)
19. Brasil: Norma Regulamentadora 36. Segurança e Saúde no Trabalho em Empresas de Abate e Processamento de Carnes e Derivados, Ministério do Trabalho e Emprego, Portaria MTE n. 555, de 18 de abril de 2013, Diário Oficial da União (2013)
20. Sundstrup, E., Jakobsen, M.D., Jay, K., Brandt, M., Andersen, L.L.: High intensity physical exercise and pain in the neck and upper limb among slaughterhouse workers: cross-sectional study. BioMed Res. Int. **2014**, 1–6 (2014). 218546

# Application of SHERPA (Systematic Human Error Reduction and Prediction Approach) as an Alternative to Predict and Prevent Human Error in Manual Assembly

Yaniel Torres[1]([⊠]) (iD), Sylvie Nadeau[1] (iD), and Kurt Landau[1,2]

[1] Department of Mechanical Engineering, École de technologie supérieure (ÉTS), 1100 Notre-Dame St W, Montreal, QC H3C 1K3, Canada
yaniel.torres-medina.1@ens.etsmtl.ca, sylvie.nadeau@etsmtl.ca
[2] Institute of Ergonomics and Human Factors, Technische Universität Darmstadt, Otto-Berndt-Straße 2, 64287 Darmstadt, Germany
office@ioa-online.at

**Abstract.** Human reliability analysis (HRA) has been identified as a key approach to improve quality in the manufacturing sector. This paper presents the results of the application of SHERPA to a manual assembly task case in the electronic industry, i.e., the assembly of a printed circuit board. It also compares the use of SHERPA with other HRA techniques in a manufacturing context. A total of 16 subtasks were obtained from the breakdown of the task that was the object of study and 12 error modes were identified based on SHERPA taxonomy: eight action errors, two checking errors, and two selection errors. The use of SHERPA provides a useful framework for identifying human errors in manual assembly even though this technique was not specifically developed for manufacturing. The analysis of human errors in manufacturing needs to consider and integrate a vocabulary harmonized with production planning. Comparison between SHERPA and other HRA techniques shows that the focus of the analysis should be placed on error identification rather than the calculation of error probabilities. A semi-quantitative index could help to reconcile these approaches by identifying and evaluating error modes in their propensity to occur, without the need for an accurate estimation of error probabilities.

**Keywords:** Human error · Manual assembly · Quality · Human reliability · Manufacturing

## 1 Introduction

Manual work and particularly manual assembly tasks are sensitive to human error and represent a potential source of quality issues. Many error-related quality issues are frequently found in manual assembly, including loose connections, missing components, installation of wrong components, or wrong torque applications [1]. In this regard, Bubb [2] argues that human reliability analysis (HRA) represents a key element to improve

© The Author(s), under exclusive license to Springer Nature Switzerland AG 2021
N. L. Black et al. (Eds.): IEA 2021, LNNS 221, pp. 445–453, 2021.
https://doi.org/10.1007/978-3-030-74608-7_56

quality in the manufacturing sector. Despite this, human reliability research has been mostly focused on safety-critical domains and less attention has been placed on the manufacturing sector [3]. According to Embrey [4], the essence of human reliability analysis (HRA) is the prediction and mitigation of error to optimize safety, reliability and productivity. The present paper shows the application of SHERPA (Systematic Human Error Reduction and Prediction Approach) to a case study of an electronic assembly task found in the literature [2]. Similar to the research conducted by Torres et al. [5], we assume that classic HRA techniques can provide a structured framework for the analysis of human error in manual assembly. The paper aims to explore the advantages and limitations of using SHERPA in manufacturing and compares it with other alternatives.

## 1.1  The SHERPA Technique

SHERPA is intended to provide guidelines for human error reduction and quantification in a wide range of human-machine systems [6]. Once the task to be analyzed is selected, Hierarchical Task Analysis (HTA) is used to break down the task [7]. Subsequently, a taxonomy of human error is used to identify specific error modes as illustrated in Table 1. The general methodology is similar to both FMEA [8] and HAZOP [9], techniques used in engineering risk analyses. SHERPA includes a second module for quantifying human error probabilities. The main steps in the application of SHERPA are as follows:

1. Breakdown of the task using Hierarchical Task Analysis (HTA)
2. Identification of error mode using TACT (Table 1)
3. Error mode description
4. Risk evaluation (Consequence x Probability)
5. Identification of corrective strategies

**Table 1.**  Task Activity Classification Taxonomy (TACT)

| Actions | Checking | Communication |
|---|---|---|
| A1 Operation too long/short | C1 Check omitted | R4 Information incorrectly interpreted |
| A2 Operation mistimed | C2 Check incomplete | I2 Wrong information communicated |
| A3 Operation in wrong direction | C3 Right check on wrong object | I3 Information communication incomplete |
| A4 Operation too little/too much | C4 Wrong check on right object | I4 Information communication unclear |
| A5 Operation too fast/too slow | C5 Check too early/late | |

(*continued*)

**Table 1.** (*continued*)

| Actions | Checking | Communication |
|---|---|---|
| A6 Misalign | Information retrieval | Selection |
| A7 Right operation on wrong object | R1 Information not obtained | S1 Selection omitted |
| A8 Wrong operation on right object | R2 Wrong information obtained | S2 Wrong selection |
| A9 Operation omitted | R3 Information retrieval incomplete | |
| A10 Operation incomplete | R4 Information incorrectly interpreted | |
| A11 Operation too early/late | | |
| A12 Operation in wrong order | | |
| A13 Misplacement | | |

## 2   Material and Methods

SHERPA was used as the methodology framework to conduct an analysis of human error. This choice is based on considerations crucial to the manufacturing context: time, simplicity, availability of information, levels of validation and an analyst-oriented approach all of these previously evaluated in different reviews [10, 11]. Only the module for human error identification was used and risk evaluation was excluded. The case represents the assembly of a printed electronic board by a worker on a production line in the electronic industry. This assembly case is taken from Bubb [2] who already used it to illustrate the application of HRA technique THERP (Technique for Human Error Rate Prediction).

### 2.1   Assembly Case

A group of components is to be assembled and fixed by soldering onto a small printed circuit board (PCB). The components are one connection socket S, two different resistors R1 and R2, a capacitor (C), and an integrated circuit (IC) coupled to the socket. All these parts are placed in storage containers on the workstation while the PCB is placed directly on the workstation. The PCB structure and the main general steps in the execution of the task can be seen in Fig. 1.

The assembler takes socket S from the storage container on the workstation and places it on the printed circuit board (PCB). Similarly, the assembler takes resistor R1 from the storage container, bends the resistor's wire ends, and puts the resistor on the circuit board. He/she proceeds in the same way for resistor R2. Then, capacitor C is taken from a storage container and placed on the PCB. Once all these parts are placed on the PCB, the assembler carefully turns the printed circuit over, careful not to make any loose elements fall off. At this point, the assembler verifies that all pins are in place.

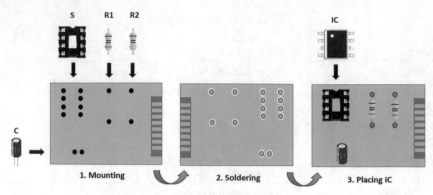

**Fig. 1.** Schematic representation of the assembly task in a series production line in the electronic industry. The task was initially presented by Bubb (2005).

Then, he/she solders the 14 wire pins using an electric soldering iron and soldering filler. After this, the assembler verifies that the wire pins are solidly affixed before turning over the PCB back to its initial position. Finally, the assembler takes the IC from the storage container and affixes it to the PCB by applying force.

## 3   Results

The breakdown of the task was done using HTA. A total of 16 subtasks were obtained in the last level of the hierarchy diagram which is presented in Appendix A. Then, using SHERPA, a total of 12 error modes were identified: eight action errors, two checking errors and two selection errors. These error modes were associated with seven out of the 16 subtasks analyzed. Table 2 shows a condensed description of the output obtained with SHERPA.

**Table 2.**   SHERPA output – human error analysis table

| Task step | Error mode | Description | Consequence | Recovery | Remedial strategy |
|---|---|---|---|---|---|
| 1.1.2 | A6 A3 | Possibility of bending a pin Socket installed in wrong direction | Damage to socket/need to replace Circuit not functional | Immediate Check correct sides | Check the pins before soldering Error-proofing design |
| 1.2.1 | S2 | Take wrong resistors from storage containers | Wrong resistors installed | Check serial number | Use colour codes on storage bins |

(*continued*)

**Table 2.** (*continued*)

| Task step | Error mode | Description | Consequence | Recovery | Remedial strategy |
|---|---|---|---|---|---|
| 1.3.1 | S2 | Take wrong resistor from storage containers | Wrong resistor installed | Check serial number | Use colour codes on storage bins |
| 2.1 | A10 | Poor hold. Elements fall out when the PCB is turned over | Damage to one or more components | | Use temporary glue to keep components in place |
| 2.2 | A9 A4 A4 | Omission of some soldering pins Not enough heat with soldering iron Too much heat with soldering iron | Circuit not functional Wire pins not solidly affixed Damage to the circuit board | 2.3 2.3 2.3 | Better tracking and guidance Semi-automatic soldering iron Idem |
| 2.3 | C1 C2 | Omission to verify soldering Omission to verify one or more soldered pins | Quality issues not detected Quality issues not detected | Final test Final test | Automated visual inspection/human redundancy Idem |
| 3.2 | A3 A4 | IC installed in wrong direction Too much force used to couple the IC to socket | Circuit not functional Electric connection damaged | Check white dot markers Final test | Direction arrow symbol |

# 4  Discussion

The results shown in Table 2 provide a portrait of the different error modes associated with the task object of analysis including possible remedial strategies. For example, a semi-automatic soldering iron can be used to gain better control of the soldering process [12]. The temperature can be set according to the task's parameter and the speed at which the solder wire is fed can be adjusted. This can support the assembler and increase the performance of the soldering. Similarly, clear identifiable labels can decrease the possibility of the wrong selection of resistors, although barcode systems and RFID technology are other more sophisticated alternatives used in manufacturing to prevent sequencing errors [13, 14]. Errors during the visual verification of the product result from the limitations of humans as visual inspectors [15]. Although human redundancy can improve this operation's reliability, it seems that automated visual inspection should be used whenever possible. With the introduction of artificial intelligence within Industry 4.0, machine vision is expanding its applications and some systems can assist in the inspection and thus support the assembler by providing tracking and guidance during the assembly process. This can be achieved using augmented reality glasses [16] or a light-guided system [17], depending on the task's characteristics. On another note, the use of SHERPA proves to be a useful framework for the analysis of human error in the context of manual assembly. Table 3 shows the advantages and limitations of three HRA techniques that have been used for the analysis of errors in manual assembly tasks. The information presented is based on applications found in the literature (THERP and MTQM) and the results from the application of SHERPA presented in this paper.

**Table 3.** Comparison of three HRA techniques used in manual assembly.

| HRA technique | Advantages | Limitations |
| --- | --- | --- |
| THERP [2] | High availability of information about the technique, including the tables with probabilities. Well-known technique | It was developed for the nuclear sector. Error probability tables may not be completely suitable for manufacturing |
| MTQM [18] | Developed explicitly for manufacturing context and integrates well with MTM system. It allows precise estimation of HEP in production planning. Cost analysis can be performed | It is an expert-oriented technique. Demands high resources in training and application time. Detailed information is not easily available (e.g., tables with probabilities of assembly errors) |
| SHERPA | High availability of information about the technique. It follows the structure of the well-known FMEA technique. Enables the performance of qualitative and quantitative analysis | Error mode categories for qualitative analysis are generic. The calculation of error probability is based on expert judgment, so staff participation is needed (values are not in tables) |

It should be noted that SHERPA was initially developed for the process industry. For example, one could say that a proportion of the 28 error modes proposed in the Task Activity Classification Taxonomy are irrelevant to a manual assembly context. Similarly, the linguistic descriptors of error modes are generic, meaning the vocabulary used in the taxonomy is incongruous with that used in manual assembly. In production planning, predetermined motion and time systems (PMTS) are widely used for the analysis of manual tasks. In factories, different stakeholders are familiarized with PMTS approaches. These system descriptors include reach, grasp, move, turn, apply pressure, position and release, eye travel and eye focus, among others (e.g., MTM or MOST). Estimation of human error probabilities is only justifiable in specific cases like probabilistic safety analysis (PSA) within safety-critical domains or for production planning purposes within manufacturing contexts [18]. In the latter case, the estimation of precise error probabilities helps to base decision-making on the costs of modifications in the structure of the work cycles (productivity vs. quality). If the objective is to identify the type of errors and why they occur, as it is often the case, then, the focus should be placed more on error identification than error prediction.

## 5    Conclusions

As exemplified in this paper, the use of SHERPA methodology provides a useful framework for the analysis of human error in manual assembly. It makes possible the identification of several error modes and the proposition of remedial strategies. However, this methodology was specifically developed for the process industry and safety-critical domains, and as such, it does not consider the specific context of manual assembly. Future developments for the specific context of manual assembly need to consider using vocabulary (linguistic descriptors) harmonized with production planning and manufacturing in general. A specific taxonomy of human errors seems necessary. Predetermined motion and time systems (PMTS) could be used as a reference. A technique more focused on error identification than error estimation (probabilities) seems more suited to the general analysis of human error in assembly. A detailed and precise estimation of human error probabilities is time-consuming and a challenge for practitioners.

## Appendix A. Hierarchical Task Analysis (HTA) of the Assembly of the Printed Circuit Board (PCB)

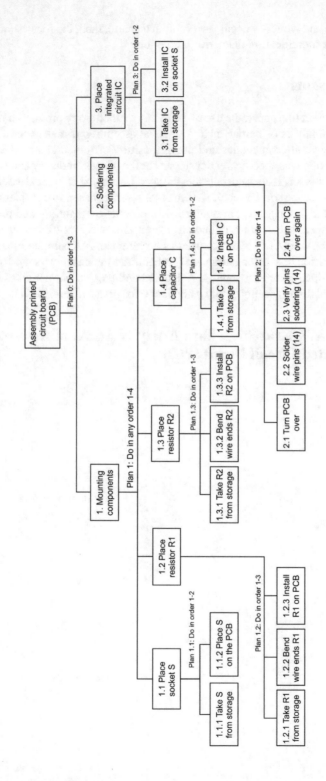

# References

1. Falck, A.-C., Örtengren, R., Rosenqvist, M.: Assembly failures and action cost in relation to complexity level and assembly ergonomics in manual assembly (part 2). Int. J. Ind. Ergon. **44**(3), 455–459 (2014)
2. Bubb, H.: Human reliability: a key to improved quality in manufacturing. Hum. Factors Ergon. Manuf. Serv. Ind. **15**(4), 353–368 (2005)
3. Pasquale, V.D., et al.: Human reliability in manual assembly systems: a systematic literature review. IFAC-PapersOnLine **51**(11), 675–680 (2018)
4. Embrey, D.: Assessment and prediction of human reliability (chap. 4). In: Nicholson, A.S., Ridd, J.E. (eds.) Health, Safety and Ergonomics, pp. 33–47. Butterworth-Heinemann, London (1988)
5. Torres, Y., Nadeau, S., Landau, K.: Classification and quantification of human error in manufacturing: a case study in complex manual assembly. Appl. Sci. **11**(2), 749 (2021)
6. Embrey, D.: SHERPA: a systematic human error reduction and prediction approach. In: Proceedings of the International Topical Meeting on Advances in Human Factors in Nuclear Power Systems, 21–24 April, pp. 184–193. American Nuclear Society, Knoxville (1986)
7. Anett, J.: Hierarchical task analysis. In: Hollnagel, E. (ed.) Handbook of Cognitive Task Design, pp. 33–51. CRC Press, Boca Raton (2003)
8. Stamatis, D.H.: Failure Mode and Effect Analysis: FMEA from Theory to Execution. ASQ Quality Press, Milwaukee (2003)
9. Kletz, T.A.: Hazop—past and future. Reliab. Eng. Syst. Saf. **55**(3), 263–266 (1997)
10. Holroyd, J., Bell, J.: Review of Human Reliability Assessment Methods. Health and Safety Laboratory, London (2009)
11. Lyons, M.: Towards a framework to select techniques for error prediction: supporting novice users in the healthcare sector. Appl. Ergon. **40**(3), 379–395 (2009)
12. AWS: B2.3/B2.3M Specification for soldering procedure and performance qualification. American Welding Society, Doral, FL (2018)
13. Chao, S., et al.: Research on mistake proofing technology for airbag flexible assembly line based on barcode and database. In: International Conference on Electronic; Mechanical Engineering and Information Technology (EMEIT 2011), 12–14 August 2011. IEEE, Piscataway (2011)
14. Yong-Shin, K., Hyoennam, K., Yong-Han, L.: Implementation of an RFID-based sequencing-error-proofing system for automotive manufacturing logistics. Appl. Sci. **8**(1), 109 (2018)
15. See, J.E., et al.: The role of visual inspection in the 21st century. Proc. Hum. Factors Ergon. Soc. Ann. Meet. **61**(1), 262–266 (2017)
16. Ryznar, P.: Vision systems and augmented reality error-proof assembly. https://bit.ly/Vision_Systems_AR. Accessed 15 Mar 2019
17. Mayrhofer, W., Rupprecht, P., Schlund, S.: One-fits-all vs. tailor-made: user-centered workstations for field assembly with an application in aircraft parts manufacturing. Proc. Manuf. **39**, 149–157 (2019)
18. Refflinghaus, R., Kern, C.: On the track of human errors - procedure and results of an innovative assembly planning method. Proc. Manuf. **21**, 157–164 (2018)

# Part VI: Human Factors/Ergonomics in Supply Chain Design and Management (Edited by Fabio Sgarbossa)

# The SRA Index (Sustainable Risk Awareness Index): A New KPI for Management Support

Helena Franzon[1,2] and Linda M. Rose[2(✉)]

[1] Praktikertjänst, Adolf Fredriks Kyrkogata 9, Stockholm, Sweden
Helena.franzon@ptj.se
[2] KTH Royal Institute of Technology, Stockholm, Sweden
lrose@kth.se

**Abstract.** The objective with this project is to develop a key performance indicator (KPI) related to work environment deviations, such as risk observations, near misses and injuries. This as a support for managers decision making in steering companies towards higher risk awareness as well as to contribute to the development of safer and more sustainable work environments and jobs. In addition, the aim is to contribute to a work environment (WE) reporting standard with a KPI related to the severity of WE deviations. Based on a literature study an iterative development of such a KPI has resulted in the Sustainable Risk Awareness Index (the SRA Index) and a visualization of it and its components using the Risk Awareness Triangle, also developed in this project. The development of the SRA Index is described and the index is exemplified with data from the electrical installation sector, the healthcare industry and one of Sweden's largest private health company. Also the Risk Triangle is exemplified. The need for and the advantages of standardized methods to report WE deviations in companies sustainability reports are discussed. It is concluded that initial use of this KPI, according to management, fills an identified gap, it provides the management with a usable tool for systematic work environment overview and it supports their informed decision-making.

**Keywords:** Decision-making · Risk management · Work environment · Deviations · Risk awareness · Risk awareness triangle

## 1  Introduction

### 1.1  Background

Work-related injuries are a burden and lead to negative consequences for those injured, for organisations as well as for societies. The ILO estimates that some 2.3 million women and men around the world succumb to work-related accidents or diseases every year, which corresponds to over 6000 deaths every day. Worldwide, around 340 million occupational accidents occur 160 million work-related illnesses occur annually [1]. Solely within the European Union, the costs of work-related injuries are estimated to exceed 3% of the gross domestic product [2]. With changing demographics, there is a need for prolonged working life to match peoples increased lifespan, which, in turn, leads to an increased need for sustainable jobs [2]. One important part to achieve such jobs is to reduce the risks of work related injuries.

Different strategies and methods have been used in the attempts to reduce the risks of such injuries. They include using tools to gain relevant data (e.g. via surveys, interviews, work environment group meetings, audits, measurements and assessments e.g. [3] and tools to identify and to assess risks e.g. [4, 5]. Further they also include tools for reporting work environment (WE) deviations (such as risk observations, near misses and injuries) and other statistical injury related data (e.g. sick leave days per diagnose) [6, 7]. In addition, they also include tools to develop and implement risk reduction measures (e.g. organisational and technical measures) [5, 8] and to evaluate the effects of the implemented changes (e.g. by follow-ups) [5, 9]. Few methods are aligned to the ISO-standard for systematic risk management process [5, 10].

One approach to reduce the risks is to systematically promote increased risk awareness within organisations. There is no single dominating definition of "Risk Awareness." In the health care sector, for example it is defined as *"the recognition of the potential for hazards, risks, and incidents that occur within the healthcare environment and result in patient harm."* [11]. Sometimes risk awareness is interpreted as that there is knowledge regarding of risk management within an organisation [12]. This paper uses the definition *"Risk awareness is the raising of understanding within the population of what risks exist, their potential impacts, and how they are managed."* [13]. In addition, we operationally specify three types of work environment deviations: *risk observations, near misses* and *injuries*. Here "risk observations" denote that risks in a system (e.g. within an organisation) are identified and observed. Further, "near misses" in this context denotes incidents when no injury happened, but was "close" to happen, (e.g. when a machine accident almost occurred, or an employee was working in a Covid-19 virus high alert area without sufficient personal protective equipment (PPE), but was not infected by the virus). The third type of work environment deviations, "injuries" is composed of accidents and diseases.

In the 1930s, Heinrich [14] established a well-known and widely spread accident prevention theory in the form of a "safety triangle". He concluded that severe occupational safety and health (OSH) incidents are preceded by numerous less severe incidents and near misses. The triangle has since been widely used and updated [15]. For example, in a campaign in Sweden a large employer organisation systematically promoted reporting near misses into the industrial sectors work environment deviation system. This resulted in a considerably larger number of reported near misses and a considerable reduction in accidents [16].

In Sweden the work environment incident reporting system, IA, is used by many companies across many industrial sectors [6]. In the IA system the abovementioned three work environment deviation types are used as input data to the database. In the IA system selected data among an organisations own work environment data can be displayed by the users (the organisations using the system) and compared with other data within the company and the company's industrial sector. The results in the IA system can solely be displayed and extracted at detailed level, e.g. generating reports per unit, organization and company's industrial sector in relation to different causes for the deviations as one example injury risks.

However, for effective risk management, risk data (whether they are risk assessments or work environment (WE) deviation data, or other) need to be available at different level of detail and scope within the different hierarchical levels in the organisation. To be able to decide on and to take relevant measures to reduce the risks close to their sources, details about the risks per se are important, while when the aim is to get *an overview* of the WE deviations and risks, the data need to be analysed and presented at a detailed level but with a larger scope. Such presentation of the data enables a more comprehensive view of the "state of the art" regarding the WE of the whole company and can be used to follow trends over time, as well as in the strategic planning. The communication between different hierarchical levels is important. E.g. Törner et al. found that high-quality interaction between different organizational functions and hierarchical levels stood out as important aspects of safety [17].

At least in Sweden there has been, up until now, no such system or method to display the WE deviation data at an overview level for the top management in a condensed, easy to understand and easy to follow way. A key performance indicator (KPI) that company managements can use to follow the development trend regarding the work environment within the company and also benchmark the own company in relation to others would be an asset. In addition, since it in Sweden is mandatory since the turn of the year 2017/2018 to report non-financial KPI in the sustainability report as part in the company's annual financial report [18]. However, there is no standardized way neither on what companies include in the different WE deviation types, nor on how they report this type of data. A method, preferably a KPI, that enables a standardized, well defined and easy to use way to calculate and present WE deviations has been high on the wish-list for several companies in different industrial sectors in Sweden.

This gap between on the one hand the need for such a method and on the other hand the lack of such a method was identified and clearly articulated by the management of one of Sweden's largest organisations in the health care sector, Praktikertjänst. The company has approximately 6,500 employees and has clinics all over Sweden. Praktikertjänst is owned and operated by experts like doctors, dentists, nurses, psychologists and physiotherapists etc., who are also responsible for managing the clinics. This is a concept that creates great commitment among the managers in the company and therefore the work environment is often prioritized. Based on discussions with several stakeholders, including other companies in different industrial sectors, insurance organisations, authorities and researchers, a project was initiated to develop a method to calculate and visualize a work environment KPI related to the severity of WE deviations, which reflects, at least to some extent, the risk awareness within an organisation.

## 1.2 Objective

The specific objective of the project is to develop a method for calculating and visualizing a work environment KPI related to the severity of WE deviations. In a larger time perspective, the aim is to disseminate, implement and evaluate the method and to contribute to the development of safer and more sustainable work environments and jobs. In addition, the aim is to contribute to a work environment reporting standard with a KPI related to the severity of WE deviations.

## 2 Methods

As a first step to reach the objective a literature study was performed. This was carried out in four parts. The focus on one part of the literature study was on risk management/risk awareness literature, including methods. In another part, the focus was on Heinrich's Safety Triangle method and methods developed from the Safety Triangle [14, 15]. These two parts of the literature study search were in the databases Scopus and PubMed. Combinations of the following search terms were used: In part one: (Risk observation AND deviation), (Risk awareness AND deviation). Here inclusion criteria were research publications written in English, published any time. Exclusion was made manually, and the exclusion criteria were risk awareness in traffic, risk awareness in data protection (Scopus) and risk awareness in catastrophe medicine (PubMed). In part two: ("Herbert Heinrich" OR "safety pyramid" OR "safety triangle"). Here inclusion criteria were research publications written in English.

A third part of the literature study was based on research papers recommended by researches linked to the project and the fourth part was grey literature on current methods and companies' sustainability reports 2019. The latter type of publications were either recommended by practitioners or researches linked to the project or found via internet searches.

The literature study result was used as a base for developing the method for risk awareness KPI and in a user guide development. This was done iteratively in collaboration with several stakeholders and intended users with different competences, including mathematical, systems, product design and work environment competences. Within the health care company initiating the project, an interdisciplinary group with 21 employees from different parts of the company, such as HR, quality, nurses, senior managers and union representatives participated in providing feedback. The project is still ongoing and in the development of the visualization of the method and its results also IT and design specialists are involved. Activities in the iterative development have so far also included usability workshops with Praktikertjänst's top management team.

As part of the work to reach the aim of disseminating the method, discussions with a broad range of stakeholders including stakeholders at different industrial sectors, insurance agencies and authorities have been held, presenting prototypes of the method and inquiring data from different organisations and industrial sectors. In addition, data for illustrating the developed KPI with an example was provided by the IA system. The data used in that example are from Praktikertjänst, the private healthcare sector (26 companies) and the electrical installation sector.

## 3 Results

Among the results from the literature study, several methods and their basis were studied and used as a base for the development of the KPI and its visualization. Mainly three sources were used in the development. One of them was the HME Index [19], which is an index for Sustainable Employee Engagement. This HME Index displays three areas: motivation, leadership and strategic management on a 0–100 scale, where higher numbers indicate high employee engagement while lower numbers indicate low employee engagement. Further Heinrich's Safety Triangle was studied, as were related articles [14, 15], and these were used as inspiration for the development of visualization of the KPI and its components. In addition, the IA system for work environment deviations management was studied regarding the work environment deviation classification as well as for retrieving data for the example illustrating the developed KPI. Further large companies' sustainability reports for 2019 from different industry sectors were studied, focusing on what types of WE deviations the companies included and how the results were presented.

## 3.1   The SRA Index

Based on the sources mentioned above and the requirements from Praktikertjänst a new KPI was developed, the Sustainable Risk Awareness Index (SRA Index). The index is the ratio between the number of risk observations divided by the number of work environment deviations during a certain period of time for parts of, or for a whole organisation. This can also be expressed as:

$$SRA\ Index = \left[No.\ of\ risk\ observations/No.\ of\ work\ environment\ deviations\right] * 100$$

where the number of work environment deviations are the sum of the risk observations, near misses and injuries (accidents and illnesses) and based on [6, 20] these are explained in Table 1.

**Table 1.** Expressions used in the SRA Index and their explanations.

| Expression | Explanation |
| --- | --- |
| Risk observation | Means that an employee has identified a risk that could lead to a near miss or an accident/work-related illness |
| Near miss | Means that something has happened that could lead to an accident, but no injury occurs or a work-related illness, but no sick leave occurs |
| Work related accident | Means that something has happened at work that caused an injury to a person |
| Work related illness | Means a disease caused by a harmful effect at work |
| Injuries | The sum of work related accidents and work related illnesses |
| Work environment deviations | The sum of risk observations, near misses and injuries |

The SRA index is constructed in a way so that its lowest possible value is zero and its highest possible values is 100. A low SRA Index signals low risk awareness while a high SRA Index signal high risk awareness in an organization. The SRA Index shows the percent risk observations in relation to all work environment deviations.

In addition, the Risk Awareness Triangle was developed to visualize the distribution between the three types of work environment deviations, namely risk observations, near misses and injuries. The current prototype version of the Risk Awareness Triangle is illustrated in Fig. 1 with data for year 2020 for the company Praktikertjänst. The Risk Awareness Triangle visualization is still under iterative development, e.g. regarding the layout of the SRA Index. In the triangle, the sections heights are proportional to the number of reported cases in each of the three types of work environment deviations.

The SRA Index and the Risk Awareness Triangle can be calculated and visualized, respectively by using the interactive method version accessible via: www.kth.se/mth/erg onomi/forskning/sustainable-risk-awareness.

In Fig. 1 the WE deviations from Praktikertjänst are visualized in the Risk Awareness Triangle for the time period January 1$^{st}$ to December 31$^{st}$, 2020. For that time period the SRA Index is 44. Figure 2 summarizes some features of the index.

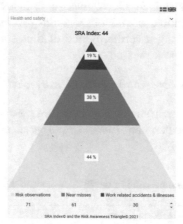

**Fig. 1.** Illustration of the current version of the SRA Index$^{©}$ and the Risk Awareness Triangle$^{©}$, available via: www.kth.se/sv/mth/ergonomi/forskning/sustainable-risk-awareness

Regarding the Risk Awareness Triangle, the developers and all in the intended user group found percentage distribution in height of the three types of work environment deviations to be more user-friendly than percentage distribution of the area.

During the development of the SRA Index feedback on it has been collected from the intended users and the initiating health-care company's management. This will be reported more in detail elsewhere. However, in summary the company's management is positive to the SRA Index, partly because the index enables reporting deviations as a KPI to steer towards increased risk awareness. In addition, they perceive that the SRA Index enables the management to make decisions that can at least to some extent affect the risk awareness within the organisation and its different parts.

### 3.2 An Example Illustrating the SRA Index

In 2019 the healthcare industry, including Praktikertjänst, started the implementation of the incident reporting system IA. This enabled easy access to and extraction of the company's WE deviation data. These data were used to calculate the SRA Index. As an illustration of the SRA Index an example is provided in Fig. 2. An analysis comparing the SRA Index between the two years reveals that the index increased slightly for both Praktikertjänst and the private healthcare sector (26 companies) in general from 2019 to 2020, indicating a slight increase in risk awareness. Praktikertjänst's SRA Index increased from 38 in 2019 to 44 in 2020. The corresponding values for the private healthcare sector were 44 and 48, respectively.

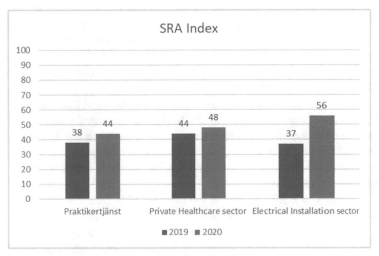

**Fig. 2.** Illustration of the SRA Index with data from Praktikertjänst, Private Healthcare sector and the Electrical Installation sector. Data for 2019 and 2020.

Figure 2 shows an illustration of how the SRA Index can be presented, enabling comparisons within the company as well as between industrial sectors over time.

## 4   Discussion

### 4.1   Discussion of Results

In this, still ongoing, project a method for calculating and visualizing a key performance indicator, the SRA Index, has been developed. It displays the proportion of the least severe type of work environment deviations, the risk observations, in relation to the sum of the three types of WE deviation often used in deviation report systems, where the other two types are near misses and injuries (accidents and work related illnesses). The SRA Index is intended as a support for management teams to support their informed decision making regarding the WE and its effects on the company. Although risk observations are common to report, as best to our knowledge, there is little or no research support about the effects that reporting risk observation contributes to reduced injuries, in a similar way as reporting near misses does [16]. The literature study resulted in finding risk awareness literature related to traffic safety [22], as well as data protection in the Scopus searches and risk awareness in catastrophe medicine in PubMed. Research on the effect that reporting risk observations has on the frequency of injuries is needed. Follow-up studies of the effects of implementing the SRA Index are suggested.

During the development of the SRA Index examples from different companies show that different companies use different definitions of the term "accident" in their sustainability report. For example, some companies classify only accidents that lead to sick-leave or death as accidents, while others also include accidents with no sick-leave. It is important that the risks and the deviations are "handled" in the same way to make it possible to compare results within the company and also benchmark the own company's result in relation to others. Greig et al. [22] found that organizations need guidance on assessing and reporting the status of their work environment and identified a need for improved standardization to report WE. The SRA Index provides a standardized way to measure and present the results and enables comparisons between companies regardless of company size and type of sector.

Although the SRA Index is not launched yet, it has received positive feedback from several types of stakeholders in Sweden, including managers and union representatives.

This way of defining and calculating a work environment related KPI and visualizing it could be used for presenting also other results in this type of format. Calculating and presenting different WE KPIs in the same way as the SRA Index could be a way to standardize WE data reporting.

The SRA Index is a KPI related to the severity of WE deviations, which reflects, at least to some extent, the risk awareness within an organisation. However, it should be noted, that although the SRA Index "catches" reported data regarding the three WE deviation types, it does not display all relevant aspects of an organisations risk awareness.

As mentioned in the results section, the health-care company's management perceives that the SRA-index enables them to make informed decisions that can at least to some extent affect the risk awareness in a positive direction within the organisation. However, to investigate if this is the case, follow-up studies are needed. As mentioned above it should be investigated if there is a relationship between risk observations and the more severe types of work environment deviations.

The choice of including "sustainable" in the index's name was motivated by several factors. For one, work environment deviation reports are mandatory to include in the sustainability report. Thus, the index name is intended to signal that it can be used in forming these reports. In addition, *if* the SRA Index is implemented at a considerable amount of organisations and *if* evaluations of the effects of using it show that the number of reported risk observations increase and the numbers of injuries decrease the method proposed here may contribute to reduce work related injuries and support the development of sustainable jobs and working lives. Thereby it may also contribute to achieving several of the United Nation Sustainable Development Goal (SDG), such as No. 8, "Decent work and economic growth" and SDG No. 3, "Good health and well-being" [23]. It also then contributes in the work to achieve the goals in the Swedish Government's new work environment strategy 2021 [24].

## 4.2   Future Work

Further development within the current project includes clear instructions and visualisation on how to insert input data regarding time span for which the SRA Index is calculated, as well as the scope of the data (e.g. a work station, a department or a whole company). The next steps in the project include finishing the development of the SRA Index and the Risk Awareness Triangle, and thereafter disseminate the method, support and follow its implementation and thereafter evaluate the results. Validation studies in which the SRA Index is compared with safety culture measures are suggested.

In this project the initiating company's need for a method displaying the WE deviations and their engagement affected the development of the model.

## 5 Conclusions

The objective of this project is to develop a method for calculating and visualizing a work environment KPI related to the severity of WE deviations. Although the project is still ongoing, such a method has been developed in form of the Sustainable Risk Awareness Index (the SRA Index) and visualized with the Risk Awareness Triangle. Initial feedback from users is positive and there is an articulated interest for the method from stakeholders from different companies and organisations. The management team at the company initializing the project perceive that the method fills the identified gap and provides the management with a usable tool for systematic work environment overview and that it supports their informed decision-making. Once the development is finished and the method launched the dissemination, implementation and evaluation phases will follow. One important research topic is to evaluate what, if any, effects the implementation of the SRA Index has on risk awareness and in a larger perspective, risk management.

## References

1. ILO: World statistics, work-related accidents or diseases. https://www.ilo.org/moscow/areas-of-work/occupational-safety-and-health/WCMS_249278/lang–en/index.htm. Accessed 05 Feb 2021
2. Tan, B.K., Tan Wee, J., Remes, J., Takala, J.: Cost Estimates Based on ILO Global Estimates on the Burden of Accidents and Diseases at Work and Disability Adjusted Life Years. Workplace Safety and Health Institute, Singapore (2017)
3. Osvalder, A.-L., Rose, L., Karlsson, S.: Methods (chap. 9). In: Bohgard, M., et al. (eds.) Work and Technology on Human Terms. Prevent. (Work Environment in Association with the Confederation of Swedish Enterprise, LO & PTK), Stockholm, Sweden (2009). ISBN 978-91-7365-058-8
4. Garg, A., Moore, J.S., Kapellusch, J.M.: The revised StrainIndex: an improved upper extremity exposure assessment model. Ergonomics 60(7), 912–922 (2017). https://doi.org/10.1080/001 40139.2016.1237678
5. Rose, L.M., Eklund, J., Nord Nilsson, L., Barman, L., Lind, C.M.: The RAMP package for MSD risk management in manual handling – a freely accessible tool, with website and training courses. Appl. Ergon. 86, 103101 (2020)
6. IA-system, a web-based risk Management system. Developed by AFA Insurance in collaboration with the Confederation of Swedish Enterprise, the Swedish Trade Union Confederation (LO), the Council for Negotiation and Co-operation (PTK) and the sectors. https://www.afa forsakring.se/forebyggande/ia/informationsmaterial/. Accessed 05 Feb 2021
7. AFA Insurance, Occupational injury statistics 2020. https://www.afaforsakring.se/forebygga nde/analys-och-statistik/arsrapport-skadestatistik/. Accessed 05 Feb 2021

8. Goggins, R.W., Spielholz, P., Nothstein, G.L.: Estimating the effectiveness of ergonomics interventions through case studies: implications for predictive cost-benefit analysis. J. Saf. Res. **39**, 339–344 (2008)
9. Systematic Work Environment Management (AFS 2001:1Eng), Provisions. https://www.av. se/en/work-environment-work-and-inspections/publications/foreskrifter/systematic-work-environment-management-afs-20011-provisions/. Accessed 05 Feb 2021
10. International Organization for Standardization (ISO), ISO 31000:2009, Risk Management - Principles and Guidelines
11. Haxby, E., Hunter, D., Jaggar, S.: An Introduction to Clinical Governance and Patient Safety. Published to Oxford Scholarship Online (2011)
12. Borys, D.: University of Ballarat, Australia. Exploring risk-awareness as a cultural approach to safety: exposing the gap between work as imagined and work as actually performed (2009)
13. Jen, R.: How to increase risk awareness. Paper Presented at PMI® Global Congress 2012—North America, Vancouver, British Columbia, Canada. Newtown Square, PA: Project Management Institute, (2012). https://www.pmi.org/learning/library/increase-risk-awaren ess-6067. Accessed 05 Feb 2021
14. Heinrich, H.W.: Industrial Accident Prevention: A Scientific Approach. McGraw-Hill Book Company, New York (1931)
15. Yorio, P.L, Moore, S.M.: Examining Factors that Influence the Existence of Heinrich's Safety Triangle Using Site-Specific H&S Data from More than 25,000 Establishments. Risk Analysis, vol. 38, no. 4 (2018)
16. Bohgard, M., et al. (eds.): Work and technology on human terms. Prevent. (Work Environment in Association with the Confederation of Swedish Enterprise, LO & PTK), Stockholm, Sweden, pp. 621–622 (2009). ISBN 978-91-7365-058-8
17. Törner, M., Pousette, A.: Safety in construction – a comprehensive description of the characteristics of high safety standards in construction work, from the combined perspective of supervisors and experienced workers. J. Saf. Res. **40**(6), 399–409 (2009)
18. The Swedish Agency for Growth Policy Analysis. From voluntary to mandatory sustainability reporting. https://www.tillvaxtanalys.se/in-english/publications/pm/pm/2018-12-14-from-voluntary-to-mandatory-sustainability-reporting.html. Accessed 05 Feb 2021
19. Swedish Association of Local Authorities and Regions, Sustainable Employee Engagement (HME – Modell in Swedish, HME survey in English). https://skr.se/arbetsgivarekollektiv avtal/uppfoljninganalys/hallbartmedarbetarengagemanghme/enkatfragorhme/hmeenkatenpa engelska.588.html. Accessed 05 Feb 2021
20. The Swedish Work Environment Authority and the Swedish Social Insurance Agency's e-service for reporting work-related injuries, definition of injuries. https://anmalarbetsskada.se/. Accessed 05 Feb 2021
21. The National Society for Road Safety. https://ntf.se/sok?q=risk%20awareness. Accessed 05 Feb 2021
22. Greig, M., Searcy, C., Neumann, W.P.: "Exploring the Need for a Work Environment Reporting Standard – Development of a Prototype Assessment Approach" Public Report for the Canadian Standards Association Group (CSA) (2020). https://www.csagroup.org/wp-content/ uploads/CSA-Group-Research-Work-Environment-Reporting-Standard.pdf. Accessed 05 Feb 2021
23. United Nations Sustainable Development Goals. Cited 2018, October 26. https://www.un. org/sustainabledevelopment/sustainable-development-goals/. Accessed 05 Feb 2021
24. The Swedish Government's work environment strategy 2021. https://www.regeringen.se/reg eringens-politik/arbetsmiljostrategin/en-ny-arbetsmiljostrategi—folj-regeringens–arbete/. Accessed 08 Feb 2021

# Interventions to Improve Occupational Safety and Health in the Garment Industry – Development of New Integrated Strategies

Peter Hasle[✉] and Jan Vang

Global Sustainable Production, University of Southern Denmark, Odense, Denmark
hasle@iti.sdu.dk

**Abstract.** International efforts to improve occupational safety and health (OSH) in garment suppliers in developing countries have so far had little impact. External pressure from international buyers and multi-stakeholder initiatives tends to result in window-dressing changes decoupled from OSH practice on the shop floor. Experience from interventions in the garment industry in Bangladesh shows that using lean as a tool to integrate OSH with productivity can create considerable improvements, and thereby offers prospects for new strategies to secure safety and health in the garment industry in emerging economies.

**Keywords:** Apparel · Decoupling · Lean · Decent work

## 1 Introduction

In recent decades and especially since the Rana Plaza accident, international efforts have pushed for the development of decent working conditions in global suppliers in emerging countries. International buyers now require suppliers to comply with codes of conduct and/or international standards and multi-stakeholder agreements (Nakamba et al. 2017). However, international buyer interest in keeping prices down and the firm belief of suppliers that low salaries and poor working conditions are the road to competitiveness have created a decoupling between policies and practices that has led to very little improvement in OSH on the shop floor in the supplier factories (Ählström 2010). New strategies are clearly needed, yet there remains a research gap in the literature about how these decoupling challenges can be overcome.

This paper presents experience from interventions aimed at overcoming the decoupling problem in the production of garment factories in Bangladesh (see further details in Hamja et al. 2019a; Hasle and Vang 2021; Hoque et al. 2020). The interventions used lean as a tool to study the opportunities to integrate OSH and productivity improvements. We contribute to closing the research gap by showing that integration of OSH and productivity can be an important strategy to supplement the present external pressure strategies to secure safety and health in global suppliers in emerging economies.

© The Author(s), under exclusive license to Springer Nature Switzerland AG 2021
N. L. Black et al. (Eds.): IEA 2021, LNNS 221, pp. 467–474, 2021.
https://doi.org/10.1007/978-3-030-74608-7_58

## 2 Decoupling of OSH and Operations

The external pressure approach is the currently dominant international buyer strategy for securing OSH and decent working conditions in the garment and other industries with production outsourced to emerging countries. Compliance requests are typically presented as corporate social responsibility (CSR) requirements assessed by auditors, and decoupling refers to the gap between the CSR requirements and the supplier's actual practices (Bartley and Egels-Zandén 2016). Despite relying on auditing of codes of conduct, for example, companies increasingly recognise that such requirements lead to decoupling. The literature is, therefore, rather critical of the approach unless it is integrated with pressure from multiple groups simultaneously, such as NGOs, government, and customers. The positive example in this respect is the Accord agreement following the Rana Plaza accident in Bangladesh, which has resulted in considerable improvements in building, fire and electrical safety (James et al. 2019).

As suggested above, the decoupling problem reflects the fact that the main drivers behind offshore outsourcing to emerging countries are cost-related, so that both buyers and suppliers focus mainly on keeping costs down without compromising too much on quality, flexibility, and deliverability (Anner 2020). However, as the literature points out, hazardous conditions in their suppliers in developing countries expose global buyers to reputation risk, so they impose social compliance on suppliers. Yet, as also underscored in the literature, neither of the two parties has decent working conditions as a critical interest, so the consequence is the prevalence of decoupling, both internally in the global buyer companies and in relation with their the suppliers (Ählström 2010; Behnam and MacLean 2011).

The result is inconsistent practices in global buyers, where CSR departments emphasise codes of conduct while purchasing departments focus on the usual cost priority (Villena 2019), and CSR and sustainability become non-strategic activities, as described in the 'sidecar' argument in OSH research (Frick 1990). CSR departments are also lower in the internal status hierarchy in global buyers and internal communication between departments is limited, which facilitates their own decoupling strategies (Kiron et al. 2017). Moreover, the CSR departments' conceptualisation of sustainability typically echoes 'weak sustainability' (Michelsen et al. 2016), which implicitly encourages suppliers to believe sustainability is not a core priority. Weak sustainability can be translated as only going after low-hanging fruit and not changes that require fundamental transformations of the global supply chains.

We conclude that the external pressure strategy has had little positive impact on compliance with codes of conduct by suppliers located in emerging countries. The most important explanations are the weak institutional setting and the decoupling between the formal requirements and the real-life practice in both international buyers and suppliers. This conclusion does not mean that external coercive pressure is not necessary for the development of decent working conditions. The pressure is needed, but if it stands alone and is not complemented by hands-on supplier development initiatives, the impact is quite limited. In the worst cases, pressure can even lead to reduced openness and transparency in the dialogue between buyer and suppliers and worsened conditions for collaboration about improvements on OHS (Hasle and Vang 2021).

## 3   Integration as a New Intervention Strategy

Discussion on how to integrate OSH and operations in supply chain management has a long history in both OSH research (Frick 1990) and operations and supply chain management research (Brown 1996; Pagell and Wu 2009). The claim is that integration is the key to both health and safety on the one hand, and productivity on the other. Yet in practice, the fields are separated in different pillars with little interaction (Hasle et al. 2021). Operations and supply chain management are seen as the core business activities, while OSH is considered as a troublesome side activity that disturbs efficient operations, so responsibility is pushed to OSH managers with little influence on the actual operations that determine the OSH level in practice.

The non-integration problem is further worsened by the tendency to focus on only limited aspects of OSH. This is particularly true in the garment industry, where OSH is often reduced to technical aspects related to building, fire, and electrical safety. This ignores the actual work process where employees are exposed to a wide range of health risks, of which the most common are muscular-skeletal disorders and respiratory diseases (Kabir et al. 2019; Shazzad et al. 2018). These risks are closely related to the actual production and work processes in the form of the ergonomic arrangement of workstations, the organisation of work, and the raw materials used in the the production.

Our interventions were designed on the basis of integrating productivity and OSH in the production set-up on the shop floor in supplier factories. We utilised knowledge from action research (Coughlan and Coghlan 2002) and change management (Cummings and Worley 2015). Figure 1 shows an overview of the design (Hasle and Vang 2021).

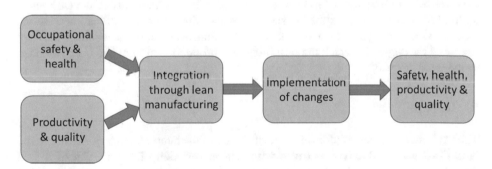

**Fig. 1.** The integrated intervention design

Inspired by the literature on operations management that emphasises the need to integrate OSH and productivity-enhancing measures (Hasle et al. 2021; Shevchenko et al. 2018), our interventions used lean to introduce operations management approaches to facilitate synergies between OSH and productivity.

Early research on lean indicated adverse consequences for health and safety (Harrison 1994; Landsbergis et al. 1999; Palmerud et al. 2012), but research since 2010 has shown that the OSH consequences of lean depend on the actual implementation (Håkansson et al. 2017; Hasle 2014). Even in the garment industry in emerging economies, it has now been documented that lean can be used to improve OSH (Hamja et al. 2019b). The advantage of lean in this perspective is that lean focuses on the specific work processes which in the garment industry are simultaneously the source of safety and health risks and low productivity. Key tools such as value stream mapping, 5S (improvement of housekeeping and layout), and kaizen (for continuous improvement) are designed in a manner that makes it easy to integrate both risk identification and control measures. Integrative tools have been developed for this specific purpose (Jarebrant et al. 2016). In other words, lean makes it possible not only to avoid the traditional conflict between OSH and productivity, but also to stop limiting OSH to the issues of building, fire and electrical safety.

## 4  Methodology

We selected 12 garment factories, using a snowball sampling method where factories were requested to join voluntarily in the lean intervention. Most of the factories were identified with the help of one global buyer, who suggested their suppliers should participate. Each factory designated a sewing line where, in collaboration with the company, we created and implemented a series of intervention activities (e.g., value stream mapping, 5S, workstation and job design, safety measures, and quality improvement). The intervention for each factory lasted approximately six months and included approximately 30 site visits to each factory. Production KPIs, OSH assessments, and employee questionnaires were collected before and after each intervention. We conducted interviews and made observations to collect qualitative data before, during and after each intervention. The interventions were carried out in two waves, with the second wave adjusted for experience from first wave. We were able to assess the sustainability of the changes in eight of the factories approximately six months after the completion of the intervention. The assessment included the maintenance and/or improvement of the results in the pilot lines and the degree to which the new integrated production system had been extended to the whole factory.

## 5  Results

The outcome of the intervention indicates that most of the intervention factories improved both OSH and productivity but also with a large variation (Table 1). Out of the 12 factories, three achieved considerable improvement, 5–6 some improvement, and 4–5 very little improvement.

We found the greatest improvement in the second wave of six factories, where we used the experience from the first wave to adjust the intervention strategy. The changes we made focused in stronger top management support for the implementation, increased training in lean and OSH, more structured project management, and stronger involvement of employees.

It is particularly important to note that employees in the pilot lines of all factories in the second wave indicated that they had experienced a reduction in muscular fatigue and pain (see details in Hamja et al. 2019a).

In the eight factories assessed for the sustainability of changes, the results show a relatively weak outcome. Only two factories continued to improve in the pilot line and

**Table 1.** Span of improvements

| Measure | Change | |
| --- | --- | --- |
| | Lowest | Highest |
| Efficiency | 0% | 26% |
| Value stream addition | −33% | 100% |
| Reduction in defects per hundred units (DHU) | 0% | 92% |
| Reduction in change-over time (SMED) | 2% | 25% |
| Machine safety (application of guards) | 3% | 70% |
| Workstations with improved ergonomics | −4% | 194% |
| Reduction in fatigue and acute muscle pain | 16% | 34% |

(See more details about results in Hamja et al. 2019a; Hoque et al. 2020)

started to roll out the changes in the whole factory. Four factories had more or less sustained results in the pilot line but had not rolled out the changes to the whole factory, and in two factories, the initial results in the pilot line had decreased and there was no roll-out to the rest of the factory.

## 6  Discussion and Conclusion

In contrast to the dominant trend among both policymakers and many scholars in pointing towards external pressure as critical for creating safe and healthy jobs in global supply chains, we argue that external pressure is at best a precondition for the development of decent working conditions in suppliers in developing countries. What is needed is development in which OSH is linked more closely to the business goals of the suppliers.

We tested an intervention design for supplier development based on integrating OSH and productivity using lean as a key tool. Our experience shows that the integrated approach can be an important source of inspiration for designing interventions that avoid the traditional focus on limited elements of OSH, which risks putting OSH in a sidecar with little influence on operations. We therefore recommend that all stakeholders with an interest in improving OSH and working conditions should develop more integrated approaches: buyers should encourage their suppliers to develop integrated improvements, and multi-stakeholder initiatives should include business goals in their social compliance programmes.

Our results further support earlier findings indicating that lean does not necessarily have a negative impact on OSH. Its impact depends on the context (Hasle et al. 2012), and where there is an explicit integration of OSH in the lean application, as in our case, it is possible to achieve improvements. Without such integration, as earlier findings indicate (Distelhorst et al. 2017), lean does not lead to OSH improvements.

Nevertheless, it is also an approach with questions and limitations. Only some of the factories fully benefitted from the intervention – especially in the longer term. It is certainly not a new experience that large change programmes, in particular those related to lean, have only limited success (see Hopp (2018) for an overview). Further research is therefore required to learn more about how the promise of the integrated approach can be more fully realised. Such research should focus on creating greater agency and ownership in the changes for both managers and workers in the factories. We tried to involve these stakeholders, but our design of the intervention limited the local influence. Increased local agency could help fit the intervention better to the local context and the prevalent understanding on how to run efficient production.

The paper also indicates broader research challenges. The interventions demonstrated that improvements in OSH can be achieved. Yet, the research also shows that improvements do not equate to the broader concept of decent work (Pereira et al. 2019), which includes a living wage, limits on working hours, and freedom of association. There is still a research gap concerning the role the integrated approach can play in the broader development of social sustainability. This issue relates to the emergence of the global sustainable development goals (SDGs), which indicate possible synergies and tensions between the economic, green and social sustainability goals. The transition literature has argued that regime actors, such as global buyers, are enforcers of the status quo, not agents for deeper sustainable transitions (Bauer and Fuenfschilling 2019; Fuenfschilling and Binz 2018). This issue has not yet been thoroughly investigated in the context of developing countries.

The conclusion is that an intervention design using lean to integrate OSH and productivity moves occupational safety and health closer to the business agenda and thereby increases the possibility of creating OSH improvements in suppliers to global supply chains – improvements that are sorely needed.

# References

Ählström, J.: Corporate response to CSO criticism: decoupling the corporate responsibility discourse from business practice. Corp. Soc. Responsib. Environ. Manag. **17**(2), 70–80 (2010). https://doi.org/10.1002/csr.232

Anner, M.: Squeezing workers' rights in global supply chains: purchasing practices in the Bangladesh garment export sector in comparative perspective. Rev. Int. Polit. Econ. **27**(2), 320–347 (2020). https://doi.org/10.1080/09692290.2019.1625426

Bartley, T., Egels-Zandén, N.: Beyond decoupling: unions and the leveraging of corporate social responsibility in Indonesia. Socio-Econ. Rev. **14**(2), 231–255 (2016). https://doi.org/10.1093/ser/mwv023

Bauer, F., Fuenfschilling, L.: Local initiatives and global regimes – multi-scalar transition dynamics in the chemical industry. J. Clean. Prod. **216**, 172–183 (2019). https://doi.org/10.1016/j.jclepro.2019.01.140

Behnam, M., MacLean, T.L.: Where is the accountability in international accountability standards?: A decoupling perspective. Bus. Ethics Q. **21**(1), 45–72 (2011). https://doi.org/10.5840/beq20112113

Brown, K.A.: Workplace safety: a call for research. J. Oper. Manag. **14**(2), 157–171 (1996). https://doi.org/10.1016/0272-6963(95)00042-9

Coughlan, P., Coghlan, D.: Action research for operations management. Int. J. Oper. Prod. Manag. **22**(2), 220–240 (2002). https://doi.org/10.1108/01443570210417515

Cummings, T.G., Worley, C.G.: Organization, Development, and Change, 10th edn. South-Western Publishing, Cincinnati (2015)

Distelhorst, G., Hainmueller, J., Locke, R.M.: Does lean improve labor standards? Management and social performance in the Nike supply chain. Manag. Sci. **63**(3), 707–728 (2017). https://doi.org/10.1287/mnsc.2015.2369

Frick, K.: Can management control health and safety at work? Econ. Ind. Democracy **11**(3), 375–399 (1990). https://doi.org/10.1177/0143831X90113005

Fuenfschilling, L., Binz, C.: Global socio-technical regimes. Res. Policy **47**(4), 735–749 (2018). https://doi.org/10.1016/j.respol.2018.02.003

Håkansson, M., Holden, R.J., Eriksson, A., Dellve, L.: Managerial practices that support lean and socially sustainable working conditions. Nordic J. Work. Life Stud. **7**(3), 63–84 (2017). https://doi.org/10.18291/njwls.v7i3.97091

Hamja, A., Maalouf, M., Hasle, P.: Assessing the effects of lean on occupational health and safety in the Ready-Made Garment industry. Work **64**(2), 385–395 (2019a). https://doi.org/10.3233/WOR-192982

Hamja, A., Maalouf, M., Hasle, P.: The effect of lean on occupational health and safety and productivity in the garment industry - a literature review. Prod. Manuf. Res. **7**(1), 316–334 (2019b). https://doi.org/10.1080/21693277.2019.1620652

Harrison, B.: Lean and Mean. The Changing Landscape of Corporate Power in the Age of Flexibility. The Guildford Press, New York (1994)

Hasle, P.: Lean production - an evaluation of the possibilities for an employee supportive lean practice. Hum. Factors Ergon. Manuf. **24**(1), 40–53 (2014). https://doi.org/10.1002/hfm.20350

Hasle, P., Bojesen, A., Jensen, P.L., Bramming, P.: Lean and the working environment: a review of the literature. Int. J. Oper. Prod. Manag. **32**(7), 829–849 (2012). https://doi.org/10.1108/01443571211250103

Hasle, P., Madsen, C.U., Hansen, D.: Integrating operations management and occupational health and safety: the necessary future of safety science? Saf. Sci. (2021, in press)

Hasle, P., Vang, J.: Designing better interventions: insights from research on decent work. J. Supply Chain Manag. **57**(2) (2021)

Hopp, W.J.: Positive lean: merging the science of efficiency with the psychology of work. Int. J. Prod. Res. **56**(1–2), 398–413 (2018). https://doi.org/10.1080/00207543.2017.1387301

Hoque, I., Hasle, P., Maalouf, M.: Lean meeting buyer expectations for enhanced supplier productivity and compliance capabilities in the garment industry. Int. J. Prod. Perform. Manag. **69**(7), 1475–1494 (2020). https://doi.org/10.1108/IJPPM-08-2019-0410

James, P., Miles, L., Croucher, R., Houssart, M.: Regulating factory safety in the Bangladeshi garment industry. Regul. Gov. **13**(3), 431–444 (2019). https://doi.org/10.1111/rego.12183

Jarebrant, C., Winkel, J., Hanse, J.J., Mathiassen, S.E., Öjmertz, B.: ErgoVSM: a tool for integrating value stream mapping and ergonomics in manufacturing. Hum. Factors Ergon. Manuf. Serv. Ind. **26**(2), 191–204 (2016)

Kabir, H., Maple, M., Usher, K., Islam, M.S.: Health vulnerabilities of readymade garment (RMG) workers: a systematic review. BMC Public Health **19**(1), 1–21 (2019). https://doi.org/10.1186/s12889-019-6388-y

Kiron, B.D., Unruh, G., Kruschwitz, N., Reeves, M., Rubel, H., Meyer, A., Felde, Z.: Corporate sustainability at a crossroads. MIT Sloan Manag. Rev. (2017)

Landsbergis, P.A., Cahill, J., Schnall, P.L.: The impact of lean production and related new systems of work organization on worker health. J. Occup. Health Psychol. **4**(2), 108–130 (1999). refman0266

Michelsen, G., Adomßent, M., Martens, P., von Hauff, M.: Sustainable development – background and context. In: Heinrichs, H., Martens, P., Michelsen, G., Wiek, A. (eds.) Sustainability Science - An Introduction, pp. 5–30. Springer, Heidelberg (2016)

Nakamba, C.C., Chan, P.W., Sharmina, M.: How does social sustainability feature in studies of supply chain management? A review and research agenda. Supply Chain Manag. **22**(6), 522–541 (2017). https://doi.org/10.1108/SCM-12-2016-0436

Pagell, M., Wu, Z.: Building a more complete theory of sustainable supply chain management using case studies of 10 exemplars. J. Supply Chain Manag. **45**(2), 37–56 (2009). https://doi.org/10.1111/j.1745-493X.2009.03162.x

Palmerud, G., Forsman, M., Neumann, W.P., Winkel, J.: Mechanical exposure implications of rationalization: a comparison of two flow strategies in a Swedish manufacturing plant. Appl. Ergon. **43**(6), 1110–1121 (2012). https://doi.org/10.1016/j.apergo.2012.04.001

Pereira, S., Dos Santos, N., Pais, L.: Empirical research on decent work: a literature review. Scand. J. Work Organiz. Psychol. **4**(1), 1–15 (2019). https://doi.org/10.16993/sjwop.53

Shazzad, M.N., Ahmed, S., Haq, S.A., Islam, M.N., Abu Shahin, M., Choudhury, M.R., Hasan, A.T.M.T., Abdal, S.J., Rasker, J.J.: Musculoskeletal symptoms and disorders among 350 garment workers in Bangladesh: a cross-sectional pilot study. Int. J. Rheum. Dis. **21**(12), 2063–2070 (2018). https://doi.org/10.1111/1756-185X.13423

Shevchenko, A., Pagell, M., Johnston, D., Veltri, A., Robson, L.: Joint management systems for operations and safety: a routine-based perspective. J. Clean. Prod. **194**, 635–644 (2018). https://doi.org/10.1016/j.jclepro.2018.05.176

Villena, V.H.: The missing link? The strategic role of procurement in building sustainable supply networks. Prod. Oper. Manag. **28**(5), 1149–1172 (2019). https://doi.org/10.1111/poms.12980

# Reality-Based Laboratory for Exoskeleton Studies in Logistics

Semhar Kinne[(✉)], Nicole Bednorz, Veronika Kretschmer, and Luisa Griese

Fraunhofer Institute for Material Flow and Logistics, Joseph-von-Fraunhofer-Str. 2-4,
44227 Dortmund, Germany
{Semhar.Kinne,Nicole.Bednorz,Veronika.Kretschmer,
Luisa.Griese}@iml.fraunhofer.de

**Abstract.** The exoskeleton technology is discussed as a promising approach in order to relieve physical work in logistics and thereby contribute to health prevention. In recent years, several models have come onto the market that are designed to support specific manual activities. However, especially the work in logistics is characterized by changing activities that cause different physical strains. An exoskeleton test center is being set up at Fraunhofer IML to investigate the effect of exoskeletons in realistic workplaces under laboratory conditions. In a logistics course consisting of typical main and secondary activities of logistics workers, exoskeletons of different categories will be compared in participant studies. Objective and subjective methods are used to analyze movement behavior and performance effects as well as to determine user impression. In a preliminary study, two participants tested a powered exoskeleton over a four-week period in a selected area of the logistics course while their movements were analyzed with motion capturing. The findings will be used to design the planned studies with a larger study sample. After evaluation of the exoskeleton test center and the experimental design, it can be used by future users as well as for exoskeleton manufacturers.

**Keywords:** Exoskeleton · Logistics · Manual order picking · Physical workload · Cognitive ergonomics · Technology acceptance

## 1 Introduction

As automated handling systems in logistics cannot meet the requirements of flexibility and reliability, essential handling operations are still performed manually. Repetitive work, heavy loads and incorrect body postures and movements increase the risk of musculoskeletal disorders [1]. The need for innovative solutions for improved ergonomics during manual load handling has highlighted the possibilities of exoskeleton technology. The rapid development of these wearable assistance systems caused various available solutions for relief of the upper and lower extremities as well as the back to support logistical activities [2]. Local efficacy in the affected areas of the body has been demonstrated in our field and laboratory research [3, 4], but possible negative long-term effects

N. L. Black et al. (Eds.): IEA 2021, LNNS 221, pp. 475–482, 2021.
https://doi.org/10.1007/978-3-030-74608-7_59

cannot yet be excluded [5, 6]. In operative use, complicated fitting processes, restricted movement, pressure marks and increased sweating are the reasons why only few employees can imagine wearing an exoskeleton all day long. In addition, there is a wide range of secondary activities in logistics, where exoskeletons tend to make the work more difficult [7]. No research results or industrial experience are known so far that confirm a preventive effect of exoskeletons on musculoskeletal complaints or disorders [8]. In order to successfully establish exoskeletons as work equipment in companies, further knowledge is required to define suitable conditions of use.

## 2  Objective

To create a data basis for the design of work systems with physical assistance systems an exoskeleton test center is implemented at Fraunhofer Institute for Material Flow and Logistics (IML) in Dortmund (Germany). In order to create conditions for an accepted daily use, application-oriented knowledge of available exoskeletons is required. The following questions will be investigated in the test center:

– Which exoskeleton is suitable for which activity requirements?
– Does an exoskeleton hinder activities for which it is not recommended?
– Which organizational aspects need to be considered in terms of donning/doffing, individualization, and performance?
– Are there gender differences regarding fit and functionality?
– Can exoskeletons contribute to preventive health promotion by training ergonomic movement patterns?

To meet this challenge, the logistics course is based on a sequence of realistic workplaces, that represent typical tasks in logistics. This contains manual load handling (in particular lifting and carrying), working in forced postures (overhead work and working in a stooped posture) and pulling and pushing aids. A standardized test procedure allows the comparison of different exoskeletons in terms of operating mode (passive, powered), supported body part, and type of assistance (relief, enhancement, stabilization). The methodology is based on a combination of movement analyses, vital data measurement as well as subjective methods. Muscle activity as well as the specific support strength of the exoskeletons are not addressed within the test center.

Since this is a young technology, no generalized statements can be made about functionality, wearing comfort and experienced effectiveness. Even exoskeletons that are supposed to relieve the same body region evoke highly different sensations among users. For this reason, all exoskeletons that address the typical complaints of logistics employees (pain in the lower back, shoulder-neck region, arms and legs) can be investigated in the exoskeleton test center. The models shown in Fig. 1 are currently conceivable for this purpose, however, their availability on the German market has not yet been clarified.

Back Support (passive)

**Fig. 1.** Appropriate exoskeleton models for the exoskeleton test center (as of January 2021)

## 3 Methodology

### 3.1 Procedure

The logistics course consists of four workstations for manual work activities that are run through in a continuous process (see Table 1). The main activities are order picking (A) from shelving racks, pallet racks and mesh boxes, palletizing and pallet wrapping (B) and loading and unloading (C) of containers and delivery vans. Secondary activities are transport processes (D) using pallet trucks, forklifts, walking without aids and or stair climbing.

In the process, cardboard boxes of different sizes and weights are moved. In activity C2, beverage crates are also handled. To enable all test persons to drive in the forklift truck (D2), this is done in a simulator. Activity D3 is performed with and without load, activity D4 only without load for safety reasons.

### 3.2 Preliminary Study

As part of a preliminary study on a partial section of the test center two male participants used the active exoskeleton Cray X for order picking from shelving racks and from mesh boxes. The participants went through the program daily over a period of four weeks and were recorded and analyzed 5 to 10 min per day. Two research conditions were conducted: working with the help of an exoskeleton and as a control condition working without using a mechanical device. Exclusion criteria for participation were based on the exoskeleton manufacturer's specifications.

**Table 1.** Overview of workstations in the exoskeleton test center.

| No. | Work Station | Location/ Resources | Activity | Primary Strain | Appropriate Exoskeleton Category |
|---|---|---|---|---|---|
| A1 | order picking | shelving rack | manual load handling overhead work | lower back: high strain on lumbar spine discs when lifting loads and bending forward shoulders: high strain when picking from awkward rack heights arms: high strain when handling high load | back support (passive) back support (active) back and arm support shoulder support |
| A2 | | pallet rack | manual load handling | lower back: high strain on lumbar spine discs when lifting loads and bending forward forced body posture due to poor accessibility and unfavorable working | back support (passive) back support (active) |
| A3 | | mesh boxes | manual load handling | Lower back: high strain on the back in the L5/S1 area due to leverage effect while leaning into the box arms: high strain when handling high load weights | back support (passive) back support (active) back and arm support |
| B1 | palletizing and pallet wrapping | ground level | manual load handling | lower back: high strain on lumbar spine discs when lifting/lowering loads and bending forward arms: high strain when handling heavy loads forced body while wrapping repetitive task | back support (passive) back support (active) back and arm support |
| B2 | | ergonomic height | manual load handling | arms: high strain when handling heavy loads forced body posture while wrapping repetitive task | back support (passive) back and arm support |
| C1 | loading and unloading | shipment container | manual load handling overhead work | lower back: high strain on lumbar spine discs when lifting loads shoulders: high strain when picking from awkward rack heights arms: high strain when handling high load weights | back support (passive) back support (active) back and arm support shoulder support |
| C2 | | delivery van | manual load handling overhead work working in stooped position | lower back: high strain on lumbar spine discs when lifting loads arms: high strain when handling high load weights forced body posture when ceiling height is low | back support (passive) back support (active) back and arm support leg support |
| D1 | transportation | pallet truck | pulling and pushing | full body | - |
| D2 | | forklift | - | full body: vibration | - |
| D3 | | walking without aids | manual load handling | arms: high strain when carrying loads | back and arm support |
| D4 | | stair climbing without aids | - | knees | - |

It was revealed from other studies that acclimatization to the tasks with exoskeleton is necessary for the study results to gain significance [8, 9]. Within five acclimatization days, the exoskeleton was adapted to fit the individual body dimensions and practice was given in putting on and taking off the exoskeleton independently. In addition, a preferred level of support was determined, and the participants could already get used to the measurement procedures. The exoskeleton was evaluated subjectively by using questionnaires and objectively by using digital motion capturing and vital data measurement. The results showed several differences for the two test conditions in terms of calculated physical workload and subjectively perceived stress. On the one hand the exoskeleton reduced physical workload, e.g. a reduction of the calculated disc compression of the lumbar spine, and on the other hand it revealed new issues like additional load due to increased readjustment of the exoskeleton. Moreover, the study has determined the increase of the required time to fulfill the work task while wearing the Cray X by 16 to 19%.

The study results lead to the conclusion that the exoskeleton has a positive impact on the musculoskeletal system and that the motion capturing combined with vital data measurement and the evaluation questionnaire is a promising approach pointing out the effects from exoskeletons on the subjective and objective physical workload.

### 3.3 Improvements from the Preliminary Study

Due to the variety of body dimensions and despite the acclimatization period and the possibility of adaptability to individual body dimensions, frequent readjustment of the exoskeleton was necessary during the testing. To ensure that the movements resulting from the initial adjustment of the exoskeleton do not weigh too heavily, investigations and analyses for longer periods of work are essential for the exoskeleton test center. In the preliminary study no lifting technique was prescribed, but the assumption was made, that prescribing a lifting technique for back-supporting exoskeletons creates better comparability among the participants.

In case of performing several work activities in succession, it is important to implement breaks in the test sequence, especially for vital data measurement, so that measured loads are not wrongly assigned to the subsequent workstations and the different workstations can be evaluated separately. The aim is to provide recommendations for individual use cases and to evaluate the activities each exoskeleton is suitable for. As for preliminary study only two participants were chosen, for the planned test course a larger study sample is required to generate representative results.

### 3.4 Subjective Measurements

With the focus on laboratory evaluations of exoskeletons, various subjective measurement methods can be used. As realistic intralogistics tasks are simulated in the exoskeleton test center (see Sect. 3.1), working tasks can be combined with experimental paradigms from the behavioral sciences by setting additional cognitive tasks in an experimental control group design, such as conditions with time pressure, task interruptions or task changes [10].

To assess the overall workload, the performance of test persons can be measured objectively (e.g. errors, duration of task completion) or subjectively with quantitative questionnaires. An internationally recognized method for recording workload is the NASA Task Load Index [11], which can be used to assess the overall workload as well as mental demands, time demands, own performance, effort and frustration. In addition, the task difficulty can be measured subjectively [6].

Furthermore, the concept of usability is used to evaluate the design quality according to the international standard DIN EN ISO 9241. A mechanical assistance system has good usability if it can be used in a specific context of use and the persons using it achieve their work goals effectively, efficiently and satisfactorily during performing a work task [12]. An established usability measurement method is, for example, the System Usability Questionnaire [13].

User experience, which is positively associated with usability, focuses primarily on emotional and aesthetic factors when using a product. During the human technology interaction, aspects such as attitudes, expectations, trust or well-being are evaluated. A well-known questionnaire is the user experience questionnaire [14], which records attractiveness, goal-oriented pragmatic quality aspects, such as efficiency, transparency and reliability, and non-goal-oriented hedonic quality aspects, such as stimulation and originality.

Furthermore, explorative individual interviews can be conducted to gather subjective knowledge. Especially with regard to the individually assessed advantages and disadvantages of the respective assistance as well as with regard to difficulties encountered during usage or also with regard to detailed suggestions for improvement, a greater gain in knowledge can be achieved with this method.

In addition to subjective cognitive impressions, physical work demands or strain can also be queried subjectively. User impression can be assessed regarding the general wearing comfort of an exoskeleton, the adjustment possibilities of the hardware or the range of movement during the work activity [6]. Wearing characteristics include, for example, handling, donning and doffing, size adjustability or range of motion [6].

### 3.5 Objective Measurements

For an all-encompassing evaluation, objective measurements can be carried out in addition to subjective methods. One objective method is the Xsens system that is a full-body motion capture system whose interface to the software Industrial Athlete (IA, scalefit) allows automated analysis of the measurement data according to ergonomic and biomechanical evaluation criteria. Xsens will be used to compare differences in body postures and movements during work activities with and without wearing the exoskeletons. It is a wearable technology using wireless sensors that can be worn on work clothing which qualifies the system for measurements under real working conditions. The IA software processes and visualizes the body movements recorded by Xsens motion trackers in real time. Workloads, disc compression and moments of force are calculated based on biomechanical principles and the joint positions of the head, trunk, arms, knees and hands. Work above shoulder height is also shown in animated representation.

To record and recognize stress, physiological data is measured with sensor wristbands worn by the test persons [15]. The vital parameters that allow conclusions about physical stress reactions during the performance of work activities are, for example, heart and pulse information, electrodermal activity, peripheral temperature and movement information [16]. The physiological measurement data is evaluated using artificial intelligence methods, so that conclusions can be drawn from combinations of different vital parameters to the underlying type of stress or strain.

## 4 Outlook

It is anticipated that with the help of the exoskeleton test center, it will be possible to prioritize the various exoskeletons in relation to the workstations. Thus, a traffic light representation is possible, which indicates for which workstation an exoskeleton is well, moderately or not at all suitable. In combination with new findings on individualization as well as donning and doffing, concepts for practical use can be made considering the set-up times for exoskeleton use between the different tasks. Recommendations can also be developed for a daily maximum wearing time that would be accepted by future users. Furthermore, we expect new findings on gender aspects with respect to wearing comfort, adjustment effort and technology acceptance.

Due to Covid-19, the completion of the exoskeleton test center and execution of first studies are planned for the end of 2021. The test environment can also be used by employees of companies as well as by exoskeleton manufacturers.

## References

1. de Looze, M.P., Bosch, T., Krause, F., Stadler, K.S., O'Sullivan, L.W.: Exoskeletons for industrial application and their potential effects on physical workload. Ergonomics **59**, 671–681 (2016)
2. Young, A.J., Ferris, D.P.: State of the art and future directions for lower limb robotic exoskeletons. IEEE Eng. Med. Biol. Soc. **25**, 171–182 (2017)
3. Bednorz, N., Kinne, S., Kretschmer, V.: Ergonomieunterstützung in der Logistik –Industrieller Einsatz von Exoskeletten an Palettier- und Kommissionierarbeitsplätzen zur körperlichen Entlastung von Mitarbeitern. In: GfA-Frühjahrskongress, B.4.1 (2019)
4. Kinne, S., Kretschmer, V., Bednorz, N.: Palletising support in intralogistics: the effect of a passive exoskeleton on workload and task difficulty considering handling and comfort. Hum. Syst. Eng. Design **II**, S.273–S.279 (2019)
5. Motmans, R., Debaets, T., Chrispeels, S.: Effect of a passive exoskeleton on muscle activity and posture during order picking. In: Advances in Intelligent Systems and Computing, vol. 820, pp. 338–346 (2019)
6. Baltrusch, S.J., van Dieën, J.H., van Bennekom, C.A.M., Houdijk, H.: The effect of a passive trunk exoskeleton on functional performance in healthy individuals. Appl. Ergon. **72**, 94–106 (2018)
7. Schulz, H., Bednorz, N., Lückmann, P., Hauser, S.: Anwendung von passiven Exoskeletten in der Intralogistik - Ergebnisse und Tendenzen aus ersten Piloteinsätzen. In: FOM ild Schriftenreihe, vol. 66 (2020)
8. Steinhilber, S., Luger, T., Schwenkreis, P., Middeldorf, S., Bork, H., Mann, B., von Glinski, A., Schildhauer, T.A., Weiler, S., Schmauder, M., Heinrich, K., Winter, G., Schnalke, G., Frener, P., Schick, R., Wischniewski, S., Jäger, M.: Einsatz von Exoskeletten im beruflichen Kontext zur Primär--, Sekundär--, und Tertiärprävention von arbeitsassoziierten muskuloskelettalen Beschwerden. Deutsche Gesellschaft für Arbeitsmedizin und Umweltmedizin e.V. (Hrsg) (2020)

9. Nussbaum, M.A., Kim, S., Alabdulkarim, S., Alemi, M.M., Esfahani, M.I.M., Rashedi, E.: Assessing the influence of a passive, upper extremity exoskeletal vest for tasks requiring arm elevation: part I – "expected" effects on discomfort, shoulder muscle activity, and work task performance. Appl. Ergon. **70**, 315–322 (2018)

10. Bröde, P., Rinkenauer, G., Jaschinski, W., Schütte, M.: Effectiveness in cognitive task performance under time pressure and elevated ambient temperature. In: Cotter, J.D., Lucas, S.J.E., Mündel, T. (eds.) Environmental Ergonomics XV: Proc. of the 15th International Conference on Environmental Ergonomics, Queenstown, New Zealand, 11–15th Feb 2013, pp. 89–93. International Society for Environmental Ergonomics, Otago (2013)

11. Staveland, L.E., Hart, S.G.: Development of NASA-TLX (task load index): results of empirical and theoretical research. Adv. Psychol. **52**, 139–183 (1988)

12. ISO 9241-11:2018, Ergonomics of human-system interaction - Part 11: Usability: Definitions and concepts (ISO 9241-11:2018)

13. Brook, J.: SUS: a retrospective. J. Usabil. Stud. **8**(2), 29–40 (2013)

14. Laugwitz, B., Schrepp, M., Held, T.: Construction and evaluation of a user experience questionnaire. In: HCI and Usability for Education and Work: 4th Symposium of the Workgroup Human-Computer Interaction and Usability Engineering of the Austrian Computer Society, Graz, Austria, 20–21 November 2008 (2008)

15. Anusha, A.S., Sukumaran, P., Sarveswaran, V., Surees Kumar, S., Shyam, A., Tony, J.Akl., Preejith, S.P., Sivaprakasam, M.: Electrodermal activity based pre-surgery stress detection using a wrist wearable. IEEE. J. Biomed. Health Inform. **24**(1), 92–100 (2020)

16. Aigrain, J., Spodenkiewicz, M., Dubuisson, S., Detyniecki, M., Cohen, D., Chetouani, M.: Multimodal stress detection from multiple assessments. IEEE Trans. Affect. Comput. **9**(4), 491–506 (2016)

# Dynamic Break Management in Logistics on the Basis of Individual Vital Data: Designing the User Interface of an AI-Based Mobile App for Employees in Order Picking

Veronika Kretschmer[1]($\boxtimes$), Benedikt Mättig[1], and Michael Fiolka[2]

[1] Fraunhofer Institute for Material Flow and Logistics IML, Dortmund, Germany
{Veronika.Kretschmer,Benedikt.Maettig}@iml.fraunhofer.de
[2] Chair of Enterprise Logistics, Technical University of Dortmund, Dortmund, Germany
Fiolka@LFO.tu-dortmund.de

**Abstract.** Frequently occurring mental and physical workloads as well as increased break absences represent a health risk for warehouse workers and a cost risk for companies in the long term. The project "Dynamic Break Management" aims to maintain health, productivity and safety of warehouse workers with the help of individual break recommendations. Using a sensor wristband, a smartphone application and methods of artificial intelligence (AI), stress is to be predicted on the basis of physiological data and breaks are to be recommended individually. The breaks are coordinated with the company's internal processes. The app is developed in accordance with internationally applicable ergonomics standards. Both, the presentation of information and the interaction between human and technology, should be user-friendly in order to increase the acceptance of the technology application and its regular use. The article gives an overview of the IT architecture of the research project "Dynamic Break Management" and the current state of development. Furthermore, different user interface (UI) concepts for the smartphone app are discussed based on the state of research on the ergonomic design of the UI of apps.

**Keywords:** Order picking · User interface design · App design · Wearable device · Artificial intelligence · Stress prevention

## 1 Problem Statement and Motivation

Along with the global change in the working world, the organization of work and especially of breaks in logistics is facing new challenges. In the field of logistics and supply chain management, the demands for flexibility are becoming even greater due to the increasingly heterogeneous and rapidly growing product portfolio, shorter delivery times and fast changing customer requirements. These permanent demands for change are reflected in the increasing digitization of processes, the introduction of new technologies or IT systems, as well as in changed information structures in the company [10].

N. L. Black et al. (Eds.): IEA 2021, LNNS 221, pp. 483–490, 2021.
https://doi.org/10.1007/978-3-030-74608-7_60

In the meantime, humans are recognized as a valuable resource in the company that needs to be integrated into the digitized logistics processes. Particularly in order picking, the majority of processes are still performed manually, as this can increase the degree of flexibility in process design [8]. Against this background, one economic success factor is to maintain and promote the human abilities, skills and existing knowledge of employees. In addition to the expertise and factual knowledge of an employee (so-called explicit knowledge), such as the level of knowledge of work instructions, internal specifications and rules, it is above all the knowledge that is gained through experience by working over years in the company (so-called implicit knowledge) that is decisive in reacting to the flexible and dynamic requirements of logistics.

In the area of warehouse management, there are still rigid structures of working time organization and resource management that are neither adapted to the characteristics and potential of the employees nor to the flexible, dynamic requirements of customers in intralogistics. Along with this, work breaks are often cancelled, interrupted or taken too late. Work breaks are defined as intentional work interruptions that serve the purpose of rest during daily working hours, balancing activities, motivation, social interaction and the perception of cultural and individual needs [16].

In addition, employees are faced with an increasing intensification of work demands in the warehouse: multitasking, working overtime and constant availability go along with a high time and performance pressure [10]. Furthermore, employees only have little scope for action and decision-making. It is found that frequently occurring physical and psychological work demands are associated with negative stress consequences, such as dissatisfaction, impaired health status or reduced productivity in the short term and with an increased risk of errors, sick leaves, staff turnover or industrial accidents in the long term. Numerous studies in the field of occupational science have already shown that work breaks not only have a positive impact on the physical and mental well-being of employees, but also have positive effects on work performance and safety in the company [16].

## 2   Research Objective

Against this background, the idea arose to dynamically design the key variable "work break" in order to meet the various flexibility requirements in the intralogistics sector on the one hand and to align breaks to the individual needs of employees on the other. The project "Dynamic Break Management" is being implemented as part of a national research initiative "Silicon Economy". The general objective is to develop a data and platform economy in which people, companies, robots, autonomous vehicles and IoT devices may interact.

The aim of the research project "Dynamic Break Management" is to develop a solution, which should make it possible to provide employees with individual break recommendations. As a result of timely controlled break recommendations, peaks of negative mental and physical stress of the employees during the work process are to be prevented. An appropriate tool for recording continuously vital data are commercially available sensor wristbands [7]. For the detection and prevention of negative stress, various physiological parameters are of interest, for example, pulse rate, electrodermal activity, peripheral skin temperature and movement data. The use of machine learning may also enable conclusions from combinations or patterns of different vital parameters in order to assess the underlying types of stress.

The long-term objective of this research project is to establish a dynamic break organization that positively influences the well-being and health of the employees and at the same time maintains the performance of the company. Furthermore, sickness rates, error rates and accidents at work are to be reduced. The complete architecture of the envisaged system is shown in Fig. 1.

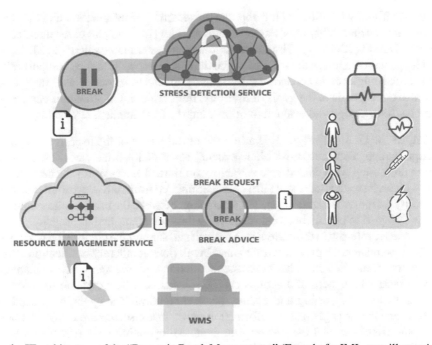

**Fig. 1.** IT architecture of the "Dynamic Break Management" (Fraunhofer IML, own illustration).

The targeted system consists of three main components. The first step is to collect vital data from the employee during the work process via a sensor wristband, which, in combination with a smartphone app, performs the direct interaction with the employee as well as the transfer of the vital data for the subsequent analysis.

Second, the analysis of the data takes place in a protected cloud service, more precisely the stress detection service, where the testing for stress indicators is performed with AI algorithms. If mental or physical stress is detected, a break request is sent to a service that manages the availabilities of the respective employees, which is called the resource management service. On the one hand, this service has the goal of transparently displaying the availabilities of the employees and thus enabling the warehouse supervisor to optimally deploy the human resources in the warehouse.

Finally, the resource management service has an interface to warehouse management systems (WMS) to manage orders and required resources. If the break recommendation is approved on duty, the employee receives a notification of a break recommendation via the smartphone app. The break advice can be accepted or rejected. In addition to the automated break recommendation, the system also offers the employee the possibility to independently request and take breaks.

## 3  Methodology

### 3.1  Principles of Human Information Processing in the Design of User Interfaces

For a user-friendly handling of the app, the presentation of information and the dialog between human and technology was designed according to principles of the international standard DIN EN ISO 9241 "Ergonomics of human-system interaction" [2, 3].

The principles address the ways in which the design of user interfaces supports effectiveness and efficiency in achieving the task and can lead to increased user satisfaction. This also corresponds to the goals of usability. Furthermore, the principles can be used in the analysis, design and evaluation of user interfaces of interactive systems.

**Principles for Dialog Design.**  Regarding the development of the user interface of the smartphone app "Dynamic Break Management", seven dialog principles of human information processing were considered: suitability for the task, self-descriptiveness, conformity with user expectations, suitability for learning, controllability, error tolerance and suitability for individualization [2]. The interaction between the user and the technology used is designed to be suitable to the task. Only those elements and information are displayed that are relevant in the current task context and support the completion of the work task (e.g. permanent display of working and break time, temporary notification when a break is recommended). Furthermore, the interaction with the app is self-explanatory, i.e. it is clear which steps and actions can be selected and how they are to be carried out (e.g. buttons for starting and ending the working day). The operating procedures, symbols and the arrangement of information on the main screen are designed consistently and therefore meet the user expectations. All operating steps and places where certain information, settings or functions are arranged are easy to understand and follow a learnable principle. With the help of buttons, icons and pop-up notifications, the user is guided to the goal of the task with simple and flexible dialog paths (e.g. gear wheel icon for the settings menu). The user can control the speed and type of input. It is also ensured that the user has control over the processing of the system, i.e. there is the possibility to interrupt or cancel a running process [13]. The dialog of the app application is designed to be error-tolerant. The user is notified of input errors and receives auditory and haptic reminders. Furthermore, logging in to the system is done via a simple but data-protected query of the user name and password. To create a degree of individualization, the system recognizes the user ID when logging in and automatically sets the user's language.

**Principles for the Presentation of Information.**  The ergonomic design principles for the software-driven presentation of information at the user interface are based on the three main human sensory modalities (visual, auditory, tactile/haptic) typically addressed in information and communication technology [3]. These principles are detectability, freedom from distraction, discriminability, unambiguous interpretability, conciseness and consistency. When designing the user interface, it was ensured that the required information is detectable and legible and that the perception of information is free of distractions. Important information is arranged centrally, the text is displayed in dark letters on a white background and in mixed upper/lower case letters in an easily readable font size [13]. For a better visual differentiation of information, e.g. the two buttons "start workday" and "end workday" were placed at different places on the screen [13]. The information presentation of the user interface is compact and consistent. Only necessary information elements are displayed. Information elements with similar intentions are presented similarly, information elements with different intentions in different styles and forms.

## 3.2    Research Findings on Ergonomic App Design

According to research regarding user interface design of mobile apps, the presentation of information of work time and break time, the recommendations to take a break or continue working were purposefully implemented [6]. Icons have the advantage of holding the user's attention, it is also beneficial to use familiar icons which makes the processing of the visuals on the screen easier and more appealing [9]. Gao and Sun conducted a study in 2015 evaluating several screen gestures in a smartphone context [5]. Their results suggest that button sizes of at least 15.9 mm × 9.0 mm lead to better performance and user satisfaction. They also concluded that the button spacing should be at least 6.0 mm for big buttons, small buttons should have at least a 3.0 mm spacing. Downward and rightward dragging motions were preferred over upward and leftward [5]. The app has to perform proficiently in a working environment and different types of smartphones as well, which brings up the factor of performance and responsiveness of the app. Study results demonstrate that already very brief delays of human-computer interaction can have considerable detrimental effects on behavioral performance and emotional wellbeing [14].

A minimalistic design provides a very responsive and fast loading experience, which could be called one of the fundamental objectives for maximizing efficiency of mobile applications [4]. This is one futile aspect for mobile applications, which heavily rely on focused and rapid actions, instead of long lasting sessions known from desktop computers [11].

## 4    Results

### 4.1    Current Development Status of the App "Dynamic Break Management"

The entire structure of the app is based on the existing structures of a typical working day. Starting with logging in with their own user data, through the beginning of the working day to the breaks taken and the end of the working day, all the typical components of a natural daily routine are depicted in the app. The aim of this structure is to offer employees a logically structured and familiar environment in which they feel comfortable and which they can understand straight away.

All functions and buttons in the app were designed to fulfil a clear function in the respective context. The amount of information presented was reduced to a necessary minimum in order to keep the cognitive effort of the employee low when using the app. After logging into the app, the employee is given access to the main screen. All the required functions can be called up via this screen. The employee can start his or her working day via a corresponding button. In the course of this, the recording of the working time and the employee's vital data starts. During the course of the working day, the employee can proactively request a break at any time. If he does so, he immediately receives feedback on the processing of this request. If the requested break is approved, the employee is notified via the app. The employee's measured vital data is evaluated throughout the entire working day and analyzed for stress characteristics. Machine learning methods are used to perform this analysis, which was trained in advance to detect specific stress features in the vital signs. If a corresponding stress level is detected or predicted, the employee receives a break recommendation via the app. He can accept this recommendation or postpone it to a later time. If the employee decides to take the break later, he or she will be reminded again after a certain time. As soon as a break is in progress, the data displayed on the main screen changes. Thus, information on the used and remaining break time is displayed to the employee, so that the employee has an overview of how much break time is left at any time. Either the employee ends the break at his or her own request or the app suggests an end of break and continuation of work. In addition to the legal and ergonomic requirements, the vital data are also used for this purpose. The measured data is used to determine the employee's recovery process during their break.

### 4.2 Different Mockups for a Research-Based App Design

The first design prototype was based on minimal-design and flat-design principles. The minimal design is characterized mostly through the generous use of white space and only little use of colours. Flat design principles focus mostly on the typography, waiving of high-fidelity graphics and the use of big and simple icons [15]. Several UI designs were developed on the basis of the first prototype (Fig. 2). One features a large circular button in the center, which switches between the "play" and "break" symbols, referring to start worktime or engaging breaktime. The button is surrounded by a circular progress bar, which indicates the progress of the working day. A version with a horizontal progress bar has also been designed. Additionally, there is a digital clock for work and break times, which is changing between the two modes. For the buttons "start workday" and "end workday", the results of Gao and Sun (2015) were used [5]. Another UI demonstrates a dragging motion that switches between the respective modes for "work time" and "break time". This design was fueled by the assumption, that a dragging motion would be less prone to unintentional button presses, with the downward dragging motion switching from "work" to "break", providing the more the satisfying experience [5]. The layout of time information was done in accordance with an international DIN standard, which provides guidelines for the layout and information processing of times [1].

**Fig. 2.** UI design concepts for the app "Dynamic Break Management" (Fraunhofer IML, own illustration).

## 5 Conclusion

A dynamic break management enables the company to manage orders and the workforce in a smart manner. The challenges in measuring highly sensitive vital data are to guarantee data protection and, in conclusion, to create trust and acceptance among the workforce [12]. In addition, health, the ability to work and productivity of the employees are to be maintained or improved in the long term. This digital health prevention helps the company to increase the performance of the employees, optimize processes and reduce the operative costs in the warehouse. On the other hand, the employee also benefits from the use of the dynamic break management. Breaks are individually tailored and oriented to the demands of each employee. This enables greater employee satisfaction and, conversely, better acceptance of the corresponding system. But this digitized endeavor has to be implemented with the lowest common denominator in mind regarding intuitiveness of interaction, individual digital competences and device performance. Apps in the industrial context have to be easy to understand and ensure a stable and satisfactory operation at all times to guarantee a consequent application and approval of the user.

**Funding.** The project "Silicon Economy Logistics Ecosystem" is funded by the Federal Ministry of Transport and Digital Infrastructure.

## References

1. DIN EN ISO 5008:2020-03: Rules for writing and layout of word and information processing (ISO 5008:2020); German version EN ISO 5008:2020-03
2. DIN EN ISO 9241-110:2008–09: Ergonomics of human-system interaction - Part 110: Dialogue principles (ISO 9241–110:2006); German version EN ISO 9241-110:2006

3. DIN EN ISO 9241-112:2017: Ergonomics of human-system interaction - Part 112: Principles for the presentation of information (ISO 9241-112:2017); German version EN ISO 9241-112:2017

4. Fui-Hoon Nah, F., Siau, K., Sheng, H.: The value of mobile applications: a utility company study. Commun. ACM **48**(2), 85–90 (2005)

5. Gao, Q., Sun, Q.: Examining the usability of touch screen gestures for older and younger adults. Hum. Factors Ergon. Soc. **57**(5), 835–863 (2015)

6. Ghafurian, M., Reitter, D., Ritter, F.E.: Countdown timer speed: a trade-off between delay duration perception and recall. ACM Trans. Comput. Hum. Interact. **27**(2), 1–25 (2020)

7. Giannakakis, G., Grigoriadis, D., Giannakaki, K., Simantiraki, O., Roniotis, A., Tsiknakis, M.: Review on psychological stress detection using biosignals. IEEE Trans. Affect. Comput. 1 (2019). https://doi.org/10.1109/TAFFC.2019.2927337

8. Grosse, E.H., Glock, C.H., Neumann, W.P.: Human factors in order picking: a content analysis of the literature. Int. J. Prod. Res. **55**(5), 1260–1276 (2017)

9. Jylhä, H., Hamari, J.: An icon that everyone wants to click: how perceived aesthetic qualities predict app icon successfulness. Int. J. Hum.-Comput. Stud. **130**, 73–85 (2019)

10. Kretschmer, V.: Die rolle des menschen in der digitalen arbeitswelt: erkenntnisse industrienaher forschungsprojekte am Beispiel der Logistik. In: Herbstkonferenz der Gesellschaft für Arbeitswissenschaft e. V. (GfA) 2020 "Stellenwert menschlicher Arbeit im Zeitalter der digitalen Transformation", 17–18 September 2020. GfA-Press, Dortmund (2020)

11. Kuusinen, K., Mikkonen, T.: On designing UX for mobile enterprise apps. In: Proceedings of the 40th Euromicro Conference on Software Engineering and Advanced Applications, SEAA 2014, 27–29 August 2014, Verona, Italy, pp. 221–228. IEEE (2014)

12. Orji, R., Lomotey, R., Oyibo, K., Orji, F., Blustein, J., Shahid, S.: Tracking feels oppressive and 'punishy': exploring the costs and benefits of self-monitoring for health and wellness. Digit. Health **4**, 1–10 (2018)

13. Scapin, D.L., Bastien, J.M.C.: Ergonomic criteria for evaluating the ergonomic quality of interactive systems. Behav. Inf. Technol. **16**(4–5), 220–231 (1997)

14. Szameitat, A.J., Rummel, J., Szameitat, D.P., Sterr, A.: Behavioral and emotional consequences of brief delays in human-computer interaction. Int. J. Hum.-Comput. Stud. **67**(7), 561–570 (2009)

15. Ullrich, D., Diefenbach, S.: Minimal design, maximum confusion - wie das minimal design dogma die usability aushebelt. In: Hess, S., Fischer, H. (eds.) Mensch und Computer 2018 - Usability Professionals, pp. 203–216. Gesellschaft für Informatik e.V. und German UPA e.V., Bonn (2018)

16. Wendsche, J., Lohmann-Haislah, A.: Psychische Gesundheit in der Arbeitswelt - Pausen. Dortmund: Bundesanstalt für Arbeitsschutz und Arbeitsmedizin (Hrsg.) (2016)

# Occupational Safety and Health Education and Training: A Latent Dirichlet Allocation Systematic Literature Review

Guido J. L. Micheli$^{(\boxtimes)}$ (iD), Gaia Vitrano, and Antonio Calabrese (iD)

Department of Management, Economics and Industrial Engineering, Politecnico di Milano,
Piazza Leonardo da Vinci, 32, 20133 Milan, Italy
{guido.micheli,gaia.vitrano,antonio.calabrese}@polimi.it

**Abstract.** Education and training play an increasingly meaningful role in recent research on Occupational Safety and Health (OSH) through the whole companies' supply chains. However, considering the extent of the subject, most research works focus on specific issues, which are not easily replicable in other contexts. Therefore, this work gathers the main results achieved by researchers and systematically identifies leading research paths and trends for future works. A review and systematic categorisation of the existent literature have deemed essential for achieving the scope. The Latent Dirichlet Allocation (LDA) technique has been chosen to extract meaningful information on education and/or training and cluster articles, which have been grouped into eight topics. This analysis has brought out several key factors (industry hazards, workers' motivation, availability of technologies, etc.) that influence the success or failure of implementing OSH education and training programs. This work pays particular attention to human factors which, if effectively managed, would induce a great step forward for OSH education and training. There is still little or no evidence of education and training's effectiveness through time since monitoring the outcomes has been often neglected by the management. Nonetheless, Industry 4.0 technologies will help to fill this gap by enabling real-time and continuous tracking of outcomes, which will pave the way for several future works.

**Keywords:** Occupational safety and health · Education · Training · Literature review

## 1 Problem Setting

Work-related injuries and diseases did not use to be the primary concern of managers and company leaders who have neglected the Safety and Health of their workers. The science of OSH appeared and developed as a consequence of several and tragically work-related accidents, which have produced adverse economic and social effects over time. Today OSH is considered a science of anticipation, recognition, evaluation and control of hazards, affecting the wellbeing of workers [1].

© The Author(s), under exclusive license to Springer Nature Switzerland AG 2021
N. L. Black et al. (Eds.): IEA 2021, LNNS 221, pp. 491–502, 2021.
https://doi.org/10.1007/978-3-030-74608-7_61

Non-Safety and Health activities generate human and social pain and, above all, an immense social and economic cost, at an individual, company, supply chain, and community level. However, luckily, most accidents are due to wrong actions or behaviours, so they can be prevented by implementing corrective measures. A good OSH management reduces injuries, diseases and fatalities among employees, and, in turn, has a positive impact on the costs occurring across the entire supply chain (i.e., at a system level).

Education and training provide theoretical and practical knowledge crucial for spreading OSH culture, or simply safety culture, which is widely acknowledged to be of paramount importance and strongly entangled with successful OSH management. Although to a different extent, education and training are essential for Safety and Health work environments by controlling (preventing and minimising) those hazards that cannot be eliminated. This theoretical and practical knowledge must be transferred to any worker considering their background and responsibilities [1, 2]. Education can be seen as a process of conceptualisation, this means an "*organized and sustained instruction designed to communicate a combination of knowledge, skills and understanding valuable for all activities of life*" [3]. Training is complementary to education, which can sometimes result too theoretical and hard to put into practice. Training, in fact, focuses on mastering workers in performing specific tasks or roles by avoiding improper actions and, thus, reducing accidents [4]. The study performed by Burke et al. [5] showed that the choice of the method for OSH education and training affects safety performance and injuries' reduction; in particular, experimentally based methods (training) generate higher knowledge acquisition than theoretical learning processes (education).

Considering the extent of the subject, this work wants to analyse the current state of the art of OSH education and training by identifying the main lines of research, inherent limitations and then the paths and trends for future works. In particular, the goal can be reached by answering the following questions: (1) What kinds of workers are mainly considered in the literature? (2) Which are the key contextual factors that shape different kinds of OSH education and training? (3) Which are the promising research areas in OSH education and training according to questions 1 and 2?

## 2   Methodology

A consistent and broad systematic literature review is deemed essential to answer the three questions stated above. Articles selection has been performed on Scopus, the world's largest database, following a detailed search protocol (Fig. 1).

First, a list of journals has been identified including all those which have in their title the word *safety*, *ergonomics* or *accident* and positively reply to the following questions: (a) Is the journal coverage starting, at least, in 2012? (b) Is it related to social science and health? (c) Has it an SJR index [6] higher or equal to 1? If not, has it an SJR index lower than 1 and higher than 0.2 with publications highly related to the research area? As a result, eight journals have been selected: Accident Analysis and Prevention; Ergonomics; Applied Ergonomics; Safety Science; Journal of Safety Research; International Journal of Industrial Ergonomics; Safety and Health at Work; International Journal of Occupational Safety and Ergonomics.

As a second step, for articles selection, three research areas have been considered: education/training, occupational and accident. Therefore, a specific query string has been created: *(education OR training) AND (occupational OR industrial OR work-related OR job-related) AND (accident OR risk OR safety OR health OR hazard)*. The identified keywords were selected in the title, abstract and keywords. Then, the research has been narrowed down considering only recent articles published starting from 2008. Since the number of publications was still quite large, a manual analysis has been performed by reading titles, keywords and abstracts to identify articles that were closely related to OSH education and training. In the end, 54 publications have been chosen and the most significant will be mentioned to drive the discussion.

Once the papers were selected, a Text Mining (TM) technique has been identified for extracting meaningful information and clustering articles. TM technique considers terms and their frequency and creates a matrix called Document-Term Matrix, in which the terms for each article are weighted according to their frequency. However, to increase the accuracy of the method, sections or terms that do not provide any relevant information for generating topics and classifying articles should be removed from the text before proceeding (the whole references section, numbers, punctuations, words like articles, conjunctions, etc.).

A dimension reduction technique has been applied to merge terms with the same semantics (synonymy) and to distinguish those with multiple meanings (polysemy): for this work, the Latent Dirichlet Allocation (LDA) technique [7] has been used. LDA takes as input the Document-Term matrix and a set of desired topics (arbitrarily chosen, then iteratively confirmed), generates a set of keywords for each topic and provides the likelihood (in per cent) between articles and created topics.

The articles have been grouped in eight categories and each of them has been assigned to the topic in which it scored the highest likelihood. If the likelihood was higher than 0.5, papers have been accepted in the cluster assigned by the LDA model. When the likelihood for the first topic was lower than 0.5 and the likelihood for the second topic was lower than 0.1, the article has been still allocated to the first topic. Whereas when the likelihood for the first topic was again lower than 0.5 but the likelihood of the second topic was higher than 0.1, a manual cluster allocation in one of the two topics was envisaged by reading full papers.

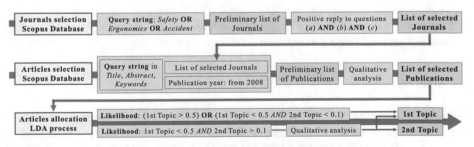

**Fig. 1.** Methodology – Articles selection and clustering.

## 3   Results

The eight topics got through the LDA process and resulted from the analysis of the articles with the highest likelihood are reported below:

- Topic 1: training methods to increase workers' knowledge of OSH and industry performance [8–16].
- Topic 2: training experiments based on accident scenarios to evaluate workers' hazard and risk perception before and after interventions [17–19].
- Topic 3: studies on safety commitment of managers, owners and leaders, which impacts on safety outcomes [20–25].
- Topic 4: studies on the effects of safety education and training on workers, which consider behaviour change, situation awareness and other measures for efficacy [26–34].
- Topic 5: studies on education programs provided to young or inexperienced workers to increase their level of knowledge and risk awareness [35–39].
- Topic 6: training methods and results in the construction industry, which mainly focus on risks related to falling from altitudes [40–45].
- Topic 7: training methods to improve workers' safety behaviour, reducing Musculoskeletal Disorders (MSDs) [46–51].
- Topic 8: training methods and ergonomic interventions to improve workers' well-being in office and decrease MSDs [52–61].

The selected publications for OSH education and/or training have been classified into three main groups according to the type of study:

- Methods: articles which proposed new methodologies for OSH education and training, experimental methods implemented and tested in specific industry settings, and evaluation methods to measure the outcomes of these procedures already implemented in organisations.
- Theoretical researches: articles focusing on evaluating procedures, methods to detect weaknesses or to accept hypotheses regarding OSH education and training.
- Literature reviews: articles reviewing and synthesising the OSH education and training literature applied in specific contexts.

## 4   Discussion

Legislations and organisations establish mandatory education and training programs for workers, which should be set according to the environment where they are implemented by adapting to several determining factors such as types of industry hazards, workers' motivation, culture and background education, availability of technologies, management commitment to safety. Therefore, the end-users, i.e., the workers, are crucial for the intervention outcomes. Papers developing or testing education and training programs usually address one specific category of workers and the most relevant groups are set out below.

Young and inexperienced workers, deemed more open to behavioural changes and knowledge acquisition, are one of the most frequent targets in the literature (as stated in Topic 5). They are at risk because they lack experience and proper training to recognise and avoid hazards. It seems, according to some researches (e.g., [35, 36]), that there is no systematic and efficient approach on young workers' instruction, foreseeing the need for further research and improvement in this matter. The choice of the method is crucial for obtaining high effectiveness of the intervention. The education methods used on vocational and educational institutions like technical high schools, universities and colleges can make the difference in transferring knowledge to young and inexperienced workers.

Although methods and programs for young and inexperienced workers still need further developments, old and experienced workers should not be neglected. In fact, employers often do not realise that this category of workers has no perception of the hazard's level [19]. Therefore, companies are invited to arrange different sessions of training considering the workers' expertise and their perception of hazards to achieve higher awareness among employees and reduce the overall risk level at the workplace.

Instead of focusing on the age and experience level of workers, other authors, to enhance Safety and Health and reduce injuries and diseases, designed programs and set interventions based on specific activities performed by workers, since the nature of the tasks largely shapes work-force requirements, risks and hazards. In fact, education and training usually result more effective if tailored to specific industries and task settings. Authors, in this literature review, have mainly pointed out three workers' categories: office, construction and manufacturing workers. The largest work-related risk for office workers is being affected by MSD, a disease characterised by discomfort and pain in joints, muscles and soft tissues, which is the leading contributor to disability worldwide and affects between one-fifth and one-third of the whole population [62]. Construction workers are exposed to a high risk of falling from altitudes, while for manufacturing workers machinery operations cause most of the injuries and diseases. Topic 6 (e.g., [40]) and Topic 8 (e.g., [56]), referring to construction and office workers respectively, mostly propose education and training interventions to reduce the impact of work-related risks. The 7th is a broader Topic as it includes literature reviews, such as [47] and [51], of articles, which mostly refer to ergonomics interventions in different work contexts, including manufacturing activities.

Considering the wide workers' diversity, education and training programs should take into account factors related to workers' cultural/professional background and the field they work in, by designing activities based on the most frequent and serious hazards for that category of workers.

Most of the articles evaluate education and training methods and interventions for workers neglecting managers, owners and leaders. However, some studies, clustered in Topic 3, explained that higher management commitment to safety positively affects safety climate and outcomes by reducing injuries and diseases. According to some authors (e.g., [20, 25]), implementing training on managers determines transformational leadership, contingent rewards and safety self-efficacy, which, in turn, produce positive control behaviours and safe environment. Luckily, recent research trends show an increasing interest in this topic.

The success of education and training activities closely relies on adopted techniques which are mainly analysed by articles belonging to Topics 1, 4 and, to a lesser extent, 8. Many methods are available, and their efficacy partially depends on the context, in which they are applied. The analysis of the literature addressed two main categories of programs to foster workers' knowledge:

- Conventional methods: normally based on theoretical presentations and classrooms training.
- New methods: aimed at increasing the level of gained knowledge by supporting worker's change of behaviour and, above all, maintaining the effectiveness of training through time. These recently developed methods (e.g., e-learning techniques and 3D simulation software) show promising results on transferring knowledge by improving hazard and risk perception and situation awareness.

According to some authors (e.g., [8, 29]), simulation tools, by representing non-routine tasks and abnormal situations, have proven to be efficient methods (comparatively faster than conventional ones) to increase workers' safety awareness. Moreover, these methods are helpful when training under real situations is not feasible due to high potential Safety and Health risks for workers.

To increase the effectiveness of education and training through time, as mentioned in Topic 2, authors after the formal training session have applied methods like notifications, toolbox meetings, reminders and rehearsals. As clearly said by Molesworth et al. [18]: *"even a single, brief rehearsal [...] will be worthwhile".*

As explained in the previous lines, several contextual factors influence the design and the following success of an education or training activity. Therefore, it is not possible to shape an activity theoretically and in advance, but it has to be developed in the specific field where it is meant to be applied. When activities for OSH improvement are developed, indicators like the number of fatalities, injury frequency rate, severity rate and all the potential affected OSH variables should be tracked over time to monitor how they get changed (positively or negatively) by implemented actions. Contextual factors and their combinations can enhance or hinder the initial desired outcome and these factors can be even improved after the intervention itself.

The complexity of variables that come into play with OSH education and training has been briefly depicted on a structured framework (Fig. 2) which synthetically gathers data collected from the literature. Figure 2 shows key elements to bear in mind when designing and implementing OSH education and training interventions.

In past years, it seems that researchers have focused mostly on shaping interventions and defining their key characteristics neglecting, however, to monitor the results over time. Today, there is still weak evidence of beneficial safety outcomes related to education and training programs [24], since the results can be only observed in the long run. Besides, most of the improvements in the OSH field need a combined action of many different activities, which makes hard to establish direct and univocal relationships between performed activities and following obtained results.

Assessing outcomes of education and training programs over time is crucial for designing and developing future activities, which will try to keep effective solutions and avoid others. Monitoring the results of interventions allows to clearly show managers, leaders and owners when a program was successful and, thus, encouraging them to actively carry out formative activities (education and training). Therefore, it turns out to be a promising research area, which would deserve greater attention, but which still needs new technological solutions to show its full potential. New education and training techniques, previously mentioned, are developing in this sense as they will be of great help for measuring the outcomes of OSH interventions. Industry 4.0 technologies (augmented reality, real-time monitoring adaptable workstations, etc.) play a crucial role in the entire supply chain by enhancing worker's activities and enabling better OSH activities' implementation, like education and training. They also help to continuously monitor achieved outcomes. These technologies are the enablers that, in the following years, will allow identifying a direct relationship between reached safety outcomes and past implemented education and training activities.

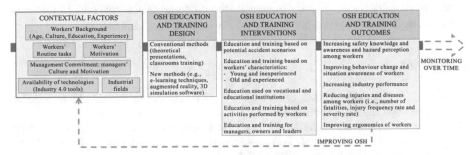

**Fig. 2.** A structured framework – Key elements for OSH education and training.

## 5   Conclusions

The proposed analysis, through the systematic literature review and LDA technique, stands above other researches (issue-specific) because it identifies the main research paths for education and training in OSH and the open-fields to be investigated.

The structured framework proposed above brings together data from the literature by detecting key factors that influence and shape education and training in OSH.

From the literature review, it has emerged that human factors (such as workers' knowledge, behaviour change, situation awareness and risk perception) and industrial settings are extremely relevant for designing education and training interventions and determining their success. It implies that good OSH management should start from the well-being of each individual. Hence, education and training methods will not be efficient enough if they are not customised upon workers' characteristics and do not stimulate and encourage workers and managers' interest. Workers' characteristics and industrial settings are accurately analysed to detect criticalities in the working environment and state which factors can foster and boost the implementation and the outcomes of education and training programs.

The literature mostly agrees that new Industry 4.0 technologies will be the break-through allowing the joint management of complex factors and situations and ensuring high efficacy of education and training in OSH in the next future. Implementing new OSH education and training methods, such as e-learning techniques, aims at increasing the level of gained knowledge and risk perception, supporting worker's change of behaviour and, above all, maintaining the effectiveness of training over time. Industry 4.0 technologies, through further research, will enable to overcome the current gap in the literature, in which, although the importance of training's effectiveness through time is often stressed, little or no evidence of it has been provided [63].

Due to some choices made in the systematic literature review process, this work carries around few main limitations which refer to the journals' selection, the decided time interval for papers' extraction and the applied method (LDA) needed to define main research fields (topics) that stood out from the collected papers. In particular, the major shortcoming related to LDA lies in the arbitrary choice of the clusters' number, eight in this work, which significantly influences the outcome of the analysis. In this case, however, eight seems to be a good trade-off for ensuring sensible results.

# References

1. Alli, B.O.: Fundamental Principles of Occupational Health and Safety, 2nd edn. International Labour Organization, Geneva (2008)
2. Cagno, E., Micheli, G.J.L., Jacinto, C., Masi, D.: An interpretive model of occupational safety performance for Small- and Medium-sized Enterprises. Int. J. Ind. Ergon. **44**, 60–74 (2014). https://doi.org/10.1016/j.ergon.2013.08.005
3. Jarvis, P.: An International Dictionary of Adult and Continuing Education, 1st edn. Routledge, London (1990)
4. Tight, M.: Key Concepts in Adult Education and Training, 2nd edn. Taylor & Francis, London (2002)
5. Burke, M.J., Sarpy, S.A., Smith-Crowe, K., Chan-Serafin, S., Salvador, R.O., Islam, G.: Relative effectiveness of worker safety and health training methods. Am. J. Public Health **96**, 315–324 (2006). https://doi.org/10.2105/AJPH.2004.059840
6. González-Pereira, B., Guerrero-Bote, V.P., Moya-Anegón, F.: A new approach to the metric of journals' scientific prestige: the SJR indicator. J. Informetr. **4**, 379–391 (2010). https://doi.org/10.1016/j.joi.2010.03.002
7. Blei, D.M., Ng, A.Y., Jordan, M.I.: Latent Dirichlet allocation. J. Mach. Learn. Res. **3**, 993–1022 (2003). https://doi.org/10.5555/944919.944937
8. Crichton, M.T.: Improving team effectiveness using tactical decision games. Saf. Sci. **47**, 330–336 (2009). https://doi.org/10.1016/j.ssci.2008.07.036
9. Thamrin, Y., Pisaniello, D.L., Stewart, S.K.: Time trends and predictive factors for safety perceptions among incoming South Australian university students. J. Saf. Res. **41**, 59–63 (2010). https://doi.org/10.1016/j.jsr.2009.11.003
10. Pisaniello, D.L., Stewart, S.K., Jahan, N., Pisaniello, S.L., Winefield, H., Braunack-Mayer, A.: The role of high schools in introductory occupational safety education - teacher perspectives on effectiveness. Saf. Sci. **55**, 53–61 (2013). https://doi.org/10.1016/j.ssci.2012.12.011
11. Haas, E.J., Hoebbel, C.L., Rost, K.A.: An analysis of trainers' perspectives within an ecological framework: factors that influence mine safety training processes. Saf. Health Work **5**, 118–124 (2014). https://doi.org/10.1016/j.shaw.2014.06.004

12. Stuart, A.: A blended learning approach to safety training: student experiences of safe work practices and safety culture. Saf. Sci. **62**, 409–417 (2014). https://doi.org/10.1016/j.ssci.2013. 10.005

13. Lee, Y.J., Lee, D.: Factors influencing learning satisfaction of migrant workers in Korea with e-learning-based occupational safety and health education. Saf. Health Work **6**, 211–217 (2015). https://doi.org/10.1016/j.shaw.2015.05.002

14. Gummesson, K.: Effective measures to decrease air contaminants through risk and control visualization - a study of the effective use of QR codes to facilitate safety training. Saf. Sci. **82**, 120–128 (2016). https://doi.org/10.1016/j.ssci.2015.09.011

15. Terwoert, J., Verbist, K., Heussen, H.: An intervention study on the implementation of control banding in controlling exposure to hazardous chemicals in small and medium-sized enterprises. Saf. Health Work **7**, 185–193 (2016). https://doi.org/10.1016/j.shaw.2015.12.002

16. Freitas, A.C., Silva, S.A.: Exploring OHS trainers' role in the transfer of training. Saf. Sci. **91**, 310–319 (2017). https://doi.org/10.1016/j.ssci.2016.08.007

17. Lesch, M.F.: Warning symbols as reminders of hazards: impact of training. Accid. Anal. Prev. **40**, 1005–1012 (2008). https://doi.org/10.1016/j.aap.2007.11.009

18. Molesworth, B.R.C., Tsang, M.H., Kehoe, E.J.: Rehearsal and verbal reminders in facilitating compliance with safety rules. Accid. Anal. Prev. **43**, 991–997 (2011). https://doi.org/10.1016/ j.aap.2010.11.026

19. Horswill, M.S., Taylor, K., Newnam, S., Wetton, M., Hill, A.: Even highly experienced drivers benefit from a brief hazard perception training intervention. Accid. Anal. Prev. **52**, 100–110 (2013). https://doi.org/10.1016/j.aap.2012.12.014

20. Huang, Y.H., Verma, S.K., Chang, W.R., Courtney, T.K., Lombardi, D.A., Brennan, M.J., Perry, M.J.: Management commitment to safety vs. employee perceived safety training and association with future injury. Accid. Anal. Prev. **47**, 94–101 (2012). https://doi.org/10.1016/ j.aap.2011.12.001

21. Brahm, F., Singer, M.: Is more engaging safety training always better in reducing accidents? Evidence of self-selection from Chilean panel data. J. Saf. Res. **47**, 85–92 (2013). https://doi. org/10.1016/j.jsr.2013.09.003

22. Farina, E., Bena, A., Dotti, A.: Impact on safety of a preventive intervention in metalworking micro-enterprises. Saf. Sci. **71**, 292–297 (2015). https://doi.org/10.1016/j.ssci.2014.05.021

23. Olivieri, A., Benacchio, L., Bizzotto, R., Zecchin, F., Barizza, M., Squarcina, V., Bottacin, G., Venturini, C., Beccastrini, S., Potì, M., Baldasseroni, A.: Empowering employers in work-related injuries prevention: a pragmatic trial. Saf. Sci. **74**, 122–127 (2015). https://doi.org/10. 1016/j.ssci.2014.08.015

24. Taylor, E.L.: Safety benefits of mandatory OSHA 10 h training. Saf. Sci. **77**, 66–71 (2015). https://doi.org/10.1016/j.ssci.2015.03.003

25. Von Thiele Schwarz, U., Hasson, H., Tafvelin, S.: Leadership training as an occupational health intervention: improved safety and sustained productivity. Saf. Sci. **81**, 35–45 (2016). https://doi.org/10.1016/j.ssci.2015.07.020

26. Guo, H., Li, H., Chan, G., Skitmore, M.: Using game technologies to improve the safety of construction plant operations. Accid. Anal. Prev. **48**, 204–213 (2012). https://doi.org/10. 1016/j.aap.2011.06.002

27. Langer, T.H., Iversen, T.K., Andersen, N.K., Mouritsen, O.Ø., Hansen, M.R.: Reducing whole-body vibration exposure in backhoe loaders by education of operators. Int. J. Ind. Ergon. **42**, 304–311 (2012). https://doi.org/10.1016/j.ergon.2012.03.001

28. Grabowski, A., Jankowski, J.: Virtual Reality-based pilot training for underground coal miners. Saf. Sci. **72**, 310–314 (2015). https://doi.org/10.1016/j.ssci.2014.09.017

29. Nazir, S., Sorensen, L.J., Øvergård, K.I., Manca, D.: Impact of training methods on Distributed Situation Awareness of industrial operators. Saf. Sci. **73**, 136–145 (2015). https://doi.org/10. 1016/j.ssci.2014.11.015

30. Suleiman, A.M., Svendsen, K.V.H.: Effectuality of cleaning workers' training and cleaning enterprises' chemical health hazard risk profiling. Saf. Health Work **6**, 345–352 (2015). https://doi.org/10.1016/j.shaw.2015.10.003

31. Misiurek, K., Misiurek, B.: Methodology of improving occupational safety in the construction industry on the basis of the TWI program. Saf. Sci. **92**, 225–231 (2017). https://doi.org/10.1016/j.ssci.2016.10.017

32. Vidal-Gomel, C.: Training to safety rules use. Some reflections on a case study. Saf. Sci. **93**, 134–142 (2017). https://doi.org/10.1016/j.ssci.2016.12.001

33. Cecchini, M., Bedini, R., Mosetti, D., Marino, S., Stasi, S.: Safety knowledge and changing behavior in agricultural workers: an assessment model applied in central Italy. Saf. Health Work **9**, 164–171 (2018). https://doi.org/10.1016/j.shaw.2017.07.009

34. Nie, B., Huang, X., Xue, F., Chen, J., Liu, X., Meng, Y., Huang, J.: A comparative study of vocational education and occupational safety and health training in China and the UK. Int. J. Occup. Saf. Ergon. **24**, 268–277 (2018). https://doi.org/10.1080/10803548.2016.1270042

35. Chin, P., DeLuca, C., Poth, C., Chadwick, I., Hutchinson, N., Munby, H.: Enabling youth to advocate for workplace safety. Saf. Sci. **48**, 570–579 (2010). https://doi.org/10.1016/j.ssci.2010.01.009

36. Andersson, I.M., Gunnarsson, K., Rosèn, G., Moström Åberg, M.: Knowledge and experiences of risks among pupils in vocational education. Saf. Health Work **5**, 140–146 (2014). https://doi.org/10.1016/j.shaw.2014.06.002

37. Laberge, M., MacEachen, E., Calvet, B.: Why are occupational health and safety training approaches not effective? Understanding young worker learning processes using an ergonomic lens. Saf. Sci. **68**, 250–257 (2014). https://doi.org/10.1016/j.ssci.2014.04.012

38. Ouellet, S., Vézina, N.: Work training and MSDs prevention: contribution of ergonomics. Int. J. Ind. Ergon. **44**, 24–31 (2014). https://doi.org/10.1016/j.ergon.2013.08.008

39. Kintu, D., Kyakula, M., Kikomeko, J.: Occupational safety training and practices in selected vocational training institutions and workplaces in Kampala, Uganda. Int. J. Occup. Saf. Ergon. **21**, 532–538 (2015). https://doi.org/10.1080/10803548.2015.1085226

40. Kaskutas, V., Dale, A.M., Lipscomb, H., Gaal, J., Fuchs, M., Evanoff, B.: Changes in fall prevention training for apprentice carpenters based on a comprehensive needs assessment. J. Saf. Res. **41**, 221–227 (2010). https://doi.org/10.1016/j.jsr.2010.01.006

41. Williams, Q.L., Jr., Ochsner, M., Marshall, E., Kimmel, L., Martino, C.: The impact of a peer-led participatory health and safety training program for Latino day laborers in construction. J. Saf. Res. **41**, 253–261 (2010). https://doi.org/10.1016/j.jsr.2010.02.009

42. Hung, Y.H., Winchester, W.W., Smith-Jackson, T.L., Kleiner, B.M., Babski-Reeves, K.L., Mills, T.H.: Identifying fall-protection training needs for residential roofing subcontractors. Appl. Ergon. **44**, 372–380 (2013). https://doi.org/10.1016/j.apergo.2012.09.007

43. Kaskutas, V., Dale, A.M., Lipscomb, H., Evanoff, B.: Fall prevention and safety communication training for foremen: Report of a pilot project designed to improve residential construction safety. J. Saf. Res. **44**, 111–118 (2013). https://doi.org/10.1016/j.jsr.2012.08.020

44. Evanoff, B., Dale, A.M., Zeringue, A., Fuchs, M., Gaal, J., Lipscomb, H.J., Kaskutas, V.: Results of a fall prevention educational intervention for residential construction. Saf. Sci. **89**, 301–307 (2016). https://doi.org/10.1016/j.ssci.2016.06.019

45. Jeschke, K.C., Kines, P., Rasmussen, L., Andersen, L.P.S., Dyreborg, J., Ajslev, J., Kabel, A., Jensen, E., Andersen, L.L.: Process evaluation of a Toolbox-training program for construction foremen in Denmark. Saf. Sci. **94**, 152–160 (2017). https://doi.org/10.1016/j.ssci.2017.01.010

46. Kim, S.L., Lee, J.E.: Development of an intervention to prevent work-related musculoskeletal disorders among hospital nurses based on the participatory approach. Appl. Ergon. **41**, 454–460 (2010). https://doi.org/10.1016/j.apergo.2009.09.007

47. Van Eerd, D., Cole, D., Irvin, E., Mahood, Q., Keown, K., Theberge, N., Village, J., St. Vincent, M., Cullen, K.: Process and implementation of participatory ergonomic interventions: a systematic review. Ergonomics **53**, 1153–1166 (2010). https://doi.org/10.1080/00140139.2010.513452

48. McDermott, H., Haslam, C., Clemes, S., Williams, C., Haslam, R.: Investigation of manual handling training practices in organisations and beliefs regarding effectiveness. Int. J. Ind. Ergon. **42**, 206–211 (2012). https://doi.org/10.1016/j.ergon.2012.01.003

49. Pęciłło, M.: Results of implementing programmes for modifying unsafe behaviour in Polish companies. Int. J. Occup. Saf. Ergon. **18**, 473–485 (2012). https://doi.org/10.1080/10803548.2012.11076954

50. Szeto, G.P.Y., Wong, T.K.T., Law, R.K.Y., Lee, E.W.C., Lau, T., So, B.C.L., Law, S.W.: The impact of a multifaceted ergonomic intervention program on promoting occupational health in community nurses. Appl. Ergon. **44**, 414–422 (2013). https://doi.org/10.1016/j.apergo.2012.10.004

51. Hogan, D.A.M., Greiner, B.A., O'Sullivan, L.: The effect of manual handling training on achieving training transfer, employee's behaviour change and subsequent reduction of work-related musculoskeletal disorders: a systematic review. Ergonomics **57**, 93–107 (2014). https://doi.org/10.1080/00140139.2013.862307

52. Robertson, M., Amick, B.C., DeRango, K., Rooney, T., Bazzani, L., Harrist, R., Moore, A.: The effects of an office ergonomics training and chair intervention on worker knowledge, behavior and musculoskeletal risk. Appl. Ergon. **40**, 124–135 (2009). https://doi.org/10.1016/j.apergo.2007.12.009

53. Wu, H.C., Chen, H.C., Chen, T.: Effects of ergonomics-based wafer-handling training on reduction in musculoskeletal disorders among wafer handlers. Int. J. Ind. Ergon. **39**, 127–132 (2009). https://doi.org/10.1016/j.ergon.2008.04.006

54. Levanon, Y., Gefen, A., Lerman, Y., Givon, U., Ratzon, N.Z.: Reducing musculoskeletal disorders among computer operators: comparison between ergonomics interventions at the workplace. Ergonomics **55**, 1571–1585 (2012). https://doi.org/10.1080/00140139.2012.726654

55. Sigurdsson, S.O., Artnak, M., Needham, M., Wirth, O., Silverman, K.: Motivating ergonomic computer workstation setup: sometimes training is not enough. Int. J. Occup. Saf. Ergon. **18**, 27–33 (2012). https://doi.org/10.1080/10803548.2012.11076912

56. Taieb-Maimon, M., Cwikel, J., Shapira, B., Orenstein, I.: The effectiveness of a training method using self-modeling webcam photos for reducing musculoskeletal risk among office workers using computers. Appl. Ergon. **43**, 376–385 (2012). https://doi.org/10.1016/j.apergo.2011.05.015

57. Elfering, A., Arnold, S., Schade, V., Burger, C., Radlinger, L.: Stochastic resonance whole-body vibration, musculoskeletal symptoms, and body balance: a worksite training study. Saf. Health Work **4**, 149–155 (2013). https://doi.org/10.1016/j.shaw.2013.07.002

58. Meinert, M., König, M., Jaschinski, W.: Web-based office ergonomics intervention on work-related complaints: a field study. Ergonomics **56**, 1658–1668 (2013). https://doi.org/10.1080/00140139.2013.835872

59. Abareshi, F., Yarahmadi, R., Solhi, M., Farshad, A.A.: Educational intervention for reducing work-related musculoskeletal disorders and promoting productivity. Int. J. Occup. Saf. Ergon. **21**, 480–485 (2015). https://doi.org/10.1080/10803548.2015.1087729

60. Bulduk, S., Bulduk, E.Ö., Süren, T.: Reduction of work-related musculoskeletal risk factors following ergonomics education of sewing machine operators. Int. J. Occup. Saf. Ergon. **23**, 347–352 (2017). https://doi.org/10.1080/10803548.2016.1262321

61. Robertson, M.M., Huang, Y.H., Lee, J.: Improvements in musculoskeletal health and computing behaviors: effects of a macroergonomics office workplace and training intervention. Appl. Ergon. **62**, 182–196 (2017). https://doi.org/10.1016/j.apergo.2017.02.017

62. WHO (World Health Organization): Musculoskeletal conditions. https://www.who.int/news-room/fact-sheets/detail/musculoskeletal-conditions. Accessed 15 Jan 2021
63. Li, J., Pang, M., Smith, J., Pawliuk, C., Pike, I.: In search of concrete outcomes–a systematic review on the effectiveness of educational interventions on reducing acute occupational injuries. Int. J. Environ. Res. Public Health **17**(18), 6874 (2020). https://doi.org/10.3390/ijerph17186874

# The Entropic Complexity of Human Factor in Collaborative Technologies

Sotirios Panagou[1]([⊠]), Fabio Fruggiero[1], W. Patrick Neumann[2], and Alfredo Lambiase[3]

[1] School of Engineering, University of Basilicata, 85100 Potenza, Italy
sotirios.panagou@unibas.it
[2] Department of Mechanical and Industrial Engineering, Ryerson University, 350 Victoria Street, Toronto, ON M5B 2K3, Canada
[3] Department of Industrial Engineering, University of Salerno, Fisciano, SA, Italy

**Abstract.** In recent years manufacturing and assembly lines are undergoing workplace changes with a scope to adapt to the Industry 4.0 (I4.0) design principles. Automation of manufacturing, collaborative robots (cobots), interconnection of cyber physical systems (CPS), cloud computing, big data analytics and Augmented/Virtual reality (AR/VR) are some of the technologies that are being introduced in industry. Human operators are required to adapt and integrate into those new environments. Human operators should be flexible in their work-tasks, upgrade their skillset and be able to act as a safeguard entity in this complex and dynamic environment. A recent shift in paradigms, the Industry 5.0 concept, focus on the sustainability of the human factor inside the technologies that I4.0 framework introduced, and relates to the ageing workforce issue and the change in individuals' capabilities. Productivity and safety of the ageing operators in the new workplace environment is causally related to their capabilities. In this research paper, we (i) study the interactions of human operator inside the "smart" workplace and (ii) develop a model using the entropy concept of statistical mechanics. This model can be utilized in the evaluation of human factor inside the complex environment by computing the probability of error based on human operator capabilities.

**Keywords:** Entropy · Complex · Collaborative · Human factor · Ageing workforce · Statistical mechanics

## 1 Introduction

The main theme of I4.0 is automation in the industrial chain of operations such as in manufacturing lines, logistics, supply chains and maintenance. For the workplace to change according to this thematic, it must follow the design principles of interoperability, virtualization, decentralization, real-time capability, service-orientation, modularity and sustainability. The emerging Industry 5.0 theme [1] focuses in using those technologies to assist the human operators inside the workplace. Those principles introduce smart technologies inside the workplace environment that human operators should learn to

© The Author(s), under exclusive license to Springer Nature Switzerland AG 2021
N. L. Black et al. (Eds.): IEA 2021, LNNS 221, pp. 503–510, 2021.
https://doi.org/10.1007/978-3-030-74608-7_62

cooperate and interact with (Fig. 1). AR/VR tools (that can assist in work-tasks with information regarding the tasks, potential or critical issues), cyber systems (such as RFID, cloud computing), human-robot communication or machine-machine communication and cobots are some of the smart technologies that human operators should learn how to cooperate and work with to meet product requirements. Real-time data concerning process evaluation, product process, and synchronization status will be conveyed to human operators who in turn should be able to evaluate as useful information, critical information or as simple information and act upon, react on arising/critical situations or ignore. A concern in this scenario is the rising trend of ageing workforce and the new demands these technologies place on that workforce.

The ageing workforce issue is recognized and acknowledged by government officials and global economic institutions [2]. In a report published by EU-OSHA in 2019, the proportion of workers aged over 55 accounts in roughly a quarter of the overall human workforce (from 21% in 2014 to close to 26% in 2019), where the younger workforce percentage fall from 35% in 2005 to 30% in 2015. Older workers in manufacturing and industry in general faces new challenges due to the evolution and introduction of new smart technologies inside the workplace and raises the question of how vulnerable in comparison with their younger counterparts the older workers are due to decline of their capabilities [3]. The decline of those capabilities can lead to increased errors, loss of performance and a probability of safety accidents. Although human errors (HEs) have been classified through research and methods (such as THERP, [4]), and through human reliability analysis (HRA) which study human error probability due to human factors [5], age is not taken into consideration as a factor that influences error and performance. This gives rise to the question of how can we evaluate those declining capabilities due to age in the I4.0 context and benefit from it.

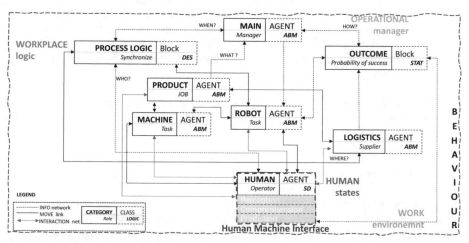

**Fig. 1.** "Smart" workplace. Human operator in his working environment interacts with machine, based on workplace logic indicated by operational management. Interaction and environment affect behavior and states of human operators.

The aim of our research is to study how human workers interact with their workplace environment and how they are affected by it. The statistical mechanic concept of entropy was used to develop a computational method in estimating the probability of human error. Entropy in statistical mechanics is considered as the measurement of a system's disorder, randomness, or uncertainty and can be used in various and diverse fields. In our work, entropy is used as a tool to quantify the uncertainty of an outcome from a process or the uncertainty of the system. In that regard, identifying the rules and variables that govern and define the system, such as the emotion of human operators, fatigue, cognitive load and motor resilience is necessary and requires the understanding of their connection to the macro-states of the systems (Physical, Behavior, Mental, Psychosocial); the entropy concept can be used to analyze the system and draw the connections between those states. In that regard, entropy is utilized as an asset in the understanding of human operators' reactions and behaviors inside the workplace environment. In this report, Sect. 2 address the changes in the human-robot interaction inside the workplace based on I4.0 collaborative theme, Sect. 3 address the initial formulation of the probability of error based on the macro states of our system, followed by Sect. 4 in which a brief discussion is presented based on results from testing the formula on initial data of our work.

## 2   Industry 4.0 Collaborative Workplace Scenario

Human robot collaboration – cobotics – in the workplace is a fundamental theme in the Industry 4.0 framework [6]. It requires an intense workplace transformation that aims in an environment that consists of connected people, processes, services, systems, and big data using Internet of Things (IoT). The goal is by using the collected data and information from those connections, to achieve an ecosystem of innovation and human-robot collaboration. Several technologies and tools are considered vital for this transformation: Cloud computing and platforms, big data analytics in cooperation with artificial intelligence (AI), cognitive computing and data analysis, mobile and RFID technologies, human to machine communication, advanced robotics and cybersecurity. The CPS are used as the main tool used to enable human operators to monitor changes inside the workplace, react to critical situations and direct communication with the end-customer (feedback, order placement, market needs). CPS assist in the information exchange between all the links of the market chain (between shop floors), maintenance and warehouse management which aims in operational efficiency and cost reduction. In general, the waste of production cycle is reduced. Digitization along with cloud computing create transparency and efficiency in the human-robot collaboration. Cyber-security is vital in data security and creating trust between human operators and cobots, and prevention of unauthorized use/access or illegal attempt of access, malicious use of the information or workplace safety risks.

In this complex and dynamic workplace, human operators remain an integral part, as human expertise in many areas is an invaluable asset for management (such as production, customer requirements and development of new trends). In this workplace, human workforce interacts dynamically with the entities (cobots, CPS, AR tools) that are part of the workplace through information exchange and physical interactions (Fig. 2). Human operators interact with cobots and CPS in their work tasks; production and quality assurance of product, safety entity inside the workplace and maintenance. In this scenario, operators receive real-time data from sensors, CPS, AR/VR tools, from logistic entities or from management for maintenance status, possible arising situation, error, simple status information and product requirements. The operator in turn, need to react to information that need his attention, take quick decisions, respond, or not act at all depending on the status of information he receives. Those interactions and the decisions that need to be made affect the demand on human operators' perception, emotions, fatigue, cognitive load and motivation.

Human operators have limitations to their abilities and are affected by several issues. Workplace changes, lack of social interaction, cognitive capacity, emotion-driven decisions in certain cases and are prone to errors when their fatigue reaches certain levels. Training of human operators can prove effective in minimizing risks and safety concerns but overcoming all the weaknesses in the design of systems and workplaces requires further measures. The needs of human operators from the side of system operations must be addressed as well. In the human robot interaction for example, cobots can be designed to create trust and meet the needs, preferences and capabilities of the human operators. To this end, we designed a simple input-output human-robot interaction map based on the following principles. Human perception and age group plays a major role on how human operators react to their environment (Fig. 3). Perception of the environment then affects the mental state, behavior, and psychosocial state of the human operator. Physical interaction while in a state of emotional discomfort can affect productivity or lead to safety risks. Although technological advances in ergonomic designs can smooth the interaction and perception of cobots, the probability of human-system interaction error is affected by more variables. Age is a variable that needs to be addressed.

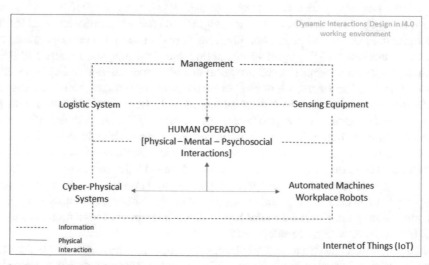

**Fig. 2.** Dynamic Interactions inside I4.0 workplace (Information data is exchanged between every agent inside workplace).

Elder workers as a term refers to employees over the age of 55 years. Furthermore, the term ageing worker/operator is used to signify when changes start to occur in a significant way in the working capacity after a certain age (usually after age 30) and will become critical in the span of the next 15–20 years if the work demands of the person do not decrease. Physical injuries tend to hinder those workers if their working tasks are heavily physical [7, 8]. Moreover, decision making becomes slower and environment changes impact older workers more than their younger counterparts [9, 10]. Despite the decline of certain capabilities, older workers are considered valuable due to the work experience and skills they possess. Their knowledge is valuable to the organization and they can transfer that knowledge to their younger counterparts [11, 12]. Older workers tend to be better prepared and use their safety equipment more effectively than their younger counterparts [13]. Furthermore, they are more autonomous and can quickly identify situations before they become critical [14]. In that extent, management and decision-making of organizations can use the knowledge of those workers either by training them for management positions or by using job scheduling and work tasks to lower the load the demands placed on workers, and by introducing to their workplace ergonomic designs for safety and assist in work tasks. Knowing the advantages and disadvantages of older workers, assisted in the development of the model to quantify the probability of error.

## 3   Entropy Concept and Human Factor

Entropy is a probabilistic measurement of the uncertainty of a system based on its states. If the probability of a certain state is equal to 1, then we have certainty, and the entropy is not defined. Human operators can be defined as a natural system. It is defined by macro states that categorized as psychosocial (PS), mental (M), behavior (B) and physical (PH). Each state affects the system and is affected by it. Furthermore, those states affect and are affected by each other. Each state is defined by several parameters and variables. The human operator at a workplace scenario is characterized by traits that are summarized as: (i) the dynamic and complex interactions between human and machine inside the workplace are the dynamics of the workplace system and affect the human through perception, (ii) initial conditions of the system are the human operator state and the machine state, (iii) initial condition of the human operator are non-consequential in the time evolution (work-shift) of the system and (iv) the probabilities of the system states are measurable.

In the human-robot interaction (Fig. 1), humans perceive the workplace (environment, operational concepts, machine and logic), thus affecting their psychosocial state. Motivation is affected by the perception and interaction, which is affecting the Skill-Rule-Knowledge based decision making of the operator and thus his behavioral state. Fatigue affects the cognitive load of the operator (linked with his mental state) and motor resilience (linked with his physical state and is linked with the training experience and ergonomics of the workplace). The above variables affect and are affected by all states of human operators. The above are part of the foundational principles of our formulation, which can be stated by the following: the human operator as a system (i) has four states, which are Psychosocial (PS), Mental (M), Behavior (B), Physical (PH) and (ii)

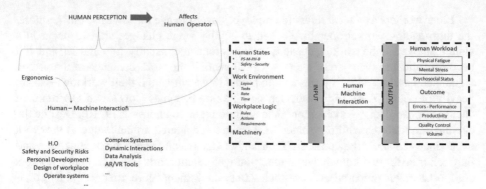

**Fig. 3.** Human-Machine Interaction Environnent. Left scheme represents how perception affects human operators and right scheme depicts the input-output of the h-r-i environment. (Ps-Psychosocial, M-Mental, PH-Physical, B-Behavior).

is affected by the age criteria. With those principles and the parameters set above the probability of error can be calculated by:

$$hfpe = exp\left[-\frac{(PHxM)}{(PSxB)}\right]^{a}$$ (1)

The HFPE notation stands for human factor probability of error. Each state and parameter have its own weight determined by the individuals' operators' parameters and can be seen in Fig. 4.

$$PS = w_{PS}xf(I, EM, P)$$ (2)

$$M = w_{M}xf(F, C)$$ (3)

$$B = w_{B}xf(SRK, M)$$ (4)

$$PH = w_{PH}xf(Erg, MR, TE)$$ (5)

| LEGEND | |
|---|---|
| **Acronyms** | **Description** |
| I | Interaction |
| EM | Emotion |
| P | Perception |
| F | Fatigue |
| C | Cognition |
| SRK | Skill Rule Knowledge |
| M | Motivation |
| Erg | Ergonomics |
| MR | Motor Resilience |
| TE | Training Experience |

**Fig. 4.** Computational equation of states with weights determined by individuals' parameters.

In Eqs. (2) to (5), the states with their weights and variables are set. Factor $a$ in Eq. 1 symbolizes the age index which for this initial study we set to 1 for young workers and − 1 for older workers. To demonstrate the application of the proposal (Eq. 1), we used the Constrained Non-Informative prior (CNI) distribution [15]. Entropy, in our case, can be defined as the expectation on the logarithm scale of the HFPE distribution. We excited the HFPE state in order to have overall mean and variance of possible configurations. This means we are investigating configurations where states mutual influence affects the overall HFPE. The statistical "moment" method is then applied to fit the approximate mean and variance to a beta distribution. To investigate the stability in error probability we plotted the HFPE over cases of the percentile variation of beta distribution (Fig. 5):

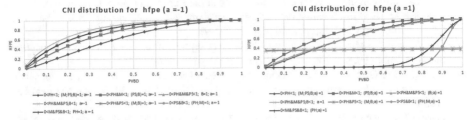

**Fig. 5.** CNI distribution of HFPE-PVBD (percentile variation of beta distribution) for old workers (a = −1) and young workers (a = 1).

The results of our test show how the probability of error changes based on how "controllable" the states are, level of control varies from 1 (control) to 0 (no-control). It reports, the span of uncertainty distribution. The model was tested for both younger and older workers. Younger workers have better stability, even when control status of one or more of their states is close to 0.

## 4  Discussion

In this work, the changes in human-robot interaction (HRI) due to the advancement of Industry 4.0 technologies, such as CPS and IoT, is presented. Integration of human operators, and older workers in particular, is essential in the advancement to the new workplace environment. The statistical mechanics concept of entropy was used to determine the connections between the input variables of the HRI. A formula was developed to compute the probability of error, based on the notion that human factor is a system consisted by four states, Mental, Psychosocial, Physical, Behavior. Weights are adjusted to those states, based on individuals' attributes. CNI distribution was used for risk assessment based on Eq. 1. The constrained non informative distribution implies that we know the posterior expected values and it does not limit the application of causal diagram or Bayesian methods. For the controllability of HFPE we require a set of rules and interaction analysis those could be mapped in a particular risky scenario with doubtful generalization. Results from the CNI distribution, show the areas where older workers and their younger counterparts are more prone to errors. There are states-based situations where controllability for young workers is inopportune (we cannot present probability of error that is more oriented to a uniform shape). On the counterpart, an older worker will report leptokurtic distribution of error. The cyber physical system of cobots assessment can excite the causal loop relations in state of human factors. These will report performances and error probability as per the constrained non informative distribution related with the maximum entropy. The future agenda of our study is to conduct a larger scale validation, using different states of control in different workplace scenarios with various ergonomic designs, robotics and AR/VR tools.

# References

1. Breque, M., De Nul, L., Petridis, A.: Industry 5.0. towards a sustainable, human-centric and resilient european industry. Publications Office of the European Union, Luxembourg (2021)
2. EU-OSHA: Third European survey of enterprises on new and emerging risks. Publications Office of the European Union, Luxembourg (2019)
3. Di Pasquale, V., Miranda, S., Neuman, P.W.: Ageing and human-system errors in manufacturing: a scoping review. Int. J. Prod. Res. **58**(15), 4716–4740 (2020)
4. Swain, A.D., Guttmann, H.E.: Handbook of human-reliability analysis with emphasis on nuclear power plant application. Final report. No. NUREG/CR-1278. Sandia National Labs (1983)
5. Boring, R.L., Hendrickson, S.M.L., Forester, J.A., Tran, T.Q., Lois, E.: Issues in benchmarking human reliability analysis methods: a literature review. Reliab. Eng. Syst. Saf. **95**(6), 591–605 (2010)
6. Fruggiero, F., Lambiase, A., Panagou, S., Sabattini, L.: Cognitive human modeling in collaborative robotics. Procedia Manuf. **51**, 584–591 (2021)
7. Neumann, P.W., Winkel, J., Palmerud, G., Forsman, M.: Innovation and employee injury risk in automotive disassembly operations. Int. J. Prod. Res. **56**(9), 3188–3203 (2018)
8. Verma, S.K., Lombardi, D.A., Chang, W.-R., Courtney, T.K., Brennan, M.J.: A matched case-control study of circumstances of occupational same-level falls and risk of wrist, ankle and hip fracture in women over 45 years of age. Ergonomics **51**(12), 1960–1972 (2008)
9. Gilles, M.A., Guélin, J.-C., Desbrosses, K., Wild, P.: Motor Adaptation capacity as a function of age in carrying out a repetitive assembly task at imposed work paces. Appl. Ergon. **64**, 47–55 (2017)
10. Nardolillo, A.M., Baghdadi, A., Cavuoto, L.A.: Heart rate variability during a simulated assembly task: influence of age and gender. In: Proceedings of the Human Factors and Ergonomics Society, pp. 1853–1857, October 2017
11. Guvernator IV, G.C., Landaeta, R.E.: Knowledge transfer in municipal water and wastewater organizations. EMJ – Eng. Manag. J. **32**(4), 272–282 (2020)
12. Massingham, P.R., Massingham, R.K.: Does knowledge management produce practical outcomes? J. Knowl. Manag. **18**(2), 221–254 (2014)
13. Lombardi, D.A., Verma, S.K., Brennan, M.J., Perry, M.J.: Factors influencing worker use of personal protective eyewear. Accid. Anal. Prev. **41**(4), 755–762 (2009)
14. Fruggiero, F., Fera, M., Iannnone, R., Lambiase, A.: Revealing a frame to incorporate safe human behavior in assembly process. IFAC PapersOnLine **51**(11), 661–668 (2018)
15. Atwood, C.L.: Constrained noninformative priors in risk assessment. Reliab. Eng. Syst. Saf. **53**(1), 37–46 (1996)

# The Influence of an Ergonomic Storage Location Assignment on Human Strain in Manual Order Picking

Tim Steinebach[✉], Jurij Wakula, and Asim Mehmedovic

Institute for Ergonomics and Human Factors, Technical University Darmstadt,
64287 Darmstadt, Germany
t.steinebach@iad.tu-darmstadt.de

**Abstract.** Order picking is the most labor-intensive task in a warehouse with high risks for the development of musculoskeletal disorders. However, ergonomic planning models in order picking are still rare. This article presents a new ergonomic storage location assignment (SLA) algorithm based on a biomechanical model ("The Dortmunder") which reduces the mechanical load of the lumbar spine.

In order picking experiments in a laboratory with 12 subjects the derived ergonomic SLA is compared to a SLA minimizing the travel distance of the operator. For the evaluation of the physiological strain of the operators in both approaches, the subjects are equipped with an EMG-System, measuring electrical activity of four muscles of the back and the shoulder-arm system. Furthermore, perceived exertion (Borg RPE scale) and the cycle time needed to complete all picks are collected.

The mean and dynamic electrical activity is significantly lower in almost all examined muscles with the ergonomic SLA. Also, the perceived exertion at the end of the picking trial is significantly reduced with the ergonomic SLA. The cycle time recorded shows no difference between the two assignment strategies.

The storage location assignment algorithm presented here is able to reduce the physiological strain and perceived exertion of operators. Further studies are recommended to evaluate, if it can be used in real warehouses to reduce the risk of developing musculoskeletal disorders without losing efficiency.

**Keywords:** Order picking · Storage location assignment · Physiological strain · Borg RPE scale

## 1 Introduction

### 1.1 Workload in Order Picking Systems

Due to the increase in e-commerce and advancing customer requirements, efficient warehouse operations are crucial for companies in production and service industry to remain competitive. For this reason, appropriate planning models are increasingly important in modern supply chains in order to be able to ensure high availability of products in short shipping times [1].

© The Author(s), under exclusive license to Springer Nature Switzerland AG 2021
N. L. Black et al. (Eds.): IEA 2021, LNNS 221, pp. 511–521, 2021.
https://doi.org/10.1007/978-3-030-74608-7_63

Nowadays, warehouse operations still require a high amount of manual material handling – especially order picking is most often performed manually [2]. During the handling of loads, e.g. lifting of heavy products, often in awkward postures, the operator is exposed to a high risk of developing musculoskeletal diseases. Lower back pain is a particularly frequently occurring health risk in manual order picking and can lead to long sick leaves of employees [3]. However, planning models in order picking mainly concentrate on (short-term) economic criteria, such as minimizing travel distance and costs only [4]. Approaches that take ergonomic criteria into account, e.g. the mechanical load on the spine of the operator, are rare [1].

Typical planning problems in order picking are the routing of operators through the warehouse, the batching of customer orders into picking orders, the determination of a efficient warehouse layout and the assignment of products to storage locations [5]. In the present paper, we focus on the latter one, which is called the storage location assignment (SLA) problem. It is further defined as the allocation of specific stock keeping units (SKU) into a specific storage space [4, 6].

## 1.2 Ergonomic SLA - Literature Review

As mentioned, most often SLA planning models are only based on economic criteria, such as picking performance or storage costs [1, 4]. In the following, papers are presented that have considered human factors in their SLA research models.

Petersen et al. [6] were among the first to include human characteristics in their mathematical models and were able to show that a "golden zone" approach, i.e. the storage of fast movers at shelf heights between shoulder and hip, leads to higher performances. However, the workload of the operator was not evaluated.

Furthermore, the energy expenditure model [7] often was used in mathematical models or simulative studies to estimate the "metabolic costs" of order picking [5, 8]. Battini et al. [5] derived a bi-objective SLA method. They combined two objectives – the first to minimize the picking time and the second to minimize the energy consumption, which led to Pareto efficient solutions. Calzavara et al. [8] added the OWAS method to evaluate body postures when picking from pallets to cost models in manual order picking. A heuristic approach supports assignment decisions of SKU to certain pallets.

In an approach by Larco et al. [9], the influence of shelf height, SKU weight and picked quantity on physical discomfort of order pickers is quantified in a regression model. The physical discomfort was collected with the Borgs CR-10 scale [10]. Similar to [5], these values were then implemented in a bi-objective SLA optimization model in order to minimize the discomfort or the picking time, respectively.

Otto et al. [11], on the other hand, used the Revised Lifting Equation from NIOSH [12] to quantify the workload of SKU picking at certain shelf heights. With a taboo search and two different heuristics, workload minimizing solutions are found. Efficiency or cost aspects were not examined.

Bortolini et al. [13] analysed a similar problem in an "assembly line balancing problem" in a manufacturing context. With the help of the REBA method [14] and the consideration of the SKU characteristics, e.g. weight and geometric dimensions, individual SKU could be assigned to specific storage locations at the assembly line with Pareto optimums of time-efficiency and REBA score.

The majority of the presented publications are mathematical models that were only evaluated in computer simulations and numerical experiments. An application of these SLA algorithms in a warehouse with test subjects and the analysis of workload or physical strain of the operators was not carried out.

## 2 Methods

### 2.1 Development of the Ergonomic SLA Algorithm

As shown in Sect. 1, there are few publications on a SLA algorithm that take into account biomechanical workload or specifically the mechanical load of the spine. In addition, the OWAS and NIOSH methods used can only be used to a limited extent in order picking. The NIOSH equation was only developed for slow and steady [15] two-handed lifting with a constant weight and unchanged postures [12]. However, in order picking manual material handling rarely is slow and the SKU weights and different postures of the operators often vary significantly. The OWAS procedure is also not further pursued in this article, as it does not consider the absolute frequency of certain material handling, although this is a crucial factor for the overall workload [16].

One of the most detailed methods for determining the workload on the spine is the biomechanical model "The Dortmunder". It takes into account three-dimensional body postures, the skeletal structure and the relevant muscles and uses this to calculate static and dynamic compressive forces in the intervertebral disc L5-S1 [17]. Numerous tables with compression forces on L5-S1 for various load handlings are available. [16] used this approach to specifically determine the load on L5-S1 for manual material handling in order picking. These compression forces, depending on the shelf height and SKU weight, are used in this article for the ergonomic SLA algorithm.

The algorithm has the goal of assigning the individual SKU to a storage location in such a way that the overall spinal load of the operator caused by the picking processes is minimized. The following mathematical objective is formulated in Eq. (1):

$$min \sum_{i=1}^{I} \sum_{j=1}^{J} L_{i,j} \cdot x_{i,j} \tag{1}$$

where

$$\sum_{i=1}^{I} x_{i,j} = 1 \, \forall j \tag{2}$$

$$\sum_{j=1}^{J} x_{i,j} = 1 \, \forall i \tag{3}$$

$$x_{i,j} \in \{0, 1\} \forall i \tag{4}$$

Here, $L_{i,j}$ describes the spinal load, resulting from a picking of SKU i from storage location j. Similarly, $x_{i,j}$ is a binary variable, which takes the value one when SKU i is assigned to storage location j. The developed algorithm is suited to any warehouse layout and shelf type regardless of the total number of SKU, if all necessary $L_{i,j}$ have been determined.

## 2.2    Evaluation of the Ergonomic SLA Algorithm

**Participants**
Twelve young individuals (7 male, 5 female; age = 23.8 ± 3.2 years) without previous picking experience from the university environment took part in the study. The test persons did not have any apparent health restrictions that would affect their activities during order picking. All subjects read an ethics statement and signed an informed written consent before the order picking trials.

**Experimental Design and Procedure**
The experiments took place in a controlled environment in a laboratory with constant temperature and lighting conditions. A one-block warehouse with a total of four rows of shelves and two aisles was set up on an area of 6 m × 8 m. For each row of shelves, three SKUs were stored next to one another in the horizontal direction (see Fig. 1).

The shelves each had five shelving levels at heights of 10 cm, 50 cm, 90 cm, 130 cm and 170 cm. In total, the picking zone contained 60 storage locations – each marked with a unique code. The picking zone was kept relatively small in comparison with real warehouses in order to be able to achieve a high picking frequency, since this study focused primarily on the evaluation of the physical strain and only secondarily on the evaluation of travel times.

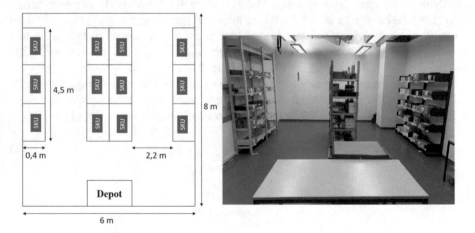

**Fig. 1.**  Layout of the picking zone

The SKU portfolio was based on a real pick list of an automotive supplier. The mean value and the standard deviation of the load weight (5.5 kg ± 3.9 kg; max: 12.6 kg) and the turnover rate of each SKU (2.1 ± 1.2 picks in one trial; max: 5 picks) remained unchanged in comparison to the real SKU portfolio. Only the total number of SKUs was reduced to 60 in accordance with the warehouse size in this experiment. Each SKU was provided as a cardboard box with approximately constant dimensions (20 cm × 20 cm × 30 cm).

After a 5-min training run, each subject executed two order picking trials, which differ in the allocation of storage locations. In a permuted sequence, the distance-minimizing SLA was used first and the ergonomic SLA in the second trial, or vice versa. The SKU had to be re-sorted into the shelves after each trial.

The individual SKU had to be collected according to a pick list and transported to the depot with a handcart. Four individual SKU were allowed to be transported on the handcart per tour (from the depot to the warehouse and back). In order to prevent the muscle fatigue of the first trial from affecting the measurement results of the second trial, there was a 15-min break between these both runs.

## Instrumentation

Surface electromyography was used to determine the physiological strain. For this purpose, self-adhesive "Blue Sensor P" electrodes from the company "Ambu" were positioned on four selected muscles (dominant side of the body) according to the recommendations of SENIAM [14]. The used Noraxon TeleMyo 2400 G2 EMG device measured the electrical activity (EA) of the following muscles with a sampling frequency of 1500 Hz: m. trapezius pars descendens and m. deltoideus acromialis in the shoulder-neck area, m. triceps brachii in the upper arm and the m. erector spinae in the lower back. This selection of crucial muscles is similar to those of other studies in manual material handling in logistics [15, 16].

The Borg RPE scale was used to determine the subjectively perceived exertion [17]. For this purpose, the test subjects were asked before the trial, after half of all picked SKU and immediately after finishing the trial about their exertion according to the RPE scale.

In addition, with a stopwatch the required cycle time was measured that was needed to complete all picks. The picking frequency could be calculated accordingly. All trials were furthermore recorded with a video camera.

## Data Processing and Analysis
### EMG Data

After rectifying and smoothing (root mean square) the EMG-signal, the EA was normalized in relation to the maximum voluntary contraction (MVC) determined beforehand with defined exercises. Both, the mean EA and the dynamic EA were determined for each SLA trial.

In addition, the EMG signals were calculated in two different ways: On the one hand, the entire order picking trial ("EA entire trial") was evaluated and, on the other hand, only the periods in which the SKU were manually removed from the shelf ("EA picking only") were considered. For this purpose, marker were set at the beginning and end of the contact between the hand and the SKU and only this part of the EA was evaluated.

Due to technical problems with the EMG equipment, the data records of one subject had to be excluded, so that only eleven data sets relating to the EMG are available.

*Statistical Data Processing*

All results obtained (EMG, perceived exertion and cycle time) were checked for statistical significance with IBM SPSS.

For the comparison of means of the two SLA trials (dependent sample), it was first necessary to check whether the corresponding data was normally distributed. If this was the case, a t-test was used. Otherwise, the Wilcoxon signed-rank test was chosen. Both tests were run at a level of significance of $\alpha = 0.05$ (0.01 for high significance).

## 3   Results

### 3.1   EMG

Figure 1 and 2 show the mean and dynamic EA for the four muscles examined in comparison between a distance-minimized SLA and an ergonomic SLA. Statically significant differences are marked with asterisks (* = significant, ** = highly significant). It can be seen that all muscles experience lower EA in the ergonomic SLA - but not significantly in most cases, except for the dynamic EA in m. trapezius and m. erector spinae (Fig. 3) .

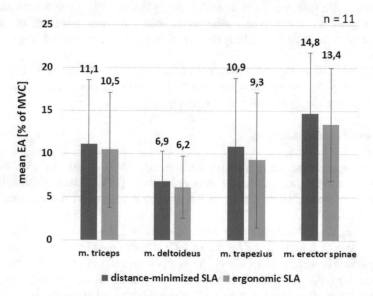

**Fig. 2.**  Mean EA (% of MVC) for the entire trial with distance-minimized and ergonomic SLA

Furthermore, the results when only evaluating EMG data during the SKU removal (EA picking only) are shown in Fig. 4 for the mean EA and in Fig. 5 for the dynamic EA. Both, mean EA and dynamic EA, are significantly reduced in the m. trapezius and m. triceps, as well as the m. deltoideus (mean EA) and the m. erector spinae (dynamic EA), when the ergonomic SLA is applied.

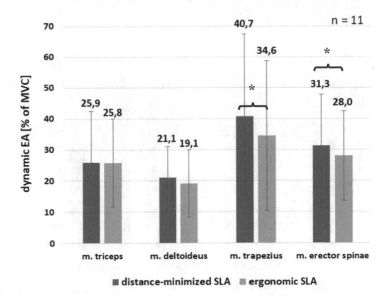

**Fig. 3.** Dynamic EA (% of MVC) for the entire trial with distance-minimized and ergonomic SLA

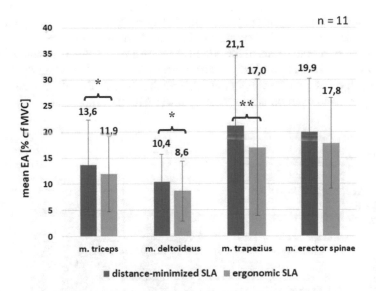

**Fig. 4.** Mean EA (% of MVC) for picking only with distance-minimized and ergonomic SLA

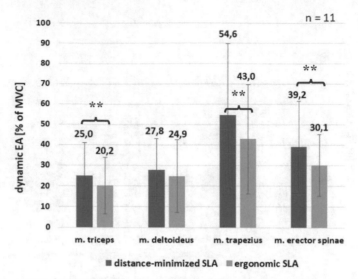

**Fig. 5.** Dynamic EA (% of MVC) for picking only with distance-minimized and ergonomic SLA

## 3.2   Perceived Exertion

The perceived exertion of the subjects immediately before, halfway through and at the end of the order picking trial is shown in Fig. 6 and increases over time.

Before the start of the trials of the two SLAs there are no differences and the exertion level is low. After half of all picks, no differences are apparent between the two SLA - the exertion level is, however, higher at 12, 8 on the Borg RPE scale. At the end of the trials, the perceived exertion is significantly lower with the ergonomic SLA.

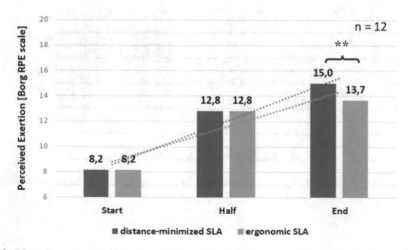

**Fig. 6.** Mean Perceived Exertion for picking trials with distance-minimized and ergonomic SLA

## 3.3  Cycle Time

The average cycle time of the order picking trials is 878 s (14:38 min) for the ergonomic SLA and 891 s (14:51 min) for the distance-minimized SLA. The difference is relatively small and not significant.

The cycle time for each subject in the second trial is about 90 s shorter than the first run, regardless of which SLA is tested first.

# 4  Discussion

## 4.1  Discussion of Results

The EMG results of the order picking clearly indicate that physiological strain can be significantly reduced when applying the ergonomic SLA. The reason for this is that the frequently picked and heavy SKUs are more likely to be stored on convenient shelf heights instead of low or high levels. This corresponds to the golden zone approach of [6]. In these shelving levels not only is the mechanical stress on the spine lower, but the muscular strain is also reduced.

This is particularly noticeable when looking at the EA for picking only. The high EA are not attenuated by the lower EA during travelling through the warehouse, so that differences in manual material handling are more visible. The average reduction in EA in picking only is between 10 and 25%, with particularly high reductions in dynamic EA in the m. erector spinae (25%) and m. trapezius (21%). The SLA thus seems to have an important influence on the strain of the muscles of the upper arm-shoulder system as well as the neck and back.

A similar picture emerges when it comes to the perceived exertion - the ergonomic SLA results in significantly lower values on the RPE scale. Subjectively, without knowing the differences between the two trials, the subjects estimate the exertion to be lower with an ergonomic arrangement. According to the Borg RPE scale, a level of exertion of "somewhat hard" is achieved with the ergonomic SLA and "hard (heavy)" with the distance minimizing SLA, after starting the trial with a level of exertion of "very light" in both SLA [21].

On the other hand, no significant differences can be found in cycle times between the two SLA, although slightly longer travel distances exist with the ergonomic SLA. The cycle time with the ergonomic SLA was even marginally shorter. The time disadvantages of the longer walking routes in the ergonomic SLA have apparently been compensated by the more frequent picks in the golden zone, in which picking is faster [6] than, for example, at low or very high storage locations that more often occur in the distance-minimized SLA.

However, when interpreting these results, one must take into account that the warehouse considered in this experiment is very small. In larger warehouses with longer walking distances, these walking routes would have a stronger influence on the cycle time.

## 4.2  Limitations

Only two different SLA are regarded in this article. The two targets (spine load and travel distance) could also be considered together in a bi-objective optimization approach [5, 9] in order to find Pareto optimal solutions between the two one criterial solutions presented here.

In addition, further investigations must be undertaken to investigate the influence of an ergonomic SLA on the cycle time, especially in larger warehouses or in practical studies.

As described, regardless of which SLA is tested first in the experiment, the first trial was significantly slower in terms of cycle time. This indicates a strong training effect in the second trial. This can be explained by the fact that inexperienced subjects took part in the study - a longer training session before the start of the experiments or more experienced order pickers could have counteracted this limitation.

## 5  Conclusion

In this article, a SLA algorithm is derived that minimizes the mechanical load on the spine. Order picking experiments show that this SLA reduces the physiological strain and subjectively perceived exertion in comparison to a distance-minimized SLA.

The ergonomic SLA presented here is therefore potentially suitable as an alternative for logistics managers to implement ergonomic planning parameters into warehouse processes.

In the future, further studies with bi-objective optimization approaches should be carried out, to evaluate both the influence of the SLA on the stress and strain of operators and on cycle time.

## References

1. Grosse, E.H., Glock, C.H., Neumann, W.P.: Human factors in order picking: a content analysis of the literature. Int. J. Prod. Res. **55**(5), 1260–1276 (2017)
2. Hanson, R., Medbo, L., Jukic, P., Assaf, M.: Manual picking from large containers-time efficiency and physical workload. IFAC-PapersOnLine **49**(12), 1703–1708 (2016)
3. Gajšek, B., Dukić, G., Butlewski, M., Opetuk, T., Cajner, H., Kač, S.M.: The impact of the applied technology on health and productivity in manual "picker-to-part" systems. Work 1–12 (2020)
4. Reyes, J., Solano-Charris, E., Montoya-Torres, J.: The storage location assignment problem: a literature review. Int. J. Ind. Eng. Comput. **10**(2), 199–224 (2019)
5. Battini, D., Glock, C.H., Grosse, E.H., Persona, A., Sgarbossa, F.: Human energy expenditure in order picking storage assignment: a bi-objective method. Comput. Ind. Eng. **94**, 147–157 (2016)
6. Petersen, C.G., Siu, C., Heiser, D.R.: Improving order picking performance utilizing slotting and golden zone storage. Int. J. Oper. Prod. Manag. **25**, 997–1012 (2005)
7. Garg, A., Chaffin, D.B., Herrin, G.D.: Prediction of metabolic rates for manual materials handling jobs. Am. Ind. Hyg. Assoc. J. **39**(8), 661–674 (1978)

8. Calzavara, M., Glock, C.H., Grosse, E.H., Sgarbossa, F.: An integrated storage assignment method for manual order picking warehouses considering cost, workload and posture. Int. J. Prod. Res. **57**(8), 2392–2408 (2019)
9. Larco, J.A., De Koster, R., Roodbergen, K.J., Dul, J.: Managing warehouse efficiency and worker discomfort through enhanced storage assignment decisions. Int. J. Prod. Res. **55**(21), 6407–6422 (2017)
10. Borg, G.: A category scale with ratio properties for intermodal and interindividual comparisons. In: Psychophysical Judgment and the Process of Perception, pp. 25–34 (1982)
11. Otto, A., Boysen, N., Scholl, A., Walter, R.: Ergonomic workplace design in the fast pick area. OR Spectrum **39**(4), 945–975 (2017)
12. Waters, T.R., Putz-Anderson, V., Garg, A.: Applications manual for the revised NIOSH lifting equation (1994)
13. Bortolini, M., Faccio, M., Gamberi, M., Pilati, F.: Multi-objective assembly line balancing considering component picking and ergonomic risk. Comput. Ind. Eng. **112**, 348–367 (2017)
14. Hignett, S., McAtamney, L.: Rapid entire body assessment (REBA). Appl. Ergon. **31**(2), 201–205 (2000)
15. Pope, M.H., Magnusson, M.L., Wilder, D.G., Goel, V.K., Spratt, K.: Is there a rational basis for post-surgical lifting restrictions? 2 possible scientific approach. Eur. Spine J. **8**(3), 179–186 (1999)
16. Goldscheid, C.: Ermittlung der Wirbelsäulenbelastung in manuellen Kommissioniersystemen. Shaker, Germany (2008)
17. Jäger, M., Luttmann, A., Göllner, R., Laurig, W.: "The Dortmunder" - biomechanical model for quantification and assessment of the load on the lumbar spine. SAE Trans. **110**, 2163–2171 (2001)
18. SENIAM. https://www.seniam.org/. Accessed 22 Jan 2021
19. Christmansson, M., Medbo, L., Hansson, G.Å., Ohlsson, K., Byström, J.U., Möller, T., Forsman, M.: A case study of a principally new way of materials kitting—an evaluation of time consumption and physical workload. Int. J. Ind. Ergon. **30**(1), 49–65 (2002)
20. Oliveira, A.B., Silva, L.C., Coury, H.J.: How do low/high height and weight variation affect upper limb movements during manual material handling of industrial boxes? Braz. J. Phys. Ther. **15**(6), 494–502 (2011)
21. Borg, G.: Borg's Perceived Exertion and Pain Scales. Human Kinetics (1998)

# Analysis of the Physical Workload and Ergonomic Design of Workstations for "Goods-to-Person" Order Picking

Jurij Wakula[1][✉], Tim Steinebach[1], Verena Klaer[1], Willibald Rabenhaupt[2], and Gernot Maier[2]

[1] Institute for Ergonomics and Human Factors, Technical University Darmstadt, 64287 Darmstadt, Germany
{wakula,t.steinebach}@iad.tu-darmstadt.de

[2] SSI Schäfer Automation GmbH, Fischeraustraße, 8051 Graz, Austria

**Abstract.** Goods-to-person picking is a dynamic, semi-automated or fully automated picking method. The main physical workloads are caused by standing work postures and repetitive movements of the upper extremities.

This paper presents the results of the ergonomic analysis of the physical workloads during picking at eight mock-up workstations for intralogistics. Workloads resulting from the standing work postures and repetitive movements of the upper extremities were analyzed and evaluated in laboratory studies using EAWS - method and the Captiv Motion Capture system. The weights of the picked products, picking frequencies and arrangement of storage and order totes were varied. Results show that order picking with exclusively low load weights ($<3$ kg) and not very high picking frequency ($<700$ picks/h) does not lead to high physical stress at the stations. However, higher pick frequencies ($>700$ picks/h) or higher weights result in increased physical workloads (EAWS values $>25$ points).

**Keywords:** Order picking · Goods-to-person; workstation · EAWS · Motion Capture

## 1 Introduction

With the one-level and two-level stations developed by SSI Schäfer Automation GmbH, innovative "goods-to-person" workstations for intralogistics were developed.

In addition to ensuring high process efficiency, the design-focus is placed on ergonomic design quality of the picking stations. Particularly with regard to demographic change and the associated "war for talents", as well as growing absenteeism due to musculoskeletal disorders, it will become increasingly important for employers in the future to incorporate ergonomic criteria into the product development process. In this study, the following process and design parameters are considered in the ergonomic analysis of order picking stations:

- Load weights of the picked articles
- Picking frequency
- Characteristics of the picked articles, e.g. droppable or non-droppable
- Postures adopted by the order picker due to the geometric dimensions of the workstation (arrangement and inclination of the storage or order totes)

The aim of the ergonomics studies was to determine the physical workloads (e.g. awkward postures, manual material handling) caused by working at the one- and two-level stations with an EAWS evaluation. In addition, 3D simulations were used to check reaching spaces and visibility for various human models and populations.

## 2  Methods

### 2.1  Captiv Motion Capture System

In order to record the movements performed by the order pickers in experiments, the Motion Capture system Captiv L7000 Premier from TEA was used (Steinebach et al. 2020). This sensor-based IMU system records at 128 Hz. The wireless sensors contain gyroscopes, magnetometers and accelerometers and are attached to 15 points on the body with the help of straps. The corresponding software evaluates the joint angles taken. It is also possible to determine the exact length of the order picker's walking paths and number of steps. The joint angle data obtained with this methodology is used to generate accurate and objective input variables for a load assessment procedure.

### 2.2  EAWS – Experts-Screening Method for Analysis of Physical Work Loads

The Ergonomic Assessment Worksheet (EAWS, Schaub et al. 2013) was used to evaluate the physical workload in the study. It is based on international ergonomics norms and standards, e.g. EN 1005 parts 1–5, ISO 11226 and ISO 11228-2 and assesses all physical types of workload that can potentially occur during activities at the analyzed workstations (manual material handling: "lifting/holding/carrying", static postures or high frequency movements, repetitive activities of the upper extremities). In contrast to other procedures such as the NIOSH lifting equation (Waters et al. 1994) or the key indicator methods, it enables a summative assessment of various workloads.

The performed analysis were additionally supported by 3D simulations with the CAD programme CATIA, in which the anthropometric design of the picking stations can be evaluated by means of digital human models.

### 2.3  Evaluation Procedure of Analysis Data

The Motion Capture data was first processed with the Captiv software and thus angles were calculated for all relevant joints. These were converted into a share of time spent in a specific posture, e.g. bending forward of the trunk.

These values were integrated into the EAWS form, particularly to EAWS Sect. 1 "postures" (standing/walking, standing with trunk bending forward, standing with elbows at shoulder height, standing with trunk rotation and trunk lateral bending), EAWS Sect. 3 "manual material handling" as well as EAWS Sect. 4 "upper limb load in repetitive tasks". For manual material handling, the load points resulting from the load weights which had to be entered manually. There were no "action forces" (EAWS Sect. 2) to take into account.

A couple of assumptions were made for the assessment. At first, values for female operators were used in order to receive a conservative assessment, which leads to higher EAWS points in manual material handling. For the upper limb load in repetitive tasks (EAWS Sect. 4), some parameters had to be determined: grip type, number of dynamic (real) actions per pick and the force required during order picking. Furthermore, regarding the duration of the repetitive activities, the net duration of a shift was set to 7 h with sufficient breaks and work interruptions possible at any time.

Thus, EAWS ratings can be assigned (see Fig. 1) to the analyzed variants of the one- and two-level stations depending on the load weights used, different picking performances and the postures adopted during picking. The resulting score indicates a risk level, see Fig. 1:

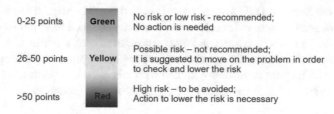

**Fig. 1.** EAWS – Overall evaluation (3 risk levels for MSDs)

## 2.4 Experimental Design and Procedure

The lab studies were carried out in a laboratory with eight test subjects without previous picking experiments (6 male and 2 female). The test persons did not have any apparent health restrictions that would affect their activities during order picking.

For experimental purposes a mock-up in a laboratory was created. Electrically height-adjustable tables were used to set the workstation to the optimum height for each subject. In addition, storage and order totes with a length of 600 mm, a width of 400 mm and a height of 220 mm were provided - as they are often used in real warehouses. The replication of a functioning conveyor system was not established.

In the laboratory studies, various influencing factors of the both stations were varied:

- one or two-level station
- length- or widthwise orientation of the storage or order totes
- with and without inclination of the storage totes
- two different article weights

In total, eight different station designs were tested in order picking trials with the mock-ups – six one-level (V1–V4, V7, V8) and two two-level versions (V5, V6). The one-level stations were characterized by the fact that the storage and order totes are at the same height. With two-level stations the storage and order totes are located at different heights. The storage totes (upper level) are tilted by 30° towards the order picker and are orientated widthwise to ensure better reaching and visibility. All stations could be adjusted in height by ±130 mm, which corresponds to anthropometric requirements.

Furthermore, the variants 1–4 only differ in the arrangement of the totes, with the storage and order totes either being arranged lengthwise or widthwise.

Each subject carried out two runs with low load weights (few grams) and heavier load weights (2–3 kg). The test subjects' task was to pick from a storage tote into an order tote - information about the totes to be selected was given on a display. In total, 128 Motion Capture data sets were tracked and transferred into the EAWS analysis.

## 3  Results

Figure 2 shows all EAWS results for light and heavy articles (≥3 kg) at a picking frequency of 600 picks/h or 100 picks/h, respectively, if women handle the loads. The figure shows that while picking low weights, all stations are below 25 EAWS points and therefore in the green area. Heavier loads, on the other hand, increase the physical workload significantly, even with lower picking frequencies. The both two-level stations have values close to 50 points but all stations remain in the yellow range.

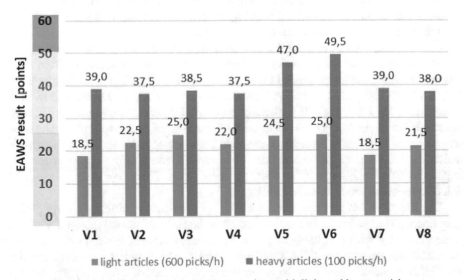

**Fig. 2.** EAWS results for 8 mock-up versions with light and heavy articles

Furthermore, in Fig. 3 EAWS results for one-level stations in dependence of picking frequencies are presented. The curves for two-level stations are very similar and increase significantly a little over 700 picks/h as well.

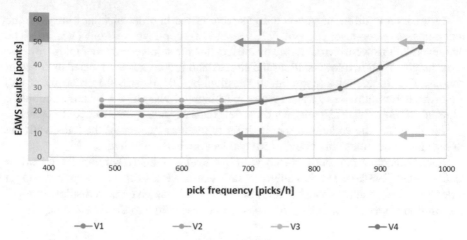

**Fig. 3.** EAWS values depending on the pick frequency for low loads (one-level stations)

## 4 Discussion

### 4.1 EAWS Analysis

With low weights, all variants can be seen as uncritical from an ergonomic point of view and are in the green area at the working point of 600 picks/h. Musculoskeletal disorders are therefore unlikely. Captiv Motion Capture data shows that only few working postures with trunk forward/lateral bending or rotation were required when working at the height-adjustable one- and two-level picking stations.

Furthermore, according to EAWS results (Fig. 3), the handling of low load weights at the picking stations only becomes relevant when the points resulting from upper limb loads (repetitive tasks) exceed those of the "whole body". Here, very high picking frequencies (>700 picks/h) result in increased loads (EAWS values in the yellow range according to DIN EN 614). The working point of 900 picks/h exemplifies this: when handling light weights, this results in an EAWS rating of about 40 points. The green dashed line also indicates the limit of the pick frequency of just over 700 picks/h, above which the EAWS rating increases due to the repetitiveness of the upper extremities, regardless of the orientation of the order and storage totes. This range indicates a possible risk of developing musculoskeletal diseases.

The EAWS values for heavier items are higher even with significantly lower picking frequencies. The reason for this is that Sect. 3 of the EAWS (manual material handling) comes into play with weights ≥3 kg. For these heavy articles, a one-level solution is preferable and leads to lower EAWS results. Here, the heavy articles do not have to be handled at shoulder height. In order to prevent EAWS values of more than 50 points and thus an increased risk of developing musculoskeletal disorders, combinations of high load weights and picking frequencies must be avoided.

Furthermore, it was also found that an inclination of the storage totes towards the order picker according to the EAWS method hardly leads to a reduction of the physical workload, as postures adopted during the picking process do not change significantly due. This becomes clear when comparing versions V1 and V7 or V2 and V8, whose design only differs in terms of inclination of the storage totes.

As well, it was investigated to what extent the EAWS assessment changes depending on the length- or widthwise orientation of the storage and order totes. Basically, the arrangement of the totes has only a minor influence on the physical loads.

However, the results show that for products that are "droppable", a lengthwise orientation is recommended. The reason for this is that in this situation the order picker will not walk directly in front of the order tote, but will drop the product with a lateral trunk bending or rotation into the target tote. Using Captiv Motion Capture data, it could be shown that with smaller distances between the centers of the totes - i.e. with lengthwise orientation - slightly smaller rotations or lateral bending occur in the trunk. With non-droppable SKUs, on the other hand, it was found that the order pickers are more likely to move directly in front of the order totes in order to be able to place the product in a more controlled manner. This hardly results in any additional lateral trunk bending or trunk rotations.

However, it should be noted, that all EAWS assessments refer to a healthy person and are therefore dependent on individual constitution. The boundaries between the green, yellow and red ranges according to DIN EN 614 should not be regarded as rigid limits in individual cases.

Furthermore, the stations enable a dynamic way of working, as at least for the outer order totes, some steps have to be taken to complete the picking process. From an ergonomic point of view, this "walking and standing" is preferable to "permanent standing" (e.g. at stations with 1 to 1 relationship between storage and order totes). This is also visible in the EAWS assessment by comparing the point values between "standing and walking in alteration" and "standing (without support)" in Sect. 1 - the points for alternating between standing and walking are significantly lower.

On the other hand, there are no long walking distances that could lead to an increased energetic load on the order picker. This could be shown by measuring the walking distances with the Motion Capture system and a subsequent calculation with the energy expenditure model according to Spitzer et al. (1982) on a basis of 1000 picks/h. Here it was assumed that each of the totes of a station with four order totes has to be served equally often. The calculated energy consumption was compared with a lower limit value for women of 5300 kJ/shift, which is not exceeded at all stations.

## 4.2  3D Simulation

An anthropometric 3D simulation of the gripping space and field of vision with the CAD program Catia, (Fig. 4), also demonstrated the good accessibility and visibility of the storage and order totes - even for very small persons like the female Japanese or French fifth percentile.

Generally, it is recommended to use this station with a height-adjustable platform to enable the order picker to reach both the upper storage totes and the lower order totes at a two-level station without significant work on shoulder height or without severe trunk forward bending, respectively.

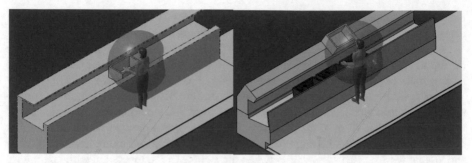

**Fig. 4.** Visualization of the gripping space for one- (left) and two-level picking (right) of a female person using CAD simulation - (here: 50th percentile female, French population)

## 5   Conclusion

Overall, the EAWS analysis showed that the analyzed one- and two-level order picking stations comply very well with the current ergonomic standards for working posture (ISO 11226), load handling (ISO 11228-1) and repetitive loads on the upper extremities (EN 1005-5) when handling loads below 3 kg and with picking frequencies below 700 picks/h. The corresponding EAWS results are below 25 points.

For high load weights, a one-level picking station is recommended. Furthermore, the inclination of the storage totes did not significantly reduce physical workloads.

In order to avoid high loads during picking (EAWS results > 50 points) and thus an increased risk of musculoskeletal disorders, combinations of high load weights and picking frequencies must be avoided.

## References

EN 614 (2009): Safety of machinery - Ergonomic design principles - Part 1: Terminology and general principles

EN 1005-1:2001. Safety of machinery - Human physical performance - Part 1: Terms and definition

EN 1005-2 (2003-09) Safety of machinery. Human physical performance. Part 2. Manual handling of machinery and component parts of machinery

EN 1005-3/A1 – 2008-04 Safety of machinery - Human physical performance - Part 3: Recommended force limits for machinery operation

EN 1005-4 (2008-04): Safety of machinery - Human physical performance - Part 4: Evaluation of working postures and movements in relation to machinery

EN 1005-5 (2007): Safety of machinery - Human physical performance - Part 5: Risk assessment for repetitive handling at high frequency

ISO 11226 - (2000): Ergonomics: Evaluation of Static Working Postures

ISO 11228-1 – (2003): Ergonomics—Manual handling—Part 1: Lifting and carrying

ISO 11228-2 - (2003): Ergonomics - Manual handling - Part 2: Pushing and pulling

Schaub, K., Caragnano, G., Britzke, B., Bruder, R.: The European assembly worksheet. Theoret. Issues Ergon. Sci. **14**(6), 616–639 (2013)

Spitzer, H., Hettinger, T., Kaminsky, G.: Tafeln für den Energieumsatz bei körperlicher Arbeit, Beuth (1982)

Steinebach, T., Grosse, E.H., Wakula, J., Glock, C.H., Lunin, A.: Evaluation der Accuracy evaluation of two markerless motion capture systems for measurement of upper extremities: kinect V2 and Captiv. Hum. Factors Ergon. Manuf. Serv. Ind. **30**(4), 291–302 (2020)

Waters, T.R., Putz-Anderson, V., Garg, A.: Applications manual for the revised NIOSH lifting equation (1994)

# Part VII: Transportation Ergonomics and Human Factors (Edited by Peter Burns)

# Exploring Cyclist-Vehicle Interaction – Results from a Naturalistic Cycling Study

Claudia Ackermann[✉], Daniel Trommler, and Josef Krems

Faculty of Behavioral and Social Science, Institute of Psychology,
Chemnitz University of Technology, Chemnitz, Germany
claudia.ackermann@psychologie.tu-chemnitz.de

**Abstract.** Automated driving is an ever-fast developing technology which is going to change the traffic system fundamentally. This development raises the question about how to interact in urban, less-regulated situations involving automated vehicles (AV) and vulnerable road users (VRU) like cyclists and/or pedestrians. Thus, it is essential to gain an understanding of interactions between VRU and current, mainly non-automated vehicles. This study focusses on cyclist-vehicle interaction and raises the questions whether there are typical interaction parameters. To address these issues, data of a previous Naturalistic Cycling Study (NCS), was re-analyzed. The selected sample consisted of 11 cyclists (ranging from 24 to 48 years, 8 males, 3 females). The subjects' bicycles were instrumented with two cameras (forward view and face of the rider) that recorded a four-week lasting cycling period. In total, 69 interactions between cyclists and vehicles in less-regulated traffic context were analyzed. As a result of this descriptive approach, we identified common cyclist maneuvers (e.g., avoiding) and behavioral parameters (e.g., keeping constant speed) in the light of different infrastructural context. The discussion addresses the functionality of different behavioral patterns and the arising challenges for AV technology.

**Keywords:** Naturalistic cycling study · Cyclist vehicle interaction · Qualitative study · Automated vehicles

## 1 Introduction

Automated Vehicles (AVs) are supposed to enter the existing traffic system gradually. However, researchers assume a long transition period, in which fully and partly AVs, manually driven vehicles as well as non-motorized road users like cyclists and pedestrians have to share the same urban traffic space [1, 2]. This assumption leads to a great challenge for AV development which is to enable the interaction between AVs and non-automated road users, especially the vulnerable ones, like cyclists and pedestrians [1, 3]. Little is known yet about interactions between vulnerable road users, (partly) AVs and conventional vehicles [1, 4] in complex, urban areas.

For that reason, this study addresses the cyclists' point of view when it comes to interactions with conventional vehicles. Based on this approach, the study aims to gain a

© The Author(s), under exclusive license to Springer Nature Switzerland AG 2021
N. L. Black et al. (Eds.): IEA 2021, LNNS 221, pp. 533–540, 2021.
https://doi.org/10.1007/978-3-030-74608-7_65

deeper understanding of parameters affecting cyclist-vehicle interactions and to recommend on AV development. This approach is not yet a common research topic, although car manufactures take cyclists into account, but merely by developing systems to avoid collisions with cyclists [1]. That means, a vehicle basically reacts to cyclist behavior, but it does not interact so far.

Current traffic interactions are affected by individual expectations, experience and routine actions [5] and mutual exchange [3]. Further, the infrastructure, traffic regulations and the behavior of other present road users determine decision-making processes as well as behavioral adaption [1]. Hence, research results which are linked to cyclists typical traffic behavior are briefly described subsequently.

Cyclists are well-studied with regard to safety issues due to the fact, that they are physically unprotected which leads to relatively high injury risks [1]. For example, the amount of deadly injured cyclists in Germany raised by almost 17% compared to 2010 [6]. Another cyclist characteristic, which is known already is the velocity of cyclists. Studies indicated a typical cyclist velocity ranging from 12 to 18 km/h [7, 8]. Further, a considerable proportion of 45% of German cyclists admit violating a red light every once in a while, [9] which leads to the assumption of different risk tolerance among cyclists. Studies concerning cyclists' route choice showed that designated cycling infrastructure is preferred in contrast to other infrastructure types, especially by older cyclists [10, 11]. Another route choice determinant is less motorized and non-motorized traffic [12]. Furthermore, studies showed a cyclists' preference for routes with less intersections and traffic lights [13]. In general, cycling is an important mode of transport especially for shorter commuting distances in towns and cities [1, 12]. Cycling is often mentioned to be environmentally friendly, flexible, healthy and popular [1]. Hence, the importance of cycling is expected to increase [14], which will also lead to more cyclist-vehicle interaction in the future.

In summary, there is probably no average cyclist [2] which makes it hard to develop a standard interaction mode for the car manufacturers. Here, it becomes even more important to understand cyclist-vehicle interaction parameters during comfortable, everyday maneuvering [15]. Those interactions will account for the bigger number of interactions compared to safety critical situations. Thus, this study focused on non- to less-regulated interactions, infrastructural aspects and cyclist/vehicle dynamics and maneuvers using Naturalistic Cycling Data (NCS).

# 2   Methods

As mentioned before, this study re-analyzed existing NCS[1] data, which was conducted in 2012. The original study addresses aspects of mobility and safety behavior of cyclists. The main aspect of this NCS approach is the instrumentation of bicycles with cameras over a 4-week period of time, to capture riders' "normal" cycling and mobility behavior. Overall, the original NCS recruited 90 participants (51 cyclists) how performed more than 4000 trips with a total length of more than 17000 km within four weeks. Based on the huge amount of collected data within the original study, it was necessary to select

---

[1] For more information about the original Naturalistic Cycling Study, see: [17].

and reduce the sample, to assess the video quality and to define and analyze interaction sequences between cyclists and vehicles. Thus, the following paragraphs address the stepwise approach to create and analyze the final data set.

## 2.1   Sample Selection

The sample of the original NCS data we were able to access, included video data from cyclists ($n = 22$) and e-bike riders ($n = 39$ pedelec riders, n = 7 S-pedelec riders) representing different age groups (younger than 40 years, 41 to 64 years, older than 65 years). Preliminary studies showed different riding behavior of e-bike users compared to traditional cyclists [16, 17] which led to the exclusion of e-bike data from further analyzes. Furthermore, cyclists also differ in riding behavior with regard to their age. Several studies pointed out the preference to use pedestrian crossings or signalized intersections among older cyclists [11]. Thus, we decided to exclude older cyclists as well and focused the analyzes on the group of younger cyclists.

The sample of younger cyclists consisted of 12 participants. Due to insufficient video quality we had to remove one participant. Finally, the sample included evaluable video data of 11 participants (8 males, 3 females) with a mean age of 35 years ($SD = 8.6$). The number of trips per person varied widely between 11 to 138 trips within four weeks. As a result, the mean kilometers driven per day within four weeks also varied around an average value of 3.6 km ($SD = 1.8$). All participants were residents in the city of Chemnitz (Federal State of Saxony, Germany) or of nearby small towns and thus, most of the trips were recorded within the city area of Chemnitz.

## 2.2   Data Preparation and Editing

In a first step, the video quality was assessed. Each bicycle from the original NCS was equipped with two cameras recording the front view and the face of the rider. The face view footage was excluded from further analyses, due to quality problems (e.g., direct sunlight led to reduced visibility).

The second step addressed a rough screening of each video to identify any interaction sequence between cyclists and vehicles in less or non-regulated situations. That means, intersections with traffic light regulation or intersections with separated pedestrian or cyclist crossing or cycle paths were excluded.

Then, the definition of cyclist-vehicle interaction scenes was added with more detailed criteria. The aim was to identify 1:1-situations (1 cyclist vs. 1 vehicle) in traffic situations with less or no regulation. Further, the intention to cross trajectories or an actual crossover of trajectories must have been visible. Videos with bad weather conditions, otherwise bad visibility or at night were also excluded.

The fourth step was the development of a category system which was transferred to ELAN (a free annotation software: https://archive.mpi.nl/tla/elan). This step included several iterative adaptions until the best fit to the video data was reached. Table 1 gives an overview of the main categories that were used to describe the bicycle-vehicle interactions.

The annotations were gathered by three raters, who were involved in the development process of the category system. To reach a high interrater reliability, they trained

**Table 1.** Selected main categories for annotation.

| Super-category | Subcategory |
|---|---|
| Level of regulation | No regulation, regulation via common priority rules, regulation via priority road signs |
| Bicycle maneuver | Go straight, turn left, urn right, avoid an obstacle, overtake, starting, stopping |
| Bicycle speed | Constant speed, decelerate, accelerate |
| Bicycle riding area | Cycle path, pedestrian way, combined cycle/pedestrian way, trail, roadside, middle of the road, parking area, intersection |
| Vehicle maneuver | Go straight, turn left, turn right, avoid an obstacle, overtake, starting, stopping, take the parking space, leave the parking space, turn around |
| Vehicle speed | Constant speed, decelerate, accelerate |
| Vehicle driving area | Driving lane, cycle path, pedestrian way, combined cycle/pedestrian way, parking area, intersection |
| Irregularities | By cyclist, by driver, by both |
| Goal achievement | Without complication, cede the right of way (by vehicle/by cyclist), demand the right of way (by vehicle/by cyclist) |

themselves using sample data and compared the results among them. Thus, a substantial agreement among the three raters was reached (*Fleiss' Kappa* = .74). In order to apply the category system, the raters identified the time stamp of a trajectory crossing or the intention to cross trajectories first. Then, a ten second lasting interval before and after this timestamp was enriched with annotations from the category system.

# 3   Results

The rough screening of the chosen video data revealed 433 interactions between cyclists and vehicles in less or non-regulated situations (step two of data preparation). The more detailed definition of interactions led to 69 cycle-vehicle interaction scenes, which were analyzed. Within these 69 interactions, 18 scenes were categorized as non-regulated and are described separately and more detailed in the following paragraph.

## 3.1   Non-regulated Cyclist-Vehicle Interactions

The non-regulated cyclist-vehicle interactions took either place at traffic calmed ($n = 10$) areas with connected parking spaces or at parking areas (e.g., nearby to a supermarket; $n = 8$). As a consequence, the most frequent vehicle maneuver was taking or leaving the parking space ($n = 10$) followed by maneuvers that characterized the search for a parking space (go straight, $n = 5$, turn left, $n = 2$, turn around, $n = 1$). When trajectories crossed, the cyclists solved the situation more often than the vehicle driver. Here the cyclist showed avoiding or overtaking behavior ($n = 11$) at a constant or slightly accelerating speed level ($n = 14$). There were three situations where the vehicle driver accelerated to solve the interaction. In total, 16 situations were solved without complication. The two situations with complications were caused in equal shares by cyclist and vehicle. One time, the cyclist was riding at the center of the lane and thus, avoided the left turn of the vehicle. The other situation with complications was caused by the driver leaving the parking space with accelerating speed so that the cyclist had to decelerate (which happened in general only once). There was no situation where the cyclist came to a halt at all. The vehicle speed level was also constant for the most interactions ($n = 7$), unless the driver intended to take a parking space. Then, the vehicle mostly stopped or decelerated clearly ($n = 5$). In case of leaving the parking space, the driver accelerated and decelerated alternately (e.g., whilst the cyclist avoided/overtook the car, $n = 4$).

### 3.2  Less Regulated Cyclist-Vehicle Interactions

We defined the less-regulated interactions to be left-yields-to-right situations ($n = 45$) or exit ramps with lowered curb ($n = 6$). Within all 51 less-regulated cyclist-vehicle interactions, we found three different mainly performed cyclist maneuvers: going straight ($n - 20$), turning left ($n = 20$) and avoiding the vehicle ($n = 11$).

Those maneuvers, where the cyclist intended to go straight, were mostly performed at constant cycling speed ($n = 18$). Within these 20 interactions, 14 interactions were performed without any complications. Here, the driver also went on a constant speed level. During the remaining six interactions, vehicle drivers ignored the cyclist's right of way signalizing it by accelerating ($n = 3$), a stop and go behavior ($n = 2$) or keeping constant speed ($n = 1$). There were two situations, where the cyclist had to decelerate.

When the cyclist intended to turn left, they also mostly kept their speed constant ($n = 14$). Other observes cyclist speed was accelerating ($n = 4$) and decelerating ($n = 2$). Vehicle drivers kept their speed level as well in most cases ($n = 16$), regardless of their intended maneuver (turn left, turn right, go straight). Further, there were three situations, where the cyclists cede it's right of way (however, cycle speed was constant). Within one cyclist left turn maneuver, the right of way was considered correctly to the cyclist; here, the vehicle came to a halt. In 16 remaining cases, the vehicle had the right of way and it was considered correctly by the cyclist.

The last group of common cycling maneuver within our sample was characterized by avoiding the vehicle with constant speed ($n = 11$). Within this category, we found the most irregularities (in terms of proportion). In three situations, the vehicle intended to turn around; one time the cyclist's right of way was ignored and one time the vehicles right of way was ignored. Within two further situations, the vehicle ignored the cyclist's right of way and there is one situation, where the cyclist ignores the vehicle's right of way. In the remaining six interactions, the cyclist avoided the vehicle for example when it left the intersection area to slow.

## 4  Discussion

This study aimed to gain a deeper understanding of parameters affecting cyclist-vehicle interactions in non- to less-regulated traffic situations. Therefore, we used a qualitative approach to explore and describe those defined interactions on the basis of already existing NCS data.

Within the data of 11 participants, we identified more than 400 interactions between cyclists and vehicles apart from highly regulated traffic (like intersections with separated cycling/pedestrian crossing). This finding in general supports the research goal to understand "everyday" cyclist-vehicle interaction, because obviously there is an already high and probably arising demand for automated vehicles to manage those situations [1, 14, 15].

Further, we identified 69 interactions to be non- or less regulated (which means ca. 6% from previously 433 situations). Nevertheless, even this comparatively small sample revealed important insights in cyclist behavioral adaptation. Hence, we found different maneuvers depending on the infrastructural context. In non-regulated areas, avoiding the vehicle with constant speed was the most common cyclist behavior. Regarding less-regulated traffic, we could distinguish three kinds of common maneuvers in terms of going straight, turning left and -at least often- avoiding the vehicle. Using the example of avoiding behavior, it seemed to have different functions depending on the infrastructure. On parking areas, cyclists clear the area maybe to facilitate the parking progress. In less-regulated situations, we got the impression that avoiding the vehicle is more associated to safety issues (due to the fact, that we found more irregularities here).

Regardless of the level of traffic regulation and maneuver, cyclists and vehicles mostly kept their speed on a constant level. Probably, this is the most comfortable way to manage their daily trips. On the AV perspective, this steady kind of cycling behavior will be challenging to interpret. Here, there must be experimental controlled studies on further parameters like the frequency of pedaling or the steering (Lee et al., 2020), ideally using realistic setups [1, 15, 18].

A really interesting finding was that even irregular behavior did not lead to any crashes or risky situations within our sample. We categorized irregular behavior, when either the vehicle or the cyclist ignored the right of way (which happened as expected also on cyclist side; [9]). Surprisingly, this kind of behavior did not change the speed adaption dramatically, neither on cyclist nor on vehicle side. In these situations, the faster agent or the one with the better road position simply took its chance and cleared the situation. Such kind of behavior (ignore the right of way) will probably not be shown by future AVs, which might lead to traffic congestion or misusing behavior on the cyclists' side [4]. This assumption is also supported by Hagenzieker et al. (2020), who found cyclists to be more confident of being noticed by an AV in situations with cyclists right of way [1]. Here, the question arises on how to meet cyclists' expectation about the upcoming AV action in a functional way that supports cyclists' decision making [5].

The limitations of this study address the naturalistic approach of collecting data. Thus, while interpreting our data we had to take into account, that there is a lack of internal validity. That is why we decided to keep the analysis on a descriptive level. Due to the lack of internal control, we cannot derive conclusion based on causality, but identified tendencies. Further, all information we analyzed was simply rated by video which probably leads to vague results (for example regarding speed adaption which could not be measured).

Nevertheless, our study reached the aim of gaining first insights into cyclist-vehicle interaction using NCS data. Further studies are needed to address 1) more naturalistic data, also from the drivers' perspectives [1, 15], 2) investigate cyclist behavioral parameter in more detail (e.g., body posture, head posture, pedaling, steering, accelerating, deceleration), 3) samples at different age and different bicycle types (pedelec, s-pedelec, e-scooter [15]) and 4) the possibilities of informal and explicit AV-cyclist communication [4].

**Acknowledgement.** This study was funded by the Federal Ministry of Education and Research (grant no.: 16ES1035). We also would like to thank German Insurers Accident Research (UDV) who gave us the chance to re-analyze the original NCS data.

# References

1. Hagenzieker, M.P., van der Kint, S., Vissers, L., van Schagen, I.N.G., de Bruin, J., van Gent, P., Commandeur, J.J.: Interactions between cyclists and automated vehicles: results of a photo experiment. J. Transp. Saf. Secur. **12**(1), 94–115 (2020)
2. Vissers, L., van der Kint, S., van Schlagen, I., Hagenzieker, M.: Safe interaction between cyclists, pedestrians and automated vehicles. What do we know and what do we need to know? Technical Report The Hague, Netherlands: SWOV Institute for Road Safety Research (2016)
3. Ackermann, C., Beggiato, M., Bluhm, L.F., Löw, A., Krems, J.F.: Deceleration parameters and their applicability as informal communication signal between pedestrians and automated vehicles. Transp. Res. Part F: Traffic Psychol. Behav. **62**, 757–768 (2019)
4. Tabone, W., de Winter, J., Ackermann, C., Bärgman, J., Baumann, M., Deb, S., Emmenegger, C., Habibovic, A., Hagenzieker, M., Hancock, P.A., Happee, R., Krems, J., Lee, J.D., Martens, M., Merat, N., Norman, D., Sheridan, T.B., Stanton, N.A.: Vulnerable road users and the coming wave of automated vehicles: expert perspectives. Transp. Res. Interdisc. Perspect. **9**, 100293 (2021)
5. Räsänen, M., Summala, H.: Car drivers' adjustments to cyclists at roundabouts. Transp. Hum. Factors **2**, 1–17 (2000)
6. Statistisches Bundesamt (Destatis). Kraftrad- und Fahrradunfälle im Straßenverkehr 2019 (2020)
7. Dozza, M., Werneke, J.: Introducing naturalistic cycling data: what factors influence bicyclists' safety in the real world? Transp. Res. Part F **24**, 83–91 (2014). https://doi.org/10.1016/j.trf.2014.04.001
8. Thompson, D.C., Rebolledo, V., Thompson, R.S., Kaufman, A., Rivara, F.P.: Bike speed measurements in a recreational population: validity of self reported speed. Inj. Prev. **3**(1), 43–45 (1997)
9. Alrutz, D., Bohle, W., Müller, H., Prahlow, H., Hacke, U., Lohmann, G.: Unfallrisiko und Regelakzeptanz von Fahrradfahrern (Heft 184). Bergisch-Gladbach: Bundesanstalt für Straßenwesen (2009)
10. Chen, C.F., Chen, P.C.: Estimating recreational cyclists' preferences for bicycle routes–evidence from Taiwan. Transp. Policy **26**, 23–30 (2013)
11. Bernhoft, I.M., Carstensen, G.: Preferences and behaviour of pedestrians and cyclists by age and gender. Transp. Res. Part F: Traffic Psychol. Behav. **11**(2), 83–95 (2008)
12. Broach, J., Dill, J., Gliebe, J.: Where do cyclists ride? A route choice model developed with revealed preference GPS data. Transp. Res. Part A: Policy Pract. **46**(10), 1730–1740 (2012)

13. Menghini, G., Carrasco, N., Schüssler, N., Axhausen, K.W.: Route choice of cyclists in Zurich. Transp. Res. part A: Policy Pract. **44**(9), 754–765 (2010)
14. Pucher, J., Buehler, R.: Cycling towards a more sustainable transport future. Transp. Rev. **37**(6), 689–694 (2017)
15. Lee, O., Rasch, A., Schwab, A.L., Dozza, M.: Modelling cyclists' comfort zones from obstacle avoidance manoeuvres. Accid. Anal. Prev. **144**, 105609 (2020)
16. Dozza, M., Piccinini, G.F.B., Werneke, J.: Using naturalistic data to assess e-cyclist behavior. Transp. Res. part F: Traffic Psychol. Behav. **41**, 217–226 (2016)
17. Schleinitz, K., Petzoldt, T., Franke-Bartholdt, L., Krems, J., Gehlert, T.: The german naturalistic cycling study-comparing cycling speed of riders of different e-bikes and conventional bicycles. Saf. Sci. **92**, 290–297 (2017)
18. Tafidis, P., Pirdavani, A., Brijs, T., Farah, H.: Can automated vehicles improve cyclist safety in urban areas? Safety **5**(3), 57 (2019)

# Human-Machine Interfaces for Automated Driving: Development of an Experimental Design for Evaluating Usability

Deike Albers[1]([envelope]) [iD], Jonas Radlmayr[1] [iD], Niklas Grabbe[1] [iD], Sebastian Hergeth[2] [iD], Frederik Naujoks[2] [iD], Yannick Forster[2], Andreas Keinath[2] [iD], and Klaus Bengler[1] [iD]

[1] Chair of Ergonomics, Technical University of Munich, Boltzmannstr. 15, 85748 Garching, Germany
deike.albers@tum.de
[2] BMW Group, Knorrstr. 147, 80937 Munich, Germany

**Abstract.** The introduction of conditionally automated driving [25] implies repeated transitions of the driving task between the human operator and the automated driving system (ADS). Human-machine interfaces (HMIs) facilitating these shifts in control are essential. Usability serves as an important criterion to assess the quality of an HMI design. This paper derives a study design for assessing the usability based on the best practice advice by [1]. The paper covers the applied definitions of usability, the sample characteristics, the test cases, the HMIs, the dependent variables, the procedure, the conditions of use, and the testing environment. The study design will be applied in a driving simulator and three test track experiments in different countries within an ongoing project. This involves a number of safety, technical and resource constraints in the development of the study design. This paper describes the challenges and limitations of applying a generic best practice advice to the varying test settings. Furthermore, two HMI concepts are developed and evaluated in an expert assessment. The two concepts will serve as the research subjects in the series of experiments. The proposed study design is suitable for application in different test settings. Therefore, the comparability between the experiments is high. This paper provides a first step in a validation project with the overall goal to propose a practical approach to usability testing of ADS HMIs that covers different constructs of usability and appropriate dependent variables within their application areas.

**Keywords:** Usability · Study design · Human-machine interface · Automated driving

## 1 Introduction

The increasing level of automation in vehicles has a strong influence on the role of the human in the car. With the introduction of conditionally automated driving (L3), the driving task is completely handed over to the automated driving system (ADS), while the human operator remains responsive to intervene in cases of ADS-issued requests

© The Author(s), under exclusive license to Springer Nature Switzerland AG 2021
N. L. Black et al. (Eds.): IEA 2021, LNNS 221, pp. 541–551, 2021.
https://doi.org/10.1007/978-3-030-74608-7_66

or system failures [25]. The associated paradigm change of the human operator, e.g. in partially automated systems (L2, [25]), towards a passenger affects the design of the human-machine interface (HMI) in the car [19]. Transitions between higher and lower levels of automation require an HMI facilitating the interaction between the human in the car and the ADS with a strong focus on the communication of the current responsibility for the driving task.

Automotive HMIs generally comprise output channels (e.g. displays, auditory signals), input channels (e.g. buttons, pedals), and a dialogue logic to ensure the appropriate interaction between drivers and their vehicles [2]. While the field of automated driving has seen developments into speech-based HMIs or haptic feedback, the following paper and study design focus on the development and evaluation of a mainly visual/manual HMI.

In a literature review, [1] identify common research methods in the context of usability assessments for ADS HMIs. The authors critically discuss the findings using the structure of study characteristics and derive a best practice advice for planning a usability evaluation. In addition to other methods, [1] propose to conduct usability assessments in driving simulators pointing out the advantage of driving simulators as being an efficient and risk-free alternative to real-driving environments [4]. However, [1] remind that results on usability assessments of ADS HMIs obtained in driving simulators have not yet been reviewed for their validity, i.e. transferability towards the real world.

Another important aspect is the potential impact of culture on the usability assessment. The growing body of research stresses the importance of culture when designing or evaluating user-interface design in general [12] and usability with a focus on automotive HMIs [16]. Therefore, cultural effects should be kept in mind when developing methodological recommendations for usability testing in the context of ADS HMIs.

This paper develops a study design based on the advice on user studies for usability evaluations provided by [1]. Furthermore, two HMI concepts are developed to serve as the research subjects. The study design presented will be applied to a series of four experiments within an ongoing project. The project pursues three objectives: (1) to evaluate the best practice advice by [1] in practical use; (2) to assess the validity of driving simulators; and (3) to investigate the influence of cultural factors on usability assessments. To conclude, the project will propose a practical approach to usability testing of ADS HMIs that covers different constructs of usability and appropriate dependent variables within their application areas. The first step in this project is presented in this paper. It comprises the development of two HMI concepts serving as research subjects. Furthermore, this paper outlines a study design describing the challenges of applying it to four experiments with varying test settings.

## 2   Design of Experiment

This chapter covers the study design that will be applied in a series of four experiments. The design practically applies the best practice advice provided by [1]. Therefore, the structure of this chapter takes up the structure of their paper and comprises the subsections *Definition of Usability*, *Sample Characteristics*, *Test Cases*, *Dependent Variables*, *Conditions of Use*, and *Testing Environment*. Additionally, the decision for two HMI concepts, their development and design are presented (*Human-machine interfaces*). The procedure of the experiment is outlined in subsection *Procedure*.

The study is developed to be suitable for the application in four different experiment settings. These cover one driving simulator experiment and three test track experiments in different countries. The study design considers constraints due to safety aspects or resources available at the different testing sites, e.g. length of test tracks or surrounding traffic. This results in four highly comparable experiments that feature only necessary and minor differences, e.g. language adaptations. The repetition of the study design will allow conclusions on the impact of the testing environment and potential cultural effects to be drawn.

## 2.1 Definition of Usability

This study design applies the ISO 9241, defining usability as the "extent to which a system, product or service can be used by specified users to achieve specified goals with effectiveness, efficiency and satisfaction in a specified context of use" [14] (p. 2). Furthermore, the NHTSA minimum requirements towards an HMI for automated driving shall be considered in the study design. The requirements state that an HMI must be designed in such a way that the user understands that the ADS is "(1) functioning properly; (2) currently engaged in ADS mode; (3) currently "unavailable" for use; (4) experiencing a malfunction; and/or (5) requesting control transition from the ADS to the operator" [23] (p. 10). The definitions will be applied to the selection of test cases [23] and dependent variables [14, 23]. The resulting usability assessment is limited to the basic functions provided by an ADS. The results implore the participants' understanding of the ADS and their interaction with the ADS.

## 2.2 Sample Characteristics

The target sample for this study design represents the potential user population, therefore, the car-driving population. For other target populations, different sample distributions might be appropriate. As recommended by [20] affiliations with study-related organisations or the tested HMI are avoided. The majority of participants shall have little or no experience with automated driving. By testing naïve participants, the intuitive usability of the ADS HMIs can be assessed. The age range is between 18 and 75. The goal is to ensure an even distribution that covers different age groups such as the age groups proposed by the NHTSA visual-manual distraction protocol (18–24, 25–39, 40–54, > 54) [22]. Gender distribution is balanced. A sociodemographic survey inquires further aspects such as visual impairments. Data on driving experience in general, prior experience with driving assistant systems, and the familiar manufacturing brands are recorded. The samples should be of great resemblance among the different experiments to ensure comparability. The target sample presented shows a great variety in its characteristics. The size of subgroups, e.g. age, is not sufficient for inferential statistical analysis. Nevertheless, important trends could be uncovered motivating future research.

## 2.3  Test Cases

The selection of test cases comprises mostly non-critical situations due to safety aspects of the test track experiments. Critical situations, e.g. with a limited time budget for take-overs, are important for safety-related assessments of ADS, such as controllability assessments [11], and have a low probability of occurrence. For evaluating the usability, especially the constructs efficiency and satisfaction [14], frequently recurring situations are of greater importance. The test cases cover standard situations, i.e. transitions between different automation modes and changes in the availability of automation modes as recommended by [1]. This allows an assessment of the basic functions provided by an ADS. Additionally, one critical situation requiring immediate intervention by the participant (TC12) is included. The selection of test cases allows conclusions related to the NHTSA minimum requirements [23]. Table 1 shows the assignment of the NHTSA minimum requirements to the specific test cases based on the information provided by the HMI concepts.

**Table 1.** Description of the twelve test cases and their linkage to the NHTSA minimum requirements [23] (p. 10): "(1) functioning properly; (2) currently engaged in ADS mode; (3) currently "unavailable" for use; (4) experiencing a malfunction; (5) requesting control transition from the ADS to the operator."

| Test case | Description | Active mode [higher modes available] [25] | NHTSA minimum requirements [23] |
|---|---|---|---|
| 1 | Continuous ride in L0, no events | L0 [−] | 1, 2, 3 |
| 2 | Change in availability | L0 [−] → L0 [L2, L3] | 1, 2, 3 |
| 3 | Transition: initiated by participant | L0 [L2, L3] → L3 | 1, 2, 3 |
| 4 | Continuous ride in L3, no events | L3 | 1, 2, 3 |
| 5 | Transition: initiated by participant | L3 → L2 [L3] | 1, 2, 3 |
| 6 | Change in availability (malfunction) | L2 [L3] → L2 [−] | 1, 2, 3, 4 |
| 7 | Continuous ride in L2, no events | L2 [−] | 1, 2, 3 |
| 8 | Change in availability | L2 [−] → L2 [L3] | 1, 2, 3 |
| 9 | Transition: initiated by participant | L2 [L3] → L3 | 1, 2, 3 |
| 10 | Change in availability (planned) Transition: system-initiated | L3 → L0 [−] | 1, 2, 3, 5 |
| 11 | Change in availability Transition: initiated by participant | L0 [−] → L3 | 1, 2, 3 |
| 12 | Change in availability (malfunction) Transition: system-initiated | L3 → L0 [−] | 1, 2, 3, 4, 5 |

In the HMIs to be tested information on the active automation mode and the availability of the different automation modes is constantly displayed. Therefore, in all test cases the participant receives information on the first three requirements "functioning properly", "currently engaged in ADS mode", and "currently unavailable for use". The requirements "experiencing a malfunction" and "requesting control transition from the ADS to the operator" are addressed by two test cases each. No permutation of the test cases is planned because specific test cases build on precedent test cases, e.g. a take-over request requires the prior activation of L3 automated driving.

## 2.4 Human-Machine Interfaces

The two HMI concepts serve as the research subjects. The concepts have the purpose of increasing the variance of results within each experiment. This provides insights into relative validity and identifies metrics sensitive to differences in HMI design. In two previous within-subject studies [9, 10], two HMI concepts were tested that varied in their compliance with several items (Items 2, 3, 7, 8, 9, and 14) of [21]. The study results confirmed differences between the two concepts in both, behavioural and self-reported measures on usability and acceptance. Therefore, a similar procedure is applied here.

The concepts are based on the HMI of [5] and adjusted for the twelve test cases and the three automation modes L0, L2, and L3 [25]. Both concepts provide information on the active automation mode, the availability of automation modes and possibly malfunctions and transition requests. Infotainment is displayed on the right side of the HMIs, though it is not functionally implemented. One HMI concept was designed following recommendations of the NHTSA minimum guidelines [23] and the HMI guidelines listed by [21], therefore called high-compliance HMI. The HMI is limited to a mainly visual HMI, comprising the instrument cluster, LED-strips on the steering wheel and warning sounds. The other concept comprises only the instrument cluster. It deviates from the high compliance HMI by deliberately violating eight items of the guidelines of [21], therefore called low-compliance HMI. Figure 1 shows snapshots of the English HMI concepts visualising the differences. The violations concern the effective communication of transitions (Item 3), the functional grouping of icons and notifications (Item 5), the colour contrast (Item 7) and the general colour selection of symbols (Items 14, 15), the size and style of texts and icons (Item 8), the supplement of non-standard symbols with text explanations (Item 9), and the multimodality of high-priority notifications (Item 18) [21].

The HMI is controlled by two buttons on the steering wheel. The left button allows the transitions L0 → L2, L2 → L0, and L3 → L0. The right button toggles L2 ↔ L3. When pressed in L0, the high-compliance HMI provides textual feedback on its function while the low-compliance HMI does not show any reaction. Additionally, the participant can deactivate L2 and L3 by steering or braking.

An expert assessment is conducted with six researchers working in the field of HMIs for three to seven years ($M = 4.5$). First, the experts assessed the two HMI concepts by using ten heuristics collated from [24] and [21] and rated the severity of violated heuristics. Afterwards, the experts were interviewed on the colours, icons, and the icons' positioning. The experts were able to express further feedback and comments in the final interview. The results confirm the different degrees of compliance of the two HMI concepts. Improvement suggestions were implemented to further increase the difference in compliance between the concepts. The control logic (toggle) of both HMI concepts was criticised by two experts. However, this was not changed due to technical constraints and because both HMI concepts applied the same control elements and logic.

The participants experience one HMI concept each and provide data on its usability. A between-subject design is chosen to avoid learning effects that are expected to be considerable due to the similarity of the concept basic structure.

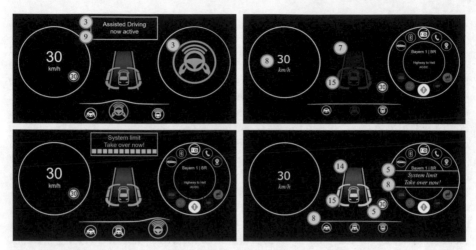

**Fig. 1.** Snapshots from high-compliance HMI (left) and low-compliance HMI (right) just after a transition to L2 (top) and in the middle of a planned take-over request by the ADS (bottom). Items violated in the low-compliance HMI are indicated with their respective number [21].

## 2.5 Dependent Variables

The experiment collects both self-reported and observational data. Table 2 provides an overview of the dependent variables and connects them to the items of [21] violated in the low-compliance HMI that potentially affect the dependent variables. Furthermore, the dependent variables are associated with the NHTSA minimum requirements [23] and the constructs of effectiveness, efficiency, and satisfaction of the ISO 9241 [14]. This allows a more in-depth assessment of the usability of the HMIs.

**Observational Measures.** Eye-tracking data is collected to calculate the attention ratios (percentage of time on area of interest) to the street, the instrument cluster, the control buttons on the steering wheel, and the tablet. The Surrogate Reference Task [13] on the tablet serves as a non-driving related activity only permitted when driving L3 automation. In automated driving research, attention ratios are used to assess trust [17] or mode awareness [6]. In this study design, attention ratios are applied to reveal whether the HMI is effectively communicating the active automation mode to the participant. Furthermore, gaze paths, gaze attention times, glance numbers and glance durations are analysed for test cases containing notifications by the HMI feedbacking how efficiently users receive the information.

Button presses for transitions, braking and steering behaviour are recorded. Takeover times and hands-off detections during L2 are analysed. The data show whether participants reach the intended goals and if they do so efficiently. The driving behaviour mostly covers the constructs of effectiveness and efficiency of usability, but also provides information on the fulfilment of the NHTSA minimum requirements [23].

After each test case, the experimenter rates the quality of the participants' interaction with the ADS on a 5-point Likert scale ranging from "no problem" to "help of experimenter" [8].

**Table 2.** List of the dependent variables and their linkage to the items of [21] violated in the low-compliance HMI, the linkage to the three constructs of usability (a) effectiveness, (b) efficiency, and (c) satisfaction of the ISO 9241 [14] and the linkage to the NHTSA minimum requirements [23] (p. 10): "(1) functioning properly; (2) currently engaged in ADS mode; (3) currently "unavailable" for use; (4) experiencing a malfunction; (5) requesting control transition from the ADS to the operator."

| Dependent variable | Items of [21] violated in low-compliance HMI | ISO 9241 [14] | NHTSA minimum requirements [23] |
|---|---|---|---|
| **Eye-Tracking [15]** | | | |
| Attention ratios (TC1, TC4, TC7) | all* | a | 1, 2 |
| Gaze paths; gaze attention times; glance numbers; (mean) glance durations (TC2, TC6, TC8, TC10-TC12) | 5, 8, 18 | b | 1, 2, 3, 4**, 5*** |
| **Driving Behaviour** | | | |
| Button presses for transitions (TC3, TC5, TC9) | 3 | a, b | |
| Takeover paths (TC10, TC12) | | a, b | |
| Takeover times (TC10, TC12) | 5, 8, 18 | b | 4**, 5 |
| Hands off detections in L2 (TC6, TC7, TC8) | 3, 7, 8, 9, 15* | a | 2 |
| **Experimenter rating after each test drive** | | | |
| Transitions and other interactions with ADS | | a, b | 1, 2, 3, 4**, 5*** |
| **Short interviews after each test drive** | | | |
| Last active automation mode | 3, 7, 8, 9, 15* | a | 2 |
| Allocation of driving task | 3, 7, 8, 9, 15* | a | 2 |
| Availability of the automation modes | 5, 8 | a | 3 |
| Transition problems (TC3, TC5, TC9-TC12) | 5, 8, 18 | all | |
| General feedback | all* | all | |
| **Questionnaires** | | | |
| System Usability Scale [3]; Usability Metric of User Experience [7]; User Experience Questionnaire [18] | all* | all | |
| Trust (1-item); acceptance (1-item) | all* | c | |
| **Final interview** | | | |
| Positive & negative feedback; improvement suggestions & general feedback | all* | all | |

*exceptions for yellow-blue colour-blind persons; **TC12 only; ***TC10 & TC12 only

**Self-reported Measures.** Participants are requested to indicate the last active automation mode, and the availabilities of different modes. In order to investigate the mental model of the allocation of the driving task, participants are asked whether they were permitted to take their hands off the steering wheel or answer e-mails. The short interviews provide valuable information on the effectiveness of the HMI concept and whether it comprehensively communicates the currently active automation mode and availability of other automation modes. When changing between automation modes, the experimenter asks about problems and encourages the participant to express feedback and thoughts.

After completion of the test drive, the participants fill out the system usability scale [3], the usability metric of user experience [7], the user experience questionnaire [18], and 1-item questions on trust and acceptance. A short interview gathers further insights of the participants' experience with the HMI.

## 2.6  Procedure

The experimental setup describes the overall study procedure to provide a better understanding of the general setup. The procedure is oriented to typical usability studies and shall enable the systematic collection of multifaceted data on human-machine interaction in this complex and dynamic context.

Prior to the test drive, participants consent to the experiment and fill out a sociodemographic questionnaire followed by a familiarisation drive. Participants are informed that their simulated car is equipped with an ADS providing the three automation modes called "manual driving", i.e. L0; "assisted driving", i.e. L2; and "automated driving", i.e. L3 [25]. Participants are instructed to engage in the Surrogate Reference Task [13] when L3 is active. Participants are instructed to initiate transitions only if explicitly requested by the ADS or the experimenter. The test drive comprises twelve test cases in a fixed order. Each test case starts at the beginning of the straight and ends in standstill at the turn-around for a short interview. The experiment ends with the questionnaires and the final interview.

Due to safety constraints and technical constraints of the underlying driver assistance system in the test track vehicles, participants must manually accelerate and decelerate in between the test cases. Thus, the participants are required to pre-set the automation mode that is needed for the respective test case themselves. Consequently, data collection on observational measures is limited to the centre of a straight (route metres 200 m–700 m) which excludes the participants' manual acceleration and deceleration. Test case events such as system notifications and transition requests are triggered at three different locations along the route (325 m, 450 m, 575 m), permutating across the test cases. Neither the range for data collection nor the trigger locations are visible to the participant. The speed limit for the automation and the driver is set to 30 km/h. This results in about 60 s of data recorded for each test case.

## 2.7  Conditions of Use

As described in the subsection *Sample Characteristics* the study design is intended to cover the intuitive usability of the HMI concepts. Participants receive written information about the three automation modes of the ADS and their respective allocation of the driving task. The experimenter verbally repeats this information and answers questions.

He indicates the two buttons on the steering wheel needed for changing the automation modes but does not give any operating instructions. A familiarisation drive is conducted prior to the test drive. However, it does not cover handling the ADS. Consequently, the test drive collects data on the first contact with the ADS.

## 2.8 Testing Environment

The experiment is repeatedly conducted in different testing environments. The first experiment is conducted in a static driving simulator consisting of a BMW 6-series convertible with front and back view projectors enabling an immersion with a front field of view of about 180°. The simulation software is SILAB. The simulated track consists of a three-lane straight about 900 m in length with opportunities to turn-around at both ends. Lane changes or surrounding traffic are not involved.

The simulated test track equals the real driving test track used in the second experiment that is conducted at the *Universität der Bundeswehr München* in Neubiberg, Germany. In the three test track experiments, the instrumented vehicle is a BMW 3series model equipped with *Driving Assistant Professional*. The vehicle is modified to enable L3 automation and the free programming of the HMI. The other two test track experiments are planned to be conducted on test tracks with similar features in the USA and Japan.

## 3    Limitations

The study design presented is limited to the usability assessment in terms of evaluating the users' intuitive understanding and interaction with the ADS. Only basic functions of the ADS are covered. Furthermore, the study design is subject to several constraints that arise from the goal of maximum comparability between experiments and overall project goals. The proposed study design is applicable for all four test sites to cover intercultural aspects. However, due to safety considerations and limits in the local conditions of the different test tracks, the overall setting is rather simple, e.g. speed of 30 km/h, no surrounding traffic. To meet the claim of developing a recommendation for usability testing in the context of ADS HMIs, a large number of dependent variables is applied. This imbalance between experiencing a system and assessing it might increase the effort of the participants and negatively impact the quality of results. The HMI concepts that serve as the research subject are mainly visual. The concepts differ from each other only in the visual design and the usage of auditory warnings. Control elements and the handling are kept constant. The design of HMIs regarding their modalities and options for interaction should be subject to future considerations.

## 4    Summary and Outlook

This paper outlines a study design that builds on the best practice advice by [1], and adapts the latter to the practical application in a series of four experiments in different locations. Additionally, the development process and the design of two HMI concepts is described. This paper gives an insight into the challenges of designing comparable driving experiments across different test settings. It proposes different measurements and metrics to quantify the various aspects of usability. The development of an appropriate study design is the first step in proposing a practical approach to usability testing of ADS HMIs that encompass different constructs of usability and appropriate dependent variables within their application areas.

**Acknowledgement.** This work was funded by the BMW Group.

# References

1. Albers, D., Radlmayr, J., Loew, A., Hergeth, S., Naujoks, F., Keinath, A., Bengler, K.: Usability evaluation—advances in experimental design in the context of automated driving human-machine interfaces. Information **11**(5), 240 (2020)
2. Bengler, K., Rettenmaier, M., Fritz, N., Feierle, A.: From HMI to HMIs: towards an HMI framework for automated driving. Information **11**(2), 61 (2020)
3. Brooke, J.: SUS: a 'quick and dirty' usability scale. In: Jordan, P.W., Thomas, B., Weerd-meester, B.A., McClelland, I.L. (eds.) Usability Evaluation in Industry, pp. 189–194. Taylor & Francis, London (1996)
4. Caird, J.K., Horrey, W.J.: Twelve practical and twelve practical and useful questions about driving simulation. In: Fisher, D.L., Rizzo, M., Caird, J.K., Lee, J.D. (eds.) Handbook of Driving Simulation for Engineering, Medicine, and Psychology. CRC Press, Boca Raton (2011)
5. Feierle, A., Danner, S., Steininger, S., Bengler, K.: Information needs and visual attention during urban, highly automated driving—an investigation of potential influencing factors. Information **11**(2), 62 (2020)
6. Feldhütter, A., Härtwig, N., Kurpiers, C., Hernandez, J.M., Bengler, K.: Effect on mode awareness when changing from conditionally to partially automated driving. In: IEA 2018: International Ergonomics Association, pp. 314–324 (2018). https://doi.org/10.1007/978-3-319-96074-6_34
7. Finstad, K.: The usability metric for user experience. Interact. Comput. **22**(5), 323–327 (2010)
8. Forster, Y., Hergeth, S., Naujoks, F., Beggiato, M., Krems, J.F., Keinath, A.: Learning to use automation: behavioral changes in interaction with automated driving systems. Transp. Res. Part F Traffic Psychol. Behav. **62**, 599–614 (2019)
9. Forster, Y., Hergeth, S., Naujoks, F., Krems, J.F., Keinath, A.: Empirical validation of a checklist for heuristic evaluation of automated vehicle HMIs. In: AHFE 2019: Advances in Human Factors of Transportation, vol. 964, pp. 3–14. https://doi.org/10.1007/978-3-030-205 03-4_1
10. Forster, Y., Hergeth, S., Naujoks, F., Krems, J.F., Keinath, A.: Self-report measures for the assessment of human–machine interfaces in automated driving. Cogn. Technol. Work **22**, 703–720 (2019)
11. Gold, C.: Modeling of Take-Over Performance in Highly Automated Vehicle Guidance (2016)
12. Heimgärtner, R., Mandl, T., Womser-Hacker, C.: Zur Forschung im Bereich der Entwicklung interkultureller Benutzungsschnittstellen. In: Boll, S., Maaß, S., Malaka, R. (eds.) Workshopband Mensch & Computer 2013, pp. 441–449. Oldenbourg Verlag, München (2013)
13. ISO: Road Vehicles—Ergonomic Aspects of Transport Information and Control Systems—Calibration Tasks for Methods which Assess Driver Demand Due to the Use of In-Vehicle Systems, 14198. ISO, Geneva, Switzerland (2012)

14. ISO: Ergonomics of human-system interaction. Part 11: Usability: Definitions and concepts, Geneva, pp. 9241–11 (2018)
15. ISO: Road vehicles - Measurement of driver visual behaviour with respect to transport information and control systems, 15007:2018(E) (2018)
16. Khan, T., Williams, M.: A study of cultural influence in automotive HMI: measuring correlation between culture and HMI usability. SAE Int. J. Passeng. Cars – Electron. Electr. Syst. **7**(2), 430–439 (2014)
17. Körber, M., Baseler, E., Bengler, K.: Introduction matters: Manipulating trust in automation and reliance in automated driving. Appl. Ergon. **66**, 18–31 (2018)
18. Laugwitz, B., Held, T., Schrepp, M.: Construction and evaluation of a user experience questionnaire. In: HCI and Usability for Education and Work, pp. 63–76 (2008)
19. Lorenz, L., Kerschbaum, P., Hergeth, S., Gold, C., Radlmayr, J.: Der Fahrer im Hochautomatisierten Fahrzeug. Vom Dual-Task zum Sequential-Task Paradigma. 7. Tagung Fahrerassistenz, München (2015)
20. Naujoks, F., Hergeth, S., Wiedemann, K., Schömig, N., Forster, Y., Keinath, A.: Test procedure for evaluating the human-machine interface of vehicles with automated driving systems. Traffic Inj. Prev. **20**(sup1), S146–S151 (2019)
21. Naujoks, F., Wiedemann, K., Schömig, N., Hergeth, S., Keinath, A.: Towards guidelines and verification methods for automated vehicle HMIs. Transp. Res. Part F: Traffic Psychol. Behav. **60**, 121–136 (2019)
22. NHTSA: Visual–Manual NHTSA Driver Distraction Guidelines for In-Vehicle Electronic Devices (2014)
23. NHTSA: Automated Driving Systems 2.0: A Vision for Safety (2017)
24. Nielsen, J.: Usability inspection methods. In: Conference Companion on Human Factors in Computing Systems, pp. 413–414. Association for Computing Machinery, New York (1994)
25. SAE International: (R) Taxonomy and Definitions for Terms Related to Driving Automation Systems for On-Road Motor Vehicles, J3016 (2018)

# I Spy with My Mental Eye – Analyzing Compensatory Scanning in Drivers with Homonymous Visual Field Loss

Bianca Biebl[✉] [iD] and Klaus Bengler [iD]

Chair of Ergonomics, Technical University of Munich, 85748 Garching, Germany
Bianca.Biebl@tum.de

**Abstract.** Drivers with visual field loss show a heterogeneous driving performance due to the varying ability to compensate for their perceptual deficits. This
paper presents a theoretical investigation of the factors that determine the development of adaptive scanning strategies. The application of the Saliency-Effort-
Expectancy-Value (SEEV) model to the use case of homonymous hemianopia in
intersections indicates that a lack of guidance and a demand for increased gaze
movements in the blind visual field aggravates scanning. The adaptation of the
scanning behavior to these challenges consequently requires the presence of adequate mental models of the driving scene and of the individual visual abilities.
These factors should be considered in the development of assistance systems and
trainings for visually impaired drivers.

**Keywords:** Driver impairment · Visual field loss · Compensation · Mental model

## 1 Theoretical Background

Due to demographic change, the prevalence of visual impairments up to a partial or
complete visual field loss will increase in the future [1]. One severe form of visual field
loss is homonymous hemianopia, which describes a lack of perception of the left or right
visual field in both eyes after postchiasmatic cerebral damage [2]. Since vision is the most
pertinent modality for information uptake within the driving context, such impairments
result in a loss of the driver's license in many countries. On-road studies have however
reported that between 14% [3] and 90% [4] of drivers with homonymous visual field loss
(HVFL) are rated as safe drivers by driving examiners. While the exact numbers vary
due to methodological differences, these results indicate that some drivers perform well
in a driving task while others with similar visual field defects perform poorly. In general,
the potential behavioral differences between drivers with HVFL and normally sighted
drivers fall into three categories: lateral guidance, longitudinal guidance and hazard
recognition/scanning. Concerning lateral guidance, on-road and simulator studies have
found deviations in lane position, lane keeping abilities and steering stability [5, 6].
While some studies report a deficient speed adaptability and faulty spatial judgements
[5, 6], reports concerning a general increase or decrease of speed are inconclusive [7,

N. L. Black et al. (Eds.): IEA 2021, LNNS 221, pp. 552–559, 2021.
https://doi.org/10.1007/978-3-030-74608-7_67

8]. One area of particular importance for driving safety is hazard detection because an overlooking of other road users can have fatal consequences. Both on-road and simulator studies have found higher miss rates and prolonged reaction times to static and moving objects, especially on the blind side for drivers with HVFL [6, 7]. [9] furthermore reports more collisions among drivers with HVFL compared to normally sighted drivers and more collisions on the blind than on the seeing side. These deficits in hazard detection and response execution are closely related to the underlying scanning performance. Since scanning is inherently related to visual perception, it is not surprising that studies consistently report a compromised gaze allocation in low performing drivers with HVFL. These deviations in scanning are reflected in reduced amplitude, horizontal variance and speed of gaze movements, a belated first fixation of hazards and fewer scans or more scans with a reduced accuracy particularly in the blind field [5, 7].

While the challenges in vehicle stabilization and scanning are evident in some drivers with HVFL, others adapt to their perceptual deficits with compensatory strategies. One compensatory strategy found among drivers with HVFL is the dislocation of the lane position towards the blind side to allow for a safety margin. This can however present an increased collision risk due to the proximity to other traffic or the curb [10]. Another commonly reported compensatory strategy is a shifting of the scanning behavior towards the blind side. Drivers who elicit good driving performance tend to show more head and eye movements, larger scans and an increased accuracy of scans in their blind field (e.g. [5, 9, 11]). Since scanning behavior is correlated to collisions [9], such an adaptation of scanning patterns can be considered to be one of the most important compensatory strategies for drivers with HVFL.

In summary, we find compensatory scanning movements applied by some but not by all drivers suffering from HVFL. According to [12], it is still unknown in detail which strategies are best suited to compensate for visual field loss. Furthermore, there is currently little evidence on the processes behind the development of compensatory strategies [13]. This paper aims to contribute to this question by firstly analyzing the mechanisms of visual attention that differ between normally sighted drivers and drivers with HFVL. This will then serve as a basis to derive the characteristics required to overcome those challenges. The identification of such determinants can contribute to the elucidation of the large heterogeneity of compensatory abilities in drivers with HFVL. The analysis will focus on the use case of homonymous hemianopia in intersections. The large extent of this visual field loss in combination with the existence of multiple potential hazards at great eccentricities is particularly suitable to reveal the challenges of drivers with peripheral visual field loss.

## 2   Analysis of Visual Attention in Drivers with HVFL

### 2.1   The SEEV Model of Attention

One model that aims to explain the general process of perception and attention is the Saliency-Effort-Expectancy-Value (SEEV) model by [14]. This model proposes linear computation of the probability of attention allocation to an area of interest (AOI), consisting of saliency and effort (bottom-up) as well as expectancy and value (top-down). While saliency, expectancy and value additively contribute to the attractiveness of a stimulus, effort works as an inhibitory factor. Due to its simple and intuitive nature, this model has received great utilization in different disciplines, ranging from its original context of aviation to infotainment systems and driver behavior in the automotive context [15]. Within the SEEV model, *effort* refers to the mental or physical effort of moving visual attention to an AOI. By approximation, this effort evaluation can be regarded as a linear metric according to distance or stimulus eccentricity. This is however not entirely the case, since the additional requirement of a head movement for gaze dislocations of more than 15° increases effort excessively [16]. Effort can be described as a bottom-up factor since it is driven by the physical characteristics of the stimulus. The same applies to *saliency*, which describes how physically salient a stimulus is in a certain AOI. This mainly refers to contrast but can also concern characteristics such as color or movement. *Expectancy* is a top-down component that represents the expected information bandwidth, i.e. the estimation as to whether a scan to a certain AOI will yield new information. As such, expectancy is highly dependent on the driver's cognitive representation of the environment. Contrarily to the other factors, *value* can only be estimated subjectively and has two potential points of reference. Firstly, a stimulus can have value in itself by the negative effect of staying unnoticed. Secondly, value describes the importance of the task and the relevance of the (expected) stimulus for this task.

## 2.2    Analysis of Attention Allocation in Drivers with HVFL

In the following, the SEEV model of attention will be utilized to derive which aspects of scanning are impacted by an HVFL and require compensation. Drivers with HVFL do not perceive any information on their blind side (Fig. 1a), which has two effects on the guidance of scans. Firstly, indicators for hazards like blinking lights or fast movements do not attract or pull the driver's attention. The benefit of salient stimuli for early hazard detection and avoidance are thus not given. This missing input of *saliency* in the attentional process could be the cause of the belated first fixation of hazards reported by [12] and [17]. Secondly, the lack of visual information from the blind field affects the guidance of scanning movements itself. Usually, peripheral markers serve as reference to calculate the required amplitude of scans and as feedback on the scan's sufficiency. As noted by [11], drivers with HVFL do not have such peripheral guidance for gazes into their blind field and therefore show more, but inaccurate and unsystematic gaze movements. The reduced amplitude of these gaze movements reported by [5] and [7] or [17], can be ascribed to a potential minimization of *effort* in the SEEV model. Coincidentally, the effort for a sufficient scan is increased in drivers with HVFL, which represents the third impact of HVFL on scanning. In a rectangular intersection, normally sighted drivers need to scan an area of 65° on both sides [11]. The residual visual acuity in the periphery allows perception of all relevant information even without foveal fixations. The reduction or deficiency of this peripheral information requires drivers with HVFL like homonymous hemianopia to perform scans of up to 85° into their blind field [11] (Fig. 1b). An additional impact of HVFL on the effort calculation stems from the increased time and workload of these large scans, since cognitive demand provokes smaller gaze movements [9]. In contrast to these challenges in the bottom-up process, HVFL does not directly affect expectancy or value, since these top-down processes do not depend on the (impaired) visual input of the scene but on mental representations.

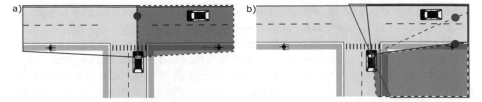

**Fig. 1.** An illustration of fixations (dots), central visual axes (dotted line) and visual fields (squares) shows that scanning in drivers with HVFL is challenged due to the lack of peripheral information to pull attention to salient stimuli such as approaching cars or cyclists (a). Compared to normally sighted drivers (blue), they furthermore need to elicit larger scans (red) in order to perceive all information without peripheral guidance on the required gaze location (b).

## 3   Derivation of Factors Influencing Compensatory Scanning

The last section provided a systematic analysis of challenges drivers with HVFL face when scanning a driving scene against the backdrop of the SEEV model, which yielded three affected bottom-up processes:

a) Requirement for increased amplitudes of gaze shifts to the blind side
b) Lack of peripheral information to guide scanning movements to the blind side
c) Lack of peripheral information to pull attention to salient hazards

Since the top-down processes were found to be unimpeded, it can be assumed that they are crucial for the adaptation of the impaired bottom-up process. [14] supports this notion by arguing that a strong involvement of top-down processes is vital for an effective and efficient scanning performance, particularly in complex situations. The specific top-down factors relevant for compensating HFVL are derived in the following. The missing peripheral information on the blind side aggravates the identification of relevant AOIs and the early recognition of arising hazards. To some degree, the location and timing of pertinent information for safe driving and hazard detection can alternatively be derived cognitively by activation of mental models. Generally, mental models refer to a cognitive representation of the current driving situation and determine how a driver perceives and interprets the world [18]. Exceeding mere knowledge, the structures within mental models allow drivers to form expectations and gauge the different courses of action in an *if-then* comparison. Activating a cognitive representation of the driving situation ahead based on already perceived input enables the anticipation of where and when relevant information will arise. This in turn allows a calculation of areas that hold information relevant to the scanning task at each moment. Drivers with an extensive mental model of the situation are therefore able to guide their scanning behavior based on anticipatory top-down information without reliance on the peripheral information that additionally supports normally sighted drivers. While this theory-driven estimation of pertinent locations at each time point is vital to compensate for the lack of peripheral information, drivers with HVFL also need to consider how far they must look to perceive this information. The second prerequisite for compensatory scanning is therefore an extensive mental model of one's visual abilities. This incorporates the extent of the blind field and the resulting requirement for eye, head and torso rotations to perceive information in the different areas of the environment.

In summary, the extent and correctness of mental models of the driving situation and of the driver's visual ability determine the ability to plan and execute compensatory scans to the blind side. They furthermore represent the basis for compensatory scanning patterns on a higher level. In normally sighted drivers, scanning patterns in T-intersections mostly follow a look left – look right – look left pattern [11]. Making a first and last scan to the left in this case is the best strategy to account for the more urgent hazards that arise on the left side. Contrarily, drivers with HVFL compensate for their deficits by initiating the gaze sequence with a first scan to the blind side irrespective of its laterality and by adding another scan to the blind side later on [11]. The increased risk of missing hazards on the blind side thus shifts the cost-benefit analysis for the different scanning patterns to emphasize the blind side. It can be assumed that this weighting of scanning sequences and the identification of supporting strategies also builds on and/or verifies in the mental models of the situation and the individual visual abilities to estimate the informative content and effort of each scan.

## 4 Discussion

The investigation of scanning mechanisms in drivers with HVFL in this paper aims at elucidating the heterogeneity in compensatory abilities. The analysis of the SEEV model reveals that impaired peripheral vision leads to an increased effort for information uptake in the blind visual field and a lack of peripheral information to guide scanning or attract attention. The investigation further indicates that the intact top-down processes are indispensable for the planning and execution of respective compensatory scanning. Firstly, drivers need an extensive and correct mental model of the driving situation to identify the location and timing of relevant AOIs. Secondly, drivers need a good mental model of their visual abilities to calculate the required eye, body or torso movement to perceive information in these AOIs.

In the past, different factors that allow discrimination between drivers with high and low compensatory abilities have been proposed. These results support our conclusion that the driver's mental model of the situation is important for the adaptation of scanning. [5] states that drivers generally attribute traffic from the right to be less dangerous, which is why they focus their attention to the left side. [19] further reports that the expectation to find pedestrians at a location due to the existence or non-existence of a crosswalk changes the timing of gaze behavior in direction of this AOI. The relevance of an adequate mental model of the visual abilities is also supported since many studies mention the awareness of the individual visual deficit to impact compensation and its correlation with driving performance and accidents (e.g. [7, 20]). Other proposed influencing factors are related to the process of forming and updating the mental models from experience as well as the feedback system to optimize strategy planning. These mainly focus on driving experience before and after the onset of the visual field loss, the time since onset especially within the first six months, and the current driving status [2, 16, 21]. Lastly, multiple factors for discrimination between high performing and low performing drivers with HVFL are proposed that describe general cognitive or physical characteristics.

Since age encompasses a multitude of characteristics, it is very frequently mentioned that it influences driving abilities in drivers with and without HVFL (e.g. [21, 22]). One pertinent feature that declines with age are executive functions. The relation to drivers' awareness of their deficit, anticipatory abilities, self-regulation and impulsivity explains their relevance to the introduction of compensatory top-down strategies for driving [23, 24]. Altogether, the factors reported to correlate with compensatory scanning seem to be related to or directly reflected in the determinants proposed in this paper.

The mechanisms behind compensatory scanning in drivers with HVFL in this paper are derived by analyzing the challenges of drivers with homonymous hemianopia in intersections. The focus on hemianopia provides a point of reference for the identification of deviations from normally sighted drivers. Due to the great number and eccentricities of relevant AOIs, intersections are especially prone to elicit differences in compensatory abilities of high and low performers [23]. The derived factors nevertheless aim at describing the requirements for compensatory scanning irrespective of the type of visual field loss or context. It should however be mentioned, that the optimal compensatory strategies for visual field loss can vary. [21] notes that while adaptive scanning is best suited for peripheral impairments, speed adaptation is the best strategy for central impairments. Therefore, the derived determinants might not be applicable for impairments that mainly affect driving due to a loss of central vision.

This paper presents a methodological consideration of factors that can explain the difference in compensatory abilities of drivers with visual field loss. It is of great relevance to do so because a deeper understanding of the mechanisms behind the individual needs and abilities of drivers provides a richer basis for assistive technologies and training. The tailored support of visually impaired drivers either in the form of additional information and warning systems in the vehicle or targeted trainings provides an opportunity for more inclusive mobility in the future. It must however be noted that the theoretical approach in the process behind compensatory scanning presented in this paper is the basis for experimental evaluations of the proposed factors. This should help to validate their impact on the adoption of compensatory strategies. The factors furthermore do not provide information on the long-term formation of compensatory strategies, which should be addressed in future studies.

## 5   Conclusion

This paper provides a theoretical approach for a systematic analysis of the mechanisms that underlie compensatory scanning among drivers with peripheral visual field loss. An adaptation of the SEEV model reveals that two top-down factors determine the ability to adapt scanning behavior to the impeded bottom-up processes. More precisely, we find that extensive and correct mental models of the situation and the individual visual abilities can account for the missing guidance of scans and the increased effort for information intake. The extent of such mental models as a determining factor provides a first explanation for the great heterogeneity in compensatory behaviors and driving performances in drivers with visual field loss. Future research should focus on an experimental evaluation of the proposed factors.

# References

1. Gilhotra, J.S., Mitchell, P., Healey, P.R., Cumming, R.G., Currie, J.: Homonymous visual field defects and stroke in an older population. Stroke **33**, 2417–2420 (2002). https://doi.org/10.1161/01.str.0000037647.10414.d2
2. Goodwin, D.: Homonymous hemianopia: challenges and solutions. Clin. Ophthalmol. (Auckland, NZ). **8**, 1919–1927 (2014). https://doi.org/10.2147/OPTH.S59452
3. Tant, M.L.M., Brouwer, W.H., Cornelissen, F.W., Kooijman, A.C.: Driving and visuospatial performance in people with hemianopia. Neuropsychol. Rehabil. **12**, 419–437 (2002). https://doi.org/10.1080/09602010244000183
4. Dow, J.: Visual field defects may not affect safe driving. Traffic Inj. Prev. **12**, 483–490 (2011). https://doi.org/10.1080/15389588.2011.582906
5. Wood, J.M., McGwin, G., Elgin, J., Vaphiades, M.S., Braswell, R.A., DeCarlo, D.K., et al.: Hemianopic and quadrantanopic field loss, eye and head movements, and driving. Invest. Ophthalmol. Vis. Sci. **52**, 1220–1225 (2011). https://doi.org/10.1167/iovs.10-6296
6. Elgin, J., McGwin, G., Wood, J.M., Vaphiades, M.S., Braswell, R.A., DeCarlo, D.K., et al.: Evaluation of on-road driving in people with hemianopia and quadrantanopia. Am. J. Occup. Ther. **64**, 268–278 (2010). https://doi.org/10.5014/ajot.64.2.268
7. Bahnemann, M., Hamel, J., de Beukelaer, S., Ohl, S., Kehrer, S., Audebert, H., et al.: Compensatory eye and head movements of patients with homonymous hemianopia in the naturalistic setting of a driving simulation. J. Neurol. **262**, 316–325 (2015). https://doi.org/10.1007/s00415-014-7554-x
8. Kasneci, E., Sippel, K., Aehling, K., Heister, M., Rosenstiel, W., Schiefer, U., Papageorgiou, E.: Driving with binocular visual field loss? A study on a supervised on-road parcours with simultaneous eye and head tracking. PloS One **9**, e87470 (2014)
9. Papageorgiou, E., Hardiess, G., Mallot, H.A., Schiefer, U.: Gaze patterns predicting successful collision avoidance in patients with homonymous visual field defects. Vis. Res. **65**, 25–37 (2012). https://doi.org/10.1016/j.visres.2012.06.004
10. Bowers, A.R., Mandel, A.J., Goldstein, R.B., Peli, E.: Driving with hemianopia, II: lane position and steering in a driving simulator. Invest. Ophthalmol. Vis. Sci. **51**, 6605–6613 (2010). https://doi.org/10.1167/iovs.10-5310
11. Bowers, A.R., Ananyev, E., Mandel, A.J., Goldstein, R.B., Peli, E.: Driving with hemianopia: IV. Head scanning and detection at intersections in a simulator. Invest. Ophthalmol. Vis. Sci. **55**, 1540–1548 (2014). https://doi.org/10.1167/iovs.13-12748
12. Coeckelbergh, T.R.M., Brouwer, W.H., Cornelissen, F.W., van Wolffelaar, P., Kooijman, A.C.: The effect of visual field defects on driving performance: a driving simulator study. Arch. Ophthalmol. **120**, 1509–1516 (2002). https://doi.org/10.1001/archopht.120.11.1509
13. Howard, C., Rowe, F.J.: Adaptation to poststroke visual field loss: a systematic review. Brain Behav. **8**, e01041 (2018). https://doi.org/10.1002/brb3.1041
14. Wickens, C.D.: Noticing events in the visual workplace: the SEEV and NSEEV models. In: The Cambridge Handbook of Applied Perception Research, vol. II, pp. 749–768. Cambridge University Press, New York (2015). https://doi.org/10.1017/CBO9780511973017.046
15. Gollan, B., Ferscha, A.: SEEV-Effort-Is it enough to model human attentional behavior in public display settings. In: Future Computing, pp. 8–14 (2016)
16. Bowers, A.R., Bronstad, P.M., Spano, L.P., Goldstein, R.B., Peli, E.: The effects of age and central field loss on head scanning and detection at intersections. Transl. Vis. Sci. Technol. **8**, 14 (2019). https://doi.org/10.1167/tvst.8.5.14
17. Alberti, C.F., Peli, E., Bowers, A.R.: Driving with hemianopia: III. Detection of stationary and approaching pedestrians in a simulator. Invest. Ophthalmol. Vis. Sci. **55**, 368–374 (2014). https://doi.org/10.1167/iovs.13-12737

18. Svenson, O., Eriksson, G.: Mental models of driving and speed: biases, choices and reality. Transp. Rev. **37**, 653–666 (2017). https://doi.org/10.1080/01441647.2017.1289278
19. Lehsing, C., Ruch, F., Kölsch, F.M., Dyszak, G.N., Haag, C., Feldstein, I.T., et al.: Effects of simulated mild vision loss on gaze, driving and interaction behaviors in pedestrian crossing situations. Accid. Anal. Prev. **125**, 138–151 (2019). https://doi.org/10.1016/j.aap.2019.01.026
20. Owsley, C., Ball, K., Sloane, M.E., Roenker, D.L., Bruni, J.R.: Visual/cognitive correlates of vehicle accidents in older drivers. Psychol. Aging **6**, 403–415 (1991). https://doi.org/10.1037//0882-7974.6.3.403
21. Patterson, G., Howard, C., Hepworth, L., Rowe, F.: The impact of visual field loss on driving skills: a systematic narrative review. Br. Ir. Orthoptic J. **15**, 53–63 (2019). https://doi.org/10.22599/bioj.129
22. Bowers, A.R.: Driving with homonymous visual field loss: a review of the literature. Clin. Exp. Optom. **99**, 402–418 (2016). https://doi.org/10.1111/cxo.12425
23. Brenner, L.A., Homaifar, B.Y., Schultheis, M.T.: Driving, aging, and traumatic brain injury: Integrating findings from the literature. Rehabil. Psychol. **53**, 18–27 (2008). https://doi.org/10.1037/0090-5550.53.1.18
24. de Haan, G.A., Melis-Dankers, B.J.M., Brouwer, W.H., Bredewoud, R.A., Tucha, O., Heutink, J.: Car driving performance in hemianopia: an on-road driving study. Invest. Ophthalmol. Vis. Sci. **55**, 6482–6489 (2014). https://doi.org/10.1167/iovs.14-14042

# A Matter of Trust – Identification and Evaluation of User Requirements and Design Concepts for a Trust Label in Autonomous Driving

Hannah Biermann[(⊠)] [iD], Ralf Philipsen[iD], and Martina Ziefle[iD]

Chair for Communication Science, RWTH Aachen University, Aachen, Germany
{biermann,philipsen,ziefle}@comm.rwth-aachen.de

**Abstract.** Human trust is a key factor in the adoption of autonomous vehicles. The development of trustworthy automation design offers the opportunity to address users' concerns well in advance. However, uncertainties may remain due to the novelty of the technology. Hence, concepts are needed that foster users' trust also during and after the rollout. In this survey, we introduce a user-centered trust label for autonomous shuttles. In an empirical mixed methods approach, we identified and evaluated label requirements and trust criteria from the perspective of prospective users as a basis for design concepts. Key findings show that the idea of a trust label is well received and has the potential to foster users' trust towards autonomous shuttles. Trust in the label requires, above all, an independent awarding institution. To increase the trustworthiness of the autonomous shuttle service through the label, it must in particular make safety-relevant aspects visible and enable user participation. Design drafts show concepts for an analog trust label attached to the vehicle as well as interactive app features. Findings are useful to researchers in the field of human-automation interaction as well as to developers and providers of innovative mobility services to enhance passenger experience.

**Keywords:** Human-automation trust · Trust label · Autonomous driving · On-demand mobility · Shuttle service

## 1 Introduction

As the vision of autonomous driving is partly entering real-world environments (e.g., public transport [1]), users get the chance to experience innovative mobility services in their role as passengers firsthand. Expected usage benefits are large and appreciated by the public, especially in terms of road safety [2]. However, perceived disadvantages and fears appear, e.g., with regard to violations of data protection in information distribution [3]. Hence, beyond interest and curiosity, the idea of being transported by a driverless vehicle may lead to perceived uncertainties from the user's perspective, including constraints on technology acceptance.

N. L. Black et al. (Eds.): IEA 2021, LNNS 221, pp. 560–567, 2021.
https://doi.org/10.1007/978-3-030-74608-7_68

Human trust was shown to determine the adoption of autonomous vehicles [4] and may be considered as a key to overcome perceived uncertainties in the context of mobility innovation. The challenge is to find practical and effective solutions to foster users' trust in automation, which requires a deep and broad understanding of the origins and formation of trust and distrust, respectively. The role of social science is to carefully identify relevant trust factors and evaluation criteria under consideration of user-specific characteristics, needs, and demands. A recent review on human trust in automation and autonomous vehicles is provided by Raats et al. [5].

So far, the state of research has provided valuable insights into trust-decisive factors in the context of autonomous driving, particularly as regards concerns about security (e.g., hacker attacks) and privacy (e.g., surveillance) as well as the perceived reliability of the vehicle [6], which need to be taken into account: first, in the engineering process in order to design trustworthy mobility services that are adapted to user needs; second, in communication and information strategies to increase public awareness. We assume that in this way many relevant concerns on the part of future and potential users can already be addressed, but also that uncertainties may remain due to the novelty of the technology, e.g., related to lacking user experience. Therefore, in this survey, we focused on the perception and evaluation of a trust label. Since labelling is already receiving a lot of attention in other application fields to foster users' trust (e.g., food industry) [7], we further assume that such a label qualifies to compensate for persisting uncertainties and to increase the perceived trustworthiness of an autonomous mobility service in the rollout. We discuss user-centered design concepts to visualize trust-decisive factors (which we have identified and measured before) as a feasible idea to address users' distrust and improve the passenger experience.

## 2  Research Objective and Questions Addressed

The research aim was to identify and evaluate user requirements and design concepts for a trust label in autonomous driving. Our use case was an on-demand mobility service (i.e., no fixed timetables or stops) with autonomous vehicles capable of carrying up to 15 passengers who shall decide on pick-up times and locations, destinations, route maps, and vehicle equipment. According to automation level 5 of the SAE International standard [8], *autonomous* was referred to as the vehicle's capability to perform all tasks of driving and parking under all on-road conditions without human operation. We addressed the following research questions:

1. How is a trust label for autonomous shuttles perceived and evaluated?
2. May a trust label increase users' trust towards an autonomous shuttle?
3. Which usage requirements are there for a trust label for autonomous shuttles?
4. What are users' designs for a trust label for autonomous shuttles?

## 3 Empirical Research Approach

The survey was conducted in Germany in 2020. Due to the Covid-19 pandemic, most of the data were collected remotely or online. We developed a three-step, consecutive empirical research approach using qualitative and quantitative methods.

### 3.1 Methodology

Initially, we conducted guided interviews (via phone, partly face-to-face) to explore general attitudes towards product or service labels as well as trust criteria, awarding requirements, and label design in regard to the implementation of a trust label for autonomous shuttles. Interviews were audio-recorded and transcribed verbatim.

Interview results were operationalized, transferred into Likert items, and quantified in an online questionnaire on the label's usage perception and evaluation, requirements, and trust perceptions. We used 5-point Likert scales with min $= 0$ "full disagreement" to max $= 4$ "full agreement". Cronbach's alpha $> .7$ indicated an overall satisfying internal scale consistency [9].

Key findings of the preceding studies formed the basis for the development of user-centered design concepts in an online workshop using a digital whiteboard, paper and pencil for illustration. Two groups developed drafts (in individual work) for an analog label attached to the vehicle, as well as app features and designs for users to participate, evaluate, and communicate their trust and passenger experience on a digital platform. The workshop was recorded (audio and video) and documented in a protocol of results.

Presentations of the autonomous shuttle as an application for the implementation of a trust label were scenario-based in text form. In the workshop, due to its creative nature, a video was additionally shown.

### 3.2 Data Collection and Procedure

Survey participation was voluntary and out of interest, without monetary or other incentive. Interviewees were acquired in the personal environment of the research team. Questionnaire participants were acquired online in social networks. Workshop participants were students at RWTH Aachen University.

Before the start of each study, the participants were informed that there are no "right" or "wrong" answers. According to ethical research standards, we guaranteed for privacy and anonymity of the data. At the beginning of each study, the participants' socio-demographics were collected in regard to age, gender, and education in order to assess the representativeness of the sampling.

### 3.3 Participants

The number of participants by study and a comparison of socio-demographics are shown in Table 1. Overall, gender distribution was balanced. The average age was below the German population average, whereas educational levels were above average [10, 11].

**Table 1.** Number of participants and socio-demographics by study.

|  | Study I Interviews | Study II Questionnaire | Study III Workshop |
|---|---|---|---|
| N | 12 | 160 | 9 |
| Gender |  |  |  |
| Female | 50% (n = 6) | 55% (n = 88) | 55.6% (n = 5) |
| Male | 50% (n = 6) | 45% (n = 72) | 44.4% (n = 4) |
| Age | M = 42 (SD = 15.2) | M = 31.4 (SD = 12.0) | M = 26.4 (SD = 3.8) |
| Range | 25–80 years | 19–79 years | 22–34 years |
| Education degree |  |  |  |
| No degree | – | 0.6% (n = 1) | – |
| Secondary school | 25% (n = 3) | 10.6% (n = 17) | – |
| High school | – | 19.4% (n = 31) | 44.4% (n = 4) |
| University | 75% (n = 9) | 69.4% (n = 111) | 55.6% (n = 5) |

## 4  Results

Next, we describe our results. Qualitative data (study I and III) were analyzed using qualitative content analysis by systematically reducing the material to essential meanings (inductive categorization) [12]. Quantitative data (study II) were analyzed by descriptive and inferential statistics. The level of significance was set at 5%.

### 4.1  Study I: Understanding Users' Perceptions of a Trust Label

**General Perception and Evaluation.** To better understand the public acceptance, we asked the participants about their perception and evaluation of labelling with regard to the quality of products and services. Using labels was generally considered beneficial, e.g., in the food industry. The interest in a trust label for autonomous shuttles was great, especially with regard to the time during or shortly after market launch to compensate for uncertainties, e.g., due to the lacking users' experience. In this regard, the label was seen as a decision-making aid for use.

**Trust Criteria.** To increase the trustworthiness of an autonomous shuttle service, the label shall include measurable evaluation criteria and display them transparently. These referred to the production site and the vehicle manufacturer, as well as information on vehicle and road safety with regard to vehicle equipment (e.g., airbags), the number of successful test drives, or accident rates. Also, control options shall be specified in regard to human intervention while driving.

**Perceived Concerns and Requirements.** Fears of economic interests and lacking supervision limited the perceived trustworthiness of a label. As precaution, it shall be comprehensible who is involved in label issuing. A consortium of several independent institutions was preferred (for awarding and monitoring). For quality assurance, the label shall be state controlled, legally valid, and up to date through regular revision. The participants wished to be involved in labelling by sharing their user experience. For increased transparency and comparability, the label was requested to be mandatory for all shuttle providers and to be as standardized as possible, i.e., there should be only a few (international) issuers, also to enable a cross-national recognition value.

**Design.** Trustworthy label design shall be recognizable, clear, and simple. For one thing, there shall be an analog label, e.g., in the form of a sticker using symbols and texts, which is placed on the vehicle (e.g., on the front or back). For another, there shall be additional information and the opportunity for user participation, preferably online (e.g., in the booking app). Overall, the participants agreed that the design shall be comprehensive, i.e., it has to show relevant evaluation criteria in a transparent way.

### 4.2 Study II: Measuring Users' Attitudes Towards a Trust Label

The participants considered the idea of using a trust label for autonomous shuttles as desirable ($M = 3.0$; $SD = 1.0$), useful ($M = 2.9$; $SD = 0.9$), and reasonable ($M = 2.9$; $SD = 1.0$). They indicated that labelling would increase their trust towards an autonomous shuttle ($M = 2.8$; $SD = 0.8$). It was rather rejected that trust cannot be labeled ($M = 1.8$; $SD = 1.1$).

The evaluation of label requirements for autonomous shuttles was affirmative, i.e., all of them were considered important. Regarding *granting and awarding*, a trust label shall be issued by an institution independent of the vehicle manufacturer and ride operator ($M = 3.4$; $SD = 0.7$) and the process should be under regular, unannounced, and independent revision ($M = 3.4$; $SD = 0.8$). In addition, it shall become clear and transparent which conditions were fulfilled ($M = 3.3$; $SD = 0.7$). User participation (e.g., via surveys) was also agreed to, but comparatively with the least consent ($M = 2.6$; $SD = 1.0$). Concerning *quality and safety control* of a trust label, compliance with legal safety standards received high levels of agreement ($M = 3.4$; $SD = 0.7$), followed by state control ($M = 3.1$; $SD = 0.9$). Regarding the *vehicle positioning* of a trust label, a well-visible location was agreed to, although with comparatively less approval ($M = 2.8$; $SD = 0.9$).

Correlation analysis showed that the evaluation of the label in terms of desirable, useful, and reasonable was related to increasing trust perceptions regarding the autonomous shuttle ($r = .778$; $p < .001$), i.e., the more positive the overall evaluation of the label, the more likely it was expected contributing to vehicle trust (and vice versa). Furthermore, correlations in regard to label requirements became apparent, particularly: The greater the agreement with a highly visible vehicle positioning of the label ($r = .421$; $p < .001$), an independent awarding institution ($r = .395$; $p < .001$), and conformity to the law with regard to safety standards ($r = .382$; $p < .001$), the greater the expectation of an increase in trust through the label with regard to the autonomous shuttle (and vice versa).

### 4.3 Study III: User-Centered Design Concepts of a Trust Label

**Analog Label.** Seriousness and comprehensibility were highlighted as relevant design criteria. Common to all designs were short slogans and icons. Interestingly, none of them contained the word "trust". Instead, trustworthiness was visualized by associated factors, in other words, connotative meanings. Recurring reference was made to the vehicle's safety, in some cases specified by naming the technical inspection or the inspector in person including contact data. Further attributions referred to the opportunity of shared mobility and the sustainability of the service. Figure 1 shows example designs.

**Fig. 1.** Example designs for an analog trust label in autonomous driving (on-demand shuttles).

**App Features and Designs.** Considering design requirements for app features corresponding to an analog trust label, consensus was reached on simplicity, clarity, and a small number of input fields to evaluate trust experiences. Evaluation criteria referred to the perceived safety, passengers on board, as well as the shuttle's equipment, comfort, punctuality, and cleanliness. Polls based on familiar rating systems, e.g., scores, thumb signals (up/down), or emoticons (laughing, crying, etc.), yes-no questions (e.g., "Did you enjoy the ride?"), selecting from predefined keywords ("What did you (not) like?"), and free text fields for detailed feedback. App participation shall be voluntary, possibly encouraged by incentives (e.g., discounts for future trips). All users shall be able to view the ratings of others and to mark individual posts as helpful in order to filter ratings, e.g., with regard to relevance or recency (by date). Figure 2 shows example designs.

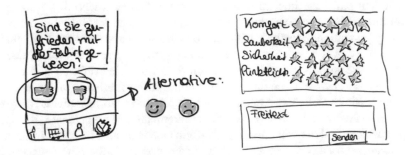

**Fig. 2.** Example app design (in German). Left: Push message "Are you satisfied with the ride?" (brief feedback). Right: Star rating of "comfort", "cleanliness", "safety", and "punctuality". Below: Text field for detailed feedback and send button.

## 5  Discussion

In this survey, we explored the user-centered assessment of a trust label for autonomous shuttles. Our empirical approach provided broad, deep, and validated insights into perceptions and evaluations of prospective users. Key findings show that a trust label was appreciated and related to increased trust perceptions towards autonomous driving.

In general, it was exciting to see that labelling trust was through associated factors. Literally stating that the shuttle service is "trustworthy" (as with some trust labels in online retailing) is apparently considered insufficient in the context of mobility innovation. Instead, consensus was that the label shall be comprehensive and transparent. Relevant evaluation criteria with regard to the trustworthiness of the shuttle service that need to be considered and operationalized in labelling referred to safety, information transparency (manufacturer, passengers on board, etc.), and vehicle features (e.g., equipment, hygiene, reliability). These aspects are consistent with those already identified in the state of research for assessing trust and acceptance of autonomous vehicles [2, 3, 6]. Label requirements (i.e., for the label to be trustworthy) related to independence in the awarding and quality assurance (through state control, legal conformity, supervision). Besides, users wished to be involved in their role as passengers.

Two label designs were preferred: first, a clearly visible analog label attached to the vehicle and, second, complementary app features on a digital platform for user participation and the assessment of the trustworthiness of the shuttle service. Label drafts were discussed in terms of an intuitive, clear, easy to read and handle (interface) design. Label designs (analog and digital) were based on familiar forms, e.g., slogans, icons, and star ratings, which, due to their conventionality, can be considered useful for labelling here.

Overall, the results of our survey indicate a high potential of the trust label to foster users' trust in autonomous vehicles, especially in the context of market introduction when users have not yet had substantial previous experience. However, in order to generalize the findings obtained here, these will have to be validated and extended in further studies. Firstly, with regard to sample construction as the participants were on average considerably younger and highly educated compared to the German population. In this regard, it is of particular interest to acquire older participants who may have specific label requirements due to cognitive and/or physical limitations, but also due to their technology generation (especially with regard to the use of app features). Only this way, the accessibility of a trust label can be guaranteed for diverse user groups. Secondly, our use case scenario as example application for a trust label referred to the concept of "mobility as a service". The on-demand shuttle service presented to the participants offers the possibility of shared mobility, which was reflected in individual logos (cf. Fig. 1) and evaluation criteria (e.g., passenger information). In this regard, it is the task of future work to find out what passenger information is needed in order for the shuttle service to appear trustworthy (e.g., number of passengers). Furthermore, our results can be compared with different autonomous vehicles (e.g., passenger cars), but also with other cultural settings, in order to identify context-specific characteristics and usage conditions of a trust label, also with regard to the recognition value of its design. Finally, empirical-experimental studies (preferably in real-life environments) are necessary in order to continue to obtain well-founded conclusions about the effect of a label on users' trust in autonomous driving.

**Acknowledgments.** The authors thank all participants. Special thanks are given to Ines Güldenberg and Britt Tapken for research assistance. This work has been funded by the Federal Ministry of Transport and Digital Infrastructure (BMVI) within the funding guideline "Automated and Networked Driving" under the project APEROL with the funding code 16AVF2134B.

# References

1. Iclodean, C., Cordos, N., Varga, B.O.: Autonomous shuttle bus for public transportation: a review. Energies **13**, 2917 (2020)
2. Schmidt, T., Philipsen, R., Ziefle, M.: Safety first? V2X – percived benefits, barriers and trade-offs of automated driving. In: Proceedings of the 1st International Conference on Vehicle Technology and Intelligent Transport Systems (VEHITS-2015), pp. 39–46 (2015)
3. Biermann, H., Philipsen, R., Brell, T., Ziefle, M.: Rolling in the deep. User perspectives, expectations, and challenges of data and information distribution in autonomous driving. Hum.-Intell. Syst. Integr. **1**, 53–70 (2020)
4. Choi, J.K., Ji, Y.G.: Investigating the importance of trust on adopting an autonomous vehicle. Int. J. Hum. Comput. Interact. **31**, 692–702 (2015)
5. Raats, K., Fors, V., Pink, S.: Trusting autonomous vehicles: an interdisciplinary approach. Transp. Res. Interdiscip. Perspect. **7**, 100201 (2020)
6. Kaur, K., Rampersad, G.: Trust in driverless cars: investigating key factors influencing the adoption of driverless cars. J. Eng. Technol. Manag. **48**, 87–96 (2018)
7. Tonkin, E., Wilson, A.M., Coveney, J., Webb, T., Meyer, S.B.: Trust in and through labelling – a systematic review and critique. Br. Food J. **117**, 318–338 (2015)
8. SAE: Taxonomy and definitions for terms related to driving automation systems for on-road motor vehicles. J3016. (2018).
9. Field, A.: Discovering Statistics Using SPSS. Sage Publications Ltd., London (2009)
10. Destatis (Federal Statistical Office): Altersdurchschnitt der Bevölkerung sank 2015 auf 44 Jahre und 3 Monate. https://www.destatis.de/DE/Presse/Pressemitteilungen/2017/06/PD17_197_12411.html
11. Destatis (Federal Statistical Office): Educational Level. https://www.destatis.de/EN/FactsF igures/SocietyState/EducationResearchCulture/EducationalLevel/AcademicDegree.html
12. Mayring, P.: Qualitative Inhaltsanalyse. Grundlagen und Techniken, 12th edn. Beltz, Weinheim (2015)

# Pedestrians-Automated Vehicles Interaction: Toward a Specific Trust Model?

Flavie Bonneviot[1,2](✉), Stéphanie Coeugnet[1,2], and Eric Brangier[2]

[1] VEDECOM Institute, 78000 Versailles, France
{flavie.bonneviot,stephanie.coeugnet-chevrier}@vedecom.fr
[2] PErSEUs, University, 54074 Metz, France
eric.brangier@univ-lorraine.fr

**Abstract.** According to Hoff and Bashir (2015), who developed a theoretical model of trust in automation, this study deals with pedestrians' adoption of automated vehicles (AVs) and their trust in the AVs. External HMI (Human Machine Interface) integrated into AV is known to increased pedestrians' trust during road crossing. To empirically apply this model and evaluate the trust potential of eHMI's, we conducted a study with 49 participants in a virtual reality environment. The study manipulated two factors: vehicle type (conventional, automated, and automated with eHMI) and road infrastructure (unmarked, pedestrian crossing with and without traffic lights). Participants self-rated their trust in automation before and after the study. Trust and emotions were retrieved after each road crossing. Preliminary results indicated a positive impact of eHMI on pedestrian's behaviors, trust and emotional levels. Infrastructure was also enhancing positive emotions and trust. During an uncertain situation such as pedestrian crossing, pedestrians felt more control with a conventional vehicle than an automated vehicle. The theoretical application of Hoff and Bashir's model is discussed regarding the results. Further research is needed to clarify dynamic contexts' implications and eHMI efficiency on automation trust.

**Keywords:** Automated vehicles · Trust in automation · External communication display · Pedestrian-vehicle interaction · Emotion · User study

## 1 Introduction

This communication is part of prospective ergonomics research on the future interaction of trust between pedestrians and automated vehicles. From a theoretical point of view, this work applies the theoretical model of Hoff and Bashir (2015) on trust in automation. The aim is to empirically measure its relevance and adapt it to dynamic contexts of human-machine interaction. Concretely, this approach involves measuring the effectiveness of the human-machine interfaces of automated vehicles on the crossing activity, the emotional and trust feelings to guarantee pedestrians' safety in this interaction.

The integration of automated vehicles (AVs) aims to make roads safer, regulate traffic by clearing throat, and reduce accidents. To achieve these objectives, it must integrate

N. L. Black et al. (Eds.): IEA 2021, LNNS 221, pp. 568–574, 2021.
https://doi.org/10.1007/978-3-030-74608-7_69

into the urban environment and ensure secure interactions with vulnerable road users, in particular pedestrians. As such, there is growing interest in how VAs (Level 4/5, Society of Automobile Engineers) should communicate and interact with pedestrians in urban settings [2]. Indeed, road users' problems can arise when the different protagonists of a given situation act according to diverging formal or informal traffic rules. Since the machine cannot predict human intentions, it is essential to establish a dialogue and a relationship of trust to guarantee both the objectives and the safety of the protagonists. Communication of vehicle intentions can be done by explicit means (e.g., turn signals) or implicit means (e.g., deceleration). To meet this goal, automakers and researchers have explored traditional methods of explicit communication. They used various external human-machine interfaces (eHMI) to communicate with pedestrians, such as screens, a smile, a hand, or even an LED strip (see review of [3]). Current research has shown that these eHMIs integrated with AVs can help pedestrians make safer crossing decisions, while in contrast, others have not found conclusive behavioral improvements and claim that HMIs are unnecessary. Research shows that the information implicitly communicated by vehicle behavior, such as deceleration [2], and sometimes road infrastructure (e.g., pedestrian traffic lights), would be sufficient to communicate the intentions of the vehicle and allow a safe and appropriate interaction with pedestrians [4]. However, the fundamental problem in designing useful and acceptable systems is in the trust that humans place in robots. Beyond the lack of a user-centric approach to the design of these HMIs [5], few studies have assessed their potential gain in terms of trust in such interactions.

Thus, trust is an essential condition of the relationship between partners, human or with artificial. Trust in the machine influences an individual's decision to use it or not [6]. It is a dynamic process in which each actor "considers the other as a resource capable of preserving their interests in a given situation" [7]. Hoff and Bashir (2015) proposed a trust model specific to the relationship between humans and automation comprising four levels of trust: dispositional, situational, and learned trust - initial and dynamic -. **Dispositional trust** is the general tendency to trust automation, referring to variations in culture, age, gender, and personality traits. **Situational trust**, on the other hand, is specific to the "context of interaction". Indeed, if the environment exerts a strong influence on situational trust, the individual's mental state can affect this trust in the situation. Finally, the **initial learned trust** is based on the preliminary knowledge of the system, whether or not it has come from previous experiences (for example, the reputation of the system's brand). Then, new knowledge is continuously created during the first interaction and feeds the so-called "**dynamic learned**" trust in the system. Experience is at the center of many decision-making models, particularly in the three levels of Rasmussen's double scale [8]: the "Skill-based" level (Skill-based behavior), the "Rule-based" level (Rule-based behavior), and the "knowledge-based" level (knowledge-based behavior). Hence, situational trust and learned trust - initial and dynamic - are closely related. The distinction between these three levels of trust depends on the perceived relevance and perceived usefulness of certain information to the individual. In short, the four levels of trust; dispositional, situational and learned - initial and dynamic - are interdependent. They are influenced by the environment and the individual's subjective perception resulting from his knowledge and experiences with the automated system.

All in all, the trust would be a dynamic process explicitly linked to the context, which is marked by the characteristics of the automated system, by the characteristics and knowledge - prior and learned - of the individual. However, this model is based on fixed human-machine interactions (e.g., computer), and since its creation, it has not been empirically proven in a dynamic interaction situation such as in the road environment [9].

## 1.1 Research Objectives

Establishing a situation of trust with pedestrians is crucial for the integration of automated vehicles into traffic. Little studied, this trust is identified as a critical factor influencing the use of an automated vehicle [10] and especially uncertain situations [11] such as crossing a street. To satisfy this, explicit communication by external HMI integrated into AVs has been one of the avenues most explored by the automotive industry. However, additional new empirical evidence is needed to clarify their impacts on pedestrian safety. The objective of our work is thus twofold.

On a practical level, this involves measuring the effectiveness of the eHMI integrated into the automated vehicle on pedestrian crossing activity, with a double vision both on the crossing behaviour and the levels of emotions and trust of pedestrians. We hypothesize that AVs' eHMI communication affects the behavior and emotions of pedestrians as they cross.

On a theoretical level, it contributes to the validation and adaptation of Hoff and Bashir's theoretical model for dynamic man-machine interaction contexts, with a particular focus on the situational and dynamic trust learned. We hypothesize that applying the theoretical model in a dynamic context will allow the model to evolve towards a more realistic representation of dynamic human-machine interaction contexts.

To achieve these goals, pedestrians were confronted with conventional vehicles (CVs), AVs and AVs equipped with eHMI (eHMI-AV) with three different crossing configurations (i.e., without pedestrian crossing, with pedestrian crossing with or without infrastructure). After each crossing, the pedestrians self-assessed their level of trust and their emotions.

## 2   Method

Participation in the study was open only to people with valid driving licenses and had normal vision. A set of data collected from 49 participants (24 females and two age range; 20–35 years and 45–60 years) were analyzed (M = 41.02, SD = 12.3; age range = 20–60 years).

The participant was seated in front of a computer placed 2.5 times the 'screen's size and moved around the virtual environment using an Xbox controller joystick. The virtual city was modeled in 3D via *Unity* with conventionals or automated vehicles. It consisted of four intersections and five buildings of interest, which he could enter to answer questionnaires projected on one of the entrance hall walls.

Counterbalanced, each participant crossed in front of 5 different vehicles: a conventional vehicle (CV; with a driver's avatar looking at the front), an automated vehicle without eHMI (without-eHMI-AV), and three automated vehicles with an eHMI (eHMI-AV) by LED strips, pictograms, or diffused LED net. These three communication systems result from a preliminary study that combined approaches through interviews, focus groups, questionnaires, benchmarks, and co-design. All vehicles were programmed to slow down as soon as the pedestrian reached the sidewalk (4 s of time gap) and stopped in the same way. The eHMIs displays four messages "I m starting", "I am driving", "I slow down to stop," and "I am stopped and patent" and, depending on the road configuration (presence or absence of pedestrian) and road regulations (e.g., red light). The participant will be confronted with different signaling levels to cross: pedestrian crossing with lights (PCL), pedestrian crossing without lights (PC), and no infrastructure (n).

Participants answered several questionnaires throughout the study and end with an individual interview. In the first phase, participants filled socio-demographic information. Initial and learned trust in automation was also measured using the same questionnaire before and three weeks after the study (*Trust in Automation Scale*; [12]). Trust in drivers was also measured before the study with an adapted version.

On the day of the study, participants read and accept the free and informed consent form. They are then invited to participate in a familiarization phase with the equipment of about ten minutes (i.e., controllers). The participant performed three virtual reality immersion sessions of approximately 25 min. Each session aims to test an eHMI (LED strip, pictograms, LED net) whose meaning has been learned beforehand. A session is made up of 5 crossings. Participants are invited to go to 5 buildings to act to verify a fire extinguisher's presence. The path they take requires them to cross the road between each building once. As soon as they enter a building located immediately after crossing, the participants responded orally to a questionnaire on their perception of the vehicle encountered before the crossing (e.g., identifying the type of vehicle, understanding the messages if applicable; Fig. 1). In terms of trust, emotions according to the three valence/activation/control scales from the Self-Assessment Manikin [13]. The questions about trust and emotional feelings were visual analog scales answered by line bisection on paper.

**Fig. 1.** On the left an example of an encounter' scene between the pedestrian and an AV without HMI at a pedestrian crossing. On the right an example of the general trust measurement.

Crossing behavior in front of or behind the vehicle was counted to assess the importance of avoidance, reflecting suspicious behavior depending on each vehicle. The semi-guided interview was composed of open questions to collect participants' opinions on their experiences with automation, eHMIs, their crossing strategies, and their immersion levels. The study lasted on average of 2 h and 30 min.

## 3  Preliminary Results

In overall analyzes, there are no significant differences between age or gender. Initially, participants felt less trust in drivers than for AVs ($M_{drivers} = 2.68$; $M_{AVs} = 4.08$ out of 7; $t(49) = -10.38$, $p < .001$). Participants had a high trust level (i.e., initial) in automation that did not increase significantly after the study ($M = 4.49$ out of 7; i.e., learned).

From a frequency table of crossing's behavior, the behavior of skirting the vehicle from the rear appeared significantly more frequently when pedestrians encountered vehicles without an eHMI (i.e., without-HMI-AV and the CV) than when it was equipped with eHMI ($N = 721$; $\chi^2 = 12.959$, $p < .001$).

During the crossings, the participants had dynamic trust levels modulated by road infrastructure ($N = 49$; $\chi^2 = 50.0$, $p < .001$). The more guided infrastructure, the more the trust increased ($p < .001$ for all comparisons).

The pedestrians' trust in our sample was influenced by the type of vehicle encountered ($N = 49$; $\chi^2 = 41.3$, $p < .001$). Pedestrians were significantly more trustful when encountered an eHMI-AV than a CV, and even less without an eHMI on the automated vehicle ($p < .05$ for all comparisons). Participants' emotions were also influenced by the type of vehicle (respectively; $N = 735$; $\chi^2 = 38.5$, $p < .001$; $N = 735$; $\chi^2 = 34.9$, $p < .001$; $N = 735$; $\chi^2 = 13.7$, $p < .001$). Without HMI, the AV induced a greater intensity, more negative emotions, and a lower emotion of control than the CV or the eHMI-AV ($p < .001$ for both comparisons). Pedestrians felt similar emotional levels when confronted with eHMI-AV and CV ($p = ns$).

The crossing analysis with infrastructure's level showed a difference in pedestrian's emotions between AVs and CV ($N = 49$; $\chi^2 = 13.7$, $p < .001$). At the pedestrian crossing without lights, participants had a better sense of situational control confronting a conventional vehicle than an AV (i.e., with and without eHMI; respectively, $p < .05$ and $p < .001$).

## 4  Discussion

The present study is based on Hoff & Bashir's (2015) model in evaluating the effectiveness of automated vehicles equipped with eHMI on the crossing activity and the feelings - emotional and trust - of pedestrians. These first results underline the need for clear communication from AVs to improve pedestrians' feelings of trust and safety in their future crossings. They also indicate behavioral modifications of pedestrians.

Consistent with Hoff and Bashir's model, dynamic trust was influenced by system characteristics, infrastructure, and prior knowledge (e.g., verbatim: "I was suspicious of the driver, I know they drive like crazy."). During the interaction, trust level has mainly been modulated by an HMI's addition to the system to achieve a similar level to that obtained with vehicles with a driver. These results are consistent with current research, which shows an increase in trust when AVs are equipped with a communication HMI [14].

Likewise, confrontation with an automated vehicle, whether or not equipped with an HMI, changed pedestrians' behavior during their crossings. Without HMI, AV caused more avoidance behavior in the pedestrians of ours sample. With the HMI, this behavior was significantly less than those seen with a conventional vehicle. In line with previous results, the eHMI would facilitate the crossing of pedestrians [15] since it will make it possible to defuse, just like the non-verbal communication of current drivers [16], situations of uncertainty, and will allow pedestrians to anticipate their crossing [17].

The street-crossing is one of those uncertain situations from a pedestrian's perspective since drivers do not always yield to them. Across three European countries, Lee et al. [18] demonstrated that 36% of observed drivers did not allow pedestrians to cross at pedestrian crossings. Our results showed that pedestrians perceived a better control sense at the pedestrian crossing in front of a conventional vehicle than with automated vehicles. We attribute this result to the participants' low level of familiarity with the automated vehicle. The vast majority of respondents (79%) said they were not familiar with automated vehicle technologies. Not having defined automated vehicles and their behavior to participants is one of our observations' limits. It would have modified the results since prior knowledge of the system is a situational factor influencing trust in automation [1].

Contrary to what was expected, there was no significant change in the level of trust in AV after the study. Also, although the drivers' initial trust level was lower than that in the automated vehicles, this difference was not observed in the results. We assume that this high level of initial/learned trust and these deviations from measurements are related to the current over-trust phenomenon in automation [19] and the difference in quality with the natural situation caused by the virtual reality method. Note that the small number of participants did not allow any conclusion on the impact of dispositional factors such as gender or age.

From a theoretical point of view, applying the model of Hoff and Bashir (2015) in a dynamic context made it possible to specify the effective inter-level influences during human-machine interaction. Given the preliminary results, the interconnection between situational trust and learned trust - initial and dynamic - seems to be the critical point in understanding the dynamics of trust in automation in a dynamic environment. However, these results do not allow us to claim an adaptation of Hoff and Bashir's theoretical model for dynamic human-machine interaction contexts.

Thus, the study of the relevant elements [19] - before and during - the interaction with automated systems is of paramount importance in a dynamic context, especially when it has an adverse potential for users. We encourage future research to apply and test this theoretical model in dynamic contexts to refine the understanding of trust in automation and ensure users' safety. Real-life research could clarify the effectiveness of these HMIs on the real activity of pedestrian crossing and guarantee their future safety when being confronted with automated vehicles.

# References

1. Hoff, K.A., Bashir, M.: Trust in automation: integrating empirical evidence on factors that influence trust. Hum. Factors **57**(3), 407–434 (2015)

2. Clamann, M., Aubert, M., Cummings, M.L.: Evaluation of vehicle-to-pedestrian communication displays for autonomous vehicles (No. 17-02119) (2017)
3. Dey, D., Habibovic, A., Löcken, A., Wintersberger, P., Pfleging, B., Riener, A., Martens, M., Terken, J.: Taming the eHMI jungle: a classification taxonomy to guide, compare, and assess the design principles of automated vehicles' external human-machine interfaces. Transp. Res. Interdiscip. Perspect. **7**, 100174 (2020)
4. Ackermann, C., Beggiato, M., Bluhm, L.F., Löw, A., Krems, J.F.: Deceleration parameters and their applicability as informal communication signal between pedestrians and automated vehicles. Transp. Res. Part F: Traffic Psychol. Behav. **62**, 757–768 (2019)
5. Florentine, E., Ang, M.A., Pendleton, S.D., Andersen, H., Ang Jr., M.H.: Pedestrian notification methods in autonomous vehicles for multi-class mobility-on-demand service. In: Proceedings of the Fourth International Conference on Human Agent Interaction, pp. 387–392. ACM, October 2016
6. Muir, B.M.: Trust in automation: Part I. Theoretical issues in the study of trust and human intervention in automated systems. Ergonomics **37**, 1905–1922 (1994)
7. Barcellini, F., Grosse, C., Karsenty, L.: Quelle démarche pour favoriser la construction de relation de confiance dans un projet de conception ? Karsenty Laurent (dir.). La confiance au travail, Octares, pp. 187–207 (2013)
8. Rasmussen, J.: Skills, rules, and knowledge; signals, signs, and symbols, and other distinctions in human performance models. IEEE Trans. Syst. Man Cybern. **3**, 257–266 (1983)
9. Hoc, J.M.: Supervision et contrôle de processus: la cognition en situation dynamique. Presses universitaires de Grenoble (1996)
10. Choi, J.K., Ji, Y.G.: Investigating the importance of trust on adopting an autonomous vehicle. Int. J. Hum.-Comput. Interact. **31**(10), 692–702 (2015)
11. Lee, J.D., See, K.A.: Trust in automation: designing for appropriate reliance. Hum. Factors **46**(1), 50–80 (2004)
12. Jian, J.Y., Bisantz, A.M., Drury, C.G.: Foundations for an empirically determined scale of trust in automated systems. Int. J. Cogn. Ergon. **4**(1), 53–71 (2000)
13. Bradley, M.M., Lang, P.J.: Measuring emotion: the self-assessment manikin and the semantic differential. J. Behav. Ther. Exp. Psychiatry **25**, 49–59 (1994)
14. Sucha, M., Dostal, D., Risser, R.: Pedestrian-driver communication and decision strategies at marked crossings. Accid. Anal. Prev. **102**, 41–50 (2017)
15. De Clercq, K., Dietrich, A., Núñez Velasco, J.P., De Winter, J., Happee, R.: External human-machine interfaces on automated vehicles: effects on pedestrian crossing decisions. Hum. Factors **61**(8), 1353–1370 (2019)
16. Kitazaki, S., Myhre, N.J.: Effects of non-verbal communication cues on decisions and trust of drivers at an uncontrolled intersection (2015)
17. Lagström, T., Malmsten Lundgren, V.: AVIP-Autonomous vehicles' interaction with pedestrians-An investigation of pedestrian-driver communication and development of a vehicle external interface. Master's thesis (2016)
18. Lee, Y.M., Madigan, R., Giles, O., Garach-Morcillo, L., Markkula, G., Fox, C., Camara, F., Rothmueller, M., Vendelbo-Larsen, S.A., Rasmussen, P.H., Dietrich, A., Nathanael, D., Portouli, V., Schieben, A., Merat, N.: Road users rarely use explicit communication when interacting in today's traffic: implications for automated vehicles. Cogn. Technol. Work, 1–14 (2020)
19. Wilson, D., Sperber, D.: Relevance theory (2002)

# Information Depth in a Video Tutorial
# on the Intended Use of Automated Driving

Annika Boos[1]([⊠]) [iD], Birte Emmermann[1] [iD], Bianca Biebl[1] [iD], Anna Feldhütter[2] [iD],
Martin Fröhlich[2], and Klaus Bengler[1] [iD]

[1] Chair of Ergonomics, Technical University of Munich, Boltzmannstraße 15,
85748 Garching, Germany
annika.boos@tum.de
[2] BMW AG, Knorrstraße 147, 80788 Munich, Germany

**Abstract.** To ensure the safe and correct use of conditionally automated driving functions, users need to be given appropriate information about the system's limitations and their responsibilities. This study compares the effect of two interactive driver education video tutorials with varying levels of information relating to the intended use of SAE Level 3 (Lvl 3) automated driving. The results indicate that drivers benefit more from a greater information depth with specific examples than from high-level, generalised information. In conclusion, it is recommended that current driver information and training practise is revised in line with the new requirements arising from the introduction of automated driving.

**Keywords:** Driver education · Training · Automated driving · Intended use

## 1 Introduction

The introduction of automated driving, allowing hands-off-wheel and eyes-off-road use, is leading to changes in drivers' responsibilities. According to [16], drivers may engage in non-driving-related activities when using a Lvl 3 driving automation, but are required to take over active driving either responding to a request to intervene or reacting to a kinaesthetically apparent vehicle failure. This includes cases when a vehicle system failure has occurred that the driving automation may not be monitoring, such as a broken suspension component. Insufficient knowledge of system limitations can cause dangerous situations if the driver does not intervene [17]. The design of information material is crucial to an adequate understanding of the system [5, 9] and the ability to responsibly employ driving automation [17]. The need to provide conclusive driver information material on the intended use of a driving automation including system capabilities, limitations as well as driver responsibilities is also highlighted in [12, 16].

This study investigates the depth of information that a driver tutorial for Lvl 3 [16] driving automation has to provide. The objective is to find an appropriate depth of information for maximising the driver's understanding and enabling a transfer of the acquired knowledge to new situations and contexts. This is all the more important as it is simply not possible to compile an exhaustive list of situations that might necessitate

© The Author(s), under exclusive license to Springer Nature Switzerland AG 2021
N. L. Black et al. (Eds.): IEA 2021, LNNS 221, pp. 575–582, 2021.
https://doi.org/10.1007/978-3-030-74608-7_70

an unprompted take-over, which means that the driver bears a residual responsibility for recognising situations that do not fall within the intended use of the automated system [3, 16].

## 1.1 How Do We Learn Best? Insights from Cognitive Psychology

There is an extensive body of research on the psychology of learning that addresses fundamental questions of how people acquire knowledge and skills. For example, [14] introduced the theory of dual coding, suggesting that verbal explanations accompanied by pictorial representations elicit the best understanding of learning material. The same effect was also shown to apply to mechanical understanding [11]. Furthermore, [13] indicate that many people are unwilling to read printed instructions, and even prefer abandoning a task over referring to instructions in the form of a printed text. It is assumed that the same applies to the information written in a vehicle's operating manual. In contrast, [4] found video-based and text-based automated driving instructions to be of similar effectiveness. The authors argue that this effect might be due to the laboratory conditions under which such material is usually tested. It can be assumed that participants behave differently under study conditions than they naturally would. Study participants are likely to pay more attention to information given to them by a researcher—regardless of whether it is in text or video form. In summary, it is advisable to develop engaging, multi-modal information that either accompanies or substitutes printed manuals.

Content can be presented either abstractly in the form of high-level information (HLI) or by giving specific examples of unintended use. On the one hand, example-based information (EBI) might initially seem more appropriate since addressing specific use cases potentially leads to a more refined knowledge of the subject and higher compliance [6]. This is of high relevance, because a broader set of use cases might result in better or quicker recognition of scenarios that do not comply with the intended use. On the other hand, a video tutorial can only present a limited number of use cases. Giving specific examples instead of high-level information could potentially lead to a decrease in knowledge transfer if the acquired knowledge is being confined to the specific examples given instead of broadened to the understanding of concepts. According to [8], knowledge transfer can be better promoted with high-level material than with specific examples. Accordingly, to optimise the effectiveness of driver information, it is necessary to define an appropriate information depth for promoting knowledge acquisition, information transfer, and the ability to identify scenarios that are not covered by the intended use of the system.

Research indicates that learning is more effective with active involvement on the part of the learner [1]. This was also shown for automated driving [2]. By the same token, tested information is more likely to be memorised than rehearsed information [7]. Whether this testing effect also applies to automated driving and whether an interactive tutorial provides an additional learning advantage is the second objective considered in this study. Furthermore, information depth potentially interacts statistically with the interactivity of the tutorial. For example, HLI could lead to higher knowledge transfer to new situations that do not comply with the intended use when including interactive scenarios while EBI does not. Accordingly, the research questions (RQ) addressed in this paper are as follows:

RQ I How does information depth influence system understanding and the transfer of acquired knowledge to new situations?
RQ II Does the interactive section of the tutorial have an additional advantage over and beyond the video-based information?

## 2    Method

### 2.1    Design and Implementation of the Interactive Video Tutorial

The video tutorial evaluated in this study combines visual (video) representations with verbal explanations on the intended use of the automated system. It comprises two parts: (1) instructional video footage with voice-overs with a duration of 1 min 54 s (EBI) and 1 min 44 s (HLI), explaining the intended use and the system's capabilities and (2) an interactive section in which participants are asked to judge whether the shown situations comply with the intended use of the driving automation function. The interactive situations comprise a large cloud of smoke hovering over the lanes, a construction site, a policeman standing at the side of the road, heavy rain with a risk of aquaplaning, a traffic jam with an approaching ambulance, a build-up of condensation on the windscreen, a lane closure necessitating a lane change, and a pothole damaging the undercarriage. Following each scenario, the correct behaviour and the underlying system capabilities are explained using text and voice-over. The depth of the information in the explanations varies in both parts of the video tutorial. The first variant only contains HLI to explain system capabilities, while the second variant uses EBI, for instance by adding specific examples to the explanation:

**HLI:** *'Should you perceive sounds that require you to continue driving manually, please take over control from the automation.'*
**EBI:** *'Should you perceive warning signals, such as emergency vehicle sirens or the hooting of car horns that can indicate hazardous situations ahead, please take over control from the automation.'*

The video sequences in the tutorial were the same for both groups. They comprised traffic scenarios that had not been mentioned before and were thus new to both groups. In the interactive section, animated scenarios were presented in randomized order, all shown from the driver's perspective. Lvl 3 automation function was activated in the depicted vehicle at all times.

### 2.2    Study Procedure and Measures

Informed consent was obtained before the study. To control for the learning environment, the video-based tutorial and the corresponding data collection took place in a parked BMW (3 Series Touring). None of the vehicle's systems were turned on. The tablet computer showing the video tutorial was placed in front of the centre information display. Subjects viewed one of the two variants of the tutorial, either containing HLI or EBI information. After first collecting demographic data, a structured interview was conducted to determine the subject's knowledge of automated vehicles (MP [measuring point] 1). The instructional video sequence was followed by a structured interview and a questionnaire (MP 2). In the interactive part of the tutorial, subjects were asked to tap the tablet screen to indicate any situation that they deemed to be outside the system's capabilities (MP 3). After each traffic scenario, subjects were questioned on their behaviour. They were then given either HLI or EBI information as to whether an intervention was needed. The video tutorial was followed by an interview and two questionnaires (MP 4). Figure 1 depicts an overview of the measuring points.

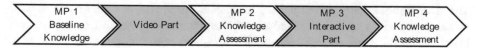

**Fig. 1.** Timeline depicting the experimental sequence of measuring points.

**MP 1 – Baseline Measurement:** Participants were interviewed to elicit their knowledge and expectations of Lvl 3 automation, which was described as the automation level currently under development and expected to be available on the German market in the coming year. Participants also rated their perceived knowledge of automated driving on a six-point Likert scale.

**MP 2 – Measuring Gained Knowledge:** A number of system capabilities were stated in a custom-designed questionnaire, e.g. *'I have to ensure that I am able to assume manual driving at all times'*. Subjects were asked to mark the statements as correct or incorrect and also to state as a percentage how confident they were of their judgement. The questionnaire did not contain any explicit examples of unintended use. Correct and incorrect answers were coded as either 1 or −1, respectively, this value then being multiplied by the level of confidence indicated (0–100) for the answer. This resulted in an overall score between −100 and +100 for each participant.

**MP 3 – Interactive Part:** In the interactive part of the tutorial, the time stamps of the interventions were recorded. The timing of the interventions during each scenario was categorised into a scoring system: optimal (3), late (2), very late (1), too late (0), too early (0), or unnecessary (0). The evaluation was based on events in the video. For example, an intervention in the event of heavy rain was only assigned the maximum score if the street was sufficiently wet for the vehicles' wheels to produce a spray. An overall performance score was calculated by multiplying the interference scores with a reasoning score that depended on whether the interference or non-interference was assessed as correct (1) or incorrect (0). Accordingly, interventions scored higher if they took place within an optimal time frame and if participants intervened for the correct reason. For example, a participant intervening late, but for a wrong reason would score zero points for this intervention: 2 (late) x 0 (incorrect) = 0.

**MP 4 – Measuring Gained Knowledge:** The questionnaire on general system understanding (see MP 2) was repeated. In a second custom-designed questionnaire, participants were asked to state what the appropriate behaviour of the driver would be in various

situations, such as *'the automation is active under roadwork conditions'*. The questionnaire included scenarios that were familiar from examples given in the EBI information
and others that were unknown to both groups. Answer categories included the options
to indicate as to a) whether an intervention is deemed necessary (either by assuming
manual control or by not activating the automation), b) whether the situation should be
monitored, or c) whether the situation does not imply non-adherence to the system's
intended use. For items that entailed a description of the driver's behaviour itself, such
as *'You're closing your eyes for a couple of minutes without falling asleep'*, participants
were asked to state whether such behaviour was permitted. The overall percentage of
correct and incorrect answers was calculated.

### 2.3   Sample Description

A total of 33 participants (mean age $= 41$ years, SD $= 13$ years, 39% female) took part
in the study. There were 16 and 17 participants in the HLI and EBI groups, respectively.
The mean self-reported knowledge of automated driving systems was 2.64 (SD $= 1.49$)
on a six-point Likert scale and was equally distributed between groups.

## 3   Results

**Qualitative Interview on Pre-experiment Lvl 3 Expectations:** The clusters derived
from the answers given in MP 1 indicate a varied knowledge of Lvl 3 driving automation.
While the majority of subjects were not able to give an exhaustive description of the
system, many displayed a rough understanding of it. However, many frequently stated
concepts indicate an overestimation of the system's capabilities, such as claiming that the
driver had no responsibilities in the driving task, assuming that the system would operate
autonomously (in general) or operate autonomously on highways (Table 1). Concepts
that were indicated four times or less are not reported.

**Table 1.** Participants' expectations at MP 1 (baseline knowledge) assessed before the information
material was given out. ([N] $=$ number of participants expressing the expectation)

| System Capabilities | [N] | Driver Responsibilities | [N] |
|---|---|---|---|
| Performing the whole driving task | 10 | Supervising the system | 10 |
| Taking over longitudinal guidance | 10 | May engage in non-driving-related tasks | 9 |
| Driving the car autonomously | 7 | Staying alert and ready for take-over-requests | 7 |
| Taking over lateral guidance | 7 | There is nothing the driver has to do | 6 |
| Driving autonomously on highways | 6 | Taking over in emergencies | 6 |

**Intervention Times During the Interactive Tutorial Part.** Regarding MP 3, participants in the EBI group achieved a mean score of 1.62 points (SD = 1.33) and the HLI group achieved a mean of 1.24 points, (SD = 1.27) (scale ranging from 0 – 3). A Wilcoxon-Mann-Whitney test indicated that this group difference is statistically significant $U = 68$; $p = .039$; with a medium effect size of $r = .37$. Two participants (one from each group) were excluded from this analysis due to missing data.

**Questionnaire-Based Knowledge Assessment:** Gained knowledge was assessed using a questionnaire at two measurement points: First after the instructional part of the tutorial (MP 2) and second after the interactive section (MP 4). A 2 × 2 mixed ANOVA was calculated taking the individual subject's effect, the group differences between the HLI and EBI information, and the measurement point into account. No significant between-subject group differences on the basis of tutorial information type were found: $F(1,31) = 0.964$, $p = .334$; no within-subject effects based on the measurement point (before or after the interactive tutorial part): $F(1,31) = 0.280$, $p = .869$; and no significant interaction: $F(1,31) = 0.266$, $p = .610$ could be shown. Subjects also completed an additional questionnaire on examples of system limitations after the two parts of the tutorial. No meaningful group difference was found between HLI and EBI ($\Delta = 1.4\%$ correct answers).

# 4  Discussion

The qualitative assessment of the participants' initial (pre-study) expectations with regard to the capabilities of a Lvl 3 system suggests that these capabilities are overestimated. The group receiving the tutorial with EBI information outperformed the HLI information group in the interactive part of the tutorial. This difference was not apparent in the questionnaire data. One of the main limitations is that non-validated custom questionnaires about Lvl 3 system capabilities and limitations were used. The absence of group differences based on questionnaire data suggests that the questionnaires were not sufficiently sensitive to detect the medium-sized effect that was apparent in intervention data regarding the interactive tutorial part. As the difference between the two levels of detail was not conclusive in all measures, further research on the identification and development of sensitive measures is encouraged. Furthermore, intervention times in the interactive part of the tutorial were processed using a custom logic (see MP 3). This processing could also explain the group differences found for interventions. The absence of differences before and after the interactive tutorial part contradicts the concepts of cognitivist design as well as the testing effect, according to which active involvement of the learner increases retention performance [1, 7], something which could be clarified in further research. It was argued in [8] that high-level learning material can promote knowledge transfer. As the group with EBI information outperformed the group with HLI information for interventions in the interactive scenarios, and these had not been introduced to either group during the instructional part of the tutorial, this effect cannot be confirmed in this study. Participants who received the EBI were able to identify situations in which the intended use of the Lvl 3 system was infringed more correctly and faster. Participants with HLI, on the other hand, missed more scenarios or intervened either too late, too early or unnecessarily. This dissociation supports the postulation that the level of detail in instructions for Lvl 3 systems is relevant to the attendant behaviour. Nevertheless, tapping a pre-recorded video on a tablet cannot be directly generalised to actual behaviour in road traffic, something that requires evaluation in future on-road and high-fidelity simulator studies. The positive effect of training and a correct mental automation model on trust and safety in use has been investigated in studies [9, 10] and [15], in which it was found that appropriate information on and experience with a technical system as well as directed training can improve the reaction to hazardous situations when using an automated system.

In summary, the gathered data are not conclusive on all measures concerning the raised research questions. RQ I: As the EBI group performed better during the interactive part and no disadvantages of EBI compared to HLI were found, the use of EBI is recommended. RQ II: As the questionnaire-based knowledge assessment revealed no differences before and after the interactive tutorial part, the used questionnaire should be revised—otherwise it may be concluded that there was no additional benefit of the interactive part.

## 5  Conclusion

This study contributes to a framework of driver instruction for Lvl 3 automation, with the aim of paving the way for an intended use of the system. The results imply that driver education methods should be reconsidered and adapted in view of the advent of driving automation. The results of the present study, together with the literature enable the following general recommendations for designing driver information material:

**Use Example-Based Information Material:**  In this study, example-based information improved the recognition of unintended use during the interactive part of the tutorial. Accordingly, giving explicit examples of unintended use seems preferable to providing high-level information.

**Consider Different Media:**  Research suggests that text-based automated driving manuals have no benefit over video-based ones [4] and printed instructions seem to be the least preferred information format [13]. Accordingly, animated instructional videos should be considered in addition to or instead of text-based manuals.

**Take into Account Different Knowledge Bases and Information Channels:**  In this study, the participants' expectations of Lvl 3 system sophistication differed substantially from the real-world picture. This is in line with other research suggesting that such expectation mismatches persist and can foster over-trust [17]. Adequate trust in automation can be influenced by the information that is presented [9]. To prevent false expectations, general concepts of driver education should be taken into consideration throughout the communication process, in marketing strategies and customer communication at car dealerships and rental companies, in driving schools and in-car information distributed prior to driving.

# References

1. Coomey, M., Stephenson, J.: Online learning: it is all about dialogue, involvement, support and control–according to the research. In: Teaching and Learning Online: Pedagogies for New Technologies, pp. 37–52 (2001)
2. Ebnali, M., Hulme, K., Ebnali-Heidari, A., Mazloumi, A.: How does training effect users attitudes and skills needed for highly automated driving? Transp. Res. Part F: Psychol. Behav. **66**, 184–195 (2019)
3. Edwards, M., Seidl, M., Tress, M., Pressley, A., Mohan, S.: Study on the Assessment and Certification of Automated Vehicles. European Commission, Brussels (2017)
4. Forster, Y., Hergeth, S., Naujoks, F., Krems, J., Keinath, A.: User education in automated driving: owners manual and interactive tutorial support mental model formation and human-automation interaction. Information **10**(4), 143 (2019)
5. Forster, Y., Hergeth, S., Naujoks, F., Krems, J.F., Keinath, A.: What and how to tell beforehand: the effect of user education on understanding, interaction and satisfaction with driving automation. Transp. Res. Part F: Traffic Psychol. Behav. **68**, 316–335 (2020)
6. Frantz, J.P.: Effect of location and procedural explicitness on user processing of and compliance with product warnings. Hum. Factors **36**(3), 532–546 (1994)
7. Johnson, C.I., Mayer, R.E.: A testing effect with multimedia learning. J. Educ. Psychol. **101**(3), 621 (2009)
8. Kaminski, J.A., Sloutsky, V.M., Heckler, A.F.: The advantage of abstract examples in learning math. Science **320**(5875), 454 (2008)
9. Körber, M., Baseler, E., Bengler, K.: Introduction matters: manipulating trust in automation and reliance in automated driving. Appl. Ergon. **66**, 18–31 (2018)
10. Larsson, A.F., Kircher, K., Hultgren, J.A.: Learning from experience: familiarity with ACC and responding to a cut-in situation in automated driving. Transp. Res. Part F: Traffic Psychol. Behav. **27**, 229–237 (2014)
11. Mayer, R.E., Anderson, R.B.: Animations need narrations: an experimental test of a dual – coding hypothesis. J. Educ. Psychol. **83**(4), 484 (1991)
12. NHTSA: Federal automated vehicles policy: Accelerating the next revolution in roadway safety. US Department of Transportation (2016)
13. Novick, D.G., Ward, K.: Why don't people read the manual? In: Proceedings of the 24th International Conference on Design of Communication, pp. 11–18 (2006)
14. Paivio, A.: Mental Representations: A Dual Coding Approach. Oxford University Press, Oxford (1990)
15. Payre, W., Cestac, J., Delhomme, P.: Fully automated driving: impact of trust and practice on manual control recovery. Hum. Factors **58**(2), 229–241 (2016)
16. SAE International: Taxonomy and definitions for terms related to driving automation systems for on-road motor vehicles. SAE International (J3016) (2016)
17. Victor, T.W., Tivesten, E., Gustavsson, P., Johansson, J., Sangberg, F., Ljung Aust, M.: Automation expectation mismatch: incorrect prediction despite eyes on threat and hands on wheel. Hum. Factors **60**(8), 1095–1116 (2018)

# Driving a Partially Automated Car with the Hands On or Off the Steering Wheel: Users' Subjective Experiences

Beatrice Cahour[1]([✉]), Forzy Jean-Francois[2], and Koustanaï Arnaud[3]

[1] C.N.R.S. i3 Telecom, Paris, France
beatrice.cahour@telecom-paristech.fr
[2] Renault DEA IRI, Guyancourt, France
[3] Lab PSA Renault, Nanterre, France

**Abstract.** Which are the subjective feelings and objective risks of driving in an automatic mode when holding the steering wheel or not holding it? Two conditions of simulated driving of a partially automated car have been tested (hands-on and hands-off), in two situations of driving on highways including critical events forcing the driver to take over. The user subjective experiences were compared: the situation awareness, feelings of safety, control, attention, on-board activities, psychological and physical comfort were analyzed on the basis of in-depth interviews right after the activity. For the critical situations designed, the performance results indicate a negative impact of the hands-off condition on the takeover. The hands-off condition is appreciated for its comfort and the multi-activity it allows, but the hands-on condition is objectively and subjectively safer in critical situations.

**Keywords:** Automated driving · Take-over · Subjective user experience · Risk · Hands-on/off · Awareness · Comfort

## 1 Problem Statement

Driving a partially automated car of level 2 (automatic control of trajectory and speed) can be risky in critical situations when the driver needs to take over (Morales-Alvarez et al. 2020; Zhang et al. 2019). A level 2 automation was defined by the Society of Automotive Engineers as a partial automation, i.e. a driver assistance system of both steering and acceleration/deceleration, using information about the driving environment, and expecting that the driver completes the event detection responses. Level 2 assumes an attentive driver supervising the driving adequacy. The difficulty for the driver is to maintain vigilance with a low level of stimulation and action (Molloy and Parasuraman 1996) and this is a major issue for partially automated cars, when the driver must take over in situations that the system cannot manage.

The issue is here to know if, when driving without holding the steering wheel (Hands-off), a driver is less attentive and less reactive than a driver who is holding it (Hands-on). The Hand-off system at level 2 is currently allowed on the market in the USA and in Japan, whereas it is not allowed presently in Europe, but it could be in the future.

© The Author(s), under exclusive license to Springer Nature Switzerland AG 2021
N. L. Black et al. (Eds.): IEA 2021, LNNS 221, pp. 583–592, 2021.
https://doi.org/10.1007/978-3-030-74608-7_71

The objective of this study is to bring empirical results and to answer some of these questions in terms of ergonomic safety and comfort. Our research questions are:

- Which are the impacts of the hands-on versus hands-off driving on the drivers' attention?
- Is it safer when the drivers keep the hand(s) on the wheel or not? How do they react, cognitively and bodily, in a critical situation when they must take over?
- Do the drivers feel more comfortable when holding the steering wheel or not?

## 2  Methodology

Fifty eight persons drove a car with a level 2 of autonomy in the dynamic simulator ULTIMATE of Renault.

### 2.1  Population

The population (58) is on average 40 years old (from 20 to 59) and 20% are women. They are Renault employees but their jobs are varied (part of them are administrative staff) and some are not especially interested in assistance systems. They were not recruited as participants if they had a current professional activity related to the tested systems. They live in Paris or its suburb.

### 2.2  Conditions and Critical Events

Two *conditions* were tested:

(COND.1) hands-on, the drivers were asked to drive with at least one hand always on the steering wheel,
(COND.2) hands-off, the drivers were asked to drive with no hand on the steering wheel, except to take over control. A variant of this condition was added for a group with monitoring of the eyes[1].

Two *critical events* occurred during the drive, with take-over need:

(EVENT.1) There is a loss of assistance in a high-speed right turn on the highway, a silent failure. The deactivation was indicated by change on the dashboard (a symbol disappears), by a slight deceleration and a slight change in the steering wheel (less hard). The drivers must take over not to deviate their trajectory on the left (Fig. 1).

---

[1] The driver's gaze was monitored by an eyes tracker; if the deviation of the gaze from the driving scene exceeded 5 s, an audible alert was emitted to encourage the participant to look back at the road.

**Fig. 1.** Event 1 (EV1) Incidental loss of assistance in a high-speed turn (130 km/h)

(EVENT.2) The car is on the right lane of the highway, at 110 km/h. A truck is stopped on the low side, and a vehicle is stopped beside, on the right lane of the highway, indicated by a traffic cone; but this obstacle is hidden for a while by a truck which is driving in front of the driver, when this truck is changing lane and makes the obstacle visible, the driver has 8 s to react and take control. Another car is driving behind on the left lane, far enough for the driver to move to the right lane. The system cannot handle the situation and the loss of assistance (deactivation) is indicated by a change on the dashboard and an alarm (Fig. 2).

**Fig. 2.** Event 2 (EV2) sudden breakdown of assistance followed by an obstacle on the roadway

## 2.3 Experimental Protocol

The temporal development of the experimentation was the following:

– Presentation of the system. It is specified that the driver is responsible of the vehicle behavior and must remain vigilant; if any problem he/she must take over.
– Appropriation: 10 mn driving on the highway and testing the automated system.
– Fist drive: The participants were driving during 20 mn on the highway with condition 1or 2; then incident-1 or 2 occurred; right after, they stopped the drive, were getting out of the car and were interviewed about what happened during the event, and then during the whole drive. The interview lasted 20 to 45 mn.
– Second drive: The participants were driving during 20 mn on the highway with the other condition; then the other incident occurred; they stopped the drive and were interviewed about what happened during the event, and then during the whole drive. The interview lasted 20 to 45 mn.

The order of the incidents and of the conditions varied.

## 2.4 Interviews

The interviews were based on Vermersch's Explicitation (or elicitation) Interview technic[2] to gather the drivers' phenomenological experiences during the drive (Vermersch 1994; Cahour et al. 2016). Firstly the driver described what happened at the end of the drive. The Explicitation Interview is used to help the drivers describe precisely their subjective experience during the events which lasted less than one minute. The instruction was: "*In relation to the incident that has just taken place, can you describe what happened to you, what you perceived, thought, did, felt, during those few seconds just before and after the incident, what comes back to you spontaneously; then we'll go back chronologically to what happened*". Non-inductive questions were used afterwards, following the chronology of the experience, to clarify: actions, awareness of the situation, sensorial perceptions such as gazes, perceived sounds, body movements and gestures, emotions, and thoughts such as hesitations, hypotheses, evaluations. This part of the interview is focused on a very specific moment of a few seconds.

Once the critical event had been described, the more general experience during the driving session was explored, the global impressions, sensations, mental states experienced during the 20 mn of drive before the critical event. At the end of the interview, the driver was asked which condition he preferred, Hands-on or Hands-off.

## 2.5 Analysis of the Verbal and Behavioral Data

The *interviews* were transcribed and analyzed: the verbal protocol of each participant was analyzed in two steps: (1) firstly an analysis of the description of the critical event, its temporal development and the cognitive, emotional and bodily processes during the

---

[2] 25% are in-depth explicitation interviews lasting 30 to 45 min, the others are a bit shorter but inspired by the technics of this interview.

few seconds of identification of the problem and reaction. (2) Secondly the first and "normal" part of the drive has been analyzed with the following thematic categories: control and security, attention and vigilance, bodily sensations, preferences, others.

The *measures of the observable behaviors* are: (cf. Forzy et al. 2021, for more details).

– For Event-1, the lateral offsets trajectories,
– For Event-2, the delay before the lane change and the acceleration.

The conditions were compared using statistical tests (analysis of variance, Chi-squared).

## 3   Results

During the incidents, the users lived experiences gathered with the interviews indicate several interesting elements about the situation awareness, the reconnection process, the roles representations, the deactivation perceptions and prereflective adjustments, the global feelings and sensations with hands-on or hands-off, and the global preferences.

In a second step, we will develop the main results of the objective measurements comparing the different conditions.

### 3.1   The Users' Subjective Experience

**Situation Awareness and Bodily/Cognitive Reconnection.**  Drivers may be so deeply immerged in their on-board activities (reading, writing, …) that they have no awareness at all of the road situation, and then feel totally surprised when an incident occurs. Hands-on, 23% of the participants said they were not aware of the traffic around at the time of the event. Hands-off, 39% of the participants were not aware of the traffic; the difference does not appear significant (p = 0.15).

> 7 EV2 ON (Participant 7, Event 2, ON condition): I had almost forgotten that I was on a two lane road. I didn't know if there were any cars next to me, or on the other side.
>
> 36 EV1 OFF: I had no awareness of the vehicles around me.

When they become aware of the deactivation, they need to reconnect cognitively and bodily for acting. Two drivers describe how they firstly recovered the awareness of their need of action on the steering wheel and in a second step, the awareness of their need of action on the brake pedal.

> 36 EV1 OFF: It took me a bit of time for my brain to reconnect and say: you're in a car, you have to put your hands back on the steering wheel, your foot on the accelerator.... I had no awareness of the vehicles around me... I wasn't thinking about the pedals at all, just the steering wheel. Which is very strange, one forgets that there were pedals to manage... when I get back to the driving situation, I first get the steering wheel and then the pedals.

**Doubts About the Roles Distribution.** Despite the instructions, several drivers have doubts about the roles distribution and feel firstly uncertain and perplex (Boelhouwer et al. 2019).

> 30 EV2 Off: is the vehicle going to change by itself or brake by itself? Finally, I hesitated to... I asked myself questions: what should I do? Should I take over or was the vehicle going to do something?

> 7 EV2 ON: It beeped and in my head I thought everything was automatically managed. So I didn't pay any attention to what was happening in front of me. I told myself that he was warning me that there was certainly a problem, I felt that he was slowing down, that he was doing something. I thought: it's good, he's slowing down because there's an obstacle ahead...

A particularly interesting phenomenon is the link established between the hands on/off position and the distribution of roles between the driver and the vehicle. Many participants tell us that when they were Hands-off, they thought the system would manage alone; whereas when they had their hands on the wheel, they thought they had to manage themselves. So they associate bodily position and role: if I have my hands on the wheel, I am still a driver, otherwise I am like a passenger. The passenger is the one who can do something else while the other controls the driving. Having the steering wheel in one's hands therefore induces a higher responsibility, an actor's position as usual in driving, whereas the hands-off position induces a passive role, one of non-responsible and non-intervening person.

**Perceptions of the System Deactivation.** Once they have perceived cues indicating the system deactivation, they have partially reconnected cognitively. These sensorial cues are:

– *Visual* cues of the screen and road.

> 4 EV2 OFF: I saw that there was the green light for autonomous driving on the dashboard which was no longer displayed ... I thought it's something not normal, it's up to me to avoid the obstacle.

> 33 EV1 OFF: it was in a bend, and as I always had my eyes on the road a little bit, I could see that at some point I was no longer between my lines

– *Auditory* alarm, in event 2 (obstacle): 52% did not perceive it, and some misinterpreted it (cf. §3.1.2 ex.7.1)
– *Kinesthetic* cues such as deceleration, deviation, and steering wheel movements.

> 36 EV1 OFF: There's really a different feeling between "the vehicle is managing the exit of the corner" and "the vehicle is not managing the exit of the corner". I felt the difference and that's what alerted me. It's a bit like climbing, you're held by a rope and all of a sudden, for a microsecond, you're in free fall. A sort of free fall effect. First of all, there was a loss of acceleration, because there is a

speed maintenance when you are in autonomous driving, and on top of that, the trajectory. So it's a rather brutal double effect, where you have a loss of speed and a trajectory that varies quite rapidly. It's a somewhat brutal movement in relation to driving, which is very smooth in autonomous driving with trajectories that are quite linear. There, it makes a small break.

Holding the steering wheel allows pre-reflected adjustments. For incident-1 (curve), drivers are often unaware of the deactivation at the beginning. In the hands-on condition 38% are not aware of the deactivation but adjust the trajectory in a pre-reflected way, not being reflectively conscious of these adjustments by the hands. Of course these adjustments are not possible when they do not hold the steering wheel. The following participant was clearly not aware of the deactivation but he adjusted the trajectory.

37 EV1 ON: Interviewer: - you have never had to take over at any time?. Participant: - It was imperceptible if it was the case.

**On-board Activities and Vigilance.** Drivers' verbalisations often go in the following direction: 'I do more on-board activities Hands-off than Hands-on, or activities that are more absorbing and that I don't usually do while driving'. No verbatim goes the other way (I do more activities Hands-on than Hands-off).

When Hands-off, drivers say they allow themselves activities they do not usually do, such as reading a full article, looking at the landscape in detail (a hot air balloon), looking at the back seat as if there were their grandchildren.

1 EV2 OFF: I was really absorbed in the radio, feeling like I was in passenger mode, being able to do something else.

45 EV2 OFF: I played a bit with my phone in the first test (OFF). I didn't feel I could do it in the second (ON).

Some mistrustful drivers who avoid on-board activities feel more bored or drowsy with Hands-off.

### Different Feelings Hands-On and -Off: Attention, Control, Responsibility, Risk

– *Hands-on*, 77% say spontaneously that they feel safer, more in control and more attentive, like a responsible actor, but some talk of an unsatisfying "hybrid solution".

11 ON : I felt more attentive and I felt more in control with hands-on

09 ON: you feel like you're still on the road, more ready to react, whereas in Off mode you don't care about driving.

06 ON: Holding the steering wheel limits what else you want to do, it's not very pleasant, it's not really comfortable; you're not completely at ease with driving and you're not completely at ease with what you're doing; it's a hybrid solution, a bit bastard; you're tempted to do something else but you can't really do it; you react faster but you're not as free.

– *Hands-off* they feel more relaxed, freer and more comfortable, also more passive, less attentive and less responsible, like a passenger. 36% of the participants spontaneously said they felt less in control and less attentive with Hands-off than with Hands-on; some even felt "completely out of control (off the hook; "décrochés" in French).

04 OFF: More relaxed because you don't have hands. We tell ourselves that a priori we don't have to intervene at all. We are freer to do something else

01 OFF: my attention was a bit lower (in OFF); since I let myself be driven, I feel like I'm in passenger mode so I can do something else

24 OFF: On the negative side, I would tend to be more distracted, which certainly requires, in terms of risk, more reaction time.

To keep control, with hands on or off, drivers remain sensitive to the vehicle's movements (trajectories, decelerations and accelerations), or even, when Hands-on, they try to turn the steering wheel instead of the car.

**Physical Sensations.** Hands-on, the physical sensations of the steering wheel moving in the hands may be unpleasant, with muscular tension in the hands to hold it.

22 ON: Depending on the density with which you hold the steering wheel, you will feel its reactions for lane correction more strongly. One tends to create constraints on the steering wheel without realizing it, so that the system reacts in opposition to possibly correct.. it is not particularly pleasant, this feeling of constraint, in opposition, is a little annoying. Sometimes I've had a lighter hand, barely able to hold the steering wheel, you don't stay there very long. It's true that you tend to get lost in it and to take the wheel in a varied manner.

Even if hands-off is more comfortable, some drivers do not know how to position their legs and arms and would like the car to be better designed for this new situation.

**Global Preferences.** In terms of global preferences, 51% of our drivers prefer the hands-off driving, 35% prefer the hands-on driving and 14% neither. It should be pointed out that this evaluation is given after $2 \times 20$ min of drive in a simulator, maybe it would change over time and in a real driving environment.

### 3.2 Observable Measures: The Objective Risk

In this article we focused on the subjective experience results obtained with the interviews, but we also obtained results from observable measures. We summarize the results of the observable conducts, and refer to Forzy et al. (2021) for a more complete description.

For Event-1 (loss of assistance in a curve) we found a significantly negative impact of the Hands-off condition on the trajectories deviations, compared to hands-on. The drivers produce a significantly larger deviation on the left lane when they do not hold the steering wheel than when they hold it. A gaze monitoring system[3], with an alarm when the driver in hands-off condition does not look at the road during more than 5 s, does not compensate totally this negative effect but it limits the more distractive behaviors (cf. means Fig. 3).

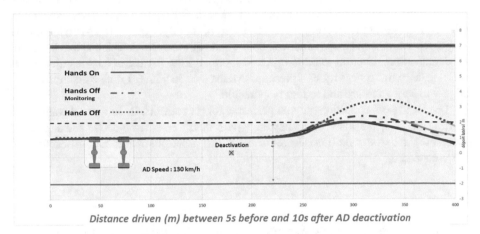

Fig. 3. EV1 incidental loss of assistance in a high-speed turn

For incident-2 (obstacle) we observe a significantly longer delay of reaction to avoid the obstacle in the Hands-off condition and significantly more accidents or near accident (cf. means Fig. 4).

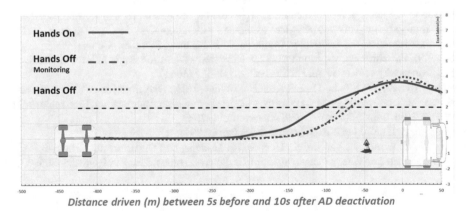

Fig. 4. EV2 sudden breakdown of assistance followed by an obstacle on the roadway

We can then conclude that the objective risk is higher when the drivers do not hold the steering wheel than when they hold it and that the eyes monitoring compensates slightly this effect.

---

[3] cf. Forzy et al. (2021).

## 4 Discussion

This study shows the richness of the complementarity of objective measures and of the users' verbalizations about their subjective experience of the driving situations (Gustavson et al. 2018), to understand how they interpret, feel, and perceive the environment. Beyond the differences in take-over performance, the Elicitation Interviews indicate the gains from holding the steering wheel (Hands-on), mainly: (a) Hands-on driving allows the perception of kinesthetic feedback on the state of the system. This feedback enables the deactivation situation to be interpreted more rapidly. (b) It can enable adjustments to be made to the trajectory in a prereflective manner (EV1). (c) It also encourages the subject to stay attentive and to feel responsible.

The Hands-off condition may be preferred for its comfort, feeling of relaxation and the multi-activity it allows "as if they are a passenger", but the objective and subjective risk in the Hands-on condition is lower in the critical situations of automation deactivation that we studied.

## References

Boelhouwer, A., Van den Beukel, A.P., Van der Voort, M.C., Martens, M.H.: Should I take over? Does system knowledge help drivers in making take-over decisions while driving a partially automated car? Transp. Res. Part F: Traffic Psychol. Behav. **60**, 669–684 (2019)

Cahour, B., Salembier, P., Zouinar, M.: Analyzing lived experience of activity. Le Trav. Hum. **79**(3), 259 (2016). https://doi.org/10.3917/th.793.0259

Forzy, J.F., Ojeda, L., Cahour, B., Koustanaï, A.: Which impacts of the hands-off modality on drivers' disconnection for level automation driving systems? In: Proceedings of the DDI Conference on Driver Distraction and Inattention, Lyon, France, October 2021

Gustavson, P., Victor, T.W., Johansson, J., Tivesten, E., Johansson, R., Aust, M.L.: What were they thinking? Subjective experiences associated with automation driving mismatch. In: DDI Driver, Distraction and Inattention Conference, Gothenburg, Sweeden, October 2018

Molloy, R., Parasuraman, R.: Monitoring an automated system for single failure: vigilance and task complexity effects. Hum. Factors **38**(2), 311–322 (1996)

Morales-Alvarez, W., Sipele, O., Léberon, R., Tadjine, H.H., Olaverri-Monreal, C.: Automated driving: a literature review of the take-over request in conditional automation. Electronics **9**(12), 2087 (2020). https://doi.org/10.3390/electronics9122087

Vermersch, P.: L'entretien d'explicitation. ESF, Paris (1994)

Zhang, B., de Winter, J., Varotto, S., Happee, R., Martens, M.: Determinants of take-over time from automated driving: a meta-analysis of 129 studies. Transp. Res. Part F **64**, 285–305 (2019)

# Effect of Time Length of Eye Movement Data Analysis on the Accuracy of Mental Workload Estimation During Automobile Driving

Takanori Chihara[✉] and Jiro Sakamoto

Kanazawa University, Ishikawa, Japan
chihara@staff.kanazawa-u.ac.jp

**Abstract.** We investigated the appropriate time window duration for calculating eye and head movement parameters in mental workload (MWL) estimation during automobile driving. Participants performed driving tasks on a driving simulator, and eye and head movements were measured by controlling their MWL using the N-back task, which required them to keep answering aloud the N-th previous digit in a sequence of digits. The eye and head movement parameters were calculated by changing a time window from 30 s to 150 s in increments of 30 s. An anomaly detector of MWL was constructed using the one-class support vector machine (OCSVM) with the no N-back task ("None") data. In each window length condition, we calculated the area under curve (AUC) for the binary classification between None and the highest MWL condition, the percentage of anomaly data, and the distance from the decision boundary. The results showed that a time window of 30 s had significantly lower AUC compared with other time windows. In addition, the correlation coefficient between the subjective MWL score and the distance of each eye movement parameter data from the decision boundary monotonically increased in the time window 30 s to 120 s and decreased at 150 s. Therefore, we concluded that 60 s to 120 s is an appropriate time window duration for MWL evaluation.

**Keywords:** Driver monitoring · Mental workload · Eye tracking · Machine learning · Anomaly detection · One-class support vector machine

## 1 Introduction

Distracted driving is one of the most common causes of fatal traffic accidents in Japan [1]. To prevent distracted driving, it is necessary to evaluate the mental state of drivers. To this end, we focused on the eye movement of the drivers for a quantitative evaluation of mental workload (MWL); tracking eye movements is practical and may indicate comfort, stress, and various other biological states of the driver. In our previous research, the following effective eye movement parameters were selected: the standard deviation (SD) of the horizontal gaze angle, the SD of the horizontal eyeball rotation angle, the sharing rate of head movement against the eyeball rotation in a gaze movement, and the brink frequency [2]. These parameters were calculated in a time window of 60 s, which was determined

© The Author(s), under exclusive license to Springer Nature Switzerland AG 2021
N. L. Black et al. (Eds.): IEA 2021, LNNS 221, pp. 593–599, 2021.
https://doi.org/10.1007/978-3-030-74608-7_72

intuitively. However, the duration of the time window may affect the accuracy of MWL estimation. A longer time window may improve the estimation accuracy as the effect of the surrounding noise is reduced; however, the temporal resolution of MWL tracking decreases as it takes time to estimate MWL. Therefore, the effect of the time window duration should be investigated to maximize the accuracy of MWL estimation. The aim of this study is to investigate the appropriate time window range for calculating eye movement parameters in mental workload (MWL) estimation during automobile driving. Furthermore, the accuracy of MWL estimation and correlation between the subjective and estimated MWL are compared for different time windows using experimental data obtained in the previous study [2].

## 2  Methods

### 2.1  Experimental Conditions

Twelve Japanese students with an average age of $21.6 \pm 0.51$ years and having drivers' licenses participated in this experiment. They performed driving tasks in an urban city course on a driving simulator (UCwin/Road Ver.13 Driving Sim, FORUM8 Inc.) (see Fig. 1); their eye and head movements were simultaneously measured with an image sensor (B5T-007001, Omron Inc.) by controlling their MWL through the N-back task [3]. In the N-back task, the participants were required to keep answering aloud the N-th previous digit in a sequence of digits that was read out consecutively. The N-back task had five difficulty levels: none, 0-back, 1-back, 2-back, and 3-back. The subjective MWL was measured using the national aeronautics and space administration task load index (NASA-TLX) [4, 5]. The adaptive weighted workload (AWWL) score [5] was used as the total score. The AWWL score is calculated as the weighted sum of the six scales with the weights of 6, 5, 4, 3, 2, and 1 in a decreasing order of the scales. The higher the value, the higher is the subjective MWL.

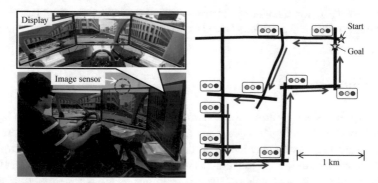

**Fig. 1.** Driving simulator and driving route.

## 2.2   Quantification of MWL by One-Class Support Vector Machine

The gaze angle, head angle, and degree of eye closure during the driving task were measured using an image sensor. Thereafter, the four eye movement parameters (i.e., SD of gaze angle, SD of eyeball rotation angle, sharing rate of head movement, and blink frequency) were calculated by changing the time window to 30–150 s in increments of 30 s (Fig. 2). Anomaly detectors for MWL were constructed using the one-class support vector machine (OCSVM) for each participant and each increment of the time window. The OCSVM creates a decision function that takes a non-negative value in the area containing a large volume of training data and a negative value in the other areas. We used the OCSVM implemented in scikit-learn 0.23.2. The radial basis function (RBF) kernel was used as the kernel function, and the coefficient of the kernel $\gamma$ was set as $\gamma = 0.25$ . In addition, the upper bound on the fraction of training errors $\nu$ was set as $\nu = 0.01$. The two hyper parameters of the OCSVM were heuristically determined.

In total, 50% of the "none" data were randomly used as the training data for the OCSVM, and the remaining "none" and "0-back" to "3-back" data were used as test data. Note that the training and the test data were normalized based on the means and SDs of the four eye movement parameters in the training dataset.

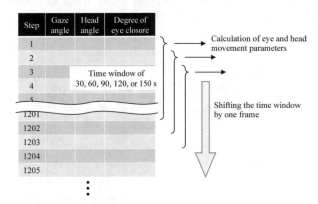

**Fig. 2.**   Calculation of eye and head movement parameters.

## 2.3   Analysis

For each window length condition, we calculated the area under the curve (AUC) for the binary classification between "none" and "3-back" data, the percentage of anomalous data, and the distance of each eye movement parameter data from the decision boundary. A one-way analysis of variance (ANOVA) was conducted to investigate the effects of the time window on the AUC; Tukey's post-hoc tests were carried out to compare the levels of the time window.

## 3   Results

Figure 3 shows the average AUCs for each time window. The ANOVA revealed that the effect of time window was significantly associated with the AUC at 1% significance level. The time window of 30 s had significantly lower AUC compared with other time windows.

The ratios of the anomalous data for each time window are shown in Fig. 4. The ratio of the anomalous data monotonically increased with the increase in the task difficulty in the range from "0-back" to "3-back." In addition, the anomaly ratio also increased with the increase in the duration of the time window with respect to the same task difficulty except "None." Especially for the time window duration of 150 s, the ratio of the anomalous data became almost 100% for "1-back" to "3-back" tasks.

Figure 5 shows the correlation coefficients between the subjective MWL (i.e., AWWL score of NASA-TLX) and the distance of each eye movement parameter data from the decision boundary of OCSVM ($N = 5$ task difficulties $\times$ 12 participants = 60). The correlation coefficients were significant at 1% significance level irrespective of the time window. The correlation coefficient monotonically increased between 30 s and 120 s and decreased at 150 s. Figure 6 shows the relationship between AWWL scores and the distance of each eye movement parameter data from the decision boundary at 120 s time window, which has the highest correlation coefficient.

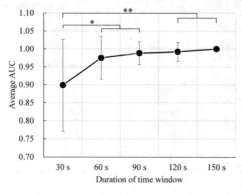

**Fig. 3.** Relationship between the time window and average AUC. Error bars represent the standard deviations. This graph includes the results of the post-hoc test; * and ** represent $p < 0.05$ and $p < 0.01$, respectively.

## 4   Discussion

As shown in Fig. 4, the ratio of the anomalous data monotonically increased with the task difficulty irrespective of the time window; therefore, the time window of 30–150 s can quantify the MWL during driving. The participants showed different abilities for the N-back task; thus, MWL from the same N-back task is different for each participant. Therefore, the ratio of the anomalous data is expected to have some variability among

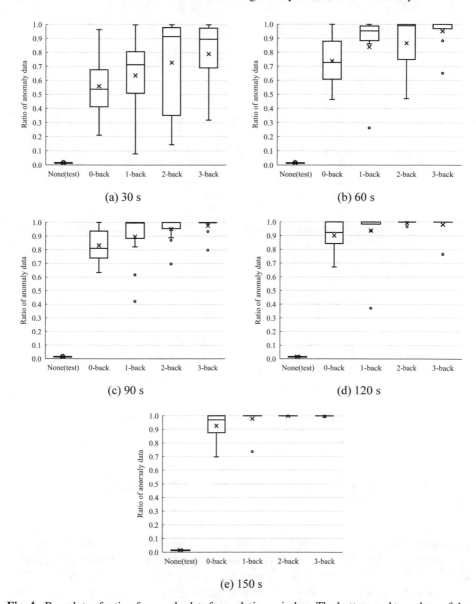

**Fig. 4.** Box plots of ratio of anomaly data for each time window. The bottom and top edges of the box represent the first and third quartiles (Q1 and Q3), respectively, and the band in the box is the second quartile (Q2) or the median. The white dot represents an outlier; the threshold for outlier determination was less than Q1 − 1.5 × IQR (IQR = interquartile range) and higher than Q3 + 1.5 × IQR. The bottom and top of the whisker represent the maximum and minimum excluding the outliers, and the cross represents the average value.

the participants, especially in the relatively easy N-back task. By contrast, the "3-back" task was the most difficult one, resulting in a considerably high MWL for almost all the

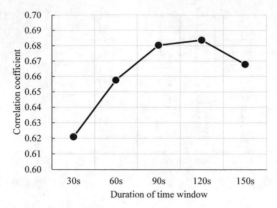

**Fig. 5.** Correlation coefficient between the normalized AWWL score and the distance from the decision boundary for each time window.

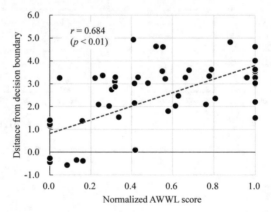

**Fig. 6.** Relationship between the normalized AWWL score and the distance from the decision boundary for the time window of 120 s.

participants. However, the average of the ratio of the anomalous data for the "3-back" was approximately 80% when the time window was 30 s (Fig. 4(a)). In addition, the detection ability for the time window of 30 s is lower compared with other time windows. This is because 30 s is relatively short for calculating the eye movement parameter, and the detection accuracy decreases due to the effect of the noise. Therefore, the time window should be more than 30 s.

The time window 120–150 s has approximately 100% anomalous data ratios, not only for the "3-back" but also for the "1-back" and "2-back" tasks. It would be more natural for the ratio of the anomalous data to increase gradually with the N-back task because the MWL from the relatively low-difficulty task may have variability across the participants. In addition, too long a window length (i.e., 150 s) impairs the correlation between the objective and subjective MWL evaluation. The time window of 150 s masks the difference for "1-back" to "3-back" tasks, whereas the anomaly ratio should increase gradually. Therefore, 150 s is slightly too long as the time window.

Considering the aforementioned points, we concluded that 60 s to 120 s is an appropriate time window duration for MWL evaluation.

## 5    Conclusions

We found that the range of 60 s to 120 s is the appropriate time window duration for calculating eye movement parameters in mental workload (MWL) estimation during automobile driving.

## References

1. Statistics about Road Traffic/Traffic accidents situation. https://www.e-stat.go.jp/en/stat-sea rch/files?page=1&layout=datalist&toukei=00130002&tstat=000001027458&cycle=7&year= 20190&month=0&stat_infid=000031910507&tclass1val=0. Accessed 21 Jan 2021
2. Chihara, T., Kobayashi, F., Sakamoto, J.: Evaluation of mental workload during automobile driving using one-class support vector machine with eye movement data. Appl. Ergon. **89**, 103201 (2020)
3. Ross, V., Jongen, E.M.M., Wang, W., Brijs, T., Brijs, K., Ruiter, R.A.C., Wets, G.: Investigating the influence of working memory capacity when driving behavior is combined with cognitive load: an LCT study of young novice drivers. Accid. Anal. Prevention **62**, 377–387 (2014)
4. Hart, S.G., Staveland, L.E.: Development of NASA-TLX (Task Load Index): results of empirical and theoretical research. Adv. Psychol. **52**(C), 139–183 (1988)
5. Miyake, S., Kumashiro, M.: Subjective mental workload assessment technique – an introduction to NASA-TLX and SWAT and a proposal of simple scoring methods. Jpn. J. Ergon. **29**(6), 399–408 (1993). (in Japanese)

# A User-Centered Approach to Adapt the Human-Machine Cooperation Strategy in Autonomous Driving

Stéphanie Coeugnet[1(✉)], Franck Mars[2], Mercedes Bueno[1], Chouki Sentouh[3], Jean-Christophe Popieul[3], Arnaud Koustanaï[4], Annie Pauzié[5], and Hélène Tattegrain[5]

[1] VEDECOM Institute, 78000 Versailles, France
stephanie.coeugnet-chevrier@vedecom.fr
[2] Université de Nantes, Centrale Nantes, CNRS, LS2N, 44000 Nantes, France
[3] LAMIH, UPHF, 59300 Famars, France
[4] Laboratory of Accidentology, Biomechanics and Driver Behavior, 92000 Nanterre, France
[5] Gustave Eiffel University, LESCOT, 69500 Bron, France

**Abstract.** Using an integrative user-centered approach, the research project aimed at designing and assessing an adaptive HMI to improve the safety and the quality of the take-over in a level-3 automated vehicle.

Future autonomous driving users confirmed the need for the monitoring systems to improve safety as long as they are simple and not intrusive. They request specific information to understand and initiate appropriated actions in case of a critical situation. However, to avoid overloading and detrimental effects, it is important that the system limits the amount of information at the right moment.

**Keywords:** Autonomous driving · Driver monitoring · HMI · Adaptive system

## 1 Introduction

The autonomous vehicle should increase driving comfort and road safety [1]. In this way, level-3 SAE systems should allow the driver to cede full control of all safety-critical function under specific conditions [2]. However, the driver is intended to respond appropriately to a request to intervene as a fallback to perform the dynamic driving task. Given this requirement to re-engage in the vehicle control loop and limitation that driver has in the monitoring road environment, a key issue is how to design time, modality, and frequency of transfer of control requests [3].

Studies on partial and conditional automation have already shown that an incorrect understanding of the system's current actions can lead to inappropriate or unsafe drivers' behaviors [4]. The profound change in driver activity brought about by automation (i.e., supervision, management of transitions, management of conflicts of intent) will require the design of new modalities of interaction with the vehicle. Designing a better dialogue between the driver and the vehicle will be essential to guarantee the acceptance, safety, and more generally, the quality of use of the autonomous vehicle [5]. To this end, the

N. L. Black et al. (Eds.): IEA 2021, LNNS 221, pp. 600–606, 2021.
https://doi.org/10.1007/978-3-030-74608-7_73

driver needs to receive information about the system's functioning and limits (e.g., the period of autonomous mode). Similarly, the vehicle needs to receive some information about the driver's state using an integrative monitoring system. The research project within the framework of which the work reported in this paper was carried out sought to respond to these issues with a multidimensional approach to ergonomics. The overall objective was to adapt the HMI of a level 3 automated vehicle to the driver's state. The initial steps of the project consisted in a series of studies that will be briefly outlined here. In a first objective, six focus groups completed large-scale questionnaires involving 2619 participants. The results showed that the higher the drivers' acceptance of automated vehicles, the more they reported trust in the high automation levels. The results also highlighted an essential need for a progressive level of information in the case of a planned take-over and the guidance of the relevant actions to be taken in unplanned take-over using visual and auditory information [6]. The driver profiles analysis, including age and driving experience, was conducted and showed a need for an advanced HMI according to the skill driving level and use time. Then, in a second objective, a set of three driving simulator studies investigated specific aspects of driver monitoring (i.e., visual, postural, and physiological indicators). The visual behavior study used partial-least-square regressions to model drivers' visual strategies during autonomous driving to determine the characteristic patterns of an out-of-the-loop driver. The results showed that beyond the time spent looking at areas of interest crucial for maintaining situational awareness (road center, adjacent traffic lane, left rear-view mirror, in particular), it is necessary to consider indicators of gaze dynamics (transitions between areas) to obtain the most predictive models [7]. Postural studies have tested the position of the joint centers and the distribution of contact pressure in order to define the best postural indicator for monitoring. The results showed that pressure measurements can be used to extract relevant parameters to detect changes in posture [8]. The study on the internal state of the driver aimed to highlight physiological indicators of the driver's attentional state as a function of cognitive distraction induced by increased cognitive load or sadness. The results showed that it was possible to differentiate the driver's activity and emotional state with different physiological measurements: cardiac variability to detect emotion, breathing amplitude to distinguish the type of activity of the driver in a state of sadness, and the breathing period to differentiate activity in a neutral emotional state [9]. This paper follows the conclusions of the previous studies, starting with the objective to develop a global diagnostic of the driver state based on the three types of indicators (i.e., gaze, postural, and physiological indicators). In parallel, a new HMI has been designed taking into account the recommendations of the focus group study. The HMI and the driver monitoring system were implemented on a Wizard of Oz (WOz) vehicle (active commands managed by a professional driver without awareness of the driver). In addition to those developments, this paper also presents the preliminary results of a final study using this vehicle on open roads, which was performed to assess both the impact and the acceptance of the system.

## 2    Indicators and Diagnose of the Driver's State

The implementation of several treatments allowed us to identify the state graph management of the vehicle that controls the different modes of automation. Initially, we designed the signals of the various sensors used to measure the driver's state and the vehicle's actions:

- the visual activity monitoring system, which provided diagnostics on the collection of perceptive information in the road scene from eye-tracking data,
- the postural monitoring system that provided diagnostics of the driver's posture, hand and foot positions from camera data,
- the physiological monitoring system that provided diagnostics on the attentional level of the driver from cardiac, respiratory, and electrodermal data,
- the system for reporting information on driving actions on the vehicle.

The Fig. 1 shows the processes of the diagnostics fusion and the related monitoring functions.

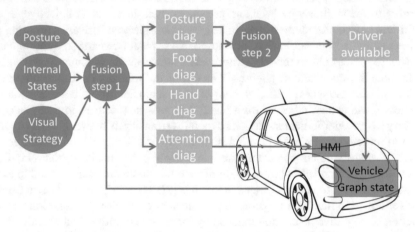

**Fig. 1.** Organization of monitoring and fusion processes.

From these indicators, the first step of merging the data using decision tables to create three diagnostics indicated whether the conditions on the body's positions, hands, and feet were correct. Finally, a fourth diagnosis considered that the attentional level was sufficient by exploiting the diagnoses of visual strategies and internal states. The second phase of fusion used these diagnostics to define a global diagnosis of the driver's ability to regain vehicle control.

## 3   Design of the HMI

The designed HMI served and communicated to the driver information related to both the driving situation and the autonomous driving system's operation. The objective was to warn the driver in the case of a potentially dangerous condition detection such as drowsiness or distraction, especially when taking back control. When returning to manual driving, when requested by the system, the HMI's role was to highlight the contextual elements that the driver must consider in order to regain control safely:

– **Entry into delegation:** before activating automated driving, the HMI allowed the driver to check that the system correctly perceived the driving environment (e.g., lanes, traffic). It supported the transition between the driver and the autonomous driving system by clearly indicating authority transfer.
– **Road monitoring during automated driving:** the HMI displayed the elements of the driving scene analyzed by the system (e.g., headway distance), thus allowing the driver not only to check the operation of the system but also to be able to make an immediate diagnosis of the driving situation and anticipate a possible need for planned or unplanned take-over request.
– **Control resumption by the driver:** during planned control recovery, the HMI informed the driver in advance, allowing him/her to prepare appropriately. During unplanned (sudden) take-over request, the HMI warned the driver with an adequate level of importance, indicating the situation to be managed imminently (identification of critical events).

The Fig. 2 presents the final HMI.

**Fig. 2.** Final designed HMI.

The HMI specifications were defined using the "five W method": What, Where, hoW, When and Who. Regarding the type of information to be displayed on the interface (What to display?), five groups were defined: the activation command (button), the driving mode indicator, the information contributing to a good "situational awareness", GPS navigation, and alert messages. To facilitate the understanding and urgency of the messages by the driver, a color code was defined. The fifth question, "Who?", aimed to identify the conditions for the HMI content evolution. The driver monitoring module diagnosed the driver's condition based on indicators related to his/her visual strategies, posture, and internal state described above. It also identified the driver's actions (e.g., resume a driving posture by putting the hands on the steering wheel and bringing the feet to the pedals). To do this, the driver monitoring manager interacted with the HMI manager module to request the display of visual messages on the screen and/or the broadcasting of voice messages. The HMI module was also in charge of not overloading the driver by managing the sequencing of visual or audio messages.

# 4 Experimental Assessment of the System – A WOz Study

## 4.1 Method

Fifty-two drivers (26 men, Mean age = 38.5 years) participated in the WOz study on public roads. The WOz vehicle could be driven by the copilot (or wizard) with a joystick hidden to the participants, thus simulating the level-3 automated driving. A simplified version of the HMI presented in the previous section was used in this study. Specifically, the HMI provided about the activation command (button), the driving modes (manual driving, automated driving), GPS navigation, and alert messages (take-over requests). During the automated driving, participants were able to engage in non-driving related activities (e.g., reading, playing a game on a tablet), and they received two types of take-over requests: unplanned (budget time = 8 s) and planned (budget time = 45 s). Drivers' visual behavior, posture, and physiological measures (heart rate, skin conductance, respiration), were recorded using the Smart-Eye Pro dx remote eye-tracking system, two Time of flight cameras (PMD Pico Monstar and Softkinetic DepthSense DS325), and the BIOPAC acquisition system, respectively. The information about the driver state was processed offline. At the end of the drive, a semi-directive interview was conducted to explore drivers' opinions following the automated driving and their expectations about the monitoring system's functioning (only the results related to the monitoring will be presented in this article).

## 4.2 Results

Analysis of interview data revealed that almost all participants (97.7%) considered that the system should assist drivers depending on their state. Most of them mentioned that it would be useful in case of drowsiness, annoying or lengthy trips (see Fig. 3).

Participants themselves were willing to be monitored with sensors (86.1%), but the system must be more simple, less intrusive, and less restrictive to be accepted (e.g., bracelet or sensors integrated into the steering wheel). 57.1% considered that the monitoring system would be relevant during the whole driving for security reasons and more reassurance. However, 40.5% would prefer to be assisted only during more complex contexts (e.g., urban driving) or specific situations that may affect their vigilance (e.g., highway).

Concerning the monitoring feedback, the visual and auditory combination was elicited by 44% of the participants. Most of them signaled that the visual modality would not be useful by itself in case of drowsiness or inattention to the HMI. However, 27.9% of the participants preferred the single visual mode because they considered it less aggressive and less disturbing to the other passengers (e.g., sleeping children). Besides, they were asked about their preferences regarding the pictogram type associated with the driver's state. They were shown and could decide between a general red pictogram ("improper driver state", see Fig. 4a) or specific red pictogram informing about

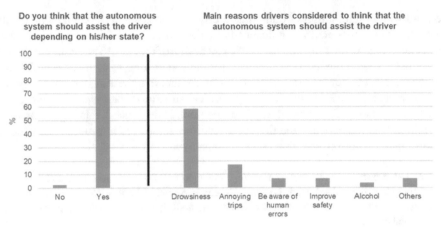

**Fig. 3.** Participants' opinion about the assistance of the autonomous system depending on the driver state.

an improper posture (Fig. 4b), hands-off (Fig. 4c), foot-off (Fig. 4d), eyes-off (Fig. 4e), and drowsiness (Fig. 4f).

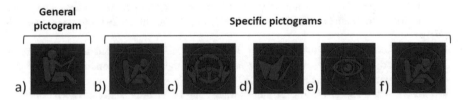

**Fig. 4.** General and specific pictograms about driver state.

More than half of the participants (61.9%) preferred the specific pictograms to be aware of the problem and correct it. However, some of them were concerned about receiving warnings too frequently, and others indicated that only the drowsiness pictogram would be relevant. Participants opting for the general pictogram cited that specific pictograms would involve too much information to process, which could be irritating.

## 5   Discussion

Based on the users' needs studies and the final assessments, main implications emerged from this research project: (1) monitoring systems should be favored - or even integrated systematically - in vehicles with automated driving; (2) the presence of driver monitoring systems must be justified by a significant gain in terms of comfort and safety; (3) a positive point of view of autonomous vehicles improve the acceptance of the monitoring and its related HMI. Using a user-centered design approach helped identify and consider the most relevant future autonomous vehicles' expectations and needs. This approach could be used to design monitoring and cooperative systems. Carrying out experiments on the road with potential users of automated driving systems and implementing suitable methodologies constituted a significant advance proposed by this research project. These assessments lead to the safer and more efficient design of the Level 3 autonomous vehicle. Future users seem convinced of the need for the monitoring systems as useful aids to improve safety. However, to be accepted, it is necessary that these systems are integrated into the vehicle and easy to use. In case of critical situations, the system should provide specific information about the cause of the problem. Nevertheless, it is important to find an optimal balance between the frequency and the amount of information provided to the system to avoid it from being counterproductive.

**Acknowledgment.** This research project (AUTOCONDUCT - ANR-16-CE22-0007) was supported by grants from the French National Research Agency (ANR – Agence Nationale pour la Recherche). The authors are grateful to the different study participants for their commitment, interest, and cooperation.

# References

1. Reimer, B.: Driver assistance systems and the transition to automated vehicles: a path to increase older adult safety and mobility? Public Policy Aging Rep. **24**(1), 27–31 (2014)
2. SAE International: Taxonomy and definitions for terms related to driving automation systems for on-road motor vehicles. SAE Standard J3016, Report No. J3016-201806, Warrendale, PA (2018)
3. Roche, F., Somieski, A., Brandenburg, S.: Behavioral changes to repeated takeovers in highly automated driving: effects of the takeover-request design and the nondriving-related task modality. Hum. Factors **61**(5), 839–849 (2019)
4. Carsten, O., Martens, M.H.: How can humans understand their automated cars? HMI principles, problems and solutions. Cogn. Technol. Work **21**, 3–20 (2019)
5. Hartwich, F., Beggiato, M., Krems, J.F.: Driving comfort, enjoyment and acceptance of automated driving–effects of drivers' age and driving style familiarity. Ergonomics **61**(8), 1017–1032 (2018)
6. Bel, M., Pauzié, A., Fehat, L., Kraiem, S.: Needs analysis, design assistance and acceptability of the automated vehicle. In: EPIQUE, Ergonomics Psychology Conference, Lyon, France (2019)
7. Schnebelen, D., Charron, C., Mars, F.: Predicting the out-of-the-loop phenomenon from visual strategies during highly automated driving. Accid. Anal. Prev. **148**, 105776 (2020)
8. Zhao, M., Beurier, G., Wang, H., Wang, X.: In vehicle diver postural monitoring using a depth camera Kinect. SAE Technical Paper 2018-01-0505 (2018). https://doi.org/10.4271/2018-01-0505
9. Hidalgo-Muñoz, A., Jallais, C., Evennou, M., Ndiaye, D., Moreau, F., Ranchet, M., Derollepot, R., Fort, A.: Hemodynamic responses to visual cues during attentive listening in autonomous versus manual simulated driving: a pilot study. Brain Cogn. **135**, 103583 (2019)

# Citizen Centered Mobility Planning: The Case of the Speed Limits Reduction of São Paulo Highways

Raquel Cordeiro[1]([⊠]) (iD), Fábio Corrêa Cordeiro[2] (iD), and Manuela Quaresma[1] (iD)

[1] Department of Arts and Design, Pontifical Catholic
University of Rio de Janeiro, Rio de Janeiro, Brazil
`raquelcordeiro@aluno.puc-rio.br`
[2] School of Applied Mathematics, FGV, Rio de Janeiro, Brazil

**Abstract.** The mobility data available in any city allows the urban managers to create models for the traffic flow and increase the streets' safety. However, a small group of technical people often creates these models without the citizens' participation, the core beneficiary of any public policy. A Human Smart City is only possible with the population engaged in the co-creation of solutions for collective social change. In this paper, we review the case of the speed limits reduction on the two main highways in São Paulo, in 2015. Despite the positive results on accidents and traffic jams indicators, a major part of society did not approve the new policy, and two years later, the speed limits returned to the previous values. This example shows the importance of the population's participation in the creation of urban policies. Conclusively, we discuss the impact of communication for success in public policy planning and its implementation.

**Keywords:** Smart city · Mobility · Urban planning · Citizen centered design · Traffic modelling

## 1 Introduction

In recent decades, the availability of data, and sensor information throughout the city influenced decisions in urban planning. The term smart city has become famous as a synonym for the technologically advanced city. With the wide use of cameras, traffic light sensors, smartphones, and location apps, traffic engineers can monitor and manage urban mobility at a level of detail unimaginable decades ago.

Public managers had created mobility models trying to optimize some aspects of city life, such as the average travel time or the number of road accidents. However, there is insufficient citizen participation in the creation of these models. Consequently, some public policies are not as effective as they should be because they do not consider citizens' needs and expectations.

Mobility plays a central role in the discussions on how to make cities friendlier to the population. In this paper, we show some traffic models and discuss how to integrate it with qualitative research and citizen participation. We selected the case study of the

N. L. Black et al. (Eds.): IEA 2021, LNNS 221, pp. 607–614, 2021.
https://doi.org/10.1007/978-3-030-74608-7_74

reduction of the maximum speed allowed on the two main highways that cross the city of São Paulo, in Brazil. We show what happened when the city administration implemented a public policy without the population point of view.

## 2 Traffic Models

When the São Paulo administration reduced the speed limits of the two main highways, they aimed to decrease accidents and traffic jams rates. They reviewed the traffic models to set new speed limits. Thus, in this section, we present some mathematical models for traffic flow, studies about the relation of speed and risk on vehicular traffic, and a bibliography about co-design in public policies.

### 2.1 Traffic Flow Theory

We can divide the mathematical models for traffic flow based on the scale of the observation. Bellomo et al. [1] define these three scales:

- Microscopic description: all vehicles are identified. The position and velocity of each one define the system state as a dependent of the time.
- Kinetic description: the position and velocity of the vehicles identify the system state. It does not refer to each vehicle but a suitable probability distribution.
- Macroscopic description: locally averaged quantities describe the state.

From the microscopic point of view, we deal with every single lane of road or highway as a complete system. Each vehicle is at a dimensionless position with a specific velocity. We model it as a Newtonian system of particles. They usually are described using ordinary differential equations (ODE), that is, an equation that relates functions and their derivatives for only one independent variable.

For the kinetic description, a statistical distribution defines the position and velocity for the whole system. $f^j = f^j(t, x, V)$ defines the position $x$ and velocity $V$ for each vehicle at time $t$. We also define this distribution for a single lane.

Modeling position and velocity as a distribution function, allows us to find interesting information about the traffic, as local density $u$. When we integrate the function $f^j$ under the velocity $V$, we find the density function for each position $x$ and time $t$. $u(t, x) = \int_0^{1+u} [f(t, x, V) \, dV]$.

Similarly, it is possible to find other important properties such as total number of vehicles, mean velocity, and speed variance. When the modeler adjusts a good distribution function, he/she can predict, at a certain level of confidence, the traffic behavior.

Finally, macroscopic models use average quantities - density $u$, velocity $V$ and energy $e$ - as dependent variables with respect to time $t$ and space $x$. We can model it as a partial differential equation (PDE), like an ordinary differential equation (ODE), but with more than one independent variable.

Curves that relate quantities are useful tools for traffic engineers. We can generate these quantities by models or observations in real situations. Two famous charts are flow-density and speed-density curves (see Fig. 1). The flow-density curve, also called the fundamental traffic diagram, presents how the flow evolves (vehicles per time) in different density scenarios (vehicles per space). For small density, the flow is low, and it increases as density increases. However, the flow reaches a maximum when the vehicles disturb how the drivers conduct and decreases until zero in a heavy traffic jam.

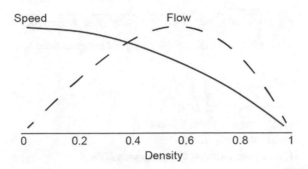

**Fig. 1.** Charts of flow-density and speed-density curves (adapted from Bellomo et al. [1]).

The velocity diagram correlates density and speed. Free speed is the average speed when the vehicle is alone on the road (zero density). When the density grows, each vehicle must adjust its free speed to the speed of other cars. When the density is too high, all cars stop.

## 2.2 Traffic Safety

These three kinds of models explain how a vehicle moves in a lane but without safety information. Some researchers focus their studies on understanding how to become streets safer. Most of these are empirical studies that relate the speed and accidents.

In a collision, the energy transmitted from vehicle to vehicle, or to pedestrian, is proportional to speed and vehicles' weight. So, the more speed implies a more severe accident (see Fig. 2). However, this relation is not linear. The "Power Laws of Nilsson" is the rate between velocity and accidents variations [2]. When the velocity changes from $V_1$ to $V_2$, crashes changed in a proportion of $\left(\frac{V_2}{V_1}\right)^2$, but injuries and fatalities changed more significantly, respectively in a proportion of $\left(\frac{V_2}{V_1}\right)^3$ and $\left(\frac{V_2}{V_1}\right)^4$. In other words, the risks of injuries and fatalities increase - or decrease - rapidly than the changes of speed.

Besides the effect of energy dissipation in a collision, the reaction of the drive varies at different speeds (see Fig. 3). If the driver spends the same time to react, this implies bigger distances when the speed is higher. In addition, the distance until completely stopping the vehicle is also bigger.

Castro et al. [5] compiled a few examples of road speed reduction and a decrease in accidents. At the beginning of the 1990s, London installed street radars that reduced speed at an average of 6 mph. It caused a 40% decrease in fatal accidents. In the US, the Insurance Institute for Highway Safety analyzed the increase of speed on some roads. There were 1.900 deaths caused by this increase, which was near the same as the death

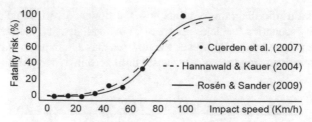

**Fig. 2.** The relation between fatality risk and speed (adapted from Rosén et al.) [3].

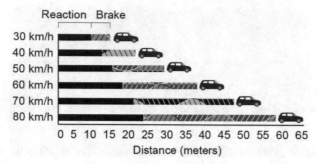

**Fig. 3.** Reaction and brake distance with different speeds (adapted from Australian Transport Safety Bureau) [4].

evicted by front airbags in the same year. This study found that an increase of 8 km/h on urban streets grows 4% the number of fatalities and 8% on interstates and highways.

## 3 Human Smart City

Mobility models are useful to understand how people move through the cities. However, there is little citizen participation in the creation of these models. The lack of participation limits the analysis, and it becomes very focused on technological aspects instead of the citizens' demands. For this reason, Oliveira and Campolargo [6] issued the term "Human Smart City", they claimed that new technologies are not an end, but they should be implemented with the engagement of the population in the co-creation of solutions for collective social change.

The concept appears to value a smart environment for smart living, with smart governance. The engagement between citizens and government is fundamental for the Human Smart City concept. For this, the city government should promote an ecosystem of urban innovation, which applies co-design and co-production of social innovation. The citizens' involvement in the idea generation is essential to build a trusted environment. If citizens collaborate actively with city administration, their ability to contribute to urban and social issues increase [6].

Co-creative partners could participate in multiple initiatives, which allows them to act as connectors that strengthen the social fabric. Mulder [7] believes that when a core group is shaped from a bottom-up initiative, it has support and remains representative for the community. "Co-creative partnerships benefit from strategic embeddedness and enhanced social learning through role-modelling which again enables a more powerful interplay between the bottom-up and top-down" [7].

An advantage of this concept is that the co-design and co-production of solutions become the city administration processes lighter and more transparent. However, a challenge ahead is how to involve the public sphere in civic life. Cities administrations need to build trust with the community and encourage citizens' collaboration. Therefore, it is crucial to identify different needs of the community. The city administration should not get feedback from a small number of citizens, but it is also important to "listen and talk" with all groups.

Manzini [8] defines co-design as a multifaceted conversation among individuals and groups who set design initiatives. In other words, a social conversation in which different actors interact in different ways (from collaborating to conflicting) and at different times (in real-time or off-line). For him, every co-design process includes the co-creation of shared ideas that emerge from a conversation between the social actors.

In this new process arises a shift from "city management" to "participatory city-making." A participatory city-making envision livable and sustainable urban environments with political, organizational, and cultural implications. The opportunities to engage with citizens, empower them and enable a social fabric to be increasingly reflexive and responsive [7].

In the case study that we present below, the technicians of the municipal traffic company knew the main theory behind traffic flow, however they probably are unaware of the potential of the communication and participation of São Paulo's citizens.

## 4 The São Paulo Case Study

In 2015, the São Paulo mayor changed the speed limits in the two main highways based on a traffic model in order to reduce the road accidents, which has changed accidents and traffic indices. However, this new policy generated conflict in part of civil society. As a consequence, after a new municipal election, the new administration returned the speed limits to the preview values.

As recorded in 2011, the transit fatalities rate in São Paulo was 12 deaths/100.000 inhabitants. Gradually, the municipality implemented speed limit reduction to halve the losses. In a context of a broader policy of speed reduction, in 2015 they changed the limits in two highways that cross the biggest Brazilian metropolis. They decreased the speed limits from 90 km/h to 70 km/h for light vehicles, and from 70 km/h to 60 km/h for heavy vehicles. In the arterial lanes, the limits decreased from 70 km/h to 50 km/h [9, 10].

The accident rates, as usually happens in other cities, decreased after the reduction of the speed limits. A counterintuitive consequence was the decrease of traffic congestion indices. It occurs because low speed demands less reaction time from drivers and less space for maneuvers. The results are fewer "slow traffic waves" and a less turbulent flow. The TomTom Traffic Index [11], which compares the traffic in the main cities, showed that the average travel time in São Paulo in 2015 was the smallest (see Fig. 4).

Despite the positive results of the new speed limits, the São Paulo government did not consider the annoyances generated by the limits reduction when they planned the policy.

Possibly, the perception of risk of fines was more impactful than the decrease in traffic lethality and fluidity. Public decisions did not regard the awareness of the population.

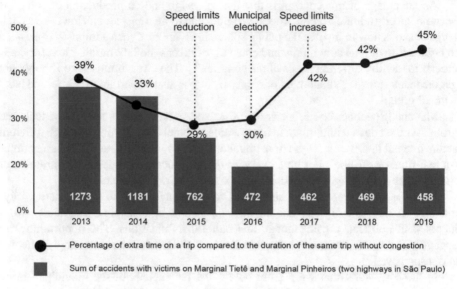

**Fig. 4.** Traffic index and accidents of São Paulo city [11, 12].

As soon as the municipality implemented the new limits, some entities tried to reverse the policy in the courts. They alleged lack of technical studies and public debate to support the new speed limits. They also claim the risk of becoming the traffic worst and an increase of robbery. In one petition, the Commercial Association wrote:

*"There is no way to escape the logic that the traffic in the Highways will flow 30% less."[...] "The reduction of the speed limits negatively impacts free circulation of people and products through the city"* [13].

In contrast, organizations of the civil society presented studies to support the reduction. Two examples of these organizations are São Paulo Urban Cycler Association and Brazilian Traffic Medicine Association.

After a few months, the first reports showed some results in the accidents and the traffic. Nonetheless, these good indices did not reflect the general view of the population. Opinion polls showed that 53% of people are against speed reduction, strengthening the position who questioned the policy [13].

The political opposition noticed the sentiment against the actions implemented by the municipality administration. In the second semester of 2016, the election campaign for mayor started and speed limits was one of the central subjects. São Paulo is a big city with more than 12 million people and has plenty of problems to solve. Speed limits are a technical parameter that usually does not appear in political speeches. In 2012, none of the candidates mentioned speed limits. Four years later, five candidates made explicit their intentions for this subject, three against reduction and two in favor - one of them was the mayor that implemented the policy [14].

The São Paulo population elected a new mayor with 53,29% of the votes with the slogan "Speed Up, São Paulo." Even after the election, some associations tried to maintain the limit, but in 2017, the speed returned to the former values.

## 5 Discussion

According to previous mathematical models, the flow goes down in a heavy traffic jam. Also, the accidents increase quicker with speed changes [1, 2]. Corroborating this data, the speed reduction in São Paulo presents slowness dropped 10% and accidents 35% [11, 12].

However, the Human Smart City concept presents the value of citizen participation in public decisions. Even with the interest of various groups in São Paulo society, there was no consensus. The population was divided, returning to changes and deteriorating mobility conditions. If the population had been called to participate in the discussions and decision making, the scenario would probably have been different. A core issue was the failed communication with the population. Generic messages, which try to reach everyone, reach only a few, especially when they intend to affect attitudes and behavior. When the government does not relate to various audience motivations, they do not speak to anyone.

For Frascara [15], this kind of problem occurs because it tries to affect ingrained attitudes. There is always a small group that is impossible to change through communications. Social interest needs that the target audience has been achievable. It requires identifying the subgroup that justifies a communication effort.

Frascara also presents a successful road safety campaign based on an extensive study of the arguments related to the local values and sensibilities. Despite this, only the information contained in a message does not motivate people to act in a given way, but a factor combination: the relationship of the values perceived in the communication with the public purpose, the source credibility, changes in legislation, and policy control.

The São Paulo disagreement caused a political opposition that was used in the campaigns of the following municipal election. A co-design process could open a dialogue with different interested parties. It engages with citizens and empowers them, changing the relationship to a "participatory city-making."

In this work, we studied the impact of speed reduction in only two highways. However, this same policy affected more streets and some of them maintain the slower limits until today. The long term effect of this policy is subject for future research. Another unanswered question is why the accidents rates in the two highways did not increase after the election - when the speed limits returned to the former value? This question also deserves more investigation.

## 6 Conclusion

The example of reducing the maximum speed of highways in São Paulo city shows the importance of people's participation in urban policies in a Human Smart City. Despite adequate modeling and positive results, a significant part of the population rejected the speed reduction policy, being reversed by the subsequent mayor. Understand the goal of different groups and adequate communication is essential for the construction of urban models and the implementation of public policies.

# References

1. Bellomo, N., Delitala, M., Coscia, V.: On the mathematical theory of vehicular traffic flow I Fluid dynamic and kinetic modelling. Math Model Methods Appl. Sci. **12**, 1801–1843 (2002)
2. Afukaar, F.K.: Speed control in developing countries: issues, challenges and opportunities in reducing road traffic injuries. Inj. Control Saf. Promot. **10**, 77–81 (2003)
3. Rosén, E., Stigson, H., Sander, U.: Literature review of pedestrian fatality risk as a function of car impact speed. Accid. Anal. Prev. **43**, 25–33 (2011)
4. Global Road Safety Partnership, World Health Organization, FIA Foundation for the Automobile and Society, World Bank. Speed management: a road safety manual for decision-makers and practitioners (2008)
5. Castro, C.P., Moita, R., Monteiro, B., Santos, E., Santos, G., Ribeiro, I.: Devagar e sempre: os efeitos da redução no limite de velocidade nos acidentes de São Paulo. In: 47° ENCONTRO Nac Econ – Econ Reg e Urbana [Internet] (2019)
6. Oliveira, Á., Campolargo, M.: From smart cities to human smart cities. In: Proceedings of Annual Hawaii International Conference on System Sciences. IEEE Computer Society, pp. 2336–44 (2015)
7. Mulder, I.: Co-creative partnerships as catalysts for social change. Strateg. Des. Res. J. **11**, 178–85 (2018)
8. Manzini, E.: Design, When Everybody Designs: An Introduction to Design for Social Innovation. MIT Press, Cambridge (2015)
9. Sarno, C.: Benefícios imediatos da redução das velocidades máximas permitidas: o caso das Marginais Tietê e Pinheiros, pp. 1–23 (2016)
10. Jardim, F.B.: Estimando o impacto da redução da velocidade máxima nas vias de São Paulo e o valor estatístico de uma vida Estimando o impacto da redução da velocidade máxima nas vias de São Paulo e o valor estatístico de uma vida. Fundação Getulio Vargas (2017)
11. TomTom Traffic Index. https://www.tomtom.com/en_gb/traffic-index/sao-paulo-traffic/
12. CET-SP: Relatório anual de acidentes de trânsito (2019)
13. da Silva Bastos, A.F., de Mello, S.C.B.: Lutas por significação do espaço viário: o caso da redução de velocidade nas marginais da cidade de São Paulo. Regimes Urbanos e Governança Metrop, Natal (2017)
14. Passos, A.B.G.: Limites de velocidade nas vias Marginais de São Paulo: Qual o papel do Direito na definição de uma política pública? Fundação Getulio Vargas (2017)
15. Frascara, J.: Diseño gráfico para la gente. Comunicaciones de masa y cambio social, 2nd edn. Ediciones Infinito, Buenos Aires (2000)

# Vibration Transmission at Seat Cushion and Sitting Comfort in Next-Generation Cars

Francesco D'Amore[⊠] [iD] and Yi Qiu

Institute of Sound and Vibration Research,
University of Southampton, Southampton SO17 1BJ, UK
{F.DAmore,Y.Qiu}@soton.ac.uk

**Abstract.** Sitting comfort in next-generation cars was explored using a key objective measure of vibration transmission. Connected, autonomous, shared, and electric vehicles (CASE mobility) will allow users to engage in several on-board activities. Within a laboratory experiment, the arrangement of the seat–occupant system was characterized with reference to performed activities in terms of "sitting configuration". Six males and six females occupying a car seat were exposed to four whole-body vibrations in four sitting configurations matching four pairs of activities. Primary-resonance modulus of vertical in-line transmissibility at seat cushion was calculated from acceleration measurements and used as the response variable of an ANOVA model. The model showed an appreciable main effect of both vibration magnitude and sitting configuration as well as a limited interaction between them. Conversely, it failed to show a main effect of sex and any sex-related interactions; nevertheless, for all treatments, the within-group mean value of the response variable was greater for males than for females. Results suggest that not only vibration magnitude but also sitting configuration and possibly sex affect sitting comfort in next-generation cars for CASE mobility.

**Keywords:** Connected autonomous shared electric vehicles (CASE mobility) ·
Posture · Secondary activities (non-driving tasks) · Whole-body vibration ·
Automotive human factors and ergonomics · Seating dynamics · Biomechanics

## 1 Introduction

Coming times will see the advent of connected, autonomous, shared, and electric vehicles (CASE mobility) [1]. On board, users will engage not only in primary activities (i.e., traveling and driving) but also in secondary activities (e.g., self-entertaining, socializing, relaxing, sleeping, working, and eating) [2]. In next-generation cars for CASE mobility, sitting comfort will be more relevant than ever; however, so far, the topic has received little attention in applied research [3–6].

Car-seat designers strive to improve sitting comfort by controlling vibrations transmitted through the seat–occupant system. To quantify vibration transmission objectively, it is customary to use frequency-domain response functions known as *transmissibility functions* [7]. The key local feature of a system's transmissibility function is its *primary*

© The Author(s), under exclusive license to Springer Nature Switzerland AG 2021
N. L. Black et al. (Eds.): IEA 2021, LNNS 221, pp. 615–622, 2021.
https://doi.org/10.1007/978-3-030-74608-7_75

*resonance*, which corresponds to the strongest vibration amplification; to characterize it, both *primary-resonance frequency* and *primary-resonance modulus* need to be specified. Within the frequency domain, these two quantities reveal respectively "where" the strongest vibration amplification occurs and "how strong" the vibration amplification is therein.

Several studies have been conducted to investigate the effects on transmissibility functions of features of motion environment (e.g., vibration magnitude [8]), seat (e.g., foam properties [9]), occupant (e.g., demographic and anthropometric characteristics [10]), and arrangement of the seat–occupant system (e.g., seat-back reclination and torso angle [11]). However, to date, the many parameters needed to specify the arrangement of the seat–occupant system have been considered separately and without any reference to performed activities [11, 12].

To explore sitting comfort in next-generation cars for CASE mobility, the arrangement of the seat–occupant system was characterized with reference to performed activities in terms of *sitting configuration* (defined as "activity-related overall arrangement of the seat–occupant system specified by seat position, seat orientation, occupant posture, occupant support, and occupant restraint"). Sitting configuration was adopted as a single compendious factor to facilitate the analysis of interactions with factors such as sex and vibration magnitude. In a previous study [6], a statistical model of *primary-resonance frequency of vertical in-line transmissibility at seat cushion* showed an appreciable main effect of both vibration magnitude and sitting configuration but failed to show a main effect of sex and any interactions.

For this study, the focus was shifted to *primary-resonance modulus of vertical in-line transmissibility at seat cushion*. Main effects and interactions of sex, vibration magnitude, and sitting configuration were examined. Main effects were well known for vibration magnitude [8], unclear for sex [10, 12], and hypothesized for sitting configuration. Little was known about interactions.

## 2    Method

A production car seat (NHK front passenger seat for right-hand-drive Subaru Outback) was rigidly mounted on the vibration table of the Six-Axis Motion Simulator of the University of Southampton. A handcrafted configurable footrest was mounted in front of the seat.

Four sitting configurations, labeled (self-) entertaining/socializing (ES), relaxing/sleeping (RS), traveling/driving (TD), and working/eating (WE), were selected to match respectively one pair of primary activities and three pairs of secondary activities [6]. The four sitting configurations are shown in Fig. 1.

Four excitations, labeled 0d28w, 0d45w, 0d71w, and 1d12w, were generated to perform an appropriate frequency-domain characterization of the seat–occupant system under "baseline" conditions, corresponding in order to the likely subjective reactions *not uncomfortable, a little uncomfortable, fairly uncomfortable,* and *uncomfortable* [13]. The four excitations were whole-body vibrations differing only in severity (vibration-magnitude values being 0.28, 0.45, 0.71, and 1.12 $m·s^{-2}$ in terms of root-mean-square value of $W_k$-weighted acceleration [13]); for the rest, they had simple direction (vertical in the direction of the earth's gravity), well-behaved waveform (stationary random with pseudo-white-noise power spectral density), wide frequency band (between 0.5 and 50 Hz), and sufficiently long duration (60 s).

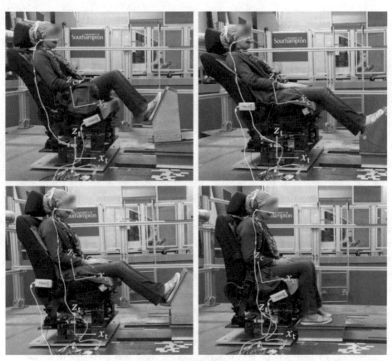

**Fig. 1.** Sitting configurations: ES (*top left*), RS (*top right*), TD (*bottom left*), and WE (*bottom right*). Coordinate systems: $\{x_t, y_t, z_t\}$ (*at vibration table*) and $\{x_c, y_c, z_c\}$ (*at interface between seat cushion and occupant buttocks*).

## 2.1 Participants

This study was approved by the Faculty Ethics Committee of Engineering and the Environment at the University of Southampton (ERGO II submission reference 41143). Ideally, participants were sampled from the target population of users of next-generation cars for CASE mobility. Twelve healthy adults (six males and six females) were recruited among students and staff members of the University of Southampton to form two independent groups organized by sex, namely male (M) and female (F). Major demographic and anthropometric characteristics of groups are shown in Table 1.

**Table 1.** Major demographic and anthropometric characteristics of groups.

| Group | Age / years | | Body Mass (Weight) / kg | | Stature (Body Height) / cm | | Body Mass Index / kg·m$^{-2}$ | |
|---|---|---|---|---|---|---|---|---|
| | *Mdn* | *IQR* | *Mdn* | *IQR* | *Mdn* | *IQR* | *Mdn* | *IQR* |
| Male | 28 | 3 | 79 | 14 | 180 | 4 | 23.8 | 2.8 |
| Female | 30 | 9 | 68 | 11 | 167 | 6 | 23.6 | 5.2 |

*Note.* $N = 12$ ($n = 6$ for each group). *Mdn* = median; *IQR* = interquartile range.

## 2.2 Measures

Acceleration was measured along the axes of the $\{x_t, y_t, z_t\}$ coordinate system at the vibration table and of the $\{x_c, y_c, z_c\}$ coordinate system at the interface between seat cushion and occupant buttocks. The two coordinate systems are shown in Fig. 1.

The frequency-domain response function was vertical in-line transmissibility at seat cushion (namely, $\{z_t, z_c\}$ transmissibility); it was calculated from auto and cross power spectral density of acceleration along $z_t$-axis (input) and $z_c$-axis (output) [14]. The response variable for statistical analysis was primary-resonance modulus of vertical in-line transmissibility at seat cushion; it was determined by inspection from the calculated modulus of vertical in-line transmissibility at seat cushion.

## 2.3 Research Design

A (balanced) three-factor mixed design was implemented with 1 two-level between-subjects factor (sex) and 2 four-level within-subjects factors (vibration magnitude and sitting configuration); accordingly, each participant received 16 treatments. Each treatment was replicated three times with each participant. Randomization was completely implemented for within-subjects factors and replicate; specifically, a different random sequence was used for the 48 tests of each participant. In total, 576 tests were performed.

A three-way mixed-design univariate analysis of variance (ANOVA) was used for statistical analysis. In accordance with the latest recommendations of the American Statistical Association (ASA) [15], no declarations of statistical significance are issued in this paper. Instead, to assess practical significance, $p$ values and point estimates are complemented respectively by numerical measures of effect size (eta-squared $\eta^2$, partial eta-squared $\eta_P^2$, and generalized eta-squared $\eta_G^2$) and by graphical representations of interval estimates (within-subjects or between-subjects confidence intervals at 95 % confidence level).

## 2.4 Experimental Manipulations

For each participant, tests were performed within two sessions held on two different days (each lasting between 2.5 and 3 h). After receiving instructions and training, participants would be secured with a safety harness, would be given ready access to an emergency stop control, and would be exposed to vibration while sitting relaxed but unmoving. To ensure that sitting configurations would be reproduced consistently across different tests, seat-back reclination and footrest configuration would be adjusted by using respectively an inclinometer and a set of reference stickers on the vibration table.

Measurements were performed at vibration table with one uniaxial accelerometer (Silicon Design 2260-005) and at the interface between seat cushion and occupant buttocks with a special-purpose triaxial accelerometer (HVLab SIT-pad-3-10g). Signals were acquired in MATLAB (version 8.5.1.959712) via the HVLab Human Response to Vibration Toolbox (version 2.0) at a sampling frequency of 512 Hz.

## 3   Results

Data processing was performed in MATLAB with a frequency resolution of 0.25 Hz. Statistical analysis was performed in RStudio (version 1.2.5033) running against R (version 3.6.2) [16]. The data set was composed of median values of the response variable (primary-resonance modulus of vertical in-line transmissibility at seat cushion) calculated across the three replicates of each treatment with each participant. There were neither missing data nor deleted cases. Within the data set, the response variable was between 1.5 and 2.7 (with median 1.9 and interquartile range 0.4).

A three-way mixed-design univariate ANOVA model of the response variable was fit by means of the R package afex (version 0.26-0) [17]. To protect against violation of the sphericity assumption, Greenhouse–Geisser corrections were applied to eligible statistical degrees of freedom. To mitigate the multiple-comparisons problem inherent in multiway ANOVA [18], $p$ values were adjusted using the Holm–Bonferroni method. Diagnostic plots indicated no obvious violation of the normality assumption for the model residuals.

The model showed an appreciable main effect of both vibration magnitude, $F(2.10, 21.01) = 61.98$, $p < .001$, $\eta^2 = .13$, $\eta_P^2 = .86$, $\eta_G^2 = .23$, and sitting configuration, $F(2.10, 20.99) = 44.28$, $p < .001$, $\eta^2 = .43$, $\eta_P^2 = .82$, $\eta_G^2 = .50$, as well as a limited interaction between them, $F(3.49, 34.87) = 3.99$, $p = .06$, $\eta^2 = .01$, $\eta_P^2 =$

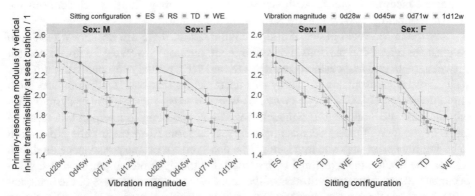

**Fig. 2.** Three-way interaction plots: primary-resonance modulus of vertical in-line transmissibility at seat cushion vs. vibration magnitude (*left*) and vs. sitting configuration (*right*). $N = 12$ ($n = 6$ for each group). Points are offset horizontally for clarity. Error bars represent within-subjects 95 % confidence intervals (not to be used for comparisons across different levels of sex).

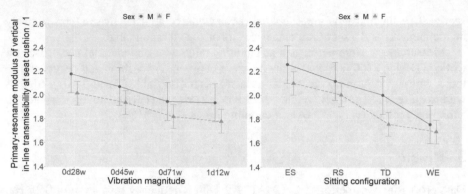

**Fig. 3.** Two-way interaction plots: primary-resonance modulus of vertical in-line transmissibility at seat cushion vs. vibration magnitude (*left*) and vs. sitting configuration (*right*). $N = 12$ ($n = 6$ for each group). Points are offset horizontally for clarity. Error bars represent between-subjects 95 % confidence intervals (not to be used for comparisons across different levels of vibration magnitude and sitting configuration).

.29, $\eta_G^2 = .03$. Conversely, it failed to show a main effect of sex, $F(1, 10) = 3.90$, $p = .31$, $\eta^2 = .07$, $\eta_P^2 = .28$, $\eta_G^2 = .17$, and any sex-related interactions, $p \geq .67$, $\eta^2 \leq .02$, $\eta_P^2 \leq .14$, $\eta_G^2 \leq .04$; nevertheless, for all treatments, the within-group mean value of the response variable was greater for males than for females. Three-way and two-way interaction plots are shown respectively in Fig. 2 and Fig. 3.

## 4   Discussion

The observed values of the response variable (primary-resonance modulus of vertical in-line transmissibility at seat cushion) are comparable with those obtained in previous studies [8–12]. The main effect of vibration magnitude is well known [8]; indeed, primary-resonance modulus decreases with increasing vibration magnitude, which confirms the known "softening" behavior of the seat–occupant system.

Regarding the main effect of sitting configuration, there are no known results to be used for direct comparisons. For sitting configurations involving complete contact between thighs and seat cushion (i.e., RS, TD, and WE), primary-resonance modulus (as well as primary-resonance frequency [6]) decreases as seat-back reclination and torso angle decrease [11]. If a single-degree-of-freedom mass–spring–damper system with moving base were adopted as a model, it would be tempting to interpret this result in terms of variation of mass in contact with the seat cushion. However, for this explanation to be legitimate, an opposite trend should be observed for primary-resonance modulus. Rather, the result can be justified by recalling that the dynamic properties of the seat–occupant system (dynamic stiffness of the seat [19] and apparent mass of the occupant [20]) change as the weight supported by the seat cushion increases. For the ES sitting configuration, the limited contact between thighs and seat cushion may account for results out of the general trend.

The interaction between vibration magnitude and sitting configuration is just limited; however, the effect of vibration magnitude appears to decrease as seat-back reclination and torso angle decrease (and hence as the weight supported by the seat cushion increases). This suggests that the softening behavior reaches "saturation" with increasing load.

The model does not support a main effect of sex; however, mixed experimental designs are less sensitive to effects of between-subjects factors than they are to effects of within-subjects factors. Indeed, despite inconclusive previous observations [10, 12], the consistent trend of the experimental data may be justified considering the influence of body composition and fat distribution; specifically, given that dynamic response at resonance is governed by damping, within-group mean values of primary-resonance modulus greater for males than for females may be explained by males having proportionally more lean mass and by females having proportionally more fat mass (especially at buttocks and thighs, right at the measurement interface) [19]. If a single-degree-of-freedom mass–spring–damper system with moving base were adopted as a model, lower damping for males than for females should correspond not only to the observed higher resonance modulus, but also to an unobserved [6] higher resonance frequency; if damping is insufficient, though, the difference in resonance frequency can be small and go undetected. In any case, it should be noted that a possible main effect of sex would be confounded with the main effects of uncontrolled demographic and anthropometric characteristics such as age and body mass (weight).

## 5   Conclusion

This study supports adopting sitting configuration to characterize the arrangement of the seat–occupant system with reference to performed activities. Results suggest that not only vibration magnitude but also sitting configuration and possibly sex affect sitting comfort in next-generation cars for CASE mobility. By using a larger sample size, these findings may be generalized to the target population of users of next-generation cars for CASE mobility. Future research should consider different seat designs, motion environments, response functions, and response variables.

**Acknowledgments.** This study was supported by NHK Spring Company (Japan).

## References

1. D'Amore, F., Qiu, Y.: Whole-body oscillatory motion and road-transport innovations: a human-factors-and-ergonomics perspective within a ride-quality framework. In: Zioupos, P. (ed.) 52nd UK Conference on Human Responses to Vibration, pp. 1–14. Cranfield University Press, Shrivenham (2017)
2. Pettersson, I., Karlsson, I.C.M.-A.: Setting the stage for autonomous cars: a pilot study of future autonomous driving experiences. IET Intell. Transp. Syst. **9**, 694–701 (2015)
3. Reed, M.: Applicability of occupant packaging and interior ergonomics tools to highly automated vehicles. SAE Technical Paper Series 2018-01-0845, pp. 1–7 (2018)

4. Parida, S., Mallavarapu, S., Abanteriba, S., Franz, M., Gruener, W.: Seating postures for autonomous driving secondary activities. In: Chen, Y.-W., Zimmermann, A., Howlett, R.J., Jain, L.C. (eds.) Innovation in Medicine and Healthcare Systems, and Multimedia, pp. 423–434. Springer, Singapore (2019)
5. Burkhard, G., Vos, S., Munzinger, N., Enders, E., Schramm, D.: Requirements on driving dynamics in autonomous driving with regard to motion and comfort. In: 18th Stuttgart International Symposium. Automotive and Engine Technology, pp. 683–697. Springer, Wiesbaden (2018)
6. D'Amore, F., Qiu, Y.: Next-generation cars, secondary activities, and sitting configurations: in-line transmission of vertical vibration at seat cushion. In: 54th UK Conference on Human Responses to Vibration. Edinburgh Napier University, Edinburgh, UK (2019)
7. ISO 2041:2018: Mechanical vibration, shock and condition monitoring. Vocabulary. International Organization for Standardization, Geneva, Switzerland (2018)
8. Walton, K.A.J.: Effect of vibration magnitude on the transmission of vertical vibration through car seating. In: 42nd UK Conference on Human Responses to Vibration, Chilworth Manor, Southampton, UK (2007)
9. Zhang, X., Qiu, Y., Griffin, M.J.: Transmission of vertical vibration through a seat: effect of thickness of foam cushions at the seat pan and the backrest. Int. J. Ind. Ergon. **48**, 36–45 (2015)
10. Toward, M.G.R., Griffin, M.J.: The transmission of vertical vibration through seats: influence of the characteristics of the human body. J. Sound Vib. **330**, 6526–6543 (2011)
11. Houghton, T.J.C.: The effect of backrest inclination on the transmission of vertical vibration through an automotive seat. In: 38th UK Conference on Human Responses to Vibration. Institute of Naval Medicine, Gosport, UK (2003)
12. Corbridge, C., Griffin, M.J., Harborough, P.R.: Seat dynamics and passenger comfort. Proc. Inst. Mech. Eng. Part F: J. Rail Rapid Transit **203**, 57–64 (1989)
13. ISO 2631-1:1997: Mechanical vibration and shock. Evaluation of human exposure to whole-body vibration. Part 1: General requirements. International Organization for Standardization, Geneva, Switzerland (1997)
14. ISO 18431-1:2005: Mechanical vibration and shock. Signal processing. Part 1: General introduction. International Organization for Standardization, Geneva, Switzerland (2005)
15. Wasserstein, R.L., Schirm, A.L., Lazar, N.A.: Moving to a world beyond "$p < 0.05$". Am. Stat. **73**, 1–19 (2019)
16. R Core Team: R. A language and environment for statistical computing. R Foundation for Statistical Computing, Vienna, Austria (2019)
17. Singmann, H., Bolker, B., Westfall, J., Aust, F., Ben-Shachar, M.S.: afex. Analysis of factorial experiments. R package (2020)
18. Cramer, A.O.J., van Ravenzwaaij, D., Matzke, D., Steingroever, H., Wetzels, R., Grasman, R.P.P.P., Waldorp, L.J., Wagenmakers, E.-J.: Hidden multiplicity in exploratory multiway ANOVA: prevalence and remedies. Psychon. Bull. Rev. **23**, 640–647 (2016)
19. Wei, L.: Predicting transmissibility of car seats from the seat impedance and the apparent mass of the human body. Institute of Sound and Vibration Research. Doctoral thesis. University of Southampton, Southampton, UK (2000)
20. Toward, M.G.R., Griffin, M.J.: Apparent mass of the human body in the vertical direction: effect of seat backrest. J. Sound Vib. **327**, 657–669 (2009)
21. Karastergiou, K., Smith, S.R., Greenberg, A.S., Fried, S.K.: Sex differences in human adipose tissues. The biology of pear shape. Biol. Sex Differ. **3**, 1–12 (2012)

# Why is the Automation Not Available and When Can I Use It?

Simon Danner$^{(\boxtimes)}$ (iD), Tobias Hecht(iD), Benjamin Steidl, and Klaus Bengler(iD)

Chair of Ergonomics, Technical University of Munich, Garching, Germany
simon.danner@tum.de

**Abstract.** To this point, research regarding Human-Machine Interfaces (HMIs) and information needs in automated vehicles has focused on the period when the automation is active whereas this study investigated information needs regarding an AutomSSSated Driving System (ADS) while the same is not available. A driving simulator study ($N = 34$) was conducted to measure the effects of displaying the time until the automation will be available as well as reasons for non-availability on subjective ratings of the system and perceived system understanding. No effects were found for subjective ratings as usability, acceptance and workload, but there was a significant increase in perceived system understanding. Even though acceptance and usability showed no significant increase, participants ranked HMI concepts containing additional information higher than the baseline concept. The results indicate that HMIs giving information on the automation while it is not available are perceived favorably by participants and can increase transparency of the automation.

**Keywords:** Automated driving · Driving simulator study · Human-machine interface · Automation availability · Mental model

## 1 Introduction

Lower levels of automated driving are available today, while higher levels such as SAE Level 3 and 4, which allow users to conduct non-driving related activities (NDRAs) [1] are estimated to hit the market in near future. In fact, the possibility to conduct NDRAs seems to be one of the main reasons to use such ADS [2]. Even though future users have no experience with automated vehicles (AVs), their mental models regarding AVs are based upon their expectations towards the usage. It is important to investigate those expectations and mental models and therefore ways of correcting them, since in some cases they might not correspond to the reality and the correctness of mental models could affect the quality of human-machine interaction [3]. Giving information on the availability of ADS while driving manually is a possibility to correct users' mental models, which is investigated in this study with special focus on periods of non-availability.

© The Author(s), under exclusive license to Springer Nature Switzerland AG 2021
N. L. Black et al. (Eds.): IEA 2021, LNNS 221, pp. 623–632, 2021.
https://doi.org/10.1007/978-3-030-74608-7_76

## 1.1 System Understanding and Mental Models

Automated vehicles will be more complicated than advanced driver-assistance systems (ADAS) [4] and human operators will not always understand when an ADS is not available [5] and could even believe that SAE level 3 automated driving functions have to be available continuously, at least on highways [2]. Future users might initially use an ADS without experience but with having expectations leading to an internal representation of the system's functionalities, which might not correspond to the actual ADS capabilities [6]. This is in accordance with the finding that drivers over-rely on automated driving functions [7] resulting from a lack of understanding of how the systems work and what their limitations are [8]. The expectations towards and the understanding of the ADS are part of the users' mental models, as a mental model is the representation of a process or a system with its functionalities and dependencies in a person's mind [9]. When it comes to new experiences, existent mental models are compared to the perceived reality and in case the model was incorrect, it is adapted [3, 10]. Therefore, functionalities or limitations of a system as part of the mental model are not necessarily constant, since not experienced limitations can be erased from the model. Beggiato & Krems (2013) [3] found that known limitations of an ACC got forgotten after five rides without experiencing this limitation. This can lead to a mismatch between the expectations and the actual situation potentially causing ADS surprise [5] and frustration [11].

## 1.2 Information on the ADS When Not Available to Enhance System Understanding

Future users of SAE Level 3 and 4 automated driving functions will most likely lack of a deep understanding of the ADS and its limitations due to a lack of training [8] and reasons for non-availability of the function will not always be obvious for drivers, analogue to reasons for requests to intervene (RtIs) [12].

In an exploratory driving simulator study investigating potential information needs regarding an ADS, participants asked for a display of the reasons for non-availability as well as for a display of the time until the ADS will be available again [2]. Danner, Pfromm & Bengler (2020) [13] conducted a study showing that the display of the availability duration of a SAE Level 3 automation before activating the same influences drivers' behavior and rating of the system. Wandtner, Schömig & Schmidt (2018) [14] investigated information on the duration of availability and non-availability periods while driving manually and automatically, but the effect of this display while driving manually was not questioned in this study.

Information on the reasons for RtIs were shown to enhance perceived system understanding during a transition to manual driving [12]. Furthermore, the display of the availability duration before and after activating the ADS can have positive effects on subjective ratings of the system [13, 15–17]. Thus, these types of information shall be adapted to design an HMI giving information on the ADS while the same is not available. Hence, the newly designed HMI gives information on when the ADS will be available and displays the reasons for the current non-availability. Consequently, giving these information is hypothesized to correct the mental model and therefore might enhance the perceived system understanding and the subjective ratings of the ADS and its HMI.

## 2    Research Objectives

Based on considerations outlined above, this study aims at investigating the effect of additional information regarding an ADS when it is not available. Therefore, three HMI concepts were designed containing different amounts of information. One baseline concept (BC) is compared to two advanced concepts. Advanced concept one (AC1) contains information on how long it takes until the ADS will be available. Advanced concept two (AC2) contains the same information as AC1 but additionally informs about the reasons the ADS is not available. Furthermore, as reasons for non-availability are not always obvious, these concepts are compared on routes where the reasons are either visible for the driver or not. The concepts are investigated regarding acceptance, usability, workload, which are important measures for evaluating HMIs [18], and perceived system understanding.

Hence the following research questions are aimed to be answered in this work:

1. Is there a difference in the perceived system understanding in dependency of the presence or absence of information on the ADS when it is not available?
2. Is there a difference in the subjective ratings of the system in dependency of the presence or absence of information on when the ADS will be available?
3. Is there a difference in the subjective ratings of the system in dependency of the presence or absence of information on the reasons for non-availability of the ADS?
4. Is there a difference in the subjective measures (acceptance, usability and workload) in dependency of the obviousness of reasons for non-availability of the ADS?

## 3    Methods

### 3.1    Experimental Design, HMI Concepts and Procedure

To answer the research questions a $2 \times 3$ mixed design was chosen. The three HMI concepts served as within-factor while the obviousness of the reasons for non-availability served as between factor. The study participants were randomly assigned to either the group "obvious reasons" (OR) or to the group "non-obvious reasons" (NOR). The obvious reasons were a construction work on the highway and afterwards a missing lane marking. The non-obvious reasons were sensor error and missing map data. Moreover, in both conditions an additional reason (connection problem) was displayed. The participants experienced three rides with three different HMI concepts, always on the same route. The order of the HMI concepts was randomized to minimize sequence effects. The participants started on a highway resting area and joined the highway. The ADS was not available at the beginning. The BC gave no information on the ADS, AC1 displayed the time until the ADS will be available and AC2 displayed the duration as well as the reasons for non-availability. The manual drive took about 5 min. Subsequently, the ADS became available and the participants could drive automatically. When driving automatically, the participants were instructed to conduct an NDRA, which consisted of the game "2049" presented on a tablet computer simulating the central information display (CID). The automated drive took about three minutes. Afterwards, a highway exit appeared and an RtI requested the participants to take over the control over the vehicle again. The reason for this RtI was the highway exit, which should be taken to be able to follow the route. The rest of the track led over a country road into a small city, where the participants stopped the car at a parking lot. After each experimental drive, subjective questionnaires were administered.

Regarding the HMI, the availability duration of the ADS was given when active [15, 17] and when available but still not activated [13]. Therefore, during the automated drive all concepts were the same. Figure 1 shows the HMI-concept displayed while the ADS was not available for AC2. The duration until the ADS will be available was shown in the top left corner for AC1 and AC2, explained by the words "automation available in X min". For AC2 the reasons for non-availability were displayed in the top right corner. An icon and a descriptive text was given, as in this example "impediment due to construction site", along with the text " +1 further". Participants had the chance to press the ADS button on the steering wheel while the ADS was not available to access a pop-up window displaying further reasons (also shown in Fig. 1). Since the participants were not instructed to try this button when the ADS was not available, it was anticipated that not all participants would see the pop-up. For this reason, a short drive was conducted after filling in the last standardized questionnaire and rating the perceived system understanding, where participants were instructed to try the button when the ADS was not available. Afterwards the pop-up as well as the interaction was rated.

**Fig. 1.** The left picture shows the HMI for AC2 during a period of non-availability. AC1 was the same only without the reason for non-availability in the upper right corner. BL was the same as AC1 but without the time until availability in the top left corner. The right picture shows the pop-up in AC2 ("no automation available, due to insufficient map data and loss of connection").

### 3.2   Apparatus and Measures

**Driving Simulator:** The study was conducted in the driving simulator of the Chair of Ergonomics offering a 120° view due to three 55″ displays. The simulator is equipped with a motion platform, capable of simulating pitch and role motions. Side mirrors were displayed by smaller displays while the view of the rare mirror was integrated in the top of the middle screen. An additional display behind the steering wheel served as the Instrument Cluster (IC). For this study, the driving simulator was equipped with an ADS of SAE Level 3, which was only available on highways. To activate the ADS, the participants had to press a button on the steering wheel. To deactivate the ADS, the same button as for the activation could be used as well as the accelerator or brake paddle.

**Acceptance:** Acceptance was measured by means of the acceptance scale [19], using a semantic differential. The questionnaire consists of nine items and two dimension, satisfaction and usefulness.

**Usability:** Usability was measured using the System Usability Scale (SUS) [20]. This scale consists of 10 items, answered on a 5-point Likert scale. The overall score is built by summing the single answers (having scores from 0 to 4) and multiplying the sum by 2.5. Therefore, the highest possible value is 100.

**Workload:** NASA-rTLX is used for measuring the perceived workload. This is the short form of the NASA TLX. It has shown to be equally sensitive like the original. It consists of 6 scales answered from 0 to 20. The overall score is built by building the mean of the 6 different scales [21].

**Perceived System Understanding:** Perceived system understanding is investigated by administering two questions answered on a 5-point Likert scale. The first question referred to the time until the ADS will be available again ("I asked myself when the automation will be available again") and the second one referred to the reasons of non-availability ("It was clear at any point of time why the automation was not available").

### 3.3  Sample and Statistical Analysis

The sample consisted of $N = 34$ participants with an average age of $M = 30.59$ ($SD = 6.96$) years. Thirteen participants were female (38%). The mean duration of possession of a driver's license was $M = 12.35$ ($SD = 14.7$). Ten of the participants (29%) had already taken part in a driving simulator study and eight (24%) had already taken part in a driving simulator study concerning automated driving.

To answer the aforementioned research questions, mixed ANOVAs were conducted if the assumptions for parametric testing were not violated. If the condition of normal distribution was not fulfilled, the ANOVA was still performed, since this method is considered robust against this violation [22]. The alternative for ANOVA was the Friedman-Test. The statistical analysis was conducted using JASP.

Two questions regarding the perceived transparency or system understanding were asked. To answer them, a Friedman-Test was conducted for each question, since single item Likert scales cannot be considered interval scaled.

## 4  Results

**Perceived Transparency/System Understanding**
The first question referred to the understanding of when the ADS will be available. A significant effect was found for the within factor concept (Chi-Square(2) = 12.13; $p = .002$; Kendall's $W = .29$). Post-hoc tests by means of Wilcoxon-Tests revealed a moderate significant difference ($p_{holm} = .006$; $r = 0.50$) between BC ($Mdn = 4$) and

AC1 ($Mdn = 2$) and a strong significant difference between BC and AC2 ($Mdn = 2$) ($p_{holm} < .001$; $r = .63$), but no effect for the comparison between AC1 and AC2 ($p_{holm} = .25$). Higher values in this question indicate less understanding.

The second question referred to the understanding of why the ADS was not available. The Friedman test showed a significant effect for the concept factor (Chi-Square(2) $= 19.61$; $p < .001$; Kendall's $W = 0.54$). The post-hoc tests showed no significant effects ($p_{holm} = .056$) for the comparisons BC ($Mdn = 3$) vs. AC1 ($Mdn = 4$), but a large significant effect for BC vs AC2 ($Mdn = 5$) ($p_{holm} < .001$; $r = .70$) and a moderate significant effect for AC1 vs AC2 ($p_{holm} = .02$; $r = 0.47$). Here, higher values indicate more understanding.

**Acceptance:** Based on the literature regarding the acceptance scale [19], acceptance consists of two dimensions. Since our data did not fit the factor structure, an overall value for acceptance was used. This value was formed by adding the single item values and then dividing them by the number of items.

We conducted a mixed ANOVA to investigate the differences between the different HMI concepts, the difference between the two conditions (OR vs. NOR) as well as an interaction effect. The sphericity assumption was violated and therefore a Greenhouse-Geisser correction was used for the analysis. Homogeneity was given in all measures of acceptance. The ANOVA showed no significant results for the main effect of the condition (Greenhouse–Geisser $F(1.50, 46.63) = 2.57$, $p = 0.10$) and the group factor ($F(1, 31) = 0.60$, $p = 0.44$). Furthermore, no significant interaction could be found (Greenhouse–Geisser $F(1.50, 46.63) = 0.94$, $p = 0.38$). On a descriptive level is a tendency towards the AC1 ($M = 1.30$, $SD = 0.50$) concept, which received the highest rating, followed by the AC2 ($M = 1.17$, $SD = 0.65$) concept. The baseline concept achieved the lowest mean value ($M = 1.07$, $SD = 0.63$). The same order of subjective ratings can be observed when investigating the mean values dependent of the between-factor. The ratings of AC1 and AC2 are less different for the OR condition, while the difference becomes stronger in the NOR condition. The values for each condition are shown in Table 1.

**Usability:** For investigating effects on usability we conducted a mixed ANOVA. Homogeneity was given for every condition, while the sphericity assumption was not met and therefore a Greenhouse-Geisser correction was used. The ANOVA showed no significant main effect for the concept (Greenhouse–Geisser $F(1.4, 43.8) = 0.392$; $p = .646$) and no significant main effect for the conditions ($F(1, 31) = 3.058$; $p = .090$) and no significant interaction effect (Greenhouse–Geisser $F(1.4, 43.8) = 0.446$; $p = .575$). On a descriptive level, the averaged ratings are the highest for the BC ($M = 82.35$, $SD = 9.86$), followed by AC 1 ($M = 81.82$, $SD = 18.31$) and AC2 ($M = 79.62$, $SD = 17.40$). For the OR condition, AC1 is rated best, followed by the BC concept. For the NOR condition, the BC is rated best, followed by AC1.

**Workload:** A mixed ANOVA was conducted to investigate the workload in dependency of the conditions and concepts. The homogeneity and sphericity assumptions were met, so no correction was used for the analysis. The ANOVA showed no significant main effects for the concepts ($F(2, 62) = 0.270$; $p = .764$) and the conditions ($F(1, 31) =$

0.006; $p = .938$). Furthermore, no significant interaction could be found ($F(2, 62) = 1.436$; $p = .246$). Investigating the mean values on a descriptive level, workload was highest for the BC ($M = 5.32, SD = 2.61$), followed by AC2 ($M = 5.15, SD = 2.73$) and AC1 ($M = 5.09, SD = 2.83$). For the OR condition AC2 concept showed least workload, followed by BC. For NOR condition the AC1 concept evoked least workload, followed by BC. The single means for every group are shown in Table 1.

**Table 1.** Means and standard deviations for every group.

|  | Acceptance | | Usability | | Workload | |
|---|---|---|---|---|---|---|
|  | OR | NOR | OR | NOR | OR | NOR |
| BC | 1.17 (0.64) | 0.94 (0.69) | 83,38 (12.31) | 83.25 (6.58) | 25.45 (14.13) | 25.73 (13.64) |
| AC1 | 1.29 (0.61) | 1.32 (0.36) | 86.03 (14.28) | 77.34 (21.36) | 26.91 (14.74) | 24.51 (12.54) |
| AC2 | 1.28 (0.62) | 1.06 (0.69) | 83.09 (14.32) | 75.94 (19.98) | 23.91 (13.75) | 27.03 (15.02) |

**Qualitative Statements:** The participants had the possibility to comment on the different concepts. After each ride with the different concepts, they were asked if they had any thoughts regarding the ADS or if something was not clear during the ride. After the ride with BC, 8 participants stated they wondered when the ADS will be available and 2 stated they would have wanted to know the reasons for non-availability, while 4 participants stated that everything was clear. After the ride with AC1, 4 participants stated they would have wanted to know the reasons for non-availability displayed while 5 participants stated that everything was clear. After the ride with AC2 5 participants stated that everything was clear, two participant noted, that the non-availability was easily understandable. One of those participants remarked that the user interface was overloaded due to the display of the reasons.

After driving the three experimental drives the participants were asked to rank the experienced concepts by putting them into an order; the first rank for the concept they considered the best and the third rank for the concept they considered the worst. For the analysis, a concept on the first rank received 3 points, on the second rank 2 and on the last rank one point. The more points a concept received in sum, the better it was ranked. AC1 received the best rating with 78 points, followed by AC2 (75) and BC (45).

The answers on the question if the participants considered the ADS activation button on the steering wheel as adequate for accessing the pop-up with further reasons for non-availability revealed overall approving rating with a median of $Mdn = 5$. The question, if the display " +1 further" was adequate was also answered approvingly with a median of $Mdn = 4$.

## 5 Discussion and Limitations

The results of this study show, that additional information has a positive significant effect on the perceived system understanding. Transparency, whose increase is shown through the increased system understanding, is associated with trust in automation [23]. In this study, the displays which contribute to transparency do not contain safety relevant information and therefore no correlation with trust is investigated, since the definition of trust includes a vulnerability aspect [24]. Furthermore, there is no relation between the perceived system understanding and the subjective ratings of the system, which is why the effect of transparency on users' attitudes should be investigated in future studies.

Even though the additional information on the system aims on enhancing usefulness of the system, no significant effect on acceptance, which contains the aspect usefulness [19], could be found, but as described in the results section there is a small tendency for better acceptance ratings for the advanced concepts on a descriptive level. Even if both advanced concepts are rated higher, the acceptance does not seem to be increased in dependency of the amount of information, since concept AC2 is rated worse than AC1. An explanation could be that participants perceive the information of when the ADS will be available actually as useful as it helps for example with the planning of NDRAs, while the information on why the ADS is not available does not contribute to this construct. This is in accordance with the findings of [12], who have shown that displaying reasons for RtIs has no significant effect on acceptance and trust, but on perceived system understanding. Future research should investigate, if giving information on the reasons for non-availability helps users calibrate their trust in automation or if it is helpful to ensure a safe human-machine-interaction due to the formation of an adequate mental model of the system [25]. Furthermore, displaying reasons for non-availability might have a negative influence on the aspect of satisfaction, which is also contained in the construct of acceptance. Especially in the condition of non-obvious reasons for non-availability, the subjective ratings are worse in comparison to the other condition. Participants might simply accept when the ADS is not available and do not have the need to know why, especially in an artificial study context. The steady confrontation with technical reasons for why the ADS does not work might seem not helpful but could even be annoying. Therefore, it can be concluded that this display should not be shown permanently. Nonetheless, for users who want to learn about system limitations, this information should be accessible.

In addition, no significant effects could be found for usability, but a tendency on a descriptive level was observed. Independent of the condition (OR vs. NOR), BC was rated the best, followed by AC1 and then AC2. When the condition is taken into account, AC1 was rated best when the reasons for non-availability were obvious. In the NOR condition the usability decreased for AC1 and AC2. Participants might have felt an inconsistency in the NOR condition, since they perceived a road where they would expect an ADS to work while the displays in the IC signalized that it did not. Furthermore, the rating could be in favor of BC, since, regarding the information content, it is more similar to ICs in present vehicles. Nonetheless, especially for usability, the differences in the means were very small and the standard deviations in AC1 and AC2 were rather large, which is why these tendencies should be interpreted very cautiously.

There were also no significant effects for workload and only little differences between the means. This could be explained by the HMI concepts not being too distracting. For AC1 and BC, workload was lower when the reasons for non-availability were not obvious. This might be due to the more comfortable ride, as no road works were passed. On the other hand, for AC2 workload was higher in the NOR condition. This could be explained again by the discrepancy between the subjectively perceived suitability of the road for driving automated and the displays giving reasons for non-availability. This would be in accordance with findings indicating that discrepancies between a mental model and actual events – and as result updating the mental model – lead to cognitive effort [26]. Future research should investigate how non-obvious reasons affect the workload as well as the subjective ratings of the system over time.

It could be shown that the HMIs giving additional information were more popular than a basic HMI. One reason for missing significant effects could be that the information were not really useful to the participants, since they could not use the ADS the way they might would have used it in reality, meaning choosing NDRAs themselves which might be important to them. Due to the artificial setting in the driving simulator and the dictated NDRA, the participants might not have felt the urge to use the ADS and consequently, the information when they could use it and why it was not available had no effect on acceptance und usability. In future studies, participants should be in a situation where they really want to use or have to use the ADS to investigate effects on these standardized constructs again, since this research has shown that participants prefer the HMIs with additional information.

# References

1. SAE: Taxonomy and Definitions for Terms Related to Driving Automation Systems for On-Road Motor Vehicles (J3016_201806) (2018)
2. Danner, S., Pfromm, M., Limbacher, R., Bengler, K.: Information needs regarding the purposeful activation of automated driving functions - an exploratory study. In: de Waard, D., Toffetti, A., Pietrantoni, L., Franke, T., Petiot, J.F., Dumas, C., et al. (eds.) HFES Europe, Nantes, FR (2020)
3. Beggiato, M., Krems, J.F.: The evolution of mental model, trust and acceptance of adaptive cruise control in relation to initial information. Transp. Res. Part F: Traffic Psychol. Behav. **18**, 47–57 (2013). https://doi.org/10.1016/j.trf.2012.12.006
4. Parasuraman, R., Riley, V.: Humans and automation: use, misuse, disuse. Abuse. Hum Factors **39**, 230–53 (1997). https://doi.org/10.1518/001872097778543886
5. Carsten, O., Martens, M.H.: How can humans understand their automated cars? HMI principles, problems and solutions. Cogn. Tech. Work. **29**, 415 (2018). https://doi.org/10.1007/s10111-018-0484-0
6. Ebnali, M., Hulme, K., Ebnali-Heidari, A., Mazloumi, A.: How does training effect users' attitudes and skills needed for highly automated driving? Transp. Res. Part F: Traffic Psychol. Behav. **66**, 184–95 (2019). https://doi.org/10.1016/j.trf.2019.09.001
7. Naujoks, F., Kiesel, A., Neukum, A.: Cooperative warning systems: the impact of false and unnecessary alarms on drivers' compliance. Accid. Anal. Prev. **97**, 162–75 (2016). https://doi.org/10.1016/j.aap.2016.09.009
8. Walker, G.H., Stanton, N.A., Salmon, P.: Trust in vehicle technology. IJVD **70**, 157 (2016). https://doi.org/10.1504/IJVD.2016.074419

9. Bach, N.: Mentale Modelle als Basis von Implementierungsstrategien. Deutscher Universitätsverlag, Wiesbaden (2000)
10. Stanton, N.A., Young, M.S.: A proposed psychological model of driving automation. Theor. Issues Ergon. Sci. **1**, 315–31 (2000). https://doi.org/10.1080/14639220052399131
11. Ochs, M., Pelachaud, C., Sadek, D.: An Empathic virtual dialog Agentto improve human-machine interaction. In: Padgham, L. (ed.) Richland, pp. 89–96. International Foundation for Autonomous Agents and Multiagent Systems, SC (2008)
12. Körber, M., Prasch, L., Bengler, K.: Why do i have to drive now? Post hoc explanations of takeover requests. Hum Factors **60**, 305–23 (2018). https://doi.org/10.1177/0018720817747730
13. Danner, S., Pfromm, M., Bengler, K.: Does information on automated driving functions and the way of presenting it before activation influence users' behavior and perception of the system? Information. **11**, 54 (2020). https://doi.org/10.3390/info11010054
14. Wandtner, B., Schömig, N., Schmidt, G.: Secondary task engagement and disengagement in the context of highly automated driving. Transp. Res. Part F: Traffic Psychol. Behav. **58**, 253–63 (2018). https://doi.org/10.1016/j.trf.2018.06.001
15. Hecht, T., Kratzert, S., Bengler, K.: The effects of a predictive HMI and different transition frequencies on acceptance, workload, usability, and gaze behavior during urban automated driving. Information **11**, 73 (2020). https://doi.org/10.3390/info11020073
16. Richardson, N.T., Flohr, L., Michel, B.: Takeover requests in highly automated truck driving: how do the amount and type of additional information influence the driver-automation interaction? MTI **2**, 68 (2018). https://doi.org/10.3390/mti2040068
17. Holländer, K., Pfleging, B.: Preparing drivers for planned control transitions in automated cars. In: Abdennadher, S., Alt, F. (eds.) The 17th International Conference, Cairo, Egypt, 25.11.2018–28.11.2018, pp. 83–92. ACM Press, New York (2018). https://doi.org/10.1145/3282894.3282928
18. François, M., Osiurak, F., Fort, A., Crave, P., Navarro, J.: Automotive HMI design and participatory user involvement: review and perspectives. Ergonomics **60**, 541–52 (2017). https://doi.org/10.1080/00140139.2016.1188218
19. van der Laan, J.D., Heino, A., de Waard, D.: A simple procedure for the assessment of acceptance of advanced transport telematics. Transp. Res. - Part C: Emerg. Technol. **5**, 1–10 (1997)
20. Brooke, J.: SUS: a "quick and dirty" usability scale. In: Jordan, P.W., Thomas, B., McClelland, I.L., Weerdmeester, B. (eds.) Usability Evaluation in Industry. Chapman and Hall/CRC, Boca Raton (1996)
21. Hart, S.G.: Nasa-task load index (NASA-TLX); 20 years later. In: Proceedings of the Human Factors and Ergonomics Society Annual Meeting, pp. s904–908 (2006)
22. Blanca, M.J., Alarcón, R., Arnau, J., Bono, R., Bendayan, R.: Non-normal data: is ANOVA still a valid option? Psicothema **29**, 552–7 (2017). https://doi.org/10.7334/psicothema2016.383
23. Kraus, J., Scholz, D., Stiegemeier, D., Baumann, M.: The more you know: trust dynamics and calibration in highly automated driving and the effects of take-overs, system malfunction, and system transparency. Hum. Factors **62**, 718–36 (2020). https://doi.org/10.1177/0018720819853686
24. Lee, J.D., See, K.A.: Trust in automation: designing for appropriate reliance. Hum. Factors **46**, 50–80 (2004). https://doi.org/10.1518/hfes.46.1.50.30392
25. Bullinger, H.-J. (ed.): Software-Ergonomie '85: Mensch-Computer-Interaktion. Teubner, Stuttgart (1985)
26. Zwaan, R.A., Radvansky, G.A., Hilliard, A.E., Curiel, J.M.: Constructing multidimensional situation models during reading. Sci. Stud. Read. **2**, 199–220 (1998). https://doi.org/10.1207/s1532799xssr0203_2

# Modeling the Orientation of Take-Over Trajectories Using Mixed Linear Effects Models

Martin Fleischer$^{(\boxtimes)}$ (iD), Johannes Elbauer, and Klaus Bengler (iD)

Chair of Ergonomics, Technical University of Munich, Munich, Germany
martin.fleischer@tum.de

**Abstract.** As automation of driving emerges, the driver becomes a passenger. If an automation reaches its system limits, the driver is obliged to retake the control over the vehicle. Grabbing the steering wheel is essential to assume lateral control, however non-driving related activities enabled by the automation may interfere with this process. This paper showcases the method modeling the orientation of hand trajectories while grabbing four different handles. In a study presented in [1] the hand trajectories of 48 participants grabbing four different handles were recorded and modelled using a mixed linear effects approach. The present paper extends this research by modeling the orientation of these trajectories. As the grasping trajectories appear to lie on a two-dimensional plane, the angle between the trajectory plane and a reference plane was modeled in a mixed linear effects model with "lme4" [2] and "afex" [3]. The maximal deviation from the plane is 10.7 mm with a mean of 2.3 mm (SD = 1.3 mm). The data shows the small influence of individual (gender, age, dominant hand, body height) and the high influence of environmental (position and type of the grasping handles) factors.

**Keywords:** Digital human modeling · Take-over · Automated driving · Mixed linear effects models

## 1 Introduction

The automation of future vehicles brings new challenges for interior designers. Digital human models (DHM) such as RAMSIS [4] are used to include humans into digital environments streamlining the design process [5]. Project INSAA funded by the Federal Ministry of Education and Research seeks to add needed features to RAMSIS. One aspect is the modeling of the human motion executed during the take-over happening during the transition from automated driving to manual vehicle control.

Research indicates, that the take-over performance is influenced by individual and environmental factors [6]. However, factors influencing the grabbing trajectory in a take-over are not well studied yet. Motion simulation is often based on kinematic models. These give a detailed insight into the forces and momentums during the movement, but require motion capturing data, when using inverse kinematics. This is not feasible for the presented use case as one of the main purposes of the DHMs used for interior design is the reduction of participant studies. Thus, empirical models are the used. The motions

N. L. Black et al. (Eds.): IEA 2021, LNNS 221, pp. 633–638, 2021.
https://doi.org/10.1007/978-3-030-74608-7_77

modeled through this method can be for example grasping motions [7–9] or car in- and egress [10]. The important aspect is the leading body part. This is typically the hand or the foot, but could be any body part. The leading body part is modeled through empirical methods. The rest of the body is then "dragged" along through inverse kinematics.

[8, 10] describe a phenomenon that will also be exploited in the paper: Human movement seems to take place inside of two dimensional planes that define the orientation of the trajectory. This leads to a model consisting of two sub-models:

1. Plane model

   The first model defines the orientation of the motion. Since start and end point of the trajectory, which are located on the plane by definition, are known, only one orientation is needed to define the plane. The trajectory will be in this two-dimensional space.

2. Trajectory model

   The trajectory is modeled through a quartic polynomial function. This is described in detail in [1].

## 2  Methodology

The data presented in this paper has already been evaluated in [1], where the modeling of the trajectory and the participant study are described in detail. 48 participants were invited to perform grasping movements in a test stand while being recorded with the VICON motion capturing system at 120 Hz. To model the trajectories in [1] the plane model is not needed as the orientation of the plane is irrelevant to the trajectory model itself. The motion capturing data generated in the study is used to model the plane on which the trajectories lie with the procedure described below.

### 2.1  Modeling the Data

The trajectory plane is parametrized through the angle $\Phi$ between the trajectory plane and a reference plane. Future users of the model know, where the starting and the end point of their simulated movement are. Thus, it is sufficient to only model the planes orientation and not the position as it is defined by tart and end point. The following steps describe the modeling procedure in detail and are executed separately for each trajectory.

### Step 1: Finding Start and End Points
Two of the three features defining the plane are start and end point. The actual movement is just a fragment of the captured data, the rest is the resting participant at the start and end points. To get rid of the data that is not part of the movement the 50 first and last data points were defined as start and end points. All data that is within a 10 mm radius

around the start and end point is regarded as data that is not part of the movement and are scraped from the data set.

**Step 2: Determine Orientation of the Plane**
After the definition of start and end point a plane is fitted to have the least square of the normal distance to the trajectory points. The resulting orientation of the plane in combination with start and end point defines the plane completely.

**Step 3: Generate Reference Plane**
To parametrize the plane where the movement takes place a second plane is generated. The reference plane connects the start and end point of the trajectory and is perpendicular to the ground. The angle $\Phi$ between the reference plane und the trajectory plane describes the plane for the model as seen in Fig. 1.

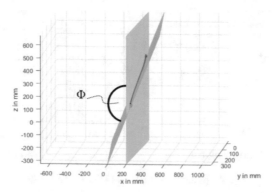

**Fig. 1.** The reference plane (cyan), the trajectory plane with trajectory (green) and the angle $\Phi$

**Step 4: Fit Linear Mixed Effects Model**
Through the "lme4"-package [2] a mixed linear effects model is fitted to the angles in RStudio:

$\Phi \sim$ Gender + Age + Dominant Hand + Body Height + Handle Position + Handle Type + (1|Participant).

Then the "afex"-package [3] is used to conduct a model comparison.

**2.2   Distance of the Trajectory from the Plane**

To test the presumption that grasping movements take place on a plane the absolute distance between the individual planes and the corresponding trajectories is calculated for every point. The maximum distance and the mean distance is analyzed.

Besides the individual trajectory planes another eight planes are fitted through the same method described in Step 2. The difference is that the eight planes are fitted to all the data within the same environmental conditions (e.g. cylinder, straight beneath the target, see [1]. The maximum distance and the mean distance is analyzed for all the 144 (three repetitions for 48 participants) datasets the plane was fitted to. This facilitates insight to how the interpretation would look, if individual factors were discarded and only environmental factors were looked at.

## 3   Results

### 3.1   The Plane Model

The scaled residuals show three or four groups (see Fig. 2). The same manifests in the Histogram (see Fig. 2). $R^2_m$ and $R^2_c$ of the model are .61 and .64.

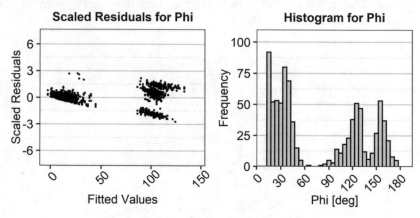

**Fig. 2.** Scaled residuals and Histogram for Φ

The ANOVA results from "afex" are shown in Table 1. The environmental factors "Handle Position" and "Handle Type" are significant with $F(1, 1097.07) = 4.7$, $p < .001$ and $F(1,1097.08) = 4.7$, $p = .003$. The individual factors ("Gender", "Age", "Dominant Hand" and "Body Height") have no significant influence on the model.

**Table 1.** Results of the ANOVA model comparison

| Effect | df | F | p-Value |
| --- | --- | --- | --- |
| Gender | 1, 42.95 | 0.56 | .458 |
| Age | 1, 43.09 | 0.34 | .562 |
| Dominant hand | 1, 43.10 | 0.20 | .657 |
| Body height | 1, 43.02 | 1.38 | .247 |
| Handle position | 1, 1097.07 | 1914.39 | <.001 |
| Handle type | 1, 1097.08 | 4.7 | .003 |

## 3.2 Distance of the Trajectory from the Plane

The mean distance of the individual trajectories to their respective planes is 2.3 mm (SD = 1.3 mm). The 99th percentile of the distance is 6.5 mm and the maximum is 10.7 mm.

The analysis of the other eight plane-trajectory distances shows that the configuration with the highest deviations is the 3-finger-contact handle positioned straight under the target handle. The other configurations lie closely below it. The mean distance between the plane and the 144 trajectories is 11.3 mm (SD = 15.3 mm). The 99th percentile is at 39.9 mm and the maximum is 53.6 mm.

# 4  Discussion

The scaled residual and the histogram show that three or four groups have formed for $\Phi$ during the modeling. This indicates a lack of variables in the model. The environ-mental factors are highly influential on $\Phi$. These two aspects suggest that the categorical type of the environmental factors corrupts the integrity of the model. Metric scales for the environmental factors might counter the grouping. It is unlikely that other factors lead to a grouping effect. Factors already included in the model show no significant effect and since $R^2m$ and $R^2c$ are very close to each other, the influence of the random factor is marginal. This means that it is improbable for the individual factors to have a large impact on the model. Both $R^2m$ and $R^2c$ indicate a strong effect since they are large than .64 [11].

Comparing these finding to the trajectory model [1] the impact of the different factors is similar to the plane model. For both models the environmental factors are dominant, while individual factors play a minor role. The most notable difference is the influence of the body height. This factor seems to play a bigger role for the trajectory itself than the orientation of the trajectory (the plane).

Similar to the model the analysis of the distances between the eight planes and the trajectories shows the importance of environmental factors for the plane on which the trajectory lies. Compared to the average precision of the RAMSIS model [12] the deviation of the trajectories from the eight planes is sufficient.

The premise that humans move on a plane during grasping movements can also be accepted. For safety critical applications the 99th percentile is usually regarded as sufficient and leaving a corridor of less than 10 mm around the moving hand should be easily achievable in the interior package of highly automated vehicles.

# 5  Conclusion

When modeling grasping movements the trajectory can be handled as a two-dimensional. The plane on which the trajectory lies is heavily influenced by environmental factors and barely influenced by individual factors. It is to be researched if the grouping effects can be dissolved by switching to from categorical to metric environmental factors. Deviation of the trajectory from the planes is negligible and are equally or higher performant than the existing RAMSIS model.

**Acknowledgments.** This study was conducted in the context of the project INSAA funded by the Federal Ministry of Education and Research of the Federal Republic of Germany.

# References

1. Fleischer, M., Hetzenecker, A., Bengler, K.: Modelling take-over hand trajectories using linear mixed effects models. In: Hanson, L., Högberg, D., Brolin, E. (eds.) DHM2020. Proceedings of the 6$^{th}$ International Digital Human Modeling Symposium, pp. 178–186. IOS Press, Amsterdam (2020)
2. Bates, D., Maechler, M., Bolker, B., Walker Steven, Christensen, R.H.B., Singmann, H., Dai, B., Scheipl, F., Grothendieck, G., Green, P., et al.: lme4 (2020)
3. Singman, H., Bolker, B., Westfall, J., Aust, F., Ben-Shachar, M., Højsgaard, S., Fox, J., Lawrence, M., Mertens, U., Love, J., et al.: afex (2020)
4. van der Meulen, P., Seidl, A.: Ramsis – the leading cad tool for ergonomic analysis of vehicles. In: Duffy, V.G. (ed.) Digital Human Modeling. First International Conference on Digital Human Modeling, ICDHM 2007, held as part of HCI International 2007, Beijing, China, proceedings, 22–27 July 2007, vol. 4561, pp. 1008–1017. Springer, Berlin (2007)
5. Bullinger-Hoffmann, A.C., Mühlstedt, J. (eds.): Homo Sapiens Digitalis - Virtuelle Ergonomie und digitale Menschmodelle. Springer, Heidelberg (2016)
6. Gold, C.: Modeling of Take-Over Performance in Highly Automated Vehicle Guidance. München (2016)
7. Reed, M.P., Zhou, W., Wegner, D.M.: Automated Grasp Modeling in the Human Motion Simulation Framework. https://www.semanticscholar.org/paper/Automated-Grasp-Modeling-in-the-Human-Motion-Reed-Zhou/151ce68a1932ffc92be1abb6e78b56ab9b94e94a?navId=extracted
8. Arlt, F.: Untersuchung zielgerichteter Bewegungen zur Simulation mit einem CAD-Menschmodell. Herbert Utz Verlag (1999)
9. Faraway, J.J.: Regression modeling of motion with endpoint constraints. J. Visual. Comput. Animat. **14**, 31–41 (2003)
10. Cherednichenko, A.: Funktionales Modell der Einstiegsbewegung in einen PKW. München (2007)
11. Ferguson, C.J.: An effect size primer: a guide for clinicians and researchers. Prof. Psychol.: Res. Pract. **40**, 532–538 (2009)
12. Bulle, J., Dominioni, G.C., Wang, X., Compigne, S.: Comparing RAMSIS driving posture predictions with experimental observations for defining optimum task constraints. In: 2nd International Digital Human Modelling Symposium (2013)

# Driving Posture Assessment: A New Approach

Yanlong Gao[1,2](✉) ⓘ, Ralf Kaiser[1], Peer-Oliver Wagner[1], Bettina Abendroth[2], and Susanne Paternoster[1]

[1] BMW Group, Knorrstraße 147, 80788 Munich, Germany
yanlong.gao@bmw.de
[2] Institut Für Arbeitswissenschaft, Technische Universität Darmstadt, Darmstadt, Germany

**Abstract.** In this paper, a new theoretical model for driving posture assessment is proposed. Other than many models that focused on sitting (dis-)comfort evaluation, our model evaluates both sitting and driving activities such as steering and pedal control. By regarding both subjective and objective posture evaluation methods, we summarized several findings from literature in this field and extracted three aspects for driving posture evaluation, i.e., accommodating various sitting strategies, reducing physical strain, and allowing the optimum physical performance of drivers. Essential impact factors were selected accordingly to determine the essential parameters for a more holistic evaluation process. These could be used for further development of digital human modeling software like RAMSIS. The new model would potentially allow a more effective and ergonomic occupant packaging.

**Keywords:** Driving posture assessment · Occupant packaging · Digital human modeling · Biomechanics · RAMSIS

## 1 Introduction

One crucial task in the occupant packaging process is to place digital human models (DHM) in ergonomic driving positions to create a solid foundation for further cockpit development. However, it is not easy to define an "ergonomic" driving posture since it involves both subjective and objective factors.

The primary concern of using subjective evaluation results like preferred postures is that they could be influenced by many factors such as experimental setups, test subjects, or driving tasks [1–3]. Therefore, researchers have developed various methods to objectify the posture assessment. Nevertheless, a purely objective optimum posture would not always be accepted [4]. It could presumedly overlook some important subjective factors.

The sitting strategy could be one of them. Many studies have shown that different drivers tend to have different postures, which can be classified into various sitting strategies [5–8]. They are affected by both vehicle dimensions and the driver's body size. In practice, for example, RAMSIS uses its Posture Model to represent the influences of vehicle types and dimensions. Nonetheless, within a Posture Model, RAMSIS has only one sitting strategy called Neutral Posture. For inexperienced users, using one posture standard to evaluate drivers with different body sizes could lead to unreliable results.

N. L. Black et al. (Eds.): IEA 2021, LNNS 221, pp. 639–646, 2021.
https://doi.org/10.1007/978-3-030-74608-7_78

There is potential for improvement to consider the variation in sitting strategy during posture assessment.

In terms of objective evaluation methods, many sitting (dis-)comfort models have been established, using objective parameters such as pressure distribution or muscle activation to predict discomfort [9, 10].

Two widely used parameters are joint angle and joint range of motion (ROM). By measuring the joint angle to joint ROM ratio, passive muscle stretch can be evaluated. There are two limitations: first, the muscle activation cannot be evaluated using joint angle only. More parameters like joint load are needed [11]. Second, a joint ROM has several impact factors which are often not represented in DHM applications accurately. In RAMSIS, for example, the joint ROM are independent of each other. In reality, they are not for those joints crossed by multi-joint muscles of which the finite muscle length could limit the range of movement of the involved joints [12]. For a proper objective posture evaluation using biomechanics, DHM applications should have an appropriate physiological representation and corresponding parameters.

In recent years, more research about the optimum posture for driving has been done by using biomechanics regarding both physical strain and physical performance [13–15]. They have introduced a new aspect to the driving posture assessment that not solely focuses on SITTING discomfort but also considers DRIVING activities. It can be beneficial since optimizing the driver's biomechanical condition would potentially increase driving safety.

This paper proposes a new theoretical model for driving posture assessment that combines subjective and objective evaluation methods. We analyzed several important works in this field and arranged the findings into three sections: sitting strategy, physical strain, and physical driving performance. As a result, we extracted few key parameters and merged them into our model.

## 2   Analyses

### 2.1   Sitting Strategy

A driving posture is a result of the interaction between driver and vehicle interior. Therefore, it is affected by the characteristics of both [3]. Studies using subjective evaluation methods to examine preferred posture will have the results that imply these influences.

As an example, we visualized five preferred driving postures from four studies [2, 5, 7, 16] and compared them to RAMSIS Neutral Posture of the Posture Model "Car", as Fig. 1 illustrates. Each posture was reconstructed in RAMSIS using the mean joint angles of each recommended angle range, respectively. The torso reclination was set at 27° for all (same as the RAMSIS mannequin) for better comparability. Note that only [2] and [7] provided H30 values of their setups, while RAMSIS and [5] only documented vehicle types. The study [16] reported neither H30 nor vehicle type. Studies [2] and [5] measured both sides of the body; the others provided only symmetrical recommendations. Figure 1 clearly demonstrates the impacts of the experimental setup on driving postures. These posture variations could also be viewed as different sitting strategies under influences of interior dimensions, which confirms Park et al. [6] that H30 has a significant effect on lower body sitting strategy.

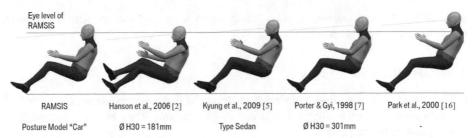

**Fig. 1.** Comparison between the RAMSIS Neutral Posture of the Posture Model "Car" and preferred driving postures from four studies [2, 5, 7, 16].

Furthermore, Kyung & Nussbaum [5] and Porter & Gyi [7] found that female drivers would have more flexed elbow and erect back, indicating that they might adjust the seat to sit closer to the steering wheel and more upright than male drivers, as Fig. 2 shows. Similar results can be found in the study of Park et al. [6], showing that gender has a significant effect on the upper-body strategy. Therefore, even though RAMSIS Posture Models like "Car" or "Heavy Truck" presented the H30 impact, other factors of the driver like gender or body dimension should be considered.

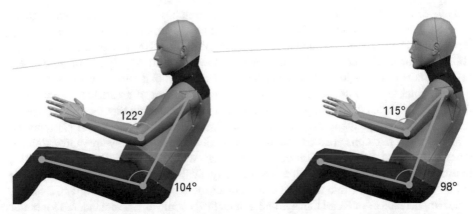

**Fig. 2.** Visualization of the preferred driving postures of a medium-sized male (left) and a medium-sized female (right) from Porter & Gyi [7]. The male driver has a more reclined upper body posture while the female driver has a more upright posture.

More importantly, a sitting strategy can reflect the driver's prioritization of requirements for basic driving activities. Wang & Bulle [8] found that, for most test drivers, the primary factor to adjust driving posture was pedal accessibility; for short and medium-sized drivers, the second factor would be road visibility, while for taller drivers, it would be steering wheel accessibility. If engineers are not aware of such differences of requirements and solely use one sitting strategy like the Neutral Posture to assess all mannequins, faulty evaluation results could occur. It can be an issue, particularly for the drivers with extreme body sizes, which will reach the seat and steering wheel's adjustment limits more likely. Accommodating various sitting strategies would ensure a driving posture to retain in a reasonable range.

## 2.2  Physical Strain

Physical strains like soft tissue compression, muscle stretch, and muscle activation should be reduced to minimize physical discomfort and fatigue. They can be grouped into passive and active responses.

### Passive Response

*Soft Tissue Compression.* Compression of soft tissue such as nerves or blood vessels is often considered as a reason for discomfort [17]. It could be represented by measuring surface pressure distribution, a commonly used method for discomfort evaluation and probably the most effective one [10]. Nevertheless, it can still be complex for ergonomic engineers to use this kind of information at an early stage of vehicle development, where the driver seat is usually not yet completely developed. Though, engineers can qualitatively examine whether there is enough contact area between the seat cushion and thighs while also ensuring that the cushion front does not interfere too much during pedal operation.

*Muscle Stretch.* An effective indicator of muscle stretches is joint usage (joint angle to joint ROM ratio) since joint ROM is often limited by insufficient muscle length during stretching. Therefore, it is crucial to represent the ROM in DHM properly. An effect that should not be neglected is multi-joint muscles since the human body has many of them [12], especially in the lower body. NASA [18] explained that "the movement range of a single joint is often drastically reduced by the movement of an adjacent joint" with multi-joint muscles due to their passive insufficiency, indicating that the ROM of these joints are not independent. For driving posture specifically, Porter & Gyi [7] reported that no subject had chosen a small trunk-thigh angle when the knees were more extended since the hip flexion could be limited by hamstrings, which are two-joints muscles. Thus, to evaluate passive muscle stretch more precisely, DHM applications should integrate a Joint Angle/Muscle Length function that includes the multi-joint muscle effect. Besides, other impact factors of ROM like age and gender [19] should also be considered for better accuracy.

### Active Response

Since human driving operations are performed through muscles, muscle activation (active muscle tension to max. isometric tension ratio) is a major factor to evaluate to prevent physical discomfort [11]. Other than passive muscle stretch, muscle activation cannot be assessed solely using joint usage without other biomechanical parameters.

One example is the lower leg muscle activation by accelerator control. If we only measure the joint usage, dorsiflexion of the right ankle between 5° and 10° would have about 16% to 32% joint usage, according to RAMSIS. It would be acceptable if the foot only rests on a surface without exerting force actively, which is not the case during accelerator operation. In a study we conducted in early 2020, 12 subjects sitting in a sedan configuration with 70° knee flexion, and 5° foot dorsiflexion experienced on average moderate to intense discomfort on the right lower leg during accelerator pedal control. Our surface EMG results indicated that they contracted the tibialis anterior (TA) at a higher level more often. It can be assumed that within such a posture, the TA was first shortened by the foot dorsiflexion and would have to contract more often and intensely to hold the foot in place actively. Therefore, it would lead to local discomfort more quickly than one with the foot in plantar flexion, where the TA was then passively stretched and no longer needed a high activation. Since plantar flexors are much larger than the TA, their activation level should also be much lower for accelerator control. Thus, to evaluate muscle activation more accurately, a reasonable biomechanical representation of the human muscular system and parameters such as joint load and muscle length should be considered.

Joint load changes with posture, and therefore the muscle activation also changes. During steering, for example, the shoulders with more stretched arms need a greater torque than a more flexed elbow due to the longer moment arm. However, the joint load alone cannot represent the muscle activation level, as Seitz et al. [11] discussed. Another essential parameter is muscle length. According to the Force-Length characteristic [12], the maximum isometric muscle contraction changes with muscle length, and the optimum is often at its resting length. For a given load, if the muscle is shortened or lengthened from its optimum length, the maximum isometric muscle contraction decreases, and accordingly, the muscle activation level increase.

### 2.3 Physical Driving Performance

In addition to a rational sitting strategy and lower physical strain, we suggest that an optimum posture should also allow drivers to achieve the optimum physical performance for primary driving tasks, which would benefit driving safety.

In addition to the Force-Length relation, the Force-Velocity relation [20] evaluates muscle contraction velocity. By concentric contraction, the higher the muscle load, the lower the contraction velocity. Therefore, to ensure an optimum muscle contraction velocity, i.e., reaction speed during driving, a posture should have optimal biomechanics to reduce the muscle load while keeping the muscles in the optimal length range to ensure a low muscle activation. In the study of Schmidt et al. [15], for example, the steering velocity of the more stretched arm with an elbow angle at 145° was significantly lower than that of a more flexed elbow at 95°. While the shoulders would generate more torque to steer and many arm muscles would also be lengthened beyond their optimum range and therefore activated at a higher level. Accordingly, the muscle contraction velocity would be lower, and the steering velocity could therefore be affected. However, this assumption needs to be examined by conducting more experiments, especially about lower extremities during pedal control, since few studies have been found regarding this aspect.

## 3 Theoretical Model

Based on the analyses above, the primary goal of our model is to provide a theoretical basis for a holistic yet practical driving posture assessment. As Fig. 3 illustrates, this three-level hierarchy is described as following:

First, sitting strategy: driving posture is influenced by characteristics of both vehicle interior and driver. It is essential to understand that drivers have different prioritizations of requirements for basic driving activities, and accordingly, they tend to use different sitting strategies. Accommodating various sitting strategies would ensure that the most basic but crucial driving abilities of different drivers could be met, such as accessibility of both pedals and steering wheel or road visibility. It would be the foundation of a realistic posture assessment.

Second, physical strain: if the first level is fulfilled, physical strain should be reduced to a lower level. On the one hand, passive physical strains like local tissue compression or muscle stretch should be minimized; on the other hand, muscle activation level should be reduced to a minimum level, which can only be assessed by introducing proper biomechanical parameters like joint load and muscle length.

Third, physical driving performance: if the second level is fulfilled, the optimum driving posture should allow a higher level of physical driving performance like faster or even more precise handling. Regarding Force-Length and Force-Velocity relations, engineers should determine whether a posture would deliver the optimum muscle condition to perform the primary driving tasks.

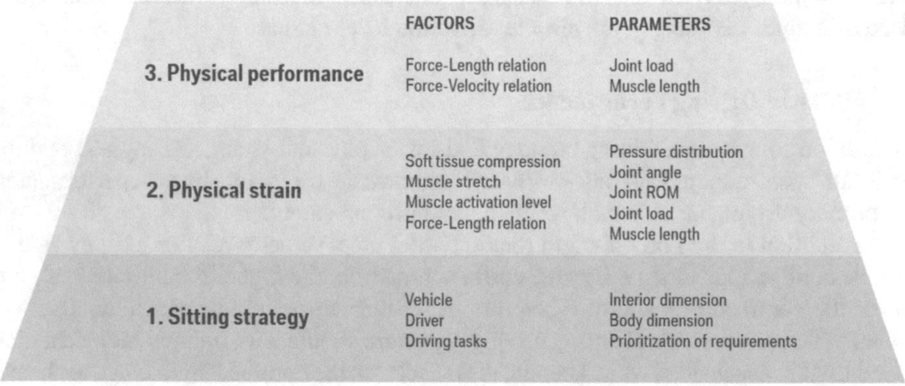

| | FACTORS | PARAMETERS |
|---|---|---|
| **3. Physical performance** | Force-Length relation<br>Force-Velocity relation | Joint load<br>Muscle length |
| **2. Physical strain** | Soft tissue compression<br>Muscle stretch<br>Muscle activation level<br>Force-Length relation | Pressure distribution<br>Joint angle<br>Joint ROM<br>Joint load<br>Muscle length |
| **1. Sitting strategy** | Vehicle<br>Driver<br>Driving tasks | Interior dimension<br>Body dimension<br>Prioritization of requirements |

**Fig. 3.** Illustration of the proposed three-level model for driving posture assessment.

## 4 Summary

In this paper, a theoretical model for driving posture assessment is proposed. Unlike many previous (dis-)comfort models for sitting evaluation, this model incorporates both sitting and driving activities regarding subjective and objective evaluation methods. It also includes the latest perspective in this field, which uses biomechanics to examine physical performance for primary driving tasks like steering and pedal control.

Nonetheless, further investigation and evaluation are needed. We will conduct an experiment on how lower body posture could affect physical strain and driving performance during pedal operations. Then, we will combine this result with the previous research about upper body posture. Ultimately, a dedicated tool for whole-body driving posture assessment could be developed based on our model for more effective and ergonomic occupant packaging.

# References

1. Fröhmel, C.: Validierung des RAMSIS-Krafthaltungsmodells. Technische Universität München, München (2010)
2. Hanson, L., Sperling, L., Akselsson, R.: Preferred car driving posture using 3-D information. Int. J. Veh. Des. **42**, 154–169 (2006)
3. Schmidt, S., Amereller, M., Franz, M., Kaiser, R., Schwirtz, A.: A literature review on optimum and preferred joint angles in automotive sitting posture. Appl. Ergon. **45**, 247–260 (2014)
4. Lorenz, S.: Assistenzsystem zur optimierung des sitzkomforts im fahrzeug. Technische Universität München, München (2011)
5. Kyung, G., Nussbaum, M.A.: Specifying comfortable driving postures for ergonomic design and evaluation of the driver workspace using digital human models. Ergonomics **52**, 939–953 (2009)
6. Park, J., Choi, Y., Lee, B., Jung, K., Sah, S., You, H.: A classification of sitting strategies based on driving posture analysis. J. Ergon. Soc. Korea **33**, 87–96 (2014)
7. Porter, J.M., Gyi, D.E.: Exploring the optimum posture for driver comfort. Int. J. Veh. Des. **19**, 255–266 (1998)
8. Wang, X., Bulle, J.: Identifying the factors affecting automotive driving posture and their perceived importance for seat and steering wheel adjustment. In: Advances in Applied Digital Human Modeling and Simulation, pp. 35–44. Springer, Florida (2017)
9. Hiemstra-van Mastrigt, S., Groenesteijn, L., Vink, P., Kuijt-Evers, L.F.: Predicting passenger seat comfort and discomfort on the basis of human, context and seat characteristics: a literature review. Ergonomics **60**, 889–911 (2017)
10. Looze, M.P.D., Kuijt-Evers, L.F.M., Dieën, J.V.: Sitting comfort and discomfort and the relationships with objective measures. Ergonomics **46**, 985–997 (2003)
11. Seitz, T., Recluta, D., Zimmermann, D., Wirsching, H.-J.: FOCOPP - An Approach for a Human Posture Prediction Model Using Internal/External Forces and Discomfort. SAE International, Warrendale, PA (2005)
12. Winter, D.A.: Biomechanics and Motor Control of Human Movement. Wiley, Hoboken (2009)
13. Kishishita, Y., Takemura, K., Yamada, N., Hara, T., Kishi, A., Nishikawa, K., Nouzawa, T., Tsuji, T., Kurita, Y.: Prediction of perceived steering wheel operation force by muscle activity. IEEE Trans. Haptics **11**, 590–598 (2018)
14. Pannetier, R.: Developing biomechanical human models for ergonomic assessment of automotive controls: application to clutch pedal. Université Claude Bernard-Lyon I, Lyon (2012)
15. Schmidt, S., Seiberl, W., Schwirtz, A.: Influence of different shoulder-elbow configurations on steering precision and steering velocity in automotive context. Appl. Ergon. **46**(Pt A), 176–183 (2015)
16. Park, S.J., Kim, C.-B., Kim, C.J., Lee, J.W.: Comfortable driving postures for Koreans. Int. J. Ind. Ergon. **26**, 489–497 (2000)
17. Reed, M.P.: Survey of auto seat design recommendations for improved comfort (1994)
18. NASA: Human Integration Design Handbook. National Aeronautics and Space Administration, Washington, DC (2014)

19. Amereller, M.: Die Gelenkbeweglichkeit des Menschen im Altersgang als Fokus wissenschaftlicher Forschung im automobilen Kontext. Technische Universität München, München (2014)

20. Hill, A.V.: The heat of shortening and the dynamic constants of muscle. Proc. Roy. Soc. Lond. Series B-Biol. Sci. **126**, 136–195 (1938)

# Goal-Directed Task Analysis for Situation Awareness Requirements During Ship Docking in Compulsory Pilotage Area

Karima Haffaci[1(✉)], Mia-Claude Massicotte[2], and Philippe Doyon-Poulin[1]

[1] Polytechnique Montréal, Montréal, QC 3T 1J4, Canada
karima.haffaci@polymtl.ca
[2] Montreal University, Montréal, QC 3T 1C5, Canada

**Abstract.** In this paper we present the results from a Goal Directed Task Analysis (GDTA), a variant of cognitive task analysis techniques, to extract the operator's situation awareness requirements. This analysis is done with 8 pilots from the Mid Saint-Laurence Pilots Corporation (CPSLC) on a ship docking scenario in a compulsory pilotage area. These findings are used to develop a tool to measure the pilot's situation awareness during the maneuver using SAGAT questionnaire.

**Keywords:** Situation awareness · SAGAT · GDTA · Pilotage · Ship · Marine navigation · Docking

## 1 Introduction

Marine navigation is a cognitively demanding task that requires the pilot to anticipate maneuvers long in advance, as the ship can take up to 30 min to come to a full stop due to its inertia. The pilot's situation awareness (SA) of the ship's surroundings and upcoming maneuver – or lack thereof – has been identified as a major factor in maritime accidents, but to this day only few studies have identified SA requirements for ship navigation and even fewer studies proposed a reliable tool to measure it [1, 2]. Moreover, there exist no study on pilot's SA in compulsory pilotage area, where the bridge authority is put under the responsibility of an expert pilot to maneuver in challenging seas, such as the Saint-Lawrence river in Qc, Canada.

In this study, we conducted a goal-directed task analysis (GDTA) during docking to identify the SA requirements and strategies adopted by pilots in a compulsory pilotage area. The article is organized as follows. Section 2 reviews previous works on situation awareness on ship pilotage. Section 3 presents the docking scenario and the interviewing methods used for data collection and Sect. 4 presents the main situation awareness requirements found using GDTA. Section 5 puts the results into perspective and offers direction for future works.

© The Author(s), under exclusive license to Springer Nature Switzerland AG 2021
N. L. Black et al. (Eds.): IEA 2021, LNNS 221, pp. 647–654, 2021.
https://doi.org/10.1007/978-3-030-74608-7_79

## 2   Previous Work

### 2.1   Situation Awareness

SA is defined as a person's perception of the elements in the environment within a volume of space and time, the understanding of their meaning, and the projection of their status in the near future [3].

This definition is based on a three-nested-level model developed by Endsley [3]. Level 1 consists of perceiving and attending the status and dynamics of element in the environment and is o fundamental in achieving SA. Level 2 is the comprehension of the perceived information. This phase involves integrating all cues collected in level 1 to determine their operational significance in view of pilot's goals. Level 3 is the highest in term of cognitive effort since it requires anticipating near future events based on the information collected from level 1 and 2.

Amongst the various cognitive task analysis methods, GDTA is a reliable method to extract SA requirements [4]. Rather than studying the pilot's task as with common task analysis methods (i.e., what the pilot does), GDTA focuses on the pilot's goals, decisions, and information requirements to fulfill the goals at the three levels of SA.

### 2.2   Ship Pilotage

So far, the SA research in the maritime navigation domain is in an early exploratory stage. For example, Okazaki and colleagues [5] proposed the Situation Awareness Global technique (SAGAT) as a method for evaluating the performance of apprentice pilots. To this end, he considered a dense traffic scenario and the key variable was to evaluate the pilots' recognition of the surrounding vessel during a crossing manoeuvre. Results showed the importance of integrating SAGAT technique in pilots' training programs. However, the research has tended to focus on one information to measure the SA (the recognition rate of crossing ships).

Chauvin and colleagues [1] measured the SA of officer-in-training having less than 2 year of sea time using goal-directed probes with 11 SA requirements in a crossing scenario in open sea on a ship simulator. Participants were exposed to a challenging interaction situation in which they need to make a decision among various options. The study demonstrates that perception of the elements of the environment is not a significant factor in the decision-making process. Interpretation of the rules and anticipation of the other vessel's intention seemed to have a higher priority in the decision-making process. Both of studies [1] and [5] are putting more emphasis on the impact of a poor recognition of the key elements in the decision making process. However, it's not clear whether the findings generalize to the work of more experienced pilots. Sharma and colleagues [2], who qualified their study as exploratory given the novelty of research in the maritime domain, conducted a GDTA analysis with 7 experienced officers during pilotage phase in open sea and presented SA information requirements at all three levels. However, the docking maneuver was not analyzed, neither was the context of compulsory pilotage.

## 2.3  Compulsory Pilotage

Compulsory pilotage areas are challenging navigation regions where incoming ships are required to be boarded and conducted by a marine pilot to its port of call. Marine pilots are highly trained officers who are intimately familiar with the coastlines, inland waters, shoals and ports of the pilotage area in which they are licensed. The bridge authority is put under the pilot's responsibility whose role is equally important to the captain.

The Saint-Lawrence river is one of the four compulsory pilotage areas in Canada spanning over 500 km of navigable water. It is administered by the Laurentian Pilotage Authority and licenses pilots are membered of one of two professional corporations: Mid Saint-Lawrence Pilots Corporation and Lower Saint-Lawrence Pilots Corporation.

# 3  Method

We conducted a GDTA study during docking at Trois-Rivières port, wharf 16 to collect the pilot's SA information requirements at all three levels.

## 3.1  Participants

8 pilots from the Mid Saint-Lawrence Pilots Corporation (*Corporation des Pilotes du Saint-Laurent Central, CPSLC*) took part in the study, with an average experience of 13.9 years of pilotage (std 8.3). They all had class-A pilotage license (ship over 210 m in length). The study received the approval of Polytechnique Montréal Ethics Research Board (CER-1920-05-D).

## 3.2  Scenario

The scenario used for the analysis is the docking at Trois-Rivières port, wharf 16. This docking is particularly challenging as the wharf is perpendicular to the river requiring 90 deg gyration to enter the dock and requires tugboats when the ship is longer than the wharf - Fig. 1.

An incident report that occurred in this section [6] summarizes the recommended docking maneuver as taught to all CPSLC apprentice pilots as follows:

1. *The approach* where the vessel should be brought from section 10 of the river until the entrance of the basin at an approximate distance of 3 vessel widths off the docks while maintaining a very low speed. At this point the pilot can decide whether to call for the help of tugs or wait for a closer point from the berthing zone;
2. *The use of anchor* near section 11, to reduce the vessel's speed;
3. *The turn* to be performed at 20 m from the corner of sections 16 and 17 with the help of tugs and the pilot's maneuvers (helm, engine propulsion);
4. *Final position,* decreasing gradually the vessel's speed and maintaining the bow on position with tugs assistance.

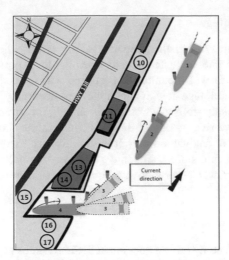

**Fig. 1.** Layout at wharf 16 and recommended berthing maneuver (from [6]).

### 3.3 Interviews

We conducted individual semi-structured interviews remotely using videoconference software to respect COVID-19 limitations. Interviews lasted from 60 min to 120 min and were recorded. Semi-structured interviews allowed us to extract a maximum of information from pilots and elicit their decision-making and cognitive processes during the maneuver. We used an interview guide that covered the main themes of SA requirements during a docking maneuver.

We constructed a preliminary interview guide and a hierarchical task analysis (HTA) of the docking with the help of a subject matter expert (SME) having over 20 years of experience. It was improved by making sure it covered themes from existing interview guides in literature [1, 2, 7].

The interview guide structure is illustrated in Table 1.

To support the pilot's recollection of the docking, we presented a video recording of the docking alongside navigation maps of wharf 16.

### 3.4 Goal Directed Task Analysis (GDTA)

The interview transcripts were analyzed to identify the three main elements of the GDTA: the goal hierarchy, decisions about goal achievement, and information requirements. The distinction between these elements was made according to the definitions and criteria provided by Endsley and Jones [4]. Each goal was broken down into sub-goals, decisions, and ultimately requirements needed for its execution. The requirements of situational awareness have also been divided into three levels: perception (L1), comprehension (L2) and projection (L3). Similar goals and decisions were grouped together to avoid redundancy. During interviews, we also presented to participants the intermediary GDTA results to validate the analysis and the vocabulary used.

**Table 1.** Interview guide structure

| Phase | Themes | Comments and data collection |
|---|---|---|
| 1 | Briefing | Presenting the research, record verbal authorization |
| 2 | Presentation | Determining the pilot's profile |
| 3 | Summary of the maneuver | Extracting the main goals and the priorities |
| 4 | Questionnaire based on the recorded video | Participants describe the video and answers to the SA questionnaire |
| 5 | Preliminary GDTA presented | Adapt the GDTA according participants' perspective |

## 4 Results

For the situation awareness requirements, we found 8 main goals, 50 sub-goals and decisions, 80 level-1, 26 Level-2 and 10 level-3 information requirements. The main goals are presented in Table 2.

**Table 2.** Main goals of the docking maneuver at wharf 16

| Overall main goal: Perform a safe docking mission in a reasonable delay |
|---|
| 1. Prepare a safe and efficient docking plan |
| 2. Obtain docking permission |
| 3. Moor the tugs to the vessel |
| 4. Maneuver the vessel on the established approach course |
| 5. Perform a 180deg turn to position against the current |
| 6. Make the turn in the basin according to the chosen approach |
| 7. Enter the basin safely |
| 8. Position the vessel at the dock |

An extract of the information requirements is presented at Table 3.

For decision-making processes, we found that pilots use two strategies for docking when coming downstream. The traditional method implies to overpass the wharf and to complete a 180 deg gyration with the tugboat or the anchor to position the ship upstream, whereas in the non-traditional method the gyration is done downstream such that the ship is perpendicular to the river current when facing the dock and the tugboat is used to stop the ship from drifting. The decision criteria for the method selection are the ship dimension and weight – where larger and heavier ships would benefit from the non-traditional method as their gyration speed could be insufficient for such a swift turn –,

**Table 3.** Extract of the information requirements

| |
|---|
| **Extract of the information requirements from the sixth main goal** |

**6. Make the turn in the basin based on the chosen approach**

    6.1. Determine the target location where the vessel begins its turn (at which position to start the vessel's gyration?)

        *Level 1 queries (L1)*

        6.1.1.Visual exploration

        6.1.2.Electronic Chart Display and Information System (ECDIS)

        6.1.3.Feedback from the officer at the bow of the vessel

    6.2. Make the turn

        *Level 1 queries (L1)*

        6.2.1.Force and direction of flow

        6.2.2.Wind force and direction

        6.2.3.Vessel manoeuvrability

        6.2.4.Current/desired vessel position

        6.2.5.Speed over the current/desired background

        6.2.6.Steering wheel

        6.2.7.Engine power

        *Level 2 queries (L2)*

        6.2.7.1.  Impact of external conditions on vessel drift and extent of turning: low, neutral, high

        6.2.7.2.  Impact of the vessel's performance and characteristics on the rate of turn: unfavorable, neutral, favorable

        6.2.7.3.  Impact of ground speed on the speed and magnitude of turning: unfavourable, neutral, favourable

        6.2.7.4.  Deviation between current and desired bottom speed

        6.2.7.5.  Control of engine power to correct the difference between the actual and desired ground speed: low, neutral, high

        *Level 3 queries (L3)*

        6.2.7.5.1.  Expected speed over the ground at the turn

        6.2.7.5.2.  Expected position at the turn

        6.2.7.5.3.  Magnitude and speed of the expected gyration

wind speed and water speed – traditional method is preferred with increased speed –, traffic, draught, manoeuvrability, propeller rotation and ship propulsion. When coming from upstream, the pilot can stay close to the wharf and start the gyration nose-in when the tugboat is midway into the dock; or stay further away from the wharf with negligible ground speed such that the gyration is done almost stationary.

# 5 Discussion

The semi-structured interviews provided us with a rich and detailed insight into how decisions were made and allowed us to collect a large amount of relevant information in order to develop a highly comprehensive GDTA structure.

It is interesting to note that even though there are two different strategies that can be used for docking when coming downstream, the 8 main goals and the information requirements are similar among all pilots.

To this day, few studies have identified situation awareness requirements for ship navigation and even fewer studies proposed a reliable tool to measure it [1, 2]. In both of these studies, the participants were unexperienced [1] or experienced [2] navigators. Sharma and his colleagues [2] noted a significant dependency upon pilot to provide certain information that would have a major impact on the navigators' SA. Therefore, it seemed fundamental to have access to the pilot SA in order to fully understand the impact of SA and information requirements on the decision making. To the best of our knowledge, our study is the first to target a specific maneuver (i.e. docking) in compulsory pilotage area, where the bridge authority is put under the responsibility of an expert pilot to maneuver in challenging seas.

There are three limitations to our study. First, pilots relied on their retrospective memory and explicit knowledge to describe the maneuver and we were unable to make direct observations due to COVID-19 constraints. This could introduce a recollection bias of SA requirements related to implicit knowledge. Second, our participants pool was only composed of highly experienced pilots (i.e., range A) which could have an impact on the evaluation of the situation awareness. Pilots with more experience may not orient their attention to the same elements and in the same way of pilots with less experience. Finally, it is important to mention that even though communicational aspect is a major element of the situation awareness as mentioned before, we did not analyze shared situation awareness between bridge officers and the tugboat, as we focused on the pilot's situation awareness.

Altogether, the results of this study will allow us to develop the first Situation Awareness Global Assessment Technique (SAGAT) questionnaire evaluating the pilot's situation awareness for the maneuver of docking. The questionnaire will be validated on a ship simulator in future work.

# 6 Conclusion

In this study, we conducted a goal-oriented task analysis to extract the SA information requirements of marine pilots in compulsory pilotage area during the docking at Trois-Rivières port wharf 16. We identified 80 level-1, 26 Level-2 and 10 level-3 information requirements and found that pilots use two berthing strategies based on the environmental conditions. The SA information requirements found will be used to develop a SAGAT questionnaire to measure the pilot's SA during docking.

**Acknowledgements.** The study was supported financially in equal parts by the Mitacs Accelerate program and the Laurentian Pilotage Authority. This research was also carried out as part of the activities of the IVADO Institute, thanks, in part, to financial support from the Canada First Research Excellence Fund.

# References

1. Chauvin, C., Clostermann, J.-P., Hoc, J.-M.: Situation awareness and the decision-making process in a dynamic situation: avoiding collisions at sea. J. Cognit. Eng. Decis. Making **2**, 1–23 (2008). https://doi.org/10.1518/155534308X284345
2. Sharma, A., Nazir, S., Ernstsen, J.: Situation awareness information requirements for maritime navigation: a goal directed task analysis. Saf. Sci. **120**, 745–752 (2019). https://doi.org/10.1016/j.ssci.2019.08.016
3. Endsley, M.R.: Toward a theory of situation awareness in dynamic systems. Hum. Factors **37**(1), 32–64 (1995). https://doi.org/10.1518/001872095779049543
4. Endsley, M.R., Jones, D.G.: Designing for Situation Awareness : An Approach to User-Centered Design, Second Edn. CRC Press (2012)
5. Okazaki, T., Ohya, M.: A study on situation awareness of marine pilot trainees in crowded sea route, p. 1530 (2012)
6. Transportation Safety Board of Canada: Government of Canada, Marine Investigation Report M12L0095 - Transportation Safety Board of Canada, January 2014. https://www.tsb.gc.ca/eng/rapports-reports/marine/2012/M12L0095/m12l0095.html
7. Lallemand, C., Gronier, G.: Méthodes de design UX : 30 méthodes fondamentales pour concevoir des expériences optimales, 2e édn. (2018)

# The Effect of Driving Automation on Drivers' Anticipatory Glances

Dengbo He, Dina Kanaan, and Birsen Donmez$^{(\boxtimes)}$

University of Toronto, Toronto, ON M5S3G8, Canada
donmez@mie.Toronto.ca

**Abstract.** In this paper, we report a secondary analysis of data collected from two driving simulator experiments to understand the effects of SAE-Level 2 driving automation on drivers' glances in anticipation of traffic events. *Background*: Current state-of-the-art consumer vehicle automation requires drivers to monitor the road and intervene when automation fails. Limited research has investigated the effects of automation on drivers' anticipation of upcoming traffic events. We recently reported two driving simulator studies that focused on drivers' glance behaviors before such events; however, we did not compare the results of these two studies. *Methods*: In this paper, we report statistical analyses comparing the glance data from these two studies that had 32 participants each, half of whom were novices and the other half were experienced drivers. The two experiments were comparable in terms of the driving scenarios that required anticipation: the first experiment focused on driving without automation; while the second focused on driving with automation consisting of adaptive cruise control and lane keeping assistance. Further, half of the participants in each experiment were provided with a self-paced visual-manual secondary task. *Results*: In the no-secondary-task condition, drivers in the automation experiment spent a higher percent of time glancing at anticipatory cues that indicated an upcoming traffic event than did drivers in the no-automation experiment. In the secondary-task condition, no such difference was observed between the two experiments. *Conclusion*: When there is no distraction to engage in, it appears that automation can allow drivers to have increased visual attention to anticipatory cues.

**Keywords:** Driving automation · Anticipatory driving · Driver behavior · Visual attention · Driving simulator

## 1 Introduction

Although recent advances in technology have enabled the automation of lateral and longitudinal vehicle control, driving automation currently implemented in consumer vehicles still requires driver supervision and intervention. Previous research has found that compared to non-automated driving, driving automation that provides longitudinal and lateral control of the vehicle is associated with slower reactions to events without environmental precursors (e.g., sudden lead vehicle braking) that require driver intervention [e.g., 1, 2]. However, driving involves not only reacting to such unexpectedly-onset events,

N. L. Black et al. (Eds.): IEA 2021, LNNS 221, pp. 655–663, 2021.
https://doi.org/10.1007/978-3-030-74608-7_80

but also the anticipation of and reaction to traffic events [3]. Cues in the environment can enable the drivers to anticipate how the traffic can develop. For example, a slow-moving vehicle in relation to a faster vehicle approaching it from behind, can indicate that the approaching vehicle may change lanes before it starts signaling. Here, the signaling would indicate the approaching vehicle's intention to change lanes unambiguously, whereas the cues leading up to it can facilitate anticipation. Even when relieved from physically controlling the vehicle in automated vehicles, anticipatory drivers (i.e., drivers who can anticipate upcoming traffic events) would be better prepared for situations that require their intervention.

Through a driving simulator study investigating anticipation in non-automated driving, our group has found that experienced drivers glanced more toward anticipatory cues that indicated upcoming traffic events and exhibited more control actions in anticipation of upcoming traffic events (i.e., had more anticipatory actions) [4, 5]. Further, secondary task engagement was found to reduce drivers' attention to anticipatory cues, and thus impede their anticipatory actions [5]. Our group conducted a follow-up driving simulator study investigating anticipation, this time in automated driving, in the form of adaptive cruise control (ACC) and lane keeping assistance (LKA) combined. The results are currently under review by a journal but have also been reported in the PhD dissertation of He [6]. It was found that secondary task engagement impeded drivers' visual attention toward cues, while no effect of driving experience was observed. In the current paper, we report a secondary analysis on data collected from these two driving simulator experiments, investigating the effects of automation, and the moderating effects of driving experience and distraction, on drivers' glances on anticipatory cues.

In a simulator experiment by Merat and Jamson [7], it was found that compared to non-automated driving, driving automation in the form of ACC and LKA was associated with slower responses to a lead vehicle braking event that could have been predicted 3 s in advance based on the behavior of nearby traffic agents. However, we could not identify studies in the literature that compared drivers' visual attention toward anticipatory cues in vehicles with and without driving automation. Thus, the secondary analysis reported in the current paper provides further insights to the literature on the effects of driving automation on driver anticipation.

The two experiments that we compare in the current paper had very similar experimental designs. Half of the drivers in each experiment were allowed to engage in a self-paced visual-manual secondary task, and half of the drivers in each experiment were experienced drivers and the other half were novice drivers. In both experiments, each participant performed four drives, each of which included a scenario that enabled drivers to anticipate a traffic event based on relevant cues in the environment. The driving automation in the second experiment could navigate these events without the driver's intervention. This was done to avoid over-exposing drivers to automation failures, which are generally rare in a real-world setting [8]. In the first experiment (no automation), however, drivers had to take action to avoid collisions. Thus, a comparison of drivers' actions in response to the traffic events across the two experiments would be unfair and the analysis presented in this paper only focused on drivers' glances towards cues that signal these events before event-onset.

# 2 Methods

## 2.1 Experiment Designs

As shown in Table 1, a 2 × 2 factorial design was used within each experiment, with driving experience (experienced vs. novice), and secondary task availability (yes vs. no) as between subject variables. In addition to these two variables, automation (Experiment 1: no automation vs. Experiment 2: automation with ACC and LKA combined) was included as an additional factor in the analysis presented in this paper.

**Table 1.** Experiment designs and participant age

| Automation | Experience | Secondary task availability | Mean age (min-max, SD) |
|---|---|---|---|
| Experiment 1: No automation (n = 32) | Experienced (n = 16) | Yes (n = 8) | 30.3 (25–36, 3.9) |
| | | No (n = 8) | 33.9 (26–47, 7.1) |
| | Novice (n = 16) | Yes (n = 8) | 21.8 (19–27, 2.9) |
| | | No (n = 8) | 25.3 (19–33, 5.2) |
| Experiment 2: ACC and LKA (n = 32) | Experienced (n = 16) | Yes (n = 8) | 37.4 (28–58, 9.4) |
| | | No (n = 8) | 39.3 (28–52, 9.6) |
| | Novice (n = 16) | Yes (n = 8) | 21.1 (18–27, 3.2) |
| | | No (n = 8) | 21.6 (18–24, 1.9) |

Thirty-two participants completed each experiment, leading to 64 participants total. The novice drivers were required to have held a G2 license in Ontario (or equivalent in Canada or the U.S.) for less than 3 years, and to have driven less than 10,000 km in the past year; experienced drivers were required to have held a full license in Ontario (or equivalent in Canada or the U.S.) for more than 8 years, and to have driven more than 20,000 km in the past year. Participants were randomly assigned to secondary task levels, with 8 participants (4 female and 4 male) under each experimental condition. The secondary task used in the experiments was a self-paced visual-manual task developed by Donmez et al. [9] that simulates searching through options on an infotainment system.

The experiment was conducted in a NADS MiniSim fixed-base driving simulator. Participants wore a Dikablis head-mounted eye-tracker to record their eye movements. Driving and eye-tracking data were collected at 60 Hz. Each participant completed four drives (each around 5 min long; two on rural roads with a speed limit of 50 mph and two on the highway with a speed limit of 60 mph), each including a distinct anticipatory scenario in which an upcoming traffic event could be anticipated based on the cues in the environment. The four anticipatory scenarios were repeated across the two experiments and they were always presented in the same order; the only difference between the two experiments was that in Experiment 1 participants controlled the vehicle whereas in Experiment 2 driving automation did. These scenarios include cues that indicate upcoming traffic events and the events themselves. For example, in the scenario depicted in

Fig. 1, the participant vehicle (in blue) followed a lead vehicle on a rural road. The vehicle behind it signaled left with high beams on, pulled into the opposite lane, and accelerated to overtake the participant vehicle. Because of an oncoming truck, the overtaking vehicle had to slow down and cut in front of the participant vehicle abruptly after signaling right. In this scenario, the anticipatory cues are the left signal of the overtaking vehicle and its move to the opposite lane, followed by the emergence of the oncoming truck. The event onset is indicated by the right turn signal of the overtaking vehicle, clearly indicating its intention to change lanes, leading to a potential conflict with the participant vehicle. More details on these scenarios and the experiment procedures can be found in the PhD dissertation of He [6].

**Fig. 1.** Example anticipatory driving scenario used in the experiments.

## 2.2   Data Analysis

In this paper, we focused on drivers' glances to two areas of interest (AOIs), the roadway and the anticipatory cues, as previous research has shown that glances to these AOIs are related to driving safety in general [e.g., 10] and drivers' anticipation of upcoming traffic events in particular [4, 5, 11]. The two metrics reported in this analysis are the percent of time spent looking at each AOI, and the time until the first glance at the cues after cue onset (i.e., first cue becoming visible to the driver). Other glance metrics (e.g., the mean glance duration and the rate of glances) have been reported in the PhD dissertation of He [6], but are excluded from this paper, as they did not provide any additional insights. A glance was defined following the ISO 15007–1:2014(E) standard [12], i.e., from the moment at which the gaze started to move toward an AOI, to the moment it started to move out of the AOI. Glances shorter than 100 ms were excluded from the analysis [13]. Roadway glances include any glances to the forward roadway, the side mirrors, and the rear-view mirror. The roadway glances also include glances to the cues.

The data extraction period for glances towards the cues starts from the cue onset; the data extraction period for the glances toward the roadway is from 20 s before cue onset. The data extraction periods for both glances at the cues and glances at the roadway end at the event onset in Experiment 1 (no automation); while in Experiment 2, the data extraction period ends at the event onset or automation disengagement, whichever happened earlier. For glances that partially fall in a data extraction period, a fraction of the glances was utilized following the method in Seppelt et al. [14] (e.g., if 0.7 s of a 1-s glance fell in the period of interest, then this glance was counted as 0.7 glances). Percent of time looking at an AOI was the total time glanced at an AOI within the data extraction period divided by the length of the data extraction period. Further, if a participant never looked at an anticipatory cue before the event onset, their time until first glance to an anticipatory cue was from the first cue becoming visible (cue onset) to event onset.

All statistical analyses were conducted in SAS on-demand V3.8. Both dependent variables were modeled using mixed models with participants introduced as a random factor and variance-covariance structure chosen based on the Bayesian Information Criterion. For glances to anticipatory cues, the independent variables include automation, experience, secondary task availability, and their two-way interactions. In addition, for percent of time looking at the roadway, to investigate whether drivers' behavior changed after cues became visible (i.e., after cue onset), an independent variable, "cue-onset", was created. The cue-onset divided the data extraction period into two: before-cue-onset period, i.e., from 20 s before cue onset to cue onset; and after-cue-onset period, i.e., from cue onset to the end of the data extraction periods.

## 3   Results

Given that the focus of this paper is on automation, in the following text, we only discuss the significant main and interaction effects related to automation (Fig. 2, Table 2). Other main and interaction effects have been reported in our previous publications [5, 15].

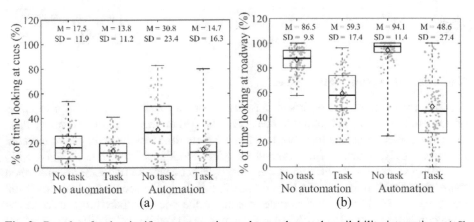

**Fig. 2.** Boxplots for the significant automation and secondary task availability interaction: a) % time looking at cues; b) % time looking at roadway. Boxplots present the five-number summary, along with the mean depicted through a hollow diamond. Mean (M) and standard deviation (SD) values are presented at the top of each figure.

**Table 2.** Statistical model results with significant effects (p < .05) bolded.

| Predictor variables | Time until first glance at cues (s) | % time looking at cues | % time looking at roadway |
|---|---|---|---|
| Automation | $F(1, 57.1) = 0.21$<br>$p = .6$ | **$F(1, 57.2) = 7.85$**<br>**$p = .007$** | $F(1, 57.1) = 0.39$<br>$p = .5$ |
| Experience | $F(1, 57.1) = 3.38$<br>$p = .07$ | **$F(1, 57.2) = 6.91$**<br>**$p = .01$** | $F(1, 57.1) = 1.13$<br>$p = .3$ |
| Secondary task | **$F(1, 57.1) = 10.81$**<br>**$p = .002$** | **$F(1, 57.2) = 18.33$**<br>**$p < .0001$** | **$F(1, 57.1) = 188.80$**<br>**$p < .0001$** |
| Automation *<br>Experience | $F(1, 57.1) = 0.19$<br>$p = .7$ | $F(1, 57.2) = 0.45$<br>$p = .5$ | $F(1, 57.1) = 0.02$<br>$p = .9$ |
| Automation *<br>Secondary task | $F(1, 57.1) = 3.64$<br>$p = .06$ | **$F(1, 57.2) = 4.62$**<br>**$p = .04$** | **$F(1, 57.1) = 11.80$**<br>**$p = .001$** |
| Experience *<br>Secondary task | $F(1,57.1) = 3.04$<br>$p = .09$ | $F(1,57.2) = 0.25$<br>$p = .6$ | $F(1, 57.1) = 0.01$<br>$p = .9$ |
| Cue-onset | – | – | **$F(1, 57.1) = 14.04$**<br>**$p = .0002$** |
| Automation *<br>Cue-onset | – | – | $F(1, 429) = 1.58$<br>$p = .2$ |
| Experience *<br>Cue-onset | – | – | $F(1, 429) = 0.00$<br>$p = .95$ |
| Secondary task *<br>Cue-onset | – | – | **$F(1, 429) = 5.69$**<br>**$p = .02$** |

### 3.1 Glances to Anticipatory Cues

An interaction effect was observed between secondary task and automation in terms of percent of time spent looking at cues (Fig. 2a). When there was no secondary task, drivers in Experiment 2 (automation) spent 10% more time looking at the cues compared to drivers in Experiment 1 (no automation), 95% Confidence Interval (CI): 4, 16, t(57) = 3.50, p = .0009. No difference was observed between the two experiments when there was a secondary task. In Experiment 2, drivers in the secondary task condition spent 13% (95% CI: 7, 19) less time looking at the cues compared to drivers in the no-secondary-task condition, t(56.6) = 4.56, p < .0001; while such a difference was not observed in Experiment 1.

### 3.2 Glances to Roadway

An interaction effect between secondary task and automation was also observed for percent of time looking at the roadway (Fig. 2b). When there was a secondary task, drivers in Experiment 2 (automation) spent 11% (95% CI: 3, 18) less time looking at the roadway compared to drivers in Experiment 1 (no automation), t(56.9) = 2.87, p = .006; while no such effect was observed when there was no secondary task. In

Experiment 1 (no automation), secondary task was associated with 27% (95% CI: 20, 35) less time spent looking at the roadway, $t(57) = 7.29$, $p < .0001$. However, in Experiment 2 (automation), secondary task was associated with 46% (95% CI: 38, 53) less time looking at the roadway, $t(57.2) = 12.14$, $p < .0001$.

## 4   Discussion

We conducted a secondary analysis on glance data collected in two comparable driving simulator experiments. The first experiment investigated anticipation of traffic events in non-automated driving, while the second investigated anticipation of traffic events with driving automation, in particular ACC and LKA combined. When there was no secondary task, drivers using ACC and LKA (combined; Experiment 2) spent a higher percent of time looking at anticipatory cues compared to those who did not have any driving automation (Experiment 1). As they were relieved from the physical demands of controlling the vehicle, it is possible that these drivers may have had more spare attentional capacity to observe the traffic situation, which may have enabled them to allocate more attention to areas of importance (i.e., anticipatory cues) that are relevant to the anticipation of traffic. However, when given the opportunity to engage in a visual-manual secondary task, drivers with automation seemed to shift their attention away from the driving task, as indicated by the drop in the percent of time looking at the roadway. Given the secondary task, these drivers' level of attention to anticipatory cues was no different than that of drivers without automation. This agrees with findings in previous research [e.g., 16, 17], in which an increased secondary task engagement was observed with the introduction of driving automation.

Interacting effects between automation and distraction have also been observed in previous research. For example, in a simulator study [18], it was found that when drivers were not distracted, the proportion of drivers who changed lanes in response to a critical event was the same in conditions with and without ACC and LKA. On the other hand, when drivers were distracted, few lane changes were made overall, especially in conditions without the ACC and LKA. Our results, which focus on glance behaviors, indicate that an interaction effect between distraction and automation exists also for glance behaviors, particularly anticipatory glances. This suggests that driver distraction can counteract the potential benefits of driving automation in terms of anticipation of traffic events. Given that drivers are more likely to be distracted when using automation like ACC and LKA [19, 20], interventions (such as display design and training) are needed to prevent and mitigate the effects of distraction on driver anticipation of traffic events when automation is being used.

Although this paper has provided some insights on the influence of automation on drivers' anticipatory glances, we have focused on scenarios that did not require drivers' intervention to avoid a crash when using ACC and LKA. Future research may be needed to explore more scenarios with different criticality as driver behavior might differ in scenarios where an intervention is needed to avoid collisions [21].

# References

1. Shen, S., Neyens, D.M.: Assessing drivers' response during automated driver support system failures with non-driving tasks. J. Saf. Res. **61**, 149–155 (2017)
2. Louw, T., et al.: Driver inattention during vehicle automation: how does driver engagement affect resumption of control? In: Proceedings of the 4th International Conference on Driver Distraction and Inattention (DDI2015). 2015, Sydney, New South Wales. ARRB Group, Australia (2015).
3. Tanida, K., Poppel, E.: A hierarchical model of operational anticipation windows in driving an automobile. Cognit. Process. **7**, 275–287 (2006)
4. Stahl, P., Donmez, B., Jamieson, G.A.: Eye glances towards conflict-relevant cues: the roles of anticipatory competence and driver experience. Accident Anal. Prevent. **132**, 105255 (2019)
5. He, D., Donmez, B.: The influence of visual-manual distractions on anticipatory driving. Hum. Factors: J. Hum. Factors Ergon. Soc. (2020). **In Press**
6. He, D.: Understanding and Supporting Anticipatory Driving in Automated Vehicles 2020, University of Toronto, Canada (2020)
7. Merat, N., Jamson, A.H.: Is drivers' situation awareness influenced by a fully automated driving scenario? In: Proceedings of Human Factors and Ergonomics Society Europe Chapter Annual Meeting, 2009, Soesterberg. Shaker Publishing, The Netherlands (2009)
8. Blanco, M., et al.: Automated Vehicle Crash Rate Comparison Using Naturalistic Data, 2016. Virginia Tech Transportation Institute, Blacksburg (2016)
9. Donmez, B., Boyle, L.N., Lee, J.D.: Safety implications of providing real-time feedback to distracted drivers. Accident Anal. Prevent. **39**(3), 581–590 (2007)
10. Victor, T., et al.: Analysis of Naturalistic Driving Study Data: Safer Glances, Driver Inattention, and Crash Risk. 2015, Transportation Research Board (2015)
11. He, D., Donmez, B.: The effect of distraction on anticipatory driving. In: Proceedings of the Human Factors and Ergonomics Society 62nd Annual Meeting, 2018. SAGE Publications, Philadelphia (2018)
12. International Organization for Standardization: Road vehicles - Measurement of Driver Visual Behaviour with Respect to Transport Information and Control Systems - Part 1: Definitions and Parameters. Switzerland, Geneva (2014)
13. Crundall, D., Underwood, G.: Visual attention while driving: measures of eye movements used in driving research. In: Porter, B.E. (ed.) Handbook of Traffic Psychology, pp. 137–148. Academic Press, Sandiego (2011)
14. Seppelt, B.D., et al.: Glass half-full: on-road glance metrics differentiate crashes from near-crashes in the 100-Car data. Accident Anal. Prevent. **107**, 48–62 (2017)
15. He, D., Donmez, B.: The influence of manual driving experience on secondary task engagement behaviours in automated vehicles. Transp. Res. Rec. **2673**(9), 142–151 (2019)
16. de Winter, J.C.F., et al.: Effects of adaptive cruise control and highly automated driving on workload and situation awareness: a review of the empirical evidence. Transp. Res. Part F: Traffic Psychol. Behav. **27**, 196–217 (2014)
17. Jamson, A.H., et al.: Behavioural changes in drivers experiencing highly-automated vehicle control in varying traffic conditions. Transp. Res. Part C: Emerg. Technol. **30**, 116–125 (2013)
18. Merat, N., et al.: Highly automated driving, secondary task performance, and driver state. Hum. Factors: J. Hum. Factors Ergon. Soc. **54**(5), 762–771 (2012)
19. Carsten, O., et al.: Control task substitution in semiautomated driving: does it matter what aspects are automated? Hum. Factors: J. Hum. Factors Ergon. Soc. **54**(5), 747–761 (2012)

20. Gaspar, J., Carney, C.: The effect of partial automation on driver attention: a naturalistic driving study. Hum. Factors: J. Hum. Factors Ergon. Soc. **61**(8), 1261–1276 (2019)
21. Eriksson, A., Stanton, N.A.: Takeover time in highly automated vehicles: noncritical transitions to and from manual control. Hum. Factors: J. Hum. Factors Ergon. Soc. **59**(4), 689–705 (2017)

# Pedestrians' Attitudes Towards Automated Vehicles: A Qualitative Study Based on Interviews in Germany

Philip Joisten[1(✉)], Pia Niessen[1,2], and Bettina Abendroth[1]

[1] Department of Mechanical Engineering, Institute of Human Factors and Ergonomics, Technical University of Darmstadt, Otto-Berndt-Straße 2, 64287 Darmstadt, Germany
{p.joisten,abendroth}@iad.tu-darmstadt.de
[2] Fraunhofer Institute for Systems and Innovation Research ISI, Breslauer Straße 48, 76139 Karlsruhe, Germany
pia.niessen@isi.fraunhofer.de

**Abstract.** For the successful implementation and acceptance in road traffic, pedestrians' attitudes towards safety, interaction and compatibility of AVs are important factors. The aim of this study is to investigate general attitudes towards AVs and to generate knowledge about aspects of safety and compatibility of AVs as well as interaction with AVs from the viewpoint of pedestrians. Semi-structured interviews with 24 participants were conducted in Germany between May and July 2020. Interviews were recorded, transcribed and analysed using Qualitative Content Analysis. The classification of participants regarding their general attitude towards AVs resulted in four categories, ranging from enthusiastic to rejecting attitudes. Our results revealed that safety attitudes are a major factor underlying pedestrians' general attitudes towards AVs. Confidence to cross the road in front of AVs was influenced by the ability of AVs to successfully interact and communicate with pedestrians. We conclude that pedestrians' attitudes towards AVs may change with increasing interaction experience.

**Keywords:** Pedestrian · Automated vehicle · Attitude · Street-crossing decision-making

## 1 Introduction

As innovation in transportation proceeds, automated vehicles (AVs) with varying technological capabilities ranging from conditional automation (SAE Level 3) to full automation (SAE Level 5) are approaching [1]. AVs could significantly reduce traffic accidents and reduce traffic congestion [2]. With the introduction of AVs, a mixed traffic environment will emerge which require interaction between automated and human road users [3]. Among all human road users, pedestrians are especially vulnerable [4]. To date, the implications of an increasingly automated vehicle fleet on pedestrians have not been studied extensively [5].

N. L. Black et al. (Eds.): IEA 2021, LNNS 221, pp. 664–673, 2021.
https://doi.org/10.1007/978-3-030-74608-7_81

Initial insight into how pedestrians perceive and interact with AVs indicate an impact of road infrastructure and socio-demographic variables (i.e., age and gender) on the type of interaction between pedestrians and AVs [6]. Deb et al. [7] showed that pedestrians with higher violation, lapse and aggression scores (as measured by the pedestrian behaviour questionnaire [8]) feel more confident about crossing in front of AVs. It is important to understand a pedestrians' attitude towards AVs, as it is a decisive factor in understanding the decision-making process when interacting with AVs [9].

Attitudes towards AVs have mainly been studied from the perspective of users of AVs [9, 10]. Only a few studies on attitudes towards AVs which take the perspective of pedestrians are available [11–13]. In US based surveys, Penmetsa et al. [12] and Das et al. [14] showed that pedestrians with direct experience interacting with AVs reported higher expectations of the safety benefits of AVs than respondents with no direct interaction experience. Findings of a survey in the UK indicate that pedestrians perceive autonomous cars as less risky compared to human-operated cars [11]. In contrast, AVs were perceived as more risky than human-operated cars from the passengers' point of view [11], stressing the need to take the type of road user into account when studying attitudes towards AVs.

This study examines attitudes towards AVs from the perspective of pedestrians in Germany. Using data from a qualitative interview study, we explore attitudes regarding safety, interaction and compatibility of AVs in a mixed traffic environment. Therefore, this work aims to contribute to a better understanding of the decision-making process of pedestrians when interacting with AVs.

## 2  Methodology

To achieve the research aim on pedestrians' attitudes towards AVs, semi-structured interviews were conducted in Germany between May and July 2020.

### 2.1  Participants

Twenty-four participants (50% female) aged between 18 and 81 years (mean $\pm$ SD = 44.9 $\pm$ 18.3 years) were recruited through the defined criteria of gender and age. Children and adolescents under the age of 18 years were excluded from participation in this study because they represent a unique group of road users with a variety of different behaviours that distinguishes them from adult pedestrians [15]. The interviewees were not compensated and no requirements regarding their previous knowledge of AVs were set for their participation in the study.

Two of 24 participants did not hold a driving license, while 18 participants owned a car. On average, the participants indicated using 1.7 main travel modes for work trips and 2.5 main travel modes for leisure trips. For leisure trips, walking (as a pedestrian) was more often indicated as a primary travel mode than the other modes. Participation in road traffic as a pedestrian (i.e. walking at least 500 m on foot in public road traffic) ranged from 1–2 days per week up to daily walking activities (Table 1).

**Table 1.** Sociodemographic data of the study participants.

| ID | Gender | Age | Driving license | Main travel mode(s) - work | Main travel mode(s) - leisure | Walking (days/week) |
|---|---|---|---|---|---|---|
| 1 | Female | 58 | Yes | Bike | Car, Bike, Walking | Daily |
| 2 | Male | 29 | Yes | Bike, Walking | PT, Bike | Daily |
| 3 | Female | 31 | Yes | Car, PT | Bike, Walking | 5–6 |
| 4 | Male | 60 | Yes | Bike, PT, Walking | Bike, Car, Walking | Daily |
| 5 | Female | 22 | Yes | PT, Walking | Bike, Car, PT, Walking | 3–4 |
| 6 | Male | 25 | No | PT, Walking | Bike, PT, Walking | Daily |
| 7 | Male | 57 | Yes | Car | Walking | 3–4 |
| 8 | Male | 40 | Yes | Car, Walking | Car, PT, Walking | Daily |
| 9 | Female | 56 | Yes | Car | Walking | 5–6 |
| 10 | Female | 19 | Yes | Car, PT | Bike, Car, PT, Walking | 1–2 |
| 11 | Male | 41 | Yes | Car | Car, PT, Walking | 1–2 |
| 12 | Male | 52 | Yes | Car | Bike, Car, TW | 1–2 |
| 13 | Male | 71 | Yes | Walking | Bike, Car | 5–6 |
| 14 | Male | 81 | Yes | Bike, Car, PT, Waling | Bike, Car, PT, Walking | 5–6 |
| 15 | Female | 36 | Yes | Car | Bike, Car, PT, Walking | 1–2 |
| 16 | Female | 47 | Yes | Bike, PT | Bike, Car, Walking | 5–6 |
| 17 | Male | 30 | Yes | Bike | Bike | Daily |
| 18 | Female | 36 | Yes | Bike | Bike, Car | 3–4 |
| 19 | Female | 71 | Yes | Bike | Bike | 5–6 |
| 20 | Female | 72 | Yes | Bike | Bike | Daily |
| 21 | Female | 27 | Yes | Car, Walking | Bike, Car, Walking | 3–4 |
| 22 | Male | 18 | No | PT | PT | 3–4 |
| 23 | Female | 50 | Yes | Car, PT | Car, PT, Walking | 1–2 |
| 24 | Male | 49 | Yes | Bike, PT, Walking | Bike, Walking | 3–4 |

*Note.* PT = powered two-wheeler

## 2.2  Data Collection

The semi-structured interview guideline contained three parts, starting with an introduction in which participants were greeted, their consent on participation obtained and a short briefing regarding the procedure of the interview was given.

The main part of the interview consisted of an opening question in which participants were asked to describe a road traffic situation in which they had interacted with a car in the past. The purpose of this question was to set up the topic and get the participants into talking. In the following the participants were asked (1) to express their attitudes towards AVs from the viewpoint of a pedestrian and (2) to describe their intended behaviour and decision factors when interacting with an AV in a predefined scenario (street-crossing under time pressure; AV has the right of way). As an intended stimulus the participants looked at a picture, which included various road users and an AV with no driver present (SAE Level 5) in an urban traffic scene. This stimulus was given after the opening question. In the third and final part of the interview, the participants were debriefed.

The main part of the interview lasted between 18 and 27 min (24 min on average). The interviews were held by means of remote communication. The visual stimulus (picture) was presented by sharing the interviewer's desktop screen or was sent beforehand to the participants by email, which was opened when prompted.

## 2.3  Data Analysis

The interviews were recorded, transcribed and analysed using Qualitative Content Analysis [16]. The software MAXQDA 2020 was used to code the qualitative data. General attitudes of participants were classified using the categories of rejector, conservative, pragmatist and enthusiast introduced by Hilgarter and Granig [17] (see Table 2 for definitions). Safety, interaction and compatibility were taken as main categories influencing behavioural intentions of pedestrians to cross the road in front of AVs [7].

# 3  Findings

## 3.1  General Attitude Towards AVs

The classification of participants regarding their general attitude towards AVs is presented in Table 2. Each category had numerous quotes of which a limited number was selected to maintain the clarity of the study. The category mentioned by 1–6 participants was represented by two quotes, the category mentioned by 7–12 participants by three quotes and the one mentioned by more than 12 participants by four quotes.

**Table 2.**  General attitudes towards AVs: definitions (according to [17]) and findings.

| Category [17] | Definition [17] | Participants' IDs |
|---|---|---|
| Enthusiast | Very open-minded about AVs and appreciate the new technology | 6, 12 |
| Pragmatist | Mostly open-minded and positive about AVs and mostly speak positively about them | 2, 3, 4, 8, 9, 11, 17, 20, 21, 22, 23 |
| Conservative | Sceptical and negative about the AVs but do not totally reject the new technology | 1, 5, 7, 10, 15, 16, 18, 19, 24 |
| Rejector | Totally reject AVs or only have negative associations about the new technology | 13, 14 |

The majority of participants (11 participants or 45.8% of the sample) held a pragmatic attitude towards AVs. They expressed benefits of the introduction of AVs regarding general road safety, traffic efficiency and the potential to eliminate dangerous behaviour of human road users (e.g. speeding).

*'If it is an automated car, it has somehow detected the dangerous situation beforehand.'* [ID 8, male, 40 years]

*'The traffic might also flow a little faster in general and we would get from A to B more quickly as a result.'* [ID 11, male, 41 years]

*'Maybe we would get the reckless speeders off the road and people would really learn to look at a vehicle as a mere means of transport and not as a showcase object.'* [ID 20, female, 72 years]

Nine participants (37.5% of the interviewees) were sceptical towards AVs and expressed distrust as well as discomfort. Conservatives highlighted missing interaction experience with AVs as a reason for their attitude.

*'I think there will certainly be a certain scepticism at first, as long as one has not yet had any or not yet many experiences with such cars.'* [ID 24, male, 49 years]

*'I would not trust AVs until I have seen it a few times.'* [ID 18, female, 36 years]

*'It definitely triggers curiosity in me but it's also unsettling for me in this situation.'* [ID 19, female, 71 years]

Rejectors (2 participants or 8.3% of the sample) were negative towards AVs and refused to accept AVs without a human supervisor. They emphasized the complexity of road traffic, missing transparency of AVs and technical errors as the main cause for their rejection of AVs.

*'When they are in traffic (...) there are situations that cannot be programmed in any way.'* [ID 13, male, 71 years]

*'I am extremely sceptical about the technology. Which of course also has to do with the fact that I can't see through the technology and that I have to rely here on things that cannot be directly influenced.'* [ID 14, male, 81 years]

In contrast, two participants (8.3% of the interviewees) were enthusiastic about AVs, expressed trust in AVs and benefits for general road safety.

*'The likelihood of an accident would be much higher if a human was driving the car and the responsiveness slower than that of the technology.'* [ID 6, male, 25 years]

*'If the system works the way it is supposed to work, I would rather it be an automated vehicle if I were the pedestrian.'* [ID 12, male, 52 years]

## 3.2   Attitudes Regarding Safety, Compatibility of AVs and Interaction with AVs

After classifying participants in accordance to their general attitude towards AVs, further analysis concerning safety and compatibility of AVs as well as interaction with AVs was conducted. The data analysis resulted in the identification of 132 quotes in total. 83 quotes were assigned to the successful control and operation of AVs (i.e., safety), 25 quotes to the ability to successfully implement AVs within the existing traffic system (i.e., compatibility) and 24 quotes to the confidence to cross the road in front of AVs (i.e., interaction). Each category was then analysed for sub-categories. In the following, sub-categories mentioned by 1–6 participants are represented by one quote, sub-categories mentioned by 7–12 participants by two quotes and sub-categories mentioned by more than 12 participants by three quotes.

**Attitudes Regarding Safety of AVs.** Regarding the successful control and operation of AVs (i.e. safety), four sub-categories emerged. The most quotes (57 quotes of 24 participants) were assigned to the perception and anticipation of human behaviour in the environment of AVs. To feel safe around AVs, participants expected the technology to perceive its whole environment, analyse and understand behaviour of other traffic participants as well as anticipate critical situations.

*'I assume that an AV has an overview of its environment and the events taking place in it.'* [ID 4, male, 60 years, pragmatist]

*'It should be able to analyse the movement of people in such a way that it can recognise whether someone is about to enter the street.'* [ID 11, male, 41 years, pragmatist]

*'It should somehow recognise dangerous situations beforehand, reduce speed and or could even take avoiding actions.'* [ID 8, male, 40 years, pragmatist]

The second sub-category influencing attitudes towards safety of AVs was described by a defensive and considerate driving behaviour of AVs (22 quotes of 14 participants). Participants expected AVs to give way in critical situations and be more considerate in choosing their speed than human drivers.

*'An AV should act defensively and calmly.'* [ID 24, male, 49 years, conservative]

*'The car should always comply with the pedestrian and give way in conflict situations.'* [ID 6, male, 25 years, enthusiast]

*'In potential conflict situations, the AV should drive slower than a driver would normally do.'* [ID 18, female, 36 years, conservative]

Two Participants (two quotes) expected the AV to operate emotionless in traffic, e.g. *'without any emotion in its driving behaviour'* [ID 24, male, 49 years, conservative]. Further, two participants (two quotes) perceived an influence of weather conditions on the successful control of AVs, e.g. *'The AV could do (...) even better when it is not snowing, raining, icy or foggy'* [ID 1, female, 58 years, conservative].

**Attitudes Regarding Compatibility of AVs.** Three sub-categories were assigned to the successful implementation of AVs in the existing traffic environment. Thirteen Participants (16 quotes) mentioned AVs should comply with the rules and laws in traffic and/or referred to situations of importance.

*'First of all, they should behave as prescribed by the law.'* [ID 2, male, 29 years, pragmatist]

*'They should adapt to the traffic situation and the traffic regulations therein.'* [ID 12, male, 52 years, enthusiast]

*'At bus stops, for example, the speed must be reduced because pedestrians could cross the road.'* [ID 3, female, 31 years, pragmatist]

The ability to integrate (and not disturb) the traffic flow was pointed out by five participants in seven quotes, e.g. *'blend into traffic flow'* [ID 19, female, 71 years, conservative]. Two participants described the ability to be up-to-date as a perquisite for the compatibility of AVs, e.g. *'AVs should be kept up to date so that destinations can be found even if the cityscape changes'* [ID 17, male, 30 years, pragmatist].

**Attitudes Regarding Interaction with AVs.** Attitudes regarding the confidence to cross the road in front of AVs (i.e., interaction) were assigned in 24 quotes, which resulted in two sub-categories. Therein, 15 quotes of 13 participants contained the need for active confirmations of AVs in the street-crossing process of pedestrians. Without a driver present, participants stressed the movement behaviour of AVs as confirmation for their behaviour.

*'When I cross the road, I always look to see if the approaching cars are somehow registering it.'* [ID 23, female, 50 years, pragmatist]

*'Brake ahead of time so that you can cross the road more safely as a pedestrian.'* [ID 22, male, 18 years, pragmatist]

*'If there is no one in the car I can get confirmation that I can walk now I would be more hesitant and wait until the vehicle is stopped.'* [ID 21, female, 27 years, pragmatist]

Regarding their confidence to cross the road in front of AVs, five participants (9 quotes) referred to missing communication channels and abilities of AVs. Within this sub-category, participants were concerned about not being able to communicate with AVs and not receiving signals to support their crossing decision.

*'Because I can't really communicate with it. It will be able to take some information from me, but I make a decision based on the information I receive. And I don't get any information from it.'* [ID 15, female, 36 years, conservative]

## 4 Discussion

Pedestrians' attitudes towards AVs are important for technology acceptance and are a decisive factor in understanding the decision-making process of pedestrians when interacting with AVs. This study investigates general attitudes towards AVs from the viewpoint of 24 pedestrians and generates knowledge about aspects of safety and compatibility of AVs as well as interaction with AVs.

The findings show that pedestrians' general attitudes can be classified using the approach of enthusiast, pragmatist, conservative and rejector which has been applied by Hilgarter and Granig [17]. During the period of our study, pedestrians were equally open-minded and sceptical towards AVs. In comparison, Hilgarter and Granig [17] found a predominantly positive attitude towards AVs of passengers after riding an autonomous shuttle. One explanation for this difference could be the higher risk exposure of pedestrians in traffic, which leads to cautious attitudes towards AVs. The type of road user, i.e. interacting pedestrian or passenger of AVs, should be distinguished when taking attitudes towards AV into account. Assumingly, a person could have different attitudes towards AVs in dependence of their current road user type. Further research could look into interdependencies of intrapersonal attitudes of pedestrians towards AVs and resulting consequences in intention and behaviour.

Our results reveal that attitudes of safety are a major factor underlying pedestrians' general attitudes towards AVs. Traffic safety attitudes can be dependent on experiences [18] and the context of the situation [19]. While concerns of safety can change with increasing experience, attitudes may also not be stable over time. Depending on experiences made in different traffic situations, attitudes may adapt dynamically. Therefore, we assume the classification regarding types of general attitudes not to be stable over time. More knowledge should be generated to discover types of experiences and the underlying situations that lead to more accepting or more rejecting attitudes. Thereby, other approaches to classify pedestrians' attitudes [20] should be explored, taking behavioural characteristics of pedestrians into account, e.g. used travel modes.

So far, there is only limited knowledge of pedestrians' attitudes towards AVs. In order to explore new or unknown phenomena qualitative studies are of high value. Interview participants may not have a clear conceptual understanding of AVs, especially regarding their different automation levels as proposed by SAE [1, 5]. To control conceptual misunderstandings of AVs, we used a visual stimulus of an AV that functioned as an anchor in the interviews. In this study, a car with full automation (SAE Level 5) was used. While this stimulated the discussion about the new technology, it can be assumed that AVs being introduced to road traffic in the next years will be under human supervision.

Some participants in our study held concerns regarding the communication capability of AVs. The difference in automation level assumingly affects the perceived interaction and communication capability of AVs. Meanwhile, research and industry are working on different communication concepts for AVs, resulting in a jungle of external human-machine interfaces [21]. It will be important to provide information about AVs communication capabilities to adjust attitudes of pedestrians accordingly.

For the successful implementation of AVs in road traffic, pedestrians' attitudes towards safety, interaction and compatibility of AVs in a mixed traffic environment are important factors to consider by designers, planners and regulators. The potential of attitudinal and behavioural changes of pedestrians is not yet fully discovered.

**Acknowledgements.** This work is a result of the research project @CITY – Automated Cars and Intelligent Traffic in the City. The project is supported by the Federal Ministry for Economic Affairs and Energy (BMWi), based on a decision taken by the German Bundestag, grant number 19A18003M. The authors are solely responsible for the content of this publication.

# References

1. SAE: Taxonomy and Definitions for Terms Related to Driving Automations Systems for On-Road Motor Vehicles, Washington, D.C. (2018)

2. Fagnant, D.J., Kockelman, K.: Preparing a nation for autonomous vehicles: opportunities, barriers and policy recommendations. Transp. Res. Part A: Pol. Pract. **77**, 167–181 (2015)
3. Schieben, A., Wilbrink, M., Kettwich, C., Madigan, R., Louw, T., Merat, N.: Designing the interaction of automated vehicles with other traffic participants: design considerations based on human needs and expectations. Cogn. Tech. Work **21**(1), 69–85 (2019)
4. Adminaité-Fotor, D., Jost, G.: How Safe is Walking and Cycling in Europe? PIN Flash Report (2020). https://etsc.eu/how-safe-is-walking-and-cycling-in-europe-pin-flash-38/. Accessed 06 Feb 2021
5. Botello, B., Buehler, R., Hankey, S., Mondschein, A., Jiang, Z.: Planning for walking and cycling in an autonomous-vehicle future. Transp. Res. Interdisc. Perspect. **1**, 100012 (2019)
6. Madigan, R., Nordhoff, S., Fox, C., Ezzati Amini, R., Louw, T., Wilbrink, M., Schieben, A., Merat, N.: Understanding interactions between automated road transport systems and other road users: a video analysis. Transp. Res. Part F: Traffic Psychol. Behav. **66**, 196–213 (2019)
7. Deb, S., Strawderman, L., Carruth, D.W., DuBien, J., Smith, B., Garrison, T.M.: Development and validation of a questionnaire to assess pedestrian receptivity toward fully autonomous vehicles. Transp. Res. Part C: Emerg. Technol. **84**, 178–195 (2017)
8. Deb, S., Strawderman, L., DuBien, J., Smith, B., Carruth, D.W., Garrison, T.M.: Evaluating pedestrian behavior at crosswalks: Validation of a pedestrian behavior questionnaire for the U.S. population. Accid. Anal. Prev. **106**, 191–201 (2017)
9. Rahimi, A., Azimi, G., Jin, X.: Examining human attitudes toward shared mobility options and autonomous vehicles. Transp. Res. Part F: Traffic Psychol. Behav. **72**, 133–154 (2020)
10. Tennant, C., Stares, S., Howard, S.: Public discomfort at the prospect of autonomous vehicles: building on previous surveys to measure attitudes in 11 countries. Transp. Res. Part F: Traffic Psychol. Behav. **64**, 98–118 (2019)
11. Hulse, L.M., Xie, H., Galea, E.R.: Perceptions of autonomous vehicles: relationships with road users, risk, gender and age. Saf. Sci. **102**, 1–13 (2018)
12. Penmetsa, P., Adanu, E.K., Wood, D., Wang, T., Jones, S.L.: Perceptions and expectations of autonomous vehicles – a snapshot of vulnerable road user opinion. Technol. Forecast. Soc. Change **143**, 9–13 (2019)
13. Ackermans, S., Dey, D., Ruijten, P., Cuijpers, R.H., Pfleging, B.: The effects of explicit intention communication, conspicuous sensors, and pedestrian attitude in interactions with automated vehicles. In: Proceedings of the 2020 CHI Conference on Human Factors in Computing Systems, pp. 1–14. ACM, New York (2020)
14. Das, S., Dutta, A., Fitzpatrick, K.: Technological perception on autonomous vehicles: perspectives of the non-motorists. Technol. Anal. Strateg. Manage. **32**(11), 1335–1352 (2020)
15. Elliott, M.A., Baughan, C.J.: Developing a self-report method for investigating adolescent road user behaviour. Transp. Res. Part F: Traffic Psychol. Behav. **7**(6), 373–393 (2004)
16. Mayring, P.: Qualitative content analysis: theoretical foundation, basic procedures and software solution (2014). https://www.ssoar.info/ssoar/handle/document/39517. Accessed 06 Feb 2021
17. Hilgarter, K., Granig, P.: Public perception of autonomous vehicles: a qualitative study based on interviews after riding an autonomous shuttle. Transp. Res. Part F: Traffic Psychol. Behav. **72**, 226–243 (2020)
18. McIlroy, R.C., Nam, V.H., Bunyasi, B.W., Jikyong, U., Kokwaro, G.O., Wu, J., Hoque, M.S., Plant, K.L., Preston, J.M., Stanton, N.A.: Exploring the relationships between pedestrian behaviours and traffic safety attitudes in six countries. Transp. Res. Part F: Traffic Psychol. Behav. **68**, 257–271 (2020)
19. Dinh, D.D., Vũ, N.H., McIlroy, R.C., Plant, K.A., Stanton, N.A.: Effect of attitudes towards traffic safety and risk perceptions on pedestrian behaviours in Vietnam. IATSS Res. **44**(3), 238–247 (2020)

20. Papadimitriou, E., Theofilatos, A., Yannis, G.: Patterns of pedestrian attitudes, perceptions and behaviour in Europe. Saf. Sci. **53**, 114–122 (2013)
21. Dey, D., Habibovic, A., Löcken, A., Wintersberger, P., Pfleging, B., Riener, A., Martens, M., Terken, J.: Taming the eHMI jungle: a classification taxonomy to guide, compare, and assess the design principles of automated vehicles' external human-machine interfaces. Transp. Res. Interdiscip. Perspect. **7**, 100174 (2020)

# The Importance of the Approach Towards the Curb Before Pedestrians Cross Streets

Luis Kalb[(✉)] and Klaus Bengler

Chair of Ergonomics, Technical University of Munich, Munich, Germany
`luis.kalb@tum.de`

**Abstract.** Multi pedestrian scenarios are the next step towards more realistic traffic research. We conducted a traffic observation with uninformed pedestrians to find differences in behavior depending on the pedestrians group sizes. We found out that most of the pedestrian's behavior occurs while they approach the street curb which hasn't been reported in previous research yet. This paper reports several objective data concerning pedestrians' positions, actions and their timings during the approach towards the curb. We identify potential differences between single pedestrians and two pedestrian groups. The results lay the basis for a future controlled experiment where the found differences will be statistically evaluated.

**Keywords:** Pedestrian · Observation · Automated driving · Traffic · Street crossing

## 1 Introduction

Pedestrian behavior has been researched for traffic safety for decades. [1] present an extended overview of publications that studied pedestrian behavior while [2] evaluate future methodologies. Previous results gain new relevance today with the introduction of automated vehicles (AVs) into traffic. Researchers need an extended understanding of pedestrian's behavior to develop AVs accordingly. The study at hand is the first step in a research effort that aims to investigate the street crossing behavior of multiple pedestrians at the same time instead of just one when an AV is approaching (Fig. 1).

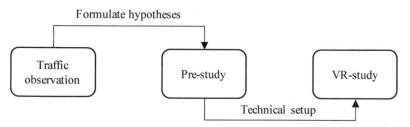

**Fig. 1.** Overall research effort and role and position of the traffic observation at hand.

AVs are not part of everyday traffic yet, so first indications for multi-pedestrian behavior come from manual traffic. These results can be used to formulate hypotheses about pedestrian behavior that can be tested in a controlled experimental environment with AV prototypes. The study described in this publication initially focused on the difference between single pedestrian and multi pedestrian street crossing scenarios as previously described in the literature in real manual traffic.

We discovered a second interesting fact during the analysis of our observation: Much of the expected pedestrian behavior happened while they were still approaching the curb instead of stopping at the curb and then executing expected behavior like looking up and down the street to check for oncoming traffic. This was not reported in other studies yet to the best knowledge of the authors which is why it became the main focus of this publication. Pedestrian behavior is described by objective data from an observation concerning the pedestrian's position in relation to the curb, the oncoming vehicle and the timing of these positions.

## 2   Method

### 2.1   Scenario

We collected video footage of an unmarked street in the inner city of Munich (Germany – right lane traffic) with uninformed pedestrians crossing while single vehicles approached (Fig. 2). The camera was positioned on a bridge approx. 5 m above ground. The focus laid on the phase when pedestrians approached a street prior to a crossing. Data acquisition was in line with German general data protection regulations.

**Fig. 2.** Screenshot from the video footage with a grid overlay. The yellow lines on the left and right show the distances from the curb of the street in one-meter steps, the red lines show the distances along the street in one-meter and five-meter steps. The background colors symbolize different areas in which the speed of the vehicle was calculated.

We measured several distances on-site and used them to create a grid. We were able to situate pedestrians and vehicles with an accuracy of one meter based on the high video resolution of 2704 × 1520 pixels (GoPro Hero 6) and the on-site measurements.

All videos were recorded during daylight and mostly shortly after rainfall. The weather conditions were not chosen on purpose but taken as-is on the days of the recordings. The selected street is usually busy and used by a lot of pedestrians. We analyzed scenarios where only one vehicle was present and the number of pedestrians crossing the street was clearly observable. The analysis also only included pedestrians crossing the street within the first 18 m from the bottom of the screen, as indicated in Fig. 2, where the grid allowed the most precise localization of pedestrians and vehicles. All vehicles drove on the right-hand side of the street, which was six meters wide in total, with respect to their driving direction (downwards from the cameras perspective). The pedestrians approach phase was determined as eight meters starting from the curb on either side because this area was sufficiently covered by the camera.

## 2.2   Data Set

We went chronologically through approx. ten hours of video footage and chose a scenario for analysis when the number of crossing pedestrians was clearly observable. The decision included no other bias regarding the pedestrians involved. As a result, we analyzed 80 scenarios with either one single pedestrian (54 scenarios, 54 pedestrians) or two separate pedestrians (26 scenarios, 52 pedestrians) crossing from the same side or opposing sides.

## 2.3   Raters

A first rater reviewed the video footage and encoded the pedestrian's positions and times using the software INTERACT (Mangold International GmbH). A second separate rater reviewed the same video footage afterwards and marked differences in encoding compared to the first rater. The two raters agreed on every time/position code yet had different views on eleven of 85 scenarios regarding the number of pedestrians that should be considered for the observation. A third rater reviewed only the disagreements between the first two raters and made the definitive decision. Five scenarios were dismissed from analysis as a result with 80 scenarios remaining.

## 2.4   Metrics

We focused on distances and times of vehicles and pedestrians at five points: (I) the point the pedestrian could see the vehicle for the first time (in most cases approx. eight meters), (II) the point the pedestrian moved his or her head towards the vehicle for the first time, (III) the point the pedestrian moved his or her head towards the vehicle for a second time, (IV) the point the pedestrian slowed down or came to a standstill, (V) the point the pedestrian reached the street (Fig. 3).

We report distances of the pedestrians to the vehicle (DPTV), the distances of the pedestrians to the street (DPTS) and the time pedestrians took for their activities (TFABP). The times (A–D) correspond to the distance points (I–IV), i.e. A is how long pedestrians walked without interruption from the beginning of the observation, B is how long pedestrians had their had turned towards the vehicle for the first time, C is how long pedestrians had their had turned towards the vehicle for the second time, D is how long pedestrians walked noticeably slower or stood still.

The distance of the pedestrian to the street is zero per definition at point V. No time is reported for this point because it's a single event and not a time span. Vehicle distances

>50 m were treated as 50 for all calculations. Data preparation and analysis was carried out using Excel (Microsoft Inc.) and MATLAB (The MathWorks Inc.)

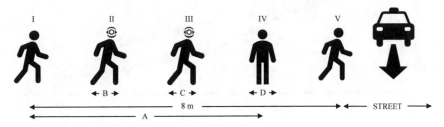

**Fig. 3.** Overview of the different analyzed data points.

## 3 Results

### 3.1 Sample

Fifty-four pedestrians were observed as single pedestrians crossing. 22 crossed the street from the left from the camera's perspective and 32 from the right. The two separate pedestrians crossed the street from the same side in 15 scenarios and from opposing sides in eleven scenarios. Pedestrians crossed five times from the left and ten times from the right in the same side scenarios for two pedestrians. Figure 4 gives an overview of the sample sizes.

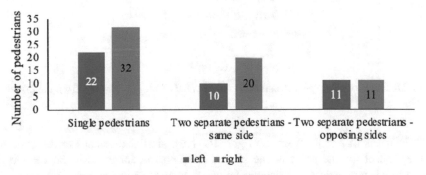

**Fig. 4.** Number of pedestrians in the observed scenarios.

### 3.2 Distance Between Pedestrian and Vehicle (DPTV)

Figure 5 shows an overview of the distance between the oncoming vehicle and pedestrians crossing from (a) the left and (b) the right at the specified points in time from 2.4. Pedestrians in Fig. 5(a) are all approaching the street from the left, pedestrians in Fig. 5(b) all from the right.

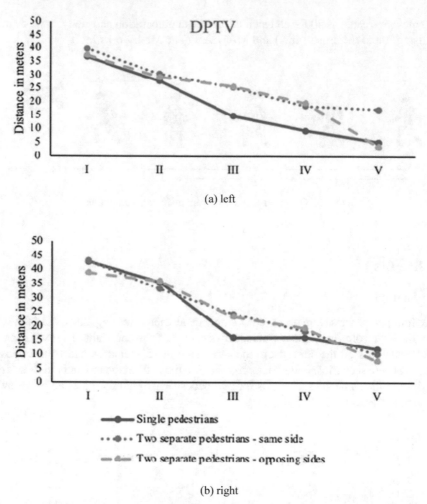

(a) left

(b) right

**Fig. 5.** Distances between pedestrians and vehicles (DPTV) for pedestrians from the (a) left and (b) right.

Pedestrians that cross from the right side have similar distances to the oncoming vehicle, except for the point of the second head movement towards the vehicle (III) where there is noticeably less distance between the vehicle and single pedestrians. This difference is present for pedestrians that cross from the left, too, but it also exists for the point when pedestrians slowed down or came to a standstill (IV). Two separate pedestrians that both cross from the left side reach the road with a distinctively larger distance to the oncoming vehicle (V) than the other two groups.

## 3.3   Distance Between Pedestrian and Street (DPTS)

Figure 6 shows an overview of the distance between the street curb and pedestrians crossing from (a) the left and (b) the right at the specified points in time from 2.4.

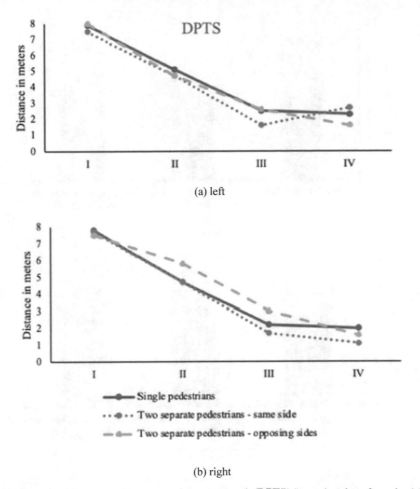

(a) left

(b) right

**Fig. 6.** Distances between pedestrians and the street curb (DPTS) for pedestrians from the (a) left and (b) right.

Single pedestrians have very similar positions for the point of the second head movement (III) and the time where they slowed down or came to a standstill (IV), while the multi pedestrians group show larger changes. It is noticeable that two pedestrians from the same side (left) on average slowed down or came to a standstill before turning their head towards the vehicle a second time.

### 3.4 Time for Activity by Pedestrian (TFABP)

Figure 7 shows an overview of the times pedestrians spent on their activities when they crossed from (a) the left and (b) the right at the specified points in time from 2.4.

Single pedestrians from the left side differ in the time they stand still before crossing the road. The difference is the largest compared to two pedestrians that both cross from the left side – 3.3 s compared to 1.8 s.

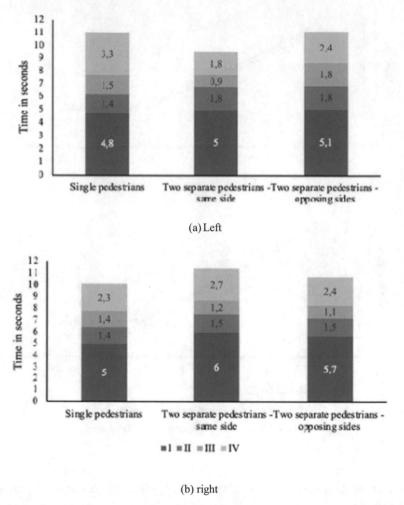

(a) Left

(b) right

**Fig. 7.** Times for activities by pedestrians (TFABP) for pedestrians from the (a) left and (b) right.

Single pedestrians from the right walked up to one second less than two pedestrians before turning their head towards the oncoming vehicle for the first time. Their second head movement towards the oncoming vehicle remains the same length as the first one in contrast to shorter second head movements by two pedestrians.

## 4   Discussion and Conclusion

We collected data from a traffic observation with pedestrian participants that were not informed that they were part of an observation, meaning their behavior was not influenced by the experiment. We collected objective data concerning the positions and timing of pedestrian's actions which hasn't been done extensively in research so far.

The downside of our approach are unknown interfering variables that could influence pedestrian behavior besides our classification by group size and crossing direction, i.e., distraction by mobile devices. Our reported results are also mean values that don't fully account for the variation across all observed participants.

Our goal was to identify potential differences between single pedestrian and multi pedestrian behavior. We found that the approaching phase towards the street curb covered a lot of pedestrian behavior before the actual street crossing took place, which was not reported in the literature so far. Our investigation subsequently focused on this area.

We found differences between the two groups in all our reported metrics. This emphasizes a) the importance of the approach before pedestrians cross a street and b) the initial assumption that pedestrian behavior would differ depending on the group size.

Our results will lead to several hypotheses that will be tested in a controlled experimental environment next (Fig. 1), e.g. (i) pedestrians turn their head towards an oncoming vehicle for the first time earlier when they are alone compared to a scenario where another pedestrian is present or (ii) pedestrians combine slowing down with a second head movement towards an oncoming vehicle when they are alone compared to leaving some spatial distance between the two actions when a second pedestrian is present. The upcoming experiment will focus a) on the proof of these hypotheses for manual driven vehicles as well as b) on the investigation of potential differences in pedestrian behavior between manual vehicles and automated vehicles when it comes to pedestrian group sizes.

# References

1. Rasouli, A., Tsotsos, J.K.: Autonomous Vehicles that Interact with Pedestrians: A Survey of Theory and Practice. https://arxiv.org/pdf/1805.11773v1 (2018)
2. Maruhn, P., Schneider, S., Bengler, K.: Measuring egocentric distance perception in virtual reality: influence of methodologies, locomotion and translation gains. PloS One **14** (10), e0224651 (2019)

# Pilot is a Pilot is a Pilot?: Exploration of Effects of Professional Culture in Helicopter Pilots

Anna Kaminska[1]([✉]), Amy Irwin[1], Devin Ray[1], and Rhona Flin[2]

[1] University of Aberdeen, Aberdeen, UK
anna.kaminska.14@aberdeen.ac.uk
[2] Robert Gordon University, Aberdeen, UK

**Abstract.** Culture has been identified as a factor influencing the way people communicate and behave. Though often imperceptible by its members, cross-cultural interactions can lead to misunderstandings and conflicts. Despite ex-military and civilian trained pilots frequently flying together, there has been a lack of research describing each professional sub-culture. The current study aims to bridge that gap by exploring how professional culture interacts in the cockpit and how it affects pilots' safety behaviours. The study used in-depth semi-structured interviews with 15 participants (14 helicopter pilots) to collect data on effects of professional culture. The data were analysed using conventional content analysis. Content analysis indicated five separate categories relevant to perceptions of professional culture. The findings indicate that pilots acknowledge the cultural differences present between themselves and others, and that culture can have an effect on their and other's safety behaviours. The participants suggested that various sub-culture types can have impact on flight safety through their effects on communication and the way people interact, but not through technical skills of flying the aircraft. The differences between military and civilian training and flying were discussed in depth. This research highlights the various ways in which culture affects pilots' safety behaviours and interactions with one another. It also provides an in-depth look at the way pilots perceive and experience cross-cultural interactions in the cockpit.

**Keywords:** Helicopters · Culture · Safety · Cross-cultural interactions · Military

## 1 Culture in the Cockpit

Culture is often imperceptible by its members, while seen by outsiders as unpredictable and even 'nonsensical' (Helmreich and Merritt 1998). Thus, it is possible for cross-cultural interactions to lead to misunderstandings and conflicts. However, the role of culture in aviation has received relatively little empirical attention since the seminal book by Helmreich and Merritt (1998), and few advances have been made in understanding how various combinations of cultures might interact in the cockpit. More importantly, despite the large amount of ex-military pilots being employed in the civil sector, the respective cultures of each pilot group and their interactions have received no mention in the academic literature. The current study aims to bridge that gap by exploring how

© The Author(s), under exclusive license to Springer Nature Switzerland AG 2021
N. L. Black et al. (Eds.): IEA 2021, LNNS 221, pp. 682–690, 2021.
https://doi.org/10.1007/978-3-030-74608-7_83

sub-groups of professional culture interact in the cockpit and how it potentially affects pilots' safety behaviours.

## 1.1 Professional Culture

While there are three (national, organisational and professional) culture types thought to be relevant for flight safety, professional culture has been underlined as being the most salient (Helmreich and Merritt 1998). Professional culture is based on job role and training background, forming a sense of community. The professional culture of fixed-wing pilots is exemplified by personality, intelligence and skills, and good social skills (Omole et al. 2016). Professional culture in aviation is still very masculine: in 2018, out of 890 helicopter pilot licence holders in the UK, only 24 were women (CAA 2019).

However, it is likely that the professional culture within aviation is not uniform and subcultures develop through various personal factors, for instance, type of flying (Helmreich and Merritt 1998) and, by association, training background. There are two general avenues to becoming a pilot (helicopter or fixed-wing): through the military (state-funded route) vs. civilian (self-funded) training. While all pilots are qualified masters of their profession once they leave training, it can be argued that the culture 'implanted' through training differs between the two.

While there are certain similarities between military and civilian flying (e.g., predominantly male, strict organisational structure, framework and rules; Redmond et al. 2015), there are also key differences between the two professional subcultures. Cooper et al. (2018) outline that military culture is grounded in strict discipline, determination and commitment to duty (e.g., 'leave no man behind' and never quitting the mission). This philosophy is indoctrinated through bootcamps and emphasises the value of the team. Civilian fields, on the other hand, differ in important ways from these rules and logic of the military field, being far more centred around safety and regulations (Hörmann 2001), and profit (Leaver and Reader 2019). Thus, not surprisingly perhaps, military pilots are described as feeling higher sense of community with other ex-military pilots than with civilian pilots, whereas civilian pilots often identify more with other pilots who fly for similar organisations.

Despite the significant contribution of ex-military personnel to many civil industries (e.g., healthcare), certain transition difficulties due to the specific military culture have been identified, for example, inability to find work due to misconceptions from employers about military job roles or lack of job opportunities at an appropriate skill level (Watts et al. 2016). In aviation it appears to be less of an issue with military veterans, having a higher status as the technically outstanding pilots. Nevertheless, due to the specific and strict indoctrination of military lifestyle at the beginning of service (i.e. boot camp), service persons in transition may find it difficult to adopt to civilian culture (Redmond et al. 2015) and start reproducing military cultural attitudes and behaviour without being aware of it.

This involuntary (and often unacknowledged) reproduction of military attitudes and behaviours can lead to culture clashes and misunderstandings. Helicopter pilots do not work alone – they are part of a team in the cockpit or a larger rescue team in Search and Rescue (SAR pilots work together with rear crew who are medics, crane operators, etc.). Moreover, typically pilots do not work in the same team every day due to shift and rotation patterns, training requirements, working time restrictions etc. (Flin 2010). Thus, unexpected culture clashes form the potential to have an adverse effect on safety critical behaviours like situation awareness (i.e., pilot's mental model of the world around him) which is crucial for mission success, as it depends on sharing mental models with each other through communication and team cooperation (Endsley 1990).

## 1.2 The Current Study

Professional culture could influence safety behaviours either through risking safety to save others (military 'leave no man behind' custom) or perhaps being too focused on following all rules (heavily regulated civil aviation). However, not only are cross-cultural interactions rarely studied, but there also is no scientific literature that examines both civilian and military culture, how they intertwine and how they affect people's safety behaviours.

The current exploratory study examined how professional culture[1] affects helicopter pilots' safety-related behaviours. Semi-structured interviews were chosen to suit the exploratory nature of the first study and to allow for more in-depth examination of all three culture types. The study had three main aims: (1) to explore pilots' views on the effects of culture on safety behaviours; (2) to determine which aspects of culture are perceived as potential factors that might influence safety behaviours, performance and training; and (3) to determine which aspect of culture is perceived as the most important and/or most likely to influence safety behaviours and performance.

## 2    Methods

### 2.1    Participants

Three groups of oil and gas pilots (pilots, trainers and management team) were contacted internally by the company's training lead (in Aberdeen), and an invitation poster was hung in the break room at the heliport. In total 15 participants (2 female) were interviewed: 5 pilots, 6 trainers and 4 managers. One participant (pilot group) was excluded as the interview was very short (less than 10min). Remaining participants ($n = 14$) age ranged from 36 to 64 ($M = 47.20$, $SD = 7.98$). Interviews were conducted both in person ($n = 11$), over video call ($n = 2$) and over the phone ($n = 2$). Most participants (all but one who was only involved in training pilots) were current pilots with varying flight experience. Ten were ex-military trained (including non-pilot) and five were civilian trained pilots. Nine participants were trained in the UK, and six pilots received their training in other countries (e.g., USA, Netherlands, etc.)

The study was approved by the University of Aberdeen, School of Psychology Ethics committee.

---

[1] The effects of organisational and national culture were also explored but are not reported here due to space constraints. National culture findings are reported elsewhere.

## 2.2 Interviews

Semi-structured interviews designed to investigate the research questions took place over two collection periods (due to COVID-19). The first wave of data collection took place January-February 2020, and second wave was June-July 2020. The in-person interviews took place in various private meeting rooms at the company's Aberdeen training department offices, over-the-phone interviews were conducted at the University of Aberdeen lab, and video call interviews were conducted from home (both researcher and the participants).

For all interviews, after initial study participation invitation from an internal contact, participants emailed the researcher directly and picked a suitable interview time using a private Doodle poll. Interviews lasted an average of 33 min (from 16 to 61 min).

In each interview after a small introduction, the purpose of the interview was explained, and the participants were given two consent form to complete along with time to ask any questions. Participant demographic information was sampled. Then participants were asked pre-prepared questions in 3 sections, each relevant to a culture type, and one overall question. In the second wave (after COVID-19), three additional overall questions were added in relation to the company's perceived handling of the crisis and any potential changes in the company culture. If participants misunderstood any questions, they were clarified. Participants were encouraged to give full answers and provide examples, where appropriate. Occasionally, follow up questions were asked, where answers were brief. This procedure was followed until all questions were covered, whereby participants were asked if there was anything else that they would like to bring up that had not been covered by the interview questions.

Throughout the interview process, the researcher remained neutral and inviting, being aware as to not provide physical or verbal (dis)approval to the answers given, apart from context specific facial expressions.

## 2.3 Analysis Strategy

A conventional content analysis (Hsieh and Shannon 2005) was performed. Codes were generated in primarily inductive coding (i.e., the analysis was data-driven (bottom-up) rather than theory-driven (top-down)) with some aspects of deductive coding (i.e., only information related to culture and safety was coded).

Data saturation, the point at which no new categories were developed on the basis of the data (Guest et al. 2006) was reached by $14^{th}$ interview, and last two interviews were conducted to confirm that.

# 3   Results

Content analysis generated five themes relevant to professional culture (Table 1).

## 3.1 Military Culture

Participants described military culture as underpinned by taking risks and doing anything to 'get the job done' attitude:

*'The priorities for military pilots are- are slightly different. They are very much focused on 'we must get this task done'. Almost come what may.' (Participant #5)*

Participants noted that ex-military pilots come with a much broader range of experience and skills, as they are trained for a different job with different requirements compared to a civilian:

*'There's guys who've been trained in the army [..] they've done some quite exciting stuff, compared to what the civilian pilots have done. Because they, [..] have to go into war zones or, they fly low level, [..] they use the helicopter for quite a lot of different tasks, not just personnel carrying, but also, erm, lift, load lifting, low level flying, all that sort of stuff. So, they come with, um, a completely different set of skills ...' (Participant #4)*

Participants mentioned that it's comfortable flying with ex-military pilots due to perceived 'quality assurance' of their skills and training.

**Table 1.** Themes and codes relevant to professional culture.

| Theme (definition) | Code |
|---|---|
| *Military culture*: Pilots describe military culture and characteristics of (ex-)military pilots. Most interviewees stress the 'get the job done' attitude and broad experience range of (ex-)military pilots | Risks and finding ways to get the job done (efficiency over safety) ($n = 10$) |
| | Military pilots have broader experience ($n = 8$) |
| | Strict hierarchy & steep cockpit gradient ($n = 7$) |
| | Military pilots 'stand out' ($n = 5$) |
| | Military pilots have better training and more invested in them ($n = 5$) |
| | 'Quality assurance' of military pilots ($n = 4$) |
| | Military pilots can be cocky ($n = 5$) |
| | Military pilots are taught to be autonomous ($n = 3$) |
| | Subconscious bond between ex-military pilots ($n = 3$) |
| | Military pilots are more resilient ($n = 3$) |
| *Civilian culture*: Pilots describe the characteristics of civilian-trained pilots as technically able, rule-following and highly motivated | Civilian pilots can be as good as military, or better, but there's more variation ($n = 8$) |
| | Civilian pilot flying is more rule-based ($n = 3$) |
| | Self-funded pilots are more motivated ($n = 2$) |
| | Civilian pilots are more individualist ($n = 1$) |
| *Characteristics and limitations of civil aviation*: Pilots describe civilian flying as 'safety above all', but a financially driven, potentially boring operation. Participants also mention that it is hard to use people's expertise and changes in rules and procedures take a long time | Safety above efficiency ($n = 6$) |
| | Civilian aviation is financially driven ($n = 5$) |
| | Civilian flying as a bus service ($n = 5$) |
| | Civilian flying is boring for military pilots ($n = 4$) |
| | In civil aviation job roles are separate ($n = 2$) |
| | Changes in rules and procedures take a long time ($n = 3$) |
| | It's hard to use each person's expertise in civil aviation ($n = 10$) |
| *Professional culture of pilots*: Pilots describe their professional culture as similar, irrespective of experience, but highlight that a broader range of experience makes pilots more understanding and better | Pilot is a pilot is a pilot ($n = 2$) |
| | Variety of jobs make pilots more understanding ($n = 4$) |
| | Pilots have big egos and personalities ($n = 2$) |
| *Early influences on development of professional culture:* | Single-pilot pilots fly differently ($n = 4$) |
| | Culture of the first job stays with you ($n = 3$) |

### 3.2  Civilian Culture

Participants described civilian pilots as just as technically able as military (in terms of their actual flying skills once they are on the job), but noted that there is more variation due to unlimited attempts to pass:

> 'There's their minimum standard that they set and anybody who's got the deter-mination and money and the perseverance, and a basic level of skill, can probably pass the exam if they try hard enough. [..] when you meet them for the first time, you've got no idea how good they're gonna be…'(Participant #3)

Participants also describe civilian pilots as also more reliant on the rules in their approach to flying, i.e., not seeing other options to approach the task other than those described in the rule book:

> 'A lot of the civilian guys become more rule-based… purely because they- they develop the skills to a certain point… [..]the rules are then written to allow them to operate the aircraft, erm, without the reliance on the skill that you might need to operate the aircraft in if the rules weren't so narrow' (Participant #13)

### 3.3  Characteristics and Limitations of Civil Aviation

Civil aviation was described as highly regulated and safe, with 'safety above efficiency' culture:

> 'We're always looking for, erm, the safest outcome, not necessarily the most efficient outcome.' (Participant #5)

It was also noted that civilian flying is financially driven and can be at times boring:

> 'We're a costumer orientated service, we're a bus service effectively, and we're trying to get guys safely from A to B, and we're offering a service…' (Participant #4)

### 3.4  Professional Culture of Pilots

Pilots described that irrespective of different training backgrounds, there are certain overarching characteristics of pilots:

> 'The thing with pilots, we're quite a highly motivated bunch, but we're also quite goal orientated, we wanna try and do things efficiently' (Participant #4)

Participants mentioned that a diversity of experiences and jobs made pilots better in terms of skills and understanding of rules.

### 3.5   Early Influences on Development of Professional Culture

Pilots highlighted that training background and culture of the first job shaped their attitudes to flying and prevailed in some form even after changing jobs.

*'I think, any job, when you first start a job, the culture that you first enter has a great effect for the rest of your career.' (Participant #1)*

Finally, it was also mentioned that if a pilot learned and flew in a single-pilot aircraft, it influenced the way they approached flying as a crew as well, meaning that they often struggle to share responsibilities and communicate.

## 4   Discussion

The qualitative data from this study provides extensive insight into helicopter pilots' perceptions of culture and its influence on performance, safety behaviours and training. Key themes discussed importance of standardisation (to eliminate or reduce the impact of culture), international differences, language barriers, and different characteristics and limitations of military and civilian cultures.

### 4.1   Research Questions and Findings

It appears that most pilots do not believe that professional culture affects their or others' general flight behaviours. The actual skills involved in day-to-day operations (e.g., flying the aircraft to a rig and back) do not differ between pilots as that is what they are trained to do. However, the broader the experience of a pilot (from their military training or simply because they have worked in many different jobs) can come in useful during unexpected situations (e.g., emergencies), where skills and quick thinking outside of the rulebook is required.

One of the most novel findings of this study is the complexity of comparisons that the pilots drew between military and civilian aviation and profound impact of training background on pilots for the rest of their careers. This research contributes to the very limited amount of literature on ex-military/civilian interactions despite the fact that the aviation industry employs a great amount of ex-military pilots. The most highlighted disparity between military and civilian flying was the safety vs. efficiency difference between the two. Almost every participant mentioned that in the military the most important thing is to 'get the job done' and being comfortable with taking risks in order to do that. It is a stark contrast to civilian operations where safety is 'above all'. While civilian pilots obviously also want to complete their flights successfully, they have no reservations about turning back if the minimum acceptable risk threshold is breached. It is clear that this disparity stems from the inherently different mission types in these environments: military pilots are trained for the worst-case scenario (i.e., war), whereas civilians would never want to put any life at risk (a single accident can destroy a company financially). However, it is interesting that some ex-military pilots admitted to still occasionally falling back into thinking of potential workarounds to get the job done even years after leaving the military. It is important to note, though, that captains stressed they would not do anything without the agreement of their co-pilot, even if it meant going back.

Another common comparison drawn was the difference in depth and quality of training between military and civilian worlds. Ex-military pilots described that the military training was much more in-depth due to the fact that they were required to fly the aircraft in more extreme weather and use less automation than their civilian counterparts. They suggested that this difference in training structure created a difference in approach to flying: pilots reflected that civilian flying is more rule-based (looking at checklists and following SOPs), whereas in the military you were expected to be more flexible and reactive to changing situations.

Interestingly, participants suggested a multitude of benefits of having multi-cultral crews. Different training background was suggested to benefit both skills (i.e., showing new things to each other) as well as broadening perspectives (e.g., suggesting new ways of thinking about issues).

Combined, the present findings demonstrate the underlying influence of culture on pilots' performance, safety behaviours and team interactions. However, participants underlined the importance of standardisation to eliminate or reduce impact of culture, for instance, using standard language in the cockpit to avoid confusion.

## 4.2 Limitations and Future Directions

The overall positive attitudes towards culture types might be questionable. Due to the fact that an internal contact was used for recruitment, it may be possible that only people with positive attitudes were recruited. It is also possible that participants exhibited social desirability bias, enhanced by the face-to-face interviews and the politically correct nature of British respondents. Future studies will employ a third person vignette design online, which will help to reduce the effect of social desirability bias, as well as expand the participant pool to hopefully broaden the opinions present in the sample. However, it also important to note that perhaps pilots interviewed genuinely enjoy their job and are happy with their workplace, as it has been previously found that pilots do overwhelmingly like their work and are proud of their profession (Helmreich and Merritt 1998).

The current study has provided a wealth of qualitative data that describes specific cultures (e.g., military culture and civilian culture) which have not been explicitly described before, especially from rotary aviation point of view.

## 5    Conclusion

The current study aimed to explore how professional culture interacts in the cockpit and how it affects pilots' safety behaviours by conducting in-depth semi-structured interviews with managers, trainers and pilots. The findings of the study provide a rich picture of how various sub-culture types present themselves in the cockpit and how they interact. Pilots also reflected on culture's effect on their and other's safety behaviours.

# References

Civil Aviation Authority: Pilot licence holders by age and sex 2018 [Data file] (2019). https://www.caa.co.uk/uploadedFiles/CAA/Content/Standard_Content/Data_and_analysis/Datasets/Licence_holders_by_age_and_sex_by_year/Pilot%20licence%20holders%20by%20age%20and%20sex%202018.pdf

Cooper, L., Caddick, N., Godier, L., Cooper, A., Fossey, M.: Transition from the military into civilian life: an exploration of cultural competence. Armed Forces Soc. **44**(1), 156–177 (2018)

Endsley, M.R.: Predictive utility of an objective measure of situation awareness. In: Proceedings of the Human Factors Society Annual Meeting, vol. 34, no. 1, pp. 41–45 (1990)

Flin, R.: CRM (non-technical) skills – applications for and beyond the flight deck. In: Kanki, B.G., Helmreich, R.L., Anca, J. (eds.) Crew Resource Management, 2nd edn., pp. 181–202. Academic Press, San Diego, CA (2010)

Guest, G., Bunce, A., Johnson, L.: How many interviews are enough? An experiment with data saturation and variability. Field Methods **18**(1), 59–82 (2006)

Helmreich, R.L., Merritt, A.C.: Culture at Work in Aviation and Medicine: National, Organizational and Professional Influences. Ashgate, Aldershot (1998)

Hörmann, H.J.: Cultural variation of perceptions of crew behaviour in multi-pilot aircraft. Le Travail Humain **64**(3), 247–268 (2001)

Hsieh, H.F., Shannon, S.E.: Three approaches to qualitative content analysis. Qual. Health Res. **15**(9), 1277–1288 (2005)

Leaver, M.P., Reader, T.W.: Safety culture in financial trading: an analysis of trading misconduct investigations. J. Bus. Ethics **154**, 461–481 (2019)

Omole, H., Walker, G., Netto, G.: Exploring the role of culture in helicopter accidents. In: Di Bucchianico, G., Vallicelli, A., Stanton, N.A., Landry, S.J. (eds.) Human Factors in Transportation: Social and Technological Evolution Across Maritime, Road, Rail, and Aviation Domains, pp. 271–296. CRC Press, Boca Raton, FL (2016)

Redmond, S.A., Wilcox, S.L., Campbell, S., Kim, A., Finney, K., Barr, K., Hassan, A.M.: A brief introduction to the military workplace culture. Work **50**(1), 9–20 (2015)

Watts, B., Lawrence, R.H., Schaub, K., Lea, E., Hasenstaub, M., Slivka, J., Kirsh, S.: Transitioning former military medics to civilian health care jobs: a novel pilot program to integrate medics into ambulatory care teams for high-risk patients. Mil. Med. **181**(11–12), e1464–e1469 (2016)

# Investigation of Driver Behavior During Minimal Risk Maneuvers of Automated Vehicles

Burak Karakaya[✉] and Klaus Bengler

Chair of Ergonomics, Technical University of Munich, Munich, Germany
{burak.karakaya,bengler}@tum.de

**Abstract.** Minimal Risk Maneuvers (MRMs) are introduced to reduce the risk of an accident during the transition from automated to manual driving. In this paper, we present the results of a dynamic driving simulator study with 56 participants with the control authority as the independent variable, i.e. allowing and blocking driver input during the MRM. In order to not communicate wrong information, input blocking was established by disabling the brake and gas pedal but not the steering wheel. The latter turned according to the performed MRM and participants had to overcome high counterforces to change the vehicle's direction. Two scenarios on a highway were investigated with the ego vehicle located in the right lane and only differing in the implemented MRM, i.e. stopping in the own lane or maneuvering to the shoulder lane combined with a standstill. Our results show a high intervention rate in both groups. Participants intervened mainly by maneuvering into the middle lane and after the Human-Machine-Interface announced the upcoming maneuver. In total, four accidents and five dangerous situations occurred due to interventions in both groups. Trajectories during re-entering into traffic showed that participants favored the middle lane over the shoulder lane here as well. To conclude, allowing or blocking driver intervention did not reduce the risk of an accident and more countermeasures need to be taken.

**Keyword:** Minimal Risk Maneuver · MRM · Level 4 · Driver behavior

## 1 Introduction

Minimal Risk Maneuvers (MRMs) are part of the functionalities of vehicles at higher levels of automation that correspond to level 3 and higher according to the SAE taxonomy [1]. Whenever these automated vehicles reach their boundaries, MRMs are employed to reach a Minimal Risk Condition (MRC) to reduce the risk of an accident. The requirement for these maneuvers is that the automated system is still functional, otherwise a failure mitigation strategy would take place. For level 3 systems, the driver is mainly responsible to achieve an MRC and the system could execute MRMs only in some circumstances. This is opposed to level 4 systems, in which the automated system itself is responsible for this in every situation. Nevertheless, the literature [1–4] still leaves some questions unanswered by stating that MRMs could start either after requesting the driver to take-over control or immediately. Furthermore, it is still under discussion if intervening in these automated maneuvers should be allowed or not. Since these aspects

© The Author(s), under exclusive license to Springer Nature Switzerland AG 2021
N. L. Black et al. (Eds.): IEA 2021, LNNS 221, pp. 691–700, 2021.
https://doi.org/10.1007/978-3-030-74608-7_84

are not regulated by law, different interpretations and implementations are possible. As an example, Honda announced together with their receipt of a type designation for level 3 automated driving, that an MRM is a key safety standard for their vehicles. In this case, the automated system must safely stop the vehicle whenever a transition of control cannot be made [5].

Karakaya et al. [6] showed the discrepancy between the literature's versus the driver's idea of an MRM, i.e. stopping the ego vehicle in-lane or on the shoulder lane versus overtaking from the left. These findings were considered for the design of a Human-Machine-Interface (HMI). From a risk assessment point of view, the risk during a transition phase with MRMs is the occurrence of an accident times its probability. This risk in turn is apparent if either the MRM has malfunctions, or if the driver can intervene intermediately. Hence, we conducted a driving simulator study to contribute to the discussion about the design of transition phases with MRMs with the research question: does the discrepancy between the driver's and literature's perspective of an MRM [6] lead to interventions if input is allowed or blocked – and if there is an intervention, is the risk still reduced?

## 2    Method

### 2.1    Scenarios

In total, two scenarios were used for the transition phase of the 25 min-long experimental drive. Both had in common that the ego vehicle is driving at 80 km/h in the right lane of a three-lane highway with a shoulder lane and right-hand drive. The obstacle causing the MRM, i.e. a stranded vehicle with activated hazard lights, was in the same lane as the ego vehicle at a distance of 200 m. That corresponds to a TTC of 9 s at the time the upcoming MRM was announced, later referred as the Announcement of Maneuver (AoM). The MRM itself was performed by the system after the AoM was finished. The two scenarios differed only in the performed MRM by the system, i.e. a standstill maneuver in the own lane ("MRM stop") and an evasive maneuver to the right combined with a full stop in the shoulder lane ("MRM evasive"). Since the vehicle came to a standstill after both maneuvers and marked the end of an MRM, the drivers were told to continue driving manually and therefore had to re-enter into traffic. After a short period of time, automation was available again and the participants were instructed to activate it. An uncritical scenario was implemented for the training drive, where participants were driving in the middle lane with no obstacle or other traffic participants. To familiarize themselves, the "MRM stop" was triggered and led to a full stop in the own lane.

### 2.2    Apparatus

The study was conducted on a modular dynamic driving simulator with a 120° horizontal field of view provided by three 55-in. screens with Ultra HD resolution. A rear mirror is integrated into the front view of the middle screen, while side mirrors are in two additional displays. An additional display located behind the steering wheel was used as a freely programmable instrument cluster (IC). Driving simulation was implemented via SILAB 6.0 from the Würzburg Institute of Traffic Sciences. For video recording of the experimental drive, a GoPro HERO 4 Silver Edition was mounted on a tripod and positioned behind the driver. A Sony Xperia Z Ultra was used for the non-driving related task during the automated drive, i.e. the Surrogate Reference Task (SuRT).

### 2.3 Participants

The experiment consisted of fifty-six participants and all fulfilled the requirements of possessing a valid driver's license, having a minimum age of 18 years and proficient German skills. The latter was important to minimize misunderstandings of the designed HMI. All participants were randomly allocated to the two groups, i.e. "Input Allowed" and "Input Blocked", which had 28 participants in each case. The sample consisted of 17 female and 39 male participants with an average age of 25.64 years (SD = 4.75), ranging from 18 to 50 years. Two participants in the "Allowed" group anticipated the obstacle even before a transition was initiated and took over manual control for the "MRM evasive" scenario. They were assigned as not intervening participants for the analysis of the number of interventions and excluded from the remaining analysis.

### 2.4 Experimental Design and Dependent Variables

This study used a between-subject design with the control authority, i.e. driver input being allowed or blocked during an MRM, as the independent variable. Conditions to disengage automation for the allowed group were braking, accelerating, or pressing a button on the steering wheel. Due to the implementation of the automation, it is not possible to distinguish an applied steering angle between the driver and automation during the drive. Therefore, a steering angle condition would also disengage the automation during the "MRM evasive". For the blocked group, automation would not disengage until the vehicle is close to standstill. However, the steering wheel was not decoupled in order to not communicate a malfunction and could be turned by applying high counterforces. Every participant experienced both scenarios with the sequences permuted.

Dependent variables were the decision to intervene and if they intervened, the time and manner of intervention. An intervention was defined as any brake or gas pedal input or a difference of the steering angle over time greater than 2 degrees*second between the participant's maneuver and the MRM, while driving faster than 10 km/h. Furthermore, the criticality of the encountered situation due to an intervention was assessed by the TTC to other road users and accidents. The intervention was classified as dangerous if the TTC was below 2 s or the distance was less than 54 m. These rules are part of driver training in Germany, where a fine can be issued if the driver falls below the named distance.

Due to technical issues, the distance data to road users in the middle lane could not be completely recorded and were therefore reconstructed in case the participants decided to overtake on the left. Thus, the time it took the ego vehicle to change lanes to the middle lane was retrieved from the participant's data. This time was used to calculate the new positions of other traffic participants, since they were always located behind the ego vehicle and drove at a constant velocity of 108 km/h. Consequently, the distance and

TTC to these traffic participants could also be calculated. Video material was watched subsequently by the investigator for verification.

Re-entering into traffic was analyzed via the ego vehicles' trajectories of those participants who did not intervene in an MRM and came to a full stop. In addition, subjective data was collected by a semi-structured interview and questionnaires.

Statistical tests were carried out in JASP (Version 0.14) with a significance level of $\alpha = .05$. Data analysis was conducted in MATLAB (The MathWorks Inc.) and Excel (Microsoft Inc.).

## 2.5   HMI

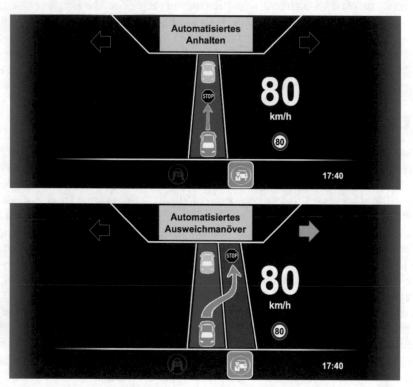

**Fig. 1.** Information on the IC during the transition phase with (I) "MRM stop" and (II) "MRM evasive". Grey boxes mean translated (I) "Automated Stop" and (II) "Automated Evasive Maneuver" (from top to bottom).

The HMI for this study was designed primarily for the transition phase to communicate relevant information regarding the upcoming MRM. Therefore, an existing HMI concept from [7–10] served as the basis and was adapted to our use case.

As soon as the obstacle is detected, the AoM is triggered and marks the beginning of the transition phase. It consists of visual and acoustic information. Visual information is shown on the IC in addition with pulsing blue edges at 1 Hz (see Fig. 1). Acoustically, two beep sounds are played followed by a computer-generated speech output with a female voice in German. It either contains the translated message "automated stop in the own lane" or "automated evasive maneuver to the right". Both acoustic messages have an approximate duration of 3 s. Without interventions, both maneuvers come to a standstill and the automated system requests to continue driving manually by displaying a grey text box and activated hazard lights at the top of the IC.

A short quiz between the training and experimental drives was conducted to ensure that participants understood the HMI correctly. Participants were asked about perceived visual and audio messages and their meaning, and were corrected in case of wrong answers.

# 3 Results

## 3.1 Number of Interventions

As shown in Fig. 2, participants intervened regardless of their group, but more interventions were performed in the "Allowed" group. The number of interventions for the "MRM evasive" and "MRM stop" were approximately the same within each group. The proportion of intervening drivers for both of these MRMs was 25.00% in the "Allowed" group and 17.86% in the" Blocked" group. In contrast, this proportion was nearly three times larger for at least one of the MRMs, i.e. 71.43% in the "Allowed" group and 57.14% in the "Blocked" group.

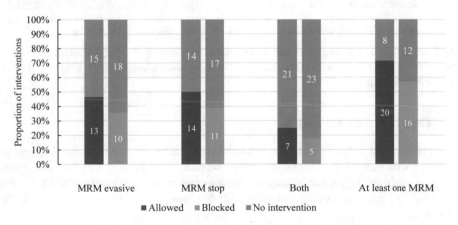

**Fig. 2.** Number of interventions per group and MRM.

## 3.2 Manner of Intervention

Participants of both groups clearly favored intervention by maneuvering to the left (see Fig. 3). One participant in each group decided to slowly overtake by using the shoulder lane during the "MRM evasive" scenario. Furthermore, the maneuver to the left started during the evasive MRM in both groups only after the vehicle started to steer to the right.

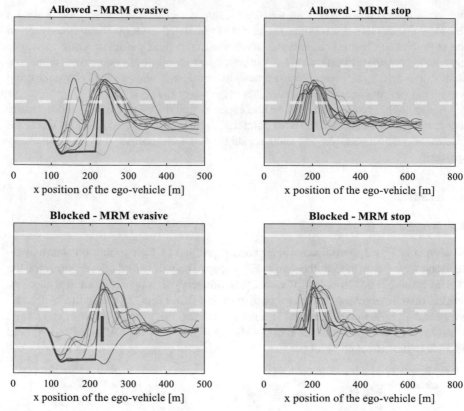

**Fig. 3.** Ego vehicle trajectories of participants who intervened during the transition phase. The blue thick line represents the trajectory that the automated system follows for the respective MRM. The AoM was triggered at 0 m.

### 3.3 Time of First Intervention

Every participant performed his/her first intervention after the AoM was finished except for one participant in the "Allowed" group and during the "MRM Stop" scenario (see Fig. 4). In this individual case, the participant noticed the obstacle before the AoM was triggered and took over manual control with one hand while holding the tablet in the other hand.

To exclude random effects, although the scenario order was permuted, the time of the first intervention between the first and second scenario was analyzed within a group via a paired samples t-test. In the "Allowed" group, no significant difference between the first ($M = 6.47$, $SD = 2.50$) and second scenario ($M = 6.12$, $SD = 1.84$) was found ($t(12) = 0.67$, $p = .515$). Also, no significant difference between the first ($M = 5.91$, $SD = 1.62$) and second scenario ($M = 5.56$, $SD = 1.46$) was found ($t(6) = 0.952$, $p = .378$) in the "Blocked" group.

Furthermore, differences between the time of first intervention during the "MRM evasive" and "MRM stop" scenario were analyzed with a paired samples t-test and showed no significant results in the "Allowed" ("MRM evasive": $M = 6.28, SD = 2.19$, "MRM stop": $M = 6.29, SD = 2.18; t(12) = 0.299, p = .770$) as well as in the "Blocked" group ("MRM evasive": $M = 5.65, SD = 1.59$, "MRM stop": $M = 5.70, SD = 1.46$; $t(9) = -0.066, p = .949$).

Therefore, the times of first intervention during the "MRM evasive" and "MRM stop" scenario within a group were combined to compare between the "Allowed" ($M = 6.29$, $SD = 2.14$) and "Blocked" group ($M = 5.68, SD = 1.45$). An independent samples t-test showed no significant difference ($t(46) = -1.112, p = .272$).

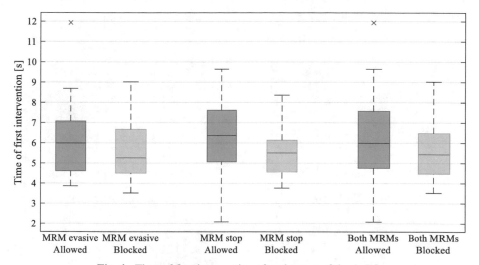

**Fig. 4.** Time of first intervention after the start of the AoM.

### 3.4 Criticality Because of Driver Intervention

None of the participants had an accident with the obstacle causing the MRM. However, several critical situations occurred due to maneuvering to the left, i.e. the middle lane. Approaching vehicles were not always detected, leading to one accident in the "Allowed" and three accidents in the "Blocked" group. Two dangerous situations as defined in Sect. 2.4 occurred in the "Allowed" group. Additionally, one participant ended up in another dangerous situation due to performing two lane changes and getting to the median strip, approximately 20 cm from the guardrail (see also Fig. 3). Two participants in the "Blocked" group got into dangerous situations as well.

### 3.5 Reasons for (Not) Intervening

On the one hand, participants stated that the reasons for their intervention were because of a disagreement with the MRM strategy by the automated system (67%), not trusting the automation (13%), not having enough time (13%) or not trusting other vehicles (7%). On the other hand, not intervening was justified since the non-driving related task was too distracting (32%), since there was not enough time for a decision (28%), since they did not trust the automation (20%) or since they did not perceive the situation urgent enough and since they wanted to observe the automated vehicle's response (20%).

## 3.6   Re-entering into Traffic

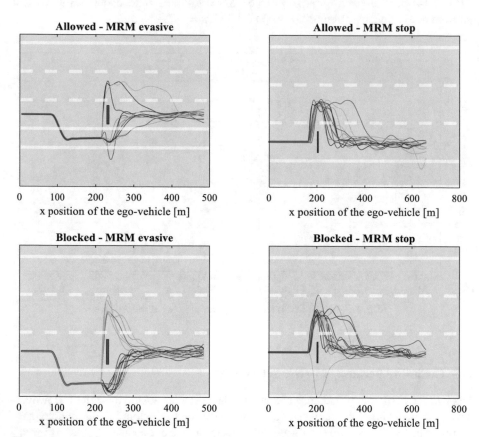

**Fig. 5.** Ego vehicle trajectories of participants re-entering into traffic after the MRM is finished. The blue thick line represents the trajectory that the automated system follows for the respective MRM. The AoM was triggered at 0 m.

Accelerating from a standstill position and re-entering into traffic happened only into the middle lane during the "MRM stop" scenario except for one participant in the "Blocked" group. Even in the "MRM evasive" scenario, two lane changes were accepted by participants in both groups in order to not have to overtake the obstacle by means of the shoulder lane (see Fig. 5).

## 4  Discussion and Conclusion

The results of our research show that the proportion of drivers intervening in an MRM is high regardless of their authority. Furthermore, participants in the "Blocked" group overcame the counterforces on the steering wheel to accomplish their desired maneuver.

We confirmed the study results of the video-based experiment from Karakaya et al. [6], where participants preferred a maneuver to the left over right and standstill. Except for two participants, everyone decided to overtake the vehicle on the left even though it would require one or two lane changes. It seems that driving in an emergency lane is avoided by any means. According to the self-stated reasons for intervention, disagreement with the MRM strategy was the main reason. The possible explanation could be traffic law and driver education in Germany, where driving on the shoulder lane is only allowed in case of an accident or emergency. This in turn means that drivers do not assess the presented situations critically enough.

According to our analysis, the order of the two implemented MRM strategies and the strategy itself do not have an impact on the time of the first intervention within a group. Also, no difference was found between the two groups. Consequently, drivers perform their first intervention regardless of the MRM strategy and control authority. The first intervention was made on average 6 s after the start of the AoM, which in turn means that participants intervened after the AoM was finished (approximately 3 s) in the case that the obstacle was not independently detected.

Investigating MRMs requires not only an analysis of the transition phase but also of the process of re-entering into traffic. Results show that even for that purpose, drivers avoid the shoulder lane and accept an overtaking maneuver at low speed through the middle lane. These results may be different for naturalistic driving studies and should be explored further.

In conclusion, the risk of an imminent collision was not reduced by introducing MRMs and simply allowing or disallowing driver intervention under the experimental conditions and based on our results. With intervention rates up to 70% in at least one of the MRMs during a 25 min drive, we can expect that drivers will tend to take over manual control in the future as well. This in turn leads to the known problems of transition phases of level 3 automation [11, 12] that were observed in our study. Therefore, more countermeasures need to be taken in the future.

**Acknowledgment.** This research was conducted within the project "CADJapanGermany: HF" which is funded by the Federal Ministry of Education and Research of Germany. We would like to acknowledge Zehui Cheng for his assistance in data collection. The experiment was approved by the Ethics Commission of the Technical University of Munich.

## References

1. Proposal: SAE International: Surface Vehicle Recommended Practice: Taxonomy and Definitions for Terms Related to Driving Automation Systems for On-Road Motor Vehicles. J3016. Warrendale, PA (2018)

2. UNECE ACSF-24–05. Revised (consolidated) proposal based on the discussions at the last IWG session (ACSF-23) and the #1–#3 web meetings, using ACSF-23–02r4 as a base. Clean version (2019). https://wiki.unece.org/display/trans/ACSF+25th+session. Accessed 4 Dec 2019
3. Gasser, T. M., Frey, A. T., Seeck, A.., Auerswald, R.: Comprehensive definitions for automated driving and ADAS. In: 25th International Technical Conference on the Enhanced Safety of Vehicles (ESV) National Highway Traffic Safety Administration (2017)
4. Wood, M., Robbel, D.P., Maass. D.M., et al.: Safety First for Automated Driving (2019)
5. Honda Motor Co. Ltd. Honda Receives Type Designation for Level 3 Automated Driving in Japan (2020). https://global.honda/newsroom/news/2020/4201111eng.html. Accessed 2 Feb 2021
6. Karakaya, B., Kalb, L., Bengler, K.: A video survey on minimal risk maneuvers and conditions. In: Proceedings of the Human Factors and Ergonomics Society Annual Meeting, vol. 64, pp. 1708–1712 (2020). https://doi.org/10.1177/1071181320641415
7. Kalb, L., Streit, L., Bengler, K.: Multimodal priming of drivers for a cooperative take-over. In: 2018 21st International Conference on Intelligent Transportation Systems (ITSC), 04. 11. 2018–07. 11. 2018, pp. 1029–1034. IEEE, Maui (2018). https://doi.org/10.1109/ITSC.2018.8569619.
8. Götze, M.: Entwicklung und Evaluation eines integrativen MMI Gesamtkonzeptes zur Handlungsunterstützung für den urbanen Verkehr [Dissertation]. Technical University of Munich, Munich (2018)
9. Feierle, A., Bücherl, F., Hecht, T., Bengler, K.: Evaluation of display concepts for the instrument cluster in urban automated driving. In: Ahram, T., Karwowski, W., Pickl, S., Taiar, R. (eds.) pp. 209–215. Springer, Cham (2020)
10. Feierle, A., Danner, S., Steininger, S., Bengler, K.: Information needs and visual attention during urban, highly automated driving—an investigation of potential influencing factors. Information. 11, 62 (2020). https://doi.org/10.3390/info11020062
11. Zhang, B., Winter, J.D., Varotto, S., Happee, R., Martens, M.: Determinants of take-over time from automated driving: a meta-analysis of 129 studies. Transp. Res. Part F: Traffic Psychol. Behav. 64, 285–307 (2019). https://doi.org/10.1016/j.trf.2019.04.020.
12. Gold, C.G.: Modeling of Take-Over Situations in Highly Automated Vehicle Guidance [Doctoral dissertation]. Technical University of Munich, Munich (2016)

# An Innovative Seat Ventilation Concept: Does the Seat Provide Overall Thermal Comfort in Autonomous Vehicles?

Manuel Kipp[(⊠)], Andreas Rolle, and Klaus Bengler

Institute of Ergonomics, Technical University of Munich, Boltzmann str. 15, 85748 Garching b. München, Germany
{manuel.kipp,a.rolle,bengler}@tum.de

**Abstract.** With regard to autonomous driving and associated new interior concepts of the vehicle, the focus will be on innovative and efficient air-conditioning concepts concerning the seat. The seat offers the opportunity to provide air-conditioning close to the body of the passenger. A new seat ventilation which generates a directed air flow to the passenger is developed. In the following investigation, an outlet air duct concept at the side of the seat is objectively assessed. Furthermore, the thermal comfort regarding different climate conditions is investigated. When evaluating the results according to the comfort zone diagrams of ISO14505-2:2006 the seat outlets perform well for hot climate conditions during a pull-down. Cold ambient temperatures are less suitable for this outlet system. More investigations are necessary to test whether this concept, in combination with other air-conditioning systems, can result in potential energy savings and increasing thermal comfort.

**Keywords:** Thermal comfort · Seat ventilation · Air-conditioning · Autonomous driving

## 1 Introduction

Future mobility trends such as autonomous driving, connectivity or electromobility are setting new focuses in the automotive industry. The transfer of the driving function to the vehicle will lead to variable seating arrangements, which leads to new vehicle interior concepts. In view of highly automated driving and the associated changes in the vehicle interior, the aspects of comfort, ergonomics and air-conditioning will become increasingly important. In light vehicles the air-conditioning system is the largest secondary energy consumer and especially in electric vehicles the driving range can be significantly reduced by heating and cooling [1]. Therefore, it is necessary to enhance the energy efficiency of air-conditioning systems by improving and developing new concepts. The challenge is to enable an individual air-conditioning for each occupant in all possible sitting and sleeping positions. Due to longer driving times and the focus on non-driving related tasks, the customers' demand for thermal comfort will thus become increasingly important. In this context, the vehicle seat represents the largest contact sur-face between passengers and vehicle. Especially during the summer months, the thermal comfort of the vehicle interior plays an important role. The aim of this investigation is to develop an innovative ventilated seat based on a conventional driver's seat, which provides optimized thermal comfort close to the body. The main research question is:

- Can the seat play a dominant role to provide the thermal comfort?

In this paper an outlet concept which generates an air curtain around the seat is evaluated. Furthermore, the seat will be verified to evaluate the overall concept.

## 2   Fundamentals

During the development of new air-conditioning concepts, the thermal comfort of the occupants in the vehicle has to be considered. Different heat transport mechanisms such as conduction, convection and radiation are used to enhance the thermal comfort of the occupants in the vehicle. According to the Comfort Pyramid by Bubb [2], thermal wellbeing- and comfort play a significant role in the driver's safety at all times and contributes to the overall feeling of comfort.

The expression thermal comfort is defined in ISO 7730:2005 [3]. It describes a subjective perception that depends on the individual physiology of the person and has a significant influence on his well-being. In order to measure thermal comfort for the assessment of workplaces and for complex technical applications such as vehicle interi-ors, the equivalent temperature $T_{eq}$ is used. It reflects the thermal perception of humans. The ISO 14505-2:2006 [4] forms the standard for assessing the thermal environment in vehicles. The equivalent temperature aims to project the thermal perception based on the sensitive heat exchange by radiation and convection between the person in his actual environment to a standardized environment with a homogeneous temperature distribution and in the absence of wind. Due to the complex thermal conditions in the vehicle interior, there are comfort zones to evaluate the current thermal conditions of the occupant. The definition of these comfort zones for summer- and winter conditions is based on experiments done by Nilsson [5]. These are integrated in ISO 14505-2:2006 as a recommended evaluation scheme of the expected subjective thermal perception. The evaluation is possible for the whole body as well as for individual body regions. Objec-tive evaluation methods are currently used in the automotive sector for the application process of vehicle air-conditioning concepts and it is used in the following investigation.

## 3   State of Research

With increasing automation in the passenger vehicle, the role of the driver in the vehicle will change. The driver will spend more time and attention on non-driving-related tasks (NDRTs). A major challenge for the automotive industry is to identify individual user needs. The aim of current studies is to predict user behavior in autonomous vehicles, especially with regard to secondary activities [6, 7].

Highly automated and autonomous vehicles enable different seating postures. Driver's behaviour while conducting the NDRTs in a highly automated vehicle is investigated in studies by Fleischer, Kamp et al. and Köhler et al. [8–10]. Space in front of the seat allows the passenger more range for movement and postures. Moreover, these studies contribute to the space managements of interior design in the future and show, that new air-conditioning concepts have to be developed regarding the flexible sitting postures and seat constellations. These should be able to ensure the thermal comfort of the occupants during non-driving activities.

Accordingly, climatization systems have to be developed that start locally and also supply or dissipate heat by means of heat conduction or radiation. Stuke [11] evaluates the influence of local air-conditioning on the overall comfort with an overhead air conditioning concept. It is shown, that local thermal sensation in one body region can have a significant impact on the global thermal comfort of the whole body [12].

One possibility of local climatization is at the seat and backrest, which allow a local temperature control close to the body of the occupant. The vehicle seat is particularly suitable for local measurements. In winter, it can provide thermal energy with the aid of a seat heater. This leads to heat exchange due to conduction between the body and the seat surface. In summer, it is possible to use forced convection to extract air from the seat or the contact surface with fans in order to create a pleasant microclimate. Fan [13] shows an interesting approach to close to the body climate control concerning a seat with personalized inlets in an aircraft. The seat ventilation system supplies fresh air by fans which are located at the armrest and the bottom of the seat. In order to provide a pleasant microclimate, it is also essential to dissipate perspired moisture from the contact area between seat and occupant. There are the use of hygroscopic climate materials or textiles [14] and a vented cushion, which is state of the art in most current automotive seats.

## 4 Methodology

A new innovative ventilated seating concept is developed to meet future usage requirements. The main objective of the development is to improve thermal comfort of the seat and to introduce new innovative concepts for future vehicle interiors and flexible seating positions.

### 4.1 Seat Design

The prototype is based on a conventional climate control seat of an upper-class vehicle. The seat is divided into seven different ventilation zones. Furthermore, the flexible active venting and ventilation of the seat and backrest by reversible fans provide local dehumidification. The integrated ventilation system in the side bolsters also provides efficient cooling of the thighs and upper back area. A new development is the implementation of air outlets on the side of the seat which can be adjusted axially and thus influence the outflow direction. The outlets can create a lateral air curtain, whereby cold air with a higher density blows from above onto the passenger and envelops the seat. In this case, the occupant is still climatized from the side and from the front, even if the seat position direction changes. The prototype and the outlet concept are shown in Fig. 1.

In addition to the CAD design, a CFD simulation of the inlet and outlet components are carried out. The digital human model RAMSIS™ is used to define critical dimensions including sitting persons of different anthropometric typologies. Furthermore, a control system for the electrical components like fans and seat heating is developed.

The seat is equipped with a 3D spacer fabric instead of foam. This highly vapor-permeable material acts as an air distribution layer to ensure that the extracted air is distributed over the entire seat surface. Even if the fans are not operating, passive convection will allow a comfortable microclimate at the contact areas between passenger and seat. Test subjects are required to evaluate the individual ventilated zones on the seat and backrest surfaces. This paper focuses on the concept of seat outlets. These can be objectively tested in the climate chamber with a dummy to investigate thermal comfort.

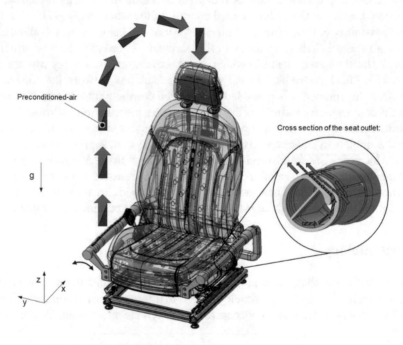

**Fig. 1.** Prototype of the ventilated seat concept and the outlets.

## 4.2  Experimental Setup

The experiments are conducted in a climate chamber at the Institute of Ergonomics, Technical University of Munich, with ambient temperatures of −20 °C and +40 °C for the winter and summer mode. A climate dummy with 16 equivalent temperature sensors attached on the surface is used. The dummy corresponds to the 50th percentile man [15]. A vehicle mock-up is used where various climate conditions for the interior can be adjusted (see Fig. 2). In this way different climate scenarios can be investigated to acquire an objective thermal perception regarding the influence of different temperatures, radiation and convection in the vehicle cabin.

The outlet vents are positioned straight up (see Fig. 1) for winter and summer temperatures during the whole experiment. The seat concept is evaluated with the extreme case for the winter and summer condition. The parameter conditions of Table 1 are kept for 60 min until stationary conditions are reached. For more realistic conditions sun simulation is generated by heat foils in the front and sides of the mock-up for the summer mode.

**Fig. 2.** Vehicle mock-up in the climate chamber for the experiment to generate individual interior climate for comfort studies.

## 4.3 Experimental Parameters

An overview of the different parameters for the climate chamber and the mock-up is given in Table 1. The ambient conditions and the temperatures of the heating foils for the summer mode are constant. The other parameters are adjusted during the test till steady state condition are achieved.

**Table 1.** Parameter settings during the investigation.

|  | Parameter setting | Winter condition | Summer condition |
|---|---|---|---|
| Backrest angle | Constant | 68° | 68° |
| Environment temperature | Constant | −20 °C | 40 °C |
| Humidity | Constant | 40% | 40% |
| Blower speed | Stepwise | 4000, 3000, 2000 rpm | 4000, 3000, 2000 rpm |
| Cooling circuit | Stepwise | – | 5, 10, 15 °C |
| Heating circuit | Stepwise | 50, 45, 40, 35, 30 °C | – |
| Heat foils front/sides | Constant | 0 °C | 52, 42, 35, 30 °C |

## 5   Results

Different values for the equivalent temperatures and air velocities are reached depending on the change of the parameter settings. The graph in Fig. 3(a) shows the averaged equivalent temperature of the sensor areas over the duration of the experiment for the pull-down. The first setting of 4000 rpm and 5 °C cooling temperature leads to a temperature gradient of 11 °C in the head area and 8 °C in the lower body area. After about 30 min the conditions become stationary. An example of the evaluation of thermal comfort according to ISO 14505-2:2006 for the dummy is given in Fig. 3(b). The colored zones in Fig. 3(b) correspond with the 16-measuring positions of the equivalent temperature sensors on the surface of the dummy. The asymmetric thermal perception results from the radiation of the heating foil from the left side panel. Further adjustments by increasing the temperature and reducing the fan speed cannot improve the thermal comfort conditions.

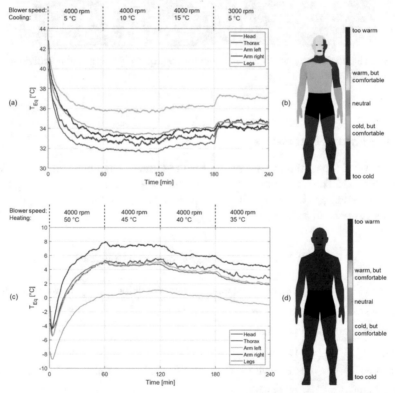

**Fig. 3.** Section from the averaged equivalent temperature over the 16 sensors for summer (a) and winter (c) mode. Thermal comfort zones of the dummy after 30 min, 4000 rpm and 10 °C outlet temperature (b) for summer condition and after 60 min, 4000 rpm and 50 °C outlet temperature (d) for winter condition.

The conditions for the winter scenario are shown in Fig. 3(c). There is a slight slope of the equivalent temperature at the beginning of the experiment at a discharge temperature of 50 °C and a blower speed of 4000 rpm. The maximum is reached after about 60 min. An evaluation of the dummy according to the comfort values of ISO 14505-2:2006 in Fig. 3(d) illustrates the thermal perception after 60 min with an outlet temperature of 50 °C. The equivalent temperature rises to a maximum of 4 °C in the head area and 0 °C in the leg area, which is 'too cold' for all body regions. Further parameter settings in the winter scenario cannot improve the thermal comfort.

# 6 Discussion

The driver seat can provide limited thermal comfort with the seat outlets. In summer condition, the implementation of seat outlets leads to a temperature difference and creates an enveloping air curtain around the seat in the upper body area. The seat outlets are only simulated in extreme climatic conditions and can partially displace the warm ambient air by the impulse from the outlets. The conditioned air moves from top to bottom and achieves a 'warm, but comfortable' thermal perception for the head region and the upper body. In a colder environment the whole body region is 'too cold'. The greatest effect for both climatic scenarios is achieved at the highest blower speed as well as the lowest cooling or the highest heating power. The parameter settings are not optimal for an efficient operation, but these are important with regard to an electric vehicle and the use of energy. In a vehicle, under normal operating conditions of the air-conditioning system, thermal comfort should be ensured for the occupant. The presented concept of the seat outlets cannot provide global thermal comfort under extremely hot and cold conditions. During the pull-down, only the upper body is climatized while the conditions of the lower body are still 'too warm'. The comfort zone 'warm, but comfortable' for the head area and upper body area becomes stationary after about 30 min. In the cold environment, the warm conditioned air could not displace the cold air. This can be influenced through cooling or heating power losses in the air duct and the non-optimal outflow from the outlets which causes flow losses. The small cross-section of the outlets can cause a too small impulse which influences the displacement of the ambient air around the occupant. Long air ducts leading to the seat should be avoided here in order to prevent heat loss.

In this investigation, only one seat posture and seat angle are examined and objectively measured. The ISO 14505-2:2006 only allows the subdivision of comfort zones into 'summer' and 'winter' while different population, anthropometries, secondary activities and seating postures are not considered. In this context these parameters has to be approached in order to evaluate the concept for future interior concepts. The objectively measured comfort zones can be subjectively evaluated in investigations with test subjects. Here, the various zones of seat ventilation combined with the individually set direction of the airflow of the seat outlets should also be investigated. In order to provide air-conditioning in different seating positions, the concept of the outlets can be transferred to the backrest so that the occupant's upper body can also be climatized in a reclining position. In the automotive sector, it is important to test extreme climate scenarios and unsteady conditions. But further parameters for the test design should be climate scenarios oriented to average temperature in Europe, in order to determine the feasibility of the seat outlets for these environmental conditions. Combinations with an overhead ventilation concept [11] or radiant elements could increase thermal comfort and should be investigated regarding energy saving potential and different seating positions.

# 7 Conclusion

This paper presents a new innovative ventilated seat being developed for new vehicle interiors regarding new seating positions and postures. A seat ventilation concept with division into seven different ventilation zones is presented. An outlet concept at the seat surface is investigated, which can climatize the occupant from the side and can be adjusted independently from the seat position. The equivalent temperature according to ISO 14505-2:2006 is used as basis for the evaluation. First results indicate that the seat system has good potential for new interior concepts. For warm environments, good results can be achieved for the head and upper body. However, in cold environments the outflow concept is less suitable.

# References

1. Großmann, H., Böttcher, C.: Pkw-Klimatisierung. Springer, Heidelberg (2020)
2. Bubb, H., Bengler, K., Grünen, R.E., Vollrath, M.: Automobilergonomie. Springer Fachmedien Wiesbaden, Wiesbaden (2015)
3. Ergonomie der thermischen Umgebung – Analytische Bestimmung und Interpretation der thermischen Behaglichkeit durch Berechnung des PMV- und des PPD-Indexes und Kriterien der lokalen thermischen Behaglichkeit (ISO 7730:2005); Deutsche Fassung EN ISO 7730:2005 (2005)
4. Ergonomie der thermischen Umgebung – Beurteilung der thermischen Umgebung in Fahrzeugen – Teil 2: Bestimmung der Äquivalenttemperatur (ISO 14505-2:2006); Deutsche Fassung EN ISO 14505-2:2006 (2007)
5. Nilsson, H.O.: Comfort Climate Evaluation with Thermal Manikin Methods and Computer Simulation Models. National Institute for Working Life (2004)
6. Pfleging, B., Schmidt, A.: (Non-) driving-related activities in the car: defining driver activities for manual and automated driving. In: Workshop on Experiencing Autonomous Vehicles: Crossing the Boundaries between a Drive and a Ride at CHI 2015 (2015)
7. Hecht, T., Darlagiannis, E., Bengler, K.: Non-driving related activities in automated driving – an online survey investigating user needs. In: Ahram, T., Karwowski, W., Pickl, S., Taiar, R. (eds.) Human Systems Engineering and Design II, 1026, pp. 182–188. Springer International Publishing, Cham (2020)
8. Fleischer, M., Chen, S.: How do we sit when our car drives for us? In: Duffy, V.G. (ed.) Digital Human Modeling and Applications in Health, Safety, Ergonomics and Risk Management. 11th International Conference, DHM 2020, held as Part of the 22nd HCI International Conference, HCII 2020, Copenhagen, Denmark, 19–24 July 2020, Proceedings, vol. 12198, pp. 33–49. Springer, Cham (2020)
9. Kamp, I., Kilincsoy, U., Vink, P.: Chosen postures during specific sitting activities. Ergonomics **54**, 1029–1042 (2011)
10. Köhler, A.-l., Prinz, F., Wang, L., Becker, J., Voß, G.M.I., ladwig, S., Eckstein, L., Schulte, T., Depner, N.: How will we travel autonomously? User needs for interior concepts and requirements towards occupant safety. In: 28th Aachen Colloquium Automobile and Engine Technology (2019)
11. Stuke, P., Bengler, K.: Interior air conditioning for electric vehicle EVA. New approach on vehicle interior cooling to increase comfort and reduce energy consumption. CoFat (2014)
12. Zhang, H.: Human Thermal Sensation and Comfort in Transient and Non-Uniform Thermal Environments. Berkely (2003)

13. Fan, J., Zhou, Q.: A review about thermal comfort in aircraft. J. Therm. Sci. **28**, 169–183 (2019)
14. Climatex: Climatex. Der Stoff für gute Gefühle. https://www.climatex.com/anwendungen/tra nsportation-automotive/ (2018)
15. Rolle, A., Schmandt, B., Guinet, C., Bengler, K.: How can the thermal sensation be objectively determined in order to analyse different vehicle air conditioning concepts? In: Roaf, S., Nicol, F., Finlayson, W. (eds.) Windsor 2020. 11th Winsor Conference: Resilient Comfort, 16th–19th April 2020, Proceedings, pp. 343–357. Windsor (2020)

# Design of External Human-Machine Interfaces for Different Automated Vehicle Types for the Interaction with Pedestrians on a Shared Space

Merle Lau[✉], Duc Hai Le, and Michael Oehl

German Aerospace Center (DLR), Lilienthalplatz 7, 38108 Braunschweig, Germany
{merle.lau,duc.le,michael.oehl}@dlr.de

**Abstract.** Future traffic will be determined by the joint interaction of automated vehicles and other traffic participants in mixed traffic environments. For an overall safe and efficient traffic flow, the communication between automated vehicles and pedestrians must be ensured. An external human-machine interface (eHMI) serves as a communication channel between automated vehicles and other traffic participants. However, it remains unclear how information needs may differ for different vehicle types and how this should be considered in the eHMI design. This experimental online study investigates the pedestrians' interactions with two different automated vehicle types (car vs. bus) on a shared space. Both vehicles were equipped with the same eHMI communication strategies (mode awareness, intention-based, perception-based, combination) based on a LED light-band eHMI. Short video sequences from a pedestrians' perspective were shown in which the participants interacted with both vehicle types. Results showed that participants felt significantly safer and more comfortable when interacting with the car compared to the bus. Furthermore, participants felt significantly safer and better informed when an eHMI communication strategy was presented vs. mere mode awareness vs. no eHMI at all for both vehicle types (car vs. bus).

**Keywords:** Traffic psychology · Human factors · Human-machine interaction · External human-machine interface

## 1 Theory

The integration of automated vehicles (AV) into urban traffic can be seen as a fundamental change in mobility [1]. While nowadays, the human driver is in charge of executing the driving task, in highly and fully AV, the driver's role will change from an active driver to a more passive on-board user [2]. Therefore, today's dyad of interaction between human driver and other traffic participants (TP) will shift to a triad of interaction between on-board user, AV and other TP. The introduction of AV will take place in mixed traffic environments in which the AV will coexist with, e.g., pedestrians, cyclists and manual vehicles [3]. For a safe interaction, AV need to be able to communicate with the traffic

N. L. Black et al. (Eds.): IEA 2021, LNNS 221, pp. 710–717, 2021.
https://doi.org/10.1007/978-3-030-74608-7_87

participants and to inform them about the vehicle's intention and behavior [3–6]. In particular, explicit communication in urban traffic becomes particularly important during low speed and low distance [7]. This applies exemplary to the use case of a shared space which describes a traffic-calmed area in which all traffic participants have equal rights [8].

As possible solution, an external human-machine interface (eHMI) as communication tool positioned on the AV's outside seems to be a promising approach to transmit explicit information to other TP, i.e., about the vehicle's future behavior and maneuvers [9]. So far, several eHMI designs have been developed using different technologies, e.g., displays or light-bands [e.g., 5, 9, 10]. As one example, [9] developed a 360° LED light-band eHMI for an AV which showed different eHMI communication strategies to illustrate the vehicle's intention (intention-based), and perception of other TP (perception-based). Results indicate that participants felt safer when interacting with an automated car equipped with eHMI compared to no eHMI. All eHMI communication strategies were well-accepted and perceived as useful [9, 11]. The question that arises is how information requirements may differ for different vehicle types and how this should be considered in the eHMI design. Focusing on the interaction between AV and pedestrian, current research has shown that vehicle appearance can influence pedestrians' expectations and consequently their behavior, e.g., when crossing the street [12]. The authors showed that participants were more likely to cross the street in front of a small vehicle compared to a larger vehicle. Furthermore, participants reported a higher perceived risk when interacting with a larger vehicle compared to a smaller vehicle [12]. These findings are in line with [10] who showed that larger vehicles are perceived as less safe compared to smaller vehicles. As a first step into eHMI design for different vehicle types, the present experimental online study investigates different eHMI communication strategies based on [9] by focusing on the interaction between different AV types (car vs. bus) interacting with a pedestrian on a shared space.

## 2 Method

An experimental online study (N = 101; 39 female) with ages between 16 and 77 years (M = 33.52; SD = 15.91) was conducted using a mixed design. The participants' affinities for technology were rated M = 3.93 (SD = 0.59) on a 6-point scale (from "completely disagree" to "completely agree") with the ATI questionnaire [13]. The independent variables were eHMI communication strategy (intention-based, n = 34; perception-based, n = 33; both combined, n = 34) as between-subjects-factor and vehicle type (car vs. bus) as within-subjects-factor. The eHMI communication strategies were based on a LED light-band eHMI developed and evaluated for a car by [9] (Fig. 1). When the automated mode was activated, the LED light-band eHMI was continuously lightened up (*mode awareness*). The *intention-based* eHMI communication strategy includes mode awareness and additionally gives further explicit information about the AV's current and future vehicle maneuvers and cooperation capability by the pulsation of the LED light-band. The slowly pulsation of the LED light-band indicates the braking process and the fast pulsation demonstrates the acceleration process of the AV. The *perception-based* eHMI communication strategy also includes mode awareness and additionally gives explicit communication information to TP that they are detected by the AV. The detection is demonstrated by a light segment that moves with the TP when crossing the shared space. The *both combined eHMI* communication strategy combined both, i.e., the pulsation of the LED light-band for the braking and acceleration process (intention-based eHMI communication strategy) and the detection of other TP (perception-based eHMI communication strategy). Both vehicle types were equipped with equal eHMI communication strategies.

**Fig. 1.** Intention-based (left) and perception-based (right) eHMI communication strategies for the car and bus.

By using the example of a shared space, different video sequences were designed in virtual reality using the 3D creation software "Unreal Engine" (Version 4.24.2). In the beginning, information about the use case shared space were provided and the eHMI communication strategies were explained. Hence, participants were not naïve throughout the experiment. Moreover, participants were instructed that the egocentric video perspective represented their field of view. They were told that they are pedestrians who want to cross the shared space and that a car and a bus would approach from the left. In the beginning of each video, the participants stood on the same position and looked to the left from where the vehicle (car vs. bus) drove towards them. Both vehicle types drove with the same speed of 20 km/h, decelerating to 5 km/h before coming to a full stop in a distance of 7,38 m (measured from the front of the stopped vehicle) in front of the pedestrian (Fig. 2). After this, the pedestrian in the video crossed the shared space and turned around to see the vehicle driving away.

In total, six experimental video sequences (within design) were shown to each participant. The first four video sequences (1–4) were the same for all participants. In video 1 (car) and 2 (bus), the eHMI was off. In video 3 (car) and 4 (bus), the LED light-band eHMI was continuously lightened up showing that the vehicle is driving in automated mode (mode awareness). Video 5 (car) and 6 (bus) differed for participants (between design) depending on the eHMI communication strategy (intention-based vs. perception-based vs. both combined). After each video presentation, the participants were asked to rate the *feeling of safety* ("For my personal safety, I found the behavior of the vehicle to be safety enhancing.") on a seven-point Likert scale (from "totally disagree" to "totally agree") and the *perceived quality of information* ("How well did you feel informed by

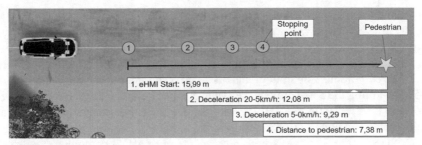

**Fig. 2.** Vehicle behavior in relation to the distance of the pedestrian from the bird's eye perspective.

the vehicle?") on a seven-point Likert scale (from "bad" to "good"). Additionally, the Self-Assessment Manikin (SAM) by [14] was used to obtain the non-verbal assessment of the three dimensions *affective valence, affective arousal* and *affective dominance*. All three dimensions were rated on a nine-point Likert scale ranging for *affective valence* from "unpleasant" to "pleasant", for *affective arousal* from "aroused" to "calm" and for *affective dominance* from "no subjectively perceived control over the situation" to "full control".

## 3   Results

In the following, the collected data is presented. A two-way analysis of variance (ANOVA) with Greenhouse-Geisser correction with eHMI communication strategy as between-subjects-factor and vehicle type as within-subjects-factor was conducted. Prerequisites for the calculation were checked and were given. All results with $p < .05$ are reported as significant. Means and standard deviations for all variables are reported in Table 1. Descriptive results showed higher scores for the highly automated car vs. highly automated bus for all variables.

**Table 1.** Means (M) and standard deviations (SD) for feeling of safety, perceived quality of information and the SAM dimensions affective valence, affective arousal, affective dominance.

| | Car | | | Bus | | |
|---|---|---|---|---|---|---|
| | M | SD | 95 % CI | M | SD | 95 % CI |
| Feeling for safety | 5.64 | 1.36 | [5.37, 5.91] | 5.47 | 1.46 | [5.17, 5.75] |
| Quality of information | 5.72 | 1.30 | [5.47, 5.98] | 5.62 | 1.26 | [5.37, 5.87] |
| Affective valence (SAM) | 6.95 | 1.85 | [6.59, 7.30] | 6.62 | 2.11 | [6.20, 7.04] |
| Affective arousal (SAM) | 3.54 | 2.09 | [3.14, 3.95] | 3.65 | 2.13 | [3.23, 4.07] |
| Affective dominance (SAM) | 6.04 | 2.16 | [5.62, 6.46] | 5.93 | 2.22 | [5.50, 6.37] |

*Note.* CI = confidence interval.

For the *feeling of safety*, results showed that vehicle type had a significant effect on the *feeling of safety,* $F(1, 98) = 4.84$, $p < .05$, $\eta^2 = .047$. Participants felt significantly safer when interacting with the car (M = 5.64, SD = 1.36) compared to the bus (M = 5.46; SD = 1.46). There was no significant effect of eHMI communication strategy and no significant vehicle type x eHMI communication strategy interaction (p > .05). For *perceived quality of information*, the results did not show significant effects of vehicle type, eHMI communication strategy and the eHMI communication strategy interaction (p > .05). Regarding the SAM dimensions, vehicle type had a significant effect on *affective valence*, $F(1, 98) = 6.04$, $p < .01$, $\eta^2 = .058$. The affective valence was significantly higher when interacting with the car (M = 6.95, SD = 1.85) compared to the bus (M = 6.62, SD = 2.11). There was no significant effect of eHMI communication strategy and no significant vehicle type x eHMI communication strategy interaction (all p > .05). Additionally, no significant differences were found for the other SAM dimensions *affective arousal* and *affective dominance* (all p > .05).

To investigate if there is a general difference between eHMI off vs. mode awareness vs. eHMI communication strategy (intention-based, perception-based, both combined), repeated-measures ANOVAs with Greenhouse Geisser correction were conducted. For *feeling of safety*, significant differences were found when participants interacted with a

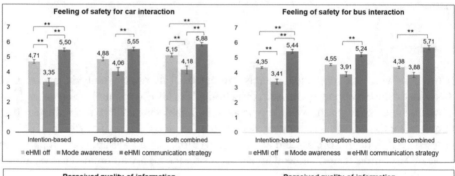

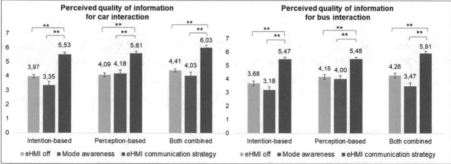

*Notes.* * p < .05; ** p < .01

**Fig. 3.** Pairwise comparisons using Bonferroni correction within the condition *intention-based* (eHMI off vs. mode awareness vs. intention-based), *perception-based* (eHMI off vs. mode awareness vs. perception-based), *both combined* (eHMI off vs. mode awareness vs. both combined) for car interaction and bus interaction for feeling of safety (top left and right) and for perceived quality of information (bottom left and right).

car and with a bus (all $p < .01$), $\eta^2$ from .184 to .417. For *perceived quality of infor-mation*, significant differences were found for the car and bus interaction (all $p < .01$), partial $\eta^2$ from .261 to .484. Pairwise comparisons using Bonferroni correction showed consistently higher scores for *feeling of safety* and *perceived quality of information* for the eHMI communication strategy compared to mode awareness and eHMI off for the car and the bus interaction (Fig. 3). Referring to *affective valence, affective arousal* and *affective dominance* (SAM), significant differences were found for eHMI off vs. mode awareness vs. intention-based eHMI for the car and bus interaction (all $p < .01$), $\eta^2$ from .332 to .484 and for eHMI off vs. mode awareness vs. both combined for the car and bus interaction (all $p < .01$), $\eta^2$ from .346 to .473. No significant differences were found for perception-based vs. mode awareness vs. eHMI off (all $p > .05$).

## 4   Discussion

The present experimental online study investigated the interaction between pedestrian and two different AV types (car vs. bus) both equipped with equal eHMI communication strategies on a shared space. Regarding the comparison between car and bus, descriptive results showed higher scores for the highly automated car vs. the highly automated bus for the feeling of safety, perceived quality of information and for the affective valence as well as for the affective dominance. This became significant for the feeling of safety and the SAM dimension affective valence which shows that participants felt safer and a higher affective valence when interacting with a highly automated car compared to a highly automated bus. However, no clear conclusions can be drawn to what extent these findings are related to the eHMI communication strategies or, e.g., vehicle movement and appearance. Generally, vehicle movements are highly relevant for the pedestrian' decision to cross the street [11]. Therefore, future studies should further focus on the interplay between implicit and explicit communication for the interaction between pedestrian and AV on a shared space and how this needs to be considered in the design of eHMI communication strategies.

Overall, the results indicate that eHMI communication strategies previously evaluated for a highly automated car [12] are also applicable for a highly automated bus and the use case shared space. There have been no significant differences between the intention-based, perception-based and both combined eHMI communication strategy which supports the assumption that all three eHMI communication strategies can contribute to a well-working interaction between pedestrian and highly automated car and bus on a shared space. This is supported by the fact that participants felt safer and better informed when the vehicle was equipped with eHMI communication strategies vs. mere mode awareness or no eHMI et all.

As a limitation of the study, the experimental online setting could lack immersion, i.e., to let the participants fully immerse in the role as pedestrians interacting with different types of AV and especially experiencing the different vehicle sizes. The used stimulus material consisted of short video sequences which can only reflect a realistic interaction to a small extent. The conduction as online study can be a possible explanation that no differences were found for the affective arousal and dominance. Future studies are planned in VR to create a more immersive environment and to enable a more realistic interaction with different vehicle types. As work-in-progress, the present study goes one step further into the design of eHMI communication strategies for different vehicle types revealing that people felt safer and more comfortable with a highly automated car compared to a highly automated bus.

**Acknowledgements.** This research was conducted within the project "CADJapanGermany: HF" which is funded by the Federal Ministry of Education and Research of Germany.

# References

1. Kauffmann, N., Winkler, F., Naujoks, F., Vollrath, M.: "What makes a cooperative driver?" Identifying parameters of implicit and explicit forms of communication in a lane change scenario. Transp. Res. Part F: Traffic Psychol. Behav. **58**, 1031–1042 (2018). https://doi.org/10.1016/j.trf.2018.07.019
2. Society of Automotive Engineers: Taxonomy and definitions for terms related to driving automation systems for on-road motor vehicles (J3016_201806) (2018)
3. Schieben, A., Wilbrink, M., Kettwich, C., Madigan, R., Louw, T., Merat, N.: Designing the interaction of automated vehicles with other traffic participants: design considerations based on human needs and expectations. Cognit. Tech. Work **21**(1), 69–85 (2019). https://doi.org/10.1007/s10111-018-0521-z
4. Färber, B.: Communication and communication problems between autonomous vehicles and human drivers. In: Maurer, M., Gerdes, J.C., Lenz, B., Winner, H. (eds.) Autonomous Driving, pp. 125–144. Springer, Berlin Heidelberg, Berlin, Heidelberg (2016)
5. Habibovic, A., Lundgren, V.M., Andersson, J., Klingegård, M., Lagström, T., Sirkka, A., Fagerlönn, J., Edgren, C., Fredriksson, R., Krupenia, S., Saluäär, D., Larsson, P.: Communicating intent of automated vehicles to pedestrians. Front. Psychol. **9**, 1336 (2018). https://doi.org/10.3389/fpsyg.2018.01336
6. Wilbrink, M., Schieben, A., Kaup, M., Willrodt, J.-H., Weber, F., Lee, Y.M., Markkula, G., Romano, R., Merat, N.: Preliminary interaction strategies for the interACT Automated Vehicles. interACT Deliverables 4.1. (2018)
7. Lee, Y.M., Madigan, R., Giles, O., Garach-Morcillo, L., Markkula, G., Fox, C., Camara, F., Rothmueller, M., Vendelbo-Larsen, S.A., Rasmussen, P.H., Dietrich, A., Nathanael, D., Portouli, V., Schieben, A., Merat, N.: Road users rarely use explicit communication when interacting in today's traffic: implications for automated vehicles. Cognit. Tech. Work **5**(9), 145 (2020). https://doi.org/10.1007/s10111-020-00635-y
8. Monderman, H., Clarke, E., Baillie, B.H.: Shared space: the alternative approach to calming traffic. Traffic Eng. Control **47**(8), 290–292 (2006)
9. Schieben, A., Wilbrink, M., Kettwich, C., Dodiya, J., Oehl, M., Weber, F., Sorokin, L., Lee, Y.M., Madigan, R., Merat, N., Dietrich, A., Bengler, K., Kaup, M.: Testing external HMI designs for automated vehicles - An overview on user study results from the EU project interACT. 9. Tagung Automatisiertes Fahren, Munich, Germany (2019)
10. De Clercq, K., Dietrich, A., Núñez Velasco, J.P., De Winter, J., Happee, R.: External human-machine interfaces on automated vehicles: effects on pedestrian crossing decisions. Hum. Factors **61**(8), 1353–1370 (2019). https://doi.org/10.1177/0018720819836343
11. Kettwich, C., Dodiya, J., Wilbrink, M., Schieben, A.M.: Light-based communication of automated vehicles with other traffic participants - a usability study in a Virtual Reality environment. In: Khanh, T.Q. (ed.) Proceedings of the 13th International Symposium on Automotive Lightning. Darmstädter Lichttechnik, vol. 18 (2019)

12. Dey, D., Martens, M., Eggen, B., Terken, J.: The impact of vehicle appearance and vehicle behavior on pedestrian interaction with autonomous vehicles. In: Löcken, A., Boll, S., Politis, I., Osswald, S., Schroeter, R., Large, D., Baumann, M., Alvarez, I., Chuang, L., Feuerstack, S., Jeon, M., van Huysduynen, H.H., Broy, N. (eds.) the 9th International Conference, Oldenburg, Germany, pp. 158–162 (2017). https://doi.org/10.1145/3131726.3131750
13. Franke, T., Attig, C., Wessel, D.: A personal resource for technology interaction: development and validation of the affinity for technology interaction (ATI) scale. Int. J. Hum.-Comput. Interact. **35**(6), 456–467 (2018). https://doi.org/10.1080/10447318.2018.1456150
14. Bradley, M.M., Lang, P.J.: Measuring emotion: The self-assessment manikin and the semantic differential. J. Behav. Therapy Exp. Psychiatry **25**(1), 49–59 (1994). https://doi.org/10.1016/0005-7916(94)90063-9

# Negative Effect of External Human-Machine Interfaces in Automated Vehicles on Pedestrian Crossing Behaviour: A Virtual Reality Experiment

Jieun Lee[1(✉)] [iD], Tatsuru Daimon[1], and Satoshi Kitazaki[2]

[1] Keio University, Yokohama 223-8522, Kanagawa, Japan
lee@keio.jp
[2] National Institute of Advanced Industrial Science and Technology, Tsukuba 305-8560, Ibaraki, Japan

**Abstract.** Communication between pedestrians and automated vehicles is playing a key role in enhancing the safety of future traffic environment. The current study attempted to suggest new insights into designing external human-machine interfaces (eHMIs) in automated vehicles for traffic safety as examines negative effects of the eHMI on pedestrian crossing behaviour in a situation where an automated vehicle yields to pedestrian. Virtual Reality systems simulated three experimental conditions: baseline (no eHMI), showing "After you" and "I'll stop" via eHMI on an automated vehicle in residential areas. The experiment using human participants resulted that conveying information via eHMI led pedestrians to do less careful exploratory behaviour toward other traffic. The result also showed the greater number of traffic collisions when the eHMI showed information compared to non-eHMI condition. The findings of this study are also being used to help how to design the eHMI on automated vehicles in shared spaces.

**Keywords:** Driving automation · External human-machine interface · Pedestrian crossing · Interface design · Virtual reality

## 1 Introduction

Driving automation is expected to bring new paradigms to surface transportation. This technology has promised a myriad of benefits, including energy resumption, traffic efficiency, and reducing traffic accidents. Following levels of driving automation defined by SAE International [1], automated vehicles with low levels of driving automation are already realised in the current market via several motor companies. Unlike the low levels that demand human drivers to intervene vehicle controls if necessary or when the automation issues a request to intervene in system failure, high levels of automation are able to undertake all dynamic driving tasks themselves. The highly developed automated vehicle is considered to be one of Mobility as a Service for improving quality of life in rural areas as well as to reduce drivers' workload produced by vehicle controls.

N. L. Black et al. (Eds.): IEA 2021, LNNS 221, pp. 718–725, 2021.
https://doi.org/10.1007/978-3-030-74608-7_88

As driving automation develops, communication between road users and automated vehicles has become an important research topic to improve traffic safety. Implicit communication among road users, such as making hand signals and eye-contact, enables them to communicate their intention, resulting in traffic efficiency and safety. However, considering symbiotic traffic environments with pedestrians and vehicles equipped with high levels of driving automation, the lack of communication possibly occurs due to the absence of human drivers. Developing explicit communication tools for effective human-vehicle communication is expected to address such problems.

Presenting information via external human-machine interfaces (eHMIs) on automated vehicles is considered to be one of solutions to reduce latent accident risk by failure in communication between road users and automated vehicles. Accordingly, interface design concept has been suggested with respect to several factors, such as display colour [2, 3], message voice [4], interpretability [4], location [5], and screen size [6] and communication partner [7]. In recent years, a myriad number of studies on eHMIs have emerged with expected benefits to road users as automated vehicles feature the eHMI.

However, it cannot affirm that information from the eHMI produces positive outcomes. One possible concern is that pedestrians are likely to shape inappropriate attitude towards the automated vehicle. Crossing after checking road situations is essential role of traffic participants, however, if they judge to cross relying on the information via eHMIs, they might not deal with latent traffic risk. Whilst pedestrian attitude towards automated vehicles, including trust or acceptance, has been widely investigated [8], the research to date has tended to focus on positive effects of eHMI rather than negative effects.

The current study seeks to address negative effects of eHMIs on automated vehicles. Virtual reality (VR) experiments using human participants were conducted to observe pedestrians' crossing behaviour when the eHMI on automated vehicle is projected.

## 2  Methods

### 2.1  Participants

Fifty-seven non-elderly participants (30 females) aged between 22 and 45 years ($M = 30.39$ years, $SD = 8.35$) took part in the current study. All participants were monetarily reimbursed JPY 3000 for their partaking. This experiment using human participants complied with the ethics code of Keio University and was approved by the ethical review board (REF No. 2020-63). Written informed consent was obtained from each participant.

### 2.2  Apparatus

We used HTC Vive VR systems to simulate a Japanese residential road environment (e.g., [9]). A head mount display presented the simulated road, with two screens (90 FPS, 2160 × 1200 binocular resolution, a field of view of 110°). Two controllers included a trigger and clip buttons, and a trackpad. Lighthouse that is a tracking system on two HTC base stations beamed infrared lasers to the HMD and controllers in order to track participants' movement and orientation data. As each base station has a 150° horizontal field of view and a 110° vertical field of view, distance between two base stations was 3.6 m. The participant was positioned between the two base stations. To run the materials, we used two computers (DELL Alienware Aurora R7 with Intel Core i7-8700 CPU, 16 GB RAM, and NVIDIA GeForce GTX 1080 GPU and Alienware Area-51 R5 with Intel Core i9-7940X CPU, 32 GB RAM, and NVIDIA GeForce GTX 1080 Ti). Figure 1 indicates the experimental environment setup at Keio University.

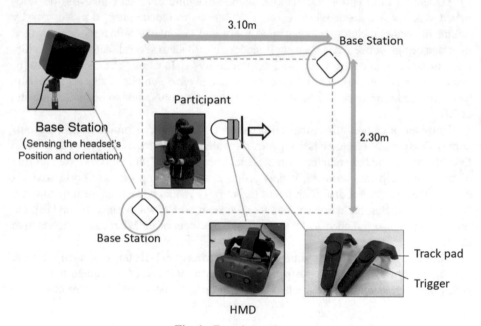

**Fig. 1.** Experimental setup.

## 2.3 Experimental Design

A between-subject design was used, with eHMI manipulations: no eHMI (Baseline), displaying a text message of "After you" (eHMI-A), and displaying a text message of "I'll stop" (eHMI-E) (see Fig. 2). As text-based eHMIs do not require participants to learn what displayed information means like anthropomorphic symbols [10], the current study prepared two types of text messages (eHMI-E and eHMI-A) [4]. Eleven experimental events were simulated on a two-way two-lane residential road. The participant experienced a critical event after the exposure to ten traffic events which were designed to shape pedestrian attitude towards the eHMI. In the critical scenario, there were two trucks and an automated vehicle on the road when the participant was on the start point. Here, the two trucks and the automated vehicle stopped in the left and right side of the participant respectively. The automated vehicle yielded the road to the pedestrian, with projecting two types of text messages or not displaying any signals, the participant then started to cross the zebra crossing as shown in Fig. 3.

no eHMI (Baseline)          "After you" (eHMI-A)          "I'll stop" (eHMI-E)

**Fig. 2.** The three eHMI manipulation types

Careful exploratory behaviour of pedestrians is required to cope with an approaching vehicle from the left side. The pedestrian could not find the vehicle without looking toward the left side because a large truck obstructed to have a wide view of traffic environment, consequently, collisions occurred for the pedestrians who could be not aware of the vehicle. As the reason why the pedestrian did not check the left side, pedestrians' decision-making depending on only information via the eHMI on the automated vehicle from the right side is considered (see Fig. 3). More specifically, if the participant crosses the zebra crossing with decisions based on information via the eHMI, they might have collisions with the approaching vehicle due to reliance on the eHMI. This can be considered to be a negative effect as providing information via the eHMI on automated vehicles.

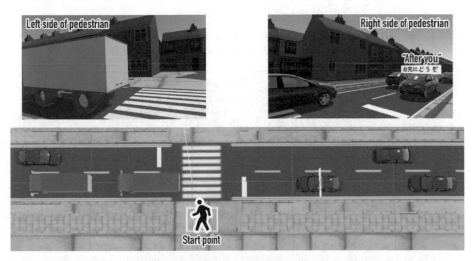

**Fig. 3.** Experimental road environment.

## 2.4  Procedure

Upon arrival, the overview of experiment was briefly explained by an experimenter, and informed consent was obtained from each participant. A practice was provided to become familiar with the VR setup, such as using controller and checking motion sickness. After the practice, participants moved on the experimental trial. In total, eleven critical events on the residential road were presented to the participant, and participants were asked to cross after checking traffic environment by pressing the trigger on the controller. Each participant responded three subsequent questionnaire items with 5 Likert-scale on the screen after the trial. The duration of the experiment was around 40 min.

## 2.5  Statistical Analyses

To look into negative effects of the eHMI on pedestrian crossing behaviour, we classified three types of pedestrian behaviour: looking toward the left during crossing, stopping on the middle of zebra crossing, and having near misses with the oncoming vehicle. Here, the pedestrian behavioural data collected from the VR system were used to examine the negative effect across three experimental conditions (Baseline, eHMI-A, eHMI-E). More specifically, data in the 11th event were facilitated for statistical analyses as the participant shaped their attitude towards the automated vehicle throughout the ten events. The data collection was submitted to Chi-squared analysis. As data from 11 participants were not tracked correctly, these data were eliminated. All statistical analyses were implemented in IBM SPSS version 26.

# 3  Results

**Table 1.** The cases whether pedestrians did look toward the left, stop on the zebra crossing, and avoid collisions with the vehicle from the left side or not ($Y = Yes$; $N = No$).

| Condition | Looked | | Stopped | | Collided | |
|---|---|---|---|---|---|---|
| | Y | N | Y | N | Y | N |
| Baseline | 16 | 1 | 14 | 3 | 3 | 14 |
| eHMI-A | 11 | 5 | 11 | 5 | 5 | 11 |
| eHMI-E | 11 | 2 | 11 | 2 | 3 | 10 |

As aforementioned, we set three time points with respect to pedestrian crossing process. Looking toward the left side and stopping on the zebra crossing during the crossing, and whether the pedestrian was able to avoid collisions with a vehicle from the left side. Table 1 describes the number of pedestrians according to their behaviour at three time points: looking toward the left during crossing, stopping on the zebra crossing during crossing, and having collisions with an approaching vehicle from the left. The observed cases for each time point were 17, 16, and 13 in the Baseline, eHMI-A, and eHMI-E respectively.

### 3.1 The Ratio of Pedestrians Who Looked Toward the Left During Crossing

As shown in Table 1, relatively small number of looking toward the left during crossing was observed in the Baseline compared to two eHMI conditions. Data provided a favourable difference in the ration of pedestrian who looked toward the left during crossing between the Baseline and eHMI-A conditions, $\chi^2(1) = 3.57, p = .059$. This indicates that the ratio of pedestrians who performed scanning behaviour was higher in the Baseline than the eHMI-A.

### 3.2 The Ratio of Pedestrians Who Stopped on the Crosswalk During Crossing

In the process of crossing which a vehicle is coming from the left, pedestrians should stop to avoid collision with the vehicle. Whilst there was no change in the cases for the eHMI-A and -E conditions between time points of looking and stopping during crossing, two more cases were observed in the Baseline between these two time points (see Table 1). However, the ratio of pedestrians who stopped on the crosswalk during crossing and did not have collisions with the oncoming vehicle was also the highest in the Baseline compared to those of eHMI-E and -A. For the stopped cases, the ratio of the Baseline, eHMI-E, and eHMI-A was 0.82, 0.85, and 0.69 respectively. The Chi-squared test did not find significant differences among all experimental conditions.

### 3.3 The Ratio for no Collision Cases

The ratio for no collision cases was 0.82, 0.77, and 0.69 respectively (Table 1). Data in terms of collision number provided that providing the intention of automated vehicles via the eHMI possibly provokes higher collision risk compared to when no information is displayed on the automated vehicle. This tendency seems similar to the observation for the stopped cases during crossing. Likewise, data did not provide significance, all $\chi^2 < 0.98, p > 0.32$.

## 4 Discussions

The main objective of this study was to observe a negative effect of eHMI messages in automated vehicles on pedestrian crossing behaviour. We classified three types of behaviour with regard to pedestrian crossing process (looking the left side, stopping on the middle of crosswalk, and collision with the upcoming vehicle).

Results found that pedestrians are likely to allocate their attention on the sides during crossing when automated vehicles do not project any signs via eHMIs. In comparison with this case, the lesser number of scanning behaviour was observed in both eHMI conditions. As the participant had more exploratory gaze behaviour in the Baseline than the eHMI-A, providing information via eHMIs with road users may lead relatively high reliance on automated vehicles, resulting in careless crossing behaviour without comprehensive understanding of traffic situations. Also, no significance in terms of stopping and collisions may indicate that the eHMI has a substantial impact on the beginning of crossing process. Next study should collect data of pedestrians' gaze behaviour to investigate their cognitive process to make decision in crossing [11].

One possible concern tangled with negative effects of the eHMI on crossing behaviour is pedestrians' attitudes towards automated vehicles. The higher levels of trust or reliance, the lesser careful crossing behaviour, resulting traffic accidents. This study provided empirical findings as analysed the number of pedestrians who checked traffic environment, made stopping after being aware of the approaching vehicle from the left side, and avoided vehicle collisions. Several participants in the post-experiment interview reported that they thought that the yielding vehicle displayed the message via the eHMI with comprehensive understanding of encountering traffic environment. This tendency indicates pedestrians' inappropriate trust towards the automated vehicle. Future study is expected to investigate pedestrian attitude towards eHMIs with questionnaire items, such as users' trust or acceptance [8].

These findings should be highlighted with several limitations. First, even though the participant experienced eleven traffic events in this VR study, all prepared events were very similar. This VR environment was limited in observing the precise number of near misses. Lastly, an equal participant number for each experimental condition is also important to bring convincing statistical findings. However, aforementioned findings can contribute to designing the eHMI for automated vehicles as well as developing training methods for road users who will share the road with automated vehicles.

This study found that displaying allocentric messages via eHMIs contributed to pedestrians' relatively careless scanning behaviour toward the left before crossing compared to when non-information was provided from automated vehicles. Findings from this study suggest a different point of view in terms of negative effects of eHMIs in certain traffic situations inconsistent with positive effects of eHMIs on road safety reported in previous studies.

# References

1. Society of Automotive Engineers (SAE): Taxonomy and Definitions for Terms Related to Driving Automation Systems for On-Road Motor Vehicles, Standard J3016 (2018)
2. Bazilinskyy, P., Dodou, D., de Winter, J.: External human-machine interfaces: which of 729 colors is best for signaling 'please (Do not) cross'?. In: 2020 IEEE International Conference on Systems, Man, and Cybernetics (SMC) on Proceedings, pp. 3721–3728. IEEE, Toronto (2020)
3. Rettenmaier, M., Schulze, J., Bengler, K.: How much space is required? Effect of distance, content, and color on external human–machine interface size. Information 11, 346 (2020)
4. Bazilinskyy, P., Dodou, D., de Winter, J.: Survey on eHMI concepts: the effect of text, color, and perspective. Transp. Res. Part F: Traffic Psychol. Behav. 67, 175–194 (2019)
5. Eisma, Y.B., van Bergen, S., ter Brake, S.M., Hensen, M.T.T., Tempelaar, W.J., de Winter, J.C.F: External human-machine interfaces: the effect of display location on crossing intentions and eye movements. Inf. (Switz.) 11(1), 13 (2020)
6. Ackermann, C., Beggiato, M., Schubert, S., Krems, J.F.: An experimental study to investigate design and assessment criteria: what is important for communication between pedestrians and automated vehicles? Appl. Ergon. 75, 272–282 (2019)
7. Rettenmaier, M., Albers, D., Bengler, K.: After you?!—use of external human-machine interfaces in road bottleneck scenarios. Transp. Res. Part F: Traffic Psychol. Behav. 70(2020), 175–190 (2020)

8. Kaleefathullah, A.A., Merat, N., Lee. Y.M., et al.: External human–machine interfaces can be misleading: an examination of trust development and misuse in a CAVE-based pedestrian simulation environment. Hum. Factors (2020)

9. Burns, C.G., Oliveira, L., Hung, V., Thomas, P., Birrell, S.: Pedestrian attitudes to shared-space interactions with autonomous vehicles - a virtual reality study. Adv. Intell. Syst. Comput. **964**, 307–316 (2020)

10. De Clercq, K., Dietrich, A., Pablo, J., Velasco, N., de Winter, J., Happee, R.: External human-machine interfaces on automated vehicles: effects on pedestrian crossing decisions. Hum. Factors **61**(8), 1353–1370 (2019)

11. Dey, D., Walker, F., Martens, M., Terken, J.: Gaze patterns in pedestrian interaction with vehicles: towards effective design of external human-machine interfaces for automated vehicles. In: Proceedings - 11th International ACM Conference on Automotive User Interfaces and Interactive Vehicular Applications, AutomotiveUI 2019, pp. 369–378 (2019)

# Personality Influences on Drivers' Decision to Take Back Manual Control: A Simulator Study on Automated Driving

Jasmin Leitner[✉], Philipp Hock, and Martin Baumann

Institute of Psychology and Education, Department of Human Factors,
Ulm University, Ulm, Germany
jasmin.leitner@uni-ulm.de

**Abstract.** Automated driving aims to enhance traffic safety. However, as long as drivers have the opportunity to take back manual control of the automated vehicle, they can disable automation to drive manually at any time. For an increase in traffic safety, this driver-initiated driver control should not occur in safety-critical situations when the automated system works faultlessly. In this driving simulator study, factors influencing the decision to take back manual control of an automated vehicle were investigated. Participants ($N = 46$) were driven by an automated system on a two-lane country road behind a slow vehicle. The visual range was restricted by fog. Therefore, the automation did not perform an overtaking maneuver. The automation could be disabled by the driver to overtake the preceding vehicle by performing a safety-critical maneuver. The influences of impulsivity and sensation seeking as well as three automation feedback systems on the decision to take back manual control were examined. Results indicated that high sensation seeking as well as high impulsivity were associated with an earlier deactivation of the automation. Though, driver-initiated driver control was not influenced by the different automation feedback systems. This experiment provides insights into factors influencing driver-initiated driver control, which might be useful for the development of automated driving systems and guidelines for automated driving.

**Keywords:** Automated driving · Driver-initiated driver control ·
Decision-making · Impulsivity · Sensation seeking

## 1 Introduction

Over the last years, the development of automated vehicles (AVs) gained increasingly in importance. Since the majority of car accidents are caused at least partly by the human driver [1], AVs should enhance traffic safety [2]. Depending on the automation level, the driver has to be able to take back manual control if the AV requests for it [3]. However, as long as drivers have the opportunity to take back manual control of the AV, they can disable automation to drive manually at any time. This voluntary transition is referred to as driver-initiated driver control (DIDC) [4]. When the automated system

© The Author(s), under exclusive license to Springer Nature Switzerland AG 2021
N. L. Black et al. (Eds.): IEA 2021, LNNS 221, pp. 726–733, 2021.
https://doi.org/10.1007/978-3-030-74608-7_89

works faultlessly and no transition is necessary, DIDCs could be a potential source for accidents in automated driving because of possible human errors. In order to decrease risky DIDCs, it is important to understand which factors influence drivers' decision to resume control in safety-critical situations that can be handled by the AV safely.

The decision of whether to use or not to use an automated system is affected by personality variables [5]. Important personality variables in manual driving are impulsivity and sensation seeking. In the driving context, impulsivity can be defined as acting quickly without thinking about future consequences [6]. Results of a systematic review in [6] indicated that impulsivity negatively influences driving behavior, such as aberrant driving, in manual driving. Sensation seeking, which can be defined as seeking experiences and being willed to take risks for these [7], also influences driving behavior in manual driving. Results in [8] showed that high sensation seeking was related to a riskier driving style. In the context of automated driving, the authors in [9] found that sensation seeking increases the intention to use a fully AV. However, the authors stated that this association might only occur in the beginning. When the feeling of novelty is gone, a lack of driving pleasure and boredom could affect the intention to use a fully AV [9]. Then, sensation seeking could have an influence on DIDC. Based on previous research, it was expected that more impulsive drivers disable automation earlier than less impulsive drivers in a safety-critical situation in automated driving. Moreover, drivers scoring high in sensation seeking were assumed to disable automation earlier compared to drivers scoring low in sensation seeking.

Besides these internal variables, also external factors, such as the automated system, can influence the decision to take back manual control. The authors in [10] used automation feedback to persuade drivers to maintain automation in highly automated driving. Results indicated that persuasive feedback has a positive influence on automation usage in a safety-critical situation. In our study, the effect of automation feedback was further investigated. Since a human-machine interface (HMI) should be developed to be adaptive to the driver's characteristics [11], an adaptive feedback system, which provides feedback individually depending on the driver, was expected to persuade drivers more to maintain automation than a non-adaptive feedback system.

## 2  Method

### 2.1  Participants

The final sample consisted of $N = 46$ participants (80% female) after the exclusion of four participants because of technical problems with either the driving simulator or data recording and one participant who had not adhered to the ban on passing. The average age was $M = 24.50\,(SD = 4.88)$ years. The sample owned their valid driver's license for $M = 7.17\,(SD = 4.24)$ years. For their participation, they received either credit points or 20 € and could get an additional amount of up to 3 €. They were instructed that they would receive more money the more kilometers they achieved in a fixed duration, but only if they obeyed the traffic rules and did not cause an accident.

## 2.2  Apparatus

A driving simulator of Ulm University was used to conduct the experiment. A vehicle mockup equipped with an automatic transmission was positioned in front of three screens (2.10 m height and 3.30 m width each) with a field of vision of approximately 190°. Three projectors with an overall resolution of 5760*1080 pixels simulated the driving scenario, which was programmed using the simulator software SILAB version 6.0. The HMI (0.27 m width and 0.34 m height) with a resolution of 1024*1280 pixels was positioned in the middle of the vehicle's dashboard. For the adaptive automation feedback, an ultrasonic sensor, which measured the distance to the vehicle's roof (approximately 0.70 m), was positioned in the center console.

## 2.3  Procedure

The experiment lasted approximately 2.5 h per participant. After signing the consent form, participants were familiarized with the driving simulator. They performed two practice drives to become acquainted with the driving behavior of the simulator as well as to become familiar with the automation and the use of the HMI. The task was to overtake three slower vehicles and to follow the fourth vehicle. Participants drove manually during the first and automated during the second practice drive. Although participants were informed that the highly AV had all functions of an ordinary vehicle and could execute overtaking maneuvers, they were instructed to disable automation to overtake the three vehicles manually during the second practice drive to get to know the deactivation and activation process of the automation.

The main experiment, which was based on the study in [10], consisted of three drives. Each of these three drives included three trials and took approximately 20 min. Hence, participants passed through the same driving scenario nine times. They were driven highly automated a slight left turn on a two-lane country road with 100 km/h. Because of a ban on passing, a slow preceding vehicle (60 km/h) was not overtaken by the automation. In this section, oncoming traffic was implemented for the participants to learn that upcoming traffic had to be expected. When the ban on passing was dissolved, the visual range was restricted by fog and enlarged stepwise (Table 1). Because of the restricted visual range, the slow vehicle could not be overtaken by the automation safely. In this section, participants received either no feedback, non-adaptive feedback or adaptive feedback. The automation feedback informed the driver about the reason for following the vehicle. Participants could disable automation in order to overtake the slow vehicle by executing a safety-critical maneuver. During the study, electrodermal activity, heart rate and the performance in a repeated task on a laptop were recorded, which were not in the scope of this paper.

After the successful completion of the three experimental drives, participants had to fill out questionnaires including impulsivity and sensation seeking. Finally, they were shortly interviewed about conspicuities during the study, their impression of the automation and the reason why they decided to overtake the vehicle.

**Table 1.** Time passed in seconds, ban on passing and associated visual range in meters since the drive's beginning.

| Time passed | Ban on passing | Visual range |
|---|---|---|
| 0 s | Present | 840 m |
| 90 s | Dissolved | 100 m |
| 130 s | Not present | 175 m |
| 170 s | Not present | 250 m |
| 210 s | Not present | 325 m |
| 250 s | Not present | 400 m |

## 2.4 Experimental Design

A one factorial within-subject design with repeated measures was used for the driving simulator experiment. The independent variable was the automation feedback system including three factor levels (none, non-adaptive or adaptive). The feedback conditions were randomized between the three experimental drives. Analog to the auditory feedback condition of the study in [10], the non-adaptive feedback was provided whenever the fog level changed. In contrast, the adaptive feedback was provided individually dependent on the behavior of the driver. The feedback always started when participants intended to disable automation. This intention was measured with the ultrasonic sensor. When participants moved their hand towards the HMI and the distance values, which the ultrasonic sensor measured, were between 0.20 m and 0.40 m, the automation feedback started. The feedback informed the driver that the automation was not overtaking the preceding vehicle because of the poor visibilities. It was the same for the non-adaptive and the adaptive feedback.

The main dependent variable was the initiation of a DIDC, which was operationalized by the point in time when the automation was disabled by the driver in order to overtake the slow vehicle.

## 2.5 Materials

**HMI.** To switch between automated and manual driving, an HMI was used. Participants activated the automation by pressing a blue button *activate automation*. During the automated drive, an *UNLOCK* dwell button was visible. To disable automation, participants had to press this button for 5 s until the blue circle was filled completely. The dwell time was used to ensure that participants heard the automation feedback completely in the adaptive feedback condition before they could disable automation. After the blue circle was filled, a red button *deactivate automation* appeared. Pressing this button disabled automation and participants drove manually.

**Questionnaires.** After the three experimental drives, participants had to answer different questionnaires and demographics. Impulsivity was measured with the German short version of the *Barratt Impulsiveness Scale (BIS-15)* [12]. For sensation seeking, items were adapted from an English version [13].

## 2.6 Data Processing

The deactivation times were calculated from the point on which the ban on passing was dissolved and the three trials of each feedback condition were averaged. To consider all participants in the analyses, the time point when the preceding vehicle drove off after the last fog level was used as deactivation time for participants who did not overtake the vehicle. The involved variables were z-scored in all regression analyses.

The internal consistencies of the two personality variables, impulsivity ($\alpha = 0.70$) and sensation seeking ($\alpha = 0.76$), were sufficient. According to [12], the overall *BIS-15* score was calculated as the sum of all impulsivity items for each participant. For sensation seeking, the respective items were averaged. The two variables were not significantly correlated, $r(44) = .20, p = .184$, and thus considered as separate constructs in the analyses.

Because of the within-subject design with repeated measures, participants experienced the same driving scenario nine times. In the interview at the end of the experiment, the majority of participants stated that the driving situation was predictable for them (54%), which partly influenced their behavior. A hierarchical model showed that participants deactivated the automation independently of the feedback condition in the first experimental drive ($M = 128.26, SD = 68.01$) significantly later compared to the average of the second ($M = 107.04, SD = 72.07$) and the third ($M = 104.23, SD = 73.18$) experimental drive, $\beta = .-32, t(91) = -3.87, p < .001$. Although the feedback conditions were randomized, the validity of the second and the third experimental drive seemed to be limited based on this. Thus, analog to a between-subject design, only the first condition of each participant was analyzed.

# 3   Results

## 3.1   Influences of Personality Variables

Regarding impulsivity, more impulsive drivers were expected to disable automation earlier than less impulsive drivers. On average, the *BIS-15* score of the sample was $M = 29.28$ ($SD = 4.77$). Descriptively, impulsivity and the deactivation time were negatively associated meaning that a higher *BIS-15* score was associated with an earlier deactivation time of the automation. To test the hypothesis, a linear regression was used with impulsivity as the predictor and the deactivation time as the criterion. The linear regression indicating a negative association between impulsivity and the deactivation time of the automation was significant, $\beta = -.35, F(1, 44) = 6.16, p = .017$.

Drivers scoring high in sensation seeking were assumed to deactivate automation earlier in comparison to drivers scoring low in sensation seeking. On a seven-point Likert scale, the average sensation seeking score of the sample was $M = 4.57$ ($SD = 1.06$). There was descriptively a negative association between sensation seeking and the deactivation time. The assumption was tested by means of linear regression. As a result, sensation seeking significantly predicted the deactivation time of the automation, $\beta = .-36, F(1, 44) = 6.42, p = .015$.

## 3.2 Influence of Automation Feedback

An adaptive feedback system was assumed to persuade drivers more to maintain automation in comparison with a non-adaptive feedback system. As depicted in Fig. 1, the automation was disabled the earliest in the condition without feedback ($M = 120.21, SD = 61.36$, $n = 17$), the latest with the non-adaptive feedback ($M = 136.80, SD = 72.99, n = 12$) and in between with the adaptive feedback ($M = 130.28, SD = 73.85, n = 17$). An analysis of variance (ANOVA) was used to analyze differences between the deactivation times. As a result, the ANOVA showed no significant difference between the three feedback conditions, $F(2, 43) = 0.21, p = .809$.

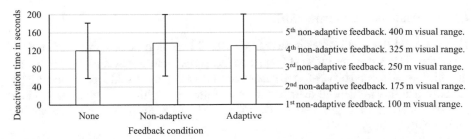

**Fig. 1.** Deactivation times in seconds for the three feedback conditions. Error bars represent standard deviations.

## 4  Discussion

This study examined the influences of impulsivity, sensation seeking and three automation feedback systems on DIDC. The results indicated that DIDC was influenced by impulsivity and sensation seeking. More impulsive drivers deactivated the automation significantly earlier compared to less impulsive drivers. Thus, impulsivity seems to not only influence driving behavior in manual driving negatively [6], but also decisions in automated driving. As expected, participants scoring high in sensation seeking disabled automation significantly earlier than participants with a low score in sensation seeking. This is in line with the results in [8], which showed a negative relation between sensation seeking and risky driving in manual driving, and extends them to automated driving. Moreover, this study provides evidence for the assumption in [9] that the intention to use an AV is affected by sensation seeking when the feeling of novelty is gone. Both results suggest that the decision to resume control of an AV in a safety-critical situation might be related to self-regulation processes, since participants were not able to inhibit their impulse to overtake the slow vehicle although an overtaking maneuver was critical due to the poor visibilities in this study.

Contrary to expectations, no differences between the deactivation times of the implemented feedback systems occurred. A comparison of the deactivation times of the study in [10] and our study showed that the deactivation times of the conditions with feedback were similar, but the baseline condition differed. Whereas participants disabled automation on average during the first fog level in the study in [10], participants maintained automation until the fourth fog level in our study. An explanation for this finding could be that the fog levels were tightened in the presented study, which increased the safety-criticality of the situation. Hence, drivers maintained automation independently of the feedback condition. With regards to the adaptive feedback, some participants stated that the timing of the feedback was too late and that they perceived it as irritating since it was provided when their decision was already taken. This stands in line with the results in [14], which reveal that additional reflections are precluded after a decision has been taken. This could be a reason for the descriptively earlier DIDC with the adaptive compared to the non-adaptive feedback.

### 4.1 Limitations and Future Work

This is one of the first studies investigating DIDC in a high-fidelity driving simulator experiment. However, the effects of repeated measures limited the validity of the second and third experimental drive of each participant as participants could forecast the driving scenario and this influenced their behavior. In future work, the driving scenario could be varied between the different trials. Therefore, oncoming traffic could be applied sporadically in single trials.

Prior to the experimental drives, participants were not informed about the automation feedback. In order to reduce the feeling of irritation, the feedback system could be introduced prior to the main experiment in future studies as the authors in [10] did.

This study provides evidence that impulsivity and sensation seeking have an influence on DIDC in highly automated driving. In future studies, the influences of these factors as well as of additional driver characteristics on DIDC could be further investigated using different driving scenarios.

## 5   Conclusion

The aim of this experiment was the investigation of DIDC with a focus on the influences of impulsivity and sensation seeking in a safety-critical situation. In addition, the effect of different automation feedback systems on the decision to take back manual control of an AV was examined. For that, a driving simulator experiment was conducted in which drivers could disable automation to overtake a slow vehicle by performing a safety-critical maneuver. Results indicate that high impulsivity and high sensation seeking were associated with an earlier deactivation of the automation and thus reduced traffic safety. Hence, the personality variables impulsivity and sensation seeking play a potentially important role in drivers' decision to resume control of an AV in a safety-critical situation that could be handled by the automated system safely.

**Acknowledgment.** This work was funded by the German Federal Ministry of Education and Research under the funding code 03IHS024D and within the project "CAD Japan Germany: HF" as well as by the Carl-Zeiss-Scholarship for PhD students. The authors are responsible for the content of this publication.

# References

1. Singh, S.: Critical reasons for crashes investigated in the National Motor Vehicle Crash Causation Survey. Traffic Safety Facts Crash•Stats DOT HS 812 506. National Highway Traffic Safety Administration, Washington, DC (2018)
2. Jeong, E., Oh, C., Lee, S.: Is vehicle automation enough to prevent crashes? Role of traffic operations in automated driving environments for traffic safety. Accident Anal. Prevent. **104**, 115–124 (2017)
3. SAE International: Taxonomy and definitions for terms related to driving automation systems for on-road motor vehicles. SAE Standard J3016_201806, pp. 1–35 (2018)
4. Lu, Z., de Winter, J. C. F.: A review and framework of control authority transitions in automated driving. In: Ahram, T., Karwoski, W., Schmorrow, D. (eds.) AHFE 2015, pp. 2510–2517. Procedia Manufacturing, Amsterdam (2015)
5. Kraus, J., Scholz, D., Messner, E.-M., Messner, M., Baumann, M.: Scared to trust? - Predicting trust in highly automated driving by depressiveness, negative self-evaluations and state anxiety. Front. Psychol. **10**, 1–15 (2020)
6. Bıçaksız, P., Özkan, T.: Impulsivity and driver behaviors, offences and accident involvement: a systematic review. Transp. Res. Part F: Traffic Psychol. Behav. **38**, 194–223 (2016)
7. Zuckermann, M.: Behavioural Expressions and Biosocial Bases of Sensation Seeking. Cambridge University, Cambridge (1994)
8. Jonah, B.A., Thiessen, R., Au-Yeung, E.: Sensation seeking, risky driving and behavioral adaption. Accident Anal. Prevent. **33**(5), 679–684 (2001)
9. Payre, W., Cestac, J., Delhomme, P.: Intention to use a fully automated car: attitudes and a priori acceptability. Transp. Res. Part F: Traffic Psychol. Behav. **27**, 252–263 (2014)
10. Hock, P., Kraus, J., Walch, M., Lang, N., Baumann, M.: Elaborating feedback strategies for maintaining automation in highly automated driving. In: Green, P., Pfleging, B., Burnett, G., Gabbard, J., Oswald, S. (eds.) AutomotiveUI 2016, pp. 105–112. Association for Computing Machinery, New York (2016)
11. Andreone, L., Amditis, A., Deregibus, E., Damiani, S., Morreale, D., Bellotti, F.: Beyond context-awareness: Driver-vehicle-environment adaptivity. From the comunicar project to the AIDE concept. In: Proceedings of the 16th Triennial World Congress, pp. 109–114. Elsevier IFAC Publications, Prague (2005)
12. Meule, A., Vögele, C., Kübler, A.: Psychometrische Evaluation der deutschen Barratt Impulsiveness Scale – Kurzversion (BIS-15). Diagnostica **57**(3), 126–133 (2011)
13. Hoyle, R.H., Stephenson, M.T., Palmgreen, P., Lorch, E.P., Donohew, R.L.: Reliability and validity of a brief measure of sensation seeking. Pers. Individ. Differ. **32**(3), 401–414 (2002)
14. Heckhausen, H., Gollwitzer, P.M.: Thought contents and cognitive functioning in motivational versus volitional states of mind. Motiv. Emot. **11**(2), 101–120 (1987)

# Is Interacting with Partial Automation System with a Joystick a Potential Option?
## Investigating Drivers' First Impressions of the Joystick Control

ChoKiu Leung[1](✉) ⓘ and Toshihisa Sato[2] ⓘ

[1] University of Tsukuba, Tsukuba, Ibaraki 305-8573, Japan
liang@css.risk.tsukuba.ac.jp
[2] National Institute of Advanced Industrial Science and Technology, Tsukuba, Ibaraki 305-8560, Japan

**Abstract.** This study presents the challenge of considering a joystick to safely control a vehicle with partially automated system. This study answered two research questions. One is related to the safety of joystick control, the other is related to the functionality. 24 elderly drivers who had not been trained in joystick control participated in the driving simulation experiment. The driving simulator with joystick device simulated the highway scenario for collecting the driver behavior when they control the vehicle with ADAS support. The result showed that most of the participants were able to control the vehicle by joystick to safely overtake and lane changes under certain road condition. Also, this study found that the characteristic of using joystick for choosing to change the lane is about 1.6 s longer than conventional steering wheel condition, and the mental workload of the joystick control was significantly higher than when the driver using steering wheel.

**Keywords:** Automated system · Human-machine interaction · Driver performance · Joystick

## 1 Introduction

### 1.1 Research Background

Recently, in some manufacturers' concept vehicles, the joystick or control stick device is considered as a potential alternative to the conventional pedal or/and steering wheel. This is not inconceivable because in air and marine transportation such as cruise ship and aircraft, the joystick as the control device is reliable [1]. Beyond that, a joystick device is compact that is also beneficial when considering the universal design of the driving control and interior space of the future vehicle. Related to the past research reported how joystick control affects driver performance in manual driving [2]. For example, drivers' lane tracking performance with the conventional steering wheel was superior to that with the joystick. Besides, the joystick and conventional steering wheel controls are comparable in terms of the driver's performance such as the situation of avoiding obstacles on the road. The conclusion as to whether the joystick is safe to

© The Author(s), under exclusive license to Springer Nature Switzerland AG 2021
N. L. Black et al. (Eds.): IEA 2021, LNNS 221, pp. 734–741, 2021.
https://doi.org/10.1007/978-3-030-74608-7_90

control the future vehicle such as the vehicle with driver-assistance system (ADAS) or SAE level 1/2 automation system [3] is still superficial [4, 5] and unclear. Therefore, the first problem should be considered for developing joystick control or support in future vehicle is related to safety when the driver using the joystick to share control the vehicle with ADAS. The second problem is related to functionality. With the develop of the ADAS or automated driving technology, it is believed that in addition to operate the vehicle, the joystick device might provide other form/function(s) such as haptic warning feedback support or as a directional trigger device for ordering the system to automatic lane changing. Therefore, which form, and function of joystick control is more easily familiar and acceptable by the driver, should also be considered.

## 1.2  Research Questions

This study focuses on the case of using joystick on partial automated vehicle which the system can perform the longitudinal control. The following two purpose/questions are considered.

- Is the joystick safe for drivers to control partially automated vehicle in no matter of road environment?
- What form/design of joystick control is more familiar and acceptable by the driver?

## 2  Method

### 2.1  Participants and Apparent

24 participants (12 male/12 female, $M = 67/SD = 4.3$) took part in the experiment. All participants, with valid Japanese driver's licenses, were over 60-year-old who have long experience of using conventional steering wheel and daily habit of driving.

**Fig. 1.** Interior of the driving simulator

The dynamic driving simulator simulate the graphic, vibration and sound of the driving. The size of the joystick device is 15 cm tall, 10 cm long and 10 cm wide. The joystick device set on the left side of the driver's seat (see Fig. 1).

## 2.2  Experiment Design

Related to experiment design, this experiment was conducted separately for three times (Day 1–3) within a month. Each time for within two hours includes the rest time, total duration is 6 h. The study used 2 × 4 design. The first factor is related to the first question and conduct as a between-participant design. To evaluate whether the driver can safely control the vehicle even under different road environment, the 24 participants were divided into 2 groups, 8 people experience simple road environment called test group A and 16 people experience complicated and dynamic road environment called test group B (see Table 1).

**Table 1.** The road environment setting in Day 1–3

| Test group | Day 1 | Day 2 | Day 3 |
|---|---|---|---|
| Group A (N = 8) | Straight highway | Straight highway | Straight highway |
| Group B (N = 16) | Straight highway | Highway with shallow curves | Highway with sharp curves |

Different group participants experienced different road environment (straight/curved) during the three-day experiment (see Table 1).

**Table 2.** Functionality of each control method

| | Cruise Control (CC) | Lane Keeping Assist (LKA) | Haptic feedback support | Automated lane change function |
|---|---|---|---|---|
| s-method | Yes | No | No | No |
| j-method | Yes | No | No | No |
| jf-method | Yes | No | Yes | No |
| ja-method | Yes | Yes | No | Yes |

The second factor is related to the second question. This factor is called the control method and conduct as a within-participant design. All participants experienced 4 forms of control method which with single/multi-function support. 3 forms/designs which the joystick is possible able to be provided have been considered for investigating what form/design of joystick control we considered is more familiar and acceptable:

1. Conventional steering wheel (s-method/baseline)
2. Lateral moving via joystick control (j-method)
3. Haptic warning feedback support via joystick (jf-method)
4. Joystick trigger with automated lane change function (ja-method)

The functions and overview of each control method are shown in Fig. 2 and Table 2. The description of each function is as follows:

- Cruise Control (CC) function: The system keeps the vehicle move forward in constant speed.
- Lane Keeping Assist function (LKA): The system keeps the vehicle within the lane by sensing the white line on the road.
- Haptic Feedback Support function: The system can provide a haptic warning feedback via joystick device to driver's hand if the ego-vehicle have a potential risk occur the collision during lane changing (see Fig. 2).
- Automatic lane change function: The system can control the vehicle change to next lane when the driver interacts the system via joystick device.

## 2.3  Scenario

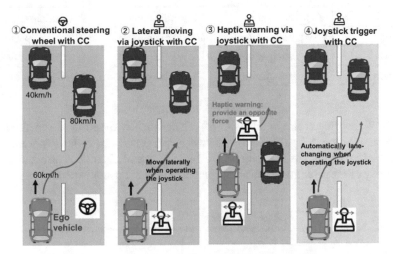

**Fig. 2.** Driving scene and introduction of 4 conditions

The sequence of the experiences conditions was randomized. Participants experience lane changing and overtaking scenes using four control methods, and their task is to safely control the vehicle (see Fig. 2) and reach the endpoint. Participants need to overtake the 16 vehicles in front of them and safely lane changing to reach the endpoint. The situation simulates a highway with 2 lanes of simple traffic, and each scene takes about 10 min. Related to scenario setting shown as Fig. 2 and the vehicles are separated from each other by approximately 100 to 250 m and travel at a fixed speed and distance.

## 3  Results and Discussion

The result showed that there is small percentage that the participant occurred accident when using j-method in a straight road environment (see Table 3 and 4). It should be mentioned that the cruise control system in this experiment forced the speed of the vehicle to be fixed. It did not slow down when approaching the vehicle in front, as the

**Table 3.** Results of the number of participants in Group A who occurred a collision.

| Test group A | Day 1 | Day 2 | Day 3 |
|---|---|---|---|
| s-method | 0/8 participant(s) | 0/8 participant(s) | 0/8 participant(s) |
| j-method | 0/8 participant(s) | 1/8 participant(s) | 0/8 participant(s) |
| jf-method | 2/8 participant(s) | 1/8 participant(s) | 1/8 participant(s) |
| ja-method | 5/8 participant(s) | 5/8 participant(s) | 6/8 participant(s) |

**Table 4.** Results of the number of participants in Group B who occurred a collision.

| Test group B | Day 1 | Day 2 | Day 3 |
|---|---|---|---|
| s-method | 0/8 participant(s) | 0/8 participant(s) | 2/8 participant(s) |
| j-method | 1/16 participant(s) | 4/16 participant(s) | 7/16 participant(s) |
| jf-method | 9/16 participant(s) | 1/16 participant(s) | 8/16 participant(s) |
| ja-method | 8/16 participant(s) | 7/16 participant(s) | 13/16 participant(s) |

function of adaptive cruise control (ACC). Under the set situation of j-method, only 1 participant in group A (see Table 3) had an accident during the 3-day experiment. Also, among the 16 participants in group B (see Table 4), 1 participant had an accident during the first day of the situation of straight road environment using j-method.

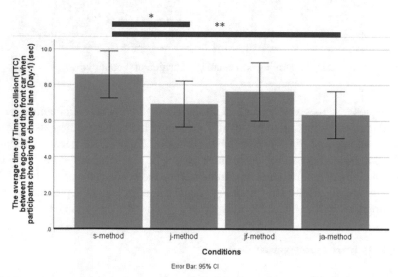

**Fig. 3.** The average time of time to collision (TTC) between the ego-car and front car (all cases averaged) when participants choosing to change lane (only day-1) (in second)

Lane changing behavior is one of the important parameters for understand the driver reaction in different control method. The reason for discussing only day 1 result is that this data allows us to understand the characteristics of joystick control, and this data had not any consider related to road environment. A one-way analysis of variance (ANOVA) for repeated measures used for analysis the lane changing behavior in 4 conditions (see Fig. 3). The results showed a significant difference among 4 conditions ($F(3, 60) = 6.1$, $p < .01$). Additionally, for pairwise comparisons, Bonferroni's adjustment for multiple comparisons was used. The conditions between s-method using a conventional steering wheel ($M = 8.5$ s) and j-method using a joystick ($M = 6.9$ s) for lateral control showed the lane changing behavior have a significant different ($p < .05$) in day-1. There is also a difference between s-method and ja-method ($M = 6.3$ s) ($p < .01$).

The meaning of above results, we believe that j-method is the control method that can be potentially considered in a straight road environment because of j-method in the case of a driver with a low accident rate in first time. Therefore, the professional training and effective collision avoidance system support might maintain more safely of joystick lateral control. Related to drivers' lane change behavior, although the time when choosing to change the lane is about 1.6 s longer than s-method, the data we obtained does not indicate whether this is a benefit or a disadvantage. Because this if has two meanings,

1. The driver using j-method needs an extra 1.6 s of load such as monitoring the traffic environment before deciding to change lanes.
2. The control method of j-method is easier to change the lane than s-method, so they can get closer to the car in front, close to 1.6 s more TTC before they think they need to change the lane.

Related to the result of other conditions, the result of ja-method and jf-method showed more participants occurred collision in the scenario. It should be noted that the difference between jf-method and j-method is that the j-method system does not provide haptic feedback warning support. Therefore, this result implies that this kind of haptic support such as providing reverse force by joystick might affect the driver's judgment and input/control of changing lanes and overtaking, causing accident. The haptic feedback support function provided by this study is not a mandatory prevent of lane changing process even if the risk of collision is increasing, it only provides as momentary warning.

The raw NASA-TLX [6] is also considerate for investigate the driver's evaluation of the mental workload when using conventional steering wheel and the three joystick controls (see Fig. 4). The Friedman's repeated measures ANOVA found that the workload of the conventional steering wheel was significantly lower than the other joystick control methods (see Fig. 4).

The questionnaire for asking the user feeling of what the users' ratings would be if these designs use on real roads in the future. The Friedman's repeated measures ANOVA used for analysis their user acceptance of the question, but the result showed that there was no significant difference (see Fig. 5).

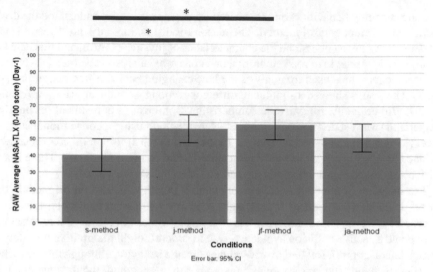

**Fig. 4.** Average raw NASA-TLX (0–100 score) (day-1)

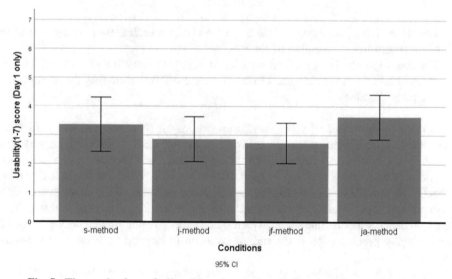

**Fig. 5.** The result of user feeling (if used on real road) (7-point Likert scale) (day-1)

## 4   Conclusion

To conclude, this study answered 2 research questions, 1. Is the joystick safe for drivers to control partially automated vehicle in no matter of road environment? 2. What form/design of joystick control is more familiar and acceptable by the driver? 24 elderly drivers who had not been professionally trained in joystick control participated in the experiment and showed that they were able to use the joystick to safely overtake and lane changes under certain road condition. The result of low percentage of accidents suggested that the j-method might be a potential safely control method, however only in specific traffic environment for example straight road environment. Because comparing with the result in straight road environment, there is high percentage of accident occurred when using j-method in a curved road environment.

The driver using jf-method and the ja-method cause more accidents than j-method. In the case of ja-method, drivers might estimate current situation and predicting future situation to decision trigger the automatic lane changing for overtaking. The wrong decision making might cause critical accident. The collision prediction system for ja-method might avoid these types of human error. Related to user feeling to joystick control, we summarized that j-method should be more familiar than jf-method and ja-method because there was no system-side intervene the human decision of lane changing. Related to user acceptance, the results showed that there was no significant difference in user acceptance among the conditions.

# References

1. Haslbeck, A., Gontar, P., Schubert, E.: The way pilots handle their control stick – effects shown in a flight simulator study. In: 30th European Annual Conference on Human Decision-Making and Manual Control, Braunschweig, pp. 1–7 (2012)
2. SAE International: Taxonomy and definitions for terms related to driving automation systems for on-road motor vehicles (SAE Standard J3016, Report No. J3016-201806) (2018)
3. Wang, C., Wang, Y., Wagner, J.: Evaluation of a robust haptic interface for semi-autonomous vehicles. SAE Int. J. Connect. Autom. Veh. 2(2), 99–114 (2019)
4. Wang, C., Wang, Y., Wagner, J.: Evaluation of alternative steering devices with adjustable haptic feedback for semi-autonomous and autonomous vehicles. SAE Technical Paper 2018-01-0572 (2018)
5. Andonian, B., Rauch, W., Bhise, V.: Driver steering performance using joystick vs. steering wheel controls. SAE Technical Paper 2003-01-0118 (2003)
6. Byers, J., Bittner, A., Hill, S.: Traditional and raw task load index (TLX) correlations: are paired comparisons necessary? In: Mital, A. (ed.) Advances in Industrial Ergonomics and Safety, pp. 481–485. Taylor & Francis, London (1989)

# Solving Cooperative Situations: Strategic Driving Decisions Depending on Perceptions and Expectations About Other Drivers

Linda Miller[✉], Johannes Kraus, Jasmin Leitner, Tanja Stoll, and Martin Baumann

Department of Human Factors, Institute of Psychology and Education,
Ulm University, 89081 Ulm, Germany
`linda.miller@uni-ulm.de`

**Abstract.** Cooperative traffic situations, in which at least two agents interact, represent not only safety-critical situations but also relevant situations for maintaining traffic flow. The successful solution of cooperative situations depends on the decisions of involved road users and their mutually expected reactions. A video-based online study ($N = 116$) was conducted to compare the dependence between drivers' decisions and expectations about other drivers in a narrow passage and lane change scenario. The effect of the perceived conflict between involved drivers' outcomes and the perceived power to influence these outcomes were examined. Besides, perceived own and other drivers' cooperativeness were analyzed. In most cases, drivers decided in accordance with their expectations. A tendency towards defensive decisions and a positivity bias in self-attributed cooperative driving in contrast to other drivers was observed. Varying perceptions of the situation on the inter-social level provide indications for mismatches between decisions, expectations, and preferences. The results give insights into expectation-based decision-making processes and associated factors that could influence traffic behavior.

**Keywords:** Cooperative driving · Decision-making · Expectations · Narrow passage · Lane change

## 1 Introduction

### 1.1 Cooperative Situations

On a daily basis, drivers encounter situations in which their goals conflict with those of other drivers [1]. To resolve the interference, involved drivers need to coordinate their actions accordingly. These situations are commonly described as cooperative [2, 3] and pose a high risk of accidents [4]. A narrow passage and a lane change as examples of cooperative traffic scenarios are illustrated in Fig. 1. Among others, these situations can be classified according to their degree of regulation. While in the narrow passage cooperative behavior is required, and drivers have to negotiate to resolve the situation [2, 5], in the lane change, the driver in the fast lane has to give the vehicle in the slower lane the opportunity to change (alternately merging traffic) [6].

© The Author(s), under exclusive license to Springer Nature Switzerland AG 2021
N. L. Black et al. (Eds.): IEA 2021, LNNS 221, pp. 742–750, 2021.
https://doi.org/10.1007/978-3-030-74608-7_91

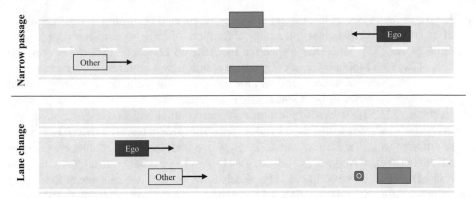

**Fig. 1.** Schematic illustration of the investigated cooperative driving scenarios. Obstacles were parked cars in the narrow passage and a parked van with a traffic cone in the lane change.

However, also in regulated situations, behavioral variance with regard to performed driving maneuvers can be observed [2, 7, 8]. To explain interindividual variance in cooperative traffic situations, situation- and driver-related as well as other road users' characteristics can be referred to. For instance, the time to arrival (TTA) at a narrow passage was observed to determine the driving order [9]. Besides, the time to collision (TTC) between a driver in the fast lane and a driver in the slower lane and the latter's intention communication was found to influence the preferred behavior in lane changes [7, 8]. However, the results still pose behavioral variance that cannot be explained exclusively by situational factors. Therefore, subjective perceptions and expectations about other drivers could provide further insights into underlying decision-making processes.

### 1.2 Expectations About Other Drivers

Cooperative situations are characterized by the dependence between the actions of at least two agents [1]. Consequently, each agent's outcome depends partly on the other's actions, resulting in social interdependence [10]. In the interpersonal domain, the role of expectations about other people for cooperative decisions was emphasized [10]. Similarly, driving behaviors in cooperative traffic situations were found to be related to the expected behaviors of other drivers [2]. Expectations thereby refer to anticipated decisions and behaviors of other drivers (e.g., drive first and accelerate in a narrow passage), which affect the own driving decision (e.g., drive first or drive second) and the selection of an associated behavior [2]. The presented research aimed to elaborate whether drivers act in accordance with their expectations and preferences in a narrow passage and lane change scenario. It was hypothesized that the individual driving decision and the expected driving decision of the other driver correspond to one another in a complementary manner.

### 1.3 Conflict and Power as Perceptions of Cooperative Situations

To add an additional aspect, conflict and power perceptions as attributes of cooperative situations were examined within the research scope. Situations with diverging self and collective interests (social dilemmas) can be distinguished according to their degree of conflict [10]. In interpersonal interactions, conflicts often arise between people with unequal power [11]. Since the respective incentive to cooperate differs between the person of high and low power, a cooperative solution of a conflict could be hindered [12]. Both attributes of interdependent situations were shown to be negatively related to cooperative behavior in both social dilemma games and more natural interpersonal interactions [12, 13]. It was found that a higher conflict and power perception was associated with a lower willingness to cooperate. The present research strived to transfer these findings to traffic interactions to improve the understanding of how cooperative situations between drivers are perceived. Two research questions were addressed: 1) Do drivers who decide more cooperatively perceive less conflict and less power in a traffic situation? 2) How does the regulation of the right of way affect the conflict and power perception in traffic situations?

## 2  Method

The presented research examined expectation-based decision-making processes in cooperative traffic situations. In a video-based within-subjects online study, the relation between decisions, expectations about other drivers, and conflict and power perceptions were investigated.

### 2.1  Sample Characteristics

Participants were invited to an online survey about driving behavior. Legal age and possession of a valid driver's license were prerequisites for participation. The final sample included $N = 116$ participants (78 female), with a mean age of $M = 31.26$ ($SD = 19.07$) years. Overall, participants held their driver's license for $M = 12.21$ ($SD = 10.74$) years and drove $M = 9\ 247$ ($SD = 13\ 072$) kilometers per year. They either received credits or could take part in a lottery as compensation.

### 2.2  Procedure

After answering questions on demographics and general driving habits, participants experienced the two cooperative scenarios of Fig. 1 (narrow passage and lane change) in randomized order. At the end of each video, they had to answer questions about their driving decision, their expectations about the other driver, and their perception of the experienced scenario. An evaluation of their own and other drivers' cooperativeness followed. Like other studies about cooperative driving [3, 7, 8], the term cooperation was only addressed at the end of the survey to avoid socially desirable responses. The survey ended with a personality questionnaire. The average study duration was around 30 min.

### 2.3  Materials and Measurements

Videos of the narrow passage and lane change were presented from an ego-perspective of a driver with an additional short description of each scenario. Both scenarios took place in a city environment. The length of the videos was six (narrow passage) and eight seconds (narrow passage). In both videos, the other driver communicated neither implicitly nor explicitly. Both videos stopped a few meters before the ego-vehicle reached the obstacle. The videos were created with Unity (version 2018.4.14f1) and had a $1920 \times 1080$-pixel resolution.

After each video, participants answered 1) how they would behave in this situation, 2) how they expect the other driver to behave in this situation, and 3) which behavior they would prefer from the other driver. The following options were presented: drive first vs. Let other driver drive first/drive second for narrow passage, let other driver merge vs. Let other driver not merge for lane change. Additionally, participants indicated which behavior they would most likely perform in real traffic: accelerate vs. Continue unchanged vs. Decelerate vs. go off the gas vs. Decelerate and stop.

Conflict and power perceptions were measured with the short version of the SIS on a 5-point Likert scale [13]. Higher values indicate more conflict and more power of the interaction partner. Cooperativeness was measured in different ways. First, participants rated their self-attributed cooperativeness as a driver on four items on a 7-point Likert scale. Second, participants indicated whether other drivers were more, equally, or less cooperative compared to themselves. Lastly, participants classified whom their and others' driving style benefits most (themselves, other drivers, or all road users).

## 3  Results

Descriptive results for decisions, expectations, and preferences were compared within and between scenarios. Conflict and power depending on individual decisions and across scenarios were analyzed with univariate ANOVAs and Wilcoxon-tests, respectively. Lastly, cooperative self-ratings and ratings of other drivers were compared.

### 3.1  Driving Decisions, Expectations, and Preferences

The distribution of driving decisions, expectations about other drivers, and preferences about the situation's solution can be seen in Fig. 2. A clear majority indicated to let the other driver drive first in the narrow passage and let the other driver merge in the lane change, which might be seen as the defensive or cooperative decisions. The other way around, comparatively fewer participants expected the other driver to drive first or merge before themselves. This resulted in a mismatch between own and expected decision in 29.3% of cases in the narrow passage and 10.3% in the lane change. Most of these combinations (29 out of 34 participants in narrow passage, 10 out of 11 participants in lane change) comprised a defensive ego-decision and an expected defensive decision from the other driver.

When looking at the preferences, a balanced distribution of almost 50% for each decision could be found in both scenarios. A preference-incongruent decision occurred

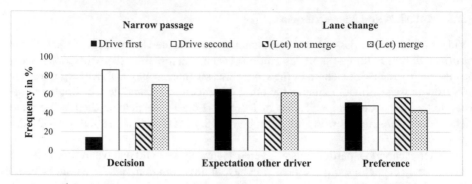

**Fig. 2.** Frequency distribution of decisions, expectations about the other driver, and preferences for narrow passage and lane change. Preference ratings have been reversed, so that depicted values correspond to the driving preference from the ego-perspective.

in 41.4% of cases in the narrow passage, but only in 17.2% in the lane change. In detail, 46 (narrow passage) and 18 (lane change) participants would prefer to drive first or let the other not merge but decided the opposite. On the behavioral level, most participants chose to reduce speed in some way in both situations (94.8% narrow passage, 69.6% lane change).

### 3.2 Perception of Cooperative Scenarios

Perceived situational conflict and power were analyzed for each scenario. Therefore, the sample was split by driving decisions within each scenario. Associated descriptive statistics can be seen in Table 1.

**Table 1.** Mean values and standard deviations of conflict and power perceptions.

| Dimension | Narrow passage | | | Lange change | | |
| | Drive first | Drive second | Overall | Let not merge | Let merge | Overall |
| --- | --- | --- | --- | --- | --- | --- |
| Conflict | 3.34 (1.00) | 2.74 (0.98) | 2.82 (1.00) | 2.97 (0.96) | 2.37 (0.93) | 2.54 (0.97) |
| Power | 2.97 (0.64) | 3.08 (0.52) | 3.06 (0.54) | 3.75 (0.64) | 3.74 (0.58) | 3.74 (0.73) |

For the narrow passage, results showed a significant difference of conflict between drivers who decided to drive first and driver who decided to drive second, $F(1,114) = 5.32, p = .023, \eta^2 = .045$. No significant results occurred for power, $F(1,114) = 0.54, p = .464, \eta^2 = .005$. For the lane change, analyses showed the same pattern. Drivers who would let the other driver not merge had significantly higher conflict perceptions than drivers who would let the other merge, $F(1,114) = 9.97, p = .002, \eta^2 = .080$. No effect for power was found in the lane change scenario either, $F(1,114) = 0.01, p = .935, \eta^2 < .001$.

Conflict and power perceptions were also compared between cooperative scenarios along the mean values across all participants. Results indicated significant differences for both dimensions ($z = -2.05, p = .040, r = 0.191$ for conflict, $z = -6.93, p < .001, r = 0.644$ for power). Conflict perception was higher in the narrow passage compared to the lane change. In contrast, power asymmetry was more balanced in the narrow passage, while more shifted towards the fast lane driver (ego) in the lane change.

### 3.3 Cooperativeness and Evaluation of Other Drivers

Overall, participants assessed themselves as cooperative drivers with $M = 5.59$ ($SD = 0.95$). In contrast, other drivers were mainly evaluated as equally cooperative (49.1%) or less cooperative (47.4%). Only four participants indicated other drivers to be more cooperative than themselves, with their self-rating being on a medium level ($M = 3.60$, $SD = 1.30$). Furthermore, the majority classified their driving behavior to benefit all road users (87.1%), whereas other drivers were mostly assumed to drive according to their own benefit (65.5%).

## 4 Discussion

Driving decisions and expectations about other drivers were investigated in two cooperative traffic scenarios. In addition, perceived conflict and power were examined.

### 4.1 Driving Decisions Depending on Expectations and Preferences

Taken together, in both scenarios, the majority of participants decided complementary to their expected decision by the other driver. This is in accordance with the findings from Imbsweiler and colleagues [2]. However, some mismatches were observed, which were higher in the narrow passage than in the lane change. These results illustrate that expectation-based decision-making represents a potential explanation for failures to successfully solve such interferences in real traffic, provided that other drivers behave as expected. In these cases, both drivers would have to reevaluate the situation, possibly communicate with each other, and negotiate how to solve the situation, which would be time-consuming and inefficient. This is important for automated vehicles, as corresponding driving strategies could be implemented to support a more efficient solution to these scenarios and increase traffic flow [14].

Beyond that, preference-compliant decisions were made even less, especially in the narrow passage, where almost half of participants decided against their preference. Possible explanations might be provided by the structural differences of the investigated scenarios and associated situational perceptions as well as the general evaluation of other drivers' (cooperative) driving behavior. These are discussed in more detail below.

### 4.2 Comparison of Cooperative Scenarios Based on Conflict and Power

The presented study compared two cooperative scenarios, which differed in several aspects. One of these was the degree of regulation and the associated right of way, which was regulated in the lane change but not in the narrow passage. This difference was represented in the subjective situational perceptions. Both conflict potential and power symmetry were perceived higher in the narrow passage than in the lane change. The higher conflict, which refers to both drivers' possibility to achieve their preferred outcomes in the situation, reflects that this scenario cannot be solved equally satisfactorily for both involved drivers. At least one driver has to accept an individual disadvantage (and wait) in the narrow passage. Contrary, in the lane change, the slower lane driver could accelerate and change lanes, which would not even affect the driver on the fast lane.

This is supported by the perceived power, which was almost equally distributed between both drivers in the narrow passage but shifted towards the fast lane driver in the lane change scenario. The results suggest that the subjective power perception reflects the degree of regulation and diffusion regarding the right of way. This is emphasized by the non-significant difference of power perception based on driving decisions, which could imply that power represents a stable property of the situation (regulated by official traffic rules). Furthermore, the unequal power perception between scenarios could explain the higher proportion of both expectation- and preference-incongruent decisions in the narrow passage. Drivers might have felt less powerful to perform and assert their preferred decision. In contrast to the interpersonal domain [12], power imbalance did not lead to less, but rather to more cooperative and defensive decisions in cooperative traffic situations. This could be justified by the fact that uncooperative behavior in road traffic might lead to severe consequences, as an accident could be provoked.

Beyond this, the combination of conflict and power shows that in conflict-prone situations with an unclear distribution of power, reducing speed is the most likely behavior. Lowering speed could be seen as a safety strategy, helping to gain time, gather more information, and reduce uncertainty. Implicit or explicit communication of one's intention or taking initiative and drive offensively might be especially relevant in such situations, also for automated vehicles [2, 8, 15].

### 4.3   Relationship Between Driving Decisions and Conflict Perception

While participants perceived the same distribution of power regardless of their decision, the conflict perception differed based on the decision in both scenarios. Drivers who decided to drive first or not let the other driver merge, which might be interpreted as the more uncooperative decisions, perceived a higher conflict. These results are in line with the findings from Gerpott and colleagues [11] from interpersonal interactions. This can be interpreted in the way that participants were well aware that this decision was the more beneficial one from an individual perspective, but not the best for all involved drivers. Therefore, a seemingly selfish decision would mean that both drivers could not achieve the best result for themselves at the same time.

### 4.4   Biases in Cooperativeness Evaluations

Considering the cooperativeness assessment of themselves and other drivers, two-thirds of participants expected others to drive according to their own benefit, which corresponds to an individualistic or egoistic orientation [16]. The results further indicate a highly positive perception of their own cooperativity in driving compared to other drivers, which matches the (often unrealistically) self-positivity biased picture people hold about themselves in various domains [17]. The more negative evaluation of other drivers is consistent with the high proportion of drivers indicating to give priority to the other driver. In contrast, other drivers were mainly expected to decide uncooperatively. This, in turn, fits in with the higher conflict perception when participants decided uncooperatively themselves, since other drivers were assumed to prefer the same.

### 4.5 Strengths, Limitations, and Future Work

A strength of this research is the integration of two cooperative scenarios that differ structurally from another. The cross-situational comparison of conflict and power as situational attributes provides a first indication for why cooperative driving behavior is shown in some situations but not in others. Based on this, a classification of driving scenarios in a framework along situational perceptions could represent a promising approach to increase the understanding of the nature of heterogeneous traffic scenarios. Furthermore, the interpersonal perceptions support that road traffic involves characteristics of social interactions, emphasizing challenges that automated vehicles must overcome to be successfully integrated into existing social systems.

In terms of limitations of this research, the design allows no conclusion about the causal and chronological relationship between one's own decision, expectations about other road users, and situational perceptions. Future research might expand this focus by experimentally investigating the causal link between these (and other relevant) perceptual dimensions and expectation-based decision-making processes. A further limitation of this study was the one-time subjective assessment of decisions, which might impair the reliability and external validity. It might be considered that the self-reported decision in the online survey may differ from actual driving maneuvers in real traffic. Nevertheless, the results provide an indication of why (near) collisions or inefficient and time-consuming interactions occur in some situations.

Primarily, this research's results depict decision-making processes and metacognitive expectations that take place before observing other road user's actions or performing driving maneuvers. Self-evidently, drivers can directly observe the outcome of their and others' actions and adapt their behavior accordingly in real traffic, which is then more likely to be adequate. Future studies could further explore the dynamic of cooperative situations and the temporal evolution of cooperative traffic decisions.

**Acknowledgment.** This research was conducted within the project "CADJapanGermany: HF" which is funded by the Federal Ministry of Education and Research of Germany.

# References

1. Hoc, J.M.: Towards a cognitive approach to human–machine cooperation in dynamic situations. Int. J. Hum. Comput. Stud. **54**(4), 509–540 (2001)
2. Imbsweiler, J., Stoll, T., Ruesch, M., Baumann, M., Deml, B.: Insight into cooperation processes for traffic scenarios: modelling with naturalistic decision making. Cogn. Technol. Work **20**(4), 621–635 (2018)

3. Stoll, T., Strelau, N.R., Baumann, M.: Social interactions in traffic: the effect of external factors. In: Proceedings of the Human Factors and Ergonomics Society Annual Meeting, pp. 97–101. SAGE, Thousand Oaks (2018)
4. Statistisches Bundesamt (Destatis): Verkehr, Verkehrsunfälle 2019. Fachserie 8 Reihe 7 (2020)
5. German Road Traffic Regulation (StVO): §11 Special traffic situations (2013)
6. German Road Traffic Regulation (StVO): §7 Use of lanes by motor vehicles (2013)
7. Stoll, T., Müller, F., Baumann, M.: When cooperation is needed: the effect of spatial and time distance and criticality on willingness to cooperate. Cogn. Technol. Work **21**(1), 21–31 (2019)
8. Stoll, T., Lanzer, M., Baumann, M.: Situational influencing factors on understanding cooperative actions in automated driving. Transport. Res. F: Traffic Psychol. Behav. **70**, 223–234 (2020)
9. Rettenmaier, M., Witzig, C.R., Bengler, K.: Interaction at the bottleneck–a traffic observation. In: Ahram, T., Karwowski, W., Pickl, S., Taiar, R. (eds.) IHSED 2019, Human Systems Engineering and Design II, pp. 243–249. Springer, Cham (2019)
10. Balliet, D., Van Lange, P.A.: Trust, conflict, and cooperation: a meta-analysis. Psychol. Bull. **139**(5), 1090–1112 (2013)
11. Rubin, J.Z., Brown, B.R.: The Social Psychology of Bargaining and Negotiation. Academic Press, New York (1975)
12. Tjosvold, D., Okun, M.: Effects of unequal power on cooperation in conflict. Psychol. Rep. **44**(1), 239–242 (1979)
13. Gerpott, F.H., Balliet, D., Columbus, S., Molho, C., de Vries, R.E.: How do people think about interdependence? A multidimensional model of subjective outcome interdependence. J. Pers. Soc. Psychol. **115**(4), 716–742 (2018)
14. Zhao, C., Li, L., Pei, X., Li, Z., Wang, F.Y., Wu, X.: A comparative study of state-of-the-art driving strategies for autonomous vehicles. Accid. Anal. Prev. **150**, 105937 (2021)
15. Rettenmaier, M., Albers, D., Bengler, K.: After you?!–Use of external human-machine interfaces in road bottleneck scenarios. Transport. Res. F: Traffic Psychol. Behav. **70**, 175–190 (2020)
16. McClintock, C.G.: Social motivation—a set of propositions. Behav. Sci. **17**(5), 438–454 (1972)
17. Fields, E.C., Kuperberg, G.R.: Loving yourself more than your neighbor: ERPs reveal online effects of a self-positivity bias. Soc. Cogn. Affective Neurosci. **10**(9), 1202–1209 (2015)

# Aspects of Brazilian Pedestrian Behavior: A Questionnaire Study

Claudia Mont'Alvão[1]([⊠]) [iD], Carolina Esteves[2] [iD], and Mariana Dias[2] [iD]

[1] Graduate Program in Design, Laboratory of Ergodesign and Usability of Interfaces, Pontifical Catholic University of Rio de Janeiro, Rua Marquês de S. Vicente 225, Gávea, Rio de Janeiro, RJ, Brazil
cmontalvao@puc-rio.br

[2] Undergraduate Program in Design, Laboratory of Ergodesign and Usability of Interfaces, Pontifical Catholic University of Rio de Janeiro, Rua Marquês de S. Vicente 225, Gávea, Rio de Janeiro, RJ, Brazil

**Abstract.** This paper presents a study that aimed to evaluate aspects of Brazilian pedestrian behavior. The considerable number of collisions with pedestrians in low and middle-income countries is a governmental concern considering its impact on the economic and health system. A survey was conducted based on a self-report questionnaire. Two rounds of pre-tests were necessary to adapt the English version of the questionnaire into Brazilian Portuguese. This effort was necessary to make respondents comfortable and understand clearly the 122 questions presented in the questionnaire. Data collection activities are still on-going at the time of writing.

**Keywords:** Pedestrian behavior · Road safety attitudes · Beliefs · Risk perceptions

## 1 Problem Statement and Context

Road safety is a significant issue globally, and especially so in low- and middle-income countries. Although many factors contribute to road trauma, road user behavior is highly influential in transport mode choice and public safety [1]. In Brazil, an upper-middle-income country [2], these problems can be seen when analyzing the reports of collisions and deaths in traffic, among other data.

Road traffic collisions in Brazil affect 1,25 million people each year, and in 2015 38,651 deaths and 174,833 hospital stays were registered, costing around USD 60.5 million to the Brazilian Health System [3]. Based on this data and many others, Brazil's Institute for Applied Economic Research [4] estimates that Brazilian people lose about BRL$ 50 billion (USD 9.4 billion) a year due to traffic collisions. Another report [5] showed that men represent 67.1% of the casualties, and young adults between 20 and 39 years are over-represented. Considering just Rio de Janeiro State, traffic collisions resulted in 675 fatalities, mostly men, of whom 137 were aged 18 to 29.

Pedestrians are not the main ones responsible for accidents and violence, but they are the primary victims in Brazil, mainly children and aged people. Considering this second group, the third part of the occurrences, when falls or runs over, dies immediately or, as a result of the accident, in the first year after. Traffic education must be part of the citizen's abilities [6].

'What happens in traffic is a social relationship in where someone has power and others, not' [7] and for those who live in low-income countries, traffic risk is there times higher than for those in developed countries. It means that in a hundred dead people in traffic accidents worldwide, seventy are from low-income countries.

Fernandes and Boing [8] analyzed the mortality coefficient trend for road traffic colli-sions involving pedestrians in Brazil between 1996 and 2015 and verified that pedestrian deaths corresponded to 26.5% of deaths due to road traffic collisions, as shown in Fig. 1. Although pedestrians' mortality is decreasing in all country regions, the numbers are still high compared to high-income countries. They indicate the significant impact of traffic collisions on the Brazilian economy and health system [4]. Although there are many road trauma contributors, this research focuses on just one; pedestrian behavior and its antecedents.

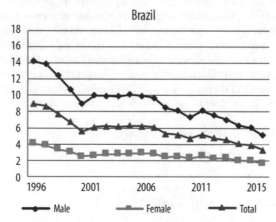

**Fig. 1.** Pedestrian accident collision standardized mortality coefficient time series (per 100,000 inhabitants), by sex and macroregions, Brazil, 1996–2015. (Fernandes and Boing [8])

## 2   Objective and Method of This Study

This study aims to verify in what way are road safety attitudes, risk perceptions, and general beliefs related to a person's self-reported behaviors as a pedestrian. Research in other countries has addressed these questions, yet there is a lack of similar effort in Brazil. This research fills that gap.

The research uses a self-report questionnaire to study the road safety attitudes, risk perceptions, general beliefs, and pedestrian behaviors of Brazilian road users. The Pedes-trian Behaviour Questionnaire (PBQ), first developed in English [9] and [10], comprises sections on demographics, transport choices and experience, attitudes to traffic safety, beliefs, and (of interest here) self-reported pedestrian behaviors.

It is part of a larger project that takes a sociotechnical perspective of global road safety, explicitly focusing on road safety in low- and middle-income countries. The project involves researchers from universities in Bangladesh, China, Kenya, the UK, Vietnam and an additional researcher from Thailand [9].

The first step of this research was the translation of this questionnaire. Following Brislin (1970) and adopting the same methodology of the partners in this research, translation considered the following steps:

1. first, the original English version is translated to the target language (here, into Brazilian Portuguese),
2. then, this translated version is viewed by a separate bi-lingual individual, one who has not seen the original English version, and it is translated back into English,
3. The original and back-translated versions are then compared, and any discrepancies are discussed between the researchers involved.

Three certified translators (English/ Brazilian Portuguese) were contacted to perform these steps, having the research team as pairs of discussions. It was noticed that this translation process was not enough to reach the research volunteers. The questionnaire should be accessible, using appropriate terms to make respondents comfortable to answer, it means, in Plain Language, considering both cultural and life aspects. Here the focus was not changing intentions, always committed to the original questionnaire (in English).

## 3   Preliminary Results

Data collection was initiated in August 2020. Due to the pandemic in Brazil, at this time, an extended in-person interview was not possible. The research team started to reach the sample using the snowball approach, as Naderifar et al. [11] explain. Once adopting this purposeful sampling, it was possible to reach people from all around the country in an inclusive approach, considering age, gender, academic background, and religion. All contacts were done using the *Whatsapp* application, while the researchers filled an online form.

Two rounds of pre-tests were necessary before arriving at the final format for the questionnaire. The first was carried out with ten volunteers (eight answers valid). Some questions formulated for 'monthly', 'weekly', or 'annual' answers were changed to 'daily'. This change was necessary to be more straightforward to answer considering Brazilian society's aspects.

The second pre-test round, undertaken once the changes mentioned above were implemented, again considered ten volunteers (seven answers valid). Here, it was noted that the questions were in an unusual way of speaking, being very formal, with some participants suggesting they were confusing. A Plain Language approach was applied, producing changes in some questions. Once changes were done to fit questions into a more reader-friendly way, it indicated the need for a new round of testing.

Considering the changes needed to understand the questions better, 25 volunteers (25 answers valid) were interviewed. It was then confirmed that the questionnaire was ready to be applied with a larger sample.

The final version of the questionnaire was inputted into a Survey Monkey form. It presents six sessions, as follows:

- Section 1 – The consent term;
- Section 2 – Demographics – about you/*Sobre você*, to obtain demographic data from respondents, as gender, age, level of education, personal annual income, religion, representativeness in society, mode of transport etc.
- Section 3 - Attitudes towards traffic safety/*Atitudes sobre a segurança de tráfego*, twenty-two sentences, 5-point Likert scale, about traffic rules and self-reported behaviour;
- Section 4 –General beliefs/*Crenças gerais*, thirty sentences, 5-point Likert scale, related with fatalism, internality, Divine/God's control of life, luck and helplessness;
- Section 5 - Risk perception on the road/*Percepção de risco nas vias*, fifteen situations in 5-point scale (from 'extremely unlikely' to 'extremely likely') of the likelihood of incidents occurs and general likelihood of a person being seriously or fatally injured;
- Section 6 - General risk perception/*Percepção de risco no dia-a-dia,* nineteen situations in 5-point scale (from 'extremely unlikely' to 'extremely likely') of the general likelihood of a person's health being badly affected;
- Section 7 - Pedestrian Behaviour Scale/*Escala de comportamento como pedestre*, twenty sentences, 6-point scale (from 'extremely infrequently or never' to 'extremely often or always'), related with violations, transgressions, aggressions, lapses, and positive behaviours.

Given the length of the questionnaire, at 122 questions with all steps necessary, it is challenging to keep volunteers connected and engaged until the last question. Another critical point is that the questionnaire is also being applied in person in addition to online. This is in order to improve the sample in both size and representativeness.

The questionnaire is currently being disseminated in the Rio de Janeiro Metropolitan area, in-person and around the country, online.

Until December 2020, a total of 313 people had attempted the questionnaire, but just 207 were completed. Some respondents gave up answering, alleging that the questionnaire was too long.

Although data collection has not yet been completed, we expect to perform similar analyses to those presented in [9–11].

The results will be valuable for validating the pedestrian behavior questionnaire in Brazil, understanding road safety attitudes, risk perceptions, and beliefs, and indicating how these factors are related.

## 4  Discussion and Future Steps

By understanding pedestrian behavior's antecedents, we can better design interventions and countermeasures to affect that behavior and therefore influence road safety. Although results are not yet in, it will be interesting to see how attitudes or beliefs of luck and divine influence are related to behavior and whether these could be targets in future road safety campaigns, including driver and conductor training. These results will also be essential to drive public safety actions that can assure pedestrians' well-being.

As a limitation in this study, once a self-report questionnaire is conducted, we must consider the potential for biases in responding. Results from the previous applications of this questionnaire point out that a more comprehensive investigation, including low-income countries in America, would help to build a better understanding of regional similarities and differences and shed light on the differing effects of national income, development, and cultural factors on traffic safety and pedestrian behavior [8].

On the other hand, some comments were valuable, giving a perception about the traffic safety and variables explored in this questionnaire, as we can read below:

*"I believe that this research is interesting, and it made (me) reflect about my attitudes in traffic, as pedestrian and as a driver."*

*'On the questions involving God and the plans and events in people's lives: God does have a plan for people; however, we have freedom in all our choices, and our choices have consequences. Evil is not present in God. God is love, and the New Testament in the Bible discusses it. We are not careful or not cared for by merit or punishment. God loves us regardless of what we do, but he wants us to have a good heart and follow Christ's example of humility and have a relationship with him. Finally, we are saved not because we deserve it but by the grace of God. Free of charge. Abundant. Real."*

This last statement highlights a point to be explored and mentioned in the previous studies [9, 10, 12], which is fatalism. Martin-Baró [14] explains this concept as "behavior of conformism and resignation before any circumstance," and it is defined by three ideas: that life is predestined, without individualities weighing in the process; that the forces of others define this life; and religion as a frame of reference, with the attribution of destiny to God.

'It is noteworthy that liberal doctrine also influences the formation of Brazilian social thinking, with many of the speeches, although they say they are aimed at reducing social inequalities, contributing to their naturalization. In this way, theories that start from reality and turn to it are urgent, in an intention not only to understand it but also to contribute to its transformation' [15].

It is expected that the results will also contribute to a better understanding of the fatalism concept and traffic safety, considering the Brazilian context as a Latin American country.

**Acknowledgements.** The authors would like to thank the Brazilian National Council for Scientific and Technological Development (CNPq), Coordenação de Aperfeiçoamento de Pessoal de Nível Superior - Brasil (CAPES - Finance Code 001), Pontifical Catholic University of Rio de Janeiro (PUC-Rio) and University of Southampton/NIHR for supporting this study.

# References

1. Santos, P., Andurand, T., Meira, L., Maia, L.: A influência da segurança pública nos desloca-mentos a pé: estudo de caso na Região Metropolitana do Recife. Anais do 7° Congresso Luso Brasileiro para o Planejamento Urbano, Regional, Integrado e Sustentável: Pluris: contrastes,

contradições, complexidades: desafios urbanos no Século XXI. Gianna M. Barbirato et al. [Org.] Maceió: Viva Editora, 2016, 176 p. (2016)

2. World Bank: Data & Research by county (2020). https://data.worldbank.org/country/brazil. Accessed 27 Jan 2021
3. Brasil: Ministério da Saúde. Projeto Vida no Trânsito. Brasília: MS (2019). https://www.saude. gov.br/saude-de-a-z/acidentes-e-violencias/41896-projeto-vida-no-transito. Accessed 27 Jan 2021
4. IPEA. Custos dos acidentes de trânsito no Brasil: estimativa simplificada com base na atualização das pesquisas do IPEA sobre custos de acidentes nos aglomerados urbanos e rodovias. Texto para discussão / Instituto de Pesquisa Econômica Aplicada. Carlos Henrique Ribeiro de Carvalho (org.) Brasília: Rio de Janeiro: IPEA (2020)
5. VIVA Inquérito 2019 Vigilância de Violências e Acidentes em Serviços Sentinelas de Urgência e Emergência – Capitais e Municípios / Ministério da Saúde, Secretaria de Vigilância em Saúde, Departamento de Análise em Saúde e Vigilância de Doenças Não Transmissíveis. – Brasília: Ministério da Saúde 2019, 132 p. ISBN 978-85-334-2736-5 (2019)
6. Minayo, M.C.S.: Conceitos, teorias e tipologias de violência: a violência faz mal à saúde. In: Njaine, K., Assis, S.G., Constantino, P. (orgs) Impactos da Violência na Saúde [online]. Rio de Janeiro: Editora FIOCRUZ, 2007, 418 p. ISBN: 978-85-7541-588-7 (2007). https://doi. org/10.7476/9788575415887
7. Peres, AC.: Velozes e vulneráveis. https://radis.ensp.fiocruz.br/phocadownload/revista/Rad is197_web.pdf. Accessed 27 Jan 2021
8. Fernandes, C.M., Boing, A.C.: Pedestrian mortality in road traffic accidents in Brazil: time trend analysis, 1996–2015 Epidemiologia e Serviços de Saúde. Brasília 28(1), e2018079 (2019)
9. McIlroy, R.C., Plant, K.L., Jikyong, U., Nam, V.H., Bunyasi, B., Kokwaro, G.O., Stanton, N.A.: Vulnerable road users in low-, middle-, and high-income countries: validation of a Pedestrian Behaviour Questionnaire. Accid. Anal. Prev. 131, 80–94 (2019). https://doi.org/ 10.1016/j.aap.2019.05.027
10. McIlroy, R.C., Kokwaro, G.O., Wu, J., Jikyong, U., Hoar, N.V., Hoque, S., Preston, J.M., Plant, K.L., Stanton, N.: How do fatalistic beliefs affect the attitudes and pedestrian behaviours of road users in different countries? A cross-cultural study. Accident Anal. Prevention (2020). https://doi.org/10.1016/j.aap.2020.105491
11. Naderifar, M., Goli, H., Ghaljaie, F.: Snowball sampling: a purposeful method of sampling in qualitative. ResearchStrides Dev Med Educ. 14(3), e67670 (2017). https://doi.org/10.5812/ sdme.67670
12. Dinh, D.D., Vu, N.H., McIlroy, R.C., Plant, K.A., Stanton, N.A.: Examining the roles of multidimensional fatalism on traffic safety attitudes and pedestrian behaviour. Saf. Sci. 124, 104587 (2020). https://doi.org/10.1016/j.ssci.2019.104587
13. Mcilroy, R.C., Nam, V.H., Bunyasi, B.W., Jikyong, U., Kokwaro, G.O., Wu, J., Hoque, M.S., Plant, K.L., Preston, J.M., Stanton, N.A.: Exploring the relationships between pedestrian behaviours and traffic safety attitudes in six countries. Transp. Res. Part F: Traffic Psychol. Behav. (2019). https://doi.org/10.1016/j.trf.2019.11.006
14. Martin-Baró, I.: O latino indolente: Caráter ideológico do fatalismo latino-americano. In: Lacerda Júnior F., (Org.) Crítica e Libertação na Psicologia, pp. 173–203. Petrópolis: Vozes. (2017)
15. Da Costa, P.H.A., Mendes, K.T.: Fatalism Dialectics: from the Fatalism of Individuals to that of the Order. Estudos e Pesquisas em Psicologia 2020 02 (2020). https://doi.org/10.12957/ epp.2020.52593

# Systematic Development and Evaluation of a User-Oriented System for Public Transport Vehicles Identification

Alexander Mueller[1](✉), Adrian Kemper[2], Ingrid Bubb[3], Nour Sakr[3], Gerhard Kopp[4], and Robert Hahn[4]

[1] Hochschule Esslingen – University of Applied Sciences, Esslingen, Germany
Alexander.mueller@hs-esslingen.de
[2] in2p GmbH, Fellbach, Germany
[3] Lehrstuhl für Ergonomie, Technische Universität München, Munich, Germany
[4] Institut für Fahrzeugkonzepte, Deutsches Zentrum für Luft- und Raumfahrt e.V., Stuttgart, Germany

**Abstract.** This paper describes how a user-oriented system for identification of public transport vehicles can be developed and evaluated. For this purpose, a vehicle design is first scaled with respect to the project requirements using a proven method and with decided consideration of customer and accessibility requirements. In a next step, it is demonstrated why the recognition of the bus by public transport users at bus stops has to be identified as critical. The following section systematically generates concepts for bus identification and presents them virtually. Finally, it is described how the concept evaluation can succeed with a pedestrian simulator and which results are obtained: For example, a number should do the primary bus identification, the route should be displayed at the boarding and the individual stop destination should be clearly highlighted on the route.

**Keywords:** User modelling · Information exchange · Display and control design · Demand responsive public transport · Autonomously operated public transport · Vehicle identification · User-centered vehicle design

## 1 Introduction

### 1.1 Status Quo and Problem Statement

The high share of individual passenger transport by car leads to traffic jams and high exhaust emissions, especially in urban areas. In order to improve this situation, there is a high level of interest in innovative, individual, environmentally friendly and thus attractive transport systems in society and subsequently among transport operators. One promising approach is to organize public transport according to demand. Advances in the fields of digital networking, autonomous driving and e-mobility are helping to make demand-responsive public transport attractive from a business perspective as well. At present, these systems are supplementing established regular transport services in the form of pilot projects [1] (see Fig. 1).

N. L. Black et al. (Eds.): IEA 2021, LNNS 221, pp. 757–765, 2021.
https://doi.org/10.1007/978-3-030-74608-7_93

**Fig. 1.** Examples of progressive and proven public transport applications in Berlin from left to right: 1. Highly automated vehicle (red route), 2. Driving routes Berlin Center, 3. Interior of a current city bus (blue/purple route)

However, since autonomous public transportation operating models eliminate the bus driver as a companion and contact person, the interaction between the user and the public transportation system must be clear and free of misunderstandings.

### 1.2 Objective

On the one hand, this leads to the question, which interactions have to be considered as critical. In addition, questions are raised regarding the development of possible interface concepts that enable the design-critical interactions with minimal errors, as well as how users evaluate them.

These questions were investigated within the research project RAMONA (**R**ealisierung **A**utomatisierter **M**obilitätskonzepte im **O**effentlichen **N**ahverkehr = Realization of Automated Mobility Concepts in Public Transportation). Through the application of development methods, layout critical design solutions were generated and partially evaluated using virtual reality. This publication especially focuses on the design process and evaluation of the display and operating concept. In particular, it focuses on the interaction between the user and the public transport system at stops and stations.

### 1.3 Input Parameter Vehicle Design Methodology

As the input variable, a generic development approach for generating a vehicle concept for demand-responsive and autonomous public transport, which was defined in the context of the research project Reallabor Schorndorf [2], was used [3]. This method is based on user-centered modeling of the dimensional layout on the basis of main requirements. As a result, the design-critical user scenario is first mapped, taking into account the technical functional assemblies, and then the vehicle geometry is systematically designed inside out by the application of the proven product development method described in VDI 2221 [4].

Due to the changed boundary conditions of the present research project, a variation of the requirements took place. This variation essentially leads to the presentation of a dimensional layout and in consequence, to a vehicle concept with smaller capacity, i.e. 10 seats and standing places including the provision for a wheelchair transport.

In comparison to the previous work, the requirements definition was extended by integrating the Quality Function Deployment (QFD) approach. In first order, requirements and wishes were derived from the user and operator perspective. For example, the desire for vehicles that can be deployed flexibly and in a demand-driven manner and that are consequently small and maneuverable contrasts with the largest possible capacity, which enables operation with few empty runs.

## 2  Identification of Critical Interactions

### 2.1  Information Flow Analysis of a Typical Public Transport Usage

For the analysis of the information flow, the fundamental schema of human-machine interaction is used as a basis [5]. The sequence and the number of information flows in a public transport use can be variant. For an effective analysis, premises (e.g.: demand-driven & autonomous operation, ordering via smartphone, etc.) were defined to narrow down the numerous variants in a meaningful way. As an approach, a typical public transport usage was divided over time into sub-processes and their individual interaction loops. Dividing into the sub-processes 1. "Ordering process", 2. "Finding the departure point", 3. "Waiting at the bus stop", 4. "Identification & preparation for entry", 5. "Boarding", 6. "Ride" and 7. "Exit" has proven to be successful. For these individual sub-processes, the multisensory information exchange was depicted and analyzed. Figure 2 shows an extract of the "Identification" and "Preparation for entry" subprocesses.

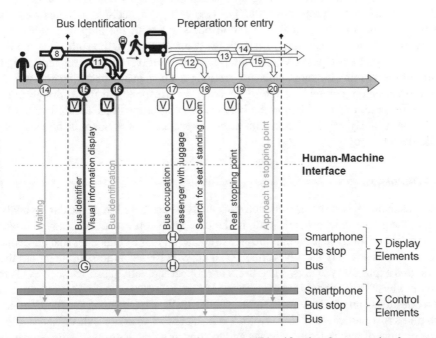

**Fig. 2.** Information flow diagram of the sub processes "Identification & preparation for entry".

In this figure, the perception and behavior of the user is shown at the top, and the display and user interface of the public transport system is shown at the bottom. Interactions across the human-machine interface are distinguished by the colors red and green, depending on the direction. The individual interactions are numbered with circles, where the identification of the perception processes is done by hexagons and the display contents are visualized with letters in circles. Information that is processed during an interaction can originate from directly preceding interaction loops or already from preceding subprocesses, which is represented by arrows above the time axis. As an example, in the "Identification (16)" interaction loop, the bus identifier information from the booking process (8) and the display content of the arriving bus (10) are compared with each other.

Based on these diagrams, the evaluation of the complexity of individual interactions can be determined. The following three hypotheses serve as evaluation criteria: Experience values with the interaction at hand, runtime/duration of the interaction loop, and number of parallel interaction loops. Since these three criteria only apply to the sub-process "Identification & boarding preparation" for the typical public transportation use described, this sub-process is considered particularly design-critical [6].

## 2.2   Observational Study

Additionally, to the methodical analysis, the authors conducted an observation study to identify interaction difficulties between conventional busses and users. The focus of the study was on minibuses transporting up to 10 people, as this best fitted the objectives and conditions of the project RAMONA. One observer recorded 121 bus stops and the behavior of 432 users at two different bus stops with the help of a self-created observation catalog. Regarding the descriptively analyzed data, the authors defined five main categories of critical passenger patterns: concentration of the passenger during the waiting time, waiting location, behavior reaching the bus, behavior during boarding and exit and necessary communication to the bus. In corresponds to the information flow process the authors could identify the location of departure and the identification of the bus as particularly critical interaction points especially if the bus will be used as an on-demand bus [6].

## 2.3   Discussion

The considerations on the information flow analysis are based in particular on analytical and theoretical background. Also, in the case of the observational study, a limiting factor is that the derived problems are an extrapolation to the challenges that on-demand autonomous buses may face. Nevertheless, it appears to the authors through both theoretical and exploratory analyses that users are concerned with questions such as "Is this really my bus?" or "Where is my bus located?" when it comes to public transportation. Such questions can justify why one of the routine tasks of a bus driver is to communicate with and assist passengers [7]. Therefore, it is necessary to address those needs as well in the context of autonomous vehicles and to conceptualize helpful solutions for users.

## 3   Conception of Control and Display System

According to the critical interaction point "identification of the bus" identified in Chapter 2, concepts for the information representation were systematically created. The concept creation also followed the procedure published in VDI 2221 [4] and was combined with a morphological product development method [8]. An essential approach was to make the relevant identification contents available to the users in different ways at the right time and partly also in parallel. Essentially, concepts for information encoding and presentation were developed using different display systems (visual displays at the front, side and inside the vehicle as well as mobile phone displays).

**Fig. 3.** Chosen information sources from left to right: 1. Mobile phone display (APP), 2. External Bus Interface (eHMI), 3. Interior lighting as feedback (e.g. green light correct bus) (iHMI).

Figure 3 shows the different chosen information levels. The first source of information is a mobile phone display including all necessary information, such as the unique identifier of the bus, route information as well as departure time and location and destination – hereafter referred to as *APP*. The second source is the unique bus identification on the bus (depending on the concept with more or less content) – henceforth called *eHMI*. The last source is a feedback system to confirm the correct entry of the passenger – hereinafter *iHMI*. If a passenger enters the correct bus, a green light flashes for confirmation in the interior of the bus; if they enter the wrong bus, a red light appears.

## 4   Concept Evaluation in Pedestrian Simulator

The authors evaluated the developed concepts by means of a virtual reality (VR) study from the perspective of a bus passenger (i.e. a pedestrian simulator). Subjects experienced a bus arrival and boarding scenario via a head-mounted display (HTC Vive Pro Eye). In the *VR* world, test persons could make use of an *APP* with all information concerning their travel whenever they needed, different *eHMIs* on the front and side of the bus with different degrees of content and an *iHMI* feedback system inside the bus (see Fig. 3). The *VR* simulation was programmed in Unity and the experimental scenario placed participants at a virtual bus stop in Munich city center. To investigate the research questions the authors chose a between-subjects design with different degrees of content for the *eHMI*. Table 1 summarizes the various interface designs as well as the utilized measures. Each subject experienced only one of the three *eHMI* identifiers.

**Table 1.** Collected data of study.

| eHMI/iHMI | Measures |
|---|---|
| 1. Number on front and side of the bus | **Efficiency** – based on how often the virtual smartphone *APP* needed to be prompted for each concept |
| 2. Number and symbol on front and side of the bus | **Effectiveness** – based on test subjects' entry into the correct or wrong bus |
| 3. Number and symbol on front and side of the bus with an additional schematic route showing the next stops on the side of the bus | **Preferred concept** – Test subjects from each group could indicate which of the three concepts types they prefer after the experiment |
| 4. Light in the interior for bording confirmation | **iHMI** – Helpfulness of the feedback system (Five-Point Likert Scale) |
| | **Qualitative feedback and design recommendations** |

## 4.1  Experimental Setup

After an initial training phase, test subjects received a written instruction, that they had ordered a bus to a specific address. The booking confirmation (APP) was presented to the subjects, so they could use it to identify the bus in the VR scenario. Subsequently, participants were asked to play a puzzle game on a mobile phone to allow for distraction. Five minutes later, they entered the *VR* and were told to board the bus that led to their destination. In the *VR* there was already a bus waiting at the stop. It had a different identifier from the one on the *APP*. Subjects could then decide whether to enter this bus or wait for the right one. The latter arrived one minute later. Using a remote control, subjects could call up the *APP* with information about the identifier of their bus. As soon as a subject boarded a bus, they received visual feedback on whether they were on the right or wrong bus via the *iHMI*. Figure 4 illustrates the starting condition of a subject for the Concept 3 group.

**Fig. 4.** Wrong automated bus waiting at the bus stop with an *eHMI*.

## 4.2  Results

Sixty subjects (46.67% women) participated on the experiment. They were manually divided into three groups of 20 persons each. There were 65% students in each group. The age of the test persons ranged between 20 and 60 years (M = 27.4 years, MdN = 25). 80% of the subjects already experienced some form of on-demand mobility (e.g. Uber). Based on the measures described in Table 1, the following results could be reported:

*Efficiency* - 30% of all subjects boarded the wrong bus. However, logistic regression shows no significance between the concepts (($\beta$ = .24; p = .49; Wald = 0.688).
*Effectiveness* - The number of *APP* views per user group was examined. A Kruskal-Wallis test identifies no significance (Chi-Square(2) = 3.42, p = .181).
*Preferred concept* - Across all groups, the third concept could be identified as the preferred concept (75%). A Kruskal Wallis test confirms this with significance (Chi-Square (2) = 7.60, p = .022). The second *eHMI* concept was only chosen by Group 2, i.e. only those who had experienced it.
*iHMI* –the majority of participants (78%), who had made an error when boarding the bus, strongly agreed that the *iHMI* lighting was helpful. No subject, who entered the wrong bus, disagreed that the *iHMI* was helpful. Of those who only experienced the green light (correct bus), only 10% disagreed that the lighting was helpful (7% strongly disagreed, 2% disagreed).

*Qualitative feedback and design recommendations.*

1. *eHMI* - the subjects prefer an interface including a number and route. As the bus is on-demand, the passenger's individual stop destination should be clearly highlighted on the route display.
2. *iHMI* - additionally to the responsive lightning (correct bus - green vs. Wrong bus - red) a route display should be visible inside the vehicle, including all the stops of all passengers.
3. *APP* - participants would like a signal on their smartphone to let them know when their bus is arriving. They also requested to be able to track the movement of the bus on their smartphones.

## 4.3  Discussion

In order to be useful, a product should fulfil the pillars of efficiency, effectiveness, and satisfaction [9]. Even though the *eHMI* concepts did not have statistically significant differences in terms of efficiency and effectiveness, the results showed significant differences in terms of satisfaction across the groups (preferred concept). Nonetheless, according to the subjective feedback the proposed concepts, especially Concept 3, seem to fulfil their purpose successfully.

Applying a between-subjects design was necessary to avoid learning effects. Evidently, all participants recognized the correct bus after making an error with the first one. That is why due to the nature of the experiment, repeated measures were not possible. This also led to a reduced number of data points and test persons per experimental group (n = 20), which does not allow any large generalizations to be made.

## 5 Conclusion

As a result of the research activities outlined, the following conclusions emerge:

1. The existing development methodology for the systematic generation of the vehicle concept was successfully applied on the basis of specified main requirements.
2. Using two independent methods to detect critical interaction behaviors between users and the public transportation system, bus identification was identified as design-critical.
3. The control and display conception with the general product development method according to VDI 2221 in combination with a morphological approach has proven to be target-oriented.
4. According to the results to Section 4 the authors suggest four fallback levels for identification (cp. Fig. 5):

1. Level: mobile application with information about the ordered bus (display number, individual routing information).

2. Level: vehicle number for primary identification of the vehicle (in front, rear and on door sides)

3. Level: route information of the bus on the door (individualized to the respective user: clear highlighting of the own stop) for additional security.

4. Level: feedback system to confirm that the user has boarded the right bus (response light upon entering, feedback on the mobile phone as well as route information in the interior).

| 1. Level | 2. Level | 3. Level | 4. Level |
|---|---|---|---|
| Mobile Application | Vehicle Number | Individualized Route Information | Different Feedback Systems |

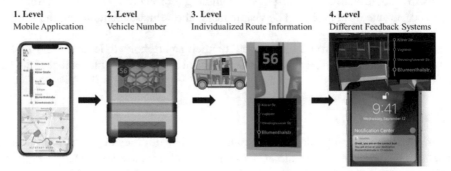

**Fig. 5.** Proposed fallback levels for correct bus identification.

**Acknowledgement.** The RAMONA research project was funded by the German Federal Ministry of Transport and Infrastructure. The authors would like to thank on behalf of all project participants for the generous funding.

# References

1. Springer Medizin. BVG und Charité testen autonome Kleinbusse. Heilberufe 69, 39 (2017). https://doi.org/10.1007/s00058-017-2966-5
2. Brost, M., Klötzke, K., Kopp, G., Deißer, O., Fraedrich, E.-M., Karnahl, K., Sippel, T., Müller, A., Beyer, S.: Development, implementation (pilot) and evaluation of a demand responsive transport system. World Electr. Veh. J. **9**, 4 (2018)
3. Mueller, A., Beyer, S., Kopp, G., Deisser, O.: User-centered development of a public transport vehicle operated in a demand-responsive environment. In: Stanton, N. (ed.) Advances in Human Factors of Transportation. AHFE 2019. Advances in Intelligent Systems and Computing, vol. 964, pp. 545 – 555. Springer, Cham (2019)
4. Standard VDI 2221: Design of technical products and systems. Model of product design. Duesseldorf, Germany (2019)
5. Seeger, H.: Basiswissen Transportation Design. Anforderungen, Lösungen, Bewertungen. Wiesbaden, Germany: Springer Fachmedien (2014)
6. Kemper, A., Bubb, I., Kriebel, E., Müller, A.: Identifikation von kritischen Interaktionen des bedarfsgerechten ÖPNV mit autonom betriebenen Fahrzeugen (2020)
7. Salmon, P.M., Young, K.L., Regan, M.A.: Distraction 'on the buses': a novel framework of ergonomics methods for identifying sources and effects of bus driver distraction. Appl. Ergon. **42**(4), 602–610 (2011)
8. Feldhusen, J., Grote, K.-H. (eds.): Pahl/Beitz Konstruktionslehre. Methoden und Anwendung erfolgreicher Produktentwicklung. 8. Auflage. Berlin, Heidelberg, Gernmay: Springer, Heidelberg (2013)
9. ISO/IEC. 9241–11. Ergonomic requirements for office work with visual displayterminals (VDTs). The international organization for standardization. 45(9) (1998)

# Driver's Cardiac Activity Measurement Using Capacitive ECG Measurements from Realistic Driving on City and Highway Roads

Priyadarshini Natarajan, Ananthakumar Balukkannu,
and Venkatesh Balasubramanian$^{(\boxtimes)}$

Indian Institute of Technology Madras, Chennai 600036, India
chanakya@iitm.ac.in

**Abstract.** A major concern in the transportation sector is that of road accidents and fatalities occurring due to driver fatigue. In this study, we have developed tin-coated copper active electrodes embedded onto the vehicle seat cover that can ubiquitously measure driver cardiac parameters. The proposed cECG sensor system was evaluated with conventional ECG system in static and dynamic real-time driving scenarios. Experimental results from filtering and R peak detection show an improved determination coefficient higher than 98% for highways driving conditions and 93.7% for city driving conditions when compared to conventional ECG measurements. The decrease in cECG signal detection for city driving could be attributed to frequent upper body movements required for steering, gear shifting, and braking in city traffic as compared to highways. This is evident from the improvement in R peak detection accuracy for cECG measurements from the passenger's seat when compared to the driver's seat. Since the number of fatalities due to road traffic accidents are biased on highways than on city roads, the developed cECG system would be ideal for long-term driver health and fatigue monitoring with high accuracy.

**Keywords:** Capacitive ECG Measurement System · Ubiquitous health monitoring · Driver fatigue · Realistic driving condition · R-peak detection accuracy

## 1 Introduction

Road accident deaths are determined to be the 7th leading cause of death for people of all ages and the number 1 cause of death in children and young adults between the ages of 5–29 [1]. As per the MoRTH 2019 report, the total number of road accidents across the country is reported as 4,49,002 causing injuries to 4,51,361 persons and claiming 1,51,113 lives in the country. About 65% of road fatalities are reported in the National and State Highways which account to only about 5% of the total Nation's road length. A progressive decrease in the driver physical and cognitive resources during long hours of driving is one of the main causes of driver errors on the highways and accidents [2]. Insufficient sleep, fatigue and excessive speed are the most common risk factors in

N. L. Black et al. (Eds.): IEA 2021, LNNS 221, pp. 766–777, 2021.
https://doi.org/10.1007/978-3-030-74608-7_94

road traffic fatalities and injuries [3]. These were commonly observed in the highway drivers irrespective of age, gender, marital status or socio-professional categories and reduces the reaction time for decision-making [4, 5]. Ubiquitous monitoring of driver's vital signs using non-contact capacitive coupled electrocardiography (cECG) has proved effective in continuous monitoring and detection of driver fatigue and drowsiness without interfering with driving performance [6–8]. cECG sensors provide unobtrusive cardiac measurement through the clothes without any preparation, making the system ideal for continuous driver health monitoring in an automobile. However, one of the main requirement for capacitive based measurements is to maintain driver contact with the sensor and the vehicle vibrations upon driving limits the practicability of the system for cardiac measurements.

The capacitive sensors are embedded into the driver seat and upon driver contact with the seat, a resistance and capacitive coupling is formed between the driver and the electrodes enabling cardiac measurements [6]. During driving any movements between the seat and the driver causes a disturbance to this coupling leading to noise and movement artefacts [9]. It is not possible to limit driver movements and vehicle vibrations are dependent on the road and the vehicle conditions. Hence improvements to the sensor design and signal processing methods enable distinguishing cardiac parameters from artefacts.

Good signal quality and high accuracy in heart rate detection were observable in real-time on-road driving studies in highway driving conditions, driving at low speeds and when the vehicle was stationary [10, 11]. City driving conditions were more prone to motion artefacts due to frequent steering movements, braking, acceleration, and road layout and surface conditions [11, 12].

Driver stress levels and state detection systems were employed to estimate fatigue and distraction. A simulated driving platform with realistic traffic conditions was used to evaluate driver state detection system based on cellular neural networks (CNNs) [13]. Pattern recognition and machine learning programs are used in improving signal detection in the presence of artefacts. To improve sensor contact with the driver, flexible conductive fabric electrodes were embedded onto the driver seat [14].

In this study, we have developed a capacitive ECG system that is embedded into a mat which can be fastened to the driver seat for cardiac monitoring. Real-time on-road validation of the cECG system under different driving scenarios is conducted to evaluate the practicability of the developed system on-road driver cardiac monitoring.

## 2    Materials and Methods

### 2.1    cECG Sensors and Measurement Setup

The capacitive ECG sensor system consists of two active electrodes and a right-leg driven ground electrode. The active electrodes were made up of a tin-coated copper plate of dimensions 8 cm x 5 cm. The tin coating provides a protective layer against sweat and humidity that can otherwise corrode the active electrodes [15]. The electronics required for a charge to voltage conversion and unity gain pre amplification with a very high input impedance of 10GW are mounted behind the active electrode.

To enable flexibility of using the cECG electrode system in the lab and any type of automobile, the electrodes are embedded on a cushioned seat cover that can be strapped to any car seat as shown Fig. 1. The sensor seat cover was adjusted such that the active electrodes were positioned at 25 cm above the seat base with 8 cm apart from seat symmetry line. This positioning of the sensors had provided an optimum signal to noise ratio, validated through one of our prior studies [6]. The sensors and the seat cover is fastened to the driver or passenger seat as required and held in place with Velcro straps. The right leg driven electrode made of flexible copper strip was placed on the driver seat as reference electrode through which the common-mode signals are actively compensated [12, 16].

**Fig. 1.** Capacitive active electrodes incised on the seat cover and secured using Velcro straps to the car used in on-road testing. The capacitive driven right leg electrode is placed on the car seat to reduce common-mode interference.

To validate the practicability of using cECG for real-time driver cardiac measurements, simultaneous conventional ECG measurements were also recorded using ECG poly-channel provided in Mitsar EEG Amplifier. Gel-based Ag/AgCl electrodes were placed on the subject slightly below the left and right collar bone with 4 cm away from the sternum. The reference electrode was placed on the right ankle. The signals were recorded using the data acquisition software provided along with the Mitsar device at a default sampling rate of 2000 samples/second. A block diagram of the cECG sensor system, required signal conditioning unit and signal processing methods are given in Fig. 2.

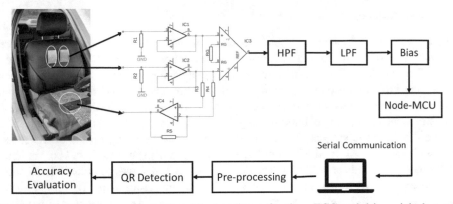

**Fig. 2.** Block Diagram representation of the locations of active cECG and driven right leg reference electrode embedded into a flexible mat. The blocks include a signal acquisition system, conditioning using, data acquisition system, serial communication and signal processing units.

## 2.2 Signal Conditioning Unit

Instrumentation amplifier AD620 was used for signal amplification with high input impedance and low noise. To prevent any saturation of the DC potential between electrode and skin, the gain was set to 248 in this study. The CMRR would be affected by the body size, curvature/shape of the seat, thickness of the cloth, and power line interferences. The driven right leg circuit as negative feedback provides an effective noise reduction [6].

The cECG signal from the instrumentation amplifier is then passed through 4th order bandpass Sallen-key filter of 0.5–40 Hz with unity gain. NodeMCU ESP-8266, a 32-bit microcontroller with an operating voltage of 3.3 V was used for data acquisition [17]. Since cECG is a biphasic signal, a bias voltage of 1 V is added to shift the filtered signal to be monophasic for NodeMCU controller. Using wired serial communication, the data is transferred to a laptop at the baud rate of 115200. The serial data was received using a Python program at a sampling rate of 80 samples/ second and stored locally.

## 2.3 QRS Detection and Validation

The most common artefact encountered in the experiment was due to vehicle vibrations and subject lateral movement while steering the car, shifting gears, and leg movements for braking and accelerating. Baseline wandering correction through mean subtraction especially for smaller movements of the subject were implemented. cECG QRS detection was implemented using the Pan-Tompkins algorithm [18] which applies filtering, differentiation, squaring, and windowing operations providing a higher accuracy of peak detection. The detected RR intervals were used to calculate the heart rate of ECG and cECG signals using their respective sampling frequencies.

The validation was conducted in two steps, the first was to validate cECG R-peak detection accuracy through analysis of correlation with ECG signals measured through conventional Mitsar system. The second part was a comparison of mean squared errors between the detected R-peaks under different driving conditions.

## 2.4 Test Protocol

The developed cECG sensor system was set up on a Maruti Swift car and the measure-ments were carried out from the driver seat and passenger seat. Both the test subjects were male. The car was driven on road by a healthy male subject aged 46 with over 20 years of driving experience and the passenger was a healthy male subject aged 22. Static and dynamic test protocols were designed to validate the accuracy of the capacitive ECG measurement system in realistic driving conditions. Two static tests were conducted. In the first one, the subjects were seated on the car seat leaning on the cECG sensor mat with the engine turned off. Simultaneous measurements of cECG and conventional ECG were recorded for two minutes. The second static test was to record cECG when the car engine was turned on with the vehicle remaining stationary. This provides the signal quality with baseline vehicle vibration. The dynamic test consisted of a defined path in Chennai, Tamil Nadu, where the test started with driving on city continuing onto highways and returning to the city. The driving time was about 25 min to cover a total distance of about 11 kms. The timestamps of vehicle moving between city and high-ways were manually noted. Simultaneous cECG and ECG measurements were recorded throughout the entire duration of the test from both the driver seat and the passenger seat.

## 3   Results

### 3.1   Static Test Measurements

The measurements were carried out for two minutes in each of the static test condition with the engine off and engine on. Correlation between the detected R peaks from the conventional ECG and cECG system was calculated. It is evident from Fig. 3 and Fig. 4 that both ECG and cECG signals are correlated with each other since the coefficient is 99.8% (Fig. 7a).

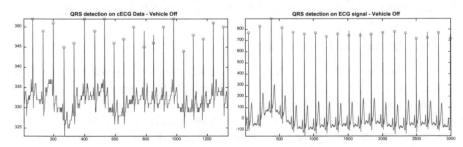

**Fig. 3.** cECG signal (left) and conventional ECG signal (right) recorded from Passenger seat during the static condition where the vehicle was at rest and the engine was off.

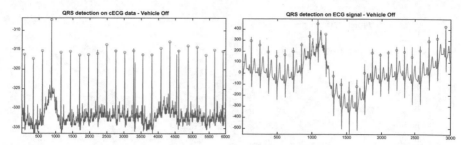

**Fig. 4.** cECG signal (left) and conventional ECG signal (right) recorded from Driver seat during the static condition where the vehicle was at rest and the engine was off.

Upon turning the vehicle engine on, an additive vibration was introduced in the cECG signal, which dropped the correlation coefficient to 96.9% (Fig. 7b) as observed from the driver and passenger seats (Fig. 5 and Fig. 6).

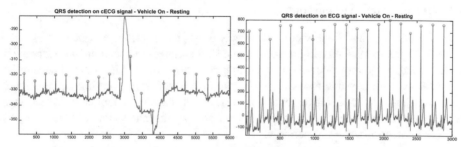

**Fig. 5.** cECG signal (left) and conventional ECG signal (right) recorded from Passenger seat during the static test condition where the vehicle was at rest and the engine was turned on.

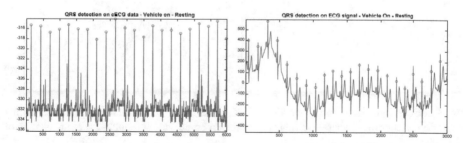

**Fig. 6.** cECG signal (left) and conventional ECG signal (right) recorded from Driver seat during the static test condition where the vehicle was at rest and the engine was turned on.

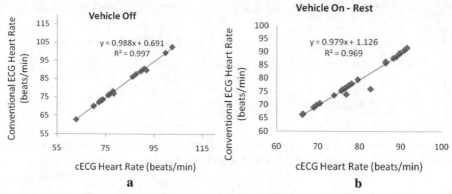

**Fig. 7.** Correlation between cECG and ECG signal recorded during the static test when the vehicle was off and stationary provided high linearity and goodness of fit of 99.7% and reduced to 96.9% when the vehicle was turned on due to vibration noise.

## 3.2 Dynamic Test Measurements

The city driving conditions were characterized by heavy traffic, lots of stop signals, increased vehicle manoeuvring, frequent gear shifts, increased speed breakers, frequent braking and, relatively poor road conditions as compared to highways. The motion artefacts were mainly due to the upper body movements while steering and changing the gear. Small steering movements only resulted in baseline changes however large movements such as while braking, U-turns and sharp turns lead to loss of cECG signals and QRS detection were not possible.

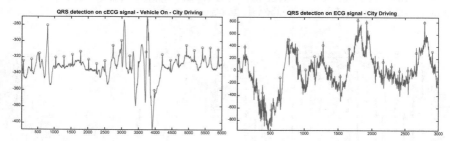

**Fig. 8.** cECG signal (left) and conventional ECG signal (right) recorded from Driver seat during dynamic test condition where the vehicle was driven on city traffic conditions at an average of 35 km/hr.

An increase in the signal noise level could be observed in both capacitive ECG and conventional ECG measurement systems in city driving conditions (Fig. 8 and 9). The average speed that could be maintained while driving was 35 km/hr frequented by braking and lane shifting. An increase in the noise level could be observed in the measurements from the driver seat as compared to the passenger seat caused due to motion artefacts from driving.

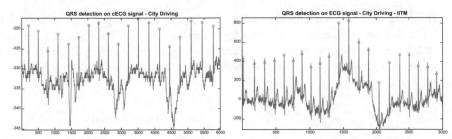

**Fig. 9.** cECG signal (left) and conventional ECG signal (right) recorded from Passenger seat during dynamic test condition where the vehicle was driven on city traffic conditions at an average of 35 km/hr.

The highway road condition was characterized by better quality straight road with no traffic signals and fewer speed breakers. This resulted in only slight movements by the driver to manoeuvre the car and hence a reduction in the noise levels could be observed as compared to city driving conditions (Fig. 10 and Fig. 11). A similar increase in movement artefacts of cECG and ECG signals measured from the driver as compared to the passenger could be seen in the plots.

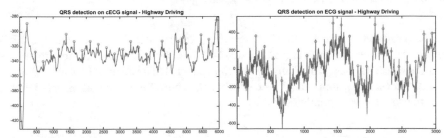

**Fig. 10.** cECG signal (left) and conventional ECG signal (right) recorded from Driver seat during dynamic test condition where the vehicle was driven on highway traffic conditions at an average of 60 km/hr.

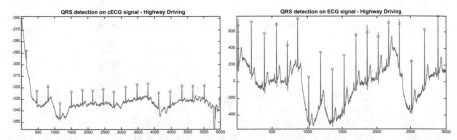

**Fig. 11.** cECG signal (left) and conventional ECG signal (right) recorded from Passenger seat during dynamic test condition where the vehicle was driven on highway traffic conditions at an average of 60 km/hr.

The QRS detection correlation of 93.7% (Fig. 12a) for city driving and 98.2% (Fig. 12b) for driving on highway driving was calculated. The correlation results of the measurements from the highway are closer to that of the accuracy from static test conditions and hence will be ideal to integrate with the vehicle for ubiquitous driver cardiac monitoring.

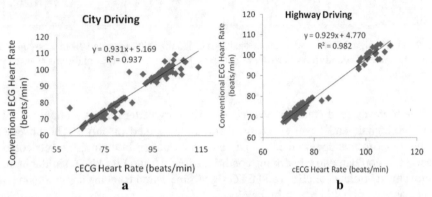

**Fig. 12.** Correlation between cECG and ECG signal recorded during the dynamic test when the vehicle was driven on city roads with 93.7% fit and highways with 98.2% fit.

The mean square error (MSE) between the QRS peak detections of measured cECG signal and conventional ECG signal, shows the highest error of 12.2 beats for city driving as compared to 4.2 beats for highway driving (Fig. 12). The error values are still lower in the static test conditions with 2.2 beats when the vehicle ignition was on and 0.3 beats when the vehicle was completely at rest.

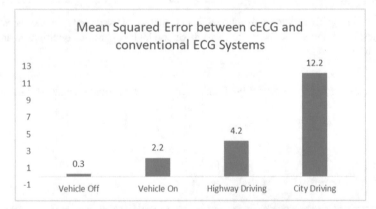

**Fig. 13.** Mean Squared Error between the computed heart rates of cECG and conventional ECG system. City driving has the highest error of 12.2 MSE as compared to 4.2 MSE for highway driving due to increased noise and motion artefacts from upper body movements while steering and frequent gear shifts.

# 4  Discussion

In this study, we have attempted to validate the performance of cECG signal acquisition system in comparison to conventional ECG system for driver cardiac monitoring in realistic driving condition. The results indicate that a single lead configuration would be sufficient for a reliable measurement of heart rate from cECG. It is evident from Fig. 8 to Fig. 13 that R peak detection from cECG signals measured during highway driving had a higher correlation of 98.2% with conventional ECG R peaks as compared to 93.7% correlation got with city driving.

The measurements taken from passenger seats had fewer missed R peaks as compared to the measurements from the driver seat. This indicates the possibility of improving detection accuracy by establishing good electrode contact and fewer subject movement. The city driving conditions were characterized by heavy traffic, increased vehicle manoeuvring, frequent braking, gear shifts, stop signals, increased speed breakers and, relatively poor road conditions as compared to highways. The frequent change in task demands in city driving could lead to physical fatigue, but very fewer accidents are caused on the city roads due to fatigue. Excessive monotonous driving time of greater than 80 min, which is most commonly observed on the highways are the significant causes of fatigue-related accidents [19]. The current cECG system would be ideal to ubiquitously monitor driver health on the highways to detect the early onset of fatigue [6].

An adaptive thresholding of parameters is applied in Pan Tomkins algorithm that is used for QRS detection in the cECG system. However, in the presence of vehicle vibrations and movement artifacts, QRS peak detection will be impossible and hence it would be beneficial to have an additional algorithm which identifies noise corrupted intervals and exclude them from analysis [10]. The most common movement artefact due to car vibration is caused by vertical accelerations and hence a combination of cECG active electrodes to perform multiple simultaneous recordings followed by signal fusion can enable greater spatial coverage of charges to reduce noise levels [12, 20].

In this study, we have proposed an unobtrusive capacitive ECG system and validated it practicability in monitoring driver performance under realistic driving conditions. Correlation of the developed cECG system with conventional ECG shows high performance in detecting R peaks from highway driving conditions which will provide to be a vital indicator of driver fatigue. Further in-depth data collection and heart rate variability study could provide findings in the identification of the onset of driver fatigue in creating suitable alarm systems.

# 5  Conclusion

In this study, we have developed a ubiquitous driver cardiac health monitoring system which could be embedded as part of the vehicle seat. The practicability of the proposed system in measuring cECG and heart rate is validated in comparison to conventional ECG system under real-time on-road driving conditions. The cECG system was validated under static and dynamic test scenarios and it was found that both the signals have greater than 95% correlation with each other in static and highway driving conditions. Due to increased body movements required in city driving conditions, the correlation between the signals reduced to 93.7% as compared to highways. In future, this work could be extended to include more drivers to conduct a larger study in identifying driver behaviour and causal factors of fatigue.

**Acknowledgment.** The authors would like to show gratitude to all the members of Rehabilitation Bioengineering Group (RBG) at the Indian Institute of Technology Madras, India, and other volunteers for their participation in this study.

# References

1. Global status report on road safety 2018: summary. Geneva: World Health Organization; 2018 (WHO/NMH/NVI/18.20). Licence: CC BY-NC-SA 3.0 IGO)
2. Jagannath, M., Balasubramanian, V.: Assessment of early onset of driver fatigue using multimodal fatigue measures in a static simulator. Appl. Ergon. **45**(4), 1140–1147 (2014)
3. Abdulbari, B., Erol, Y., Türker, O., Timo, L.: Driver sleepiness, fatigue, careless behavior and risk of motor vehicle crash and injury: population based case and control study. J. Traffic Transp. Eng. **4**(5), 496–502 (2017)
4. Philip, P., Sagaspe, P., Taillard, J., et al.: Fatigue, sleep restriction, and performance in automobile drivers: a controlled study in a natural environment. Sleep **26**(3), 277–280 (2003)
5. Philip, P., Sagaspe, P., Lagarde, E., et al.: Sleep disorders and accidental risk in a large group of regular registered highway drivers. Sleep Med. **11**(10), 973–979 (2010)
6. Bhardwaj, R., Balasubramanian, V.: Viability of cardiac parameters measured unobtrusively using capacitive coupled electrocardiography (cECG) to estimate driver performance. IEEE Sens. J. **19**(11), 4321–4330 (2019)
7. Wang, L., Wang, H., Jiang, X.: A new method to detect driver fatigue based on EMG and ECG collected by portable non-contact sensors. Traffic Transp. **29**(5), 479–488 (2017)
8. Sun, Y., Yu, X.: An innovative nonintrusive driver assistance system for vital signal monitoring. IEEE J. Biomed. Health Inform. **18**(6), 1932–1939 (2014)
9. Ottenbacher, J., Heuer, S.: Motion artefacts in capacitively coupled ECG electrodes. In: IFMBE Proceedings World Congress on Medical Physics and Biomedical Engineering, pp. 1059–1062. Springer, Berlin (2010)
10. Wartzek, T., Eilebrecht, B., Lem, J., et al.: ECG on the road: robust and unobtrusive estimation of heart rate. IEEE Trans. Biomed. Eng. **58**(11), 3112–3120 (2011)
11. Matsuda, T., Makikawa, M.: ECG monitoring of a car driver using capacitively-coupled electrodes. In: Annual International Conference of the IEEE Engineering in Medicine and Biology Society, pp. 1315–8. IEEE-EMBS, Canada (2008)
12. Leonhardt, S., Aleksandrowicz, A.: Non-contact ECG monitoring for automotive application. In: 5th International Summer School and Symposium on Medical Devices and Biosensors, pp. 183–185. Hong Kong (2008)
13. Mühlbacher-Karrer, S., Mosa, A.H., Faller, L.M., et al.: A driver state detection system—combining a capacitive hand detection sensor with physiological sensors. IEEE Trans. Instrum. Measur **66**(4), 624–636 (2017)
14. Sidikova, M., Martinek, R., Kawala-Sterniuk, A.: Vital sign monitoring in car seats based on electrocardiography, ballistocardiography and seismocardiography: a review. Sensors (Basel). **20**(19), 5699 (2020)
15. Norlin, A., Pan, J., Leygraf, C.: Investigation of interfacial capacitance of Pt, Ti and TiN coated electrodes by electrochemical impedance spectroscopy. Biomol. Eng. **19**, 67–71 (2002)

16. Winter, B.B., Webster, J.G.: Driven-right-leg circuit design. IEEE Trans. Biomed. Eng. **30**(1), 6265 (1983)
17. NodeMCU ESP-8266 Datasheet. https://www.espressif.com/
18. Pan, J., Tompkins, W.J.: A real-time QRS detection algorithm. IEEE Trans. Biomed. Eng. **BME-32**(3), 230–236 (1985)
19. Ting, P.H., Hwang, J.R., Doong, J.L., Jeng, M.C.: Driver fatigue and highway driving: a simulator study. Physiol. Behav. **94**, 448–53 (2008)
20. Wartzek, T., Czaplik, M., Antink, C.H., et al.: UnoViS: the MedIT public unobtrusive vital signs database. Health Inf. Sci. Syst. **3**(2) (2015)

# Pedestrian Behavior and Its Influence to Improve Road Safety in Ecuador

Esteban Ortiz-Prado[1]([✉]), Simone Cordovez[1], Rich McIlroy[2], and Katherine Simbaña[1]

[1] One Health Research Group, Universidad de Las Américas, Quito, Ecuador
esteban.ortiz.prado@udla.edu.ec
[2] Transportation Research Group, University of Southampton, Southampton, UK

**Abstract.** According to WHO [1] data, about 1.4 million people die each year from road traffic collisions. Traffic collisions continue to be the one of the main causes of death in the world, which reflects that the lack of road safety is still a serious global problem, especially in low- and middle-income countries, where road safety policies they have not been as closely studied or implemented, resulting in a strong social impact.

Ecuador is a developing country, and with a high mortality rate due to traffic collisions, it currently does not have the research base necessary to implement a properly informed management and intervention plan in order to improve road safety. This is the reason of this study.

This project is mainly focused on the analysis of a pedestrian's attitude and behavior as factors that are linked to minor, serious and moderate collisions on the roads. The analysis of these factors gives us extremely important information, which in turn includes those points where more attention should be paid from the health perspective.

An interesting information of data obtained after analyzing the results of this project is that 60% of the population analyzed, whether as a pedestrian, driver or passenger, has been in a situation that could end in a serious collision, but did not end up injuring people. In other words, a large percentage of the population runs the risk of being harmed in a collision on the road due of the lack of road safety.

**Keywords:** Pedestrian behavior · Road safety attitudes · Beliefs · Risk perceptions · Ecuador

## 1 Road Safety in Ecuador

According to the revised data of the PAHO [2], the Andean Zone, where Ecuador is located, has the highest mortality rate caused by traffic collisions in the Central and South American regions, with 23.4 deaths per 100,000 inhabitants, followed by the Southern Cone and the Latin Caribbean.

The topic of this research is pedestrian behavior and its antecedents, in an Ecuador context. Much of the work into road user behavior concerns drivers. This excludes larges parts of the world's population who do not drive, especially in low- and middle-income countries where motorization rates are lower, and pedestrian fatalities higher. We describe here the application of a questionnaire survey looking into road safety attitudes, risk perceptions, and general beliefs, and how they contribute to explain variance in self-reported pedestrian behaviors.

In developing countries, education on road regulations and road safety depends mainly on the possibility of access that the population has to it; understanding in this way that since not all the population has access to it, priority is given to those who drive, either in their own car or as a driver for a company. However, this population is a minority compared to the population that does not drive and therefore does not receive any type of training on road laws and road safety.

Another point of focus is demographic growth, since in the last decade and according to the records obtained in the INEC database [3], the population mass has increased, generating greater expansion of cities, and reducing the limit between urban areas and rural areas, which in turn also exposes this rural population to contact with motorized vehicles.

As we already know, road safety represents a global problem that puts the population at risk, both individually and collectively. The attitude of the pedestrian on the road provides us with a lot of information about the variants to be analyzed in this study, such as: the hours of greatest and least vehicular traffic, areas of greatest influx, types of collisions, types of risk for pedestrians; whether these are modifiable or not modifiable, as well as information such as the type of urban traffic, signage used, minimum and general knowledge of pedestrians about traffic laws and road safety, rights and duties of pedestrians, urban planning, demographic expansion, type of both objective and subjective beliefs and perspectives of pedestrians about mobility within the city, among many others that will be reviewed in the results section.

Through the analysis of the perspectives of pedestrians, we have managed to understand in a deeper way the thinking that encompasses their behavior. In many cases, especially in developing countries, religion remains deeply rooted, and beliefs on which people rely to give meaning to their actions.

## 2  Analysis

To carry out this descriptive cross-sectional study, we used a questionnaire hat was disseminated through different platforms for this purpose in order to reach the largest number of participants. In the period of time used to carry out the data, a total of 287 responses were obtained.

The questions are oriented to inquire about the level of education, average income, access and knowledge about road safety, respect and understanding of traffic laws. All these variables have allowed us to show which are the situations and conditions that can put people's lives at risk according to their perspectives.

### 2.1  Results

For the analysis of the results of this study we have relied on the information available from a previous work by McIlroy et al. 2019, 2020a and 2020b [4] and by Heydari et al. 2019 [5], through which we have been able to make a comparison with the data obtained in our questionnaire, obtaining information of great importance and relevance both for the development of this document and for future research on this topic.

Definitely the degree of education has a very close link with the probability of having greater access to an approach to information on road safety. However, it is interesting to observe how in the population analyzed it is evident that despite having the necessary resources to access a decent education, they do not have the necessary training in road safety issues.

This has been evident when evaluating the importance given to this specific knowledge versus people's beliefs when acting. Undoubtedly, this type of information allows us to see the lack of importance given to road safety, which in turn significantly impairs the safety of society.

In the questionnaire, in one of the questions we asked the participants to indicate if they have ever been involved in a situation that resulted in a traffic collision or if they have been involved in a situation that could have resulted in a traffic collision, but which was avoided. This question yields a lot of important information that has allowed us to evaluate the content of the following questions used since we can observe that 59% of the population has been more than once in a situation that could have ended in a traffic collision and 10% of the population has been present in more than one traffic collision that has required the hospitalization of one of those involved in it. In the breakdown of this information, as we can see below (Fig. 1), about 60% of the population, as a pedestrian, driver, copilot, occupant, is at risk of suffering a traffic accident given the high possibility of being involved in one.

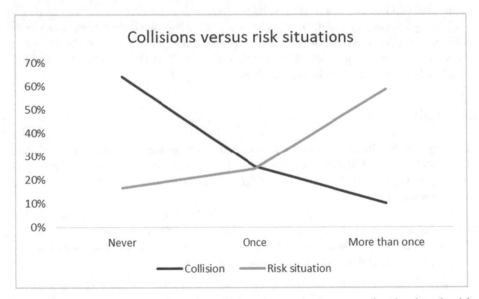

**Fig. 1.** The presence of pedestrians in collisions versus the presence of pedestrians in risk situations that could end in a collision.

Despite observing that a large percentage of the population is at risk of probably being present in a traffic accident, 5.5% of the population indicated in the survey that it is possible to take risks and break some rules if there are no people involved without necessarily be a bad driver and 76% indicated that they could not risk their life. This information, although it is certainly contradictory, to some extent, allows us to identify that there is a true lack of information about road safety and the laws or that despite having knowledge about them, in many situations people consider that they can ignore them.

Focusing directly on the responses obtained that include information regarding the beliefs and perspectives of the population as a pedestrian, we find these interesting data: 21% of the population indicated that everything that happens in their lives is part of God's plan. Therefore, if it is part of your destiny, any accident can happen to you despite taking safety measures. Regarding the subject of fortune and luck, 32% indicate that luck is a predetermining factor of their days, of these, 5% indicated that some people are born with more luck than others. On the other hand, 34% indicate that it is in their hands to make the right decisions in life to avoid taking risks, the remaining percentage fluctuated among other factors such as the consequence of negative acts and thoughts as responsible for events that may threaten health.

In the data collection carried out, we are struck by the trend that we present in the Table 1, which synthesizes the factors that the population mentions as protective and on which they base the consequences of their actions.

**Table 1.** Protective factors according to population

| Factor | Mention percentage |
|---|---|
| Self-care | 46% |
| Destiny or chance | 33% |
| Luck | 11% |
| God | 10% |

The question related to this answer includes road safety education as one of the points of focus, and based on this, what would be the protective factor in case of being present in a possible risk situation on the roads. We can see that 46% of the population indicates that self-care is paramount, followed by the destiny, mentioned by 33% of the population. Luck is one of the factors that the pedestrian population blames with 11% and finally the belief of God, as the main protector, is present in 10% of responses obtained in the survey.

This information is extremely important as it allows us to identify that there is a real problem in terms of the importance given to knowledge and self-care that must be taken as citizens and as pedestrians to reduce the probability of suffering a situation that may result in a collision on the roads.

## 3   Conclusions

Ecuador is a developing country with high collision rates on public roads. Despite having stipulated regulations to better control this problem, the figures continue to increase, so, analyzing this information from the pedestrian's perspective yielded valuable information to achieve the changes that are desired to be established in society in order to improve quality of road safety that is provided.

The behavior of pedestrians on the roads is, without doubt, a factor of great influence on road safety. For this reason, by specifically understanding this behavior, its variants, reasons, and causes, we can better design interventions and countermeasures with a better perspective that can generate a change in the population and positively influence road safety.

Through the results obtained in this project, it has been interesting to analyze how certain specific attitudes of the culture and beliefs of the population such as: luck, divine influence, destiny, among others, can be directly related to the behavior of pedestrians.

Undoubtedly, this project allows us to reflect a poor studied reality, and through the integration of the already known information with the information obtained it is possible to make the necessary changes to cover this situation objectively and proposing effective solutions in the medium and long term.

Although the results obtained through this research project show us information of great magnitude, it is just as important to propose education and training policies based on road safety, in addition to implementing lines of research that allow analysis of each of the indicated factors and through these develop an action plan to initiate awareness, education, prevention, and precaution campaigns in order to improve road safety.

At the moment and with the information obtained so far, it has been possible to give visibility to this great problem that was being minimized, but that since now has created interest in authorities of different entities to promote not only the development of a plan to implement measures road safety, but in addition to developing a permanent line of research on this important topic. At the time of writing, this work is still on-going, with data collection still underway.

**Acknowledgements.** This research was funded by the National Institute for Health Research (NIHR; 16/137/122) using UK aid from the UK Government to support global health research. The views expressed in this publication are those of the author(s) and not necessarily those of the NIHR or the UK Department of Health and Social Care.

## References

1. World Health Organization, Road Traffic Injuries 2020, WHO (2020). https://www.who.int/es/news-room/fact-sheets/detail/road-traffic-injuries
2. Pan American Health Organization, Road safety in the Region of the Americas 2016, PAHO. https://iris.paho.org/bitstream/handle/10665.2/28565/9789275319123-spa.pdf?sequence=6
3. Instituto Nacional de Estadísticas y Censos, Population and demographic expansión 2018, INEC. https://www.ecuadorencifras.gob.ec/censo-de-poblacion-y-vivienda/

4. McIlroy, R., Plant, K., Hoque, M., Wu, J., Kokwaro, G., et al.: Who is responsible for global road safety? A cross-cultural comparison of Actor Maps. Accident Anal. Prevention. **122**, 8–18 (2019)

5. Heydari, S., Hickford, A., McIlroy, R., Turner, J., Bachani, A.: Road safety in low-income countries: state of knowledge and future directions. Sustainability **11** (2019). https://doi.org/10.3390/su11226249

# Mediating Role of Driving Stress in the Relation Between Reaction Time and Risky Driving

Swathy Parameswaran[1], Aswin Ramesh[2], and Venkatesh Balasubramanian[1(✉)]

[1] Indian Institute of Technology Madras, Chennai 600036, India
chanakya@iitm.ac.in
[2] Cleartax, Bengaluru 560068, India

**Abstract.** Psychophysiological studies have illustrated the role of stress in altering the reaction time in an individual. However, studies relating to driving stress and changes in driver's reaction time are scarce. This study's importance stems from the observation that driving stress is a critical causal factor of risky driving and on-road crashes. The study attempted to quantify the role of driving stress in altering the reaction time in drivers. Thirty subjects (Mean age = 24.56 ± 1.46 years, 18 males) volunteered to the study. The driving stress was induced by a highly congested urban simulated driving experiment. The reaction time before and after the simulated driving correlated with violations made during the simulated driving. The results suggest that risky behavior in driving stress could be attributed to impaired reaction time in drivers. The work highlights the importance of driving stress in congested roads and its implications of risky driving.

**Keywords:** Reaction time · Driving stress · Urban traffic · Congested roads

## 1 Introduction

Driving requires sensory information interpretation, cognitively evaluating the information perceived and a coordinated motor task as an output of the phases mentioned above. The cognitive evaluation phase of driving remains critical as it serves as an indicator of safe driving (Anstey et al. 2005). The coordination between evaluation and acting upon a situation indexed by psychomotor activities has been widely studied in driving research. Reaction Time (RT), defined as the time interval between onset of stimuli and initiation of a response to the stimuli, has been among the indicators of risky driving behavior given its relationship with accidents (Kuang et al. 2015). Several mediating factors like sleep time (Philip et al. 1999), alcohol usage (Laude and Fillmore 2015), work shift (Saadat et al. 2018) have been shown to affect RT during driving and a cause for risky driving.

Driving stress has also been a cause for risky driving. Several studies have reported the prevalence of driving stress and its association with dangerous driving in highly congested urban road conditions (Bitkina et al. 2019). Studies quantifying the causes of urban road crashes indicate that risky driver behavior has been the leading cause of accidents in congested roads (Summala 1996). Given that the number of casualties is multifold in congested roads than free-flowing traffic (Zheng 2012), this work pertains to exploring the variables in congested road driving conditions.

The association between driving stress and RT stems from the observation that stress has been linked to impaired psychomotor activations (Carter 2017). Studies have shown that RT impaired by stress can be detrimental in critical motor movements (Arora, Sevdalis, Aggarwal et al. 2010). Driving is one of such activities with critical motor movements. This work aims to quantify the effect of stress on RT during driving. The study hypothesizes that driving stress mediates driver's RT, which could indirectly lead to risky driving behavior.

The key objectives of the study are (i) to induce driving stress by simulating congested urban roads, (ii) to study the effect of induced driving stress on risky driving (iii) correlate the risky driving to driver's reaction time.

## 2  Methodology

### 2.1  Subjects

30 (Mean age $= 24.56 \pm 1.46$ years, 18 males) subjects volunteered to the study. All participants had a valid Indian driving license for at least three years. The participant's age was limited to $< 0$ years as the age group poses the highest risk for crash risk and has limited emotion regulation (Scott-Parker et al. 2009). Eight hours of sleep for the night before data collection and no caffeine were mandated. Volunteers with any prescribed drugs that would alter cardiac rhythm were excluded from the study. For having control over the homogeneity of traffic exposure, subjects were limited to the origin of the same city (Chennai, Tamil Nadu, India).

### 2.2  Experiment Protocol

The experiment design is shown in Fig. 1. On arrival, all the subjects were given 15 min of test driving to get acquainted with the setup. After the orientation session, the experiment consisted of 45 min of driving in simulated urban congested roads using Midtown Madness, a gaming software. The number of signals, pedestrian crossings, and vehicle density was kept high in order to replicate the congested urban roads and induce driving stress. Reaction time was measured just before the start and at the end of driving.

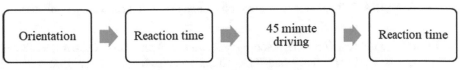

**Fig. 1.** Experiment design

## 2.3  Equipment

The driving simulation was done using Logitech G29 Driving Force Racing Wheel for PC and Consoles steering wheel with accelerator and brake pedal as shown in Fig. 2. The driving console was connected to a 15.6-inch laptop screen. The software used for the city traffic simulation was Midtown Madness II. This choice of the simulation was chosen because it allows left side road driving so as to mimic the driving conditions in India.

**Fig. 2.**  Driving simulator with logitech G29 driving force racing wheel for PC and consoles

Stress perceived is indexed by Heart Rate (HR) changes indexed by beats per minute (BPM) and was measured by the MEDIAID 160p Pulse oximeter shown in Fig. 3. The setup was mounted on to subjects throughout the study, and HR was measured for 45 min driving period.

**Fig. 3.**  MEDIAID 160p Pulse oximeter for measuring Heart Rate in Beats per Minutes

To measure the reaction time, a setup made with an Arduino UNO board, as shown in Fig. 4, was used. The setup had three LEDs connected to individual switches (2 footswitches, one hand button). The LEDs were programmed to glow randomly, and the subject was instructed to press the corresponding switches as soon as LED glows. The time taken between the onset of LED glow and the subject pressing the switch is calculated as the reaction time.

The subjects were made aware of the violations possible during simulation that will be considered risky driving. While the subjects were driving, two expert administrators

**Fig. 4.** Setup to measure Reaction Time

were present to note down the violations made during the simulated driving. The traffic violations that were indexed as risky driving are given in Table 1.

**Table 1.** List of behaviors marked as violations

| List of traffic violations |
| --- |
| Speeding above limit |
| Traffic signal violations |
| Turns without indications |
| Violating right of way for pedestrians |
| Stop line violations |
| Abrupt lane change |

## 2.4   Statistical Analysis

SPSS v16.0 (SPSS, Inc., Chicago, IL) was used to analyze the data collected. The subjects were grouped into two groups based on hours of driving in the city per day. Group 1 consisted of 14 subjects driving through the city every day for work, and group 2 consisted of 16 subjects who knew driving but seldom drove to work. The variables (RT, violations, BPM) were normally distributed, and hence a t-test was used to compare the means of two groups. Pearson $r$ correlations were used to test for the relationships between variables of interest. For all tests, $p < 0.05$ was considered statistically significant.

# 3   Results

To verify if the experiment induced stress in the participants, a 2-way t-Test was conducted to test the difference in BPM between the groups and across the conditions -before and after driving. The difference in BPM across the conditions and between the groups in shown in Fig. 5. Results indicated that BPM across conditions was recorded to be statistically significant while there were no differences between the groups. This observation could be inferred that the experiment successfully induced stress in both groups.

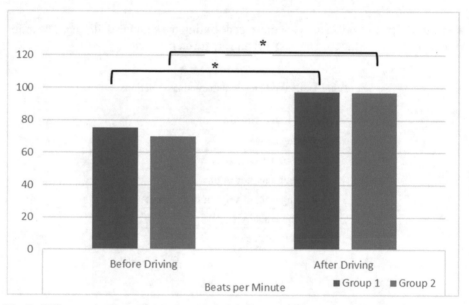

**Fig. 5.** Difference in Heart Rate indexed by BPM between group 1 and 2. **Note:** * indicates p < 0.05.

The t-Test to compare the means of collected variables between the two groups presented a statistically significant difference only in RT after driving. Group 1 had higher RT compared to group 2 as shown in Fig. 6. This difference could be attributed to stress perceived as the literature indicates that stress reduces the RT to improve alertness (Desiderato 1964).

Pearson r correlations were computed to check for relationships between RT and violations made. A statically significant positive correlation was obtained only between violations made during the driving and the difference in the RT between driving conditions for both the groups. This observation indicates that increasing RT could possibly be linked to increasing violations made.

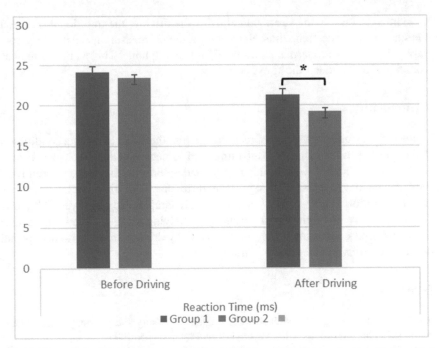

**Fig. 6.** Difference in RT between group 1 and 2 measured before and after driving. **Note:** * indicates p < 0.05.

## 4  Discussion

The study was preliminary conducted to test the hypothesis if driving stress impairs RT and resulting in risky driving. The results indicated that simulated experiment of driving through congested roads induced stress in subjects with varying driving hours. Group 1 subjects who drove on a regular basis showed higher RT and made higher violations indicating exhaustion due to stress-induced (Jonsdottir et al. 2013). While, group 2 showed relatively lesser RT and violations indicating alertness due to stress (Desiderato 1964).

Risky driving has been well documented by studies evaluating driver stress in congested urban roads. Reaction time, being one of the critical driver's ability to act in a situation, needs to be studied to better quantify risky driving as the stress response. This study has attempted to quantify the relationship between reaction time mediated by stress and risky driving behavior. It is critical to study the response time since it contributes significantly to on-road crashes (Droździel et al. 2020). It has been well registered that chronic stress and burnout cause adverse effects while the psycho-physiological manifestations of acute stress are currently being explored. Low levels of stress have been observed to enhance alertness, task efficiency (Leblanc 2009), and motor skills (Arora, Sevdalis, Nestel, et al. 2010). But prolonged exposure to acute stress has shown unfavorable effects (Plieger et al. 2017). In tasks like driving, where there is particular importance for integration of complex cognitive processes with manual dexterity, measuring the effect of stress on psychomotor coordination becomes critical.

In addition, to assess the stress perceived while driving, the traditional techniques include standardized questionnaires, electrophysiological measurements like Electrocardiography (ECG), Electrodermal Activity (EDA), smartphone. This work has indicated the usability of RT to index the stress perceived.

## 5  Conclusion

The results of the study are the first of its kind to report the effect of driving conditions on RT. This study is limited in terms of the number of subjects and the effect size observed. A simulator study is pilot work in this regard, and an on-road study is required for the efficient conclusion. A statistically significant difference in traffic violations made over the driving duration is noteworthy given the small sample size employed. The results of the current study highlight the importance of studying reaction time in drivers. The emotional toll that congestion costs in terms of risky driving are important, especially for urban road safety policies and planning.

## References

Anstey, K.J., Wood, J., Lord, S., Walker, J.G.: Cognitive, sensory and physical factors enabling driving safety in older adults. Clin. Psychol. Rev. **25**(1), 45–65 (2005)

Arora, S., Sevdalis, N., Aggarwal, R., Sirimanna, P., Darzi, A., Kneebone, R.: Stress impairs psychomotor performance in novice laparoscopic surgeons. Surg. Endosc. **24**(10), 2588–2593 (2010)

Arora, S., Sevdalis, N., Nestel, D., Woloshynowych, M., Darzi, A., Kneebone, R.: The impact of stress on surgical performance: a systematic review of the literature. Surgery **147**(3) (2010)

Bitkina, O.V., Kim, J., Park, J., Park, J., Kim, H.K.: Identifying traffic context using driving stress: a longitudinal preliminary case study. Sensors (Switzerland) **19**(9) (2019)

Carter, B.: Acute stress impacts psychomotor performance. J. Neurosurg. Am. Assoc. Neurol. Surg. **126**(1), 69 (2017)

Desiderato, O.: Effect of anxiety and stress on reaction time and temporal generalization. Psychol. Rep. **14**(1), 51–58 (1964)

Jonsdottir, I.H., Nordlund, A., Ellbin, S., Ljung, T., Glise, K., Währborg, P., Wallin, A.: Cognitive impairment in patients with stress-related exhaustion. Stress **16**(2), 181–190 (2013)

Kuang, Y., Qu, X., Weng, J., Etemad-Shahidi, A.: How does the driver's perception reaction time affect the performances of crash surrogate measures? PLOS ONE **10**(9), e0138617 (2015)

Laude, J.R., Fillmore, M.T.: Simulated driving performance under alcohol: effects on driver-risk versus driver-skill. Drug Alcohol Dependence **154**, 271–277 (2015)

LeBlanc, V.R.: The effects of acute stress on performance: implications for health professions education. Acad. Med. **84**(10), S25–S33 (2009)

Philip, P., Taillard, J., Quera-Salva, M.A., Bioulac, B., Åkerstedt, T.: Simple reaction time, duration of driving and sleep deprivation in young versus old automobile drivers. J. Sleep Res. **8**(1), 9–14 (1999)

Plieger, T., Felten, A., Diks, E., Tepel, J., Mies, M., Reuter, M.: The impact of acute stress on cognitive functioning: a matter of cognitive demands? Cogn. Neuropsychiatry **22**(1), 69–82 (2017)

Saadat, S., Karbakhsh, M., Saremi, M., Alimohammadi, I., Ashayeri, H., Fayaz, M., Sadeghian, F., Rostami, R.: A prospective study of psychomotor performance of driving among two kinds of shift work in Iran. Electron. Phys. **10**(2), 6417–6425 (2018)

Scott-Parker, B., Watson, B., King, M.J.: Understanding the psychosocial factors influencing the risky behaviour of young drivers. Transp. Res. Part F: Traffic Psychol. Behav. **12**(6), 470–482 (2009)

Summala, H.: Accident risk and driver behaviour. Saf. Sci. **22**(1–3), 103–117 (1996)

Zheng, Z.: Empirical analysis on relationship between traffic conditions and crash occurrences. Procedia-Soc. Behav. Sci.s **43**, 302–312 (2012)

# Differences in Driving Performance Between Different Road Environment and Emotions

Shih-Yun Peng[✉], Min-Chun Hsu, and Yung-Ching Liu

Department of Industrial Engineering and Management, National Yunlin University of Science and Technology, 123, University Rd. Sec. 3, Douliu 640, Yunlin, Taiwan

**Abstract.** The study uses different types of music to induce different emotions of the subjects, then checks if the emotions affect driving behavior in different road environments. 30 subjects used the STISIM driving simulator to con-duct the experiments. A mixed factor design of 3 music types (positive vs negative vs no music) * 2 road environments (urban vs rural). After filling out an emotion scale, subjects listened to positive or negative music, recalled relevant memories that matched the emotion, and then filled out the emotion scale again. After reaching the conforming emotion, they listened to the mu-sic and followed a car while completing the driving task. The data collected driving behavior and the duration of TTC < 2.5(time to collision). The results show that an existing interaction between the environment and the music type: in the urban environment, the lane departure offset in non-music sce-narios is greater than that of positive and negative music—same goes for the rural environment. The total time of TTC < 2.5 s in the urban environment is longer than the rural environment; the longitudinal acceleration variation in the urban is higher than the rural environment.

**Keywords:** Music type · Road environment · TTC · Following task · Driving behavior

## 1 Introduction

Traffic collisions remain one of the most common causes of accidental death in developed nations. Risky driving behaviors include speeding, vehicle trailing, lack of a fastened seatbelt, and drunk and fatigue driving. Inexperience and mechanical failure also contribute to many traffic accidents.

Emotions affect driving performance, behavior and safety. According to previous studies, stress causes a decrease in driving performance (Mesken 2002), anger leads to aggressive driving behavior (Carmona et al. 2016), and frustration and sadness reduces attention levels (Du et al. 2018). Therefore, the occurrence of traffic accidents are related to emotions, and an analysis of emotions can help prevent the risk of possible accidents.

Different types of music may affect the mood of the driver (Brodsky 2001). Relaxed and pleasant music cause drivers to demonstrate more positive driving behaviors. Conversely, sad music causes drivers' thoughts to be disordered and affect their driving concentration. Different road driving environments affect the driver's emotions in different ways (Healey and Picard 2005; Mesken 2002).

© The Author(s), under exclusive license to Springer Nature Switzerland AG 2021
N. L. Black et al. (Eds.): IEA 2021, LNNS 221, pp. 792–797, 2021.
https://doi.org/10.1007/978-3-030-74608-7_97

This study compared the driving behaviors for different emotions on various road environments. In this study, music type is divided into a positive (pleasant), negative (sad), or no music (base line) environment. The road environment is divided into a complex (urban) and simple (rural) one. Ultimately, the effects different emotions and road environments have on driving behaviors and their interactions with one another are explored. Results were collected for future goals of an improvement of human-computer interactions, based on said emotional and environmental factors.

## 2    Methods

### 2.1    Participants

A total of 30 subjects (15 males, 15 females) between the ages of 21 and 30 were included the study. The subjects were students from the National Yunlin University of Science and Technology in Douliu, Taiwan. All held qualified driving licenses and drive on the road at least once a week. They had normal vision or above 0.8 vision after correction. All were required to fill out an informed consent beforehand.

### 2.2    Apparatus

A STISIM® driving simulator (System Technology, Inc) was used in the study. SDL (Scenario Definition Language V.8.1) was used to write the road environment script that was to be simulated. The created road is projected on a 100-inch curved Mocom projection screen through a BenQ projector. Three wooden speakers of EDIFIER C3X 2.1 channel were installed in the car to simulate the environmental sound effects of the engine and speakers, both inside and outside the car.

### 2.3    Tasks

Before the experiment, subjects listened to music (positive or negative), and recalled the corresponding event such as: when they heard pleasant music, they needed to recall events that made him feel happy, but when they heard negative music, they needed to recall things that made him feel sad (Steinhauser et al. 2018). Afterwards, they were asked to fill in the profile of mood states, and their own emotional feelings to ensure their emotion achieved the requirements. Finally, in the driving task, subjects needed to drive in the designated vehicle and fol-low the road speed limit according to the experimental requirements, while avoiding collision accidents.

### 2.4    Simulation Road Environment

The environment was divided into urban and rural sections. The script scenes were all daytime. The road was a two-way two-lane road with sidewalks on both sides. In the urban environment, there were high-density and tall buildings on both sides of the road, and more congested traffic conditions. In the rural setting, the buildings on both sides were low-density and bungalows, with low-density traffic flow. The total length of the road was 23,000 feet. The following task was carried out throughout the experiment. The speed of the target vehicle is mainly 55 to 75 miles per hour, and the amplitude of the above and below speed is 10 miles per hour to make sine wave speed changes. Subjects followed the tar-get vehicle at a safe distance they determined. When the distance was too far, the simulator reminded the test subject to keep up with the target vehicle in front. Each driving time is about 5–6 min.

## 2.5  Experiment Design

The study used a 3 (music types: positive, negative, and no music)*2 (road environment: urban and rural) factorial design to collect driving behavior through a driving simulator. The data included (1) The total number of occurrences of TTC $< 2.5$ s (2) The total time of TTC $< 2.5$ s (3) Lane position variation (4) Longitudinal acceleration. Music type and road environment were all factors within the group. The experiment used a counter-balanced method to arrange the experiment sequence to avoid the sequence affecting the driving expectations and caused the learning effect.

## 2.6  Process

The researcher would inform the subjects of the experiment process and ask the subjects to sign the informed consent form before the experiment. Before the start of the formal experiment, the subject practiced operating the driving simulator to make sure the subject was familiar with and perform the experiment naturally. In the formal experiment, the subject listened to music (positive or negative), and asked the subject to recall the event corresponding to the emotion. During the listening process, the subject was also asked to the profile of mood states. After that, the subject began the driving tasks. The subject needed to follow the vehicle in front and maintain a safe distance they deemed reasonable. During the driving task, the music continued to be played until the end of the experiment. After the experiment, the subjects filled out the profile of mood states again. The experiment was carried out on two days, one day for environ-mental tasks without music and positive music; and the other day for environ-mental tasks without music and negative music. After driving a section of road, the subjects were allowed to rest for 5 min. The experiment was carried out 4 times in total, each time about 10 min, with the total experiment time being about 60 min.

# 3  Results

There were no statistically significant differences in gender and age between the subjects. Since the p-value in the sphere test was $< 0.05$, which violated the assumption of the sphere test, Greenhouse-Geisser was used to modify the degree of freedom for statistical analysis.

### 3.1 The Total Number of Occurrences of TTC < 2.5 s

This study explores the number of occurrences of TTC transition from a safe following state to TTC < 2.5 s when the subject is following a car. In terms of the total number of occurrences of TTC < 2.5 s, there was no sig-nificant interaction between the music type and the environment, and neither the music type nor the environment had a sig-nificant impact on the number of occur-rences. We conclude that music genre or road environment, no matter the type, generally does not affect driving behavior.

### 3.2 The Total Time of TTC < 2.5 s

In road driving, the average reaction time of a person was 2.5 s, and the reaction time was the shortest time for driving in an environment specified for avoiding chasing and collision. Reaction time less than 2.5 s were judged as a dangerous driving behavior. The main effect of environmental factors was significant $F(1,29) = 6.026$, $p = 0.02$. The total time of TTC < 2.5s when driving in the urban setting (average = 59.598) was significantly longer than the total time of TTC < 2.5s of driving in the rural setting (average = 52.735).

### 3.3 Lane Position Variation

For each subject in an environment without music, the average lane offset was greater in urban than compared to rural. While in an environment with music, the average lane offset in the rural was greater than that in urban. It can be seen from the table that there were significant differences in the music types * road environment, $F(1.494, 43.327) = 9.951$, $p = 0.001$. There was no significant difference in music types; and there was no significant difference in the road environment. This means the subjects in different road environments and music types have no significant affect on the lane offset.

In terms of road environment, there was an interaction between environment and music type, $F(2, 43.327) = 9.951$, $p = 0.001$(see Fig. 1). In the urban cnvironment, the position offset of the test subject in the lane without music was larger than that of the positive music ($p = 0.003$) and negative music ($p = 0.047$); while in the rural environment, the test subject was in no music. The lane position offset is less than that of positive music ($p = 0.038$) and negative music ($p = 0.006$).

### 3.4 Longitudinal Acceleration

The longitudinal acceleration of the subjects in the urban environment was greater than the longitudinal acceleration of the rural environment. There was a significant difference in the environment, $F(1,29) = 7.042$, $p = 0.013$, which means that the longitudinal acceleration of the subject in different road environments were significantly different. The longitudinal acceleration variation when driving in the urban (average value = 15.014) was significantly higher than the longitudinal acceleration variation when driving in the rural (average value = 13.603). There was no significant difference in music type; there was no significant difference in interaction.

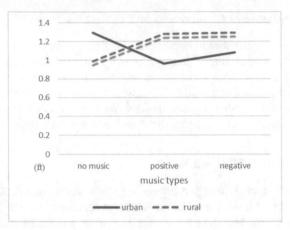

**Fig. 1.** Interaction between environment and music type. In the case of no music, the lane offset in the urban is larger than in the rural; however, whether it is positive or negative music, the lane offset in the urban is less than that in the rural.

## 4    Conclusions

Regardless of whether the subjects were in any road environment or emotional music, there was no significant difference in the total number of occurrences of TTC < 2.5 s. The analysis of the duration of the total time of TTC < 2.5 s found that the duration of the total time of TTC < 2.5 s in urban conditions was more than that in rural situations. Although there was no significant difference in the number of possible hazards in different environments, the number of seconds that the subject may have a collision hazard increases significantly in urban conditions. This may be because the subject is in a more complicated urban environment and the load is heavier. Compared with the rural environment, they were less likely to realize that their driving distance was too close to the vehicle in front, and accidents were more likely to occur if the current vehicle has emergency braking.

For the lane offset, it was found that in the urban environment, the offset of the test subject in the lane without music was greater than the offset of the positive music and negative music; while in the rural environment, the test subject was in the absence of music. The lane position offset was less than that of positive music and negative music. This study predicts that driving performance will be better in an environment without music. This expected result is valid in a rural environment. It is consistent with Zimasa et al. (2017) and Zimasa et al. (2019) that less emotional participation can lead to better driving performance.

The results found that the longitudinal acceleration of the subjects in different road environments will be significantly different, and the longitudinal acceleration variation in urban driving is significantly higher than the longitudinal acceleration variation in rural driving. Faur et al. (2016) and Weber et al. (2019) proposed that the psychological load of the urban environment will be higher than that of the rural environment, and in the urban environment, it may be difficult for the subjects to judge that they are too far or too close to the vehicle in front, and instant acceleration or instant deceleration will occur. There are many conditions, so it is in line with the expected results of this study.

# References

Brodsky, W.: The effects of music tempo on simulated driving performance and vehicular control. Transp. Res. Part F: Traffic Psychol. Behav. **4**(4), 219–241 (2001)

Carmona, J., García, F., de Miguel, M.Á., de la Escalera, A., Armingol, J.M.: Analysis of aggressive driver behaviour using data fusion. In: VEHITS, pp. 85–90 (2016)

Du, X., Shen, Y., Chang, R., Ma, J.: The exceptionists of Chinese roads: the effect of road situations and ethical positions on driver aggression. Transp. Res. Part F: Traffic Psychol. Behav. **58**, 719–729 (2018)

Faure, V., Lobjois, R., Benguigui, N.: The effects of driving environment complexity and dual tasking on drivers' mental workload and eye blink behavior. Transp. Res. Part F: Traffic Psychol. Behav. **40**, 78–90 (2016)

Healey, J.A., Picard, R.W.: Detecting stress during real-world driving tasks using physiological sensors. IEEE Trans. Intell. Transp. Syst. **6**(2), 156–166 (2005)

Mesken, J.: Measuring emotions in traffic (No. D-2002-3). Leidschendam, The Netherlands: SWOV Institute for Road Safety Research (2002)

Hayley, A.C., de Ridder, B., Stough, C., Ford, T.C., Downey, L.A.: Emotional intelligence and risky driving behaviour in adults. Transp. Res. Part F: Traffic Psychol. Behav. **49**, 124–131 (2017)

Steinhauser, K., Leist, F., Maier, K., Michel, V., Pärsch, N., Rigley, P., Wurm, F., Steinhauser, M.: Effects of emotions on driving behavior. Transp. Res. Part F: Traffic Psychol. Behav. **59**, 150–163 (2018)

Weber, M., Giacomin, J., Malizia, A., Skrypchuk, L., Gkatzidou, V., Mouzakitis, A.: Investigation of the dependency of the drivers' emotional experience on different road types and driving conditions. Transp. Res. Part F: Traffic Psychol. Behav. **65**, 107–120 (2019)

Zimasa, T., Jamson, S., Henson, B.: Are happy drivers safer drivers? Evidence from hazard response times and eye tracking data. Transp. Res. Part F: Traffic Psychol. Behav. **46**, 14–23 (2017)

Zimasa, T., Jamson, S., Henson, B.: The influence of driver's mood on car following and glance behaviour: using cognitive load as an intervention. Transp. Res. Part F: Traffic Psychol. Behav. **66**, 87–100 (2019)

# Strategies for User-Centered Adaptation of Future Vehicles

Florian Reichelt[✉], Daniel Holder, Andreas Kaufmann, and Thomas Maier

Institute for Engineering Design and Industrial Design, Department of Industrial Design Engineering, University of Stuttgart, Pfaffenwaldring 9, 70569 Stuttgart, Germany
florian.reichelt@iktd.uni-stuttgart.de

**Abstract.** Future vehicle design is mainly driven by the technology changes and the results of this transformation. Automated driving in particular creates completely new potential for vehicle design solutions. But also, future mobility means shared mobility: The classic form of mobility known as individual transport is increasingly moving into the background, thus being replaced by new mobility approaches such as car-sharing or ride-hailing. Unlike public transport, this specific change in passenger cars collides with the still strong desire for individuality. Adaptive elements in the vehicle context provide a solution to this conflict. The term adaptivity is a diversely used principle and does not generally offer any guidance for a user-centered development in the vehicle context. Within this contribution we derive necessary strategies for the development of user-centered adaptivity and describe them exemplarily. The three core strategies are Contextual Adaptation, Psychographical Adaptation and Anatomical Adaptation. These strategies create a guidance for the goal-oriented development of adaptive elements. In addition, several technologies and innovations were examined and potentials for further development are provided.

**Keywords:** User-centered design · Autonomous driving · Vehicular adaptation

## 1 Introduction

The transformation of today's mobility encompasses numerous facets. Automated vehicles are one of the most important technological developments of this transformation. Due to this technology new possibilities arise to radical redesign the vehicle interior and exterior design in passenger and freight traffic [1].

Especially with regard to the interior design automated vehicles evolve the interior of the future to the $3^{rd}$ living space besides home and work [2]. Therefore, the megatrends of individualization, customization and personalization gain increasingly more importance [2–4]. In response to this trend, automotive manufacturers focus primarily on modularization strategies and an extensive expansion of the model range [5].

However, these trends in particular are in contrast to another key aspect of the mobility of the future: shared mobility. Whether car-sharing, ride-sharing or ride-pooling, owning your own vehicle is becoming increasingly less important [6].

Ultimately, the developers of new vehicles and mobility concepts are faced with a central conflict between the demands of the trends for individualization on the one hand and shared mobility on the other hand that must be resolved.

Vehicular adaptation constitutes one of the most promising solutions for solving this trade-off. Especially a dynamic adaptivity can enable a fast and person-specific adaptation to the user. Therefore, an increase of adaptivity within future vehicle designs can be observed. [7]

However, adaptivity has broad applications in a variety of disciplines. Purposeful integration therefore requires a specification of the term to provide guidance in the development of adaptive elements in the vehicle. Furthermore, a precisely definition of adaptivity is currently lacking for a more extensive user-oriented development. In this contribution we evolve the idea of adaptive vehicle design and present strategies for the development of a user-centered adaptation based on the identified potentials.

## 2 Methodology

In order to approximate the described problem, a basic literary classification and presentation of the terms adaptation and adaptivity is given in a first step. Furthermore, the correlation between these terms and technical systems is determined. We then specify the terms in the automotive context and derive a general definition of vehicular adaptivity.

The deduction of a user-centered and -focused development of adaptive individualizable vehicle elements requires the consideration of the correlations between the user and the product. As a specification of the general definition of vehicular adaptivity, the basic scheme for product perception and human-machine interface (HMI) is used to identify dedicated approaches and strategies. For each strategy definitions are presented and examples are provided to exemplify these strategies.

In conclusion, various innovative technologies, concepts, and systems related to user-centered adaptivity are analyzed and assigned to these three strategies.

## 3 Vehicular Adaptation

The demands placed on the automobile have been subject to constant change from the very beginning. While the original aim was solely transport, modern passenger cars are placing more and more demands on the vehicle interior. [8]

In order to fulfill these demands, it is possible to create an adaptive user environment via adaptations. The focus here is on comfort adaptations, task-specific adaptations and user-specific adaptations. In order to pursue this approach of adaptation further, a clarification of terms is necessary.

The term of adaptation or adaptivity is a wide spread term in literature and practice use [9]. Basically, a distinction can be made between adaptive and adaptable. If the user is able to change certain parameters to adapt the systems behavior it is an adaptable system. If there is an automatically adaption triggered by the system to support the user and his needs it is an adaptive system. [10, 11]

In terms of adaptation used in an automotive context, an additional distinction needs to be made between the form of adaptation and the form of activation. Figure 1 outlines vehicular adaptation, using the seat adjustment in the vehicle as an example.

The *form of adaptation* can be differed into passive, active, and smart adaptation [12]. In the example of seat adjustment, passive adaptation is manual or electric adjustment without any support from the system. In the case of active adaptation, the seat adjustment is activated by the user with the help of saved profile settings. Smart adaptation in this case would be automated seat adjustment using sensor-based information about the user.

The *form of activation* ranges from user initiated adaptability which implies fully user control over adaptation, to system initiated adaptivity which implies no user control. [13]

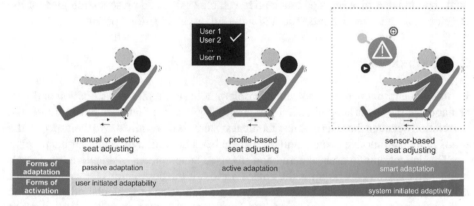

**Fig. 1.** Interrelations between forms of adaptations and forms of activations using the seat adjustment as an example.

In a preceding study Reichelt et al. investigated general potentials of vehicular adaptation by analyzing concept cars. As a result, the potential of adaptivity in an early stage of the development process could be identified. Therefore, a distinctive consideration needs to be made for supporting the development of vehicular adaptation [7].

Especially in order to ensure that individual requirements are taken into account in the future development there is a need for a specification of user-centered adaptation.

## 4    Strategies for User-Centered Adaptation

In order to provide adequate support for the user-centered development of user-specific individualization by adaptation, it is important to examine the relationships between the user and the product in detail. For this purpose, the so-called basic scheme exists [14, 15]. This basic approach has been used successfully for years for research and industry projects at the Institute for Engineering Design and Industrial Design (IKTD) and is based on the considerations of Seeger [16].

Figure 2 illustrates the correlations of the product perception. The user perceives the product by interacting therewith and he processes his sensory impressions cognitively. Based on the result of his cognitive information processing, a mindset is created - the attitude of the user. This attitude causes the user to interact with the product in a reactive way. Besides the stimuli of the product and the user's mindset the environment also affects the kind of product perception.

The purpose of user-centered design is to ensure the needs and requirements of the user. The basic scheme provides information about the necessary interrelation between user and product and therefore provides guidance for the developers.

Especially with regard on adaptation these interactions have to be taken into account to advance an increase of usability, comfort and health throughout individual adaptation. As key factors for user-centered adaptation the following three factors can be determined: Contextual, Anatomical and Psychographical Adaptation. The environmental influences and relevant use cases lead to Contextual Adaptations. The Anatomical Adaptation takes into account different physical constitutions of the user. Finally, different personal preferences are addressed by using Psychographical Adaptations.

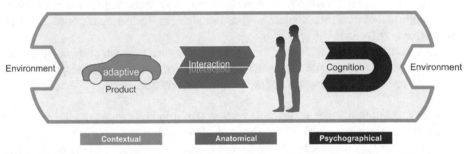

**Fig. 2.** Variation of the basic scheme for the description of the product design and the human-machine interaction for vehicular adaptation.

With these three types of adaptivity, corresponding strategies for the user-oriented development of adaptive elements in vehicles can be derived:

Anatomical Adaptation (AN): This kind of adaptation is based on the anatomical needs and conditions of the user. In terms of this adaptation, the direct human-machine interface is adapted to the individual anthropometry, demographics and constitution of the user. It can typically be initiated by the user. For example, the seat adjustment and geometrical morphing of the seat shell is done by adapting to the anthropometry of the occupant. An adjustment of the HMI layout in the vehicle to enable accessibility of entertainment or steering wheel and pedals can also be considered as Anatomical Adaptation.

Contextual Adaptation (CO): This adaptation occurs due to a change in environmental influences, use cases or user tasks. Based on altering influences, the control element also changes in terms of function, modality, etc. One example is improving driver attention by changing the seat position or adjusting the ambient lighting. This adaptation starts primarily from the system, which sees an adaptation as necessary.

Psychographical Adaptation (PS): This adaptation primarily addresses the psychographic user needs and the associated individual attitudes and preferences. Based on the preferences, for example, the ambient lighting can reflect the favorite color. Additionally, the driving style of the autonomous vehicle as well as the corresponding graphical user interface (GUI) designs can be adapted. In addition to an adaptation in the context of a user switch, this adaptation can be initiated by the system or the emotional mood of the user. For example, the music selection or the atmosphere in the vehicle can be adapted according to the detected mood of the passenger by the system.

With the help of these three strategies all major needs of the user can be targeted. An increase of health, comfort and safety can be assumed. How these strategies are already recognizable will be examined in detail below. Based on this analysis further potential of vehicular adaptivity is derived.

## 5    Analysis of Current Technologies for Individual Adaptation

Following the deduction and definition of strategies, the results of an analysis of current vehicle implementation technologies and innovations with regard to individual adaptation to the user are presented below. The analysis focuses on technologies and innovations that directly affect the HMI: vehicle steering, implement control, seat posture, seating position, and advanced vehicle controls.

The results presented in Table 1 show several examples for each of these categories that represent the current state of research and development in vehicular adaptation. The examples were examined concerning the following characteristics:

- Form of adaptation: According to the general definition of vehicular adaptation, the examples were categorized in the forms passive, active and smart. To reduce the amount of data, this paper only considers technologies that involve collaborative human-system interaction. Since this interaction will increase in the future, passive adaptation is not considered any further.
- Strategy of user-centered adaptation: The examples were assigned in terms of recognizable adaptation strategies to the three identified types of Anatomical, Contextual, or Psychographical Adaptation.
- Realization: The kind of realization was also examined. A differentiation between primely hardware-based and software-based changes was distinguished.

Technologies from current production cars as well as innovations from research projects and concept cars were used for the analysis. The data basis for the evaluation of these concepts is based on officially provided information. Speculations and own interpretations are not included in the evaluation.

The analysis showed that active adaptation is currently being focused as a form of vehicular adaptation. As for the determined strategies both anatomical and psychographical strategies could be identified mostly within cars in serial production. Concept vehicles, on the other hand, focus in particular on the strategy of Contextual Adaptation. With regard to the realization, changes are mainly applied to the hardware. Software changes are used sporadically. In this context, it needs to be mentioned that a GUI change, as it currently exists, is classified as passive adaptation, since it is initiated exclusively by the user.

**Table 1.** Selection of analyzed technologies and innovations in the vehicle for individual adaptation with regard to the characteristics of vehicular adaptation.

| Technology Innovation | Examples | form of adaptation | | strategy of adaptation | | | realization | |
|---|---|---|---|---|---|---|---|---|
| | | active | smart | AN | CO | PS | hardware | software |
| vehicle steering | Audi AI:ME [17] | X | | | X | | X | |
| | BMW next 100 [18] | X | | | X | | X | |
| | MB S-Class [19] | X | | X | | | X | |
| implement control | aISA-Armrest [20] | X | | | X | | X | |
| | Liebherr INTUSI [21] | X | | | X | | | X |
| | RAFI Flexscape [22] | X | | | X | | X | X |
| seat posture | Bosch Perfectly Keyless [23] | X | | X | | X | X | X |
| | MB S-Class [19] | X | | X | | | X | |
| seating position | BMW next 100 [18] | X | | | X | | X | |
| | Volvo 360c [24] | X | | | X | | X | |
| advanced vehicle controls | Bentley Flying Spur [25] | X | | | | X | X | |
| | Bosch Perfectly Keyless [23] | X | | X | | X | X | X |
| | Mercedes MBUX [26] | X | | X | | X | | X |
| | Samsung Digital Cockpit [27] | X | | X | X | | X | X |

The lack of recognized smart adaptation can be seen both as most promising and complex challenge. Smart adaptation requires a detailed and reliable connectivity of different sensors, e.g. passenger monitoring. Especially, a reliable monitoring and interpretation of passengers needs to be developed. As this technology becomes available, an increase of smart adaptation can be anticipated.

Furthermore, the findings in the concept cars indicate that the future development of adaptive elements is currently pursuing a contextual strategy. An extension to the other strategies also depends on the reliable identification of passenger preferences.

Especially in the case of Anatomical Adaptation, familiar technologies such as seat and steering wheel adjustment in combination with the memory function have often been used up to now. Currently, there is no link between sensors for detecting the user's anatomy to trigger corresponding reactions of actuators.

The results regarding the realization suggest that there is great potential for software-based adaptation. Software-based adaptivity tends to be faster and easier to implement than hardware adaptivity. But despite a higher complexity, hardware-based adaptivity however is more predictable.

## 6 Conclusion and Outlook

After deriving the essential need for adaptivity in the vehicle, the concept of vehicular adaptation was sharpened in this paper. In a first step, the technical possibilities and the relations between humans and systems were presented.

Based on the human-product interaction, which is elementary for user-centered development, the necessary distinction of vehicular adaptation became apparent. Hence, three strategies for user-centered development of individual adaptation were derived and defined.

These different strategies are important and helpful for a user-centered and user-friendly development, especially in the context of future automated vehicles. The derivate forms of adaptivity and the corresponding requirements were worked out in this paper and will serve as a foundation for the development and design of adaptive interior design for fully automated vehicles (SAE L4).

In addition, the analysis of existing and future vehicle technologies shows the potential of individual adaptivity for the future of mobility. In particular, a stronger connectivity of sensors in and around the vehicle can create a basis for smart adaptation.

This development enables the expansion from the currently focused Contextual Adaptation to Anatomical and Psychographical Adaptation.

Ultimately, an increase in the development of adaptive vehicle elements will lead to an increase in development complexity. Especially in case of vehicular adaptation, the interaction between human, design, and technology is in the core of this specific development. Appropriate methodological support is therefore essential and will be investigated in the following.

# References

1. Laakmann, F., Zink, L., Seyffert, M.: New interior concepts for occupant protection in highly automated vehicles. ATZ Worldwide **121**, 48–53 (2019)
2. Dattatreya, P.H.: Future automotive interiors-the 3rd living space. In: SID Symposium Digest of Technical Papers, vol. 47, no. 1 (2016)
3. Braess, H.H., Fritzsche, E., Gail, J.C., Lorenz, B., Seeck, A., Seiffert, U.: Anforderungen, Zielkonflikte. In: Braess, H.H., Seiffert, U. (eds.) Vieweg Handbuch Kraftfahrzeugtechnik pp. 11–55. Springer, Wiesbaden (2016)
4. Chen, T., Fritz, S., Shea, K.: Design for mass customization using additive manufacture: case-study of a balloon-powered car. In: DS 80–4 Proceedings of the 20th International Conference on Engineering Design (ICED 15), vol. 4, pp. 245–254 (2015)
5. Helmers, E.: Die Modellentwicklung in der deutschen Autoindustrie: Gewicht contra Effizienz. Gutachten im Auftrag des BUND und des VCD. Trier (2015)
6. Clewlow, R.R., Gouri, S.M.: Disruptive Transportation: The Adoption, Utilization, and Impacts of Ride-Hailing in the United States. Institute of Transportation Studies, University of California, Davis, Research Report UCD-ITS-RR-17–07 (2017)
7. Reichelt, F., Holder, D., Inkermann, D., Krasteva, P., Maier, T., Vietor, T.: Potenziale anpassbarer Fahrzeuggestalten im Zusammenspiel des Exterieurs und Interieurs. In: Stuttgarter Symposium für Produktentwicklung 2019 (2019)
8. Spies, R.: Entwicklung und Evaluierung eines Touchbedienkonzepts mit adaptiv haptisch veränderlicher Oberfläche zur Menübedienung im Fahrzeug. TU München: Fakultät für Maschinenwesen (2013)
9. Hein, A., Patzer, E., Maier, T.: Improving HMIs of vehicle exterior design using adaptive structures and systems. In: International Conference on Applied Human Factors and Ergonomics, pp. 261–273. Springer, Cham (2017)
10. Oppermann, R.: Adaptive User Support – Introduction. In: Oppermann, R. (ed.) Lawrence Erlbaum Associates, pp. 1–13. Hillsdale, New Jersey (1994)
11. Gullà, F., Ceccacci, S., Germani, M., Cavalieri, L.: Design adaptable and adaptive user interfaces: a method to manage the information. In: ForItAAL, Conference Paper (2014)

12. Friedrich, H.E., Treffinger, P., Kopp, G., Knäbel, H.: Werkstoffe und Bauweisen ermöglichen neue Fahrzeugkonzepte. In: Schindler, V., Sievers, I. (eds.) Forschung für das Auto von morgen. Springer, Heidelberg (2008)
13. Oppermann, R., Rashev, R.: Adaptability and Adaptivity in Learning Systems. In: Behrooz, A. (ed.) Knowledge Transfer, vol. II, pp. 173–179. pAce, London (1997)
14. Schmid, M., Maier, T.: Technisches Interface Design: Anforderungen. Springer, Bewertung und Gestaltung (2017)
15. Holder, D.: Gefallensurteil und Blickanalyse zum Fahrzeugdesign zukünftiger Aufbaugestalten anhand einer technischen Prognose. Institut für Konstruktionstechnik und Technisches Design, Stuttgart (2016)
16. Seeger, H.: Design technischer Produkte. Produktprogramme und-systeme. Springer, Heidelberg (2005)
17. Audi AI: ME Concept. https://www.audi-mediacenter.com/de/audi-aime-2019-11455. Accessed 04 Feb 2021
18. BMW next 100 Concept. https://www.bmwgroup.com/en/company/the-next-100-years/brandvisions.html. Accessed 04 Feb 2021
19. Mercedes-Benz S-Class. https://moba.i.daimler.com/baixn/cars/222.0_comand_2017/de_DE/page/ID_c702ae40e2532d26354ae36513ba6b0b-2da31f14daaadcb354ae36544dcc585-de-DE.html. Accessed 04 Feb 2021
20. Kaufmann, A., Schempp, T., Stöhr, I., Schmid, M., Maier, T.: Managing complexity-adaptive control armrest. ATZheavy Duty Worldwide **13**(2), 22–29 (2020)
21. Liebherr INTUSI. https://www.liebherr.com/shared/media/corporate/images/events/bauma-2019/magazine/liebherr-bauma-magazine-2019.pdf. Accessed 04 Feb 2021
22. RAFI Glasscape. https://www.rafi.de/en/glasscape/. Accessed 04 Feb 2021
23. Bosch Perfectly Keyless. https://www.bosch-mobility-solutions.com/en/products-and-services/passenger-cars-and-light-commercial-vehicles/connectivity-solutions/perfectly-keyless/. Accessed 04 Feb 2021
24. Volvo 360c Concept. https://www.volvocars.com/intl/cars/concepts/360c?redirect=true. Accessed 04 Feb 2021
25. Bentley Flying Spur Roating Display. https://www.bentleymotors.com/en/world-of-bentley/news/2020-news/the-flying-spur-in-detail-the-bentley-rotating-display.html
26. Mercedes-Benz MBUX. https://www.mercedes-benz.de/passengercars/technology-innovation/mbux/highlights.module.html. Accessed 04 Feb 2021
27. Samsung Digital Cockpit. https://www.samsung.com/de/explore/experiences/ces2021. Accessed 04 Feb 2021

# Assessment of Thermal Comfort in Different Vehicle-Classes – The Suitability of ISO 14505-2:2006-12

Andreas Rolle[1]([⊠]), Bastian Schmandt[2], Cyril Guinet[2], and Klaus Bengler[1]

[1] Chair of Ergonomics, Technical University of Munich, Munich, Germany
a.rolle@tum.de
[2] I/EK-432, Audi AG, Ingolstadt, Germany

**Abstract.** Future mobility is changing so that new requirements concerning air conditioning in vehicles arise. With the increase of electric- and the development of autonomously driving vehicles, classical air conditioning concepts ought to be adapted to fulfil new requirements. During the development of new climate concepts, the thermal wellbeing of the occupants in the vehicle need to be kept in mind. New air conditioning concepts will only prevail if they ensure adequate thermal comfort with reduced energy consumption. Objective evaluation methods are currently used to a limited extent during the application process for vehicle air conditioning. In the following investigation the interior climate for two vehicles (mid-range and upper-class) is objectively assessed and compared for a wide range of ambient temperatures from $-20\,°C$ to $+40\,°C$. During this investigation the ISO 14505-2:2006-12 is tested to find out whether it is suitable to assess and evaluate the thermal perception by measuring the equivalent temperature. When evaluating the results according to the comfort zone diagrams of ISO 14505-2:2006-12 the mid-range vehicle has a better interior climate than the upper-class vehicle. This paper will show that it is necessary to adapt the comfort zone diagrams to demographic differences that influence the thermal perception of humans.

**Keyword:** Thermal comfort assessment · Human thermal modelling · Objective evaluation

## 1 Introduction

Thermal wellbeing and comfort play a significant role in the driver's alertness at all times and contribute to the overall feeling of comfort perceived by all the occupants in a vehicle. This is also illustrated by the comfort pyramid according to Bubb (see Fig. 1) [1]. The pyramid shows that the influence of different factors, of which thermal comfort is only one contributor, on the so-called overall comfort. Furthermore, it illustrates the hierarchy of the different contributors with respect to the overall comfort. Only when the following factors – odor, light, vibration and noise – have no negative influence, the comfort will be positively affected by a pleasant climate. The influence of the climate, which has to guarantee a high standard of wellbeing during travelling, is greater than the effect of

© The Author(s), under exclusive license to Springer Nature Switzerland AG 2021
N. L. Black et al. (Eds.): IEA 2021, LNNS 221, pp. 806–813, 2021.
https://doi.org/10.1007/978-3-030-74608-7_99

the anthropometric factors. However, air conditioning is the greatest secondary energy consumer in cars and especially in electric vehicles the driving range can be significantly reduced by heating and cooling the car cabin [2]. Therefore, it is necessary to enhance the energy efficiency of air conditioning systems by improving and developing new concepts. In the field of research, various evaluation methods are developed to simulate and assess thermal comfort in a vehicle. Most of these methods are rarely used in the car industry and are not integrated in the developing process.

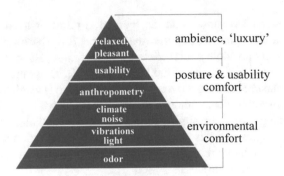

**Fig. 1.** Comfort pyramid according to Bubb [1].

## 1.1 Evaluation of Thermal Comfort in a Vehicle

The evaluation of thermal comfort in a vehicle ought to be discussed from two different perspectives. On the one hand air conditioning has to consider safety issues, like defrosting and defogging during winter. The air supply and airflow through the cabin also has to conform to legal requirements. The above-mentioned requirements of the heating, ventilation and air conditioning system (HVAC) are therefore coordinated and objectively tested step by step to optimize it during an extensive test phase. In this phase the application of a new vehicle project builds onto the experiences of previous projects [3].

On the other hand, methods used to assess the thermal comfort are based on an empirical approach. This evaluation is mostly based on subjective evaluation methods with the support of conventional temperature measuring equipment. Individual factors influencing the thermal perception of the test engineer may lead to adverse effects while the HVAC-System is adjusted, as the main objective of the test engineer is to secure an average thermal wellbeing satisfying a large group of customers. In future objective measurements should assist or even substitute subjective evaluation methods used so far to provide a wider range of quantitative and reliable results on thermal perception.

## 1.2 Objective Evaluation of Thermal Comfort

The most applied model in thermal comfort studies, developed for buildings, is the Predicted Mean Vote model (PMV) based on Fanger's equation for human body heat exchange. As people perceive thermal sensation differently, he also introduced the Predicted Percentage Dissatisfied (PPD) for the evaluation of conditions of discomfort. The PPD is thus giving information about how many people are experiencing the given conditions as too cold or too hot. The model, described above, is sometimes used in the car industry but is unsuitable to evaluate thermal comfort in vehicles because only the global comfort of the occupants is determined neglecting the conditions of individual body parts. The PMV and PPD model are taken over by the American ASHRAE-55 and the European EN ISO 7730 as a suggested standard to mainly assess thermal comfort in buildings [4, 5].

However, research has shown that the thermal comfort of local body parts has a significant influence on global body thermal comfort [6]. These findings lead to the development of thermophysiological models. Important examples of these models are the Berkeley Comfort Model, Tanabe and the Fiala Model [7]. These models' predictability cannot really be measured and are often questioned because it is validated by the results of the developer's own experiment without comparing them with independent experimental data. This leads to a gab between simulated results and the validation of thermal comfort [7]. Thermophysiological models are not recognized by international standards. These are a few reasons why they are not really used to assess the thermal comfort in a car cabin during the application process.

When comparing the established measuring methods, it is found that the equivalent temperature is the most suitable climate index to evaluate thermal environments in cars and to assess the thermal comfort [8]. The equivalent temperature is defined as 'The temperature of an imaginary enclosure with the mean radiant temperature equal to air temperature and still air in which a person has the same heat exchange by convection and radiation as in the actual condition' [5]. Therewith nearly all the physical factors of the thermal environment, which have a major influence on the thermal comfort in a car cabin, are considered. In this paper the directed equivalent temperature is used as the index to measure thermal comfort.

Based on the equivalent temperature Nilsson [9] conducted different surveys with test subjects to enable an interpretation of their thermal wellbeing. He used 20 male subjects in a climate chamber where asymmetries were produced by vertical air temperature gradients and sun radiation. Two different sets of clothing were used to investigate the effect of summer and winter clothing. The subjects were exposed to 30 different climate conditions for 60 min. Their subjective responses were correlated with the measured equivalent temperatures. Nilsson developed 'Comfort Zone Diagrams' for a simple interpretation of thermal comfort. Figure 2 shows the 'Comfort Zone Diagrams' for summer and winter conditions [9].

The equivalent temperature in °C is presented on the x-axis and the whole body with 16 different body segments are presented on the y-axis. The colored comfort zones ('cold, but comfortable', 'neutral' and 'warm, but comfortable') present limits of the equivalent temperatures where the occupants still feel comfortable. The two white zones ('too cold' and 'too warm') present limits where occupants feel discomfortable. In the 'Comfort Zone Diagrams' two evaluations are considered, the equivalent temperature of the whole body as well as the equivalent temperature for 16 different body zones, which correspond with the body segments measured on the climate dummies used in this investigation.

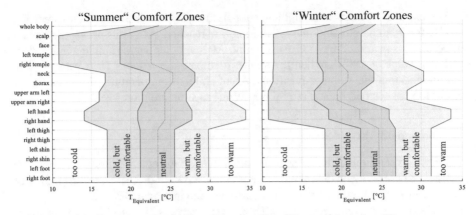

**Fig. 2.** Summer and winter 'Comfort Zone Diagram' based on [5].

### 1.3 Objectives

The thermal comfort of two current car classes are compared with each other, considering the following hypothesis:

H1: Are the measured equivalent temperature values of the climate dummies adequate to assess all thermal effects in the car cabin?
H2: Are the comfort zone diagrams suitable to assess the cabin climate of a mid-range and upper-class vehicle?
H3: Does the test show any class specific differences concerning the cabin climate?

## 2 Methodology

The experiments are done in the climate wind channel to allow reproducible results. Both the mid-range and upper-class vehicle are tested at the same environmental conditions and over the same period of time. The test is done at a wide range of ambient temperatures from $-20$ °C to $+40$ °C. In this way the response of the two vehicles to a variety of 'normal' temperatures as well as 'extreme' conditions can be measured.

### 2.1 Experimental Design and Procedure

Each vehicle is supplied with three climate dummies seated on the passenger seat and on the left and right back seats. A detailed description of the climate measuring dummy can be found in [10]. Additionally, the air temperatures of all vents, as well as headspace and footwell are measured by standard temperature sensors. Furthermore, surface temperatures of the windowpanes and the dashboard are also measured. The air vents are positioned in a defined way for winter and summer temperatures. In both vehicles the climate control is adjusted to 'AUTO 22'. The test driver keeps the vehicle at a constant speed of 50 km/h. He also answers a standardized questionnaire about his subjective thermal comfort as published in DIN EN ISO 14505-3:2006-09 [11].

The experiment starts at an ambient temperature of −20 °C. Both vehicles are kept at −20 °C for 90 min until stationary conditions are reached. After this phase, the ambient temperature is increased by 1 °C every 6 min. After another 6 h the ambient temperature reaches a value of 40 °C. When the ambient temperature reaches 16 °C, the air vents are changed into the summer positions. At an ambient temperature of 20 °C, the sun simulation is switched on at a rate of 600 W/m² to simulate more realistic conditions.

## 2.2 Dependent Variables

During the experiment different surface and air temperatures and different air velocities are reached depending on the change of the ambient temperature. The resulting influences of the different temperatures, radiation and convection in the car cabin can be assessed by measuring the equivalent temperature. These measurements give an objective description of the climate in the car interior. Furthermore, answering the questionnaire by the driver enables a plausibility check on the measured values.

## 3 Results

During the experiment three different sets of results are obtained. The standardized questionnaire answered by the driver shows a correlation between the driver's subjective thermal perception and the objective equivalent temperature measurements of the climate dummies.

A selection of 13 environmental conditions are evaluated, starting with −20 °C and assessing the conditions in 5 °C steps (−20 °C, −15 °C … 35 °C, 40 °C). The results for 10 °C will be presented as this temperature is statistically relevant and about equal to the average temperature measured in Germany during the last 30 years [12]. The second set of results obtained are the measurements of the standard temperature sensors. The measured outlet temperature of all vents and several surface temperatures of the windowpanes, dashboard and footwell show that the temperatures are slightly higher in the upper-class vehicle.

The measured equivalent temperature values are converted to comfort values between −2 (too cold) to + 2 (too warm) according to ISO 14505-2:2006-12. An example of this evaluation for all three dummies seated in the car cabin, are given in Fig. 3. The colored zones in Fig. 3 correspond with the 16-measuring positions of the equivalent temperature sensors on the surface of the dummy.

The green body segments are 'neutral', the light blue zones are cold but comfortable and the yellow zones correspond with a warm but comfortable thermal perception. Body zones which are colored blue or red are discomfortable and correspond with a 'too cold' respectively 'too warm' thermal perception. In the case of the mid-range vehicle 29 body zones are rated as 'neutral' and 16 zones are 'warm, but comfortable'. At the back the thighs of the right dummy as well as the left thigh of the left dummy are 'cold, but comfortable'. In the case of the upper-class vehicle there are less 'neutral' body zones (22) and more 'warm, but comfortable' body regions (26). No 'cold, but comfortable' regions are measured.

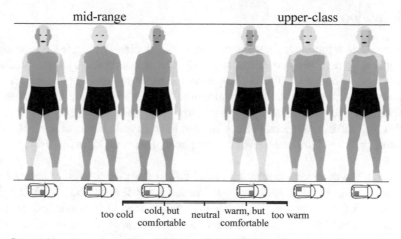

**Fig. 3.** Comparison thermal comfort of the dummies at 10 °C in mid-range and upper-class vehicle

These comfort values, for each of the 16 body segments, are rated according to a summary evaluation as given in the following Eq. (1). Top credits are given for a neutral thermal perception:

$$P = 0 \cdot TC + 1 \cdot C + 2 \cdot N + 1 \cdot W + 0 \cdot TW \tag{1}$$

P = 'score'; TC = 'too cold'; C = 'cold, but comfortable'; N = 'neutral'; W = 'warm, but comfortable'; TW = 'too warm'.

The results of the credit evaluations for the 13 environmental conditions are summarized on a percentage scale in Fig. 4. The front passenger seat in the mid-range vehicle attains 74,9% which is a 3,4% higher value than in the case of the evaluation for the upper-class vehicle. Compared to the upper-class vehicle with a value of 76,2% the mid-range vehicle attains a value of 78,7% for the left back seat. For the right back seat, the mid-range vehicle attains 6,3% more credits than the upper-class vehicle with a total value of 79,4%.

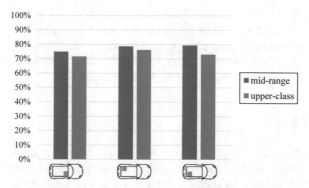

**Fig. 4.** Credit evaluation on thermal comfort for each dummy in mid-range and upper-class vehicle

# 4 Discussion

The asymmetric temperature field in the car cabin is clearly detected by the equivalent temperature measurement sensors. Firstly, this is confirmed by the evaluation of the questionnaire and secondly by comparing the measured thermal environment with equivalent temperature values. This is also illustrated in Fig. 3 as the side of the specific dummy seated next to the door and window is by tendency slightly colder than the other side. All measured thermal effects exceed the measuring inaccuracies. Hence, the measured equivalent temperature values adequately assess all thermal effects in the car cabin.

By using the summary evaluation based on the thermal comfort values the cabin climate of the mid-range vehicle performs better, according to ISO 14505-2:2006-12. When comparing the average equivalent temperatures of the 13 environmental conditions the upper-class vehicle is warmer than that of the mid-range vehicle. The warmer car cabin of the upper-class vehicle leads to a different profile in favor of the mid-range vehicle according to the credit evaluation based on the ISO 14505-2:2006-12 (see Fig. 4). The above-mentioned results do not correlate with the technical effort which is done to ensure a good interior climate in upper-class vehicles for example there are additional vents in the B-pillar to improve air conditioning for the second seat row. Even more technical differences are found when mid-range and upper-class vehicles are compared with each other so that a reverse result would be expected. Air conditioning systems not only have to satisfy a manifold of technical but also customer-specific requirements. Contrary to this, the evaluation of the conducted experiment is based on the ISO standard and is using the same evaluation criteria for both vehicles. In the application phase, though, vehicles are not only technically tested but also adapted for a specific market. The car cabin of the upper-class vehicle is especially implemented warmer to meet the requirements of estimated customers who are in general older people and prefer a warmer climate.

Therefore, the evaluation following the ISO 14505-2:2006-12 leads to a misleading interpretation. The ISO 14505-2:2006-12 only allows the subdivision of comfort zones into 'summer' and 'winter' which is inadequate for the comparison of mid-range and upper-class vehicles as other demographic characteristics and ethnic influences are not considered. On the other hand, these influences are important during the development process. A user-oriented scaling of the comfort zones for various age groups, gender, or their origin is therefore necessary. Consequently, hypotheses H2 is declined and hypothesis H3 confirmed. Should two vehicles of the same class be evaluated, a direct comparison according to the ISO 14505-2:2006-12 is possible.

# 5 Conclusion

This analysis of the climate application requirements shows that the ISO 14505-2:2006-12 is restricted in its suitability for the evaluation of thermal comfort in current vehicles with different application goals and user characteristics. Further studies with test subjects will follow to allow a more differentiated evaluation. The spectrum of test subjects should be extended by including representative gender issues and a larger age spectrum.

# 6 Outlook

Studies with numerous test subjects will be conducted at the Chair of Ergonomics, Technical University of Munich using a vehicle mock-up where various climate conditions for the interior can be generated. In this way the subjective thermal perception of the test subjects can be determined. These values can then be compared with the objective measurements of the equivalent temperature. This should allow an improved correlation between subjective and objective measurements.

# References

1. Bubb, H.: "Komfort und Diskomfort", Ergonomie Aktuell, 4. Technische Universität München, Lehrstuhl für Ergonomie (2003)
2. Großmann, H.: Pkw-Klimatisierung: Physikalische Grundlagen und technische Umsetzung, 2nd edn. Springer, Heidelberg (2013)
3. Thomschke, C., Bader, V., Gubalke, A., van Treeck, C.: Bewertung der transienten thermischen Behaglichkeit in einer realen Fahrzeugumgebung. In: IBPSA Conference (2014)
4. ASHRAE 55, Thermal environmental conditions for human occupancy. Atlanta Ga.: ASHRAE (2013)
5. ISO 14505–2:2006–12, "Ergonomics of the thermal environment - Evaluation of thermal environments in vehicles - Part 2: Determination of equivalent temperature"
6. Zhang, H., Arens, E., Huizenga, C., Han, T.: Thermal sensation and comfort models for non-uniform and transient environments: Part II: local comfort of individual body parts (2009)
7. Katić, K., Li, R., Zeiler, W.: Thermophysiological models and their applications: A review. Build. Environ. **106**, 286–300 (2016). https://doi.org/10.1016/j.buildenv.2016.06.031
8. Schwab, R., Grün, G. (eds.): Ableitung eines messbaren Klimasummenmaßes für den Vergleich des Fahrzeugklimas konventioneller und elektrischer Fahrzeuge. Hannover, Berlin, FAT-Schriftenreihe, Berlin (2013)
9. Nilsson, H.: Comfort climate evaluation with thermal manikin methods and computer simulation models," Dissertation, Department of Civil and Architectural Engineering, Royal Institute of Technology, Stockholm (2004)
10. Rolle, A., Schmandt, B., Guinet, C., Bengler, C.: How can the thermal sensation be objectively determined in order to analyse different vehicle air conditioning concepts? In: Windsor Conference, pp. 343–357 (2020)
11. DIN EN ISO 14505–3:2006–09, "Ergonomie der thermischen Umgebung – Bewertung der thermischen Umgebungen in Fahrzeugen – Teil 3: Bewertung der thermischen Behaglichkeit durch Versuchspersonen"
12. DWD, "Entwicklung der Jahresmitteltemperatur in Deutschland in ausgewählten Jahren von 1960 bis 2020" (2021)

# Identifying Human Factors and Other Characteristics that Contribute to Injury Severity in Single-Vehicle Four-Wheeler Crashes in Tamilnadu, India

Sathish Kumar Sivasankaran and Venkatesh Balasubramanian[✉]

RBG Lab, Department of Engineering Design, IIT Madras, Chennai 600036, India
chanakya@iitm.ac.in

**Abstract.** Single-vehicle crashes are of major concern in developed and developing nations due to the severity of injuries. According to the Ministry of Road Transport and Highways (MoRTH, 2018) report, a total of 4,67,044 accidents have been reported by the states and union territories in which have claimed 1,51,417 lives. However, a clearer picture of single-vehicle crashes is unavailable. The present study's objective is to obtain a more precise understanding concerning the injury severity of the out-of-control single-vehicle four-wheeler crashes with the drivers being at fault. Contributory factors, including driver, roadway, and environmental characteristics, are investigated and discussed. The crash dataset for the present study was prepared from the police-reported single-vehicle crashes for the past nine years that occurred within Tamilnadu. The research team retrieved all the single-vehicle out-of-control four-wheeler crashes for the period between 2009 and 2017. To deal with that of the ordered categorical variable, ordinal logistic regression analysis was carried out. The brant test was carried out to check for the proportional odds assumption being valid or not. Younger and working-age group drivers, violation of rules, number of lanes, median separators, highways, and village roads were significantly associated with increased crash severity. Based on the above results' findings, targeted countermeasures may be designed in light of the driver's injury severity. For example, drivers who violate the law are prone to more severe injuries; awareness to strictly avoid such behaviors and strict law enforcement is need of the hour in those crashes.

**Keywords:** Road traffic accidents · Crash severity · Single vehicle crashes · Ordered logit model · Transportation human factors

## 1 Introduction

A disproportionate number of serious and fatal crashes are often associated with single-vehicle crashes. Single-vehicle collisions pose rising traffic safety challenges. Single-vehicle crashes are of major concern in developed and developing nations due to the severity of injuries. For example, in developed nations like the US, fatalities in single-vehicle accidents increased by 5.9% rise nationally during 2016, whereas multi-vehicle crash fatalities increased by a smaller proportion [1]. According to the Ministry of Road Transport and Highways [2] report, a total of 4,67,044 accidents have been reported by the states and union territories in which have claimed 1,51,417 lives. However, a clearer picture of single-vehicle crashes is unavailable. These figures indicate that significant research efforts are needed to understand better important causal factors in single-vehicle collisions and their effects on injury severity. Previous studies have compared single-vehicle crashes to multi-vehicle crashes and found major variations between these two types of crashes.

Single-vehicle crashes are generally classified into two types: one in which the vehicle collides with the pedestrians and the other where the vehicle does not collide with other road users. The drivers themselves simply contribute to the collision in single-vehicle crashes. The vehicles do not collide with other vehicles or pedestrians involved due to causes such as self-skidding, hitting stationary objects and trees are majorly referred to as single-vehicle crashes. Such type of accidents that the drivers themselves contribute is referred to as out-of-control single-vehicle crashes. The influence of roadway and environmental factors play a major role in these crashes.

Many studies have been conducted regarding the contributing factors to single-vehicle crash severity; however, a small number of these studies focused on single-vehicle four-wheeler crashes and their characteristics. Most studies in India are concentrated on the analysis of fatal road traffic crashes and pedestrian road crashes. Although attempts have been made to study vulnerable road user crashes in India, studies evaluating contributing factors to single-vehicle four-wheeler crashes are limited in the literature. This study is the first to be studied in India as per the author's knowledge. Hence, there exists a knowledge gap that needs to be filled. Facts are available with respect to developed nations; these findings from western nations may not be directly applicable due to the differences in roadway features, roadside environments, policies and practices, and, more importantly, driver's behavior compared to developing nations.

More studies focusing on single-vehicle crash severity in different geographical regions must average the geographical bias related to crash severity. Also, there is a huge potential for four-wheeler issues in India to increase due to the substantial growth of the four-wheeler population in many states and lack of sufficient infrastructure. This article attempts to fill that knowledge gap.

The present study's objective is to obtain a more precise understanding concerning the injury severity of the out-of-control single-vehicle four-wheeler crashes with the drivers being at fault. The present study's four-wheelers include light motor vehicle, light goods van, SUV, light goods vehicle. Special vehicles, buses, heavy goods trucks, earth moving equipment, heavy articulated vehicles, heavy goods vehicles, agricultural vehicles were excluded from the present study. Contributory factors, including driver, roadway, and environmental characteristics, are investigated and discussed.

## 2  Methods and Materials

### 2.1  Data

Tamil Nadu is the tenth largest Indian state by area and the sixth-largest by population. Over 50 of the state is urbanized, accounting for 9.6 of the country's urban population, while only comprising 6 of India's total population. According to the 2011 India census, Tamil Nadu had a population of 7.2 crores. Tamilnadu was chosen for the study as it has a high incidence of Road Traffic Crashes (RTC's). The recent reports by MORTH highlight that Tamilnadu has recorded the highest number of road crashes for the past few consecutive years, contributing to 14.1 of its total RTCs in the country.

The data for the present study was extracted from the state accident database maintained by the Additional Director General of Police (ADGP), State Traffic Planning Cell (STPC) Tamilnadu, referred to as the Road Accident Database management System (RADMS) database. Tamilnadu police compile reports of accidents on state roads, and the police officials record information about the accident, the persons and the vehicles involved after a detailed investigation process. The entire dataset consists of three sub-datasets, including the crash dataset, the vehicle dataset, and the driver dataset. The crash dataset documents crash-level information regarding collision types, crash location, road geometric, and environmental conditions. The vehicle dataset illustrates detailed characteristics of each vehicle, occupant injury outcomes, and vehicle-specific information. The driver dataset demonstrates the demographic and behaviour information of each driver involved in crashes. Each crash data has a unique crash identification number common in different datasets to link the records together.

The crash dataset for the present study was prepared from the police-reported single-vehicle crashes for the past nine years that occurred within Tamilnadu. The research team retrieved all the single-vehicle out-of-control four-wheeler crashes for the period between 2009 and 2017. To focus on this study's prime objective, the research team identified contributory factors that influence the severity of crashes. The identified variables include driver characteristics (driver gender, age, license status, alcohol/drug status, driver error), crash-related factors (accident severity, collision type, central divider, number of lanes, road category, road conditions), traffic-related factors (traffic movement, traffic control), vehicle (vehicle maneuver) and environment-related factors (population setting, weather condition, light condition, region, season, day of the week and location).

There were four categories of outcome concerning motorcyclists in these crashes: fatal (K), incapacitating injury (A), non-incapacitating injury (B), possible injury (C). Property damage only (PDO) crashes were not considered as this study is focused on injurious crashes. According to Indian practice, fatal crashes (K) referred to road users involved in a vehicle crash and died within 30 days of a traffic crash. The incapacitating injury (A) is determined when the person is hospitalized for 24 h or more, and non-incapacitating injury (B) is designated when the road user suffers from traffic injury and is hospitalized for less than 24 h. Possible injury (C) injury means that a person was injured in the crash, but there was no evident injury, and he or she was able to walk away from the scene of the crash.

The dataset includes 17,882 single-vehicle two-wheeler reported crashes for which injury severity levels were reported. To ensure that each category has a decent number of observations, they have regrouped into three categories (1) fatal injury (K), (2) incapacitating injury (A) (3) possible injury/non-incapacitating injury (B/C). Possible injury and non-incapacitating injury were combined into one group because they share most of the crash characteristics. To simplify the following presentation, incapacitating injury is referred to as severe injury; possible injury/non-incapacitating injuries referred to a minor injury, and fatal injuries were retained in the study. The final proportion of categories was 4091 (22.9) fatal, 2449(13.7) serious crashes, and 11342(63.4) minor injuries. The number of crashes involving no injuries is highly unreported in India and has already been reported in the works of [3–5].

## 2.2 Methodology

The highest level of driver injury typically measures crash severity in single-vehicle crashes. When the response variable is categorical and ordinal, the distance between categories is unknown [6]. To deal with an ordered categorical variable, an ordered logit model is more appropriate. One of the important assumptions for such a model is the proportional odds assumption, which considers the parameter estimates constant across all severity levels. The brant test is usually applied for checking the proportional odds assumption. If the proportional odds assumption holds good, ordered logistic regression models can be applied.

Methodologies used in this study follow the processes described by other researchers (e.g., [7–9]. We used an ordered logit model to determine the possible factors influencing the severity of single-vehicle motorcycle crashes. The assumptions of the ordered logit/proportional odds model were met in this study. This type of model's choice was also influenced by the polytomous nature of the response variable (motorcycle crash severity) and the response variable's ordinal nature.

The ordered logit model is derived by specifying a latent variable, Z, which is specified as a linear function for each injury severity observation, such that

$$Z = \beta X + \varepsilon \tag{1}$$

where: Z: latent variable used as the basis for modeling the ordinal ranking of the observed injury severity data, X: vector of variables determining the discrete ordering for each injury severity observation, $\beta$: vector of estimable parameters, $\varepsilon$: disturbance term.

With this specification, the observed ordered data, y, for each occupant injury observation is defined as

$$y = 1 \text{ if } Z \le \mu_0 \text{ (Minor Injury)}$$
$$y = 2 \text{ if } \mu_0 \le Z \le \mu_1 \text{ (Serious Injury)}$$
$$y = 3 \text{ if } \mu_1 \le Z \le \mu_2 \text{ (Fatal Injury)} \tag{2}$$

Where; $\mu_i$ are unknown estimable parameters (refer to as thresholds) that define crash severity.

For testing the goodness-of-fit, the likelihood ratio (LR) test is used to evaluate model performance. This test result shows whether the null hypothesis for a specific model should be rejected or not. The corresponding equation is

$$\eta^2 = 1 - \frac{l(\beta)}{l(0)} \tag{3}$$

Where; $l(\beta)$ is the log-likelihood value of the developed model and $l(0)$ is the log-likelihood value of the model without predictive variable included. The descriptive statistics of the dataset is provided in Table 1.

**Table 1.** Descriptive statistics of the crash dataset

| Variable description | Fatal injuries | | Serious injuries | | Minor injuries | | Total |
|---|---|---|---|---|---|---|---|
| | Count | % | Count | % | Count | % | |
| **Crash severity** | 4091 | 22.9 | 2449 | 13.7 | 11342 | 63.4 | 17882 |
| **Season** | | | | | | | |
| Monsoon | 1343 | 21.90 | 829 | 13.50 | 3961 | 64.60 | 6133 |
| Post Monsoon | 576 | 22.10 | 337 | 12.90 | 1696 | 65.00 | 2609 |
| Summer | 1198 | 24.20 | 691 | 13.90 | 3070 | 61.90 | 4959 |
| Winter | 974 | 23.30 | 592 | 14.20 | 2615 | 62.50 | 4181 |
| **Day of the week** | | | | | | | |
| Weekend | 1251 | 23.70 | 725 | 13.70 | 3298 | 62.50 | 5274 |
| Workday | 2840 | 22.50 | 1724 | 13.70 | 8044 | 63.80 | 12608 |
| **Region** | | | | | | | |
| Central | 702 | 21.60 | 346 | 10.70 | 2195 | 67.70 | 3243 |
| North | 1210 | 22.10 | 681 | 12.40 | 3582 | 65.40 | 5473 |
| South | 1065 | 23.50 | 568 | 12.50 | 2905 | 64.00 | 4538 |
| West | 1114 | 24.10 | 854 | 18.50 | 2660 | 57.50 | 4628 |
| **Collision type** | | | | | | | |
| Hit animal | 14 | 10.20 | 19 | 13.90 | 104 | 75.90 | 137 |
| Hit object | 568 | 20.60 | 430 | 15.60 | 1753 | 63.70 | 2751 |
| Hit parked vehicle | 19 | 25.00 | 12 | 15.80 | 45 | 59.20 | 76 |
| Hit Tree | 461 | 26.30 | 215 | 12.30 | 1076 | 61.40 | 1752 |
| Others | 1598 | 23.50 | 987 | 14.50 | 4217 | 62.00 | 6802 |
| Ran off road | 175 | 24.10 | 99 | 13.70 | 451 | 62.20 | 725 |
| Side swipe | 292 | 22.60 | 168 | 13.00 | 830 | 64.30 | 1290 |
| Skidding | 964 | 22.20 | 519 | 11.90 | 2866 | 65.90 | 4349 |
| **Number of lanes** | | | | | | | |
| Multiple | 644 | 40.60 | 137 | 8.60 | 805 | 50.80 | 1586 |
| Single | 1519 | 12.70 | 1901 | 15.90 | 8557 | 71.40 | 11977 |
| Two | 1928 | 44.60 | 411 | 9.50 | 1980 | 45.80 | 4319 |
| **Central divider** | | | | | | | |
| No | 2235 | 41.90 | 574 | 10.80 | 2520 | 47.30 | 5329 |
| Yes | 1856 | 14.80 | 1875 | 14.90 | 8822 | 70.30 | 12553 |
| **Traffic control** | | | | | | | |

(*continued*)

Table 1.  (*continued*)

| Variable description | Fatal injuries | | Serious injuries | | Minor injuries | | Total |
|---|---|---|---|---|---|---|---|
| | Count | % | Count | % | Count | % | |
| Functioning | 71 | 18.20 | 65 | 16.60 | 255 | 65.20 | 391 |
| No control | 493 | 24.10 | 275 | 13.50 | 1275 | 62.40 | 2043 |
| None | 3527 | 22.80 | 2109 | 13.70 | 9812 | 63.50 | 15448 |
| **Road category** | | | | | | | |
| District road | 727 | 53.50 | 138 | 10.20 | 494 | 36.40 | 1359 |
| Highways | 2913 | 20.00 | 2008 | 13.80 | 9680 | 66.30 | 14601 |
| Other roads | 246 | 24.00 | 167 | 16.30 | 614 | 59.80 | 1027 |
| Village roads | 205 | 22.90 | 136 | 15.20 | 554 | 61.90 | 895 |
| **Light conditions** | | | | | | | |
| Darkness-lighted | 841 | 22.90 | 503 | 13.70 | 2334 | 63.50 | 3678 |
| Darkness-unlighted | 505 | 26.30 | 213 | 11.10 | 1204 | 62.60 | 1922 |
| Daylight | 2458 | 22.20 | 1569 | 14.20 | 7025 | 63.60 | 11052 |
| Dusk/Dawn | 287 | 23.30 | 164 | 13.30 | 779 | 63.30 | 1230 |
| **Weather condition** | | | | | | | |
| Fine | 3968 | 22.80 | 2393 | 13.70 | 11074 | 63.50 | 17435 |
| Inclement | 123 | 27.50 | 56 | 12.50 | 268 | 60.00 | 447 |
| **Road condition** | | | | | | | |
| Good | 4037 | 22.90 | 2403 | 13.60 | 11215 | 63.50 | 17655 |
| Others | 54 | 23.80 | 46 | 20.30 | 127 | 55.90 | 227 |
| **Traffic movement** | | | | | | | |
| One-way | 351 | 25.20 | 156 | 11.20 | 885 | 63.60 | 1392 |
| Two-way | 3740 | 22.70 | 2293 | 13.90 | 10457 | 63.40 | 16490 |
| **Population** | | | | | | | |
| Rural | 3661 | 23.20 | 2071 | 13.10 | 10043 | 63.70 | 15775 |
| Urban | 430 | 20.40 | 378 | 17.90 | 1299 | 61.70 | 2107 |
| **Location** | | | | | | | |
| Business area | 2179 | 21.60 | 1476 | 14.60 | 6450 | 63.80 | 10105 |
| Open area | 616 | 27.10 | 303 | 13.30 | 1357 | 59.60 | 2276 |
| Others | 1090 | 23.50 | 547 | 11.80 | 3002 | 64.70 | 4639 |
| Residential area | 206 | 23.90 | 123 | 14.30 | 533 | 61.80 | 862 |

(*continued*)

**Table 1.** (*continued*)

| Variable description | Fatal injuries | | Serious injuries | | Minor injuries | | Total |
|---|---|---|---|---|---|---|---|
| | Count | % | Count | % | Count | % | |
| **Driver gender** | | | | | | | |
| Female | 10 | 23.30 | 6 | 14.00 | 27 | 62.80 | 43 |
| Male | 4081 | 22.90 | 2443 | 13.70 | 11315 | 63.40 | 17839 |
| **Driver age** | | | | | | | |
| <17 | 8 | 57.10 | 1 | 7.10 | 5 | 35.70 | 14 |
| >65 | 27 | 34.60 | 6 | 7.70 | 45 | 57.70 | 78 |
| 18–25 | 750 | 24.00 | 413 | 13.20 | 1960 | 62.80 | 3123 |
| 25–64 | 3306 | 22.50 | 2029 | 13.80 | 9332 | 63.60 | 14667 |
| **License type** | | | | | | | |
| Invalid | 27 | 20.90 | 19 | 14.70 | 83 | 64.30 | 129 |
| No license | 759 | 27.20 | 342 | 12.30 | 1689 | 60.50 | 2790 |
| Valid | 3305 | 22.10 | 2088 | 14.00 | 9570 | 64.00 | 14963 |
| **Alcohol/drug** | | | | | | | |
| Alcohol | 16 | 36.40 | 10 | 22.70 | 18 | 40.90 | 44 |
| Drug | 5 | 29.40 | 1 | 5.90 | 11 | 64.70 | 17 |
| None | 4070 | 22.80 | 2438 | 13.70 | 11313 | 63.50 | 17821 |
| **Driver error** | | | | | | | |
| Carelessness | 306 | 23.00 | 207 | 15.50 | 820 | 61.50 | 1333 |
| Distraction | 80 | 23.10 | 41 | 11.80 | 226 | 65.10 | 347 |
| None | 678 | 22.80 | 429 | 14.50 | 1861 | 62.70 | 2968 |
| Others | 163 | 21.70 | 114 | 15.20 | 474 | 63.10 | 751 |
| Not specified | 1145 | 22.40 | 778 | 15.20 | 3199 | 62.50 | 5122 |
| Violation of rule | 1719 | 23.40 | 880 | 12.00 | 4762 | 64.70 | 7361 |
| **Vehicle maneuver** | | | | | | | |
| Crossing traffic stream | 41 | 20.70 | 29 | 14.60 | 128 | 64.60 | 198 |
| Diverging/merging | 1037 | 23.60 | 548 | 12.50 | 2806 | 63.90 | 4391 |
| Going ahead | 1181 | 23.10 | 670 | 13.10 | 3270 | 63.90 | 5121 |
| Making U turn | 110 | 21.60 | 65 | 12.80 | 334 | 65.60 | 509 |
| Others | 218 | 26.00 | 100 | 11.90 | 519 | 62.00 | 837 |

(*continued*)

**Table 1.**  (*continued*)

| Variable description | Fatal injuries | | Serious injuries | | Minor injuries | | Total |
|---|---|---|---|---|---|---|---|
| | Count | % | Count | % | Count | % | |
| Overtaking from left | 128 | 21.10 | 96 | 15.80 | 382 | 63.00 | 606 |
| Parked/while parking | 32 | 29.60 | 20 | 18.50 | 56 | 51.90 | 108 |
| Starting from near/ off side | 42 | 19.90 | 37 | 17.50 | 132 | 62.60 | 211 |
| Sudden start/stop | 540 | 20.40 | 413 | 15.60 | 1688 | 63.90 | 2641 |
| Turning right/left | 388 | 23.50 | 236 | 14.30 | 1026 | 62.20 | 1650 |
| Not specified | 374 | 23.20 | 235 | 14.60 | 1001 | 62.20 | 1610 |

# 3  Results and Discussions

We employ the polr () function in the MASS package associated with [10], one of R-software's recommended packages. The brant test was carried out to check for the proportional odds assumption being valid or not. The poTest function in R implements Brant's (1990) [11] tests for proportional odds for logistic models. From the result, it can be concluded that the parallel assumption holds since the probability (p-values) for all variables are greater than alpha = 0.05. The output also contains an Omnibus variable, which stands for the whole model, and it is still greater than 0.05. Therefore, the proportional odds assumption is not violated, and the model is a valid model for this dataset [12].

The Ordered Logistic technique was applied to the dataset, and Table 2 depicts the impact of the associated variables on crash severity level. Out of the nine (20) variables considered as explanatory variables to the model, the study reveals that only ten (10) were statistically significant. The result presents the estimated b coefficients of ordered logistic regression analysis. Interpretation of the coefficients as indicated in Table 2 is difficult; therefore, it is recommended to convert the log of odds into the odds ratio for easier comprehension. Table 2 also shows the odds ratio for 25 and 95 confidence interval of each coefficient. In Table 2, the number of lanes' coefficient is 1.575 for single lane and 0.327 for two-lane roads, and the odds ratios were 4.829 and 1.387, respectively. The odds ratio means that a crash resulting in fatal/serious/minor injury is 4.829 higher for single-lane roads and 1.387 times higher for two-lane roads than multiple-lane roads.

The results show that the number of driver-related factors was found to be significant with respect to four-wheeler drivers. Compared to younger drivers less than 17 years, young adults (18–25 years) (OR = 3.22; 95 CI = 1.09 – 10.17) and adults (26-64years) (OR = 3.21; 95 CI = 1.09–10.11) were at higher odds of a crash being fatal/serious/minor. Regarding driver errors, violation of rules 1.23 (OR = 1.23; 95 CI = 1.08–1.40) times more likely to result in fatal/serious/minor injuries than careless driving behaviour among four-wheeler crashes. Considering the vehicle maneuver at the time of the accident, parked /parking of vehicle was 0.55 (OR = 0.55; 95 CI = 0.34–0.91) times less likely to result in fatal/serious/minor injuries compared to crossing traffic stream.

Locations of crash occurrences in the urban areas have lower odds of 0.699 times resulting in fatal/serious/minor injuries compared with rural areas. From the study, the road category is seen to be statistically significant with crash severity. Highways, other district roads and village roads are about 3.496, 2.174 and 2.499 times more likely to result in fatal/serious/minor injuries than major district roads. Among the collision type, hit parked vehicles, hit trees, others and ran off-road are about 0.433, 0.652, 0.587, 0.611 times less likely to result in fatal/serious/minor injuries than hit animals. The median separator (central divider) was 1.857 times more likely to result in fatal/serious/minor injuries than the absence of median separators.

**Table 2.** Results of ordered logit model for single-vehicle four-wheeler crashes in Tamilnadu.

| | Estimate | Std. Error | t- value | p-value | OR | Confidence interval | |
|---|---|---|---|---|---|---|---|
| | | | | | | 2.5 | 97.5 |
| **Region(ref: Central)** | | | | | | | |
| South | − 0.210 | 0.055 | − 3.844 | < 0.001*** | 0.811 | 0.729 | 0.902 |
| West | − 0.339 | 0.052 | − 6.493 | < 0.001*** | 0.712 | 0.643 | 0.789 |
| **Collison type (ref: Hit animal)** | | | | | | | |
| Hit Parked Vehicle | − 0.837 | 0.316 | − 2.653 | 0.008** | 0.433 | 0.233 | 0.804 |
| Hit Tree | − 0.427 | 0.212 | − 2.012 | 0.044* | 0.652 | 0.424 | 0.978 |
| Others | − 0.532 | 0.207 | − 2.567 | 0.01* | 0.587 | 0.385 | 0.871 |
| Ran Off Road | − 0.492 | 0.221 | − 2.230 | 0.026* | 0.611 | 0.392 | 0.932 |
| **Number of Lanes (ref: Multiple)** | | | | | | | |
| Single | 1.575 | 0.058 | 27.201 | < 0.001 | 4.829 | 4.311 | 5.409 |
| Two | 0.327 | 0.062 | 5.247 | < 0.001*** | 1.387 | 1.228 | 1.568 |
| **Central Divider (ref: No)** | | | | | | | |
| Yes | 0.697 | 0.039 | 17.672 | < 0.001*** | 2.007 | 1.857 | 2.168 |
| **Road Category (ref: District road)** | | | | | | | |
| Highways | 1.252 | 0.062 | 20.283 | < 0.001*** | 3.496 | 3.098 | 3.946 |
| Other roads | 0.777 | 0.089 | 8.770 | < 0.001*** | 2.174 | 1.829 | 2.587 |
| Village roads | 0.916 | 0.091 | 10.119 | < 0.001*** | 2.499 | 2.094 | 2.986 |
| **Population Setting (ref: Rural)** | | | | | | | |
| Urban | − 0.255 | 0.053 | − 4.849 | < 0.001*** | 0.775 | 0.699 | 0.859 |
| **Driver Age (ref: < 17)** | | | | | | | |
| 18–25 | 1.172 | 0.558 | 2.102 | 0.036* | 3.228 | 1.097 | 10.172 |
| 25–64 | 1.168 | 0.557 | 2.098 | 0.036* | 3.215 | 1.094 | 10.114 |
| **Alcohol/Drug status (ref: Alcohol)** | | | | | | | |
| None | 0.644 | 0.293 | 2.198 | 0.028* | 1.905 | 1.066 | 3.382 |
| **Driver error (ref: Carelessness)** | | | | | | | |

*(continued)*

**Table 2.** (*continued*)

| | Estimate | Std. Error | t- value | p-value | OR | Confidence interval | |
|---|---|---|---|---|---|---|---|
| | | | | | | 2.5 | 97.5 |
| Not Specified | − 0.147 | 0.069 | − 2.133 | 0.033* | 0.863 | 0.753 | 0.988 |
| Violation of rule | 0.212 | 0.066 | 3.211 | 0.001** | 1.236 | 1.086 | 1.406 |
| **Vehicle Maneuver (ref: Crossing traffic stream)** | | | | | | | |
| Parked/While parking | − 0.584 | 0.250 | − 2.335 | 0.02* | 0.558 | 0.342 | 0.911 |
| **Threshold value** | | | | | | | |
| Fatal ǀ Serious | 2.735 | 0.794 | 3.444 | 0.000*** | | | |
| Serious ǀ Minor injury | 3.514 | 0.794 | 4.423 | 0.000*** | | | |
| Log-likelihood at Zero | 32133.9 | | | | | | |
| Log-likelihood at Convergence | 29147.10 | | | | | | |
| AIC | 29261.1 | | | | | | |
| BIC | 29705.22 | | | | | | |
| Pseudo R2 | 0.092 | | | | | | |

*Significant at 0.01. **Significant at 0.05. ***Significant at 0.001

# 4 Conclusions and Limitations

The findings of this study shed considerable light on the factors causing Single vehicle four-wheeler crashes in India. These results will help road engineers, road safety experts, and relevant authorities design suitable countermeasures. To test the spatial transferability of the model developed in this study, the future research scope may include the compilation of a detailed multi-state dataset. In single-vehicle four-wheeler collisions, including seat belt use, lower speed limits, improved speed compliance in high-risk areas, and in-vehicle stability-enhancing systems can mitigate crash severity. It is important to continue efforts to encourage seat belt use as the first line of defense. In education programs, policy decisions, and community awareness events, driver's behavioural traits, such as those with a history of unsafe driving, may be targeted. In developing and deploying successful countermeasures, additional research on the effects of driver education, behaviour may also be useful.

One major limitation of the analysis is that the primary source of traffic accident data used to make official estimates of fatalities in road traffic accidents is crash reports registered by India's police. This will result in predictable underreporting. A more comprehensive list of variables may also boost the study's liability. This is the first macroscopic study of crash severity for single-vehicle accidents in India to the best of our knowledge.

# References

1. National Highway Traffic Safety Administration (NHTSA). n.d.a. Department of Transportation. Washington, DC. https://www.nhtsa.gov/
2. Ministry of Road Transport and Highways (MoRTH, 2019). Road accidents in India (2019). MoRTH

3. Mohan, D., Tiwari, G., Bhalla, K.S.: Road safety in India: status report. Transportation Research and Injury Prevention Programme, Indian Institute of Technology, Delhi (2015)
4. Mohan, D., Tsimhoni, O., Sivak, M., Flannagan, M.J.: Road safety in India: Challenges and opportunities. University of Michigan, Ann Arbor, Transportation Research Institute (2009)
5. Gururaj, G.: Road traffic deaths, injuries and disabilities in India: current scenario. Natl. Med. J. India **21**(1), 14 (2008)
6. Quddus, M.A., Wang, C., Ison, S.G.: Road traffic congestion and crash severity: econometric analysis using ordered response models. J. Transp. Eng. **136**(5), 424–435 (2010)
7. Lu, J.J., Xing, Y., Wang, C., Cai, X.: Risk factors affecting the severity of traffic accidents at Shanghai river-crossing tunnel. Traffic Injury Prevention **17**(2), 176–180 (2016)
8. Gujarati, D.N., Porter, D.C.: Basic Econometrics. McGraw-Hill, New York (2003)
9. Greene, W.H., Hensher, D.A.: Modeling Ordered Choices: A Primer. Cambridge University Press (2010)
10. Venables, W.N., Ripley, B.D.: Modern Applied Statistics with S-PLUS. Springer, Heidelberg (2013)
11. Long, J.S., Freese, J.: Regression models for categorical dependent variables using Stata. Stata Press (2006)
12. Brant, R.: Assessing proportionality in the proportional odds model for ordinal logistic regression. Biometrics 1171–1178 (1990)

# Severity of Pedestrians in Pedestrian - Bus Crashes: An Investigation of Pedestrian, Driver and Environmental Characteristics Using Random Forest Approach

Sathish Kumar Sivasankaran and Venkatesh Balasubramanian[✉]

RBG Lab, Department of Engineering Design, IIT Madras, Chennai 600036, India
chanakya@iitm.ac.in

**Abstract.** Bus- pedestrian crashes typically result in more severe injuries and deaths than any other type of crashes due to physical characteristics such as heavy-weight, large size and maneuvering restrictions. The statistical data report by the Ministry of Road Transport and Highways (MoRTH, 2017) highlights that bus crashes alone account for about 6.9% of the total crashes occurring within the country. 10,651 (7.2%) persons have been killed, and 44,330(9.4%) persons have been injured in bus-involved collisions during 2017. The purpose of this research is to investigate the factors that significantly contribute to the severity of pedestrian injuries resulting from pedestrian- bus crashes using a random forest approach. Contributory factors, including the driver, pedestrian, and environmental characteristics, are investigated and discussed. The crash dataset for the present study was prepared from the police-reported pedestrian- bus crashes for the past nine years that occurred within Tamilnadu. The research team retrieved all the single-vehicle out-of-control four-wheeler crashes for the period between 2009 and 2017. Random Forest method is an ensemble method for classification problems that is a collection of decision trees. It aggregates all the predictions made by the decision trees into one final prediction. The complete dataset (11735) was divided into two separate datasets: the training dataset (9388) for the development of the model and the testing dataset (2347) for the performance evaluation of the model. The most significant variables in RF were found to be the number of lanes (both single and two-lane), presence of median separators, crashes occurrence at the intersection was unknown and pedestrians aged above 55 years. Based on the findings of the above results, targeted countermeasures may be designed in light of the injury severity of the pedestrians in pedestrian- bus collisions.

**Keywords:** Road Traffic Accidents · Pedestrian –Bus crashes · Random Forest · Transportation Human factors

## 1 Introduction

Road Traffic Crashes (RTC's) continue to be a public health concern and the leading cause of death, killing more than 1.35 million people worldwide. This has made RTCs

© The Author(s), under exclusive license to Springer Nature Switzerland AG 2021
N. L. Black et al. (Eds.): IEA 2021, LNNS 221, pp. 825–833, 2021.
https://doi.org/10.1007/978-3-030-74608-7_101

the eighth leading cause of death globally and the number one cause of death among 15- to 29-year-olds [1]. Buses include one of the major modes of public transport and are responsible for a significant proportion of the RTC, directly or indirectly [2]. In developing countries, bus transport plays a major role in ensuring adequate and affordable mobility for the vast majority of the population; bus safety is a major concern. Although the prevalence seemed to be lower than those of trucks, bikes and cars, the fatalities and damage caused by bus-related accidents also significantly affect the community.

Bus- pedestrian crashes typically result in more severe injuries and deaths than any other type of crashes due to physical characteristics such as heavyweight, large size and maneuvering restrictions. The statistical data report by the Ministry of Road Transport and Highways [3] highlights that bus crashes alone account for about 6.9% of the total crashes occurring within the country. A total of 10,651 (7.2%) persons have been killed, and 44,330(9.4%) persons have been injured in bus-involved collisions during 2017. The majority of them were identified to be vulnerable road users, particularly pedestrians. There are several incidents between pedestrians and buses because of access for passengers to get on and off buses, resulting in a significant number of fatalities. The protection of buses and pedestrians should be enhanced in order to create a sustainable transportation system. Despite several pedestrian-oriented countermeasures to improve pedestrian safety in several countries, pedestrians continue to be exposed to the risk of bus crashes. Hence, this necessitates the need for identifying the variables contributing to bus-pedestrian collisions and continue to make efforts to remove those variables.

In most of the bus-involved crashes, a significant probability exists that vulnerable road users such as pedestrians, motorcyclists and bicyclists will sustain an injury due to their unprotected nature. At the same time, the likelihood is small that the bus drivers and occupants will be injured. The large numbers of pedestrian fatalities and injuries from bus crashes highlight the necessity of analyzing such crashes. Different factors cause Bus-pedestrian crashes. Several studies have considered these factors, such as drivers, vehicles, roadways, and environmental factors. Pedestrians are more vulnerable in crashes with buses than in crashes with other lighter vehicles. The severity of the injuries, therefore, to some degree, will rely on the condition of the driver of the bus and his/her ability to cope with dangerous situations, working conditions, company policies etc. earlier studies have also highlighted that safety attitude, safety-oriented work culture, the behaviour of bus drivers, regional characteristics can affect bus- pedestrian crashes.

Interestingly, the rising emphasis on bus safety is not reflected in the literature. As a result, many fundamental factors influencing pedestrian severity in pedestrian- bus crashes remain widely ignored. Specifically, the question regarding the risk factors associated with bus crashes. This research identifies the variables that affect pedestrian injury severity in bus-pedestrian crashes, including pedestrian, driver, roadway, environmental, vehicle, crash variables. However, the variables of the regional and company community are not considered in this study.

# 2  Methods and Materials

## 2.1  Data

Tamil Nadu is the tenth largest Indian state by area and the sixth-largest by population. Over 50% of the state is urbanized, accounting for 9.6% of the country''s urban population, while only comprising 6% of India's total population. According to the 2011 India census, Tamil Nadu had a population of 7.2 crores. Tamilnadu was chosen for the study as it has a high incidence of RTCs. The recent reports by MORTH highlight that Tamilnadu has recorded the highest number of road crashes for the past few consecutive years, contributing to 14.1% of its total RTCs in the country.

Bus accident data were extracted from the state accident database maintained by Additional Director General of Police (ADGP), State Traffic Planning Cell (STPC) Tamilnadu, referred to as Road Accident Database management System (RADMS) database. Tamilnadu police compile reports of accidents on state roads, and the police officials record information about the accident, the persons and the vehicles involved after a detailed investigation process. The entire dataset consists of three sub-datasets, including the crash dataset, the vehicle dataset, and the driver dataset. The crash dataset documents crash-level information regarding collision types, crash location, road geometric, and environmental conditions. The vehicle dataset illustrates detailed characteristics of each vehicle, occupant injury outcomes, and vehicle-specific information. The driver dataset demonstrates the demographic and behaviour information of each driver involved in crashes. Each crash data has a unique crash identification number common in different datasets to link the records together.

Given the focus of the present study, accidents involving buses between 2009 and 2017 were extracted initially. After removing samples with incomplete records and retaining crashes involving pedestrians only, 11,735 valid observations were retained for further analysis and sufficiently guaranteed an adequate sample size. Though the dataset is taken from the state accident database, there exists restriction common to all police report-based datasets, namely the possibility of under-reporting, nevertheless satisfies the scope of the current analysis. Firstly, it should be remembered that police reports are the key source of data in the road safety literature for accident severity analysis due to their rich data source by linking with the hospital data. Secondly, it should be remembered that bus accidents are not likely to go unnoticed, and therefore the possibility of under-reporting is far less apparent.

The severity of injuries has been categorized in this database into five levels, as per the KABCO scale developed by the National Safety Council, i.e., fatal injuries, major/ grievous injuries and minor/simple injuries (hospitalized and non-hospitalized). According to Indian practice, fatal crashes referred to road users involved in a vehicle crash and died within 30 days of a traffic crash. The grievous injury is determined when the person is hospitalized for 24h or more, and simple injuries are designated when the road user suffers from traffic injury and is hospitalized for less than 24 h. Due to the low frequency of some crash severity categories using the KABCO scale, Injury (K- Fatalities) and (A–major/grievous injuries) were combined and referred to as Fatal/Grievous Injuries) whereas Injury B category (minor/simple injuries hospitalized) and (C- minor/simple injuries non-hospitalized) cases were combined and referred to as simple injuries.

The identified variables include bus driver characteristics (driver gender, age, license status), pedestrian characteristics (pedestrian gender, pedestrian age, pedestrian action, pedestrian position), crash-related factors (pedestrian severity, collision description, road separation, number of lanes, road category, intersection), traffic-related factors (traffic movement, traffic control), vehicle (bus type, vehicle maneuver) and environment-related factors (population setting, weather condition, light condition, region, season and day of the week).

## 2.2 Random Forest

Random Forest (RF) is an ensemble method for classification and regression problems. The decision made by a random forest model is based on the ensemble of decisions made by numerous decision trees such as CART (Classification And Regression Tree). RF overcomes the disadvantages of a decision tree with a low prediction and a possibility of over-fitting. Further, RF's unique advantage is that no processing of data is required; both numerical and categorical data can be handled, with large data sets functioning well. A single decision tree is created by dividing the dataset into subsets using all of the variables to create two child nodes by a statistical approach. If the target value is categorical, the Gini index is used. The Gini index (or the mean-decrease-impurity) is a measure of how often a randomly chosen component from the set would be incorrectly labeled if it was randomly labeled according to the distribution of target values in the subset.

The combination of several weak learners to create a final learner with more randomness is referred to as an ensemble, the most common being bagging (bootstrap aggregation) and boosting techniques. RF method combines bootstrapping and random feature selection. In the bootstrapping, each tree grows with a different training sample randomly selected from the training dataset with replacement. Some observations might appear more than once through sampling with replacement, while others will be left out in the bootstrap sample. A random selection chooses the splitting variables in each tree from the full set of explanatory variables. In every single tree, splitting is continued until the tree reaches the maximum depth. After estimating base tree models, the majority voting strategy is employed to compute the result. The final predicted outcome is the one that is predicted most across the ensemble.

The development of an RF will include four steps:

1. Using the bootstrapping method to randomly resample a sample with the same size as the full dataset or the training dataset.
2. Using the random subspace method to select L variables from total M explanatory variables in the study, $L << M$.
3. Building a decision tree by using the bootstrapping sample and chosen attributes from steps 1 and 2.
4. Repeating steps 1 to 3 to build many trees until reaching the desired RF.

The confusion matrix is applied to evaluate the RF for classifying the crash injury severity. After obtaining the confusion matrix, the classification accuracy is calculated as the proportion of the total number of correctly predicted crashes. However, the accuracy does not measure the prediction accuracy in each target class. Precision, recall and F1 score index are also introduced as metrics. Precision describes how good a model is at predicting the positive class. It evaluates the percentage of correct positive predictions in relation to the model's total positive predictions. The recall represents the ratio of positive samples correctly detected by the classifier; this is also known as the sensitivity or true positive rate (TPR). The recall measures how many of the total positive samples are classified as true positive (TP) rather than false negative (FN), where the total positive samples are the sum of these values (TP + FN). The recall is used as a performance indicator when all positive samples need to be identified. It is important to avoid false negatives. The precision and recall are used as indices of the F1-score, which is a harmonic mean. As it takes into account both precision and recall, it is a better indicator of accuracy than an imbalanced binary classification dataset.

## 3   Results and Discussions

The dataset is divided into two parts: a data set containing 80% of randomly selected observations for training, and the remaining 20% of observations become the dataset for testing. The number of observations in the training dataset is 9,388, and the number of observations in the testing dataset is 2347. There are 23 variables in the dataset, including one response and 22 attributes. Every node splitting for a tree in the RF model using five randomly selected attributes; the same procedure is repeated for all trees in the RF model. Since each tree in the RF model will stop growing when either all attributes have been applied, or the node is with zero information gain, 22 attributes will be used to construct the RF model. Because the response variable, Fatal/grievous or simple injuries, is a categorical variable, the classification trees are used to build the RF model. The python language is employed to do the analysis, and "RandomForestClassifier" from Scikitlearn is used to construct the RF Model.

The RF algorithm was implemented to classify the crash injury severity by growing 100 trees for all datasets, as suggested in previous studies [4, 5]. The algorithm also set the number of variables randomly selected as candidates at each split as the square root of the number of explanatory variables $\sqrt{22} \approx 5$, as suggested in previous studies [6].

The RF was fitted as follows. The accuracy score of the fitted RF Model is 98.64% for the training dataset and 71.83% for the test dataset. However, since classification problems do not favor accuracy as a measure of performance, a different evaluation technique is used. To ensure that the model is generalized, we predicted the learned model using the test set and visualized the confusion matrix's result. The target values are classified as Fatal/Grevious, Simple Injuries, as shown in Fig. 1.

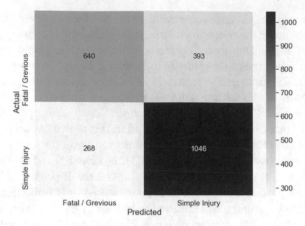

**Fig. 1.** Confusion matrix

After implementing the RF classifier, the importance of the various variables in classifying the crash injury severity was ranked. Figure 1 summarizes the variable importance score and its standard error for the variables. It can also be observed that the top ten importance rank of the variables is as follows: Number of lanes = Single, Road Separation = Yes, Number of lanes = Two, Day of Week = Workday, Pedestrian Gender = Male, Season = Winter, Season = Summer, Light Conditions = Daylight, Population Setting = Urban, Season = Post Monsoon. The VIM for the basic model is provided in Fig. 2.

Results show that certain environment and road-related variables are of high importance, including the number of lanes, road separators, day of the week, season, light

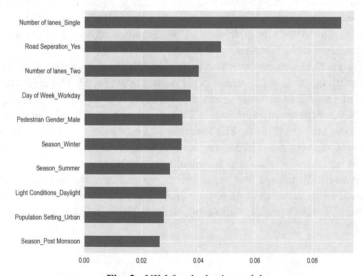

**Fig. 2.** VIM for the basic model

conditions and urban areas. Two variables related to the number of lanes and two variables related to the season are ranked among the most important features. Feature related to the time of the accident (workday and daylight condition) is also the most important variable in this context, particularly ransom forest models. The bottom five attributes in terms of importance are animals involved in the collision, Rail crossing, male drivers, inclement weather conditions such as hail/sleet and smoke/dust. Features related to light conditions, road category, pedestrian position, pedestrian action at the time of the accident are found to be of minor importance.

Hyperparameter-tuning is done for the model independently. Tuning of the random forest models is straightforwardly achieved using a randomized search with cross-validation. To optimize the model, it is critical to know the effects of different parameters on the model's performance. Based on this information, we can set the optimal parameters to achieve higher prediction accuracy. Typically, the classic parameters in a random forest that we would like to tune include the number of trees in the forest (n_estimator), max number of features used to split a node (max_feature), maximum number of levels in each tree (max_depth), minimum number of data points placed in a node before the node is split (min_samples_split), minimum number of data points allowed in a leaf node (min_samples_leaf). This different parameters which was considered were n_estimator = 100,200,300,400,500, min_samples_split = 2,4,6,8,10, the min_samples_leaf = 2,4,6,8,10 and max_depth = 200,400,600,800,1000 using the training data. Finally, we compare the train/test scores to decide which combination is the best to use in our final model. The values of best parameters found out by the hyperparameter tuning were 'n_estimators':300, 'min_samples_split': 2, 'min_samples_leaf': 4, 'max_depth': 800.

The accuracy score of the hyper-tuned RF Model is 78.48% for the training dataset and 73.32% for the test dataset. After implementing the RF classifier with the best hyperparameters, the various variables' importance in classifying the crash injury severity was

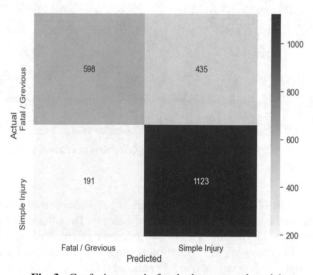

**Fig. 3.** Confusion matrix for the hyper-tuned model

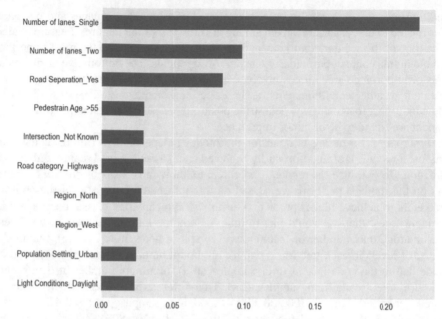

**Fig. 4.** VIM for the hyper-tuned model.

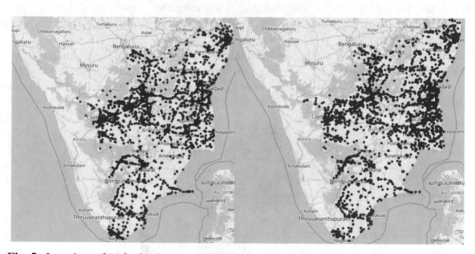

**Fig. 5.** Locations of (a) fatal/grievous and (b) minor pedestrian-bus Crashes in Tamilnadu between 2009 and 2017.

ranked. It can also be observed that the top ten-importance rank of the variables is as follows: Number of lanes = Single, Number of lanes = Two, Road Separation = Yes, Pedestrian Age = >55 yrs, Intersection = unknown, Road Category = Highways, Region = North, Region = West, Population Setting = Urban, Light condition = Daylight. Unsurprisingly, pedestrians above 55 years old (elderly pedestrians) prevails as the most important feature with respect to pedestrian characteristics. The Confusion matrix and the VIM for the hyper-tuned model are shown in Fig. 3 and Fig. 4, respectively. The Locations of fatal/grievous and minor pedestrian-bus crashes are shown in Fig. 5(a) and 5(b), respectively.

## 4 Conclusions and Limitations

We have deduced the various factors influencing pedestrian crash severity by examining crash data to analyze pedestrian-bus collisions in Tamilnadu. We suggested a model that could, in the future, predict and avoid crashes. The model showed a 73% accuracy of prediction. We constructed a model to derive feature importances and verified the prediction correctness. Key factors have been proposed based on the findings, making a big contribution to assessing accident severity for both practitioners and researchers in the road safety industry. The variable importance measures highlight that number of lanes is a major factor in determining the crash severity. Hence, introducing separate bus lanes can reduce the severity of crashes and have proved beneficial in other developed nations based on previous research. There are no specific bus lanes available exclusively in Tamilnadu; hence, they use the roads with other road users. The present study results also highlight exclusive bus lanes are essential on the highways, including state, national, and express highways, especially in urban areas.

This paper's contribution to the existing literature is two-fold: the paper's first important contribution is related to pedestrian safety analysis in collisions with heavy vehicles such as buses and one of its first kind to be done in LMIC's. Also, certain driver and bus-related variables such as the size of the bus, age of the bus, length of the bus, restraint system of bus drivers, travel time of the bus before the accident, bus ownership or company size, buses/companies registered locally versus other areas, history of crashes and convictions among bus drivers were found to be associated with crash severity in earlier studies. Their effects were not considered in the current study due to limitations in the dataset.

## References

1. World Health Organization (WHO). Road traffic injuries (2019). https://www.who.int/en/news-room/fact-sheets/detail/road-traffic-injuries
2. Muhlrad, N., Lassarre, S.: Systems approach to injury control. The way forward: transportation planning and road safety, pp. 52–73. Macmillan India Ltd. New Delhi (2005)
3. Ministry of Road Transport and Highways (MoRTH, 2019). Road accidents in India (2019). MoRTH
4. Harb, R., Yan, X., Radwan, E., Su, X.: Exploring precrash maneuvers using classification trees and random forests. Accident Anal. Prevention **41**(1), 98–107 (2009)
5. Abdel-Aty, M., Haleem, K.: Analyzing angle crashes at unsignalized intersections using machine learning techniques. Accident Anal. Prevention **43**(1), 461–470 (2011)
6. Iranitalab, A., Khattak, A.: Comparison of four statistical and machine learning methods for crash severity prediction. Accident Anal. Prevention **108**, 27–36 (2017)

# Towards the Management and Mitigation of Motion Sickness – An Update to the Field

Joseph Smyth[✉], Jonathan Robinson, Rebecca Burridge, Paul Jennings, and Roger Woodman

WMG University of Warwick, Coventry CV4 7AL, UK
j.smyth.4@warwick.ac.uk

**Abstract.** Almost everyone can experience motion sickness and one third of the population are highly susceptible. With growing development and popularity of technologies such as self-driving cars, simulators and virtual reality (VR), motion sickness management will be more of a consideration in the future than ever before. People who are susceptible to motion sickness may not gain the full benefits of self-driving cars (e.g., increased productivity), have access to vocations involving significant simulator-based training (e.g., airplane pilots), or have access to the increased opportunities that VR headsets may bring (e.g., vocational training or job roles involving VR). Further, with demographic variance within susceptibility to motion sickness, it is known some demographic groups are far more susceptible to motion sickness than others (e.g., females vs. Males), which further identifies an inclusivity aspect to these technologies. This report evidences the strong motivation towards the mitigation of motion sickness and discusses the associated benefits. Working towards the objective of enhanced motion sickness management, this paper presents a new model to detail the onset of motion sickness syndrome and discusses the causal relationship between sensory conflict and the physiological and psychological effects of motion sickness. In doing so we identify within the existing literature many methods towards the management (both prevention and mitigation) of motion sickness and provide a direction for further study.

**Keywords:** Motion sickness · Wellbeing · Treatment and prevention · Carsickness · Nausea

## 1 Introduction

Motion sickness is not a new phenomenon – humans have been documenting motion sickness as early as 800 BC [1] and there is no evidence to suggest humans have become more resilient or adept to overcome this condition today [2]. Early theories of motion sickness included that of the 'blood and guts theories', which suggested changes in flow of blood in the brain, specifically the cerebral cortex, and/or disruption to the viscera was the cause of motion sickness. These theories were eventually disproved in 1882 [3] and it was not until 1975 that we were presented with the sensory conflict theory – which

© The Author(s), under exclusive license to Springer Nature Switzerland AG 2021
N. L. Black et al. (Eds.): IEA 2021, LNNS 221, pp. 834–840, 2021.
https://doi.org/10.1007/978-3-030-74608-7_102

we hold today as the most widely accepted theory of motion sickness. The 'sensory conflict theory' [4] explains that mismatches between vestibular, visual and somatosensory motion cues are responsible for motion sickness. For example, the vestibular system senses motion, yet the visual system detects none; there is a conflict between senses and motion sickness can prevail. The body's reaction to this conflict in motion sense(s) is similar to that of a self-preservation response. Offering an explanation to this, the evolutionary hypothesis [5] proposes that when the body senses a mismatch between motion cues, the body assumes a poison has been ingested and it is that poison which is responsible for the incoherent sensory information. Thus, people often experience stomach churning, fatigue, increased sweat rate and other thermoregulatory responses as the body attempts to mitigate the effects of the suspected poison before ejecting it through the most widely known symptom of motion sickness – vomiting.

## 2   Background

Motion sickness affects the majority of the population, in fact it is known that everyone (besides those who are profoundly deaf) can be affected by motion sickness, and according to the U.S. National Library of Medicine, around one third of the population are highly susceptible to motion sickness [6]. It is prevalent in many domains, including in car travel (carsickness), boat travel (seasickness), in simulators (simulator sickness), in planes (airsickness) and even in virtual reality (cybersickness). Furthermore, with the growth and development in technologies such as simulation, virtual reality and automated vehicles, motion sickness is likely to become a greater problem in the future than it is today. Combining this knowledge with the evidence of the sex-effect within motion sickness opens up an interesting area for accessibility and inclusivity. Specifically, females are known to be more than twice as susceptible to motion sickness than their male counterparts as evidenced in multiple studies [7–9] and across various sectors including airsickness [10], seasickness, [11] and car sickness [12]. The implications of this identify that the many benefits and expected use cases for technology which has motion sickness as a factor are drastically more limiting for some more than others. In consideration of this, we are provided with a strong motivation to tackle motion sickness.

The issue of discomfort and aversion to certain travel methods due to motion sickness is well established and documented. As such there is clear benefit in managing motion sickness to improve comfort and wellbeing. However, we also have strong evidence to show that motion sickness affects human performance and productivity in a negative way. In industries where motion sickness is a factor (e.g., navy crew, pilot simulator training or VR training tools), this is potentially limiting to not only recruitment prospects but also job performance [13–16].

Clearly there is a strong motivation to mitigate motion sickness across many sectors and this paper will summarize and discuss these efforts in the automotive domain. Motion sickness in cars (i.e., carsickness) has been a longstanding issue, although one which is fairly easily overcome through constantly looking ahead, in the direction of travel at all times. However, with the exciting potential use cases of automated vehicles, and with occupant comfort and wellbeing giving manufactures a competitive edge, there is growing demand in this sector to tackle this area of motion comfort. In doing so we may enable car passengers today, and in future vehicles to have a better and more productive travel experience, affording opportunities other than just staring at the horizon.

## 3   Motion Sickness Prevention and Mitigation

In order to examine the various methods and attempts to mitigate motion sickness we must first consider the onset the condition:

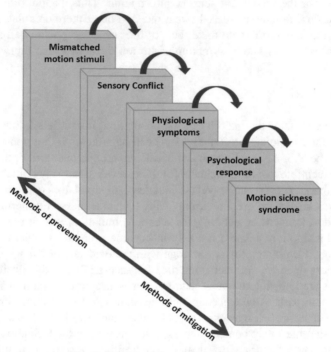

**Fig. 1.** Motion sickness domino model

The model presented in Fig. 1 is useful for detailing the stages and causality of motion sickness onset. As was introduced previously, the first stage (the 'instigator') of motion sickness is known to be related to the presence of various motion cues that are received by the visual, vestibular or somatosensory systems. If there is a noticeable difference between these motion cues, sensory conflict [4] prevails. This leads to various physiological self-preservation responses, related to the evolutionary hypothesis [5]. The implications of this result in a thermoregulatory response [17] as well as the onset of gastrointestinal related activity [18] leading to nausea [19]. When the human becomes conscious of the onset of motion sickness and notices these physiological symptoms (e.g., stomach churning, nausea or sweating) this manifests in a psychological stress/alarm response [20]. It is the totality of these processes that we can think about as motion sickness syndrome. The interconnected nature of these (i.e., physiological symptoms both affect, and are affected by, psychological response) is part of the reason why motion sickness is so difficult to measure objectively [20]. Further, the variance within humans, for example related to thermoregulatory ability (correlated with physical fitness) [21], and psychological perseverance and self-efficacy [22] make the actual onset of motion sickness syndrome highly variable within and between individuals [20].

Figure 1 maps not only the onset of motion sickness, but also identifies the difference between prevention of motion sickness (i.e., stopping the onset) and mitigation of motion sickness (i.e., reducing the impact of effects). With a spectrum of opportunities for intervention identified, it becomes apparent that interventions can theoretically sit between dominoes to prevent or mitigate the onset of motion sickness. For example, highly effective suspension and vehicle dynamics to limit nauseating low frequency vibrations in a car may prevent the onset of motion sickness between the 1st and 2nd domino; or using airflow over the skin may begin to mitigate symptoms related to sweat rate and prevent or delay the psychological identification of motion sickness onset.

With the conception of motion sickness onset identified, and areas of prevention/mitigation highlighted, the literature can be reviewed to begin to understand some previous successes within the management of motion sickness (with a specific focus on carsickness). Given the range of implementation opportunities of the various methods of motion sickness management and the variety of testing environments, this paper does not seek to identify the effectiveness of specific methods, but instead work towards a greater understanding of the concepts and theories behind motion sickness mitigation strategies.

### 3.1 Mismatched Motion Stimuli

There have been studies investigating the provision of additional motion-related information in an attempt to prevent sensory conflict theory. Methods have been investigated involving the provision of visual cues using lights around or within interfaces [23, 24] and audio-based cues to give information about direction of travel [25–27]. Methods of haptic interventions have also been evidenced using various 'vibrotactile' methods to give motion cues [28] and seat vibration [29]. The degree of success of such methods are varied, but the concept remains, if accurate motion-related information can be provided (consciously or otherwise) it is conceivable that sensory conflict may not happen and thus motion sickness can be prevented.

### 3.2 Sensory Conflict

Still within the remit of motion sickness prevention, if it is possible to stop the brain from registering mismatched motion cues according to 'sensory conflict theory' then it is theoretically possible to stop the onset of physiological symptoms. Methods have been evidenced involving training visuospatial reasoning to self-resolve motions as an effective means of motion sickness prevention [30]. Other research uses bone conducting vibration (BCV) to disrupt vestibular-related motion cues in an attempt to prevent sensory conflict, which falls into this same preventative classification category [31]. Most famously the use of prescribed medication such as scopolamine [32] is an effective prevention method of motion sickness, which blocks the action of acetylcholine through disturbing vestibular communication with the brain.

### 3.3 Physiological Symptoms

If sensory conflict cannot be avoided, we move towards mitigation methods to limit the physiological response. Natural remedies for motion sickness mitigation often involve the use of ginger. The anti-motion sickness features of ginger are not well evidenced [33], however the 'stomach calming' effect of ginger is known. Ginger therefore may act as an anti-motion-sickness strategy [34] through mitigating physiological symptoms and reducing the likelihood of a psychological stress/alarm response. Other mitigation strategies may involve the treatment of motion sickness symptoms to prevent discomfort and limit psychological distress. For example, using a vehicle's HVAC (heating, ventilation, and air conditioning) system to cool the occupant and limit sweat-related discomfort, particularly on the face [35].

### 3.4 Psychological Response

The role of psychology in motion sickness has been known for some time [36] and given the power of psychological some may argue it should sit above the entire 'domino chain' as presented in Fig. 1. Where, for example, methods of increasing self-efficacy [37], distraction [38] or even relaxation through calming music [39] seem to have a positive preventative effect on motion sickness. However, it stands also as the final domino where the realization or awareness of the onset of motion sickness triggers responses linked to stress and alarm [40]. The nature of being aware of motion sickness onset exacerbates the condition [38], and we see evidence for motion sickness mitigation through cognitive-behavioral management of motion sickness [41].

### 3.5 Motion Sickness Syndrome

At the stage of motion sickness syndrome onset there appears to be few mitigation or prevention opportunities remaining. At this stage, the human is in a self-repeating cycle of physiological discomfort, psychological distress, and physiological responses. Avoiding the motion sickness-inducing stimulus is the only remedy at this stage, such as stopping reading a book in a car and focusing visual attention on the direction of travel.

## 4   Conclusive Thoughts

Motion sickness syndrome is a complex multi-factorial condition consisting of self-effecting physiological symptoms and psychological stressors. Without considerable intervention, it is likely that many of the benefits of technologies such as self-driving cars, simulators and virtual reality will not be fully achieved equally across society. We identify a significant motivation to mitigate the unwanted effects of motion sickness and introduce literature working towards this goal. This paper has presented a motion sickness domino model to detail the 'stages' of motion sickness onset and therefore providing a visual representation of prevention/mitigation opportunities with a specific focus on the automotive sector. Many methods currently discussed within the literature focus on the mitigation of motion sickness onset (e.g., treating the symptoms). However, working towards solutions for the prevention of motion sickness through specific intervention and technology design will have the greatest utility and is where future research should focus.

# References

1. Huppert, D., Benson, J., Brandt, T.: A historical view of motion sickness–a plague at sea and on land, also with military impact. Front. Neurol. **114**(8), 1–5 (2017)
2. Schmidt, E.A., Juiper, O., Wolter, S., Diels, C., Bos, J.E.: An international survey on the incidence and modulating factors of carsickness. Transport. Res. F: Traffic Psychol. Behav. **71**, 76–87 (2020)
3. James, W.: The sense of dizziness in deaf-mutes. Am. J. Ontol. **4**(4), 239–254 (1882)
4. Reason, J.T., Brand, J.J.: Motion Sickness. Academic Press, New York (1975)
5. Treisman, M.: Motion sickness: an evolutionary hypothesis. Science **197**(4302), 493–495 (1977)
6. U.S. National Library of Medicine, "Motion Sickness," U.S. National Library of Medicine, Washington DC, USA (2019)
7. Flanagan, M.B., May, J.G., Dobie, T.G.: Sex Sifferences in Tolerance to Visually-Induced Motion Sickness, viation, Space, and Environmental Medicine, pp. 642–646 (2005)
8. Leung, A., Hon, K.L.: Motion sickness: an overview. Drugs in Context (2019)
9. Dobie, T., McBride, D., May, J., Dobie, T.J.: The effects of age and sex on susceptibility to motion sickness. Aviat. Space Environ. Med. **72**, 13–20 (2001)
10. Lindseth, G., Lindseth, P.D.: The relationship of diet to airsickness. Aviat. Space Environ. Med. **66**, 537–541 (1995)
11. Grunfeld, R., Gresty, M.A.: Relationship between motion sickness, migraine, and menstruation in crew members of a "round-the-world" yacht race. Brain Res. Bull. **47**, 433–436 (1998)
12. Turner, M., Griffin, M.J.: Motion sickness in public road transport: passenger behaviour and susceptibility. Ergonomics **42**, 444–461 (1999)
13. Smyth, J., Jennings, P., Mouzakitis, A., Birrell, S.: Too sick to drive: how motion sickness severity impacts human performance. In: The 21st IEEE International Conference on Intelligent Transportation Systems, Maui, Hawaii (2018)
14. Smyth, J., Birrell, S., Mouzakitis, A., Jennings, P.: Motion sickness and human performance – exploring the impact of driving simulator user trials. In: 9th International Conference on Applied Human Factors and Ergonomics, Orlando Florida, USA (2018)
15. Bos, J.E.: How motions make people sick such that they perform less: a model based approach. In: Symposium on Habitability of Compact and Transport Vehicles: Noise Vibration and Motion. Czech Republic, Prague (2004)
16. Bos, J.E., Valk, P.L., Hogervorst, M.A., Munnoch, K., Perrault, D., Colwell, J.L.: TNO contribution to the Quest 303 trial - Human performance assessed by a Vigilance and Tracking Test, a Multi-Attribute Task, and by Dynamic Visual Acuity. TNO Defence, Security and Safety, Soesterberg The Netherlands (2008)
17. Mekjavic, I.B., Tipton, M.J., Gennser, M., Eiken, O.: Motion sickness potentiates core cooling during immersion in humans. J. Physiol. **535**(2), 619–623 (2001)
18. Thornton, W., Linder, B., Moore, T., Pool, S.: Gastrointestinal motility in space motion sickness. Aviation Space Environ. Med. **58**(9 Pt2), 16–21 (1987)
19. Lackner, J.R.: Motion sickness: more than nausea and vomiting. Exp. Brain Res. **232**(8), 2493–2510 (2014)

20. Smyth, J., Birrell, S., Woodman, R., Jennings, P.: Exploring the utility of EDA and skin temperature as individual physiological correlates of motion sickness. Appl. Ergon. **92** (2021)
21. Cheung, B.S., Money, K.E., Jacobs, I.: Motion sickness susceptibility and aerobic fitness: a longitudinal study. Aviation, Space, and Environmental Medicine, March 1990
22. Dov, E., Yaakov, Z.: Seasickness as a self-fulfilling prophecy: raising self-efficacy to boost performance at sea. J. Appl. Psychol. **80**(5), 628–635 (1995)
23. Karjanto, J., Nidzamuddin, Y.M., Wang, C., Terken, J., Delbressine, F., Rauterberg, M.: The effect of peripheral visual feedforward system in enhancing situation awareness and mitigating motion sickness in fully automated driving. Transp. Res. Part F: Traffic Psychol. Behav. (2018)
24. de Winkel, K.N., Pretto, P., Nooij, S.A., Cohen, I., Bulthoff, H.H.: Efficacy of augmented visual environments for reducing sickness in autonomous vehicles. Applied Ergonomics, vol. 90 (2021)
25. Galvesz-Garcia, G.: A comparison of techniques to mitigate Simulator Adaptation Syndrome. Ergonomica **58**(8), 1365–1371 (2015)
26. Galvez-Garcia, G., Aldunate, N., Bascour-Sandoval, C., Barramuno, M., Fonseca, F., Gomez-Milan, E.: Decreasing motion sickness by mixing different techniques. Appl. Ergon. **82** (2020)
27. Kuiper, O., Bos, J.E., Diels, C., Schmidt, E.A.: Knowing what's coming: anticipatory audio cues can mitigate motion sickness. Appl. Ergon. **85**, 103068 (2020)
28. Yusof, N.M.: Comfort in Autonomous Car: Mitigating Motion Sickness by Enhancing Situation Awareness through Haptic Displays (2018)
29. D'Amour, S., Bos, J.E., Keshavarz, B.: The efficacy of airflow and seat vibration on reducing visually induced motion sickness. Experimental Brain Res. 2811–2820 (2017)
30. Smyth, J., Jennings, P., Benett, P., Birrell, S.: A novel method for reducing motion sickness susceptibility through training visuospatial ability – a two-part study. Appl. Ergon. **90** (2021)
31. Salter, S., Diels, C., Kanarachos, S., Thake, C.D., Herriotts, P., Depireux, D.: Increased bone conducted vibration reduces motion sickness in automated vehicles. Int. J. Hum. Factors Ergon. **6**(4), 299–318 (2020)
32. Wasiak, S.A.B.J., Villanueva, E.V., Bernath, V.: Scopolamine for preventing and treating motion sickness. Cochrane Database Systematic Reviews (2004)
33. Grontved, A., Brask, T., Kambskard, J., Hentzer, E.: Ginger root against seasickness: a conctrolled trial on the open sea. Acta Otolaryngol. **105**(1–2), 45–49 (1988)
34. Lien, H.C., Sun, W.M., Chen, Y.H., Kim, H., Hasler, W., Owyang, C.: Effects of ginger on motion sickness and gastric slow-wave dysrhythmias induced by circular vection. Internal Med. – Gastroenterol. Mol. Integrative Physiol. **284**, 481–489 (2003)
35. Vulcu, V.G.: Systems and methods for mitigating motion sickness in a vehicle. Southfield , MI (US) Patent US 2020/0353934 A1, 10 May 2019
36. Zerling, I.: Psychological factors in susceptibiliy to motion sickenss. J. Psychol. 219–239 (1947)
37. Eden, D., Zuk, Y.: Seasickness as a self-fulfilling prophecy: raising self-efficacy to boost performance at sea. J. Appl. Psychol. **80**(5), 628–635 (1995)
38. Bos, J.E.: Less sickness with more motion and/or mental distraction. J. Vestib. Res. **25**(1), 22–33 (2014)
39. Keshavarz, B., Hecht, H.: Pleasant music as a countermeasure against visually induced motion sickness. Appl. Ergon. Elsevier Ltd **45**(3), 521–527 (2014)
40. Harm, D.L.: Physiological of Motion Sickness Symptoms. In: Motion and Space Sickness, p. 165. Florida, USA, CRC Press, Boca Raton (1990)
41. Dobie, T.G., May, J.G.: Cognitive-behavioral management of motion sickness. Aviat. Space Environ. Med. **65**, 1–20 (1994)

# Determining How Long Truck Driver Whole Body Vibration Exposure Data Has to Be Collected to Estimate Actual Daily Exposures

Richard Taing, Debra Cherry, and Peter W. Johnson[✉]

University of Washington, Seattle, WA, USA
petej@uw.edu

**Abstract.** Exposure to Whole body Vibration (WBV) has been associated with an increased prevalence of low back pain in occupational settings. Current WBV directives, guidelines and standards are devoid of any recommendations for the length of time needed to accurately and reliably characterize a vehicle operator's daily, full-shift exposure to WBV. Using full-shift, seat-measured, tri-axial WBV exposures from a group of 64 regional truck drivers, the daily WBV exposures were cut to simulate different lengths of measurement (5, 7.5, 10, 15, 30, 60, 120, 240 and 480 min). The differing lengths of the data (5 to 240 min) were then normalized to reflect 8-h of vehicle operation [A(8) and VDV(8)]. The analysis of the data demonstrated that the z-axis was the predominant exposure axis and a measurement duration of 30-min or longer would be required to accurately estimate a truck driver's daily, full-shift A(8) and VDV(8) exposures. Determining the minimum required measurement duration can help reduce the costs associated with WBV exposure assessment.

**Keywords:** Exposure assessment · VDV · Average weighted vibration

## 1 Introduction

Exposure to Whole body Vibration (WBV) has been associated with an increased prevalence of low back pain (LBP) in occupational settings [1]. A recent cross-sectional study on truck drivers indicated that 72.5% of truck drivers reported experiencing LBP [2]. Not only does exposure to WBV have a high personal cost for workers who experience chronic pain, but it also has a high impact on the costs of workers' compensation claims, worker productivity and well-being. Current WBV directives, guidelines and standards are devoid of any recommendations for the length of time needed to accurately and reliably characterize a vehicle operator's daily, full-shift exposure to WBV [3, 4]. Determining and optimizing the required measurement duration to characterize daily, full-shift WBV exposures is needed.

Using daily, full-shift WBV exposures from semi-truck drivers, the purpose of this study was to determine the minimum measurement duration needed to accurately characterize a truck driver's daily, full-shift, 8-h WBV exposures. Determining the minimum measurement duration necessary to assess WBV exposures can reduce the costs associated with WBV exposure assessment.

N. L. Black et al. (Eds.): IEA 2021, LNNS 221, pp. 841–844, 2021.
https://doi.org/10.1007/978-3-030-74608-7_103

## 2  Methods

Following the ISO 2631–1 standard [3], this study used tri-axial seat-pad accelerometers placed on top of the seats to measure 64 daily, full-shift, 8 h WBV exposures in a group of regional truck drivers. Truck GPS data were also collected over the full shift. Two WBV exposure parameters were evaluated: root mean square weighted acceleration ($A_w$) and vibration dose value (VDV). Using the GPS data, the VDV(8) exposures were calculated in two ways: 1) based on all the WBV exposure data (truck movement and idle periods), and 2) based solely on periods of truck movement.

Seat exposure measurements were collected in 3 axes (x, y, and z) and the full-shift samples were broken into segments of 5, 7.5, 10, 15, 30, 60, 120, 240 and 480 min. For each exposure axis, the various segments of the data (5 to 240 min) were normalized to reflect 8-h of vehicle operation [A(8) and VDV(8)].

Using a repeated-measures analysis of variance methods and Tukey-Kramer follow-up tests, the minimum segment length needed to approximate the actual full-shift, 8-h daily exposures was determined. P-values less than 0.05 were used to identify differences that were significant The 480 min measures were the gold-standard measures for the 8-h, daily WBV exposures.

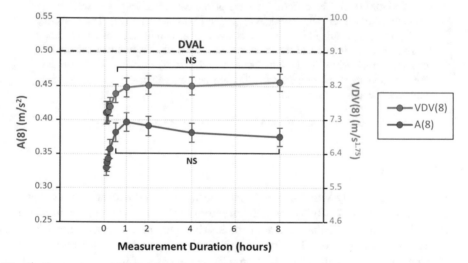

**Fig. 1.** Comparisons of daily equivalent weighted average vibration ($A_w$) and vibration dose value (VDV) exposures collected for different durations and normalized to reflect daily, full-shift, 8-h exposures [A(8) and VDV(8)]. The red dashed line is the European Union's Daily Vibration Action Limit (DVAL) which is 0.5 $m/s^2$ for A(8) and 9.1 $m/s^{1.75}$ for VDV(8). The brackets indicate the exposure measures that are not significantly different from the daily, full-shift, 8-h exposure measurements.

## 3  Results

The z-axis was the predominant axis of exposure. As shown in Fig. 1., when the z-axis $A_w$ and VDV exposures of different durations were normalized to 8-h daily exposure equivalents [A(8) and VDV(8)], the WBV exposures slowly increased during the first 60 min. After 60 min, the VDV(8) exposures slightly increased and the A(8) exposures decreased. As shown by the brackets in Fig. 1., the follow-up test indicated that measurement durations of 30 min or longer would be needed to accurately characterize daily, full-shift, predominant z-axis A(8) and VDV(8) exposures. The time trends for the non-predominant x-axis exposures mirrored the trends of the predominant z-axis exposures. However, the time trends of the non-predominant y-axis exposures differed and were dependant on how the VDV(8) exposures were measured and calculated. When the y-axis VDV(8) exposures were based solely on when the truck was in motion, the exposures were highest at the beginning and end of the daily, 8-h shifts. When the y-axis VDV(8) exposures were based on all the exposure data (truck movement and idle periods), the time trends were similar to the x- and z-axis exposure data.

## 4  Discussion and Conclusions

Using different durations of $A_w$ and VDV exposures, normalized to reflect daily, full-shift, 8-h exposures [A(8) and VDV(8)], this study systematically determined the minimum measurement duration needed to characterize full-shift WBV exposures. The ISO 2631–1 standard [3] recommends that the predominant exposure axis, if present, be used for exposure assessment purposes.

In this study of regional truck drivers, the z-axis was the predominant exposure axis and the $A_w$ and VDV analyses demonstrated measurements of 30 min or longer would be needed to accurately characterize the daily, full-shift, 8-h WBV exposures. The VDV exposures, which are a cumulative measure, were relatively stable and the z-axis VDV(8) exposures only increased slightly after 30 min of measurement. However, the $A_w$ exposures, are an average measure, and the z-axis A(8) exposures gradually decreased after 60 min. This gradual decrease in the A(8) exposures was likely due to the truck stopping sometime after the first 60 min of travel to deliver their cargo before their return trip back to the truck terminal.

The y-axis VDV(8) exposures had a more complex relationship with time and depended on how y-axis VDV(8) exposures were measured and calculated. When the y-axis, VDV(8) exposures were based solely on truck movement, the exposures were highest at the beginning and end of the daily, 8-h shift. These higher impulsive exposures at the beginning and end of the shift were thought to be associated with periods where the trucks were either coupling or uncoupling their trailers. The x-axis VDV(8) exposures did not have this same high beginning and end of the shift, time-dependent, exposure behavior.

Due to the z-axis resonant frequencies of the truck seat often matching the resonant frequencies of the low back [5], the z-axis exposures have been most prominently associated with the onset and development of low back pain. The non-predominant x- and y-axis exposures appear to play less of a role in truck driver low back pain.

This study determined the minimum measurement duration necessary to characterize daily, full-shift WBV exposures in regional truck drivers. Determining the minimum required measurement duration can help reduce the costs associated with WBV exposure assessment. This methodology may be employed for other operators of other vehicle types and in other industry sectors.

# References

1. Bovenzi, M., Rui, F., Negro, C., D'Agostin, F., Angotzi, G., Bianchi, S., Bramanti, L., Festa, G.L., Gatti, S., Pinto, I., Rondina, L., Stacchini, N.: An epidemiological study of low back pain in professional drivers. J. Sound Vib. **298**(3), 514–539 (2006)
2. Kim, J., Zigman, M., Aulck, L., et al.: Whole body vibration exposures and health status among professional truck drivers: a cross-sectional analysis. Ann. Occup. Hyg. **60**, 936–948 (2016)
3. International Organization for Standardization. ISO 2631–1: Mechanical vibration and shock—evaluation of human exposure to whole-body vibration—Part I: general requirements (1997)
4. European Union: Directive 2002/44/EC of the European Parliament and of the Council of 25 June 2002 on the minimum health and safety requirements regarding the exposure of workers to the risks arising from physical agents (vibration) (sixteenth individual Directive within the meaning of Article 16(1) of Directive 89/391/EEC). Official Journal of the European Communities L 177, 13–19 (2002)
5. Pope, M.H., Wilder, D.G., Magnusson, M.: Possible mechanisms of low back pain due to whole-body vibration. J. Sound Vib. **215**(4), 687–697 (1998)

# How Does Instructed Knowledge Influence Drivers' Decision-Making in Conditional Driving Automation?

Huiping Zhou[1]($\boxtimes$), Makoto Itoh[1], and Satoshi Kitazaki[2]

[1] Faculty of Engineering, Information and Systems, University of Tsukuba, Tsukuba, Japan
zhouhp@css.risk.tsukuba.ac.jp
[2] Automotive Human Factors Research Center, National Institute of Advanced Industrial Science and Technology, Tsukuba, Japan

**Abstract.** This study aimed to reveal how instructed knowledge influences human drivers to make decisions in complex driving-task traffic environments when they use conditional driving automation (CDA). A driving simulator experiment was conducted to collect data in resuming car control from automation; 54 individuals (mean age = $40.9 \pm 16.8$ years old) participated. According to the experimental results, imparting knowledge of the request to intervene (RtI) helped to reduce the reaction time (RT) to the RtI to 1.22 s on average, but also caused 20% of drivers to resume vehicle control who failed to choose the correct route in terms of the issued route guidance. This ratio was significantly higher than the 3% of drivers who were unfamiliar with the RtI, but were only instructed on the necessity of taking over car control due to functional limitations. On the other hand, 28% of those drivers resumed control for responding to the guidance before the system limitation occurred. Further, subjective assessment suggests that the drivers tended to over-rely on their instructed knowledge, and were prone to overlooking other important details when the knowledge was restricted to the specified concept. Conveying knowledge appropriately not only contributes to driver interventions, but also greatly impacts other kinds of decision-making performance.

**Keywords:** Decision-making · Knowledge · Takeover control · Request to intervene · Conditional driving automation · Safety

## 1 Introduction

Driver takeover control in driving automation is an important issue because of the limitations of systems' capabilities. As defined in SAE 3016 [1], conditional driving automation (CDA) does not require a driver to monitor the driving task. Hence, non-driving related activity is allowed in the CDA; for example, watching TV, reading books, and even playing games. On the other hand, once the CDA issues a request to intervene (RtI), the driver must take over vehicle control from the CDA and halt whatever he/she has been doing. Hence, traditional issues of human factors become more critical, such as

© The Author(s), under exclusive license to Springer Nature Switzerland AG 2021
N. L. Black et al. (Eds.): IEA 2021, LNNS 221, pp. 845–852, 2021.
https://doi.org/10.1007/978-3-030-74608-7_104

the problem of "out-of-the loop" degradation of situational awareness [2], a decline in manual skills [3], and over-reliance [4].

The above challenges make it difficult for human drivers to perceive functional limitations, malfunctions, or failures when they need to take control from ADS. In fact, driver reactions are delayed, and inappropriate responses become frequent due to these problems [5, 6]. According to Körber et al. [5], driver reactions were delayed by up to 5 s, as compared to reactions in the case of manual control for the same situation. Also, the takeover time was extended by 1.2 s, and the minimum time-to-collision was 0.9 s shorter on average in terms of a critical hazard [6]. These studies also provided evidence that the use of automation deeply impacts drivers' gaze behavior. Moreover, changes in trust and reliance on driving automation have been reported [5, 7].

Many studies have been conducted to resolve these obstacles and to support human drivers to safely take over car control from an automated driving system (ADS) [8–10]. These studies have focused their efforts on the concept of the human-machine interface (HMI) [8, 10] and optimal takeover time [9]. In addition, introductory information has been pointed out as important when using an ADS. Our previous studies have primarily discussed the influence of education/learning on driver takeover performance [11, 12]. Zhou et al. demonstrated the influence of instructed knowledge and driving experience on system malfunction in relation to the driver taking over control at the training stage in CDA [12], as well as partial driving automation [11]. Their results revealed that teaching the concept of the HMI in advance contributed largely to the driver's reaction time (RT) to an RtI. Note that the test scenarios were designed to examine drivers' simple decision-making when responding to an RtI. However, in more realistic traffic environments, human drivers would face more complex situations and have to make multiple decisions for different driving tasks almost simultaneously.

**Fig. 1.** Fixed-base driving simulator used in the experiment. This system provides simulated longitudinal (accelerator and brake pedals) and lateral (steering wheel) control.

The goal of the present study was to focus on the driver's decision-making performance in a relatively complex driving environment in terms of instructed knowledge. A driving simulator (DS) experiment was carried out to collect data during the transition of resuming vehicle control from the CDA to test the following two hypotheses:

**Hypothesis-1.** Appropriately instructing drivers to improve driving safety in a relatively complex driving environment.

**Hypothesis-2.** Instructed knowledge influences driver decision-making (on what to do and when to do it) in complex situations.

# 2 Method

## 2.1 Apparatus

A fixed-base DS (D3sim; Mitsubishi Precision Co., Ltd., Tokyo, Japan) is used in the data collection phase (see Fig. 1). This system provides simulated longitudinal and lateral direction control on a multilane expressway. Automated vehicle control can be implemented as a CDA in which automatic lane changing is not operative. The system's

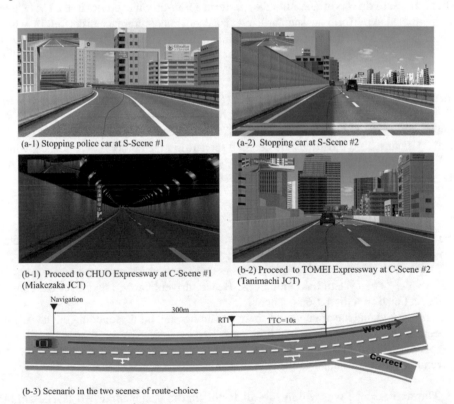

(a-1) Stopping police car at S-Scene #1    (a-2) Stopping car at S-Scene #2

(b-1) Proceed to CHUO Expressway at C-Scene #1 (Miakezaka JCT)    (b-2) Proceed to TOMEI Expressway at C-Scene #2 (Tanimachi JCT)

(b-3) Scenario in the two scenes of route-choice

**Fig. 2.** Two simple test scenes (*S-scenes*) (a-1 & a-2) and two complex test scenes (*C-scenes*) (b-1 & b-2), and driver decisions in the *C-scenes* (b-3). In terms of the announced navigation at 300 m in front of the junction, the green route was correct, while the red one was incorrect.

control would be automatically cancelled if a driver did not take control of the car within 10 s after the RtI is issued. The concept of HMI consists of both visual and acoustic messages. When an RtI is triggered, the visual message in the HMI changes to amber and blinks at 5 Hz, and an acoustic message is presented for approximately 1 s.

## 2.2 Participants

In total, 54 individuals (32 females, 22 males; mean age: $40.9 \pm 16.8$ years) participated in the data collection conducted in the DS. All participants—each of whom held a valid driver's license—were recruited from a local society and agreed to participate in the experiment. This study has been approved by the Research Ethics Committee from the University of Tsukuba's Faculty of Engineering, Information and Systems.

## 2.3 Driving Task and Non-driving Related Activity

The participants are asked to operate a virtual vehicle on a simulated expressway as safely as they would operate a real vehicle. After the system was engaged, they are allowed to release their feet from the pedals and to remove their hands from the steering wheel. Because drivers are permitted to perform a non-driving activity in the CAD, they are instructed to perform the standardized visual surrogate reference task (SuRT), which is presented on a touch monitor on the left side of the steering wheel, as shown in Fig. 1.

## 2.4 Scenes and Scenarios

There are four test scenes: two simple ones (*S-scene #1*: stopping police car, and *S-scene #2*: stopping car), as displayed in Fig. 2a (1 & 2), and two complex scenes (*C-scene* #1: Miakezaka Junction (JCT), and *C-scene #2*: Tanimachi JCT), as portrayed in Fig. 2b (1 & 2). Figure 2b-3 illustrates the detailed scenario in the complex JCT scenes, which include the following events: a navigation system issues route guidance, and the CAD gives an RtI.

## 2.5 Experimental Design

The study is a two-factorial design (instructed knowledge × traffic scene). The instructed knowledge is a between-subject factor with the following three levels:

– *Baseline:* "The system has limitations. Hence, drivers have to take over car control once a functional limitation occurs."
– *+HMI:* "A visual message would change to amber and blink, sounding out a warning beep, in the case of a functional limitation."
– *+Scenes:* "The functional limitation would occur in scenes such as confluence, bad weather, pylon ahead, and sudden cutting-in."

The traffic scene is a within-subject factor that is designed at two levels: simple and complex, called *S-scene* and *C-scene*, respectively. Hence, a two-factor ($3 \times 2$) analysis of variables (ANOVA) is performed. A significance level of $p = 0.05$ is used. All participants are divided into *Baseline*, *+HMI*, and *+Scenes* groups.

## 2.6  Dependent Variables

To determine the effect of instructed knowledge on drivers taking over car control from the system, the RT is recorded from the moment when the system issues the RtI to the moment when the driver initiates taking over the car control by manipulating the steering wheel or depressing the accelerator/brake pedal.

Next, driver decision-making performance is categorized in terms of their consequences, crashes, wrong choices without crashes, delayed takeover but correct choice without a crash, successful takeover of the RtI, and takeover prior to the RtI. The ratios of the consequences are calculated to establish how instructed knowledge influenced their decision-making. Note that the correct/wrong choice denotes that a driver does (not) proceed on the route corresponding to the guidance (refer to Fig. 2b-3); successful takeover is defined as cases in which drivers take over car control before the system automatically cancels the control.

A questionnaire consisting of two items is administered to all participants. One item is: *"Did you have any trouble in taking over car control from the automated driving system?"* of a 2-point scale (0 = No; 1 = Yes). The other is *"To what extent did you trust the system"* on an 11-point scale (0 = do not trust at all; 11 = trust deeply).

## 2.7  Procedure

First, all participants who agree to participate sign an informed consent form after receiving explanations of the experiment's primary aim and the driving tasks. Next, a 5-min manual exercise is carried out for participants to familiarize themselves with the DS. Then, further instructions are given, consisting of the ADS manual, driving exercises to be familiarized with the ADS. Subsequently, half of the participants in each of the three groups are instructed to experience these scenes in the order of *S-scene #1, C-scene #1, S-scene #2, and C-scene #2*. The other half of them experience the other different order of *S-scene #1, S-scene #2, C-scene #1, and C-scene #2*.

Finally, the participants are instructed to fill out the questionnaire.

# 3  Results

## 3.1  Rt

A total of 187 valid RT data were gathered, but other RTs failed to collect data in 30 trials due to prior takeover or event failure. According to an ANOVA of the RTs, as outlined in Fig. 3, the interaction between instructed knowledge and the traffic scene was not significant (F $(2, 181) = 0.32$, $p = .72$, partial $\eta^2 = .004$). The main effect of the traffic scene was statistically significant (F $(1, 181) = 4.45$, $p < 0.05^{**}$, partial $\eta^2 = .02$); the main effect of the instructed knowledge was also significant (F $(2, 181) = 6.22$, $p < 0.01^{**}$, partial $\eta^2 = .06$). According to Tukey's test on the effect of knowledge, significant differences were revealed between *baseline* and *+scene* ($p < 0.01^{**}$), but not between *baseline* and *+HMI* ($p = 0.11$). The result revealed that drivers' response under the conditions of *Baseline* was delayed on average by 1.22 s to *+HMI*, and on average by 1.73 s to *+ Scenes*.

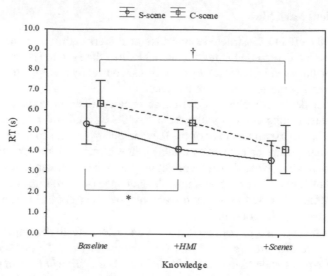

**Fig. 3.** Time of taking over car control from/to an RtI. Note that the value is negative in cases that a driver took over the control prior to an unissued RtI, and the value is positive after an issued RtI

## 3.2 Drivers' Decision-Making

Figure 4 depicts the ratios of the consequences of decision-making in/after the resuming process from the system to drivers. In the simple scenes, 97% and 92% of successful takeovers were achieved for +HMI and +Scenes, respectively, which were significantly higher than 72% for Baseline (see Fig. 4a). In the complex scenes, 28% of the participants under Baseline intervened in car control before the system issued an RtI, which was greater than +HMI (6%) (see Fig. 4b); that is, those drivers reacted to the route guidance.

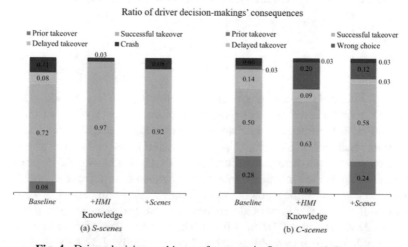

**Fig. 4.** Driver decision-making performance in *S-scenes* and *C-scenes*.

Meanwhile, 63% of the participants under +HMI safely reacted to the issued RtI, which was the highest among the three conditions (Baseline, 50%; +Scene, 58%). Further, + HMI yielded a 20% failure rate in choosing the route in accordance with the guidance, which was also the highest (Baseline, 3%; +Scenes, 12%). This outcome suggests that highlighting conveying the concept of the HMI causes drivers to greatly depend on the issued RtI, and hence to miss other important details, such as route guidance.

### 3.3 Questionnaire

According to the questionnaire, 15 of the 18 participants in the *Baseline* group thought they had trouble taking control over the car from the system, which was largely more than the other two conditions (*+HMI*: 9 of 18; *+Scenes*: 10 of 18). According to the self-rating on the item *driver trust*, the participants in the *Baseline* group who had relatively low confidence in resuming car control also expressed correspondingly low trust in driving automation (*Baseline*, 6.06 ± 1.66; *+HMI*, 6.50 ± 1.38; *+Scenes*, 6.50 ± 1.76).

## 4   Discussions and Conclusions

This study focused on the effect of instructed knowledge on driver decision-making in the transition from automated to manual driving under relatively complex driving conditions. First, the concept of the HMI in instructed knowledge (*+HMI*) largely advanced drivers' reactions to the RTI for approximately 1.73 s in a simple driving environment (see Fig. 3), and contributed to a significant increase in the ratio (+25%) of successful takeover in comparison to a lower level of knowledge (see Fig. 4); that is, only teaching about functional limitations. These findings support Hypothesis 1: that appropriately conveying knowledge contributes to driving safety in a relatively complex driving environment.

Second, instructed knowledge greatly influences driver decision-making in complex driving conditions (see Fig. 4b). More specifically, drivers who have not been instructed about the RtI would be apt to be aware of various details, such as route guidance, as well as the RtI. On the other hand, those who were familiar with the RtI tended to rely on the message of the RtI and missed other important information, failing to proceed to the right route. Meanwhile, the reduction of the ratio for the wrong choice (−8%) from +HMI to +Scenes hinted that teaching drivers about the sample scenes might enhance their situational awareness and reduce over-reliance on the RtI. The above findings agree with Hypothesis 2: that instructed knowledge influences driver decision-making consequences besides taking over car control.

On the other hand, drivers in the +HMI group showed relatively higher self-rated confidence in their takeover performance, as well as a higher extent of trust in the CAD, although many of them failed to choose the right route. This outcome implies that a higher level of instructed knowledge induces over-reliance on knowledge.

Although we aimed to discuss complex driving environments, critical hazards were not designed for all scenes, such that we could not investigate accidents. Our future work will expand our discussion to a more critical situation. Our future research will try to address how to prevent over-relying on the system to support driver decision-making in resuming car control from driving automation.

**Acknowledgments.** This study was conducted as part of the Cross-Ministerial Strategic Innovation Promotion Program, which advances automated driving for a universal service (SIP-adus) project entitled "Human Factors and HMI Research for Automated Driving."

# References

1. SAE: Society of Automotive Engineers: Taxonomy and Definitions for Terms Related to Driving Automation Systems for On-Road Motor Vehicles. SAE International, Warrensdale, PA (SAE Standard J3016_201609) (2016)
2. de Winter, J.C.F., Happee, R., Martens, M.H., Stanton, N.A.: Effects of adaptive cruise control and highly automated driving on workload and situation awareness: a review of the empirical evidence. Transp. Res. Part F: Traffic Psychol. Behav. **27**, 196–217 (2014). ISSN 1369–8478. https://doi.org/10.1016/j.trf.2014.06.016
3. Seppelt, B.D., Victor, T.W.: Potential solutions to human factors challenges in road vehicle automation. In: Meyer, G., Beiker, S. (eds.) Road Vehicle Automation, vol. 3, pp. 131–148. Springer, Heidelberg (2016). https://doi.org/10.1007/978-3-319-40503-2_11.
4. National Transportation Safety Board (NTSB). Collision between a car operating with automated vehicle control systems and a tractor-semitrailer truck. Williston, F. L. (May 7, 2016). Highway Accident Report NTSB/HAR-17/02. Washington, DC (2017)
5. Körber, M., Baseler, E., Bengler, K.: Introduction matters: manipulating trust in automation and reliance in automated driving. Appl. Ergon. **66**, 1–31 (2017)
6. Eriksson, A., Stanton, N.A.: Takeover time in highly automated vehicles: noncritical transitions to and from manual control. Hum. Factors **59**(4), 689–705 (2017). https://doi.org/10.1177/0018720816685832
7. Gold, C., Körber, M., Hohenberger, C., , Lechner., D., & Bengler, K. : Trust in automation – before and after the experience of take-over scenarios in a highly automated vehicle. Procedia Manuf. **3**, 3025–3032 (2015)
8. Naujoks, F., Forster, Y., Wiedemann, K., Neukum, A.: A Humanhuman--machine interface for cooperative highly automated driving. Adv. Intell. Syst. Comput. **585–595** (2017). https://doi.org/10.1007/978-3-319-41682-3-49
9. Zeeb, K., Buchner, A., Schrauf, M.: What determines the take-over time? An integrated model approach of driver take-over after automated driving. Accid. Anal. Prevent. Anal. Preven. **78**, 212–221 (2015)
10. Petermeijer, S.M., de Winter, J.C.F., Bengler, K.J.: Vibrotactile displays: a survey with a view on highly automated driving. IEEE Trans. Intell. Transp. Syst. **17**, 897–907 (2016). https://doi.org/10.1109/TITS.2015.2494873
11. Zhou, H., Itoh, M., Kitazaki, S.: Effect of instructing system limitations on the intervening behavior of drivers in partial driving automation. Cogn. Technol. Work **22**, 321–334 (2020). https://doi.org/10.1007/s10111-019-00568-1
12. Zhou, H., Itoh, M., Kitazaki, S.: How do levels of explanation on system limitations influence driver intervention to conditional driving automation? IEEE Trans. Hum.-Mach. Syst.

# Correction to: Conscious Ergonomics in Architecture: Energy, Matter, and Form from Theory to Practice

María Araya León⬤, Ricardo Guasch, Alberto T. Estévez⬤, and Javier Peña

**Correction to:**
**Chapter "Conscious Ergonomics in Architecture: Energy, Matter, and Form from Theory to Practice"**
**in: N. L. Black et al. (Eds.):** *Proceedings of the 21st Congress of the International Ergonomics Association (IEA 2021),* **LNNS 221, https://doi.org/10.1007/978-3-030-74608-7_37**

The original version of the book was inadvertently published with error as "EGG and Menez", and this has been corrected as "EEG and Mendez" in Page "299" of Chapter "Conscious Ergonomics in Architecture: Energy, Matter, and Form from Theory to Practice".

The updated version of this chapter can be found at
https://doi.org/10.1007/978-3-030-74608-7_37

# Author Index

N. L. Black et al. (Eds.): IEA 2021, LNNS 221, pp. 853–856, 2021.
https://doi.org/10.1007/978-3-030-74608-7